Curiosities of London

C. Cook, sc.

Yours faithfully,
John Timbs.

From a Painting by J. Gilbert

CURIOSITIES

OF

LONDON:

EXHIBITING THE MOST

RARE AND REMARKABLE OBJECTS OF INTEREST

IN THE METROPOLIS;

WITH

Nearly Fifty Years' Personal Recollections

By JOHN TIMBS, F.S.A.

LONDON:

DAVID BOGUE, FLEET STREET.

CURIOSITIES

OF

LONDON:

EXHIBITING THE MOST

RARE AND REMARKABLE OBJECTS OF INTEREST IN THE METROPOLIS;

WITH

Nearly Fifty Years' Personal Recollections.

By JOHN TIMBS, F.S.A.

AUTHOR OF A PICTURESQUE PROMENADE ROUND DORKING; AND EDITOR OF
LACONICS, THE YEAR-BOOK OF FACTS, ETC.

Charter granted by William the Conqueror to the City of London,
A.D. 1067. (See page 460.)

LONDON: DAVID BOGUE, 86 FLEET STREET.
MDCCCLV.

LONDON:
PRINTED BY LEVEY, ROBSON, AND FRANKLYN,
Great New Street and Fetter Lane.

PREFACE.

LITTLE need be said to bespeak the interest of readers in the *staple* of the present work—the Notable Things in the History of London through its Nineteen Centuries of accredited antiquity. Still, I am anxious to offer a few words upon the origin and growth of this volume; and the means by which I have striven to render it as complete as the extent and ever-varying nature of the subject will allow.

Twenty-seven years since (in 1828), I wrote in the parlour of the house No. 3 Charing Cross (then a publisher's), the title and plan of a volume to be called "CURIOSITIES OF LONDON;" and the work here submitted to the public is the realisation of that design. I then proposed to note the most memorable points in the annals of the Metropolis, and to describe its most remarkable objects of interest, from the earliest period to my own time,—for the Present has its "Curiosities" as well as the Past. Since the commencement of this design in 1828,—precisely midway in my lifetime,—I have scarcely for a day or hour lost sight of the subject; but, through a long course of literary activity,* have endeavoured to profit by every fair opportunity to increase my stock of materials; and by constant comparison, "not to take for granted, but to weigh and consider," in turning such materials to account. In this labour I have been greatly aided by the communications of obliging friends, as well as by my own recollection of nearly Fifty Years' Changes in the aspects of "enlarged and still increasing London."

"Thinking how different a place London is to different people," I have, in this volume, studied many tastes; but its leading cha-

* WORKS BY THE AUTHOR OF THE PRESENT VOLUME: A Picturesque Promenade round Dorking in Surrey, 1822. The same, 2d edit., 1823.—Laconics; or, the Best Words of the Best Authors, 3 vols. 1826.—Mirror, edited, 1827-1838 (Twenty-two vols.).—Signs before Death, 1828.—Cameleon Sketches, 1828.—Companion to the Theatres, 1829.—Arcana of Science and Art, 1828-1838 (Eleven vols.).—Wine-drinker's Manual, 1830.—Family Manual, 1831.—Knowledge for the People; or, the Plain Why and Because, 4 vols. 1831-2.—Popular Zoology, 1834.—Domestic Life in England, 1835.—The Instructor, Vol. 2 (written for the Society for Promoting Christian Knowledge), 1835.—Family Handbook, 1837.—Literary World, 3 vols. 1839, 1840.—London Anecdotes, 2 vols. 1848.—Illustrated Year-book, 2 vols. 1850, 1851.—Wellingtoniana, 1852.—Year-book of Facts, 1839-1855. (Seventeen vols.)

racteristics will be found to consist in what Addison's *Freeholder* calls " the Curiosities of this great Town." Their bibliographical illustration, by quotations from Old Poets and Dramatists, Travellers and Diarists, presents a sort of literary chequer-work of an entertaining and anecdotic character ; and these historic glimpses are brought into vivid contrast with the Social Statistics and other Great Facts of the London of to-day.

The plan of the book is in the main alphabetical. Districts and localities are, however, topographically described; the arrangement of streets being generally in a *sub-alphabet*. The Birth-places, Abodes, and Burial-places of Eminent Persons—so many sites of charmed ground—are specially noted, as are existing Antiquities, Collections of Rare Art and Virtu, Public Buildings, Royal and Noble Residences, Great Institutions, Public Amusements and Exhibitions, and Industrial Establishments; so to chronicle the renown of Modern as well as Ancient London. The articles describing the Churches, Exchanges, Halls, Libraries and Museums, Palaces and Parks, Parliament-Houses, Roman Remains, and the Tower of London, are, from their importance, most copious in their details.

The utmost pains has been taken to verify dates, names, and circumstances ; and it is trusted that no errors may be found in addition to those noted at the close of the volume, with the changes in the Metropolis during the progress of the printing of the work.* The reader, it is hoped, will regard these inaccuracies with indulgence, when the immense number of facts sought to be recorded in this volume is considered. Lastly, it has been my aim to render the "Curiosities" useful as well as entertaining, and with that view are introduced several matters of practical information for Londoners as well as visitors.

JOHN TIMBS.

88 SLOANE-STREET, CHELSEA,
    Jan. 16, 1855.

* See ADDITIONS AND CORRECTIONS, pp. 782-784.

THE FRONTISPIECE.—This Portrait has been engraved from a painting by Thomas John Gullick ; exhibited at the Royal Academy in 1854, and pronounced to be the work of an artist of great promise.

THE VIGNETTE.—This Charter, described at page 460, is in English as follows:

" William the King friendly salutes William the Bishop, and Godfrey the Portreve, and all the Burgesses within London, both French and English. And I declare, that I grant you to be all law-worthy, as you were in the days of King Edward; and I grant that every child shall be his father's heir, after his father's days; and I will not suffer any person to do you wrong. God keep you."

SUBSCRIBERS TO THE PRESENT WORK.

His Grace the Duke of Norfolk, K.G. *Norfolk House, St. James's-square.*
His Grace the Duke of Sutherland, K.G. *Stafford House, St. James's.*
Her Grace the Duchess of Sutherland, *Stafford House, St. James's.*
The Most Hon. the Marquis of Lansdowne, K.G., D.C.L., F.R.S. *Lansdowne House, Berkeley-square.*
The Right Hon. the Earl of Carlisle, F.R.S.L. *Grosvenor-place.*
The Right Hon. Lord Londesborough, K.C.H., F.R.S., F.S.A. *Carlton-House-terrace.*
The Lord Edward George Fitzalan Howard, M.P. *Rutland Gate.*
The Right Hon. Lord Braybrooke, LL.D., F.S.A. *New Burlington-street.*
Sir Edward Bulwer Lytton, Bart., M.P. *Knebworth, Herts.*
Lieut.-General Sir Henry G. W. Smith, Bart., G.C.B. *Plymouth.*
The Right Hon. F. G. Moon, Lord Mayor, F.S.A. *Four copies.*
Sir Charles Barry, R.A , F.R.S. *Old Palace-yard.*
Sir Joseph Paxton, M.P , F.L.S. *Sydenham.*
Sir J. Bernard Burke, Ulster King-at-Arms, *Record Tower, Dublin Castle.*

Abraham, H. R. Esq. *Howard-street, Strand.*
Ainsworth, W. Harrison, Esq. *Arundel-terrace, Kemp Town, Brighton.*
Angell, C. F. Esq. F.S.A. *Grove-lane, Camberwell.*
Ashton, Henry, Esq. *Great George-street, Westminster.*
Badger, Benjamin, Esq. *Eastwood House, Rotherham.*
Badger, Joseph, Esq *Rotherham.*
Badger, Thomas S Esq. *Lincoln's Inn.*
Baker, Edward D. Esq. *Newcastle-street, Strand.*
Bank of England Library and Literary Association.
Barnard, Samuel, Esq. *Holborn-hill.*
Barnett, Miss, *Mornington-crescent, Hampstead-road.*
Batt, James S. Esq. *Oxford-street.*
Battam, Thomas, Esq F.S.A. *Heron Cross, Stoke-upon-Trent.*
Bayley, W. H. Esq. *Madras.*
Bell, Robert, Esq F.S.A. *The Nook, Irthington, Cumberland.*
Bennett, Miss, *Sloane-street. Two copies.*
Bennoch, Francis, Esq. *Blackheath Park.*
Bleaden, John, Esq. *The Monument, London.*
Britton, John, Esq. *Burton-street, Burton-crescent.*
Brooks, Shirley, Esq. *New Inn.*
Buckstone, J. B. Esq. *Suffolk-street, Pall Mall East. Two copies.*
Burges, Alfred, Esq. F S.A. *Blackheath.*
Bury, Talbot, Esq. *Welbeck-street, Cavendish-square.*
Cabbell, Benjamin Bond, Esq M.P. *Portland place. Two copies.*
Calder, George A. Esq. *Bathurst-street, Hyde Park.*
Carter, Mr. Alderman, *Cornhill.*
Caslon, H. W. Esq. *Chiswell-street, Finsbury.*
Chaffers, W. jun. Esq. F.S.A. *Old Bond-street.*

Churchill, H. Blencowe, Esq. *Raymond-buildings, Gray's Inn.*
Cole, Henry, Esq. C.B. *Gore House, Kensington.*
Cooke, Nathaniel, Esq *Ladbroke-terrace, Notting-hill.*
Collingridge, W. H. Esq. *Long-lane, Smithfield. Two copies.*
Collins, Samuel, Esq. *Denmark-hill.*
Cooper, C. H. Esq. F.S.A. Town Clerk of *Cambridge.*
Crace, F. Esq. *Vine Cottage. Blythe-lane, Hammersmith.*
Crossley, Luke T. Esq. *Hankelow Hall, Nantwich, Cheshire.*
" Crowquill, Alfred." *Portland-place North, Clapham-road.*
Cunningham, Peter, Esq F S.A. *Victoria-road, Kensington.*
Dalziel, Edward, Esq. *Camden-street North.*
Dalziel, George, Esq. *Albert-street, Mornington-crescent.*
Davies, Robert, Esq F.S.A. *The Mount, York.*
Delamotte, Philip H. Esq. F.S.A. *Newton-road, Bayswater.*
Dick, W. Robertson, Esq. *Simsby, Derby.*
Dodd, John, Esq. *Rickmansworth, Herts.*
Doudney, Rev. J. A. *Bonmahon, Waterford, Ireland. Two copies.*
Duncan, Edward, Esq. *Mornington-place, Hampstead-road.*
Dyott, Captain John P *Knowle Lodge, Lichfield*
Edwards, F. Howarth, Esq *Gloucester-place, Kentish Town.*
Edwards, James Alton, Esq. *Camden-road Villas.*
Evans, Edmund, Esq. *Roquet court, Fleet-street.*
Fairholt, F. W. Esq. F.S A. *Mon'pellier-square, Brompton.*
Fitz-Cook, Henry, Esq. *New Ormond-street, Queen-square.*
Fletcher, Angus, Esq. *Oxton. Tadcaster, York.*
Forteath, G. A Esq. *Bunny Park, Notts.*
Foster, Birket, Esq *Clifton-road, St. John's Wood.*
Francis, Charles Larkin, Esq *Eccleston-square.*
Fuller, Francis, Esq. *Abingdon-street, Westminster.*
Garle, Thomas, Esq *Hamilton-terrace, St. John's Wood.*
Gatty, Robert, Esq. *Angel court, Throgmorton-street.*
Geldard, John, Esq. *Great Portland street.*
Geldard, Mrs. *Norman terrace, Willington-road, Clapham.*
Gener, R. Esq. *Osnaburg-terrace, Regent's Park.*
Gibson, W. Sidney, Esq. F S.A. *Newcastle-upon-Tyne.*
Gilbert, John, Esq. *Blackheath. Two copies.*
Gilks, Thomas, Esq. *Fleet-street.*
Glaisher, James, Esq. F R.S. *Lewisham.*
Godsell, George, Esq. *Magdalen Hall, Oxford.*
Godwin, George, Esq. F.R.S., F.S.A. *Alexander-square, Brompton.*
Gooch, John, Esq. *River-terrace, Islington.*
Gould, John, Esq. F.R S., F.L S *Broad-street, Golden-square.*
Gruneisen, C. Lewis, Esq. *Surrey-street, Strand.*
Gullick, Thomas, Esq. *Pall Mall.*
Gullick, Thomas John, Esq *Sloane-street.*
Gutch, John, Esq. *Clifton Villas. Warwick-road, Paddington..*
Gwilt, George, Esq. F.S.A. *Union-street, Southwark.*
Haes, John, Esq. *Park-road, Stockwell.*
Hall, S. Carter, Esq. F.S.A. *Lancaster-place, Strand.*
Halliwell, J. O. Esq. F.R S., F.S.A. *Avenue Lodge, Brixton-hill.*
Hands, Decimus, Esq. *Dory't-square.*
Harding, C. T. Esq. *Clifford-street, Bond-street.*
Hardy, Benjamin, Esq *Brompton.*
Hargreaves, E. H. Esq. *Upper Spring-street, Portman-square.*

Harvey, C. S. Esq. *Buenos Ayres.*
Harvey, William, Esq. *The Vineyard, Richmond.*
Hawkins, Walter, Esq. F.S.A. *Leonard-place, Kensington.*
Heigham, T. Esq. *Grove-place, Brompton.*
Hewitt, John, Esq. *Office of Ordnance, Pall Mall.*
Hill, Henry, Esq. *Garrick Club.*
Hoare, Charles, Esq. *Edenbridge, Kent.*
Hogg, Jabez, Esq *Gower-street, Bedford-square.*
Hope, A. J. B. Beresford, Esq. F.S.A. *Arklow House, Connaught-place.*
   Three copies.
Hope, Henry Thomas, Esq. *Piccadilly. Five copies.*
Huddlestone, J. W. Esq. *Garrick Club.*
Ingram, Herbert, Esq. F.S.A. *Strand. Two copies.*
Jackson, Mason, Esq. *Cardington-street, Hampstead-road.*
Jay, Captain, *Regent-street.*
Jerdein, John Inglis, Esq. *St. George's-terrace, Hyde Park Corner.*
Jerrold, Douglas, Esq *Circus-road, St. John's Wood.*
Keon, Miles Gerald, Esq. *Oxford terrace, Hyde Park.*
Landells, Ebenezer, Esq *Holford-square, Pentonville.*
Langford, J. M. Esq. *Raymond-buildings, Gray's Inn.*
Lemon, Mark, Esq *Gordon-street, Gordon-square.*
Lings, Mrs. Deborah, *Hampstead-road.*
Little, William, Esq. *Strand.*
Mackay, Charles, Esq. LL D., F.S.A. *Camden-square.*
Macready, W. C. Esq *Sherborne House, Sherborne, Dorset.*
Mair, George G. Esq F.S.A. *Upper Bedford-place, Russell-square.*
Manby, Charles, Esq. F.R.S. *Great George-street, Westminster.*
Martin, W. C L Esq. F.L.S. *Dacre-Park-terrace, Lee.*
Martiny, E. Esq. *Office of Ordnance, Pall Mall.*
Mather, James, Esq. *The Grove, South Shields.*
Mawe, T. J. Esq. *Carlton Villas, Maida Vale. Two copies.*
Mayer, Joseph, Esq. F S.A. *Liverpool.*
Merewether, Mr. Serjeant, Town Clerk of *London.*
Minister, E. W. Esq. *Arragon Villas, Twickenham.*
Monte Video Consul, *London. Two copies.*
Moses, Mrs. *Hanway-street, Oxford-street.*
Munro, Alexander, Esq. *Upper Belgrave-place.*
Noble, Matthew, Esq. *Bruton-street, Berkeley-square.*
Ottley, Henry, Esq. *Vale of Health, Hampstead.*
Owen, Rev. O. Freire, F.S.A. *Maida-hill West.*
Parkyns, Mansfield, Esq. *Woodborough Hall, Notts.*
Parry, Thomas, Esq. *Slenford, Lincoln.*
Pellatt, Apsley, Esq. M.P. *Southwark. Two copies.*
Penson, R. Kyrke, Esq. F.S.A. *Oswestry, Salop.*
Pepper, J. H. Esq. *Polytechnic Institution, Regent-street.*
Phillips, Richard M. Esq *Brompton.*
Piper, Captain, *Cumberland House, Shepherd's Bush.*
Pollard, George, Esq *Watling-street.*
Prior, James, Esq. R.N., F.S.A. *Norfolk-crescent, Hyde Park.*
Purland, Theodosius, Esq *Mortimer-street, Cavendish-square. Two copies.*
Reach, Angus B. Esq. *Albert-street, Mornington-crescent.*
Read, Samuel, Esq. *New Cavendish-street, Portland-place.*
Redwood, H. B. Esq. *Sloane-street.*
Richards, Rev. Joseph, M.A. *Calcutta.*

Roots, William, Esq. M.D., F.S.A. *Surbiton, Kingston-upon-Thames.*
Rose, William, Esq. *Coalport, Salop.*
Russell, John Scott, Esq. F.R S. *Great George-street, Westminster.*
Salmón, Frederick, Esq. F.S.A. *Lower Berkeley-street.*
Sargent, Mrs. *Ely Lodge, Stoke Newington.*
Savill, T. C. Esq. *South Villas, Campden-hill, Kensington.*
Scott, G. Gilbert, Esq. F.S.A. *Spring-gardens.*
Scott, John, Esq. *Coventry-street.*
Shepard, E. Clarence, Esq. *Onslow-square, Brompton.*
Sidney, Samuel, Esq. *Chaplin Villa, Forest-hill. Two copies.*
Simpson, Henry, Esq. *Philpot-lane, Eastcheap.*
Simpson, T. Bridge, Esq. *Leadenhall-street.*
Smee, Alfred, Esq. F.R.S. *Finsbury-circus.*
Smith, Albert, Esq. *Percy-street, Bedford-square. Two copies.*
Smith, William, Esq. F.S.A. *Upper Southwick-street, Hyde Park.*
Smith, W. H. Esq *Strand. Two copies.*
Spalding, Thomas, Esq. *Drury-lane.*
Spencer, Joseph Frowd, Esq. *Brompton.*
Staunton, Howard, Esq. *Mill Hill House, Barnes Common, Surrey.*
Tennant, James, Esq. F.G.S. *Strand.*
Thackeray, W. M. Esq. *Young-street, Kensington.*
Thomas, John, Esq. *Church-street, Paddington. Three copies.*
Thomas, John Evan, Esq. *Lower Belgrave-place.*
Tucker, Charles, Esq. F S.A. *Marlands, Heavitree, Exeter.*
Tudor, E. Owen, Esq. F.S.A. *Westbourne-terrace.*
Tupper, Martin Farquhar, Esq. D.C.L., F.R S. *Albury, Surrey.*
Tussaud, Joseph, Esq *Baker-street, Portman-square.*
Tymbs, John, Esq *Worcester.*
Veall, J. R. Esq *Waterloo-road, Wolverhampton.*
Virtue, George H. Esq F.S.A. *Finsbury-square.*
Walesby, Thomas, Esq. *Waterloo-place, Pall Mall.*
Ward, E. M. Esq. A.R A. *Upton Villas, Slough.*
Waterton, Edmund, Esq. F.S.A. *Walton Hall, Yorkshire.*
Way, Albert, Esq F.S.A. *Wonham Manor, Surrey.*
Weir, W. Harrison, Esq. *Lyndhurst Villas, Peckham. Two copies.*
Whitty, E. M. Esq. *Great College-street, Westminster.*
Williams, John M. Esq. *Palsgrave-place, Strand.*
Williams, Joseph L. Esq. *Victoria-road, Kensington.*
Williamson, Joseph, Esq. *Princess-terrace, Caledonian-road.*
Wilson, James H. Esq. *Onslow-square, Brompton.*
Wire, Mr. Alderman, *St. Swithin's-lane.*
Worster, Major, *Observatory, Madras.*
Wright, Thomas, Esq. M.A., F.S.A. *Sydney-street, Brompton.*

CURIOSITIES OF LONDON.

ADELPHI, (THE),

A SERIES of streets in the rear of the houses on the south side of the Strand, reaching east and west from Adam-street to Buckingham-street, and facing the Thames on the south—a grand commencement of the architectural embankment of the river in 1768. It is named Adelphi (αδελφος, *brother*) from its architects, the four brothers Adam, who built vast arches over the court-yard of old Durham House, and upon these erected, level with the Strand, *Adam*-street, leading to *John*, *Robert*, *James*, and *William* Streets; the noble line of houses fronting the Thames being the Adelphi Terrace. The view from this spot is almost unrivalled in the metropolis for variety and architectural beauty: from Waterloo Bridge on the east, with the majestic dome and picturesque *campanili* of St. Paul's, to Westminster Bridge on the west, above which rise the towers of Lambeth Palace, and Westminster Abbey, and the pinnacles and bristling roofs of the New Houses of Parliament. At No. 5, the centre house of the Terrace, David Garrick died, Jan. 20, 1779; and here his remains lay in state, previous to their interment in Westminster Abbey, Feb. 1. Garrick's widow also died here in 1822. At No. 1 Adam-street, lived Dr. Knox, the "British Essayist." At Osborne's Hotel, John-street, in 1824, sojourned Kamehameha II., King of the Sandwich Islands, and his sister the Queen, with their suites: the Queen died here of measles, July 8; and the King died of the same disease, at the Caledonian Hotel, on the 14th: their remains lay in native pomp at Osborne's, and were then deposited in the vaults of St. Martin's Church, prior to their being conveyed in the *Blonde* frigate to the Sandwich Islands for interment. The poor King and Queen were wantonly charged with gluttony and drunkenness while here; but they lived chiefly on fish, poultry, and fruit, and their favourite drink was some cider presented to them by Mr. Canning.

In John-street, also, is the house built for the Society of Arts by the Adams. In the second-floor chambers at No. 2 James-street, lived, for nearly thirty years, Mr. Thomas Hill, the "Hull" of Theodore Hook's *Gilbert Gurney*. Hill died here Dec. 20, 1841, in his 81st year; and left a large collection of curiosities, including a cup and a small vase formed from the mulberry-tree planted by Shakspeare at Stratford-upon-Avon. Neither of these, however, is the Shakespeare Cup presented to Garrick by the Mayor and Corporation of Stratford at the time of the Jubilee. This celebrated relic was bought on May 5, 1825, for 121 guineas, by Mr. J. Johnson; and by him sold, July 4, 1846, for 40*l.* 8*s.* 6*d.*, to Mr. Isaacs, of Upper Gower-street.

The Adelphi vaults, occupied as cellars and coal-wharfs, in their grim vastness, remind one of the Etruscan Cloaca of old Rome. Beneath the "dry arches," the most abandoned characters have often passed the night, nestling upon foul straw; and many a street-thief escaped from his pursuers in these subterranean haunts, before the introduction of gas-light and a vigilant police.

ADMIRALTY OFFICE, (THE),

forms the left flank of the detachment of Government Offices on the north side of Whitehall. It occupies the site of Wallingford House, from the roof of which Archbishop Usher saw King Charles I. led out to execution in the front of Whitehall Palace, and swooned at the sight.

The Admiralty Office, built by Ripley, about 1726, is a tasteless pile: to conceal its ugliness, the court-yard was fronted with a stone screen, by the Adams, in the reign of George III. This screen is a very characteristic composition: its sculptured hippocampi, and prows of ancient vessels, combining with an anchor in the pediment of the portico of the main building, to denote the purposes of the office—the administration of the affairs of the Royal Navy. In one of the large rooms the remains of Lord Nelson lay in state, Jan. 8, 1806; and next day, took place the solemn funeral procession, with a military force of nearly 8000 men, from this spot to St. Paul's Cathedral.

On the roof of the Admiralty Office, many years since, was placed a Semaphore, (the invention of Sir Home Popham); the arms of which, extending laterally at right angles, communicated orders and intelligence to and from the sea-ports; previous to which was used the shuttle telegraph, invented by R. L. Edgeworth. The Semaphore has, however, been superseded by the Electric Telegraph, of which nine wires are laid from the office in Whitehall to the Dockyard at Portsmouth; the Admiralty paying the Electric Telegraph Company 1200l. a-year.

ALCHEMISTS.

The last true believer in Alchemy was, according to Mr. Brande, Peter Woulfe, who occupied chambers in Barnard's Inn, Holborn, while residing in London, and usually spent the summer in Paris: he died in 1805. About 1801, an adept lived, or rather starved, in the metropolis, in the person of an editor of an evening journal, who expected to compound the alkahest if he could only keep his materials digested in a lamp-furnace for the space of seven years. The lamp burnt brightly during six years, eleven months, and some odd days besides, and then, unluckily, it went out. Why it went out the adept never could guess; but he was certain that if the flame could only have burnt to the end of the septenary cycle his experiment must have succeeded.—(*Paper on Astrology and Alchemy, by Sir Walter Scott; Quarterly Review,* 1821.)

In Catherine-street, Strand, lived for many years one John Denley, a bookseller, who amassed here a notable collection of the works of alchemist, cabalist, and astrologer: he is the individual referred to by Sir E. Lytton Bulwer in the introduction to his *Zanoni.*

ALDERMAN,

The oldest office in the Corporation of London, and derived from the Ealdorman, or superior Saxon noble; but not mentioned as presiding over gilds or wards until Henry II. In some cases, the wards were the Aldermen's heritable property, and received their own names. The present ward of Farringdon was bought by William Faryngdon in 1279, and remained in his family upwards of eighty years; it was held by the tenure of presenting at Easter a gillyflower, then of great rarity. Each of the twenty-six City wards elects one Alderman for life, or "during good behaviour." The fine for the rejection of the office is 500l.; but it is generally sought as a stepping-stone to the Mayoralty, each Alderman being *in rotâ* Lord Mayor, he having previously served as Sheriff of London and Middlesex. The Aldermen form a court, the Lord Mayor presiding; and sit in a superb apartment of the Guildhall, which has a rich stucco ceiling painted mostly by Sir James Thornhill; in the cornice are carved and emblazoned the arms of all the Mayors since 1780: each Alderman's chair bears his name and arms, and he wears a scarlet cloth gown, hooded and furred; and a gold chain, *if he has served as Mayor.* Upon state visits of sovereigns to the City, the several Aldermen ride in procession on horseback. At the opening of the New Royal Exchange, October 28, 1844, ten Aldermen rode thus, wearing their gowns and chains and cocked hats, carrying wands, and preceding the Queen's procession from Temple Bar.

The office of Alderman has rarely been filled by men of intellectual mark. Alderman Fabian, who wrote the "Chronicles of England and France," early in the 16th century, is an exception. Alderman Barber, the first printer Lord Mayor (1733), was the friend of Bolingbroke, Swift, and Pope; and in 1721 erected a cenotaph to Samuel Butler in Westminster Abbey, notwithstanding Butler's satiric "Character" of an Alderman. The notorious John Wilkes was a man of talent, though profligate and unprincipled. Alderman Boydell was a generous and discriminating promoter of the fine arts, and was honoured with a public funeral. The Court of Aldermen, in 1850, consisted of—

2 wharfingers, 2 auctioneers, 1 potter, 1 grocer, 1 publisher, 1 ship-broker, 1 wine-merchant, 1 tea-dealer, 1 print-seller, 2 general merchants, 1 solicitor, 1 dealer in hides, 1 iron-master; 10 of independent property, and mostly retired traders = 26.

Five of the Aldermen sit in Parliament, one for his own City. The above list, however, does not include one banker, and only two "merchant-princes:" the dignity of the office has unquestionably been trifled with by the choice of retail traders; for an Alderman to sell a pound of candles or a penny tart will not increase the respect for his magisterial or corporate position. The histories of the Aldermen of our time exhibit some melancholy instances of reverse of fortune: upwards of 1300*l.* is paid annually, in pensions or allowances, by the Court of Aldermen, to the widows or descendants of their less prosperous brethren.

ALMACK'S

Assembly Rooms, on the south side of King-street, St. James's, were built by Mylne, for one Almack, a Scotsman; and were opened Feb. 12, 1765, with an Assembly, at which the Duke of Cumberland, the hero of Culloden, was present. The large ball-room is about one hundred feet in length by forty feet in width; it is chastely decorated with gilt columns and pilasters, classic medallions, mirrors, &c., and is lit with upwards of five hundred wax-lights in five cut-glass lustres. The largest number of persons ever present in this room at one ball was 1700.

The Assembly is regulated by Ladies Patronesses, who in the season of 1850 were the Duchess of Norfolk, the Marchioness of Ely, Marchioness of Londonderry, Marchioness of Westminster, the Countess of Jersey, Countess of Kinnoull, Countess of Lichfield, Viscountess Palmerston, and Lady Clinton. The series consisted of six assemblies, on alternate Thursdays after Easter, subject to the following regulations: "Each Lady Patroness to have on her list a limited number of subscribers. The Lady Patronesses to have a limited number of non-subscribers for each ball. No Lady Patroness can give a subscription or a ticket to a lady she does not visit, or to a gentleman who is not introduced to her by a lady whose name is upon her visiting-list. No gentlemen's tickets can be transferable."

The rooms are let for public meetings, dramatic readings, concerts, balls, and occasionally for dinners. Here Mrs. Billington, Mr. Braham, and Signor Naldi gave concerts from 1808 to 1810, in rivalry with Madame Catalani at Hanover Square Rooms; and here Mr. Charles Kemble gave his Readings from Shakspeare, in 1844. Almack's Rooms are often called "Willis's," from the name of their present proprietor.

Almack's has declined of late years; "a clear proof that the palmy days of exclusiveness are gone by in England; and though it is obviously impossible to prevent any given number of persons from congregating and re-establishing an oligarchy, we are quite sure that the attempt would be ineffectual, and that the sense of their importance would extend little beyond the set."—(*Quarterly Review*, 1840.)

ALMONRY, (THE),

Or Eleemosynary, now corruptly, (as in Stow's time,) the Ambry, was named from its being the place where the alms collected in the Abbey Church at Westminster were distributed to poor persons. It was situated at the east end of the Sanctuary, and was divided into two parts: "the Great Almonry, consisting of two oblong portions, parallel to the two Tothill streets, and connected by a narrow lane (the entrance being from Dean's Yard); and the Little Almonry, running southward, at the eastern end of the other Almonry."—(*Walcot's Westminster*, 1849.)

In the Almonry the first printing-press ever known in England was set up by William Caxton, according to Stow, in an old chapel near the entrance of the Abbey; but a very curious placard, in Caxton's largest type, and now preserved in the library of Brasenose College, Oxford, shews that he printed in the Almonry; for in this placard he invites customers to "come to Westmonester in to the Almonestrye at the Reed Pale," the name by which was known a house in which Caxton is said to have lived. It stood on the north side of the Almonry, with its back against that of a house on the south side of Tothill-street. Bagford describes this house as of brick, with the sign of the King's Head: it is stated to have fallen down in November, 1845, before the removal of the other dwellings in the Almonry, to form a new line (Victoria-street) from Tothill-street to Pimlico. A beam of wood was saved from the materials of the house, and from it have been made a chess-board and two sets of chessmen, as appropriate memorials of Caxton's first labour in England—*The Game and Playe of the Chesse*, 1474, folio, believed to be the first book printed in England—(See *Illustrated London News*, June 5, 1847). According to a view of Caxton's House, engraved by G. Cooke, in 1827, it was three-storied, and had a gallery or balcony to the upper floor, with a window in its bold gable.

In one of the almshouses built by King Henry VII., north of the Almonry, lived Thomas Barker, who aided Izaak Walton in writing *The Complete Angler*. And in the Little Almonry was the house of Harrington, the poet, who attended Charles I. on the scaffold; and who was here often visited by Roger l'Estrange and Andrew Marvell.

There is an old brick house in Tothill-street, opposite Dartmouth-street, which was probably at one time connected with the Almonry. It has upon its front, sunken in the brickwork, the letters E. (Eleemosynaria?), T. A. (perhaps the initials of the almoner's name), with, however, a late date, 1571. A heart, which is above the inscription, was the symbol used in the old Clog Almanacks for the Annunciation, the Purification, and all other Feast-days of Our Lady.—(*Walcot's Westminster*, 1849.)

ALMONRY, ROYAL.

This Office, in Middle Scotland Yard, Whitehall, is maintained expressly for the distribution of the Royal Alms, or Bounty, to the poor. The duties of the Hereditary Grand Almoner, first instituted in the reign of Richard I., are confined to the distribution of alms at a Coronation. The office of the High Almoner is of a more general description. In the reign of Edward I., his office was to collect the fragments of the royal table, and distribute them daily to the poor; to visit the sick, poor widows, prisoners, and other persons in distress; to remind the King about the bestowal of his alms, especially on Saints' Days; and to see that the cast-off robes were sold, to increase the King's charity.

For more than a century the office of Lord High Almoner was held by the Archbishops of York; but on the death of Archbishop Harcourt, in November, 1847, the office was conferred upon Dr. Samuel Wilberforce, Bishop of Oxford.

The distribution of Alms on the Thursday before Easter, or *Maundy Thursday*, takes place in Whitehall Chapel; that at Easter, Whitsuntide, and Christmas, at the Office in Middle Scotland Yard. Thus, on Easter Monday, 1850, "upwards of 500 men and women were presented with 5s. each, all being above sixty, and many upwards of ninety years of age." The pious Queen Adelaide, who died in 1849, and is known to have expended one-third of her large income in private and public charity, maintained in her household an Almoner, whose duty it was to investigate all applications for the royal benevolence.

ALMSHOUSES,

Built by Public Companies, Benevolent Societies, and private individuals, for aged and infirm persons, are very numerous in the metropolis and its suburbs. The Companies' Almshouses were originally erected next their Halls, that the almspeople might be handy to attend pageants and processions; but these almshouses have mostly been removed, owing to the increased value of ground in the City.

Almshouses succeeded the incorporated Hospitals dissolved by King Henry VIII. Among the earliest erected were the Almshouses founded by Lady Margaret, mother of King Henry VII., for poor women: they were afterwards converted into lodgings for the singing men of the Abbey, and called Choristers' Rents: they were taken down about 1800. Westminster has several of these munificent foundations: as the Red Lion Almshouses, in York-street, founded in 1577, for eight poor women, by Cornelius Van Dun, of Brabant, a soldier who served under King Henry VIII. at Tournay. Next are, in the same neighbourhood, the Almshouses for twelve poor housekeepers of St. Margaret's, with a school and chapel—the boys clad in black: these were founded in 1566, by the Rev. Edward Palmer, B.D., many years preacher at St. Bride's, Fleet Street, and who used to sleep in the church-tower. Emmanuel Hospital, James Street, was founded by the will of Lady Ann Dacre, in 1601, for aged parishioners of St. Margaret's: and in one of its almshouses, on January 22, 1772, died Mrs. Windimore, cousin of Mary (consort of William III.,) and of Queen Anne.

In 1720, the Drapers' Company maintained Almshouses at Tower Hill, Beach Lane, Greenwich, Stratford-le-Bow, Shoreditch, St. George's Fields, St. Mary Newington, and Mile End. Whittington's College, or Almshouses, founded in 1621, on College Hill, were rebuilt by the Mercers' Company, at the foot of Highgate Hill, about 1826. The Fishmongers' Company's Almshouses, or St. Peter's Hospital, Newington Butts, founded 1618, consisted of three courts, dining-hall, and chapel: and were rebuilt on Wandsworth Common, in 1850.

Richard Alleyn, the distinguished actor, and friend of Ben Jonson and Shakspeare, besides founding Dulwich College, built and endowed three sets of Almshouses in the metropolis: in Lamb Alley, Bishopsgate Street; in Bath Street, St. Luke's; and in Soap Yard, Southwark.

Traditionally, we owe the foundation of Dame Owen's School and Almshouses, at Islington, to Archery. In 1610, this rich brewer's widow, in passing along St. John-street Road, then Hermitage Fields, was struck by a truant arrow, and narrowly escaped "braining;" and the old lady, thinking such close shooting dangerous, in commemoration of her providential escape, built, in 1613, a free school and ten almshouses upon the scene of her adventure. Since 1839, they have been

The Trinity House Almshouses, in the Mile End Road, founded in 1695, for decayed commanders of ships, mates, or pilots, and their wives and widows, have characteristic ornaments of shipping on their roofs, and a statue of Captain Saunders, a benefactor to the charity; died 1721.

Bancroft's Almshouses and School, Mile End, were built in 1735, with the ill-gotten fortune bequeathed by Francis Bancroft, grandson of Archbishop Bancroft, and an officer of the Lord Mayor's Court; and so hated for his mercenary and oppressive practices, that at his funeral, a mob, for very joy, rang the church bells of St. Helen's, Bishopsgate, where is a tomb to his memory, erected in his life-time. The almsmen are twenty-four poor old members of the Drapers' Company; and the school boards, clothes, educates, and apprentices 100 boys. In May, 1850, there was a public dinner of persons brought up in Bancroft's School.

The Almshouses erected of late years are mostly picturesque buildings, in the old English style, with gables, turrets, and twisted chimney-shafts, of red brick, with handsome stone dressings.

The Marylebone Almshouses, built in St. John's Wood Terrace, Regent's Park, in 1836, originated in a legacy of 500*l.* from Count Woronzow; the site being leased for ninety-nine years, at a peppercorn rent, by Colonel Eyre, with two presentations to the Charity.

The London Almshouses were erected at Brixton, in 1833, to commemorate the passing of the Reform Bill, instead of by illumination.

The King William Naval Asylum, at Penge, opened 1849, for the widows of Commanders, Lieutenants, Masters, and Pursers in the Royal Navy, was built by Queen Adelaide, to the memory of William IV.

AMUSEMENTS, PAST AND PRESENT.

ARCHERY is mentioned among the summer pastimes of the London youth by Fitzstephen, who wrote in the reign of Henry II.; and the repeated statutes from the 13th to the 16th centuries, enforcing the use of the Bow, invariably ordered the leisure time upon holidays to be passed in its exercise. Finsbury appears to have been a very early locality for Archery; for in the reign of Edward I. there was formed a society entitled the Archers of Finsbury, subsequently known as the Artillery Company. In the reign of Henry VII., all the gardens in Finsbury were destroyed by law, " and of them was made a plain field for archers to shoote in ;" this being the appropriation of what is now called " the Artillery Ground." Among the curious books on Archery are the *Ayme for Finsburie Archers*, 1628; and the *Ayme for the Archers of St. George's Fields*, 1664.

Henry VIII. shot with the longbow as well as any of his guards: he chartered a society for shooting; and jocosely dignified a successful archer as Duke of Shoreditch, at which place his Grace resided. This title was long preserved by the Captain of the London Archers, who used to summon the officers of his several divisions under the titles of Marquis of Barlo, of Clerkenwell, of Islington, of Hoxton, of Shacklewell, &c., Earl of Pancras, &c. We read of a grand pageant in this reign, of three thousand archers, guarded by whifflers and billmen, pages and footmen, proceeding from Merchant Taylors' Hall, through Broad-street, the residence of their captain; thence into Moorfields by Finsbury, and so on to Smithfield, where they performed evolutions, and shot at a target for honour.

Stow, (who died in 1605) informs us, that before his time it had been customary at Bartholomew-tide for the Lord Mayor, with the sheriffs and aldermen, to go into the fields at Finsbury, where the citizens were assembled, and shoot at the standard with broad and flight arrows for games; and this exercise was continued for several days.

Edward VI. was fond of archery; and in his reign the scholars of

St. Bartholomew, who held their disputations in cloisters, were rewarded with a bow and silver arrows. Charles I. was an excellent archer, and forbade by proclamation the inclosure of shooting-grounds near London. Archery, however, seems then to have fallen into disrepute. Sir William Davenant, in a mock poem, entitled *The Long Vacation in London*, describes the attorneys and proctors as making matches in Finsbury Fields:

> "With loynes in canvas bow-case tied,
> Where arrows stick with mickle pride;
> Like ghosts of Adam Bell and Clymme:
> Sol set for fear they'll shoot at him!"

Pepys records (1667), that, when a boy, he used to shoot with his bow and arrows in the fields at Kingsland.

In 1781, the remains of the "Old Finsbury Archers" established the Toxophilite Society, at Leicester House, then in Leicester Fields; it is stated, principally through Sir Ashton Lever, who shewed his Musuem there. The Society held their meetings in Bloomsbury Fields, behind the present site of Gower-street. In about twenty-five years they removed on "target days" to Highbury Barn; from thence to Bayswater; and in 1834, to the Inner Circle, Regent's Park, where they have a rustic lodge, and between five and six acres of ground. The Society consisted in 1850 of 100 members; terms, 5l. annually, entrance-fee 5l., and other expenses. They meet every Friday during the Spring and Summer; the shooting is at 60, 80, and 100 yards; and many prizes are shot for during the season; Prince Albert, patron. They possess the original silver badge of the old Finsbury Archers.

The most numerous Society of the kind now existing is, however, "The Royal Company of Archers, the Queen's body-guard of Scotland," whose captain-general, the Duke of Buccleuch, rode in the coronation procession of Queen Victoria.

In 1849, the Society of Cantelows Archers was established; their shooting-ground is at Camden Square, Camden New Town; the prize, a large silver medal.

There was a fine display of Archery at the Fête of the Scottish Society of London, in Holland Park, Kensington, June 20 and 21, 1849, when 300l. worth of prize plate was shot for.

BALLAD-SINGING, the vestige of the minstrelsy which Cromwell, in 1656, silenced for a time, was common in the last century. "The Blind Beggar" had conferred poetic celebrity upon Bethnal Green; "Black-eyed Susan," and "'Twas when the seas were roaring," were the lyrics that landsmen delighted to sing of the sea; and "Jemmy Dawson," (set to music by Dr. Arne,) grew into historic fame elsewhere than on the scene of the tragedy, Kennington Common. To these succeeded the sea-songs of Charles Dibdin, which were commonly sung about the streets by the very tars who had first felt their patriotic inspiration: a sailor, who wore a model of the brig Nelson upon his hat, long maintained a vocal celebrity upon Tower Hill. Hogarth, in his "Wedding of the Industrious Apprentice," has painted the famous ballad-singer "Philip in the Tub;" and Gravelot, a portrait-painter in the Strand, had several sittings from ballad-singers. The great factory of the ballads has long been Seven Dials, where Pitts employed Bat Corcoran, the patron of "slender Ben" and "over-head-and-ears Nic." Among its earlier lyrists were "Tottenham Court Meg," the "Ballad-singing Cobler," and "oulde Guy, the poet." Mr. Catnach, another noted printer of ballads, lived in Seven Dials; and, at his death, left a considerable fortune. He was the first ballad-printer who published *yards of songs for one penny*, in former days the price of a single ballad;

and here he accumulated the largest stock on record of whole sheets, last-dying speeches, ballads, and other wares of the flying-stationers.

BEAR AND BULL BAITING.—A map of London, three centuries ago, gives the "Spitel Field" for archers; "Fynsburie Fyeld," with "Dogge's House," for the citizens to hunt in; "Moore Fyeld," with marks, as if used by clothiers; "the Banck" by the side of the River; "the Bolle Bayting Theatre," near "the Beare Baitynge House," nigh where London Bridge now commences. Pepys describes a visit to the "beare-garden" in 1666, where he saw "some good sport of the bull's tossing of the dogs, one into the very boxes. But it is a very rude and nasty pleasure." Hockley-in-the-Hole, Clerkenwell, was styled "His Majesty's Bear-Garden" in 1700, and was the scene of bull and bear baiting, wrestling, and boxing; but it was neglected for Figg's Amphitheatre, in Oxford Road:

> "Long liv'd the great Figg, by the prize-fighting swains
> Sole monarch acknowledged of Marybone plains."

At Tothill Fields, Westminster, was, in 1793, a noted bear-garden, a portion of which now forms Vincent Square.

BOWLS was formerly a popular game in the metropolis: it succeeded archery before Stow's time, when many gardens of the City and its suburbs were converted into bowling-alleyes; our author, in 1579, wrote:—"Common bowling-alleyes are privy mothes that eat up the credit of many idle citizens, whose gaynes at home are not able to weigh downe theyr losses abroad;" elsewhere he says:—"Our bowes are turned into bowls." The game of bowls, however, is as old as the 13th century, and in the country was played upon greens; but the alleys required less room, and were covered over, so that the game could be played there in all weathers, whence they became greatly multiplied in London. Bowls was played by Henry VIII., who added to Whitehall "tennise-courtes, bowling-alleys, and a cock-pit."

Spring Garden, St. James's, had its ordinary and bowling-green kept by a servant of Charles the First's Court, and Piccadilly Hall, at the corner of Windmill-street and Coventry-street, had its upper and lower bowling-greens.

In the last century, Bowls was much played in the suburbs, especially at Marybone Gardens, mentioned by Pepys in 1668 as "a pretty place." Its bowling-greens were frequented by the nobility, among whom was Sheffield, Duke of Buckingham, to whose partiality for the game Lady Mary Wortley Montague refers in the line—

> "Some dukes at Marybone bowl time away."

The place grew into disrepute, and was closed in 1777; it is made by Gay a scene of Macheath's debauchery in the *Beggar's Opera.*

The grave John Locke, in one of his private journals (1679) records "bowling at Marebone and Putney by persons of quality; wrestling in Lincoln's Inn Fields on summer evenings; bear and bull baiting at the Bear-Garden; shooting in the longbow and stob-ball in Tothil Fields."

Greens remain attached to a few old taverns round London. In the town, bowling-alleys were abolished in the last century, and gave rise to long-bowling, or bowling in a narrow inclosure at nine pins upon a square frame. The ball-games next merged into cricket.

Bowling-street, Westminster, commemorates the spot where the members of the Convent of St. Peter amused themselves at bowls.

CARD-PLAYING would appear to have become early a favourite pastime with the Londoners; for in 1643 a law was passed, on a petition of the cardmakers of the city, prohibiting the importation of playing-cards. It was a very fashionable court amusement in the reign of Henry VII.; and so general, that it became necessary to prohibit by law apprentices from using cards, except in the Christmas holidays, and then only in their masters' houses. Agreeable to this privilege, Stow, speaking of the customs at London, says, "From Allhallows Eve to the day following Candlemas-day, there was, among other sports, playing at cards, for counters, nails, and points, in every house, more for pastime than for gayne." Whist, in its present state, was not played till about 1730, when it was much studied by a set of gentlemen who frequented the Crown coffee-house in Bedford Row.

The name of "Hells," applied in our time to gambling-houses, originated in the room in St. James's Palace formerly appropriated to Hazard being remarkably dark, and on that account called "hell."

A few years ago there were more of these infamous places of resort in London than in any other city in the world. The handsome gas-lamp and the green or red baize door at the end of the passage (as well known a sign as the Golden Cross or Spread Eagle) were conspicuous objects in the vicinity of St. James's; and of St. George's, Hanover Square: and the nuisances still linger about the Regent's Quadrant and Leicester Square; notwithstanding, for the suppression of gaming, the police are armed with the power of breaking into the houses of her Majesty's lieges at all hours of the day and night.

COCK-FIGHTING was a London pastime in 1190, and very fashionable from *temp.* Edward III. almost to our time. Henry VIII. added a cock-pit to Whitehall Palace, where James I. went to see the sport twice a-week; this pit being upon the site of the present Privy Council Office: hence the Cockpit Gate, built by Holbein, across the road at Whitehall. Besides this Royal Cockpit, there were formerly a Cockpit in Drury Lane, now corrupted to Pitt-place, and where was the Cock-pit or Phœnix Theatre. There were other Cockpits, in Jewin-street, Cripplegate, and near Bedford Row, whence the Cockpit Yards there; and another in Shoe Lane, *temp.* James I., whence Cockpit Court in that neighbourhood; and another noted Cockpit was "behind Gray's Inn." Hogarth's print best illustrates the brutal refinement of the Cock-fight-ing of the last century; and the barbarous sport is, we believe, encouraged at some low haunt in Westminster, not far distant from the spot where in kindred pastime Royalty relieved the weighty cares of state. Cock-fighting is now forbidden and punishable by statute.

CRICKET.—This noble game, first mentioned in 1719, was played by the "White Conduit" and other clubs before 1780, when the Maryle-bone Club was formed, and Lord's Ground was established by Thomas Lord. The latter is in St. John's Wood Road, and is about 7¼ acres in extent, and devoted almost exclusively, in May, June, and July, to the matches and practice of the Marylebone Club; in 1850, consisting of 578 members, with Prince Albert as patron; at the annual meeting, early in May, the Laws of Cricket are revised, and matches for the season arranged. Attached to Lord's Ground are a Tennis Court and Baths.

Among the other principal Cricket Grounds are the Oval (larger than Lord's), near Kennington Church: the Royal Artillery Ground, Finsbury, is, perhaps, the oldest Ground in London; for here a match was played between Kent and All England in 1746. There are also grounds in Copenhagen Fields; at the Brecknock Arms, Camden Town; at Brixton, near the church; adjoining the New Cattle Market, Isling-ton; in Lord Holland's Park, Kensington; and the Scholars' Ground, Vauxhall Bridge Road: here "the Westminster Boys" play: their cricket-flag bears "R. S. W.," surrounded by the motto, *In Patriam Populumque.* (See *The Cricketer's Manual,* by "Bat," 1850.)

DUCK-HUNTING with Dogs was a barbarous pastime of the last century in the neighbourhood of London, happily put an end to by the want of ponds of water. St. George's Fields was a notorious locality for this sport; hence the infamous Dog and Duck Tavern and Tea Gardens, from a noted dog which hunted ducks in a sheet of water there: Hannah More makes it a favourite resort of her Cheapside Apprentice. The premises were afterwards let to the School for the Indigent Blind, and were taken down in 1812, when Bethlem Hospital was built upon the site; in its front wall is preserved the original sign-stone of a Dog with a Duck thrown across his back. Ingenious lesson this, of setting up a memorial of profligacy and cruelty upon a site devoted to the restoration of reason!

EQUESTRIANISM appears to have been a favourite amusement with the Londoners for nearly a century past. One of the first performers was Thomas Johnson, who exhibited in a field behind the Three Hats, at Islington, in 1758; he was succeeded by one Sampson, in 1767, whose wife was the first female equestrian performer in England. In the same year, rode one Price at Dobney's Gardens, nearly opposite the Belvidere Tavern, Pentonville, and where Wildman exhibited his docile Bees, in 1772. About this time, Hughes established himself in St. George's Fields, and Astley in Westminster Bridge Road, the latter being succeeded by Ducrow and Batty. Horses in England were taught dancing as early as the 13th century; but the first mention of feats on horseback occurs in the Privy Purse expenses of Henry VIII.

FAIRS.—The three great Fairs of old London belonged, in Catholic times, to the heads of religious houses: Westminster to its abbot; and St. Bartholomew and Southwark, (or St. Mary Overie, as it is oftener called,) to the priors of those monasteries.

Westminster, or St. Edward's, Fair, (held on that Saint's Day,) was commanded by proclamation of Edward III. in 1248; it was first held in St. Margaret's Churchyard, and then was removed to Tothill Fields, where the Fair continued to be held so lately as 1823.

Two Fairs were held in Smithfield at Bartholomew-tide: that within the Priory precincts was one of the great Cloth Fairs of England: the other Fair was held in the field, and granted to the City of London, for cattle and goods. The latter remains, but is limited to one day, and has nearly as few booths and stalls.

Southwark Fair was held on St. Margaret's Hill, on the day after Bartholomew Fair; and was by charter limited to three days, but usually lasted fourteen. Evelyn records among its wonders, monkeys and asses dancing on the tight rope, and the tricks of an Italian wench, whom all the Court went to see. Pepys tells of its puppet-shows, especially that of Whittington, and of Jacob Hall's dancing on the ropes. The Fair was suppressed in 1762; but it lives in one of Hogarth's prints.

St. James's Fair, held in the month of May, in Brook Field, gave name to "May Fair." It was abolished in 1709; but was revived, and was not finally suppressed until late in the reign of George III.

Fairs have been occasionally held in Hyde Park; as at Coronations, and the Peace Commemoration in 1814.

FIREWORKS, for pastime, are rarely spoken of previous to the reign of Elizabeth; when the foyste, or galley, with a great red dragon, and "wilde men casting of fire," accompanied the lord-mayor's barge upon the Thames. A writer in the reign of James I. assures us there were then "abiding in the city of London men very skilful in the art of pyrotechnie, or of fireworkes:" which were principally displayed by persons fantastically dressed, and called Green Men. In the last century, the train of Artillery displayed annually a grand firework upon Tower Hill on the evening of His Majesty's birthday. Fireworks were exhibited regularly at Marybone Gardens and at Ranelagh; but not at

Vauxhall until 1798, and then but occasionally. At Bermondsey Spa, and various tea-gardens, they have since been displayed, in inferior style. There have been some grand exhibitions at the Government expense: as in the Green Park at the Peace of Aix-la-Chapelle, in 1748; and on August 1, 1814, in celebration of the general Peace, and the Centenary of the accession of the Brunswick family to the British throne; these Fireworks being by Sir William Congreve, of "rocket" celebrity. There have been similar Firework galas in Hyde Park at coronations. At the Coronation of King William IV. and Queen Adelaide, Sept. 1831, the amount expended for Fireworks and for keeping open the public theatres was 3,034*l*. 18*s*. 7*d*.

At the Surrey Zoological Gardens, Walworth, there have been Fireworks since 1837.

FOOT-BALL was played in the twelfth century by the youth of the City in the fields; and five centuries later, we find foot-ball players in Cheapside, Covent Garden, and the Strand.

HUNTING.—"The Common Hunt" dates from a charter granted by Henry I. to the citizens to "have chaces, and hunt;" and Strype, so late as the reign of George I., reckons among the modern amusements of the Londoners, "riding on horseback, and hunting with my Lord Mayor's hounds, when the Common Hunt goes out." The Epping Hunt was appointed from a similar charter granted to the citizens.

Stow describes a visitation of the Lord Mayor Harper, and other civic authorities, to the Tyburn Conduits, in 1562, when "afore dinner they hunted the hare and killed her," at the end of St. Giles's, with great hallooing and blowing of horns.

MASQUERADES were introduced into England from Italy in 1512-13, by Henry VIII. They were frequent among the citizens at the Restoration. In 1717-18, a very splendid masquerade was given at the Opera House by Heidegger, at which there was high play; heaps of guineas passing about with as little concern in the losers as in the winners. Soon after, the Bishops preached against these amusements, which led to their suppression, 9 George I., 1723. They were, however, revived, and carried to shameful excess by connivance of the Government, and in direct violation of the laws. At Ranelagh, and the Pantheon in Oxford Road, the most costly masquerades were given. At the Pantheon, in 1783, a masquerade was got up by Delpini, the famous clown, in celebration of the Prince of Wales attaining his majority; tickets, three guineas each. In the same year, Garrick attended a masked fête at the Pantheon as King of the Gipsies. In the present day, a masquerade is a dull affair: as Steele remarks: "the misfortune of the thing is, that people dress themselves in what they have a mind to be, and not what they are fit for."

MAYINGS AND MAY-GAMES were celebrated by "the citizens of London of all estates" with Maypoles and warlike shows, "with good archers, morrice-dancers, and other devices for pastime, all day long; and towards evening they had stage-plays and bonfires in the streets." The games were presided over by the Lord and Lady of the May, decorated with scarves, ribands, and other finery; to which were added Robin Hood and Maid Marian.

May-poles were regularly erected in many parts of London on May-day morning: as in Leadenhall Street (then Cornhill), before the south door of St. Andrew's Church, therefore called *Under-Shaft;* this pole being referred to by Chaucer as "the great Shaft of Cornhill:" it was higher than the church-steeple (91 feet). After Evil-May-day, in 1517, the pole was, in 1549, sawn into pieces, and burnt as "an idol." Another celebrated May-pole was that placed in the Strand, upon the site of the present church of St. Mary : this pole was 134 feet high, and was set up with great pomp and festivity in 1661 ; but, becoming old and decayed, in 1717 it was obtained by Sir Isaac Newton, then of the parish, and conveyed in 1718 to Sir Richard Child's park at Wanstead, as a stand for a telescope presented by Mons. Hugon to the Royal Society. The custom of milkmaids wearing head-dresses of silver dishes, tankards, and crosses, intermixed with flowers, on May-day, is certainly as old as the reign of Queen Anne. Yet, how different is all this from the youths of the city on May-morning going out into the fields, which then stretched just outside the city-walls, to "fetch in May ;" and the city maidens gathering May-dew ; and the sober citizens all up betimes, walking forth into the "green meadows to rejoice their hearts with the sweet melody of the birds," as worthy Master Stow says.

THE PARKS had their pastimes upwards of two centuries ago. The French game of Paille-mall, (striking a ball with a wooden mallet through an iron ring,) was introduced in the reign of Charles I. Skating was first introduced into England on the new canal in St. James's Park. Evelyn enters it, 1st Dec. 1662, "with scheets after the manner of the Hollanders." Pepys records, 10th Aug. 1664, Lords Castlehaven and Arran running down and killing a stout buck in St. James's Park for a wager, before the King ; and Evelyn enters, 19th Feb. 1666-67, a wrestling match for 1000*l.* in St. James's Park, before his Majesty, a world of Lords, and other spectators, 'twixt the western and northern men, when the former won. At this time, there were in the Park flocks of wild fowl breeding about the Decoy, antelopes, an elk, red-deer, roebucks, stags, Guinea fowls, Arabian sheep, &c. ; and here Charles II. might be seen playing with his dogs and feeding his ducks. In one of St. James's Park walks, in 1770, Tom Brown tells us, there walked a beau bareheaded, here a French fop, there a cluster of senators talking of state affairs and the price of corn and cattle, disturbed by cries of "A Can of Milk, Ladies ; A Can of Red Cows' Milk, Sir."

St. James's Park has long been deserted as a fashionable promenade, which it was sixty years since. "The Mall," wrote Theodore Hook, "is now only useful as a thoroughfare from Whitehall to Pimlico ; and evening promenade there is none, for the strongest possible reason, that the class of persons who give the tone to society dine at the hour at which their grandfathers supped, and dress for dinner at the period when their ancestors, two centuries since, were undressing for bed. But the beautiful garden has superseded the swampy meadow, and the Dutch canal within the inclosure is thronged in the summer evenings with those who *have* dined, and enjoy themselves as much as those who have not."

Hyde Park was celebrated for its deer-hunts, foot and horse races, musters and coach races, boxing-matches, and Mayings.

Poaching was common in the metropolis three centuries since ; for, in a proclamation of Henry VIII., 1546, (preserved in the library of the Society of Antiquaries), the King is desirous to have the "Games of Hare, Partridge, Pheasant, and Heron," preserved from Westminster palace to St. Giles's-in-the-Fields, &c.

PIGEONS are kept in vast numbers in and round the metropolis : many persons convert the spaces between the garrets and roofs of their houses into lofts, by making an aperture in the tiling, which opens on a platform fixed on the outside. The cats should, however, be kept out by fences. But there are other enemies : pigeon-poachers set traps to decoy their neighbours' pigeons ; and "it is calculated that we have in London upwards of 2000 men thus graduating for the penal settlements." Hundreds of pigeon-traps are set on a Sunday morning : the gains are small, but the excitement is great, much artifice and patience being essential to success; at the utmost, "a green dragon" may produce 2s., or "a fine pouter" 5s. Great numbers of pigeons, too, are lost during the winter, by the slight falcon taking up its abode every year, from October and November until the spring, upon Westminster Abbey, and other churches. Pigeons build about these and other edifices; they have made nests at Somerset House, both on the side towards the water and inland, for the last sixty years; the birds are blue, but whether originally wild, or returned to their wild habits from the domesticated state, is uncertain. Carrier-Pigeons are kept in London as messengers to the race-course and the prize-ring, and for stock-jobbing transactions: in 1830, a pigeon flew from London to Maestricht, 260 miles, in 6½ hours. In Hogarth's print of the Execution of the Idle Apprentice, a pigeon is flying off with the intelligence of the felon's death. Pigeon-shooting is extensively practised in the neighbourhood of London : the crack shots assemble at the Red House at Battersea on matches of importance, when rarely a single bird escapes the shooter. To describe the varieties of tame pigeons, as tumblers, croppers, jacobins, runts, spots, turbits, owls, nuns, &c., would fill a volume.

PRISON BARS, OR BASE, is as old as the reign of Edward III., when it was, by proclamation, prohibited to be played in the avenues of the Palace at Westminster during the session of Parliament, from its interruption of the members and others in passing to and fro. About 1780, a grand match at base was played in the fields behind Montague House, by twelve gentlemen of Cheshire against twelve of Derbyshire, for a considerable stake.

PUPPET-SHOWS were common at the suburban fairs in the early part of the last century; they also competed with the larger theatres, until they were superseded by the revival of pantomimes. But the Italian Fantoccini was popular early in the present century. The puppet-showman, with his box upon his back, is now rarely seen in the street; but we have the artist of Punch, with his theatre. Clockwork figures appeared early in the last century. In the reign of Queen Anne, a celebrated show of this kind was exhibited at the great house in the Strand over against the Globe Tavern, near Hungerford Market. A saraband, danced with castanets, and throwing balls and knives alternately into the air and catching them as they fall, with catching oranges upon forks, formed part of the puppet-showman's exhibition.

Men and monkeys dancing upon ropes, or walking upon wires; dogs dancing minuets, pigs arranging letters so as to form words at their master's command, hares beating drums, or birds firing off cannons,— these were favourite exhibitions early in the last century. Raree-shows, ladder-dancing, and posturing, are also of this date.

"PUNCH" has for nearly two centuries delighted the Londoners; there being entries of Punchinello's Booth at Charing Cross, 1666, in the Overseers' Books of St. Martin's-in-the-Fields. (Cunningham's Handbook, 2d edit.). His costume closely resembles the Elizabethan peasecod-bellied doublets. Covent Garden was another of Punch's early locations, where Powel's performances thinned the congregation in St. Paul's Church, as we learn from No. 14 of the Spectator; and in 1711-12, he lessened the receipts at the opera and the national theatres : the showman worked the wires, and by a thread in one of Punch's chops, gave to him the appearance of animation. Such was the olden contrivance: at present, the puppets are played by putting the hand under the dress, and making the middle finger and thumb serve for the arms, while the fore finger works the head. Mr. Windham, when one of the Secretaries of State, on his way from Downing Street to the House of Commons, was seen to stop and enjoy the whimsicalities of Punch; and in 1850, we frequently saw Punch exhibiting for the special amusement of an infant Duke in Piccadilly.* Punch has not, however, been always a mere puppet; for we read of a farce called " Punch turned Schoolmaster ;" and in 1841, was commenced " Punch; or the London Charivari," which attained circulation co-extensive with our language, and is known to have effected high moral service, besides giving a tone to our lighter literature. George Cruikshank's " Punch and Judy," published in 1828, and Haydon's picture, painted in 1830, are truthful illustrations of Punch.

RACKETS is nearly coeval with Tennis, which it so much resembles; Rackets being striking a ball against a wall, and Tennis dropping a ball over a central net. There are Racket-grounds at the Belvidere, Pentonville; and in the Queen's Bench Prison. Rackets was also much played in the Fleet Prison, taken down in 1844.

At Westminster School is a paved court for playing the game.

SKITTLES, corrupted from kayles of the fourteenth century, and afterwards kettle, or kittle-pins, was much played in and near London until 1780, when the magistrates abolished all Skittle-grounds. To this succeeded Nine-holes, or " Bubble-the-justice," on the supposition that it could not be set aside by the justices, as it was not named in the prohibitory statutes: it is now called " Bumble-puppy," and the vulgarity of the term is well adapted to the company who play it. Nine-pins, Dutch-pins, and Four-corners are but variations of Skittles; and as these games originated in the covering of open grounds in London and its neighbourhood with houses, they will probably be forgotten when additional parks and walks are provided for public recreation.

TEA-GARDENS were the favourite resorts of the middle classes in the last century; and, in most cases, they succeeded the promenades of mineral springs. Such was Bagnigge Wells, Cold Bath Fields, taken down a few years since: we remember its concert-room and organ, its grottoes, and fountains, and grotesque figures, and bust of Nell Gwynne, who is said to have had a country-house near this spot. Next were "Sadler's Wells Music House," before it became a theatre; Tunbridge Wells, or Islington Spa; and the Three Hats, at Islington, mentioned in Bickerstaff's comedy of the *Hypocrite*: the house remained a tavern until 1839, when it was taken down. White Conduit House, Pentonville,

* Street Shows and Performers have become very numerous in the present day. Such are Punch, Fantoccini, Chinese Shades, and Galantee Shows; jugglers, conjurors, balancers, posturers, stiff tumblers, pole-balancers, salamanders or fire-eaters, and sword and snake swallowers; street dancers; and performances of trained animals, as dancing dogs, acting birds, and mice. The street musicians include brass and other bands, Ethiopians, farm-yard fiddlers, horse organs, Italian organ-boys, hurdy-gurdy players, blind and crippled fiddlers, and violoncello and clarionet players. Next are the peep-showmen and the proprietors of giants, dwarves, industrious fleas, alligators, "happy families," and glass ships; together with street telescopes, microscopes, thaumascopes, and weighing, lifting, and measuring machines. Porsini and Pike were celebrated Punch exhibitors: the former is said to have frequently taken 10l. a-day; but he died in St. Giles's workhouse. A set of Punch figures costs about 15l., and the show about 3l. The speaking is done by a "call," made of two curved pieces of metal about the size of a knee-buckle, bound together with black thread, and between them is a thin metal plate. Porsini used a trumpet. The present artists maintain that "Punch is exempt from the Police Act." The most profitable performance is that in houses; and Punch's best season is in the spring, and at Christmas and Midsummer: the best " pitches" in London are in Leicester-square, Regent-street (corner of New Burlington-street), Oxford Market, and Belgrave-square. There are sixteen Punch and Judy frames in England, eight of which work in London. *Fantoccini* are puppets, which, with the frame, cost about 10l. *Chinese Shades* consist of a frame like Punch's, with a transparent curtain and movable figures; shewn only at night, with much dialogue.—*Selected from a Letter by Henry Mayhew; Morning Chronicle*, May 16, 1850.

was originally built in the fields, in the reign of Charles I., and named from a conduit in an adjoining meadow: here Topham, the Strong Man, frequently exhibited his feats; it was originally a small ale and cake house, but was lately so extensive as to dine upwards of 2000 persons in its largest room. An association of Protestant Dissenters, formed in the reign of Queen Anne, met at this house; the Wheel Pond, close by, was a famous place for duck-hunting; Sir William Davenant describes a city wife going to the fields to "sop her cake in milke;" and Goldsmith speaks of tea-drinking parties, with hot rolls and butter, at White Conduit House. A description of the place in 1774 presents a general picture of the Tea-Garden of that period: " The garden is formed into walks, prettily disposed. At the end of the principal one is a painting, which seems to render it (the walk) longer in appearance than it really is. In the centre of the garden is a fish-pond. There are boxes for company, curiously cut into hedges, adorned with Flemish and other paintings. There are two handsome tea-rooms, one over the other, and several inferior ones in the house." The fish-pond was soon after filled up, and its site planted, the paintings removed, and a new dancing and tea saloon, called the Apollo-room, built. In 1826, the gardens were opened as a " Minor Vauxhall;" and here Mrs. Bland, the charming vocalist, last sung in public. In 1832, the small house, the original tavern, was taken down, and rebuilt upon a much larger plan; but in 1849 these premises were also taken down, and re-erected on a smaller scale, and the garden-ground let on building leases.

Next we reach Highbury, where originally stood the *Barn* of the Monks of Clerkenwell: hence the old name of the Tavern, Highbury Barn. Opposite Pentonville Prison is Copenhagen House, (Coopen Hagen, in Camden's *Britannia*, 1695,) first opened by a Dane.

Toten Hall, at the north-west extremity of Tottenham Court Road, was the ancient court-house of that manor, and subsequently a place of public entertainment. In the parish books of St. Giles's-in-the-Fields, year 1645, is an entry of Mrs. Stacye's maid and others being fined "for drinking at Tottenhall Court on the Sabbath daie, xij*d*. a-piece." The premises next became the Adam and Eve Tea-Gardens. Before the house is laid the scene of Hogarth's March to Finchley; and in the grounds, May 16, 1785, Lunardi fell with his burst balloon, and was but slightly injured. The Gardens were much frequented by respectable company; but the place falling into disrepute, the music-house was taken down, and upon the site of the Skittle-grounds and Gardens was built Eden Street, Hampstead Road, the public-house being rebuilt.

Chalk Farm was "the White House," to which, in 1678, the body of Sir Edmundberry Godfrey was carried, after it had been found about two fields distant, upon the south side of Primrose Hill. Chalk Farm is still a white-washed tavern, with a tea-garden, and a field where wrestling is occasionally exhibited. Several duels have been fought here: here John Scott, (of the *London Magazine*), was shot by Mr. Christie, Feb. 16, 1821; and here the poet Moore, and Jeffrey, of the *Edinburgh Review*, met in 1806.

The above were the most celebrated Tea-Gardens north and north-west of London. Westward lay Marybone Gardens, opened for public breakfasts and evening concerts to high-class company; fireworks being added. In 1777-8 these gardens were shut up, and the site let to builders; the ground being now occupied by Beaumont and Devonshire Streets, and part of Devonshire Place. Next were the Bayswater Gardens, once the " Physic Garden" of Sir John Hill; and Ranelagh, the costly rival of Vauxhall, but a Tea-Garden in the present century. Mulberry Garden, upon the present site of Buckingham Palace and its gardens, dates from *temp*. Charles I.; Pimlico was noted for its tea-gardens and ale to our day. Southward were Cumberland Gardens, the site now occupied by Price's Candle Company's Works, Vauxhall Bridge; Spring Garden, Vauxhall; the Dog and Duck, and Apollo Gardens, St. George's Fields; Cuper's Gardens, through the site of which runs Waterloo Bridge Road. Bermondsey had its Spa Gardens in the Grange Road; and Cupid's Gardens upon Jacob's Island, the ill-fated locality in which the cholera (1848-9) first broke out in the metropolis, and where it lingered last.

Few of these old Tea-Gardens remain. In the increase of London within the last half century, the environs have lost their suburban character, and have become part of the great Town itself; and steamboats and railways now, for very small sums, convey the over-worked artisan out of its murky atmosphere into pure air and rural scenery.

TENNIS, from the French Hand-ball or Palm-play, was played in London in the sixteenth century, in covered courts erected for the purpose. Henry VII. and VIII. were fond of Tennis; and the latter added to the palace of Whitehall "tennise-courts." James I. recommended Tennis to his son, as becoming a prince. Charles II. was an accomplished Tennis-player, and had particular dresses for playing in. We have a relic of these times in the Tennis-court in James Street, Haymarket, which bears the date 1676, and was formerly attached to the gaming-house, or Shavers' Hall, or Piccadilly Hall. Another famous Tennis Court was Gibbon's, in Clare Market, where Killigrew's comedians performed for some time. There are in Holborn, Blackfriars, and Southwark thoroughfares known as "Tennis Court," denoting the game to have been formerly played there.

THAMES SPORTS.—Fitzstephen relates of the ancient Londoners. fighting "battles on Easter holidays on the water, by striking a shield with a lance." There was also a kind of water tournament, in which the two combatants, standing in two wherries, rowed and ran against each other, and fought with staves and shields. In the game of the water quintain, the shield was fixed upon a post in the river, and the champion, stationed in a boat, struck the shield with a lance. Justing upon the ice was likewise practised by the young Londoners. Each mansion upon the Thames banks had its private retinue of barges and wherries, and the sovereign his gilded and tapestried barge. Stow. computes there to have been in his time 2000 small boats, that there were 40,000 watermen upon the rolls of the company, and that they could furnish 20,000 men for the fleet. All that we have left of the gay water pageants are the state barges of the Sovereign and the Admiralty, the Lord Mayor, and a few of the wealthier City companies. In 1850, the old Barge of the Goldsmiths' Company was let at Richmond, "for Pic-nic, Wedding, and Birthday Parties," at 5l. 5s. per day.

Of Boat-races, the oldest is that for Dogget's Coat and Badge, on August 1. We have also Regattas and Sailing Matches, to aid in the enjoyment of which steamers are employed.

THEATRES originated in Miracle Plays, such as were acted in fields and open places and inn-yards. The playhouse dates from the age of Elizabeth; and between 1570 and 1629, London had seventeen theatres. (See THEATRES.)

APOLLONICON, (THE),

A magnificent musical machine, constructed upon the principle of the organ; the sound being produced by a current of air urged by bellows through several series of vertical pipes, so as closely to imitate all the most admired wind instruments, with the effect of a full orchestra. It is the invention of Messrs. Flight and Robson, who spent five years in its completion. There are about 250 keys, upwards of 1900 pipes,

45 draw-stops, and 2 kettle-drums : the largest double-diapason pedal-pipe is twenty-four feet long and twenty-three inches square, being eight feet longer than the corresponding pipe in the great organ at Haarlem. The mechanism is enclosed in a case twenty-four feet high, embellished with pilasters and paintings of Apollo, Clio, and Erato. The Apollonicon was first exhibited at the inventors' house, 101 St. Martin's Lane, in June 1817.

APOTHECARIES' HALL,

In Water Lane, Blackfriars, at the east end of Union Street, Bridge-street, was built for the Company of Apothecaries, in 1670. Here are several portraits, including James I., Charles I., William and Mary, and a bust of Gideon Delaune, who brought about the separation of the Company from the Grocers'. Adjoining the Hall are laboratories, warehouses, drug-mills, and a retail shop for the sale of medicines to the public. Here are prepared medicines for the army and navy.

On June 4, 1842, Mr. H. Hennell, the principal Chemical Operator to the Apothecaries' Company, met a terrific death in the laboratory-yard, by the explosion of between five and six pounds of fulminating mercury, which he was manufacturing for the East India Company.

The Apothecaries rank as the 58th in the list of City companies. Their arms are azure, Apollo in his glory, holding in his left hand a bow, and in his right an arrow, bestriding the serpent Python; supporters, two unicorns; crest, a rhinoceros, all or; motto, *Opiferque per orbem dicor.*

ARCADES.

Only a few of these covered passages (series of arches on insulated piers,) have been constructed in London; although Paris contains upwards of twenty *passages* or *galleries* of similar design.

BURLINGTON ARCADE, on the west side of Burlington House, and leading from Piccadilly to Burlington Gardens, was built by Samuel Ware, in 1819. It consists of a double row of shops, with apartments over them, a roof of skylights, and a triple arch at each end; it is about 210 yards long, and the shops, seventy-two in number, produce to the noble family of Cavendish 4000*l*. a-year; though the property, by sub-letting and otherwise, is stated to yield 8640*l*. a-year.

EXETER CHANGE (the second building of the name, but on a differ-ent site from the first,) is on the estate of the Marquis of Exeter, and runs obliquely from Catherine-street to Wellington-street North, Strand. It was designed by Sydney Smirke; and consists of a polygonal compart-ment at each extremity, the intermediate passage being about twelve feet in width, by sixty in length, and twenty in height, coved and groined, and lighted from above, and containing ten neat shops, with dwellings over. The cove, fascia, piers, &c., have polychromic arabesque deco-rations; at each entrance to the Arcade is an imitation bronze gate; and the fronts in Catherine-street and Wellington-street are of fine red brick, with stone dressings, in the style of the street architecture of the reign of James I.

LOWTHER ARCADE (named from Lord Lowther, Chief Commis-sioner of the Woods and Forests when it was built,) leads from the triangle of the West Strand to Adelaide-street, north of St. Martin's Church. It was designed by Witherden Young, and far sur-passes the Burlington Arcade in architectural character: the ceiling vista of small pendentive domes is very beautiful, and the caducei in the angles are well executed. The length is 245 feet, breadth 20 feet, and height 35 feet. The sides consist of twenty-five dwellings and shops, principally kept by dealers in foreign goods, who, by mu-tual consent, hold in the avenue a sort of fair for German and French

C

toys, cheap glass, and jewellery, &c. At the north end of the Arcade is the Adelaide Gallery, where Mr. Jacob Perkins exhibited his Steam Gun; and a living Electrical Eel was shewn from August, 1838, to March 14, 1843, when it died; and in 1832 was formed here a Society for the Exhibition of Models of Inventions, &c. The rooms were subsequently let for concerts; dancing, &c.

THE PIAZZA OR ARCADE OF COVENT GARDEN was designed about 1631, for Francis Earl of Bedford; but only the north and east sides were built, and half of the latter was destroyed by fire about the middle of the last century. The northern was called the Great Piazza, the eastern side, the Little Piazza: Inigo Jones probably took his idea from an Italian city, Bologna, for instance. "The proportions of the arcades and piers, crossed with elliptical and semi-circular arches into groins, are exquisitely beautiful, and are masterpieces of architecture." (*Elmes*.)

The elevation was originally built with stone pilasters on red brick, which have been for many years covered with compo' and white paint. Properly speaking, the term *Piazza* (place, Ital.) is only applicable to the enclosed area or square, the covered portion being strictly an Arcade.

The Arcade in the rear of Her Majesty's Theatre has no architectural pretension; but the Arcade in the front of this theatre is a good specimen of Italian architecture, by Nash; and the colonnades of fluted Doric columns in the centre and sides are of iron, cast at the Butterley Foundry, Derbyshire, and worth notice.

ARCHÆOLOGICAL SOCIETIES.

There are two Societies to aid the study of the Arts and Monuments of the Middle Ages: 1. The British Archæological Association, established 1843 (apartments, 32, Sackville-street, Piccadilly). 2. Archæological Institute of Great Britain and Ireland, established 1843 (apartments, 26, Suffolk Street, Haymarket). Each Society holds weekly or monthly meetings; publishes its Journal; has local secretaries; and meets annually in a different cathedral town, where a Museum of Antiquities is exhibited, and whence excursions are made to sites of archæological interest in the neighbourhood. Subscription to each Society, one guinea a-year.

ARCHES.

London differs essentially from many other European capitals in the paucity of its Arches, or ornamental gateways. It has only three grand triumphal Arches; whereas Paris, not half the size of our metropolis, has four magnificent Arches, and the principal entrances are graced with trophied gateways and storied columns. The last erected of the Parisian arches is the *Arc de l'Etoile*, without exception, the most gigantic work of its kind either in ancient or modern times; within its centre arch would stand eight such structures as Temple Bar, that is, four in depth, and as many above them: it cost 416,666*l.*

BUCKINGHAM-PALACE ARCH, St. James's Park, reserved for the especial entrance of the Sovereign and the Royal Family, was the largest work of mere ornament ever attempted in Great Britain. It was adopted by Nash from the arch of Constantine at Rome, and has a centre gateway and two side openings; the larger archway, as first designed, was not sufficiently wide to admit the royal state-coach; fortunately, the blunder was discovered in time to be remedied. The material is Carrara marble, which soon became discoloured by smoke and damp, so as to resemble in appearance dirty sugar. In each face are four Corinthian columns; the other sculpture being a keystone to the centre archway, and a pair of figures in the spandrils, a panel of figures over each side entrance, and wreaths at each end: these are by Flaxman, Westmacott, and Rossi. The centre gates, designed and cast by Samuel Parker of Argyll-street, are the largest and most superb in Europe, not excepting those of the Ducal Palace at Venice, and of the Louvre at Paris. They are of a beautiful alloy, the base refined copper, bronzed; design, scroll-work, with six circular openings, two filled with St. George and the Dragon, two with G. R., and above, two lions *passant-gardant;* height to the top of arch, 21 feet; width, 15 feet; extreme thickness, 3 inches; weight 5 tons 6 cwt.; cost, 3000 guineas, including a frieze and semicircle, to fill up the archway, the most beautiful portion of the design, but irretrievably mutilated in removal from the foundry. This Arch was not included in the design for building the new front to the Palace.

THE GREEN PARK ARCH, at Hyde Park Corner, was built by Decimus Burton in 1828. It is Corinthian, and each face has six fluted pilasters, with two fluted columns, flanking the single archway, raised upon a lofty stylobate, and supporting a richly-decorated entablature, in which are sculptured alternately G. R. IV. and the imperial crown, within wreaths of laurel. The soffite of the arch is sculptured in sunk panels. The gates, by Bramah, are of massive iron scroll-work, bronzed, with the royal arms in a circular centre. Within the pier of the arch are porter's apartments, and stairs ascending to the platform, where, upon a vast slab, laid upon a brick arch, the colossal equestrian statue of the Duke of Wellington was placed Sept. 30, 1846. The height of the arch, its attic, and platform is about 90 feet; of the statue, 30 feet. (*See* STATUES.)

Opposite the above arch is the elegant entrance to Hyde Park, by three carriage archways and sides, in a screen of fluted Ionic columns, of 107 feet frontage, designed and built by Decimus Burton, in 1828. The blocking of the central archway has a beautiful frieze (Grecian naval and military triumphal processions), designed by the son of Mr. Henning, known for his successful models of the Elgin marbles. The gates, by Bramah, are a beautiful arrangement of the Grecian honeysuckle in bronzed iron; the hanging, by rings of gun-metal, is very ingenious.

Altogether, these two Park entrances, with St. George's Hospital north, and the Duke of Wellington's palatial mansion south, form the finest architectural group in the metropolis, and its most embellished entrance. Sir John Soane, however, proposed two triumphal arches, connected by a colonnade and arches, stretching across the main road— a design of superb grandeur. (*See* TEMPLE BAR.)

ARGYLL ROOMS,

Regent Street, a large house purchased by Col. Greville, of sporting notoriety, and converted into a place of public entertainment, where balls, concerts, and masquerades were much patronised by the *haut ton.* In 1818, the Rooms were rebuilt in handsome style, by Nash, at the north corner of Little Argyll Street, Regent Street: they were burnt down in February, 1830, when Mr. Braithwaite first publicly applied steam-power to the working of a fire-engine; it required eighteen minutes to raise the water in the boiler to 212°, when the engine threw up from thirty to forty tons of water per hour to a height of ninety feet.

At the Argyll Rooms, June 9, 1829, Signor Velluti, the *contralto* singer, gave a concert. In the same year, M. Chabert, "the Fire-King," exhibited here his power of resisting the effects of poisons, and withstanding extreme heat. He swallowed 40 grains of phosphorus, sipped oil at 333° with impunity, and rubbed a red-hot shovel over his tongue, hair, and face unharmed. Sept. 23, on a challenge of 50*l.*, Chabert repeated these feats, and won the wager; he next swallowed a piece of a burning torch; and then, dressed in coarse woollen, entered an oven heated to 380°, sang a song, and cooked two dishes of beef-steaks! Still, the performances were suspected, and in part proved, to be a chemical juggle.

ARTESIAN WELLS

Have been bored in various parts of the metropolis, the London basin being thought well adapted for them; there being on it a thick lining of sand, and a deep bed of "London blue clay," on boring which the water rises to various heights. With this view the New River Company sunk a vast well at the foot of their reservoir in the Hampstead Road: the excavation was steined with brick, 12 ft. 6 in. in diameter, and then reduced and continued with iron cylinders, (like those of a telescope), to 183 feet. The expense was 12,412*l.*; but the supply of water was too inconsiderable for the purpose.

Artesian Wells are mostly formed by boring and driving pipes, varying from 6 to 10 inches or more in diameter; but many of these only enter the sand immediately below the clay, instead of obtaining the supply of water from the chalk. Thus, an Artesian Well sunk in Covent Garden for more than fourteen years failed to supply the ordinary wants of the Market; but having been deepened and carried ninety feet into the chalk, it yielded an abundant supply, and is constantly worked, without materially reducing the level of the water, or lowering it in neighbouring wells, as in cases where the chalk is not reached. It has been long known that Calvert's well, in the Thames-street Brewery, and Barclay's well at the Southwark Brewery, affect each other so much—even though the Thames lies between them—that the two firms have agreed not to pump at the same time.

The following are the depths of a few of the Wells bored in London: Berkeley Square, 320 feet; Meux's Brewery, 180 feet; Reid and Co.'s, Liquorpond-street, 260 feet; Whitbread and Co.'s, Chiswell-street, 160 feet; Combe and Co.'s, Castle-street, Long Acre, 190 feet; Covent Garden Market, 340 feet; Calvert and Co.'s, 240 feet; Barclay and Co.'s, 367 feet; Piccadilly (St. James's Church), 240 feet; Elliot's Brewery, Pimlico, 390 feet; Royal Mint, Tower Hill, 400 feet. The Trafalgar Square Wells, 300 feet and 400 feet deep, supply the two *jets d'eau* at the rate of 500 gallons a minute; and the Admiralty, Treasury, Houses of Parliament, &c., at the rate of 100 gallons a minute, for ten hours in the day, at an outlay of 9000*l.*, and an annual rental of 500*l.*

Dr. Buckland, the eminent geologist, states that, although there are from 250 to 300 so-called Artesian Wells in the metropolis, there is not one *real Artesian Well* within three miles of St. Paul's; such being a well that is always overflowing, either from its natural source or from an artificial tube; and when the overflowing ceases, it is no longer an Artesian Well. The wells which are now made by boring through the London clay are merely common wells. It has been said that a supply of water, if bored for, will rise of its own accord; but the water obtained for the fountains in Trafalgar Square does not rise within forty feet of the surface, and is pumped up by means of a steam-engine—the same water over and over again. Dr. Buckland maintains that the supply of water formerly obtained from the so-called Artesian Wells in London has been greatly diminished by the sinking of new wells; of the more than 250 wells, one-half have broken down, and others are only kept in action at an enormous expense. The average depth at which water can be obtained from these defective wells is 60 feet below the Trinity House water-mark.

ARTILLERY COMPANY (ROYAL).

This Company originated in the body of volunteers known as the City Trained Band, raised in 1585, at the period of the menaced Spanish invasion; and within two years there were enrolled nearly 300 merchants and others, capable of training and teaching the common soldiers. They exercised in "the Old Artillery Ground," originally a field called Tassel Close, then let for archery practice, and next enclosed with a wall for the Gunners of the Tower to exercise in. After 1588, the City Artillery neglected their discipline; but in 1610 they formed anew, and in a few years numbered nearly 6000. In 1622, they removed to a larger Ground, without Moorgate, the present Artillery Ground, west of Finsbury Square.

In the Civil War, the Company "behaved themselves to wonder" against the King. In 1657, they numbered 12,000; and at the Restoration 18,000, when they were disbanded. They, however, still continued their evolutions; and the King and the Duke of York became members, the latter taking upon himself the command, and naming it his own Company. The sovereign or heir-apparent has usually been the Captain-General: Prince George of Denmark, George I. (who gave the Company 500*l.*), George II., and George IV. (when Prince of Wales), held the command; as did William IV., succeeded by the Duke of Sussex, upon whose death the command was accepted by Prince Albert.

The last time the Company were in active service was at the Riots of 1780, when they aided in saving the Bank of England from the pillage of the mob. In case of civil disturbances being apprehended, they muster at their head-quarters, the Artillery Ground, Finsbury. Here are the spacious Armoury House, finished in 1735; and some fine pieces of ordnance, including a pair of very handsome brass field-pieces, presented by Sir William Curtis, Bart., President; besides portions of the ancient costume and arms of the corps, as caps and helmets, pikes and banners. The motto of the Company's ensign is *Arma Pacis fulcra*—Arms are the maintenance of Peace. The corps comprises six companies of Infantry, besides Artillery, Grenadiers, Light Infantry, and Yagers. They exercise on occasional field-days in the Artillery Ground, and meet for rifle practice in the vicinity of the metropolis, the prize being a large gold medal.

Upon royal visits to the City, the Artillery Company attend as a guard of honour to the sovereign: as, on Nov. 9, 1837, when Queen Victoria dined in Guildhall; and Oct. 28, 1844, when Her Majesty opened the New Royal Exchange.

ART-UNION OF LONDON,

A Society established 1836, and incorporated by 9th and 10th Vict., c. 48, "to aid in extending the love of the Arts of Design within the United Kingdom, and to give encouragement to artists beyond that afforded by the patronage of individuals." The annual subscription is one guinea, which entitles the subscriber to one chance for a prize in a scheme, in 1850 ranging from 10*l.* to 200*l.*, to be selected from one of the London exhibitions of the year. There are also prize medals and statuettes; and every subscriber is entitled to a print or prints.

In 1836, when the Art-Union was organised, the subscriptions did not amount to 500*l.*; in 1837, they were 757*l.* 1*s.*; 1839, 1295*l.* 14*s.*; 1840, 2244*l.* 18*s.*; 1841, 5562*l.* 18*s.*; 1842, 12,905*l.* 11*s.*; 1845, 15,440*l.* 5*s.*; and in 1847 (the largest amount), 17,871*l.*; 1850, 11,180*l.* 8*s.*; the works of art allowed as prizes varying from 13 to upwards of 700. The Society has about 400 local Honorary Secretaries in the provinces, in the British Colonies, in America, &c., including Canton; it has expended about 150,000*l.* in the purchase and production of works of art; and in one morning, one of its Honorary Secretaries (Mr. G. Godwin, F.R.S.) has paid to artists of the metropolis no less than 10,000*l.* The drawing of the prizes is usually held in Drury Lane Theatre, in April, and the subscribers are admitted by tickets: office, 445 West Strand.

ASHBURNHAM HOUSE,

Little Dean's Yard, Westminster, is one of the best specimens of the mansions built by Inigo Jones, though omitted by his biographers. It is named from John Ashburnham, the faithful attendant of King Charles I.: it was purchased by the Crown, in 1730, of John Earl of Ashburnham, when the Cottonian Library was removed here from a house in Essex-street; and upwards of two hundred volumes were lost or irretrievably damaged in a fire, Oct. 23, 1731, when also Dr. Bentley lost some valuable MSS. which he had been collecting for ten years for his Greek Testament.

Ashburnham House was long the prebendal residence of the Rev. H. H. Milman, appointed to the deanery of St. Paul's in 1849. The small garden alcove, the ornamental ceiling of the drawing-room, the finely-proportioned dining-room, and an exquisite staircase, lighted by an elegant cupola, denote the taste of Inigo Jones. " In the cellars, it is said, were some remains of conventual buildings, and a capital of the time of King Edward the Confessor, which was built into the modern wall." (Walcott's *Westminster*, 1850.)

AVIARIES.

A few ingenious individuals in the metropolis and its suburbs constructed Aviaries in or adjoining their houses, long before " Zoological Gardens" were thought of. Such was the Aviary of Mr. Purland, 59 Mortimer-street, Cavendish Square—a room 18 by 19 feet, lit from above, and seen from the verandah of his Museum of Antiquities. In this space, from forty to fifty song-birds flew about and sung; the walls were painted with landscapes, and the floor hidden by imitative rocks, hills, forests, and paddocks, intersected by a mimic river, in which were living fish. Interspersed were models of celebrated houses, castles, and ruins, windmills in activity, soldiers, country-people, with cows and sheep, crossing bridges, and other automata; all to be enjoyed with the songs of the lark, robin, siskin, linnet, redpole, bulfinch, greenfinch, thrush, &c. Another Aviary was constructed by Mr. W. A. Foster in the house wherein Mrs. Barbauld wrote her beautiful Hymns, in Church-street, Stoke Newington. This Aviary was more *native* than Mr. Purland's: it was 25 feet long, 8 feet wide, and 12 feet high, had net-work sides and top, and was placed in a flower-garden, so that the birds enjoyed grassy banks, gravel paths, live shrubs, stumps of trees, rock-work, a stream, a pool, and a fountain. Here were blackbirds, thrushes, skylarks, woodlarks, titlarks, siskins, redstarts, linnets, robins, nightingales, canaries, with nearly all " the finches of the grove;" and here a skylark has bred—very unusual in captivity.

In the Saracenic Conservatory of the Pantheon in Oxford Street are Aviaries, with Java sparrows, canaries, and other birds of brilliant plumage, for sale; and fine collections of birds are to be seen at dealers'.

BALLOON ASCENTS.

The following are the more memorable Balloon Ascents made from the metropolis since the introduction of aerostation into England. In most cases, the aeronauts were accompanied by friends, or persons who paid for the trip various sums.

Nov. 25, 1783, the first Balloon, (filled with hydrogen), launched in England, from the Artillery Ground, Finsbury, by Count Zambeccari.

Sept. 15, 1784, Lunardi ascended from the Artillery Ground, Moorfields; being the first voyage made in England.

Mar. 23, 1785, Admiral Sir Edw. Vernon, accompanied by Count Zambeccari.

June 29, 1785, ascent of Mrs. Sage, the first Englishwoman aeronaut.

July 5, 1802, M. Garnerin made his second ascent in England, from Lord's Cricket Ground; the same year he ascended three times from Ranelagh Gardens.

Sept. 21, 1802, M. Garnerin descended successfully from a Balloon by a Parachute, near the Small-pox Hospital, St. Pancras.

1811, James Sadler ascended from Hackney; his two sons, John and Windham, were also aeronauts; the latter killed, Sept. 29, 1824, by falling from a balloon.

July 19, 1821, Mr. Charles Green first ascended in a Balloon inflated with coal gas, on the Coronation-day of George IV. Cost of inflation, from 25*l.* to 50*l.* This was Mr. Green's first aerial voyage. Up to May 1850 he had made 142 ascents from London only. Ten persons named Green have ascended in balloons.

May 25, 1824, Lieut. Harris, R. N., ascended from the Eagle Tavern, City Road, with Miss Stocks; the former killed by the too rapid descent of the balloon.

July 2, 1833, Mr. Graham ascended from Hungerford Market; day of opening.

Sept. 17, 1835, Mr. Green ascended from Vauxhall Gardens, and remained up during the night.

August 22, 1836, the Duke of Brunswick.

Sept. 9, 1836, Mr. Green's first ascent in his great Vauxhall Balloon.

Nov. 7, 1836, Mr. Green, Mr. Monck Mason, and Mr. Holland ascended in the great Vauxhall Balloon, and descended, in eighteen hours, at Weilburg in Nassau.

July 24, 1837, Mr. Green ascended in his great Balloon, with Mr. Cocking in a parachute, from Vauxhall Gardens; the latter killed in descending.

May 24, 1838, unsuccessful attempt to ascend with a large Montgolfier Balloon from the Surrey Zoological Gardens. The balloon destroyed by the spectators. It was the height of the York Column, and half the circumference of the dome of St. Paul's; and would contain, when fully inflated, 170,000 cubic feet of air.

Sept. 10, 1838, Mr. Green and Mr. Rush ascended from Vauxhall Gardens in the Nassau Balloon, and descended at Lewes, Sussex; having reached the greatest altitude ever attained,—27,146 feet, or 5 miles 746 feet.

July 17, 1840, the Vauxhall, or Great Nassau Balloon, sold to Mr. Green for 500*l.*, in 1836 it cost 2100*l.*

August 19, 1844, Mr. Hampton ascended from White Conduit House.

July 6, 1847, Perilous night descent of Mr. Gypson's Balloon, from bursting, at Vauxhall. Night ascents, with displays of fireworks, are now common.

May 24, 1850, Mr. H. Bell ascended from the Phœnix Gas Works, Kennington, in an "Aerial Machine," shaped like an elongated egg, which he propelled with a single screw, and steered by an apparatus for nearly thirty miles, and descended safely at High Laver, Essex; though a lad, in assisting him, was so injured by the grapnel that he died.

BANK OF ENGLAND (THE)

Is an insulated assemblage of buildings and courts, occupying three acres, on the north side of the Royal Exchange, Cornhill; bounded by Prince's-street, west; Lothbury, north; Bartholomew-lane, east; and Threadneedle-street, south. Its exterior measurements are 365 feet south, 410 feet north, 245 feet east, and 440 feet west. Within this area are nine open courts, a spacious rotunda, numerous public offices, court and committee-rooms, an armoury, engraving and printing offices, a library; apartments for officers, servants, &c.

The Bank, "the greatest monetary establishment in the world," was projected, in 1691, by Mr. William Paterson, a Scotsman: established by a company of Whig merchants, and incorporated by William III., July 27, 1694, Paterson being placed on the list of Directors for this year only; the then capital, 1,200,000*l.*, being lent to Government.

The first Governor was Sir John Houblon, whose house and garden were on the site of the present Bank; and the first Deputy-Governor was Michael Godfrey, who, July 17, 1695, was shot at the siege of Namur, while attending King William upon the Bank affairs.

The Bank commenced business at Mercers' Hall, and next removed to Grocers' Hall, then in the Poultry; at this time the secretaries and clerks numbered but 54, and their united salaries amounted to 4350*l.* In 1734, they removed to their own establishment, part of the present Bank, built by Sampson. On Jan. 1, 1735, was set up the marble statue of William III., by Cheere, in the Pay Hall, 79 feet by 40 feet, which, in the words of Baron Dupin, would "startle the administration of a French bureau, with all its inaccessibilities."

In 1757, the Bank premises were small, and surrounded by St. Christopher-le-Stocks Church, (since pulled down), three taverns, and several private houses: and the first chest used (somewhat larger than a seaman's,) was shewn to visitors. Between 1766 and 1786, east and west wings were added by Sir Robert Taylor, upon whose death, in 1788, Sir John Soane was appointed Architect to the Bank; and, without any interruption to the business, he completed the present Bank of brick and Portland stone, of incombustible materials, insulated, one-storied, and without external windows. The general architecture is Corinthian, from the Temple of the Sybil at Tivoli, of which the south-west angle exhibits a fac-simile portion. The Lothbury court is very fine; and the chief cashier's office is from the Temple of the Sun and Moon at Rome. The embellishments throughout are very beautiful; and the whole well planned for business. The Rotunda has a dome 57 feet diameter; and the Bank-Parlour, where the Governor and Company meet, is a noble room by Taylor. Here the Dividends are declared; and here the Directors are *baited* half-yearly by every Proprietor who has had 500*l.* Bank stock in his possession for six months. In the Parlour lobby is a portrait of Daniel Race, who was in the Bank service for more than half a century, and thus amassed upwards of 200,000*l.* In the ante-chamber to the Governor's Room are fine busts of Pitt and Fox, by Nollekens. The ante-room to the Discount Office is adapted from Adrian's Villa at Tivoli. The private Drawing Office, designed in 1836, by Cockerell (Soane's successor), is original and scenic; and the Drawing Office, completed by the same architect in 1849, is 138 feet 6 inches long, and lit by four large circular lanterns. In 1850, the Cornhill front was heightened by an attic; and a large room fitted up as a library for the clerks.

The entrance to the Bullion Yard is copied from Constantine's Arch at Rome, and has allegories of the Thames and Ganges, by T. Banks, R.A. The Bullion Office, on the northern side of the Bank, consists of a public chamber and two vaults,—one for the public deposit of bullion, free of charge, unless weighed; the other for the private stock of the Bank. The duties are discharged by a Principal, Deputy-Principal, Clerk, Assistant-Clerk, and porters. The public are on no account allowed to enter the Bullion Vaults. Here the gold is kept in bars, (each weighing 16 lbs., and worth about 800*l.*,) and the silver in pigs and bars, and dollars in bags. The value of the Bank bullion in May 1850 was sixteen millions. This constitutes, with their securities, the assets which the Bank possess against their liabilities, on account of circulation and deposits; and the difference between the several amounts is called "the Rest," or balance in favour of the Bank. For weighing, some admirably constructed machines are used: the larger one, invented by Mr. Bate, for weighing silver in bars from 50 lbs. to 80 lbs. troy; second, a balance, by Sir John Barton, for gold; and a third, by Mr. Bate, for dollars, to amounts not exceeding 72 lbs. 2 oz. troy.

In the Weighing Office, established in 1842, to detect light gold, is the ingenious machine invented by Mr. W. Cotton, then Deputy-Governor of the Bank. About 80 or 100 light and heavy sovereigns are placed indiscriminately in a round tube; as they descend on the machinery beneath, those which are light receive a slight touch, which moves them into their proper receptacle; and those which are of legitimate weight pass into their appointed place. The light coins are then defaced by a machine, 200 in a minute; and by the weighing-machinery 35,000 may be weighed in one day. There are six of these machines, which from 1844 to 1849 weighed upwards of 48,000,000 pieces without any inaccuracy. The average amount of gold tendered in one year is nine millions, of which more than a quarter is *light*. The silver is put up into bags, each of one hundred pounds value, and the gold into bags of a thousand; and then these bagsful of bullion are sent through a strongly guarded door, or rather window, into the Treasury, a dark gloomy apartment, fitted up with iron presses, supplied with huge locks and bolts.

The Bank-note machinery invented by the Oldhams, father and son, exerts, by the steam-engine, the power formerly employed by the mechanic in pulling a note. The Bank-notes are numbered on the dexter and sinister halves, each bearing the same figures, by Bramah's machines: as soon as a note is printed, and the handle reversed to take it out and put another in its place, a steel spring attached to the handle alters the number to that which should follow.

The Clock in the roof is a marvel of mechanism, as it is connected with all the clocks in the Stock Offices: the hands of the several dials indicate precisely the same hour and second, by means of connecting brass-rods, (700 feet long, and weighing 6 cwt.,) and 200 wheels; the principal weight being about 350 lbs.

The Bank has passed through many perils: it has been attacked by rioters, its notes have been at a heavy discount, it has been threatened with impeachment, and its credit has been assailed by treachery. In 1696 (the great re-coinage), the Directors were compelled to suspend the payment of their notes. They then increased their capital to 2,201,271*l.* The Charter has been renewed, 1697 to 1711; 1708 to 1733; 1712 to 1743; 1742 to 1765; 1763 to 1786; 1781 to 1812; 1800 to 1833; and 1833, by Act of 3 and 4 Wm. IV., c. 98, the Charter was renewed until 1855.

The earliest panic, or *run*, was in 1707, upon the threatened invasion of the Pretender. In the run of 1745, the Corporation were saved by their agents demanding payment for notes in sixpences, and who paying in the same, thus prevented the *bonâ-fide* holders of notes presenting them. Another memorable run was on February 26, 1797, upon an alarm of invasion by the French, when the Privy Council Order and the Restriction Act prohibited the Bank from paying cash, except for sums under 20*s.* During the panic of 1825, from the evidence of Mr. Harman before Parliament, it appears that the quantity of gold in the treasury, in December, was under 1,300,000*l.* It has since transpired that there was not 100,000*l.*, probably not 50,000*l.*! The Bank then issued one-pound notes, to protect its remaining treasure; which worked wonders, though by sheer good luck: "because one box containing a quantity of one-pound notes had been overlooked, and they were forthcoming at the lucky moment."

The Bank is the treasury of the Government; for here are received the taxes, the interest of the National Debt paid, the Exchequer business transacted, &c.; for all which the Bank is paid a per-centage or commission, annually about 120,000*l.*; with the profit derived from a floating balance due to the public, never less than four millions sterling, which, employed in discounting mercantile bills, yields 160,000*l.* yearly.

"The Old Lady of Threadneedle Street," applied to the Bank, is a political *sobriquet* now almost forgotten.

The forgeries upon the Bank supply a melancholy chapter in its history. The first forger of a note was a Stafford linendraper, who, in 1758, was convicted and executed. Through the forgeries of one person, Robert Astlett, the Bank has lost 320,000*l.*; and by another, (Fauntleroy,) 360,000*l.*

In the Riots of 1780, the Bank was defended by military, the City volunteers, and the officers of the establishment, when the old inkstands were cast into bullets. It was attacked by the mob, when Wilkes rushed out and seized some of the ringleaders. Since this date, a military force has been stationed nightly within the Bank; a dinner is provided for the officer on guard and two friends. In the political tumult of November, 1830, provisions were made at the Bank for a state of siege. At the Chartist Demonstration of April 10, 1848, the roof of the Bank was fortified by Sappers and Miners, and a strong garrison within.

The Committee of Treasury sit weekly, and is composed of all the Directors who have passed the chair, except Mr. George Warde Norman, whose great information as to the circulation qualifies him to sit, although he has never been Governor. The Accountant, the Secretary, and the Cashier reside within the Bank; and a certain number of Clerks sit up nightly to go the round of the building, in addition to the military guard. The number of Clerks was, in 1850, 700; and the salaries amounted to about a quarter of a million annually.

The Bank possess a very fine collection of ancient coins. Visitors are shewn some bank-notes for large amounts which have passed between the Bank and the Government, including a single note for One Million sterling.

Notes of the Bank, at its establishment, 20 per cent discount; in 1745 under par. Bank Bills paid in silver, 1745. Bank Post Bills first issued, 1754. Small Notes issued, 1759. Cash Payments discontinued, Feb. 25, 1797, and Notes of 1l. and 2l. put into circulation. Cash Payments partially resumed, Sept. 22, 1817. Restriction altogether ceased, 1821. May 14, 1832, upwards of 300,000l. weighed and paid to bankers and others. Quakers and Hebrews not eligible as Directors. Qualification for Director, 2000l. Bank Stock; Deputy-Governor, 3000l.; Governor, 4000l. Highest price of Bank Stock, 299; lowest 91. The Bank has paid Dividends at the rate of 21 per cent, and as low as 4½ per cent, per annum. Silver Tokens issued, Jan. 1798. Issue on paper securities not permitted to exceed 14,000,000l. Capital Punishment for forgery, excepting only forgeries of wills and powers of attorney, abandoned in 1832. — (See Francis's popular *History of the Bank of England*, 3d edit. 1848.)

BANK, LONDON AND WESTMINSTER.

This banking-house, facing the north-east angle of the Bank of England, in Lothbury, has some striking architectural merits. It was completed in 1838; architects, Cockerell and Tite. It occupies eighty feet frontage, and ninety feet depth: the front, of Portland stone, is one plane, or general face, and proves that a splendid building may be erected without columns or pilasters. The windows are set, as it were, between piers; the lower ones divided by bronzed candelabra, and the upper ones having side-panels, decorated with caducei and fasces, expressive of the *vis unita fortior* of the joint-stock association of the establishment. The attic story has a cornice and balustrade, which give dignity to the whole façade. At the extremities are bold piers, surmounted by sitting figures—the City of London at the east end, and the City of Westminster at the west; both modelled by Cockerell, and executed by Nichol.

The interior is very original: the principal apartment, the "Town Bank," exceeds even the offices of the Bank of England in height; it is a square of about thirty-four feet, as high as the entire building, fifty-nine feet six inches. East and west are aisles to a portion of this height, with balustraded galleries; their sides being divided from the centre by an arcade springing from Doric columns; and the vast hall, surrounded closely with lofty buildings, is mainly lighted by a dome and semicircular Diocletian windows from above. Cost of the building, about 50,000l.

BARBICAN,

A spacious thoroughfare, connecting Finsbury Square with Aldersgate-street, and named from a burgh-kenin, barbican, or watch-tower, where now is the Watchhouse; the same being built on high ground, and of some good height: from thence "a man," says Stow, "might behold and view the whole city towards the south, and also into Kent, Sussex, and Surrey, and likewise every other way, east, north, or west." Here also were the mansions of the Bridgewater family and Sir Thomas Wriothesley, Garter-King-at-Arms; whence *Brackley*-street and *Garter*-court.

BARCLAY AND PERKINS' BREWERY,

In Park-street, Southwark, is the largest establishment of its class in the kingdom, or in the world. It may be inspected by a letter of introduction to the proprietors; and a large number of the foreigners of distinction who visit the metropolis avail themselves of such permission.

The Brewery and its appurtenances occupy about twelve acres of ground, immediately adjoining Bankside, and extending from the land-arches of Southwark Bridge nearly half of the distance to those of London Bridge. Within the Brewery walls is said to be included the site of the famous Globe Theatre, "which Shakspeare has bound so closely up with his own history:" in a history of the neighbourhood, dated 1795, it is stated that "the passage which led to the Globe Tavern, of which the playhouse formed a part, was, till within these few years, known by the name of Globe-alley, and upon its site now stands a large storehouse for porter." We are inclined to regard this evidence as traditional. However, the last Globe Theatre was taken down about the time of the Commonwealth; and so late as 1720, Maid-lane (now called New Park-street), of which Globe-alley was an offshoot, was a long straggling place, with ditches on each side, the passage to the houses being over little bridges, with little garden-plots before them.— (*Strype's Stow.*)

Early in the last century there was a Brewery here, comparatively very small: it then belonged to a Mr. Halsey, who, on retiring from it with a large fortune, sold it to the elder Mr. Thrale; he became Sheriff of Surrey and M.P. for Southwark; and died in 1758, leaving his property to a son, the friend of Dr. Johnson, who, from 1765 to the brewer's death, lived at the Brewery, and at his villa at Streatham. Before the fire at the Brewery, in 1832, a room was pointed out, near the entrance gateway, which the Doctor used as a study, and wherein he wrote part of his Dictionary. In 1781, Mr. Thrale died; and as he had no sons, his executors, of whom Dr. Johnson was one, sold the Brewery jointly to Mr. Barclay and Mr. Perkins (the latter of whom had been superintendent of the Brewery,) for the sum of 135,000*l.*; and the property is now held by the descendants of those gentlemen. The concern in Thrale's time must have been comparatively small, for he did not brew annually more than one-twelfth part of the quantity now brewed by the same establishment. Nevertheless, we remember it of considerably less extent, about thirty years since. In 1832 a great portion of the old premises was destroyed by fire, but was rebuilt; mostly of iron, stone, and brick.

Having crossed by Southwark Bridge to the Surrey side, we descend from Bridge-road to New Park-street, which is flanked by lofty buildings, connected by a covered bridge or passage; these are ranges of malthouses, extending northward, with a wharf to Bankside. At the termination of New Park-street we proceed southward, through Park-street, both sides of which are the Brewery buildings, connected by a light suspension-bridge; to the right is the vast brewhouse and principal entrance. From the roof of nearly the middle of the premises may be had a bird's-eye view of the whole.

The water used for brewing is that of the river Thames, pumped up by a steam-engine through a large iron main, which passes under the malt warehouses, and leads to the "liquor-backs," two cisterns, which, as well as their supporting columns, are of cast-iron, and reach an elevation of some 40 feet. By this means the establishment may be supplied with water for brewing to the extent of a hundred thousand gallons daily. There is on the premises an Artesian well 367 feet deep; but its water, on account of its low temperature, is principally used for cooling the beer in hot weather.

The machinery is worked throughout the Brewery by steam; there are two of Boulton and Watt's engines, of 45 and 30 horse power, the latter constructed in 1780. The furnace-shaft is 19 feet below the surface, and 110 feet above; and, by its great height, denotes the situation of this gigantic establishment among the forest of Southwark chimneys.

The malt is carried from barges at the river-side by porters, and deposited in enormous bins, each of the height or depth of an ordinary three-storied house. There are few rats here, for they betake themselves to the strong drinks elsewhere on the premises; but they are all kept in check by a standing army of cats, some forty-five in number, who are regularly fed and maintained.

The malt is conveyed to be ground in tin buckets upon an endless leather band, ("Jacob's Ladder"); and thus carried to the height of 60 or 70 feet, in the middle of the Great Brewhouse. This stupendous room is built entirely of iron and brick, and is lighted by eight large and lofty windows. There is no continuous floor; but looking upwards, whenever the steamy vapour permits, there may be seen at various heights, stages, platforms, and flights of stairs, all subsidiary to the cyclopean piles of brewing vessels. The coals, about 20 tons per day, are drawn up from below by tackle, and wheeled along a railway; and the smoke from all the furnaces is conveyed by a large subterranean flue to the great chimney-shaft already mentioned.

West of the Brewhouse are large buildings, with cooling floors, into which is pumped the hot wort, or beer. The surface of one floor is not less than 10,000 square feet; and, in case of need, the men wear gigantic pattens to cross the vast lakes of beer. Sometimes, the beer is more rapidly cooled by passing a refrigerator in close contact with cold spring water.

Both porter and ale are brewed in the large Brewhouse; but the ale is carried by pipes along the suspension-bridge, across Park-street, to the opposite building, and is there cooled, fermented, and tunned.

The cold beer is fermented in vast rooms, or squares, one of which will hold 1500 barrels. The surface of one of these squares nearly filled is a strange sight; the yeast rises in rock-like masses, which yield to the least wind, and the gas hovering in pungent mistiness over the ocean of beer.

The beer is next conveyed to the tun-room, where are nearly 300 cylindrical vessels, or rounds, each holding upwards of 300 gallons; and sunk in the floor is a tank, 100 feet by 20 feet. The beer is then conducted through large pipes to "No. 9," where are 180 stupendous tuns, in 16 storehouses. One of the largest of these vats will contain about 3500 barrels of porter, which, at the selling price, would yield 9000l. The "Great Tun of Heidelberg" holds but half this quantity. The average capacity of the vats, large and small together, is upwards of 30,000 gallons. From them the beer is drawn by hose into butts, of 108 gallons each. The aggregate number of casks used by the Brewery exceeds 60,000.

The Large Brewhouse has been known to work throughout the

year, Sundays and seven breaking-days excepted. Often 600 quarters of malt are brewed daily.

There are 180 horses employed in the cartage department. They are brought principally from Flanders, and cost from 50l. to 80l. each. There are annually consumed by these horses 5000 quarters of oats, beans, or other grain, which are bruised, 450 tons of clover, and 170 tons of straw for litter. The manure, spent hops, and other refuse, are let yearly ; and the lessee employs a railway company to take them from the premises to his farm. There are four partners in this house : they pay their head brewer a salary of 1000l. The following is a statement of the malt used by several of the principal London brewers in 1849, which is an average for some years past :—

	Qrs.		Qrs.
Barclay, Perkins, and Co.	115,542	Calvert and Co.	29,630
Hanbury and Co.	105,022	Mann and Co.	24,030
Meux and Co.	59,617	Charrington and Co.	22,023
Reid and Co.	56,640	Thorne and Co.	21,016
Whitbread and Co.	51,800	Taylor and Co.	15,870
Combe and Co.	43,282		

BAROMETER (THE) IN LONDON.

The average monthly readings of the Barometer in London, as found from the observations made at the Royal Society, are as follow :

	inches.		inches.		inches.
Jan.	29·82	May	29·85	Sept.	29·83
Feb.	29·80	June	29·88	Oct.	29·81
March	29·84	July	29·86	Nov.	29·76
April	29·82	Aug.	29·86	Dec.	29·79

Hence the greatest monthly mean reading of the Barometer occurs in June, and the least in November.

The following table shews the difference of the mean reading of the Barometer in different years in the same months :

Month.	Mean reading.		Diff. of readings.	Month.	Mean reading.		Diff. of readings.
	Greatest.	Least.			Greatest.	Least.	
	inches.	inches.	inches.		inches.	inches.	inches.
Jan.	30·26	29·45	0·81	July	30·12	29·62	0·50
Feb.	30·26	29·40	0·86	Aug.	30·08	29·59	0·49
March	30·22	29·39	0·83	Sept.	30·05	29·59	0·46
April	30·17	29·48	0·69	Oct.	30·15	29·44	0 71
May	30·10	29·63	0·47	Nov.	30·20	29·40	0·80
June	30·13	29·75	0·38	Dec.	30·28	29·43	0·85

Thus, we see that the mean monthly reading of the Barometer in the winter months, between one year and another, exceeds three-quarters of an inch; and that in the summer months the difference is less than half an inch. The month of February seems to be subject to the greatest change, and the month of June to the least.

The annual range of readings is nearly two inches. The reading is sometimes almost as low as 28 inches, and at times as high as 31 inches nearly. In February, 1849, the reading of the Barometer was unusually high; and for a long time its mean reading, from the 1st to the 18th, was 30·55 inches, or fully half an inch above its average value. On the day this very high reading ended at London, the Barometer reading at Boston in America began to increase; and during the following eighteen days, the reading there was at the same value as it was at London from Feb. 1 to Feb. 18. This great atmospheric wave, therefore, seems just to have reached from England to America; and its rate of motion appears to have been the same whilst passing over both countries.

Barometers, hitherto rare, and confined to the cabinets of virtuosi, were first sold publicly in the metropolis by Jones, a clockmaker, of Inner Temple Lane, who made the instrument at the suggestion of Lord Keeper Guildford.

BARTHOLOMEW FAIR

Originated in two Fairs or Markets, proclaimed on the Eve of St. Bartholomew, and continued during the next day and the next morrow. One Fair was granted to the Priory of St. Bartholomew, in Smithfield, for the clothiers of England and the drapers of London, who had their booths and standings within the Priory churchyard (the site now Cloth Fair), the gates of which were locked every night and watched, for the safety of the goods and wares. The grant is by some referred to Henry II.; but there is a charter from Henry I., granting "free peace" to all persons frequenting the fair of St. Bartholomew. Within its limits was also held a Court of Pie-poudre, by which persons infringing upon the laws of the Fair, its disputes, debts, &c., were tried the same day, and the punishment of the stocks or whipping-post summarily inflicted. The second Fair, for cattle, stands and booths for goods, with tolls and profits, was granted to the City of London, to be held "in the field of West Smithfield." At the dissolution of religious houses, the right in the first-mentioned Fair was sold to Sir John Rich, the then Attorney-General, and was enjoyed by his descendants till the year 1830, when it was purchased of Lord Kensington by the Corporation. It greatly declined as a "Cloth Fair" from the reign of Queen Elizabeth; and the Corporation granted licenses to mountebanks, conjurors, &c., and allowed the Fair to be fourteen days, the sword-bearer and other city officers being paid out of the emoluments. Hentzner, in 1578, describes a tent pitched for the proclamation, and wrestling after the ceremony, with the crowd hunting wild rabbits for the sport of the mayor and aldermen. There was formerly a burlesque proclamation on the night before, by the drapers from Cloth Fair, snapping their shears and shouting in Smithfield.

Ben Jonson, in his play of *Bartholomew Fair*, tells us of its motions, or puppet-shows, of Jerusalem, Nineveh, and Norwich; and "the Gunpowder Plot, presented to an eighteen or twenty pence audience nine times in an afternoon." The showman paid three shillings for his ground; and a penny was charged for every burden of goods and little bundle brought in or carried out. A rare tract of the year 1641 describes the "variety of Fancies, the Faire of Wares, and the several enormityes and misdemeanours" of the Fair of that period. At these, the sober-minded Evelyn was shocked; and Pepys (Aug. 30, 1667,) found at the Fair "my Lady Castlemaine at a puppet-show," her coach waiting, "and the street full of people expecting her." The sights and shows included wild beasts, dwarfs, and other monstrosities; operas, and tight-rope dancing, and sarabands; dogs dancing the Morrice, and the hare beating the tabor; a tiger pulling the feathers from live fowls; the humours of Punchinello, and drolls of every degree. The public theatres were closed during the fair-time, the drolls finding St. Bartholomew's more profitable than Dorset Garden or old Drury Lane. An ox roasted whole, and piping-hot roast pig, sold in savoury lots, were among the Fair luxuries, the latter called Bartholomew Pigs.

At length, the fourteen days' carnival proved too long. According to Strype, in 1708, it was again restricted to three days; and in 1735, the Court of Aldermen resolved that no acting should be permitted in the Fair ; but, in 1760, the Deputy City Marshal lost his life in enforcing this regulation.

The proclamation of the Fair before the entrance to Cloth Fair was a state ceremony ; the Lord Mayor proceeding thither in his gilt coach, " with city officers and trumpets;" and on his way calling upon the Keeper of Newgate, to partake of "a cool tankard of wine, nutmeg, and sugar;" but this custom has been discontinued since the second mayoralty of Alderman Wood, in 1818.

In 1840, the entire suppression of the Fair was proposed ; when, upon the recommendation of the City Solicitor, the duration was restricted, and the prices of ground raised, so as to reduce the Fair, in 1849, to one or two stalls for ginger-bread, gambling-tables for nuts, a few fruit-barrows, toy-stalls, and one puppet-show.

Hone, in his *Every-day Book*, describes (with wood-cuts,) the Bartholomew Fair of 1825, with the minuteness of Dutch painting ; not forgetting Richardson's Show, which held nearly a thousand persons, and the rabble-rout of " Lady Holland's Mob."

BARTHOLOMEW'S (ST.) HOSPITAL,

In West Smithfield, is one of the five Royal Hospitals of the City, and the first institution of the kind established in the metropolis. It was originally a portion of the Priory of St. Bartholomew, founded by Rahere, in 1102, who obtained from Henry I. a piece of waste ground, upon which he built an hospital, for a master, brethren and sisters, sick persons, and pregnant women. Both the Priory and the Hospital were surrendered to Henry VIII., who, at the petition of Sir Richard Gresham, Lord Mayor, and father of Sir Thomas Gresham, re-founded the latter, and endowed it with an annual revenue of 500 marks, the City agreeing to pay an equal sum; since which time the Hospital has received princely benefactions from charitable persons. It was first placed under the superintendence of Thomas Vicary, sergeant-surgeon to Henry VIII., Edward VI., Mary, and Elizabeth ; Harvey was physician to the Hospital for thirty-four years; and here, in 1619, he first lectured on his discovery of the Circulation of the Blood.

The Hospital buildings escaped the Great Fire in 1666; but becoming ruinous, were taken down in 1730, and the great quadrangle rebuilt by Gibbs: over the entrance next Smithfield is a statue of Henry VIII., and under it, " St. Bartholomew's Hospital, founded by Rahere, A.D. 1102, re-founded by Henry VIII., 1546;" on the pediment are two reclining figures of Lameness and Sickness. The cost of these buildings was defrayed by public subscription, to which the munificent Dr. Radcliffe contributed largely ; besides leaving 500*l.* a-year for the improvement of the diet, and 100*l.* a-year to buy linen.

The principal entrance, next Smithfield, was erected in 1702.

The Museums, Theatres, and Library of the Hospital are very extensive; as is also the New Surgery, built in 1842. The Lectures of the present day were established by Mr. Abernethy, elected Assistant-Surgeon in 1787. Prizes and honorary distinctions for proficiency in medical science were first established in 1834; and their annual distribution in May is an interesting scene. In 1843 was founded a Collegiate Establishment for the pupils' residence within the Hospital walls. The Charity is ably managed by the Corporation : the president must have served as Lord Mayor ; the qualification of a governor is a donation of 100 guineas. The Hospital receives, upon petition, cases of all kinds free of fees ; and accidents, or cases of urgent disease, without letter at the Surgery, at any hour of the day or night. There is also a " Samaritan Fund," for relieving distressed patients. The several wards contain 580 beds; in 1849-50, patients admitted, cured, and discharged,

6146, (including 478 cases of cholera,) in-patients; besides 71,564 medical and surgical out-patients; and many of them being destitute, were supplied with money, clothes, and other necessaries, to enable them to return to their habitations.

The interior of the Hospital, besides its cleanly and well-regulated wards, has a grand staircase; the latter painted by Hogarth, for which he was made a life-governor. The subjects are the Good Samaritan; the Pool of Bethesda; Rahere, the founder, laying the first stone; and a sick man carried on a bier, attended by monks. In the Court Room is a picture of St. Bartholomew holding a knife, as the symbol of his martyrdom; a portrait of Henry VIII. in Holbein's manner; of Dr. Radcliffe, by Kneller; Perceval Pott, by Reynolds; and of Abernethy, by Lawrence.

In Jan. 1846, the election of Prince Albert to a Governorship of the Hospital was commemorated by the president and treasurer presenting to the foundation three costly silver-gilt dishes, each nearly twenty-four inches in diameter, and richly chased with a bold relief of—1. The Election of the Prince; 2. The Good Samaritan; 3. The Plague of London.

BATHS, OLDEN.

The most ancient Bath in the metropolis is "*the old Roman Spring Bath*" in Strand Lane; but evidently unknown to Stow, though he mentions the locality as "a lane or way down to the landing-place on the bank of the Thames." This Bath is in a vaulted chamber, and is formed of thin tile-like bricks, layers of cement and rubble-stones, all corresponding with the materials of the Roman wall of London: the water is beautifully clear and extremely cold.

St. Agnes-le-Clair Baths, Tabernacle Square, Finsbury, are supposed to have been of the above age, from finding the Roman tiles through which the water was once conveyed. Stow mentions them as "Dame Anne's the clear." The date assigned to these Baths is 1502.

Peerless Pool, Old-street Road, is referred to by Stow as near St. Agnes-le-Clair, and "one other clear water, called Perillous Pond, because divers youths, by swimming therein, have been drowned." In 1743, it was enclosed, and converted into a bathing-place.

Cold Bath, said to be "the most noted and first about London," is a "cold spring," discovered about 160 years since, near the top of Mount Pleasant, in Cold Bath Square, Clerkenwell.

The Duke's Bath is in Old Belton-street, now Endell-street, Long Acre; it was new-fronted in 1845, but the original exterior had red brick pilasters and cornice, in the style of Inigo Jones. There was a large plunging-bath, paved and lined with marble, the walls lined with small Dutch tiles; the water supplied from a well on the premises. This has been popularly known as "Queen Anne's Bath."

The Queen's Bagnio, in Long Acre, was on the south side, nearly opposite the door of Long Acre Chapel.

The Bagnio, in Bagnio Court (altered to Bath-street in 1843), Newgate Street, was built by Turkish merchants, and first opened in December, 1679, for sweating, hot bathing, and cupping. The bath has a cupola roof, marble steps, and Dutch tile walls, and is now used as a cold Bath. In the *Spectator*, No. 332, is mentioned another Bagnio, in Chancery Lane.

The Hummums, in Covent Garden, now an hotel, with baths, was formerly "a Bagnio, or Place for Sweating;" in Arabic "Hammam."

The Floating Baths upon the Thames in plan remind one of the Folly described by Tom Brown as "a musical summer-house," usually anchored opposite Somerset House Gardens. The Queen of William III. and her court once visited it; but it became a scene of low debauchery, and the bath building was left to decay, and be taken away for firewood.

Queen Elizabeth's Bath formerly stood among a cluster of old buildings adjoining the King's Mews, at Charing Cross, and was removed in 1831. This Bath was of fine red brick, and had a groined roof, apparently of the date of the fifteenth century. It is engraved in the *Archæologia*, xxv. pp. 588-90.

BATHS AND WASH-HOUSES

For the Working Classes originated, in 1844, with an " Association for promoting Cleanliness among the Poor," who fitted up a Bath-house and a Laundry in Glass-house Yard, East Smithfield; where, in the year ending June 1847, the bathers, washers, and ironers amounted to 84,584; the bathers and washers costing about one penny each, and the ironers about one farthing. The Association also gave whitewash, and lent pails and brushes, to those willing to cleanse their own wretched dwellings. And so strong was the love of cleanliness thus encouraged, that women often toiled to wash their own and their children's clothing, who had been compelled to *sell their hair* to purchase food to satisfy the cravings of hunger. This successful experiment led to the passing of an Act of Parliament (9 and 10 Vict. c. 74), " To Encourage the Establishment of Baths and Wash-houses." A Committee sit at Exeter Hall for the same object; a Model Establishment has been built in Goulston Square, Whitechapel; and Baths and Wash-houses have been established in St. Pancras, Marylebone, St. Martin-in-the-Fields, and other large parishes.

These measures have contributed, though not so extensively as could be wished, to better acquaintance with the art of Swimming, the neglect of which leads to much loss of life in the metropolis. It is calculated that 500 deaths occur annually in the river Thames between Richmond and Gravesend; of which one third are in the Pool. In Christ's Hospital, the scholars are sent, at stated intervals, with proper attendants, to a public bath (generally Peerless Pool), and taught to swim. Mr. J. T. Finnimore, one of the best swimmers in England, and who has won several prizes in matches across the Thames, Serpentine, &c., was educated at Christ's Hospital.

BATTERSEA,

Three miles S.W. of London, on the Surrey bank of the Thames, was the birthplace of Henry Viscount Bolingbroke, at the ancient seat of the St. Johns, a spacious mansion containing forty rooms on a floor. This was once the resort of Pope, Swift, Arbuthnot, Thomson, Mallet, and other contemporary genius of England. Bolingbroke died here in 1751, and, with his second wife, niece of Madame de Maintenon, lies in the family vault in St. Mary's Church, where there is an elegant monument by Roubiliac, with busts of the great lord and his lady; the epitaphs on both were written by Bolingbroke: that upon himself is still extant, in his own handwriting, in the British Museum. The greater part of Bolingbroke House was taken down in 1778, and on the site were erected an horizontal air-mill (now removed,) and a malt-distillery. In the wing of the mansion, left standing, a parlour of brown polished oak, with a grate and ornaments of the age of George I., was long pointed out as the apartment in which Pope composed his *Essay on Man*.

In 1816, there was living at Battersea a Mrs. Gilliard, who well remembered Lord Bolingbroke; that he used to ride out every day in his chariot, and had a black patch on his cheek, and a large wart over his eyebrows; she also had often seen Mallet the poet walking in

D

the village, while visiting at Bolingbroke House. (See Sir Richard Phillips's *Morning's Walk from London to Kew*, p. 54.)

The *horizontal mill* was erected by Captain Hooper, who also built a similar one at Margate. It consisted of a circular wheel, with large boards or vanes fixed parallel to its axis, and arranged at equal distances from each other. Upon these vanes the wind could act, so as to blow the wheel round. But if it were to act upon the vanes at both sides of the wheel at once, it could not, of course, turn it round; hence one side of the wheel must be sheltered, while the other was submitted to the full action of the wind. For this purpose it was enclosed in a large cylindrical framework, with doors or shutters on all sides, to open and admit the wind, or to shut and stop it. If all the shutters on one side were open, whilst all those on the opposite side were closed, the wind acting with undiminished force on the vanes at one side, whilst the opposite vanes are under shelter, turned the mill round; but whenever the wind changed, the disposition of the blinds must be altered, to admit the wind to strike upon the vanes of the wheel in the direction of a tangent to the circle in which they moved.—(Dr. Paris's *Philosophy in Sport*.) This mill resembled a gigantic packing-case, which gave rise to an odd story, that when the Emperor of Russia was in England, he took a fancy to Battersea Church, and determined to carry it off to Russia, and had this large packing-case made for it; but as the inhabitants refused to let the church be carried away, the case remained on the spot where it was deposited.

St. Mary's Church, a tasteless brick edifice, was rebuilt in 1776: the east window contains some finely painted glass, replaced from the old church. Christchurch, at South Battersea, is an elegant Decorated structure, designed by C. Lee, erected by subscription, and opened in 1849. Battersea Bridge was built of wood in 1771, by fifteen proprietors, but is unworthy of its position across a river spanned by some of the finest bridges in the world. In the rich alluvial soil of Battersea great quantities of asparagus are grown.

In 1846, two Acts of Parliament were passed for forming a Park and constructing a Bridge and Embankment at Battersea.

BAYNARD'S CASTLE,

A stronghold, "built with walls and rampires," on the banks of the Thames, below St. Paul's, by Bainiardus, a follower of William the Conqueror. In 1111, it was forfeited, and granted by Henry I. to Robert Fitzgerald, son of Gilbert Earl of Clare; from whom it passed, by several descents, to the Fitzwalters (the chief bannerets of London, probably in fee for this castle), one of whom, at the commencement of a war, was bound to appear at the west door of St. Paul's, armed and mounted, with twenty attendants, and there receive from the Mayor the banner of the City, a horse worth 20*l.*, and 20*l.* in money. In 1428, the castle became, probably by another forfeiture, crown property; it was almost entirely burnt, but was granted to Humphrey Duke of Gloucester, by whom it was rebuilt; upon his attainder, it again reverted to the Crown. Here Stafford, Duke of Buckingham, presented to Richard Duke of Gloster a parchment purporting to be a declaration of the three estates in favour of Richard; and in "the Court of Baynard's Castle" Shakspeare has laid scenes 3 and 7, act iii., of *King Richard III.*; the latter between Buckingham, the Mayor, Aldermen, and citizens, and Gloster. Baynard's Castle was repaired by Henry VII., and used as a royal palace until the reign of Queen Elizabeth, when it was let to the Earls of Pembroke; and here, in 1553, the Privy Council, "changing their mind from Lady Jane," proclaimed Queen Mary. The castle subsequently became the residence of the Earls of Shrewsbury. Pepys records King Charles II. supping here, 19th June, 1660; and six years after, the castle was destroyed in the Great Fire. The buildings surrounded two court-yards, with the south front to the Thames, and the north in Thames-street, where was the principal entrance. Two of the towers, incorporated with other buildings, remained till the present century, when they were pulled down to make way for the Carron Iron Company's premises.

The ward in which stood the fortress-palace is named Castle Baynard, as is also a wharf upon the site; and a public-house in the neighbourhood long bore the sign of " Duke Humphrey's Head."

BAYSWATER,

In the parish of Paddington, was long noted for its springs and conduits, which, until the present century, partly supplied London with water. In *Notes and Queries*, No. 11, it is shewn that Bainiardus, who gave his name to Baynard's Castle, held land here of the Abbot of Westminster; and in a grant of 1653 is described " the common field at Paddington," (now Bayswater Field,) as being " near to a place commonly called *Baynard's Watering*." Hence it is concluded " that this portion of ground, always remarkable for its springs of excellent water, once supplied water to Baynard, his household, or his castle; that the memory of his name was preserved in the neighbourhood for six centuries;" and that this watering-place is now Bayswater. Here was Sir John Hill's " Physic Garden;" and facing Hyde Park is a Chapel of Ease to St. George's Hanover Square, in the burial-ground of which lies Lawrence Sterne, his grave denoted by a head-stone set up by two Freemasons, and restored by a shilling subscription in 1846.

BAZAARS.

The Bazaar is an adaptation from the East, the true principle of which is the classification of trades. Thus, Paternoster-row, with its books; Newport Market, with its butchers' shops; and Monmouth-street, with its shoes; are more properly Bazaars than the miscellaneous stalls assembled under cover, which are in London designated by this name. Exeter 'Change was a great cutlery bazaar; and the row of attorneys' shops in the Lord-Mayor's Court Office, in the old Royal Exchange, were a kind of legal bazaar, the name of each attorney being inscribed upon a projecting sign-board.

The introduction of the Bazaar into the metropolis dates from 1816, when was opened the Soho Bazaar, at 4, 5, and 6, Soho-square. It was planned solely by the late Mr. John Trotter, with a benevolent motive. At the termination of the late war, when a great number of widows, orphans, and relatives of those who had lost their lives on foreign service were in distress and without employment, Mr. Trotter conceived that an establishment in the hands of Government would promote the views of the respectable and industrious, (possessing but small means,) by affording them advantages to begin business without great risk and outlay of capital. Mr. Trotter having at that time an extensive range of premises unoccupied, without any idea of personal emolument, offered them to Government, free of expense, for several years, engaging also to undertake their direction and management on the same disinterested terms. His scheme was, however, considered visionary, and his offer rejected. Mr. Trotter then undertook the whole responsibility himself; and, by excellent management, the establishment has flourished for thirty-four years, having been opened 1st February, 1816. This success is mainly attributable to the selection of persons of respectability as its inmates, for whose protection an efficient superintendence of several matrons is provided. The rent of the counters, mostly for fancy goods, is 3d. per square foot, paid daily. To obtain a tenancy, it is requisite that a testimonial, signed by eight persons, be presented, on application, to the Managers of the Bazaar. The establishment is in two floors, and, in 1850, there were from 160 to 170 tenants. These, together with many more persons employed at their homes, in connexion with the Bazaar, come within the range of its influence; and means are constantly used to afford each an opportunity of profiting by religious counsel and guidance.

The success of the Soho Bazaar led to similar establishments; and for a short time Bazaars flourished, to the injury of shopkeepers.

The WESTERN EXCHANGE, Old Bond-street (with an entrance from the Burlington Arcade), was burnt down, and not re-established.

The QUEEN'S BAZAAR, on the north side of Oxford-street, the rear in Castle-street, was destroyed, May 28, 1829, by a fire which commenced at a dioramic exhibition of "the Destruction of York Minster by Fire." The Bazaar was rebuilt; but proving unsuccessful, was taken down, and upon the site was built the present Princess' Theatre.

The PANTHEON BAZAAR, on the south side of Oxford-street, with an entrance in Great Marlborough-street, was constructed in 1834, from the designs of Sydney Smirke, A.R.A., within the walls of the Pantheon Theatre, built in 1812; the fronts to Oxford-street and Poland-street being the only remains of the original structure. The magnificent staircase leads to a suite of rooms, in which pictures are placed for sale; and thence to the great Basilical Hall or Bazaar, which is 116 feet long, 88 feet wide, and 60 feet high; it is mostly lighted from curved windows in the roof, which is richly decorated, as are the piers of the arcades, with arabesque scrolls of flowers, fruit, and birds; the ornaments of papier-maché by Bielefield. The style of decoration is from the loggias of the Vatican. The galleries and the floor are laid out with counters, and promenades between. From the southern end of the hall is the entrance to an elegant conservatory and aviary, mostly of glass, ornamented in Saracenic style. Here are birds of rich plumage, with luxuriant plants, which, with the profusion of marble, gilding, and colour, have a very pleasing effect in the heart of smoky town.

The BAZAAR in BAKER-STREET, Portman-square, was originally established for the sale of horses; but carriages, harness, furniture, stoves, and glass are the commodities now sold here. Madame Tussaud's Wax-work Exhibition occupies the greater part; and here, annually, early in December, the Smithfield-Club Cattle-Show takes place.

The PANTECHNICON, Halkin-street, Belgrave-square, is a Bazaar chiefly for carriages and furniture. Here, too, you may warehouse furniture, wine, pictures, and carriages, for any period, at a light charge compared with house-rent.

The LOWTHER BAZAAR, nearly opposite the Lowther Arcade, Strand, is a repository of fancy goods, besides a "Magic Cave," and other exhibitions. The establishment was frequently visited by Louis Philippe from 1848 to 1850. This and the house adjoining, eastward, have fronts of tasteful architectural design.

ST. JAMES'S BAZAAR, King-street, St. James's-street, was built for Mr. Crockford in 1832, and has a saloon nearly 200 feet long by 40 wide. Here were exhibited, in 1841, three dioramic tableaux of the second obsequies of Napoleon, in Paris, in December, 1841. And in 1844 took place here the first exhibition of Decorative Works for the New Houses of Parliament.

The most imposing Bazaar display was, however, that made in the spring of 1845, when the auditory and stage of Govent-Garden Theatre were fitted up as a BAZAAR for the ANTI-CORN-LAW LEAGUE, who, in six weeks, cleared 25,000*l.* by the speculation, partly by admission-money. The Theatre was painted as a vast Tudor Hall by Messrs. Grieve, and illuminated with gas in the day-time; the goods being exhibited for sale on stalls, appropriated to the great manufacturing localities of the United Kingdom. At this time, the Theatre was let to the League at 3000 guineas for the term of holding the Bazaar, and one night per week for public meetings throughout one year.

BEGGARS.

Begging, although illegal, and forbidden by one of our latest statutes, is followed as a trade in the metropolis, perhaps, more systematically than in any other European capital. It has been stated that the number of professional Beggars in and about London amounts to 15,000, more than two-thirds of whom are Irish.

The vigilance of the Police, and the exposure of Beggars' frauds by the press and upon the stage (from the *Beggar's Opera* to *Tom and Jerry*), have done much towards the suppression of Begging. The Mendicity Society, in Red Lion Square, Holborn, established in 1818, has also moderated the evil by exposing and punishing impostors, and relieving deserving persons. The receipts of this Society are upwards of 4000*l.* a year: in 1839, the applicants were 16,785; in 1840 (a severe winter), 23,117; in January and February, 1841, there were 20,903 applicants, many with large families, when 104,352 meals were given, and 1385 begging-letters investigated; and in 1840, the number of these letters was 5074. The Society has a mill, stone-yard, and oakum-room, in which, during one day, there have been employed 763 persons, who would otherwise have been begging in the streets. The Society keep a record of all begging-letter cases, from which police-magistrates obtain information as to the character of persons brought before them.

Many years ago, there died in Broad Street Buildings, aged 81, John Yardley Vernon, who wore in the streets the garb of a beggar, though he possessed 100,000*l.*, which he had realised as a stockbroker.

BELGRAVIA

Was originally applied as a *sobriquet* to Belgrave and Eaton Squares and the radiating streets, but is now received as the legitimate name of that "City of Palaces." In 1824, its site was "the Five Fields," intersected by mud-banks, and occupied by a few sheds. The clayey swamp retained so much water, that no one would build there; and the "Fields" were the terror of foot-passengers proceeding from London to Chelsea after nightfall. At length, Mr. Thomas Cubitt found the strata to consist of gravel and clay, of inconsiderable depth : *the clay he removed, and burned into bricks; and by building upon the substratum of gravel, he converted this spot from the most unhealthy to one of the most healthy,* to the immense advantage of the ground-landlord and the whole metropolis. This is one of the most perfect adaptations of the means to the end to be found in the records of the building art. In 1829, the same land, consisting of about 140 acres, was nearly covered with first and second-class houses, the nucleus being Belgrave Square, designed by George Basevi; the detached mansions, at the angles, by Hardwick, Kendall, and others; the area of the square occupying about ten acres. The level is low; for it has been ascertained that the ground-floor of Westbourne Terrace, Hyde Park Gardens, 70 feet above the Thames highwater mark, is on a level with the attics of Eaton and Belgrave Squares. Yet Chelsea acquired a proverbial salubrity in the last century by Doctors Arbuthnot, Sloane, Mead, and Cadogan residing there.

BELLS AND CHIMES.

The following are the principal peals of Church Bells in London:

BELLS.

St. Giles, Cripplegate; St. Saviour, Southwark; St. Bride, Fleet Street; St. Martin-in-the-Fields; St. Leonard, Shoreditch 12
Christchurch, Spitalfields; St. Sepulchre, Skinner Street . . . 11
St. Mary-le-Bow, Cheapside; St. Magnus', Lower Thames Street; St. Dionis', Fenchurch Street; All Saints, Poplar; St. Dunstan, Stepney; St. John, Horsleydown; St. James, Bermondsey; St. Giles, Camberwell; St. Luke (New), Chelsea 10
St. George in the East 9

We find the Curfew mentioned to a very late period as a common and approved regulation. Among the charges directed for the wardmote inquests in London, in the mayoralty of Sir Henry Colet, A.D. 1495, it is said: "Also yf there be anye paryshe clerke that ryngeth curfewe after the curfewe be ronge at Bow Chyrche, or St. Bryde's Church, or St. Gyles-without-Cripelgate, all suche to be prevented." —(Knight's *Life of Dean Colet*, p. 6.) The same charge remained in the wardmote inquest as printed in 1649.

"Bow Bells" are of olden celebrity: the Citizens' love of them led to persons born within their sound being called genuine "Cockneys." In 1469, by an Order of Common Council, Bow Bell was to be rung nightly at nine o'clock, and lights were to be exhibited in the steeple during the night, to direct the traveller towards the metropolis. The present Bells, bought by subscription, were first rung June 4, 1762, the birthday of George III. They are not allowed to be rung in the scientific method, but only in set changes, lest the vibration should cause the fall of the new spire! The twelve bells of St. Saviour's, Southwark, were not rung at the opening of New London Bridge, in 1831, on account of the alleged insecurity it would occasion to the tower. The tenor of this peal weighs 52½ cwt.; that of Bow, 53 cwt.

St. Sepulchre's Bell has a melancholy history. In 1605, Mr. R. Dowe left 50*l*. to this parish, on condition that a person should go to Newgate in the still of the night before every execution-day, and, standing as near as possible to the cells of the condemned, should, with a hand-bell, (which he also left,) give twelve solemn tolls, with double strokes, and then deliver this impressive exhortation:

> "All you that in the condemned hole do lie,
> Prepare you, for to-morrow you shall die;
> Watch, all, and pray, the hour is drawing near
> That you before the Almighty must appear;
> Examine well yourselves, in time repent,
> That you may not t' eternal flames be sent.
> And when St. Sepulchre's Bell to-morrow tolls,
> The Lord have mercy on your souls!
>   Past twelve o'clock!"

Dowe likewise ordered that the great Bell of the church should toll on the morning; and that, as the criminals passed the wall to Tyburn, the bellman or sexton should look over it and say, "All good people, pray heartily unto God for these poor sinners, who are now going to their death;" for which he who says it is to receive 1*l.* 6*s.* 8*d.* The place of execution being changed, a part of this ceremony has been long discontinued; and let us hope that the gift ere long will be a free one.

Christchurch, Spitalfields', Bells are scarcely inferior to any in the kingdom; the tenor weighs 44 cwt., or 4928 lbs. Occasionally, some fine feats of Bell-ringing are executed. On Monday evening, March 13, 1843, the Society of Cumberland rang a complete peal of Cinques on "Stedman's principle," consisting of 5146 changes, in four hours, two minutes, at St. Bride's, Fleet Street; it being the first peal in that scientific method ever performed on the Bells.

St. Paul's Cathedral has four Bells,—one in the northern, and three in the southern or clock-tower: the former is tolled for prayer three times a-day, and has a clapper; but neither of the four can be raised upon end and rung, as other church bells. In the clock-tower are hung two Bells for the quarters, and above them is hung the Great Bell, on gudgeons or axles, on which it moves when struck by the hammer of the clock. It weighs 11,474 lbs., and its diameter is nine feet. It was cast principally from the metal of the Bell in the clock-tower opposite Westminster Hall Gate, which, before the Reformation, was named "Edward," after the Royal Confessor; subsequently to the time of Henry VIII., as appears by two lines in Eccles's *Glee*, it was called "Great Tom," as Gough conjectures, by a corruption of "Grand Ton," from its deep, sonorous tone. On August 1, 1698, the clochard, or clock-tower, was granted by William III. to St. Margaret's parish, and was taken down; when the Bell was found to weigh 82 cwt. 2 qrs. 21 lbs., and was bought at 10*d.* per lb., producing 385*l.* 17*s.* 6*d.*, for St. Paul's. While being conveyed over the boundary of Westminster, under Temple Bar, it fell from the carriage; it stood under a shed in the Cathedral Yard for some years, and was at length re-cast, with additional metal, in 1716, the inscription stating it to have been "brought from the ruins of Westminster."

"The key-note (tonic) or sound of this Bell is A flat, (perhaps it was A natural, agreeably to the pitch at the time it was cast,) but the sound heard at the greatest distance is that of E flat, or a fifth above the key-note; and a musical ear, when close by, can perceive several harmonic sounds." (*W. Parry.*)

The Great Bell is never used, except for the striking of the hour, and for tolling at the deaths and funerals of any of the Royal Family, the Bishop of London, the Dean of the Cathedral, and the Lord Mayor, should he die in his mayoralty. The same hammer which strikes the hours has always been used to toll the Bell, on the occasion of a demise; but the sound produced on the latter occasions is not so loud as when the hour is struck, in consequence of the heavy clock-weight not being attached when the Bell is tolled, and causing the hammer to strike with greater force than by manual strength.

It was the Westminster "Great Tom" which the sentinel on duty at Windsor Castle, during the reign of William III., declared to have struck thirteen instead of twelve times at midnight, and thus cleared himself of the accusation by the relief-guard of sleeping upon his post. The story is told of St. Paul's Bell; but the Cathedral had no heavy Bell until the above grant by King William, who died in 1702; the circumstance is thus recorded in the *Public Advertiser*, Friday, June 22, 1770:

Mr. John Hatfield, who died last Monday at his house in Glasshouse Yard, Aldersgate, aged 102 years, was a soldier in the reign of William and Mary, and the person who was tried and condemned by a court-martial for falling asleep on his duty upon the Terrace at Windsor. He absolutely denied the charge against him, and solemnly declared that he heard St. Paul's clock strike thirteen; the truth of which was much doubted by the court, because of the great distance. But whilst he was under sentence of death, an affidavit was made by several persons, that the clock actually did strike thirteen instead of twelve; whereupon he received his Majesty's pardon."

Chimes.—The only Chimes now existing in the metropolis are those of St. Clement Danes, in the Strand; St. Giles's, Cripplegate; and St. Dionis, Fenchurch Street. The Cripplegate chimes are the finest in London; they were constructed by a poor working man. Formerly, several churches in London, including those of St. Margaret and St. Sepulchre, had chime-hammers annexed to their bells.

In each Royal Exchange, the business has been regulated by a bell: in Gresham's original edifice was a tower "containing the bell, which twice a-day summoned merchants to the spot—at twelve o'clock at noon, and at six o'clock in the evening." (Burgon's *Life and Times of Sir T. Gresham*, ii. 345.)

The Chimes at the Royal Exchange, destroyed by fire in 1838, played, at intervals of three hours, "God save the Queen," "Life let us cherish," the old 104th Psalm, (on Sundays,) and "There's nae luck about the house," which last air they played at twelve o'clock on the night of the fire, just as the flames reached the chime-loft.

In the new Exchange, Chimes have not been forgotten. The airs have been arranged by Mr. E. Taylor, the Gresham Professor of Music; which Mr. Dent has applied on the Chime-barrel. The airs are:—

1. A Psalm tune, by Henry Lawes, the friend of Milton; it is in the key of B flat, so as to exhibit the capability of the chimes to play in different keys.

2. God save the Queen, in E flat. 3. Rule Britannia.

4. An air selected by Professor Taylor to exhibit the power of the bells. The key in which the bells are set is E flat. There are fifteen bells, and two hammers to several, so as to play rapid passages. There are frequently three hammers striking different bells simultaneously, and sometimes five. The notes of the bells are as follow: B flat, A natural, A flat, G, F, E flat, D natural, D flat, C, B flat, A natural, A flat, G, F, and E flat. The first bell, B flat, weighs 4 cwt. 26 lbs., and its cord, 8 cwt. 2 qrs. 5 lbs; the four bells, A flat, G, F, and E flat, weigh severally, 10 cwt. 1 qr. 9 lbs., 12 cwt. 2 qrs. 27 lbs., 15 cwt. 2 qrs. 14 lbs., and 23 cwt. 2 qrs. 24 lbs. The united weight of them is 131 cwt. 1 qr. They were cast by Messrs. Mears, of Whitechapel.

BERMONDSEY,

Is a large parish in Surrey, adjoining the Borough of Southwark; and named *Beormund's eye*, or island, from its having been the property of some Saxon or Danish Thane, and the land being insulated by water-courses connected with the Thames. In 1082, a wealthy citizen built here a convent, wherein some Cluniac Monks settled in 1089, to whom William Rufus gave the manor of Bermondsey; and numerous donations and grants followed, until this became one of the most considerable alien priories in England. From its vicinity to London, the monastery occasionally became the residence of some of our kings. Katherine of France, widow of Henry V., retired to this sanctuary, and died here, Jan. 3, 1437; and Elizabeth Widvile, relict of Edward IV., was committed to the custody of the monks by her son-in-law, Henry VII., and ended her days here, in penury and sorrow, in 1492. Among the persons of note interred here is said to have been Margaret de la Pole, executed by Henry VIII. in 1513. The Abbey occupied the ground between Grange Walk (where was a farm) and Long Walk, which was a passage between the monastic buildings and the conventual church; the latter a little south of the present parish church of St. Mary Magdalene, originally founded by the Priors of Bermondsey for their tenantry, rebuilt in 1680, and since repaired. Among the communion plate is an ancient silver alms-dish, supposed to have belonged to the Abbey.

A drawing in the late Mr. Upcott's collection shewed the Monastery as rebuilt early in the reign of Edward III., and the cloisters and refectory in 1380. After the surrender of the establishment to Henry VIII., he granted it to Sir Robert Southwell, Master of the Rolls: it was by him sold to Sir Thomas Pope, who, in 1545, pulled down the ancient Priory Church, and with the materials built Bermondsey House, where died Thomas Ratcliffe, Earl of Sussex (Lord Chamberlain to Queen Elizabeth), in 1583. The east gate of the monastery was taken down about 1760; the great gate-house was nearly entire in 1806, shortly after which all the ancient buildings were removed, and Abbey-street built on their site. Bermondsey-square now occupies the great close of the Abbey, and Grange-road was its pasture-ground, extending to the farm or Grange; the ancient water-course, the Neckinger, was formerly navigable from the Thames to the Abbey precincts.

Adjoining the monastery was an Almonry, or Hospital, for "indigent children and necessitous converts," erected by Prior Richard in 1213, but not to be traced after the Reformation.

There is also, in the Spa Road, a Grecian church, opened in 1829: the altar-piece is a large picture of "the Ascension," painted by John Wood in 1844, and the prize picture selected from among eighty competitors for 500l. bequeathed for this purpose by Mr. Harcourt, a parishioner, and awarded by Eastlake and Haydon. St. Paul's Gothic Church and Schools were opened in 1848; and Christ Church and Schools, Neckinger Road, (Romanesque,) in 1849.

The Roman Catholic population of Bermondsey exceeds 5000 persons; they have a large church near Dockhead, opened in 1835. Precisely three centuries after the Dissolution of the Monasteries, was founded here, in 1838, a Convent for "the Sisters of Mercy." The inmates are mostly ladies of fortune, and support a school for 200 children. Sister Mary, the Lady Barbara Eyre, second daughter of the sixth Earl of Newburgh, took the vows December 12, 1839; with Miss Ponsonby, now Sister Vincent.

At Bermondsey, perhaps, is carried on a greater variety of trades and manufactures than in any other parish of the kingdom. It has been the seat of the Leather Market for nearly two centuries; its series of tidal streams from the Thames twice in twenty-four hours supplying water for the tanners and leather-dressers. At the Neckinger Mills here, nearly half a million of hides and skins are converted into leather yearly; and in the great Skin Market are sold the skins from nearly all the sheep slaughtered in London. Steam-machinery is much employed in the manufactories; and in Long-lane is an engine chimney-shaft 175 feet high. Here is Christy's Hat Manufactory, employing 500 persons, and considered the largest establishment of the kind in the world. Here, too, abound paper and lead mills, chemical works, boat and ship builders, mast and block makers, rope and sail makers, coopers, turpentine works, &c. The tidal ditches, with their filthy dwellings, produced cholera in 1832 and 1848-9; in the latter year 189 deaths occurred in 1000 inhabitants. Here was Jacob's Island, so powerfully pictured in Dickens's novel of *Oliver Twist*. There were till lately thirty miles of tidal ditches in the district; but these nuisances have been abated by the exertions of the General Board of Health.

Bermondsey Spa, a chalybeate spring, discovered about 1770, was opened, in 1780, as a minor Vauxhall, with fireworks, and a picture-model of the Siege of Gibraltar, painted by Keyse, and occupying about four acres. He died in 1800, and the garden was shut up about 1805. There are *Tokens* of the place extant, and the *Spa-road* is named from it.

In the parish was born Mary Johns, the daughter of a cooper, in 1752, who wrote the Lord's Prayer in the compass of a silver penny.

Viewed from the Greenwich Railway, which crosses its north-eastern side, Bermondsey presents a curious picture of busy life, amid its streams and tan-pits, its narrow streets, close rents and lanes, by no means tributary to the public health. Yet the district has long been noted for longevity; and from 90 to 105 years are not uncommon in the burial registers.

In the Registers, 1604, is "the forme of a solemne *Vowe* made betwixt a Man and his Wife, having been longe absent, through which occasion the Woman beinge married to another Man, took her again."

BETHLEHEM, OR BETHLEM HOSPITAL,

Originated in an establishment founded as a " priory of canons, with brethren* and sisters," in 1246, by Simon Fitz-Mary, a sheriff of London; towards which he gave all his lands in St. Botolph without Bishopsgate, being the spot afterwards known as Old Bethlem, now Liverpoolstreet. This priory stood on the east side of Morefield, from which it was divided by a deep ditch. It is described as " an Hospital " in 1330; in 1346 it was received under the protection of the City of London, who purchased the patronage, lands, and tenements in 1546; and in the same year, Henry VIII. gave the Hospital to the City, though not before he had endeavoured to sell it to them.

Bethlem is, however, first mentioned as an hospital for lunatics in 1402. The earliest establishment of the kind in the metropolis appears, from Stow, to have been "by Charing Cross," though when founded is unknown; "but it was said that some time a king of England, not liking distraught and lunatic people to remain so near his palace, caused them to be removed farther off to Bethlem;" to which Hospital the site of the house in question belonged till 1830, when it was exchanged with the Crown to make way for the improvements at Charing Cross.

The priory buildings becoming dilapidated, another Hospital was built in 1675-76, on the south side of Moor Fields, north of the London Wall, on ground leased to the Governors by the Corporation for 999 years, at 1s. annual rent, if demanded. This, the centre of Old Bethlem Hospital, cost 17,000l., raised by subscription: it was designed by Robert Hooke; but there is no foundation for the traditional story of its so closely resembling the palace of the Tuileries, that Louis XIV., in retaliation, ordered a copy of our King's palace at St. James's to be built for his offices.

This second Bethlem was 540 feet in length and 40 feet in breadth; it was surrounded by gardens, in one of which the convalescent lunatics were allowed to walk: the whole was enclosed by a high wall and gates, the posterns of the latter surmounted with two finely-sculptured figures of Raving and Melancholy Madness, by Caius Gabriel Cibber.

In 1733, two wings were added for incurable patients. In 1754, the Hospital is described as consisting chiefly of two galleries, one over the other, divided in the middle by two iron gates, so that all the men were placed at one end of the house and all the women at the other; there was also "a bathing-place for the patients, so contrived as to be a hot or cold bath." The Hospital then held 150 patients. The favourite resort of the poor inmates was the Fore-street end of the building, from the windows of which they could look out upon the unafflicted passengers in the streets below.

Nat Lee, the tragic poet, to madness near allied, was confined here four years, and did not live long after his release.

Here, too, was confined Oliver Cromwell's gigantic porter, who is traditionally said to have been the original of one of Cibber's figures.

Hannah Snell, out-pensioner of Chelsea Hospital, for wounds received at the siege of Pondicherry, died a patient of Bethlem, Feb. 8, 1792.

" Tom o' Bedlams " was the name given to certain out-door patients, or pensioners, for whom room could not be found in the Hospital; they wore upon their arms metal plates, licensing them to go a-begging,

---

* They wore the order of Bethlem, or the Star, and a star upon their mantles, and were subject to entertain the Bishop of Bethlem whenever he came to London: hence the name of the Hospital. " St. Theodosius, (born 423, died 529,) established near Bethlehem a monastery, to which were annexed three infirmaries,—one for the sick, one for the aged and feeble, and the other for such as had lost their senses,—in which all succours, spiritual and temporal, were afforded with admirable order, care, and affection." Butler's *Lives of the Saints.*

which many cunning impostors adopted, until a notice from the Hospital put an end to the fraud.

In 1799, the Hospital was reported by a committee to be in a very bad condition: it had been built in sixteen months, upon part of the City ditch filled in with rubbish, so that it was requisite to shore-up and underpin the walls. At length, it was resolved to rebuild the Hospital; and in 1810 its site, 2½ acres, was exchanged for about 11 acres in St. George's Fields, including the gardens of the infamous Dog and Duck. The building fund was increased by grants of public money, benefactions from the Corporation, City companies, and private individuals. The first stone of the new edifice, for 200 patients, was laid in April 1812, and completed in August 1815, at a cost of 122,572l. 8s., the exact sum raised for the purpose. It was built from three prize designs, superintended by the late Mr. Lewis: it consists of a centre and two wings, the entrance being beneath a hexastyle Ionic portico of six columns, with the royal arms in the pediment, and underneath the motto :—HEN. VIII. REGE ' FUNDATVM.' CIVIUM ' LARGITAS ' PERFECIT. Two wings, for which the Government advanced 25,144l., are appropriated to criminal lunatics. Other buildings have since been added, for 166 patients, by Sydney Smirke, A.R.A. the first stone of which was laid July 26, 1838, when a public breakfast was given at a cost of 464l. 8s. to the Hospital, and a narrative of the proceedings was printed at a charge to the charity of 140l. The entire building is three stories in height, and 897 feet in length. To the centre was added a large and lofty dome in 1845; the diameter is 37 feet, and it is about 150 feet in height from the ground. The Hospital and grounds extend to eight acres; the adjoining three acres being devoted to the House of Occupations, a branch of Bridewell Hospital.

In the entrance-hall are placed Cibber's two statues, from the old Hospital: they are of Portland stone, and were restored by the younger Bacon in 1814; they are screened by curtains, which are only withdrawn upon public occasions: some of the irons formerly used are also shewn as *curiosities.* The basement and three floors are divided into galleries. The improved management was introduced about 1816. The patients employ themselves in knitting and tailoring, in laundry-work, at the needle, and in embroidery; the women have pianos, and occasionally dance in the evening; the men have billiard and bagatelle tables, newspapers, and periodicals; and they play in the grounds at trap-ball, cricket, fives, leap-frog, &c. Others work at their trades, in which, though dangerous weapons have been entrusted to them, no mischief has ensued, and the employment often induces speedy cure. The railed-in fire-places and the bone knives are almost the only visible peculiarities; there are cells lined and floored with cork and India-rubber for refractory patients. The building is fire-proof throughout, and warmed by hot air and water.

From the first reception of lunatics into Bethlem, their condition and treatment was wretched in the extreme. In a visitation of 1403 are mentioned iron chains with locks and keys, and manacles and stocks. In 1598, the house was reported so loathsome and so filthily kept, as not fit to be entered; and the inmates were termed prisoners. In a record of 1619 are expenses of straw and fetters. Up to the year 1770, the public were admitted to see the lunatics at 1d. each, by which the Hospital derived a revenue of at least 400l. a year: hence Bethlem became one of "the sights of London;" and such was the mischief occasioned by this brutal and degrading practice, that, to prevent disturbances, the porter was annually sworn a constable, and attended with other servants to keep order. So late as 1814, the rooms resembled dog-kennels; the female patients were chained by one arm or leg to the wall, were covered by a blanket-gown only, the feet being naked; and they lay upon straw. The male patients were chained, handcuffed, or locked to the wall; and chains were universally substituted for the strait-waist-coat. One Norris, stated to be refractory, was chained by a strong iron ring, riveted round his neck, his arms pinioned by an iron bar, and his waist similarly secured, so that he could only advance twelve inches from the wall, the length of his chains; and thus he had been "encaged and chained more than twelve years;" yet he read books of various kinds, the newspapers daily, and conversed rationally: a drawing was made of Norris in his irons, and he was visited by several members of Parliament, shortly after which he died, doubtless from the cruel treatment he had received. This case led to a Parliamentary inquiry, in 1815, which brought about the adoption of a new method of treatment in Bethlem; although, in two years, 660l. were expended from the Hospital funds in opposing the bill requisite for the beneficial change.

The last female lunatic released from her fetters was a most violent patient, who had been chained to her bed eight years, her irons riveted, she being so dangerous that the matron feared being murdered if she released her; in May 1838, she was still in the New Hospital, and was the only patient permitted to sleep at night with her door unlocked; the slightest appearance of restraint exasperated her; but on her release she became tranquil, and happy in nursing two dolls given to her, which she imagined to be her children.

The criminal lunatics are maintained and clothed at the expense of Government, and cost nearly 4000l. a year; they are charged 13s. 6d. a week, or 35l. per annum, whereas the average charge for pauper lunatics in country asylums is but 7s. Most of the criminals are confined for murder, committed or attempted. Among them was Margaret Nicholson, for attempting to stab George III.; she died here in 1828, having been confined forty-two years. Here is confined Oxford, for shooting at Queen Victoria, in St. James's Park, June 10, 1840; he is idiotic rather than insane. Here, too, is M'Naughten, for shooting Mr. E. Drummond, at Charing Cross, January 20, 1843. In 1841, died James Hadfield, who had been confined here since 1802, for shooting at George III., at Drury Lane Theatre. He was a gallant dragoon, and his face was seamed with scars got in battle before his crime: he employed himself with writing poetry on the death of his birds and cats, his only society in his long and wearying imprisonment.

Bethlem is not visited by Commissioners, but is managed by the officers and Governors. The following cases are inadmissible: lunatics who have been insane for more than twelve months; who have been discharged uncured from other hospitals; afflicted with idiotcy, palsy, or epileptic or convulsive fits, or any dangerous disease. The patients are not allowed to remain more than one year; they are classed as "curable," "incurable," and "criminals." Patients are admitted by petition to the Governors from a near relation or friend; forms to be obtained at the Hospital. The visiting days are two Mondays in each month; for taking in and discharging patients, every Friday. In 1849, there were admitted 150 males, 194 females. Discharged cured 70 males, 106 females. The annual rate of mortality in Bethlem is 7 per cent; in other asylums, from 13 to 22 per cent.—(*Registrar-General's Report*, 1850.)

The income of Bethlem and Bridewell Hospitals amounts to about 33,000l. per annum, mostly the accumulation of private benevolence.

From November 22, 1841, Bethlem Hospital, with its purlieus and approaches, was considered to be within the rules of the Queen's Bench, by an order of that Court, until their abolition.

Strangers are admitted, on Tuesdays, Wednesdays, Thursdays, and

Fridays, to view the Hospital by Governors' orders; and foreigners and Members of Parliament by orders from the president, treasurer, or Secretary of State; but the average yearly number of visitors does not exceed 550. Still, few sights can be more interesting than the present condition of the interior of Bethlem. The scrupulous cleanliness of the house, the decent attire of the patients, and the unexpectedly small number of those under restraint, (sometimes not one person throughout the building,) lead the visitors, not unnaturally, to conclude that the management of lunatics has here attained perfection; while the quiet and decent demeanour of the inmates might almost make him doubt that he is really in a madhouse. The arrangements, however, are comparatively, in some instances, defective: the building being partly on the plan of the old Hospital in Moorfields, in long galleries, with a view to the coercive system there pursued, is, consequently, ill adapted to the present improved treatment.

Above the door of the entrance-lodge are sculptured the arms of the Hospital,—*Argent, two bars sable, a file of five points gules, on a chief azure en étoile of sixteen rays or, charged with a plate, thereon a cross of the third, between a human skull placed on a cup, on the dexter side, and a basket of Wastell bread, all of the fifth, on the sinister.*

BETHNAL GREEN,

A village or large green, formerly a hamlet of Stepney, but made a parish (St. Matthew) in 1743. The old English ballad of *The Blind Beggar of Bednall Green* has given the district a long celebrity; the story "decorates not only the sign-posts of the publicans, but the staff of the parish beadle."—(*Lysons*). The story has been cleverly wrought into a drama by Sheridan Knowles. The mansion traditionally pointed to as "the Blind Beggar's Home" was, however, built by John Thorpe, in 1570, for a citizen of London, and called, after him, "Kirby's Castle." Here was a mansion said to have been a palace of Bishop Bonner's, and taken down in 1849, in forming Victoria Park. Between 1839 and 1849, there were built here ten district churches, principally through the exertions of Dr. Blomfield, Bishop of London : the tenth of these churches (St. Thomas's) was built at the sole cost of a private individual. Silk-weavers live in great numbers at Bethnal Green.

BILLINGSGATE

Is stated to take its name from having been the gate of King Belin, a king of the Britons, about 400 B. C. But this rests upon no better authority than Geoffrey of Monmouth, and is doubted by Stow, who suggests that the gate was called from some owner named Beling or Biling : Stow describes it as "a large water-gate, port, or harborough for ships and boats, commonly arriving there with fish, both fresh and salt, shell-fishes, salt, oranges, onions, and other fruits and roots, wheat, rye, and grain of divers sorts, for the service of the city." It has been a quay, if not a market, for nearly nine centuries,—since the customs were paid here under Ethelred II., A.D. 979; and fishing-boats paid toll here, according to the laws of Athelstan, who died 940. Its present appropriation dates from 1699, when, by an Act of William III., it was made "a free and open market for all sorts of fish ;" and was fixed at the western extremity of the Custom House, on the northern bank of the Thames, a short distance below London Bridge.

The Market, for many years, consisted of a collection of wooden pent-houses, rude sheds, and benches; it commenced at three o'clock in the summer and five in the winter; in the latter season it was a strange scene, its large flaring oil lamps shewing a crowd struggling amidst a Babel din of vulgar tongues, such as rendered "Billingsgate" a byword for low abuse: "opprobrious, foul-mouth language is called Billingsgate discourse."—(Martin's *Dictionary*, 1754, second edit.) In Bailey's *Dictionary* we have "a Billings*gate*, a scolding, impudent slut." Tom Brown gives a very coarse picture of her character; and Addison refers to "debates which frequently arise among the ladies of the British fishery." She wore a strong stuff gown, tucked up, and shewing a large quilted petticoat; her hair, cap, and bonnet flattened into a mass by carrying a basket upon her head; her coarse, cracked cry, and brawny limbs, and red, bloated face, completing a portrait of the "fish-fag" of other days.

Not only has the virago disappeared, but the market-place has been rebuilt, and its business regulated by the City authorities, with especial reference to the condition of the fish; and in 1849 was commenced the further extension of the market. There is no crowding, elbow-ing, screaming, or fighting, as heretofore; coffee has greatly superseded spirits; and a more orderly scene of business can scarcely be imagined. The market is daily, except Sundays, at five A.M., summer and winter, announced by ringing a bell, the only relic of the olden rule. The fish-ing-vessels reach the quay during the night, and are moored alongside a floating wharf, which rises and falls with the tide. The oyster-boats are berthed by themselves, the name of the oyster cargo is painted upon a board, where they are measured out to purchasers. The other fish are carried ashore in baskets, and there sold, by Dutch auction, to fishmongers, whose carts are waiting in the adjoining streets. The wholesale market is now over; but there remain the *bummarees*, who supply the costermongers, &c.

All fish is sold by tale, except oysters and shell-fish, which are sold by measure, and salmon by weight. In February and March, about thirty boxes of salmon, each one cwt., arrive at Billingsgate per day; the quantity gradually increases, until it amounts, in July and August, to 1000 boxes; (during one season it reached 2500 tons)—the fish being finest when it is lowest in price. Of lobsters, Mr. Yarrell states a twelvemonth's supply to be 1,904,000; of turbots, 87,958. The specu-lation in lobsters is very great; in 1816, one Billingsgate salesman is known to have lost 1200l. per week, for six weeks, by lobsters! Pe-riwinkles are shipped from Glasgow, fifty or sixty tons at a time, to Liverpool, and sent thence by railway to London, where better profits are obtained, even after paying so much sea and land carriage. Some-times there is a marvellous glut of fish: thus, in two days from 90 to 100 tons of plaice, soles, and sprats have been landed at Billingsgate, and sold at two and three lbs. a penny; soles, 2d.; large plaice 1d. each.

A full season and scarce supply, however, occasionally raise the price enormously; as in the case of four guineas being paid for a lobster for sauce, which, being the only one in the market, was divided for two London epicures! During very rough weather, scarcely an oyster can be procured in the metropolis. In the height of the season, a fine cod-fish has been sold for a guinea and a half.

Mackerel were, in 1698, first allowed to be cried through the streets on a Sunday; but, by the 9 and 10 Victoria, passed August 3, 1846, the sale of mackerel on a Sunday was declared illegal.

At Billingsgate is the "Three Tuns Tavern," with a fine view of the river, where a *table d'hôte* dinner of three kinds of fish, with meat, &c., may be had for 1s. 6d.: hours, one and four.

BIRDS OF LONDON.

Birds, for the most part, avoid cities and large towns; but there have been some remarkable exceptions to this rule noted in the metro-polis by careful observers.

The House-Sparrow is to be seen in nearly every locality. In 1850, there was a numerous colony of sparrows upon the west side of the court-yard of No. 94 Piccadilly, the residence of the Duke of Cambridge. Another nesting-place for sparrows was the capitals of the Corinthian columns of the portico of Carlton House.

There was, too, a noted rookery in the lofty trees of the grounds of Carlton House: on these being cut down, the birds removed, in 1827, to some trees in the rear of New-street, Spring-gardens. Perchance, few remember the satirical lament of Tom Hudson's song : "Now the old rooks have lost their places." Rooks build in the south church-yard of St. Dunstan-in-the-East, Tower-street. The rookery, before the last church was removed, consisted of upwards of twenty nests; and they were annually supplied with osier-twigs, and other materials for building. The colony migrated to the Tower of London, when disturbed for the pulling down of the church in 1817; they built in the White Tower, but returned as soon as the noise of axes and hammers had ceased. In 1849, their building-materials were hospitably provided for them by Mr. Crutchley, the assistant-overseer: the trees are plane. There was also, formerly, a rookery on some large elm-trees in the College Garden, behind the Ecclesiastical Court, in Doctors' Commons. There is, too, a rookery in the fine trees near Kensington Palace.

"We have rooks in the very heart of London, on a noble plane-tree which grows at the corner of Wood-street, Cheapside. There are now, -(May, 1850,) signs of four nests in that tree; but I am unable to state whether they have reared their young in that locality. Rooks, how-ever, build in the crowns surmounting the highest pinnacles of the turrets of the Tower of London; and there is another rookery in Gray's-Inn Gardens. Pigeons have lately taken to build on the tops of the pillars of the Bank of England and the Royal Exchange: so that London can now boast of three kinds of birds which rear their young, viz. sparrows, pigeons, and rooks. We have every year a robin or two at Finsbury Circus, but it does not build; and we are frequently favoured with a visit from starlings." (*Instinct and Reason*, by A. Smee, F.R.S., 1850.)

The Swallow, Swift, and Martin seem to have almost deserted Lon-don, although they are occasionally seen in the suburbs. The scarcity of the Swallow is referred to most of the chimneys having conical or other contracted tops to them, which is no inducement for this bird to build in them. In 1826, Mr. Jennings observed Martins' nests in Goswell-street Road, and on Islington Green.

The Redbreast has been occasionally seen in the neighbourhood of Fleet Market and Ludgate Hill: in November 1825, Mr. Jennings saw it in the City Road; where, in November 1826, he saw the Wren.

The Thrush is often heard in the Regent's Park. Some of the mi-gratory birds approach much nearer London than is generally imagined. The Cuckoo and Wood-pigeon are heard occasionally in Kensington Gardens. The Nightingale is often heard at Hornsey-wood House, Hackney, and Mile-end. (See Jennings's *Ornithologia*, 1829.)

The London gardens are much more injured by insects than those in the country, on account of the smaller number of insectivorous birds, the great number of bird-catchers, and, in some respects, the cats, in and about the metropolis; and their scarcity is not, as is frequently alleged, owing to the smoke, the number of houses, the want of trees and food, because every kind of bird will live and thrive in cages in the heart of London.

In James-street, on the north side of Covent Garden, a Bird Mar-ket was formerly held on Sunday mornings.

The Canary is much reared in the metropolis; there are Societies for this purpose, the principal being the Friendly, the Royals, the Amateurs, and the Hand-in-Hand. Several varieties are distinguished; and there is a "London criterion of a perfect Canary." The Fancy hold their principal Shows in November and December, at the Gray's Inn Coffee-house, Holborn, and the British Coffee-house, Cockspur-street.

BLACKFRIARS,

The district between Ludgate Hill and the river Thames; and anciently a monastery of Black or Dominican Friars, who removed here from Holborn in 1276, to a piece of ground given them by Gregory Rocksley, Mayor. The monastery, church, and a mansion were built with the stone from the tower of Montfichet, and from part of the City wall. Edward I. and his Queen Eleanor were great benefactors to the new convent. Here the King kept his charters and records; and great numbers of the nobility dwelt in the precinct. In the church, divers parliaments and other great meetings were held. In 1522, the Emperor Charles V. of Spain was lodged here by Henry VIII.; and here, in 1524, was begun the sitting of a parliament, adjourned to the Black monks at Westminster, and therefore called the Black Parliament. Henry's divorce from Katherine of Arragon was decided here; and the parliament which condemned Wolsey, assembled at Blackfriars. The precinct was very extensive, was walled in, had four gates, and contained many shops, the occupiers of which were allowed to carry on their trades, although not free of the city, privileges maintained even after the dissolution of the monasteries. In the View of London (1543), in the Sutherland Collection, the church of Blackfriars is shewn with a lofty tower and spire, and the end towards the Fleet river flanked with two large turrets. Part of this church was altered and fitted up for parochial use; it was destroyed by the Great Fire of 1666, and the church of St. Andrew by the Wardrobe erected in its place.

Taking advantage of the sanctuary privilege, Richard Burbage and his fellows, when ejected from the City, built a playhouse in the Blackfriars precinct, and here maintained their ground against the powerful opposition of the City and the Puritans. Shakspeare had a share in this theatre, and part of its site is now Playhouse Yard. The poet possessed other property here; for in the City of London Library, at Guildhall, is preserved a deed of conveyance to Shakspeare of a house bought by him March 10, 1612-13, and bequeathed by him to his daughter, Susannah Hall. This document was sold by auction, May 24, 1841, for 165l. 15s.

Three eminent painters resided in Blackfriars: Isaac Oliver, the celebrated miniature-painter, who died in 1617, and is buried in St. Anne's; Cornelius Jansen, the portrait-painter, employed by King James I.; and Van Dyck, during his nine years' abode in England.

At Hunsdon House, in the Friary, on Sunday, Oct. 26, 1623, there perished 59 persons by the falling of a floor, during the preaching of a sermon by Father Drury; the catastrophe is recorded as "the Fatal Vespers."

In 1735, the right of the City to the jurisdiction of the precinct was decided in their favour in an action against a shalloon and drugget seller, tried in the Court of King's Bench; since which Blackfriars has been one of the precincts of Farringdon Ward.

BLACKWALL,

On the north bank of the Thames, and at the eastern extremity of the West India Docks, is said to have been originally called Bleakwall, from its exposed situation on the artificial bank or wall of the river, through the winding of which it is nearly eight miles from the City, though less than half that distance by land. Here, on the Brunswick Wharf or Pier, is the handsome Italianised terminus (by Tite) of the Blackwall Railway from Fenchurch-street, 4½ miles in length.

To the large taverns at Blackwall and Greenwich *gourmets* flock to eat Whitebait, a delicious little fish caught in the Reach, and directly netted out of the river into the frying-pan. They appear about the end of March or early in April, and are taken every flood-tide until September.

Pennant describes Whitebait as esteemed by the *lower order of epicures*. If this account be correct, there must have been a strange change in the grade of the epicures frequenting Greenwich and Blackwall since Pennant's days; for at present the fashion of eating Whitebait is sanctioned by the highest authorities, from the court of St. James's in the West to the Lord Mayor and *his* court in the East; besides the philosophers of the Royal Society; and her Majesty's Cabinet Ministers, who wind up the Parliamentary session with their "annual fish dinner," whither they go in an Ordnance barge, or a Government steamer.

Whitebait are taken by a net in a wooden frame, the hose having a very small mesh. The boat is moored in the tideway, and the net fixed to its side, when the tail of the hose, swimming loose, is from time to time handed in to the boat, the end untied, and its contents shaken out. Whitebait were thought to be the young of the shad, and were named from their being used as bait in fishing for whitings. By aid of comparative anatomy, Mr. Yarrell, however, proved Whitebait to be a distinct species, *Clupea alba.*

Perhaps the famed delicacy of Whitebait rests as much upon its skilful cookery as upon the freshness of the fish. Dr. Pereira has published the mode of cooking in one of Lovegrove's "bait-kitchens" at Blackwall. The fish should be dressed within an hour after being caught, or they are apt to cling together. They are kept in water, from which they are taken by a skimmer as required; they are then thrown upon a layer of flour, contained in a large napkin, in which they are shaken until completely enveloped in flour; they are then put into a colander, and all the superfluous flour is removed by sifting; the fish are next thrown into hot lard contained in a copper cauldron or stew-pan placed over a charcoal fire; in about two minutes they are removed by a tin skimmer, thrown into a colander to drain, and served up instantly, by placing them on a fish-drainer in a dish. The rapidity of the cooking process is of the utmost importance; and if it be not attended to, the fish will lose their crispness, and be worthless. At table, lemon-juice is squeezed over them, and they are seasoned with Cayenne pepper; brown bread and butter is substituted for plain bread; and they are eaten with iced champagne, or punch.

An important thing to be noticed is the vast extent of iron ship-building carried on here, an art of construction but of twenty years' growth. A great portion of Blackwall and the Isle of Dogs is occupied in this building trade, with its clanking boiler-works, and its Cyclopean foundries and engineering shops, in which steam is the *primum mobile.* Then, what a range of size have these steamers—from the huge troop-ship, or war-vessel (for foreign as well as British service), to the half-penny "bread-and-butter boats," which flit about above bridge from the City to Chelsea.

In the East India Docks, at Blackwall, arrived, April 1848, a large Chinese Junk, the first ever seen in England; and here it was exhibited until May 1850.

BLIND-SCHOOL (THE),

Or the School for the Indigent Blind, was established in 1799, at the Dog and Duck premises, St. George's Fields; and for some time received only fifteen blind persons. The site being required by the City of London for the building of Bethlem Hospital, about two acres of ground were allotted opposite the Obelisk, and there a plain school-house for the blind was built. In 1826, the School was incorporated; and in the two following years three legacies of 500*l.* each, and one of 10,000*l.*, were bequeathed to the establishment. In 1834, additional ground was purchased, and the school-house remodelled, so as to form a portion of a more extensive edifice in the Tudor or domestic Gothic style, de-

E

signed by John Newman, F.S.A. The tower and gateway in the north front are very picturesque; the School will now accommodate 220 inmates. The pupils are clothed, lodged, and boarded, and receive a religious and industrial education; so that many of them have been returned to their families able to earn from 6s. to 8s. per week. Applicants are not received under twelve, nor above thirty, years of age; nor if they have a greater degree of sight than will enable them to distinguish light from darkness. The admission is by votes of the subscribers; and persons between the age of twelve and eighteen have been found to receive the greatest benefit from the instruction.

The pupils may be seen at work between ten and twelve A.M., and two and five P.M., daily, except Saturdays and Sundays. The women and girls are employed in knitting stockings and needlework; in spinning, and making household and body linen, netting silk, and in fine basket-making; besides working baby-hoods, bags, purses, watchpockets, &c. of tasteful design, both in colour and form. The women are remarkably quick in superintending the pupils. The men and boys make wicker baskets, cradles, and hampers; rope door-mats and worsted rugs; and they make all the shoes for the inmates of the School. Reading is mostly taught by Alston's raised or embossed letters, in which have been printed the Old and New Testament, and the Liturgy. Both males and females are remarkably cheerful in their employment: they have great taste and aptness for music, and they are instructed in it, not as a mere amusement, but with a view to engagements as organists and teachers of psalmody; and once a year they perform a concert of sacred music in the chapel or music-room: the public are admitted by tickets, the proceeds from the sale being added to the funds of the institution. An organ and piano-forte are provided for teaching; and above each of the inmates of the males' working-room usually hangs a fiddle. They receive, as pocket-money, part of their earnings; and on leaving the school, a sum of money and a set of tools, for their respective trades, are given to them.

Among the other Charities for the Blind is the munificent bequest of Mr. Charles Day, (of the firm of Day and Martin, High Holborn), who died in 1836, leaving 100,000l. for the benefit of persons afflicted, like himself, with *loss of sight;* the dividends and interest to be disbursed in sums of not less than 10l., or more than 20l., per year, to each blind person, the selection being left to Trustees. In 1850, there were 271 recipients of these pensions. The Treasurer of this Charity, ("the Blind Man's Fund,") is Mr. John Simpson, 29 Savile Row, Old Burlington-street.

BOTANIC GARDENS.

The earliest Botanic Garden in the suburbs was that of John Tradescant (gardener to Charles I.), in the South Lambeth Road, now the site of the Nine Elms Brewery.

THE BOTANIC GARDEN, OR "PHYSIC GARDEN," OF THE APOTHECARIES' COMPANY, upon the Thames Bank at Chelsea, is maintained by the Company for the use of the medical students of London. The ground was first laid out in 1673. Evelyn saw here, in 1685, a tulip-tree and a tea-shrub, and the first hot-house known in England; "the subterranean heat conveyed by a stove under the conservatory, all vaulted with brick," so that "the doores and windowes" are open in the hardest frosts, excluding only the snow. On Sir Hans Sloane purchasing the manor of Chelsea in 1721, he granted the freehold of the Garden to the Apothecaries' Company, on condition that the Professor who gave lectures to the medical students should deliver annually to the Royal Society fifty new plants, well cured and specifically described, and of the growth of the Garden, till the number should amount to 2000. This condition was complied with, and a list of the new plants published yearly in the *Philosophical Transactions*, for about fifty years, when, 2500 plants having been presented, the custom was discontinued. The Garden is about three acres in extent: it contains a marble statue of Sir Hans Sloane, by Rysbrack, set up in 1733; and two noble cedars, planted in 1683, then about three feet high: in 1766, they measured more than twelve feet in circumference at two feet from the ground, and their branches extended forty feet in diameter. One of these cedars is said to have been brought from Lebanon for Sir Hans Sloane. The Apothecaries' Company give annually a gold and silver medal to the best informed students in botany who have attended this Garden; and they still observe an old custom of summer *herbarising*, or simpling excursions to the country, when the members are accompanied by apprentices or pupils. The Garden is open daily, from eight to eleven; admission from May to July, by order from the Apothecaries' Company.

THE HORTICULTURAL SOCIETY'S GARDENS at Chiswick are thirty-three acres in extent, and were commenced in 1821: they comprise Orchard and Kitchen, Hot-house and Tender and Hardy departments, the latter containing the arboretum and flower-garden; besides a conservatory, 184 feet long, 25 feet high, and about 30 feet wide. Here the Society hold exhibitions on a Saturday of May, June, and July, when medals and smaller prizes are awarded for the finest flowers and fruit. Visitors are admitted by tickets, obtainable at the Society's Office, 21 Regent Street, by personal or written order of a Fellow of Society, at 5s. each, prior to the Exhibition-day; or 7s. 6d. each on that day, at the Gardens. In 1849, there were issued 18,517 tickets; in 1844, 24,480. Formerly, costly public breakfasts were given at these Exhibitions: the weather is often unfavourable; of nine meetings in 1847, 8, and 9, five were more or less stormy; the tents erected for the occasion now provide as much as possible for such *contretems*. The Gardens are also open daily from nine to six, except Sunday, to Fellows; and by their personal introduction or order, to visitors. The arboretum contains the richest collection of trees and shrubs in Europe; the orchard is the most perfect ever formed; and the forcing-houses and hot-houses are complete. The Society distributes plants, seeds, and cuttings, to Members, foreign correspondents, and the British colonies.

THE ROYAL BOTANIC GARDENS at Kew are considered the richest in England. They are open to the public from one till six every day, except Sundays: the entrance being from Kew Green. The new Palm-House is 362 ft. 6 in. long; the ribs and columns are of wrought iron, and the roofs are glazed with sheet glass, slightly tinged green; the floor is of perforated cast-iron, under which are laid the pipes, &c. for warming by hot water; and the smoke is conveyed from the furnaces by a flue, 479 feet, to an ornamental shaft or tower, 60 feet in height. The cost of this magnificent Palm-House has been upwards of 30,000l. The Gardens, under the judicious curatorship of Sir W. J. Hooker, have been greatly extended and improved. Among the rarities here is a weeping-willow, raised from that which overshadowed Napoleon's remains at St. Helena;[*] the Egyptian papyrus; the bread-fruit-tree from the South-Sea Islands; the cocoa-nut, coffee, and cow trees; the banana

---

[*] Willows from slips brought from Napoleon's trees at St. Helena were, in the year 1836, flourishing in the garden of Captain Stevens, Beaumont-square, Mile End; in the grounds of the late Sir Thomas Farquhar at Roehampton; in the garden of the Roebuck Tavern, Richmond Hill; at No. 1 Canonbury-place, Islington; in Mr. Bentley's garden, Highbury Grange; at No. 10 King-street, St. James's: in the Surrey Zoological Gardens; at Kew; and at No. 11 Brompton-row.—*J. H. Fennell*, in Loudon's *Arboretum Britannicum*.

and cycas (sago); the gigantic tussack grass, &c. The Gardens are the richest in the world in New Holland plants. Here is also a Museum of specimens of raw and manufactured produce of the vegetable kingdom, and a variety of objects of kindred interest.

LODDIDGE'S NURSERY, at Hackney, was commenced in 1765; and contains a large house for Orchids, varying from five to twenty guineas each specimen; also air-plants and Chinese pitcher-plants. The Palm Stove is 45 ft. high, and twice as long; and here may be seen growing the palmetto, bamboo, cycas, cocoa-nut, arrow-root, plantain, &c.; cinnamon, clove, coffee, nutmeg, tamarind, cocoa, tea, camphor, and caoutchouc. The Camellia House is a splendid spectacle in March and April, when the plants are in bloom. Admission free, with references.

THE GARDENS OF THE ROYAL BOTANIC SOCIETY OF LONDON, (incorcorporated in 1839,) occupy the centre of the Inner Circle, Regent's Park: they consist of about eighteen acres, (including the site of Jenkins's Nursery,) and contain a Winter Garden; besides a Conservatory, entirely of glass and iron, covering 15,000 square feet, which cost about 6000l., and will contain 2000 visitors. The Society hold three Exhibitions annually, on Wednesdays in May, June, and July, when prize medals are distributed. Admission by tickets, to be had at the Society's office. Visitors are admitted daily from six to five, by Member's order. The Rock, Winter, and Landscape Garden, with their lake and artificial mound, are very picturesque.

There are several other botanical displays in the environs. Tulipshows and Prize Exhibitions of Floricultural Societies take place in the season. Mr. Groom, of Clapham Rise, exhibits a bed of tulips containing hundreds of varieties. The smoke of London is, however, a great impediment to the rearing of choice plants. In a report made to the House of Commons, Mr. Chandler, camellia-grower at Wandsworth, stated that on account of the great increase of chimneys from manufactories in that vicinity, plants now soil the hands. China roses, rhododendron hirsutum, rhododendron Virginium, and many other of the prettiest varieties, will not grow here as they formerly did. Mr. Anderson, the curator of the Physic Garden at Chelsea, testifies to the noxious effects of the "bitter smoke" upon the evergreens there.

BRIDEWELL HOSPITAL.

The ancient palace of Bridewell, which extended nearly from Fleetstreet to the Thames at Blackfriars, was founded upon the remains of a building supposed to be Roman, and inhabited by the Kings of England previous to the Conquest. Here our Norman Kings held their courts: Henry I. gave stone towards rebuilding the palace; and, in 1847, in excavating the site of Cogers' Hall, in Bride-lane, was discovered a vault with a groined roof, a Norman pellet-moulding, a cherub's head, and other remains of the same date: and in the rubbish was found a bull of Pope Nicholas V., a small jetton or abbey-piece, and some early pottery, glass, and tiles.

The palace afterwards came into the possession of Cardinal Wolsey, upon whose downfall it again reverted to the crown. It was here that Henry VIII. summoned to appear before him the heads of all the religious houses in England, to acknowledge his supremacy. In 1522, Henry, upon the site of the tower or castle of Montfiquet, rebuilt the palace, "a stately and beautiful house, giving it the name Bridewell, of the parish and well there:" it was purposely erected for the reception of Charles V. of Spain, though only his suite were lodged here,—Charles preferring the house of the Blackfriars, on the other side of the river Fleet, over which a temporary bridge was thrown, so as to pass through the city wall, and communicate with the palace. In 1528, Cardinal Campeius "was brought to ye Kinges presence, then living at Brydewel, by ye Cardinal of Yorke;" and the King "caused all his nobilitie, judges, and counsaylors, w^t· divers other persons, to come to his palace of Brydewel on sonday the viii. day Nouêber, at after none, in his great chamber," (*Hall's Chronicle*, fol. 180,) and there delivered a speech to them, touching his marriage with Katharine of Arragon. Next year, Henry and his Queen resided here while the question of their marriage was pending, (see Shakspeare's *Henry VIII.*, act 3); subsequent to which, taking a dislike to the place, the King let it fall to decay.

After the suppression of the monasteries, " the wide, large, empty house" was begged of Edward VI. by Bishop Ridley and the citizens, as a Workhouse and House of Correction; it was granted by the king, and confirmed only ten days before his death; and confirmed also by Queen Mary, who gave the Palace, and endowed it with great part of the revenues of the Savoy,—the City taking possession in 1555. In 1608, they erected here twelve large granaries, capable of containing 6000 quarters of corn, and two storehouses for coals. In 1620, the ancient chapel was enlarged and beautified: here was a portrait of Edward VI., with these lines:

> " This *Edward*, of fair memory the Sixt,
> In whom with Greatness Goodness was commixt,
> Gave this *Bridwell*, a *Palace* in old times,
> For a Chastening House of vagrant crimes."

Fuller has thus quaintly commemorated the gift :

" The House of Correction is the fittest hospital for those cripples whose legs are lame through their own laziness. Surely King Edward VI. was as truly charitable in granting Bridewell for the punishment of sturdy rogues, as in giving St. Thomas's Hospitall for the relief of the poore."

The Hospital was almost entirely destroyed in the Great Fire of 1666, but was rebuilt in two quadrangles, the principal of which fronted the Fleet River, now a vast barrel-like sewer under the roadway of Bridge-street. The Hall still remains, but the committee-room, prisons, chapel, &c. have been built in the present century; and the whole now forms only one large quadrangle, with a handsome entrance from Bridge-street, above which is a bust of Edward VI. Here are the offices and residence of the Chamberlain, Keeper of the City cash, and Treasurer of Bridewell. The Hall is a handsome wainscotted apartment, 85 feet 4 inches by 29 feet 8 inches, and 24 feet 9 inches high: beneath is a large kitchen, used once a year for dressing the dinner for the Governors, in June, at the expense of the twelve stewards. Above one of the fire-places, at the west end of the Hall, is a large and nearly square picture, by Holbein, of Edward VI. delivering his charter for this Hospital to the Lord Mayor (Sir George Bowes) and citizens ; the head of Holbein is painted in one corner. Opposite is a clever cartoon of " the Good Samaritan," by the youthful artist, Dadd. Here also are full-lengths of Charles II., by Lely ; George III. and Queen Charlotte, by Reynolds ; portraits of several Presidents of the Hospital; and of Mr. Chamberlain Clark, who died in 1832, in his 92d year.

The prison of Bridewell has one hundred cells. The prisoners sentenced to hard labour work on the treadwheel and grind corn, or they pick junk, and clean the wards. The women wash and mend the prisoners' linen or pick junk, and clean their side of the prison. Offences within the walls are punished by diminution of food and solitary confinement, and irons in extreme cases; but not with whipping. Formerly, prisoners for offences outside the prison were flogged, both men and women, on their naked backs, before the Governors, until the President's hammer fell. Hogarth has pictured the place, with hemp-beating, stocks, &c., in the fourth plate of the Harlot's Progress. The boys of Bridewell originally wore a peculiar dress, and attended fires with an engine belonging to the Hospital; but in 1755 they had become so turbulent that the practice was discontinued, and their costume laid aside.

In 1829, was built, adjoining Bethlem, in Lambeth, a "House of Occupations," whither young prisoners are sent from Bridewell, to be taught useful trades. In 1849 there were received into Bridewell, under the commitments by the Lord Mayor and Aldermen, as criminal or disorderly persons, who were kept to hard labour or received correction, 812; refractory apprentices sent by the Chamberlain for confinement, 25; persons found wandering abroad and begging in the City, 287; admitted to the House of Occupations, 130.

"To Bridewell are weekly and daily committed the young, the depraved, and the criminal, of every age and class. But even here humanity steps in to receive the unfortunate and the reclaimable. A Refuge of Occupations has been formed, whither the unprotected orphan, the child made guilty by bad example, and a necessity which truly exempts the offenders from moral responsibility,—thither they are taken and taught to labour industriously for their maintenance in the world, to fear God, and to keep His commandments. Many brands are thus rescued from the fire of destruction, and, from the abysses of vice, made useful and virtuous members of society. Girls are sent to service, and rewarded for the continued maintenance of fair characters; boys are bound to trades, and have the rewards of good conduct placed within their reach. Assuredly this is a purely philanthropic and Christian work. There are gifts of hundreds, and thousands, and tens of thousands of pounds inscribed upon the boards which surround the hall; there are fine portraits, too, of patriotic benefactors."—*Literary Gazette*, No. 1277.

BRIDGES.

There is no feature of the metropolis calculated to convey so enlarged an idea of the wealth, enterprise, and skill, of its population, as the *Seven* magnificent *Bridges*, which have been thrown across the Thames within the last hundred years, and five of these within the present century. Until the year 1750, the long narrow defile of Old London Bridge formed the sole land communication between the City and the suburbs on the Surrey bank of the Thames; whereas now, westward of the structure built to replace this ancient Bridge, and almost equidistant from each other, are Southwark, Blackfriars, Waterloo, Hungerford, Westminster, and Vauxhall Bridges.

LONDON BRIDGE, the first Bridge across the Thames at the metropolis, was of wood, erected in the year 994, opposite the site of the present St. Botolph's Wharf: it is mentioned in a statute of Ethelred II., fixing the tolls to be paid by boats bringing fish to "Bylynsgate."

This first wooden bridge is stated to have been built by the pious Brothers of St. Mary's monastery, on the Bankside; which house was originally a convent of sisters, founded and endowed with the profits of a ferry at this spot, by Mary, the only daughter of the ferryman, who is traditionally said to be represented by an antique monumental figure in St. Saviour's Church. This bridge is described with turrets and roofed bulwarks in the narrative of the invasion of the fleet of Sweyn, King of Denmark, in 994; and it was nearly destroyed by the Norwegian Prince Olaf in 1008. It was rebuilt before the invasion of Canute in 1016, who is said to have sunk a deep ditch on the south side, and dragged his ships to the west side of the bridge. It was easily passed by Earl Godwin in 1052; but it was swept away by flood in 1091; rebuilt in 1097; burnt in 1136; and a new one erected of elm timber in 1163, by Peter, chaplain of St. Mary Colechurch, Poultry.

The same pious architect began to build a *stone* bridge, a little to the west of the wooden one, in 1176; when Henry II. gave towards the expenses the proceeds of a tax on wool, which gave rise to the popular saying, that "London Bridge was built upon woolpacks." Peter of Colechurch died in 1205; but the Bridge was finished in 1209.

The new bridge consisted of a stone platform, 926 feet long and 40 in width, standing about 60 feet above the level of the water; and consisting of a drawbridge and 19 broad-pointed arches, with massive piers, raised upon strong oak and elm piles, covered by thick planks bolted together. It had a gate-house at each end; and towards the centre, on the east side, was built a beautiful Gothic chapel, dedicated to St. Thomas of Canterbury; in the crypt of which, within a pier of the bridge, was deposited, in a stone tomb, the body of Peter of Colechurch.

Norden describes the bridge, in the reign of Elizabeth, as "adorned with sumptuous buildings and statelie and beautiful houses on either syde," like one continuous street, "except certain voyd places for the retyre of passengers from the danger of cars, carts, and droves of cattle, usually passing that way," through which vacancies only could the river be seen over the parapet-walls or palings. Some of the houses had platform roofs, with pretty little gardens and arbours. Near the drawbridge, and overhanging the river on each side, was the famed Nonsuch House, of the Elizabethan age: it was constructed in Holland, entirely of timber, put together with wooden pegs only, and was four stories high, richly carved and gilt.

The chronicles of this stone bridge through nearly six centuries and a quarter form, perhaps, the most interesting episode in the history of London. The scenes of fire and siege, insurrection and popular vengeance, of national rejoicing, and of the pageant victories of man and of death, of fame or funeral,—it were vain for us to attempt to recite. In 1212, within four years after the bridge being finished, there was a terrific conflagration at each end, when nearly 3000 persons perished; in 1264, Henry III. was repulsed here by De Montfort, Earl of Leicester, and the populace attacked the Queen in her barge as it was preparing to shoot the bridge; in 1381, the rebel Wat Tyler entered the City by this road; in 1392, Richard II. was received here with great pomp by the citizens; in 1415, it was the scene of a grand triumph of Henry V., and in 1422 of his funeral procession; in 1428, the Duke of Norfolk's barge was lost by upsetting at the bridge, and his Grace narrowly escaped; in 1450—

> "Jack Cade hath gotten London Bridge; the citizens
> Fly and forsake their houses:"

but the rebel was defeated, and his head placed upon the Gate-house; in 1477, Falconbridge attacked the Bridge, and fired several houses; in 1554, it was one of the daring scenes of Sir Thomas Wyatt's rebellion; in 1632 more than one-third of the houses were consumed in an accidental conflagration; and in 1666 the labyrinth of dwellings was swept away by the Great Fire: the whole street was rebuilt within twenty years; but, in 1757, the houses were entirely removed, and parapets and balustrades erected on each side; and in this state the venerable structure remained till its final demolition in the year 1832.

In 1582, at the west side of the City end of the Bridge, Waterworks were commenced by Morice, with water-wheels turned by the flood and ebb current of the Thames passing through the purposely contracted arches, and working pumps for the supply of water to the metropolis; this being the earliest example of public water service by pumps and mechanical powers which enabled water to be distributed in pipes to dwelling-house. Previously, water had only been supplied to public cisterns, from whence it was conveyed at great expense and inconvenience in buckets and carts. These Waterworks were not removed until 1822, when the proprietors received for their interest 10,000l. from the New River Company.

The Bridge shops had signs, and were "furnished with all manner of trades." Holbein is said to have lived here; as did also Herbert, the printseller, and editor of Ames's *Typographical Antiquities*, at the time the houses were taken down. On the first night Herbert spent here a dreadful fire took place on the banks of the Thames, which suggested to him the plan of a floating fire-engine, soon after adopted. Tradesmen's Tokens furnish but few records of the Bridge shopkeepers. "As fine as London Bridge" was formerly a proverb in the City; and many a serious, sensible tradesman used to believe that heap of enormities to be one of the seven wonders of the world, and, next to Solomon's temple, the finest thing that ever art produced.

The street was also the abode of many artists: here lived Peter Monamy, the marine painter, who was taught drawing by a sign and house painter on London Bridge. Dominic Serres once kept shop here; and Hogarth lived here when he engraved for old John Bowles, in Cornhill. Swift and Pope have left accounts of their visits to Crispin Tucker, a waggish bookseller and author-of-all-work, who lived under the southern gate. One Mr. Baldwin, haberdasher, born in the house over the Chapel, at seventy-one could not sleep in the country for want of the noise of the roaring and rushing of the tide beneath, which " he had been always used to hear."

A most terrific historic garniture of the Bridge was the setting up of heads on its gate-houses: among these ghastly spectacles was the head of Sir William Wallace, 1305; Simon Frisel, 1306; four traitor knights, 1397; Lord Bardolf, 1408; Bolingbroke, 1440; Jack Cade and his rebels, 1451; the Cornish traitors of 1497; and of Fisher, Bishop of Rochester, 1535, displaced in fourteen days by the head of Sir Thomas More. In 1577, the several heads were removed from the north end of the Drawbridge to the Southwark entrance, thence called Traitors' Gate. In 1578, the head of a recusant priest was added to the sickening sight; and in 1605, that of Garnet the Jesuit, as well as those of the Romish priests executed under the statutes of Elizabeth and James I. Hentzner counted above thirty heads on the Bridge in 1598. The display was transferred to Temple Bar in the reign of Charles II.

The narrowness of the Bridge arches so contracted the channel of the river as to cause a rapid; and to pass through them was termed to "shoot the bridge," a peril taken advantage of by suicides. Thus, in 1689, Sir William Temple's only son, lately made Secretary at War, leaped into the river from a boat as it darted through an arch: he had filled his pockets with stones, and was drowned, leaving in the boat this note: "My folly in undertaking what I could not perform, whereby some misfortunes have befallen the King's service, is the cause of my putting myself to this sudden end; I wish him success in all his undertakings, and a better servant." Pennant adds to the anecdote that Sir William Temple's false and profane reflection on the occasion was, that "a wise man might dispose of himself, and make his life as short as he pleased!" In 1737, Eustace Budgell, a *soi-disant* cousin of Addison, and who wrote in the *Spectator* and *Guardian*, when broken down in character and reduced to poverty, took a boat at Somerset Stairs; and ordering the waterman to row down the river, Budgell threw himself into the stream as they shot London Bridge. He too had filled his pockets with stones, and rose no more: he left in his secretary a slip of paper, on which was written a broken distich: " What Cato did, and Addison approved, cannot be wrong." This is a wicked sophism; "there being as little resemblance between the cases of Budgell and Cato as there is reason for considering Addison's " Cato" written in defence of suicide.

Of a healthier complexion is the anecdote of Edward Osborne, in 1536, leaping into the Thames from the window of one of the Bridge-houses, and saving his master's infant daughter, dropped by a nurse-maid into the stream. The father, Sir William Hewet, was Lord Mayor in 1559, and gave this daughter in marriage to Osborne, whose great-grandson became the first Duke of Leeds.

To allow of extensive changes and repairs, a temporary wooden bridge was built on the sterlings, or ancient coffer-dams, to protect the piers; it was burnt April 10, 1758, but rebuilt in a month. The centre pier and two arches adjoining were then taken down and replaced by one large arch, the bridge widened several feet, and re-opened in 1759. These alterations are said to have cost 100,000*l.*

The annual loss of life and property that occurred through the dangerous state of the navigation under the arches, (the fall being at times five feet,) and the perpetually recurring expense of keeping the bridge in repair, suggested, about the beginning of the present century, its demolition and rebuilding; but not until 1824 was the new structure commenced, the first pile being driven March 15. It was designed by John Rennie, F.R.S., and is about 100 feet westward of the old bridge. In excavating the foundations, were discovered brass and copper coins of Augustus, Vespasian, and later Roman emperors; Venetian tokens, Nuremberg counters, and a few Tradesmen's Tokens; brass and silver rings and buckles, ancient iron keys and silver spoons, the remains of an engraven and gilt dagger, an iron spear-head, a fine bronze lamp (head of Bacchus), and a small silver figure of Harpocrates: the latter preserved in the British Museum. We may here notice, that upon the old bridge grew abundantly *Sisymbrium Irio*, or London Rocket, with small yellow flowers and pointed leaves: this plant probably appeared here soon after the Great Fire of 1666, when it sprung up from among the City ruins.

Mr. Rennie died in 1821; but the works were continued by his sons, Mr. (now Sir John) Rennie and Mr. George Rennie; the builders being Mr. W. Jolliffe and Sir Edward Banks. On June 15, 1825, the first stone was laid in a coffer-dam nearly forty-five feet below high-water mark, opposite the southern arch (fourth lock), with great ceremony, by the Lord Mayor (Garratt), in the presence of the Duke of York; and in the evening the Monument was illuminated with portable gas, to commemorate the event. Two large gold medals were also struck on the occasion. The first arch was keyed August 4, 1827; the last Nov. 19, 1828; and the bridge was opened with great state, August 1, 1831, by King William IV. and Queen Adelaide, who went and returned by water, after partaking of a banquet given on the bridge; the Lord Mayor (Key) presiding; and the King and Queen, and the Royal Family, partaking of the loving-cup.

New London Bridge is unrivalled in the world "in the perfection of proportion and the true greatness of simplicity."

"It consists of five semi-elliptical arches, viz. two of 130 feet, two of 140 feet; and the centre, 152 feet 6 inches span, and 37 feet 6 inches rise, is perhaps the largest elliptical arch ever attempted: the roadway is 52 feet wide. This bridge deserves remark, on account of the difficult situation in which it was built, being immediately above the old bridge, in a depth of from 25 to 30 feet at low water, on a soft alluvial bottom, covered with large loose stones, scoured away by the force of the current from the foundation of the old bridge, the whole of which had to be removed by dredging, before the coffer-dams for the piers and abutments could be commenced, otherwise it would have been extremely difficult, if not impracticable, to have made them water-tight; the difficulty was further increased by the old bridge being left standing, to accommodate the traffic, whilst the new bridge was building; and the restricted water-way of the old bridge occasioned such an increased velocity of the current as materially to retard the operations of the new bridge, and at times the tide threatens to carry away all before it. The great magnitude and extreme flatness of the arches demanded unusual care in the selection of the materials, which were of the finest blue and white granite from Scotland and Devonshire; great accuracy in the workmanship was also indispensable. The piers and abutments stand upon platforms of timber resting upon piles about 20 feet long. The masonry is from 8 feet to 10 feet below the bed of the river."—*Sir John Rennie, F.R.S.*

The time occupied in its erection, from the driving of the first pile on March 15, 1824, to its completion on July 31, 1831, was seven years five months and thirteen days, during which time it employed upwards of 800 men. Its building was attended with so many local difficulties, that forty persons lost their lives in the progress of the works.

The total quantity of stone in the bridge is stated at 120,000 tons; and the ends of the parapets consist of the largest blocks of granite ever brought to this country.

A single cornice runs along the upper part of the bridge, supported on dentils formed of solid beams of granite, marking externally the line of the roadway; this is surmounted by a close parapet, four feet high, upon which are lofty and massive bronzed standards, with gas lanterns.

The amount paid to Messrs. Jolliffe and Banks for this bridge was 425,081*l.* 9*s.* 2*d.*; but the whole sum expended on it, including the approaches, was 1,458,311*l.* 8*s.* 11¾*d.* The latter are very fine, especially the roadway into the City, where, at the suggestion of Mr. Alderman Gibbs, a granite statue of King William was set up, to commemorate the opening; and a bronze equestrian statue of the Duke of Wellington, in front of the Royal Exchange, was erected as an acknowledgment by the citizens of his Grace's exertions in facilitating the means of erecting the new bridge.

The old bridge was not entirely removed until 1832, when the bones of the builder, Peter of Colechurch, were found beneath the masonry of the chapel, as if to complete the eventful history of the antique structure.

At the sale of the materials of this bridge, Mr. Weiss, the cutler, of the Strand, purchased all the iron, amounting to fifteen tons, with which the piles had been shod; and such portions as had entered the ground produced steel infinitely superior to any which Mr. Weiss had ever met with. Upon examination, it was inferred that the extremities of the piles having been charred, the straps of iron closely wedged between them and the stratum in which they were imbedded, must have been subjected to a galvanic action, which, in the course of some six or seven hundred years, produced the above effects.

The stone proved finely seasoned material: a portion of it was purchased by Alderman Harmer, and used in building his seat, Ingress Abbey, near Greenhithe, and the balustrades, of good proportions, were preserved. Many snuff-boxes and other memorials were turned from the pile-wood.

The traffic across the old bridge, in one day of July 1811, amounted to 89,640 persons on foot, 769 wagons, 2924 carts and drays, 1240 coaches, 485 gigs and taxed carts, and 764 horses.—[See *Chronicles of London Bridge*, by an Antiquary (Mr. Richard Thomson), 1827; where the researches of a lifetime appear to be condensed into a single volume.]

WESTMINSTER BRIDGE was opened in 1750, until when the only communication between Lambeth and Westminster was by the ferry-boat near Lambeth Palace-Gate, the property of the Archbishop of Canterbury, granted by patent under a rent of 20*d.*; and for the loss of which ferry 2205*l.* were given to the see.

Attempts to obtain another bridge over the Thames, besides that of London, were made in the several reigns of Elizabeth, James I., Charles I. and II., and George I.; but it was not until the year 1736 (10 Geo. II.) that Parliament authorised the building of a second bridge.

The architect of Westminster Bridge was Charles Labelye, a native of Switzerland: the first stone was laid by the Earl of Pembroke, Jan. 29, 1738-9; and the bridge was opened Nov. 18, 1750. It consists of fifteen semicircular arches, the centre seventy-six feet span; it is 1223 feet long by 44 feet wide. It was originally intended for a wooden bridge, and was partly commenced on this principle. The bottom courses of the piers were laid, or built, in floating-vessels, or caissons, which, when so loaded, were conducted to their proper positions, and there sunk upon the natural alluvial bed of the river; the bottom of the caissons thus forming, when the sides had been removed, the platforms or foundations of the masonry, unsustained by under-filing, or any other support than that of the gravel or sand on which they rested. The defects and dangers of this mode of building soon appeared: in July 1747, one of the western piers had so settled, that it was thought necessary to take off the balustrades, paving, and ballast; before the bridge was completed it was indispensable to take down and rebuild two arches; and at subsequent periods the whole of the structure, more or less, settled or gave way. Labelye states the quantity of stone in this bridge to be nearly double that employed in building St. Paul's Cathedral. "The caissons contained upwards of 150 loads of timber, and were of more tonnage than a forty-gun vessel."—(*Hutton's Tracts*). The original cost of the bridge was 218,800*l.*; of the approaches, 170,700*l.*

In 1823, Telford inspected the foundations, when he found the platforms upon which the piers rest considerably sunk. Vast sums have been expended in its repair. Within the last forty years, it has cost nearly half a million of money; whereas the property of the bridge only realises 7,464*l.* 11*s.* 8*d.* In 1838, Mr. W. Cubitt found the caissons in a perfect state, the wood (fir) retaining its resinous smell. After the removal of old London Bridge, as Telford foresaw, more than one of the Westminster piers gave way; to stay their sinking, in Aug. 1846, the thoroughfare was closed; the balustrades and heavy stone alcoves were removed, the stone-work stripped to the cornice, and the roadway lowered, thus lightening it of 30,000 tons weight; timber palings were put up at the sides, and the bridge re-opened.* The proportions of the sides are stated to have been so accurate, that if a person spoke against the wall of any of the niches on one side of the way, he might be distinctly heard upon the opposite side; even a whisper was audible in the stillness of the night. This was the last metropolitan bridge which had a balustraded parapet, that of Blackfriars Bridge having been removed in 1839. At Westminster, "the swelling of each heavy balustrade exactly ranged with the eye of a foot passenger, and from a carriage, the top of the line of balustrades almost entirely obstructed the view of the river; thus hiding one of the finest rivers in Europe for the sake of preserving some imaginary form in architecture."—(*Repton.*)

The bridge is built of magnesian limestone, containing from 24 to 42 per cent of carbonate of magnesia, from which Epsom salts are obtained by the application of sulphuric acid. "If," said Dr. Ryan, in a

---

* Sir Howard Douglas observes: "The more remote dangers of the defective mode of laying the foundations of the piers were, to a certain extent, kept in suspension so long as the river remained undisturbed, in that somewhat artificial state in which it was when Westminster Bridge was constructed. But no sooner was that condition altered, first by opening the great arch of London Bridge, then by removing the London Water-works, and ultimately by taking away Old London Bridge, than all the defects and dangers of this mode of construction became active and progressive."—(*Metropolitan Bridges and Improvements*, 1845.) The increase of the current, alterations in its set and action, and the consequent scouring and deepening of the river, particularly at the waterways of the bridges, have, from time to time, perilled Westminster Bridge.

lecture before the Royal Agricultural Society, "Westminster Bridge, built of that rock, were covered with water and sulphuric acid, it would be converted into Epsom salts." Mr. Barry has proposed to substitute for this patched-up stone bridge a five-arched iron structure, in the Gothic style, to assimilate with the new Houses of Parliament.

Upon Westminster Bridge, September 3, 1803, Wordsworth composed this majestic sonnet:

> Earth has not any thing to shew more fair:
> Dull would he be of soul who could pass by
> A sight so touching in its majesty:
> This City now doth like a garment wear
> The beauty of the morning; silent, bare,
> Ships, towers, domes, theatres, and temples, lie
> Open unto the fields, and to the sky,
> All bright and glittering in the smokeless air.
> Never did sun more beautifully steep
> In his first splendour valley, rock, or hill;
> Ne'er saw I, never felt, a calm so deep!
> The river glideth at its own sweet will:
> Dear God! the very houses seem asleep,
> And all that mighty heart is lying still!

BLACKFRIARS BRIDGE originated with a committee appointed, in 1746, to examine Labelye's designs for improving London Bridge; though the architect of Blackfriars Bridge was Robert Mylne, a native of Edinburgh. "The first pile of it was driven in the middle of the Thames June 7, 1760; and the foundation-stone was laid by Sir Thomas Chitty, Lord Mayor, Oct. 31. On Nov. 19, 1768, it was made passable as a bridle-way, exactly two years after its reception of foot-passengers; and it was finally and generally opened on Sunday, Nov. 19, 1769. Until June 22, 1785, there was a toll of one halfpenny for every foot-passenger, and one penny on Sundays. The toll-house was burnt down in the riots of 1780, when all the account-books were destroyed." (Chronicles of London Bridge.) The total cost of building and completing the Bridge and avenues thereto was 261,579l. 0s. 6¼d.; including 12,250l. 17s. 6d. paid to the Watermen's Company for the Sunday ferry.

The bridge is built of Portland stone, and consists of nine semi-elliptical arches, the largest being 100 feet span, and 41 feet 6 inches rise; the total length of the bridge is 995 feet, its width 45 feet. Here the elliptical arch was introduced about the first time in this country, in opposition to Gwyn, who, in his design, proposed the semicircular arch. The columns are the most objectionable feature in Mylne's design, architecturally; for the line of the parapet being a curve, the pillars are necessarily of different heights and diameters. Between 1833 and 1840, the bridge was thoroughly repaired by Walker and Burges, at an expense of 74,035l., it is stated at a loss to the contractor. The foot and carriage ways were lowered. The removal of the balustrades, and the substitution of a plain parapet, have altogether spoiled the architectural beauty of the structure.

On the Middlesex side of the river, east of the bridge, in 1845, was constructed, by Walker and Burges, a Landing-Pier, 185 feet in length; the floating-barge, or dumby, being 100 feet long, and rising and falling with the tide, in grooves at each end, formed by piles and protected by dolphins. This pier cost 4000l., and was proposed in 1841, but was not decided on until after five persons had been drowned near the bridge, by the breaking down of a temporary pier, July 22, 1844.

VAUXHALL BRIDGE, communicating with Millbank, had, in consequence of disputes, four engineers: Ralph Dodd, Sir Samuel Bentham, John Rennie, F.R.S.; and lastly, James Walker, who carried the design into effect at the expense of a public Company. The Bridge is of cast-iron, but was originally intended to be of stone: hence the narrowness of the nine arches, which would not have been necessary for an iron structure. The first stone of the pier begun by Mr. Rennie was laid by Lord Dundas, as proxy for the Prince Regent, May 9, 1811. The building was then suspended, but transferred to Mr. Walker; the first stone of the resumed works was laid by the late Duke of Brunswick, August 21, 1813; and on June 4, 1816, the bridge was opened.

The width of the river is 900 feet at this bridge, the length of which, clear of the abutments, is 806 feet; its 9 arches are each 78 feet span, and its 8 piers, each 13 feet wide; height of centre arch, at high water, 27 feet. The Bridge cost upwards of 300,000*l.*; its half-year's clear revenue from tolls in 1849-50 was 2986*l.* 3*s.* 4*d.* The low grounds west of the Bridge, and formerly known as the Neathouse Gardens, have been elevated to a level with the Chelsea road, by transporting hither the soil excavated from St. Katherine's Docks; and upon this artificial foundation several streets have been built.

WATERLOO BRIDGE has been dignified by Canova as "the noblest bridge in the world," and by Baron Dupin as "a colossal monument worthy of Sesostris and the Cæsars." It was partly projected by George Dodd, the engineer, and designed for him by John Linnell Bond, architect, who died in 1837; but the bridge was eventually built for a public Company by John Rennie, F.R.S. It crosses the Thames from the Strand, between Somerset Place and the site of the Savoy, to Lambeth, at the centre of the site of Cuper's Gardens, where the first stone was laid by the Chairman and Directors of the Company, October 11, 1811.

This bridge consists of nine semi-elliptical arches, each 120 feet span and 35 feet high, supported on piers 20 feet wide at the springing of the arches; with "useless and inappropriate Grecian-Doric columns between the piers, surmounted by the anomalous decoration of a balustrade upon a Doric entablature."—(*Elmes.*) The width of the Thames at this part is 1326 feet at high water; the entire length of the Bridge is 2456 feet,—the bridge and abutments being 1380 feet, the approach from the Strand 310 feet, and the land-arch causeway on the Surrey side 766 feet. The roadway upon the summit of the arches is carried upon brick arches to the level of the Strand; and by a gentle declivity upon a series of brick arches over the roadway upon the Surrey bank of the river to the level of the roads near the Obelisk by the Surrey Theatre. This district, until the building of the Bridge, was known as Lambeth Marsh, was low-lying and swampy, with thinly scattered dwellings; but in a few years it became covered with houses.

The bridge is built of granite, "in a style of solidity and magnificence hitherto unknown. There elliptical arches, with inverted arches between them to counteract the lateral pressure, were carried to a greater extent than in former bridges; and isolated coffer-dams upon a great scale in a tidal river, with steam-engines for pumping out the water, were, it is believed, for the first time employed in this country; the level line of roadway, which adds so much to the beauty as well as the convenience of the structure, was there adopted."—(*Sir John Rennie, F.R.S.*) The bridge was opened by a procession of the Prince Regent and the Dukes of York and Wellington, and a grand military cavalcade, on June 18, 1817, the second anniversary of the battle of Waterloo, whence it is named. The bridge itself cost about 400,000*l.*, which, by the expense of the approaches, was increased to above a million of money; —a larger sum than the cost of building St. Paul's, the Monument, and seven of our finest metropolitan churches. It has been a ruinous speculation to the Company, the tolls scarcely amounting to 20,000*l.* per annum. The property has been offered at a low sum to the Government, to be opened as a free bridge.

Formerly, the average number of suicides annually committed from Waterloo Bridge was 40; and in September, 1841, there were nine attempts made, within a few days, to commit suicide from Blackfriars Bridge. The alteration in the law in punishing attempted self-destruction has greatly checked this wicked propensity.

SOUTHWARK BRIDGE, designed by John Rennie, F.R.S., was built by a public Company, and cost about 800,000l. It consists of three cast-iron arches : the centre 240 feet span, and the two side arches 210 feet each, about forty-two feet above the highest spring-tides : the ribs forming, as it were, a series of hollow masses, or voussoirs, similar to those of stone, a principle new in the construction of cast-iron bridges, and very successful. The whole of the segmental pieces and the braces are kept in their places by dove-tailed sockets and long cast-iron wedges, so that bolts are unnecessary; although they were used during the construction of the bridge, to keep the pieces in their places until the wedges had been driven. The spandrils are similarly connected, and upon them rests the roadway of solid plates of cast-iron, joined by iron cement. The piers and abutments are of stone, founded upon timber platforms, resting upon piles driven below the bed of the river. The masonry is tied throughout by vertical and horizontal bond-stones, so that the whole acts as one mass in the best position to resist the horizontal thrust. The first stone was laid by Admiral Lord Keith, May 23, 1815, the Bill for erecting the Bridge having been passed May 6, 1811. The iron-work, weight 5700 tons, had been so well put together by the Walkers, of Rotherham, the founders, and the masonry by the contractors, Jolliffe and Banks, that when the work was finished, scarcely any sinking was discernible in the arches. From experiments made to ascertain the extent of the expansion and contraction between the extreme range of winter and summer temperature, it was found that the arch rose in the summer about 1 inch to 1½ inch. The works were commenced in 1813, and the bridge was opened by lamp-light March 24, 1819, as the clock of St. Paul's Cathedral tolled midnight. Towards the middle of the western side of the bridge is a descent from the pavement to a steam-boat pier.

HUNGERFORD SUSPENSION-BRIDGE, from Hungerford Market to Belvedere Road, Lambeth, was constructed by I. K. Brunel, F.R.S., and is a fine specimen of mechanical skill. It consists of two lofty brick piers or towers, in the Italian style, 58 feet above the road, and built in brick-work and cement on the natural bed of the river, without piles. In the upper part of these towers, four chains pass over rollers, so as to equalise the strain; they carry the platform or roadway, in two lines, with single suspension rods, 12 feet apart; the chains being secured in tunnels at the abutments to iron girders, embedded in brickwork and cement, and strengthened with concrete. There are three spans, the central one between the piers being 676½ feet, or 110 feet wider than the Menai Bridge ; and second only to the span of the wire suspension-bridge at Fribourg, which is nearly 900 feet. The length between the abutments of the Hungerford Bridge is 1352½ feet. The roadway is in the centre 32 feet above high-water mark, or 7 feet higher than the crown of the centre arch of Waterloo Bridge. The height above the piers is 28½ feet. Thus are gained additional height for the river traffic, and a graceful curve, with the appearance of swagging prevented. The bridge was commenced in 1841, and was built without any scaffolding but a few ropes, consequently, without impediment to the navigation of the river. The iron-work, between 10,000 and 11,000 tons, is by Sandys and Co., Cornwall. The entire cost of the bridge was 110,000l., raised by a public Company. The toll is a halfpenny each person each way. The bridge was opened May 1, 1845, when, between noon and midnight, 36,254 persons passed over. Hungerford is the great focus of the Thames steam-navigation, the embarkations and landings here exceeding 2,000,000 per annum.

HAMMERSMITH SUSPENSION-BRIDGE is one of the most elegant structures of its kind; and, unlike other suspension-bridges, has part of the roadway *supported on*, and not hanging from, the main chains. The weight of the masonry abutments on each bank is 2160 tons, to resist the pull of the chains. Cost, 80,000*l.*; engineer, W. T. Clarke; first stone laid by the Duke of Sussex, May 7, 1825; finished, 1827.

BUCKLERSBURY,

A short street at the point where the Poultry meets Cheapside: here formerly stood the great conduit which brought water from Conduit Mead, near Oxford-road and Paddington. Stow writes: " Buckles bury, so called of a manor and tenements pertaining to one Buckles who dwelt there, and kept his courts." The manor-house, in Stow's time, bore the sign of the Old Barge, from its being said, that when Walbrook lay open, barges were rowed or towed out of the Thames up here: hence the present Barge Yard. Bucklersbury was a noted place for grocers and apothecaries, drugsters and furriers. In Shakspeare's days it was, probably, a herb market; for he has the comparison of smelling "like Buckler's-bury in simple-time."—(*Merry Wives of Windsor*, act iii. sc. 3.)

BUNHILL FIELDS,

The name of the great burial-ground of the Dissenters, City-road, near Finsbury-square; originally a field of Finsbury Manor Farm; next a general burial-place at the Great Plague of 1665; then walled in by the City, and subsequently leased to Dissenting sects and Tyndal, and thence called " the fanatic burying-place." Here are interred John Bunyan, author of the *Pilgrim's Progress;* George Fox, founder of the Quakers; Daniel Defoe, author of *Robinson Crusoe ;* the mother of John Wesley; Dr. Isaac Watts; Joseph Ritson, the antiquary; William Blake, painter and poet; Thomas Stothard, R.A.; Thomas Hardy, tried for high treason, in 1794, with John Horne Tooke, John Thelwall, &c.

"People like to be buried in company, and in good company. The Dissenters regarded Bunhill Fields' burial-ground as their *Campo Santo*, and especially for Bunyan's sake. It is said that many have made it their desire to be interred as near as possible to the spot where his remains are deposited."—*Southey.*

CANONBURY TOWER,

At the northern extremity of the parish of Islington, denotes the site of the country-house of the Prior of the Canons of St. Bartholomew : hence, it is supposed, the name of Canons'-bury, *bury* being synonymous with *burgh*, a dwelling. On a garden-house hard by is sculptured the rebus or device of Bolton, the last prior,—a *bolt*, or arrow for the crossbow, through a *tun ;*

"Old Prior Bolton, with his bolt and tun."

The Tower, which is of red brick, is believed to have been built by Sir John Spencer, of Crosby-place, who purchased the estate in 1570. Elizabeth, his only daughter and heiress, married William, second Lord Compton, who is traditionally said to have contrived her elopement from her father's house at Canonbury in a baker's basket. In 1618, he was created Earl of Northampton, and from him the present owner of Canonbury, who is the ninth Earl and first Marquess of Northampton, is lineally descended.

The Tower is 17 feet square, and nearly 60 feet in height, and consists of seven stories and 23 rooms. For many years it was let in lodgings. Amongst its tenants was Ephraim Chambers, whose Cyclopædia was not only the basis of Rees's work, but originated all the modern Cyclopædias in the English and the other European languages. Chambers died at Canonbury, May 18, 1740, and was buried in Westminster Abbey, under a short Latin inscription, his own composition. Newbery, the bookseller, lodged here; and in his apartments Goldsmith often lay concealed from his creditors, and under a pressing necessity he there wrote his *Vicar of Wakefield*: "he was the most diligent slave that ever toiled in the mill of Grub-street."

"A silly notion at one time prevailed that there was formerly a subterranean communication between Canonbury House and the Priory of St. Bartholomew. Similar vulgar and absurd stories are current at most of the large monasteries; as Malmesbury, Netley, Glastonbury, &c."—(*Godwin's Churches of London.*)

The ancient priory mansion covered the entire site now occupied by Canonbury-place, and had attached to it a park of about four acres, with large gardens, a fish-pond, &c.; most of which were included in the premises of Canonbury Tea-gardens and Tavern, in the middle of the last century but a small ale-house. It was enlarged and improved by a Mr. Lane, who had been a private soldier; but its celebrity was chiefly owing to the widow Sutton, who resided here from 1785 to 1808, and laid out the bowling-green and grounds.

CARLTON HOUSE,

In Pall Mall, was originally built for Lord Carlton, in 1709; bequeathed by him to his nephew, Lord Burlington, the architect; and purchased in 1732, by Frederic Prince of Wales, father of George III.; here the Princess of Wales died in 1772. The first house was of red brick; the grounds extended westward to Marlborough House, and were laid out for Lord Burlington, by Kent, with bowers and grottoes, a cascade, statues and busts, a marble saloon and bagnio.

In 1783, Carlton House was assigned to George Prince of Wales, who employed Holland the architect to enlarge the mansion; and he added a Corinthian portico and a screen of Ionic columns[*] fronting Pall-Mall: in one of the lodges dwelt "Big Sam," the royal porter, nearly eight feet high. Here was a remarkably fine collection of arms and costumes, including two swords of Charles I.; swords of Columbus and Marlborough; and a *couteau-de-chasse* used by Charles XII. of Sweden; which relics are now in the North Corridor at Windsor Castle. Carlton

* Bonomi wrote the following epigram upon this screen:
"Care colonne, che fatti quá?
Non sapiamo, in verità:"
Thus anglicised by Prince Hoare:
"Dear little columns, all in a row,
What *do* you do there?
Indeed we don't know."
Sheridan's allusion to these columns was not much more complimentary. About the time that the Duke of York took possession of Melbourne House, now Lady Dover's, near the Horse-Guards, of which the most remarkable feature is the cupola in front, some discussions were raised in Parliament about the debts of the Duke and his royal brother at Carlton House. The virtuous indignation of the Opposition was tremendous; and some of their remarks having been reported to Sheridan when he entered the House of Commons, "I wonder," said he, "what amount of punishment would satisfy some people! Has not the one got into the Roundhouse, and the other into the *Pillory?*"

House was sumptuously furnished for the Prince's ill-starred marriage in 1795: here, Jan. 7, 1796, was born the Princess, baptised Feb. 11, Charlotte-Augusta; and on May 2, 1816, married here to Leopold, now King of the Belgians. The ceremonial of conferring the Regency was enacted at Carlton House with great pomp, Feb. 5, 1811; and on June 19 following, the Prince Regent gave here a superb supper to 2000 guests; a stream with gold and silver fish flowing through a marble canal down the centre table.

In 1827, Carlton House was removed; the columns of the portico, (adapted from the Temple of Jupiter Stator at Rome,) being subsequently used in the portico of the National Gallery; and the ornamental interior details (as marble mantel-pieces, friezes, columns, &c.) transferred to Buckingham Palace. Thus has disappeared Carlton House: *sed stat nominis umbra.* Upon the site of the gardens have been built the York Column and Carlton-House-terrace; the balustrades of the latter originally extended between the two ranges of houses, but were removed to form the present entrance into St. James's Park, by command of William IV., very soon after his accession. Upon the site of the courtyard and part of Carlton House are the United Service and Athenæum Clubhouses, and the intervening area facing Waterloo-place.

Eastward is the riding-house of Carlton Palace, or Carlton Ride, long the depository of the Common Pleas, Exchequer, Land Revenue, and other records.

CARVINGS IN WOOD.

The art of Sculpture in Wood has ever been royally and nobly encouraged in England; and the metropolis contains many fine specimens of ancient and modern skill in this tasteful branch of decoration.

The figures carved upon the chestnut roof of Westminster Hall shew the degree of excellence the art had attained in this country so early as the reign of Richard II. The sculptured arms on the corbels are those of France and England, quarterly, and of St. Edward the Confessor, as borne by Richard II.; whose favourite badge, viz. the white hart, lodged, ducally gorged and chained, and his crest of a lion guardant crowned, standing on a chapeau and helmet, are also carved, in alternate succession, on the cornice.

There is every reason to suppose the timber architecture of Old London to have been elaborate and beautiful. Till about the year 1625, nearly all the houses were built of wood: the interiors of the better sort were often richly carved, particularly in the panels of rooms, chimney-pieces, ceilings, and staircases; and the exteriors displayed a similar love of ornament in the doors and barge-boards.

The Great Fire of 1666 spared few specimens of early wood-carving; but several exist in quarters not reached by the destroyer. Of existing gothic work may be mentioned the decorations of Crosby Hall, much injured, however, by "restoration." The excellently carved stalls in the Church of St. Helen, Bishopsgate, and those of the Chapel of Henry VII. at Westminster, are unusually magnificent, and were mostly executed by foreign workmen summoned to England by Henry VII.

In the reign of Elizabeth, not only the houses of the nobility were decorated, but furniture made of British woods was richly carved: the late Mr. Cottingham, F.S.A., assembled many unique specimens of this period. In the Elizabethan style may also be mentioned:—

Two splendid brackets (griffins), dated 1592, supporting the yard entrance at 21 Princes-square, Wilson-street, Finsbury.

Two house-fronts in Aldersgate-street.

Some boldly carved brackets (1595) at the Old Boar's Head, Grays' Inn-lane.

F

Panel and trusses over the mantel of the Cock Tavern, Fleet-street (*temp.* James I.). The room was formerly paneled opposite the fire-place.

Brackets (*temp.* James I.) at the back of the house, 61 Gray's-Inn-lane.

There was some fine Elizabethan paneling in the Star Chamber at Westminster, taken down 1835; but restored for the Hon. E. Cust, at Leasowe Castle.

Brackets, very fine, at the corner of Cloth Fall and Cloth Fair, Smithfield.

House-front, 94 Fenchurch-street.

Several house-fronts, rather later, in Whitechapel Market.

The Sir Paul Pindar's Head, Bishopsgate-street-without, has a finely carved front, and a carved ceiling in one of the unmodernised rooms.

The projecting house-front (now gilt), 17 Fleet-street, opposite Chancery-lane.

Mask brackets (*temp.* James I.), at the front and back of the Old Cheshire Cheese, 48 Hart-street, City; and a spirited, grotesque head (same date) within the court of Red-Lion-place, Cock-lane.

A fine staircase, attributed to Inigo Jones, (probably later,) at 96 St. Martin's-lane, Charing Cross.

At the White Horse Inn, Church-street, Chelsea, (burnt Dec. 14, 1840,) were four grotesque Elizabethan brackets, carved chimney-pieces; and a carved frame for the sign, dated 1509.

The most celebrated carver after the Great Fire was Grinling Gibbons, who, Walpole tells us, so delicately carved a pot of flowers, that they shook in the room with the motion of coaches passing in the street. Most of the interior carvings of St. Paul's Cathedral were executed by Gibbons, or by Dutch workmen under his superintendence; the cherubs in the choir are in the highest style of the art.

One of the best carvers employed by Wren was Philip Wood, who came up a poor lad from Suffolk, and carved as a specimen of his skill a sow and pigs, for which he received ten guineas. According to the Commissioners' Report, between the years 1701 and 1707, Wood was paid large sums of money for carved work in St. Paul's Cathedral.

It is not generally known that the pulpit at St. Paul's was designed by Mylne, and executed about sixty years since by one of the finest flower-carvers of the time, named Mowatt, then employed by a relative of Edward Wyatt, the present carver and gilder, in Oxford-street. The pulpit is carved in Spanish mahogany and satin-wood; the foliage is marvellously played with in the volutes.

Many of the Halls of the City Companies are decorated with Gibbons's work; as well as the interiors of most of the Churches built by Sir Christopher Wren. St. James's, Piccadilly, has some fine pulpit, altar, and pew carvings; and the Churchwardens' pews at Allhallows Barking, (with the symbols of the four Evangelists,) are amongst the most delicate decorations of their time in the metropolis. The Hall of Heralds' College is also well enriched in the Gibbons style; and a beautiful specimen of his skill in marine subjects is preserved at the New River House, Spa-Fields.

London abounds in richly-carved doorways and over-doors of the 17th and 18th centuries: there are good examples in Great Ormond-street; in Shire-lane, Temple Bar, where Gibbons once lived; in Cavendish-square, especially at No. 33; the entrance to Langbourn Chambers, Fenchurch-street; and some old mansions in Mark-lane.

A pair of exquisitely carved statuettes, (Raving and Melancholy Madness,) is shewn among the *curiosities* of Bethlem Hospital.

State Coaches present fine carving. Such are the Lord Mayor's Coach, (stated to have been designed by Angelica Kauffman,) kept at the Green Yard, Whitecross-street; the Queen's Coach, at the Royal Mews, Pimlico; and the Speaker's Coach, Prince's-street, Westminster.

In private collections, some magnificent specimens of early carving are preserved: such are the Italian bedstead-pillars of the 16th century, and the bas-relief after Rubens, in the possession of the Earl of Cadogan; and the collection, dating from the 15th to the 18th centuries, the property of G. Field, Esq., of Lister House, Clapham.

Carving received considerable check from the introduction of stucco in the reign of George II.; but the art has received a fresh impetus in the present century. Some fine church carving was executed in 1839-42 for the Temple Church; and in 1847-8 for the choir of Westminster Abbey, then refitted with canopied stalls, organ-case, screen, &c., by Messrs. Ruddle, of Peterborough. The church of St. Mary-at-Hill, Billingsgate, was redecorated in 1849-50, by W. Gibbs Rogers: the pulpit alone cost upwards of 500*l.* ; the stairs have an elaborate string-course, and all the banisters are on the rake; the bosses and flowers of the sounding-board exceed a foot in projection: the organ-gallery front has flowers festooned with musical instruments, and the pretty conceit of a crab crawling over a violin. Mr. Rogers has also carved, from a design suggested by the Queen, a box-wood cradle in rich Italian style, most delicately finished, and first used for the infant Prince Arthur, born 1850: it is cleverly engraved and described in the *Art-Journal* for August, 1850.

The interior enrichments of the New Palace at Westminster present some fine specimens of contemporary carving. Much of the work has, however, been executed by machinery, and finished by hand.

The great depository for old carvings is Wardour-street, Oxford-street, where the dealers mostly keep shop.

CATO-STREET CONSPIRACY.

In 1820, at Cato-street, John-street, Edgeware-road, Arthur Thistlewood and his fellow-conspirators met to assassinate the Ministers assembled at a cabinet dinner, on February 23d, at Lord Harrowby's, 39 Grosvenor-square, where Thistlewood proposed, as "a rare haul, to murder them all together." Some of the conspirators were to watch Lord Harrowby's house; one was to call and deliver a despatch-box at the door; the others were then to rush in and murder the Ministers as they sat at dinner; and, as special trophies, to bring away with them the heads of Lords Sidmouth and Castlereagh, in two bags provided for the purpose! They were then to fire the cavalry-barracks; and the Bank and Tower were to be taken by the people, who, it was hoped, would rise upon the spread of the news. This diabolical plot was, however, revealed to the Ministers by one Edwards, who had joined the conspirators for that purpose. Still, no notice was apparently taken. The preparations for dinner went on at Lord Harrowby's till eight o'clock in the evening; but the guests did not arrive. The Archbishop of York, who lived next door, happened to give a dinner-party at the same hour, and the arrival of the carriages deceived those of the conspirators who were on the watch in the street, till it was too late to give warning to their comrades who had assembled at Cato-street, in a loft over a stable, accessible only by a ladder. Here, while the traitors were arming themselves by the light of one or two candles, a party of Bow-street officers entered the stable; when Smithers, the first of them who mounted the ladder, and attempted to seize Thistlewood, was run by him through the body, and instantly fell; whilst, the lights being extinguished, a few shots were exchanged in the darkness and confusion, and Thistlewood and several of his companions escaped through a window at the back of the premises; nine were taken that evening with their arms and ammunition, and the intelligence conveyed to the Ministers, who, having dined at home, met at Lord Liverpool's to await the result of what the Bow-street officers had done. A reward of 1000*l.* was immediately offered for the apprehension of Thistlewood; but he was captured before eight o'clock next morning, while in bed at a friend's house, No. 8 White-street, Little Moorfields. The conspirators were sent to the Tower, and were the last persons imprisoned in that fortress. On April 20th, Thistlewood was condemned to death,

after three days' trial; and on May 1st, he and his four principal
accomplices, Ings, Brunt, Tidd, and Davidson, who had been severally
tried and convicted, were hanged at the Old Bailey, and their heads
cut off. Southey relates this touching anecdote of Thistlewood's last
hours :—

"When the desperate and atrocious traitor Thistlewood was on the scaffold,
his demeanour was that of a man who was resolved boldly to meet the fate he had
deserved; in the few words which were exchanged between him and his fellow-
criminals, he observed, that the grand question whether or not the soul was im-
mortal would soon be solved for them. No expression of hope escaped him; no
breathing of repentance, no spark of grace, appeared. Yet (it is a fact which,
whether it be more consolatory or awful, ought to be known), on the night after
the sentence, and preceding his execution, while he supposed that the person who
was appointed to watch him in his cell was asleep, this miserable man was seen
by that person repeatedly to rise upon his knees, and heard repeatedly calling
upon Christ his Saviour to have mercy upon him, and to forgive him his sins."—
The Doctor, chap. lxxi.

The selection of *Cato*-street for the conspirators' meeting was
accidental; and the street itself is associated but indirectly in name
with the Roman patriot and philosopher. To efface recollection of
the conspiracy of the low and desperate politicians of 1820, Cato-
street has been changed to Homer-street.

CEMETERIES,

Or public burial-grounds, planted and laid out as gardens around the
metropolis, are a novelty of our times; although they were suggested
just after the Great Fire of 1666, when Evelyn regretted that advantage
had not been taken of that calamity to rid the City of its burial-places,
and establish a necropolis without the walls. He deplores that " the
churchyards had not been banished to the north walls of the City,
where a grated inclosure, of competent breadth, for a mile in length,
might have served for an universal cemetery to all the parishes, distinguished by the like separations, and with ample walks of trees; the
walks adorned with monuments, inscriptions, and titles, apt for con-
templation and memory of the defunct, and that wise and excellent law
of the Twelve Tables restored and renewed."

There were, in 1850, eight Cemeteries in the suburbs, each the property of a public Company.

KENSAL GREEN CEMETERY was the first established. It lies upon
high ground, left of the Harrow Road and the hamlet of Kensal Green,
about two miles from Paddington Green. It contains fifty-three acres,
divided into two grounds: the westernmost consecrated Nov. 2, 1832;
the smaller ground being for the interment of persons whose friends
desire a funeral service differing from that of the Church of England.
The same distinction is observed in each of the Cemeteries; and each is
planted and laid out in walks, parterres, and borders of flowers, and
other styles of landscape garden. A register is kept of interments for
both portions of the grounds, and a duplicate is lodged with the registrars of parishes in the diocese. Each Company has its scale of charges
for interment in catacomb, vault, or grave.

Within three years from the opening of the Kensal-Green Cemetery,
there took place in it about 1000 interments. Each ground has its chapel
and colonnades; in the latter are placed mural tablets, and beneath are
the vaults or catacombs. The memorials in this Cemetery are very numerous: altar-tombs, "monumental urns," sarcophagi, and the broken
column; capacious tomb-houses, encompassed with flower-beds, or overhung with funereal trees; pillars, bearing urns; weeping and praying
figures, medallion portraits, and groups of insignia, are most frequent;
though emblems are borrowed alike from the Pagan temple and the

Christian church. The cross, in its picturesque varieties, and the plain but massive slab, are side by side. Among the most conspicuous is, at the entrance, a monument to Madame Soyer, by a Belgian sculptor; the pedestal and a colossal figure of Faith are upwards of twenty feet in height. The tombs of St. John Long, the "counter-irritation" surgeon; of Morison, the "hygeist;" and of Ducrow, the equestrian, are also prominent: the latter left a sum of money for flowers, shrubs, and repairs. Here is interred the Duke of Sussex, according to especial directions left by that prince: his grave, near the chapel, is covered by an immense granite tomb; and near it rest the remains of the Princess Sophia, his sister, beneath a handsome sarcophagus tomb of Sicilian marble, erected in 1850, by subscription of Queen Victoria, the King of Hanover, Adolphus Duke of Cambridge, and the Duchess of Gloucester. Several persons of rank and station are buried here; and the predominance of authors, artists, and youthful dead, is observable.

THE SOUTH METROPOLITAN and NORWOOD CEMETERY contains about fifty acres, and was consecrated Dec. 6, 1837: the chapels, by Tite, in the pointed style, are very beautiful; and the grounds are hilly, and picturesquely planted.

HIGHGATE AND KENTISH TOWN CEMETERY, twenty-two acres, consecrated May 20, 1839, lies immediately beneath Highgate Church. It has a Tudor gate-house and chapel, and catacombs of Egyptian architecture; the ground is laid out in terraces, tastefully planted; and the distant view of London from among the tombs is suggestive to a meditative mind.

ABNEY PARK CEMETERY and Arboretum, lying eastward, at Stoke-Newington, thirty acres, was opened by the Lord Mayor, May 20, 1840. It was formed from the Park of Sir Thomas Abney, the friend of Dr. Isaac Watts, to mark whose thirty-six years' residence here a statue of the Doctor, by Baily, was erected in 1845. The Abney mansion was taken down in 1844; many of the fine old trees remain.

WESTMINSTER AND WEST OF LONDON CEMETERY, Earl's Court, Fulham Road, thirty-nine acres, was consecrated June 15, 1840; it has a domed chapel, with semi-circular colonnades of imposing design. In the grounds is a large altar-tomb, with athlete figures, modelled by Baily, and erected by subscription to Jackson, the pugilist.

NUNHEAD CEMETERY, Peckham, consists of fifty acres, and was consecrated July 29, 1840.

THE CITY OF LONDON AND TOWER HAMLETS CEMETERY, about thirty acres, lies at the extremity of Mile-End Road, north of Bow Common; and VICTORIA PARK CEMETERY, about eleven acres, at Bethnal Green, north of the Eastern Counties Railway.

The public are allowed to walk in each of the Cemeteries at stated hours. They comprised, in 1850, about 282 acres of ground, of which about seventeen acres had been used for graves and vaults, exclusive of the space occupied by roads and paths, plantations and buildings.

A few suburban churchyards are planted similarly to the Cemeteries; as that of St. John's Wood Chapel, where are buried Joanna Southcott and Richard Brothers, the prophetic; and John Jackson, R.A., the portrait-painter. The churchyard of St. Giles's-in-the-Fields, Lower Pancras Road, consecrated so long ago as 1804, has many flowery graves: here is the handsome tomb of Sir John Soane, overhung with cypresses. The burying-ground of St. Martin's-in-the-Fields, Pratt-street, Camden Town, is also planted: here lies Charles Dibdin, the song-writer.

The burial-grounds for Jews are mostly laid out and planted in the "cemetery" manner. Formerly their burial-place was outside the City Wall, at Leyrestowe, "without Cripelgate."

Cemeteries have, from the costliness of interment in them, been, mostly used by the wealthier classes, and but for the reception of few of the 52,000 persons who die annually in the metropolis. Hence they have little abated the evil of intramural interments; and, as stated by Dr. Sutherland, in his Report of the Board of Health, in 1850, "the grave-yards of London are still the plague-spots of its population. The putrid drainage of them pollutes its wells, seethes beneath its dwellings, and poisons its atmosphere; and some parts of the metropolis are still honeycombed with deposits of the putrescent remains of millions of its citizens." By the Metropolitan Interment Act, passed in 1850, it is hoped these evils to Public Health will be remedied.

CHANCERY LANE,

Formerly New-lane and Chancellor's-lane, is the greatest "legal thoroughfare" in London, and extends from Fleet-street, opposite Inner Temple Gate, to Holborn, nearly opposite Gray's Inn. In Edward I.'s time it was so foul and miry as to be barred up, to prevent accidents. Entering by Fleet-street, on the left are some half-timbered houses, with projecting windows, overhanging stories, and gabled fronts. Izaak Walton kept a draper's shop at the second house on the left, taken down when that end of the lane was widened; he subsequently removed, according to Sir Harris Nicolas's *Life of Walton*, five doors higher up in the Lane. Opposite is Serjeants' Inn, rebuilt by Sir Robert Smirke in 1838; but the old Hall remains. Higher up, on the west, is the Law Institution, with a noble Grecian-Ionic portico, built of stone by Vulliamy, in 1842; it contains a library and club accommodations for the legal profession.

The Bishop of Chichester formerly had a palace in Chancery-lane, where is still Chichester Rents and Symonds Inn; the latter, to this day, owned by the see. The large old house, with low-built shops before it, and between Bream's Buildings and Cursitor-street, is said to have been the Bishop's palace. Nearly opposite is the red-brick gatehouse of Lincoln's Inn; a Tudor arch between two massive towers, built by Sir Thomas Lovell, 1518.

The survey of Aggas, in 1560, shews Chancery-lane with only a few houses at the ends, the intervening road flanked with gardens; and there is no reason to doubt Aubrey's statement that young Ben Jonson worked with his father-in-law, a bricklayer, in building the garden-wall of Lincoln's Inn, when, as Fuller says, "having a trowel in his hand, he had a book in his pocket."

The stone buildings at the northern end of the Lane are the Accountant-General's and Inrolment Offices. Opposite, upon the site of Southampton Buildings, was Southampton House, inherited by the ill-fated Lord William Russell, by his marriage with the daughter of Thomas, last Earl of Southampton.

"It was in passing this house, the scene of his domestic happiness, on his way to the scaffold in Lincoln's-Inn-Fields, that the fortitude of the martyr for a moment forsook him (Lord W. Russell); but over-mastering his emotion, he said, 'The bitterness of death is now pass d.' It is from this house that some of Lady Rachel Russell's celebrated letters are dated. A former entrance of the chapel of Southampton House appears to correspond with the moulding of the flat timbered roof, which is of the time of Henry VII. This part of the edifice retains its original proportions, except that its height is divided by a modern floor. Its length is about 40 feet by about 20. It is now used by Mr. Griffiths, a whip-maker, 322 Holborn, as his warehouse. Other portions of Southampton House have been incorporated with the surrounding dwellings, one of which contains a beautiful Elizabethan staircase. Old mouldings and paneling appear likewise in Mill's Tavern, 47 Southampton Buildings, which house seems to have been constructed upon a portion of the ancient mansion."—*J. Wykeham Archer.*

CHARING CROSS,

The large area at the meeting of the Strand, Whitehall, and Cockspur-street, with Trafalgar Square on the north, received part of its name from the stone cross erected there, 1291-1294, to Eleanor, queen of Edward I.; and was the last spot at which the Queen's body was rested, in the way to Westminster Abbey for burial. The name Charing has not been satisfactorily traced; the *chere reine* origin is traditional. Mr. Hudson Turner, in *Manners and Household Expenses of England in the 13th and 15th Centuries,* gives some curious particulars of the nine Eleanor Crosses, of which two were those at Charing and Cheap. Charing Cross was built of Caen stone, and. Dorset marble steps, by Richard and Roger de Crundale; it was highly decorated, and had paintings and metal figures, gilt; besides Eleanor and others, sculptured in Caen stone by Alexander of Abingdon, and modelled by Torel, a goldsmith, probably an Italian.

The Cross (which appears in the Sutherland View of 1543, with only a few houses near it, and St. Martin's Church, literally "in the fields,") was voted down by the Long Parliament, and removed in 1647. Part of the stone was used to pave Whitehall, and some was made into knife-handles. The site of the Cross was next used as a place of execution, and here several of the Regicides suffered. In 1674, the equestrian statue of Charles I. was placed here.—(*See* STATUES.) The spot was a favourite "pitch" for Punchinello nearly two centuries ago; and Dr. Johnson, in one of his London ruminations, thought "the full tide of human existence" to be at Charing Cross. Proclamations for ages have been read here. On June 21, 1837, Queen Victoria was proclaimed here in fitting state; the High Constable and High Bailiff of Westminster, Knight-marshalmen, drums and trumpets, sergeants-at-arms, pursuivants, heralds, and other authorities, in official costume, standing within a cordon of Life Guards, round the statue, and the Somerset Herald reading aloud the proclamation.

CHARTER-HOUSE,

Upon the north side of Charter-house-square, Aldersgate-street, comprehends a collegiate asylum for the aged, a school-house for the young, and a chapel; the whole occupying 13 acres 1 rod of land, anciently part of the estate of St. Bartholomew's 'Spital, appropriated by Sir Walter de Manny, of Hainault, and Knight of the Garter in the reign of Edward III., as a burial-place for the poor destroyed by the Plague of 1349.

In 1361, Michael de Northburgh, Bishop of London, purchased of Sir Walter the whole cemetery; and at his death, in the same year, the good Bishop bequeathed it to Sir Walter, with all his property, for the founding, building, and furnishing a monastery of Carthusians,—an order of monks instituted in 1080, by Bruno, at Chartreux, near Grenoble, in France. This Sir Walter de Manny completed in 1371: he died in the following year, and was buried in the monastery, his funeral being attended by the King and his children, many barons and prelates.

Late in the 15th century, Sir Thomas More "gave himself to devotion and prayer in the Charter-house of London, religiously living there without vow about four years." The house had flourished nearly three centuries, when it fell in the universal Dissolution; and several of the monks, with John Howghton, the last prior, were, for denying the King's Supremacy, executed at Tyburn, May 4, 1535; their heads being set upon London Bridge, and the mangled body of Howghton placed over the gate of the Charter-house itself.

The Monastery was surrendered in 1537, and within 74 years had several owners, among whom were John Dudley, Duke of Northumberland, executed in 1553; and Thomas Howard, Duke of Norfolk, executed in 1572, from whom the place was called Howard House. Queen Elizabeth, Nov. 19, 1558, two days after her accession, stayed at the Charter-house "many days;" and in July, 1561, she sojourned there four days, even after Sir Edward North, then owner of the Charter-house, had been dismissed from her Privy Council. On the entry into London of James I., May 7, 1603, he visited Lord Thomas Howard, and kept his court four days at the Charter-house, whither he was conducted, in splendid procession from Stamford Hill, through Islington.

In 1611, the estate was sold by Thomas Earl of Suffolk, for 13,000l., to Thomas Sutton, the wealthy merchant of London, who endowed it as "the Hospital of King James;" though it is now known as the Charter-house, corrupted from the Chartreux of its monastic history.

Sutton fitted up the house and buildings; but he died the same year, Dec. 12, 1611, before he had perfected his good work, characterised by Stow as "the greatest gift in England, either in Protestant or Catholic times, ever bestowed by any individual."

Sutton was buried in a costly tomb in the Hospital chapel, both which are perfect illustrations of the state of the sculptor's and builder's art in the early part of the 17th century; and here the first tribute of praise was paid by Burrell, the preacher to the Hospital, in a sermon to the memory of the pious founder, printed in 1629, but now as rare as a MS. The vault was opened in 1842, when the body of Sutton was found in lead, wrapped about it like a winding-sheet.

Over the present porter's lodge is the house formerly occupied by the physicians of the Charter-house. The wooden gates are those of the ancient monastery. The building to the right in the Entrance Court is thought to be a part of the "fair dwelling" erected by Sir Edward North on the ruins of the monastery about 1537. The middle court, now called the Master's Court, was also part of North's building. The Long Gallery, originally more than 100 feet, is now reduced to 45 feet by partitions. The Washhouse Court is one of the few remaining portions of the old monastery. The Preacher's Court is the most important in appearance. The site of the chapel, from an old plan now in existence, date about 1500, seems to be identical with that of the monastery. The south wall is probably the oldest portion of the building; but the east wall is of considerable antiquity, for on the removal of the wainscotting, in the course of repairs in 1842, an old ambrie was discovered towards its south corner. The Ante-Chapel, which, like the Evidence Room above it, has a groined roof, bears the date 1512. The Great Chamber, or Old Governors' Room, was either built or decorated by Thomas, fourth Duke of Norfolk, between 1565 and 1571: it was restored in 1838, and is now the most perfect Elizabethan apartment in London. It has a chimney-piece of wood, a centre and two wings, in two stories, Tuscan and Ionic, reaching to the ceiling, which is also elegantly ornamented. The walls are richly painted, and hung with six pieces of tapestry. The Great Hall has a screen, music-gallery, sculptured chimney-piece, and lantern in the roof; and here hangs a noble portrait of the founder, Sutton.

Upon this foundation are maintained eighty pensioners, or poor brethren, who "live together in collegiate style, provided with handsome apartments, and all necessaries, except apparel, in lieu of which they are allowed 14l. a-year and a gown each. They are nominated, in the same manner as the scholars, by the Governors, who present in rotation. In 1850, there were forty-four scholars "on the foundation," supported free of expense; and there are several exhibitions to the Universities, available for foundation scholars only.—(Low's *Charities of London*.) The total number of scholars in 1850 was about 200.

The Charter-house is under the direction of the Queen, Prince Albert, the Archbishops of Canterbury and York, and thirteen other Governors; besides the Master of the Hospital, who resides within the walls. The most distinguished Master was Dr. Thomas Burnet, author of the *Sacred Theory of the Earth :* he was elected in 1685, died here in 1715, and was buried in the chapel of the institution.

Soon after Burnet's election, James II. addressed a letter to the Governors, ordering them to admit one Andrew Popham as pensioner into the Hospital upon the first vacancy, without tendering to him any oath, or requiring of him any subscription or recognition, in conformity with Church of England doctrine, the King dispensing with any statute or order of the Hospital to the contrary. Burnet, as junior Governor, was called upon to vote first, when he maintained that by express Act of Parliament, 3 Car. I., no officer could be admitted into that Hospital without taking the oaths of allegiance and supremacy. An attempt was made, but without effect, to overrule this opinion. The Duke of Ormond supported Burnet, and on the vote being put, Popham was rejected: and notwithstanding the threats of the King and the Popish party, no member of the communion was ever admitted into the Charter-house.

In 1652, Oliver Cromwell was elected Governor; he was succeeded by his son Richard in 1658.

Among the eminent scholars, or " Carthusians," were Richard Crashaw, the poet ; Isaac Barrow, the divine : Blackstone, lord-chief-justice ; Addison and Steele, both here together ; John Wesley ; lord-chief-justice Ellenborough (buried in the chapel) ; and Lord Liverpool.

In the Old Court Room is celebrated the Anniversary of the Foundation, on December 12 ; when is always sung the old Carthusian melody, with this chorus:

> " Then blessed be the memory
>   Of good old *Thomas Sutton*;
>   Who gave us lodging—learning,
>   And he gave us beef and mutton "

In the Governors' Room in the Master's House, upon the elegant chimney-piece, is the celebrated portrait of Sutton, the founder, ætatis seventy-nine, anno 1611, in an elaborately carved frame. The other pictures comprise whole-lengths of Charles II.; Gilbert Sheldon, Archbishop of Canterbury, sitting ; William Earl of Craven, in armour ; George Villiers, second Duke of Buckingham ; George Talbot, Duke of Shrewsbury ; the ill-fated Duke of Monmouth ; Lord Chancellor Shaftesbury ; and a half-length of Dr. Thomas Burnet, by his friend Sir Godfrey Kneller, very highly finished.

The entire internal economy of the establishment is vested in the Master ; the manciple, or house-steward, provides the diet of the Hospital, for which he has " to *pay in ready money*." The grounds, which extend from the Hospital buildings to Wilderness-row and Goswell-street, include a playing-green of about three acres, a wilderness of fine trees, with gravel and grass walks, and a kitchen-garden. Southeast of the green are two courts for tennis, a favourite pastime with the Carthusians.

The history of this noble foundation has been written by Bearcroft, Herne, and Smythe: and recently (1847) in *Chronicles of Charter-house*, by a Carthusian; a clever work, with illustrations.

CHEAPSIDE,

The street extending from the Poultry and Bucklersbury to St. Paul's and Newgate-street, was, some three centuries ago, worthily called "the Beauty of London," and was famed for its " noted store of goldsmiths," linen-drapers, haberdashers, &c. It is called from the Saxon word *Chepe*, or market: the name, therefore, is the *Market-side;* and in 1331 the south side only was built upon, and the north side was an open field, where jousts, tournaments, or ridings, were often held. Stow describes one of these joustings held in the reign of Edward III., Sept. 21, 1331; when, "the stone pavement being covered with sand, that the horses might not slide when they strongly set their feet to the ground, the king held a tournament three days together, with the nobility, valiant men of the realm, and other strange knights. And to the end the beholders might with the better ease see the same, there was a wooden scaffold erected across the street, like unto a tower, wherein the Queen Philippa, and many other ladies, richly attired, and assembled from all parts of the realm, did stand to behold the jousts." This frame brake down; after which the king had a stone shed built "for himself, the queen, and other-estates, to stand on, and there to behold the joustings and other shows, at their pleasure, by the church of St. Mary Bow." This shed, or "seldam," was similarly used in after reigns, especially to behold the great watches on the eve of St. John-Baptist and St. Peter at Midsummer. In 1510, on St. John's eve, King Henry VIII. came to this place, then called the King's Head in Cheape, in the livery of a yeoman of the guard, with an halbert on his shoulder, and there beholding the watch, departed privily when the watch was done; "but on St. Peter's night next following, he and the queen came royally riding to the said place, and there with their nobles beheld the watch of the city, and returned in the morning." When Bow Church was rebuilt, Wren provided, in place of the shed or sild, a balcony in the tower, immediately over the principal entrance in Cheapside; and though the age of tournaments had passed away, the Lord Mayor's pageants were long viewed from this balcony.

Cheapside Cross, which stood facing Wood-street, was the most magnificent (except that of Charing,) of the nine crosses built by Edward I. to his queen Eleanor, and was (Mr. Hudson Turner states) the work of Alexander of Abingdon. It was "re-edified" by John Hatherly, mayor, by license procured in 1441 of Henry VI.; it was regilt in 1522, for the visit of the Emperor Charles V.; and in 1533, for the coronation of Henry VIII: and Anne Boleyn; newly burnished at the coronation of Edward VI.; and again newly gilt, 1554, against the arrival of King Philip. After this the Cross was presented by juries as standing "in the highway to the let of carriages;" but they could not get it removed; and it was by turns defaced and repaired, and its images stolen and replaced, until May 2, 1643, when it was demolished to the sound of trumpet, the workmen being protected by soldiery.

Nearly opposite Honey-lane was the Standard, the place of execution; and between Bucklersbury and the Poultry stood Westcheap, or the Great Conduit, which brought the first supply of sweet water to London, from Paddington; and facing Foster-lane stood the Little Conduit. Westward of the site of the Great Conduit, on the north side, is Mercers' Hall and chapel, rebuilt after the Great Fire of 1666; the original chapel being an hospital purchased at the Dissolution by means of Sir Richard Gresham. Westward, next No. 142, is Saddlers' Hall. Both these Halls have in their street fronts balconies for viewing the City pageants.

The handsome stone-fronted house, No. 73, built by Sir C. Wren, was, before the erection of the Mansion House, (1737,) sometimes tenanted by the Lord Mayor, during his year of office: here Mr. Tegg, the publisher, amassed great wealth. Nearly opposite, between Ironmonger-lane and King-street, is the Atlas Insurance Office, with three enriched fronts, granite basement, and stone superstructure: built in 1839.

CHELSEA,

A large and populous parish upon the north bank of the Thames: it was a village of 300 houses in the last century, but now extends from beyond Battersea or Chelsea Bridge almost to Hyde Park Corner. It lies about fifteen feet above the river; and, according to Norden, is named from its strand, "like the chesel (ceosel or cesel) which the sea casteth up of sand and pebble-stones, thereof called *Cheselsey*, briefly *Chelsey*, as is Chelsey (Selsey) in Sussex." In a Saxon charter, however, it is written *Cealchylle*; in Domesday, *Cercehede* and *Chalced*; and Sir Thomas More wrote it *Chelchith*, though it began to be written Chelsey in the 16th century. Among the possessors of the manor were Sir Reginald Bray (*temp.* Henry VII.); it was given by Henry VIII. to Katherine Parr as a portion of her marriage settlement; and it was bought of Lord Cheyne by Sir Hans Sloane in 1712, from whom it passed by marriage and bequest to Baron Cadogan, of Oakley, in whose family the property remains: hence the names of Cheyne Walk, Cadogan and Hans Places, and Sloane and Oakley Streets.

Chelsea was once a place of courtly resort: many of the nobility, as well as scholars and philosophers, resided here; and its noted taverns and public gardens were much frequented in the 17th and 18th centuries. The principal features now are its palace-hospital for soldiers, its Botanic Gardens, its Dutch-like river terrace (Cheyne-walk), mostly brick-built, and fronted by lofty trees; and its olden church, with a heavy brick tower.

At Chelsea lived Sir Thomas More, in a mansion at the north end of Beaufort-row, with gardens extending to the Thames. Here More was visited by Henry VIII., who, "after-dinner, in a fair garden of his, walked with him by the space of an hour, holding his arm about his neck;" and used to ascend with him to the house-top to observe the stars and discourse of astronomy. A more illustrious visitor was Erasmus, who describes the house as "a practical school of the Christian religion." Holbein was kindly received here by More, where the painter worked, for near three years, upon portraits of the Chancellor, his relations, and friends. More also hired a house for aged people in Chelsea, whom he daily relieved. His own establishment was large: Erasmus says, "there he converseth with his wife, his son, his daughters-in-law, his three grand-daughters with their husbands, with eleven great-grandchildren." More resigned the Great Seal in 1533; and retired to Chelsea for study and devotion; but d-smissed his retinue, and gave his barge to his successor in the Chancellorship. After his execution, July 6, 1535 (according to Aubrey), his body was buried in Chelsea Church (which he had regularly attended); and his head was placed in a vault in St. Dunstan's Church, Canterbury. More's mansion was purchased by Sir Hans Sloane, and taken down in 1740.

Sloane dwelt in the New Manor-House, nearly opposite the Pier. In the hamlet of Little Chelsea lived Sir Bulstrode Whitelocke; Mr. Pym, member of the Long Parliament; Bishop Fowler, Sir Richard Steele, Addison, and John Locke; Lord Shaftesbury, (author of the *Characteristics*,) in the house now St. George's additional workhouse; and here Dr. Smollett retired after his failure in practice at Bath. Dean Swift had lodgings "a little beyond the church;" and Sir Robert Walpole had a house adjoining Gough House: hence, Walpole-street.

Towards the western end of Cheyne Walk, the Bishops of Winchester possessed a palace from 1663, until the death of Brownlow North in 1820. Further west, near the river side, was the Chelsea China Manufactory. (See CHELSEA CHINA.)

In Cheyne-walk was the Museum and Coffee-house of Don Saltero, renowned in the swimming exploits of Dr. Franklin. The landlord, James Salter, was a noted barber, who made a collection of natural curiosities, which acquired him the name (probably first given him by Steele,) of Don Saltero. (See *Tatler*, Nos. 34, 195, and 226.) The quiet tavern remains, but the Museum was dispersed by auction about the year 1807. Another wonder was the old Chelsea Bun-house, which possessed a sort of rival Museum to Don Saltero's. (See CHELSEA BUNS.) It was taken down in 1839. Eastward is the Royal Hospital (see CHELSEA HOSPITAL); and on part of its garden was the gay Ranelagh, from 1740 to 1815. Here, too, is the Apothecaries' Company's Garden (see BOTANIC GARDENS); and nearly opposite is "the Red House" at Battersea, about fifty yards west of which Cæsar is believed by some antiquaries to have forded the Thames.

Chelsea has two churches dedicated to St. Luke. The old riverside church was built in the sixteenth and seventeenth centuries, and has an eastern chapel added by Sir Thomas More. In the chancel is a black marble tablet to More, placed there by himself in 1532, three years before his death: it was restored by Sir John Lawrence about 1644, and by subscription in 1833: the inscription, in Latin, is by More. Here are also several other memorials of eminent persons, including a monument to Jane, wife of the ambitious John Dudley, Duke of Northumberland; and to Lady Jane Cheyne, by Bernini. In the churchyard is the tomb of Sir Hans Sloane, egg-shaped and entwined with serpents; also a monument to Philip Miller, erected by the Linnæan and Horticultural Societies; and here rests Cipriani, the painter. Several eminent persons have been interred in the church without monuments. (See Cunningham's *Handbook of London*, 2d edit., p. 307.)

St. Luke's new church, between King's Road and Fulham Road, was built by Savage, in 1820, in the style of the fourteenth and fifteenth centuries, and has a pinnacled tower 142 feet high.

Above Battersea Bridge is Cremorne House, formerly the elegant villa of Lord Cremorne, who had here a fine collection of Italian and Flemish pictures; adjoining was the residence of Dr. Benjamin Hoadley (son of the bishop), the author of *The Suspicious Husband*. Cremorne has been converted into a place of public entertainment, for which the grounds are well adapted.

CHELSEA BUNS.

Chelsea has been famed for its Buns since the commencement of the last century. Swift, in his *Journal to Stella*, 1712, writes "Pray are not the fine buns sold here in our town, as the rare Chelsea buns? I bought one to-day in my walk," &c. They were made and sold at "the Old Original Chelsea Bun-house," in Jews'-row, a one-storied building, with a colonnade projecting over the foot-pavement. It was customary for the Royal Family and the nobility and gentry to visit the Bun-house in the morning. George II., Queen Caroline, and the Princesses frequently honoured the proprietor, Richard Hands, with their company; as did also George III. and Queen Charlotte; her Majesty presented Mrs. Hands with a silver half-gallon mug, with five guineas in it. On Good Friday mornings, upwards of 50,000 persons have assembled here, when disturbances often arose among the London mob; and in one day more than 250*l*. have been taken for buns. The Bun-house was also much frequented by visitors to Ranelagh, after the closing of which the bun-trade declined. Notwithstanding, on Good Friday, April 18, 1839, upwards of 240,000 buns were sold here. Soon after, the Bun-house was sold and pulled down; and at the same time was dispersed a collection of pictures, models, grotesque figures, and modern antiques, which had for a century added the attractions of a museum to the bun celebrity. Another Bun-house has been built; but the olden charm of the place has fled. In the *Mirror* for April 6, 1839, are two views of the old Bun-house, sketched just before its demolition.

CHELSEA CHINA.

The earliest manufactories of porcelain in England were those at Bow* and at Chelsea, both which have long been extinct. "The Chelsea ware, bearing a very imperfect similarity in body to the Chinese, admitted only of a very fusible lead glaze; and in the taste of its patterns, and the style of their execution, stood as low, perhaps, as any on the list." (A. Aikin; *Trans. Soc. Arts.*) This character, however, applies only to the later productions.

Faulkner, in his *History of Chelsea*, (1829,) states:

"The Chelsea China Manufactory was situate at the corner of Justice-walk, and occupied the houses to the upper end of the street. Several of the large old houses were used as shew-rooms. It has been discontinued for more than forty years, the whole of the premises pulled down, and new houses erected on the site."

Justice-walk took its name from a magistrate who resided in the house at the south corner of Church-street, whence formerly an avenue of lime-trees extended to Lawrence-street; and in the latter were the ovens of the Chelsea China Manufactory, where Dr. Johnson made experiments on tea-cups. The premises, therefore, were not far from Church-street, and near the water-side. They subsequently became a stained paper Manufactory, conducted by Messrs. Echardts and Woodmason, in 1786; afterwards by Messrs. Bowen and Co.; and in 1810 by Messrs. Harwood and Co. We have been favoured with these addenda by Mr. T. Crofton Croker, F.S.A.

In July, 1850, we saw in the stock of Mr. Heigham, Fulham-road, a set of three Chelsea vases, remarkably fine in form and colour; each bearing a view of the old church at Chelsea and river-side.

"Martin Lister mentions a manufacture at Chelsea as early as 1698, comparing its productions with those of St. Cloud, near Paris. It was patronised by George II., who brought over artificers from Brunswick and Saxony; whence, probably, M. Brongniart terms Chelsea a 'Manufacture Royale.' Its reputation commenced about 1740; and in 1745 the celebrity of Chelsea porcelain was regarded with jealousy by the manufacturers of France, who therefore petitioned Louis XV. to concede to them exclusive privileges. About 1750, it was under the direction of M. Spremont, a foreigner. The productions of the Chelsea furnaces were thought worthy to view with those of the celebrated manufactories of Germany. Walpole, in his correspondence with Sir Horace Mann, mentions a service of Chelsea porcelain sent by the King and Queen to the Duke of Mecklenburg, which cost 1200l. The Duke of Cumberland took much interest in promoting the success of this interesting manufacture. The *mark* is an Anchor, in gold, burnished on the best specimens, and red on the inferior."

We are indebted for this information to Mr. Forster's piquant notes to the Catalogue of the Sale at Stowe, in 1848, where the finest specimens "of rare old Chelsea," a pair of small vases, painted with Roman triumphs, sold for 23l. 10s. There were but few specimens of Chelsea ware sold at Strawberry Hill in 1842. At the sale of the late Sir John Macdonald's collection, in 1850, a pair of cups and saucers, beautifully painted with birds, brought 36l. 15s.

CHELSEA HOSPITAL

Occupies the site of "Chelsea College," commenced by Dr. Sutcliffe, Dean of Exeter, in the reign of James I., but only in part built. Its object was to maintain fellows in holy orders, "to answer all the adversaries of religion," and others to write the history of their own times. It was nicknamed "Controversy College" by Archbishop Laud; the whole scheme and its originator were mercilessly ridiculed by

* Bow China, formerly made at Stratford-le-Bow, is always marked with a crescent, or *bow*: it much resembles in quality the old Worcester or Derby, and is mostly of blue pattern; it is scarce, but never fine.

the wits of the day, and thus failed. It was given by Charles II. to the then newly-established Royal Society, who, in 1681-82, sold the property to Sir Stephen Fox for 1300*l.*, as a site for a Royal Hospital for aged and disabled soldiers, the building of which has been attributed to Fox, as well as to the influence of Nell Gwynne. "No matter," says Faulkner, "with whom the idea may have originated, whether with Sir Stephen Fox, with his master (Charles II.), or with Nell Gwynne; it is certain that but for his exertions the project would have come to nothing." One of these traditions is kept in countenance by the head of Nell Gwynne having been for very many years the sign of a public-house in Grosvenor-row, Pimlico. More than one entry in Evelyn's *Diary*, however, prove that Sir Stephen "had not only the whole managing" of the plan, but was himself "a grand benefactor" to it. He was mainly advised by Evelyn, who arranged the officers, "would needes have a library, and mentioned several bookes."

Sir Christopher Wren was appointed architect; and the foundation-stone was laid, Feb. 16, 1682, by Charles II., who promised to provide the funds, and was assisted by public subscription. The progress of the building is recorded in this inscription on the southern front:

"In subsidium et levamen emeritorum venio, belloque fractorum, condidit Carolus Secundus, auxil. Jacobus Secundus, perfecere Gulielmus et Maria, Rex et Regina, MDCXC."

The building, which cost 150,000*l.*, is of red brick, with stone quoins, cornices, pediments, and columns, and is remarkable for its harmonious proportions. It consists of three courts, two of which are spacious quadrangles; the third, the central one, is open on the south side, next the Thames; and in the area is a statue of Charles II., in Roman imperial armour, sculptured by Gibbons, for Tobias Rustat. In the eastern and western wings of this court are the wards of the pensioners. At the extremity of the eastern wing is the Governor's house, with a state apartment, and portraits of Charles I., his queen, and two sons—Charles, Prince of Wales, and James, Duke of York; Charles II., William III., and George III., and Queen Charlotte. The north front is of great extent, and faced by avenues of limes and horse-chestnuts. In the centre is a tetrastyle Roman-Doric portico, surmounted by a handsome lofty clock-turret in the roof.

Beneath are the principal entrances. To the right is the Chapel, the furniture and plate of which were given by James II., and the organ by Major Ingram; the altar-piece has a painting of the Ascension, by Sebastian Ricci. In the left wing is the Hall, wherein the pensioners dine: here is an equestrian portrait of Charles II., by Verrio and H. Cooke; and an allegorical picture of the victories of the Duke of Wellington, by James Ward, R.A. Both the Hall and Chapel are paved with black and white marble: in each are suspended colours captured by the British army; in the chapel are thirteen eagles taken from Napoleon, and in the Hall, fragments of the standards captured at Blenheim; in addition are dragon banners of the Chinese, and the trophies of the Sikh campaign of 1840.

The old soldiers receive pensions from funds voted by Parliament: in 1850 there were nearly 70,000 out-pensioners, who received 6*d.*, 9*d.*, and 1*s.* per diem; there were 539 in-pensioners, who were well clothed and fed in the Hospital, and were allowed 1*d.* a-day for tobacco, which is called "her Majesty's bounty." They wear long scarlet coats, lined with blue, and the original three-cornered cocked hats of the last century: undress, a foraging cap, inscribed R. H. Their ages vary from 60 to 90 years, and two veterans had in 1850 attained the age of 104. The annual rate of mortality among the pensioners is 27 per cent.

Adjoining the Hospital is a burial-ground for the pensioners, wherein are the following data:

Thomas Asbey	. . . .	died 1737,	aged	112
Captain Laurence	. . . .	„ 1765	„	95
Robert Comming	. . . .	„ 1767	„	116
Peter Dowling	. . . .	„ 1768	„	102
A soldier who fought at the battle-of the Boyne	.	„ 1772	„	111
Peter Bennet, of Tinmouth	. . . . .	„ 1773	„	107

In 1739 was interred here Christian Davis, alias Mother Ross, who had served in campaigns under William III. and the Duke of Marlborough, and whose third husband was a pensioner in the Hospital.

The Hospital Gardens are, in a measure, open to the public, but are little frequented. The river terrace is bordered with dwarf limes, and there are besides some fine old shady trees.

North of the Hospital is the Royal Military Asylum, for the support and education of the children of soldiers and non-commissioned officers: the first stone of the building was laid by the Duke of York in 1801.

The Hospital and Asylum may be seen daily, from 10 till 4: the boys parade on Fridays.

CHESS-CLUBS.

In 1747, the principal, if not the only Chess-Club in the Metropolis met at Slaughter's Coffee-house, St. Martin's-lane. The leading players of this Club were—Sir Abraham Janssen, Philip Stamma (from Aleppo), Lord Godolphin, Lord Sunderland, and Lord Elibank; Cunningham, the historian; Dr. Black and Dr. Cowper; and it was through their invitation that the celebrated Philidor was induced to visit England.

Another Club was shortly afterwards founded at the Salopian Coffee-house, Charing Cross: and a few years later, a third, which met next door to the Thatched House Tavern, in St. James's-street. It was here that Philidor exhibited his wonderful faculty for playing blindfold; some instances of which we find in the newspapers of the period:

"Yesterday, at the Chess-Club in St. James's-street, Monsieur Philidor performed one of those wonderful exhibitions for which he is so much cel·brated. He played *three different games at once* without seeing either of the tables. His opponents were Count Bruhl and Mr. Bowdler (the two best players in London), and Mr. Maseres. He defeated Count Bruhl in one hour and twenty minutes, and Mr. Maseres in two hours; Mr. Bowdler reduced his games to a drawn battle in one hour and three quarters. To those who understand Chess, this exertion of M. Philidor's abilities must appear one of the greatest of which the human memory is susceptible. He goes through it with astonishing accuracy, and often corrects mistakes in those who have the board before them."

In 1795, the veteran, then nearly seventy years of age, played three blindfold matches in public. The last of these, which came off shortly before his death, we find announced in the daily newspapers thus:

"CHESS-CLUB, 1795. PARSLOE'S, ST. JAMES'S STREET.
By particular desire, Mons. Philidor, positively for the last time, will play on Saturday, the 20th of June, at two o'clock precisely, three games at once against three good players; two of them without seeing either of the boards, and the third looking over the table. He most respectfully invites all the members of the Chess-Club to honour him with their presence. Ladies and gentlemen not belonging to the Club may be provided with tickets at the above-mentioned house, to see the match, at five shillings each."

Upon the death of Philidor, the Chess-Clubs at the West-end seem to have declined; and in 1807, the stronghold and rallying point for the lovers of the game was "the London Chess Club," which was established in the City, and for many years held its meetings at Tomm's Coffee-house, in Cornhill. To this Club we are indebted for many of the finest chess-players of the age; and even now, after the lapse of nearly a century, the Club still flourishes, and numbers among its members some of the leading proficients.

About the year 1833, a Club was founded by a few amateurs in Bedford-street, Covent Garden. This establishment, which obtained remarkable celebrity as the arena of the famous contests between La Bourdonnais and M'Donnell, was dissolved in 1840; but shortly afterwards, through the exertions of Mr. Staunton, was re-formed under the name of "the St. George's Club," in Cavendish-square, where it still continues, deservedly ranking as the most influential club of the kind in England.

In addition to the St. George's Club, at the West End, and the London Chess Club, which of late years has held its meetings at the George and Vulture Tavern, Cornhill, there are many minor institutions in various parts of the metropolis and its environs, where Chess, and Chess only, forms the staple recreation of the members. There are also the magnificent Cigar Divan, No. 100, Strand, belonging to Mr. Ries; and Kilpack's well-appointed Divan, 42 King-street, Covent Garden; at each of which the leading Chess publications are accessible to visitors, and where as many as twenty Chess-boards may often be seen in requisition at the same time.

CHRIST'S HOSPITAL,

Newgate-street, is one of the five Royal Hospitals of the City of London, and was founded for destitute children, by Edward VI., June 26, 1553, on the site of the Grey Friars' Monastery. At the same time the King founded St. Thomas's and Bridewell Hospitals: the three foundations forming part of a comprehensive scheme of charity, originating in a sermon preached before his Majesty by the pious Bishop Ridley. Besides the sites and appurtenances, Edward bestowed lands for their support to the amount of 600l. a-year; "and then said in the hearing of his Councell, 'Lord, I yield Thee most hearty thanks, that Thou hast given me life thus long to finish this work to the glory of Thy Name.' After which foundation established, he lived not above two daies; whose life would have been wished equall to the patriarches, if it had pleased God so to have prolonged it."—(Stow.)

A picture (attributed to Holbein) which hangs in Christ's Hospital Hall portrays this interesting scene. The young monarch sits on an elevated throne, in a scarlet and ermined robe, holding the sceptre in his left hand, and presenting with the other the charter to the kneeling Lord Mayor. By his side stands the Chancellor, holding the seals, and next to him are other officers of state. Bishop Ridley kneels before him with uplifted hands, as if supplicating a blessing on the event; whilst the Aldermen, &c., with the Lord Mayor, kneel on both sides, occupying the middle ground of the picture; and lastly, in front are a double row of boys on one side, and girls on the other, from the master and matron down to the boy and girl who have stepped forward from their respective rows, and kneel with raised hands before the King.

The old monastic buildings were then repaired: the citizens became animated by Edward's zeal; and, by aid of their benefactions, in Nov. 1552, 340 "poore fatherlesse children" were admitted within the ancient monastery walls. "On Christmas-day," says Stow, "while the Lord Maior and Aldermen rode to Paul's, the children of Christ's Hospitall stood from St. Lawrence-lane end in Cheape towards Paul's, all in one livery of russet cotton, 340 in number; and at Easter next they were in blue, at the Spittle, and so have continued ever since." Hence the popular name of the Hospital, "the Blue-Coat School."

Since this period, the income of the institution has known much fluctuation; and consequently, also, the number of inmates. The 340 children with which the Hospital opened had dwindled in 1580 to 150. The object of the institution has also, in the lapse of time, become materially changed, which may in a great measure be attributed to the influence of the Governors, or benefactors, its chief supporters.

The Hospital suffered materially in the Great Fire of 1666, when the church of the monastery was destroyed. It was rebuilt by Sir Christopher Wren, between the years 1687 and 1705; and here are annually preached the "Spital Sermons." There is scarcely any portion of the ancient friary remaining, except the Cloisters.

The Hospital was rebuilt by the Governors, by anticipating its revenue. The first important addition to the foundation, after the Fire, was the Mathematical School, founded by Charles II. in 1672, for forty boys to be instructed in navigation: they are called "King's Boys," and wear a badge on the right shoulder. Lest this Mathematical School should fail for want of boys properly qualified to supply it, one Mr. Stone, a Governor, left a legacy to maintain a subordinate Mathematical School of twelve boys ("the Twelves"), who wear a badge on the left shoulder; to these have been added "the Twos."

This was the first considerable extension of the system of education at the Hospital, which originally consisted of a grammar-school for boys; and a separate school for girls, where the latter were taught to read, sew, and mark. A book is preserved containing the records of the Hospital from its foundation, and an anthem sung by the first children.

The East Cloister and south front were next (1675) rebuilt by Sir Robert Clayton, alderman, and cost him about 7000l.; but it was not known who was the benefactor until the whole was finished.

The Writing-School, a large edifice, was built by Wren in 1694, at the expense of Sir John Moore, Lord Mayor in 1681, of whom a marble statue is placed in the façade. This school is situate on the west side of the playground, and being supported on columns, the under part, called the New Cloister, shelters the boys in bad weather.

The Ward over the East Cloister was rebuilt, in 1705, by Sir Francis Child, the banker. In 1795, the Grammar School, of neat yellow brick, near Little Britain, and on the north side of the ditch playground, was erected partly with a sum of money bequeathed by John Smith, Esq.

The old buildings of the Hospital had been altered, enlarged, and augmented at different periods; but, becoming ruinous and unsafe, the Governors, in 1803, determined to rebuild the whole. With a part of the general revenues of the Hospital was, therefore, established a building fund; and with that, aided by a grant of 5000l. from the Corporation of London, and many private benefactions, the grand undertaking was commenced. The architect was the late John Shaw, F.R.S. and F.S.A., who has been succeeded by his son. Of the great Dining Hall the first stone was laid by the Duke of York, April 25th, 1825. This noble structure is in the Tudor style, and is built partly on the ancient wall of London, and partly on the foundation of the refectory of the Grey Friars. The back wall stands on the site of the ditch that anciently surrounded London, and is built on piles driven 20 feet deep: in excavating for the foundation, there were found some Roman urns and coins, and some curious leathern sandals. The southern or principal front, facing Newgate-street, is supported by buttresses, and has an octagonal tower at each extremity; and the summit is embattled and pinnacled. On the ground story is an open arcade (187 feet in length, and 16½ feet in width): here also are a meeting-room for the Governors, the Hospital wardrobe, &c. Over the centre arch of the arcade is a bust of Edward VI.

The area in front, or play-ground, is enclosed by handsome metal gates, enriched with the arms of the Hospital: argent, a cross gules, in the dexter chief, a dagger of the first (*City of London*), on a chief azure, between two fleurs-de-lis or, a rose argent.

The Dining Hall, with its lobby and organ-gallery, occupies the entire upper story, which is 187 feet long, 51 feet wide, and 47 feet high: it is lit by nine large and handsome windows on the south side: next to Westminster Hall, it is the noblest room in the metropolis. The arcade beneath the Hall is built with blocks of Haytor granite, highly wrought; and the remainder of the front is of Portland stone. The basement story contains the Kitchen,—67 feet in length and 33 feet in width,—besides butteries, cellars, &c.

In the rear of the Hall is the Infirmary, a large building erected in 1822; and on the east and west sides of the Cloister are the Dormitories.

In the great Dining Hall, besides the picture of Edward VI. granting the Hospital Charter (said to be by Holbein), is a large painting, by Verrio, of James II. on his throne, receiving the "Mathematical Boys," as at the annual presentation to this day; though in this picture are girls as well as boys. It was presented to the Hospital by Verrio, who also painted a full-length of Charles II., which hangs near it. Here, too, are full-lengths of Queen Victoria and Prince Albert, by F. Grant, A.R.A.; and Brook Watson's escape, when a boy, from a shark, with the loss of a leg, while bathing, painted by J. S. Copley, R.A., the father of Lord Lyndhurst.

In this Hall are held the "Suppings in Public," on the seven Sunday evenings preceding Easter Sunday, and on that evening, to which visitors are admitted by tickets given by the Treasurer and by the Governors, each of whom issues a certain number. The tables are laid with cheese in wooden bowls; beer in wooden piggins, poured from leathern jacks; and bread brought in huge baskets. The official company then enter, the Lord Mayor or President taking a state chair made of oak from old St. Katherine's Church; a hymn is sung, accompanied by the organ; a Grecian reads the evening service from the pulpit, silence being enforced by three strokes of a hammer. After prayers, the meal commences, the visitors walking between the tables. At its close, the "trade boys" take up the piggins and jacks, baskets, bowls, and candlesticks, and pass in procession before the authorities, bowing to them; the entire 800 boys thus passing out. This interesting spectacle was witnessed by Queen Victoria and Prince Albert on Sunday evening, March 9, 1845.

The Spital Sermons* are preached in Christchurch, Newgate-street, on Easter Monday and Tuesday, before the Lord Mayor and Corporation, and Governors of the five Royal Hospitals; the Bishops in turn preaching on Monday, and usually his Lordship's chaplain on Tuesday. On Monday, the children, headed by the beadle, proceed to the Mansion House, and return in procession to Christchurch with the Lord Mayor and City authorities, to hear the sermon. On Tuesday, the children again go to the Mansion House, and pass through the Egyptian Hall before the Lord Mayor, each boy receiving a glass of wine, two buns, and a shilling; the monitors half-a-crown each, and the Grecians a guinea. They then return to Christchurch, as on Monday. The boys formerly visited the Royal Exchange on Easter Monday; but this has been discontinued since the burning of the last Exchange in 1838.

At the first Drawing-room of the year, forty "Mathematical Boys" are presented to the Sovereign, who gives them 8l. 8s. as a gratuity. To this other members of the Royal Family formerly added smaller sums, and the whole was divided among the ten boys who left the school in the year. On the illness of King George III. these presentations were discontinued; but the Governors of the Hospital continued to pay 1l. 3s., the amount ordinarily received by each, to every boy on quitting. The practice of receiving the children was revived by William IV.

Each of the "Mathematical Boys" having passed his Trinity-House

* See CHURCHES: CHRIST CHURCH, Newgate-street, with the origin of the Spital Sermons.

examination, and received testimonials of his good conduct, is presented with a *watch*, as a reward, worth from 9*l.* to 13*l.*; in addition to an outfit of clothes, books, mathematical instruments, a Gunter's scale, a quadrant, and sea-chest.

On St. Matthew's Day, (Sept. 21,) "the Grecians" deliver orations before the Lord Mayor, Corporation, Governors, and their friends; this being a relic of the scholars' disputations in the cloisters.

Christ's Hospital, by ancient custom, possesses the privilege of addressing the Sovereign on the occasion of his or her coming into the City to partake of the hospitality of the Corporation of London. On the visit of Queen Victoria in 1837, a booth was erected for the Hospital boys in St. Paul's Churchyard; and on the Royal carriage reaching the Cathedral west gate, the senior scholar, with the Head Master and Treasurer, advanced to the coach-door, and delivered a congratulatory address to her Majesty, with a copy of the same on vellum.

The dress of the "Blue-Coat" boys is the costume of the citizens of London at the time of the foundation of the Hospital, when blue coats were the common habit of apprentices and serving-men, and yellow stockings were generally worn. Mr. Brayley describes the dress as the nearest approach to the monkish costume now worn; (*Londiniana,* vol. ii. p. 153:) the dark-blue coat, with a close-fitting body and loose skirts, being the ancient tunic, and the under-coat, or "yellow," the sleeveless under-tunic of the monastery. The girdle was also a monastic appendage: the boys wear it of red leather. Yellow worsted stockings, a flat black woollen cap, (scarcely larger than a saucer), and a clerical neckband, complete the dress.

The education of the boys consists of reading, writing, and arithmetic, French, the classics, and the mathematics. There are sixteen Exhibitions for scholars at the Universities of Oxford and Cambridge, besides a "Pitt Scholarship," and a "*Times* Scholarship," the latter founded by the proprietors of that journal, with a fund subscribed by the public in testimony of their detection of the Bogle fraud, 1841. There are also separate trusts held by the Governors of the Hospital, which are distributed to poor widows, to the blind, and in apprenticing boys, &c. The annual income of the Hospital is about 50,000*l.*; its ordinary disbursements, are 48,000*l.*

There is printed annually, and freely circulated; "A True Report of the Number of Children and other poor People maintained in the several Royal Hospitals of the City of London, under the pious care of the Right Honourable the Lord Mayor, Aldermen, and Governors thereof, for the year last past." This document, in appearance, resembles a sheet almanack: it is headed by the Easter anthem set to music; and it is enclosed in a woodcut border, the design of which indicates the custom of printing these Reports to have been of long standing. In the upper portion of the border are the Royal Arms; at the sides are the City Arms, ancient and modern; in medallions at the corners are three figures of the Christ's Hospital boys, and one of a girl; at the foot is an emblematic group, with the old Hospital in the background; and beneath it is inscribed on a ribbon, "Pray remember the Poor."

There are several portraits in the Treasurer's room, including two of Edward VI. by Holbein, one of which belonged to Sir Anthony Mildmay, Queen Elizabeth's Chancellor.

The general burial-ground of the Hospital is between the south cloister and the houses in Newgate-street, where the funerals formerly took place by torch-light, and the service was preceded by an anthem, thus reviving the monastic associations of the place. The burials are now by daylight.

Among the eminent "Blues" from the present period were, Leigh Hunt; Thomas Barnes, many years editor of the *Times* newspaper; Thomas Mitchell, the translator of Aristophanes; S. T. Coleridge, the poet, and Charles Lamb, his contemporary; Middleton, Bishop of Calcutta; Jeremiah Markland, the best scholar and critic of the last century; Samuel Richardson, the novelist; Joshua Barnes, the scholiast; Bishop Stillingfleet; Camden, "the nourrice of antiquitie;" and Campion, the learned Jesuit of the age of Elizabeth. Coleridge, Charles Lamb, and Leigh Hunt have published many interesting reminiscences of their contemporaries in the school.

The subordinate establishment is at Hertford, to which the younger boys are sent preparatory to their entering on the foundation in London, which takes place as vacancies occur. The building at Hertford was erected by the Hospital Governors in 1683; when full, it will contain 416 children, of whom about 200 are taught the classics. There is likewise accommodation here for 80 girls.

Besides the Lord Mayor, Court of Aldermen, and twelve members of the Common Council, who are Governors *ex officio*, there are between 400 and 500 other Governors, at the head of whom are the Queen and Prince Albert, with the Prince of Wales and Prince Alfred, and the Duke of Cambridge. The qualification for Governor is a donation of 500*l.*; an Alderman may nominate a Governor for election at half-price. There are from 1400 to 1500 children on the foundation, including those at the branch establishment at Hertford. About 200 boys are admitted annually, (at the age of from 7 to 10 years), by presentations of the Governors; the Queen, the Lord Mayor (two presentations), and the Court of Aldermen presenting annually, and the other Governors in rotation, so that the privilege occurs about once in three or four years. A List of the Governors having presentations is published annually in March, and is to be had at the counting-house of the Hospital. "Grecians" and "King's Boys" remain in the school after they are fifteen years old; but the other boys leave at that age.

CHURCHES AND CHAPELS.

London and the suburbs, in the Middle Ages, contained, according to Fitz-Stephen, "13 churches belonging to convents, besides 126 lesser parish churches." Stow states the entire number of churches at his time, in and about London, within four miles' compass, at 139; and thus they, doubtless, remained down to 1666, when the Great Fire at once destroyed 89 of their number, 35 of which were not rebuilt. The sites of the latter are mostly, to this day, denoted by their burial-grounds; a few of which have each a tablet inscribed with the name of the late church, and stating to whom dedicated.

Pepys records this odd coincidence concerning the London churches destroyed in the Great Fire: "Jan. 7th, 1667-8. It is observed, and is true, in the late Fire of London, that the fire burned just as many parish churches as there were hours from the beginning to the end of the fire; and next, that there were just as many churches left standing in the rest of the city that was not burned, being, I think, thirteen in all of each; which is pretty to observe."

Eleven of the thirteen churches "belonging to convents" may be traced. Thus, we find in Fitz-Stephen's time, Trinity Priory, Aldgate; St. Bartholomew's, West Smithfield (see page 31); Bermondsey, Southwark (see page 40); St. James's Priory, Clerkenwell; the Priory of St. John the Baptist, Holywell, Shoreditch; St. Katherine's Hospital, by the Tower; St. Thomas Acon, at the south-west corner of King-street, Cheapside, upon the site of the birthplace of Thomas à Becket; St. John of Jerusalem, Clerkenwell; the Temple; St. Mary Overie's, Southwark; and St. Martin's-le-Grand, so named from its magnificence. All, except Bermondsey, are shewn in the Sutherland View, 1543.

We shall first describe the two "Mother Churches" of London and Westminster.

OLD SAINT PAUL'S.

The present Cathedral of St. Paul is the third church built to that about A.D. 610, by Ethelbert, King of Kent, but destroyed by fire in 1087. Its rebuilding was commenced by Bishop Maurice, whose successor completed the enclosing walls, which extended as far as Paternoster-row and Ave-Maria-lane, on one side; and to Old Change, Carter-lane, and Creed-lane, on the other. This second church, " Old Saint Paul's," was built of Caen stone: it was greatly injured by fire in 1137; but a new steeple was finished in 1221, and in 1240 a choir.

The entire edifice was 690 feet long, and 130 feet broad; and its tower and spire rose 520 feet, or 116 feet higher than the spire of Salisbury Cathedral; 64 feet loftier than that of Vienna; 50 feet higher than that of Strasburg; surpassing the height of the Great Pyramid of Egypt; and higher than the Monument placed upon the cross of the present Cathedral. It had a bowl of copper-gilt, 9 feet in compass (large enough to hold 10 bushels of corn), supporting a cross 15½ feet high, surmounted by an "eagle-cock of copper-gilt, 4 feet long." In 1314, the cross fell; and the steeple, of wood covered with lead, being ruinous, was taken down, and rebuilt with a new gilt ball. In 1444, it was nearly destroyed by lightning, and not repaired till 1462. In 1561, the Cathedral was partly burnt, but was restored by 1566, except the spire, which was never rebuilt. The church was of the Latin-cross form, with a Lady-chapel, and two other chapels, at the east end; near which, on the north side, stood Paul's or Powly's Cross, with a pulpit whence sermons were preached, the anathema of the Pope thundered forth, heresies recanted, and sins atoned for: here, in 1483, Jane Shore, with a taper in one hand, and arrayed in her "kertell onelye," did open penance:

> " Before the worlde I suffered open shame,
> Where people were as thicke as is the sand,
> A penaunce took, with taper in my hand."—*Higin's Coll.* 1587.

This famous Cross was pulled down in 1643 by order of Parliament; but its site was long denoted by a tall elm-tree. At the eastern extremity of the churchyard stood a square *clochier*, or bell-tower, with four bells, rung to summon the citizens to folkmotes held here. These bells belonged to St. Faith's under St. Paul's, a church so situated, but demolished about 1256, when part of the crypt beneath the Cathedral choir was granted to the parishioners for divine service: hence the popular story in our time of there being a church under St. Paul's, and service in it once a year. At the south-west corner was the parish-church of St. Gregory. Fuller wittily describes Old St. Paul's as being " truly the mother-church, having one babe in her body — St. Faith's — and another in her arms — St. Gregory's."

On the south side of the Cathedral, *within a cloister*, was a chapter-house, in the pointed style: and on the north, on the walls of another cloister, next to the charnel-house, was a " Dance of Death," or, as Stow calls it, "Death leading all Estates, curiously painted upon board, with the speeches of Death, and answer of every Estate," by John Lydgate. It was painted at the cost of John Carpenter, Town Clerk of London, temp. Henry V. and VI.

The interior of the church was divided throughout by two ranges of clustered columns; it had a rich screen, and canopied doorways; and a large painted rose-window at the east end. The walls were sumptuously adorned with pictures, shrines, and curiously wrought tabernacles; gold and silver, rubies, emeralds, and pearls glittered in splendid profusion; and upon the high altar were heaped countless stores of gold and silver plate, and illuminated missals. The shrine of St. Erkenwald (the fourth bishop), at the back of the high altar, had among its jewels a sapphire, believed to cure diseases of the eye. The mere enumeration of these treasures fills twenty-eight pages of Dugdale's folio history of the Cathedral.

Camden relates, that on the anniversary of the Conversion of St. Paul, January 25, held in the church, a fat buck was received with great formality at the choir-entrance by the canons, in their sacerdotal vestments, and with chaplets of flowers on their heads; whilst the antlers of the buck were carried on a pike in procession round the edifice, with horns blowing, &c. On the buck being offered at the high altar, one shilling was paid by the Dean and Chapter.

Within was the tomb of John of Gaunt, Duke of Lancaster, with the chivalric appointments of proper helmet and spear and target. Here also were monuments to Sir Nicholas Bacon and Sir Christopher Hatton, and tablets to Sir Philip Sydney and Sir Francis Walsingham; the skeleton effigies of Colet, founder of St. Paul's School; and of Dr. Donne, the poet, erect in his stony shroud. Van Dyck was buried here, but had not a monument. Here, too, in the nave, was the tomb of Sir John Beauchamp, son of Guy Earl of Warwick: it was unaccountably called " Duke Humphrey's Tomb," and the dinnerless persons who lounged here were said to dine with Duke Humphrey.

But, perhaps, the finest monument was that of Henry de Lacy, Earl of Lincoln, Edward I.'s able lieutenant in his Scottish expeditions; his portrait effigy lay upon an altar of beautiful decoration.

The state obsequies were a profitable privilege of the Cathedral: the choir was hung with black and escutcheons; and the herses were magnificently adorned with banner-rolls and other insignia of vainglory.

The floor was laid out in walks: " the south alley for usurye and poperye; the north for simony and the horse-fair; in the midst for all kinds of bargains, meetings, brawlings, murthers, conspiracies, &c." The middle aisle was called Paul's Walk, and was a lounge for idlers and hunters after news, wits and gallants, cheats, usurers, and knights of the post; the *font* itself being used as a counter. Ben Jonson has laid a scene of his *Every Man out of his Humour* in " the middle aisle in Panle's;" Captain Bobadil is a " Paul's man;" and Falstaff bought Bardolph in Paul's. Greene, in his *Theeves falling out, &c.*, says: " Walke in the middle of Paul's, and gentlemen's teeth walk not faster at ordinaries, than there a whole day together about enquiry after news." Bishop Earle, in his *Microcosmographia*, 1629, says: " Paul's Walke is the Land's Epitome, or you may cal it the lesser Ile of Great Brittaine. * * * The noyse in it is like that of Bees, in strange hummings or buzze, mixt of walking, tongues, and feet; it is a kind of still roare, or loud whisper." It was a common thoroughfare for porters and carriers, for ale, beer, bread, fish, flesh, fardels of stuff, and " mules, horses, and other beasts;" drunkards lay sleeping on the benches at the choir-door; within, dunghills were suffered to accumulate; and in the choir people walked " with their hatts on their heddes." Dekker, in his *Gull's Hornbook*, tells us that the church was profaned by shops, not only of booksellers, but of other trades, such as "the semsters' shops," and "the new tobacco office." He also mentions "Paul's Jacks," automaton figures which struck the quarters on the clock.

The desecration of the exterior of the church was more abominable. The chantry and other chapels were used for stones and lumber, as a school and a glazier's workshop; parts of the vaults were occupied by a carpenter, and as a wine-cellar; and the cloisters were let out to trunk-makers, whose " knocking and noyse" greatly disturbed the church-service. Houses were built against the outer walls, in which closets and window-ways were made: one was used " as a play-house," and in another the owner " baked his bread and pies in an oven excavated within a buttress;" for a trifling fee, the bell-ringers allowed wights to ascend the tower, halloo, and throw stones at the passengers be-

On special saints' days it was customary for the choristers of the Cathedral to ascend the spire to a great height, and there to chant solemn prayers and anthems: the last observance of this custom was in the reign of Queen Mary, when, " after even-song, the quere of Paules began to go about the steeple singing with lightes, after the olde custome." A similar tenure-custom is observed to this day at Oxford, on the morning of May 1, on Magdalen College tower.

We read, too, of rope-dancing feats from the battlements of St. Paul's exhibited before Edward VI., and in the reign of Queen Mary, who, the day before her coronation, also witnessed a Dutchman standing upon the weathercock of the steeple, waving a five-yard streamer! Another marvel of this class was the ascent of Bankes, on his famous horse Marocco, to the top of St. Paul's, in 1660. The first recorded Lottery in England was drawn at the west door in 1569.

At length, the vast pile became dilapidated; but no effectual step for its repair was taken until 1633, when Inigo Jones commenced the great work: to remove the desecration from the nave to the exterior, he built, it is stated at the expense of Charles I., at the west end, a Corinthian portico of eight columns, with a balustrade in panels, upon which he intended to have placed ten statues: this portico was 200 feet long, 40 feet high, and 50 feet deep; but its classic design, affixed to a Gothic church, must be condemned, unless it be considered as an instalment of a new cathedral. Laud was then Bishop of London. The sum collected was 101,330l.; and the repairs progressed until about one-third of the money was expended, in 1642, when they were stopped by the contests between Charles and his people: the funds in hand were seized to pay the soldiers of the Commonwealth, and barracks made in the church.

Shortly after the Restoration, the repairs were resumed under Sir John Denham; and "that miracle of a youth," Wren, drew plans for the entire renovation. In the Great Fire of 1666, the church was reduced to a heap of ruins; and books valued at 150,000l., which had been placed in St. Faith's (the crypt) for safety by the stationers of Paternoster-row, were entirely destroyed. After the Fire, Wren removed part of the thick walls by gunpowder, but most he levelled with a battering-ram: some of the stone was used to build parish churches, and some to pave the neighbouring streets; and thus was prepared the ground for the present Cathedral.

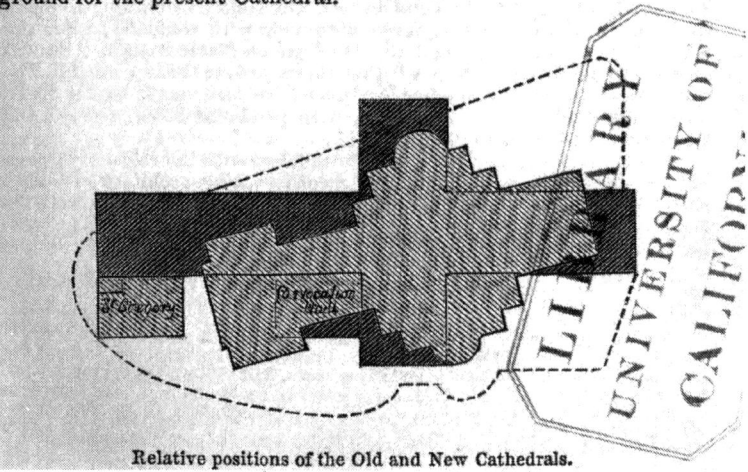

Relative positions of the Old and New Cathedrals.

St. Paul's Cathedral.

Nearly eight years elapsed after the Great Fire ere the ruins of the old Cathedral were cleared from the site. Meanwhile, Wren was instructed "to contrive a fabric of moderate bulk, but of good proportion; a convenient quire, with a vestibule and porticoes, and a dome conspicuous above the houses." A design was accordingly prepared, octagonal in plan, with a central dome and cupolettas, and affording a vast number of picturesque combinations, as shewn in the model, preserved to this day. This was rejected; and the surveyor next devised "a cathedral form, so altered as to reconcile, as near as possible, the Gothic to a better manner of architecture;" which being approved, Charles II. issued his warrant for commencing the works May 1, 1675. In digging the foundation, a vast cemetery was discovered, in which Britons, Romans, and Saxons had been successively buried; and on digging deeper, marine shells were found, thus proving that *the sea once flowed over the site of the present Cathedral.* Wren did not, however, find any remains to support the tradition of a Roman temple to Diana having once occupied this spot.

The first stone of the new church was laid June 21, 1675, by the architect and his lodge of Freemasons; and the trowel and mallet then used are preserved in the Lodge of Antiquity, of which Wren was master. In commencing the works, he accidentally set out the dimensions of the dome upon a piece of a gravestone inscribed *Resurgam* (I shall rise again); which propitious circumstance is commemorated in a Phœnix rising from the flames, with the motto *Resurgam*, sculptured by Cibber in the pediment over the southern portico. In 1678 Wren set out the piers and pendentives of the dome. By 1685, the walls of the choir and its side aisles, and the north and south semicircular porticoes, were finished; the piers of the dome were also brought up to the same height. On Dec. 2, 1697, the choir was opened on the day of thanksgiving for the peace of Ryswick, when Bishop Burnet preached before King William. On Feb. 1, 1699, the Morning Prayer Chapel, at the north-west angle, was opened; and in 1710 the son of the architect laid the last stone—the highest slab on the top of the lantern. Thus, the whole edifice was finished in thirty-five years; under one architect, Sir Christopher Wren; one master-mason, Mr. Thomas Strong; and while one bishop, Dr. Henry Compton, occupied the see. For his services, Wren obtained, with difficulty, 200*l.* per annum! "and for this," said the Duchess of Marlborough, "he was content to be dragged up in a basket three or four times a week." The fund raised for the rebuilding amounted, in ten years, to 216,000*l.*; a new duty laid on coals for this purpose produced 5000*l.* a-year; and the King contributed 10,000*l.* annually.

The Cathedral remained almost untouched until the reign of George III., when Mylne was appointed its conservating architect; an office since filled by C. R. Cockerell, R.A., who, in 1821-2, renewed the copper ball and cross,* the original ball being preserved at the Colosseum, in the Regent's Park. In 1841, the exterior of the dome was

---

* It was during these repairs that Mr. Hornor, having passed the summer of 1820, in the lantern above the dome, in executing a general view of the metropolis, next erected, at several feet above the highest portion of the present cross, an observatory, in which he drew a new series of sketches on 280 sheets of drawing-paper—a surface of 1680 square feet. From these sketches was painted the great panoramic view of London and the suburbs, first exhibited at the Colosseum, Regent's Park, in 1829. In 1848, there was put up from the Golden Gallery to the summit of the cross a scaffold supporting an observatory, as the main station for a new trigonometrical survey of the metropolis; and between 3000 and 4000 observations were taken here within three months.

repaired by the workmen resting upon a shifting iron frame. The golden gallery railing has since been regilt.

Exterior.—St. Paul's occupies very nearly the site of the old Cathedral, in the centre and most elevated part of the City; though its highest point, the cross, is 36 feet lower than the Castle Tavern, on Hampstead Heath. The plan of St. Paul's is a Latin cross, and bears a general resemblance to that of St. Peter's. Its length, from the east to the west wall, is 500 feet; north to south, 250 feet; width, 125 feet, except at the western end, where two towers, and chapels beyond, make this, the principal front, facing Ludgate Hill, about 180 feet in width. The chapels are, the Morning Prayer, north; and the Consistory Court, south.

The exterior generally is of two orders, 100 feet in height—the upper Composite, and the lower Corinthian; and the surface of the church is Portland stone, rusticated or grooved throughout. At the east end is a semicircular recess, containing the altar. At the west end, a noble flight of steps ascends to a double portico of coupled columns, twelve in the lower, Corinthian; and eight in the upper, Composite; terminated by a pediment, in the tympanum of which (64 feet long and 17 feet high) is the conversion of St. Paul, sculptured in pretty high relief by Bird; on the apex is a colossal figure of St. Paul, and on the right and left, St. Peter and St. James. Beneath the lower portico are the doors, and above them a sculptured group, in white marble, of St. Paul preaching to the Bereans. This double portico has been much censured: Wren pleaded that he could not obtain stone of sufficient height for the shafts of one grand portico; "but," says Mr. Gwilt, "it would have been far better to have had the columns in many pieces, and even with vertical joints, than to have placed one portico above another." At the extremities of this front rise, 220 feet, two

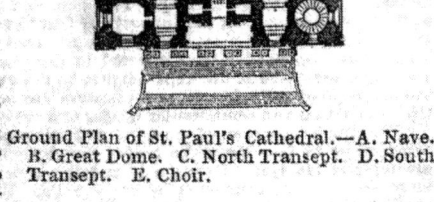

Ground Plan of St. Paul's Cathedral.—A. Nave. B. Great Dome. C. North Transept. D. South Transept. E. Choir.

campanile towers, terminating in open lanterns, "covered with domes formed by curves of contrary flexure, and not very purely composed, though, perhaps, in character with the general façade." (*Gwilt.*) Each dome has a gilt pine-apple at the apex: the south tower contains the clock, and the north is a belfry; and in the west faces are statues of the four Evangelists. At the northern and southern ends of the transepts, the lower order, Corinthian, is continued into porticoes of six fluted columns, standing, in plan, on the segment of a circle, and crowned with a semi-dome. In the upper order are two pediments, the south sculptured with the Phœnix, and the north with the royal arms and regalia; and on each side are five statues of the Apostles. The main building is surmounted with a balustrade, not in Wren's design, the obtrusion of which by the Commissioners caused the architect to say : " I never designed a balustrade : ladies think nothing well without an edging."

The Cathedral was scientifically secured from lightning, according to the suggestion of the Royal Society, in 1769. The seven iron scrolls supporting the ball and cross are connected with other rods (used merely as conductors), which unite them with several large bars descending obliquely to the stone-work of the lantern, and connected by an iron ring with four other iron bars to the lead covering of the great cupola, a distance of forty-eight feet; thence the communication is continued by the rain-water pipes to the lead-covered roof, and thence by lead water-pipes which pass into the earth; thus completing the entire communication from the cross to the ground, partly through iron and partly through lead. On the clock-tower a bar of iron connects the pine-apple at the top with the iron staircase, and thence with the lead on the roof of the church. The bell-tower is similarly protected. By these means the metal used in the building is made available as conductors; the metal employed merely for that purpose being exceedingly small in quantity.—(*Times, Sept.* 8, 1842, *abridged.*)

Construction.—The following details are by an eminent architect :

The entrances from the transepts lead into vestibules, each communicating with the centre, and its aisles formed between two massive piers and the walls at the intersections of the transepts with the choir and nave. The eight piers are joined by arches springing from one to the other, so as to form an octagon at their springing points; and the angles between the arches, instead of rising vertically, sail over as they rise and form pendentives, which lead, at their top, into a circle on the plan. Above this a wall rises in the form of a truncated cone, which, at the height of 168 feet from the pavement, terminates in a horizontal cornice, from which the interior dome springs. Its diameter is 100 feet, and it is 60 feet in height, in the form of a paraboloid. Its thickness is 18 inches, and it is constructed of brickwork. From the haunches of this dome, 200 feet above the pavement of the church, another cone of brickwork commences, 85 feet high, and 94 feet diameter at the bottom. This cone is pierced with apertures, as well for the purpose of diminishing its weight as for distributing light between it and the outer dome. At the top it is gathered into a dome, in the form of a hyperboloid, pierced near the vertex with an aperture 12 feet in diameter. The top of this cone is 285 feet from the pavement, and carries a lantern 55 feet high, terminating in a dome, whereon a ball and (aveline) cross is raised. The last-named cone is provided with corbels, sufficient in number to receive the hammer-beams of the external dome, which is of oak, and its base 220 feet from the pavement,—its summit being level with the top of the cone. In form it is nearly hemispherical, and generated by radii 57 feet in length, whose centres are in a horizontal diameter, passing through its base. The cone and the interior dome are restrained in their lateral thrust on the supports by four tiers of strong iron chains (weighing 95 cwt. 3 qrs. 23 lbs.), placed in grooves prepared for their reception, and run with lead. The lowest of these is inserted in the masonry round their common base, and the other three at different heights on the exterior of the cone. Externally, the intervals of the columns and pilasters are occupied by windows and niches, with horizontal and semicircular heads, and crowned with pediments.

Over the intersection of the nave and transepts for the external work, and for a height of 25 feet above the roof of the church, a cylindrical wall rises, whose diameter is 146 feet. Between it and the lower conical wall is a space, but at intervals they are connected by cross walls. This cylinder is quite plain, but perforated by two courses of rectangular apertures. On it stands a peristyle of thirty columns of the Corinthian order, 40 feet high, including bases and capitals, with a plain entablature crowned by a balustrade. In this peristyle, every fourth intercolumniation is filled up solid, with a niche, and connexion is provided between it and the wall of the lower cone. Vertically over the base of that cone, above the peristyle, rises another cylindrical wall, appearing above the balustrade. It is ornamented with pilasters, between which are two tiers of rectangular windows. From this wall, the external dome springs. The lantern receives no support from it. It is merely ornamental, differing entirely in that respect from the dome is of wood, covered with lead; at its summit is *The Golden Gallery*, (with gilt railing,) where the lantern commences.

The interior of the nave and choir are each designed with three arches longitudinally springing from piers, strengthened, as well as decorated, on their inner faces by an entablature, whose cornice reigns throughout the nave and church. Above this entablature, and breaking with it over each pilaster, is a tall attic from projections, on which spring semicircular arches which are formed into *arcs doubleaux.* Between the last, pendentives are formed, terminated by horizontal cornices. Small cupolas, of less height than their semi-diameter, are formed above these cornices. In the upright plane space on the walls above the main arches of the nave, choir, and transepts, a *clerestory* is obtained over the attic order, whose form is generated by the rising of the pendentives. (*Gwilt.*)

Over the entrance to the Choir is a copy of the Latin epitaph on Wren, ending with " Lector, si monumentum requiris, circumspice," (Reader, if you would behold his monument, look around you).

The screen of wrought iron which separates the Choir from the Nave is very elegant. Above this is placed the organ, built by Bernard Schmydt, in 1694, at a cost of 2000*l.*

The Choir contains some of the finest carvings in the world, by Gibbons : as, the episcopal throne; the bishop's ordinary seat, with a mitre and pelican; the lord-mayor's, with the mace and other insignia; and the dean's stall, with fruit and flowers: for the entire work Gibbons received 1333*l. 7s. 5d.* (see CARVINGS, p. 66). The lectern is a large brass-gilt eagle. The decoration of the east end is poor and mean, and was intended by Wren only to serve until he had provided for it a magnificent altar, of Greek marbles, with a stately canopy.

The side aisles, or oratories, were added to the Nave, as Wren designed it, by the Duke of York, afterwards James II., who " was willing to have them ready for the Popish service, when there should be occasion." Wren remonstrated with tears, but in vain.

The walls and massive piers are bare of ornament ; though, in 1773, Sir Joshua Reynolds, P.R.A., and five of his fellow Academicians, offered to furnish, gratis, a series of scripture pictures to be placed in the Cathedral; but the proposition was rejected.

Immediately under the centre of the dome, in the marble pavement, is a brass plate, denoting the position of Nelson's remains in the crypt.

The Monuments (exceeding forty) have been for the most part voted by Parliament in honour of naval and military officers, though there are a few also to authors and artists, and philanthropists. But, in general, while civil eminence has been commemorated in Westminster Abbey, St. Paul's has been made a Pantheon for our heroes. At the entrance of the Choir is a colossal statue of John Howard, with an inscription by Samuel Whitbread, this being the first monument erected in the church (1796); at a corresponding point is a colossal statue of Dr. Johnson, the inscription by Dr. Parr: both statues are by Bacon, R.A.: Howard, with his keys, is often mistaken for St. Peter; and Johnson, with his scroll, for St. Paul. At opposite piers are statues of Sir Joshua Reynolds, by Flaxman, R.A., and Sir William Jones, by Bacon, R.A. Under the great choir arch is a monument to Lord Nelson, by Flaxman ; the statue is characteristic, but the figures about the pedestal are absurd. Opposite is a monument to Lord Cornwallis, by Rossi, R.A.: the Indian river-gods are most admired. In the south transept are monuments to Sir Ralph Abercrombie and Lord Collingwood, by Sir R. Westmacott, R.A., and to Lord Howe, by Flaxman ; statue of Elliot, Lord Heathfield, by Rossi, R.A.; monument to Sir John Moore, by Bacon, R.A.; statue of Sir W. Hoste, by Campbell; and Major-General Gillespie, by Chantrey, R.A. In the north transept, the principal are monuments to Lord Rodney and to Captains Mosse and Rivers, by Rossi, R.A.; Capt. Westcott, by Banks, R.A.; Gen. Ponsonby, a graceful composition, by Baily, R.A.; Major-Gen. A. Gore and J. B. Skerrett, by Chantrey; statue of Earl St. Vincent, by Baily, R.A.; Gen. Picton, who fell at Waterloo, by Gahagan; Admiral Duncan, an elegant figure, by Sir R. Westmacott, R.A.; and Major-Gen. Dundas, by Bacon, R.A.

In the south aisle of the nave is a monument to Dr. Middleton, the first Protestant Bishop of India, by Lough; and in the south aisle of the choir is a kneeling figure of Bishop Heber, by Chantrey, R.A. Here also are statues of Sir Astley Cooper, by Baily, R.A., and Dr. Babington, by Behnes. Two of the finest and most touching works here are Chantrey's battle-piece monuments to Colonel Cadogan, mortally wounded at the battle of Vittoria; and Major-General Bowes, slain at the head of his men at the storming of Salamanca: these are poetic pictures of carnage closing in victory.

The Crypt is now used only as a place of interment. In the south aisle is the grave of Sir Christopher Wren, covered by a flat stone, the English inscription upon which merely states that he died in 1723, aged 91: hung on the adjoining wall is a tablet bearing the Latin epitaph, also placed over the choir entrance. Near Wren's remains are the graves of our great painters. Hence, " if Westminster Abbey has its *Poets' Corner*, so has St. Paul's its *Painters' Corner*. Sir Joshua Reynolds's statue, by Flaxman, is here, and Reynolds himself lies buried here; and Barry, and Opie, and Lawrence are around him; and, above all, the ashes of the great Van Dyck are in the earth under the Cathedral." (*C. R. Leslie, R.A.*) Here also are the altar-tombs of Robert Mylne, the architect, and John Rennie, the engineer. In the middle of the crypt, upon an altar-tomb, is Nelson's coffin, within a black marble sarcophagus made by order of Cardinal Wolsey, but left unused in the tomb-house adjoining St. George's Chapel, Windsor. It is surmounted with a viscount's coronet upon a cushion; on the pedestal is inscribed, "Horatio Viscount Nelson." The coffin, made from part of the mainmast of the ship *L'Orient*, which blew up at the battle of the Nile, was presented to Nelson by his friend Ben Hallowell, captain of the *Swiftsure*. It was deposited here January 9, 1806 (see ADMIRALTY, page 2). Nelson's flag was to have been placed with the coffin; but just as it was about to be lowered, the sailors who had borne it, moved by one impulse, rent it in pieces, each keeping a fragment. Lord Collingwood, as he requested, lies near Nelson, beneath a plain altar-tomb; and opposite lies Lord Northesk, distinguished in the victory of Trafalgar. Here too are the graves of Dr. Boyce,—next to Purcell, perhaps, the greatest English musician; and George Dance, the architect, and the last survivor of the original forty of the Royal Academy. In a dark recess of the eastern wall are some remains of the monuments of Old St. Paul's (see page 86).

The ascent to the Whispering Gallery is by 260 steps; to the outer, or highest Golden Gallery, 560 steps; and to the Ball, 616 steps.

The Library, in the gallery over the southern aisle, was formed by Bishop Compton, whose portrait it contains. Here are about 7000 volumes, besides some manuscripts belonging to Old St. Paul's. The room has some fine brackets, and pilasters with flowers, exquisitely carved by Gibbons; and the floor consists of 2300 pieces of oak, parquetted, or inlaid without nails or pegs. At the end of this gallery is a *Geometrical Staircase*, of 110 steps, built by Wren, for private access to the Library. In crossing thence to the northern gallery, a fine view is gained of the entire vista of the Cathedral from west to east. You then reach the *Model-Room*, where are Wren's first design for St. Paul's, and some of the tattered flags formerly suspended beneath the dome. Returning to the southern gallery, a staircase leads to the south-western campanile tower, where is the *Clock-Room*.

The Clock is remarkable for the magnitude of its wheels and fineness of works, and cost 300*l.* It was made by Langley Bradley in 1708: it has two dial-plates, one south, the other west; each is 51 feet in circumference, and the hour-numerals are 2 feet 2½ inches in height. The minute-hands are 9 feet 8 inches long, and weigh 75 lbs. each; and the hour-hands are 5 feet 9 inches long, and weigh 44 lbs. each. The pendulum is 16 feet long, and the bob weighs 180 lbs.; yet it is suspended by a spring no thicker than a shilling: its beat is 2 seconds,—a dead beat, 30 to a minute instead of 60.

The Clock, "going eight days," strikes the hour on the *Great Bell,*[*] suspended about 40 feet from the floor: the hammer lies on the outside brim of the bell; it has a large head, weighs 145lbs., is drawn by a wire at the back part of the clockwork, and falls again by its own weight upon the bell. The clapper weighs 180lbs. The hour struck by this clock has been heard, in the silence of midnight, on the terrace of Windsor Castle. (See page 39.) Below the Great Bell are two smaller bells, on which the clock strikes the quarters: the larger of these weighs 24cwt. 2qrs. 25lbs; the smaller, 12cwt. 2qrs. 9lbs. The northern tower contains the bell tolled for prayers.

The Whispering Gallery is reached by returning towards the dome, and again ascending. Here a low whisper, uttered on one side, may be distinctly heard at the opposite side, of the gallery. The phenomenon is thus explained by Dr. Paris:

"M shews the situation of the mouth of the speaker, and E that of the ear of the hearer. Now, since sound radiates in all directions, a part of it will proceed directly from M to E, while other rays of it will proceed from M to *u*, and from M to *z*, &c.; but the ray that impinges upon *u* will be reflected to E, while that which first touches *z* will be reflected to *y* and from thence to E; and so of all intermediate rays, which are omitted in the figure to avoid confusion. It is evident, therefore, that the sound at E will be much stronger than if it had proceeded immediately from M without the assistance of the dome; for, in that case, the rays at *z* and *u* would

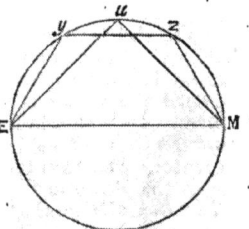

have proceeded in straight lines, and consequently could never have arrived at the point E." *Philosophy in Sport made Science in Earnest,* p. 310.

The Inner Dome (which Wren intended to have lined with mosaic) is plastered on the under side; and painted, by Sir James Thornhill, with events in the life of St. Paul: 1. His Conversion; 2. The Punishment of Elymas the Sorcerer; 3. Cure of the Cripple at Lystra; 4. Conversion of the Gaoler; 5. Paul preaching at Athens; 6. Burning of the Books at Ephesus; 7. Paul before Agrippa; 8. Shipwreck on the Island of Melita. For these paintings Thornhill only received 40*s.* per square yard: they are fast decaying from damp. Although Mr. Parris, the painter, invented an apparatus by which they could be restored at a small expense, the Cathedral funds will not "afford it."

The paintings are best seen from the Whispering Gallery, by the flood of light which pours from the lantern through the opening at the crown of the dome. When looking down into the Church, men seem but as children, and the immensity of the structure is best felt. From the Whispering Gallery, we ascend to

The Stone Gallery, outside the base of the dome, where the gigantic

* The new Great Tom of Lincoln, cast in 1834, is 6 cwt. heavier than the Great Bell of St. Paul's. Its tone is generally considered to be about the same as that of St. Paul's, but sweeter and softer. Mr. E. B. Denison, however, "thinks St. Paul's far the best of the four large bells of England, though it is the smallest of them, being about 5 tons; while York is 12, Lincoln 5½, and Oxford 7¼, which last is a remarkably bad bell." *Treatise on Clock and Watch Making* (Weale, 1850).

height of the figures (11 feet) on the western pediment, and the outlines of the campanile towers are very striking. There is a second outer gallery, still below the base of the dome; and thence you ascend to
The Outer Golden Gallery, at the summit of the dome; the *Inner Golden Gallery* being at the base of the lantern. Through this the ascent is by ladders, to the small dome immediately below the inverted consoles which support
The Ball and Cross; and ascending through the iron-work in the centre, we look into the dark Ball. It is stated to weigh 5600lbs.; thence to the Cross is 30 feet, the latter weighing 3360lbs.
The View from the Outer Golden Gallery is very minute : the occupants of the streets below " appear like mice;" London seems little else than a dense mass of housetops, chimneys, and spires ; the Thames being conspicuous from its glittering surface, but the bridges appearing as dark lines across at intervals. Here, and at the higher points, in clear weather, the metropolis is seen as in a map, with the country 20 miles round. The north division of London rises gently from the Thames, to Hampstead and Highgate. On the east and west are fertile plains extending at least 20 miles, and watered by the Thames. On the south, the view is bounded by the high grounds of Richmond, Wimbledon, Epsom, Norwood, and Blackheath; terminating in the horizon by Leith Hill, Box Hill, and the Reigate and Wrotham hills. Shooter's Hill is conspicuous eastward, and, in a more easterly direction, parts of Epping Forest and other wooded uplands of Essex.

Mr. Hornor describes the strange scene from this lofty summit at three o'clock in the morning as very impressive; for here he frequently beheld " the Forest of London" without any indication of animated existence. It was interesting to mark the gradual symptoms of returning life, until the rising sun vivified the whole into activity, bustle, and business. In high winds, the creaking and whistling of the scaffolding resembled those of a ship labouring in a storm; and once Mr. Hornor's observatory was torn from its fastenings, and turned partly over the edge of the platform.*

The Establishment of the Cathedral consists of the Dean; the precentor, or chanter; the chancellor; the treasurer; the five archdeacons of London, Middlesex, Essex, Colchester, and St. Alban's; thirty major canons, or prebendaries, four of whom are resident ; twelve minor canons; and six vicars choral, besides the children of the choir. One of the vicars-choral officiates as organist, and three of the minor canons hold the places of sub-dean, librarian, and succentor, or underprecentor.

Two of the brightest wits of their day, Sydney Smith (*Peter Plymley*), d. 1845, and R. H. Barham (*Thomas Ingoldsby*), d. 1845, were at the same period Canons of St. Paul's. In 1849, the Rev. H. H. Milman (the poet) was appointed Dean, an office hitherto held by the Bishop of Llandaff for the time being.

The lord-mayor's chaplain is the preacher on all state holidays; viz. 30th January, 29th May, 20th June, and 5th November, on the first Sunday in term, and the anniversary of the Great Fire of 1666. The Paul's Cross sermons are also still preached. Sermons are preached by the Dean and canons-residentiary on Sunday afternoons and holidays, and every Wednesday and Friday during Lent.

* An accident somewhat more perilous befel Mr. Gwyn, when measuring the top of the dome for a section of the Cathedral. While intent on his work his foot slipped, and he slid down the convex surface of the dome until his descent was fortunately obstructed by a small projecting piece of the lead. He thus remained until released from the impending danger by one of his assistants, who providentially discovered his awful situation. *Mr. Hornor's Narrative.*

The choral service is performed at a quarter before ten in the morning, and at a quarter past three in the afternoon. Divine service is likewise held in the Morning Prayer Chapel every week-day morning at eight o'clock.

The Anniversary Festival of the Sons of the Clergy is celebrated in the Cathedral about the middle of May; when the service is preceded by a performance of sacred music, selected from Handel, Boyce, Atwood, and others; aided by the choirs of St. Paul's, Westminster Abbey, and the Chapel Royal. The Anniversary of the Charity Schools is customarily held on the first Thursday in June; when 8000 of the charity-school children are generally present, upon an amphitheatre of seats erected beneath the great dome, and the effect of their united "songs of praise" is very impressive. Both these festivals are usually graced by the presence of royalty.

Admission.—Visitors are admitted to view the building daily, except during the time of divine service. The following are the charges :

	s.	d.
To view the Monuments and body of the Church	0	2
To the Whispering Galleries and the two outside Galleries . .	0	6
To the Ball	1	6
To the Library, Great Bell, Geometrical Staircase, and Model Room	1	0
Clock	0	2
Crypt, or Vaults	1	0

Or 4s. 4d. each person.

The general entrance is at the great North Door, opposite Canon-alley.

The admission-fee originated in "the Stairs-foot Money," fixed by Jennings, the carpenter, in 1707; the proceeds of which were applied to the relief of those men to whom accidents happened during the progress of the works. In 1849, the sum received from visitors to the body of the Cathedral, at 2d. each, was 430l. 3s. 8d., which was divided among the four vergers.

Nearly opposite the North Door in St. Paul's Churchyard is the Convocation or Chapter House of the Cathedral, where a kind of clerical parliament is summoned with every new Imperial Parliament.

The State processions to St. Paul's have been very imposing. Queen Anne came yearly to return thanks for the brilliant successes of Marlborough, who carried the sword of state before Her Majesty; as did Wellington before the Prince Regent, on the day of thanksgiving for peace in 1814. George III. visited St. Paul's, to return public thanks for his recovery from derangement, in 1789; and in 1797, in thanksgiving for naval victories. The last procession of this kind was on Nov. 29, 1820, when Queen Caroline went to St. Paul's, in thanksgiving for her deliverance from the Bill of Pains and Penalties.

Churchyard.—The enclosed ground-plot of the Cathedral is 2 acres 16 perches 70 feet. In the area before the west front, marking the site of St. Gregory's Church, is the statue of Queen Anne, with figures of Britain, France, Ireland, and America, at the corners of the pedestal. Sir Samuel Garth wrote some bitter lines upon this group, where

" France above with downcast eyes is seen,
The sad attendant of so good a queen."

Her Majesty's nose was struck off by a lunatic, about a century ago, and has but lately been repaired. The Churchyard is enclosed with a dwarf stone wall, on which is a noble iron balustrade, 5 feet 6 inches high; there are in it seven ornamental gates, which, with the 2500 rails, weigh 200 tons 8llbs. They were cast at Gloucester Furnace, Lamberhurst, Kent; they cost 6d. per pound, and with other charges, amounted to 11,202l. 0s. 6d.; the cost of the Church was 736,752l. 2s. 3d.;

in all, 747,954*l.* 2*s.* 9*d.*,* equal to 1,222,437*l.* present money. About nine-tenths of this sum were raised by a tax on coals received into the port of London. It has more than once been proposed to remove the wall and balustrade, or a portion of them.

Annexed is a recapitulation of the main dimensions :

	ft.	in.
Circumference of the Cathedral	2292	0
Height of Centre, exclusive of Dome	210	0
Height of Nave, Choir, and Transepts	100	0
Height from floor of Crypt to top of Cross	404	0
Height from Nave pavement to top of Cross	360	0
Height of Western Towers	220	0
Height of Western Front	138	0
Diameter of Interior Dome	100	0
Height of Dome	60	0
Height of Dome from ground-line	215	0
Diameter of opening at top of Dome	14	10¾
Height of Lantern Gallery	274	9
Diameter of opening at top of Upper Dome	8	0

The following are the comparative dimensions of St. Paul's, London, and St. Peter's at Rome :

	E. to W. within.	West end, in.	Ditto, out.	Transept.	Height to top.	
St. Paul's	500	100	138	223	360	English feet.
St. Peter's	669	226	395	442	432	,,
St. Peter's occupies an area of			227,069 superficial feet.			
St. Paul's			84,025			,,
St. Mary's, at Florence			84,802			,,

" For external elegance," says Mr. Gwilt, " we know no church in Europe which exhibits a cupola comparable with that of St. Paul's; though in its connexion with the church by an order higher than that below it, there is a violation of the laws of the art. While, notwithstanding its inferior dimensions (it would stand within St. Peter's), the external appearance of St. Paul's has been preferred by many to that of St. Peter's, it is admitted by all that the interior of the English cathedral will bear no comparison with that of the Roman. The upward view of the dome of St. Paul's, however, conveys an impression of extraordinary magnificence; though not so elevated as St. Peter's, it is still very lofty : the form of the concave, which approaches considerably nearer to that of a circle—the height being equal to a diameter and a half, while in St. Peter's it is equal to two diameters —has also been considered more beautiful than that of its rival." As a whole, however, the effect is truly magnificent, surrounded as the vast edifice is by buildings in every direction : viewed from Cheapside, it presents an imposing mass, and the western front, with its campanili and the majestic dome, is a stupendous termination to the vista of Ludgate-hill; whilst from Blackfriars Bridge, the graceful dome appears in impressive contrast with the less harmonious body of the building.

WESTMINSTER ABBEY

Occupies the site of a Church " to the honour of God and St. Peter," commenced by Sebert, about A.D. 616, on Thorney Island, " overgrown with thorns, and environed with water." This Church was not, however, completed until about 360 years after, by King Edgar, when it was named from being the " Minster West " of St. Paul's. It was destroyed by the Danes, but wholly rebuilt *circ.* 1050, by the pious King Edward the Confessor, who gave to its treasury rich vestments, a golden crown

* In more than one of the Guide-books the cost of the Cathedral is stated at a million and a half of money; which error probably arose from its first perpe-

and sceptres, a dalmatic, embroidered pall, a pair of spurs, &c., to be used on the day of the Sovereign's coronation. This injunction has been observed through a lapse of nearly eight centuries; most of these insignia having been preserved; and our sovereigns, from Harold and William the Conqueror to Queen Victoria, have been crowned here.

King Edward was buried in his new Church, which the monarchs of the next 160 years beautified and endowed with rich gifts and legacies. Henry III., in pious veneration for the memory of the Confessor, began to rebuild the Church on the same spot, 16 May, 1220: hardly was it completed, when it was almost wholly destroyed by fire; but it was restored in the reigns of Edward I. and II. Nicholas Litlington, Abbot in the reign of Edward III., added several abbatial buildings, including the Hall; a great chamber called "the Jerusalem;" the west and south sides of the Great Cloister; and the Granary. In 1502, Henry VII. pulled down the Chapel of the Virgin, at the east end, and replaced it with the beautiful Chapel now called by his name.

The dedication of the Church to St. Peter, (the tutelar saint of fishermen,) led to their offerings of salmon upon the high altar; the donor on such occasions having the privilege of sitting at the convent-table to dinner, and demanding ale and bread from the cellarer.

"The Abbey Church," says Mr. Bardwell, "formerly arose a magnificent apex to a royal palace, surrounded by its own greater and lesser sanctuaries and almonries: its bell-towers (the principal one 72 feet 6 inches square, with walls 20 feet thick), chapels, prisons, gatehouses, boundary-walls, and a train of other buildings, of which we can, at the present day, scarcely form an idea. In addition to *all the land around it*, extending from the Thames to Oxford-street, and from Vauxhall-Bridge road to the Church of St. Mary-le-Strand, the Abbey possessed 97 towns and villages, 17 hamlets, and 216 manors! Its officers fed hundreds of persons daily; and one of its priests (not the Abbot) entertained at his 'pavilion in Tothill' the King and Queen, with so large a party, that seven hundred dishes did not suffice for the first table; and the Abbey butler, in the reign of Edward III., rebuilt, at his own private expense, the stately gatehouse which gave entrance to Tothill-street, and a portion of the wall of which remains to this day." *Brief Account of Ancient and Modern Westminster*, 1839.

At the Dissolution, the Abbey was resigned to Henry VIII. by Abbot Benson; and the King ordered the Church to be governed by a Dean and Prebendaries, making Benson the Dean. In 1541, the Church was turned into an Episcopal See, having Middlesex for its diocese; but was soon again placed under a Dean and Prebendaries. Mary, in 1556, dissolved this institution, and re-appointed an Abbot and monks; but Elizabeth, on her accession, placed it under a Dean and 12 secular Canons, as a Collegiate Church, besides Minor Canons, and others of the choir, to the number of 30; 10 other officers, 2 schoolmasters, 40 scholars, and 12 almsmen, with ample maintenance for all; besides stewards, receivers, registrars, library-keepers, and other officers, the principal being the High Steward of Westminster. In the time of Cromwell, most of the revenues were devoted to the public service, but afterwards restored. As the Abbots of the Monastery had in former times possessed great privileges and honours annexed to the foundation, such as being intrusted with the keeping of the regalia for the coronation, &c., having places of necessary service on days of solemnity, and also exercising archiepiscopal jurisdiction in their liberties, and sitting as spiritual lords in Parliament,—so the Deans of the Collegiate Church succeeded to most of them, and still possess considerable privileges. The Chapter still have a jurisdiction, not only within the city and liberty of Westminster, but also the precincts of St. Martin's-le-Grand, first annexed to it by Henry VII.

From the first opening of the edifice until after the reign of Elizabeth, the Abbey was regarded as a safe Sanctuary: hither the Queen of Edward IV. fled with her five daughters and the young Duke of York when the crafty Richard Duke of Gloucester was plotting to seize the crown. "The Queen," says Sir Thomas More, "sate low on the rushes, all desolate and dismayed;" whilst the Thames was full of boats of Gloucester's servants, watching that no man should go to Sanctuary. On the reverse of Edward IV., in 1470, his Queen, Elizabeth Woodville, took shelter in the Sanctuary, where, "in great penury, forsaken of all her friends," she gave birth to Edward V.

Successive Kings and Abbots continued the building on the plan of Henry III., but so slowly, that the west end towers in 1714 were unfinished: these Sir Christopher Wren pulled down, and erected the present western towers, in Grecianised Gothic style; he also proposed a central spire, as originally intended, for its beginnings appear on the corners of the cross, "but left off before it rose so high as the ridge of the roof." Of the old west front there is a view by Hollar in Dugdale's *Monasticon*. Of the Confessor's Church, the early Anglo-Norman work under the present edifice, or buildings attached to it, may have formed a part.

" The Church, as far as rebuilt in the reign of Henry III., may be easily distinguished from the parts erected at a later period. It consists of Edward the Confessor's Chapel, the side aisles and chapels, the choir, (to somewhat lower than Sir Isaac Newton's monument,) and the transepts. The four pillars of the present choir, which have brass fillets, appear to finish Henry's work; the conclusion of which is also marked by a striped chalky stone, which forms the roof." Dugdale's *Monasticon*, vol. i. p. 273.

The Church is built upon a close fine sand, secured only by its very broad, wide-spreading foundations. It is of several varieties of stone, similar to that of Gatton or Reigate, which are much decomposed: the Caen stone is generally in a bad condition, especially on the north side; the cloisters are mouldering, except where recently restored; but the western towers, of shelly Portland oolite, are sound. The Chapel of Henry VII., originally built with Caen stone, was restored within the present century, at a cost of 42,028*l*., but with Combe Down Bath-stone, already in a state of decomposition.

The *Chapel of Henry VII.*, at the eastern end of the entire pile, is styled by Leland the "miracle of the world;" and probably in no other edifice in the world is displayed such profound geometrical skill, mingled with such luxuriance of ornament. So profuse and delicate is the tracery throughout, that "it would seem as though the architect had intended to give to stone the character of embroidery, and inclose his walls in the meshes of lace-work." With the exception of the plinth, every part is covered with sculptural decorations: the buttress towers are crowned by octagonal domes, with richly-crusted finials, and enriched by niches and elegant tracery; the cross-springers are perforated into airy forms; and the very cornices and parapets are charged, even to profusion, with armorial cognizances and knotted foliage. Prominent among these decorations are the portcullis chained, the rose barbed and seeded, the *Tudor Flower*, the *fleur-de-lis* and the radiated quartrefoil, oak and vine branches, conjoined leaves, dragons, lions, grotesque human heads, demi-angels, animals with two bodies uniting in one head, and demi-musicians playing the violin. The towers are charged with the badges and supporters of the royal founder, deeply undercut; the portcullis, the rose, and the *fleur-de-lis* alternating with the lion, the dragon, and the greyhound; whilst the niches have statue-pedestals, each labelled, in black-letter, with the name of some prophet, apostle, or saint. The first stone of this superb edifice was laid by Abbot Islip, Sir Reginald Bray, and others, in the name of King Henry VII., Jan. 24, 1503; the architect is stated to have been William Bolton, Prior of St. Bartholomew beside Smithfield.

The *Exterior* of the Abbey is best viewed from a distance: the western front from Tothill-street; the picturesque North Transept from

King-street; and the south side from College-street. St. Margaret's Church, so often condemned as a disfigurement in viewing the Abbey, renders its height much greater by contrast. " Distant peeps of the Abbey towers, springing lightly above the trees, may be caught on the rising ground of the Green Park, and from the bridge over the Serpentine; and the superior elevation of the whole Abbey is seen with great effect from the hills about Wandsworth and Wimbledon." (*Handbook*, by H. Cole.) The importance of the western towers will, however, be lessened by the loftier towers of the New Houses of Parliament.

The *North Transept*, though its niches are statueless, is remarkable for its pinnacled buttresses, its triple porch and clustered columns, and its great rose-window, 90 feet in circumference—so as to have been called, for its beauty, "Solomon's porch." From the west side of this Transept judicious restorations are in progress. At the arched doorway leading into the North Aisle terminates the portion of the Abbey completed by Edward I.

The *Western Front* bears the date 1735: the height of the towers (225 feet) tells nobly; they were used as a telegraph station during the last French war. The great west window was the work of Abbot Estney, in 1498. The base of the south tower is hidden by the gable of the Jerusalem Chamber, now used as the Chapter-House. Its northern window has some stained glass *temp*. Edward III.; and here hangs the ancient portrait of Richard II. in the Coronation Chair. Adjoining is the Deanery, where are portraits of several Deans. Parallel with the Jerusalem Chamber is the College Dining Hall and Kitchen, built by Abbot Litlington. The Westminster scholars dine in the Hall: in the centre faggots blaze on a circular stone hearth, the smoke finding egress through the lantern in the roof.

In the *Jerusalem Chamber* died Henry IV., brought from the Confessor's Shrine in the Abbey in a fit of apoplexy, March 20, 1413. Being carried into this Chamber, he asked, on rallying, where he was; and when informed, he replied, to use the words of Shakspeare, founded on history—

> " Laud be to God! even here my life must end:
> It hath been prophesied to me many years.
> I should not die but in Jerusalem."
> *King Henry IV.*, Part 2, act iv. sc. 4.

Here the body of Congreve lay in state, before his pompous funeral, at which noblemen bore the pall. Here, too, Addison lay in state, before his burial in Henry VII.'s Chapel, as pictured in Tickell's elegy:

> " Can I forget the dismal night that gave
> My soul's best part for ever to the grave?
> How silent did his old companions tread,
> By midnight lamps, the mansions of the dead:
> Through breathing statues, then unheeded things;
> Through rows of warriors, and through walks of kings," &c.

The *South Side* is approached from Dean's Yard, on the east side of which an old doorway leads into a court where is Inigo Jones's rustic entrance to the school-room of the College, refounded, in 1560, by Queen Elizabeth. To the left are the old grey *Cloisters*, with groined arches of the 14th century, surrounding a grassy area—monastic solitude in contrast with the scene on the opposite side of the Church. The Rembrandtish lights of these cloisters are very fine; and here the South Aisle of the Church, with its huge buttresses, is best seen. The North Cloister is distinguished by its trefoiled arches, with circles above them, of the 12th century. The East Cloister (*temp*. Edward III.) is rich in flowing tracery and foliations. Here is the entrance to a chapel of the Confessor's time, and now " the Chamber of the Pix," wherein are kept the standards used at the trial of the Pix, the three keys of its double doors being deposited with distinct officers of the Exchequer. The groined roofs are supported by Romanesque or semicircular arches, and thick, short, round shafts.

Eastward is the once magnificent entrance to the *Chapter-House, temp.* Henry III. Here the Commons assembled in 1377, and continued their sittings till they removed to St. Stephen's Chapel. The Chapter-House is now a treasury of Records, including the Star-Chamber proceedings. But the gem of the place is William the Conqueror's Domesday Book, in excellent condition, from searchers not being allowed to touch the text, or writing. Here, too, are Clement the Seventh's Golden Bull, confirming the title of Defender of the Faith on Henry VIII.; a treaty of perpetual peace between Henry VIII. and Francis I., with a gold seal, 6 inches diameter, said to be the work of Cellini; the original wills of Richard II., Henry V., Henry VII., and Henry VIII.; and the Indenture between Henry VII. and the Abbot of Westminster, a glorious specimen of miniature painting and velvet binding, with enamelled and gilt bosses. The Chapter-House is octagonal in plan; and on one of its sides is a statue called "St. John," said to be one of the oldest sculptures in the Abbey. This was a beautifully-decorated building, with painted walls and coloured and gilded arcades, and high-arched windows in seven of its sides, now sadly obscured. The interior is only to be viewed by permission, to be obtained from the authorities of the Public Record Office, at the Rolls House, Chancery-lane. Here is the *Library* of the Dean and Chapter, (about 11,000 volumes): it was formed from the monks' parlour by Dean Williams, whose portrait hangs at the south end.

The *South Transept* is less decorated than its fellow on the north; and the lower part is concealed by the Library and Chapter-House.

The *Chapels*, both on the north and south sides, are nearly alike, and architecturally in character with Henry III.'s structure: they are lighted by lofty windows, with arches enclosing circles, above which are windows within triangles, also enclosing circles.

At the entrance of the Little Cloisters is Litlington Tower, built by Abbot Litlington, and originally the bell-tower of the Church:* the four bells were rung, and a small flag hoisted on the top of this tower (as appears in Hollar's view), when great meetings or prayers took place in St. Catherine's Chapel, pulled down 1571. The bells (one dated 1430, and two 1598) were taken down, and, with two new bells, were hung in one of Wren's western towers. Litlington Tower has been restored by its tenant, Mr. R. Clark, one of the choir, who also erected in its front the original Gothic entrance to the Star-Chamber Court, and its ancient iron bell-pull.†

The best entrance to the Abbey is through the little door into the South Transept, or Poets' Corner; whence the endless perspective lines lead into mysterious gloom.

From Poets' Corner we see, almost without changing the point of sight, the two Transepts, and part of the Nave and Choir. The interior consists, as it were, of two grand stories, or series of groined arches of unequal height: a lower story, which comprises the outer aisles of the Transepts, of the Nave, and the ambulatory of the Choir; and a higher story, forming the middle aisles of the Nave, Transepts, and the Choir. The lower story mostly exhibits the remains of a series of three-headed arches, or trefoil-headed arcades, resting on a base-

---

* An author of the fourteenth century says: "At the Abbey of St. Peter's, Westminster, are two bells, which over all the bells in the world obtain the precedence in wonderful size and tone." We read also, that "in the monasterye of Westminster ther was a fayr yong man which was blynde, whom the monks hadde ordeyned to rynge the bellys."

† In Litlington Tower lived the noted Lady Hamilton, when servant to Mr.

ment seat: and above these arcades are pointed windows, each divided in the centre by a single mullion, surmounted by a circle. Among the marked features of the whole of the upper and inner story are the mural decorations of the spandrels of the arches; above them, the gallery or triforium; and over this, a clerestory of lofty windows. (See *Handbook*, by H. Cole, pp. 45, 46.)

There is a vague tradition that the triforium, or upper vaulting of the Abbey, was occupied by the nuns of Kilburn when they visited the Abbey, to which their house was subordinate.

The *Interior*, viewed from the western entrance, shews the surpassing beauty of the long-drawn aisles, with their noble columns, harmonious arches, and fretted vaults, "a dim religious light" streaming through the lancet windows. Altogether, Henry III.'s portions of the Abbey Church, especially the Choir, exhibit the most perfect specimens of the latest period of the Lancet, Early English, and Early Pointed style; whilst in the tombs of Crouchback and Valence, in the Choir, in the Cloisters, in the Chapels of Henry V. and VII., and in many later monuments, we may collect specimens of Pure Gothic, Decorated English, Florid Pointed or Perpendicular, Tudor, Elizabethan or Cinque-cento.

"The exquisite and airy grace of the lofty pointed arch and clustered shafts of the Early English style, the beautiful purity of design and enrichment of the Decorated, and the elaborate profusion of ornamental detail which marks the Perpendicular or Tudor work,—each and all find here most glorious representatives.

"The *Early English* is exemplified in the North Transept, the South Aisle of the Nave, and in one compartment of the Nave, the narrow lancet-shaped Arch. The elegant Windows, with their beautiful and simple tracery; the Piers, with slender shafts surrounding them, connected by moulded bands; the diaper-work covering the walls; the bold and deeply-cut mouldings; and the light, chaste groining of the ceiling,—are all indicative of the best and purest epoch of the style.

"The *Decorated Style* is shewn in the western portion of the sides of the Nave; and they differ from the eastern part only in detail, the general outline being similar.

"Of the *Perpendicular* we have a most gorgeous specimen in Henry VII.'s Chapel. The large windows, divided into stories by transoms, the head filled with tracery formed by the vertical continuation of the mullions; the *canopied* niches, with images of saints and martyrs; the profusion of panelling, shields, and badges covering the walls; and above all the stupendous roof, with its magnificent fan-tracery and pendants, are all well-recognised features of the architecture of this period, and unite to form a sublime monument, without a parallel, of the consummate skill and genius of the architects of old. The Tomb of Edward III. is also a fine specimen of Perpendicular work of earlier date, and affords a good example of the ancient canopies of wood which covered many of the old tombs." See *A Chart illustrative of the Architecture of Westminster Abbey*, by Francis Bedford, jun.

The general plan of the Church is cruciform, and, besides the Nave, Choir, and Transepts, contains 12 Chapels; the principal of which are those dedicated to St. Edward of England, to the Blessed Virgin (Henry VII.'s), the easternmost building, and those in the northern and southern sides of the building: four on the south, viz. those of St. Blaise, St. Benedict, St. Edmund, and St. Nicholas; on the north those of St. Andrew, St. Michael, St. John the Evangelist, St. Erasmus, St. John the Baptist, and St. Paul. Of these, 10 are nearly filled with monumental tombs; the Chapel of Henry VII. containing but the monument of its founder; and that of St. Paul having but one tomb.

From Poets' Corner, (where a guide accompanies visitors through the Chapels and Choir,) in passing to the first Chapel may be seen, preserved under glass, the remains of an altar-painting, including a figure, probably intended for Christ, an angel with a palm-branch on each side, and a figure of St. Peter, considered by Sir C. L. Eastlake, P.R.A., to be "worthy of a good Italian artist of the fourteenth century," yet executed in England: of the costly enrichments there remain coloured

thè order of the Chapels, only the most remarkable of their monumental *Curiosities* being noticed :

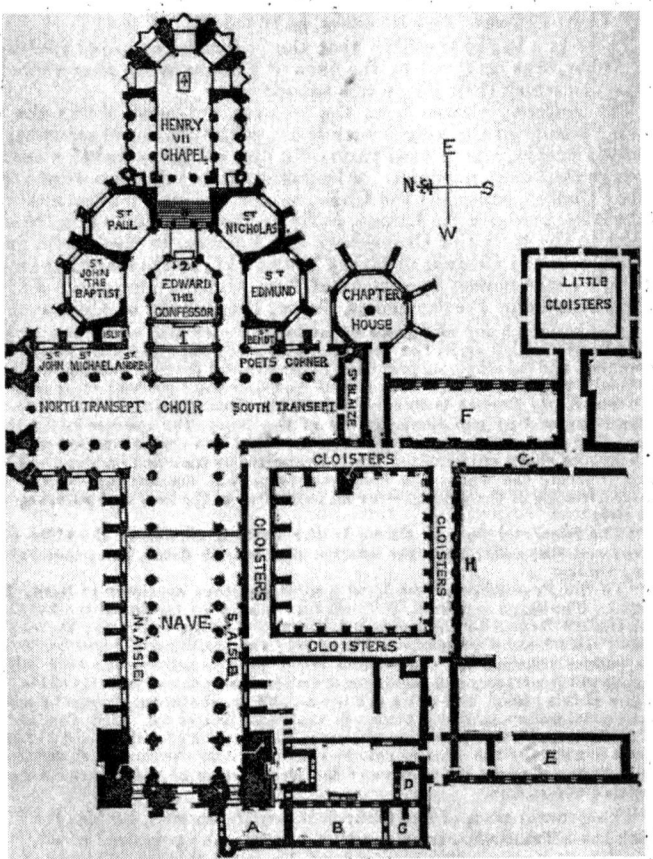

Ground Plan of Westminster Abbey.—A. Jerusalem Chamber. B. College Dining Hall. C. Kitchen. D. Larder. E. Ancient remains. F. Confessor's building (Pix). G. Dark Cloisters. H. Hall of Refectory. 1. High Altar. 2. Henry V.'s Chapel. 3. Porch to Henry VII.'s Chapel. 4. Henry VII.'s Tomb.

1. *St. Benedict's Chapel.* The oldest tomb here is that of Langham, Archbishop of Canterbury (d. 1376), with his effigies robed and mitred.

2. *St. Edmund's Chapel :* Tomb of William de Valence, Earl of Pembroke, and half-brother to Henry III. (d. 1296), the effigies encased in metal ; tomb of John of Eltham, son of Edward II. (d. 1334) ; alabaster figures of William of Windsor and Blanch de la Tour, children of Edward III., the boy in a short doublet, the girl in a horned headdress ; portrait brasses, in the area, of Eleanora de Bohun, Duchess of Gloucester, as a nun of Barking Abbey (d. 1399), and Robert de Waldeby, Archbishop of York (d. 1397) —both the most perfect in the

the guides to have died from the prick of a needle; wall monuments to Lady Jane Seymour (d. 1560) and Lady Jane Grey (d. 1553); black-marble gravestone of Lord Herbert of Cherbury (d. 1678); and Sir Bernard Brocas (d. 1470), altar statue and decorated canopy.

3. *St. Nicholas's Chapel:* Perpendicular stone screen, with quatre-foiled arches highly decorated, and embattled frieze of shields and roses, once coloured; entrance, over the grave of Spelman, the anti-quary, (d. 1641); rich in Elizabethan tombs, bright with gold and colour, alabaster, touchstone, porphyry, and variegated marbles, Gothic canopies, Corinthian pillars, kneeling and recumbent figures, &c.: marble tomb of the wife of the Protector Somerset, (d. 1578); portrait brass of Sir Humphry Stanley, (d. 1505,) knighted by Henry VII. on Bosworth Field; gorgeous monument of the great Lord Burghley to his wife Mildred, (d. 1589,) and their daughter Anne (d. 1588); costly altar-tomb of Sir George Villiers, (d. 1619,) erected for his wife, by N. Stone, cost 560*l.*, the year before her death, 1632; monument of Bishop Dudley, his original brass effigies gone, and the figure of Lady Catherine St. John in its place! Here rests Katherine of Valois, Queen of Henry V., removed on the pulling down of the old Chapel of the Virgin; her body was for nearly three centuries shewn to visitors, not being re-interred until 1776. Next is the vault of the Percys, with a large marble monument, designed by Adam: here, Feb. 22, 1847, Hugh, second Duke of Northumberland, was interred with great state.

In the Ambulatory, opposite St. Nicholas's Chapel, is the eastern side of the tomb of Edward III., and the chantry of Henry V.; looking whence, "in a few square feet, we have specimens of Gothic archi-tecture, in several of its stages, as it flourished from the time of Henry III. to Henry VII." Through a dark vestibule you ascend to

4. *Henry VII.'s Chapel,* consisting of a nave and two aisles, with five chapels at the east end. The entrance-gates are of oak, cased with brass-gilt, and richly dight with the portcullis, the crown, and twisted roses. The vaulted porch is enriched with radiated quatrefoils and other figures, roses, fleurs-de-lis, &c.; Henry's supporters, the lion, the dragon, and the greyhound; his arms and his badges; a rose frieze and embattlement. The fan-traceried pendentive stone roof of the Chapel is encrusted with roses, knots of flowers, bosses, pendants, and armorial cognizances; the walls are covered with sunk panels, with feathered mouldings: and in a profusion of niches are statues, and angels with escutcheons; and the royal heraldic devices, the Tudor rose and the fleur-de-lis under crowns. The edifice is lighted by eight clere-story windows over the aisles.

In the nave are the dark oaken canopied stalls of the Knights of the Bath, who were installed in this Chapel until 1812: these stalls are stud-ded with portcullises, falcons on fetterlocks, fruit and flowers, dragons and angels; and above each stall hangs the banner of its knight. In the centre of the apsis, or east end, within rich and massive gates of brass, is the royal founder's tomb: a pedestal, with the effigies (supposed likenesses) of Henry and his Queen Elizabeth, originally crowned; the whole adorned with pilasters, relievos, rose-branches, and images, on graven tabernacles, of the Kings and patron Saints, all copper-gilt; at the angles are seated angels. This costly tomb is the six years' work of Pietro Torrigiano, a Florentine, who received for it the immense sum of 1500*l.*: the Perpendicular brazen screen, resembling a Gothic palace, is English art: it formerly had 36 statues, of which but six remain. The only remnant of old glass in the Chapel is a figure called Henry VII. in the east window.

From Henry VII. to George II., most of the English sovereigns have been interred here. Edward VI. was buried near the high altar, but is without tomb or inscription. In the *North Aisle*, in the same tomb, lie the Queens Mary and Elizabeth, with a large monument to Elizabeth, by Maximilian Coulte, erected by James I.*

Near this royal monument is an alabaster cradle and effigy of the infant daughter of James I.; which King, with his Queen Anne, and son Prince Henry, the Queen of Bohemia, and Arabella Stuart, lie beneath. Next is a white marble sarcophagus, containing the supposed remains of Edward V. and his brother Richard, murdered in the Tower by order of their uncle, King Richard III. Near it is a recumbent figure, by Sir R. Westmacott, R.A., of the Duke of Montpensier (d. 1807), brother of Louis Philippe, King of the French. Next is the grave of Addison, whose elegant and impressive essay on the Abbey Church and its monuments is inseparable from its history; and close by is the great pyramidal monument of Addison's friend and patron, the Earl of Halifax, one of the Poets of Johnson's *Lives*. The headless corpse of Charles I. was buried at Windsor. The Protector was buried in Henry VII.'s Chapel, (1658,) but in about two years his remains were removed. In the *South Aisle* was interred (1685) Charles II., "without any manner of pomp, and soon forgotten" (*Evelyn*). James II. has no place here;† the vacant space next his brother's remains being occupied by William III. and his Queen. Anne and Prince George complete the royal occupants of the vault. In the centre of the Chapel, in another vault, are the remains of King George II. and Queen Caroline, as it were in one receptacle, a side from each coffin having been removed by the King's direction. In the same vault rests Frederick Prince of Wales, father of George III., beside the Duke of Cumberland, the hero of Culloden. In the South Aisle is the altar-tomb of Margaret Countess of Richmond, mother of Henry VII., with a brass effigy, by Torrigiano; a very fine altar-tomb, with effigy, of

* "The bigot Mary rests in the Abbey Church at Westminster, but no storied monument, no costly tomb, has been raised to her memory. She was interred, with all the solemn funeral rites used by the Roman Church, and a mass of requiem, on the north side of the Chapel of Henry VII. During the reign of her successor not the slightest mark of respect was shewn to her memory by the erection of a monument; and even at the present day no other memorial remains to point out where she lies, except two small black tablets at the base of the sumptuous tomb erected by order of King James I. over the ashes of Elizabeth and her less fortunate sister. On them we read as follow:

REGNO CONSORTES ET VRNA HIC OBDORMIMUS ELIZABETHA	ET MARIA SORORES IN SPE RESVRRECTIONIS.

Sir F. Madden; Privy-Purse Expenses of the Princess Mary, &c.

† James II. died at St. Germain-en-Laye, and his body was kept unburied until 1793 or 1794, in the church of the English Benedictine Monastery at Paris, where it was exhibited for money. It was not until 1824 that the body, or the greater portion of it, was conveyed to St. Germain, where it was buried with great pomp in the parish church, — most of the English then in Paris or the neighbourhood joining in the funeral procession. The intestines of the king were given, soon after his death, to the Irish College in Paris; where also his body lay after the destruction of the Church of the Benedictines, and before its final interment at St. Germain. The brain of the king was given to the Scotch College in Paris, and the heart to the Convent at Chaillot. In the chapel of the Scotch College in Paris is a monument, with a long Latin inscription, erected in 1703 by James Duke of Perth, to the memory of James II. An urn once stood over the monument containing the king's brain, but this was destroyed at the period of the Revolution. Near this is a slab covering the heart of his queen, and another the intestines of his daughter Louisa. A monument of white and grey marble was also erected to the King at St. Germain, by order of George IV.: it bears a Latin inscription, in which James is characterised as

"Magnus in prosperis, in adversis major."

Communicated by Dr. Wreford of Bristol to the Athenæum, Nov. 30, 1850.

Lord Darnley's mother, who "had to her great grandfather King Edward IV., to her grandfather King Henry VII., to her uncle King Henry VIII., to her cousin-german King Edward VI., to her brother King James V. of Scotland, to her son Darnley, (husband of Mary Queen of Scots,) King Henry I. (of Scotland), and to her grandchild King James VI. (of Scotland)," and I. of England. Here also is the tomb, with effigy, of Mary Queen of Scots, erected by Cornelius Cure for James I., who removed his mother's remains thither from Peterborough Cathedral. In the same aisle lies Monk, Duke of Albemarle, whose funeral Charles II. personally attended : the statue monument is by Kent. Here likewise are interred George Villiers, Duke of Buckingham (assassinated 1628), and his son, the profligate Duke.

Henry VII. did not live to see this Chapel finished ; but his will, dated A.D. 1509, contains orders and directions for its completion. In several parts of the Chapel is repeated a rebus, formed by an *eye* and a *slip* or branch of a tree, indicating the name of the founder, Islip.

5. *St. Paul's Chapel* is crowded with Cinque-cento tombs, rich in marble, gilding, and colour : the tombs of Sir Thomas Bromley, Queen Elizabeth's Chancellor, hung with banners ; of Lord Bourchier, standard-bearer to Henry V. at Agincourt ; and of Sir Giles Daubney, are among the best specimens of the period. In frigid and colossal contrast with their beauty, and hiding the Raffaelesque sculptures of Henry the Fifth's chantry, is the sitting statue of James Watt, the engineer, by Chantrey, R.A., strangely out of place in a mediæval Church : the inscription is by Lord Brougham. Next westward is

6. *St. Erasmus's Chapel*, with an enriched canopy, erected, as its rebuses shew, by Abbot Islip, and leading to

7. *St. John the Baptist's Chapel*, with a groined roof, coloured end wall, and sculptured arcades. Here are buried several early Abbots of Westminster. An altar-tomb, of freestone, bears the effigy of William de Colchester, wearing gold bracelets bordered with pearls and set with stones, and a gold mitre covered with large pearls, and crosses and stars of precious gems,—a rare piece of monumental costume. Here is a large Cinque-cento monument to Cary, Lord Hunsdon, first cousin and Chamberlain to Queen Elizabeth ; in the centre of the area is the altar-tomb of Thomas Cecil, Earl of Exeter, and his two wives, the second of whom refused to allow her statue to be laid in the left side space, still vacant. The alabaster monument to Colonel Edward Popham, "one of the Parliament generals at sea," was the only one spared at the Restoration. Nearly all the old tombs have lost their canopies. The view from here is very picturesque and varied ; and in leaving the Chapel, the eye ranges across the north transept, and down the north aisles of the choir and nave, through a high o'erarching vista of "dim religious light," brightened by a geminy lancet window.

8. *Abbot Islip's Chapel* is elegantly sculptured, and contains his altar-tomb, with an effigy of the Abbot in his winding-sheet. In this chapel was the Wax-work Exhibition, which originated in the olden custom of waxen figures of great persons being formerly borne in their funeral processions, then for a time deposited over their graves, and subsequently removed. Other figures were added ; the *sight* was called by the vulgar, "The Play of the Dead Volks," and was not discontinued until 1839. Next the Chapel is the monument to General Wolfe, by Wilton, R.A., with a lead-bronzed bas-relief of the landing at Quebec, executed by Cappizoldi. We now enter the East Aisle of the North Transept, formerly divided by enriched screens into the Chapels of St. John, St. Michael, and St. Andrew. Here is the celebrated tomb of Sir Francis Vere (*temp.* Elizabeth), his effigy recumbent beneath a canopy on which are his helmet, breastplate, &c., supported by four kneeling knights at the four corners ;

the design is said to have been borrowed from a tomb at Breda, attributed to Michael Angelo. Roubiliac was found one day with his looks fixed on one of the knights' figures; "Hush! hush!" said he to the Abbey mason, laying his hand on his arm as he approached, and pointing to the figure, "he will speak presently." Near this tomb is Roubiliac's famous monument to Mr. and Mrs. Nightingale, where Death, as a skeleton, is launching his dart at the beautiful wife, who sinks into the arms of her agonised husband: her right arm is the perfection of sculpture: "life seems slowly receding from her tapering fingers and quivering wrist." (*Allan Cunningham.*) Roubiliac died the year after its erection, 1762. This work touches every heart, but the figure of Death is too literal and melodramatic. Upon the spot, formerly the oratory of St. John the Evangelist, is a marble statue of Mrs. Siddons by Campbell; she is in her famous walking dream as Lady Macbeth. Here is also an alto-relievo, by J. Bacon, jun., to Admiral R. Kempenfeldt, drowned by the sinking of the Royal George, 1782:

> " When Kempenfeldt went down
> With twice four hundred men."

Opposite is the colossal statue of Telford, the eminent engineer (d. 1834), by Baily, R.A.; and a tablet to Sir Humphry Davy (d. 1829). Eastward is the north side of Henry the Fifth's Chantry, with its coronation ceremony, and its equestrian war group, whose poetic grandeur of sculpture so charmed Flaxman. We now ascend a small staircase, to

9. *Edward the Confessor's Chapel*, in the rear of the high altar of the Abbey. In the centre is the Shrine of the Confessor, erected at the expense of Henry III., and enriched with mosaic, priceless jewels, and images of gold and silver; and bearing a Latin inscription, now almost effaced. Northward is the altar-tomb of Edward I. (d. 1307), of Purbeck marble, "scantly fynysshed:" it was opened in 1774, when the King's body was nearly entire. Next is the canopied altar-tomb of Henry III. (d. 1272), once richly dight with glittering marbles and mosaic work of gold, and still bearing a fine brass effigies of the King. At the east end is the altar-tomb and effigies of Eleanor, Queen of Edward I.; its beautiful iron-work, wrought by a smith at Leighton Buzzard in 1293-4, was restored in 1849: the statues of the Queen and of Henry III. are concluded to be by the same artist, William Torrel. To Fabian's time, two wax tapers had been kept burning upon Eleanor's tomb, day and night, from her burial. The altar-tomb and chantry of Henry V. occupy the east end of the Chapel: the head of the King, of solid silver, was stolen at the Reformation. "In Harry the Fifth's time," says Sir Philip Sydney, "the Lord Dudley was his lord-steward, and did that pitiful office in bringing home, as the chief mourner, his victorious master's dead body, as who goes but to Westminster in the church may see." Henry's helmet (probably worn at Agincourt), his shield and saddle, are preserved here; the canopies and niches, filled with statues of kings, bishops, abbots, and saints, are very fine. The archway had formerly ornamented iron gates, made by a London smith, in 1431, and now among the Abbey stores.

Near to this Chantry is the altar-tomb, with marble effigies, of Philippa, Queen of Edward III. (d. 1369); but the tomb has been stripped of its 30 statues. Next is the highly-decorated altar-tomb and effigies of Edward III. (d. 1377), with the richest and most perfect canopy in the Abbey; beside it rest the state sword and shield "carried before Edward III. in France:"

> " The monumental sword that conquered France." *Dryden.*

Here, too, are three small tombs of children of Edward III., Edward figures of Richard II. (d. 1399-1400) and his first Queen, Anne of Bohemia (d. 1394). Also, a brass of John de Waltham, Bishop of Salisbury, and Lord High Treasurer, buried, by favour of Richard II., in this "Chapel of the Kings." The Chapel is parted from the Choir by a shrine of fifteenth-century work, its frieze bearing the following 14 sculptures, illustrative of the life of Edward the Confessor:

1. Prelates and nobles doing fealty to Edward the Confessor before he was born. 2. Birth of the Confessor. 3. The Confessor's Coronation. 4. The Confessor witnessing the Devil dancing on the Danegelt Tax in casks. 5. Edward admonishing the thief stealing his treasure. 6. Christ appearing to Edward. 7. Vision—King of Denmark falling into the sea. 8. Tosti and Harold's quarrel. 9. Vision—Emperor Theodosius, and Cave of Seven Sleepers of Ephesus. 10. Edward giving his ring to St. John Evangelist. 11. Restoration of the Blind, by use of water in which Edward had washed. 12. St. John giving Edward's ring to Pilgrims. 13. Pilgrims returning the ring to Edward. 14. Called "Dedication of Edward the Confessor's Church."

The two upper stories of the Shrine are of wainscot, and were probably erected by Abbot Feckenham, in Queen Mary's reign. The present coffin of the pious Edward, within the ancient stonework, may be seen from the parapet of Henry V.'s Chapel.

With their backs to the screen stand the two Coronation Chairs used at the crowning of the British sovereigns. One was made by order of Edward I. to hold the Scone stone, of legendary fame, and which had been for ages the coronation-seat of the Scottish kings: it is of reddish-grey sandstone, 26 by 16¾ inches, and 10½ inches thick. The companion chair was made for the coronation of Mary, Queen of William III. Both chairs are of architectural design: the ancient one, St. Edward's Chair, is supported upon four lions; and both are covered with gold-frosted tissue, and cushioned, when used at coronations.

In 1297, according to Stow, Edward offered at the Confessor's Shrine the chair, containing the famous stone; and the sceptre and crown of gold of the Scottish sovereigns, which he had brought from the Abbey of Scone. It is called the Prophetic or Fatal Stone, from the belief of the Scots that whenever it was lost, the power of the nation would decline; it was also superstitiously called Jacob's Pillow. The mosaic pavement of this Chapel, by Abbot Ware, is as old as the Confessor's Shrine: its enigmatical designs in tesseræ of coloured marbles, porphyry, jasper, alabaster, &c., are very curious.

The *Choir* has some fine canopied monuments. On the north side are the tombs of the Countess of Lancaster; of Aymer de Valence, Earl of Pembroke (best seen from the north aisle); and Edmund Crouchback, Earl of Lancaster, second son of Edward III. Flaxman speaks of the two latter monuments as "specimens of the magnificence of our sculpture in the reign of the first two Edwards. The loftiness of the work, the number of arches and pinnacles, the lightness of the spires, the richness and profusion of foliage and crockets, the solemn repose of the principal statue, representing the deceased in his last prayer for mercy at the throne of grace; the delicacy of thought in the group of angels bearing the soul, and the tender sentiment of concern variously expressed in the relations ranged in order round the basement,—forcibly arrest the attention, and carry the thoughts not only to other ages, but to other states of existence." On the south is the altar-tomb of Anne of Cleves; and above it is the tomb of King Sebert, erected in 1308, and bearing two pictures, Sebert and Henry III., in tolerable condition.

In 1848, the oak refitting of the Choir was completed; and the organ over the screen at the west entrance partly removed to the sides, and partly lowered, so as not to intercept the view of the great west window. On each side are ranged oaken stalls, with decorated gables, those for the Dean and Subdean distinguished by loftier canopies, and the western entrance being still more enriched; the pew-fronts and seat-ends are also carved, and 1000 more sittings have been provided: the carved wood-work is by Messrs. Ruddle, of Peterborough, from designs by Mr. E. Blore. The great circular or marigold window, and the triforium and other windows beneath it, in the South Transept, have been filled with stained glass by Ward and Nixon; the subjects are incidents in the life of our Saviour, with figures nearly 3 feet high. From the cross of the Transepts, the magnificent perspective of the high imbowed roof of the Nave and Choir, and the great height of the edifice, nearly 104 feet, is seen to the best advantage. The pavement is partly Abbot Ware's, and in part black and white marble, the latter given by Dr. Busby, of Westminster School. The decorations of the altar are in the Gothic style; but a classic altar disgraced the choir from the days of Queen Anne to the reign of George IV.

The *North Transept* contains some important modern monuments: such are Bacon's statue of the great Lord Chatham, with allegorical figures; and Nollekens's large group of pyramid, allegory, and medallion, to the three Captains mortally wounded in Rodney's victory of April 12, 1782: these are national tributes, erected by the King and Parliament. The memorials to naval commanders here are numerous, and their heroic suffering is usually narrated in medallion. Mrs. Warren and child, sometimes entitled "Charity," for pathetic treatment has few rivals in modern sculpture; it is by Sir R. Westmacott, R.A. One of the grandest works here is Flaxman's sitting statue of Lord Chief-Justice Mansfield, supported by figures of Wisdom and Justice; in the rear of the pedestal is the crouching figure of a condemned youth, with the torch of life reversed; or it is better described as " a criminal, by Wisdom delivered up to Justice." (Cunningham's *Handbook of Westminster Abbey*.) Lord Mansfield rests beneath this memorial: it cost 2500*l*., bequeathed by a private individual for its erection. In the pavement are buried Chatham, Pitt and Fox, Castlereagh, Canning and Grattan, Lord Colchester, and William Wilberforce:

> " Now—taming thought to human pride!—
> The mighty chiefs sleep side by side.
> Drop upon Fox's grave the tear,
> 'Twill trickle to his rival's bier;
> O'er Pitt's the mournful requiem sound,
> And Fox's shall the notes rebound." *Scott.*

Fox's memorial, by Westmacott, shews the orator dying in the arms of Liberty, attended by Peace and a kneeling negro;[*] Pitt's monument, by the same sculptor, is over the great western door of the Nave. Here, and in the north aisle of the Choir, leading to the Nave, are Chantrey's marble portrait-statues of Horner, Canning, Malcolm, and Raffles; a statue of Follett, by Behnes; John Philip Kemble (without a name), modelled by Flaxman, but executed after his death; Wilberforce, by S. Joseph; and, opposite Canning, the late Marquis of Londonderry, by J. E. Thomas,—placed here, in 1850, by the present Marquis.

Here are three monuments by Wilton: statue of General Wolfe, and figures; statue of Admiral Holmes, in Roman armour; and William Pulteney, Earl of Bath, statues and medallion.

The north aisle of the Choir, leading to the Nave, has been described as a sort of *Musicians' Corner;* for here rests Purcell, with the striking epitaph, attributed to Dryden: "Here lies Henry Purcell, Esq., who left this life, and is gone to that blessed place where only his harmony can be exceeded." On the same pillar is a memorial to Samuel Arnold:

* Canova said of the figure of the African in this group, that "neither in England nor out of England had he seen any modern work in marble which surpassed it." King George IV. subscribed 1000 guineas towards this monument.

both Purcell and Arnold were organists of the Abbey. Opposite is a tablet to Dr. Blow, and beneath it his pupil's, Dr. Burney; and close by lies Dr. Croft, another organist of the Abbey, whose death was brought on by his attendance at the coronation of George II.

The *Nave* has almost every variety of memorial—sarcophagus and statue, bust and brass, tablet and medallion, mostly modern. In the southern aisle of the Choir, leading to the Nave, is Bird's monument to Sir Cloudesley Shovel, personifying "the brave, rough English Admiral," by a periwigged beau, which is so justly complained of by Addison and the pious Dr. Watts. Opposite is Behnes's bust of Dr. Bell, the founder of the Madras System of Education; and near it is the monument to Thomas Thynne, of Longleat, Wilts: he was shot in his coach, at the end of the Haymarket, Sunday, Feb. 12, 1682, as sculptured on the tomb. Here, too, is a fine bust, by Le Sœur, of Sir Thomas Richardson, Lord Chief-Justice (*temp.* Charles I.); and a bust of Pasquale de Paoli, the Corsican chief. Here, also, are the monuments to Dr. South, the witty prebendary of the Church; Dr. Busby, master of Westminster School; and Dr. Isaac Watts, buried in Bunhill Fields.

In the two side arches of the Choir screen are the monuments of Sir Isaac Newton, and James, first Earl Stanhope; both designed by Kent, and executed by Rysbrack: Newton's is characterised by the celestial globe, with the course of the comet of 1681, and the genius of Astrology above it. In the screen niches are statues of Edward the Confessor, Henry III., and Edward I., and their respective queens.

In the north aisle is a weeping female, by Flaxman, to the memory of George Lindsay Johnstone,—a touching memorial of sisterly sorrow. One of the few old monuments here is that to Mrs. Jane Hill (d. 1651), —a kneeling figure and sheeted skeleton, and the mottoes: "Mors mihi lucrum," and "Solus Christus mihi sola salus." Near the above is the Parliamentary figure group, by Westmacott, to Spencer Perceval, the prime-minister, shot by Bellingham, in the lobby of the House of Commons, May 11, 1812; the assassination is sculptured rearward of the figures. Here also are several interesting monuments to heroes who have fallen in battle: as, Colonel Bringfield, killed by a cannon-shot at Ramilies whilst remounting the great Duke of Marlborough on a fresh horse; the three brothers Twysden, who fell in their country's service in three successive years; Captains Harvey, Hutt, and Montagu, who fell in Lord Howe's victory of June 1; Sir Richard Fletcher, killed at St. Sebastian; and the Hon. Major Stanhope, at Corunna. Here, too, is a plain tablet to Banks, the sculptor and R.A.; a monument to Sir Godfrey Kneller, the painter, by Rysbrack, after Sir Godfrey's own design, Pope furnishing the epitaph: Kneller is buried in Twickenham Church. Towards the middle of the Nave are the gravestones of Major Rennell, the geographer; and Thomas Telford, the engineer; and near Banks's tablet is buried Ben Jonson, his coffin set on its feet, and originally covered with a stone inscribed "O rare Ben Jonson!" By his side lies Tom Killigrew, the wit of Charles the Second's court; and opposite, his son, killed at the battle of Almanza, in Spain, in 1707.

Over the west door is Westmacott's statue-memorial to the Right Hon. William Pitt: it cost 6300l., the largest sum ever voted by Government for a national monument.[*]

To the left is a large marble monument to Lord Holland, by Baily, R.A., erected by public subscription in 1848: the design,—the prison-house of Death, with three poetic figures in lamentation, bassi-relievi on the two sides, and the whole surmounted by a colossal bust of the

[*] Immediately after the death of Sir Robert Peel, in 1850, the sum of 5000l. was voted by Parliament for a monument to his memory, to be placed "in the Collegiate Church of St. Peter, Westminster."

deceased Lord,—is, perhaps, the finest architectural and sculptural combination in the Abbey.

We now reach the south tower of the western front, used as the Consistory Court, and Chapel for Morning Prayers.

In the south aisle of the Nave, commencing from the west, is the tomb of Captain Cornewall, who fell in the sea-fight off Toulon, 1743; this being the first monument voted by Parliament for naval services.

Next is the statue of the Right Hon. James Craggs, the friend of Pope and Addison.

Next is Bird's bust-monument to Congreve, the great dramatic poet, erected at the expense of Henrietta Duchess of Marlborough, to whom Congreve, " for reasons not known or not mentioned," bequeathed 10,000*l.* Among the noticeable personages interred here, without memorials, is Dean Atterbury—the place his own previous choice, being, as he told Pope, " as far from kings and kæsars as the space will admit of;" also Mrs. Oldfield, the actress, buried "in a very fine Brussels lace-head, a Holland shift, with a tucker and double ruffles of the same lace, a pair of new kid gloves," &c.; to which Pope thus alludes:

" Odious! in woollen! 'twould a saint provoke,
(Were the last words that poor Narcissa spoke) :
No, let a charming chintz and Brussels lace
Wrap my cold limbs and shade my lifeless face ;
One would not, sure, be frightful when one's dead—
And—Betty, give this cheek a little red."

Eastward is the sculptural burlesque deservedly known as "the Pancake Monument," to Admiral Tyrrell, with its patchy clouds, coral rocks, cherubs, harps, palm-branches, and other allegorical absurdities. Between three successive windows are the monuments, by Roubiliac, of Lieut.-Gen. Hargrave, Maj.-Gen. Fleming, and Marshal Wade, all in the conventional school of allegory. Next is a good bust, by Bird, of Sidney, Earl of Godolphin, chief minister to Queen Anne; alto-relievo and figures to Lieut.-Col. Townsend, killed by a cannon-ball at Ticonderago, in his 28th year ; and a monument, by Bushnell, to Sir Palmes Fairborne, governor of Tangier, with inscription by Dryden. We now reach the tomb of Major André, who was executed by the Americans. as a spy in 1780; his remains were removed here in 1821 : the bas-relief shews André as a prisoner in the tent of Washington, with the bearer of a flag of truce to solicit his pardon. This monument was put up at the expense of George III.; the heads of the principal figures have been several times mischievously knocked off, but as often restored.

In *Poets' Corner (South Transept)* are the graves or monuments of the majority of our greatest poets, from Chaucer to Campbell. To the right of the entrance-door is the tomb of "the Father of English Poetry," (d. 1400): it is a dingy and greasy recess, on which may be traced with the finger Galfridus Chaucer, the only part of the inscription which was originally chiselled ; the other lines have disappeared. This memorial was partly placed here in 1556, by Nicholas Brigham, a student at Oxford, and a poet too: the altar-tomb originally covered Chaucer's remains, removed from here by Brigham, who placed over it the canopy : it is altogether in decay, but in 1850 was proposed to be restored. Nearer the door is the large monument erected by Sheffield, Duke of Buckingham, to Dryden, whose name it simply bears, with a noble bust of him by Scheemakers. Pope wrote for the pedestal this couplet :

" This Sheffield raised: the sacred dust below
Was Dryden once: the rest, who does not know?".

Next is a wreathed urn, by Bushnell, erected by George Duke of Buckingham, over Abraham Conolly, as the Latin inscription declares, the Pindar, Horace, and Virgil of England: this full-blown flattery, by

Dean Sprat, greatly provoked Dr. Johnson. From Chaucer's tomb, eastward, the monuments are placed as follows: to

John Philips, who wrote *The Splendid Shilling*, *Cider*, and other poems: profile in relief, within a wreath of apple and laurel leaves.

Barton Booth, the eminent actor, the original *Cato* in Addison's play: a bust, erected by Booth's widow.

Michael Drayton, who wrote the *Polyolbion:* a bust on pediment, with a beautiful epitaph, attributed to Dryden; erected at the expense of Clifford, Countess of Dorset, who also put up a monument to

Edmund Spenser, author of the *Faerie Queene:* tablet and pediment, renewed in marble in 1778. Spenser was the second poet interred in the Abbey: he " died for lake of bread, in King-street," Westminster; and was buried here by Devereux, Earl of Essex.

Ben Jonson: medallion on the wall, by Rysbrack, after Gibbs; " O rare Ben Jonson !", inscribed beneath the head.

Samuel Butler, author of *Hudibras:* bust, placed here by Alderman Barber, the patriotic printer (see ALDERMAN, p. 3).

John Milton, buried in Cripplegate Church: bust and tablet, erected by Mr. Auditor Benson, who, "in the inscription, has bestowed more words on himself than upon Milton."

Thomas Gray, buried at Stoke Pogeis: a figure of the Lyric Muse holding a medallion of the poet, by Bacon, R.A., with inscription by

William Mason, Gray's biographer, who lies next: profile medallion, with inscription by Bishop Hurd.

Matthew Prior: bust by Coysevox, presented to Prior from Louis XIV.; and statues of Thalia and Clio, by Rysbrack.

St. Evremond, the French Epicurean wit: bust and tablet; and below it, profile medallion, by Chantrey, R.A., of Granville Sharp, Negro Slavery Abolitionist, erected by the African Institution of London.

Thomas Shadwell, poet-laureate early in the reign of William III., buried at Chelsea: bust crowned with bays, above Prior's monument.

Christopher Anstey, author of the *New Bath Guide:* tablet on the next column; and at the back of St. Evremond's monument, a tablet to Mrs. Pritchard, the eminent tragic actress.

William Shakespeare: the subscription monument; a statue by Scheemakers, after Kent, with absurd and pedantic accessories: the lines on the scroll are from the play of the *Tempest*.

James Thomson, buried in Richmond (Surrey) Church: statue, paid for by a subscription edition of his *Seasons*, &c. in 1762.

Nicholas Rowe, dramatist and poet-laureate (George I.), and his daughter Charlotte: busts by Rysbrack; inscription by Pope.

John Gay, who wrote the *Beggar's Opera:* winged boy and medallion portrait, erected by the Duke and Duchess of Queensbury: the scoffing couplet, " Life's a jest," is Gay's own unworthy composition; the lines beneath it are by Pope.

Oliver Goldsmith, poet, dramatist, and essayist: medallion by Nollekens, R.A., over doorway to the Chapel of St. Blaise; the place chosen by Sir Joshua Reynolds; the Latin inscription written by Dr. Johnson.

John Duke of Argyll (d. 1743): statues of the warrior and orator as a Roman, with History, Eloquence, Britannia, &c., by Roubiliac. Canova said of the figure of Eloquence: " This is one of the noblest statues I have seen in England."

George Frederick Handel, the great musician: statue, beneath a winged harper and stupendous organ; the last work of Roubiliac, who took the mould from Handel's face after death. Above the niche is a record of the " Commemoration," in 1784; the gravestone is beneath.

Joseph Addison, buried in Henry VII.'s Chapel: a poor statue on pedestal, by Westmacott, R.A. Addison's visits here are ever to be remembered: "When I am in a serious humour," writes he, "I very often walk by myself in Westminster Abbey, where the gloominess of the place, and the use to which it is applied, with the solemnity of the building, and the condition of the people who lie in it, are apt to fill the mind with a kind of melancholy, or rather thoughtfulness, that is not disagreeable."

Isaac Barrow, "the unfair preacher," *temp.* Charles II.: bust and tablet. Sir Richard Coxe, Taster (of food) to Queen Elizabeth and James I.: marble tablet. Isaac Casaubon, the learned editor of *Pernices* and *Polybius*: marble monument.

Camden, the great English antiquary, and a Master of Westminster School: half-length figure; buried before St. Nicholas's Chapel.

David Garrick, the eminent actor: statue, with medallion of Shakspeare; a coxcombical piece of art, which provoked Charles Lamb to question the fitness of Shakespeare's tragedies for stage representation.

The most remarkable gravestones in the *South Transept* are those of Richard Cumberland, Richard Brinsley Sheridan, Samuel Johnson, and David Garrick and his wife; "Thomas Parr, of ye county of Sallop, born in A. D. 1483. He lived in the reignes of ten princes: viz. King Edward IV., King Edward V., King Richard III., King Henry VII., King Henry VIII., King Edward VI., Queen Mary, Queen Elizabeth, King James, and King Charles; aged 152 years, and was buryed here Nov. 15, 1635;" Sir William Chambers, architect of Somerset House; R. Adam, architect of the Adelphi; John Henderson, the actor; James Macpherson, Esq., M.P. (*Ossian* Macpherson); William Gifford, critic; Davenant (inscribed, "O rare Sir William Davenant!"), in the grave of Thomas May, the poet, whose body was disinterred, and his monument destroyed, at the Restoration; Francis Beaumont, "Fletcher's associate;" Sir John Denham, K.B., author of *Cooper's Hill.*

Near Shakespeare's monument is a bust, by Weekes, of Robert Southey, poet-laureate, (buried in Crosthwaite Church, Keswick); and next is the gravestone over Thomas Campbell, author of the *Pleasures of Hope*, with an exquisite statue of the poet, by W. C. Marshall.

Large fees are paid to the Dean and Chapter for the admission of monuments: from 200*l.* to 300*l.* for a statue, and from 150*l.* to 200*l.* for a bas-relief; for Lord Holland's monument, 20 feet square, 300*l.* The statue of Lord Byron, by Thorwaldsen, was refused admission; and after lying twelve years in the London Dock cellars, in 1845 it was placed in the Library of Trinity College, Cambridge.

On the end of the gallery westward are the remains of a supposed fresco, a White Hart, "couchant, gorged with a gold chain and coronet," the device of Richard II.

Painted and Stained Glass. — (Ancient.) North Aisle of Nave, figure, said to be Edward the Confessor; South Aisle, given to the Black Prince, Edward III. and Richard II. See also clerestory windows east of Choir, east window of Henry VII.'s Chapel, and Jerusalem Chamber.—(Modern.) Great west window, the Patriarchs; large rose window. North Transept, Apostles and Evangelists—a noble mass of brilliant colour and delicate stone tracery; marigold window in South Transept, (put up in 1847,) figures nearly three feet high; also windows above Henry VII.'s Chapel, and in east end of triforium.

Brasses.—The principal are in the Chapels of St. Edmund, St. John the Baptist, and Edward the Confessor.

Cloisters.—South lie four of the early Abbots of Westminster; and here is "Long Meg," a slab of blue marble, traditionally the gravestone of twenty-six monks who died of the plague in 1349, and were buried in one grave. Here is a tablet to William Lawrence, which records:

"Short-Hand he wrote: his Flowre in prime did fade,
And hasty Death Short Hand of him hath made.
Well cooth he Nv'bers, and well mesur'd Land;
Thvs doth he now that Grovd where on yov stand,
Wherein he lyes so Geometricall:
Art maketh some, bvt thvs will Natvre all."

This quaint conceit is in the North Walk; where also are the graves of Spranger Barry, the actor, famous in Othello, and Sir John Hawkins, who wrote a History of Music, and a Life of Dr. Johnson.

East Walk: medallion monument to Bonnell Thornton ("the Connoisseur"), inscription by Joseph Warton; monument to Lieut.-Gen. Withers, with inscription by Pope, "full of commonplaces, with something of the common cant of a superficial satirist" (*Johnson*); tablet to Sir Edmondberry Godfrey (d. 1678), buried in St. Martin's-in-the-Fields; graves of Aphra Behn, the lady dramatist (*temp.* Charles I.), and Mrs. Bracegirdle, the fascinating actress.

West Walk: bust and alto-relievo, by Banks, R.A., to William Woollett, the engraver, buried in Old St. Pancras' churchyard: tablets to George Vertue, the engraver; Dr. Buchan, who wrote on "Domestic Medicine;" and Benjamin Cooke, organist of the Abbey, with the musical score of "the Canon by twofold augmentation" graven upon the slab.

In the Cloisters, too, are interred Henry Lawes, the composer of the music of *Comus*, and "one who called Milton friend;" Tom Brown, the wit; Thomas Betterton,* who "ought to be recorded with the same respect as Roscius among the Romans;" Samuel Foote, the actor and dramatist; Mrs. Rowe, Mrs. Cibber, and Mrs. Yates: so that the Cloisters may be termed the *Actors' Corner.*

The present conserving architect of the Abbey is Mr. George Gilbert Scott. The following are the principal *Admeasurements:*

Nave.—Length, 166ft.; breadth, 38ft. 7in.; height, 101ft. 8in.; breadth of aisles, 16ft. 7in.; extreme breadth of nave and its aisles, 71ft. 9in.

Choir.—Length, 155ft. 9in.; breadth, 38ft. 4in.; height, 101ft. 2in.

Transepts.—Length of both, including choir, 203ft. 2in.; length of each transept, 82ft. 5in.; breadth, including both aisles, 84ft. 8in.; height of south transept, 105ft. 5in.

Interior.—Extreme length, from western towers to the piers of Henry VII.'s Chapel, 383ft.; extreme length, from western towers, including Henry VII.'s Chapel, 511ft. 6in.

Exterior.—Extreme length, exclusive of Henry VII.'s Chapel, 416ft.; extreme length, inclusive of Henry VII.'s Chapel, 530ft.; height of western towers, to top of pinnacles, 225ft. 4in.

Henry VII.'s Chapel. (*Exterior.*)—Length, 115ft. 2in.; extreme breadth, 79ft. 6in.; height to apex of roof 85ft. 6in.; height to top of western turrets, 101ft. 6in. (*Interior.*)—Nave: length, 103ft. 9in.; breadth, 35ft. 9in.; height 60ft. 7in. Aisles: length, 62ft. 5in.; breadth, 17ft. 1in.; height of west window, 45ft.

Admission.—The Abbey is open to the public between the hours of 11 and 3, generally; and in summer, between 4 and 6 in the afternoon. There is no charge for admission to the Nave, Transepts, and Cloisters; but the fee for admission to view the Choir and Chapels, and the rest of the Abbey, is 6d. each person, with the attendance of a guide. The entrance is at Poets' Corner. The Admission-money was originally 15d. each person, when it usually produced upwards of 1500l. per annum, mostly distributed among the minor canons, organists, and lay-clerks.

Divine Service commences in the church daily, at 10 o'clock in the morning, and at 3 o'clock in the afternoon. Also, daily, (Sundays excepted,) at a quarter before 8 in the morning there is a communion, and at 8 o'clock in the morning every Sunday, except on the first Sunday in the month, when the communion is at the 10-o'clock service.

---

* Mrs. Glover, (Julia Betterton,) the comedy actress, who died July 16, 1850, claimed descent from Thomas Betterton; and they met kindred deaths, both a few days after their second farewell benefits: Mrs. Glover through great excitement in weak health, and Betterton by a violent remedy for gout; both, nevertheless, performing to prevent disappointment to their audiences.

Music.—In 1784 took place the "Commemoration of Handel," in the Abbey nave ; and similar festivals in 1785-6-7, and 1790-91; and in 1834 was a Four Days' Festival, commencing June 24, when King William IV., Queen Adelaide, and the Princess Victoria were present.

> "It is full fifty years since I heard last,
> Handel, thy solemn and divinest strain
> Roll through the long nave of this pillar'd fane,
> Now seeming as if scarce a year had pass'd." *W. Lisle Bowles,* 1834.

Oct. 28, *St. Simon and St. Jude.* Anniversary of the birth of Thomas Tallis celebrated; his Cathedral Service performed at morning prayers. Tallis was organist to Henry VIII., Edward VI., Queen Mary and Elizabeth.

Coronations.—Harold and William the Conqueror were crowned in the new Abbey Church, as were also the succeeding sovereigns to our time. Upon most occasions, the sacred ceremony was followed by a banquet in the Great Hall of the Palace, built by William Rufus. The last of these festivities was that at the Coronation of King George IV., July 19, 1821. On the night previous, the king reposed on a couch in the tapestry-room of the Speaker's official residence in the Old Palace ; and next morning the royal procession advanced by a raised platform, covered by an awning, from Westminster Hall to the Abbey Church, where the king was crowned; and then returned to the Great Hall, when the banquet was served.* The Coronation of King William IV. and Queen Adelaide, Sept. 8, 1831, was simply the Abbey ceremonial; as was also the Coronation of Queen Victoria, June 28, 1838. Upon the latter occasion, temporary reception apartments were erected at the great western entrance to the Abbey Church; the nave was fitted with galleries and seats for spectators, as were also the choir and transepts ; the peers were seated in the north transept, and the peeresses south ; and the House of Commons in a gallery over the altar; and the orchestra of 400 performers in front of the organ. At the intersection of the choir and transepts was the theatre, or pulpitum, covered with rich carpets and cloth of gold, in the centre of which, upon a raised platform, stood the chair of homage. At the north-east corner of the theatre was the pulpit, whence "the Coronation Sermon" was preached. The crowning in St. Edward's Chair took place in the Sacrarium, before the altar, in front of St. Edward's Chapel; and behind the altar was "the Queen's Traverse," or retiring-room. (See "Coronation Chairs," described at p. 107.)

Sir Christopher Wren built, besides St. Paul's and the western towers of Westminster Abbey, Fifty Churches in the metropolis, at sums varying from less than 2,500*l.* to upwards of 15,000*l.* In "Gothic," or, as Wren proposed to term it, "Saracenic" architecture, Wren was certainly not a successful practitioner; although in the adaptation of a steeple (a form peculiar to pointed architecture) to Roman buildings, he has manifested much ingenuity, and produced some light and graceful

---

* The entire cost of this Coronation is stated to have exceeded a quarter of a million, or more than 268,000*l.* It has been commemorated in one of the most costly works of pictorial art ever produced—the *Illustrated History of the Coronation of George IV.*, by Sir George Nayler: containing forty-five splendidly coloured plates, atlas folio, price fifty guineas per copy. Sir George lost a considerable sum by the publication, although Government voted 5000*l.* towards the expenses. Sir George also undertook a much more costly memorial of this Coronation for George IV., but it was never completed. The portion executed contains seventy-three coloured drawings, finished like enamels, on velvet and white satin : the portraits are very accurate likenesses, and many of the coronets have rubies, emeralds, pearls, and brilliants set in gold; each portrait costing fifty guineas, first hand.

)rms of almost endless variety. This may be seen by reference to
Ir. Cockerell's picturesque grouping of the principal works of Wren :
he drawing of which was exhibited at the Royal Academy in 1838, and
as been engraved in line by Richardson.

In the reign of Queen Anne were built or commenced eleven churches.
n the next two reigns were completed three large churches, each dis-
nguished by a noble Corinthian portico: viz. St. George's, Blooms-
ury; St. Martin's-in-the-Fields; and St. George's, Hanover-square.
Vith the exception of St. Peter-le-Poor (1791) and St. Martin's Out-
ich (1796), not one church was built from the commencement of the reign
f George III. nearly to the Regency, an interval of more than half a
entury. The two Grecian orders, Doric and Ionic, were then adopted
i church-building; this pseudo-classic style was superseded by the Old
inglish of various periods. The increase of churches did not, however,
eep pace with the population; though the appeals to the public for
inds were, in some instances, answered with rare munificence. Thus,
i the subscription-list in 1836 for building new churches we find the
)llowing donation: "A clergyman seeking for treasure in heaven,
)00l."

In 1839, Lord John Russell stated in Parliament, that in London
*ere 34 parishes, with a population of 1,170,000, and church accommo-
ation for only 101,000; and in these 34 parishes were only 69 churches,
nd including proprietary chapels, only 100 places of worship in the
'hole; whereas, if we allot a church to every 3000, there ought to be
79, leaving a deficiency of 279. In the following year, 1840, the
iishop of London remarked to the House of Lords:—

"If you proceed a mile or two eastward of St. Paul's, you will find yourself in
ie midst of a population the most wretched and destitute of mankind, consisting
' artificers, labourers, beggars, and thieves, to the amount of 300,000 or 400,000
)uls! Throughout this entire quarter there is not more than one church for
),000 inhabitants; and in one, nay in two districts, there is but one church for
5,000 souls."

A few years since, the Rev. Dr. Cumming stated that in a radius of
ight miles around St. Paul's there was a population of two millions, of
7hom not more than 60,000 were communicants in any church or chapel
7hatever. Instead of five-eighths, or 1,300,000, of the population being
hurch-goers, the greatest extent of attendance at any place of worship
oes not exceed 400,000, and not more than 600,000 could be accom-
10dated. In a small district of Covent Garden there were 354 houses:
38 were of the most wretched description; these contained 1216 indi-
iduals, of whom only 134 attended church; and in that small locality
here were no fewer than 44 shops regularly open on the Sabbath. In
ome cases there was a population of 100,000 in the parish, with only
ne rector and one curate.

These startling statistics led to a "Metropolis Churches Fund," esta-
lished in 1836, by which means sixty-three churches have been built and
)rovided for. Meanwhile, a few of the City churches have been taken
lown: their number, in some cases, has been more than equal to the
vants of the citizens, more especially since their private residence out
f town. In 1834, Mr. Lambert Jones stated in the Court of Common
Jouncil, that the population of the City had within a century decreased
ne-half; that the number of inhabitants did not then exceed 53,000,
ind for them were 66 churches.

We now proceed to notice the more remarkable Churches of the
netropolis, and their *Curiosities.*

St. Alban's, Wood-street, Cheapside, is stated to have been named
rom its belonging to the monastery of St. Alban's. Stow thinks it to

to 941), who, as the tradition says, had his house at the east end of this church," and which gave name to Adel-street. Maitland supposes the church to have been one of the first places of worship built in London by Alfred, after he had driven out its destroyers, the Danes. It was rebuilt by Inigo Jones, but destroyed by the Great Fire of 1666, and rebuilt by Wren in 1685, "Gothic, as the same was before the Fire," with clustered columns, flat-pointed arches, and boldly groined roof. To the right of the reading-desk, within twisted columns, arches, &c., and in a frame richly ornamented with angels sounding trumpets, &c., is an hour-glass, such as was common in churches in the sixteenth and seventeenth centuries, "that when the preacher doth make a sermon, he may know the hour passeth away:" the hour-glass frame and the spiral column upon which it is mounted are of brass. The exterior of the church is ill designed, and has a pinnacled tower 92 feet high.

ALL SAINTS, New Cut, Lambeth, built in 1846, in the Anglo-Norman style, has a tower and spire 160 feet high, and upwards of 100 feet from the body of the church, with which it is connected by a passage.

· ALL SOULS, Langham-place, built by Nash in 1822-25, has been much ridiculed, but is suited to its angular plan ; the circular tower, surrounded with Ionic columns, has a Corinthian peristyle above, and a fluted stone cone or spire : it is well adapted to its situation, having the same appearance whichever way viewed. The church contains an altar-picture by R. Westall, R.A., of Christ crowned with thorns.

· ALLHALLOWS BARKING, at the east end of Tower-street, narrowly escaped the Great Fire of 1666, which burnt the dial and porch and vicarage-house. It contains a curiously-carved communion-table, font-cover, and screen, and some funeral brasses of early date. The headless bodies of the poet Surrey, Bishop Fisher (More's friend), and Archbishop Laud, who were executed on Tower Hill, were interred in Allhallows Church and churchyard, but have been removed.

· ALLHALLOWS THE GREAT, Upper Thames-street, has a richly-carved oak rood-screen the whole width of the church. It was manufactured at Hamburgh, and presented in the reign of Queen Anne to the church by the Hanse Merchants, who formerly resided in the parish.

· ALLHALLOWS, Lombard-street, destroyed by the Great Fire of 1666, and rebuilt by Wren, contains an exquisitely-sculptured white marble font ; and carved figures of Time and Death, in wood, besides a carved curtain, which seems to hide foliage behind it. The churchyard was closed in the cholera year, 1849, and laid out as a garden.

ALLHALLOWS STAINING, Mark-lane, escaped the Great Fire, and Stow thinks was called Stane church to distinguish it from others in the City of the same name built of timber. The tower and a portion of the west end alone are ancient. The Princess Elizabeth, on May 19, 1554, after her release from the Tower, performed her devotions in this church ; and afterwards is said to have dined off pork and peas at the King's Head in Fenchurch-street, where a metal dish and cover used on· the occasion are shewn ; and a commemorative dinner was held annually on Elizabeth's birthday, but discontinued twenty years since. The churchwardens' books contain payments for ringing the bells "for joye of ye execution of ye Queene of Scots ;" also for the return of King James II. from Feversham, and, two days after, on the arrival of the Prince of Orange.

ALLHALLOWS-IN-THE-WALL, Broad-street Ward, is named "of standing close to the wall of the City." (Stow.) It was built by Dance, jun., 1715-17, and contains an altar-picture, painted and presented by Sir N. Dance, of P. da Cortona's "Ananias restoring Paul to sight."

The parish books (commencing 1455) record the benefactions of an "ancker," or hermit, who lived near the church.

St. Alphage, London Wall, escaped the Great Fire of 1666, and was rebuilt in the last century: it has a porch with sculptured heads and pointed arches, a remnant of the ancient Elsing Priory. Its registers record, within a few years, about forty persons in this parish who certified that they had been *touched* by Charles II. for the evil.

St. Andrew's, Holborn, was rebuilt by Wren, upon the site of the old church, in 1686; the original tower, (date Henry VI.,) 110 feet high, being recased in 1704. It is one of the best-placed churches in London: "for as the west end is nearly at the summit of Holborn-hill, the foundation was necessarily continued throughout on this level to the east end in Shoe-lane; so that the basement is there considerably elevated above the houses." (*Godwin.*) The interior is rich in gilding and stained glass; the organ, built by Harris, is that rejected in the competition with Father Schmidt's organ for the Temple Church. St. Andrew's has been called "the Poets' Church," from the sons of Song connected with it: John Webster, the dramatic poet, a late contemporary of Shakspeare, is said to have been parish-clerk here, but this is not attested by the register; Richard Savage was christened here, Jan. 18, 1696-7; the register records, Aug. 28, 1770, "*William*" (Thomas) "Chatterton," with "the poet" added by a later hand, interred in the burial-ground of Shoe-lane Workhouse, now the site of Farringdon Market; and in the churchyard lies Henry Neele, the gravestone bearing a touching epitaph written by him to his father. Among the eminent rectors of the church were Hacket and Stillingfleet, afterwards bishops; and Sacheverel, the partisan preacher, who is buried in the chancel. In the south aisle is a tablet to John Emery, the comedian, d. 1822. Some of the registers date from 1558: the entries for five years, ending 1835, shew a daily average of one marriage, two burials, and three baptisms.

St. Andrew's Undershaft, Leadenhall-street, nearly opposite the East India House, a Tudor church, before whose south side was set up on every May-day morning a long shaft or May-pole, which was higher than the church-steeple. It was last raised in 1517, on "Evil May-day," "so called of an insurrection made by apprentices and other young persons against aliens:" it was then hung on iron hooks over the doors and under the "pentices" of Shaft-alley, until, 3d King Edward VI., when one St. Stephen, a curate, preaching at Paul's Cross, "said that this shaft was made an idol, by naming the church of St. Andrew with the addition of 'under-that-shaft.'" Stow heard this sermon, and describes how the parishioners in the afternoon lifted the shaft from the hooks whereon it had rested 32 years, sawed it in pieces, "every man taking for his share so much as had lain over his door and stall, the length of his house; and they of the alley divided among them so much as had lain over their alley-gate" (*Stow*): and thus was this idol "mangled and after burned." The present church, rebuilt 1520-1532, consists of a nave and two side aisles, with ribbed and flattened roof, painted and gilt with flowers and shields. The chancel has also paintings of the heavenly choir, landscapes, and buildings. St. Andrew's has much stained glass; and a large pointed window at the east end of the nave contains whole-length portraits of King Edward VI., Queen Elizabeth, James I., Charles I., and Charles II. The church was *pewed* soon after 1520. It contains many brasses, tablets, and monuments, the most characteristic of which is that of John Stow,* author of *A*

* John Stow was born in the parish of St. Michael, Cornhill, in the year 1525. There is abundant proof that he was by trade a tailor. In 1549, he was dwelling near the well within Aldgate, now known as Aldgate pump; where the Bailiff

Survey of London (1598). This monument is of terra-cotta, and was erected by Stow's widow; it contains the figure of the chronicler, once coloured after life: he is seated at a table, pen in hand, with a book before him, and a clasped book on each side of the alcove: above are the arms of Stow's Company, the Merchant Tailors'. In a desk in this church are preserved seven curious old books, mostly in black letter, with a portion of iron chain attached to them, by which they were formerly secured under open cages.

St. Andrew's, Wells-street, Marylebone, built by Daukes and Hamilton, in 1845-7, is fine Early Perpendicular, and has a tower and spire 155 feet high: the musical service is fully performed here.

St. Anne's, Limehouse, built by Hawksmoor, pupil of Wren, 1712-24, at a cost of 35,000*l.*, has a tower, with four angular turrets, and a more lofty one in the centre, original and picturesque. At 130 feet high is the clock, put up by Messrs. Moore in 1839: it is the highest in the metropolis, not excepting St. Paul's, and has four dials, each 13 feet in diameter; the hours being struck on the great bell (38 cwt.), inscribed:

> " At proper times my voice I'll raise,
> And sound to my subscribers' praise."

The whole of the interior of the church, including a fine organ, was destroyed by an accidental fire on the morning of Good Friday, March 29, 1850; but has been judiciously restored.

St. Ann's, Soho, was finished in 1686, and occupies a spot formerly called Kemp's Fields. The tower and spire were rebuilt about 1806 by the late S. P. Cockerell; the clock is a whimsical and ugly excrescence. The interior is very handsome, and has a finely-painted window at the east end. In this church is a tablet to the memory of Theodore Anthony Neuhoff, King of Corsica, who died in this parish in 1756, soon after his liberation from the King's Bench Prison by the Act of Insolvency. The friend who gave shelter to this unfortunate monarch, whom nobles could praise when praise could not reach his ear, and who refused to succour him in his miseries, was himself so poor as to be unable to defray the cost of his funeral. His remains were, therefore, about to be interred as a parish pauper, when one John Wright, an oilman in Compton-street, declared that *he for once would pay the funeral expenses of a king*, which he did. The tablet was erected at the expense of Horace Walpole, who inscribed upon it:

> " The grave, great teacher, to a level brings
> Heroes and beggars, galley-slaves and kings;
> But Theodore this moral learn'd ere dead;
> Fate pour'd its lesson on his living head,
> Bestow'd a kingdom, and denied him bread."

St. Anthony's (St. Antholin's or St. Antling's), in Bridge-row, at

---

of Rumford was, to use Stow's own words, "executed upon the pavement of my door, where I then kept house." Amidst the toils of business, Stow wrote his *Chronicles*, his *Annales*, and his *Survey*, a " simple and unadorned picture of London at the close of the 16th and commencement of the 17th century;" besides other works, printed and manuscript, which, to use his own words, " cost him many a weary mile's travel, many a hard-earned penny and pound, and many a cold winter night's study." He enjoyed the patronage of Archbishop Parker, the friendship of Lambarde, and the respect of Camden; yet he fell into poverty, and all he could obtain from his sovereign, James I., for the toil of near half a century, was a license to beg! Stow died a twelvemonth after, on the 6th of April, 1605, in the parish of St. Andrew Undershaft, and was buried on April 8: but, according to Maitland, in the year 1732, certain men removed Stow's " corpse, to make way for another." His collections for the *Chronicles of England*, occupying 60 quarto volumes, are now in the British Museum. Of the various editions of Stow's *Survey*, it may suffice to commend to the reader's notice the reprint from the edition of 1603, carefully edited by W. J. Thoms, F.S.A. 1842.

he corner of Size-lane, is of ancient foundation, being mentioned in the twelfth century. The church was rebuilt about 1399 and 1513; and being destroyed in the Great Fire of 1666, was rebuilt by Wren in 1682, when the parish of St. John Baptist, Watling-street, was annexed to that of St. Antholin. The interior has an oval dome, supported on eight columns; and the carpentry of the roof is a fine specimen of Wren's constructive skill. The exterior has a tower rising directly from the ground, with an octagonal spire, terminating with a Composite capital, at the height of 154 feet. In 1559, there was established, " after Geneva fashion," at St. Antholin's, an early prayer and lecture, the bells for which began to ring at five in the morning. This service is referred to by our early dramatists, and the preacher (a Puritan) and the bell of St. Antlin's were proverbially loud and lengthy. The chaplains of the Commissioners from the Church of Scotland to King Charles, in 1640, preached here; and "curiosity, faction, and humour," drew such crowds, that on Sundays, from daybreak to nightfall, the church was never empty. The Churchwardens' accounts present (in an unbroken series,) the parish expenditure for nearly three centuries.

St. Barnabas', Queen-street, Pimlico, is a portion of a College founded on St. Barnabas' Day, 1846, including schools and residentiary house for the clergy, upon ground presented by the first Marquis of Westminster. The buildings are in the Early Pointed style (Cundy, architect); and the church has a Caen-stone tower and spire 170 feet high, with a peal of ten bells, the gifts of as many parishioners. The windows throughout are filled with stained glass by Wailes of Newcastle, the subjects from the life of St. Barnabas. The open roof is splendidly painted; the rood dividing the choir from the chancel, and other fittings, are entirely of oak; the lectern is a brass eagle: the superb altar-plate, the font, illuminated office-books, the *corona lucis* in the chancel, and other costly ornaments, are the gifts of private individuals. The funds have been contributed by the inhabitants of the district of St. Paul, Knightsbridge, through the pious zeal of the Rev. W. G. Bennett, the incumbent. There is an organ by Flight, of great richness, variety, and power; and full choral service is performed. During the Anti-Papal agitation towards the close of 1850, this church was more than once the scene of disgraceful interruption by intolerant mobs, who, but for the intrepidity of the officiating clergy, would have set aside the right to undisturbed worship. The church was consecrated by the Bishop of London, on St. Barnabas' Day, (June 11,) 1850.

St. Bartholomew the Great, in West Smithfield, is part of the ancient Priory of St. Bartholomew the Great, founded about 1102, by Rahere, the King's Minstrel, who became first Prior. The Choir is Norman, and resembles the earlier portions of Winchester Cathedral, distinguished by semicircular arches and billet moulding; the clerestory above the triforium having pointed windows of later date. A large bay or oriel bears the rebus of a *bolt*, or arrow from the cross-bow, and a *tun*, of Bolton, who was Prior from 1506 to 1532. The roof is of timber, divided into compartments by a tie-beam and king-post, supported by brackets. Portions of the nave and transepts are also ancient; but the brick tower bears the date 1628. The nave is supposed to have originally extended to the house-fronts in Smithfield, where is a stone archway, with a dog's-tooth ornament; vestiges of the old foundations occur in the churchyard, within a few feet of the surface; and in the church other portions of the original building remain. Among the monuments is Rahere's, in elegant Perpendicular style, with the effigy of the Prior, an angel and monks, beneath a canopy. Besides the church, (which is comparatively little known,) a cloister and crypt of the Priory exist;* and the great Close, though now covered with modern buildings, bears the name—Bartholomew Close. .

ST. BARTHOLOMEW THE LESS is the parish church of the precinct of St. Bartholomew's Hospital, and escaped the Great Fire, but has been twice rebuilt, the tower alone being ancient. The memorials preserved from the old church include two floor brasses of Robert Balthrope, serjeant-surgeon to Queen Elizabeth, (d. 1591.)

ST. BARTHOLOMEW BY THE EXCHANGE, rebuilt by Wren after the Great Fire of 1666, mostly with the old masonry, was taken down in 1840: the tower was in eccentric taste, appearing as though the upper part had been blown down, and a door-way or window-frame been left on each side. Here was buried Miles Coverdale, our first translator of the Bible, whose remains were removed to St. Magnus' Church, London Bridge, on the taking down of St. Bartholomew's.

ST. BENET'S (Benedict), Gracechurch-street, was called Grass-church, because the herb-market was held nearly opposite the western door of the ancient church, destroyed in the Great Fire of 1666; but upon the same site was completed the present church, by Wren, in 1685. The height of the tower and spire, at the west angle, is 149 feet. In the parish books, at the accession of Queen Mary, 1553, appears:

"Paid to a plasterer, for washing oute and defacing of such Scriptures as in the tyme of King Edward VI. were written about the chirche and walls, 3s. 4d.;" and "Paid to the paynters for making ye Roode, with Mary and John, 6l." While in the first year of Queen Elizabeth, 1558, is "Payd to a carpenter for pulling downe the Roode and Mary, 4s. 2d.;" "Paid three labourers, one day, for pulling down the altars and John, 2s. 4d." In 1642 we find them selling the superstitious brasses taken off the gravestones for 9s. 6d.—*Malcolm's Londinium Redivivum*, i. p. 316.

ST. BENNET FINK, named from Robert Finke, the original founder, (as also of Finch-lane adjoining,) was destroyed in the Great Fire of 1666, rebuilt by Wren, but taken down in 1842-44. The remains were sold by auction, Jan. 15, 1846, when lot 12, the carved oak poor-box, with lock, &c. (date on the lock, 1683), fetched four guineas; and lot 17, the carved and panelled oak pulpit, with sounding-board, &c., fifteen guineas. The paintings of Moses and Aaron, the carved and panelled oak fittings of the altar, marble floor, and the two tablets with inscriptions in gold, were purchased for 50l.

ST. BOTOLPH'S is situate *without* the walls of London, near one of the ancient entrances to the City, supposed to have been built by a bishop, and thence called Bishopsgate. The old church narrowly escaped the Great Fire of 1666, and was rebuilt in 1725-29 by James Gold; its peculiarity is, that the tower rises at the east end, in Bishopsgate-street, and the lower part forms the chancel. The living is the richest in the City and Liberties of London. In the chancel is the monument to Sir Paul Pindar, whose residence in Bishopsgate-street Without is now the Sir Paul Pindar's Head public-house. He was a rich merchant (*temp.* James I. and Charles I.), and, like many other good subjects, was ruined by his attachment to the latter monarch. He was charitable and hospitable, and often gave "the parish venison"† for public dinners: yet the parishioners made him pay for a license for eating flesh.

ST. BOTOLPH, ALDGATE, at the corner of Houndsditch, opposite the Minories, was rebuilt by G. Dance, 1741-44. It contains monuments of good sculpture to Lord Dacre, beheaded 1537; and Sir Nicholas Carew, of Beddington, beheaded 1538; also an effigies monument to

* See "Vestiges of Old London," by J. W. Archer, part v. 1851.

† Sir Paul appears to have presented the parish yearly with a venison pasty; for in 1634 we find charged in the parish books 19s. 7d. for the mere "flour, butter, pepper, eggs, making, and baking." Another curious entry is in 1578: "Paid for frankincense and flowers when the Chancellor sate with us 11s."

Robert Dowe, who left the St. Sepulchre's Bell, &c. (see page 38). In the churchyard is a tomb inscribed with Persian characters, of which Stow gives the following account :

"August 10, 1626. In Petty France [a part of the cemetery unconsecrated], out of Christian burial, was buried Hodges Shaughsware, a Persian merchant, who with his son came over with the Persian ambassador, and was buried by his own son, who read certain prayers, and used other ceremonies, according to the custom of their own country, morning and evening, for a whole month after the burial ; for whom is set up, at the charge of his son, a tomb of stone with certain Persian characters thereon, the exposition thus : This grave is made for Hodges Shaughsware, the chiefest servant to the King of Persia for the space of twenty years, who came from the King of Persia, and died in his service. If any Persian cometh out of that country, let him read this and a prayer for him. The Lord receive his soul, for here lieth Maghmote Shaughsware, who was born in the town Novoy, in Persia."—(*Stow's Survey*, ed. 1633, p. 173.)

Bow Church, Cheapside. (See St. Mary-le-Bow.)

St. Bride's, or St. Bridget, Fleet-street, was built by Wren, upon the site of the old church, destroyed in the Great Fire of 1666. It was completed in 1703, cost 11,430*l.*, and is remarkable for its graceful steeple, which, as left by Wren, was 234 feet high. In June 1764 it was so damaged by lightning, that it was found requisite to take down eighty-five feet of the stone-work, and in restoring it, the height was lowered eight feet: the whole cost was 3,000*l.* In 1803 the steeple was again struck by lightning : "The metal vane, the cramps with which the masonry was secured, and the other ironwork employed in the construction, led the electric fluid down the steeple, in the absence of any continued or better conductor; and as at each point where the connexion was broken off, a violent disruption necessarily ensued, the stonework was rent in all parts, and projected from its situation. One stone, weighing nearly eighty pounds, was thrown over the east end of the church, and fell on the roof of a house in Bride-lane ; while another was forced from the bottom of the spire, through the roof of the church, into the north gallery." (*Godwin's Churches of London*, vol. ii.) The *Philosophical Transactions* for 1764 also contains two scientific investigations of the above damage. The upper part was, for a long time, preserved on the premises of a mason in Old-street Road. The entire spire is one of Wren's most beautiful designs, and consists of four stories, the two lower Tuscan, the third Ionic, and the fourth Composite, terminating in an obelisk, with a ball and vane. In height and lightness it approaches nearer to the exquisite spires of the pointed style than any other example; the details, however, (in Portland stone,) are hastening to decay. In the north face of the tower is a transparent clock-dial, first lit with gas in 1827, and one of the earliest of the kind in the metropolis. The interior is handsome ; the great eastern window, above the altar, is filled with a copy, in stained glass, of Rubens's "Descent from the Cross," in Antwerp Cathedral: this was executed by Mr. Muss in 1824-5, and is a fine production. The marble font bears the date 1615. Richardson, the author of *Clarissa Harlowe,* and who printed his own novels in Salisbury-square, is buried in the church ; and in the porch, beneath the tower, is a tablet to Alderman Waithman (interred here), who sat in five parliaments for the City of London. The registers of St. Bride's were saved at the destruction of the first church ; they commence from 1587 : and the vestry-books, which date from 1653, minutely chronicle the Great Fire, a relic of which is the doorway into Mr. Holden's vault, to the right of entering from Bride-passage. In the old church were buried Wynkin de Worde, whose printing-office was in Fleet-street ; Thomas Sackville, Earl of Dorset (d. 1608), the poet, who commenced "The Mirrour for Magistrates ;" Sir Richard Baker, the chronicler, who died in the Fleet Prison, 1644-5 ; Richard Lovelace, the poet, who died a broken cavalier, "very poor in body and purse," in Gunpowder-alley, Shoe-lane, in 1658. The register also records the burial of Ogilby, the translator of Homer (d. 1676); and Mary Carlton, or Frith, the "English Mall" of *Hudibras*, alias Moll Cutpurse, an infamous cheat and pickpocket, hanged at Tyburn 1672-3. The church and its elegant spire was hidden by houses until after a destructive fire in Bride-passage on Nov. 14, 1824, when an avenue was opened from Fleet-street: it was designed by J. B. Papworth, and the improvement cost 10,000*l.*, of which Mr. Blades, of Ludgate-hill, advanced 6,000*l.*

St. Catherine Cree, (or Christ Church,) on the north side of Leadendall-street, was rebuilt in the year 1629, and consecrated by Laud, Bishop of London, Jan. 16, 1630-31; when persons were stationed at the doors of the church to call with a loud voice on his approach, "Open, open, ye everlasting doors, that the King of Glory may enter in." When Laud had reached the interior, he fell on his knees, and lifting his hands, exclaimed, "This place is holy, the ground is holy; in the name of the Father, Son, and Holy Ghost, I pronounce it holy;" then throwing dust from the ground into the air, he bowed to the chancel, and went in procession round the church. These and other ceremonies, fully described in Rushworth, were made grave accusations against Laud, and brought about his death. The present church is debased Gothic and Corinthian. Among the monuments removed from the old church is a canopied figure of Sir Nicholas Throgmorton, (d. 1570,) from whom Throgmorton-street is named. Hans Holbein (d. 1554,) is also stated to have been buried in the first church. By the will of Sir John Gager, Lord Mayor in 1646, provision is made for a sermon to be annually preached on the 16th of October, in St. Catherine Cree's Church, in commemoration of his happy deliverance from a lion, which he met in a desert whilst travelling in the Turkish dominions, and which suffered him to pass unmolested.

Christ Church, Broadway, Westminster, was designed in 1842, in the Early Pointed style, by Poynter, upon the site of the former New Chapel. It has some good stained glass by Willement, especially in the centre window. The New Chapel was built about 1631; Archbishop Laud contributing to the funds 1000*l.* and some most curious glass. At the Rebellion, Sir Robert Harley defaced the windows, laid the painted glass in heaps upon the ground, and trod it to pieces, calling his sacrilegious antics "dancing a jig to Laud." The troopers of the Commonwealth stabled their chargers in the church aisles; and Cromwell and his officers are said to have used it as a council-room. In the adjacent ground was buried Sir William Waller, (d. 1688,) the famous Parliamentarian General in the Civil Wars. On June 26, 1739, Margaret Patten was interred here, at the age of 136 years: she was born at Lochborough, near Paisley, and was brought to England to prepare Scotch broth for King James II.; but after his abdication, she fell into poverty, and died in St. Margaret's Workhouse, where her portrait is preserved. "None would recognise the description given of this burial-ground—now so crowded upon by houses—towards the beginning of the last century, that it was 'the pleasantest churchyard all about London and Westminster.'" (*Walcott's Westminster*, p. 286.)

Christ Church, Highbury, built by T. Allom, in 1848, has a tower and spire in the angle between the north transept and nave, the spire having gabled and crocketted lucarnes. Internally, the plan is equally novel, in the centre becoming an octagon of eight arches, so as to allow the pulpit and reading-desk, placed againt the pillars of the chancel arch, to be distinctly seen from all parts of the church.

Christ Church, Newgate-street, was built by Wren, between

1687 and 1704, and occupied part of the site of the ancient Grey Friars' Church, destroyed by the Great Fire of 1666. The tower rises directly from the ground, and with the steeple is 153 feet high; the basement-story being open on three sides, and forming a porch to the church. A large gallery at the west end is appropriated for the Christ Church Boys; and here, since 1797, have been preached the "Spital Sermons." In 1799, the Spital Sermon on Easter Tuesday was preached by the celebrated Dr. Parr, who occupied nearly three hours in its delivery.

The SPITAL SERMONS originated in an old custom by which some learned person was appointed yearly by the Bishop of London to preach at St. Paul's Cross, on Good Friday, on the subject of "Christ's Passion:" on the Monday, Tuesday, and Wednesday following, three other divines were appointed to uphold the doctrines of "The Resurrection" at the Pulpit Cross in the "Spital" (Spitalfields). On the Sunday following, a fifth preached at Paul's Cross, and passed judgment upon the merits of those who had preceded him. At these Sermons, the Lord Mayor and Aldermen attended; ladies also on the Monday forming part of the procession; and at the close of each day's solemnity, his Lordship and the Sheriffs gave a private dinner to such of their friends among the Aldermen as attended the Sermon. From this practice, the civic festivities at Easter were at length extended to a magnificent scale. The children of Christ's Hospital took part in the above solemnities; so that, in 1594, when it became necessary to rebuild the Pulpit Cross at the Spital, a gallery was erected also for their accommodation. In the Great Rebellion, the pulpit was destroyed, and the Sermons were discontinued till the Restoration; after which, the *three* Spital Sermons, as they were still called, were revived at St. Bride's Church, in Fleet Street. They have since been reduced to two, and from 1797 have been delivered at Christ Church, Newgate-street. It was at their first appearance at the Spital that the children of Christ's Hospital wore the blue costume by which they have since been distinguished. Instead of the subjects which were wont to be discussed from the Pulpit Cross of St. Mary Spital, discourses are now delivered commemorative of the objects of the five sister Hospitals; and a Report is read of the number of children maintained and educated, and of sick, disorderly, and lunatic persons for whom provision is made in each respectively. On each day, the boys of Christ's Hospital, with the legend "He is risen" attached to their left shoulders, form part of the civic procession; walking on the first day in the order of their schools, the King's Boys bearing their nautical instruments; and on the second, according to their several wards, headed by their nurses.—(Abridged from the Rev. Mr. Trollope's *History of Christ's Hospital.* See also page 82 of the present volume.)

CHRIST CHURCH, Spitalfields, (originally a hamlet of St. Dunstan's, Stepney,) was built by Hawksmoor, a pupil of Wren, and consecrated July 5, 1729. It is entirely of stone, very massive, and has one of the loftiest spires in London, 225 feet high, or 23 feet higher than the Monument. It contains a peal of twelve bells, scarcely inferior in power and sweetness to any in the kingdom, the tenor weighing 4,928 lbs. It has a large organ, the master-piece of Bridge, containing 2,126 pipes. Here is a monument to Sir Robert Ladbroke, a whole-length figure, in the full dress of Lord Mayor: one of the early works of Flaxman. This church was greatly injured by fire on Feb. 17, 1836, shortly after the parishioners had finished paying 8000*l.* for repairs. On the morning of Jan. 3, 1841, the spire and roof of this church were greatly damaged by lightning, at ten minutes before seven, when the clock stopped. The lightning struck the cone, or upper part of the spire; thence it descended to a room above the clock-room, forcing the trap-door from the hinges down to the floor, melting the iron wires connected with the clock, scorching the wooden rope-conductors, breaking many of the windows, and making a considerable fracture in the wall, where the lightning is supposed to have escaped. The roof was partially covered with large stones, which broke in the lead-work by their weight in falling; and the lead near the injured masonry was melted in several places.

ST. CLEMENT'S DANES, Strand, the first church west of Temple Bar, is said by Stow to have been so called "because Harold, a Danish king, and other Danes, were buried there." Strype gives another reason : that the few Danes left in the kingdom married English wo-men, and compulsorily lived between Westminster and Ludgate; and there built a synagogue, called " Ecclesia Clementis Danorum." This account Fleetwood, the antiquary, Recorder of London in the reign of Elizabeth, reported to the Lord Treasurer Burleigh, who lived in this parish. The body of the old church was taken down in 1680, and rebuilt to the old tower in 1682, by Edward Pierce, under the gratuitous direc-tions of Wren, as recorded on a marble slab in the north aisle. In 1719, Gibbs added the present tower and steeple, about 116 feet high, with a peal of ten bells. The clock strikes the hours twice; "the hour being first struck on a larger bell, and then repeated on a smaller one, so that has the first been miscounted, the second may be more correctly observed." (A. Thomson's *Time and Timekeepers*, p. 77.) In addition to the clock is a set of chimes, which play the old 104th Psalm, though somewhat crazily. In the church are buried Otway and Nat. Lee, the dramatic poets; and Rymer, compiler of the *Fœdera*, &c.

ST. DIONIS', BACKCHURCH (behind the line of Fenchurch-street), is the third church upon this site, and was rebuilt by Wren after the Great Fire of 1666: it has a tower 90 feet high. In the vestry-room are preserved four of the large syringes at one time the only engines used in London for the extinction of fires; they are about 2 feet 3 inches long, and were attached by straps to the body of the fireman.

ST. DUNSTAN'S IN THE EAST, between Tower-street and Upper Thames-street, was nearly destroyed in the Great Fire of 1666, and was restored by Wren in 1698: it has a stone tower and spire, sup-ported on four arched ribs, springing from the angles of the tower: this is Wren's best work in the Pointed style; but it closely resembles the spire of St. Nicholas's Church, at Newcastle-upon-Tyne, built in the fifteenth century. John Carter, however, says: " St. Nicholas's tower is so lofty, and of such a girth, that, to compare great things with small, our London piece of vanity is but a mole-hill to the Newcastle ' mountain,' the pride and glory of the northern hemisphere." There is a tradition, that the plan of St. Dunstan's tower and spire was fur-nished by the architect's daughter, Jane Wren, who died in 1702, aged 26, and was buried under the choir of St. Paul's Cathedral. Lady Dio-nysia Williamson, in 1670, gave 4000*l*. towards the rebuilding of St. Dunstan's. After the dreadful storm in London through the night of the 26th November, 1703, Wren hearing next morning that some of the steeples and pinnacles had been damaged, quickly replied, " Not St. Dunstan's, I'm quite sure." The old church had a lofty leaden steeple. The body of the present church was rebuilt of Portland stone, in the Perpendicular style, by Laing and Tite, in 1817. The interior is divided into three aisles by clustered columns and pointed arches. The east window represents symbolically the Law and the Gospel; the north, Christ Blessing Little Children; and the south, the Adora-tion of the Magi. In the vestry is a wood carving, by Gibbons, of the arms of Archbishop Tenison. In the south churchyard is a Rookery. —(See BIRDS, p. 47.)

ST. DUNSTAN'S IN THE WEST, Fleet-street, was designed by John Shaw, F.R.S. and F.S.A.; in 1831-33, set back 30 feet from the site of the former church, which projected considerably beyond the street-line. It just escaped the Great Fire of 1666, which stopped within three houses of it; as did also another fire in 1730. A view in 1739 shews the oldest portion to be the tower and bell-turret, the latter containing a small bell which was rung every morning at a quarter before seven o'clock. The body of the church is Italianised Gothic, with battle-ments and circular-headed windows: shops with overhanging signs are built against the south and east walls, though previously the church-yard was thus built in, and was a permanent station for booksellers, as appears by many imprints. Thus, " Epigrams by H. P.," &c.—" and are to be soulde by John Helme, at his shoppe in St. Dunstan's Church-yarde, 1608, qto." John Smethwick had " his shop in St. Dunstan's Church-yard, in Fleet-street, under the Diall;" and here, in 1653, Richard Marriott published the first edition of Walton's *Angler*, for 18*d*. The church clock was one of London's wonders : it had a large gilt dial, overhanging Fleet-street, and above it two figures of savages, of life-size, carved in wood, and standing within an alcove, each having in his right hand a club, with which they struck the quarters upon two suspended bells, moving their heads at the same time. This clock and figures were the work of Mr. Thomas Harrys, in 1671, then living at the lower end of Water-lane, who received for his work 35*l*. with the old clock, and the sum of 4*l*. per annum to keep the whole in repair.* Originally, the clock was within a square ornamented case, with a semi-circular pediment, and the tube from the church to the dial was sup-ported by a carved figure of Time, with expanded wings, as a bracket; when altered, in 1738, it cost the parish 110*l*. Strype calls the figures " two savages, or Hercules;" Ned Ward, " the two wooden horolo-gists;" and Cowper, in his *Table Talk*, likens a lame poet to—

> " When labour and when dulness, club in hand,
> Like the two figures at St. Dunstan's, stand."

In 1766, the elegant statue of Queen Elizabeth, which stood on the west side of Ludgate, was put up at the east end of St. Dunstan's Church; and the other figures, King Lud and his two sons, were deposited in the parish bone-house. The old church was taken down in December 1829, when the materials were sold by auction : the bell-turret for 10*s*.; the flag and flag-staff for 12*s*.; and an iron standard, with copper vane, warranted 850 years old (?), weighing three-quarters of a cwt. was sold for 2*l*. 1*s*. At another sale, in 1830, the statue of Queen Elizabeth was knocked down for 16*l*. 10*s*., and a stained-glass window for 4*l*. 5*s*. The clock, figures, &c. were purchased by the late Marquis of Hertford, and placed in the grounds of his villa in the Regent's Park, where they strike the hours and quarters to this day. The new church of St. Dun-stan was consecrated July 31, 1833, which the architect did not live to witness, he having died July 30, 1832, the twelfth day after the exter-nal completion of the edifice.† It is in the latest Pointed style, and has a lofty tower, surmounted by an elegant lantern, 130 feet high, (of Ketton stone,) different from any other in the metropolis, but resem-bling St. Botolph's, Boston, Lincolnshire; St. Helen's, York; and St. George's, at Ramsgate, built in 1825. Over the entrance-porch are sculptured the heads of Tyndale, the Reformer ; and Dr. Donne, who was once vicar of the church : they are considered faithful portraits. Above is a clock, with three dials, curiously coloured and gilt in the em-bellished taste of the architectural period ; and a belfry, with eight fine bells from the old church, the sound of which receives effect from the four large upper windows, which are the main features of the tower. The enriched stone lantern is perforated with Gothic windows of two heights; the whole being terminated by an ornamental, pierced, and very rich crown parapet. The body of the church is of octagon form, and has eight

---

* So early as 1478 there was a similar piece of mechanism in Fleet-street. Stow describes a conduit erected in the above year, near Shoe-lane, with angels having " sweet-sounding bells before them; whereupon, by an engine placed in the tower, they, divers hours of the day and night, with hammers chimed such an hymn as was appointed." There is, we believe, a like contrivance to that at St. Dunstan's, in Norwich Cathedral. (See also *Paul's Jacks*, p. 86.)
† The interior was finished by his son, John Shaw.

recesses, with as many windows above, containing good stained glass. The roof is formed by eight iron spandrel-beams, projecting from an angle towards the centre, and there connected by an iron ring; and from the enriched key-stone hangs the chandelier. The *northern* recess contains the altar-table, of oak elaborately carved; and the altar-piece presents three admirably carved canopies, of foreign workmanship. Above is a large pointed window, filled with stained glass, by Williment, in the ancient manner: it contains figures of the Evangelists; the crown of thorns and the nails; the spear and sponge upon a reed; the Holy Lamb; and the inscription, in black letter, "Deo et ecclesiæ fratres Hoare dicaverunt, anno Domini MDCCCXXXII." This is, altogether, one of the most elegant church interiors in the metropolis. In May 1839, the statue of Queen Elizabeth, already mentioned, was placed in a niche, flanked with two pilasters, above the doorway of the parochial schools, east of the principal entrance to the church. On the west side is the Law Life Insurance Office, designed by John Shaw, in the style that prevailed between the last period of Pointed architecture, (of which St. Dunstan's Church is an example,) and the complete revival of the architecture of Greece and Rome. In the old church was a large hour-glass, in silver frame; of the latter, in 1723, two heads were made for the parish staves. The Rev. William Romaine was rector of the old church* in 1749, when it was generally so crowded that the pew-opener's place was worth 50*l.* per annum.

St. Dunstan's, Stepney, a Perpendicular church, is famed in story for its legend of "The Fish and Ring," and the popular ballad of "The Cruel Knight, or Fortunate Farmer's Daughter:" her identity is referred to Lady Berry, whose tomb is on the outer east wall, with the fish and amulet in the arms thereon: but the finding of a ring in a fish is an incident of much greater antiquity than Lady Berry's time (1696), and occurs in the *Arabian Nights' Entertainments*. The churchyard is noticed in the *Spectator*, by Steele, for the number and oddity of its epitaphs: here lies the father of Dr. Mead, who was born over the antique brick gateway opposite the rectory, and first began practice here; also Rev. W. Vickers, author of the *Companion to the Altar ;* and Roger Crab, who lived long on bran, dock-leaves, grass, and water. Within the church is the splendid tomb of Sir H. Colet, Lord Mayor in 1486 and 1495, and father of the founder of St. Paul's School. Here also is a marble monument of the Good Samaritan, by Sir R. Westmacott, R.A., to B. Kenton, Esq. (d. 1800), leaving 63,500*l.* to charity schools, and 30,000*l.* to his friends. In the western porch is a stone reputed to have been brought from the wall of Carthage. In 1625 and 1665, died at Stepney of the Plague 9,561 persons.

St. Edmund's (the King and Martyr), Lombard-street, has also been called St. Edmund's Grass Church, because of a grass-market held here: whence Grasschurch-street, now Gracechurch-street. The church was destroyed in the Great Fire, and rebuilt by Wren: it has a tower and incongruous steeple, 90 feet high, and a projecting bracket clock. The altar-piece has some fine carvings, and two paintings of Moses and Aaron, executed by William Etty, in 1833: above is a stained glass window, with the arms of Queen Anne, "set up in the memorable year of union, 1707;" besides two other stained glass windows, of superior excellence, representing St. Paul and St. Peter.

St. George's, Hanover-square, was completed by John James in 1724; the parish being taken out of St. Martin's-in-the-Fields. St. George's is built upon ground given by Lieut.-Gen. W. Stewart: it has a stately and august Corinthian portico, and a handsome and well-proportioned steeple; still, it can only be viewed in profile; but "were it not for two or three intervening houses, it would be seen in the noblest point of sight in the world." The interior has a large altar-picture of the Last Supper, attributed to Sir James Thornhill; above it is a painted window, foreign, of the 16th century, with the Virgin and Child, the Crucifixion, ecclesiastical personages, masonic emblems, &c.; the altar-piece in its sculptured framework, and the painted glass in its architectural recess, is effective; but this Gothic window in a Roman church is a glaring absurdity.

"The view down George-street, from the upper side of Hanover-square, is one of the most entertaining in the whole city: the sides of the square, the area in the middle, the breaks of building that form the entrance of the vista, but above all, the beautiful projection of the portico of St. George's Church, are all circumstances that unite in beauty, and make the scene perfect."—*Ralph*.

St. George's, Hanover-square, also possesses a burial-ground at a short distance on the Bayswater-road. Here is the grave of Sterne, with a stone set up by two "Brother Masons:" where too lies Sir Thomas Picton, who fell at the Battle of Waterloo in 1815. (See BAYSWATER, p. 35.)

St. GEORGE'S, Hart-street, Bloomsbury, was designed by Nicholas Hawksmoor, a pupil of Wren, and was consecrated in 1731; a district for its parish being taken out of that of St. Giles's-in-the-Fields. This church is remarkable for standing north and south; the tower and steeple are placed by the side of the main edifice, the favourite practice of Palladio. Upon the tower, on the four sides, rises a range of unattached Corinthian pillars and pediments; above is a series of steps, with lions and unicorns at the corners, guarding the royal arms, and which supports at the apex, on a short column, a statue, in Roman costume, of George I. The design is from Pliny's description of the first mausoleum, the tomb of King Mausolus, in Caria. Walpole calls this steeple a master-stroke of absurdity, and it has provoked this epigram:

"When Harry the Eighth left the Pope in the lurch,
    The people of England made him head of the Church;
    But George's good subjects, the Bloomsbury people,
    Instead of the church, make him head of the steeple."

More admired is the magnificent portico of eight Corinthian columns, which Hawksmoor added to his design, influenced by Gibbs's portico at St. Martin's-in-the-Fields, then just completed; but St. George's is the better, from its height above the level of the street. The church, altogether, is by some considered one of the most picturesque in the metropolis. Here is a tablet to the great Lord Mansfield; and a monument to Mr. Charles Grant, by Bacon, R.A.

St. GEORGE THE MARTYR, Queen-square, Bloomsbury, built in 1706, as a chapel of ease to St. Andrew's, Holborn, was declared a parish church in 1723; of which Dr. Stukeley, the Roman-British antiquary, was many years the rector: in his MS. Diary, 1749, in the possession of Mr. Britton, F.S.A., is described the then rural character of Queen-square and its vicinity. The parish burial-ground is in the rear of the Foundling Hospital: a strong prejudice formerly existed against new churchyards, and no person was interred here till the ground was broken for Robert Nelson, author of *Fasts and Festivals*, whose character for piety reconciled others to the spot: people like to be buried in company, and in good company. Nancy Dawson, the dancer, of Covent Garden and Drury-lane Theatres, (noted for hornpipes,) lies here.

St. GEORGE THE MARTYR, Southwark, was built in 1733-36, by John Price, upon the site of the old church; the parish having been orginally given by William the Conqueror to the noble family of Arderne, and for some time attached to the Priory of Bermondsey. Stow describes the former church as almost directly over against Suffolk-House, formerly the mansion of Charles Brandon, Duke of Suffolk, the brother-in-law of Henry VIII., now the site of the premises of Mr. Pigeon, the distiller. There were buried in the old church, Bonner, Bishop of London, who died in the Marshalsea ; and Rushworth, author of the *Collections*, who died in the King's Bench : both these prisons being in the parish. Edward Cocker, engraver and teacher of writing and arithmetic, is also stated upon a sexton's evidence to have been interred here : his "Arithmetic," a posthumous work, was first published "by John Hawkins, writing-master, near St. George's Church." The present church has a lofty stone spire and tower, with a fine peal of eight bells ; the large bell is tolled nightly, and thought to be a relic of the curfew. Hogarth, in his plate of Southwark Fair, represents Figg, the famous prizefighter, and a worthy named Cadman, flying by a rope from the tower of St. George's Church ; the fair being held in that part of the Mint which lies in the rear of the houses opposite. (A very interesting paper on the Statistics of St. George's parish was read to the Statistical Society of London, in 1840, by the Rev. Mr. Weight.)

St. GEORGE'S IN THE EAST, Ratcliffe Highway, built by Hawksmoor, 1715-29, in an original and massive style, has a very picturesque spire. In the churchyard is buried Joseph Ames, (d. 1759,) author of *Typographical Antiquities*, originally a plane-maker, and afterwards a ship-chandler at Wapping ; he lies in a stone coffin, in *virgin earth*, at the depth of eight feet.

In this parish are the Schools and Asylum founded by Mr. Raine, a wealthy brewer, in 1717 and 1736 ; who also provided that on May 1 and Dec. 26, annually, a marriage-portion of 100*l*. should be presented to two young women, former inmates of the School, and who have attained the age of twenty-two years. The bridegrooms must be inhabitants of St. George's-in-the-East, or of Wapping or Shadwell ; and the young women drawing lots for the portion, one hundred new sovereigns, usually put into a handsome bag, made by a young lady of St. George's parish, and presented at a dinner of the trustees. In the morning a discourse is preached in the Church, "On Diligence and Industry in our Calling;" after which the drawing takes place at the Asylum.

St. GILES'S, Camberwell, is one of the largest churches built in England since the Reformation : it occupies the site of the old brick church, burnt on Sunday, Feb. 7, 1841. The new church, designed by Scott and Moffatt, is massively built entirely of stone, and was consecrated Nov. 21, 1844 : it is in the transition style, from Early English to Decorated ; cruciform in plan, with a large central tower and spire, 207 feet high, and the tower thirty feet square ; it has a fine peal of bells, by Mears. The outside length of the church exceeds 153 feet. The interior has an open timber roof, and oak fittings ; a very powerful organ, by Bishop ; and several stained-glass windows by Ward and Nixon, the largest, over the altar, enriched with the symbolism of the thirteenth century. The edifice, within and without, has an antique and pleasing character, the sculpture and other accessories being correct in period.

St. GILES'S, Cripplegate, is the successor of a church founded in 1090, near the postern in the City wall, called Cripple-gate from an adjoining hospital for lame people (*Camden*), or from the numerous cripples begging there (*Stow*). In 1545, the church was burnt, but was soon repaired, and perhaps partially rebuilt ; and in 1682, the tower was raised fifteen feet : it has a peal of twelve bells, besides one in the turret, and a very musical set of chimes (see p. 39). In the church are buried John Fox, the martyrologist, described in the Register as "householder, preacher ;" John Speed, the historian, with his bust, once painted and gilt ; John Milton and his father, under the clerk's desk : a bust of the poet, by Bacon, R.A., with a tablet, were set up on the north parish register is : " 12 November, 1674, John Milton, gentleman, consumpcon, chancell."* The remains were scandalously disturbed in Aug. 1790, " and little boys have played with the bones of great kings."† In the chancel, too, are tablets to Constance Whitney and Margaret Lucy, both descendants of Sir Thomas Lucy, of Charlecote, Warwickshire: the former represents a female rising from a coffin, and has been erroneously supposed to commemorate a lady who, having been buried while in a trance, was restored to life through the cupidity of the sexton in digging up the body to get possession of a ring left upon her finger. Several of the actors from the Fortune Theatre, Whitecross-street, are buried here. Here, too, rests Sir Martin Frobisher, one of the earliest of the Arctic voyagers (d. 1594-5); and Henry Welby, the Grub-street hermit, yet a man of exemplary charity (d. 1636). And the register records the marriage of Oliver Cromwell with Elizabeth Bowchier, August 20, 1620.

ST. GILES'S-IN-THE-FIELDS, on the south side of High-street, was formerly *in the fields*, and the parish the village of St. Giles; the church being traceable to the chapel of a Hospital for Lepers, founded about 1117, by Queen Matilda, consort of Henry I. The ancient church was taken down in 1623, and a brick edifice erected in its place : this was removed in 1730, and the present church, designed by Henry Flitcroft, was completed in 1734. It is built of Portland stone, and has a tower and spire, 160 feet high, with eight bells. Above the entrance gateway from the street is a bas-relief of the Day of Judgment, from the Lich or " Resurrection Gate " of the former church. Here were buried Chapman, the translator of Homer; Lord Herbert of Cherbury, who lived in Great Queen-street; Shirley, the dramatist, and his wife; Sir Roger L'Estrange, the political writer; and Andrew Marvell, " a man in whose reputation the glory of the patriot has eclipsed the fine powers of the poet." The monument to Chapman, built by Inigo Jones at his own expense, is now in the churchyard, against the south wall of the church. In the churchyard, too, is the altar-tomb of Richard Pendrell, who aided in the escape of Charles II.; and a few years since was revived the custom of decorating this tomb on Restoration Day (May 29) with branches of oak. The finest monument in the present church is the recumbent effigies of the Duchess Dudley (d. 1670), preserved in grateful memory of her munificence to the parish. At the place of public execution, a short distance north-west of the church, Sir John Oldcastle, Lord Cobham, was hung in chains and roasted over faggots in 1417, during the reign of Henry V., his early friend. The phrase " St. Giles's Bowl" is referred to the custom of giving, at the Hospital gate, every malefactor on his way to Tyburn a bowl of ale, as his last worldly draught, which practice was afterwards continued at an hostel built upon the site of the monastic house; of this the Bowl Brewery, taken down in 1849, was the representative; and the bowl itself is said to be in existence. The transparent clock-dial of the church was lit with gas in 1827, the first in the metropolis; and opposite, in 1842, was made one of the earliest experiments with wood-paving. In Endell-street, in 1845, was built a district church, in the Early Pointed style, by Ferrey,—a timely provision for the spiritual destitution of the parish. St. Giles's possesses also a cemetery in the Lower St. Pancras-road; where

* Under St. Bride's (p. 121) has been omitted mention of St. Bride's church-yard as one of Milton's abodes in London: here, after his return from Italy, he lodged with one Russel, a tailor, and devoted himself to the education of his nephews, John and Edward Philips, and to the politics of the day. Thence, however, he soon removed to " a pretty garden-house" in Aldersgate-street.
† See the Diary of General Murray, in *Monthly Magazine* for August 1833.

are buried, beneath an altar-tomb, John Flaxman, R.A., the sculptor, and Sir John Soane, R.A. the architect. (See CEMETERIES, p. 69.)

ST. HELEN'S, Bishopsgate, on the east side of Bishopsgate-street Within, was once the church of the priory of St. Helen, the site of which, judging from pavements found here, was originally occupied by a Roman building. During the continuance of the priory, the church was divided by a partition, and served both the nuns and the parishioners; but after the Dissolution, this was removed: against the north wall is a range of the nuns' seats. The interior of the edifice, with its columns and pointed arches, is picturesque; it contains more monuments, perhaps, than any other church in the metropolis; and these being altar-tombs upon the floor, increase the appearance of antiquity and solemnity. They include a freestone altar-tomb, with quatrefoil panels enclosing shields; upon the ledger lie full-length alabaster effigies of Sir John Crosbie and his first wife Anneys or Agnes (see CROSBY HALL); the knight wears his aldermanic gown over plate armour. A canopied monument to Sir W. Pickering, in dress armour, reclining upon a pillow of matting (d. 1542); several kneeling figures, elaborately painted and gilt, in memory of Sir Andrew Judd (in armour) (d. 1558); a very large sculptured altar-tomb to Sir Thomas Gresham, who founded the Royal Exchange; a monument representing Martin Bond, captain of the trained bands at Tilbury when the Spanish Armada was expected—he is sitting within a tent, with sentries, &c. (d. 1643); tomb of Francis Bancroft (d. 1726), built in his lifetime, when he directed that his body should be embalmed, and placed in a coffin unfastened (see ALMSHOUSES, p. 6); and a table monument by N. Stone to Sir Julius Cæsar, Master of the Rolls to James I. (d. 1636), the monument erected in the previous year, with the Latin inscription sculptured, as if on a folded deed, an engagement of the deceased to pay the debt of nature whenever it shall please God to appoint it. In the vestibule also are several elaborate monuments, displaying figures; and an alms-box supported by a curiously-carved figure of a mendicant. The church also contains fine monumental brasses of the fifteenth and sixteenth centuries.

HOLY TRINITY, Besborough Gardens, close to Vauxhall Bridge, a district church of St. Margaret's and St. John's, Westminster, was erected at the sole expense of Archdeacon Bentinck, Prebendary of Westminster; the foundation-stone was laid by Mrs. Bentinck, Nov. 8, 1849, on which day also was founded another church, in Great Peter-street, in the same parish. Holy Trinity Church is designed in the Early Decorated style, (temp. Edward I. and II.): at the intersection of the four arms rises an enriched tower and spire, 193 feet high: the east end window of seven lights is large and fine. The church has been decorated and furnished by subscription.

HOLY TRINITY, Bishop's-road, Paddington, a Perpendicular church, built by Cundy in 1844-6; it has a richly crocketed spire and pinnacled tower, 219 feet high, and a magnificent stained chancel-window: the crypt is on a level with the roofs of the houses in Belgrave-square.

HOLY TRINITY, Brompton, a church in the Early English style, by Donaldson; with a lofty tower, and stained glass of ancient design and colour; consecrated 1829. It occupies, with the burial-ground, the site of a nursery-garden; here flowers and funereal shrubs decorate the graves. John Reeve, the comic actor (d. 1838), is buried here.

HOLY TRINITY, Hartland-road, Haverstock-hill, is a district church of St. Pancras, and was consecrated Oct. 15, 1850. It is built in the Middle Pointed style (Wyatt and Brandon, architects), and consists of a nave, with north and south aisles, chancel, and tower and spire 160 eet high: the chancel is novel, the arches producing an elegant play of lines. The church will seat 1500 persons, and cost about 10,000*l.*

St. James's, Clerkenwell, on the north side of Clerkenwell Green, ias replaced the church of a Benedictine monastery, founded about 1100; t served the nuns and inhabitants until the Dissolution of the convents, vhen it was made parochial, and dedicated to St. James the Less intead of the Virgin Mary. In the Sutherland View of 1543, we see it far n the fields. In 1623, the steeple was rebuilt upon the old tower, when ioth fell, and destroyed part of the church. In 1788, the whole was aken down, rebuilt by Carr, and consecrated in 1792. In the vaults re preserved some coffins from the old church, and among them that of Bishop Burnet, who died 1714-15 in St. John's-court, close by, though he fanatic rabble threw stones and dirt at his funeral. His handsome nural monument was also removed to the present church.

St. James's, Garlick Hithe, on the east side of Garlick-hill, Upper Thames-street, is named from its being near the chief garlick market if the City. It was rebuilt in 1326: among the persons interred iere was Richard Lyons, a wine-merchant and lapidary, beheaded in Cheapside by Wat Tyler in the reign of Richard II. Stow describes iis "picture on his gravestone very fair and large, with his hair rounded by his ears, and curled; a little beard forked; a gown girt to him down o his feet, of branched damask, wrought with the likeness of flowers: t large purse on his right side hanging in a belt from his left shoulder; t plain hood about his neck, covering his shoulders, and hanging back iehind him." The following citizens who had served Mayor were also ouried here: John of Oxenford, Mayor in 1341; Sir John Wrotch, or Wroth, 1360; William Venor, 1389; William More, 1395; Robert Chihell, 1421; James Spencer, 1527. The old church was destroyed in he Great Fire: it was rebuilt by Wren, 1676-83, with a tower and antern, 98 feet high, and a projecting clock-dial, with a carved and gilt igure of St. James: a large organ, built by Bernard Schmidt, in 1697; ind a clever altar-picture of the Ascension, by A. Geddes. In this church Steele heard the Common-Prayer service read so distinctly, so emphatially, and so fervently, that it was next to an impossibility to be inatentive. Steele proposed that this excellent reader (Mr. Philip Stubbs, ifterwards Archdeacon of St. Alban's), upon the next and every annual issembly of the clergy of Sion College, and all other convocations, should read before them.—*Spectator*, No. 147, *Saturday, August* 18, 1711.

St. James's, Piccadilly, or St. James's, Westminster, built by Wren, at the cost of Henry Jermyn, Earl of St. Alban's, whose arms are placed above the south door; and consecrated Sunday, July 13, 1684. It has a tower and spire, 150 feet high; the latter was coated with cement in 1850, when the exterior of the church was repaired throughout. The clock was the gift of Mr. H. Massey, and the original dial was gilded and painted by Mr. Highmore, H. M. Serjeant-Painter: its diameter is 10 feet. The interior, Wren's masterpiece, is separated into a nave and aisles by two ranges of Corinthian columns; and the roof is divided into sunken and enriched panels. The great east window was filled with stained glass, by Wailes of Newcastle, in 1846: the subjects are the Burial, the Resurrection, and the Ascension, the Agony, the Passion, and the Bearing of the Cross. The noble organ was built for James II., and intended for his Roman Catholic Oratory at Whitehall, but given to this parish by Queen Mary in 1691. In 1738, the Prince of Wales gave crimson velvet and gold hangings, valued at 700*l.*, for the holy table and pulpit. Facing the western entrance is the white marble font, exquisitely sculptured by Gibbons: it is nearly 5 feet high, and the bowl is about six feet in circumference.

The shaft represents the tree of life, with the serpent twining round it, and offering the forbidden fruit to Eve, who, with Adam, stands beneath : these figures are 18 inches high. On the bowl are bas-reliefs of the Baptism of the Saviour in the Jordan: the Baptising of the Treasurer of Candace by St. Philip the Deacon; and the Ark of Noah, with the dove bearing the olive-branch. The cover of this font (shewn in Vertue's engraving), held by a flying angel and a group of cherubim, was stolen about the beginning of the present century, and subsequently hung up as a sign at a spirit-shop in the neighbourhood.—(Brayley's *Londiniana*, vol. ii. p. 282.) Evelyn, in his *Diary*, thus describes the east end of the church:

" *Dec.* 16, 1684.—I went to see the new church at St. James's, elegantly built. The altar was especially adorned, the white marble inclosure curiously and richly carved, the flowers and garlands about the walls by Mr. Gibbons, in wood: a pelican, with her young at her breast, just over the altar in the carv'd compartment and border invironing the purple velvet fringed, with (black) I. H. S. richly embroidered, and most noble plate, were given by Sir R. Geere, to the value (as was said) of 200*l*. There was no altar anywhere in England, nor has there been any abroad, more handsomely adorned."

The wood is lime, with cedar for the reredos; the marble scrolls have been replaced by bronze. In the church are interred Charles Cotton (d. 1686-7), the companion of Walton in the *Complete Angler ;* Dr. Sydenham (d. 1689), with a marble tablet erected by the College of Physicians, in 1810; Hayman, the portrait-painter (d. 1696), and the two Vanderveldes, the marine painters; and Michael Dahl, the Swedish portrait-painter (d. 1743); Dr. Arbuthnot (d. 1734-5), the friend of Pope, Swift, Gay, and Prior ; Benjamin Stillingfleet, the naturalist, so touchingly deplored by Pennant, in the preface to his *British Zoology ;* Dr. Akenside, the poet (d. 1770); James Dodsley, the bookseller, with a tablet (d. 1797); G. H. Harlow, who painted " The Trial of Queen Katherine" (d. 1819); and Sir John Malcolm (d. 1833). Here also lies Thomas d'Urfey, dramatist and song-writer, to whom there is a tablet on the outer south face of the church-tower, inscribed " Tom d'Urfey, dyed February 26, 1723." In the vestry are the portraits of the St. James's Rectors, that of Dr. Birch alone missing : the first Rector, Dr. Tenison; the third, Dr. Wake; and the seventh, Dr. Secker, became Archbishops of Canterbury. (See Walcott's *Handbook of St. James's.*)

St. James's, Spa-road, Bermondsey, contains a large altar-picture, painted for 500*l.*, by John Wood, upon conditions detailed at p. 41. The subject is the Ascension of our Saviour; the figures are considerably above the natural size : on a canvass of 275 square feet (25 feet by 11), in the upper part, a full-length figure of the Saviour occupies nearly one-half of the picture, a nimbus around the head illumining the upper sky; the eleven disciples are in various positions, standing, kneeling, prostrated, with uplifted hands and faces, and bodies bent with reverential awe and devotion; and their personal identity, costume, and colouring, are very successful.

St. John's, Clerkenwell, a modern church, in St. John's-square, with an ancient crypt, (part of the Priory of St. John of Jerusalem,) in which the detection of the Cock-lane Ghost hoax was consummated.

" While drawing in the crypt of St. John's, Clerkenwell, in a narrow cloister on the north side (there being at that time coffins, and fragments of shrouds, and human remains lying about in disorder), the sexton's boy pointed to one of the coffins, and said the woman in it was ' Scratching Fanny.' This reminding me of the business of the Cock-lane Ghost, I removed the lid of the coffin, which was loose, and saw the body of a woman, which had become adipocere; the face perfect, handsome oval, with aquiline nose. [Will not arsenic produce adipocere?] She was said to have been poisoned, although the charge is understood to have been disproved. I inquired of one of the churchwardens of the time

(Mr. Bird, I believe), and he said the coffin had always been understood to contain the body of the woman whose spirit was said to have haunted the house in Cock-lane."—*Communicated by John Wykeham Archer.*

ST. JOHN'S, formerly ST. AUGUSTIN'S, at Hackney, was taken down in 1798, except the tower, of the sixteenth century, which still remains, with a clock and a peal of eight bells; eastward is the chapel of the Rowe family, built in 1614, and preserved as a mausoleum. The church-yard has thoroughfare paths, lined with lofty trees, but the funereal yew is not among them. The old church, before its demolition, was extremely rich in monuments and brasses, some of which were removed to the porches and vestibules of the new church of St. John, completed in 1797, northward of the ancient edifice.

ST. JOHN THE EVANGELIST, Charlotte-street, Fitzroy-square, designed by Hugh Smith, in the Norman or Romanesque style, was opened in 1846, its west front having a tower and spire, 120 feet high, and a large wheel-window beneath the intervening gable.

ST. JOHN THE EVANGELIST, Horsleydown, one of the Fifty New Churches (10 Anne), was finished in 1732: it has a tower, with an ill-proportioned Scamozzian Ionic column, seen to the eastward from the London and Greenwich Railway.

ST. JOHN THE EVANGELIST, Smith Square, Westminster, the second built of the Fifty New Churches (10 Anne), finished in 1728, after the designs of Archer, pupil of Vanbrugh; before which it began to settle, and a tower and lantern-turret were added at each corner to strengthen the main building; " and these would have been beautiful accompaniments to the central tower and spire intended by the architect." —(*Elmes.*) These towers reminded Lord Chesterfield of an elephant thrown on its back, with its four feet erect in the air; and Charles Mathews, of a dining-table upside-down, with its four legs and castors. Meanwhile, justice has not been done to the originality and powers of the architect: the whole composition is impressive, and its boldness loses nothing by the graceful playfulness of the outline; it has some inaccuracies of detail, but is, altogether, a very striking production of the Vanbrugh school. (*Donaldson.*) It has semicircular apses east and west, and imposing Doric porticoes north and south. The interior of the church (said to have been the first in London lit with gas), is without columns, and is highly embellished: the east window is filled with ancient painted glass brought from Normandy; and above the altar-table is a copy of the celebrated picture of Christ bearing his Cross, by Ribalta, in the Chapel of St. Mary Magdalene College, Oxford. The elegant marble font, designed by C. Barry, jun., sculptured by J. Thomas, was placed here in 1847. Churchill, the satirist, born in the parish, succeeded his father in 1758, in the curacy and lectureship of this church: he soon disgraced the holy office, and substituted for the clerical costume a blue coat, gold-laced waistcoat and hat, and large ruffles; remonstrances ensued, and he resigned.

St. John's burial-ground contains " the ashes of an Indian chief, who died of small-pox, in 1734, and was buried in the presence of the Emperor Toma, after the custom of the Karakee Creeks, sewn up in two blankets, between two deal boards, with his clothes, some silver coins, and a few glass beads."—Walcott's *Westminster*, p. 314.

ST. JOHN'S, Notting Hill, an Early English cross church, designed by Stevens and Alexander, and consecrated Jan. 22, 1845: it stands upon an elevated portion of Kensington Park, facing Ladbroke Grove, and has a tower 156 feet high, seen to picturesque advantage.

ST. JOHN OF JERUSALEM, South Hackney, Middlesex; a large and beautiful church, in the best Pointed style, 13th and 14th centuries, by

E. C. Hakewill; first stone laid May 15, 1845; consecrated July 20, 1848. The plan is cruciform, with a tower and spire of equal height, together rising 187 feet; the latter has graceful lights and broaches, and the four Evangelists beneath canopies at the four angles; the nave has side aisles with flying buttresses to the clerestory; each transept is lit by a magnificent window, 29 feet high; and the choir has an apsis with seven lancet windows: entire external length, 192 feet; materials, Kentish rag and Speldhurst stone. The principal entrance is at the west, through a screen of open arches. The roof, of open-work, is of 60 feet, highest pitch, with massive arched and foliated ribs; and the meeting of the transepts, chancel, and nave is very effective. The chancel has a stone roof, and the walls of the apse are painted and diapered—red with fleur-de-lis, and blue powdered with stars; the pulpit and reading-desk are also diapered; and the seats are of oak, and mostly formed of stall-ends with finials: the two first seats are well-carved; on one is the crest of the rector and the badge of the patron saint, and on the other side the dove with the olive-branch, and the lynx, as an emblem of watchfulness. All the windows are filled with painted, stained, or richly-diapered glass, by Wailes, Powell, &c.; and a memorial cleres-tory window, Christ Blessing Little Children, and Raising Jairus's Daughter, is beautifully painted by Ward and Nixon. The altar-floor is laid with Minton's tiles; the font is nicely sculptured; the organ is from the old church at Hackney; the tower has a fine peal of eight bells. The entire cost was 15,740*l.*; sittings, 1500.

St. Katherine's, the church of the Royal Hospital of St. Kathe-rine, rebuilt in 1827, on the east side of the Regent's Park, after the de-molition of the ancient Hospital and Church, "at the Tower," for the site of St. Katherine's Docks. The new church, designed by A. Poynter, is in the florid Gothic style, and has octagonal towers, with a large window of beautiful tracery: it contains the original pulpit, with views of the ancient Hospital and its gates, an elaborate piece of carpentry; besides monuments, &c. from the old church.

St. Lawrence Jewry, King-street, Cheapside, was commenced by Wren, in 1671, upon the site of the old church, destroyed in the Great Fire of 1666: it has a tower and steeple 130 feet high, with, for a vane, a gilt gridiron, the emblem of St. Lawrence; and the east end in King-street is so pure as to be almost Grecian. The interior has some excellent plaster-work, in wreaths and branches; and the organ-case, pulpit, and doorways, are richly-carved oak. In the centre is a large pew for the Lord Mayor and Common Council, the church being used for Corporation Sermons. Here Tillotson was Tuesday lecturer; was married 1663-4; and buried in 1694, three years after he was conse-crated Archbishop of Canterbury: his sculptured monument is on the north wall of the church. The Vestry-room walls are entirely cased with fine dark carved oak; and the ceiling has elaborate plaster foliage, and a painting, by Thornhill, of St. Lawrence. In the old church, men-tioned 1293, was buried Thomas Boleyn, Earl of Wiltshire, (d. 1471,) whose daughter Anna married King Henry VIII., and was the mother of Queen Elizabeth: here lay also the remains of Richard Rich, mercer (d. 1469), from whom descended the Earls of Warwick.

St. Leonard's, Shoreditch (anciently *Soresdich*), occupies the site of a church mentioned in grants early in the 13th century. The last church (which had four gables in a line, and a low square tower), was taken down in 1736; and the present church built by the elder Dance in 1740: it has a steeple imitated from that of St. Mary-le-Bow, Cheap-side, and a fine peal of twelve bells. The parish register records the burial of Will Sommers, Henry VIII.'s jester (d. 1560), and of several distinguished players of the age of Queen Elizabeth and James I.; for a list of whom see Cunningham's *Handbook*, 2d. ed.; p. 235. In the register, is entered, among the "Burialles, Thomas Cam, y[e] 22d inst. of Januarye, 1588, Aged 207 years, Holywell-street. George Garrow, parish clerk." [Is not 2 written for 1 in the number of years?]

ST. LUKE's, Chelsea, Old and New Churches, described at page 76. In the churchyard of the latter lie Egerton and Blanchard, the comedians; M'Leod, who wrote a Journal of the Voyage of the *Alceste* to China, in 1817; and Alexander Stephens, editor of the *Annual Biography and Obituary.*

ST. MAGNUS THE MARTYR, London Bridge, was burnt in the Great Fire of 1666, and rebuilt by Wren, 1676. It has a tower, octagon lantern, cupola, and spire, added in 1705, which are very picturesque. The footway under the tower, on the east side, was made in 1760, through the recesses and groined arches originally formed in the main building by Wren, as if he had seen its necessity whenever the street leading to Old London Bridge required widening.* There is a similar passageway through the tower of Christ Church, Newgate-street. Miles Coverdale was for a short time rector of St. Magnus: he was buried in St. Bartholomew's by the Exchange, which being taken down in 1840, Coverdale's remains were removed, and interred in St. Magnus',† where a monument to his memory had been erected in 1837. The projecting gilt dial of the clock affixed to the tower was the gift of Sir Charles Duncomb; in 1709, and cost 485*l.* 5*s.* 4*d.*: Sir Charles, it is related, when a poor boy, had once to wait upon London Bridge a considerable time for his master, whom he missed through not knowing the hour; he then vowed that if ever he became successful in the world, he would give to St. Magnus' a public clock, that passengers might see the time; and this dial proves the fulfilment of his vow. It was originally ornamented with several richly gilded figures: upon a small metal shield inside the clock are engraven the donor's arms, with this inscription: "The gift of Sir Charles Duncomb, Knight, Lord Major, and Alderman of this ward. Langley Bradley fecit, 1709." Sir Charles also presented the large organ in St. Magnus' church: it was "made and erected by Abraham Jordan, senior and junior;" and in the *Spectator*, Feb. 8, 1712, was announced the public opening of the instrument on the following Sunday. The tower has a set of ten bells. A bronzed or copper medalet, date 1676, bears on its obverse a view of old St. Magnus' Church. Here was buried Hervey Yevele, or Zenely, described by Stow as *Free-Mason* to Edward III., Richard II., and Henry IV.: he assisted to erect the tomb of Richard II. in Westminster Abbey, between 1395 and 1397, and prepared plans for raising the walls of Westminster Hall.

ST. MARGARET'S, Lothbury, destroyed in the Great Fire of 1666, and rebuilt by Wren in 1690, has a steeple 140 feet high; two carved and painted figures of Moses and Aaron, brought from St. Christopher-le-

* This improvement was made after the destruction of the church roof by fire, April 18, 1760, which began in the oilmen's premises in Thames-street, adjoining the church, and consumed seven houses and all the warehouses on Fresh Wharf. This conflagration was occasioned by the neglect of a servant, who left some inflammable substances boiling while he went to see Earl Ferrers return from his trial and condemnation for murder: before the man could get back, the shop was in flames.

† The inscription upon Coverdale's tomb states: "On the 4th of October, 1535, the first complete English version of the Bible was published under his direction." The third centenary of this event was celebrated by the clergy throughout the churches of England, October 4, 1835; and several medals were struck upon the occasion.

Stocks, when that church was taken down; and a marble font attributed to Gibbons, resembling that in St. James's Church, Piccadilly.

St. Margaret Pattens, Fenchurch-street, destroyed in the Great Fire of 1666, and rebuilt by Wren in 1687, contains a fine altar-picture—Angels ministering to Christ in the Garden—ascribed to Carlo Maratti. About the altar-piece are some exquisitely carved flowers. Against the south wall is a large monument, by Rysbrack, to Sir P. Delme, Lord Mayor in 1723.

St. Margaret's parish church, Westminster, is placed a short distance from the north door of Westminster Abbey: it was originally built about 1064, by Edward the Confessor, for the people who had thickly settled around the Abbey, and were greatly increased by those who sought here the privilege of Sanctuary. This Norman edifice was destroyed, and the church rebuilt in the reign of Edward I., of which period there exist a few remains. It was considerably altered in the time of Edward IV., when, probably, a flight of steps led up to the church-door, the surrounding level having been raised about nine feet above the original surface: a stone cross and a pulpit formerly stood here, as at St. Paul's. Soon after the ancient Chapel of St. Stephen had been given up for the sittings of the House of Commons, it is supposed the members attended Divine Service in St. Margaret's, as the Lords went to the Abbey Church. On Sept. 25, 1642, the Covenant was read from St. Margaret's pulpit, and taken by both Houses of Parliament, the Assembly of Divines, and the Scots Commissioners. Here also were preached the lengthy Fast-day Sermons; and Hugh Peters, "the pulpit buffoon," persuaded the Parliament to bring Charles " to condign, speedy, and capital punishment," while the churchyard was guarded by soldiers with pikes and muskets. St. Margaret's did not escape plunder by the Puritans; but in 1660, "the State's Arms," richly carved and gilt, were set up in the church, and they are still preserved in the vestry. In 1641, a gallery was built over the north aisle; and in 1681, another over the south aisle, "exclusively for persons of quality," the latter erected at the expense of Sir John Cutler, the miser satirised by Pope. Doctors Burnet and Sprat, old rivals, once preached here before Parliament in one morning; and on Palm Sunday, 1713, Dr. Sacheverel preached here first after the term of his suspension: 40,000 copies of this sermon were sold. In 1735, St. Margaret's was repaired at the expense of Parliament, when the tower was faced with Portland stone and raised 20 feet, being now 85 feet high: it has a fine peal of ten bells, the tenor weighing 26 cwt. In 1753 was placed on the altar-table a relievo of our Lord's Supper at Emmaus, sculptured in lime-wood, by Alken of Soho, from Titian's celebrated picture in the Louvre. In 1758, the east end was rebuilt and made apsidal; and the great east window removed, and replaced by the present beautiful cinque-cento window, said to have occupied five years executing, at Gouda in Holland, intended as a present from the magistrates of Dort to Henry VII.

This celebrated glass painting represents the Crucifixion, with angels receiving the blood-drops from the Saviour's wounds; an angel wafts the soul of the good thief to paradise, and a dragon (the devil) bears the soul of the wicked thief to eternal punishment. The six upper compartments are filled with as many angels, bearing the cross, the sponge, the crown of thorns, the hammer, the rods, and nails. In the lower compartment (right) is Arthur Prince of Wales, eldest son of Henry VII., and above him St. George and the red and white rose; and to the left is Catherine of Arragon, Arthur's bride, with above her the figure of St. Cecilia, and a bursting pomegranate, the emblem of Granada. The window is also said to have been ordered by Ferdinand and Isabella, on Prince Arthur being affianced, in 1499, to the Princess Catherine, their portraits being procured for the purpose. It was probably finished after his brother's death, to be sent as a gift to Henry VIII. The king gave it to Waltham Abbey, where it remained until the Dissolution, A.D. 1540; when the last abbot sent it for safety to his private chapel at New Hall, which, by purchase, subsequently became the property of Sir Thomas, father of Anne Boleyn, queen of Henry VIII. The chapel remained undisturbed until General Monk becoming possessor of New Hall, to save the window from destruction by the Puritans, had it buried underground. After the Restoration, Monk replaced the window in the chapel. Subsequent to his death, the seat fell into decay, and the chapel was taken down; but the window was preserved for some time cased up, until purchased by Mr. Conyers, of Copt Hall, Essex, by whose son it was sold, in 1758, to the churchwardens of St. Margaret's for 400 guineas, when it was placed in the church, re-opened in 1759, a fine anthem for the occasion being composed by Dr. Boyce. A prosecution was now instituted against the parishioners by the Dean and Chapter of Westminster, for putting up what was attempted to be proved "a superstitious image or picture." After seven years' suit, the bill was dismissed; in memory of which Mr. Churchwarden Peirson presented, as a gift for ever, to the churchwardens of the parish, a richly-chased cup, stand, and cover, silver-gilt, weighing 93oz. 15dwt., which is the loving-cup of St. Margaret's, and is produced with especial ceremony at the chief parochial entertainments.

The church is otherwise rich in painted glass: the north-east window is filled with gold mosaic designs, the Holy Monogram, the red and white roses, and portcullis, and a saint (Iago of Compostella?) bearing an open book. The crescent beside the rose, Mr. Rickman thought, denoted some "expectancy of regal amplitude;" so Shakspeare:

"*Pompey.* My power 's a crescent, and my auguring hope
Says it will come to the full." *Ant. and Cleop.* act ii. sc. 1.

In this and the south-east window are the arms of Edward the Confessor, represented as blazoned by the heralds *temp.* Henry VIII. The saint in the centre is St. Michael overcoming the dragon.—Abridged from Walcott's *Westminster.*

The chancel is decorated in polychrome by Willement: and over the reredos are crocketed canopies, coloured ruby, azure, and emerald diaper, and richly gilded. In 1802, the present beautifully carved pulpit and reading-desk, by Lenox, were erected; the Speaker's chair of state was placed in the front of the west gallery; and a new organ, by Avery, was built. Altogether, the votes of the House of Commons for the repairs of this church have been frequent and considerable. Upon certain occasions, as Restoration Day (May 29), the Chaplain of the House of Commons preaches here; when "the House" is usually represented by the Speaker, the Serjeant-at-Arms, the clerks and other officers, and some eight or ten Members. The church originally consisted of a nave and choir, with side aisles; with chapels or altars in the latter to St. Margaret, St. George, St. Katherine, St. Erasmus, St. John, and St. Cornelius, besides two to St. Nicholas and St. Christopher: the churchwardens' accounts bear evidence of the maintenance of these shrines. In the ambulatory is a carved stall of the 16th century.

Among the names of the more eminent of the Puritans who preached in St. Margaret's are those of Calamy, Vines, Nye, Manton, Marshall, Ganden, Owen, Burgess, Newcomen, Reynolds, Cheynell, Baxter, Case, (who censured Cromwell to his face, and when discoursing before General Monk, cried out, "There are some will betray three kingdoms for filthy lucre's sake," and threw his handkerchief into the General's pew,) the critical Lightfoot, Taylor, "the illuminated doctor," and Goodwyn, "the windmill with a weathercock upon the top."—Walcott's *Westminster,* p. 120.

The monuments are very numerous: among them are a tablet to Caxton the printer, by Westmacott, raised 1820 by the Roxburgh Club; alabaster figures, coloured and gilt, to Marie Lady Dudley (d. 1600); brass tablet, put up by subscription, 1845, to Sir Walter Raleigh, whose body was interred within the chancel of this church on the day he was beheaded in Old Palace-yard, Oct. 29, 1618; black marble slab to James Harrington (d. 1677), who wrote *Oceana;* monument near the porch-door to Mrs. E. Corbet, with what Johnson considered "the most valuable of all Pope's epitaphs;" monument to Captain Sir Peter Parker, Bart., R.N., with bas-relief of his death, 1814, and lines by Lord Byron, in chancel north aisle; a curious tablet of Cornelius Van

Dun (d. 1577), with a coloured bust in the uniform of the Yeomen of the Guard; and a small monument to Mrs. Joane Barnett (d. 1674), who left money for a yearly sermon and poor widows: she is said to have sold oatmeal cakes hard by the church-door, in memory of which a large oatmeal pudding is a standing dish at the "Feast." There is but one ancient brass in the church, the rest having been sold, in 1644, at 3*d.* and 4*d.* per pound, as the churchwardens' accounts attest. Weever records the burial here of John Skelton, Poet Laureate to Henry VIII. (d. 1529); and the registers contain the burial of Thomas Churchyarde, "Court Poet" (d. 1604). Soon after the Restoration, several bodies were disinterred from the Abbey, and deposited in a pit in St. Margaret's churchyard: among them was the corpse of Oliver Cromwell's mother, from Henry VII.'s Chapel; Sir W. Constable, one of the judges in the trial of Charles I.; Admiral Blake; John Pimme; Thomas May, the poet, &c. Here, too, are buried Sir William Waller, the Parliament General (d. 1668); Hollar, the engraver (d. 1677), in the churchyard, "near N.W. corner of the tower" (*Aubrey*); Thomas Blood, who attempted to steal the regalia (d. 1680); Gadbury, the Cavalier astrologer, and helpmate of Lilly (d. 1704); Frances Whate (d. 1736), a charwoman, buried in the church; John Read, the "Walking Rushlight," and the oldest general in the service (d. 1807). The churchyard is extremely crowded with bodies. In the Report on Extramural Sepulture, 1850, Dr. Reid states, "that the state of the burying-ground around St. Margaret's Church is prejudicial to the air supplied at the Houses of Parliament, and also to the whole neighbourhood;" that "these offensive emanations have been noticed at all hours of the night and morning;" and that even "fresh meat is frequently tainted" by the deleterious gases issuing from this churchyard. The removal of the church was proposed even in Stow's time, and has often been revived; it is favoured by Mr. Barry, in his design for the completion of the New Palace of Westminster: if allowed to remain, it should be restored; to harmonise with the Abbey, to which it was originally an adjunct. Among the bequests is an endowment, founded in 1781, by the will of Mr. Edward Dickenson, who left 5000*l.* stock, the interest of which was to be divided, on the first month after Easter-day, between three newly-married couples from each parish of St. Margaret and St. John the Evangelist, Westminster, and of Acton. The distribution takes place with the approbation of the Bishop of London; and petitions are taken into consideration by the trustees on the Wednesday in Easter week, when they decide on the nine couples to receive the bounty, 15*l.* each.

A celebrated heirloom of the parish is the "*Overseers' Box,*" originally purchased at Horn Fair for fourpence, and presented by a Mr. Monck to his brother Overseers, in 1713. In 1720, the Society of Past Overseers commemorated the gift by adding to the Box a silver rim; and in 1726 were added a silver side-case and bottom. In 1740, an embossed border was placed on the lid, and the bottom enriched with an emblem of Charity. In 1746, Hogarth engraved inside the lid a bust of the Duke of Cumberland, in memory of the Battle of Culloden. In 1765 was added to the lid a plate with the arms of the City of Westminster, and the inscription: "This Box is to be delivered to every succeeding set of Overseers, on penalty of five guineas." The original Horn Box thus ornamented has been placed in four additional cases, each ornamented by its several custodians, the senior Overseer for the time being, with silver plates engraved with the following subjects: Fireworks in St. James's Park (Peace of Aix-la-Chapelle), 1749; Admiral Keppel's Action off Ushant, and his Acquittal by Court Martial; Battle of the Nile, 1798; Repulse of Admiral Linois, 1804; Battle of Trafalgar, 1805; Action between San Fiorenzo and La Piedmontaise, 1808; Battle of Waterloo, 1815; Bombardment of Algiers, 1816; House of Lords at Trial of Queen Caroline, Coronation of George IV., and his Visit to Scotland, 1822. Portraits: Wilkes, Churchwarden in 1759; Nelson, Duncan, Howe, and Vincent; Fox and Pitt, 1806; the Prince Regent, 1811; Princess Charlotte, 1817; and Queen Charlotte, 1818. Views: Interior of

Westminster Hall, with Westminster Volunteers attending Divine Service, on Fast-day, 1803; the old Sessions House; St. Margaret's Church from north-east, the west front, tower, and altar-piece. In 1813 was added to the outer case a large silver plate portrait of the Duke of Wellington, commemorating the centenary of the Box. The top of the second case represents the Governors in their board-room, inscribed, "The original Box and cases to be given to every succeeding set of Overseers, on penalty of fifty guineas, 1783." Outside the first case is engraved a cripple. In 1793, a contumacious Overseer detained the Box, and it was deposited "in Chancery" until 1796, when it was restored to the Overseers' Society; this event being commemorated by the addition of a third case, of Justice trampling upon an unmasked man and a serpent, and the Lord Chancellor (Loughborough) pronouncing his decree. On the fourth, or outer case, is the Anniversary Meeting of the Past Overseers' Society, and the delivery of the Box to the succeeding Overseer, who must produce it at certain parochial entertainments, with three pipes of tobacco at least, under the penalty of six bottles of claret; and must return the whole safe and sound, with some addition, under penalty of two hundred guineas. Within the Box is a mother-of-pearl tobacco-stopper, with a silver chain.—*Abridged from* Walcott's *Westminster*, pp. 105-107.

St. Mark's, Kennington Common, a Doric church, designed by Roper, and built in 1824, on the spot formerly the place of execution for Surrey, and where several persons suffered death in the Stuart cause.

St. Mark's, Old-Street-road, St. Luke's, a beautiful Early English church, designed by Ferrey, and built in 1848: it has a noble four-storied tower and spire, rising from the ground 125 feet; and the windows throughout the edifice are fine.

St. Martin's-in-the-Fields, north of the western extremity of the Strand, is the second church built upon this site; the first having been erected by Henry VIII., from his disliking the funerals of inhabitants passing Whitehall in their way to St. Margaret's, at Westminster, as they had no parish church.[*] In the Sutherland View in 1543, St. Martin's has a low square tower, and is strictly "in the fields:" in 1607, Henry Prince of Wales added a chancel; but the whole was taken down in 1720-21, and the present church commenced from a design by Gibbs, when King George I., by proxy, laid the first stone, March 19, 1721, gave the workmen 100 guineas, and subsequently presented the parish with 1500*l.* for an organ. The church was consecrated Oct. 20, 1726: the cost of its erection was 36,891*l.* 10*s.* 4*d.* Its length, including the portico, is equal to twice its width: it is in the florid Roman or Italian style, and has a very fine western Corinthian hexastyle portico: the east end is truly elegant, and the round columns at each angle of the building render it very effective in profile. The tower and spire rise out of the roof, behind the portico. The interior is richly ornamented, "a little too gay and theatrical for Protestant worship." In 1842, 45 feet of the spire was struck by lightning, and had to be restored at the expense of 1000*l.*: the ball and vane were also regilt; the latter is 6 feet 8 inches high and 5 feet long, and is surmounted with a *crown*, to denote this the parish of the Sovereign; and in its Registers are entered the births of the royal children born at Buckingham Palace. The tower has a fine peal of twelve bells;[†] but the story of Nell Gwynn having left a legacy, paid weekly to the ringers, has no foundation in fact. The churchyard was paved in 1829; and in 1831, the vaults beneath the church were reconstructed, each vault being 10 feet high, 20 wide, and 40 long. Here is preserved the old

[*] It is probable that there was a building before this, but "only a chapel for the use of the monks of Westminster when they visited their Convent (*Covent*) Garden," which then extended to it."—*J. Gwilt.*

[†] High in the steeple hangs a small shrill bell, formerly called the Sanctus, and now the Saints' or Parson's Bell. "It was rung before the Reformation, when the Priest came to the *Sanctus*, 'Holy, holy, holy, Lord God of Sabaoth!' so that those without the church might participate in the devotions of those present at the most solemn part of the divine office."—*The Parish Choir.* No. 59.

parish whipping-post; and the monument of Sir Theodore Mayerne, the physician, (buried here,) a friend of Van Dyck, to whom he communicated valuable information relating to pigments. Here also are the coffins of Miss Reay, and Hackman, her assassin, fastened together by a chain; the former covered with crimson velvet, the latter made of rough deal. Jack Sheppard is likewise buried here; and Nell Gwynn, in the church. Among other persons of note interred here are Paul Vansomer and Laguerre, the painters; Dobson, the English Van Dyck: Hilliard, the miniature-painter; Nicholas Stone, the sculptor; Hon. Robert Boyle,* the chemist, whose funeral sermon was preached by his friend, Dr. Burnet; George Farquhar, the comic dramatist; Roubiliac, the sculptor; John Hunter, the surgeon; and Scott, the author of a *Visit to Paris*, who was killed in a duel in 1821. In the old church was buried, Oct. 31, 1679, Sir Edmundberry Godfrey, found murdered in a ditch near Chalk Farm: the corpse was brought from Bridewell Hospital with great pomp, eight knights supporting the pall, and attended by all the City aldermen, 72 London ministers, and above 100 persons of distinction. At the funeral sermon, two divines stood by the preacher, lest he should be assassinated by the Papists.

ST. MARTIN'S, LUDGATE, near the site of the City gate of that name, in Ludgate-street, was rebuilt by Wren after the Great Fire of 1666: the steeple has a small gallery, and rises 168 feet. Between Ludgate-street and the body of the church is an ambulatory, the whole depth of the tower, so as to lessen within the church the noise from the street. In the vestry-room are a carved seat (date 1690), and several curious coffers or chests. The font has a Greek inscription, a palindrome, *i. e.*, it reads the same backwards as forwards. In the old church was the following epitaph, dated 1590:

Earth goes to		As mold to mold
Earth treads on	Earth	Glittering in gold
Earth as to		Return nere should
Earth shall to		Goe ere he would
Earth upon		Consider may
Earth goes to	Earth	Passed away
Earth though on		Is stout and gay
Earth shall from		Passe poor away.

The spire of St. Martin's, backed by the campanile towers and majestic dome of St. Paul's, seen from Fleet-street, is a fine architectural group.

ST. MARTIN'S OUTWICH (Otteswich), Bishopsgate-street, was originally built in the fourteenth century, in the Pointed style, with a low tiled roof and square tower; and the churchwardens' accounts (1508 to 1545) contain entries of ancient usages previous to the Reformation: as, "Wyne on Relyks Sondaye, 1*d*.;" "Paschall or Hallowed Taper, tenebur Candell and Cross Candell, License to eate flesh," &c. This church escaped the Great Fire of 1666, but was greatly injured in a conflagration in Nov. 1765, which burnt fifty houses. In 1796, the present church was built by S. P. Cockerell. Its form is oval, with a recess for the chancel, in the ceiling of which is a light filled with stained glass, mostly from the old church, There are also several monuments from the same, including two recumbent stone figures of John Oterwich and his wife, their head-cushions supported by angels; the feet of the man resting against a lion, and those of the female against a dog. Here also is a canopied tomb, date 1500, with remains of brass figures, armorial bearings, and labels against the back; and several stone effigies to the memory of Alderman Staper (1594): "hee was the greatest merchant in his tyme, the chiefest actor in discovere of

---

* Boyle was born in the year in which Bacon died, (1627,) and Newton in that in which Galileo died (1642); Boyle being fifteen years older than Newton.

the trades of Turkey and East India, &c.;" also two brass figures of rectors of the church in the fifteenth century. Few would expect to find these monumental treasures within a church of such un-ecclesiastical design. The South Sea House, which is in this parish, was given to the church by Mrs. Margaret Taylor in 1667.

St. Mary Abbots', Kensington, the mother-church, was rebuilt about 1691: here are monuments to Edward, eighth Earl of Warwick and Holland (d. 1759), with his effigies, seated, and reposing upon an urn; and to the three Colmans: Francis Colman; his son, George, "the Elder;" and his son, "the Younger:" the two latter wrote several comedies, and were proprietors of the Haymarket Theatre. In the churchyard are monuments to Jortin, author of the *Life of Erasmus*, and Vicar of Kensington; and to Mrs. Inchbald (a Roman Catholic), a beauty, a virtue, a player, and authoress of the *Simple Story*. Here, too, is buried William Courten, the traveller and naturalist, whose curiosities, it is said, filled ten rooms in the Middle Temple: this collection he bequeathed to Sir Hans Sloane, and thus it became the nucleus of the British Museum. St. Mary's, Kensington, had a "Vicar of Bray" in one Thomas Hodges, collated to the living by Archbishop Juxon: he kept his preferment during the Civil War and interregnum, by joining alternately with either party; although a frequent preacher before the Long Parliament and one of the Assembly of Divines, he was made Dean of Hereford after the Restoration, but continued Vicar of Kensington.—Murray's *Environs of London*, page 69.

St. Mary Abchurch, Abchurch-lane, was destroyed by the Great Fire of 1666, and rebuilt by Wren in 1686: its tower and spire are 140 feet high: the interior has a large cupola, painted by Sir James Thornhill; and an altar-piece, with fruit and flowers, exquisitely carved by Gibbons, and originally painted after nature by Thornhill.

St. Mary Aldermary, Bow-lane, destroyed in the Great Fire of 1666, was rebuilt by Wren, a legacy of 5000*l.* being left for that purpose. It has rich fan-groined ceilings; a tower, with four turrets, 130 feet high, and a fine bell-tower. Among the monuments is a tablet, beautifully sculptured by Bacon, but bearing *no inscription*. In the great storm of 1703, two of the turrets were blown down.

St. Mary-at-Hill, on the ascent from Billingsgate, was partly rebuilt by Wren, between 1672 and 1677, the west-end tower being of subsequent date. In 1848-9, the interior was entirely refitted, with such an extent of carving as had not been executed before in the City for many years. The pillars supporting the organ gallery are ornamented with fruit and flowers. The great screen has a frame of oak; the rector's pew and reading-desk are enriched with carved open tracery, and brackets surmounted with the royal supporters, bearing shields with V.R. 1849. The pulpit is entirely new, and is very elaborately carved: in the sounding-board are bosses of flowers of 12-inch projection; from the eyes of the volutes garlands of flowers are suspended, which pass through the split trusses, and fall down, crossing and uniting behind; and within the pulpit, at the back, is a well-executed drop of fruit and flowers: on the front of the organ-gallery are bold clusters of musical trophies and garlands of flowers, with birds and fruit; and the royal arms, with a mantle scroll, about ten feet long, form a perforated screen on the top of the gallery. All the carved work is by Mr. W. Gibbs Rogers (see Carvings, page 67). The organ was built by Mr. Hill, on the German plan, and contains two manuals and a pedal organ. Brand, who compiled the *Popular Antiquities*, and was Secretary to the Society of Antiquaries, was Rector of St. Mary-at-Hill from 1789 till his death in 1806: he is buried in the chancel.

St. Mary's, Battersea, a church of tasteless design, built in 1776, is remarkable only for Roubiliac's elegant monument to the celebrated Lord Bolingbroke. (See pp. 33, 34.)

St. Mary-le-Bone, or St. Mary-at-the-Bourne, at the end of the High-street, verging on the New-road, was originally the mother-church of Marylebone, and was rebuilt in 1741, on the site of an edifice erected about 1400, on the removal of the ancient church of Tyburn, "which stood in a lonely place near the highway (on or near the site of the present Court House, at the corner of Stratford-place), subject to the depredations of robbers, who frequently stole the images, bells, and ornaments." (Lysons's *Environs*, vol. iii. 1795.) In Vertue's Plan, about 1560, the only building seen between the village of St. Giles's and Primrose Hill is the little solitary church of Marybone: its interior is shewn in one of Hogarth's plates of the *Rake's Progress* (the Marriage), where some ill-spelt verses on the vault of the Forset family, and the churchwardens' names, are accurately copied; this plate was published in 1735, and part of the original inscription was preserved in the present church, converted into a parish chapel in 1817, on the consecration of the church in the New-road. In the chapel are tablets to Gibbs, the architect; Baretti, the friend of Dr. Johnson; and Caroline Watson, the engraver: and in the churchyard is a monument to James Ferguson, the astronomer. Among the burials in the Register are James Figg, the prize-fighter; Vanderbank, the portrait-painter; Hoyle, aged 90, who wrote the *Treatise on Whist*; Rysbrack, the sculptor; and Allan Ramsay, portrait-painter, and son of the author of the *Gentle Shepherd*. In Paddington-street are two burial-grounds attached to this church. In 1511, the Marylebone curate's stipend was only 13s. per annum; in 1650, the impropriation was valued at 80l. per annum, and Richard Bonner was curate; and before the late separation the value of the living was 1898l.*

St. Marylebone (New Church), New Road, opposite York Gate, Regent's Park, designed by T. Hardwick, father of P. Hardwick, R.A., was originally built " on speculation" as a chapel; and was purchased by the parish, and converted into a handsome church, at the cost of 60,000l. It has a lofty stone clock-tower and portico; the interior was at first objected to as too theatrical in arrangement: it has an altar-picture of the Holy Family, painted and presented by B. West, P.R.A. Cosway and Northcote, Royal Academicians, are buried here.

St. Mary-le-Bow, Cheapside, "for divers accidents happening there, hath been made more famous than any other parish church of the whole city or suburbs." (*Stow.*) If not originally a Roman temple, as was once believed, it was one of the earliest churches built by our Norman conquerors. Stow says it was named St. Mary *de Arcubus*, from its being built on arches of stone, the semicircular-arched Norman crypt, extant to this day: and hence is named the "Court of Arches," formerly held in the church. About 1190, Longbeard, ringleader of a tumult, took refuge in the steeple, which was fired to drive him out: in 1271, part of the steeple fell, and killed several persons; and some years

---

* In a Map published in 1742, the diminutive church of St. Mary-le-Bone is shewn detached from London, with two zig-zag ways leading to it, one near Vere-street, then the western extremity of the new buildings, and the second from Tottenham-Court-road. Rows of houses, with their backs to the fields, extended from St. Giles's Pound to Oxford-market; but Tottenham-Court-road had only one cluster on the west side, and the spring-water house. The zig-zag way above mentioned, near Vere-street, still retaining its original name of Mary-le-bone lane, was the communication between the high road and the village. A friend, born in 1780, remembers his father and mother relating how they walked out *through the fields*, to be married at Marybone Church.

fter its repair, one Ducket, a goldsmith, fled here for Sanctuary, and
was murdered. The old steeple was entirely rebuilt by 1469, when the
Common Council ordered that Bow bells should be rung nightly at nine
'clock, a vestige of the Norman curfew; in 1472, two tenements in
Cosier-lane (now Bow-lane), were bequeathed "to the maintenance of
low bell," which being rung for the closing of shops somewhat late,
he young men, 'prentices, and others in Cheap, made this rhyme:

> "Clarke of the Bow bell, with the yellow lockes,
> For thy late ringing, thy head shall have knockes."

'o which the Clerk replied:—

> "Children of Cheape, hold you all still,
> For you shall have the Bow bell rung at your will."

William Copeland, churchwarden, either gave a new bell for this pur-
ose, or caused the old one to be re-cast, in 1515: Weever says the
rmer. In 1512, the arches and spire of the tower were provided with
anterns, as beacons for travellers: the latter is shewn in the View of
london, 1543 (in the Sutherland Collection); it has a central lantern, or
ell-turret, and a pinnacle at each corner. The church was rebuilt, as
e now see it, by Wren, after the Great Fire of 1666, and the belfry was
repared for twelve bells, though only eight were placed; but two were
absequently added, and the set of ten bells was first rung in 1762. (See
ELLS, p. 38.) The earliest monument in the old church was that to Sir
ohn Coventry, Mayor in 1425: Weever gives his epitaph. The pre-
ant church contains a large marble sarcophagus, with figures of Faith
nd a cherub, and a medallion bust, by Banks, R.A., of Bishop Newton,
wenty-five years rector of this parish, and interred in St. Paul's.

Independently of ordinary services in the church, prayers are read and the
acrament administered at eight o'clock in the morning on every festival through-
ut the year which does not fall on a Sunday. This is in compliance with the
ill of Mr. Robert Nelson, author of the *Companion to the Festivals and Fasts of
he Church of England*, who left for the purpose 3l. per annum. Formerly, the
oyle lectures were delivered here, but they have been discontinued for some
ears past. The Bishops elect of the province of Canterbury attend at this church,
revious to their consecration, to take the oaths of supremacy, &c.

low Church is one of Wren's finest works. The large Palladian doorways are noble; and the campanile is picturesque.

The circular peristyle, or continued range of columns, which rises from a sty-
obate on the top of the tower (a miniature representation of that around the
ome of St. Paul's), let it be viewed from what point it may be, is the most beau-
iful feature of the steeple. By the introduction of the combined scrolls at each
ngle of the tower, Wren has endeavoured to prevent that appearance of abrupt-
ess which would otherwise have resulted from the sudden transition from the
quare to the circular form, and has caused the outline to be gradually pyra-
idical from the top of the tower to the vane. The flying buttresses, which
ppear to support the columns above the peristyle, are introduced chiefly with a
iew to effect the same end.

The spire was repaired by Sir W. Staines when a young stonemason;
nd in 1820 it was in part rebuilt by George Gwilt, but was not low-
red, as generally believed. Its height is 225 feet; the dragon, ten feet
ong, was then re-gilt, and a young Irishman descended from the spire
oint on its back, pushing it from the cornices and scaffolds with his feet,
n the presence of thousands of spectators.* Over the doorway in Cheap-
ide is a small balcony, intended as a place to view processions from. (See
CHEAPSIDE, p. 74.) The present Bells are much heavier, and more

---

* One of Mother Shipton's prophecies was, that when the dragon of Bow
Church and the grasshopper of the Royal Exchange should meet, London streets
would be deluged with blood! In 1820, both these vanes were lying together in a
tonemason's yard in Old-street Road, where the upper portion of Wren's spire is
reserved to this day.

powerful in tone, than the first set. It requires two men to ring the largest (the tenor, 53 cwt., key C). The ringers belong to a society called the "College Youths," founded in 1637, and named from the College of St. Spirit and Mary, built by Sir Richard Whittington, on College-hill, Upper Thames-street, and burnt down in the Great Fire. A book recording the names of the founders and members of the "College Youths," from 1637 to 1724, was lost about the latter date, and only recovered in 1840. Another society, called the "Cumberland Society," rang for a few years at Bow Church. There is a peal called the "Whittington Peal," which can only be rung on twelve bells; and the College Youths are anxious to have two bells added to the present number, as the peal is considered incomplete.

St. Mary's, Herne Hill, between Camberwell and Dulwich, was built in 1844-5, by Stevens and Alexander, in the Perpendicular Gothic style of the 15th century. It has a lofty stone tower and spire, and a highly-decorated interior : the ceiling is divided, by moulded beams and Gothic tracery, into panels, elaborately painted; the beams have illuminated Scripture texts; all the windows are filled with stained glass; the open seats are of polished oak; the floor is laid with coloured encaustic tiles, and the chancel-steps with beautiful porcelain, by Copeland; the Decalogue, &c., is written in illuminated characters upon porcelain slabs; and the pulpit panels are filled with paintings of the Evangelists and Apostles. As this was one of the earliest specimens of modern High-Church embellishment, so it remains one of the most beautiful.

St. Mary's, Islington, "the old church," is the successor of a church upon the same site : this had an embattled tower, with a bell-turret, and was presumed to be 300 years old on being taken down in 1751, when the present church was erected by Launcelot Dowbiggin, and opened May 26, 1754. It has a tower and stone spire, 164 feet high, and a fine peal of eight bells, each inscribed with a couplet inculcating loyalty, love, and harmony. In 1787, when a lightning conductor was affixed to the spire, one Thomas Bird constructed round it a wicker-work scaffold, with steps within. The parish register dates from 1557. Among the persons buried here are Dame Alice Owen, who founded a free-school and almshouses in the parish (see p. 5); Dr. Hawes, one of the originators of the Humane Society; Earlom, the mezzotinto engraver; and John Nichols, F.S.A., the editor of the *Gentleman's Magazine*, his grave being a few yards from the house in which he was born. In this parish are three Gothic churches, with towers, built by C. Barry, R.A.: St. Paul's, Ball's Pond, and St. John's, Upper Holloway, 1828; and Trinity, Cloudesley-square, 1829.

St. Mary's, Lambeth, the mother-church of the manor and parish, stands within the patriarchal shade of Lambeth Palace, and has a Perpendicular tower, lately restored. In the Bishop's Register at Winchester, date 1377, is a commission to compel the inhabitants to erect this tower for their church, then newly built. In the church-wardens' accounts, "pewes" are mentioned as early as the reign of Philip and Mary. The eastern end of the north aisle, built 1522, by the Duke of Norfolk, is called the Howard Chapel. In the church are the tombs of these Archbishops of Canterbury : Bancroft, d. 1610; Parker, d. 1575; Tenison, d. 1715; Hutton, d. 1758; Secker, (in passage between church and palace,) d. 1768; Cornwallis, d. 1783; Moore, d. 1805.

In burying Archbishop Cornwallis, were found the remains of Thirlby, the first and only Bishop of Westminster: he died a prisoner in Lambeth Palace (*temp.* Elizabeth). The body was discovered wrapped in fine linen, the face perfect, the beard long and white; the linen and woollen garments well preserved; the cap, silk and point lace, as in portraits of Archbishop Juxon; slouched hat, under left arm; cassock, like apron with strings; and pieces of garments like a pilgrim's habit.

Here also are the tombs of Alderman Goodbehere; Madame Storace, the singer; Peter Dollond, inventor of the achromatic telescope; and Elias Ashmole, the antiquary. In the churchyard is the altar-tomb of the Tradescants, father and son:

> "These famous antiquarians, that had been
> Both gardeners to the Rose and Lily queen."—*Epitaph.*

The tomb is sculptured with palm-trees, hydra and skull, obelisk and pyramid, and Grecian ruins, crocodile, and shells. In the Register are entered the burials of Simon Forman, the astrologer; and Edward Moore, who wrote the tragedy of the "Gamester." In a window of the middle aisle is painted a pedlar with his pack and dog, said to represent the person who bequeathed to the parish of Lambeth "Pedlar's Acre," provided his portrait and that of his dog were perpetually preserved in one of the church windows. When the painting was first put up is unknown, but it existed in 1608; "a new glass pedlar" was put up in 1703, but removed in 1816.*

ST. MARY MAGDALENE, Bermondsey, was originally founded by the monks of Bermondsey, it is supposed, early in the reign of Edward III.; but taken down in 1680, when the present church was built upon the same site: in 1830, the west front was remodelled, the tower repaired, and the large pointed window restored. Among the communion plate is an ancient silver salver, supposed to have belonged to the Abbey of Bermondsey: in the centre, a knight in plate armour is kneeling to a female, about to place a helmet on his head, at the gate of a castle or fortified town: from the fashion of the armour and the form of the helmet, this relic is referred to the age of Edward II. In the church is a monument to Dr. Joseph Watson, more than thirty-seven years teacher to the first public institution in this country for the education of the deaf and dumb, established in this parish, 1792. In the churchyard is buried Mrs. S. Utton, who was tapped twenty-five times for dropsy, and had 157 gallons of water taken from her; also Mrs. S. Wood, tapped ninety-seven times, water 461 gallons; and the husband of the latter, who died 1837, aged 108 years! (See BERMONDSEY, page 40.)

ST. MARY MAGDALEN, Old Fish-street, rebuilt by Wren, after the Great Fire of 1666, contains a small brass tablet, date 1586, with the figure of a man, and the following lines in black letter:

> "In God the Lord put all your truste,
>   Repente your formar wicked waies,
>   Elizabethe our Queen moste juste
>   Bless her, O Lord, in all her daies;
>   So Lord encrease good councelers,
>   And preachers of his holie worde
> Mislike all papistes desiers
>   O Lord, cut them off with thy sworde.
> How small soever the gift shall be
>   Thank God for him who gave it thee.
> III penie loaves to III poor foulkes
>   Geve every Sabbath day for aye."

The Rev. R. H. Barham (*Thomas Ingoldsby*) was rector of this church from 1824 to his death in 1845.

* The name of the benefactor is unknown; but it has been suggested that this portrait was intended rather as a rebus upon the name "Chapman" than upon his trade: for in Swaffham Church, Norfolk, is the portrait of John Chapman, a great benefactor to that parish; and the device of a pedlar and his pack occurs in several parts of the church, which has given rise to nearly the same tradition at Swaffham as at Lambeth.—*Preface to Hearne's Caii Antiquitates,* p. 84. Besides, Pedlar's Acre was not originally so called, but the Church Hopes, or Hopys, (an isthmus of land projecting into the river,) and is entered in the Register as bequeathed by "a person unknown."—*Popular Errors Explained, &c.* p. 293.

L

St. Mary's Matfelon, Whitechapel, at the eastern end of High-street, was originally a chapel-of-ease to Stebenhith, or Stepney; its second name being from *Matfel*, in Hebrew, a woman recently delivered of a son. Stow traces the name to the wives of the parish having slain out of hand a certain Frenchman who had murdered and plundered a devout widow, by whom he had been cherished and brought up of alms. This occurred in 1428, the sixth of King Henry VI.; but Stow also finds the name as early as the twenty-first of Richard II. The old church was taken down in 1673, and rebuilt nearly as at present: it has a gas-lit clock-dial.

The Parish Register records that Richard Brandon was buried in the church-yard, June 24, 1649; and a marginal note, (not in the hand of the Registrar, but bearing the mark of antiquity,) states: " This R. Brandon is supposed to have cut off the head of Charles I." He was assisted by his man Ralph Jones, a ragman in Rosemary-lane; and a tract in the British Museum, entitled, " The Confession of Richard Brandon, the Hangman, upon his Deathbed, concerning the Beheading of His late Majesty," printed in 1649, relates that the night after the execution he returned home to his wife, living in Rosemary-lane, and gave her the money he had received, 30*l.*; that about three days before he died, he lay speechless. " For the burial whereof, great *store of wines were sent by the sheriff of the city of London*, and a great multitude of people stood wayting to see his corpse carried to the churchyard, some crying out, ' Hang him, rogue!' ' Bury him in the dunghill!' others pressing upon him, saying they would quarter him for executing the King, insomuch that the churchwardens and masters of the parish were fain to come for the suppression of them; and with great difficulty he was at last carried to Whitechapel churchyard." See Ellis's *Letters on English History*, vol. iii. second series; and the *Trials of Charles I.* vol. xxxi. *Family Library*.

St. Mary's, Newington-Butts, was built in 1791-3 by Hurlbatt, in place of a smaller church. It contains a monument with statues to Sir Hugh Brawne, buried in the old church, 1614, and who "for the space of twenty-two years was the whole ornament of the parish." Here, too, is a tablet to Dr. Fothergill; and to Captain M. Waghorn, one of the few persons who escaped from the sinking of the *Royal George*, in 1782. The parsonage-house was originally built of wood, and surrounded by a moat, now filled up. In this parish was a small water-course called the river Tigris, part of Cnut's trench; and a parishioner who died at the age of 109 years, early in the present century, remembered when boats came up as far as the church at Newington.

In the church is buried Mr. Sergeant Davy (d. 1780). He was originally a chemist at Exeter: and a sheriff's officer coming to serve on him a process from the Court of Common Pleas, he civilly asked him to drink; while the man was drinking, Davy contrived to heat a poker, and then told the bailiff that if he did not eat the writ, which was of sheepskin and as good as mutton, he should swallow the poker! The man preferred the parchment; but the Court of Common Pleas, not then accustomed to Mr. Davy's jokes, sent for him to Westminster Hall, and for contempt of their process, committed him to the Fleet Prison. From this circumstance, and some unfortunate man whom he met there, he acquired a taste for the law; and on his discharge he applied himself to the study of it in earnest, was called to the bar, made a sergeant, and was for a long time in good practice.—See Manning and Bray's *History of Surrey*.

St. Mary's, Paddington, on the Green, was rebuilt in 1788-91; and its churchyards are remarkable as the burial-place of several eminent artists; among whom are, Bushnell, the sculptor of the statues on Temple Bar; Barrett, the landscape-painter; Banks and Nollekens, the sculptors; Vivares, Hall, and Schiavonetti, the engravers: Caleb Whitefoord (see Goldsmith's *Retaliation*); Mrs. Siddons, the great actress (d. 1831); Collins, the painter; and others. Hogarth was married in this church to the daughter of Sir James Thornhill, March 23, 1729.

St. Mary's, Rotherhithe, close to the shaft of the Thames Tunnel, was rebuilt in 1736-39, upon the site of the old church, which had stood above 400 years. This new church has a lofty spire: in the vestry-room is a portrait of the royal martyr, King Charles I., in his robes, kneeling at an altar, and holding a crown of thorns, the composition resembling the frontispiece to the *Eikon Basilike*. In the churchyard is buried Prince Le Boo, a native of the Pellew Islands, d. Dec. 29, 1784, æt. 20 ; over his remains a monument has been erected by the East India Company, in testimony of his father's humane and kind treatment of the crew of the *Antelope*, wrecked off Goo-roo-raa, one of the Pellew Islands, on the night of August 9, 1783.

St. Mary-le-Savoy, a Perpendicular chapel, in the rear of the south side of the Strand, and west of Wellington-street, is all that remains of the Hospital of St. John Baptist, built by Henry VII. upon the site of the palace of Peter-le-Savoy, burnt by the Kentish rebels in 1381, when John of Gaunt was its proprietor. The other relics of the Hospital were cleared away on the building of Waterloo Bridge. The chapel was originally dedicated to the Saviour, the Virgin, and St. John the Baptist : but when the old church of St. Mary-le-Strand was destroyed by the Protector Somerset, the parishioners united themselves to those of the precinct of the Savoy ; and the chapel, being used as their church, acquired the name of St. Mary-le-Savoy. It was built in 1505, of squared stone and boulders, has a low bell-tower and large Tudor windows. The interior has a remarkably fine ceiling, with carved figures of the Holy Lamb, and emblems of the Plantagenets down to the last of the Tudors ; restored and emblazoned, in 1843, by Willement, who also reglazed the altar-window with the figure of St. John the Baptist. The altar-screen, said to have been designed by Sir Reginald Bray, has also been restored by Sydney Smirke. The chapel was endowed by Henry VII. ; and the incumbent, to this day, receives an annual fee by royal warrant. The edifice was last repaired at the expense of Queen Victoria, in 1843. Several persons of historic note are buried here, and have figure monuments ; here lies Gawin Douglas, who translated Virgil (d. 1522) ; George Wither, the poet (d. 1667) ; and D. Cameron, the last person who suffered for the Rebellion of 1745, to whom was erected a marble relief tablet, by his great grandson, in 1846, "one hundred years after the Battle of Culloden." The Savoy was the scene of the last attempt made by the State and the authorities of the Church to reconcile the Church and the Dissenters ; the Savoy Conference finally settled the Book of Common Prayer ; and here was written the preface to the Liturgy, which, it is stated, was first publicly read in this chapel. Here many of the Bishops were consecrated ; and among them, Wilson, Bishop of Sodor and Man, by Archbishop Sharpe, in 1698. A considerable part of the Hospital was burnt in the reign of Charles II. ; after which, and until the removal of the buildings, the Savoy was principally occupied as barracks for soldiers, and a prison for deserters. Where the middle Savoy gate was, is now Savoy-street, with the German Lutheran Church, of brick, and modern date, on the west side. The approach to Waterloo Bridge from the Strand, or Wellington-street and Lancaster-place, covers the entire site of the old Duchy-lane and great part of the Hospital.

St. Mary's, Somerset, (Summer's hith, or wharf,) was destroyed in the Great Fire of 1666, and rebuilt by Wren in 1695 : it has a tower, with pedestals and urns and obelisks upon the summit, 120 feet high ; and the keystones of the arches are sculptured with grotesque heads.

St. Mary's, Stoke Newington, (2½ miles north from London,) in the patronage of the Prebendary of Newington, in St. Paul's Cathedral, was repaired, or "rather new builded" (*Stow*), in 1563, of hewn stones, flint, and pebbles, but has been much modernised. It has a square embattled tower, about 60 feet high, with six bells, with an additional bell in a wooden cupola, and a clock made 1723. The chapel, and a portion of the body of the church, under two other roofs, formed the whole of the ancient structure. The painted altar-window represents the Virgin Mary and the Purification, the Birth and Preaching of St. John the Baptist, and the arms of Queen Elizabeth; and in the chancel windows are the arms of the Drapers' Company and the City of London. Among the communion plate is a large silver offertory alms-dish. In the chancel is an elegant coloured alabaster monument to John Dudley, Esq., and his widow, afterwards married to Thomas Sutton, Esq., founder of the Charterhouse: the writer of the long Latin inscription was rewarded with 10s., according to the roll of Mr. Dudley's funeral expenses: and the tomb was restored in 1808 by subscription of grateful Carthusians. Behind the church is Queen Elizabeth's Walk, a grove of tall trees; and at Newington-green is King Harry's Walk. At Stoke Newington lived many years Mrs. Barbauld, the amiable educationist, who taught Lord Denman when a boy the art of declamation; and Mr. Barbauld was for four years morning preacher to an Unitarian congregation at Newington-green.

St. Mary-le-Strand, nearly upon the site of the old Maypole, was the first built (1714-17) of Queen Anne's Fifty Churches, but is to this day called "the New Church." It was not consecrated till Jan. 1, 1723. Gibbs, the architect, was desired by the Commissioners "to beautify it," on account of its public situation: hence it is overloaded with ornament. It was originally to have had only a small bell-tower at the west end, changed to a steeple, which therefore appears to stand on the roof; it consists of three receding stories, surmounted by a vane: when it was last repaired, at an expense of 47l. 10s., the scaffolding cost 30l. The exterior of the body is of two stories, Ionic below, the lower wall " solid, to keep out noises from the street;" and Composite above, surmounted by a balustrade and urns:* the west end has a semicircular Ionic portico, and occupies the Maypole site. The interior is grand, but too florid, with Corinthian and Composite pilasters, ceiling crowded with ornaments, and the semicircular altar-part, with the triangular symbol of the Trinity glorified, and cherubim, &c. The windows are hung with crimson drapery, and in the side intercolumniations are paintings of the Annunciation and the Passion, by Brown. The old church was " next beyond Arundell House, on the street side," and was " called of the Nativitie of our Lady (St. Mary), and the Innocents of the *Strand*." (*Stow.*) Seymour states, that its site became part of the garden of Somerset House, and that when the Protector pulled down this old church, he promised to build a new one for the parishioners, but death prevented his fulfilling that engagement.

St. Mary's, Windham-place, Marylebone, was designed by Sir Robert Smirke, R.A., and consecrated Jan. 7, 1824, when the Rev. T. Frognall Dibdin, D.D., was instituted rector. This church has a large painted east window, of the Ascension, said to have cost 250 guineas. The circular tower and cupola, 135 feet high, are picturesque.

St. Mary's Woolnoth, one of the most striking and original churches in the metropolis, is between the western ends of Lombard-street and King-William-street. This has been the site of a Christian church from a very early period, and previously of a pagan temple. The church was rebuilt early in the fifteenth century, much injured by the Great Fire of 1666, and repaired by Wren in 1677; to this Alderman Sir R. Viner, living in Lombard-street, contributed liberally, to

* During the procession to proclaim Peace, in 1802, one of these urns was accidentally pushed down on the crowd below, when three persons were killed, and several others much hurt.

:ommemorate which, says Stow, " a number of *vines* were spread over hat part of the church which faced his house." In 1716, the church, is we now see it, was rebuilt by Hawksmoor: the west front, which ias an elongated tower, like two towers united, has no prototype in England; but its details are so heavy as to indicate rather a fortress ind prison than a church. The interior, on the model of a Roman trium, is nearly square: it has twelve Corinthian columns, admirably arranged, and is profusely ornamented with panels and carved nouldings. It contains an organ built by "Father Smith, in 1681." Iere is a tablet to the Rev. John Newton (d. 1807), the friend of Cow-er, and rector of this church for twenty-eight years: it bears this iscription, written by himself:

"John Newton, clerk, once an infidel and libertine, a servant of slaves in .frica, was, by the rich mercy of our Lord and Saviour Jesus Christ, preserved, :stored, pardoned, and appointed to preach the faith he had long laboured to estroy."*

:he origin of Woolnoth is uncertain; but is attributed to the beam for reighing wool, which stood in the churchyard of St. Mary's Woolchurch, i the Stocks Market, on the site of the Mansion-house: this church was urnt in 1666, and the parish is now united to St. Mary's Woolnoth.

St. Matthew's, Bethnal Green, built in 1740, has at the west end low square tower, with a large stone vase at each angle. A second hurch, *St. John's*, was built by the late Sir John Soane, and much isembles his Grecian Church of the Holy Trinity, Regent's Park. In 839, there were only these two churches for a population of 80,000, nd schools for about 1000 children. There have since been built in the arish ten churches: St. Matthew's, St. John's, St. Peter's, St. An-rew's, St. Philip's, St. James the Less, St. James the Great, St. Bar-1olomew's, St. Jude's; and St. Simon Zelotes, the latter at the sole ex-ense of Mr. W. Cotton: whilst the number of children now educated in :hools in connexion with these churches exceeds 6000.

St. Matthew's, Brixton, at the junction of the Tulse-hill and Brix-)n-hill roads, is of Grecian-Doric design, by Porden, and was conse-rated in 1824: it has a noble portico, resembling the proanos of a Irecian temple; at the east end is a tower surmounted with an ctagonal temple, from that of Cyrrhestes, at Athens. In the church-ard is a costly mausoleum of Grecian design, upwards of 25 feet high.

St. Matthew's, Oakley-crescent, City Road, built by Scott, in 348, in the Early English style, has an ornamented four-storied tower nd spire, eastern lancet windows, and other meritorious details.

St. Michael's, Bassishaw (haugh, or hall, of the Basing family), asinghall-street, was originally founded about 1140, and rebuilt in !460; here was interred Sir John Gresham, uncle to Sir Thomas Gres-

* "I remember, when a lad of about fifteen, being taken by my uncle to hear he well-known Mr. Newton (the friend of Cowper the poet) preach his wife's ιneral sermon in the church of St. Mary's Woolnoth, in Lombard-street. Newton ras then well stricken in years, with a tremulous voice, and in the costume of he full-bottomed wig of the day. He had, and always had, the entire possession f the ear of his congregation. He spoke at first feebly and leisurely, but as he rarmed, his ideas and his periods seemed mutually to enlarge: the tears trickled own his cheeks, and his action and expression were at times quite out of the rdinary course of things. It was as the 'mens *agitans* molem et magno se cor-ιore miscens.' In fact, the preacher was *one* with his *discourse*. To this day have not forgotten his text, Hab. iii. 17-18: 'Although the fig-tree shall not lossom, neither shall fruit be in the vines; the labour of the olive shall fail, and he fields shall yield no meat; the flock shall be cut off from the fold, and there hall be no herd in the stalls; yet I will rejoice in the Lord, I will joy in the God f my salvation.' Newton always preached extemporaneous."—Dibdin's *Remi-iscences of a Literary Life*, vol. i. p. 162.

ham, and Lord Mayor in 1547 : at his funeral, on a fast-day, a fish dinner was provided for all comers :

"He was buried with a standard and penon of arms, and a coat of armour of damask (Damascus steel), and four penons of arms; besides a helmet, a target, and a sword, mantles and the crest, a goodly hearse of wax, ten dozen of pensils, and twelve dozen of escutcheons. He had four dozen of great staff torches, and a dozen of great long torches. The church and street were all hung with black, and arms in great store ; and on the morrow three goodly masses were sung." *Stow.*

The old church was destroyed in the Great Fire of 1666, and rebuilt by Wren in 1676-79. It contains a beautifully sculptured monument to Dr. T. Wharton, who did so much to stay the Great Plague of 1665; and here rests Alderman Kirkman, Sheriff elect in 1780, when he died, at the age of 39, of a cold taken in aiding to suppress the Riots.

St. MICHAEL's, in Chester-square, Pimlico, is a picturesque church in the Decorated style of the fourteenth century, and has a tower and spire rising from the ground at the west end, 150 feet high. (Cundy, architect, 1844.) The details are very characteristic.

St. MICHAEL's, Cornhill, was destroyed by the Great Fire of 1666, except the great tower, which contained a celebrated set of ten bells: the body was first rebuilt by Wren, and fifty years later the tower itself, which is an imitation of the splendid chapel tower of Magdalen College, Oxford, built in the fifteenth century, and 145 feet high ; but St. Michael's is only 130 : it has a set of twelve bells. The site is presumed to have been occupied by a church since the Saxon dynasty : it had a cloister and pulpit-cross ; and here rested the remains of Fabyan the Chronicler, Alderman of London, and Sheriff in 1493.

St. MICHAEL's, Paternoster Royal, Thames-street, is partly named from its neighbourhood to the Tower Royal, wherein our sovereigns, as early as King Stephen, resided. The church was rebuilt by the munificent Whittington, who was himself buried in it, under a marble tomb with banners, but his remains were twice disturbed : once by an incumbent, in the reign of Henry VI., who fancied that money was buried with him ; and next by the parishioners, in the reign of Mary, to rewrap the body in lead, of which it had been despoiled on the former occasion (Godwin's *Churches of London*). Whittington's church was destroyed by the Great Fire of 1666, but rebuilt by Wren, and has a somewhat picturesque steeple. The interior has a beautiful altar-picture, by Hilton, R.A., of Mary Magdalen anointing the feet of Christ: this fine work was presented by the Directors of the British Institution in 1820. There is no memorial to Whittington in the present church. The rights and profits of the old church he bestowed on a College and Almshouses close by, the site of which is now occupied by the Mercers' Company's School.

St. MICHAEL's, Queenhithe, destroyed in the Great Fire of 1666, was rebuilt by Wren in 1677 : it is chiefly remarkable for its spire, 135 feet high, with a gilt vane in the form of a ship in full sail, the hull of which will contain a bushel of grain,—referring to the former traffic in corn at the Hithe.

St. MICHAEL's, Wood-street, Cheapside, stands at the corner of Huggin-lane, named from a resident there about the time of Edward I., and known as "Hugan in the lane." The old church was destroyed by the Great Fire of 1666, and the present edifice completed in its place by Wren, in 1675 : it is of very unecclesiastical design, but the Wood-street front is well-proportioned Italian. The head of James IV. of Scotland, slain at Flodden Field, Sept. 9, 1513, is said by Stow to have been buried here ; the body was conveyed, after the battle, to London, and thence to the monastery of Sheen, in Surrey, where it was seen by Stow, lapped in lead, but thrown into a waste room. "Some workmen, for their foolish pleasure, hewed off his head, which Launcelot Young, master-glazier to his Majesty, brought to his house in Wood-street, where he kept it for a time; but at length gave it to the sexton, to bury amongst other bones," &c. This statement is contradicted by the Scottish historians; but Weever is positive that Sheen was the place of James's burial.

ST. MILDRED'S, Bread-street, destroyed in the Great Fire of 1666, and rebuilt by Wren, 1677-83, is remarkable for being roofed by a large and highly-enriched cupola; and has a pulpit and sounding-board and altar-piece exquisitely carved in the style of Gibbons.

ST. MILDRED'S, Poultry, was destroyed by the Great Fire of 1666, and rebuilt by Wren; when was united with it the parish of St. Mary's, Colechurch, the church of which stood at the south end of the Old Jewry: its chaplain was "Peter of Colechurch," who in part built old London Bridge. (See p. 54.) St. Mildred's has a tower 75 feet high, surmounted by a gilt ship in full sail. In the former church was buried Thomas Tusser, who wrote the "Points of Husbandrie," and was by turns choir-ister, farmer, and singing-master.

ST. NICHOLAS COLE ABBEY, Fish-street-hill, destroyed by the Great Fire, and rebuilt by Wren in 1677, has a tasteless steeple, 135 feet high, but some fine interior carvings; the parish Register Books contain a list of persons, with their ages, whom King James II. at his coronation touched for the cure of the "Evil."

ST. OLAVE'S, Hart-street, at the corner of Seething-lane, Crutched Friars, escaped the Great Fire of 1666; and has an interesting inte-rior, with clustered columns and pointed arches and windows, and the ceilings of the aisles powdered with stars. This church is often mentioned in the Diary of Samuel Pepys, Secretary to the Navy (temp. Charles II. and James II.), who lived in a house belonging to the Navy Office, in Seething-lane; and resided subsequently in Hart-street: he was buried in St. Olave's at nine at night, "in a vault of his own makeing, by his wife and brother," "by ye Communion Table," June 4, 1703; and there is a monument to his wife in the chancel. There are also several figure tombs and brasses; and a marble figure of Sir Andrew Riccard (d. 1672), who bequeathed the advowson of the living to the parish. In the churchyard are interred a number of victims to the Great Plague: the first entry in the Register is dated July 24, 1665: "Mary, daughter of William Ramsay, one of the Drapers' Almsmen;" and there is a tradition that the pestilence first appeared in the Drapers' Almshouses, Cooper's-row, in this parish.

ST. OLAVE'S, Jewry, a brick church, rebuilt by Wren, in 1673-76, upon the site of the old church, destroyed in the Great Fire of 1666, is alone remarkable for containing the remains of Alderman Boydell, the eminent engraver and printseller, who expended a large fortune in founding the English School of Historic Painting: he was Lord Mayor in 1790 (d. 1804); and on the north wall of the church is a tablet to him, surmounted by his bust.

ST. OLAVE'S, Tooley-street, Southwark, in Bridge Ward Without, was rebuilt in 1737-39, by Flitcroft, a pupil of Kent; the funds being mostly advanced by a French emigrant, on an annuity for his life; and he dying soon after, it became a saying that the organ had cost more than the church: it had a richly-decorated interior, and a fine peal of bells. The whole was burnt almost to the walls on August 19, 1843; when also was destroyed Watson's Telegraphic Tower, originally a shot-factory. St. Olave's Church has since been handsomely restored. The former church was of the fourteenth century, and is shewn in the Sutherland View, 1543, with a low square tower and bell-house. The first church was certainly founded prior to the Norman Conquest, from its dedication to St. Olave, or Olaff, King of Norway, who, with Ethelred, in 1008, destroyed old London Bridge, then occupied by the Danes. (*See* BRIDGES, p. 54.) The present church is nearly on the site of this exploit; for the first bridge was somewhat eastward of the old bridge, taken down after the building of the present bridge. St. Olave has been corrupted to St. Oley and Tooley street.

ST. PANCRAS-IN-THE-FIELDS, one of the oldest churches in Middlesex, is situated on the north side of the road leading from King's Cross to Kentish Town. It consisted, before its enlargement in 1848, of a nave and chancel, with a low tower at the west end, built late in the twelfth century. Norden, in his *Speculum Britanniæ*, describes it, in 1593, as standing "all alone, utterly forsaken, old and wether-beten;" "yet about this structure have bin manie buildings, now decaied, leaving poore Pancras without companie or comfort." Norden adds:

"Although this place be, as it were, forsaken of all, and true men seldom frequent the same but upon devyne occasions; yet it is visited by thieves, who assemble there not to pray, but to wait for praye; and manie fall into their handes, clothed, that are glad when they are escaped naked. Walk not there late."

The church and churchyard have long been noted as the burial-place of Roman Catholics, "who," Strype says, have of late "affected to be buried here;" and many of the tombs bear the customary cross and R. I. P. (*Requiescat in pace*). Among other reasons assigned for this preference was, that the church was the last where bell tolled in England for Mass, and in which any rites of the Roman Catholic religion were celebrated after the Reformation; but the choice is believed to be a mere prejudice. The church, reconstructed and enlarged by A. D. Gough, was re-opened July 5, 1848: the style adopted is Anglo-Norman: the edifice has been lengthened westward; the old tower has been removed, and a new one built on the south side; and the west end has an enriched Norman porch, and a wheel-window in the gable above. In the progress of the works were found Roman bricks, a small altar-stone, Early Norman capitals, an Early English piscina, and Tudor brickwork. The chancel windows are filled with stained glass, by Gibbs, as is also the western wheel-window. The several old monuments have been restored, and refixed as nearly as possible in their original positions. On the north wall, opposite the baptistery, is the early Tudor marble Purbeck memorial, supposed to have belonged to the Gray family, of Gray's Inn; the recesses for brasses removed, and neither date nor arms remaining. On the south-east interior wall is the marble tablet, with palette and pencils, to Samuel Cooper, the celebrated miniature-painter (d. 1672); over the vestry are three small brasses to the daughter of A. Glover, of Tottenham Court (d. 1588): on the south side of the nave is a monument with busts to William Platt (d. 1637), and his wife, removed from the old chapel at Highgate, in 1833. The church is mostly floored with black and white marble tombs, of considerable age, and in good preservation. The ancient communion-plate, date 1638, discovered in 1848, is now again in use. In the churchyard are headstones to William Woollett, the engraver (d. 1785), and John Walker, the dictionary compiler (d. 1807); and an altar-tomb to William Godwin, the novelist (d. 1836), and his two wives. The register records the burials of Abraham Woodhead (d. 1678), and Obadiah Walker (d. 1699), both of whom were said to have written the *Whole Duty of Man*, and who both became Papists; Lady Slingsby, an actress in Dryden and Lee's plays, from 1681 to 1689; Jeremy Collier (d. 1726), who battled with Congreve and Vanbrugh, and improved the decency of the stage; Ned Ward, the "London Spy" (d. 1731); Leoni, the architect (d. 1746); Lady Henrietta, wife of Beard, the singer (d. 1753); Mazzinghi, leader of the band at Marylebone Gardens; Arthur O'Leary, the Franciscan Friar (d. 1802); Paoli, the Corsican (d. 1807); the Chevalier d'Eon (d. 1810); Packer, the comedian (d. 1806), said to have performed 4852 times; and Scheemakers, the sculptor (d. 1808). Pancras was corrupted to "Pancredge" in Queen Elizabeth's reign.

St. Pancras, near Euston-square, New-road, was built by Messrs. Inwood; the first stone being laid by the Duke of York, July 1, 1819. The cella, or body of the church, is designed from the Erectheum, dedicated to Minerva Polias and Pandrosus, at Athens; and the steeple, 168 feet high, is from the Athenian Tower of the Winds, with a cross, in lieu of the Triton and wand, symbols of the wind, in the original. The clock-dials are but $6\frac{1}{2}$ feet in diameter, though at the height of 100 feet, and therefore are much too small. The western front of the church has a fine portico of six columns, with richly-sculptured voluted capitals; beneath are three enriched doorways, designed exactly from those of the Erectheum, and exquisite in detail. Towards the east end are lateral porticoes, each supported by colossal statues of females,[*] on a plinth, in which are entrances to the catacombs beneath the church, to contain 2000 coffins: each of the figures bears an ewer in one hand, and rests the other on an inverted torch, the emblem of death: these figures are of terra-cotta (artificial stone), formed in pieces, and cemented round cast-iron pillars, which in reality support the enablatures. The eastern front varies from the ancient Temple in having a semicircular termination, round which, and along the side walls, are terra-cotta imitations of Greek tiles. The interior is designed in conformity with the general plan of ancient temples. The pulpit and reading-desk are made from the trunk of "the Fairlop Oak," in Hainhault Forest, blown down in 1820. The cost of this classic edifice, much too close a resemblance to a Pagan temple to be appropriate for a Christian church, was 76,679l.

St. Paul's, Camden New Town, St. Pancras, was built in 1848-9 (Ordish and Johnson, architects): it is majestically situated, and consists of a nave and aisles, with transepts and chancel, and a tower and spire at the west end, 156 feet high; the windows are Decorated, the roofs have crosses and crestings, and the arrangement is very picturesque: this large church, for 1200 persons, cost less than 9000l.

St. Paul's, Covent Garden, was commenced for the ground landlord, Francis Earl of Bedford, by Inigo Jones, in 1631, but not finished till 1638; this being the last of that great architect's works. The Earl's commission is stated to have been for a chapel "not much better than a barn;" when Jones replied, "Well, then, you shall have the handsomest barn in England." The truth of this anecdote has been questioned; for the fabric cost 4500l., a large sum for those days. It was built of brick, with a portico at the east front, consisting of a pediment supported by four Tuscan columns of stone, and the roof was covered with tiles: Hollar's print of it shews a small bell-turret surmounted with a cross. Within the pediment was placed a pendulum clock, made by Richard Harris in 1641, and stated by an inscription

---

* These figures are ill-executed, as may be seen by reference to the original Caryatides from the Pandrosion, in the Elgin Collection in the British Museum. The St. Pancras figures, and other artificial stone details for the church, were executed by Rossi, from Messrs. Inwood's designs, and cost 5400l.

in the vestry to be the first made.* The ceiling of the interior was beautifully painted by E. Pierce, senior, a pupil of Van Dyck. Inigo Jones was present at the consecration by Bishop Juxon, Sept. 27, 1638. The church was repaired by Lord Burlington in 1727: in 1788, the walls were cased with Portland stone; and the rustic gateways at the east front, which Jones had imitated in brick and plaster from Palladio, were then rebuilt with stone. In 1795, the church was burnt to the walls by an accidental fire, but was restored by the elder Hardwick. The altar-piece has two figures of angels, sculptured by Banks, R.A. Among the eminent persons interred here are Samuel Butler (d. 1680), author of *Hudibras*, whose friends could not afford to bury him in Westminster Abbey; Sir Peter Lely (d. 1680), the painter, to whom there was a monument, with a bust by Gibbons, destroyed with the old church; Edward Kynaston (d. 1712), the famed actor of female parts, who played Juliet to Betterton's Romeo; William Wycherley (d. 1715), the witty dramatist, who had " a true nobleman's look;" Susannah Cent-livre (d. 1723), who wrote the *Wonder*; Grinling Gibbons (d. 1721), the sculptor and wood-carver; Dr. John Armstrong (d. 1779), known by his didactic poem, *The Art of Preserving Health*; and Charles Macklin, the actor (d. 1797), at the age of 107: the two last in a vault under the communion-table. Strype mentions Marmaduke Conwey, Esq., buried here 1717, at the age of 108 years and some months: he was in the service of the royal family from the reign of King James I. to his dying day, and was much liked by Charles I. for his skill in hawk-ing. In the churchyard lies Sir Robert Strange, the engraver (d. 1792), who published his own prints at " the Golden Head," in Henrietta-street. Holland and Edwin, and many players of minor note, are also buried in the churchyard. The portico and overhanging roof of the church are picturesque in effect; and the whole building is impressive from its vastness, and agreeable from the simple rusticity of the order.

ST. PAUL'S CHURCH FOR SEAMEN OF THE PORT OF LONDON, near the London and St. Katherine's Docks, the Sailor's Home, and the Seamen's Asylum, was founded by Prince Albert, May 11, 1846, and consecrated July 10, 1847 (H. Roberts, architect). The style is Early English, with a western tower and spire 100 feet high. " In the course of a year it is computed that about 7000 seamen come to this church: a field of usefulness that can scarcely be over-rated " (Low's *Charities of London*, p. 390). St. Paul's has superseded the Episcopal Floating Church, originally the *Brazen* sloop-of-war: she was moored in the Pool, and fitted with a small organ; and boats were provided on Sun-days at the Tower-stairs for the free passage of sailors to attend the ship service, which was under the direct superintendence of the Bishop of London.

ST. PAUL'S, Shadwell, named from its being in the patronage of the Dean and Chapter of St. Paul's, was originally built in 1656; but re-built, as we now see it, in 1820-1; by Walters, who died in the latter year: it has a beautiful spire, and is throughout a very meritorious design. The parish, formerly a hamlet of Stepney, was called Chadwelle, it is

* Cunningham's *Handbook*, 2d edit. p. 386. If this inscription be correct, it negatives the claim of Huyghens to having first applied the pendulum to the clock, about 1657; although Justus Bergen, mechanician to the Emperor Ro-dolphus, who reigned from 1576 to 1612, is said to have attached one to a clock used by Tycho Brahe. Inigo Jones, the architect of St. Paul's, having been in Italy during the time of Galileo, it is probable that he communicated what he heard of the pendulum to Harris. Huyghens, however, violently contested for the priority; while others claimed it for the younger Galileo, who, they asserted, had, at his father's suggestion, applied the pendulum to a clock in Venice which was finished in 1649.—Adam Thomson's *Time and Timekeepers*, pp. 67, 68.

supposed, from a spring dedicated to St. Chad, within the church-yard.

ST. PAUL'S, Wilton-place, Knightsbridge, designed by Cundy, was consecrated by the Bishop of London, May 30, 1843. It has an Early Perpendicular and eight-pinnacled tower, 121 feet high. Within is a magnificent organ in a richly-canopied case, and the choral service is efficiently performed; the silver-gilt communion plate is very massive; the altar appointments are truly Anglican; and the font is cleverly sculptured with Scripture scenes. The cost of this church was 11,000*l.*, exclusive of fittings. The Rev. W. J. E. Bennett, M.A., of Christ Church, Oxford, appointed to the incumbency in 1843, resigned in 1850.

ST. PETER'S, Cornhill, was rebuilt of brick by Wren, after the Great Fire of 1666: it has a tower and spire 140 feet high, surmounted by an enormous key, the emblem of St. Peter. Here is a tablet recording the death by fire, Jan. 18, 1782, of the seven children of James and Mary Woodmason, of Leadenhall-street. An inscription upon a brass plate in the vestry-room describes the old church as founded A.D. 179,—a statement unsupported by facts. Stow records a murderer to have fled to St. Peter's for sanctuary in 1230; and one of its priests was murdered in 1243. The nave and chancel are separated by a carved wainscot rood-screen, set up by direction of Bishop Beveridge, who was 32 years rector of St. Peter's, and who paid special attention to the appropriateness of church furniture and repairs.

ST. PETER'S, Eaton-square, Pimlico, an Ionic church, was designed by Henry Hakewill, and consecrated by Bishop Howley, July 20, 1827. The altar-piece is "Christ crowned with thorns," painted by W. Hilton, R.A., and presented to the church by the British Institution.

ST. PETER'S, Saffron-hill, a district church of St. Andrew's, Holborn, designed by Barry, R.A., in the Anglo-Norman style, and consecrated in 1832: it has been placed in a proverbially depraved locality, with the most salutary effect.

ST. PETER'S, Sumner-street, Bankside, designed by Edmunds, and consecrated Nov. 7, 1839, is in the plain Pointed style, and has an embattled tower 84 feet high.

ST. PETER'S-LE-POOR, Old Broad-street, was taken down in 1788, rebuilt by Jesse Gibson, and consecrated by Bishop Porteus in 1792. The church is traceable to 1181: it was "sometime peradventure a poor parish" (*Stow*), but scarcely now contains one pauper.

ST. PETER'S AD VINCULA, the chapel of the Tower, situate north-west of the White Tower, was erected *temp.* Edward I., though there was a chapel within the walls, dedicated to the same saint, at a much earlier date. The present chapel is built of squared stones and flints, and has a small bell-tower. The interior consists of a chancel, nave, and north aisle, the two latter separated by flat-pointed arches springing from clustered columns; but little of the original building remains. This chapel is extremely interesting, as the burial-place of these eminent persons, executed within the Tower walls or upon Tower-hill: Queen Anne Boleyn (beheaded 1536); Queen Katherine Howard (beheaded 1542); Sir Thomas More (beheaded 1535); Thomas Cromwell, Earl of Essex (beheaded 1540); Margaret Countess of Shrewsbury (beheaded 1541); Thomas Lord Seymour, Lord Admiral, beheaded 1549, by warrant of his own brother, the Protector Somerset, who in 1552 was executed on the same scaffold; John Dudley, Duke of Northumberland (beheaded 1553).

"There lyeth before the High Altar, in St. Peter's Church, two Dukes between two Queenes, to wit, the Duke of Somerset and the Duke of Northumberland between Queen Anne and Queen Katherine, all four beheaded."—*Stow (Howes's)*.

Lady Jane Grey and her husband, Lord Dudley (beheaded 1553-4); Robert Devereux, Earl of Essex (beheaded 1600): under the communion-table lies the Duke of Monmouth (beheaded 1685); and beneath the gallery, Lords Kilmarnock and Balmerino (beheaded 1746); and Simon Lord Lovat (beheaded 1747). The Register records the burial in this chapel of Sir Thomas Overbury, poisoned in the Tower, 1613: and here lies Sir John Eliot, who died a prisoner in the Tower, his son being refused by King Charles I. permission to remove the body to Cornwall for interment. Also are buried in St. Peter's, John Roettier, "his Majesty's engraver at the Tower" (d. 1703); and Colonel Gurwood, who edited the *Wellington Despatches* (d. 1846). In the north aisle is the altar-tomb, with effigies, of Sir Richard Cholmondeley (Lieutenant of the Tower, *temp.* Henry VII.) and his wife, Lady Elizabeth. In the chancel is a rich marble monument to Sir Richard Blount and his son Sir Michael, Lieutenants of the Tower, sixteenth century; with figures of the knight and his sons in armour, and of his wife and daughters. Here also is the tomb of Sir Allan Apsley, Lieutenant of the Tower (d. 1630); and in the nave-floor is the inscribed gravestone of Talbot Edwards, (d. 1674,) Keeper of the Regalia in the Tower when Blood stole the crown. (*See* TOWER OF LONDON.)

ST PETER'S, Walworth-road, in the parish of St. Mary, Newington, was built 1823-5, and cost about 19,000*l.* It is one of Soane's classic churches; the west front decorated with Ionic columns, and the tower has two stories, the lower Corinthian and the upper Composite. The interior is in elegant and original taste.

ST. SAVIOUR'S, Southwark, a short distance from the south foot of London-bridge, ranks in magnitude and architectural character as the third church in the metropolis, and is one of the few churches in the kingdom possessing a Lady Chapel. It was originally the church of the Augustine Priory of St. Mary Overie, and was founded by the Norman knights, William Pont de l'Arche and William Dauncy. The nave of the church is attributed to Gifford, Bishop of Winchester in 1106 (7th Henry I.); and an arch, an apsis, and other remains of this date, have been uncovered by the removal of the masonry of the church, altered in the reigns of Richard II. and Henry IV. After the Dissolution of the Monasteries, this church was purchased of Henry VIII. by the people of Southwark; and in 1540, it was made parochial as St. Saviour's, and united with the two parishes of St. Mary Magdalen and St. Margaret-at-Hill. The church is cathedral or cruciform in plan, with a nave, transepts, choir, and Lady Chapel, and a lofty embattled tower at the central intersection; besides Mary Magdalen's and the Bishop's Chapels, now removed. An etching, by Hollar, executed for Dugdale's *Monasticon*, shews the church about 1660. The choir and Lady Chapel were commenced in the Lancet style, according to an ancient chronicle: "John anno X° (1208). Seynte Marie Overie was that yere begonne."* In 1618, the fine perspective of nave and choir was destroyed

---

* "A Chronicle of London from 1089 to 1483," first printed in 1827. A romantic tradition is associated with this church. Stow, in the account which he received from Linsted, the last Prior, describes it as "Saint *Mary* ouer the *Rie*, or *Overy*, that is, over the water. This church, or some other in place thereof, was (of old time, long before the Conquest,) an House of Sisters, founded by a mayden named *Mary*, unto the which House and Sisters she left (as was left to her by her parents) the ouersight and profits of a Crosse Ferrie, or trauerse ferrie ouer the Thames, there kept before any bridge was builded." (See LONDON BRIDGE, p. 54.) This story has, however, been much discredited. The shrouded figure now in the north aisle has been gossipingly assigned to Audery,

by an organ-screen, set up in place of the ancient rood-loft. In 1624, the Lady Chapel, which had been let out as a bakehouse for 60 years, was restored; and in 1689, the tower was repaired, and the pinnacles were rebuilt: height 150 feet. From the roof Hollar drew his celebrated View of London, lately rendered familiar by Martin's pen-and-ink lithograph. For a long interval, the only repairs of the church tended to its disfigurement, by barbarous brick casing and the destruction of beautiful windows; until, in 1818, the repair of the entire edifice was commenced with the tower. The pinnacles and embattled parapets were rebuilt, windows inserted, and the tower, split by the violent vibration of the bells, was secured with cast-iron ties concealed within the masonry. This restoration was superintended by George Gwilt, F.S.A., who also, in 1822-24, took down the east end of the church to the clerestory, and gave the present face to the structure—his own design—consisting of an enriched gable, with an elaborately foliated cross in its apex; pinnacled staircase turrets, with niches at the angles; and a new triple lancet window, in the more florid style of the 13th century, instead of the original window of five lights (temp. Henry VII.); and a Catherine-wheel window, of extraordinary richness and beauty. Over the vaulting a cast-iron roof was erected, and covered with copper; and the piers of the flying buttresses on each side were cased with stone, the aisle windows built anew, &c.; in all which Mr. Gwilt has rigidly adhered to the former work, "not only in the general design, but in the minutest details, wherever prototypes could be found." In 1829-30, the transepts were restored from the designs of R. Wallace, architect: groined roofs were added; and in the south was introduced a circular window, designed from that in the ruins of Winchester Palace, Bankside, discovered through a fire in 1814. In the north transept has been inserted a window of circular tracery, in the style of Westminster Abbey; but the side windows, originally of beautiful length, have been injudiciously shortened. Within, the transepts present a beautiful vista, second only to the choir. The four magnificent arches which support the tower remain unaltered. The timber roof of the nave, a fine specimen of carpentry, said to have been put up by Bishop Fox (temp. Edward IV.), was next removed "by Order of Vestry," and the organ was moved up to form a temporary end to the choir. Thus dismantled, in splendid ruin, stood the roofless walls, and the massive Tudor doorway at the west end, until, in 1838-9, the nave was rebuilt for Divine Service in poor, incongruous style; and being separated from the choir, St. Saviour's now presents the anomalous appearance of two churches in one; but had the nave been restored according to the ancient example, the groined roof of the church would exhibit an uninterrupted perspective of 208 feet. The most picturesque views are from the clerestory vaultings of the choir. The commonplace oak and plaster of the last century have been removed from the eastern end, thus unveiling the stone altar-screen, a beautiful composition of niches, &c.; and which, from its resembling that in Winchester Cathedral, and bearing Bishop Fox's device of the Pelican feeding her young, is inferred to be his workmanship: it was restored in 1833, at the cost of 700l.

---

the Ferryman, father of the foundress of St. Mary Overie's. There is a curious, although probably fabulous tract of his life, entitled, "The True History of the Life and sudden Death of old John Overs, the rich Ferry-Man of London, shewing how he lost his life by his own covetousness. And of his daughter Mary, who caused the church of St. Mary Overs in Southwark to be built; and of the building of London Bridge." There are two editions: the first, 1637, with woodcuts; the second, 1744, "Printed for T. Harris at the Looking-Glass on London Bridge." It is among Sir W. Musgrave's Biographical Tracts in the British Museum. A synopsis of the story is given in the *Chronicles of London Bridge*, pp. 40-44.

"In the fifteenth century, sculpture and painting lent their aid to complete and embellish this sumptuous display of architecture. Upon the altar and under the central canopy, in the first range, stood the crucifix; the large niche above was appropriated to the statue of the Blessed Virgin, the patroness of the church; and the corresponding niche in the upper range we may as confidently assign to the representation of the sacred Trinity; the minor niches might be occupied by the sainted bishops of the see. Above the whole, the design was carried on in the painted glass of the east window, inclosed as it were in a richly sculptured frame: in this perfect state, what a magnificent scene was displayed in the choir!"—*E. J. Carlos, Gentleman's Magazine,* Feb. 1834.

The Lady Chapel, which Bishop Gardiner used as a consistorial court in the reign of Queen Mary, was restored by subscription in 1832: the groined roof is very fine, and here is the marble tomb of Lancelot Andrewes, Bishop of Winchester, with his full-length effigies, formerly in the Bishop's Chapel, where also his leaden coffin was found. In 1555, a commission sat in St. Mary Overie's for the trial of heretics, Bishop Hooper and John Rogers being the first victims to the stake; but within four years, the Popish vestments were sold for the repairs of the church, and next the valuable Latin records of the Priory were burnt as superstitious remains of Popery. The church is very rich in painted sculpture tombs. In the south transept is the Perpendicular monument of the poet Gower, removed from the north aisle of the nave in 1832, when it was restored and coloured at the expense of Lord Francis Leveson Gower, now Duke of Sutherland, a presumed collateral descendant from the poet. Gower was married in this church, in 1397, to Alice Groundolf, by the celebrated William of Wykeham, then Bishop of Winchester, and here Gower and his wife are buried; the poet beneath the above monument, triple canopied, and richly dight with gold and colour inscription, with the recumbent effigies of Gower in prayer: his hair auburn, and long to the shoulders, and a small forked beard; on his head a purple and gold rose fillet, with the words, "Merci Ihu;" a habit of purple, damasked, down to his feet; a collar of esses, gold, about his neck; his head resting upon three gilded volumes, the "Speculum Meditantis," "Vox Clamantis," and "Confessio Amantis;" on the wall at his feet are his arms, and a hat or helmet, with a red hood, ermined, and surmounted by his crest—a dog. Opposite Gower's tomb is the coloured bust of John Bingham, saddler to Queen Elizabeth and James I. In the north transept is a richly-painted, carved, and gilt monument, with angels, rocks, suns, and serpents, to William Austin, Esq. (d. 1833), who wrote a poem of "Meditations." Next lies Dr. Lockyer, the empiric (temp. Charles II.), his reclining effigies in thick-curled wig and furred gown:

> "His virtues and his pills are so well known,
> That envy can't confine them under stone."—*Epitaph.*

In the north aisle is the monument to John Trehearne, gentleman-porter to James I., with the costumed busts of himself and wife. Opposite is the tomb of Alderman Humble (temp. James I.), with kneeling figures of himself and his two wives, and representations of their children; and an inscription, slightly varied from a poem attributed to Francis Quarles, commencing,

> "Like to the damask rose you see."

Here, too, is an oaken effigies, supposed of one of the Norman knights, founders of the church; and near it is the figure of an emaciated man, wrapped in a shroud, and finely sculptured. The Burial Register records, under 1607, "Edmond Shakspeare, player, in the church," the great dramatist's brother, and who, doubtless, was followed to the grave by *him* as chief mourner; under 1625 is "Mr. John Fletcher, a man, in the church" (Beaumont and Fletcher); and Philip Massinger, "a stranger," in the churchyard, 1638-9. The ower has a fine peal of twelve bells, and in the belfry are recorded exploits performed upon them by the College and Cumberland youths see St. Mary-le-Bow Church, p. 142); though these bells were not rung at the opening of London-bridge, in 1831, from the alleged insecurity to the masonry: the entire weight of the twelve bells is 10 tons, 15 cwt. 1 qr. 9 lbs. The clock, put up in 1795, has a dial 31 feet in circumference; length of minute-hand, 5 feet; circumference of bell, 11 feet 6 inches. The tower, east end, and Lady Chapel, originally concealed by the west side of the old High Street, were opened to view in forming the approaches to New London-bridge, thus presenting, perhaps, the finest architectural group in the Metropolis: its restoration has cost upwards of 50,000*l.*

St. Sepulchre's, anciently "in the Bailey," at the east end of Skinner-street, and adjacent to Newgate, was damaged in the Great Fire of 1666, which just reached Pye Corner, northward of the church. It was rebuilt about the middle of the fifteenth century. The south-west entrance-porch, resembling a transept, has a groined roof, with bold ribs and beautifully-sculptured bosses; adjoining is an ancient chapel, erected by the Popham family. The body of the church was re-fitted by Wren after the Fire. The organ, one of the largest and finest in London, was built in 1677, and has been recently enlarged; the pedal organ, with ten stops, or fourteen ranks of pipes throughout, is unqualled in England. The pulpit has a sounding-board, like a parabolic reflector, with ribs of mahogany, the grain radiating from the centre. Among the monuments is that of Capt. John Smith, Governor of Virginia, and a romantic traveller (d. 1631): his eccentric epitaph, recorded by Strype, has disappeared. The benefactions to the parish include that of Mr. Richard Dowe, who left a hand-bell, to be rung, with certain forms, to the condemned criminals in Newgate, and on their way to Tyburn for execution, (see St. Sepulchre's Bell, p. 38,) when it was also customary to present a nosegay to each. St. Sepulchre's tower, "one of the most ancient in the outline in the circuit of London," *Malcolm*,) has four pinnacles with vanes, rebuilt 1630-33, and is 140 feet high: it has a fine peal of ten bells; the clock regulates the hanging of criminals at Newgate. "Unreasonable people," says Howell, "are as hard to reconcile as the vanes of St. Sepulchre's tower, which ever looked all four upon one point of the heavens." On April 10, 600, one William Dorrington threw himself from the roof of this tower, leaving there a written prayer for forgiveness.

St. Stephen's, Coleman-street, was destroyed by the Great Fire of 1666, and rebuilt by Wren, as we now see it, with a tower and bell-turret 65 feet high. Among the monuments is a marble bas-relief, by E. W. Wyon, erected in 1847, to the Rev. Josiah Pratt, Vicar of the parish, whose missionary labours are personified by the Angel of the Gospel addressing an African, Hindoo, and New Zealander. The entrance-gateway from Coleman-street has a very curious sculpture, embodying the Last Judgment. In the old church was buried Master Antony Munday, (d. 1633,) who wrote a continuation of Stow's *Survey*, and for more than forty years arranged the City pageants and shows. Of this parish John Hayward was under-sexton during the Great Plague, when he carried the dead to their graves, and fetched the bodies with the Dead Cart and Bell, yet "never had the distemper at all, but lived about twenty years after it."—Defoe's *Memoirs*.

St. Stephen's the Martyr, Avenue Road, Portland Town, is a large decorated church, by Daukes, with a tower and spire 136 feet high; towards building which two individuals gave 1000*l.* each; the freehold of the site and 500*l.* being also given by the Duke of Portland.

St. Stephen's the Martyr, Rochester-row, Westminster, a stately church, built and endowed at the sole cost of Miss Burdett Coutts, as a memorial to her father, Sir Francis Burdett, Bart., M.P. for Westminster thirty years. The site was presented by the Dean and Chapter of Westminster, and is nearly opposite the almshouses founded by Emery Hill in 1674. The first stone of the church was laid by Miss Coutts, July 20, 1847; it was consecrated June 20, 1850. The style is the Decorated, of the reigns of the first three Edwards; and the architect, Ferrey. The church consists of a nave with aisles, and a chancel; and on the north side a massive tower and spire, 200 feet high, with a peal of eight bells by Mears; all the windows are richly traceried. The chancel ceiling is coloured blue, powdered with gold stars; the walls are decorated with texts; and the reredos is of the Canterbury diaper, picked out in gold and colour: the altar-cloth was presented by the Duke of Wellington, and the chancel carpet was wrought in Berlin work by forty ladies of rank, the border by the girls of St. Stephen's Schools: the design consists of shields and heraldic devices, and panels of the fleur-de-lis and Tudor rose, within a Tudor-rose border. The organ, by Hill, has a screen of diapered pipes, and cost 800 guineas. The nave and aisle roofs are of oak; and the arcade rests upon clustered shafts, with sculptured capitals. The pulpit is of stone, and enriched with tracery; and the font is sculptured with Scripture subjects. Some of the windows are filled with stained glass, by Wailes, and the others with Powell's stamped quarries. The stalls and seats are of oak, and for about 900 persons: the church is lit by gas, and has in the chancel a handsome *corona* of gas-burners and candlesticks. Adjoining are Schools, of very picturesque design, also designed by Ferrey.

St. Stephen's, Walbrook, in the rear of the Mansion House, is the third church of that name and locality: the first, according to Dugdale, stood on the *west* side of the "Brook;" the second, built in 1428, on the *east* side, was destroyed in the Great Fire of 1666; and the present church was built upon the same site, 1672-79, from the designs of Wren, at a salary of 100*l*. a-year: and the parish accounts shew that a hogshead of claret was presented to the architect, and twenty guineas to his lady. The interior is one of Wren's finest works, with its exquisitely-proportioned Corinthian columns, and great central dome of timber and lead, resting upon a circle of light arches springing from column to column; its enriched Composite cornice, the shields of the spandrels, and the palm-branches and rosettes of the dome-coffers, are very beautiful; and as you enter from the dark vestibule, a halo of dazzling light flashes upon the eye through the central aperture of the cupola. The elliptical openings for light in the side walls are, however, very objectionable. The fittings are of oak; and the altar-screen, organ-case, and gallery have some good carvings, among which are prominent the arms of the Grocers' Company, the patrons of the living, and who gave the handsome wainscoting. The enriched pulpit, its festoons of fruit and flowers, and canopied sounding-board, with angels bearing wreaths, are much admired. The church was cleansed and repaired in 1850, when West's splendid painting of the Martyrdom of St. Stephen, presented in 1779 by the then Rector, Dr. Wilson, was removed from over the altar and placed on the north wall of the church; and the window which the picture had blocked up was then re-opened. The oldest monument in the church is that of John Lilburne (d. 1678): Sir John Vanbrugh, the wit and architect, is buried here, in the family vault. During the repairs in 1850, it is stated that 4000 coffins were found beneath the church, and were covered with brickwork and concrete to prevent the escape of noxious effluvia. The exterior of the church is plain; the tower and spire, 128 feet high, is at

ie termination of Charlotte-row. The present Rector is the Rev.
eorge Croly, D.D., the eloquent poet and imaginative prose writer.
This church, unquestionably elegant, has been overpraised. The rich dome is
nsidered by John Carter to be Wren's attempt to "set up a dome, a compara-
ve imitation (though on a diminutive scale) of the Pantheon at Rome, and
hich, no doubt, was a kind of probationary trial previous to his gigantic opera-
on of fixing one on his octangular superstructure in the centre of his new St.
aul's." Mr. J. Gwilt says of St. Stephen's: "Compared with any other church
nearly the same magnitude, Italy cannot exhibit its equal; elsewhere its rival
not to be found. Of those worthy notice, the Zitelle at Venice (by Palladio), is
e nearest approximation in regard to size, but it ranks far below our church in
int of composition, and still lower in point of effect." Again: "Had its mate-
als and volume been as durable and extensive as those of St. Paul's Cathedral,
r Christopher Wren had consummated (in St. Stephen's) a much more efficient
onument to his well-earned fame than that fabric affords."

t. Stephen's serves also for the parish of St. Bennet Sherehog. Upon
ie north side of Pancras-lane is a small enclosed piece of ground, and
pon a stone on an adjoining house is inscribed, "Before the dreadful
re, anno 1666, here stood the parish church St. Bennet Sherehog."

Pendleton, the celebrated Vicar of Bray, known by his multiversations, sub-
quently became rector of St. Stephen's, Walbrook. It is related that in the
ign of Edward VI., Lawrence Sanders, the martyr, an honest but mild and
morous man, stated to Pendleton his fears that he had not strength of mind to
idure the persecution of the times; and was answered by Pendleton that "he
ould see every drop of his fat and the last morsel of his flesh consumed to ashes
e he would swerve from the faith then established." He, however, changed
ith the times, saved his fat and his flesh, and became rector of St. Stephen's,
hilst the mild and diffident Sanders was burnt in Smithfield.

St. Swithin's, London Stone, Cannon-street, was destroyed by
ie Great Fire of 1666, and rebuilt by Wren, in 1680, as we now see it.
; has a tower and spire 150 feet high; but is chiefly remarkable for
aving against its outer south wall, within a modern stone case, all that
:mains of the ancient "London Stone," a Roman *miliarium*.

Temple Church, (*St. Mary's*,) in the rear of the south side of
leet-street, was the church of the Knights Templar after their re-
oval from their chief house, on the site of old Southampton House,
ithout Holborn-bars.* It consists, first, of "the Round," built in
185, and dedicated by Heraclius, Patriarch of Jerusalem. (See in-
ription from the Saxon, inside, over western doorway.) This is one of
ie four circular churches built in England after the Templars' return
om the first and second Crusades; the other three existing at Cam-
ridge, Northampton, and Maplestead in Essex. The architecture is
idway between Romanesque and Early English Gothic: the western
ntrance semicircular arches and capitals are richly sculptured and
eeply recessed; within, Purbeck marble columns, with boldly-sculp-
ired capitals, support a gallery or triforium of interlaced Norman
rches; and the clerestory has six Romanesque windows, one filled with
tained glass, bright ruby ground, with a representation of Christ, and
mblems of the Evangelists; and the ceiling, of Saracenic character,
i coloured. On the gallery well-staircase is a "penitential cell." The
rcade in the aisle beneath has sculptured heads of astonishing variety,
opies executed by Sir R. Smirke in 1827; and here are pointed arches
ith Norman billets. Upon the pavement are figures of Crusaders,

* In the rear of the house No. 322 High Holborn, is a room or hall, for some
inexplained reason, called "the chapel:" it has a finely-panelled oak ceiling,
bout A.D. 1500; a large window opening, and a pointed doorway, now filled up.
i few yards westward may be traced the position of the Round Church of the
emplars, which they possessed previous to the erection of the present Temple
hurch in Fleet-street. Stow relates that adjoining the old Temple Church was
he inn of the Bishop of Lincoln; and afterwards a house belonging to the Earl
f Southampton, to which the room in question appears to pertain.

"in cross-legged effigy devoutly stretched;" but originally placed upon altar-tombs and pedestals.

These effigies of feudal warriors are sculptured out of freestone. The attitudes of all are different, but they are all recumbent with the legs crossed. They are in complete mail with surcoats; one only is bare-headed, and has the cowl of a monk. The shields are of the *heater* or Norman shape, but the size is not the same in all; one of them is very long, and reaches from the shoulder to the middle of the leg. Their heads, with one exception, repose on cushions, and have hoods of mail. Three of them have flattish helmets over the armour, and one has a sort of casque. They have been well restored by Mr. Richardson. The best authorities assign five of them as follow: to Geoffry de Magnaville, Earl of Essex, A.D. 1144 (right arm on his breast and large sword at his right)—he is not mentioned by Weever; William Mareschall, Earl of Pembroke, A.D. 1219, (sculptured in Sussex marble, with his sword through a lion's head); Robert Lord de Ros, A.D. 1245 (head uncovered, with long flowing hair), whose effigy is said to have been brought from Helmsley Church, Yorkshire; William Mareschall, junior, Earl of Pembroke, 1231 (with lion rampant on shield, and sheathing his sword); Gilbert Mareschall, Earl of Pembroke, 1241 (drawing his sword, winged dragon at feet).—Cole's *Glance at the Temple Church.*

In 1841 were discovered the ancient lead coffins containing the bodies of these knights, who did not appear to have been buried in their armour; and none of the coffin ornaments were of earlier date than the beginning of the 13th century.

In the Temple Round, lawyers received clients, as merchants on 'Change:

> " Retain all sorts of witnesses,
> That ply i' the Temple under trees;
> Or walk the Round with Knights o' the Posts,
> About the cross-legg'd knights, their hosts."—*Hudibras*, pt. iii. c. 3.

Dugdale says: "Item, they (the lawyers) have no place to walk in and confer their learnings but the *church;* which place all the term-times hath in it no more quietness than the Pervise of Paules, by occasion of the confluence and concourse of such as are suitors in the law." The pavement is laid with Minton's encaustic tiles, the patterns mostly from the floor of the Chapter House of Westminster Abbey. "The Round" is the nave or vestibule to the oblong portion of the church, the choir, in pure Lancet style, and almost rebuilt in the restorations and alterations made 1839-42 by Savage and Sydney Smirke. It is divided into three aisles by clustered marble columns, the groined roof being richly coloured in arabesque, and ornamented with holy emblems. Triple lancet-headed windows let in floods of light. The organ, by Bernard Schmydt, is remarkable as having quarter-tones.

Towards the end of the reign of Charles II., the Societies of the Temple determined on the erection of an organ; when the two great builders of the time, Schmydt and Harris, were competitors, and each was supported by his patrons and partisans. Each then erected an organ in the church, the Benchers promising to keep the best. Blow and Purcell performed on appointed days on Schmydt's organ, which, it was thought, must be chosen. Harris's organ was then played by Baptiste Draghi, and won many admirers; and the competition was kept up for nearly a twelvemonth: when the decision being referred to Judge Jefferies, he decided in favour of Schmydt's organ.

In the little vestry beneath the organ-gallery is a marble tablet to Oliver Goldsmith, buried in the ground east of the choir, April 9, 1774. The choir-stalls and benches are beautifully carved in oak from ancient examples: the altar is new, in the style of Edward I., and contains five canopied panels, gilt and illuminated; here are an ambry, piscina, and sacrarium or tabernacle for the Eucharist; and behind the altar are three ancient niches for sacred utensils. On the south is the monumental effigies of a bishop in pontificals, supposed to be that of Silverston de Eversdon, Bishop of Carlisle, d. 1255, and buried here. To the left is a white marble tomb over the remains of the learned Selden, d. 1654, in Whitefriars: his funeral sermon was preached by Archbishop Usher. In the triforium are the tombs of Plowden, the jurist; Howell, writer of the *Familiar Letters;* and Gibbon, the hisorian: the views of the church from this gallery are very picturesque. Here are also several memorials of eminent lawyers; and among them, a marble bust, by Rossi, of Lord Chancellor Thurlow (d. 1806). On the south wall is a tablet to Anne Littleton (d. 1623), daughter-in-law to Sir Edward Littleton, with a quaint epitaph, ending,

> "Keep well this pawn, thou marble chest;
> Till it be called for, let it rest:
> For while this jewel here is set,
> The grave is but a cabinet."

It is mentioned in Dugdale's *Monasticon* that both King Henry II. and his Queen Eleanor directed that their bodies should be interred within the walls of the Temple Chapel, and that the above monarch by his will left 500 marks for that purpose. The walls are inscribed with Scripture texts in Latin; and between the top of the stalls and the string-course beneath the windows, is the Hymn of St. Ambrose. The windows, by Willement, are among the finest specimens of modern stained glass: the altar subjects are from the life of Christ, the interspaces being deep-blue and ruby mosaic, with glittering borders. Knights Templar fill the aisle windows; but that opposite the organ has figures of angels playing musical instruments.

A brief history of the Templars in England, and of this church, may be read in the rude effigies of the successive kings during whose reigns they flourished, now painted on the west end of the chancel. At the south corner sits Henry I. (A. D. 1128), holding the first banner of the Crusaders, half black, half white, entitled "Beauseant;" white typifying fairness towards friends; black, terror to foes. This banner was changed during the reign of Stephen (A. D. 1116) for the red cross:

> "And on his brest a bloodie crosse he bore,
> The deare remembrance of his dying Lord."

Henry II. and the Round Church are represented by the third figure. Richard I., with the sword which he wielded as Crusader, and John, his brother, are the next kings; and in the north aisle is portrayed Henry III., holding the two churches; the chancel, or square part, having been added in his reign, and consecrated on Ascension-day, 1240.—Cole's *Glance at the Temple Church*.

Externally, the Round has been refaced with stone, and the groined western portico restored; the east end has three high gables, with crosses; and the bell is hung in a new stone turret on the north side. North-east of the choir is the house of the Master of the Temple, as the preacher at the church is called: it is fronted by a garden, beneath which is the Benchers' Vault. One of the most learned Masters was Hooker, author of the *Ecclesiastical Polity;* another eminent Master was Sherlock, afterwards Bishop of London.

St. Thomas, Charterhouse, Goswell-Street-road, a brick church in the Anglo-Norman style, was designed by E. Blore, and consecrated 842. A portion is set apart for the Brethren of the Charter-House.

St. Thomas's, Southwark, in St. Thomas's-street, was originally the church of the Monastery or Hospital of St. Thomas, but was made parochial after the Dissolution: in 1702 it was rebuilt of brick, with square tower, closely resembling that of the former church.

Trinity, Gray's-Inn-road, district church of St. Andrew's, Holborn, designed by Pennithorne, was built in 1837-8: it has a pedimented centre, and belfry with cupola roof and cross; and catacombs beneath for 1000 bodies. Adjoining is the old burial-ground of St. Andrew's, is crowded graves interspersed with trees.

Trinity, Minories, was originally the church of the Priory of the Holy Trinity, founded by Matilda, Queen of Henry I., in 1108. This church escaped the Great Fire of 1666; but becoming insecure, it was taken down, and rebuilt in 1706. It is stated, in a note in Strype, that Trinity pretended to privileges, as "marrying without a license." In the chancel is the tomb of the loyal William Legge, who bore the touching message of Charles I. from the scaffold to his son, the Prince of Wales, enjoining him to "remember the faithfullest servant ever prince had." Here, too, is buried Legge's son, the first Earl of Dartmouth.

St. Vedast's, Foster-lane, destroyed by the Great Fire of 1666, and rebuilt by Wren, has an original and graceful spire, in three stories. The interior has a ceiling enriched with wreaths of flowers and fruits and foliage; and a carved oak altar-piece, with winged figures, palm-branches, a pelican, &c. In the vestry-room is a print of "West Cheap" in 1585, with the church of St. Michael on the north side of Paternoster-row, the burial-place of the antiquary, Leland (d. 1552).

St. Bartholomew by the Exchange (see page 120), which was taken down in 1840, has been rebuilt in Moor-lane, Fore-street, under the direction of C. R. Cockerell, R.A. The interior details are Tuscan; the altar-piece, pulpit, &c. are richly-carved oak; and the communion end is lighted by a stained Catherine-wheel window. From the western door, the whole interior to the east is discovered through a triumphal arch, formed by a novel and ingenious construction of the choir-gallery in front of the organ.

British and Foreign Sailors' Church (the) was opened April 30, 1845, in the Danish Church, Wellclose-square, Ratcliffe Highway. An inscription over the entrance states it to have been built in 1696, by Caius Gabriel Cibber, the sculptor, at the cost of Christian V., King of Denmark, for such merchants and seamen, his subjects, who visited the port of London. The architect and his son, Colley Cibber, are buried in the vaults; and in the church is a tablet to Jane Colley. The pulpit has four sand-glasses in a brass frame, by which preachers formerly regulated the length of their sermons.

St. Luke's, near the centre of Old-Street-road, is one of the Fifty Queen Anne Churches, and was consecrated on St. Luke's day, Oct. 16, 1733. It is built of stone, and has an obelisk spire, "a master-stroke of absurdity." The parish was taken out of St. Giles's, Cripplegate.

EPISCOPAL CHAPELS.

Asylum (Female Orphan) Chapel, Westminster-road, Lambeth, was built for the Charity, established 1758, at the suggestion of Sir John Fielding, the police-magistrate. The chapel service is rendered attractive by the singing of the orphan children, and by popular preachers, thus contributing to the support of the Institution by a collection.

St. Bartholomew's, Kingsland, was an ancient and picturesque wayside chapel, near the toll-gate, and taken down in 1846. Its walls were of flint and rubble, the window-frames of stone, in the Perpendicular style, and in the roof was a wooden bell-turret. It was originally the chapel of a hospital or house of lepers, called "Le Lokas," and was long an appendage to St. Bartholomew's, to which it was a kind of outer ward till 1761, when all the patients were removed from Kingsland, and the hospital site let for building. Upon the petition of the neighbouring inhabitants, the chapel was repaired, and service performed there, the chaplain being appointed by the governors of St. Bartholomew's. It was so small as scarcely to contain 50 persons. It is engraved in Archer's Vestiges of Old London, part i. 1850.

Bentinck Chapel, Chapel-street, New-road, was built in 1772, and opened by the Rev. Mr. Hunt, father of the originator of the Examiner newspaper. The Rev. Basil Woodd was minister of this chapel 45 years.

Brompton Consumption Hospital Chapel (Lamb, architect,)

as founded by the Rev. Sir Henry Foulis, Bart., and consecrated June ', 1850. It is exclusively for the officers and patients of the Hospital, id has been built as a memorial of a relative of the founder. The hapel consists of a nave, north and south transeptal projections, and chancel; and is connected with the Hospital by a corridor, externally namented with pinnacled buttresses and gable crosses, and an octa-)nal bell-turret. The windows are traceried, and have stained glass; e roof is open timbered; the chancel has florid sedilia of stone, and is parated from the nave by a low traceried screen. The interior fittings e of oak, some bearing the arms and crest of the founder, heraldically: Arg. three bay-leaves proper; crest, a crescent arg. surmounted by cross sa.;" the motto is "Je ne change qu'en mourant." The crest is been most frequently used, as applicable to the building—"Chris- anity overcoming Paganism." The floor is partly paved with tiles of morial patterns. The seats are specially adapted for the patients.

CHAPEL ROYAL (the), St. James's Palace, is situated on the western de, between the Colour Court and Ambassadors' Court. It is oblong plan, with side galleries; the Royal Gallery being at the west end,)pposite the communion-table.

The superb ceiling, painted by Holbein in 1540, is one of the earliest speci- ens of the new style introduced by him into England. The rib-mouldings are of)oden frame-work, suspended to the roof above; the panels have plaster grounds, e centres displaying the Tudor emblems and devices. The subject is gilt, shaded ldly with bistre; the roses glazed with a red colour, and the arms emblazoned in .eir proper colours; leaves, painted dark-green, ornamented each subject; the :neral ground of the whole was light-blue. The mouldings of the ribs are painted een, and some are gilt; the under side is a dark-blue, on which is a small open .nning ornament (cast in lead), gilt. The ceiling has undergone several repairs, one of which the blue ground was painted white. In 1836, when the chapel as enlarged under the direction of Sir Robert Smirke, the blue ground was disco- :red, as were likewise some of the mottoes in the small panels: thus, "STET DIEV. ELIX: HENRICQ REX 8—H. A. VIVAT. REX. 1540. DIEV. ET. MO. DROIT," &c.

'ivine Service is performed here as at our cathedrals, by the gentlemen [the choir, and ten choristers (boys). The establishment consists : a Dean (usually the Bishop of London), the Sub-Dean, Lord High lmoner, Sub-Almoner, Clerk of the Queen's Closet, deputy-clerks, 1aplains, priests, organists, and composer; besides violist and lutanist 10w sinecures), and other officers; and until 1833, there was a "Con- :ssor to the Royal Household." Each of the Chaplains in Ordinary reaches once a year in the Chapel Royal. The hours of service are A. M. and 12 noon. There are seats for the nobility, admission-fee 2s. 'eorge III., when in town, attended this chapel, when a nobleman car- ied the sword of state before him, and heralds, pursuivants-at-arms, nd other officers, walked in procession; and so persevering was his ttendance at prayers, that Madame d'Arblay, one of the robing-women, ells us, in November 1747, the Queen and family, dropping off one by ne, used to leave the King, the parson, and His Majesty's equerry, to 'freeze it out together." In this chapel were married Prince George f Denmark and the Princess Anne; Frederick Prince of Wales and he daughter of the Duke of Saxe-Gotha; George IV. and Queen Caro- ine; and Queen Victoria and Prince Albert. Before the building f the Chapel at Buckingham Palace, Her Majesty and the Court at- ended the Chapel Royal, St. James's. The silver candelabra and other iltar plate are magnificent. The fittings of the Chapel and Palace for he last royal marriage cost 9226l.

In the *Liber Niger Domus Regni* (*temp.* Edward IV.) is an ordinance naming 'Children of the Chapelle viij. founden by the King's privie cofferes for all that ongeth to their apperelle by the hands and oversyghte of the deane, or by the naster of song assigned to teache them;" such being the origin of the present nusical establishment of the Chapel Royal. Ordinances were also issued for the *impressment of boys* for the royal choirs: in 1550, the master of the King's Chapel had license "to take up from time to time children to serve the King's Chapel." Tusser, the "Husbandrie" poet, was, when a boy, in Elizabeth's reign, thus impressed for the Queen's Chapel. The Gentlemen and Children of the Chapel Royal were the principal performers in the religious dramas or *Mysteries;* and a "master of the children," and "singing children," occur in the chapel establishment of Cardinal Wolsey. In 1583, the Children of the Chapel Royal, afterwards called the Children of the Revels, were formed into a company of players, and thus were among the earliest performers of the regular drama. In 1731, they performed Handel's *Esther,* the first oratorio heard in England; and they continued to assist at oratorios in Lent, so long as those performances maintained their ecclesiastical character entire.

"Spur-money," a fine upon all who entered the chapel with spurs on, was formerly levied by the choristers at the doors, upon condition that the youngest of them could repeat his gamut; if he failed, the spur-bearer was exempt. In a tract dated 1598, the choristers are reproved for "hunting after spur-money;" and the ancient Cheque-book of the Chapel Royal, date 1622, contains an order of the Dean, decreeing the custom. "Within my recollection," writes Dr. Rimbault, in 1850, "the Duke of Wellington (who, by the way, is an excellent musician) entered the Royal Chapel 'booted and spurred,' and was, of course, called upon for the fine. But his Grace calling upon the youngest chorister to repeat his gamut, and the 'little urchin' failing, the impost was not demanded."—*Notes and Queries,* No. 30.

CHAPEL ROYAL, WHITEHALL, the Banqueting House of the Palace, designed by Inigo Jones, commenced June 1, 1619, finished March 31, 1622, cost 14,940*l.* 4*s.* 1*d.* (See WHITEHALL.) The above hall was converted into a chapel in the reign of George I., who, in 1724, appointed certain preachers, six from Oxford and six from Cambridge University, to preach in successive months on the Sundays, at a salary of 30*l.* through the year. The edifice has, however, *never been consecrated* as a chapel. It was shut up in 1829, and remained closed till 1837, during which time it was restored and refitted as we now see it, under the direction of Sir Robert Smirke, R.A. The lower windows were then closed up, the walls were hung with drapery, (1400 yards of drugget,) and the floor carpeted, to remedy the excessive echo. The Guards formerly attended Divine Service here; they now attend at the chapel in Wellington Barracks, St. James's Park; and the gallery in which they sat at Whitehall has been removed. The organ originally placed here was sold by order of Cromwell, and is now in Stamford Church, Leicestershire; the present organ is of subsequent date. The hall is exactly a double cube, being 111 feet long, 55 feet 6 inches high, and 55 feet 6 inches wide. Over the principal doorway is a bronze bust of James I., attributed to Le Sœur; above is the organ-loft, and along the two sides is a lofty gallery. Above the altar were formerly placed eagles and other trophies taken from the French at Barossa, in Egypt, and at Waterloo; but they have been removed to Chelsea Hospital. The Whitehall ceiling is divided into panels, and painted black, and gilded in parts. These are lined with oil pictures on canvass, painted abroad by Rubens in 1635, it is stated for 3000*l.*, by commission from Charles I. There are nine compartments: the largest in the centre, oval, contains the apotheosis of James I., who is trampling on the globe, and about to fly on the wings of Justice (an eagle) to heaven.* On the two long sides of it are great friezes, with genii, who load sheaves of corn and fruits in carriages, drawn by lions, bears, and rams: each of the boys measures 9 feet. The northernmost of the large compartments represents the King pointing to Peace and Plenty, embracing Minerva, and routing Rebellion and Envy; at the south end (the altar) the King is on the throne, appointing Prince Charles his successor. The four corner pictures are allegorical representations of Royal Power and Virtue. The whole are best viewed from the south end of the apartment. Dr.

* Rubens's original sketch is in the National Gallery, Trafalgar-square.

Waagen considers these pictures to have been principally executed by he pupils of Rubens : they have undergone four restorations : in 1687, under the direction of Sir Christopher Wren ; and about 1811, by Cipriani, who was paid 200*l.* Vandyck was to have painted the sides if the Banqueting House with the history and procession of the Order of the Garter. Divine Service is performed in the chapel on Sundays, Saints' Days, &c., the gentlemen and choristers of the Chapels Royal executing the musical service.

In Whitehall Chapel, on Maundy Thursday (the day preceding Good Friday), is distributed by the Queen's Almoners the Royal Bounty to as many poor aged men and women as the sovereign is years of age. The alms-money consists of sovereigns, and silver pieces of 4*d.*, 3*d.*, 2*d.*, and 1*d.* value, (*Maundy Money,*) in purses and red and white leather bags, carried in alms-dishes by Yeomen of the Guard, preceded by the Almoners. The distribution takes place at the conclusion of the first lesson of the Morning Service : the purses are given to the women ; and the leathern bags, with stockings, shoes, and broadcloth, to the men. The service is then proceeded with, and concludes with a prayer for the Queen. The Maundy gift to each person, in coin and clothing, amounts to about 5*l.*; and it s extended to the pensioners of previous years. The gold is put in the red bags, he silver in the white. The *Maundy Money* is struck each year at the Royal Mint, and is current coin of the realm : a set may be purchased of any dealer in coins. Formerly bread, meat, and fish were also distributed in large wooden bowls, and the officers carried bouquets of flowers and wore white scarves and sashes; but the earliest custom was the King washing with his own hands the feet of as many poor men as he was years old, in imitation of the humility of the Saviour. The last prince who performed this was James II., in the ancient Chapel.

CHARLOTTE CHAPEL, Charlotte-street, Buckingham-gate, was built in 1776 for "the unfortunate Dr. Dodd," who laid the first stone in July. "Great success attended the undertaking," writes Dodd ; "it pleased and it elated me." In the following year, June 27, he was hanged at Tyburn for forgery. Charlotte Chapel, now St. Peter's, was also occupied by Dr. Dillon; and it was refitted, with great cost, in 1850.

DUKE-STREET CHAPEL, Westminster, was originally the north wing of the house built for Lord Jefferies, Lord Chancellor to King James II., who permitted a flight of stone steps to be made thence into St. James's Park, for Jefferies's special accommodation : they terminate above in a small court, on three sides of which stands the once costly mansion. One portion of it was used as an Admiralty House, until that office was removed by William III. to Wallingford House. The north wing (in which Jefferies transacted his judicial business out of term,) was formed into a chapel in 1769, with a daily service; Dr. Pettingale, the antiquary, was for some time incumbent. (See Walcott's *Westminster,* p. 72.)

ST. ETHELREDA's, Ely-place, Holborn, is all that remains of the ancient palace of the Bishops of Ely, and retains much of its original aspect : the interior roof is boldly arched; on each side is a row of noble windows, though their tracery has disappeared; the pinnacle-work between and overtopping them is very fine, and at the east end is "one fine Decorated window, of curious composition." Evelyn records the consecration here of Dr. Wilkins, Bishop of Chester, in 1668, when Dr. Tillotson preached; and April 27, 1693, Evelyn's daughter Susannah was married here to William Draper, Esq., by Dr. Tenison, then Bishop of Lincoln. Cowper thus chronicles an amusing occurrence in this chapel, at the time of the defeat of the Young Pretender by the Duke of Cumberland, in 1746 :

> " So in the chapel of old Ely House,
> When wandering Charles, who meant to be the Third,
> Had fled from William, and the news was fresh,
> The simple clerk, but loyal, did announce,
> And eke did roar right merrily two staves,
> Sung to the praise and glory of *King George.*"

The chapel, after being leased to the National Society for a school-room, was for some time closed; but on Dec. 19, 1843, was opened for the service of the Established Church in the Welsh language; this being the first performance of the kind in London.

FOREIGN PROTESTANT CHURCHES.—There are in London two branches of the Church of Foreign Protestants founded by Charter of Edward VI., July 24, 1550. The *French Branch* was at first exclusively composed of the refugees who quitted France before the revocation of the Edict of Nantes.* They first assembled with their German and Dutch brethren in the "Temple du Seigneur Jesus" in Austin Friars; but their number having greatly increased, they subsequently met for public worship in the chapel of St. Mary, dependent on the Hospital of St. Antony, in Threadneedle-street, and belonging to the Dean and Chapter of Windsor, which building was taken down in 1841. They next removed to a new church in *St. Martin's-le-Grand*, nearly opposite the General Post-Office: this church, designed by Owen, and opened in 1842, is a tasteful specimen of Gothic, and has a large east window with *flamboyant* tracery, flanked by lofty turrets. *The German, Dutch, or Flemish Branch* was at first composed of the Polish exile Jean à Lasco, and the members of his church at Embden in East Friesland. To these German Protestants were united the Dutch and Flemish refugees; they are all included in the Charter of Edward VI., as forming one sole nation, *Germanorum*; and the church was subsequently known as the Flemish Church. The "Temple du Seigneur Jesus," in Austin Friars, is occupied by the members of the *Dutch* Church: on each of its painted windows is inscribed, "Templum Jesu, 1550." It originally belonged to the house of the Augustine Friars, founded in 1243. Stow describes it as surmounted by "a most fine-spired steeple, small, high, and straight;" and adds, "I have not seen the like." At the Dissolution, the church was reserved by Henry VIII., and was granted by his son to the poor Dutch refugees from the Netherlands, France, "and other parts beyond seas, from Papist persecutors;" and the grant is enjoyed by the Dutch to this day. The church contains some very good Decorated windows.

"On the west end, over the skreen, is a fair library, inscribed thus: 'Ecclesiæ Londino-Belgiæ Bibliotheca, extructa sumptibus Mariæ Dubois, 1659.' In this library are divers valuable MSS., and letters of Calvin, Peter Martyr, and others, foreign Reformers."—*Strype*, b. ii, p. 116.

On July 24, 1850, the tercentenary of the Royal Charter of Edward VI. was solemnly commemorated in this church by a special service, as also in the French Protestant Church in St. Martin's-le-Grand; and the members of the consistories of both churches dined together in the evening, and drank "To the memory of the pious King Edward VI." Besides the above, there is a *French Protestant Chapel* in Bloomsbury-street, designed by Poynter, and built in 1846, for the congregation first established in the Savoy: it has a pointed gable and a large Decorated eastern window. In Moor-street, Soho, is a *Swiss Protestant Chapel*, where is preserved a pair of colours, thus inscribed:

"These colours were presented by King George the Second to the Swiss residents in this country, as a mark of the sense which his Majesty was graciously pleased to entertain of the offer made by them of a battalion of 500 men, towards the defence of the kingdom on the occasion of the Rebellion" (Scottish, 1745).

---

* The number of French Protestants who took refuge in England after the revocation of the Edict of Nantes is estimated at 80,000. Of these, 13,000 settled in London, in the districts of Long Acre, Seven Dials, Soho, and Spitalfields. At least one-third of these refugees joined the French Church in the years 1686, 1687, and 1688.—*Manifesto*, 1850.

FOUNDLING HOSPITAL CHAPEL, Guildford-street, was designed by Jacobson, in 1747; and built by subscription, to which George II. contributed 3000*l.* Handel gave the large profits of a performance of his music; and his "Messiah," performed in the chapel for several years under his superintendence, produced the Charity 7000*l.* At the west end of the edifice are seated the children and the choir; and in the centre is the organ, given by Handel: the altar-piece, "Christ presenting little child," is by West, who retouched the picture in 1816. Several blind "foundlings," instructed in music, by their singing, greatly added to the funds of the Charity, by pew-rents and contributions at the doors, and for several years the latter exceeded 1000*l.*; the net proceeds of the chapel at present are 687*l.* the year, after paying the professional choir. The services are on Sunday morning and afternoon, but no service in the evening. Beneath the chapel are stone catacombs : the first person buried here was Captain Coram, the founder of the Hospital. Lord-Chief-Justice Tenterden (d. 1832) is interred here; and a marble bust is placed in the eastern entrance to the chapel. Children who die in the Hospital are buried in the churchyard of St. Pancras. See FOUNDLING HOSPITAL.)

GRAY'S INN CHAPEL adjoins the Great Hall, and is provided for the public, as well as for the Benchers and residents of the Inn. It is of modern Gothic design, and is supposed to occupy the site of "the Chauntry of Portpoole," mentioned in the grant from Lord Gray of Wilton, in 1505, to Hugh Denny. Among the preachers was Richard Gibbs, author of the *Bruised Reed*, which led to the conversion of Richard Baxter, the future Puritan divine.

GROSVENOR CHAPEL, South Audley-street, contains in its vault the remains of Ambrose Philips, the Whig poet, whom Pope ridiculed, but Nickell, Warton, and Goldsmith eulogised; of Lady Mary Wortley Montagu; and John Wilkes, designated by himself on a tablet as "a Friend of Liberty."

HANOVER CHAPEL, Regent-street, between Prince's and Hanover-streets, was built in 1823-5, (C. R. Cockerell, R.A., architect,) and is of the Ionic order of the Temple of Minerva Polias at Priene: it has a well-proportioned portico extending across the footpath, and picturesquely breaking the street line; two square turrets, of less felicious design, finish the elevation. The interior is square, and mostly lighted by a large glazed cupola, surmounted with a cross; and the arrangement generally resembles that of St. Stephen's, Walbrook: the altar-piece is a splendid composition of imitative antique marbles, enriched with passion-flowers and lilies, superbly coloured.

ST. JAMES'S CHAPEL, Hampstead-road, is a chapel-of-ease to St. James's, Westminster. In the burial-ground adjoining lie George Morland, the painter (d. 1804), and his wife; John Hoppner, the portrait-painter (d. 1810); and, without a memorial, Lord George Gordon, the leader of the Riots of 1780, who died in Newgate in 1793.

ST. JAMES'S CHAPEL, Pentonville, is a chapel-of-ease to St. James's, Clerkenwell, and was built by T. Hardwick. Here is interred R. P. Bonington, the landscape-painter (d. 1828); and in the burial-ground lies poor Tom Dibdin, the playwright, close by the grave of his friend, Joseph Grimaldi, "Old Joe," the famous clown (d. 1837).

ST. JOHN'S CHAPEL, Bedford-row, at the corner of Chapel-street and Great James-street, has been the frequent scene of schism from its first erection for Dr. Sacheverel; it was subsequently occupied by the Rev. Mr. Cecil (low-church); by the Rev. Dr. Dillon, of unenviable notoriety; the Rev. Daniel Wilson (now Bishop of Calcutta); the Rev. Mr. Sibthorp, given to change; and by the Hon. and Rev. Baptist

Noel, who, after 22 years' ministry, preached his farewell sermon here, Dec. 3, 1848.; and on Aug. 9, 1849, was publicly *baptised* in John-street Chapel, of which he became minister.

KENTISH TOWN CHAPEL, or district church, is a spacious and costly edifice in the Early Decorated style (Bartholomew, architect). It has two lofty steeples, and a large painted altar-window, and four smaller windows, inscribed with the Decalogue, Creed, &c., within sacramental borders of corn and vines; the altar recess has some good sculpture.

ST. JOHN'S WOOD CHAPEL, north-west of the Regent's-park, is of the Ionic order, and was designed by the late T. Hardwick: it has a tetra-style portico, and a tower, surmounted with a Roman-Doric lantern. Here or in the adjoining cemetery, which is tastefully planted with trees and shrubs, are buried John Farquhar, Esq., of Fonthill Abbey, Wilts, with a medallion portrait (d. 1826); Richard Brothers, "the prophet" (d. 1824); Tredgold, the engineer (d. 1829); Joanna Southcott, "the prophetess" (d. 1814), with prophetic quotations from Scripture, in gilt letters upon black marble: John Jackson, R.A., the portrait-painter (d. 1831), &c. "About 40,000 persons lie interred in this cemetery."— Smith's *Marylebone*, 1833.

LINCOLN'S INN CHAPEL, one of "the Old Buildings," was built in 1621-23: Dr. Donne laid the first stone, and preached the consecration sermon, the old chapel being then in a ruinous condition. Inigo Jones was the architect of the new chapel, as stated in the print by Vertue, in 1751: it stands upon an open crypt or cloister, in which the students of the Inn met and conferred, and received their clients. Pepys records his going to Lincoln's Inn, "to *walk under the chapel,* by agreement." It is now enclosed with iron railings, and is used as a burial-place for the Benchers. The chapel has side windows and intervening buttresses, style, *temp.* Edward III.; the large eastern window has a beautifully traceried circle, divided into twelve trefoiled lights. At the south-west angle is a turret with cupola and vane, and containing an ancient bell, traditionally brought from Spain about 1596, among the spoils acquired by the gallant Earl of Essex at the capture of Cadiz. The ascent to the chapel is by a flight of steps, under an archway and porch, the latter built by Hardwick in 1843. The windows are filled with glass, unusually fine: those on the sides have figures of prophets and apostles, by Flemish artists; the great eastern and western windows have armorial embellishments. The carved oaken seats are of the time of James I., but the pulpit is later. The organ, by Flight and Robson (1820), is of great power and sweetness of tone; and the choral service is attentively performed. In the porch is a cenotaph, with Latin inscription, to the Right Hon. Spencer Perceval; and on the ascent to the chapel is a marble tablet to Eleanora Louisa (d. 1839), daughter of Lord Brougham (a Bencher of Lincoln's Inn), with a poetic inscription, in Latin, by the late Marquis of Wellesley, written in his 81st year. Among the remarkable persons buried in the cloister under the chapel are John Thurloe, Secretary of State to Oliver Cromwell; and William Prynne, who preserved many of our public records. In the list of preachers in this chapel are the great names of Gataker, Donne, Usher, Tillotson, Warburton, Hurd, Heber, &c. The Rev. J. S. M. Anderson is the present preacher. (Selected principally from a carefully-written account of *Lincoln's Inn and its Library,* by W. H. Spilsbury, Librarian. 1850.)

MAGDALEN HOSPITAL CHAPEL, Blackfriars-road, is attractive by the singing of a choir of the reclaimed women. The "Magdalen House" was originally established in Prescot-street, Goodman's-fields, in 1758; where Dr. Dodd was chaplain, and rendered great service to the Charity by his eloquent preaching.

. MARGARET-STREET CHAPEL, Margaret-street, Cavendish-square, was first converted into a chapel in 1789. Huntington preached here with Lady Huntingdon's people, when he first came to London. In 1833, the minister was the Rev. W. Dodsworth, who has since seceded to the Roman Catholic Church. At Margaret-street may be said to have been the first development of "Puseyism" in the metropolis. In 1842, the chapel was under the direction of the Rev. Frederick Oakeley, a non-resident Fellow of Balliol College, Oxford.

"Flowers, and altar-candlesticks, and Gregorian chantings, and scarce-concealed bowings, and strange modes of reading prayers, and frequent services, with a conspicuous cross over the communion-table, served to awake the suspicions of the wary; and in conjunction with a course of zealous and earnest preaching, and the self-denying lives of the chief minister and his friends, to persuade the frequenters of the chapel that here, at least, was a true 'Catholic revival,' and that by the multiplication of Margaret Chapels the whole Anglican Establishment might be at length 'un-Protestantised.' To Margaret Chapel also was due no little of that phase of the movement which consisted in the 'adapting' of Catholic books to 'the use of members of the English Church;' and by the employment of which it has done so much good in preparing the minds of its congregation for the reception of the Catholic faith. This system was soon taken up by no less important a person than Dr. Pusey himself."—*The Rambler, a Catholic Journal,* Feb. 1851.

In 1845, Mr. Oakeley resigned his license as minister of Margaret Chapel, which then fell to his curate, Mr. Richards. Mr. Oakeley subsequently joined the Roman Catholic Church; and the chapel in Margaret-street was taken down in 1850 to be rebuilt.

ST. MARK's CHAPEL, Fulham-road, attached to the National Society's Training College for Schoolmasters, was erected in 1843, in the Norman or Romanesque style; cruciform in plan, with semicircular eastern end, and twin towers with high-pitched *broche* roofs, resembling an early German church. It serves as a place of worship for the adjoining district, as well as for the inmates of the College; and the greater part of the service is chanted by the students, without organ or other accompaniment. The east end has some stained glass of olden character.

ST. MARK's, North Audley-street, a chapel-of-ease to St. George's, Hanover-square, is of original and not inelegant design, by Gandy Deering, R.A.: the order is Ionic from the Erectheum; the portico has two handsome fluted columns, with an enriched entablature; and above is a turret of Grecian design, with pierced iron-work sides and pyramidal stone roof, with gilt ball and cross. This chapel was consecrated April 25, 1828. Some of the adjoining houses are in the heavy style of Sir John Vanbrugh.

PERCY CHAPEL, Charlotte-street, was built by the Rev. Henry Matthew, an early patron of Flaxman (*Cunningham*). It has since been the scene of the eloquent preaching of the Rev. Robert Montgomery, author of "The Omnipresence of the Deity," a poem.

ST. PHILIP's CHAPEL, Regent-street, midway between Waterloo-place and Piccadilly, was built by Repton, and consecrated in 1820. It has a tower from the Lantern of Demosthenes at Athens, and a Doric portico, with sacrificial emblems on the side porticoes or wings.

ST. PETER's EPISCOPAL CHAPEL, Queen-square, Westminster, was originally a royal gift for the special use of the Judges of Westminster, and was frequented by the members of the Royal Household. In 1840, it was much injured by a fire, which originated in the adjoining mansion of Mr. Hoare; and the altar-piece, then nearly destroyed, was one of the finest specimens of ancient oak-carving in England. Here have officiated the venerable Romaine; Gunn, Basil Woodd, Wilcox, and Shepherd: the latter for 50 years held the chaplaincy, with the lectureship of St. Giles's-in-the-Fields. St. Peter's was, about 136 years ago, the chapel of the Spanish Embassy; and here preached Antonio Gavin, a secular priest, who having been converted from Popery to the Church of England, was licensed to officiate in this chapel in the Spanish language, by Dr. Robinson, then Bishop of London; and sermons in Spanish preached here by Gavin were published.—See *Gent. Mag.* Feb. 1827.

St. Peter's (formerly Oxford) Chapel, Vere-street, Oxford-street, designed by Gibbs, was built about 1724, and was once considered the most beautiful edifice of its class in the metropolis. It has a Doric portico and a three-storied steeple. The Duke of Portland was married at this chapel in 1734.

Portland Chapel, now St. Paul's, in Great Portland-street, was built in 1776, on the site of Marylebone basin, which supplied that part of the metropolis with water. The chapel was not consecrated at the time of its erection; but Divine Service was performed in it until 1831, when the consecration was performed, and it was dedicated to St. Paul. At the Portland Hotel, north of the chapel, Captain (now Sir John) Ross lodged after his return from the North Pole, in 1833.

Quebec Chapel, Quebec-street, Marylebone, was built in 1788, and is celebrated for its sweet-toned organ, and musical service.

Rolls' Chapel is attached to the Rolls House, between 14 and 15 Chancery-lane, and was originally built of flints, with stone finishings, early in the seventeenth century. Pennant states that it was begun in 1617, and that Dr. Donne preached the consecration sermon. The large west window has some old stained glass, including the arms of Sir Robert Cecil and Sir Harbottle Grimston; and here are a large organ, and presses in which the Records are kept. Among the monuments are: to Dr. John Young, Master of the Rolls temp. Henry VIII., a recumbent figure, in a long red gown and deep square cap, the face fine; above, in a recess, is a head of Christ, between two cherubim, in bold relief; this tomb is attributed to Torrigiano: to Lord Kinloss, Master of the Rolls to James I., reclining figure in a long furred robe, and before him a kneeling figure in armour, supposed his son, killed in a desperate duel with Sir Edward Sackville; also, kneeling figure in armour of Sir Richard Allington, his wife opposite, and three daughters on a tablet; and here lie Sir John Trevor, Master of the Rolls (d. 1717), and other Masters. Bishops Burnet, Atterbury, and Butler, were eloquent preachers at the Rolls'; and Burnet's volume of fifteen sermons delivered here contains the germ of his great work the *Analogy of Religion.* Rolls' Chapel occupies the site of a house founded by Henry III. for converted Jews, and in 1377, annexed by Edward III. to the new office of Custos Rotulorum, or Keeper of the Rolls, who has his chaplain and preacher: in 1837, the estate was vested by Parliament in the Crown, the salary of the Master of the Rolls being fixed at 7000*l.* a-year in lieu of fines and rents.

Tenison's Chapel, between Nos. 172 and 174, east side of Regent-street, was founded by Archbishop Tenison, who, in 1700, conveyed to trustees, (of whom Sir Isaac Newton was one,) this chapel or tabernacle, to be employed as a public chapel or oratory for St. James's parish; at the same time giving 500*l.* to be laid out in the purchase of houses, lands, or ground-rents. Out of the revenues and the Archbishop's charity were to be provided two preachers for the chapel, and a reader "to say Divine Service every day throughout the year, morning and afternoon;" a clerk to officiate; and schoolmasters to teach without charge poor boys of the parish to read, write, cast accounts, and in five years to assist them in becoming apprentices. There are forty boys on the foundation; non-foundationers pay 12*s.* 6*d.* per quarter: the school is at No. 172 Regent-street. The Archbishop of Canterbury for the time being

visitor of this excellent charity. The chapel was erected in 1702, and
was refronted in building Regent-street.

TRINITY CHAPEL, Conduit-street, now a neat brick edifice, was
originally a small wooden room upon wheels, resembling a caravan:
Evelyn describes it as "formerly built of timber on Hounslow-heath,
by King James, for the mass-priests, and being begged by Dr. Tenison,
rector of St. Martin's, was set up by that public-minded, charitable,
and pious man." Pennant writes:

"The history of Conduit-street Chapel, or Trinity Chapel, is very remarkable.
It was originally built of wood by James II., for private mass, and was conveyed
on wheels, attendant on its royal master's excursions, or when he attended his
army. Among other places, it visited Hounslow-heath, where it continued some
time after the Revolution. It was then removed and enlarged by the Rector of
the parish of St. Martin's, and placed not far from the spot on which it now stands.
Dr. Tenison, when Rector of St. Martin's, got permission of King William to rebuild it; so, after it had made as many journeys as the house of Loretto, it was by
Tenison transmuted into a good building of brick, and has rested ever since on
the present site."

YORK-STREET CHAPEL, on the north side of St. James's-square, is a
chapel-of-ease to St. James's. In 1815, it was occupied by Swedenbor-
gians. It was originally the chapel of the Spanish Embassy (then at
the present No. 7 St. James's-square); and the "Tower of Castile,"
the Arms of Spain, appears on the parapet of the front.

DISSENTERS' CHAPELS.

ALBION CHAPEL, Moorgate, next to 116 London Wall, designed by
Jay, has a pleasing diastyle Ionic portico. It belongs to a congregation of the Scotch Secession.

BAPTIST CHAPEL, Little Wild-street, Lincoln's-Inn-fields: here is
annually preached a sermon in commemoration of the Great Storm,
Nov. 26, 1703. The preacher in 1846, the Rev. C. Woollacott, in describing the damage by the storm, stated:

"In London alone, more than 800 houses were laid in ruins, and 2000 stacks of
chimneys thrown down. In the country upwards of 400 windmills were either blown
down or took fire, by the violence with which their sails were driven round by the
wind. In the New Forest, 4000 trees were blown down, and more than 19,000 in
the same state were counted in the county of Kent. On the sea the ravages of
this frightful storm were yet more distressing: 15 ships of the Royal Navy, and
more than 300 merchant vessels, were lost, with upwards of 6000 British seamen.
The Eddystone Lighthouse, with its ingenious architect, Mr. Winstanley, was
totally destroyed. The Bishop of Bath and Wells and his lady were killed by the
falling of their palace. The sister of the Bishop of London, and many others,
lost their lives."

This annual custom has been observed upwards of a century. The
chapel is built upon the site of Weld House and gardens, the mansion
of the son of Sir Humphrey Weld, Lord Mayor of London in 1608. It
was subsequently let: Ronquillo, the Spanish Ambassador, lived here
in the time of Charles II. and James II.; and in the anti-Popish riots
of the latter reign the house was sacked by the mob, and the Ambassador compelled to make his escape at a back door.

BLOOMSBURY BAPTIST CHAPEL, on the west side of Bloomsbury-
street, was designed by Gibson, and opened Dec. 2, 1848: it is in elegant Lombardic style; the central portion has a gable pediment, large
wheel-widow, flanked by two lofty spires, and is very picturesque.
South is the French Protestants' Gothic Chapel; and the tasteless pile
to the north is Bedford Chapel. Among the houses taken down near
Bloomsbury-street, and towards the centre of what is now New Oxford-street, stood the Hare and Hounds public-house, a noted resort of
the Londoners of the sixteenth and seventeenth centuries: till the reign

changed, owing to a hare having been hunted and caught there, and cooked and eaten in the house.

CONGREGATIONAL NONCONFORMIST CHURCH, Kentish Town, designed by Hodge and Butler, and opened in 1848, is in the ecclesiastical style of the 15th century, and has several richly-traceried windows filled with stained glass, including a splendid wheel-window, 15 feet diameter.

ESSEX-STREET CHAPEL, Strand, the head-quarters of the Unitarians of the metropolis, is built upon part of the site of Essex House, taken down in 1774. In a portion of it was kept the Cottonian Library from 1712 to 1730; one of its large apartments was let to Paterson, the auctioneer, and was next hired by the patrons of Mr. Lindsey and Dr. Disney (Unitarians), to preach in. In 1805, on the death of Dr. Disney, Mr. Thomas Belsham removed to Essex-street Chapel from the Gravel-pit congregation at Hackney, where he had succeeded Dr. Priestley. At Essex-street, Belsham continued pastor during the rest of his life, acquiring great popularity by his eloquent and argumentative preaching; he died in 1829, aged 80, and was succeeded by the Rev. Thomas Madge, the present minister.

HORBURY CHAPEL, Kensington-Park-road, Notting-hill, was built by subscription of the Independent denomination, and opened Sept. 13, 1849. The design, by Tarring, is transition from Early English to Decorated, with a pair of towers and spires; the principal windows are filled with stained glass.

INDEPENDENT CHAPEL, Robinson's-row, Kingsland, was built about 1792: here the Rev. John Campbell, the benevolent South-African missionary, was 37 years minister, and is buried; and an elegant marble monument to his memory has been erected by his flock.

JEWIN-STREET CHAPEL, Aldersgate-street, was built in 1808, for a congregation of English Presbyterians, who removed thither from Meeting-House-court, Old Jewry. Among the eminent pastors were the eloquent John Herries; Dr. Price, F.R.S., the writer on finance; and Dr. Abraham Rees, editor of the *Cyclopædia* which bears his name.

MORAVIAN CHAPEL, Fetter-lane, is the only place of worship belonging to the Moravians (United Brethren) in London, by whom it was purchased in 1738, on their settling in England. The interior is remarkably plain, and bespeaks the simple character of its occupants; there is a small organ, for they have church music and singing; there are no pews, but seats for males and females, apart. The chapel is capacious, but the auditory does not exceed from 200 to 300 persons: the support is voluntary. There is a burial-ground for the members, with a small chapel, at Lower Chelsea, near the Clock-house. At Chelsea, in June 1760, died Count Zinzendorf, who first introduced the Moravians into this country. The chapel in Fetter-lane lies in the rear of the houses, one of the entrances to it being through No. 32: it was possibly so built for privacy. It escaped the Great Fire of 1666, and was originally occupied by the Nonconformists. Turner, who was its first minister, was very active during the Great Plague; and having been ejected from Sunbury, he continued to preach in Fetter-lane till towards the close of the reign of Charles II. Here also Baxter, the eminent Nonconformist divine, preached after the Indulgence granted in 1672; and he held the Friday-morning lectureship until August, 1682.

NATIONAL SCOTCH CHURCH, Crown-court, Little Russell-street, Covent Garden, has a cement Norman façade, with the staircases effective outside features. The minister is the Rev. Dr. Cumming, who preached before Queen Victoria, at Crathie, Balmoral, Sept. 22, 1850; and who ably controverted the claims of Dr. Wiseman in the same year.

OLD GRAVEL-PIT MEETING-HOUSE, Hackney, was built in 1715: ere Dr. Price, F.R.S., and Dr. Priestley were ministers; next Mr. Belham, the congregation being Anti-Trinitarians; succeeded by the Rev. Robert Aspland, who remained here till the erection of the New Gravel-it Meeting-house, "Sacred to one God the Father," in Paradise-fields.

PRESBYTERIAN DISSENTERS' CHAPEL, Mare-street, Hackney, was established early in the 17th century: here Philip Nye and Adoniram Byfield, two eminent Puritan divines, preached in 1636; and Dr. W. Bates and Matthew Henry were pastors late in the 17th century. The old meeting-house has been taken down, and a new one built opposite, and occupied by Independents.

PRESBYTERIAN MEETING-HOUSE, Newington-green, established soon after the Restoration, was rebuilt about 1708: in the list of ministers are Richard Biscoe, Hugh Worthington, M.A., John Hoyle, Dr. Richard Price, F.R.S., Dr. Amory, Dr. Towers, Mr. Lindsey, Dr. Isaac Maddox (afterwards Bishop of Worcester), Thomas Rees, and Mr. Barbauld, husband of the authoress.

PROVIDENCE CHAPEL, Little Titchfield-street, Marylebone, was built by a congregation of Independents for Huntington, S S., ("the coal-heaver," as he called himself,) upon his credit with "the Bank of Faith," when he quitted Margaret Chapel: when it was finished, "I was in arrears," says Huntington, "for 1000*l.*, so that I had plenty of work for faith, if I could but get plenty of faith to work; and while some deny a providence, providence was the only supply I had." This chapel was burnt down, with seven houses adjoining, and the site became a timber-yard.

PROVIDENCE CHAPEL, on the east side of Gray's-Inn-lane, nearly opposite Guildford-street, was built for Huntington, S.S., by his flock, after the destruction of the Titchfield-street Chapel: this second edifice he named from the pulpit for these reasons: that "unless God provided men to work, and money to pay them, and materials to work with, no chapel could be erected; and if He provided all these, Providence must be its name." The chapel was, accordingly, built in Gray's-Inn-lane, and upon a larger scale than the last; it was made over to him as his own, and bequeathed in his will to his widow, who, however, resigned it to the congregation. It was subsequently altered and opened as an Episcopal Chapel, the Rev. T. Mortimer, D.D., minister.

REGENT-SQUARE CHAPEL, Gray's-Inn-road, was built for the Rev. Edward Irving, in 1824-5, Mr. Tite, the architect, adapting the principal front from York Cathedral: the twin towers are 120 feet in height. Here the "unknown tongues" attracted large and fashionable congregations.

SOUTH-PLACE CHAPEL, Finsbury, is of Ionic design, and was built for an Unitarian congregation, under the ministry of Mr. W. J. Fox, the eloquent M.P. for Oldham.

SPA-FIELDS CHAPEL, Exmouth-street, Clerkenwell, is in the hands of "Lady Huntingdon's connexion." The Spa-fields burying-ground contains 42,640 square feet, and would decently inter 1,361 adult bodies; yet within fifty years 80,000 bodies were deposited here, averaging 1500 per annum. To make room, bones and bodies were burnt for upwards of a quarter of a century, to the constant annoyance of the neighbourhood; until, in 1845, the lessees of the ground were indicted, and the pestilential nuisance stopped.

SURREY CHAPEL, corner of Little Charlotte-street, Blackfriars-road, is of octagonal form, and was built in 1783, for a congregation of Calvinistic Dissenters, the Rev. Rowland Hill pastor, who preached here in the winter season for nearly 50 years: he had a house adjoining where he died, aged 88, in 1833, and was buried in a vault under the chapel. Adjacent, in Hill-street, are alms-houses for 24 poor widows, built and maintained by the congregation.

SWEDENBORG CHURCH, Argyle-square, King's-cross, was opened Aug. 11, 1844, for the followers of Swedenborg, whither they removed from a small chapel in the City, built about forty years previously. The new church is in the Anglo-Norman style, (Hopkins, architect,) with two towers and spires, 70 feet high, each terminating with a bronze cross; the intervening gable has a stone cross, and a wheel window over a deeply-recessed doorway. The interior has a finely-vaulted roof; the altar arrangements are peculiar; and there is an organ and choir. The founder of this sect, Baron Swedenborg (d. 1772), is buried in the Swedish Church, Prince's-square, Ratcliffe Highway.

THE TABERNACLE, in Moorfields, was built in 1752; previously to which, in 1741, shortly after Whitefield's separation from Wesley, some Calvinistic Dissenters raised for Whitefield a large shed near the Foundry, in Moorfields, upon a piece of ground lent for the purpose, until he should return from America. From the temporary nature of the structure it was called, in allusion to the tabernacles of the Israelites in the Wilderness; and the name became the designation of the chapels of the Calvinistic Methodists generally. Wvitefield's first pulpit here is said to have been a grocer's sugar-hogshead, an eccentricity not improbable. In 1752, the wooden building was taken down, the site was leased by the City of London, and the present chapel was built, with a lantern roof: it is now occupied by Independents, and will hold about 4000 persons. This chapel was the cradle of Methodism; the preaching-places had hitherto been Moorfields, Marylebone-fields, and Kennington-common. Silas Told describes the Moorfields Tabernacle, in 1740, as "a ruinous place, with an old pantile covering, a few rough deal boards put together to constitute a temporary pulpit, and several other decayed timbers, which composed the whole structure." John Wesley also preached here (the Foundry, as it was called), at five in the morning and seven in the evening. The men and women sat apart; and there were no pews, or difference of benches, or appointed place for any person. At this chapel, the first Methodist Society was formed in 1740.

TRINITY CHAPEL, East-India-road, Poplar, was erected in 1840-1, from a design by Hosking, at the expense of Mr. George Green, the wealthy shipbuilder of Blackwall, principally for shipwrights in his employ, and for inducing the seamen in the neighbourhood to attend divine worship. The chapel has a Greek Corinthian portico, and façade with enrichments of shells, dolphins, and foliage; and a classic bell-tower, the summit 80 feet high. The interior has a Keene's-cement pulpit, highly decorated; and a powerful organ by Walker, with a Grecian architectural case.

WESLEYAN CHAPEL, City-road, was built in 1778, upon ground leased by the City: thither John Wesley removed from the Foundry in Moorfields, the lease of which had expired; and thenceforth the City-road Chapel became the headquarters of the Society of Methodists. Wesley laid the first stone, in which his name and the date were inserted upon a plate of brass: "This was laid by John Wesley, on April 1, 1777." "Probably," says he, "this will be seen no more by any human eye, but will remain there till the earth and the works thereof are burnt up." John Wesley, who died March 2, 1791, aged 88, was buried here in a vault which he had prepared for himself, and for those itinerant preachers who might die in London.

"During his last illness, Wesley said, 'Let me be buried in nothing but

hat is woollen; and let my corpse be carried in my coffin into the chapel.'
his was done, according to his will, by six poor men, each of whom had 20s.;
or I particularly desire,' said he, ' that there may be no hearse, no coach, no
cutcheon, no pomp, except the tears of them that love me, and are following
e to Abraham's bosom.' On the day preceding the interment, Wesley's body
y in the chapel, in a kind of state becoming the person, dressed in his clerical
bit, with gown, cassock, and band, the old clerical cap on his head, a Bible in
e hand, and a white handkerchief in the other. The face was placid, and the
pression which death had fixed upon his venerable features was that of a serene
d heavenly smile. The crowds who flocked to see him were so great, that it was
ought prudent, for fear of accidents, to accelerate the funeral, and perform it
tween five and six in the morning. The intelligence, however, could not be
pt entirely secret, and several hundred persons attended at that unusual hour."
Southey's *Life of Wesley*, 3d edit. vol. ii. p. 403.

WESLEYAN CHAPEL, Great Queen-street, Lincoln's-Inn-fields, built
1811, has a tasteful façade, added by Jenkins in 1841, consisting of a
nall Ionic tetrastyle forming a portico, crowned by a pediment; above
a Venetian triple window, and a handsome cornicione. The front is
ecuted in beautiful Talacre stone from North Wales, and is the earliest
stance of its being employed in our metropolitan buildings.

WESLEYAN MODEL CHAPEL, East-India-road, Poplar, named from
s improved plan, was built in 1848 (James Wilson, architect), by sub-
ription, to which one person gave 500l. The style is Decorated, and
e materials are Caen and rag stone. The windows are richly traceried;
ere are two turrets, each 80 feet high, and the building is finished
ith a pierced parapet, pinnacles, and roof-cresting.

WESLEYAN CHAPEL, at the angle of the Islington end of the Liver-
ool-road, is in the Decorated style : it has a turret on the front gable
feet in height, and the parapets are pierced with trefoils and quatre-
ils. The principal windows have flowing tracery; and the interior,
vided by arches and octangular columns, whence spring the roof tim-
rs, is altogether of ecclesiastical character.

" The Wesleyans have now five or six edifices in London, clothed in the
othic dress of various periods, and following the usual arrangements of a me-
æval church, except having no tower and no extensive chancel, resembling
this respect the churches erected between the Reformation and the late aban-
nment of church design. The average capacity of these buildings is for 1300
rsons. One, nearly facing St. John's, Clerkenwell, affects the complete Gothic
ove, and has a neat original front, but thin."—*Companion to the Almanac*, 1851.

WHITEFIELD'S TABERNACLE, Tottenham-Court-road, was designed
y Whitefield, and commenced building in 1756, upon a plot of ground
ear the Field of Forty Footsteps, and the Lavender Mills, Coyer's
ardens. In 1759 or 1760 was added an octangular front, which gave
the appearance of two chapels; the addition being called "the Oven,"
nd the chapel itself, " Whitefield's Soul-Trap." This enlargement is said
have been aided by Queen Caroline, consort of George II., who see-
ig a crowd at the door unable to obtain admission, observed it was a
ity that so many good people should stand in the cold, and accordingly
ent Whitefield a sum of money to enlarge the chapel; it was called "the
issenters' Cathedral." Whitefield died in America; and in 1770, John
Vesley preached here his funeral sermon. In August, 1787, the Rev.
r. Pickwell, rector of Bloxham-cum-Digby, Lincolnshire, preached
is own funeral sermon in this chapel: he had pricked his finger in
pening the body of a person who had died of consumption, and the
ound proved fatal by mortification in ten days afterwards. Attached
the chapel is a burial-ground, the mould for which is stated to have
een brought from the churchyard of St. Christopher-le-Stocks, in
780, by which the consecration fees were saved. In 1828, White-
eld's lease expired, and the chapel was closed until 1830, when it was

purchased by trustees for 20,000*l.*, and altered at a great cost, the exterior being coated with stucco. It is 126 feet by 76 feet, and 112 feet high to the crown of the dome; it is well adapted for hearing, the octagonal portion serving as a kind of funnel or trumpet to the voice; it will seat from 7000 to 8000 persons. In 1834, the trial of a long-pending Chancery suit respecting this chapel occupied between three and four days. Here are monuments to Whitefield, the founder; to Toplady, the zealous Calvinistic controversialist with John Wesley; and to John Bacon, the sculptor, who wrote his own epitaph, as follows:

"What I was as an Artist
Seemed to me of some importance while I lived;
But what I really was as a Believer
Is the only thing of importance to me now."

The chapel is now occupied by Independents.

ZOAR CHAPEL, in Zoar-street, leading from Gravel-lane to Essex-street, Southwark, is the meeting-house in which the celebrated John Bunyan was allowed to preach, by favour of his friend, Dr. Thomas Barlow, Bishop of Lincoln, to whom it belonged; and if only one day's notice were given, the place would not contain half the people that attended. 3000 persons have been gathered together there, and not less than 1200 on week-days and dark winter mornings at seven o'clock. There is a print of this chapel in Wilkinson's *Londina Illustrata*, and a woodcut vignette of it in Dr. Cheever's Memoir of Bunyan, prefixed to the *Pilgrim's Progress* (Bogue, 1850). The chapel was used as a wheelwright's shop prior to its being pulled down, when the pulpit in which Bunyan had preached was removed to the Methodist Chapel, Palace-yard, Lambeth. Another "true pulpit" is shewn in Jewin-street Chapel, Aldersgate-street. Bunyan's Pulpit Bible was purchased by Mr. Whitbread, M.P., at the sale of the library of the Rev. S. Palmer, at Hackney, in 1813.

FRIENDS' OR QUAKERS' MEETING-HOUSES.

There are six Friends' Meeting-houses in the metropolis: 1. Devonshire House (Houndsditch); 2. Gracechurch-street (White-Hart-court); 3. Peel (Peel-court, John-street, Smithfield); 4. Ratcliffe (Brook-street); 5. Southwark (Redcross-street); 6. Westminster (Peter's-court, St. Martin's-lane). The first established was that in White-Hart-court.

"The *Yearly Meeting* of the Society of Friends is held in London, opening always on a Wednesday in the latter end of May, and continuing into the month of June, generally lasting about ten days or a fortnight. Of course it is the most important event in their religious system, the most interesting season in their year. To this Great Meeting the business of all their lesser meetings points, and is here consummated. To it delegates are sent from every quarter of the island; by it committees are appointed to receive appeals against the decisions of minor meetings, to carry every object which is deemed desirable, within their body or beyond it, into effect; by it Parliament is petitioned; the Crown addressed; religious ministers are sanctioned in their schemes of foreign travel, or those schemes restrained; and funds are received and appropriated for the prosecution of all their views as a society. The City is their place of resort; and the Yearly Meeting is held in Devonshire House.

"The mingling of plain coats, broad hats, friendly shawls, and friendly bonnets, in the great human stream that ever rolls along the *pavés* of the City, is in that neighbourhood, at this season, become very predominant. Bishopsgate Within and Bishopsgate Without, Gracechurch-street, Houndsditch, Liverpool-street, Old Broad-street, Sun-street, almost every street of that district, fairly swarms with Friends. The inns and private lodgings are full of them. The White Hart and the Four Swans are full of them. They have a *table-d'hôte*, at which they generally breakfast and dine. Every Friend's house at this time has its guest; and many of the wealthy keep a sort of open house.

"At a Friends' Meeting, the men are sitting all on one side by themselves, with

eir hats on, and presenting a very dark and sombre mass; the women sitting
gether on the other, as light and attractive. In the seats below the gallery are
ting many weighty friends, men and women, still apart; and in the gallery a
ig row of preachers, male and female, perhaps twenty or thirty in number.
u may safely count on a succession of sermons or prayers. Men and women
se, one after another, and preach in a variety of styles, but all peculiar to
iends. Suddenly a man-minister takes off his hat, or a woman-minister takes
'her bonnet; he or she drops quietly on the bass before them; at the sight the
iole meeting rises, and remains on its feet while the minister enters into 'sup-
cation.' Most singular, striking, and picturesque are often the sermons you
ar."—*William Howitt.*

GREEK CHURCH.

GREEK CHURCH, London Wall, the first ecclesiastical structure
ected by the Greek residents in London, was opened in 1850, on Sun-
y, Jan. 6, o.s., and in the Greek Kalendar, Christmas-day. The
ifice is Byzantine, (from Byzantium, the capital of the Lower Greek
mpire,) with Italian interior details. The north front has three
rse-shoe arches fringed, and Byzantine columns, between which are
e entrance-doorways; and in the upper story is a similar arcade, con-
ining three windows: above is this inscription, in Greek characters:

"During the reign of the august Victoria, who governs the great people of
itain, and also other nations scattered over the earth, the Greeks sojourning
re erected this church to the Divine Saviour, in veneration of the rights of their
hers."

bove is a pediment surmounted with a cross. In plan, the church
a cross of equal parts; the ceiling is domed in the centre: on the
rth and south sides are galleries, with flower-ornamented fronts,
d supported on decorated arches and pillars, with fine capitals. The
tar-screen has these panel pictures, painted in Russia: the Annun-
ation; the Virgin holding the infant Jesus; Jesus sitting on a throne;
d St. John the Baptist. In a centre panel is inscribed, in Greek:

"O Lord, the strength of those who trust in Thee, uphold the Church which
ou hast redeemed with Thy precious blood."

ithin the iconostasis, or screen, is the altar in "the holy place,"
mbolic of the Holy of Holies in the Jewish ritual. A magnificent
andelier, with wax-lights, is suspended from the ceiling. The con-
egation stand during the whole service; but there are seats made to
rn up, as in our cathedral stalls; and knobs are placed on the upper
ms, to serve as rests. The officiating priest is richly robed, and at-
nded by boys bearing a wax taper, each in a surplice with a blue
oss on the back. Upon the high altar is placed a large crucifix, can-
labra with lights, &c. At a portion of the Mass, a curtain is drawn
fore the altar, whilst the priest silently and alone prays for the sanc-
ication of the Sacrament; he then re-appears, "bids peace to all the
ople," and blesses them. The sermon is preached in the pulpit, the
iest wearing a black robe and a black hat; this is covered with the
ελυττρα, or veil, to indicate that the wearer is under the influence of
e Gospel. The church at London Wall (designed by T. E. Owen,
Portsmouth,) cost about 10,000*l.*; yet the number of Greek residents
the date of its opening, in 1850, did not exceed 220.

JEWS' SYNAGOGUES.

The NEW SYNAGOGUE, in Great St. Helen's, Bishopsgate, was built
y Davies, in 1838. It is in rich Italian style, with an open loggia of
iree arches resting upon Tuscan columns. The sides have Doric piers,
d Corinthian columns above, behind which are ladies' galleries, fronted
ith rich brasswork. There are no pews; the centre floor has a plat-

form, and seats for the principal officers, with four large brass-gilt candelabra.

At the south end is *the Ark*, a lofty semicircular-domed recess, consisting of Italian Doric pilasters, with *verde antico*, and porphyry shafts, and gilt capitals; and Corinthian columns, with sienna shafts, and capitals and entablature in white and gold. In the upper story the intercolumns are filled with three arched windows of stained glass, arabesque pattern, by Nixon; the centre one having Jehovah, in Hebrew, and the Tables of the Law. The semi-dome is decorated with gilded rosettes on an azure ground; there are rich festoons of fruit and flowers between the capitals of the Corinthian columns, and ornaments on the frieze above, on which is inscribed in Hebrew, "Know in whose presence thou standest." The centre of the lower part is fitted up with recesses for Books of the Law, enclosed with polished mahogany doors, and partly concealed by a rich velvet curtain fringed with gold; there are massive gilt candelabra; and the pavement and steps to the Ark are of fine veined Italian marble, partly carpeted. Externally, the Ark is flanked with an arched panel; that on the east containing a prayer for the Queen and Royal Family in Hebrew, and the other a similar one in English. Above the Ark is a rich fan-painted window, and a corresponding one, though less brilliant, at the north end. The ceiling, which is flat, is decorated with thirty coffers, each containing a large flower aperture for ventilation.

This congregation had been previously established about eighty years in Leadenhall-street, and there known as the "New Synagogue."

The WEST LONDON SYNAGOGUE, Margaret-street, Cavendish-square, designed by D. Mocatta, was completed in 1850. It is square in plan, and consists of Ionic columns supporting the ladies' gallery, whence rise other columns, receiving semicircular arches, crowned by a bold cornice and lantern-light. *The Ark* composes cleverly with the semicircular arches, which hang as pendants before it, and complete the fourth side of the building; the steps, platform, stylobate, and columns, are all of scagliola, surmounted by a decorated entablature, which supports a niche-head, in which are placed the tablets of the Ten Commandments, surrounded and shadowed by the palm-leaf.

There are in London other Synagogues: the chief one, the German, is in Duke's-place, Houndsditch, in the midst of the Jewish population. The Sabbath commences at sunset on Friday, when the Synagogue is opened; and again at ten o'clock on Saturday morning. The singing, handed down from the temple service, and the chanting of the Law, said to be the manner in which it was revealed to Moses, is interesting. The Jews, and the officers in attendance, are most kind and polite to strangers. The interest of the visit is enhanced by procuring a Jewish prayer-book, with the English translation on the opposite page. Strangers are reminded not to take off their hats as they enter: it is an abomination to the Jews, who worship with their heads covered.

ROMAN CATHOLIC CHURCHES AND CHAPELS.

In London alone, exclusive of the surrounding episcopal district, there are about 200,000 Roman Catholics. This is, however, to some extent a floating population; the Irish immigrants often leaving London for work. About twenty years ago, the Roman Catholics numbered half as many: the number of their chapels in London was then twenty-four; it is now fifty. There was not then a single convent or religious house; there are now seventeen for nuns, and two for religious men; thirty-seven charity-schools, and four orphan-asylums. In the whole London District are 104 Roman Catholic Churches and Chapels, with 168 Priests on duty, nine for the urban flocks. The services are more or less the counterpart of each other; and it is merely in the eloquence of their preachers, or in their music and church-furniture, that the Churches and Chapels differ.

AMBASSADORS' CHAPELS: *Spanish Place Chapel* is attended by the members of the Spanish Embassy; *Warwick-street*, Golden-square, by the Bavarian Embassy (the former Chapel was destroyed in the Riots f 1780); *Duke-street*, Lincoln's-Inn-fields, by the Sardinian; and *Little George-street*, King-street, Portman-square, by the French. Here the Comte de Paris received his first communion, in 1850. Celebrated foreign preachers are occasionally heard here, chiefly in Lent; as Martin, Lavignan, Lacordaire, &c.

St. George's Church, St. George's Fields, nearly facing the eastern wing of Bethlem Hospital, is built upon the site of the focus of the "No Popery" Riots of 1780, and is the largest Roman Catholic church erected in England since the Reformation; and with the quaint conventual buildings (priests' houses and schools, and a convent for Sisters of Mercy) at the north end, was designed by A. W. Pugin. The church is a high example of Roman Catholic symbolic details: it is in the Decorated style, (*temp.* Edward III.,) is cruciform in plan, and consists of a nave and aisles, chancel, and two chapels; and a tower at the north-west end, to be surmounted by a rich hexagonal spire, 320 feet high.

The church is about 235 feet in length, and will seat 3000 persons. It is lit by laceried windows, some filled with stained glass, by Wailes of Newcastle; the great chancel-window was given by John Earl of Shrewsbury, and represents the root of Jesse, or genealogy of our Lord. The large window over the principal entrance, in the great tower, has figures of St. George, St. Michael, and other saints. There is no clerestory, but each roof is gabled; slender pillars and arches divide the nave and side aisles, in which are confessionals; and between the nave and chancel is a double stone screen bearing a rood-loft, with a crucifix of Belgian fifteenth-century work, and images of the Virgin and St. John, nearly life-size, and coloured. The chancel is panelled with oak, with crocketed arches round the sanctuary; the high altar has bas-reliefs of the Transfiguration, Resurrection, and Ascension; the tabernacle is richly dight and painted, the metal doors being chased and gilt, and studded with large crystals. Behind the altar is an elaborately-carved stone reredos, with niches filled with images of angels, and the Saints Peter and Paul. The high altar furniture is very superb and massive; the chancel is floored with encaustic tiles; and the chapels are superbly decorated in gold and colour. In the baptistery is an octagonal stone font, with sculpture and Gothic panelling. Outside the church, between two confessionals, is a Perpendicular chantry to the late Hon. Edmund Petre, for the repose of whose soul Mass is offered herein daily; this being the first foundation for the support of the church. "The Adorable Presence is day and night in the Chapel of the Blessed Sacrament. Look for the red light; it is there."

St. George's was opened with great pomp, July 4, 1848; and was the scene of the solemn enthronisation of Cardinal Wiseman, Archbishop of Westminster, Dec. 6, 1850. The cost of this church to July 1848 had been 38,000*l.*

Immaculate Conception Church, Farm-street, Berkeley-square, designed by Scoles, and built at the expense of Jesuits, is the first ever possessed by the Order in London: it was opened 1849. The style is the Decorated, the south front much resembling that of Beauvais Cathedral. The altar and organ-loft windows are filled with brilliant stained glass: the rose in the latter is very elegant; and each of the 22 flank windows has different tracery. The interior is large and lofty, and has no aisles or rood-screen: the high altar, designed by A. W. Pugin, cost about 1000*l.*, and was presented by Miss Monica Tempest, of Broughton Hall, Yorkshire; and her brother, Sir Charles Tempest, presented the Missal, which cost about 50*l.* "Confraternities of the Bona Mors, of the Sacred Heart of Jesus, and of the Immaculate Heart of Mary, are established in this church." The services are performed by Jesuits.

+ "Roman Catholic churches seem to be distinguished from those of the national faith, at present, only by the occupation of niches that in the latter would be left vacant. It is remarkable, however, that they all seem to affect the style of one period, viz. the first half of the fourteenth century, their designers apparently disdaining the representation of either an immature or a declining fui'n of art; but fixing always on the fully developed Gothic, just at the turning point of its career."—*Companion to the Almanac*, 1851.

St. John the Evangelist's, Duncan-terrace, Islington, was opened in 1843. It was designed by Scoles, in the Anglo-Norman style, and has an eastern gable, flanked by two spires, each 130 feet high. Under the chancel is a crypt, or mortuary chapel; and adjoining is a spacious cemetery. This church has a Holy Guild attached: the Rev. F. Oakeley (late of Margaret-street Chapel) officiates.

St. Mary's, Moorfields, corner of East-street, Finsbury Circus, opened in 1820, has an embellished entrance façade, in the pediment of which are sculptured two figures kneeling at the Cross. The interior is very superb: the semicircular altar-wall, behind a screen of marble columns, has a large painting of the Crucifixion, by Aglio, an Italian artist; it is called fresco, but is mezzo-fresco (begun upon wet plaster, and finished with tempera; but is very perishable).* This great scenic picture is effectively illumined by a subdued light from the roof, and has the touching aspect of life and reality. On the ceiling are painted the Virgin Mary, the Infant Jesus, the four Evangelists, and scenes from events in the life of the Saviour. The sacramental plate was presented by Pope Pius VII. Carl Maria von Weber was buried in the vaults of this Chapel, June 21, 1826; but his remains have since been removed to the Catholic churchyard in the Friederichstadt, Dresden.

Oratory of St. Philip Neri, King-William-street, Strand, was originally an Assembly Room; here the Rev. F. W. Faber, author of the *Cherwell Water-Lily*, and other poems, preached (in 1850) to a large and deeply-moved audience.

Our Lady's, Grove-End-road, St. John's Wood, designed by Scoles, 1834, was built and endowed by two ladies, the Misses Gallini. The site formerly belonged to the Knights of St. John of Jerusalem, (whence St. John's Wood,) whose predecessors, the Knights Templar, held the same estate; and built the Temple Church, the prototype of the present cross church, which is Early Pointed, 13th century. The western front, with its three gables and crosses, Catherine-wheel and lancet windows, and pinnacled turrets, is a fine composition. The gables of the north and south fronts are surmounted with canopied niches, containing sculptured groupes of the Madonna and Child; and the east front has a large window filled with stained glass. The interior has acutely-arched and richly-bossed roofs, springing from slender shafts; and the high altar is backed by a rich oaken screen. In the schools are educated and clothed, gratuitously, 300 poor children.

St. Patrick's, Sutton-street, Soho, is much frequented by the poor Catholic population of St. Giles's. The festival of St. Patrick (March 17) is observed here as a double of the first class, with High Mass.

Sardinian Chapel (the), Duke-street, Lincoln's-Inn-fields, is the oldest of the metropolitan places of worship now in the hands of the Roman Catholics of London. It was built in the year before King Charles was beheaded: that is, in 1648, just at the close of the Great Rebellion, and the practical commencement of Oliver Cromwell's rule. During the existence of the penal laws, the only entrance to the chapel was through the Sardinian Ambassador's house, in Lincoln's-Inn-fields. The Riots of 1780 commenced with the partial demolition of this building: the mob were especially savage in attacking it, it being the mother-chapel, the oldest in London, and at that time the resort of all the leading Roman Catholics. In derision of their worship, a cat was dressed in the miniature vestments of a priest, an imitative host or wafer was placed in its paws, and thus it was hung to the lamp-

* Eugenio Latilla on Fresco, &c., 1842. The above specimen has been unfairly referred to as an evidence of the failure of fresco-painting in this country.

post of the chapel. This edifice was rebuilt after the Riots, and was enlarged by adding to it at the west end the Ambassador's stables. It has some painted glass, a finely-toned organ, and splendid church-plate, used only on solemn festivals: the altar-furniture was presented by the late King of Sardinia, and cost 1000 guineas; and the painting over the altar, "the Taking down from the Cross," is valued at 700*l.* The choir was formerly maintained at a great expense; though on Whitsunday, during Dr. Baldaconi's chief chaplaincy, Malibran, Persiani, Lablache, and Rubini, and the principals of the Italian Opera orchestra, gave their aid gratuitously. The choir is now scarcely above mediocrity; but the services are conducted with great solemnity. All Saints' day (Nov. 1) is one of the best in the year on which to witness the splendour of the worship. About twenty years ago the district of the chapel extended to Islington, and the congregation numbered about 12,000 souls. This district has been much diminished by the building of other chapels; but the Sardinian congregation is much larger— about 15,000. There are four resident priests, one expressly for the Italians. The Savoyard organ-boys much resort here.

Sunday Services: Low Mass at 7, 8, 9, and 10, with a short discourse at 7 and 9. High Mass and sermon at 11. Vespers at 3. Service in Italian at 4. Evening service and sermon at 7. *Week-days:* Mass at 8, 9, and 10. Wednesday evening, English Prayers and Benediction. On Monday, Wednesday, and Friday, the Rosary and English prayers immediately after 10-o'clock Mass. The Chaplains attend the Confessionals every morning from 8 till 11; and on Wednesday, Friday, and Saturday evenings from 6 till 10, or later, if required. Each Roman Catholic has a right to be visited when sick; and the priest must in duty attend, however dangerous and infectious the case.

SPANISH CHAPEL, Spanish-place, Manchester-square, was built, in 1797, by Joseph Bonomi, and enlarged in 1846, when a picturesque campanile, 70 feet high, was added by C. Parker: its interior is a Lady Chapel, and forms a second south aisle. The chapel is lighted from the roof with a most captivating effect of architectural chiaroscuro, and is divided by Corinthian columns.

The two RELIGIOUS HOUSES (of men) are at the Hyde and at Clapham, and belong respectively to the Orders of Passionists and Redemptorists; of the former, or the Order of St. Philip Neri, the Rev. J. H. Newman, though stationed at Birmingham, is "Provincial." Both houses are largely recruited with recent converts.

CITY (THE).

Nearly in the centre of what is strictly the *City* of London stands the centre or dome of St. Paul's Cathedral; latitude 51° 30' 47·59", longitude 5' 48·2" west of Greenwich, which is 51° 28' 38·07" latitude. The whole area is 600 acres. London Bridge is held to be within the City, together with a plot of ground at the Surrey-end, called the Bridge-foot.

"Few unacquainted with the locality would imagine that within the confines of the Poultry, Cornhill, Threadneedle-street, Lombard-street, Lothbury, and Broad-street, the vast amount of the commerce of England may be said to be transacted; or that the dingy counting-houses discoverable every where in the nooks and corners of the intersecting thoroughfares are occupied by our first merchants and traders, many of whom hold foreign Governments as heavy and responsible creditors. Many are, of course, aware that the Stock markets are for bargains in money securities, that 'Change is the great mart of the merchant, that Lloyd's is most particularly identified with the shipping interest, and that the Jerusalem and the North and South American Coffee-houses are places where traders and captains meet each other."—*The City,* Preface, p. vii.

The bustle of City life begins at nine and ten a.m., and concludes between six and seven p.m.; at other hours the streets and courts present one vast blank. 'Change, Broad-street, Bartholomew-lane, Lombard-street, Throgmorton-street, and all the great City thoroughfares, are then deserted; and at eight p.m. the stillness of death reigns over these once busy haunts. Thus far "the City" commercially. Formerly it was the merchant's residence.

> "Those mansions of the great old burghers which still exist have been turned into counting-houses and warehouses; but it is evident that they were originally not inferior in magnificence to the dwellings which were then inhabited by the nobility. They sometimes stand in retired and gloomy courts, and are accessible only by inconvenient passages; but their dimensions are ample, and their aspect stately. The entrances are decorated with richly carved pillars and canopies. The staircases and landing-places are not wanting in grandeur. The floors are sometimes of wood, tesselated after the fashion of France. The palace of Sir Robert Clayton, in the Old Jewry, contained a superb banquetting-room wainscoted with cedar, and adorned with battles of gods and giants in fresco. Sir Dudley North expended 4000l., a sum which would have been important to a duke, on the rich furniture of his reception-rooms in Basinghall-street. In such abodes, under the last Stuarts, the heads of the great firms lived splendidly and hospitably. To their dwelling-place they were bound by the strongest ties of interest and affection. There they had passed their youth and had made their friendships, had courted their wives, had seen their children grow up, had laid the remains of their parents in the earth, and expected that their own remains would be laid. That intense patriotism which is peculiar to the members of societies congregated within a narrow space was in such circumstances strongly developed. London was to the Londoner what Athens was to the Athenian of the age of Pericles, what Florence was to the Florentine of the fifteenth century. The citizen was proud of the grandeur of his city, punctilious about her claims to respect, ambitious of her offices, and zealous for her franchises."—Macaulay's _History of England._

"The City," says Addison, "has always been the province for satire, and the wits of King Charles's time jested upon nothing else during his whole reign."

CITY WALL AND GATES.

The City Wall is believed to have been a work of the later Roman period, when London was not unfrequently exposed to hostile attacks. Its direct course was as follows:—Beginning at a fort on part of the site of the present Tower of London, the line was continued by the Minories, between Poor-Jury-lane and the Vineyard, to _Ald-gate._ Thence, forming a curve to the north-west, between Shoemaker-row, Bevis-marks, and Houndsditch, it abutted on _Bishop's-gate_, from which it extended nearly in a straight line, through Bishopsgate churchyard, and behind Bethlem Hospital and Fore-street, to _Cripple-gate._ At a short distance further, it turned southward, by the back of Hart-street and Cripplegate churchyard; and thence, continuing between Monkwell-street and Castle-street, led by the back of Barber-Surgeons' Hall and Noble-street to Dolphin-court, opposite Oat-lane, where, turning westerly, it approached _Alders'-gate._ Proceeding hence, towards the south-west, it curved along the back of St. Botolph's churchyard, Christ's Hospital, and Old _New-gate_, from which it continued southward to _Lud-gate_, passing at the back of the College of Physicians, Warwick-square, Stationers' Hall, and the London Coffeehouse, on Ludgate-hill. From Ludgate it proceeded westerly by Cockcourt to Little Bridge-street, where, turning south, it skirted the Fleet-Brook to the Thames, near which it was guarded by another fort. The circuit of the whole line, according to Stow, was two miles and one furlong nearly. Another wall, defended by towers, extended the whole distance along the banks of the Thames between the two forts. The walls were defended by strong towers and bastions; the remains of three of which, of Roman masonry, were, in Maitland's time, to be seen in the vicinity of Houndsditch and Aldgate. The height of the perfect wall is considered to have been 22 feet, and that of

e towers 40 feet. The superficial contents of the ground within the
alls has been computed at 380 acres.

The following course of the Wall is shewn in a plan drawn by order
f the Corporation of London, to ascertain the extent of the Great Fire
f 1666, and now preserved in the Comptroller's Office, Guildhall. It
ay be distinctly traced as the southern boundary of the churchyard of
. Botolph, at the back of Bull-and-Mouth Street. Hence it proceeded
ue east, across Aldersgate-street, to Aldersgate, whence it continued,
t the same direction perhaps, about 200 feet, where it formed an angle,
nd had a curious bastion. It then went rather to the north-north-east
f Falcon-square, eastward of Castle-street, where it is now standing,
cternally incorporated with the walls of the houses; and in their cellars
is still to be traced, the stone being very smooth, massive, and perct; thence it proceeds, and exhibits large remains in the churchyard
f St. Giles, Cripplegate.

"The latter, including a bastion, are the most perfect relics. The base of the
Wall is composed of small rough flints, to the height of one foot six inches, resting
n a fine loam, upon which are placed four feet six inches of rough Kentish rag-
one (the green sandstone of geologists), with pieces of ferruginous sandstone
regularly interposed. Then come two courses of bricks, each measuring eighteen
iches by twelve, and one and three-quarters thick, on which is laid more of the
igstone for two feet six inches; again a double course of tiles, and above that one
ot six inches of the ragstone. Total existing height, nineteen feet seven inches.
t is nine feet six inches in width at the base, and two feet at the top."—*Mr.*
aull, F.G.S.

In the Sutherland View, 1543, and in Tapperell and Innes's large
Iap, the Great Wall is seen entire, with its embrasures, its large and
ifty gates, and intervening towers. These gates are minutely described
y Stow. Chamberlayne, in his *Magnæ Britanniæ Notitia,* 1726, says:
Most of the gates of that old Wall still remain: those which were
urnt down at Ludgate and Newgate are rebuilt with great solidity and
aagnificence; and those which escaped, as Aldersgate, Cripplegate,
Ioorgate, Aldgate, are kept in good repair, and are shut up at every
ight, with great diligence and a sufficient watch, at ten o'clock; none
eing suffered to go in or out without examination. Most of these gates
re of good architecture, and adorned with statues of some of our kings
nd queens; as is that, likewise, called Temple Bar, in Fleet-street, near
he Middle Temple Gate.'' The Gates, except the latter, were taken
own 1760-62: a statue of Queen Elizabeth, from Ludgate, is now
laced on the outer wall of the church of St. Dunstan in the West;
nd the statues of Lud and his sons, from the same gate, are in the
rounds of St. Dunstan's Villa, Regent's Park (the Marquis of Hert-
ord's). These statues were supposed by Flaxman to have preserved
he likeness of the originals, as copies, or possibly liberal restorations,
f the actual figures. (Archer's *Vestiges of Old London,* Part IV.,
vith six views.) Four of the figures from Newgate are in the south
ront of the present prison of that name.

The City of London, properly so called, consists of that part anciently *within*
he Walls, together with that termed *the Liberties,* which immediately surrounded
hem. The Liberties are encompassed by the *Line of Separation,* the boundary
etween them and the county of Middlesex; and marked by *the Bars,* which for-
nerly consisted of posts and chains, but are now denoted by lofty stone obelisks,
earing the City arms, which may be seen, eastward, in Whitechapel, the Minories,
nd Bishopsgate-street; northward, in Goswell-street, at the end of Fan-alley, and
n St. John's-street; and westward, at Middle-row, Holborn; while at the western
nd of Fleet-street the boundary is the stone gateway called Temple Bar.—*G. J.*
Aungier.

See also a Comparative Plan of that part of the City of London which was de-
troyed by the Great Fire in 1666, and its altered condition in 1849, by Francis
Whishaw, C.E.; wherein old London is shewn by strong lines, and modern London
v dotted lines.

CLEARING-HOUSE (THE),

In Lombard-street, and opposite the Foreign Post-Office, is an establishment in which the majority of the private bankers *clear*, or settle, the accounts they have with one another. The room is fitted up with desks for each of the clearing bankers, whose names, taking the first of each firm, are arranged in alphabetical order over each desk: the rapidity with which the charges are required to be entered just before four o'clock, when the day's clearance closes, and the excitement which is created by their swift distribution through the room, are difficult to be conceived; and then the value of the alphabetical arrangement of the clearer's desk is best seen.

In "*The City; or the Physiology of London Business*," 2d edit. 1848, it is related that the origin of the Clearing-house was a post at the corner of Birchin-lane and Lombard-street, near Overend, Gurney, and Co.'s, the great bill-discounters, where two or three of the clerks of banking-houses met for years to furnish each other with the memoranda of their accounts.

CLERKENWELL.

A large parish north-east of High Holborn, and named from a well around which the parish clerks, or clerken, were wont to assemble to act Scripture plays. The whole district was originally a village, which grew up around the Priory of St. John of Jerusalem, north, and the Nunnery of St. Mary, south, of what is now Clerkenwell-green. It was then a succession of gentle pastures and slopes, with the "River of Wells," or "Fleet," flowing between two hills on its western border: and its rural character is kept in mind by its Coppice and Wilderness rows, Saffron-hill, Vineyard-gardens, Field-lane, Clerkenwell-green, and Cow-cross; whilst Turnmill-street recals the "noise of the water-wheels" mentioned by Fitzstephen in 1190. In the Sutherland View of London, 1543, we see St. John's with a lofty spire, with trees extending to St. Bartholomew's, Smithfield; and westward the village green and St. James's Church, formerly of St. Mary's Nunnery, and then just made parochial. The nave, aisles, and bell-tower of St. John's were, however, pulled down to supply materials for building the proud Protector Somerset's palace. Aggas's map, in 1563, shews us a few houses bounded on three sides by little else than fields. By 1617, however, a number of fine houses had been built in the district, and were inhabited by persons of note. Hence to the village of Islington lay through green fields and country paths; and so lately as 1780, "persons walking from the City to Islington in the evening, waited near the end of St. John's-street, in what is now termed Northampton-street (but was then a rural avenue planted with trees, called Wood's Close), until a sufficient party had collected, who were then escorted by an armed patrol." (Storer and Cromwell's *Clerkenwell*.) The whole locality is covered with crowded streets. Here is still a large house, once the town residence of the Northampton family, the garden-ground of which is now Northampton-square; and Compton, Perceval, Spencer, Wynyate, and Ashby streets are named from the titles of the Marquis of Northampton, the principal ground-landlord of the district.

Passing to olden Clerkenwell, the Priory-gate of St. John has been transformed into a public-house; and the Square, once part of the Priory precincts, and afterwards the residence of the titled and wealthy, is now mostly tenanted by watchmakers and jewellers: in this Square died Bishop Burnet. Jerusalem-passage leads to Aylesbury-street, between which and St. John's Church stood the town-house of the Earl of Aylesbury, in the reign of Charles II. At the corner of Jerusalem-passage and Aylesbury-street, Thomas Britton, the "musical small-coal man," held his music-meetings from 1678 to 1714, in a low and narrow room over the coal-shop, to which all the fashion of the age flocked; Britton himself playing in the orchestra the viol di gamba. In Woodbridge-street, branching from Aylesbury-street, was the celebrated Red Bull Theatre, conjectured to have been originally an inn-yard, used for performance late in the reign of Queen Elizabeth, and where the king's players under Killigrew acted until they removed to Drury-lane. At the Red Bull, women first acted on the English stage: its site is probably now occupied by part of a distillery. St. James's Church was rebuilt in 1788 as we now see it. The Nunnery Close became Clerkenwell-close, on the east side of which was Newcastle House, built by the Earl of Newcastle, and where the eccentric literary Duchess Margaret held a sort of academic court for many years after the Restoration. "Of all the riders of Pegasus," says Walpole, "there have not been a more fantastic couple than his Grace and his faithful Duchess, who was never off her pillion." Pepys notes a visit of Charles II. to her Grace at Newcastle House, in April 1667.

Another eccentric inhabitant of Newcastle House was Elizabeth Duchess of Albemarle, and afterwards of Montague. She was married in 1669 to Christopher Monck, second Duke of Albemarle, then a youth of 16, whom her inordinate pride drove to the bottle and other dissipation. After his death, in 1688, at Jamaica, the Duchess, whose vast estate so inflated her vanity as to produce mental aberration, resolved never again to give her hand to any but a sovereign prince. She had many suitors; but true to her resolution, she rejected them all, until Ralph Montague, third Lord and first Duke of that name, achieved the conquest by courting her as *Emperor of China:* and the anecdote has been dramatised by Colley Cibber, in his comedy of "The Double Gallant, or Sick Lady's Cure." Lord Montague married the lady as "Emperor," but afterwards played the truant, and kept her in such strict confinement, that her relations compelled him to produce her in open court, to prove that she was alive. Richard Lord Ross, one of her rejected suitors, addressed to Lord Montague on his match:

"Insulting rival, never boast   From one that's under Bedlam's laws
     Thy conquest lately won;   What glory can be had?'
  No wonder that her heart was lost,—   For love of thee was not the cause:
     Her senses first were gone.   It proves that she was mad."

The Duchess survived her second husband nearly thirty years, and at last "died of mere old age," at Newcastle House, August 28, 1738, aged 96 years. Until her decease, she is said to have been constantly served on the knee as a sovereign,

On the east side of the Close stood a large house, by unauthorised tradition said to have been inhabited by Oliver Cromwell; but Cromwell-place, built upon the house-site, has been named from this story. Another inhabitant of the Close was Weever, the antiquary, who dates the Epistle to the first edition of his "Ancient Funerall Monuments" from his "House in Clerkenwell-close," May 28, 1631: he died in the next year, and was buried in old St. James's Church. On Clerkenwell-green is the Middlesex Sessions-House (Rogers, architect), built in 1779-82: it has a handsome east front, and a large hall, with a lofty dome. Here the County Sittings were removed from "Hicks's Hall," in St. John's-street, opposite the Windmill Inn, and named after Sir Baptist Hicks, of Kensington, one of the justices of the county, afterwards Viscount Campden, who built the Hall in 1612; from this site, "the spot where Hicks's Hall formerly stood," the distances on the milestones on the Great North Road were formerly measured. In this Hall, the patriotic Lord William Russell was condemned to death, 1683. In St. John's-lane are the remains of an Elizabethan house, with the sign of the Baptist's Head (probably in compliment to Sir Baptist Hicks): it is said to have been frequented by Samuel Johnson and Oliver Goldsmith, in their transactions with Cave, the printer, at St. John's-gate; and in the tap-room is a fine old armorial chimney-piece, engraved in Archer's *Vestiges of Old London,* part iii. The Clerks' Well is in Ray-street, and was the Nunnery well; and here is a pump, with an inscription telling its history.

Upon the site of Back-hill and Ray-street was the Bear-garden of Hockley-in-the-Hole, not only the resort of the mob, but of noblemen and ambassadors, to witness the cruelties of bear and bull baiting by greater brutes, and "the noble science of defence;" for, says Mrs. Peachum (*Beggar's Opera*), "You should go to Hockley-in-the-Hole to learn valour:" but the nuisance was abolished soon after 1728. The locality, however, still retains its foul stain of moral degradation and squalid misery in its alleys and courts, several with but one narrow entrance; and three-storied houses let in tenements, where men, women, and donkeys find shelter together.

Westward of this spot, Cobham-row denotes the site of the mansion of Sir John Oldcastle, afterwards Lord Cobham, the Wickliffite burnt in 1417. The tract immediately eastward of the Fleet River was rich in springs, many of them medicinal :- hence Coldbath-fields, Bagnigge-wells, Sadler's-wells, Islington Spa, the London Spa, and the "Wells" of the earlier topographers; and Spa-fields, the hot-bed of Radical riot in 1817, but now covered with streets.

Watchmakers, clockmakers, and jewellers settled in Clerkenwell in great numbers early in the last century, and several streets are mostly occupied by them; as "escapement-maker," "engine-turner," "fusee-cutter," "springer," "secret-springer," "finisher," and "joint-finisher," inscribed upon door-plates, attest; for in no trade is the division of labour carried to a greater extent than in watchmaking. (See St. John's Gate.)

CLIMATE OF LONDON.

The temperature of the air in the metropolis is raised by the artificial sources of heat existing in it no less than two degrees on the annual mean above that of its immediate vicinity. Mr. Howard, in his work on "Climate," has fully established this fact, by a comparison of a long series of observations made at Plaistow, Stratford, and Tottenham Green, (all within five miles of London,) with those made at the apartments of the Royal Society in London, and periodically recorded in the *Philosophical Transactions.* In explanation, Mr. Howard refers to the heat induced by the population, (just as the temperature of a hive of bees), from the domestic fires, and from the foundries, breweries, steam-engines, and other manufactories. "When we consider that all these artificial sources of heat, with the exception of the domestic fires, continue in full operation throughout the summer, it should seem, that the excess of the London temperature must be still greater in June than it is in January, but the fact is otherwise. The excess of the City temperature is greater in winter, and at that period seems to belong entirely to the nights, which average 3·710° warmer than the country; while the heat of the days, owing, without doubt, to the interception of a portion of the solar rays by a constant veil of smoke, falls, on a mean of years, about a third of a degree short of that in the open plains."

In the winter of 1835, Mr. W. H. White ascertained the temperature in the City to be 3° higher than three miles south of London Bridge; and *after the gas had been lighted in the City* four or five hours, the temperature increased full 3°, thus making 6° difference in the three miles.

Dr. Prout found that when his observations were made during the prevalence of wind (his station being at the western extremity of London), the air blowing from the east contained a minute portion of oxygen less than that which blew from the west. The difference was exceedingly small; still, it tended to shew that the air which has passed over the busy streets of the metropolis differs in its amount, not only of carbonic acid, but also of oxygen, from the air which has not reached those scenes.

Change of air in the metropolis is mostly effected by the mixture of the gases composing it. There are hundreds of places in London into which the *wind* never finds admission; and even among the wider streets there are many through which a free current is rarely blown. It is only in the night, when combustion in some measure ceases, and the whole surface of the earth is cooled, that the gases are gradually removed, and the whole atmosphere of the City is brought nearly to an equality. Nothing, indeed, can be more striking than the difference even in the *sensible* qualities of the air of London in the early morning and in the evening: in the former it has a coolness and refreshing clearness, which those who know it in the heat of later hour scan scarcely imagine.—(*Medical Gazette.*)

Every one has observed upon dirty windows in the metropolis small tree-like crystallisations: these consist of sulphate of ammonia, which is produced in the atmosphere by the burning of vast quantities of coal, combining with the sulphurous acid in the atmosphere.

Owing to the smoke, many species of flowers (the yellow rose, for instance) will not bloom within ten miles of London; Paris, on the contrary (where wood is almost universally burnt), produces the finest flowers, not alone in the gardens of the Tuileries and Luxembourg, but in the nursery-grounds of the famous rose-growers, Noisette and Laffay; which, in the Fauxbourg St. Germain, enjoy advantages such as it would be necessary to retreat some miles from London to secure.

In London, in sunny weather, some fine effects of light and shade may be witnessed in the neighbourhood of the public buildings. Miss Landon refers to a bright day in spring as "a very spendthrift of sunshine, when the darkest alley in London wins a golden glimpse, and the eternal mist around St. Paul's turns to a glittering haze."

CLUBS AND CLUB-HOUSES.

Although the Club was a social feature of the last century, to the present age is due the establishment of a system of Club Living upon a scale of splendour and completeness hitherto unattainable. Formerly the Club resembled an ill-appointed coffee-house or tavern; often, however, redeemed by the brilliancy of the wit which was "wont to set the table in a roar," and animated by a conversational spirit comparatively little indulged in the present day.

It has been pleasantly observed, that Clubs are gradually working as complete a revolution in the constitution of society as they have already effected in the architectural appearance of our streets. In the year 1800, there were only White's, as old as Hogarth's time; Brooks's and Boodle's; the Cocoa-Tree, Graham's, and another: now there are upwards of thirty Clubs, each possessing a well-appointed mansion. The facilities of living have been wonderfully increased by them, whilst the expense has been greatly diminished: and for a few pounds a-year, advantages are to be enjoyed which no fortune except the most ample can procure. The numbers of members in these Clubs are limited from 500 to 1500: the entrance-fees are from 9*l.* 9*s.* to 32*l.* 11*s.*; and the annual subscriptions from 5*l.* 5*s.* to 12*l.* 12*s.*

ALFRED CLUB, the No. 23 Albemarle-street, established in 1808, is described by Earl Dudley, in his time, as the dullest place in existence, "the asylum of doting Tories and drivelling quidnuncs." It was at this club that "Mr. Canning, whilst in the zenith of his fame, dropped in accidentally at a house-dinner of twelve or fourteen, stayed out the evening, and made himself remarkably agreeable, without any of the party suspecting who he was." (*Quarterly Review*, No. cx.) Lord Byron was a member of the Alfred, with "Peel, and Ward, and Valentia."

ARMY AND NAVY CLUB-HOUSE, Pall Mall, corner of George-street, designed by Parnell and Smith, was opened February, 1851. The exterior is a combination from Sansovino's Palazzo Cornaro, and Library of St. Mark at Venice; but varying in the upper part, which has Corinthian columns, with windows resembling arcades filling up the intercolumns; and over their arched headings are groupes of naval and military symbols, weapons, and defensive armour—very picturesque. The frieze has also effective groupes symbolic of the army and navy; the cornice, likewise very bold, is crowned by a massive balustrade. The basement, from the Cornaro, is rusticated; the entrance being in the centre of the east or George-street front, by three open arches, similar in character to those in the Strand front of Somerset House. The whole is extremely rich in ornamental detail. The hall is fine; the coffee-room, 82 feet by 39 feet, is panelled with scagliola, and has a ceiling enriched with flowers, and pierced for ventilation by heated flues above; adjoining is a room lighted by a glazed plafond; next is the house dining-room, decorated in the Munich style; and more superb is the morning room, with its arched windows, and mirrors forming arcades and vistas innumerable. A magnificent stone staircase leads to the library and evening rooms; and in the third story are billiard and card rooms; and a smoking-room, with a lofty dome elaborately decorated in traceried Moresque. The apartments are adorned with an equestrian portrait of Queen Victoria, painted by Grant, R.A.; a piece of Gobelin tapestry (Sacrifice to Diana), presented to the Club in 1849 by Prince Louis Napoleon; marble busts of William IV. and the Dukes of Kent and Cambridge; and several life-size portraits of naval and military heroes. The Club-house is provided with twenty lines of Whishaw's Telekouphona, or Speaking Telegraph, which communicate from the Secretary's room to the various apartments. The cost of this superb edifice, exclusive of fittings, was 35,000*l.*; the plot of ground on which it stands cost the Club 52,000*l.*

ARTHUR's CLUB-HOUSE, 69 St. James's-street, is named from Mr. Arthur, the keeper of White's Chocolate-house, who died 1761. The present Club-house is by Hopper; the principal windows are decorated with fluted Corinthian columns.

ATHENÆUM CLUB, Waterloo-place, Pall Mall, was established in 1823: the members are chosen by ballot, one black ball in ten excluding. The present Club-house, designed by Decimus Burton, was built in 1829-30, on a portion of the court-yard of Carlton Palace; the architecture is Grecian, with a frieze exactly copied from the Panathenaic procession in the frieze of the Parthenon—the flower and beauty of Athenian youth gracefully seated on the most exquisitely-sculptured horses,—which Flaxman regarded as the most precious examples of Grecian power in the sculpture of animals. Over the Roman-Doric entrance-portico is a colossal figure of Minerva, by Baily, R.A.; and the interior has some fine casts from *chef d'œuvres* of sculpture: the style of the hall, staircase, gallery, and apartments, is grand, massive, and severe. The Athenæum is a good illustration of the Club system. The number of ordinary members is fixed at 1200; they are mostly eminent persons, civil, military, and ecclesiastical: peers spiritual and temporal; men of the learned professions, science, the arts, and commerce; and the distinguished who do not belong to any particular class. Many of these are to be met with every day, living with the same freedom as in their own houses. For 25 guineas entrance, and 6 guineas a-year, every member has the command of an excellent library (the best Club library in London), with maps; of newspapers, English and foreign; the principal periodicals; writing materials, and attendance. The building is a sort of palace, and is kept with the same exactness and comfort as a private dwelling. Every member is master, without any of the trouble of a master: he can come when he pleases, and stay away when he pleases, without any thing going wrong; he has the command of regular servants, without having to pay or manage them; he can have whatever meal or refreshment he wants, at all hours, and served up as in his own house. From an account of the expenses at the Athenæum in the year 1832, it appears that 17,323 dinners cost, on an average, 2s. 9¾d. each, and that the average quantity of wine for each person was a small fraction more than half-a-pint. The expense of building the Club-house was 35,000l., and 5000l. for furnishing; the plate, linen, and glass cost 2500l.; library, 4000l.; and the stock of wine in cellar is usually worth about 4000l.: yearly revenue about 9000l. The principal rooms are lighted by chandeliers fitted with Faraday's perfect ventilation apparatus. In the library is an unfinished portrait of George IV., which Sir Thomas Lawrence was painting but a few hours before his decease, the last bit of colour he ever put upon canvass being that on the hilt and sword-knot of the girdle.

At the preliminary meeting for the formation of the Athenæum, February 16, 1824, were present Sir Humphry Davy, Bart., P.R.S., the Right Hon. John Wilson Croker, Sir Francis Chantrey, R.A., Richard Heber, Sir Thomas Lawrence, P.R.A., Dr. Thomas Young, F.R.S., Lord Dover, Davies Gilbert, the Earl of Aberdeen, P.S.A., Sir Henry Halford, Sir Walter Scott, Bart., Joseph Jekyll, Thomas Moore, Charles Hatchett, F.R.S.; Secretary, Professor Faraday.

"The mixture of Whigs, Radicals, savans, foreigners, dandies, authors, soldiers, sailors, lawyers, artists, doctors, and Members of both Houses of Parliament, together with an exceedingly good average supply of bishops, render the *mélange* very agreeable, despite of some two or three bores, who ' continually do dine,' and who, not satisfied with getting a 6s. dinner for 3s. 6d., ' continually do complain.' "—*New Monthly Magazine,* 1834.

BEEF-STEAK SOCIETY, "the sublime Society of Beef-steaks," (but disdaining to be thought a Club,) consists of twenty-four members, noblemen and gentlemen, who dine together off beef-steaks at five o'clock on Saturdays, from November until the end of June, at their rooms in the Lyceum Theatre. The dining-room is lined with oak, and decorated with emblematic gridirons, and in the middle of the ceiling is the gridiron first used by the cook. The orthodox accompaniment to the steaks is arrack punch. Each member may invite a friend. The Society originated with George Lambert, the scene-painter of Covent Garden Theatre during Rich's management, where Lambert often dined from a steak cooked on the fire in his painting-room, in which he was often joined by his visitors. This led to the founding of the Society by Rich and Lambert, in 1735, in a room in the theatre. After its rebuilding, the place of meeting was changed to the Shakspeare Tavern, in the Piazza; afterwards to the Lyceum Theatre, and on its destruction by fire in 1830, to the Bedford Hotel; and thence to the Lyceum, rebuilt in 1834. The number of members was increased to twenty-five, to admit the Prince of Wales (afterwards George IV.); and Captain Morris was the laureat, the sun of this "jovial system:" in 1831 he bade adieu to the Society, but in 1835 revisited it, and was presented with an elegant silver bowl; at the age of 90, he sung:

> "When my spirits are low for relief and delight,
> I still place your splendid memorial in sight;
> And call to my muse, when care strives to pursue,
> 'Bring the steaks to my mem'ry, and the bowl to my view.'"

There was also a Beef-steak *Club,* which is mentioned by Ned Ward in

1709. Peg Woffington was a member, and the President wore as an emblem a gold gridiron.

BOODLE'S, 28 St. James's-street, is the noted "Savoir vivre" Club-house, designed by Holland. It contains portraits of C. J. Fox and the Duke of Devonshire. Gibbon, the historian, was one of its early members. Next door, 29, Gillray, the caricaturist, in 1815, threw himself from an upstairs window, and died in consequence.

BROOKS'S, the Whig Club-house, at 60, west side of St. James's-street, was designed by Holland, and opened in 1778; but was originally established in Pall Mall, in 1764, by the Duke of Portland, C. J. Fox, and others. It was formerly a gaming-club, kept by Almack, and then by Brooks, a wine-merchant and money-lender, who left the Club soon after the present house was built, and died in poverty about 1782. Among the early members were C. J. Fox, Burke, Sir Joshua Reynolds, Garrick, Horace Walpole, Hume, Gibbon, and Sheridan. When Wilberforce was young and gay, he played here at faro; but his usual resort was at Goosetree's, in Pall Mall, where he one night kept the bank and won 600l.; but this weaned him from gaming. On March 21, 1772, Mr. Thynne retired from Brooks's in disgust, because he had won only 12,000 guineas in two months. The Club was famous for wagers; and the old betting-book is an oddity.

CARLTON CLUB-HOUSE, Pall Mall (Tory and Conservative), was originally built in the Grecian style, by Sir Robert Smirke, R.A., but was enlarged by his brother, Mr. Sydney Smirke, in florid Italian, nearly a fac-simile of Sansovino's Library of St. Mark at Venice: the lower order Doric, the upper Ionic; the six intercolumniations occupied by arched windows, with bold keystones, and the upper window spandrels filled with sculpture; above is a decorated frieze, rich cornice, and massive balustrade. The façade is of Caen stone, but the shafts and pilasters are of polished Peterhead granite, already dimmed by London smoke. This new portion will form only one-third of the entire façade.

CHESS-CLUBS, see page 79-80.

CITY CLUB-HOUSE, 19 Old Broad-street, occupying the site of the old South-Sea House, was built in 1833, from the design of Hardwick, R.A. The style is handsome Palladian; the only sculpture is a rich festooned garland over the doorway. The Club consists of merchants, bankers, and professional men of the City.

CLUB CHAMBERS, Regent-street, west side, between Pall Mall and Piccadilly, was built in 1839, by Decimus Burton; cost 26,000l. The style is Italian; the ground-story is rusticated, and terminated by a lace band, or string-course, enriched with the Vitruvian scroll; this forms a basement to three other stories, surmounted by a bold and enriched cornice. The principal floor has handsome balconies, Corinthian columns, and pediments; but the whole façade is too narrow for its height. The entrance is beneath a portico with coupled Doric columns. The building contains 77 chambers, coffee and dining-rooms, and offices. The whole is ventilated, and warmed by hot water, with complete skill; and is supplied with water from a well 250 feet deep, which is raised to the attic story by a steam-engine, also employed for lifting coals, furniture, &c. The Chambers are let in suites by the proprietors. They occupy the site of a house built by Mr. Nash for Charles Blicke, Esq.: it was filled with articles of vertu, and superb decoration; among which was a small circular temple, supported by Corinthian columns with brass capitals; and a conservatory embellished with models from Canova. Altogether, this was one of the most elaborately-decorated houses in the metropolis.

CLUB CHAMBERS, St. James's-square, north corner of King-street (formerly the mansion of Lord Castlereagh, d. 1822), has been refronted in cement, in the Italian *palazzo* style (Johnson, architect) : the ground-floor has some good vermiculated rustic-work, and the windows of the King-street front are piquant.

CONSERVATIVE CLUB-HOUSE, on the site of the old Thatched-House Tavern, 74 St. James's-street, was designed by Sydney Smirke and George Basevi, 1845. The upper portion is Corinthian, with columns and pilasters, and a frieze sculptured with the imperial crown and oak-wreaths ; the lower order is Roman-Doric ; and the wings are slightly advanced, with an enriched entrance-porch north, and a bow-window south. The interior is superbly decorated in colour by Sang : the coved hall, with a gallery round it, and the domed vestibule above it, is a fine specimen of German encaustic embellishment, in the arches, soffites, spandrels, and ceilings ; and the hall floor is tessellated, around a noble star of marqueterie. The evening room, on the first floor, nearly 100 feet in length and 26 in breadth, has an enriched coved ceiling, and a beautiful frieze of the rose, shamrock, and thistle, supported by scagliola Corinthian columns ; the morning room, beneath, is of the same dimensions, with Ionic pillars. The library, in the upper story north, has columns and pi-lasters with bronzed capitals ; and beneath is the coffee-room. Here is no grained or imitative wood-work, the doors and fittings being wainscot-oak, bird's-eye maple, and sycamore. The baths and dressing-rooms in the entresol are very complete, and the kitchen is skilfully planned.

COVENTRY HOUSE CLUB (the AMBASSADORS') is at 106 Piccadilly : the mansion occupies the site of the old *Greyhound* Inn, and was bought by the Earl of Coventry of Sir Hugh Hunlock, in 1764, for 10,000 guineas.

CROCKFORD'S CLUB-HOUSE, 50, west side of St. James's-street, was built for Crockford in 1827 ; B. and P. Wyatt, architects. It consists of two wings and a centre, with four Corinthian pilasters with entab-lature, and a balustrade throughout ; the ground-floor has Venetian windows, and the upper story large French windows. The entrance-hall has a screen of Roman-Ionic scagliola columns with gilt capitals, and a cupola of gilding and stained glass. The coffee-room and library have Ionic columns and centre from the Temple of Minerva Polias ; the staircase is panelled with scagliola, and enriched with Corinthian columns. The grand drawing-room is in the style of Louis Quatorze : azure ground, with elaborate cove, ceiling enrichments bronze-gilt, doorway paintings *à la Watteau ;* and paneling, masks, and terminals heavily gilt. The interior was redecorated in 1849, and opened for the Military, Naval, and County Service Club, but was closed in 1851.

Crockford started in life as a fishmonger, in the old bulk-shop next door to Tem-ple Bar Without, which he quitted for "play" in St. James's. He began by taking Watier's old club-house, where he set up a hazard-bank, and won a great deal of money ; he then separated from his partner, who had a bad year, and failed. Crockford now removed to St. James's-street, had a good year, and built the mag-nificent club-house which bore his name ; the decorations alone are said to have cost him 94,000*l.* The election of the club members was vested in a committee ; the house appointments were superb, and Ude was engaged as *maître d'hôtel.* "Crockford's" now became the high fashion. Card-tables were regularly placed, and whist was played occasionally ; but the aim, end, and final cause of the whole was the hazard-bank, at which the proprietor took his nightly stand, prepared for all comers. His speculation was eminently successful. During several years, every thing that any body had to lose and cared to risk was swallowed up ; and Crockford became a *millionaire.* He retired in 1840, "much as an Indian chief retires from a hunting-country when there is not game enough left for his tribe ;" and the Club then tottered to its fall. After Crockford's death, the lease of the club-house (thirty-two years, rent 1400*l.*) was sold for 2900*l.*

DILETTANTI SOCIETY, Thatched-House Tavern, 85 St. James's-street, originated in 1734, with a party of *Dilettanti* (lovers of the fine arts), who had travelled or resided in Italy : in 1764, they commissioned certain artists to journey to the East, to illustrate its antiquities; and by the aid of the Society several important works, including Stuart's *Athens*, have been published. The Dilettanti formerly met at Parsloe's in St. James's-street, whence they removed to the Thatched-House in 1799, where they dine on Sundays from February to July. The meeting-room is hung with portraits of the early members, and two fine conversation pictures by Sir Joshua Reynolds.

The forty-two pictures include portraits of Sir Joseph Banks, Sir William Hamilton, Sir Joshua Reynolds, Sir H. Englefield, R. Payne Knight, the Earls of Sandwich and Holderness; Charles Sackville, Duke of Dorset; Lords Galloway and Le Despencer, &c.

ERECTHEUM CLUB-HOUSE, St. James's-square (entrance 8 York-street), was the house of Wedgewood, whose beautiful "ware" was shewn in its rooms. It was formerly the site of Romney House; and from its windows William III. used to witness the fireworks in the square at public rejoicings.

GARRICK CLUB-HOUSE, 23 King-street, Covent Garden, contains a Collection of Theatrical Paintings and Drawings, assembled by the late Charles Mathews, and now the property of a member of the Club: they include:

Elliston as Octavian, by Singleton; Macklin (aged 93), by Opie; Mrs. Pritchard, by Hayman; Peg Woffington, by R. Wilson; Nell Gwynne, by Sir Peter Lely; Mrs. Abington; Samuel Foote, by Sir Joshua Reynolds; Colley Cibber as Lord Foppington; Mrs. Bracegirdle; Kitty Clive; Mrs. Robinson, after Reynolds; Garrick as Macbeth, and Mrs. Pritchard, Lady Macbeth, by Zoffany; Garrick as Richard III., by Morland, sen.; Young Roscius, by Opie; Quin, by Hogarth; Rich and his Family, by Hogarth; Charles Mathews, four characters, by Harlowe; Nat Lee, painted in Bedlam; Anthony Leigh as the Spanish Friar, by Kneller; John Liston, by Clint; Munden, by Opie; John Johnstone, by Shee; Lacy in three characters, by Wright; Scene from Charles II., by Clint; Mrs. Siddons as Lady Macbeth, by Harlowe; J. P. Kemble as Cato, by Lawrence; Macready as Henry IV., by Jackson; Edwin, by Gainsborough; the twelve of the School of Garrick; Kean, Young, Elliston, and Mrs. Inchbald, by Harlowe; Garrick as Richard III., by Loutherbourg; Rich as Harlequin; Moody and Parsons in the "Committee," by Vandergucht; King as Touchstone, by Zoffany; Thomas Dogget; Henderson, by Gainsborough; Elder Colman, by Reynolds; Mrs. Oldfield, by Kneller; Mrs. Billington; Nancy Dawson; Screen scene from the "School for Scandal," as originally cast; Scene from "Venice Preserved" (Garrick and Mrs. Cibber), by Zoffany; Scene from "Macbeth" (Henderson); Scene from "Love, Law, and Physic," (Mathews, Liston, Blanchard, and Emery), by Clint; Scene from the "Clandestine Marriage" (King and Mr. and Mrs. Baddeley), by Zoffany; Weston as Billy Button, by Zoffany. The following have been presented to the Club: Busts of Mrs. Siddons and J. P. Kemble, by Mrs. Siddons; of Garrick, Captain Marryat, Dr. Kitchiner, and Malibran; Garrick, by Roubiliac; Griffin and Johnson in the "Alchemist," by Von Bleeck; miniatures of Mrs. Robinson and Peg Woffington; Sketch of Kean, by Lambert; Garrick Mulberry-tree Snuff-box; Joseph Harris as Cardinal Wolsey, from the Strawberry Hill Collection; proof print of the Trial of Queen Katherine, by Harlowe.

The Pictures may be seen by the personal introduction of a member of the Club on Wednesdays (except in September), between eleven and three o'clock. The Garrick Club was instituted in 1831, "for the general patronage of the Drama; the formation of a Theatrical Library; and Works, and Costume; and for bringing together the patrons of the Drama," &c. Members not to exceed 300; entrance, fifteen guineas; annual subscription, six guineas. The *Garrick* is noted for its summer gin-punch, thus made: Pour half-a-pint of gin on the outer peel of a lemon, then a little lemon-juice, a glass of maraschino, a pint and a quarter of water, and two bottles of iced soda-water.

GRESHAM CLUB-HOUSE, St. Swithin's-lane, King-William-street, City, was built in 1844, for the Club named after Sir Thomas Gresham, who founded the Royal Exchange. The Club consists chiefly of merchants and professional men. The style of the Club-house (H. Flower, architect) is Italian, from portions of two palaces in Venice.

GUARDS' (Officers of the Household Troops) CLUB-HOUSE, 70 Pall Mall, was designed by Henry Harrison, for the Club, who removed here from St. James's-street in 1850.

KIT-KAT CLUB, a society of thirty-nine noblemen and gentlemen, zealously attached to the Protestant succession in the House of Hanover. The Club is said to have originated about 1700, in Shire-lane, Temple Bar, at the house of Christopher Kat, a pastrycook, where the members dined: he excelled in making mutton-pies, always in the bill of fare, and called Kit-kats; hence the name of the Society.

Jacob Tonson, the bookseller, was secretary: among the members were the Dukes of Somerset, Richmond, Grafton, Devonshire, and Marlborough; and (after the accession of George I.) the Duke of Newcastle, the Earls of Dorset, Sunderland, Manchester, Wharton, and Kingston; Lords Hallifax and Somers; Sir Robert Walpole, Garth, Vanbrugh, Congreve, Granville, Addison, Maynwaring, Stepney, and Walsh. Pope tells us that "the day Lord Mohun and the Earl of Berkley were entered of the Club, Jacob said he saw they were just going to be ruined. When Lord Mohun broke down the gilded emblem on the top of *his* chair, Jacob complained to his friends, and said that a man who could do that would cut a man's throat. So that he had the good and the forms of the Society at heart. The paper was all in Lord Hallifax's writing, of a subscription of 400 guineas for the encouragement of good comedies, and was dated 1709. Soon after that they broke up." (Spence's *Anecdotes.*) Tonson had his own and all their portraits painted by Sir Godfrey Kneller: each member gave him his; and to suit the room, a shorter canvass was used (viz. 36 by 28 inches), but sufficiently long to admit a hand, and still known as the Kit-kat size. The pictures, 42 in number, were removed to Tonson's seat at Barnes Elmes, where he built a handsome room for their reception. At his death in 1736, Tonson left them to his great nephew, also an eminent bookseller, who died in 1767. The pictures were then removed to the house of his brother, at Water-Oakley, near Windsor; and on his death to the house of Mr. Baker, of Hertingfordbury, where they now remain.

Walpole speaks of the Club as "the patriots that saved Britain," as having "its beginning about the Trial of the Seven Bishops in the reign of James II.," and consisting of "the most eminent men who opposed the reign of that arbitrary monarch." Garth wrote some verses for the toasting-glass of the Club, which have immortalised four of the reigning beauties at the commencement of the last century: the Ladies Carlisle, Essex, Hyde, and Wharton. Hallifax similarly commemorated the charms of the Duchesses of St. Albans, Beaufort, and Richmond; Ladies Sunderland and Mary Churchill; and Mdlle. Spanheime.

LAW INSTITUTION (the), west side of Chancery-lane, was built in 1832, (Vulliamy, architect,) for the Law Society of the United Kingdom; and combines a valuable library with a hall and office of registry, with club accommodation. The Chancery-lane front has a Grecian-Ionic portico, with a pediment of considerable beauty; and the club front in Bell-yard resembles that of an Italian palace. The Society consists of attorneys, solicitors, and proctors practising in Great Britain and Ireland, and of Writers to the Scottish Signet and courts of justice; and certificates of attorneys and solicitors must be registered here before granted by the Commissioners of Stamps. Law lectures, limited to one hour, are delivered during term in the Great Hall.

LITERARY CLUB, or "THE CLUB," was formed by Sir Joshua Reynolds and Dr. Johnson in 1764, at the Turk's Head, in Gerard-street; whence they removed to Prince's, in Sackville-street; and next to Baxter's, afterwards Thomas's, in Dover-street; in 1792 to Parsloe's, in St. James's-street; and in 1799 to the Thatched-House Tavern. They originally supped together weekly on Mondays, which, after 1772, was changed to dining together once in every fortnight during the sitting of

Parliament. Dr. Johnson was a great encourager of clubs; he was member of one held at the King's Head, Ivy-lane, Newgate-street, now a chop-house. Johnson, in 1783, also established a minor club at the Essex Head, Essex-street, Strand, then kept by Samuel Greaves, an old servant of Mr. Thrale. The Doctor, inviting Sir Joshua Reynolds to join the club, says, "We meet twice a-week, and he who misses forfeits twopence:" Sir Joshua declined being a member; but Brocklesby, Horsley, Daines Barrington, and Windham joined this Club: its rules were drawn up by Johnson, and are printed by Boswell.

OCTOBER CLUB (the), formed in 1712, at the Bell Tavern, King-street, Westminster, was so called from being composed of High-Church Tory country gentlemen, who, when at home, drank October ale. From it the March Club took its rise.—Walcott's *Westminster*, p. 70.

ORIENTAL CLUB, 18 Hanover-square, was established in 1824 by Sir John Malcolm, the traveller and brave soldier. The members are noblemen and gentlemen associated with the administration of our Eastern empire, or who have travelled or resided in Asia, at St. Helena, in Egypt, at the Cape of Good Hope, the Mauritius, or at Constantinople.

OXFORD AND CAMBRIDGE CLUB-HOUSE, 71 Pall Mall, for Members of the two Universities, was designed by Sir Robert Smirke, R.A., and his brother, Sydney Smirke, 1835-8. The Pall Mall façade is 80 feet in width by 75 in height, and the rear lies over-against the court of Marlborough House. The ornamental detail is very rich: as the entrance-portico, with Corinthian columns; the balcony, with its panels of metal foliage; and the ground-story frieze, and arms of Oxford and Cambridge Universities over the portico columns. The upper part of the building has a delicate Corinthian entablature and balustrade; and above the principal windows are bas-reliefs in panels, executed in cement by Nicholl, from designs by Sir R. Smirke, R.A.

Centre panel: Minerva and Apollo presiding on Mount Parnassus; and the river Helicon, surrounded by the Muses. Extreme panels: Homer singing to a warrior, a female, and a youth; Virgil singing his Georgics to a group of peasants. Other four panels: Milton reciting to his daughter; Shakspeare attended by Tragedy and Comedy; Newton explaining his system; Bacon, his philosophy.

Beneath the ground-floor is a basement of offices, and an entresol or mezzanine of chambers. The principal apartments are tastefully decorated; the drawing-room is panelled with *papier-maché*; and the libraries are filled with book-cases of beautifully-marked Russian birch-wood. From the back library is a view of Marlborough House and its gardens.

PARTHENON CLUB-HOUSE (late Mr. Edwards's), east side of Regent-street, nearly facing St. Philip's Chapel, was designed by Nash: the first floor is elegant Corinthian. The south division was built by Mr. Nash for his own residence; it has a long gallery, decorated from a *loggia* of the Vatican at Rome: it is now the "Gallery of Illustration."

REFORM CLUB-HOUSE, between the *Travellers'* and *Carlton* Club-houses, has a frontage in Pall Mall of 135 feet, being nearly equal to that of the *Athenæum* (76 feet) and *Travellers'* (74 feet). The *Reform* was built in 1838-39, from the designs of Barry, R.A.; and resembles the Farnese Palace at Rome, designed by Michael Angelo Buonarotti, in 1545. The club-house contains six floors and 134 apartments: the basement and mezzanine below the street pavement, and the chambers in the roof, are not seen.

"The points most admired are extreme simplicity and unity of design, combined with very unusual richness. The breadth of the piers between the windows contributes not a little to that repose which is so essential to simplicity, and hardly less so to stateliness. The string-courses are particularly beautiful, while the cornicione (68 feet from the pavement) gives extraordinary majesty and grandeur to the whole. The roof is covered with Italian tiles; the edifice is faced throughout with Portland stone, and is a very fine specimen of masonry. In building it a strong scaffolding was constructed, and on the top was laid a railway, upon which was worked a traversing crane, movable along the building either longitudinally or transversely; by which means the stones were raised from the ground, and placed on the wall with very little labour to the mason, who had only to adjust the bed and lay the stone."—*Civil Engineer and Architect's Journal*, 1841.

In the centre of the interior is a grand hall, 56 by 50, resembling an Italian *cortile*, surrounded by colonnades, below Ionic, and above Corinthian; the latter is a picture-galley, where, inserted in the scagliola walls, are whole-length portraits of eminent political Reformers. The floor of the hall is tessellated; and the entire roof is strong diapered flint-glass, by Pellatt and Co. The staircase, like that of an Italian palace, leads to the upper gallery of the hall, opening into the principal drawing-room, which is over the coffee-room in the garden front, both being the entire length of the building; adjoining are a library, card-room, &c., over the library and dining-rooms. Above are a billiard-room and lodging-rooms for members of the Club; there being a separate entrance to the latter by a lodge adjoining the Travellers' Club.

The basement comprises two storied wine-cellars beneath the hall, besides the Kitchen Department, planned by Alexis Soyer, originally *chef-de-cuisine* of the Club: it contains novel employments of steam and gas, and mechanical applications of practical ingenuity; the inspection of which has long been one of the privileged sights of London. The *cuisine*, under M. Soyer, enjoyed European fame, fully testified in a magnificent banquet given by the Club to Ibrahim Pasha, July 3, 1846. The Club-house is ventilated by a rapidly-revolving fan driven by a steam-engine, the steam of which warms the whole building.

The Reform Club was established by Liberal Members of the two Houses of Parliament, to aid the carrying of the Reform Bill, 1830–32; the number of members is limited to 1400, exclusive of honorary, supernumerary, and life members: entrance-fee 25 guineas; annual subscription, first five years 10*l*. 10*s*., subsequently 8*l*. 8*s*.*

The south side of Pall Mall has a truly patrician air in its seven costly Club-houses, of exceedingly rich architectural character, and reminding one of Captain Morris's luxurious resource:

> " In town let me live then, in town let me die;
> For in truth I can't relish the country, not I.
> If one must have a villa in summer to dwell,
> Oh, give me the sweet shady side of Pall Mall."

ROXBURGHE CLUB (the) was founded by the Rev. T. Frognall (afterwards Dr.) Dibdin, at the St. Albans Tavern, St. James's, on June 17, 1812, immediately after the sale of the rarest lot in the Roxburghe Library, viz. *Il Decamerone di Boccaccio*, which produced 2260*l*. The number of members was limited to 24, subsequently to 31.

The President of this Club was the second Earl Spencer: among the most celebrated members were the Duke of Devonshire, the Marquis of Blandford (the late Duke of Marlborough), Lord Althorp (late Earl Spencer), Lord Morpeth (present Earl of Carlisle), Lord Gower (late Earl of Carlisle), Sir Masterman Sykes, Sir Egerton Brydges, Mr. (afterwards Baron) Bolland, Mr. Dent, Mr. Townley, Rev. T. C. Heber, Rev. Rob. Holwell Carr, Sir Walter Scott, &c.: Dr. Dibdin being secretary. The avowed object of the Club was the reprinting of rare and neglected pieces of ancient literature; and, at one of the early meetings, " it was proposed and concluded for each member of the Club to reprint a scarce piece of ancient lore, to be given to the members, one copy being on vellum for the chairman, and only as many copies as members." It may, however, be questioned whether the " dinners" of the Club were not more important than the literature. They were given at the St. Alban's, at Grillion's, at the Clarendon, and the Albion Taverns. Of these entertainments some curious details have been recorded by Mr. Joseph Haslewood, one of the members, in a MS. entitled " *Roxburghe Revels; or, an Account of the Annual Display, culinary and festivous, interspersed with Matters of Moment or Merriment:*" a selection from its rarities has ap-

* The number of Members in the different London Clubs may be about 28,000.

peared in the *Athenæum:* at the second dinner, Mr. Heber in the chair, a few tarried until, " on arriving at home, the click of time bespoke a quarter to four." Among the early members was the Rev. Mr. Dodd. one of the masters of Westminster School, who, until 1818 (when he died), enlivened the Club with Robin-Hood ditties. At the fourth dinner, at Grillion's, Sir Masterman Sykes chairman, 20 members present, the bill was 57*l*. At the Anniversary, 1818, at the Albion, Mr. Heber in the chair, 15 present, the bill was 85*l*. 9*s*. 6*d*., or 5*l*. 14*s*. each; including turtle, 12*l*. 10*s*.; venison, 10*l*. 10*s*.; and wine, 30*l*. 17*s*. " Ancients, believe it," says Haslewood, " we were not dead drunk, and therefore lie quiet under the table for once, and let a few moderns be uppermost."

The Roxburghe Club still exists; and may justly be said to have suggested the publishing Societies of the present day; as the Camden, Shakspeare, Percy, &c.

TRAVELLERS' CLUB-HOUSE, adjoining the *Athenæum*, in Pall Mall, was designed by Barry, R.A., and built in 1832. The architecture is the nobler Italian, resembling a Roman palace: the plan is a quadrangle, with an open area in the middle, so that all the rooms are well lighted. The Pall Mall front has a bold and rich cornice, and the windows are decorated with Corinthian pilasters; the garden front varies in the windows; but the Italian taste is preserved throughout, with the most careful finish: the roof is Italian tiles. The Travellers' Club originated shortly after the Peace of 1814, in a suggestion of the late Marquis of Londonderry, then Lord Castlereagh, with a view to a resort for gentlemen who had resided or travelled abroad; as well as to the accommodation of foreigners, who, when properly recommended, receive an invitation for the period of their stay. (*Quarterly Review*, No. cx. 1836.) By one of the rules, "no person is eligible to the Travellers' Club who shall not have travelled out of the British Islands to a distance of at least 500 miles from London in a direct line." Prince Talleyrand, during his residence in London, generally joined the muster of whist-players at this Club.

UNION CLUB-HOUSE, Cockspur-street, and west side of Trafalgar-square, was completed in 1824, from designs by Sir R. Smirke, R.A.* James Smith has left us a sketch of his every-day life at this Club:

" At three o'clock I walk to the Union Club, read the journals, hear Lord John Russell deified or diablerised, do the same with Sir Robert Peel or the Duke of Wellington, and then join a knot of conversationists by the fire till six o'clock, consisting of lawyers, merchants, and gentlemen at large. We then and there discuss the Three per Cent Consols (some of us preferring Dutch Two-and-a-half per Cents), and speculate upon the probable rise, shape, and cost of the New Exchange. If Lady Harrington happen to drive past our window in her landau, we compare her equipage to the Algerine Ambassador's; and when politics happen to be discussed, rally Whigs, Radicals, and Conservatives alternately, but never seriously, such subjects having a tendency to create acrimony. At six, the room begins to be deserted; wherefore I adjourn to the dining-room, and gravely looking over the bill of fare, exclaim to the waiter, 'Haunch of mutton and apple-tart!' These viands despatched, with the accompanying liquids and water, I mount upward to the library, take a book and my seat in the arm-chair, and read till nine. Then call for a cup of coffee and a biscuit, resuming my book till eleven; afterwards return home to bed."—*Comic Miscellanies.*

UNITED SERVICE CLUB-HOUSE, at the corner of Pall Mall, was built in 1826, from a design by Nash : the principal front has a Roman-Doric portico, and above it a Corinthian portico with pediment. Here is Stanfield's fine picture of the Battle of Trafalgar ; and a copy by Lane (painted 1851) of a contemporary portrait of Sir Francis Drake.

The *Wyndham* was once considered the most expensive club, and the *United Service* the cheapest; the latter, probably, from the number of absent members.

---

* The West-end clubs contribute largely to the feeding of the poor. The Union Club distributed in the year 1844, to the poor of St. Martin's in-the-Fields, no less than 3104 lbs. of broken bread, 4556 lbs. of broken meat, 1147 pints of tea-leaves, and 1158 pints of coffee-grounds.

Formerly, the Duke of Wellington might often be seen dining at this Club on a joint; "and on one occasion, when he was charged 15d. instead of 1s. for it, he bestirred himself till the odd threepence was struck off. The motive was obvious; he took the trouble of objecting to give his sanction to the principle."
—*Quarterly Review*, No. cx. 1836.

UNITED SERVICE CLUB (JUNIOR), north corner of Charles-street, Regent-street, was originally designed for the United Service Club, by Sir Robert Smirke, R.A. The Charles-street front has a large bas-relief of Britannia distributing laurels to her brave sons by land and sea.

UNIVERSITY CLUB-HOUSE, Suffolk-street, Pall Mall East, was built in 1824; Deering and Wilkins, architects. It is of the Grecian-Doric and Ionic orders; the staircase walls have casts from the Parthenon frieze. The Club is limited to 1000 members, 500 from each University.

WHITE'S (Tory) CLUB-HOUSE, 36 and 37 St. James's-street, has an elegant front, designed by James Wyatt, restored and enriched in 1851: the medallions above the drawing-room story are classic compositions. The Club, as White's Chocolate-house, was originally established about 1698, near the bottom of the west side of St. James's-street: the Club-house, then kept by Mr. Arthur, was burnt down April 28, 1773; and plate 6 of Hogarth's "Rake's Progress" shews a room at White's so intent upon their play, as neither to see the flames nor hear the watchmen, who are bursting into the room to give the alarm. Sir Andrew Fountayne's collection of pictures, valued at 3000l., was destroyed in the fire; and the King and the Prince of Wales were present, encouraging the firemen and people to work the engines. In 1736, the principal members of the club were the Duke of Devonshire, Lord Chesterfield, Sir John Cope, Bubb Doddington, and Colley Cibber: before this date it was an open chocolate-house. It soon became a gaming-club and a noted supper-house, the dinner-hour being early a century since. Betting was another of its pastimes; and a book for entering wagers was always laid upon the table.

Walpole writes to Sir Horace Mann, Sept. 1, 1750: "They have put into the papers a good story made at White's. A man dropped down dead at the door, and was carried in; the Club immediately made bets whether he was dead or not; and when they were going to bleed him, the wagerers for his death interposed, and said it would affect the fairness of the bet."

The Club, on June 20, 1814, gave at Burlington-house, to the Allied Sovereigns then in England, a ball, which cost 9489l. 2s. 6d.; and on July 6 following, the Club gave a dinner to the Duke of Wellington, which cost 2480l. 10s. 9d.—See Cunningham's *Handbook* ("White's,") for several very interesting extracts from the Club-books, and from writers of the middle of the last century, "curiously characteristic of the state of society at the time."

WHITTINGTON CLUB and METROPOLITAN ATHENÆUM, Arundel-street, originated in 1846 with Mr. Douglas Jerrold, who became its first president. It combines a literary society with a club-house, upon an economical scale, for the middle classes. The premises, formerly the Crown and Anchor Tavern, contain dining and coffee-rooms, library and reading-rooms, smoking and chess-rooms; and a large room for balls, concerts, and soirees. Lectures are given here, and classes held for the higher branches of education, fencing and dancing, &c. The members average 1600, nearly one-fourth ladies at one guinea per annum; gentlemen two guineas, and 10s. 6d. entrance. In the ball-room is a picture of Whittington listening to Bow-bells, painted by F. Newenham, and presented to the Club by its founder.

WINDHAM CLUB, 11 St. James's-square, was founded by the late Lord Nugent, for gentlemen "connected with each other by a common bond of literary or personal acquaintance:" limited to 600 members; entrance, 25 guineas; annual subscription, 8*l*. The mansion was the residence of William Windham, and of the accomplished John Duke of Roxburghe; and here the Roxburghe Library was sold in 1812, the sale commencing May 18, and extending to forty-one days. Lord Chief-Justice Ellenborough lived here in 1814; and subsequently the Earl of Blessington, who possessed a fine collection of pictures.

COFFEE-HOUSES.

Coffee was first drunk in London about the middle of the 17th century. "The first coffee-house in London," says Aubrey (MS. in the Bodleian Library), "was in St. Michael's-alley, in Cornhill, opposite to the church, which was set up by one —— Bowman (coachman to Mr. Hodges, a Turkey merchant, who putt him upon it), in or about the yeare 1652. 'Twas about four yeares before any other was sett up, and that was by Mr. Farr. Jonathan Paynter, over-against to St. Michael's Church, was the first apprentice to the trade, viz. to Bowman."

Another account states that one Edwards, a Turkey merchant, on his return from the East in 1657, brought with him a Ragusian Greek servant, Pasqua Rosee, who prepared coffee every morning for his master, and with the coachman above named set up the first coffee-house in St. Michael's-alley; but they soon quarrelled and separated, the coachman establishing himself in St. Michael's churchyard.

Sir Hans Sloane had in his Museum in Bloomsbury-square, "part of a coffee-tree, with the berries and leaves thereon; it was brought over from Moco, in Arabia, by Mr. E. Clive, of London, merchant," who has described it in *Philos. Trans.* No. 208.

Coffee is first mentioned in our statute-book anno 1660 (12 Car II. c. 24), when a duty of 4*d*. was laid upon every gallon of coffee made and sold. A statute of 1663 directs that all coffee-houses should be licensed at the Quarter Sessions. In 1675, Charles II. issued a proclamation to shut up the coffee-houses, charged with being seminaries of sedition; but in a few days he suspended this proclamation by a second.

BAKER'S COFFEE-HOUSE, 1 Change-alley, Lombard-street, is noted for its chops and steaks, broiled in the coffee-room, and thus eaten hot from the gridiron; with excellent stout and post-prandial punch.

BALTIC COFFEE-HOUSE, 58 Threadneedle-street, is the rendezvous of merchants and brokers connected with the Russian trade, or that in tallow, oil, hemp, and seeds. The supply of news to the subscription-room is, with the exception of the chief London, Liverpool, and Hull papers, confined to that from the north of Europe, and the tallow-producing countries on the South American coast. In the upper part of the Baltic Coffee-house is the auction sale-room for tallow, oils, &c.

BEDFORD COFFEE-HOUSE, Covent Garden, at the north-east corner of the arcade, or Piazza, was the favourite resort of Garrick, Quin, Foote, Murphy, and Sheridan; and here the Beef-steak Society once met.

BUTTON'S COFFEE-HOUSE, "over-against Tom's, in Covent Garden," was established in 1712, and thither Addison transferred the company from Tom's. In July 1713, a Lion's Head, "a proper emblem of knowledge and action, being all head and paws," was set up at Button's, in imitation of the celebrated Lion at Venice, to receive letters and papers for the *Guardian*. Here the wits of that time used to assemble; and among them, Addison, Pope, Steele, Swift, Arbuthnot, Count Viviani, Savage, Budgell, Philips, Davenant, and Colonel Brett; and here it was that Philips hung up a birchen rod, with which he threatened to chastise Pope for "a biting epigram." Button, the master of the coffee-house, had been a servant in the Countess of

Warwick's family; and it is said that when Addison suffered any vexation from the Countess, he withdrew the company from Button's house. The Lion's Head was removed to the Shakspeare Tavern, under the Piazza; and in 1751 was placed in the Bedford Coffee-house adjoining, as the letter-box of the *Inspector*. In 1804, it was bought by Mr. Richardson, of Richardson's Hotel : it was sold by his son to the late Duke of Bedford, and is preserved to this day at Woburn. The Lion's Head is etched in Ireland's *Illustrations of Hogarth :* it is boldly carved, and bears these lines from Martial :

> " Cervantur magnis isti Cervicibus ungues :
> Non nisi delictâ pascitur ille ferâ."

CHAPTER COFFEE-HOUSE, 50 Paternoster-row, is mentioned in No. 1 of the *Connoisseur*, Jan. 31, 1754, as the resort of "those encouragers of literature, and not the worst judges of merit, the booksellers." Chatterton dates several letters from the *Chapter*.

The late Alexander Stephens left some reminiscences of the literati and politicians who frequented the Chapter from 1797 to 1805. The box in the north-east corner was called the *Witenagemot*, and was occupied by the "Wet Paper Club." Here assembled Dr. Buchan, author of *Domestic Medicine;* Dr. Berdmore, Master of the Charter-house; Walker, the rhetorician; and Dr. Towers, the political writer; Dr. George Fordyce, and Dr. Gower of "the Middlesex," who, with Buchan, prescribed the Chapter punch; Robinson, King of the Booksellers; and his brother John; Joseph Johnson, the friend of Priestley and Paine, and Cowper and Fuseli; Alexander Chalmers, the workman of the Robinsons; the two Parrys, of the *Courier*, then the organ of Jacobinism; Lowndes, the electrician; Dr. Busby, the writer on music; Jacob, an Alderman and M.P.; Waithman, then Common Councilman; Mr. Blake, the banker, of Lombard-street; Mr. Patterson, a North Briton, who taught Pitt mathematics; Alexander Stephens; and Phillips (afterwards Sir Richard), who here recruited for contributors to his *Monthly Magazine*. The Witenagemot has long lost its literary celebrities; but the *Chapter* maintains its reputation for good punch and coffee, scarce pamphlets, and liberal supply of town and country newspapers.

CLIFFORD-STREET COFFEE-HOUSE, corner of Bond-street, had its debating club, of which Canning, Mackintosh, and "Conversation" Sharp; Charles Moore, son of the celebrated traveller; and Lord Charles Townsend, fourth son of the facetious Marquis; were distinguished members. During the debate, the refreshment was porter, to a pot of which Canning once compared the eloquence of Mirabeau, as empty and vapid as his patriotism—"foam and froth at the top, heavy and muddy within."

COCOA-TREE, 64 St. James's-street, near the Thatched House, was the Tory chocolate-house in Queen Anne's reign : " a Whig," says Defoe, " will no more go to the *Cocoa-Tree* or *Ozinda's*, than a Tory will be seen at the coffee-house of St. James's." The *Cocoa-Tree* is named in the *Spectator* and *Connoisseur;* and in 1762 by Gibbon, who describes " the first men in the kingdom, in fortune and fashion, supping at little tables covered with a napkin, in the middle of a coffee-room, upon a bit of cold meat or a sandwich, and drinking a glass of punch."

DEACON'S COFFEE AND DINING HOUSE, 3 Walbrook, has a sixty years' file of the *Times;* here also are filed the London, Provincial, Colonial, Continental (French and German), and American newspapers; with periodicals, professional publications, and directories.

DICK'S COFFEE-HOUSE (now a tavern), 8 Fleet-street, near Temple Bar, was originally called Richard's, from its tenant in 1680. Here Steele takes the "Twaddlers," in the *Tatler*. The coffee-room retains its olden paneling, and the staircase its original balusters.

"In 1737, Dick's was kept by a Mrs. Yarrow and her daughter, who were the reigning toasts with the frequenters, and were supposed to be ridiculed in the comedy of 'the Coffee-house,' by the Rev. James Miller. This was stoutly denied by the author; but the engraver having inadvertently fixed upon Dick's Coffee-house as the frontispiece scene, the Templars, with whom the ladies were great favourites, became by this accident so confirmed in their suspicions, that they united to damn the piece, and even extended their resentment to every thing suspected to be this author's for a considerable time after."—*Biographia Dramatica.*

DON SALTERO'S COFFEE-HOUSE. (See CHELSEA, p. 75.)

GARRAWAY'S COFFEE-HOUSE, 3 Change-alley, Cornhill, was established by Thomas Garway, tobacconist and coffee-man, who first sold and retailed tea, in 1657, according to his shop-bill, still extant. Garraway's is now a noted house for luncheons and punch, and property sales. ROBINS's and JONATHAN'S were two other Change-alley coffee-houses : Garraway's for people of quality who have business in the City, and for wealthy citizens; Robins's for foreign bankers, and even foreign ministers; and Jonathan's for the buyers and sellers of stock.

The consumption of sandwiches, pale ale, stout, and sherry at Garraway's is immense. The Sale-room is an antiquated first-floor apartment, with a small rostrum for the seller, and a few commonly grained settles for the buyers. Here sales of drugs, mahogany, and timber are periodically held. Twenty or thirty property and other sales sometimes take place in a day.

GEORGE'S COFFEE-HOUSE (now a hotel), No. 213 Strand, near Essex-street, is mentioned by Foote, in his *Life of A. Murphy,* as an evening meeting-place of the town wits of 1751. Shenstone was a frequenter of George's, where, for a shilling subscription, he read "all pamphlets under a three shillings' dimension."

GRECIAN COFFEE-HOUSE, Devereux-court, Strand, was originally kept by one Constantine, a Grecian. From this house Steele proposed to date his learned articles in the *Tatler ;* it is mentioned in No. 1 of the *Spectator ;* and it was much frequented by Goldsmith and the Irish and Lancashire Templars. The premises have, since 1843, been the "Grecian Chambers;" and over the door is a bust of Devereux, Earl of Essex.

JAMAICA COFFEE-HOUSE, 1 St. Michael's-alley, Cornhill, is noted for the accuracy and fulness of its West India intelligence. The subscribers are merchants trading with Madeira and the West Indies. It is the best place for information as to the mail-packets on the West India station, or the merchant-vessels making these voyages.

ST. JAMES'S COFFEE-HOUSE, St. James's-street, south-west end, was frequented by Addison, Steele, Swift, Garrick, and Joseph Warton; and Goldsmith, whose "*Retaliation*" originated in a dinner here.

JERUSALEM COFFEE-HOUSE, 1 Cowper's-court, Cornhill, is one of the oldest of the City news-rooms, and is frequented by merchants and captains connected with the commerce of China, India, and Australia.

"The subscription-room is well furnished with files of the principal Canton, Hong Kong, Macao, Penang, Singapore, Calcutta, Bombay, Madras, Sydney, Hobart Town, Launceston, Adelaide, and Port Phillip papers, and Prices Current; besides shipping lists and papers from the various intermediate stations or ports touched at, as St. Helena, the Cape of Good Hope, &c. The books of East India shipping include arrivals, departures, casualties, &c. The full business is between two and three o'clock, p.m. In 1845, John Tawell, the Slough murderer, was captured at the Jerusalem, which he was in the habit of visiting, to ascertain information of the state of his property in Sydney."—*The City,* 2d edit. 1848.

KING'S COFFEE-HOUSE, Covent-Garden Market, was kept by Tom King, beneath the portico of St. Paul's Church. Harwood's *Alumni Etonenses,* p. 293, in the account of the boys elected from Eton to King's College, contains this entry :

"A.D. 1713. Thomas King, born at West Ashton in Wiltshire, went away scholar, in apprehension that his fellowship would be denied him, and afterwards kept that coffee-house in Covent Garden which was called by his own name."

LANGBOURN COFFEE-HOUSE, Ball-alley, Lombard-street, rebuilt in 1850, has a broiling-stove in the coffee-room, whence chops and steaks are served hot from the gridiron; and here is a wine and cigar room, embellished in handsome old French style.

LONDON COFFEE-HOUSE, Ludgate-hill (now a hotel and tavern), was opened May 1731, as "a Punch House, Dorchester Beer, and Welsh Ale Warehouse, where the finest and best old Arrack, Rum, and French Brandy is made into Punch." In front of the London Coffee-house, immediately west of St. Martin's Church, stood Ludgate; and on the site of the church Wren found the monument of a Roman soldier of the Second Legion, which is preserved in the Arundelian Collection. The London Coffee-house is noted for its booksellers' sales of stock and literary copyrights: it was within the Rules of the Fleet Prison.

LLOYD'S, Royal Exchange, celebrated for its priority of shipping intelligence, and its marine insurance, originated with one Lloyd, who kept a coffee-house in Lombard-street. One of the apartments in the Exchange is fitted up as Lloyd's coffee-room. (See EXCHANGES.)

MILES'S COFFEE-HOUSE, New Palace-yard, Westminster, was the place of meeting of the noted Rota Club, founded by James Harrington in 1659, for the dissemination of republican opinions, which he had so temptingly painted in his *Oceana.* The Club was named from its plan for changing a certain number of Members of Parliament annually by rotation: Sir William Petty, the statist, was one of its members.

" 'In 1659, the beginning of Michaelmas Term,' says Aubrey, ' he had every night a meeting at the then Turke's Head, in the New Palace-yard, where they take water, the next house to the Staires, at one Miles's, where was purposely a large ovall table, with a passage in the middle for Miles to deliver his coffee. About it sat his disciples and the virtuosi. We many times adjourned to the Rhenish Wine-house. One time Mr. Stafford and his gang came in drink from the tavern, and affronted the Junto; the soldiers offered to kick them down staires, but Mr. Harrington's moderation and persuasion hindered it.' "

NEW ENGLAND AND NORTH AND SOUTH AMERICAN COFFEE-HOUSE, 59 and 60 Threadneedle-street, has a subscription-room, with news-papers from every quarter of the globe. Here the first information can be obtained of the arrival and departure of steamers, packets, and traders, engaged in the commerce of America, whether at Montreal and Quebec, or Boston, Halifax, and New York. The heads of the chief American and continental firms are on the subscription-list, and the representatives of Barings, Rothschilds, and other wealthy establish-ments, attend the room as regularly as 'Change; as do also American captains, and the "City Correspondents" of the morning and evening press. From 300 to 400 files of newspapers are kept here, ranging from America to the East or West Indies, thence to Australia, the Havana, France, Germany, Holland, Russia, Spain, and Portugal.— (Abridged from *The City,* 2d edit.)

Adjoining is the *Cock Tavern,* with a large Soup Room, named after the *Cock,* which faced the north gate of the old Royal Exchange, and was long celebrated for the excellence of its soups, served in silver. This house was taken down in 1841; when, in a claim for compensation made by the proprietor, the trade in three years was proved to have been 344,720 basins of various soups—viz. 166,240 mock turtle, 3920 giblet, 59,360 ox-tail, 31,072 bouilli, 84,128 gravy and other soups: sometimes 500 basins of soup were sold in a day.

PEELE'S, 177 and 178 Fleet-street, east corner of Fetter-lane, was one of the coffee-houses of the Johnsonian period; and here was preserved until lately a portrait of Dr. Johnson, on the keystone of a chimney-piece, stated to have been painted by Sir Joshua Reynolds. Peele's is noted for its files of newspapers from these dates: Gazette, 1759; Times, 1780; Morning Chronicle, 1773; Morning Post, 1773; Morning Herald, 1784;

Morning Advertiser, 1794; and the evening papers from their commencement. The London, Provincial, Colonial, Continental, and American newspapers are regularly filed here; and Peele's is a well-appointed coffee-house and hotel.

RAINBOW COFFEE-HOUSE (now a tavern), 15 Fleet-street, by the Inner-Temple-gate, was the second or third Coffee-house opened in London, and had its token-money, which exists.

"JAMES FARR, 1666. A rainbow. ℞ IN FLEET-STREET. In the centre, HIS HALFPENNY. It is well known that James Farr kept the Rainbow, in Fleet-street, at the time of the Great Fire, the very year of which is marked on this token. Farr was a barber; and in the year 1657 was prevented by the inquest of St. Dunstan's-in-the-West from making and selling 'a sort of liquor called 'coffee,'' which was described *as a great nuisance and prejudice to the neighbourhood!* The house known by the sign of *the Rainbow* appears to have been let off into tenements, for there were books printed at this very time 'for Samuel Speed, at the sign of the Rainbow, near the Inner Temple Gate, in Fleet Street.'"—*Tradesmen's Tokens, &c.*, by John Yonge Akerman, Sec. Soc. Antiquaries.

The Phœnix Fire Office was established at the Rainbow about the year 1682. Coffee-houses soon became very popular:

"And who would then have thought London would ever have had near 3000, such nuisances, and that coffee would have been (as now) so much drank by the best of quality and physicians."—Hatton's *New View of London*, 1708.

Mr. Moncrieff, the dramatist, states, that about 1780 this house was kept by his grandfather, Alexander Moncrieff, when it retained its original title of "the Rainbow Coffee-house." It has vaulted cellars, excellent for keeping stout, for which the house is famous; the coffee-room, which originally had a lofty bay-window at the south end, has lately been handsomely decorated and furnished in the *Renaissance* style.

SMYRNA COFFEE-HOUSE, Pall Mall, is frequently alluded to by the writers of Queen Anne's reign; and was one of the most celebrated of the west-end houses. Prior and Swift were among its most distinguished frequenters; its "seat of learning," and "cluster of wise heads."

SOMERSET COFFEE-HOUSE, 162 Strand, has a literary association, from the Letters of *Junius* having been sometimes left at the bar.

SQUIRE'S COFFEE-HOUSE, Fulwood's-rents, Gray's Inn, was opened "when coffee first came in," and was then John's Coffee-house. From "Squire's" some of the *Spectators* are dated. The house, on the west side of the court, adjoins Gray's-Inn-gate, and is of old deep-coloured brick; it has been handsome, and is roomy, with a wide staircase, but is now let in tenements.

TOM'S COFFEE-HOUSE, Birchin-lane, Cornhill, was frequented by Garrick and by Chatterton, as a place "of the best resort;" and here was first established "the London Chess-Club." (See CHESS-CLUBS, p. 79.)

TOM'S COFFEE-HOUSE, Devereux-court, Strand, was much resorted to by men of letters: among whom were Dr. Birch, who wrote the *History of the Royal Society;* and Akenside, the poet.

TOM'S COFFEE-HOUSE, 17 Great Russell-street, Covent Garden, opposite Button's, was kept by Thomas West, and was in the reign of Queen Anne, and more than half a century after, a celebrated resort. In 1764, it had a guinea subscription of nearly 700 members; and in 1768, its suite of card, conversation, and coffee rooms, in No. 17 and the two adjoining houses. Here assembled Dr. Johnson, Garrick, Murphy, Dr. Dodd, Dr. Goldsmith, and Sir Joshua Reynolds; Foote, Moody, and Beard; Count Bruhl and Sir Philip Francis; George Colman the Elder; the Dukes of Northumberland and Montague; the Marquises of Granby and Monthermor; Admiral Lord Rodney; Henry Brougham (father of Lord Brougham); George Steevens, Warner, and other Shaksperean commentators; and the subscription-rooms were kept up as late as 1814. Some books of the Club are preserved, and the tables are used, by the present tenant, Mr. Webster, the coin-dealer.

TURK'S-HEAD COFFEE-HOUSE, Strand, was a favourite supping-place of Dr. Johnson and Boswell. The house has been rebuilt as "Wright's Hotel," but is now a bookseller's, No. 142. There was another *Turk's Head* in New Palace-yard; and in a newspaper of 1662, customers and acquaintances are invited the next New Year's Day to the *Great Turk* new coffee-house, in Exchange-alley, "where coffee will be free of cost."

WILL'S COFFEE-HOUSE, on the north side of Great Russell-street, and No. 1 Bow-street, Covent Garden, was originally kept by William Urwin. Pepys records his first visit to Will's, 3 Feb. 1663-4, "where Dryden the poet (I knew at Cambridge), and all the wits of the town, and Harris the player, and Mr. Hoole of our college," with "very witty and pleasant discourse." Ned Ward calls it "the Wits' Coffee-house." Dryden had here his arm-chair, in winter by the fireside, in summer in the balcony: the company met in the first floor, and there smoked; and the young beaux and wits were sometimes honoured with a pinch out of Dryden's snuff-box. Old Cibber remembered Dryden: "a decent old man, arbiter of critical disputes at Will's."

> " Be sure at Will's the following day,
> Lie snug, and hear what critics say."—Swift's *Rhapsody on Poetry.*

Defoe wrote in 1722: "After the play, the best company generally go to Tom's and Will's Coffee-houses, near adjoining, where there is playing at picket, and the best of conversation, till midnight. Here you will see blue and green ribbons and stars sitting familiarly, and talking with the same freedom as if they had left their quality and degrees of distance at home."

There are in the metropolis about 800 Coffee-shops or Coffee-rooms; the establishment of the majority of which may be traced to the cheapening of coffee and sugar, and to the increase of newspapers and periodicals. About the year 1815, the London Coffee-shops did not amount to twenty, and there was scarcely a Coffee-house where coffee could be had under 6*d*. a cup; it may now be had at Coffee-shops at from 1*d*. to 3*d*. Some of these shops have from 700 to 1600 customers daily; 40 copies of the daily newspapers are taken in, besides provincial and foreign papers, and magazines. Cooked meat is also to be had at Coffee-shops, at one of which three cwt. of ham and beef are sometimes sold weekly.

Excellent coffee may be had at Groom's, the confectioner's, 16 Fleet-street, at 3*d*. per cup; also at Purssell's, 78 and 80 Cornhill; and Verrey's, 229 Regent-street. At Ries's Divan, 102 Strand, and at Kilpack's, 42 King-street, Covent Garden, coffee may be enjoyed with a cigar.

COLLEGES.

ST. BARNABAS COLLEGE, Queen-street, Pimlico, a church, schools, and residentiary house for the clergy, built 1846-50, in the first Pointed (Early English) style (Cundy, architect). The schools are for about 600 boys, girls, and infants; and the residentiary house is for four clergymen, who attend to the parochial duties of the district, minister in the church, teach in the schools, and superintend the twelve choristers. The schools were opened on St. Barnabas day, 1847, and the church in 1850. (See CHURCHES, page 119.*) The freehold site of the College was given by the first Marquis of Westminster, and is in the poorest part of the district. The College was built by subscription, to which

* For W. G. read W. J. E. Bennett.

the Rev. Mr. Bennett, then incumbent of the district, contributed the bulk of his fortune, and the most zealous pastoral care.

CHURCH OF ENGLAND METROPOLITAN TRAINING INSTITUTION, Highbury (late Highbury College), was instituted 1849, to train pious persons as masters and mistresses of juvenile schools connected with the Established Church, " upon principles Scriptural, Evangelical, and Protestant."

CHURCH MISSIONARY COLLEGE, 12 Barnsbury-place, Upper Islington, is an important branch of the Church Missionary Society for Africa and the East ; and here the students are trained for future missionaries. Among the early founders of this Society were Wilberforce, Scott, Cecil, Newton, Venn, and Pratt: it was chiefly matured at the "Eclectic Society" assembling then and now at the vestry of St. John's Chapel, Bedford-row. The annual cost of the College operations averages 100,000l., or about 1000l. for every station. (See Low's *Charities of London,* pp. 412-13.)

COLLEGE OF CHEMISTRY (ROYAL), 16 Hanover-square, was founded in 1845, for instruction in Practical Chemistry at a moderate expense, and for the general advancement of Chemical Science. The first stone of the three new laboratories was laid by Prince Albert, President of the College, June 16, 1846; James Lockyer, architect. The Oxford-street front has a rusticated ground-floor, and an upper story decorated with six Ionic columns. The students' fee for working daily in the session is 15l.; four days in the week, 12l.; three days, 10l.; two days, 7l.; one day, 5l.: hours, 9 to 5. Anniversary, first Monday in June.

COLLEGE FOR CIVIL ENGINEERS, on the banks of the Thames, at Putney, was established here in August 1840, in Putney House and the Cedars, which were fitted up for the institution ; the offices converted into a chemical laboratory and lecture-room, workshops, and an hospital; and a factory, with engine-shaft, smithy, and foundry, was added. The College buildings also include a chapel, hall, council-room, &c. In the ground (22 acres) are conducted the practical operations of the surveying and civil engineering departments ; and for the illustration of lectures, there are tunnel works, a lime-kiln, &c. There are also a gymnasium and cricket and racket grounds ; but boating is the favourite recreation. The students qualify for architects and surveyors, as well as civil engineers; and others for the army and navy, and colonial service : they wear a naval blue uniform and forage-cap. The College is gratuitously open to visitors, and in July is the annual distribution of prizes. The efficiency of the pupils has been attested in a late survey of the City of London, for the improvement of the City sewers. The College is proprietary, was originally founded in 1838, and commenced operations at Kentish Town.

COLLEGE OF PHYSICIANS (ROYAL), corner of Pall Mall East and Trafalgar-square, designed by Sir R. Smirke, R.A., was opened June 25, 1825, with a Latin oration by the President, Sir Henry Halford. The style is Grecian-Ionic, with an elegant hexastyle Ionic portico. The interior is sumptuous. In the dining-room are portraits of Dr. Hamey, the Commonwealth physician; of Dr. Freind, imprisoned in the Tower ; and of Sir Edmund King, who bled Charles II., in a fit, without consulting the royal physicians, and who was promised for the service 1000l. by the Council, which was never paid. In the oak-panelled Censors' Room is a portrait of Dr. Sydenham, by Mary Beale ; of Linacre, surmounted by the College arms in oak, and richly-emblazoned shield ; of the thoughtful Sir Thomas Browne, who wrote *Religio Medici ;* of the good-humoured Sir Samuel Garth, by Kneller; and of

Cardinal Wolsey, Henry VIII. (after Holbein), and Andreas Vesalius, the Italian anatomist; other portraits; and a marble bust of Sir Henry Halford. In the Library, lighted by three beautiful lanterns, is a fine portrait of Radcliffe, by Kneller; and of Harvey, by Jansen. Here is a gallery filled with cases, containing preparations, including some of the nerves and blood-vessels, by Harvey, and used by him in his lectures on the discovery of the circulation of the blood. Adjoining is a small theatre, or lecture-room, where are busts of George IV., by Chantrey; Dr. Mead, by Roubiliac; Dr. Sydenham, by Wilton; Harvey, by Schee-makers; Dr. Baillie, by Chantrey; Dr. Babington, by Behnes. Here also is a picture of Hunter lecturing on Anatomy before Royal Acade-micians (portraits), by Zoffany; besides a collection of Physicians' canes. The whole may be seen by the order of a physician, Fellow of the Col-lege. The Harveian Oration (in Latin) is delivered annually by a Fel-low, usually on June 25.

In the Library is a copy of the *Homer* published at Florence in 1488, an im-mortal work for this early period of typography: in the whiteness and strength of the paper, the fineness of the character, the elegant disposition of the matter, the exact distance between the lines, the large margin, and various ornaments.

The College of Physicians was founded in 1518, by Linacre, physician to Henry VII. and VIII., who lived in Knight-Rider-street, and there received his friends, Erasmus, Latimer, and Sir Thomas More. Linacre was the first President of the College, and the members met at his house, which he bequeathed to them; and the estate is still the property of the College. Thence they removed to a house in Amen Corner, where Harvey lectured on his great discovery, and built in the College garden a Museum, upon the site of the present Stationers' Hall. The old College and Museum being destroyed in the Great Fire of 1666, the members met for a time at the President's house, until Wren built for them a new College in Warwick-lane, Newgate-street, opened in 1689: it has a large entrance-porch, is octangular in plan, and is surmounted by a dome, as described by Garth in his satire on the quarrel between the Apothecaries' Company and the College:

> " Not far from that most celebrated place
> Where angry Justice shews her awful face,
> Where little villains must submit to fate,
> That great ones may enjoy the world in state,
> There stands a Dome, majestic to the sight,
> And sumptuous arches bear its oval height;
> A golden Globe, plac'd high with artful skill,
> Seems to the distant sight—a gilded pill."—*The Dispensary.*

" The theatre was amphitheatrical in plan, and one of the best that can be ima-gined for seeing, hearing, and the due classification of the students, and for the display of anatomical demonstrations or philosophical experiments upon a table in the centre of the arena, of any building of its size in existence." (*Elmes.*) This portion is now occupied as a meat-market, and the other College buildings by braziers and brass-founders. The buildings comprise a lofty hall, with a magnifi-cent staircase; a dining-room, with a ceiling elaborately enriched with foliage and flowers in stucco, and carved oak chimney-piece and gallery; and in the court are statues of Charles II. and Sir John Cutler,—the latter voted in acknowledgment of a sum of money presented by Sir John to the College, but attempted to be recovered by his executors. The inscription beneath the statue,

> " Omnis Cutleri cedat Labor Amphitheatro,"

has, however, been consistently removed. Here the Fellows of the College met until 1825. In the garrets were dried the herbs for the use of the Dispensary.

COLLEGE OF PRECEPTORS (the), 28 Bloomsbury-square, a proprie-tary institution, established 1847, to elevate the character of the profes-sion of Teachers, irrespective of distinctions of sects and parties; and to grant certificates and diplomas to candidates duly qualified, after exa-

---

* Old Bailey. Garth thus describes the College antagonist, Apothecaries' Hall:

> " Nigh where Fleet Ditch descends in sable streams,
> To wash his sooty Naiads in the Thames,
> There stands a structure on a rising hill,
> Where tyros take their freedom out to kill."

mination. There is a ladies' department of the College, managed by a committee of ladies.

COLLEGE OF SURGEONS (ROYAL), on the south side of Lincoln's-Inn-fields, was originally built by Dance, R.A., for the College, who removed here from their Hall on the site of the New Sessions-House, Old Bailey, on their incorporation by royal charter in 1800. It was almost entirely rebuilt by Barry, R.A., in 1835-37, when the stone front was extended from 84 to 108 feet, and a noble Ionic entablature added, with this inscription: ÆDES · COLLEGII · CHIRVRGORVM · LONDINENSIS · DIPLOMATE · REGIO · CORPORATI · A.D. MDCCC.

The interior contains two Museums, a Theatre, Library, and vestibule with screens of Ionic columns. On the staircase-landing are busts of Cheselden and Sir W. Banks. In the Library are portraits of Sir Cæsar Hawkins, by Hogarth; Serjeant-Surgeon Wiseman (Charles II.'s time); and the cartoon of Holbein's picture of the granting of the charter to the Barber-Surgeons. In the Council Room (where sits the Court of Examiners) are Reynolds's celebrated portrait of John Hunter, and other pictures: bust of John Hunter, by Flaxman; of Cline, Sir W. Blizard, Abernethy, and George III. and George IV., by Chantrey; of Pott, by Hollins; and Samuel Cooper, by Butler. The Museum, with Hunter's collection for its nucleus, was erected in 1836; and the College has since been enlarged by adding to it the site of the Portugal-street Theatre, late Copeland's China Warehouse, taken down in 1848. (See MUSEUMS.) In the Theatre is annually delivered the Hunterian Oration (in Latin), by a Fellow of the College, on Feb. 14, John Hunter's birthday.

DULWICH COLLEGE, in the pleasant hamlet of Dulwich, exactly 5 miles south of Cornhill, was built and endowed in 1613-19, by Edward Alleyn, "bred a stage-player:" he became a celebrated actor, erected the Fortune Theatre, and with Henslowe, was co-proprietor of the Paris Bear-Garden at Bankside. Alleyn named the foundation at Dulwich "the College of God's Gift;" for a master and warden, four fellows, six poor brethren, six sisters, and twelve scholars; and thirty out-members lodged in almshouses. By the founder's statutes, the master and warden should bear the name of Alleyn, or Allen, and both continue unmarried, or be removed from the College; yet the first master and warden (Alleyn's kinsmen) were both married, and Alleyn himself was twice married. He bequeathed his books and musical instruments, and his "seal-ring with his arms, to be worn by the master." The gross annual income of the College is about 8000l., or nearly tenfold the value settled by the founder. The only eminent master or warden was John Allen, one of the earliest writers in the *Edinburgh Review*. Little of the old buildings remains in the present structure, three sides of a quadrangle; the entrance gates are curiously wrought with the founder's arms, crest, and motto "God's Gift." In the centre is the Chapel, with a low tower; the altar-piece is a copy, by Julio Romano, of Raphael's *Transfiguration*; the font is inscribed with a Greek anagram, the same read either way. Alleyn (d. 1626) is buried here. Adjoining the College is "the Grammar-school of God's Gift College," built by Barry, R.A., in 1842; and the Dulwich Gallery of Pictures, famed for its Cuyps and Murillos.

In the College and Master's Apartments are several portraits, including Alleyn the founder, full-length, in a black gown; also left by Cartwright, player and bookseller, 1687, portraits of "the Actors" Richard Burbage, Nat. Field, Richard Perkins, Thomas Bond, &c.; and of the poet Drayton; Lovelace the poet, and "Althea" with her hair dishevelled; a Lady in a richly-flowered dress, large ruff, and pearls; and a Merchant and his Lady on panel, their hands resting upon a human skull placed on a tomb, below which is a naked corpse. The Library chimney-piece is made out of "the upper part of the Queen's barge," purchased by Alleyn in 1618. The books number about 4200 volumes: those relating to the theatre have been exchanged or filched away; and a very valuable collection of old plays was exchanged by the College with Garrick for modern works, and eventually purchased for the British Museum. The College possesses an original letter written by Alleyn to his first wife, Joan Woodward, from Chelmsford, in 1593, when he was one of "the Lord's strange Players." Here also is the MS. Diary and Account-Book of Philip Henslowe, printed by the Shakspeare Society; and in the old carved Treasury Chest, a memorandum-book in Alleyn's hand-writing; besides other " Dulwich papers."—See Collier's *Memoirs of Alleyn*.

When the office of Master of the College becomes vacant, the Warden imme-diately succeeds to it, and a new Warden is elected by the Master, the four Fel-lows, and six Assistants; the latter being two churchwardens from each of the parishes of St. Botolph's, Bishopsgate; St. Luke's, Old-Street-road; and St. Saviour's, Southwark. At the last election, in 1851, the ceremony was as fol-lows: Divine service having been performed in the chapel, and the names of the candidates having been previously written on a sheet of paper, the Assistants severally recorded their votes in favour of two candidates; the Fellows and Master then registered their votes; and the Master pronounced the numbers to be in favour of John Hensleigh Allen, one of the two candidates selected by the Col-lege; and Richard William Allen, the candidate named by the Assistants. These two gentlemen were then called to the front of the altar, and the Master having put into a box two rolls of paper tied with red tape, on one of which were written the words, "God's gift," and having shaken them thrice, called upon Mr. Richard William Allen, who was by a few months the senior, to select one. This he did, and Mr. John Hensleigh Allen took the other. Each paper was then unrolled, and the words, " God's gift," were found on the roll taken by Mr. Richard Wil-liam Allen, the nominee of the Assistants. It was stated by the solicitor of the College, that the course pursued by the Assistants on this occasion had not been adopted for the last seventy years. In 1851, the Archbishop of Canterbury, as official Visitor of the College, extended the education at the School to surveying, chemistry, engineering, and the allied sciences.

GRESHAM COLLEGE, Basinghall-street, corner of Cateaton-street, a handsome stone edifice, designed by George Smith, was opened Nov. 2, 1843, for the Gresham Lectures. It is in the enriched Roman style, and has a Corinthian entrance-portico. The interior contains a large library, and professors' rooms; and on the first floor a lecture-room, or theatre, to hold 500 persons. The building cost upwards of 7000*l*. The Lectures, on Astronomy, Physic, Law, Divinity, Rhetoric, Geo-metry, and Music, are here read to the public gratis, during " Term Time," daily, except Sundays; in Latin, at 12 noon; in English, at 1 p.m.; the Geometry and Music Lectures at 7 p.m. Gresham College was founded by Sir Thomas Gresham, who, in 1575, gave his mansion-house and the rents arising from the Royal Exchange, which on the death of Lady Gresham, in 1597, were vested in the Corporation of London and the Mercers' Company, who were conjointly to nominate seven professors, to lecture successively, one on each day of the week; their salaries being 50*l*. per annum : a more liberal remuneration than Henry VIII. had appointed for the Regius Professors of Divinity at Ox-ford and Cambridge, and equivalent to 400*l*. or 500*l*. at the present day. The Lectures commenced June 1597, in Gresham's mansion, which, with almshouses and gardens, extended from Bishopsgate-street westward into Broad-street. Here the Royal Society originated in 1645, and met (with interruptions) until 1710. The buildings were then neglected, and in 1768 were taken down, and the Excise Office built upon their site; and the reading of the Lectures was removed to a room on the south-east side of the Royal Exchange; the lecturers' salaries being raised to 100*l*. each, in place of the lodging they had in the old College, of which there is a view, by Vertue, in Ward's *Lives of the Gresham Pro-fessors*, 1740.* On the rebuilding of the Royal Exchange, the Gresham Committee provided a separate edifice for the College, as above.

* In Vertue's print, at the entrance archway are two figures, designed for Dr. Woodward and Dr. Mead, Professors, who having quarrelled and drawn swords,

Above the entrance portico are sculptured the following arms :

City of London.	Gresham.	Mercers' Company.
Arg. a cross, and in the dexter chief a sword erect gu.	Arg. a chev. erm. betw. three mullets pierced sa.	Gu. a demi-virgin couped below the shoulders, issuing from clouds, all ppr. veiled or crowned with an eastern coronet of the last, her hair dishevelled, all within a bordure nebuly arg.

HERALDS' COLLEGE (College of Arms), east side of Benet's-hill, Doctors' Commons, was built in 1683, from the design of Sir Christopher Wren, upon the site of the former College (Derby House), destroyed in the Great Fire; but all the valuable documents and books were fortunately saved. Sir William Dugdale, then Norroy King-of-Arms, built the north-west corner at his own expense: the hollow arch of the gateway on Benet's-hill is a curiosity. On the north side of the court-yard is the grand hall, in which the Court of Chivalry was formerly held. On the right is the old library, opening into a fire-proof record-room, built in 1844: it contains the MS. collection of Heralds' visitations, records of grants of arms, royal licenses, official funeral certificates, and public ceremonials. Here, too, are several portraits: among which are Sir Gilbert Dethick, Garter King-at-Arms; John Anstis, Garter; Peter Le Neve, Norroy; John Talbot, Earl of Shrewsbury, &c. In the grand hall is the judicial seat of the Earl Marshal; "but the chair is empty, and the sword unswayed." On the south side of the quadrangle is a paved terrace, on the wall of which are two escutcheons; one bearing the arms (and legs) of Man, and the other the Eagle's claw—both ensigns of the house of Stanley, and denoting the site of old Derby House, though they are not ancient.

The College of Arms received the first charter of incorporation from Richard III., who gave them, for the residence and assembling of the Heralds, Poulteney's Inn, "a righte fayre and stately house," in Coldharbour. They were dispossessed of this property by Henry VII., when they removed to the Hospital of Our Lady of Rounceval, at Charing Cross, where now stands Northumberland House. They next removed to Derby or Stanley House, on St. Benet's-hill, granted by Queen Mary, July 18, 1555, to Sir Gilbert Dethick, Garter King-of-Arms, and to the other Heralds and Pursuivants at Arms, and their successors. The service of the Pursuivants, and of the Heralds, and of the whole College, is used in marshalling and ordering Coronations, Marriages, Christenings, Funerals, Interviews, Feasts of Kings and Princes, Cavalcades, Shows, Justs, Tournaments, Combats, before the Constable and Marshal, &c. Also they take care of the Coats of Arms, and of the Genealogies of the Nobility and Gentry. Anciently, the Kings-at-Arms were solemnly crowned before the sovereign, and took an oath; during which the Earl Marshal poured a bowl of wine on his head, put on him a richly-embroidered velvet Coat of Arms, a Collar of Esses, a jewel and gold chain, and a crown of gold.—Chamberlayne's *Magnæ Britanniæ Notitia*, 1726.

The College has, since 1622, consisted of thirteen officers :—*Kings* : Garter, Principal; Clarencieux; Norroy. *Heralds :* Lancaster, Somerset, Richmond, Windsor, York, Chester. *Pursuivants :* Rouge Croix, Blue Mantle, Portcullis, Blue Dragon. These hold their places by appointment of the Duke of Norfolk, as Hereditary Earl Marshal. Few rulers have been insensible to the pageantry of arms : even the royalty-hating Cromwell appointed his Kings-at-Arms; and the heraldic expenses of his funeral were between 400*l.* and 500*l.* The *Court of Chivalry* was nearly as oppressive as the detestable Star Chamber ; for we read of its imprisoning and ruining a merchant-citizen for calling a swan a goose; and fining Sir George Markham 10,000*l.* for saying, after he had horse-whipped the saucy huntsman of Lord Darcy, that if

Mead obtained the advantage, and commanded Woodward to beg his life: "No, Doctor, that I will not, till I am your patient," was the witty reply; but he yielded, and is here shewn tendering his sword to Mead.

his master justified his insolence, he would horse-whip him also. The severest punishment of the Court is the degradation from the honour of knighthood, of which only three instances are recorded in three centuries : this consisted in breaking and defacing the knight's sword and gilt spurs, and pronouncing him "an infamous errant knave." In our time, the banner of a Knight of the Bath has been pulled down by the heralds, and kicked out of Henry VII.'s Chapel at Westminster. The heralds' visitations were liable to strange abuses, and ceased with the seventeenth century. Another trusty service of the Officers-at-Arms is the bearing of letters and messages to sovereign princes and persons in authority : these officers were the "Chivalers of Armës," or Knights Riders, the original King's Messengers; and adjoining the College is Knight-Rider-street.

Among the *Curiosities* of the College are, the Warwick Roll, with figures of all the Earls of Warwick from the Conquest to Richard III.; a Tournament Roll of Henry VIII.'s time; a sword, dagger, and turquois ring, said to have belonged to James IV. of Scotland, who fell at Flodden-field; portrait of the warrior Talbot, Earl of Shrewsbury, from his tomb in Old St. Paul's; pedigree of the Saxon kings, from Adam, with beautiful pen-and-ink illustrations (*temp.* Henry VIII.); and a volume in the handwriting of "the learned Camden," created Clarenceux in 1597. Among the other officers of note were Sir William Dugdale, Garter; Elias Ashmole, Windsor Herald, who wrote the *History of the Order of the Garter;* John Anstis, Garter; Francis Sandford, Lancaster Herald, who wrote an excellent Genealogical History of England; Sir John Vanbrugh, who was made Clarenceux as a compliment for building Castle Howard, but sold the situation for 2000*l.*; Francis Grose, Richmond Herald, the convivial writer on British Antiquities; and Edmund Lodge, Lancaster Herald, who has given his name to a "Peerage," and has left us "Portraits of Illustrious British Personages." (See the excellent paper by J. R. Planché, F.S.A., in Knight's *London,* vol. vi.)

A Grant of Arms is thus obtained: The applicant employs any member he pleases of the Heralds' Office, and through him, presents a memorial to the Earl Marshal, setting forth that he the memorialist is not entitled to arms, or cannot prove his right to such; and praying that his Grace will issue his warrant to the Kings of Arms authorising them to grant and confirm to him due and proper armorial ensigns, to be borne according to the laws of heraldry by him and his descendants. This memorial is presented, and a warrant is issued by the Earl Marshal, under which a patent is made out, exhibiting in the corner a painting of the armorial ensigns granted, and describing in official terms the proceedings that have taken place, and the correct blazon of the arms. This patent is registered in the books of the Heralds' College, and receives the signatures of the Garter and one of the Provincial Kings of Arms.* Thus an "Armiger" is made. The fees on a Grant of Arms amount to seventy-five guineas; an ordinary search of the records is 5*s.*; a general search, one guinea. Arms that are not held under a Grant must descend to the bearer from an ancestor recorded in the Herald's visitations. No prescription, however long, will confer a right to a coat-armour.

KING'S COLLEGE AND SCHOOL, Somerset House, extend from the principal entrance in the Strand to the east wing of the river-front, designed by Sir William Chambers, but left unfinished by him; its completion by the College being one of the conditions of the grant of the site: here reside the Principal and Professors. The College façade, designed by Sir Robert Smirke, R.A., is 304 feet in length, and consists of a centre, decorated with Corinthian columns and pilasters; and two wings with pilasters, upon a basement of piers supporting arches, which extend the whole length of the building. On the interior ground-

* If the grantee be resident in any place *north* of the Trent, his patent is signed by Garter and *Norroy* Kings of Arms; if he reside *south* of that river, the signatures are those of Garter and Clarenceux Kings of Arms.

floor are the theatres or lecture-rooms, and the hall, with two grand staircases, which ascend to the Museum and Library; the Chapel occupying the centre. Over the lofty entrance-arch in the Strand are the arms of the College; motto, " Sancte et sapienter."   (See MUSEUMS.)

King's College and School are proprietary. The College was founded in 1828, for the education of youth of the metropolis in the principles of the Established Church. There are five departments: 1. Theological; 2. General Literature; 3. Applied Sciences; 4. Medical; 5. The School. The age for admission to the latter is from 9 to 16; and each Proprietor can nominate two pupils to the School, or one to the School and one to the College at the same time. The first Conference of Degrees by the University of London took place in the hall of King's College, May 1, 1850. In connexion with the Medical Schools has been established King's College Hospital, in Portugal-street, Lincoln's-Inn-fields.

ST. MARK'S TRAINING COLLEGE, Chelsea, was established for training schoolmasters for the National Society. The College, fronting King's-road, is of Italian design; the Chapel, facing the Fulham-road, is Anglo-Norman; to the west is an octagonal Practising School; and the grounds contain about 15 acres. The term of training is three years: it comprises, with general education, the industrial system, as the business of male servants in the house, managing the farm-produce, and gardening. Still, the religious service of the Chapel is, as it were, the keystone of the system of the College. (See CHAPELS, p. 171.)

There are also other Training Institutions connected with the National Society: at Battersea, for schoolmasters; Whitelands, Chelsea, for schoolmistresses; and Manchester-buildings, Westminster, for schoolmasters and mistresses. There is likewise the Kneller Hall Training School,* at Whitton, Middlesex, to train masters for schools of Parochial Unions, or otherwise connected with the civil government; the Church of England Metropolitan Training Institution, Highbury-Park; the Home and Colonial Society, Gray's-Inn-road; and the British and Foreign Society's Central Schools, Borough-road; all which institutions are greatly improving our National System of Education. One of the most interesting examples is the Model Schools of the Home and Colonial Society, Gray's-Inn-road, which are open during the usual school hours for the inspection of the public; but on Tuesdays, from half-past 2 to 4, the complete working of the institution may be seen, from the first to the last step, under its own teachers.

NEW COLLEGE, St. John's Wood, was commenced building in 1850, when the first stone was laid, May 11, by the Rev. Dr. John Pye Smith, known as a divine, and as a man of science from his work on Scripture and Geology. The building was completed in 1851, and opened October 8. It has been erected by the Independent Dissenters for the education of their ministers, and is founded on the union of Homerton Old College and Coward and Highbury Colleges. The classes are divided into two faculties, Arts and Theology; the former open to lay students, and having chairs of Latin and Greek, mathematics, moral and mental philosophy, and natural history. The building, of Bath stone, designed by Emmett, in the Tudor (Henry VII.) style, is situated about a mile and a half north of Regent's-park, between the Finchley-road and Bellsize-lane. The frontage is 270 feet, having a central tower 80 feet high. The interior dressings are of Caen stone, and the fittings of oak; some of the ceilings are of wrought wood-work, and the windows of elaborate beauty. The main building contains lecture-room, council-room, laboratory, museum, and students' day-rooms; at the north end is the Principal's residence, and at the south a library of 20,000 volumes.

ST. PETER'S COLLEGE (WESTMINSTER SCHOOL), Dean's-yard, Westminster, was originally founded by Henry VIII., on the remodel-

* Kneller Hall (between Hounslow and Twickenham) was formerly in the possession of Sir Godfrey Kneller, who pulled down the manor-house and erected a new house on the same site, as inscribed upon a stone: "The building of this house was begun by Sir Godfrey Kneller, Bart., A.D. 1709." It had a sumptuously painted staircase, by Kneller's own hand. The Hall has been almost wholly taken down, and the Training School built upon its site.

ling of the Abbey establishment; but inadequately supported until, in 1560, Elizabeth restored its revenues, and the foundation of an Upper and Lower Master, and 40 scholars, and gave the present statutes. The College consists of a Dean, 12 Prebendaries, 12 Almsmen, and the above 40 " Queen's Scholars," with a Master and Usher; maintained, since the Restoration, by the common revenues of St. Peter's Collegiate Church (the Abbey), at 12,000*l.* a-year. These scholars wear a cap and gown; and there are four " Bishop's boys," educated free, who wear a purple gown, and have 60*l.* annually amongst them. Besides this *foundation*, a great number of sons of the nobility and gentry are educated here. Of the Queen's Scholars, an examination takes place on the first Tuesday after Rogation Sunday, when four are elected to Trinity College, Cambridge, and four to Christ Church, Oxford; scholarships, about 60*l.* a-year. The scholars from the 4th, 5th, and Shell Forms "stand out" in Latin, Greek, and grammatical questionings, to fill up the vacancies, on the Wednesday before Ascension Day; when the " Captain of the Election" is chaired round Dean's-yard. There are several other funds available to needful scholars; and the whole foundation and school is managed by the Dean and Chapter of Westminster.

Any boy may enter at Westminster School: the entire annual charges (including board and lodging) are from 76 to 83 guineas; or if he board and lodge at home, 25 guineas. From the Boarders are elected the Queen's Scholars, who, after four years' residence, have the chance of obtaining good scholarships; they are charged about 40*l.* a year.

The entrance to the school-court, Little Dean's-yard, is under a low groined gateway: the school-porch is said to have been designed by Inigo Jones; and adjoining is the paved racket-court. The venerable School was once the dormitory of the monks: it is 96 feet long and 34 feet in breadth, and has a massive open chestnut roof; at one end is the Head Master's table, and four tiers of forms are ranged along the east and western walls.* The Upper and Lower Schools are divided by a bar, which formerly bore a curtain: " over this bar on Shrove Tuesday, at 11 o'clock, the College cook, attended by a verger, having made his obeisance to the Masters, proceeds to toss a pancake into the upper school, once a warning to proceed to dinner in the Hall."—(Walcott's *Westminster,* p. 176.) Upon the walls are inscribed many great names; in the library is preserved part of the form on which Dryden once sat, and on which his autograph is cut.

In the *Census Alumnorum,* or list of *foundation* scholars, are Bishops Overall and Ravis, translators of the Bible; Hakluyt, collector of Voyages; Gunter, inventor of the Scale; "Master George Herbert;" the poets Cowley and Dryden; South; Locke; Bishops Atterbury, Spratt, and Pearce; Prior and Stepney, poets and statesmen; Rowe and "Sweet Vinery Bourne," the poets; Churchill, the satirist; Warren Hastings; Colman the Elder; Everard Home, surgeon; Dr. Drury, of Harrow School, &c.

Among the other eminent persons educated here are Lord Burghley; Ben Jonson; Nat Lee; Sir Christopher Wren; Jasper Mayne, the poet; Barton Booth, the actor; Blackmore, Browne, Dyer, Hammond, Aaron Hill, Cowper, and Southey, the poets; Horne Tooke; Gibbon, the historian; Cumberland, the dramatist; Colman the Younger; Sir Francis Burdett; Harcourt, Archbishop of York; the Marquis of Lansdowne; Lord John Russell; the Marquis of Anglesey; Sir John Cam Hobhouse (Lord Broughton), &c.

* The basement story beneath the School serves as an undercroft, has semicircular groined Saxon arches, considered to be of the time of Edward the Confessor, whose steward, Hugolin, was buried here. Here is deposited the standard money, which, when there is a new Master of the Mint, is taken out to be carried to the Exchequer, for a trial of the Pix. The outer doors have seven locks, each lock a different key, and each key a different possessor; so that the seven holders assemble on the above occasion. The last trial of the Pix was in 1851, on the admission of Sir John F. W. Herschel, Bart., to the Mastership of the Mint, which office was held by Sir Isaac Newton from 1699 until 1728.

Among the eminent Masters are Camden, "the Pausanias of England," who had Ben Jonson for a scholar; and Dr. Busby, who had Dryden; and who, out of the bench of Bishops, taught sixteen.

The College Hall, originally the Abbot's refectory, was built by Abbot Litlington, *temp.* Edward III.: its dimensions are 47 feet by 27½ feet in width; the floor is paved with chequered Turkish marble; at the south end is a musicians' gallery, now used as a pantry, and behind are butteries and hatches; upon the north side, upon a dais, is the high table; those below, of chestnut-wood, are said to have been formed out of the wreck of the Armada; and the roof-timbers spring from carved corbels, with angels bearing shields of the Confessor's and Abbots' arms. A small louvre rises above the central hearth, upon which, in winter, a charcoal fire used to burn. The Library is a modern Italian room, and contains several memorials of the attachment of "Westminsters." The old dormitory, built in 1380, was the granary of the monastery; and was replaced by the present dormitory in 1722, from the designs of the Earl of Burlington: it is 161 feet long by 25 feet broad, and its walls are inscribed with names. Here Latin plays are represented upon the second Thursday in December, and the Monday before and after that day; those acted of late years were the *Andria, Phormio, Eunuchus,* and *Adelphi,* of Terence, with Latin prologue and epilogue.* Warton mentions, "this liberal exercise is yet preserved, and in the spirit of true classical purity, at the College of Westminster." The scenery was designed by Garrick; the modern dresses formerly used were exchanged for Greek costume in 1839. Boating is a favourite recreation of the Westminsters, who have often contested the championship of the Thames with Eton. On May 4, 1837, the Westminsters won a match at Eton; when, by desire of William IV., the victors visited Windsor Castle, and were there received by the good-natured king.

QUEEN'S COLLEGE, LONDON, 67 Harley-street, was established 1848, for general female education, and for granting to Governesses certificates of qualification. The instruction is given in lectures by gentlemen connected with King's College, and other professors; there are also preparatory classes and evening classes, the latter gratuitous: the whole superintended by ladies visitors.

SION COLLEGE, London Wall, is built on the site of the Priory of Elsinge Spital, and consists of a college for the clergy of London, and almshouses for twenty poor persons, founded 1623, by the will of Dr. Thomas White, Vicar of St. Dunstan's-in-the-West; to which one of his executors, the Rev. John Simson, Rector of St. Olave's, Hart-street, added a library. "Here," says Defoe, "expectants may lodge till they are provided with houses in the several parishes in which they serve cure;" and the Fellows of the College are the incumbents of parishes within the City and Liberties of London. The library is their property: a third of the books was destroyed in the Great Fire of 1666, which consumed great part of the College. The collection contains about 35,000 volumes, mostly theological, among which are the Jesuits' books seized in 1679. By the Copyright Act, 8 Anne, c. 19, the library received a gratuitous copy of every published work till 1836, when this privilege was commuted for a Treasury grant of 363*l.* a-year, now its chief maintenance. It is open to the public by an order from one of the Fellows, daily from 10 to 4; but books are not allowed to be taken out. Here are several pictures, including a costume-portrait of Mrs. James, a citizen's wife in the reign of William and Mary.

* These performances superseded the old Mysteries and Moralities in the reign of Queen Mary, when the boy-actors were chiefly the acolytes who served at mass.

UNIVERSITY COLLEGE, east side of Upper Gower-street, was designed by Wilkins, R.A.;* the first stone laid by the Duke of Sussex, April 30, 1827; and the building opened Oct. 1, 1828. It has a bold and rich central portico of twelve Corinthian columns and a pediment, elevated on a plinth 19 feet, and approached by numerous steps, arranged with fine effect. Behind the pediment is a cupola with a lantern light, in imitation of a peripteral temple; in the great hall under which are the original models of the principal works of John Flaxman, R.A., presented by Miss Denman. In the vestibule is Flaxman's restoration of the Farnese Hercules; beneath the dome is his grand life-size Michael and Satan; and around the walls are his various monumental and other bas-reliefs: "in all the monumental compositions there is a touching story, and the sublimity of the poetic subjects is of a quality which the Greeks themselves have never excelled." (*Art Journal.*) An adjoining room contains Flaxman's Shield of Achilles, and other works.

The University building extends about 400 feet in length: in the ground-floor are lecture-rooms, cloisters for the exercise of the pupils, two semicircular theatres, chemical laboratory, museum of materia medica, &c. In the upper floor, on entering by the great door of the portico, the whole extent of the building is seen. Here are, the great hall, museums of natural history and anatomy, two theatres, two libraries, and rooms with naturo-philosophical apparatus. The principal library is richly decorated in the Italian style; here is a marble statue of Locke. The Laboratory, completed from the plan of Prof. Donaldson, in 1845, combines all the recent improvements of our own schools with that of Professor Liebig, at Giessen.

University College is proprietary, and was founded in 1828, principally aided by Lord Brougham, the poet Campbell, and Dr. Birkbeck, for affording "literary and scientific education at a moderate expense;" but Divinity is not taught. There is a Junior School. The graduates of the University of London from University College are entitled Doctors of Laws, Masters of Arts, and Bachelors of Law, Medicine, and Art. The School of Medicine is highly distinguished; and under the superintendence of its professors has been founded University College Hospital, opposite the College, in which the medical students receive improved instruction in medicine and surgery.

In the rear of the College, on the west side of Gordon-square, is *University Hall*, designed by Prof. Donaldson, 1849, and built for instruction in Theology and Moral Philosophy, which are excluded by the College. The architecture is Elizabethan-Tudor, in red brick and stone; the grouping of the windows is cleverly managed. In the great hall the students breakfast and dine; and the establishment is a sort of students' club-house, or model lodging-house.

WESLEYAN NORMAL COLLEGE, Horseferry-road, Westminster, (James Wilson, architect,) has been erected for the training of schoolmasters and mistresses, and the education of the children in the locality. It is in the late Perpendicular style, of brick, with stone dressings; and consists of a Principal's Residence, a quadrangular Normal College for 100 students, with Lecture and Dining Halls; Practising Schools, and Masters' Houses: beyond is the Model School, in Early English style, with porch and lancet windows: the buildings and playgrounds occupying upwards of 15 acres, with a large central octagonal tower, which, with the embattled parapets, pointed gables, and traceried oriel-windows, forms a picturesque architectural group.

* Wilkins also designed the National Gallery, a far less happy work than University College, which is unfinished; the original design comprised two additional smaller cupolas. The two works seem hardly to be the production of the same architect; in the National Gallery the dome being as unsightly a feature in composition as in the College it is graceful.

COLLEGIATE AND OTHER PUBLIC SCHOOLS.

CAMBERWELL FREE GRAMMAR-SCHOOL, Camberwell, Surrey, was founded 1615, by the Rev. E. Wilson, forty-one years vicar. The patronage is vested in governors, and the number of free boys limited to twelve. The seal of the school exhibits the master seated, baton in hand, with his scholars in a circle around him; and the master's dues included 5s. 3d. towards brooms and *rods*. The scholars were to play but once a-week, on Thursday; and to amuse themselves on half-holidays by learning Calvin's Catechism. Shooting with the long-bow, chess, running, and leaping, were the plays allowed. The old school-house, eastward of Camberwell Church, has been taken down; and a new school-house built, 1835, in Camberwell-grove, in the Collegiate style, with a cloister; H. Roberts, architect.

CHARTER-HOUSE SCHOOL, see page 72.

CHRIST'S HOSPITAL (Blue-Coat School), see page 80.

CITY OF LONDON SCHOOL (the) occupies the site of Honey-lane Market, in the rear of the houses facing Bow Church, and was designed by J. B. Bunning; the first stone laid by Lord Brougham, Oct. 21, 1835. The style is Elizabethan, with earlier and more enriched principal windows and entrance; the latter, a rich arched doorway, surmounted by a lofty gable pediment, and above, an open gallery of five trefoiled pointed arches on lofty pillars, flanked by buttress-turrets 76½ feet high, is novel and picturesque. The cost of the edifice, about 12,000*l.*, was defrayed by the Corporation of London, who gave the site, which produced a yearly rental of 300*l.* The school, for 400 scholars, is partly supported with 900*l.* a-year derived from certain lands and tenements bequeathed by John Carpenter, Town-Clerk and "Secretary" of London in the reign of Henry VI.; and who several times represented the City in parliament, and was "executor of the will of Richard Whityngton." Carpenter's bequest, originally but 19*l.* 10*s.* per annum, was "for the finding and bringing up of four poor men's children with meat, drink, apparel, learning at the schools, in the universities, &c., until they be preferred, and then others in their places for ever." (*Stow.*) The bequest was thus appropriated in 1633, when the boys wore "coats of London russet," with buttons; and they were accustomed from time to time to shew their copy-books to the Chamberlain, in proof of the application of the Charity. In 1827, it was extended to the education of four boys, sons of freemen, and nominated by the Lord Mayor, at the Tonbridge Grammar-School; each boy, on quitting, received 100*l.*, thus increasing the annual expense to about 420*l.* In the lapse of nearly four centuries, the value of Carpenter's estates had augmented from 19*l.* 10*s.* to 900*l.*, or nearly five-and-forty fold, when the school was established as above. The form of admission must be signed by a member of the Corporation of London: the general course of instruction includes the English, French, German, Latin, and Greek languages.

The school year is divided into three terms, at 2*l.* 15*s.* a term for each pupil. There are eight free foundation scholarships available as exhibitions to the Universities, in addition to the following: the *Times* scholarship (see CHRIST'S HOSPITAL, p. 83), three Beaufoy scholarships, the Salomons scholarship, and the Travers scholarship, and the Tegg scholarship, ("Sheriff's Fine,") varying from 35*l.* to 50*l.* a year each; and there are other valuable prizes, determinable by examination at Midsummer.

Upon the great staircase of the school is a statue, by Nixon, of John Carpenter, in the costume of his period; he bears in his left hand his *Liber Albus*, a collection of the City laws, customs, and privileges, compiled in 1419, and still preserved in the Corporation archives. The statue is placed upon a pedestal inscribed with a compendious history of the founder and his many benevolent acts.*

St. Margaret's Hospital, Palmer's Village, Westminster, was established and endowed in 1633, and consists of a large quadrangle and the master's house; with a bust of Charles I., and the royal arms in colours, and richly carved and gilt. In the panelled board-room are portraits of Charles I. by Vandyke, and Charles II. by Lely; and the windows look into a neatly-kept flower-garden. Upon this foundation are maintained twenty-nine boys, who wear a long green skirt, and a red leather girdle resembling that worn by the boys of Christ's Hospital: hence St. Margaret's is also known as the "Green-Coat School." The grace used here, attributed to Bishop Compton, is the same as that said in Christ's Hospital. (Walcott's *Westminster*, p. 295.)

Mercers' School, College-hill, Dowgate, was founded and endowed by the Mercers' Company, for seventy scholars of any age or place. It is mentioned as early as 1447, and was then kept at the Hospital of St. Thomas of Acon; but was removed to St. Mary Cole-church, next the Mercers' Chapel. After the Great Fire of 1666, the school-house was rebuilt on the west side of the Old Jewry. In 1787, it was removed to 13 Budge-row; in 1804, to 20 Red-Lion-court, Watling-street; and from thence, in 1808, to premises on College-hill. The present school, designed by George Smith, is an elegant stone structure, (adjoining St. Michael's Church,) on the site of Whittington's Almshouses, removed to Highgate to make room for it. The education, classical and general, is free; the boys being selected in turn by the Master and three Wardens of the Mercers' Company. Among the early scholars were, Dr. Colet, Sir Thomas Gresham, and Bishop Wren.

Merchant Taylors' School, Suffolk-lane, Cannon-street, was founded in 1561, by the Merchant Taylors' Company, principally by the gift of 500*l.*, and other subscriptions by members of the court of assistants, among whom was Sir Thomas White, sometime Master of the Company, and who had recently founded St. John's College, Oxford. With these funds was purchased part of "the Manor of the Rose," a palace originally built by Sir John Poultney, Knt., five times Lord Mayor of London, in the reign of Edward III.; the estate successively belonged to the De la Pole or Suffolk family (whence Suffolk-lane), and the Staffords, Dukes of Buckingham:

> "The Duke being at the Rose, within the parish
> Saint Lawrence Poultney."—*Shakspeare, Henry VIII.* act i. sc. 2.

Hence, also, "Duck's-Foot-lane" (the Duke's foot-lane, or private way from the garden to the Thames), which is hard by. These ancient premises were destroyed in the Great Fire of 1666, and the present building was erected on the same site, in 1675, by Wren: it is a large brick edifice, with pilasters; the upper school-room, and library adjoining, supported by stone pillars, forming a cloister; there are also other rooms, and the head-master's residence. The school consists of 260

---

* At the expense of John Carpenter was "artificially and richly painted" the *Dance of Death* upon the north cloister of St. Paul's, and thence called the "Dance at Paul's." (See Churches, p. 85.) It consisted of a long train of all orders of mankind; each figure having for a partner the spectral Death leading the sepulchral dance, and shaking the last sands from his hour-glass: intended as a moral memorial of the Plague and Famine of 1438. Among Carpenter's property is a lease of premises in Cornhill, granted by the City, for eighty years, at the annual service of *a red rose* for the first thirty years, and a yearly rent of 10*s.* for the remainder of the term.

boys, present charge ten guineas per annum each: they are admitted at any age, on the nomination of the forty members of the Court of the Company in rotation; and the scholars may remain until the Monday after St. John the Baptist's Day preceding their nineteenth birthday. Hebrew, Greek, and Latin have been taught since the foundation of the school; mathematics, writing, and arithmetic were added in 1829, and French and modern history in 1846. The boys are entitled to 37 out of the 50 fellowships at St. John's College, Oxford, and several other exhibitions at both the Universities; the election to which takes place annually on St. Barnabas Day, June 11, when the school prizes are also distributed: there is another speech-day, "Doctors' Day," in December. Plays were formerly performed by the Merchant Taylors' boys, who, in 1664, acted Beaumont and Fletcher's *Love's Pilgrimage* in the Company's Hall, but under order that this "should bee noe precident for the future."

Amongst the eminent scholars educated at Merchant Taylors' were, Bishops Andrewes, Dove, and Tomson, three of the translators of the Bible; Archbishop Juxon, who attended Charles I. to the scaffold; Bishop Hopkins (of Londonderry); Archbishops Sir William Dawes, Gilbert, and Boulter; Bishop Van Mildert, and eleven other prelates; Titus Oates, who contrived the "Popish Plot;" Sir James Whitelocke, Justice of the King's Bench; Bulstrode Whitelocke, who wrote his "Memorials;" Shirley, the dramatic poet, contemporary with Massinger; Charles Wheatly, the ritualist; Neale, the historian of the Puritans; Edmund Calamy, and his grandson Edmund, the Nonconformists—the former died in 1666, from seeing London in ashes after the Great Fire; the great Lord Clive; Dr. Vicesimus Knox, one of the "British Essayists;" Dr. William Lowth, the learned classic and theologian; Nicholas Amhurst, associated with Bolingbroke and Pulteney in the *Craftsman;* Charles Mathews the elder, comedian; Lieut.-Col. Denham, the explorer of central Africa; and J. L. Adolphus, the barrister, who wrote a *History of the Reign of George III.* Also, Sir John Dodson, Queen's Advocate; Sir Henry Ellis, and Samuel Birch, of the British Museum; John Gough Nichols, F.S.A. &c.

St. Olave's and St. John's Free Grammar-School (originally St. Olave's) was founded by the inhabitants in 1561; and endowed, among other property, with the "Horseydowne" field, at the yearly rent of a *red rose,* which is paid by the Churchwardens and Overseers previously to the annual commemoration sermon on Nov. 17, by presenting to each of the School Governors a nosegay of flowers with a rose in it. The school originated in the bequest of a wealthy brewer named Leeke, who, in 1561, left 8l. a-year for a free school in St. Savyor's, which bequest, however, was to go to St. Olave's, if within two years of his death a school should be built and established there. St. Olave's contrived to secure the legacy; and in 1567 the school was made free, and incorporated by Queen Elizabeth; charter extended by Charles II. 1674.

In 1579, Horseydowne, (now Horslydown,) was passed over by the parish to the use of the school. It was originally a large grazing field, *down,* or pasture, for horses and cattle, containing about sixteen acres; but having long since been covered with houses, erected on building leases, which have fallen in, the yearly income of the School from this source is upwards of 2000l. The old school, in Churchyard-alley, was taken down about 1830, for making the approaches to the new London Bridge, when a piece of ground in Duke-street was granted by the City of London as a site for a new school; but this ground was exchanged with the London and Greenwich Railway Company for a site in Bermondsey-street, where the school was rebuilt, and opened Nov. 17, 1835. It was in the latest Tudor or Elizabethan style, of red brick, with an octangular embattled tower, lantern-roofed; James Field, architect. In 1849, this new building being required for the enlargement of the terminus of the London, Brighton, and South-Coast Railway Company, they paid a considerable sum of money for it, the Governors undertaking to find another site for the school, and rebuild the same; the tuition being in the mean time carried on in a temporary building in Maze Pond.

The School is free to "children and younglings," rich or poor, inhabitants of St. Olave's and St. John's parishes, admitted by presentation from the Governors. The Classical School consists of about 320 boys; and the branch or English School, in Magdalen-street, and built in 1824, contains about 260 boys. The governors also award annually four exhibitions at Oxford or Cambridge University, besides apprentice-fees for poor scholars, and funds for other benevolent purposes. Commemoration-day, Nov. 17, (Accession of Elizabeth).

"The seal of the corporation, dated 1576, and distinguished by a rose displayed, the ancient cognizance of Southwark, represents the master sitting in a high-backed chair at his desk, on which is a book, and the rod is conspicuously displayed to the terror of five scholars standing before him."—*G. R. Corner, F.S.A.*

LADY OWEN'S SCHOOL, Owen-street, St. John-Street-road, was founded and endowed in 1613, by Dame Alice Owen, in memory of her having escaped "braining" by a stray arrow upon the site, then Hermitage Fields; the arrow having passed through her ladyship's high-crowned hat. (See ARCHERY, page 5.) The Charity, in the trust of the Brewers' Company, educates thirty poor children from Islington and Clerkenwell, to whom the master must teach Latin if required: there are also pay scholars. The school-house was rebuilt in 1840, in the Elizabethan style, of fine red brick, with stone dressings, to correspond with Lady Owen's Almshouses, opposite; Tattersall, architect.

ST. PAUL'S SCHOOL, east end of St. Paul's Churchyard, was founded in 1512, by Dr. John Colet, son of Sir Henry Colet, mercer, and lord mayor in 1486 and 1495; and it is "hard to say whether he left better lands for the maintenance of his school, or wiser laws for the government thereof" (*Fuller*). The school is for 153 boys "of every nation country, and class;" the 153 alluding to the number of fishes taken by St. Peter (*John* xxi. 2). The education is entirely classical; the presentations to the school are in the gift of the Master of the Mercers' Company; and scholars are admitted at fifteen, but eligible at any age. The original school-house was built 1508-12: this was destroyed in the Great Fire of 1666, but was rebuilt by Wren; this second school was taken down in 1824, and the present school built of stone from the designs of George Smith: it has a handsome central portico upon a rusticated base, projecting over the street pavement. The original endowment, and for several years the only endowment of the school, was 55*l.* 14*s.* 10½*d.*, the value of estates in Buckinghamshire, which now produce 1858*l.* 16*s.* 10½*d.* a-year; and with other property, make the present income of the school upwards of 5000*l.* Lilly, the eminent grammarian, the friend of Erasmus and Sir Thomas More, was the first schoolmaster of St. Paul's, and "Lilly's Grammar" is used to this day in the school: the English rudiments were written by Colet, the preface to the first edition by Cardinal Wolsey; the Latin syntax chiefly by Erasmus, and the remainder by Lilly. Colet directed that the children should not use tallow but wax candles in the school; 4*d.* entrance-money for each was to be given to the poor scholar who swept the school; and the masters were to have livery gowns "delivered in clothe." The present teachers consist of a high-master, salary 618*l.* per annum, with spacious house; sur-master, 307*l.*; under-master, or ancient chaplain, 227*l.*; assistant-master, 257*l.*: the last master only having no house. The scholars' only expense is for books and wax tapers. There are several very valuable exhibitions, decided at the Apposition, held in the first three days of the fourth week after Easter, when a commemorative oration is delivered by the senior boy, and prizes are presented from the governors. In the time of the founder, the "Apposition dinner" was "an assembly and a litell dinner, ordayned by the surveyor, not exceedynge the pryce of four nobles."

In the list of eminent Paulines are, Sir Anthony Denny and Sir William Paget, privy councillors to Henry VIII.; John Leland, the antiquary; John Milton, our great epic poet; Samuel Pepys, the diarist; John Strype, the ecclesiastical historian; Dr. Calamy, the High Churchman; the great Duke of Marlborough; R. W. Elliston, the comedian; Sir C. Mansfield Clarke, Bart.; Lord Chancellor Truro, &c.

On Apposition Day, June 4, 1851, were announced these three additional prizes: 1. "The Chancellor's Prize," by Lord Truro, 100*l.*; the interest to be applied in awarding a gold medal, value ten guineas, and a purse of twenty guineas, or books to that amount, each yearly Apposition, to the author of the best English Essay. 2. "The Milton Prize," by Sir C. M. Clarke, Bart., for English Verses on a sacred subject, annually. 3. "The Thurston Memorial," an annual prize for a copy of Latin Lyrics, given by the parent of a student named Thurston, recently deceased; the High Master to apply a portion of the endowment to keeping up the youth's gravestone in the Highgate Cemetery.

PHILOLOGICAL SCHOOL, (the,) Gloucester-place, New-road, was founded 1792; and, in union with King's College, offers first-class education gratuitously, for the sons of clergymen, naval and military officers, professional men, merchants, manufacturers, clerks in public offices, the higher order of tradesmen, and other persons whose families have been in better circumstances and are reduced. There are also contributory scholars. Admission by presentation of Governors. (Low's *Charities of London*, p. 351.)

ST. SAVIOUR'S GRAMMAR-SCHOOL, Sumner-street, Southwark-Bridge-road, was rebuilt 1830-9, nearly adjoining St. Peter's Church. The school was founded by parishioners in 1562, and chartered by Queen Elizabeth; the original endowment being 40*l.* a-year. The scheme, approved by the Court of Chancery in 1850, provides six governors to manage the school property; the instruction to comprise religion, classical learning, English composition, grammar, arithmetic, history, geography, mathematics, &c., subject to the approval of the Bishop of Winchester; the head master to be a Master of Arts, and to be appointed in conformity with the statutes of 1614. Small prizes are adjudged yearly, and there are two University exhibitions. Among the olden rules for the choice of a master is the following:

"The master to be a man of a wise, sociable, and loving disposition, not hasty or furious, or of any ill example; he shall be wise and of good experience, to discern the nature of every several child; to work upon the disposition for the greatest advantage, benefit, and comfort of the child; to learn with the love of his book." It was necessary then, as now, to add, "if such an one may be got."— The corporation seal represents a pedagogue seated in a chair, with a group of thickly-trussed pupils before him; date, 1573.

The original school-house, on the south side of St. Saviour's churchyard, was burned in 1676, but was immediately rebuilt: it had a richly-carved doorway-head. This building was taken down after the erection of the new school in Sumner-street. Among the donations is 500*l.* by Dr. W. Heberden, the celebrated physician, who is said to have been partly educated in the school.

GREY-COAT HOSPITAL, Tothill Fields, Westminster, a Charity School, was founded in 1698, and reconstituted 1706, when the school-house was built. The centre has a clock, turret, and bell, above the royal arms of Queen Anne, with the motto *Semper eadem*, flanked by figures in the former costume of the children. Here are a wainscoted dining-hall, and a handsomely panelled board-room, with a full-length portrait of Queen Anne, painted in Lely's manner, and other pictures. Upon this noble foundation are maintained sixty-seven boys, who now wear a dark-grey dress, similiar in form to that of the St. Margaret's

Hospital; and thirty-three girls, whose dress is also of a dark-grey colour, open in front and corded. (Walcott's *Westminster*, p. 323.) Three guineas or upwards annually, or thirty guineas composition, is a governor's qualification, with the right to present a child for admission as vacancies arise. In 1686, Sarah Duchess of Somerset bequeathed 1000*l.* to support six fatherless boys in the school, to be distinguished by wearing yellow caps. There is also in Tothill Fields Palmer's School, the boys of which wear black coats.

TENISON's (Archbishop) GRAMMAR SCHOOL, St. Martin's-in-the-Fields. (See page 172.)

WESTMINSTER SCHOOL. (See ST. PETER's COLLEGE, page 212.)

COLOSSEUM (THE).

The Colosseum, upon the east side of the Regent's-park, was originally planned by Mr. Hornor, a land-surveyor; and the building was commenced for him in 1824, by Peto and Grissell, from the designs of Decimus Burton. The chief portion is a polygon of sixteen faces, 126 feet in diameter externally, the walls being 3 feet thick at the ground; and the height to the glazed dome is 112 feet. Fronting the west is an entrance portico, with six Grecian-Doric fluted columns, said to be full-sized models of those of the Parthenon. The external dome is supported by a hemispherical dome, constructed of ribs formed of thin deals in thicknesses, breaking joint and bolted together, on the principle educed by M. Philibert de l'Orme in the 14th century, and stated to be introduced here for the first time in England. This second dome also supports a third, which forms the ceiling of the picture. The building resembles a miniature of the Pantheon, and has been named from its colossal size, and not from any resemblance to the Colosseum at Rome; but it more closely resembles the Roman Catholic Church at Berlin.*

The building is lighted entirely by the glazed dome, there being no side windows. Upon the canvassed walls was painted the Panoramic View of London, completed in 1829; for which Mr. Hornor, in 1821-2, made the sketches at several feet above the present cross of St. Paul's Cathedral (see pages 88 and 94). The view of the picture is obtained from two galleries: the *first* corresponds, in relation to the prospect, with the first gallery at the summit of the dome of St. Paul's; the *second* with the upper gallery of the cathedral. Upon this last gallery is placed the identical copper ball which formerly occupied the summit of St. Paul's; above it is a fac-simile of the cross; and over these is hung the small wooden cabin in which Mr. Hornor made his drawings. A small flight of stairs leads from this spot to the open parapet gallery which surrounds the domed roof of the Colosseum. The communication with the galleries is by spiral staircases, built on the outside of a lofty cylindrical core in the centre of the rotunda; within which is also

* In 1769, there was constructed in the Champs Elysées, at Paris, a vast building called *Le Colisée*, for fêtes in honour of the marriage of the Dauphin, afterwards Louis XVI. Here were dances, hydraulics, pyrotechnics, &c.; the building did not resemble the Pantheon, as ours in the Regent's-park, but the Colosseum at Rome. It contained a rotunda, saloons, and circular galleries, skirted with shops, besides trellis-work apartments and four *cafés*. In the centre of *Le Cirque* was a vast basin of water, with fountains; beyond which fireworks were displayed. The whole edifice was completely covered with green trellis-work; the entire space occupied by the buildings, courts, and gardens was sixteen acres; and the cost was two and a half millions of money. There were prize exhibitions of pictures; and Mr. Hornor projected similar displays at the Colosseum, but the idea was not taken up by the British artists. In 1778, the Parisian building was closed, and two years afterwards was taken down. It is mentioned by Dr. Johnson, in his *Tour*, in 1775.

the " Ascending Room," capable of containing ten or twelve persons. This chamber is decorated in the Elizabethan style, and lighted through a stained-glass ceiling; it is raised by secret machinery to the required elevation, or gallery, whence the company view the panorama. The hoisting mechanism is a long shaft connected with a steam-engine outside the building, working a chain upon a drum-barrel, and counter-balanced by two other chains, the ascending motion being almost imperceptible.

The painting of the picture was a marvel of art. It covers upwards of 46,000 square feet, or *more than an acre of canvass;* the dome on which the sky is painted is 30 feet more in diameter than the cupola of St. Paul's; and the circumference of the horizon from the point of view is nearly 130 miles. Excepting the dome of St. Paul's Cathedral, there is no painted surface in Great Britain to compare with this in magnitude or shape, and even that offers but a small extent in comparison. It is inferred that the scaffolding used for constructing St. Paul's cupola was left for Sir James Thornhill, in painting the interior; and his design consisted of several compartments, each complete in itself. Not so this Panorama of London, which, as one subject, required unity, harmony, accuracy of linear and aerial perspective; the commencement and finishing of lines, colours, and forms, and their nice unity; the perpendicular canvass and concave ceiling of stucco was not to be seen by, or even known to, the spectator; and the union of a horizontal and vertical surface, though used, was not to be detected. After the sketches were completed upon 2000 sheets of paper, and the building finished, no individual could be found to paint the picture in a sufficiently short period, and many artists were of necessity employed: thus, by the use of platforms slung by ropes, with baskets for conveying the colours, temporary bridges, and other ingenious contrivances, the painting was executed, but in the peculiar style, taste, and notion of each artist; to reconcile which, or bring them to form one vast whole, was a novel, intricate, and hazardous task, which many persons tried, but ineffectually. At length, Mr. E. T. Parris, possessing an accurate knowledge of mechanics and perspective, and practical execution in painting, combined with great enthusiasm and perseverance, accomplished the labour principally with his own hands; standing in a cradle or box, suspended from cross poles or shears, and lifted as required, by ropes.

The Panorama is viewed from a balustraded gallery, with a projecting frame beneath it, in exact imitation of the outer dome of St. Paul's Cathedral, the perspective and light and shade of the campanile towers in the western front being admirably managed; whilst cannot exceed the contrast of the bold and broad buildings in the foreground with the receding mid-distance, and the minuteness of the horizon. The spectator is recommended to take four distinct stations in the gallery, and then inspect in succession the views towards the north, east, south, and west; altogether representing the Metropolis of 1821, (the date of the sketches,) or thirty years since.

The North comprises Newgate-market, the old College of Physicians, Christ's Hospital (before the rebuilding of the Great Hall), St. Bartholomew's Hospital, and Smithfield Market; and the New General Post-Office, then building. These are the objects near the foreground; beyond them are Clerkenwell, the Charter-house, and the lines of Goswell-street, St. John-street, Pentonville, Islington and Hoxton. In the next, or third distance, are Primrose Hill, Chalk Farm, Hampstead, and a continued line of wooded hills to Highgate, where are the bold Archway and the line of the Great North Road from Islington; whilst Stamford-hill, Muswell-hill, part of Epping Forest, and portions of Essex, Hertfordshire, and Middlesex, bound the horizon.

The East displays a succession of objects all differing from the former view in effect, character, and associations. Whilst the north exhibits the rustic scenery f the environs of London, the east presents us with the Thames, and its massive warehouses and spacious docks; the one a scene of rural quiet, the other a focus f commercial activity. In the foreground is St. Paul's School-house; whilst the ines of Cheapside, Cornhill, Leadenhall-street, and Whitechapel carry the eye hrough the very heart of the City, and thence to Bow, Stratford, and a fine ract of woodlands in Essex. On the right and left of this line are the towers and teeples of Bow Church, St. Mary Woolnooth; St. Michael, Cornhill; St. Ethelerg, Bishopsgate, and others of subordinate height; the Bank, Mansion-house, Royal Exchange (since destroyed by fire), East India House, and several of the Companies' Halls. Another line, nearly parallel, but a little to the east extends hrough Watling-street (the old Roman road) to Cannon-street, Tower-street, and he prison, palace, fortress, and museum—the Tower. The course of the Thames, with its vessels and wilderness of masts, the docks and warehouses on its banks; he palace-hospital of Greenwich, and the beautiful country beyond it, contrasted with the levels of the Essex bank,—are all defined in this direction.

Southward, the eye traces the undulating line of the Surrey hills in the disance; and in the forepart of the picture the Thames, with its countless craft, among which are civic barges and steamers, characteristic of ancient and modern London. Here also are shewn old London Bridge, and Southwark, Blackfriars, Waterloo, Westminster, and Vauxhall Bridges; whilst the river-banks are crowded with interesting structures, among which are the old Houses of Parliament.

The Western view presents a new and different series of objects. First in effect, n beauty of execution and imposing character, are the two *campanili*, the pediment, and the roof of the western end, of St. Paul's Cathedral. The painting here s masterly and magical; it so deceives the eye and the imagination, that the pectator can scarcely believe these towers to be depicted on the same canvass and the same surface as the whole line of objects from Ludgate-hill to St. James's-ark. This view to the west embraces the long lines of Ludgate-hill, Fleet-street, and the Strand, Piccadilly, &c.; Holborn Hill and Oxford-street, with the Inns f Court; Westminster; numerous churches and public buildings, right and left; and Hyde-park, Kensington-gardens, and a long stretch of flat country to Windor.—*Brief Account*, by John Britton, F.S.A., 1829.

A staircase leads to the upper gallery, whence the spectator again commands the whole picture in a sort of bird's-eye view. Another light of stairs communicates with the room containing the copper ball and fac-simile cross of St. Paul's. A few more steps conduct to the outer gallery at the summit; where, if the weather be fine, the spectator may compare the colouring, perspective, and effects of nature with those of art within.

The Panorama was first exhibited in the spring of 1829. It was almost repainted by Mr. Parris in 1845; when also a Panorama of London by Night, essentially the same as the day view, was exhibited n front of the latter, and had to be erected and illuminated every evening: the moonlight effect upon the rippling river; the floating, fleecy clouds and twinkling stars; the lights upon the bridges, in the shops, and in the open markets, formed a rare triumph of artistic illusion. In May 1848, a moonlight Panorama of Paris, of the same dimensions as the night view of London, was painted by Danson, and was very attractive in illustration of the localities of the recent Revolution. In 1850, both views gave way to a Panorama of the Lake of Thun, in Switzerland, painted in tempera by Danson and Son; and in 1851, the Panorama of London was reproduced as a more appropriate sight for the International Exhibition season.

The Picture, however, is but one of the many features of the Colosseum. The basement of the Rotunda has a superb Ionic colonnade, as a sculpture-gallery, named the Glyptotheca: the columns and entablature are richly gilt; and the frieze, nearly 300 feet in circumference, s adorned with bas-reliefs from the Panthenaic friezes of the Parthenon, exquisitely modelled by Henning; the ribbed roof being filled with embossed glass. In hot weather, this apartment, being subterranean, s cool; and in winter, comparatively warm.

Southward and eastward of the Rotunda are large Conservatories, a

Swiss *chalet*, and mountain-scenery interspersed with real water: these were executed by Mr. Hornor, whose enthusiasm led him to project a tunnel beneath the Regent's-park road, and to anticipate a grant from the opposite enclosure to be added to the Colosseum grounds. But the ingenious projector failed: the property passed into the hands of trustees, and was next sold to Messrs. Braham and Yates, in 1831, it is believed for 40,000*l*.; it was again sold in 1835, after which it lost much of its status as a place of public amusement; but on May 11, 1843, it was bought for 23,000 guineas by Mr. David Montague, the present proprietor, who has altogether retrieved and elevated the artistic character of the establishment.

The Colosseum, as we now see it, was, with the exception of the Panorama, principally executed in 1845, from the designs of the late Mr. W. Bradwell, formerly chief machinist of Covent Garden Theatre. The eastern entrance, in Albany-street, was then added; with an arched corridor in the style of the Vatican, and leading to the Glyptotheca, the Arabesque Conservatories, and the Gothic Aviary; the exterior promenade, with its model ruins of the Temple of Vesta and Arch of Titus, the Temple of Theseus, and golden pinnacles and eastern domes,—a chaos of classic relics of the antique world, and of luxuriant and mouldering beauty from our own. Here you may almost forget the working-day world, amidst the murmur of sparkling fountains, the songs of gaily-plumed birds, the fragrance of exotic plants and flowers, and the beautiful forms and brilliancy of the embellishments. A romantic pass leads to the *chalet*, or Swiss Cottage, originally designed by P. F. Robinson: the roof, walls, and projecting fireplace are fancifully carved; and the bay-window looks upon a mass of rock-scenery, a mountain-torrent and lake,—a model picture of the sublime.

In another direction lies a large model of the Stalactite Cavern at Adelsberg, in Carniola; constructed by Messrs. Bradwell and Telbin. The countless arches in the sparry roof, and the stalagmites on the floor, glistening in the candle-light, are very effective. The illusion of height and distance is complete; and "the deep, cold, clear lake," reflecting the gorgeous scene, and fading into impenetrable darkness, is a scenic romance.

At Christmas 1848 was added a superb theatre, with a picturesque rustic armoury as an ante-room. The spectatory, designed and erected by Bradwell, resembles the vestibule of a regal mansion fitted up for the performance of a masque: it is decorated with colossal Sienna columns, and copies of three of Raphael's cartoons in the Vatican (School of Athens, and Constantine and the Pope), by Horner, of Rathbone-place; the ceilings are gorgeously painted with allegorical groups; and upon the fronts of the boxes is a Bacchanalian procession, in richly-gilt relief. Upon the stage passes the Cyclorama of Lisbon, depicting in ten scenes the terrific spectacle of the great earthquake of 1755—the uplifting sea and o'ertopping city, and all the frightful devastation of flood and fire; accompanied by characteristic performances upon Bevington's Apollonicon. The scenes are painted by Danson, in the manner of Loutherbourg's Eidophusicon, which not only anticipated, but in part surpassed, our present dioramas.

COLUMNS.

NELSON COLUMN (the), south side of Trafalgar-square, was erected between 1839 and 1852, by public subscription and the aid of the Government. It was designed by W. Railton, and is of the exact proportion of a column of the Corinthian temple of Mars Ultor at Rome: Mr. Railton choosing the Corinthian order from its being the most lofty and elegant in its proportions, and having never been used in England for this purpose; whilst it is in keeping with the surrounding buildings, and tends more than any other species of monument to bring the entire scene into general harmony, without destroying the effect of any portion of it. The foundation rests upon a 6-feet layer of concrete in a compact stratum of clay, about 12 feet below the pavement; upon which is the frustum of a brick-work pyramid, 48 feet square at the base, and 13 feet high, upon which the superstructure commences with the graduated stylobate of the pedestal, the first step of which is 33 feet 4 inches wide. From this point to the foot of the statue, the work is of solid granite, in large blocks admirably dressed; and in the shaft they are so well connected as to give the fabric almost the cohesion of a monolith. The granite was brought from Foggin Tor, on the coast of Devon; and was selected for its equable particles and intimate distribution of mica, feldtspar, and quartz. The shaft (lower diameter 10 feet) is fluted throughout, the base being richly ornamented; the lower torus with a cable, the upper with oak-leaves. The pedestal is raised upon a flight of steps; and at the angles are massive cippi, or blocks, intended to receive four recumbent African lions. The capital is of bronze, and was cast from old ordnance in the Arsenal foundry at Woolwich, from full-sized models carefully prepared by C. H. Smith. "The foliage is connected to the bell of the cap by three large belts of metal lying in grooves, and rendering it needless to fix plugs into the work, with the concomitant risk of damage from the galvanic action of metals." (*G. Godwin, jun. F.R.S.*) One of the lower tiers of leaves weighs about 900 lbs. Upon a circular pedestal on the abacus is a colossal statue of Nelson, with a coiled cable on his left; E. H. Baily, R.A., sculptor. The figure is of Cragleith stone, in three massive blocks, presented by the Duke of Buccleuch; the largest block weighing upwards of 30 tons. The statue measures 17 feet from its plinth to the top of the hat; it was raised on Nov. 3 and 4, 1843; and on October 23 previous, fourteen persons ate a rump-steak dinner on the abacus of the Column.

The scaffolding used in constructing this Column was a novelty of mechanical skill. Instead of the usual forest of small round poles, there were five grand uprights or standards on the east and west sides, in six stages or stories, marked by horizontal beams and curbs, at nearly equal intervals; the base being greatly extended, and the sides strengthened by diagonal and raking braces. By means of a powerful engine moving on a railway, and a travelling platform, blocks of stone, from six to ten tons weight, were, at a rate of progression scarcely more perceptible than the motion of a clock-weight (being only 30 feet in the hour), raised to a great elevation, and set down with less muscular exertion than would be expended on a lamp-post; one mason thus setting as much work in one day as was done in three days by the old system, even with the aid of six labourers, who are now dispensed with. The timber used in erecting this scaffold was 7700 cubic feet, and its cost was 240*l.* for labour in erecting.

The pedestal has on its four sides the following bronze reliefs:

North (facing the National Gallery), *Battle of the Nile:* designed by W. F. Woodington. Nelson, having received a severe wound in the head, was caught by Captain Berry in his arms as he was falling, and carried into the cockpit; the surgeon is quitting a wounded sailor, that he may instantly attend the Admiral. "No," said Nelson, "I will take my turn with my brave fellows." Some of the parts project 15 inches, and the figures are 8 feet high: the casting weighs 2 tons 15 cwt. 2 qrs.; and the metal is three-eighths of an inch thick.

South (facing Whitehall), *Death of Nelson at Trafalgar:* designed by C. E. Carew. Nelson is being carried from the quarter-deck to the cockpit by a marine and two seamen. "Well, Hardy," said Nelson to his captain, "they have done for me at last." "I hope not," was the reply. "Yes; they have shot me through the backbone." At the back of the centre group is the surgeon. To the left are three sailors tightening some of the ship's cordage; another kneels, holding a handspike and leaning on a gun, arrested by the conversation between the dying hero and Captain Hardy. In the front, lying on the deck, are an officer and marines, who have fallen to rise no more. Behind stand two marines and a negro sailor. One of the former has detected the marksman by whose shot Nelson fell, and is pointing him out to his companion. The latter has raised his musket, and has evidently covered his mark; whilst the black, who stands just before the two marines, is grasping his firelock. The figures are of life-size; the casting weighs about five tons. Beneath are Nelson's memorable words: "England expects every man will do his duty."

East (facing the Strand), *Bombardment of Copenhagen:* designed by the late Mr. Ternouth. Nelson is sealing, on the end of a gun, his despatch, to send by the flag of truce; a group of officers surround him, and a sailor holds a candle and lantern: in the foreground are wounded groups; and in the distance are a church and city (Copenhagen) in flames.

. *West* (facing Pall-Mall), *Battle of St. Vincent:* commenced by Watson, and finished by Woodington. Nelson, on board the San Josef, is receiving from the Spanish admirals their swords, which an old Agamemnon man is putting under his arm; in the foreground is a dying sailor clasping a broken flag-staff.

A monument to Nelson was first proposed in 1805 (the year of his death) when the Committee of the Patriotic Fund raised 1330*l.* reduced 3 per Cents, which, with the accumulated dividends, amounted in June 1838 to 5545*l.* 19*s.* Meanwhile, in 1816, the monument was proposed in Parliament, as " a duty which the nation ought, perhaps, to have discharged not less than thirty years ago." The subject, however, rested until 1838, when a subscription was raised, Trafalgar-square chosen as the site, and a column recommended by the Duke of Wellington. In January 1839, 118 drawings and 41 models were submitted, and the first prize, 250*l.*, awarded to Mr. Railton for his column; in May following, a second series of designs (167) was exhibited, but the Committee adhered to their former choice. In 1844, the subscriptions,* 20,483*l.* 11*s.* 2*d.*, had been expended; and the Government undertook the completion of the monument, estimated at 12,000*l.* additional. The column itself has cost 23,000*l.* building ; the statue, capital, and reliefs, 5000*l.*; and 2000*l.* architect's commission ; the four lions are estimated at 3000*l.* Trafalgar-square was much objected to as the site : in the Parliamentary examination, eight architects and sculptors were in favour of it, and four architects against it. Chantrey considered Trafalgar-square to be " the most favourable that could be found or imagined for any national work of art ; its aspect is nearly south, and sufficiently open to give the object placed on that identical spot all the advantage of light and shade that can be desired; to this may be added the advantage of a happy combination of unobtrusive buildings around : but to conceive a national monument worthy of this magnificent site is no easy task." Chantrey objected to a column as a monument, unless treated as a biographical volume, with the acts of the hero sculptured on the shaft, as on the columns of Trajan and Antoninus. Annexed are the comparative dimensions of the principal monumental columns :

Date.	Column.	Site.	Order.	Height to the top of Capital.	Diameter.
A.D.				Feet.	Feet.
118	Trajan . . .	Rome . .	Doric . .	115	12
162	Antoninus . .	Rome . .	Doric . .	123	13
1671	Monument . .	London .	Doric . .	172	15
1806	Napoleon . .	Paris . .	Doric . .	115	12
1832	Duke of York .	London .	Tuscan .	111	11
1839	Nelson . . .	London .	Corinthian	145·6	10·1¾—11·7½

Nelson Column, 145 feet 6 inches; statue and plinth, 17 feet; =162 feet 6 inches.

YORK COLUMN, Carlton Gardens, built 1830-33, in memory of the Duke of York (d. 1827), Commander-in-Chief of the army, and forty-six years a soldier : whose statue is placed on the summit. The building fund, about 25,000*l.*, was raised by subscription, to which each indivi-

* To which Nicholas, Emperor of Russia, had contributed 500*l.*

dual of the service contributed one day's pay. The column (Tuscan), designed by B. Wyatt, is of fine Aberdeenshire granite, the lower pedestal grey, and the shaft of red Peterhead; the surface fine-axed, or not polished. The abacus of the capital is enclosed with iron railing, and in its centre is the pedestal for the statue. Within the pedestal and shaft is a spiral staircase of 168 steps, which, with the newel, or central pillar, and outer casing, are cut from the solid block. The masonry throughout, by Nowell, is remarkably good. The statue, of bronze, by Sir Richard Westmacott, R.A., represents the Duke in the robes of the Order of the Garter. The weight is 7 tons 800lbs., or 16,480lbs.; it was raised April 8, 1834, between the column and the scaffolding, seven hours labour, at a cost of 400*l*. The column may be ascended from 12 to 4, from May to Sept. 24, 6*d*. each person: the view from the gallery of the Surrey hills and western London is fine; the latter shewing the magnificence of Regent-street, and the skill of the architect, Nash, in the junction of the lines by the Quadrant. On May 14, 1850, Henri Joseph Stephan, a French musician, committed suicide by throwing himself from the gallery, which has since been entirely enclosed with iron caging. The height of the column is 123 feet 6 inches; of the statue, 13 feet 6 inches = 137 feet; or viewed from the bottom of the steps, at the level of St. James's Park, 156 feet: upper diameter of shaft, 10 feet 1¾ inches; lower diameter, 11 feet 7½ inches. The foundation, laid in *concrete*,* is pyramidal, 53 feet square at the base.

The height of the balcony of the York Column is very nearly that of the under side of the great tube of the Britannia Bridge, over the Menai Straits, above high-water. The entire length of the bridge is 1832 feet 8 inches; considerably more than that of Waterloo Place, from the York Column to the foot of the Quadrant.—*Proceedings of the Society of Arts,* 1851.

Dr. Waagen condemns this monument as a bad imitation of Trajan's Column, very mean and poor in appearance, with a naked shaft, and without an entasis; whereas the bas-reliefs on the shaft of Trajan's Pillar give it, at least, the impression of a lavish profusion of art. Besides, the statue on the York Column, though as colossal as the size of the base will allow, appears little and puppet-like compared with the column; and the features and expression of the countenance are wholly lost to the spectator.

See also MONUMENT, THE.

COMMON-COUNCIL.

The constitution of the Corporation of London presents a remote and illusory resemblance to the constitution of the state. There are the Lord Mayor, the Court of Aldermen, and the Court of Common-Council. Strictly speaking, the Court of Common-Council includes the Chief Magistrate and the Aldermen; but in ordinary language it is understood to mean the Commons of the City, being somewhat like the House of Commons; the Court of Aldermen bearing some analogy to the House of Lords; and the Lord Mayor to the Sovereign. (*Lord Brougham, in Parliament,* March 3, 1843.)

The two corporate assemblies can be traced back to a very distant period, and there are records of disputes between the two Courts six centuries ago; but the Common-Council appears to have been first constituted in its present form only in the reign of Richard II., by a civic ordinance; whilst in an Act of Parliament of the previous reign (28 Edw. III. c. 10), the mayor, sheriffs, and aldermen are invested with the redress and correction of errors, &c. in the city of London, for default of good government.

In the reigns of Edward I. and II., a body analogous to the Common-Council was formed by the representatives from the different

* *Concrete* (of lime, sand, pebbles, &c.) is inferred, from documents dated 1292, to have been employed in the foundation of St. Stephen's Chapel at Westminster.

Wards of the City. From thence to the time of Richard II. they were returned by the Companies or Mysteries. In the Mayoralty of Nicholas Brembre, (7 and 8 Rich. II.), the election was established by Ward-mote. The original number of members, in 1384, was 96; July 31, 1384, 207; in 1549, 197; Stow's *Survey* (1717), 231; Stow (1736 and 1755), 214; 1837, 240; reduced in 1840 to 206, the present number.

From 1660 to 1676, several attempts were made by the Aldermen to limit the choice of the Wardmote to citizens of the higher class; but no permanent regulation was the result. In 1831, a Committee reported that persons convicted of defrauding in weights and measures, or having compounded with their creditors, or of having been bankrupt, without paying 20s. in the pound, were ineligible as Common-Councilmen.

The members are elected annually on St. Thomas's Day (Dec. 21) by the resident freemen of the 26 Wards, exclusive of Bridge Without. The candidates must be freemen householders of the Ward for which they declare. The Alderman of the Ward is the presiding officer at the election; and the return of the persons elected is made on Monday next after the Epiphany, *i.e.* Plough Monday.

Each Common-Councilman wears a gown of Mazarine-blue silk, trimmed with badger's fur — a costume, probably, of the reign of Edward VI. They formerly wore black gowns; and the change is thus alluded to in the chorus to a political song of 1766:

"Oh, London is the town of towns! Oh, how improved a city!
Since chang'd her Common Council's gowns from black to blue so pretty!"

They, however, discontinued wearing their gowns in court in 1775; perhaps in consequence of a Common-Councilman being called "a Mazarine." Nor has he escaped the severer whipping of the satirist:

"The cit — a Common-Councilman by place,
Ten thousand mighty nothings in his face,
By situation, as by nature, great,
With wise precision parcels out the state;
Proves and disproves, affirms and then denies,
Objects himself, and to himself replies;
Wielding aloft the politician rod,
Makes Pitt by turns a devil and a god;
Maintains, ev'n to the very teeth of pow'r,
The same thing right and wrong in half-an-hour
Now all is well, now he suspects a plot,
And plainly proves whatever is — is not:
Fearfully wise, he shakes his empty head,
And deals out empires as he deals out thread;
His useless scales are in a corner flung,
And Europe's balance hangs upon his tongue."—*Churchill.*

The Court hold their sittings in a chamber on the north side of the Guildhall, where the Lord Mayor presides in a chair of state; and visitors are admitted below the bar, at which petitions, &c. are presented in due legislative form. The entire Court were entertained by George I. at a banquet at St. James's Palace in 1727.

CONDUITS.

Spring water was formerly conveyed to public reservoirs in the City by leaden pipes from various sources in the suburbs; viz. from Tyburn in 1236, from Highbury in 1438, from Hackney in 1535, from Hampstead in 1543, and from Hoxton in 1546. For these useful works the citizens were indebted to the munificence of mayors, sheriffs, and other individuals. Stow devotes a section of his *Survey* to "ancient and present rivers, brooks, bowers, pools, wells, and conduits of fresh water, serving the City:" he also gives a long list of benefactors to the Conduits, the principal of which were in Aldgate, Leadenhall, Cornhill, West-

Cheape, Aldermanbury, Dowgate, London Wall, Cripplegate, Paul's-gate, Old Fish-street, Oldbourne, &c. In a large map and drawing* of London and Westminster, early in the reign of Queen Elizabeth, the several Conduits occupy central positions in the roadways.

The Great Conduit stood at the east end of Cheapside, at its junction with the Poultry ; and, says Stow, "was the first sweete water that was conveyed by pipes of lead under ground to this place in the citie from Paddington." Another Great Conduit stood in West Cheap, at the west end of Cheapside, facing Foster-lane and Old 'Change.

Another celebrated Conduit, "castellated in the middest" of Cornhill, opposite the south entrance to the present Royal Exchange, was called the Tun, from its being like a tun standing on one end. It was a prison-house until 1401, when "it was made a cistern for sweet water, conveyed by pipes of lead from Tiborne, was from thenceforth called the Conduit upon Cornhill." (*Stow.*) A well, which adjoined, was then planked over, and a timber cage, pillory, and stocks, set upon it ; these were removed in 1546, the well revived, and made a pump ; since renewed, with the following inscription : " On this spot a well was first made, and a House of Correction built by Henry Wallis, Mayor of London in 1285. The well was discovered, much enlarged, and this pump erected in 1799, by the contributions of the Bank of England, East India Company, and the neighbouring Fire Offices, together with the bankers and traders of the ward of Cornhill." Round the head of the pump are the devices of the Fire Offices.

"The Standard in Cornhill" was a sort of Conduit, set up in 1582, by Peter Morris, who, by an "artificial forcer," conveyed Thames water in pipes of lead over the steeple of St. Magnus' Church, and from thence to the north-west corner of London Wall, the highest ground of all the City, where the waste of the main-pipe rising into the Standard at every tide, ran by four mouths, and thus served the inhabitants, and cleansed the streets towards Bishopsgate, Aldgate, London Bridge, and Stocks Market. This Conduit appears only to have run from 1598 to 1603: from its site have since been measured distances, and hence " the Standard in Cornhill" on our milestones.

The Priory of St. Bartholomew was supplied from Canonbury ; for a water-course is specified in the grant made to Sir Richard Rich, Knight, at the Suppression, as "the water from the Conduit-head of St. Bartholomew, within the manor of Canonbury, as enjoyed by Prior Bolton and his predecessors."

Another famous Conduit stood at the south end of Shoe-lane, Fleet-street, surmounted with automaton figures, chimes, &c. (See p. 125.)

Bayswater was noted for its Conduit-Heads (see BAYSWATER, p. 36); and the association is preserved in Conduit-street in the town built between 1839 and 1849, in the rear of Hyde Park Gardens.

Tyburn furnished nine Conduits, and with Bayswater, was "viewed" periodically by the Lord Mayor on horseback, and ladies in wagons; after which they dined at the Lord Mayor's Banqueting House, at the end of Stratford-place, Oxford-road; and when the mansion was taken down in 1737, the cisterns beneath were arched over.

Strype notes that on Sept. 18, 1562, "the Lord Mayor, Aldermen, and many worshipful persons, rode to the conduit-heads to see them, according to the old custom ; and then they went and hunted a hare before dinner, and killed her; and thence went to dinner at the Banqueting House at the head of the conduit, where a great number were handsomely entertained by their Chamberlain. After dinner they went to hunt the fox. There was a great cry for a mile, and at length

* Dimensions, 6 feet 3 inches by 2 feet 6 inches, with References and Historical Notes. Published by Taperell and Innes, 2 Winchester-buildings, Old Broad-street. 1850.

the hounds killed him at the end of St. Giles's, with great hollowing and blowing of horns at his death; and thence the Lord Mayor, with all his company, rode through London to his place in Lombard-street."

The establishment of the Waterworks at London Bridge in 1512, and the subsequent introduction of the New River in 1618, having superseded the use of the Tyburn water, the Corporation let the water of these conduits on a lease for 43 years, for the sum of 700*l*. per annum. The Marylebone Waterworks were in the possession of Hugh Merchant, lessee, in 1698; they had then been established 36 years, and supplied Covent Garden and St. Martin's-lane. These Waterworks were situated at a short distance from the south end of Portland-place; Portland Chapel having been built upon the site of Marylebone Basin, which was anciently a reservoir belonging to the said Waterworks. They are often mentioned in old newspapers as the cause of many fatal accidents, and the scene of as many suicides. There is a view of this basin, by Chatelain, in the British Museum. (Smith's *Marylebone*, 1833, p. 147.)

" New Bond-street was at that time (1760) an open field, called *Conduit-mead*, from one of the conduits which supplied this part of the town with water; and Conduit-street received its name for the same reason." (*Pennant.*) Carew Mildmay, who died between 1780 and 1785, told Pennant that he remembered killing a woodcock on the site of Conduit-street, when it was open country.

On Kensington Palace green was formerly a four-gabled Conduit, built *temp.* Henry VIII.; and a Water Tower, erected by Sir John Vanbrugh, *temp.* Queen Anne; both were very fine specimens of brickwork, and communicating by pipes with the wells on the green, supplied the Palace with water, which was raised in the Tower by a horse and wheel. By forming the great sewer for " Palace Gardens" adjoining, all the wells on the green, except one, were unexpectedly drained: the Conduit and Tower were then taken down, and the Palace has since been supplied from Chelsea Water-works.

Westminster Abbey has been, from a very distant period, supplied with spring-water from a Conduit-head at Bayswater, communicating with a Gothic conduit, erected by the Dean and Chapter (bearing their arms), at the lower end of the Serpentine in Hyde Park. West of the Lodge at Hyde-Park-corner, and facing the Knightsbridge-road, is a square building, inclosing a tank filled from the above Conduit-head, for the supply of Buckingham and St. James's Palaces; the water is remarkably fine, and the building bears on a tablet "IV. G. R., 1820," the date of its repair. The leaden pipes pass through the Green Park, and the end of the ornamental water in St. James's Park, at a spot denoted by a stone, and through Queen-square to the Abbey.

The Palace at Westminster had its conduit. In the Close Rolls (Hen. III. 1244) the king commands a payment to be made out of his treasury to Edward of Westminster, on account of " our conduit;" and by a singular precept of the same year is a grant to Edward, that "from the aqueduct which the king had constructed to the Great Hall at Westminster, he might have a pipe to his own court at Westminster, of the size of a goose-quill." In a memorandum of works executed (Edw. II. 1307-1310,) is the following entry:

" The conduit of water coming into the palace, and into the king's mews, for the falcons, which in various places was obstructed and injured, and the underground pipes stolen, was completely repaired, and the water returned to its proper courses and issues, both at the palace and at the mews."

" A beautiful fountain, which fell in large cascades, and on jubilee days was made to pour forth streams of choice wine, stood rather towards the west, and on the north side of the court. Permission to make use of the surplus water which flowed from this conduit was granted, on Feb. 3 (25 Hen. VI.), to the parish. Under the date 1524, the churchwardens for the time being note, 'Mem^m. the King's charter for the Condett at the Pales'-gate remayneth in the custody of the churchwardens.' The fountain was removed in the reign of King Charles II."— Walcott's *Westminster*. Lastly, in the very curious Harleian MS. numbered 433 (Rich. III. 1484) we find mentioned " the lytell wat^r conduct."

A print by Godfrey, after a drawing by Hollar, (probably *temp.*

Charles I.,) shews a stone conduit in St. James's-square, on or near the spot now occupied by Bacon's equestrian bronze statue of William III. : the whole of Pall Mall was then clear of houses, from the village of Charing to St. James's Palace. The above conduit is mentioned by Lord Bacon (*Works*, vol. ii.) in connexion with one of his experiments. In 1720, a basin of water, with a fountain and pleasure-boat, had taken the place of the conduit ; and into this basin were thrown the keys of Newgate Prison during the Riots of 1780.

Dalston and Islington had their conduit-heads ; and the Report of a View of them, dated 1692, describes the entire course of this supply until it reaches the Conduit at Aldgate. This Report mentions " the White Conduit," fed by sundry springs, in a field at Islington, and resorted to by the Carthusian friars of the monastery upon the site of which Sutton founded the Charterhouse, supplied also from the above conduit. It likewise gave name to White Conduit House. (See AMUSE-MENTS, Tea-Gardens, p. 15.) The small stone house built over the well or conduit in 1641 was taken down in 1832. It was, however, survived by the Old Conduit at Dalston, the remains of which, in 1849, served as a tool-house in the nursery-ground of Mr. Smith.

The Charter-house Conduit was rebuilt by the executors of Thomas Sutton. It bore the date 1641, and upon it were sculptured the arms and initials of Sutton. No vestige of it now remains.

William Lamb was sometime a Gentleman of the Chapel to Henry VIII., citizen and clothworker: "neere unto Holborn," says Stow, "he founded a faire conduit and a standard, with a cocke at Holborn-bridge to conveye thence the waste. These were begun the six-and-twentieth day of March, 1577," &c. The conduit is described by Hatton, in 1708, as " near the fields (now Lamb's Conduit street), affording plenty of water, clear as chrystal, which is chiefly used for drinking. It belongs to St. Sepulchre's parish, the fountain-head being under a stone, marked S. S. P., in the vacant ground a little south of Ormond-street, whence the water comes in a drein to this conduit; and it runs thence in lead pipes (2000 yards long) to the conduit on Snow-hill, which has the figure of a lamb upon it, denoting that its water comes from Lamb's Conduit."

The sign of the Lamb public-house, at the north-east end of Lamb's Conduit-street, is the effigy of a lamb cut in stone, believed to be one of the figures which stood upon Lamb's Conduit, as a rebus on his name. When the Foundling Hospital was erected, we learn from Hatton that the conduit was taken down, and the water conveyed to the east side of Red Lion-street, at the end, (now Lamb's Conduit street;) an inscription stating the waters to be preserved "by building *an arch* over the same ;" and in 1851, Mr. J. Wykeham Archer discovered, beneath a trap-door in the pavement of the Lamb-yard, a short flight of steps, a brick vault, and the covered well ; as well as on the north wall of the next yard southward, this inscription cut in wood, over a recess now bricked up :

"Lamb's Conduit, the property of the City of London. This Pump is erected for the Benefit of the Publick."

The water is perfectly clear, and is slightly astringent; and the Mansion House is said still to derive a supply from this source.

In the garden of the house, No. 30 East-street, Lamb's Conduit street, is a pump and spring; and on the opposite wall a stone stating this to be "the head of the spring Lamb's Conduit Water."

Many of the City Conduits were destroyed in the Great Fire of 1666; and others were removed in 1728, it is stated, to compel the public to have the New River water laid on to their houses.

Upon great festal occasions, the Conduits flowed with wine instead of water: at the procession of Anne Boleyn, June 1, 1533, the Great

Cheap Conduit ran with white and claret wine all the afternoon. Probably the last of these prodigal events was in 1727, on the anniversary of the Coronation of George I., when Lamb's Conduit ran with wine.

CONVENTS.

Before we notice the Conventual establishments of the present day, we shall glance at the religious houses and hospitals which, for ages before the Reformation, occupied nearly two-thirds of the entire area of London. Independently of St. Paul's Cathedral and Westminster Abbey, the following Friaries and Abbeys existed almost immediately prior to the Reformation :—

Friaries: Black Friars, between Ludgate and the Thames; Grey Friars, near old Newgate, now Christ's Hospital; Augustine Friars, now Austin Friars, near Broad-street; White Friars, near Salisbury-square; Crouched or Crossed Friars, St. Olave's, Hart-street, near Tower-hill; Carthusian Friars, now the Charter House; Cistercian Friars, or New Abbey, East Smithfield; Brethren de Sacco, or *Bon Hommes*, Old Jewry.

Priories: St. John's of Jerusalem, Clerkenwell; Holy Trinity, or Christ Church, on the site of Duke's-place, and near Aldgate; St. Bartholomew the Great, near Smithfield; St. Mary Overie's, Southwark; St. Saviour's, Bermondsey.

Nunneries: Benedictines, or Black Nuns, Clerkenwell; St. Helen's, Bishopsgate-street; St. Clare's, Minories; Holy-well, between Holywell-lane and Norton-folgate.

Colleges, &c.: St. Martin's-le-Grand; St. Thomas of Acres, Westcheap; Whittington's College and Hospital, Vintry Ward; St. Michael's College and Chapel, Crooked-lane; Jesus Commons, Dowgate.

Hospitals (having resident Brotherhoods): St. Giles's in the Fields, near St. Giles's Church; St. James's, now St. James's Palace; Our Lady of Rounceval, near Charing-cross; St. Mary, Savoy, Strand; Elsing Spital, now Sion College; Corpus Christi, in St. Lawrence Pountney; St. Passey, near Bevis Marks; St. Mary Axe; Trinity, without Aldgate; St. Thomas, Mercers' Chapel; St. Bartholomew the Less, near Smithfield; St. Giles's, and Corpus Christi, without Cripplegate; St. Mary of Bethlehem, on the eastern side of Moorfields; St. Mary Spital, without Bishopsgate; St. Thomas, Southwark; Lok Spital, or Lazar, Kent-street, Southwark; St. Katherine's, below the Tower.

Fraternities: St. Nicholas, Bishopsgate-street; St. Fabian and St. Sebastian, or the Holy Trinity, Aldersgate-street; St. Giles, Whitecross-street; the Holy Trinity, Leadenhall; St. Ursula-le-Strand; Hermitage, Nightingale-lane, East Smithfield; Corpus Christi, St. Mary Spital; the same at St. Mary Bethlehem, and St. Mary, Poultry.

The majority of these establishments disappeared at the Reformation; but a glance at the Sutherland View of London in 1543, and at Taperell and Innes's Map (early in the reign of Elizabeth), shews us many of these important buildings entire, and others lying distant in the fields. Almost the only remains now traceable are around the Abbey Church at Westminster, where some of the monastic offices are tenanted as the School; of Grey Friars, the cloisters exist; of the Augustine Friars, the church; of the Carthusian Friars, the wooden gate and a few other relics; of St. John of Jerusalem, the gateway; of St. Bartholomew the Great, the church cloister and crypt; of St. Mary Overie's, the church-choir and lady-chapel; and at Bermondsey the great gatehouse remained nearly entire till 1807; of St. Helen's, Bishopsgate, the church remains; of St. Bartholomew's the Less, the church-tower; and St. Katherine's "by the Tower" disappeared in 1827. Such are the principal *Monastic Remains* in the metropolis.

Since the relaxation of the penal laws, a few Roman Catholic Convents have been erected in London and the suburbs. Of these, the Convent for the Order of the Sisters of Mercy was founded by subscription, at Dockhead, Bermondsey, in 1838, and opened for the Sisterhood December 12, 1839; when Sister Mary, the Lady Barbara Eyre, sister to Francis the eighth earl of Newburgh, took the vows, with five other ladies of fortune, and liberal benefactresses to the chapel and convent. In addition to the services of their religion, the Sisters devote themselves to the education of poor girls, the visitation and comfort of the sick and afflicted, and the protection of distressed reputable females.

The reception of a postulant into the sisterhood, or the "taking of the veil," is an impressive ceremony performed in the chapel of the convent, or in the church adjoining; when the whole sisterhood walk in procession, dressed in the habit of their order, each bearing a lighted taper, and followed by the postulants, in white dresses, and head-wreaths of white flowers and evergreens. The choir then chant "Gloriosa virginum;" the priest invokes the prayers of the Virgin in behalf of the postulants, to each of whom he presents a lighted taper, "as a corporal emblem of inward light." The superioress and her assistant then conduct the postulants to the celebrant, who inquires if they enter the Order by their own free will, and if it be "their firm intention to persevere in religion to the end of their lives." These questions being answered satisfactorily, the postulants withdraw with the superioress, put off their secular dress, and return wearing the sombre habit of the Order. The superioress then girds them with the cincture; and the celebrant holds a white veil over the head of each, requesting her to accept it as "the emblem of purity." They are subsequently habited with "the cloak of the Church;" each of the novices sings: "My heart hath uttered a good word; I speak my words to the King," &c.; each novice embraces the superioress and each member of the sisterhood, and they retire as they entered, in procession.

The Convent of Mercy, in Blandford-square, has school-rooms for 1000 poor children, and is situated in the centre of the parish of St. Marylebone, which has a population of nearly 20,000 Roman Catholics; this Convent is intended to afford an asylum to Roman Catholic female servants when out of situations.

Another Convent for the Sisters of Mercy was erected in Cadogan-street, Chelsea, in 1845, at the expense of Mr. Knight, the eminent botanist, of King's-road; besides the convent are a chapel and schools.

The Convent of the Order of the Faithful Companions of Jesus (Carmelite Nuns), in Clarendon-square, Somers-town, is the representative of Syon at Isleworth; and of the same order are the Convents at Hampstead and Tottenham; and Benedictine Solitaries of the Perpetual Adoration, London Abbey, London-road, St. George's-fields.

The buildings occupying the angle of the St. George's and Westminster-roads, and adjoining St. George's Cathedral, were, in part, originally designed for a convent, but will probably be adapted as a palace for the Bishop of Southwark. The edifice, with a pretty little oriel-window, buttresses, and spiral bell-turret, is a pleasing group, in combination with the gables and elegant pinnacles of the cathedral.

The Convent of our Lady of Norwood (late the Park Hotel) was established by a number of nuns from France, for Catholic orphans. In December 1851, a *paysan*, dressed in a blouse, called at the mother establishment of the above convent in France, and presented to the Lady-Superior 1500 francs (about 62l.), as a small contribution for the Orphanage at Norwood.

The Asylum of the Good Shepherd at Hammersmith consists of a convent and church, communicating by cloisters, designed by Pugin, who has also added to the old foundation cells for the nuns. There are received here nearly 100 penitents, who, on leaving the asylum, are fitted out for service; and work for the needle and laundry, and cast-off clothes, are efficient aid.

St. Mary's (Redemptorist Fathers), Park-road, Clapham, was established in 1848, in a private house, to which the Superior attached a belfry, where the bell was tolled five times a-day for five days in the week, and was subsequently increased to six bells. The noise became intolerable to the occupant of the next house, who brought an action in the Court of Exchequer in August 1851, and obtained damages 40s. and costs. On November 9 the bells were rung again (one bell weighing nine cwt.), so as effectually "to cause mischief and material injury to the comfort of those that dwell near" (*Lord Eldon*), when an injunction was sought to restrain the Superior, or any person acting under him, from ringing the bells, which was granted by Vice-Chancellor Kindersley, December 23, 1851.

The Convents of the Sisters of Notre Dame, Bedford-road, Clapham, and of the Sisters of the Christian Retreat, Manor House, Kennington-lane, are educational establishments: the latter is the only vestige of the old palace, and had for its last royal tenant Charles I. when Prince of Wales.

CORNHILL,

A principal street of the City, extending from the western end of Leadenhall-street, crossing westward to the Mansion House. It was named "of a corn-market time out of mind there holden." (*Stow.*) Here was the "Tun" prison, built in 1283, upon the spot now occupied by a pump; also a castellated conduit, and its water "Standard" (1528), near the junction of the street with Leadenhall-street. On March 25, 1748, a fire within twelve hours consumed between ninety and a hundred houses in Cornhill (200,000*l.* loss), including that in which was born the poet Gray, whose father was an Exchange broker; the house was rebuilt, and was, in 1774, occupied by one Natzell, a perfumer; and in 1824 it was still inhabited by a perfumer—No. 41, a few doors from Birchin-lane. (Brayley's *Londiniana*, vol. iii. p. 98.) Cornhill has been the site of the Merchant's Exchange for nearly three centuries. On the west side, adjoining the Bank of England, was St. Christopher-le-Stocks church, with a lofty pinnacled tower, which escaped the Great Fire of 1666: the church was rebuilt by Wren, but taken down in 1781, and its site included within the Bank. About the same time was erected Bank-buildings, in place of a block of houses built after the Great Fire; the former were removed in 1844: the end house extended to the site of the equestrian statue of the Duke of Wellington. In excavating for the new Royal Exchange, in 1841, was discovered a gravel pit, supposed by Mr. Tite, the architect, to have been sunk during the earliest Roman occupation of London; and then to have been a pond, gradually filled with rubbish. In it were found Roman work, stuccoed and painted; fragments of elegant Samian ware; an amphora, with terra-cotta lamps, 17 feet below the surface; also pine-wood table-books and metal styles, sandals and soldier's shoes, a Roman strigil, coins of Vespasian and Domitian, &c.; and almost the very foot-marks of the Roman soldier. The locality is now the most embellished area of the City, and a nucleus of new streets and sumptuous architecture.

Cornhill was formerly noted for its shops of "much stolen gear," mentioned by Lydgate early in the fifteenth century; as well as for its taverns, where was "wine one pint for a pennie, and bread to drink it" was given free in every tavern." Here was the famous Pope's-Head Tavern, whence Pope's-Head alley. No. 15, with a quaint old front, was the shop of Messrs. Birch, father and son, the celebrated cooks and confectioners: the son, born in 1757, was Alderman of Candlewick ward, and Lord Mayor in 1815-16; and annually presented to the Mansion House a splendid cake, to keep Twelfth Night. Alderman Birch wrote the *Adopted Child* and other dramatic pieces. At a corner house, between Cornhill and Lombard-street, Thomas Guy, the wealthy stationer, commenced business. (See HOSPITALS.) This "lucky corner" was subsequently Pidding's Lottery-office. There were several other lottery-offices in Cornhill, including that of Carroll, knighted as Sheriff in 1837, Lord Mayor in 1846.

Cornhill has been the scene of two calamitous fires: one in 1748, above mentioned, which commenced at a peruke-maker's in Exchange-alley, and burnt from 90 to 100 houses, including the London Assurance Office, the Fleece and Three Tuns Taverns, and Tom's and the Rainbow Coffee-houses, in Cornhill; the Swan Tavern, with Garraway's, Jonathan's, and the Jerusalem Coffee-houses, in Exchange-alley; besides the George and Vulture Tavern, and several other coffee-houses: many lives lost. The second fire commenced also at a peruke-maker's, in Bishopsgate-street, adjoining Leadenhall-street, Nov. 7, 1765; when all the houses from Cornhill to St. Martin Outwich church were burnt; and the church, parsonage-house, Merchant-Tailors' Hall, and several houses in Threadneedle-street, were much damaged. The White Lion Tavern, purchased for 3000*l.* on the preceding evening, and all the houses in White Lion Court, were burnt, together with five houses in Cornhill and others in Leadenhall-street, when several lives were lost.

COSMORAMAS.

The Cosmorama, though named from the Greek, (*kosmos,* world; and *orama,* view, because of the great variety of views,) is but an enlargement of the street peep-show; the difference not being in the construction of the apparatus, but in the quality of the pictures exhibited. In the common shows, coarsely-coloured prints are sufficiently good; in the Cosmorama a moderately good oil-painting is employed. The pictures are placed beyond what appear like common windows, but of which the panes are really large convex lenses, fitted to correct the errors of appearance which the nearness of the pictures would else produce. The optical part of the exhibition is thus complete; but as the frame of the picture would be seen, and thus the illusion be destroyed, it is necessary to place between the lens and the view a square wooden frame, which, being painted black, prevents the rays of light passing beyond a certain line, according to its distance from the eye: on looking through the lens, the picture is seen as if through an opening, which adds very much to the effect. Upon the top of the frame is a lamp, which illuminates the picture, while all extraneous light is carefully excluded by the lamp being in a box, open in front and top.

A Cosmorama is shewn at Nos. 207 and 209 Regent-street, where the most effective scenes are views of cities and public buildings. Cosmoramas also form part of other exhibitions. At the Lowther Bazaar, Strand, the "Magic Cave," (cosmoramic pictures,) has realised 1500*l.* per annum, at 6*d.* for each admission.

COVENT GARDEN,

Lying between the north side of the Strand and Long Acre, has been a locality of great interest and celebrity for six centuries past. In 1222 most of the present parish of St. Paul, Covent Garden, was occupied by the Garden of the Abbey at Westminster; *unde* Convent, corrupted to Covent Garden, which name occurs in a deed of 2 August, 9 Elizabeth. In digging for the foundations of the new Market, in 1829, a quantity of human bodies was exhumed on the north side of the area, supposed to have been the Convent burial-ground. After the Dissolution, this Garden and the lands belonging to it were granted by Edward VI. to his uncle, the Duke of Somerset, upon whose attainder they reverted to the Crown. In 1552, they were granted by patent, with seven acres, called Long Acre, of the yearly value of 6*l.* 6*s.* 8*d.*, to John Earl of Bedford, who built a town residence, principally of wood, upon the site of Southampton-street, where it remained till 1704; the garden extending northward nearly to the site of the present Market. Southampton-street was then built, and named after Lady William Russell, daughter of the Earl of Southampton; and other streets were named from the Russell family,—as Russell, Bedford, Tavistock, Chandos; King and Henrietta streets, from Charles I. and his queen; and James and York streets, from the Duke of York, afterwards James II.

In 1634 Francis Earl of Bedford cleared the area; in 1640, Inigo Jones built for his lordship the fine church of St. Paul, "the handsomest barn in England," on the west side; and lines of lofty houses upon arcades on the north and east sides, (a near imitation of the piazza at Livorno,) Tavistock-row being built, in 1704, upon the south. (*See* ARCADES, p. 18.) The area was inclosed with railings, at 60 feet from the buildings; and in the centre was a dial, with a gilt ball, raised upon a column. One of Hollar's prints, *temp.* Charles II., shews the place as above, with uniform houses, one on each side of the church. In 1671, the Earl of Bedford obtained a patent for the Market, which, however, was for a long time only held on the south side against the garden-wall of Bedford House; for we read of "bonefires" and fire-works in the square in 1690 and 1691.

Upon the site of the large house, northward, lived Sir Kenelm Digby, of "Sympathetic powder" fame, and here he had a laboratory. The mansion (now Evans's Hotel) was built for Lord Orford, who won the victory off Cape La Hogue, in 1692; the front is imagined to re-semble the forecastle of a ship. The premises were first opened as an hotel in 1774, but the upper portion was subsequently let as chambers.

From its contiguity to the Cockpit and Drury Lane theatre, Co-vent Garden became surrounded with taverns; and here, in 1711, stood "Punch's Theatre," which thinned the congregation in the church. Quacks used here to harangue the mob, and give advice gratis. These adventitious notorieties did not improve the morals of the locality—

> "Where holy friars told their beads,
> And nuns confess'd their evil deeds:
> But oh, sad change! oh, shame to tell
> How soon a prey to vice it fell!
> How?—since its justest appellation
> Is Grand Seraglio to the nation."—*Satire*, 1756.

The Piazza was formerly "a sad place." Shenstone tells us of pick-pockets in 1744, in large bodies, armed with *couteaux*, attacking parties coming out of the playhouse. At the north-east angle, in 1779, Miss Reay was shot by Hackman, as she was entering a carriage to return from Covent Garden Theatre.

Among the notorieties of "the Garden" was, beneath the church portico, "Tom King's Coffee-house," shewn in Hogarth's print of "Morning:" it was a mere shed, as Murphy described it, "well known to all gentlemen to whom beds are unknown." Upon the south side of the market sheds was the noted "Finish," kept by Mrs. Butler, the last of the Covent Garden night-taverns, and only cleared away in 1829.

In 1711, at the Bumper Tavern, in James-street, the best Port-wine was advertised at 5s. per gallon; and in this street, the Bird Market was formerly held on Sunday mornings. In 1712, Prince Eugene at-tended a musical festival at the Two Golden Balls, in Bow-street. In Great Russell-street were the three celebrated coffee-houses, "Will's," "Tom's," and "Button's," the resort of Dryden, Prior, Addison, Pope, Swift, and Gay: at Tom's, No. 8, Johnson and Boswell first met.—(*See* COFFEE-HOUSES, pp. 200, 204-5.) In 1711, Bohea tea was sold at 26s. the pound at the Barber's Pole in Southampton-street; where, No. 31, Godfrey and Cooke's, (established 1680,) is the oldest chemist and drug-gist's shop in London. At No. 27 lived David Garrick, before he re-moved to Adelphi Terrace.

The Piazza houses are still mostly occupied as hotels and coffee-houses. At the Bedford, frequented by Garrick, Quin, Foote, Murphy, and Sheridan, was held for many years the Beefsteak Society, with Cap-tain Morris for laureat: and here and at the Piazza, Richardson's, and Joy's (now Evans's), a few of the gay nobility were wont to dine. The

Piazza has had for tenants Sir Peter Lely, Sir Godfrey Kneller, Sir James Thornhill, and Richard Wilson; and Hogarth's Marriage-à-la-Mode pictures were exhibited gratis in the premises now Robins's Auction-rooms. One of the earliest records of its artistic fame is, however, that of Charles I. establishing at the house of Sir Francis Kynaston, in "the Garden," an academy called "Museum Minervæ," for the instruc-tion of gentlemen in arts and sciences, knowledge of medals, antiquities, painting, architecture, and foreign languages. Mr. Cunningham's *Hand-book* is pleasantly anecdotic of the residence of many eminent persons in this locality. Till the present century, the neighbouring streets were a fashionable quarter; and Tavistock and Henrietta streets, famed for *perruquiers*, were crowded with carriages at shopping hours.

The parish of St. Paul, Covent Garden, is completely encircled by that of St. Martin-in-the-Fields; and the boundary of each, upon the site of Bedford House and grounds, towards the lower end of South-ampton-street, has been contested since the eighteenth century.

Before the portico of St. Paul's church is erected the hustings for the election of Members of Parliament for Westminster. Contests are now restricted to one day; but in this political cockpit were fought many battles of Government and People, when "madman's holiday" extended to 15 days; the defeat of the Tory party leading to the division of the Liberals into Whigs, Radicals, and Reformers.

COVENT GARDEN MARKET. *See* MARKETS.
COVENT GARDEN THEATRE. *See* THEATRES.

CRANE-COURT,

A *cul-de-sac* on the north side of Fleet-street, and the first court eastward of Fetter-lane, was originally called Two-Crane-court. It was rebuilt immediately after the Great Fire of 1666: the house No. 5 is a fine specimen of brickwork, dated 1670; and the large top house was built by Wren. Upon its site was the mansion of the well-known Dr. Nicholas Barbon, with garden and fish-pond in the rear. In the present house, the Royal Society met from 1710 till 1782; and the room in which Sir Isaac Newton sat as president is preserved intact. In 1782, when the Society removed to Somerset-House, they sold the pre-mises in Crane-court to the Scottish Hospital and Corporation, who now occupy it. In the hall are some fine portraits: including Mary Queen of Scots, by Zucchero; and William IV., painted and presented by Sir David Wilkie. The ancient Scottish arms, cut in stone, which adorned the original hospital, is still preserved in the inner court. The house formerly included the present No. 8, in which was kept the library of the Royal Society, in cedar-wood cases. Strype describes Crane-court as "a very handsome open place, graced with good buildings, well inhabited by persons of repute." Until about 1782 it was paved with black and white marble, which was taken up by the parish, and com-mon pavement substituted. In 1754 and 1755, the Society of Arts met at a circulating library,* and subsequently at another house, in this court; and here the first premium of five pounds, offered for drawings by boys under fourteen years of age, was adjudged to Richard Cosway, afterwards R.A. In the house No. 9 was originally printed and pub-lished the *Traveller* newspaper; at No. 10 (Palmer and Clayton's) was first printed the *Illustrated London News;* and in the house immedi-ately opposite, the early numbers of *Punch*.

In Crane-court lived Dryden Leach the printer, who, in 1763, was arrested on a general warrant, upon suspicion of having printed Wilkes's libellous *North Briton*, No. 45. Leach was taken out of his bed in the night, his papers were seized, and even his journeymen and servants were apprehended; the only foun-dation for the arrest being a hearsay that Wilkes had been seen going into Leach's

* This must have been one of the earliest circulating libraries established in London, since only four existed in the metropolis in 1770.

house: he, however, subsequently obtained a verdict and 300*l.* damages from three of the king's messengers who had executed the illegal warrant.

CROSBY HALL,

In Bishopsgate-street, and north of the entrance into Crosby-square, is a portion of Crosby Place, built upon ground leased of the Prioress of St. Helen's in 1466, by Sir John Crosby, alderman, one of the sheriffs in 1471, knighted by Edward IV. in the same year, and deceased in 1475: "so short a time enjoyed he that his large and sumptuous building; he was buried in St. Helen's, the parish church; a fair monument to him and his lady was raised there."—(*Stow.*)

The next possessor of Crosby Place was Richard Duke of Gloucester, afterwards King Richard III.; and here Shakspeare* has laid a portion of his drama of that name; though "the historian is compelled to say, that neither at the death of Henry VI. in 1471, nor at the marriage of Richard with the Lady Anne in 1473, is it probable that Richard was in possession of Crosby Place;" but here he determined upon the deposition, and perhaps the death, of the young King Edward V., and here plotted his own elevation to the vacant throne.

Crosby Place was then purchased by Sir Bartholomew Read, who kept here his mayoralty, 1501. Its next possessor was Sir John Best, Mayor in 1516 (the year of Evil May-day), and by him it was sold to Sir Thomas More.† In 1523, More sold Crosby Place to his dearest friend Antonio Bonvisi, a rich merchant of Lucca, who leased the mansion to William Rastell, More's nephew; and to William Roper, the husband of More's favourite daughter Margaret. In the reign of Edward VI., Bonvisi, Rastell, and Roper were driven abroad by religious persecution, and Crosby Place was forfeited, but restored on the accession of Mary. The next proprietors were Jermyn Cioll, who married a cousin of Sir Thos. Gresham; and Alderman Bond, who added to the edifice a lofty turret, though no traces of it are now to be found.

In 1594, Sir John Spencer purchased Crosby Place, and in it kept his mayoralty that year. He greatly improved the Place, and "builded a most large warehouse near thereunto." He was "the rich Spencer," worth nearly a million of money; and here he entertained Sully, when he came on a special embassy from Henry IV. of France to James I. Sir John Spencer's daughter and sole heiress married William, the second Lord Compton, afterwards Earl of Northampton, and ancestor of the present Marquis. During Lord Compton's proprietorship, the celebrated Countess of Pembroke, "Sidney's sister, Pembroke's mother," lived many years in Crosby Place. Spencer, Earl of Northampton, son of the last-mentioned proprietor, resided here in 1638. Two years previously, the property was leased to Sir John Langham, sheriff in 1642, during whose occupation it was frequently used as a prison for Royalists. His son, Sir Stephen Langham, succeeded him; and during his tenancy, Crosby Place was so injured by fire that it was

---

* Shakspeare must have been familiar with the beauty and magnificence of Crosby Place; for in an assessment-roll for levying subsidies, dated October 1, 40th of Queen Elizabeth (1598), the name of William Shakspeare occurs in connexion with that of Sir John Spencer, and other inhabitants of the parish of St. Helen's, with the sum 5*l.* 13*s.* 4*d.*, the assessment, against the poet's name.

† More, after his marriage in 1507, resided for some years in Bucklersbury. In what year he purchased Crosby Place is uncertain; but it was probably soon after his return from his mission to Bruges, in 1514 and 1515; and as this journey forms the groundwork of the *Utopia,* there is reason to infer this charming romance to have been written at Crosby Place, to which the picture in the preface of Sir Thomas's domestic habits may apply. There is little or no doubt that More wrote his *History of Richard the Third* at Crosby Place, however it may be with the *Utopia.* Here, too, More probably received Henry VIII.; for this was just the time he was in high favour with the king, who then kept his court at Castle Baynard's, and St. Bride's,

never after used as a dwelling. In 1672, the Upper Hall was converted
into a Presbyterian meeting-house by the Rev. T. Watson; he was followed by Stephen Charnock; Dr. Grosvenor, a pupil of Benjamin Keach;
and Edmund Calamy, jun. The congregation continued to meet here
till 1769, when it was dispersed; and a farewell sermon was preached
by Mr. Jones, the predecessor of Dr. Collyer, at Peckham.

The Hall was then let as a packer's warehouse. In 1677, the present houses in Crosby Square were built on the ruins of the old mansion. In 1831, the packer's lease of the Hall expired; when public
attention was drawn to its restoration, as the finest example in the metropolis of the domestic mansion of Perpendicular work. Its long list
of distinguished tenants,—above all, its association with Richard III.,
greatly popularised the proposed restoration; and, on June 27, 1836, the
first stone of the new work was laid by Lord Mayor Copeland, alderman of Bishopsgate; when the Hall was fitted up with banners, strewed
with rushes, and an Elizabethan breakfast served upon the long tables.

On July 12, 1838, a musical performance was given in the Hall, after
service in St. Helen's Church, in commemoration of Sir Thomas Gresham: the place is fraught with musical memories, for under its shadow once lived Byrde, Wilbye, and Morley, the celebrated madrigalists.

The restoration was completed in 1842: repairs have been made, and
much of the original mansion has been rebuilt: the Hall, the Council-chamber, with the Throne-room above, remain; and the vaults are a
fine specimen of early brickwork. The entrance to Crosby Square is
through a small gateway from Bishopsgate-street. The Hall consists
of one story only, lighted by lofty and elegant windows, and a beautiful oriel window, reaching from the floor to the roof. The Council-
chamber* was stripped of many of its decorations in 1816 by the proprietor, who removed them to adorn a dairy at his seat, Fawley Court,
Bucks; but the finely coved ceiling became the property of Mr. Yar-
old of Great St. Helen's, at the sale of whose Collection, in 1825, this
lot was purchased by Mr. Cottingham, the architect, who fitted it as
the ceiling of his Elizabethan Museum at No. 43 Waterloo-Bridge-
road: at the dispersion of which, in 1851, the relic was again sold.
The Throne-room has an oak-ribbed rounded roof; and among its windows, one reaching the entire height of the apartment.

The Great Hall, the innermost sanctuary, is 54 ft. long, 27½ broad,
and 40 feet high. It has a minstrels' gallery, but not a daïs.

The glory of the place is, however, the roof, which is an elaborate architectural study, and decidedly one of the finest specimens of timber-work in existence. It differs from many other examples in being an inner-roof; it is of cork
or chestnut, of low pointed arches, approaching to an ellipse. From the main
points of intersection hang pendants, which end in octagonal ornaments, pierced
with small niches, each pendant forming the centre of four arches; so that in
whatever point it is viewed, the design presents a series of arches of elegant construction, whilst the spandrils are pierced with perpendicular trefoil-headed
niches. The principal timbers are ornamented with small flowers, or knots of
foliage, in a hollow; and the whole springs from octangular corbels of stone attached to the piers between the windows. Here the superior taste of the architect is strikingly displayed in the method by which he has avoided an horizontal
import to his ceiling, by constructing arches of timber corresponding with the ornamental portions of the roof above the lateral windows, and thus completely avoid-
ing a horizontal line, which was as much the abomination of our ancient archi-
ects, as it is the favourite of our modern ones. These arches are surmounted by an
elegant entablature, of a moulded architrave, a frieze of pierced quatrefoils in square
panels, and an embattled cornice; each quatrefoil contained a small flower, of which
fifty-six originally existed on each side of the Hall, the designs being dissimilar.

* In 1794, Mr. Capon painted for John Philip Kemble, at New Drury-lane
Theatre, the Council-chamber, for the play of *Jane Shore;* a correct restoration
of the original apartment, as far as existing documents would warrant.

The oriel, forming an ornamented recess in the side of the Hall, has ever been regarded as one of its best features: it is vaulted with stone, beautifully groined, the ribs springing from small pillars attached to the angles; while knots of foliage and bosses are at the points of intersection. Among them is a ram trippant, the crest of Sir John Crosby. This and the other windows have been, for the most part, filled with stained glass, decorated with the armorial bearings of the several personages famous in the history of Crosby Place, as well as of persons of taste who have contributed to its restoration. The lower aperture has been closed by the same piece of wood-work that was formerly elevated above it. The floor is paved with stone in small square slabs, arranged diagonally. In the north wall is a fire-place, which is at least singular, if not unique, in a Hall of this age.

Crosby Hall, in its restored state, is let for musical performances and lectures; and it was, for some time, the meeting-place of a Literary Society. The west front of the premises, next Bishopsgate-street, has been composed in the style of the timber houses of the Crosby period. Here is a statue of Sir John, by Nixon; with his arms and crest.

CRYPTS.

The Crypts, vaults, or undercrofts remaining in the metropolis, are interesting specimens of its ecclesiastical and domestic architecture.

The Crypt or Lower Chapel of Old London Bridge belongs to the past: it was constructed in the tenth or great pier, and was entered both from the upper apartment and the street, as well as by a flight of stone stairs winding round a pillar which led into it from outside the pier; whilst in front of this latter entrance the sterling formed a platform at low-water, which thus rendered it accessible from the river. This Crypt was about 60 feet in length, 20 feet high, and had a groined roof, supported by stone ribs springing from clustered columns; at the intersections were bosses sculptured with cherubs, episcopal heads, and a crowned head (probably Richard Cœur de Lion), grouped with four masks; and near the entrance was a piscina for holy water. Here was a rich series of windows looking on to the water, and the floor was paved with black and white marble: herein was buried Peter of Colechurch, the priest-architect of the bridge. The Chapel was taken down in 1700: the Crypt had been many years used as a paper-warehouse; and though the floor was always from 8 to 10 feet under the surface at high-water mark, yet the masonry was so good that no water ever penetrated. In front of the bridge-pier, a square fish-pond was formed in the sterling, into which the fish were carried by the tide, and there detained by a wire grating placed over it; and "an ancient servant of London Bridge, now (1827) verging upon his hundredth summer, well remembers to have gone down through the Chapel to fish in the pond." Thomson's *Chronicles*, p. 517.

St. Bartholomew's Crypt, Smithfield, exists in good preservation under the dining-hall or refectory of the priory, of which also there remain other appurtenances. This crypt is of great length, has a double row of beautiful aisles, with Early-Pointed arches, divided by Middlesex-passage, leading from Great to Little Bartholomew-close; a door at the extremity is traditionally said to have communicated by a subterranean passage with Canonbury at Islington. Beneath the "Coach and Horses" public-house, and probably once the *hospitium*, within the west gate of the monastery, is the remains of another crypt.

Bow Church Crypt, Cheapside, consists of columns and simple Romanesque groinings, said to be of the age of the Conqueror: it is the crypt of the ancient Norman church, but it was mistaken by Wren for Roman workmanship. It has long been used as a dead-house, is ventilated, and the coffins are put in fair order. At Messrs. Growcock's, in Bow Churchyard, is a small portion of another crypt or undercroft. It is difficult to understand how Wren was led to the belief that the above remains were Roman; unless, as was pointed out by Mr. Gwilt, in an admirable description of the crypt (*Vetusta Monumenta*, vol. v. plates 61 to 65), Wren was deceived by the fact that Roman bricks are used in the construction of the arches; or did he mean that they were *more Romano*, or in the Roman manner?

GARRAWAY'S COFFEE-HOUSE, 3 Change-alley, Cornhill, has a Crypt of fourteenth and sixteenth century architecture : it is of ecclesiastical character, and has a piscina; but is now used as the coffee-house wine-cellar.

GERARD'S HALL CRYPT, Basing-lane, was the only remaining vestige of the mansion of John Gisors, pepperer, Mayor of London in 1245; "a great house of old time, builded upon arched vaults, and with arched gates of stone brought from Cane in Normandy" (*Stow*); Gisors' Hall being corrupted to Gerard's Hall. The date of this crypt was probably late in the thirteenth century. The groined roof was supported by sixteen columns : the crypt, although generally resembling a subterranean ecclesiastical edifice, was constructed solely for the stowage of merchandise, and was thus an example of the warehouse of the wealthy London merchant of the thirteenth century. The great house called the Vintrie stood upon similar vaults, which were used for the stowage of French wines; it was likewise occupied, in 1314, by Sir John Gisors, who was a vintner. Gerard's Hall Crypt, with the modern inn which had replaced the hall, was removed in forming a new street in 1852, when some curious old merchant's marks were found.

Here was preserved the tutelar effigies of "Gerard the gyant," a fair specimen of a London sign, *temp.* Charles II. Here also was shewn the staff used by Gerard in the wars, and a ladder to ascend to the top of the staff; and in the neighbouring church of St. Mildred, Bread-street, hangs a huge tilting-helmet, said to have been worn by the said *gyant*. The staff, Stow thinks, may rather have been used as a May-pole, and to stand in the hall decked with evergreens at Christmas; the ladder serving for decking the pole and hall-roof.—*J. W. Archer.*

GUILDHALL CRYPT is the finest and most extensive undercroft remaining in London, and is the only portion of the ancient hall (erected in 1411) which escaped the Great Fire of 1666. It extends the whole length beneath the Guildhall from east to west, divided nearly equally by a wall, having an ancient Pointed door. The crypt is divided into aisles by clustered columns, from which spring the stone-ribbed groins of the vaulting, composed partly of chalk and bricks; the principal intersections being covered with carved bosses of flowers, heads and shields. The north and south aisles had formerly mullioned windows, now walled up. At the eastern end is a fine Early-English arched entrance, in fair preservation; and in the south-eastern angle is an octangular recess, which formerly was ceiled by an elegantly groined roof; height, 13 feet. The vaulting, with four-centred arches, is very striking, and is probably some of the earliest of the sort, which seems peculiar to this country. Though called the Tudor arch, the time of its introduction was Lancastrian. (See Weale's *London*, p. 159.) In 1851 the stonework was rubbed down and cleaned, and the clustered shafts and capitals were repaired; and on the visit of Queen Victoria to Guildhall, July 9, 1851, a banquet was served to her Majesty and suite in this crypt, which was characteristically decorated for the occasion. Opposite the north entrance is a large antique bowl, of Egyptian red granite, which was presented to the Corporation by Major Cookson in 1802, as a memorial of the British achievements in Egypt.

"GUY FAWKES'S CELLAR" was a crypt-like apartment beneath the old House of Lords, the ancient Parliament-chamber at Westminster, believed to have been rebuilt by King Henry II. on the ancient foundations of Edward the Confessor's reign. "The walls of this building were nearly seven feet in thickness, and the vaults below ('Guy Fawkes's Cellar') were very massive. Piers of brickwork (possibly of Charles the Second's time) had been raised to strengthen the ceiling and sustain the weight of the Parliament-chamber floor, together with strong rafters of oak, supported by twelve octagonal oak posts, on stone plinths. This building was taken down about the year 1823, when it was ascertained that the vaults had been the ancient kitchen of the Old Palace; and near the south end the original buttery-hatch was discovered, together with an adjoining pantry or cupboard." (Britton and Brayley's *Westminster Palace*, p. 421.) The Conspirators obtained access to the vaults through a house in the south-east corner of Old Palace-yard, which was at one time occupied as the Ordnance Office, and afterwards as the entrance to the House of Lords.

Since the Gunpowder Plot, Nov. 5, 1605, it has been the custom to search and carefully examine all the vaults and passages under the Houses of Parliament, previous to the Sovereign opening the Session. This precautionary inspection, which is continued to the present day, is performed by certain officers of Parliament, headed by the Usher of the Black Rod, who go through the vaults, and examine the various nooks and recesses that might, if Conspirators were so inclined, again hold combustibles, with the intent, "suddenly and with one blast, to blow up and tear in pieces" those assembled on the occasion in Parliament. The search takes place on the morning of the day of the Royal ceremonial.

HOSTELRY OF THE PRIOR OF LEWES CRYPT was discovered in Carter-lane, Tooley-street, Southwark, nearly opposite St. Olave's Church, in 1832. This vaulted chamber was supported by six demi-columns, attached to the side walls; the columns and arches of wrought stone, and the vaultings of chalk. In 1834 was discovered another crypt-like chamber, with a plain, massive, round pillar in the centre, from which sprang elliptic-ribbed arches, forming a groined roof. This vault is supposed to have been the cellar of the "Hostelry for Travellers" which had the sign the 'Walnut Tree'" (*Stow*). Both crypts originally belonged to the town lodging of the priors of Lewes; the larger crypt being under the great hall, which had been used as the grammar school-room of St. Olave's, founded by Queen Elizabeth. These crypts were destroyed in making the approaches to the New London Bridge.

LAMBETH PALACE CRYPT, or Under-chapel, is considered to be the oldest portion of the palace. It consists of a series of strongly-groined stone arches, supported centrally by a short, massive column, and by brackets in the side walls. These vaults are now converted into cellars; but might, possibly, have been originally used for divine worship, as there are two entrances to them from the cloisters.

"Lambeth Palace Chapel retains a crypt, a doorway, and windows of great beauty, but the chapel has otherwise been quite barbarised; and the remainder of this archiepiscopal residence, though founded as early as the reign of Richard Cœur-de-Lion (before which it was a residence of the Bishop of Rochester), now forms only a confused medley of buildings, with no fragment older than the fifteenth century." Weale's *London*, p. 145.

LAMB'S CHAPEL CRYPT, Monkwell-street, is a remarkably pure and finished specimen of the Norman style. The vaulted roof has been supported by nine short columns, six of which remain, with very ornate capitals; and the intersecting ribs of the groining are decorated with zig-zag moulding and a spiral ornament. The carved work is of Caen stone. The chapel was originally "the Hermitage of St. James's" in the wall, a cell to the Abbey of Quorndon, in Leicestershire, and said to have been founded by Henry III., but evidently upwards of a century earlier. The chapel and its appurtenances were granted by Henry VIII. to William Lamb, who bequeathed it and endowed it at his death for the benefit of the Clothworkers' Company, of which he was a member. (See LAMB'S CONDUIT, page 231.)

LEATHER-SELLERS' HALL CRYPT, at the east end of St. Helen's-place, Bishopsgate, adjoins the church of St. Helen on the north side, and extends beneath the present hall: it is boldly groined. In the wall which separated this crypt from the church were two ranges of small apertures, made in an oblique direction, so that the high altar might be seen by those in the crypt when mass was performing. The position of one set of these openings ("The Nuns' Grating ") is marked out within the present church by a stone-canopied altar affixed to the wall. The crypt has been engraved by J. T. Smith.

St. ETHELREDA'S CHAPEL CRYPT, Ely-place, originally a burial-place, is not vaulted, but has for its roof the chapel-floor, supported by enormous chestnut posts and girders. During the Interregnum, when Ely House and its offices were converted into a prison and hospital, this crypt became a kind of military canteen; it was subsequently used as a public cellar to vend drink in; and here were frequently revellings heard during divine service in the chapel above. (See page 167.)

St. JOHN'S CRYPT, Clerkenwell, is Early-English, and part of the magnificent Priory-Church of St. John of Jerusalem; the superstruc-ture of the present Church of St. John being mostly the patched-up remains of the choir. (See page 132.)

St. MARTIN'S-LE-GRAND CRYPT was laid open in clearing for the site of the new General Post-Office, in 1818, the area formerly occupied by the Church and Sanctuary of St. Martin. There were then found two ranges of vaults, which had served as cellars to the houses above; one of these being the crypt of St. Martin's (taken down in 1547), and afterwards the cellar of a large wine-tavern, the "Queen's Head." This was in the Pointed style of Edward III., and was most likely the work of William of Wykeham. The second or westernmost range, which must have supported the nave, was of earlier date, and was a square, vaulted chamber, divided by piers six feet square: here was found a coin of Constantine, and a stone coffin containing a skeleton; and in digging somewhat lower down, Roman remains were met with in abundance. In St. Martin's-le-Grand also, between Aldersgate and St. Anne's-lane end, was the large tavern of the "Mourning Bush," whose vaulted cellars, as they remain from the Great Fire of 1666, disclose the foundation-wall of Aldersgate, and a remarkably fine spe-cimen of early brick arch-work.

St. MARY ALDEMARY, Bow-lane.—In 1835, upon the removal of some houses in Watling-street, at the east end of this church, a build-ing, thought to be the crypt of the old church commenced by Sir Henry Keble in 1510, was brought to light. In 1851, in widening the thoroughfare by way of Cannon-street, just opposite St. Swithin's Church and London Stone, an ancient vault or crypt, of considerable length, was opened; it had stone cross-springers, forming a Pointed arch, and was vaulted with chalk.

St. MICHAEL, ALDGATE.—A subterranean passage is said to con-duct from the Tower to the ancient Chapel or Crypt of St. Michael at Aldgate, situated under the house at the south-east corner of London-Wall-street, hard by Aldgate pump. It has some marks of the semi-Norman, or Transition style, but it is assigned to Prior Norman, in 1108. The central clustered column is Norman; the bosses remain perfect, and contain roses and grotesque heads. A means of approach from the street has existed; and there are indications of two other passages, one said to have run to Duke's-place, and the other to the Tower.

St. PAUL's CRYPT extends beneath the whole of the church, and, like the body of the cathedral, is divided into three avenues by mas-sive pillars and arches; except the portion beneath the area of the dome, it is well lighted and ventilated by windows opening into the churchyard. The north aisle is a place of sepulture for the parishioners of St. Faith (See CHURCHES, St. Paul's, page 92). Here, in "Painters' Corner," near Reynolds and between Barry and Wren, was buried, Dec. 30, 1851, J. M. W. Turner, R.A., aged 79, the greatest landscape-painter the world ever produced. In the crypt of old St. Paul's (see page 85) the stationers of Paternoster-row had warehoused their stocks of books, which were destroyed in the Great Fire of 1666.

ST. STEPHEN'S CRYPT, WESTMINSTER PALACE, also called " St. Mary's Chapel in the Vaults," formed the basement of St. Stephen's Chapel, founded by King Stephen, and rebuilt by Edward I. in 1292: a roll of this date records the purchase of two shiploads of chalk, besides burnt lime, ashes, and sand, for the foundation of the chapel, thus proving it to have been raised on a *concrete* basis; and how substantially is proved by the Crypt remaining in excellent preservation, notwithstanding the superstructure has been twice destroyed by fire— in 1298 and 1834. Like other crypts, this is of low proportions, but has no division by detached pillars; the masses projecting inwards, and dividing window from window in short massive clusters, the vault-ribs and all other members partaking of the same bold, thick character; whilst the tracery of the windows is exquisitely beautiful. " Strength, solidity, fine proportions, and skilful execution, are the characteristics of this basement chapel" (*Britton and Brayley*), which " is the last fragment in London that can be decidedly classed in the first or progressive period of English architecture."—(Weale's *London*.) This crypt was fitted up as the state dining-room of the Speaker of the House of Commons: it was much damaged in the great fire of 1834, but has been restored as a chapel for the officers of the House of Commons; and during the works, on January 17, 1852, the workmen discovered, beneath a window-seat, the embalmed body of an ecclesiastic, without any coffin. The corpse lay with its feet towards the east (said to be an unusual position for an ecclesiastic); it was wrapped in several folds of waxed cloth sewn together with coarse twine; its right hand, on which was probably the ring or jewelled glove, was lying on the breast. Over the left arm was the pastoral staff—a crook—of oak, beautifully carved. On the feet were sandals, with leathern soles sharply pointed. Upon removing the cere-cloth, the face proved to be in remarkable preservation, with hair on the chin and upper lip. The remains are presumed to be those of William Lyndwoode, Bishop of St. David's, who founded a chantry in St. Stephen's Chapel, and died in 1446; and in the patent-roll of 32 Henry VI. there is a license to the bishop's executors for one or two chaplains to celebrate divine service daily "for the soul of the aforesaid bishop, whose body lies buried in the said under-chapel," &c. The relics were inspected by a deputation from the Society of Antiquaries on Jan. 31, 1852; and a cast of the face having been taken for Her Majesty, the remains were placed in an elm coffin, and buried in a grave in the north cloister of Westminster Abbey; the pastoral staff and sandals being sent to the British Museum.

TOWER OF LONDON.—The Crypt, or large range of vaults, beneath the White Tower, is half underground, and now covered by modern brickwork. These vaults have been occupied as prisons; and among the inscriptions still remaining on the walls of the subterranean cells is one cut by the unfortunate Bishop of Rochester, John Fisher, who was beheaded for his opposition to the Reformation.

CURFEW, OR COUVRE-FEU.

Although the *Couvre-feu* law* was abolished by Henry I., who re-

* The *Couvre-feu* formerly in the collection of the Rev. Mr. Gostling, and so often engraved, passed into the possession of Horace Walpole, and was sold at

tored the use of lamps and candles at night after the ringing of the Curfew-bell, which had been prohibited by his predecessors, (*Will. Malmesb.* fol. 88,) yet the custom of ringing the bell long continued; and in certain parishes of the metropolis, and in some parts of the country, to the present time

"The curfew tolls the knell of parting day."

Among the charges directed for the wardmote inquests of London, in the second mayoralty of Sir Henry Colet (A.D. 1495), it is said: " Also if there be anye paryshe clerke that ryngeth curfew after the curfewe be ronge at Bowe Chyrche, or Saint Brydes Chyrche, or Saint Gyles without Cripelgat, all suche to be presented." (Knight's *Life of Dean Colet*, p. 6.) The same charge remained in the wardmote inquest 1649.

" The church of St. Martin's-le-Grand, with those of Bow, St. Giles's, Cripplegate, and Barkin, had its Curfew-bell long after the servile injunction laid on the Londoners had ceased. These were sounded to give notice to the inhabitants of those districts to keep within, and not to wander in the streets; which were infested by a set of ruffians, who made a practice of insulting, wounding, robbing, and murdering the people whom they happened to meet abroad during the night."—*Strype's Stow*, v. i. book iii. p. 106.

" The Couvre-feu is still rung, at eight o'clock, at St. Edmund the King, Lombard-street. At Bishopsgate (St. Botolph's); St. Leonard's, Shoreditch; Christchurch, Spitalfields; St. Michael's, Queenhithe; St. Mildred's, Bread-street;* St. Antholin's, Budge-row; and in some other City churches, there are evening bells, which are popularly known as the *couvre-feu*, but some of which are really, I believe, prayer-bells. (*See* CHURCHES, St. Mary-le-bow, p. 143.)

" On the southern side of the Thames, the *couvre-feu* was, till within these six or seven years, nightly rung at St. George's Church, Borough."—Mr. Syer Cuming: *Proceedings of the British Archæological Association, April 12, 1848.*

Mr. Cuming also states that at St. Peter's Hospital, Newington (the Fishmongers' Almshouses, taken down in 1851,) "there is a bell rung every evening from eight o'clock till nine, which the old parishioners were wont to denominate the couvre-feu; but it is now said that this is rung to warn all strangers from the premises, and the almspeople to their several apartments."

The Curfew was not always rung at eight o'clock, for the sexton in the old play of the *Merry Devil of Edmonton* (4to, 1631) says:

"Well, 'tis *nine a cloke*, 'tis time to ring curfew."

The Curfew-bell, strictly as such, had probably fallen into disuse previous to the time of Shakspeare, who, in *Romeo and Juliet*, applies the term to the morning bell:

" The second cock hath crow'd,
The curfew-bell has rung, 'tis three o'clock."

At Charterhouse, the Chapel bell, (which bears the arms and initials of Thomas Sutton, the founder, and the date 1631,) is rung at eight and nine to warn the absent pensioner of the approaching hour; and this practice is, we think, erroneously adduced as a relic of Curfew-ringing.

" There is one peculiarity attached to the ringing, which is calculated to serve the office of the ordinary passing-bell; and that is the number of strokes, which

Strawberry Hill, in 1842, to Mr. William Knight. It is of copper, riveted together, and in general form resembles the "Dutch-oven" of the present day. It is stated to have been used for extinguishing a fire, by raking the wood and embers to the back of the hearth, and then placing the open part of the couvre-feu close against the back of the chimney. In February 1842, Mr. Syer Cuming purchased of a curiosity-dealer in Chancery-lane a couvre-feu closely resembling Mr. Gosting's; and Mr. Cuming considers both specimens to be of the same age, of the close of the 15th or early part of the 16th century; whereas Mr. Gostling's specimen was stated to be of the Norman period. A third example of the *couvre-feu* exists in the Canterbury Museum.

* The bell at this church was silenced by order of vestry, December 1847.

must correspond with the number of pensioners. So that, when a brother pensioner has deceased, his companions are informed of their loss by one stroke of the bell less than on the preceding evening."—*Chronicles of Charterhouse,* p. 180.

CURIOSITY-SHOPS.

The principal locality for dealers in *Curiosities,* including ancient furniture and carvings, pictures, china and enamels, painted glass, metal-work, and church-furniture, has long been in Wardour-street, Soho and Oxford-street. Formerly it was also noted for its bookstalls; but in the spreading taste for Curiosities within the last quarter of a century, the bookstalls have mostly disappeared, and the Curiosity-dealers here now number sixteen. Still, Wardour-street is especially famous for old furniture and carvings; Hanway-street (formerly Hanway-yard, at the east end of Oxford-street,) being more exclusively celebrated for its china-dealers. There is also a good specimen of a well-stocked Curiosity-shop in Bear-street, Leicester-square. These several shops are principally supplied from the Continent; but it is a profitable business to collect specimens from our provinces, where an Elizabethan bedstead has been bought for five shillings, and sold for twice as many pounds in Wardour-street. The *marks* on porcelain denote its age and manufacture, but there is no such warrant for genuine old furniture; and rough work which has just left the carver's hands, and has been pickled and charred, *ante-dated,* and even shattered, to imitate age, is often sold for the ingenuity of the two preceding centuries.

The revival of the style of Louis XV. has done much to foster this false taste; and our collectors, "not content with ransacking every pawnbroker's shop in London and Paris for old buhl, old porcelain, and old plate, old tapestry and old frames, even set every manufacturer at work, and corrupt the taste of every modern artist by the renovation of this wretched style."—*Hope's Hist. Architecture.*

The dispersion of famed collections, (as Strawberry Hill, in 1842; Mr. Beckford's, in 1845; and Stowe, in 1849,) is a benefit, direct and indirect, to Curiosity-dealers. The taste for Mediæval art in church-fittings and painted glass has also greatly encouraged this trade, as well as the copying of olden works in new materials. Certain auction-rooms are noted for the sale of Curiosities: as Christie and Manson's, King-street, St. James's, especially for pictures. Phillips's, New Bond-street; Foster's, Pall-mall; Oxenham's, Oxford-street; and Deacon's, Berners-street, are known for their sales of articles of *vertu,* and collections, as well as "importation sales." Here the accumulation of a lifetime is often distributed in a week or a day. (*See* CARVINGS IN WOOD, p. 66; and CHELSEA CHINA, p. 77.)

The Fox public-house, in Wardour-street, was formerly kept by Sam House, "publican and republican," who commenced politician in 1763, and became conspicuous in the memorable Westminster election-contest between Lord Lincoln and Mr. Fox, in 1780: a picture, with Fox arm-in-arm with House, was sold by Christie and Manson in 1845. In a pawnbroker's window in Wardour-street, the writer remembers to have seen the Ireland Shakspearean Mss. ("great and impudent forgery," *Dr. Parr*) lying for sale upon a family Bible.

CUSTOM-HOUSE (THE),

Lower Thames-street, immediately east of Billingsgate-dock, was originally designed by David Laing: the foundations were laid in 1813, upon piles driven into the old bed of the river, and extending eastward beyond the site of the Custom-House, destroyed by fire Feb. 12, 1814, when the greater part of the trade records were consumed. The northern elevation, fronting Thames-street, is plain; but the south front towards the Thames has in the wings Ionic colonnades and a projecting centre, the attic of which was decorated with terra-cotta bas-relief figures of the Arts and Sciences, Commerce and Industry; and natives of the principal countries of the globe, with emblems of their arts. The clock-dial, nine feet in diameter, was supported by colossal figures of Industry and Plenty; and the royal arms by Ocean and Commerce. Unfortunately, the piling gave way; and in 1825 the re-centre was taken down, the foundation relaid, and the Thames front erected as we now see it, by Sir Robert Smirke. The expense was 180,000*l.*, which, added to the original expenditure, 255,000*l.*, made the total cost of the edifice nearly half a milion, or two-thirds the cost of St. Paul's Cathedral. The river façade is 488 feet in length, or 90 feet longer than the General Post-Office, and exceeding by 30 feet the National Gallery. It is fronted by a noble esplanade, or quay, reminding us how many opportunities have been lost of embanking the river with public walks—from the plans of Wren to those of Sir Frederick Trench, John Martin, and Thomas Allom. As the breadth of the quay is not equal to the height of the Custom-House, its façade, which is of Portland stone, is not seen to advantage from that point, but from London Bridge or the middle of the river.

The interior contains, besides warehouses and cellars, about 170 apartments, classified for contiguity and convenience of the several departments. In the Board-room are portraits of George III. and George IV., the latter by Lawrence. The Long Room, in the centre of the building, is probably the largest apartment of its kind in Europe: its length is 190 feet, width 66 feet, and height between 30 and 40 feet; but it is not so handsome as the "Long Room" taken down after the failure of the foundation. The walls and ceiling are stone tint, and the floor is of oak; and the room is mainly warmed by a large Arnott stove. The seventy-four officers and clerks form three divisions: the inward department, with its collectors, clerks of rates, clerks of ships' entries, computers of duties, receivers of plantation-duties, wine-duties, &c.; the outward department, with its cocket-writers, &c; and the coast department. Here a Trinity-House officer sits for the collection of lighthouse dues; and here is a constant succession of ship-brokers and ship-owners, and their clerks, and of skippers and wholesale merchants. Defoe relates Count Tallard to have said, that nothing gave him so true and great an idea of the richness and grandeur of England as seeing the multitude of payments made in a morning in the Long Room; since which was said, the Customs have increased tenfold.

On the ground-floor is the Queen's Warehouse, with a diagonal-ribbed roof. The cellars in the basement form a groined crypt, and are fire-proof; the walls are extraordinarily thick; and here are kept the wines and spirits seized by the officers of the Custom-house. The condemned articles are disposed of quarterly by auctions or "Custom-House Sales," at which the lots are not produced, but have been previously viewed in the Queen's Warehouse and at the Docks. The total number of persons employed in the Custom-House is 1800, and the annual amount of salaries 200,000*l.*

The following is an average *daily report* of the principal articles passed through the Custom-House, and issued to the public for consumption; and to arrive at a year's amount these figures must be multiplied in many instances 300 times: Anchovies, 1455 lbs.; arrow-root, 101 cwt.; cattle, 172; cocoa and coffee, 78,684 lbs.; corahs, 1042 pieces; elephants' teeth, 395; gloves, 2237 pairs; gum, 450 packages; handkerchiefs, 791 pieces; hemp, 587 bales; hides, 780; honey, 17 cwt.; horns, 1500; indigo, 274 chests; iron, 5760 bars; isinglass, 6 cwt.; jute, 636 bales; leeches, 180*l.* value; lemon-peel, 20 pipes; lithographic stones, 953; manufactures, 6352*l.* value; marble, 12 blocks; molasses, 1176 cwt.; nutmegs, 414 lbs.; oil, 546 packages; oil, scented, 810 lbs.; onions, 800 bushels; pepper, 11,832 lbs.; quicksilver, 4089 bottles; rags, 67 bales; rice, 215 cwt.; sago, 70 cwt.; sheep, 65; silk, 382 bales; spelter, 638 cakes; spirits, 19,875 gallons; sugar, 11,151 cwt.;

tallow, 327 cwt.; tea, 89,742 lbs.; timber, 1900 loads; tobacco, 14,143 lbs.; whale-fins, 279 bundles; wine, 10,765 gallons; wool, 354 bales. Warehoused in one day: anchovies, 250 barrels; butter, 539 casks; coffee, 2650 bags; cork, 19 bales; hams, 500; manufactures, 168 packages; marble mortars, 50; mats, 1000; raisins, 750 drums; rice, 581 bags; rum, 111 casks; spirits, 554 cases or casks; sugar, 1345 packages; tallow, 191 packages; tobacco, 990 packages; tin, 1075 slabs; timber, 72,635 deals and pieces; wine, 896 cases or casks.

The present is the fifth Custom-House built nearly upon the same site. The *first* was erected by John Churchman, Sheriff of London in 1385. (*Stow*.) The *second* was built in the reign of Queen Elizabeth, and appears in the 1543 View of London with several high-pitched gables and a water-gate: it was burnt in the Great Fire of 1666. It was rebuilt by Wren, at a cost of 10,000*l.*; and this *third* House was consumed by fire in 1718, and was the only one of Wren's buildings that in his long life was destroyed. This Custom-House was replaced by Ripley, who introduced the "Long Room," and embellished the river-front with Ionic columns, pediments, and a Tuscan colonnade: this *fourth* House was burnt in 1814.

The taxes levied on imported and exported commodities having been repeatedly altered, to meet the necessities of the State, or serve political purposes, their amount at different periods is not of itself a correct test of the increase of trade. In 1613, the date of one of the earliest notices preserved, the Customs duties collected in London amounted to 109,572*l.*, being nearly thrice as much as was collected in all the rest of the kingdom (England), the whole Customs duties then amounting to 148,075*l.* In 1711, about the period when M. Tallard made the preceding remark, a similar proportion was observed: London then yielding 1,268,095*l.*, and all England 1,614,176*l.* In 1849, the proportion was about one-half: London paying 11,070,176*l.*, and the whole empire 22,483,956*l.* The amount collected in London reached its highest point in 1835—11,773,616*l.*; in 1848, the next highest, it was 11,193,707*l.* Notwithstanding the tenfold increase since 1711, there are now no heaps of money at the Custom-House such as excited Tallard's admiration. The duties are paid into the Receiver-General's Office in the Custom-House, and almost invariably in paper, so that only very small sums of metallic money pass in collecting the 22,483,956*l.*

The total value of the produce conveyed into and from London, including the home and foreign markets, is stated at 65 millions sterling.

DAGUERREOTYPE (THE).

The first experiment made in England with the Daguerréotype was exhibited by M. St. Croix, on Friday, September 13, 1839, at No. 7 Piccadilly, nearly opposite the southern Circus of Regent-street; when the picture produced was a beautiful miniature representation of the houses, pathway, sky, &c., resembling an exquisite mezzotint. M. St. Croix subsequently removed to the Argyll Rooms, Regent-street, where his experimental results became a scientific exhibition. One of the earliest operators was Mr. Goddard. The discovery was patented by Mr. Miles Berry, who sold the first license to M. Claudet for 100*l.* or 200*l.* a-year; and in twelve months after disposed of the patent to Mr. Beard, who, however, did not take a Daguerréotype *portrait* until after Dr. Draper had sent from New York a portrait to the editor of the *Philosophical Magazine*, with a paper on the subject.

With reference to the conditions of a London atmosphere, as regards its influence upon Daguerréotypic or Photographic processes, there are some very peculiar phenomena; for the following details of which we are indebted to Mr. Robert Hunt, the author of many valuable researches in Photography.

The *yellow* haze which not unfrequently prevails, even when there is no actual fog over the town itself, is fatal to all chemical change. This haze is, without doubt, an accumulation, at a considerable elevation, of the carbonaceous matter rom the coal-fires, &c. Although a day may appear moderately clear, if the sun ssume a red or orange colour, it will be almost impossible to obtain a good Daguerréotype. Notwithstanding in some of the days of spring our photographers btain very fine portraits or views, it must be evident to all who examine an extensive series of Daguerréotypes, that those which are obtained in Paris and New York re very much more intense than those which are generally procured in London. This is mainly dependent upon the different amounts and kinds of smoke diffused hrough the atmospheres respectively of these cities. At the same time, there is o doubt the peculiarly humid character of the English climate interferes with he free passage of those solar rays which are active in producing photographic hange. It was observed by Sir John Herschel, when he resided at Slough, that sudden change of wind to the east almost immediately checked his photoraphic experiments at that place, by bringing over it the yellow atmosphere of London: this is called by the Berkshire farmers *blight*, from their imagining that mut and other diseases in grain are produced by it.

It is a curious circumstance, that the summer months, June, July, and August, otwithstanding the increase of light, are not favourable to the Daguerréotype. This arises from the fact, now clearly demonstrable, that the luminous powers of he sunbeam are in antagonism to the chemical radiations, and as the one increases, the other diminishes. This may be imitated by a pale yellow glass, which, although it obstructs no light completely, cuts off the chemical rays, and ntirely prevents any photographic change taking place.

DAIRIES.

Little is positively known of the London Dairy system, save that iven by Mr. Youatt, who in 1834 stated the number of cows requisite or the supply of the metropolis with milk to be 12,000; and the present umber is estimated at 13,000. Elsewhere it is stated at 60,000 cows, ielding upwards of 100,000 gallons of milk per day. Again, Mr. Rugg, M.R.C.S., says, in his *Observations on London Milk* : "taking London o contain 2,000,000 individuals, and supposing each to consume on an verage half-a-pint of milk per day, it would require 50,000 cows producing ten quarts per day each to maintain the supply of 500,000 quarts er day, or 182,500,000 quarts per year." It is hard to reconcile these onflicting statements; but we are inclined to adopt the former.

Railways now bring fresh milk from the country in less time and vith less injury, for a distance of 20 miles round London, than used to e incurred in conveying it from the milkman to the consumer. The ailways have also cheapened the food. The sum of 82*l.* per cow has een given as an estimate of her produce per annum to the retail dealer; nd the gross sum expended in milk and cream in London at nearly one million sterling. The milk is sold by the dairymen to the middlemen etailers, who take off the cream and mix it with water for sale; boil he skim-milk, and sell it warm from the fire. There is no such thing as ew milk in London; it is all boiled skim-milk.

The adulteration of milk is a pestilential practice. The substances usually mployed are water, flour, starch, chalk, and the brains of sheep, oxen, or cows; he brains have been detected with a microscope, shewing the nerve-tubes, heir natural size being only about 1500dth of an inch in diameter; they are ubbed with warm water into an emulsion, and then added to the milk, or in arger proportion to London cream. This is a vile fraud imported from Paris. n Smollett's time (see *Humphrey Clinker*) London milk was described as chalk nd water, with beaten snails for froth; the milkmen of our day have added reacle, salt, whiting, sugar-of-lead, annatto, size, &c.: the sugar-of-lead is most ernicious, being formed into carbonate of lead, which is held in suspension, a, ittle giving a great bulk of water a milky appearance. A never-failing pump, or cow with the iron tail," is indispensable to a Dairy establishment, to balance the tatistics of demand and supply.

Again, the cows are often poor, lean, mangy, and feverish, are kept in dark ellars or filthy yards, and fed upon decaying vegetables, brewers' and distillers' rains, and distillers' wash. Under the Adelphi arches are cow-sheds entirely ighted by gas, and ill ventilated, so as freely to engender disease; an evil, however, which the railway supply of milk will abate.

At Islington, a few years since, there existed Laycock's Dairy, the largest in the metropolis, but since divided. It consisted of fourteen acres, surrounded by a high wall, and nearly covered with buildings. There were upwards of 400 cows, which were milked by women at three o'clock in the morning and at noon. The cows were kept in stalls; mangelwurzel was their chief food, alternating with turnips, cabbages, carrots, and clover, and oil-cake to fatten them for Smithfield Market. They were fine sleek animals, and were currycombed every day. As it was requisite to have 400 cows to milk each day, there were more than that number kept on the premises; and there was a hospital for cows to calve in, and where those unwell received medical treatment. The dairy and utensils were scoured with hot water twice a-day. Grains for the cows were kept in immense pits, where, if covered up, they would remain good for seven years. The capital locked up in this Dairy was immense, as each of the cows was worth more than 20l., and four farms were kept for supplying them with food. Within the walls also were *layers*, where great numbers of the oxen brought by steam from Ireland and Scotland were rested, sheltered, and fed for a few days; and upon Sundays upwards of 2000 animals might be seen thus provided for.

The Yorkshire cow is generally the favourite in the London dairies, because she is of more value for fattening than almost any other; and gives a larger proportion of milk, although it be of a poorer quality.

The Friern Dairy Farm, beyond Peckham Rye, in Surrey, is a novel establishment for supplying the metropolis with milk, and comprises about 250 acres. The cows have fine air and good attendance; are fed on mangel-wurzel, parsnips, turnips, and kohl-rabi (Jewish cabbage), and unlimited grass in the pastures; so that 24 quarts of milk per day is not an unusual yield for a single cow. The cow-sheds are divided into 50 stalls each; every stall is marked with a number, a corresponding number being marked on one horn of the cow to whom it belongs; and in winter-time, or any inclement season (for they all sleep out in fine weather), each cow deliberately finds out and walks into her own stall. Beside these sheds, in a cottage, live the keepers, milkers, and attendants. The first milking begins at 11 at night, and the second at ¼ past 1 in the morning. The milk is strained and put into large tin cans, which are barred across the top and sealed; and is thus conveyed in a van to the Dairy in London, between 3 and 4 in the morning. Here the seals are examined and taken off; the milkmen's tin pales are filled, fastened at top, and sealed as before; and away they go on their "walks," the milk being drawn of by a tap as required.— (See *Dickens's Household Words*, No. 33.)

Milk-street, north of Cheapside, is so called, "as is supposed, of milk sold there" (*Stow*); here was born Sir Thomas More, "the brightest star that ever shone in that *via lactea*" (*Fuller*).

The milkmaid has almost disappeared from our streets; she was never like "the country wench" of Sir Thomas Overbury:

"On doors the sallow milkmaid chalks her gains;
Ah, how unlike the milkmaid of the plains!"—Gay's *Trivia*, b. ii.

We have lost, too, the milkmaids' May-day festival, such as Pepys saw Nell Gwynne enjoying May 1, 1667. (See DRURY LANE.)

" Alack,
What's a May-day milking-pail without a garland and a fiddle?"
Col. Martin, 1685.

In Tempest's *Cryes of London* is a print of a merry milkmaid, named Kate Smith, dancing with a milk-pail, hung round with borrowed silver cups and tankards; flowers and ribbons upon her head. Later, the plate and other decorations were piled up, and carried by two chairmen upon a wooden horse, the milkmaids dancing before it. Sometimes was substituted a cow, with her horns gilt, and her body nearly covered with ribbons in bows and rosettes, interspersed with green oaken leaves and bunches of flowers.

"Milk Fair," with its lowing cows and squalling children, is held to this day near the Spring-Garden entrance to St. James's Park, by privilege granted to the gate-keepers. In Tom Brown's time, 1700, the noisy milk-folks in the park cried, *A can of milk, ladies! A can of red cow's milk, sir!*

Asses' milk is a restorative of our day, and is a fashionable conceit in Gay's London, where

> " Before proud gates attending asses bray,
>   Or arrogate with solemn pace the way;
>   These grave physicians with their milky cheer
>   The love-sick maid and dwindling beau repair."—*Trivia*, b. ii.

DAY IN LONDON AND OTHER CAPITALS.

The following Table, computed for this work by Mr. Henry Belville, of the Royal Observatory, Greenwich, shews the duration of the longest and shortest days in the principal capitals throughout the world, corrected for refraction, &c., and carried out to the nearest minute :—

Name of Place.	Latitude.	Length of the Longest Day.		Length of the Shortest Day.	
		H.	M.	H.	M.
Stockholm	59° 20' N.	18	30	5	54
Copenhagen	55 41 N.	17	20	6	54
St. Petersburg	59 56 N.	18	44	5	42
Berlin	52 31 N.	16	38	7	40
London	51 31 N.	16	32	7	44
Edinburgh	55 57 N.	17	32	6	50
Dublin	53 22 N.	16	56	7	18
Amsterdam	52 22 N.	16	44	7	33
Vienna	48 13 N.	15	58	8	17
Paris	48 50 N.	16	6	8	10
Madrid	40 25 N.	15	0	9	14
Lisbon	38 42 N.	14	50	9	24
Cairo	30 3 N.	14	0	10	10
Naples	40 50 N.	15	3	9	14
Constantinople	41 1 N.	15	4	9	12
Buda	47 29 N.	15	54	8	16
Calcutta	22 36 N.	13	26	10	42
Pekin	39 55 N.	14	58	9	16
Cape Town	33 56 S.	14	22	9	48
Boston	42 25 N.	15	16	8	58
Washington	39 0 N.	14	52	9	22
Panama	8 58 N.	12	36	11	34
St. Julian	49 10 S.	16	10	8	8
Sydney	33 51 S.	14	22	9	50

DEAF AND DUMB ASYLUM.

The first Asylum or School established in England for the Deaf and Dumb was opened in 1792, in Fort-place, Bermondsey, under the auspices of the Rev. John Townsend, of Jamaica-row Chapel; and of the Rev. H. Cox Mason, then curate of Bermondsey. The teacher was Joseph Watson, LL.D., who held the situation upwards of thirty-seven years, and taught upwards of 1000 pupils, who were thus able to read articulately, and to write and cipher. This tuition was commenced with six pupils only. In 1807 the first stone of a new building was laid in the Old Kent-road, whither the establishment was removed October 5, 1809; when the Society celebrated the event by a public thanksgiving at the church of St. Mary Magdalen, Bermondsey, the Rev. C. Crowther preaching the sermon. A memorial bust of the Rev. Mr. Townsend is placed in the committee-room. The pupils, male and female, are such children only as are deaf and dumb, not being deficient in intellect. Other children are admitted on payment of 20*l.* annually for board; and private pupils are also received. The term of each pupil's stay is five years: they are taught to read, write, draw, and cipher ; to speak by signs, and in many instances to articulate so as to be clearly understood. They are wholly clothed and maintained by the charity, are instructed in working trades, and in some cases apprentice-fees are given. About 300 children are maintained in the Asylum, which is amply supported by the wealthy; and besides its annual receipts from subscriptions, donations, and legacies, &c., nearly 10,000*l.* a-year, it has a funded stock of nearly 150,000*l.* The instructor of the Asylum is Mr. T. J. Watson, a son of the late Dr. Watson ; he is assisted by twelve male and two female teachers. The pupils are elected half-yearly, without reference to locality, sect, or persuasion. The Asylum may be inspected daily; most convenient time from eleven till one o'clock. The importance of this Asylum is attested by the fact that in 1833, in 20 families of 159 children, 90 were deaf and dumb.

There is also at 26 Red-Lion-square, Bloomsbury, an Institution for the Employment, Relief, and Religious Instruction of the Adult Deaf and Dumb ; who are taught shoemaking, tailoring, dressmaking, shoebinding, fancy-work, &c., the produce of their labour being added to the funds of the Society. In the chapel the Scriptures are expounded, and church-services regularly held, at which the deaf and dumb are ready and interested attendants.

DIORAMAS.

The Diorama, on the eastern side of Park-square, Regent's-park, was exhibited in Paris long before it was brought to London, by its originators, MM. Bouton and Daguerre ; the latter, the inventor of the Daguerreotype, died 1851. The exhibition-house, with the theatre in the rear, was designed by Morgan and Pugin: the spectatory has a circular ceiling, with transparent medallion portraits ; the whole was built in four months, and cost 10,000*l.*

The Diorama consists of two pictures, eighty feet in length and forty feet in height, painted in solid and in transparency, arranged so as to exhibit changes of light and shade, and a variety of natural phenomena; the spectators being kept in comparative darkness, while the picture receives a concentrated light from a ground-glass roof. The contrivance is partly optical, partly mechanical; and consists in placing the pictures within the building so constructed, that the saloon containing the spectators may revolve at intervals, and bring in succession the two distinct scenes into the field of view, without the necessity of the spectators removing from their seats ; while the scenery itself remains stationary, and the light is distributed by transparent and movable blinds—some placed behind the picture, for intercepting and changing the colour of the rays of light, which pass through the semi-transparent parts. Similar blinds, above and in front of the picture, are movable by cords, so as to distribute or direct the rays of light.

The revolving motion given to the saloon is an arc of about 73° ; and while the spectators are thus passing round, no person is permitted to go in or out. The revolution of the saloon is effected by means of a sector, or portion of a wheel, with teeth which work in a series of wheels and pinions ; one man, by turning a winch, moves the whole.

The space between the saloon and each of the two pictures is occupied on either side by a partition, forming a kind of avenue, proportioned in width to the size of the picture. Without such a precaution, the eye of the spectator, being thirty or forty feet distant from the canvass, would, by any thing intervening, be estranged from the object. The combination of transparent, semi-transparent, and opaque colouring, still further assisted by the power of varying both the effects and the degree of light and shade, renders the Diorama the most perfect scenic representation of nature; and adapts it peculiarly for moonlight subjects, or for shewing such accidents in landscape as sudden gleams of sunshine or lightning. It is also unrivalled for representing architecture, particularly interiors, as powerful relief may be obtained without that exaggeration in the shadows which is almost inevitable in every other mode of painting. The interior of Canterbury Cathedral, the first picture exhibited, in 1823, was a triumph of this class; and the companion picture, the Valley of Sarnen, equally admirable in atmospheric effects. In one day (Easter-Monday, 1824), the receipts exceeded 200*l.*

In viewing the Diorama, the spectator is placed, as it were, at the extremity of the scene, and thus has a view *across, or through it.* Hence the inventor of the term compounded it of the Greek preposition *dia*, through, and *orama*, scene; though, from there being two paintings under the same roof in the building in the Regent's-park, it has been supposed the term is from *dis*, twice, and *orama*; but if several paintings of the same kind were exhibited, each would be a *Diorama.* (*Black.*)

Although the Regent's-park Diorama has been artistically successful, it has not been commercially so. In September 1848, the building and ground in the rear, with the machinery and pictures, was sold for 6750*l.*; again, in June 1849, for 4800*l.*; and the property, with sixteen pictures, rolled on large cylinders, have since been sold for 3000*l.*

Dioramas have also been painted for our theatres by Stanfield and Roberts, the Grieves, and other artists. In 1828, Stanfield painted for Drury-lane Theatre a series of views on the Rhine; in the same year, a Diorama for the Christmas pantomime; and another in 1836.

Other Dioramic exhibitions have been opened in the metropolis. In 1828, one was exhibited at the Queen's Bazaar, Oxford-street; in 1829, the picture was "The Destruction of York-Minster by Fire," during the exhibition of which, May 28, the scenery took fire, and the premises were entirely burnt.

In 1841, there was exhibited at the Bazaar, St. James's-street, a Diorama, of five large scenes, of the second funeral of Napoleon; but, though most effectively painted by members of " The Board of Arts for the Ceremony," and accompanied by funereal music by Auber, the spectacle excited little interest.

At Easter 1849 was opened the Gallery of Illustration, in the large saloon of the late residence of Mr. Nash, the architect, No. 14 Regent-street, a series of thirty-one dioramic pictures of the Overland Mail Route from Southampton to Calcutta; the general scenery painted by T. Grieve and W. Telbin, human figures by John Absolon, and animals by J. F. Herring and H. Weir: in picturesqueness, aërial effect, characteristic grouping, variety of incident, richness of colour, and atmosphere skilfully varied with the several countries, this Diorama has, perhaps, scarcely been equalled: it was exhibited between 1600 and 1700 times, and visited by upwards of 250,000 persons. The same artists have produced other subjects, including a set of Illustrations of the Duke of Wellington's Campaigns.

The Great Exhibition year, 1851, was very productive of Dioramas, which we shall scarcely be expected to enumerate. The most successful was the Diorama of Jerusalem and the Holy Land, painted from sketches by Bartlett, and exhibited at the St. George's Gallery, Hyde-Park-corner; the entire cost of this Diorama was 2000*l.*

DOCKS.

The Docks of London are entirely the growth of the present century, and the result of the vast increase in the commerce of the preceding 25 years, which was as great as in the first 70 years of the century: a hundred years since, London had not one-twentieth of its present trade. Hitherto, merchandise was kept afloat in barges, from want of room to discharge it at the legal quays, when the plunder was frightful—lightermen, watermen, labourers, the crews of ships, the mates and officers, and the revenue officers, combining in this nefarious system, which neither the police nor the terrors of Execution Dock could repress. At length, in 1789, Mr. Perry, a shipbuilder, constructed at Blackwall the Brunswick Dock, to contain 28 East Indiamen and 50 or 60 smaller ships; and in ten years after, the construction of public Docks was commenced.

From near the Tower to Blackwall, or nearly four miles, is now occupied by five Docks, comprising 450 acres, and accommodation for 1200 ships and 530,000 tons of goods: the mass of shipping, the vastness of the many-storied warehouses, and the heaps of merchandise from every region of the globe, justify the glory of London as "the great emporium of nations," and "the metropolis of the most intelligent and wealthy empire the sun ever shone upon, and of which the boast is, as of Spain of old, that upon its dominions the sun never sets."

These several Docks have been constructed at the expense of Joint-stock Companies, and have been moderately profitable to their projectors, but more advantageous to the Port of London.

COMMERCIAL DOCKS, Rotherhithe, on the south bank of the Thames, are, upon the authority of Stow, said to include the commencement of Canute's trench, cut early in the 11th century from thence to Battersea; and into which the river was diverted when the first stone bridge across the Thames was built, *temp.* King John. The present Commercial Docks, however, originated in the " Howland Great Wet Dock," which existed in 1660, and extended about 10 acres in Queen Anne's time, larger than the famous basin of Dunkirk. It was then engaged for the Greenland whale-fishery vessels, next for the Baltic trade in timber, deals, tar, corn, &c.; and in 1809 was opened as the Commercial Docks. They are now five in number, and comprise about 60 acres of water and 40 acres of land; and the granaries will hold 100,000 quarters of grain. Adjoining, southward, is the EAST COUNTRY DOCK, 5 acres; and northward is the SURREY DOCK, an entrance basin to the Surrey Canal, which can accommodate 300 vessels.

EAST INDIA DOCKS, Blackwall, lie below the West India Docks, and immediately adjoin the Blackwall Railway and Brunswick Wharf. These Docks, originally constructed for the East India Company, were completed in 1808. Since the opening of the trade to India, they have been the property of the East and West India Company. Their water area is 30 acres, and their great depth (23 feet) accommodates vessels of very large size; they have a cast-iron wharf, 750 feet in length, in which are more than 900 tons of metal. Here, from 1848 to 1850, lay the Chinese Junk *Keying,* the first which ever reached Europe, or even rounded the Cape of Good Hope: she is stated to have cost her proprietors upwards of 7000*l.*

ST. KATHERINE'S DOCKS, just below the Tower, were planned by Telford, and constructed by Hardwick: in clearing the ground, the fine old church and other remains of the Hospital of St. Katherine (founded 1148 by Matilda of Boulogne, wife of King Stephen), with 1250 houses and tenements, inhabited by 11,300 persons, were purchased and pulled down: the Hospital and Church were rebuilt in the Regent's-park. (See CHURCHES, p. 134.) The Docks were commenced May 3, 1827, and upwards of 2500 men worked at them till their opening, Oct. 25, 1828; a labour of unexampled rapidity. The excavated earth was carried by water to Millbank, and there used to fill up the reservoirs of the Chelsea Water-works, upon which has been built a new town south of Pimlico. The cost of St. Katherine's Docks was 1,700,000*l.* The lofty walls constitute it a place of "special security," and surround 23 acres, of which 11 are water, and will accommodate 120 ships, besides barges and other craft. The lock from the Thames is crossed by a vast iron swing-bridge 23 feet wide: it can be filled or emptied by a steam-engine of 200-horse power, and 14 feet depth can be made by the gate-paddles in six minutes. This lock is sunk so deep that ships of 700 tons burden may enter at any time of the tide; and the depth of water at spring-tides is 28 feet, or 4 feet more than in any other dock of London: the machinery of the gates, by Bramah, is very fine. At these Docks was first provided accommodation for landing and embarking passengers without using small wherries; and in 1844 there was added an extensive foreign baggage-warehouse and wharf, for the landing and examination, or despatching, of a vast number of passengers in a very short time.

The frontage of the quays, paved with cast-iron, is 4600 feet; and the warehouses, vaults, sheds, and covered ways will contain 110,000 tons of goods. The warehouses, five and six stories high, are supported on cast-iron columns, 3 feet 9 inches diameter; they have massive granite stairs, huge machinery over the wells or shafts, and powerful cranes on the quays, so that goods can be taken at once into the warehouses from the ships, and in one-fifth of the time required in the earlier-constructed docks. A ship of 250 tons burden can be discharged at St. Katherine's in twelve hours, and one of 500 tons in two or three days. One of the cranes cost about 2000*l.*, is worked by ten or twelve men, and will raise from 30 to 40 tons. The vaults below for wine and spirits have crypt-like arches: "lights are distributed to the travellers who prepare to visit these cellars, as if they were setting out to visit the catacombs of Naples or of Rome." (*Baron Dupin.*) From the vaultings hang vinous fungi, like dark woolly clouds, light as gossamer, and a yard or more in length, a piece of which applied to the flame of a candle will burn like tinder; in the spirit-vaults the Davy safety-lamp is used. Cats are kept to destroy the rats in the warehouses, at an annual cost of more than 100*l.*

LONDON DOCKS lie immediately below St. Katherine's Docks, and were opened in 1805; John Rennie, engineer. They comprise 90 acres: 35 acres of water, and 12,980 feet of quay and jetty frontage; with three entrances from the Thames—Hermitage, Wapping, and Shadwell, where the depth of water at spring-tides is 27 feet. The Western Dock comprises 20 acres, the Eastern 7 acres, and the Wapping Basin 3 acres, besides a small dock exclusively for ships laden with tobacco. The two large Docks afford water-room for 302 sail of vessels, exclusive of lighters; warehouse-room for 220,000 tons of goods; and vault-room for 80,000 pipes of wine and spirits. The superficial area of the vault-room is 890,545 feet; of the warehouse-room, 1,402,115 feet. The enclosing walls cost 65,000*l.* The capital of the Company is four millions of money. Six weeks are allowed for unloading, beyond which period a farthing per ton is charged for the first two weeks, and then a halfpenny per week per ton.

In these Docks are especially warehoused wine, wool, spices, tea, ivory, drugs, tobacco, sugars, dye-stuffs, imported metals, and other articles. These, except the wine, tea, spices, and ivory, may be inspected by an order from the Secretary; for the wine a " tasting order" must be obtained from the owners. The shipping and people at work may be seen without any order.

Of the Wine-vaults, one alone, formerly 7 acres, now extends under Gravel-lane, and contains upwards of 12 acres: above is the mixing-house, the largest vat containing 23,250 gallons. The Wool-floors were considerably enlarged and glass-roofed in 1850: the annual importation is 130,000 bales; value 2,600,000*l.* A vast Tea-warehouse was completed in 1845; cost 100,000*l.*; stowage for 120,000 chests of tea. To inspect the Ivory-warehouse requires a special order: here lie heaps of elephant and rhinoceros tusks, the ivory weapons of sword-fish, &c.

The great Tobacco-warehouse, "the Queen's," being rented by Government for 14,000*l.* per annum, is 5 acres in extent, and is covered by a skilfully iron-framed roof, supported by slender columns: it will contain 24,000 hogsheads of tobacco, value 4,800,000*l.*; the huge casks are piled two in height, intersected by passages and alleys, each several hundred feet long. There is another warehouse for finer tobacco; and a cigar-floor, in which are frequently 1500 chests of cigars, value 150,000*l.*

Near the north-east corner of the Queen's Warehouse, a guide-post, inscribed " To the Kiln," directs you to the Queen's Pipe, or chimney of the furnace; on the door of the latter and of the room are painted the crown-royal and V.R. In this kiln are burnt all such goods as do not fetch the amount of their duty and Customs' charges: tea, having once set the chimney of the kiln on fire, is rarely burnt; and the wine and spirits are emptied into the Docks. The huge mass of fire in the furnace is fed night and day with condemned goods: on one occasion, 900 Australian mutton-hams were burnt; on another, 45,000 pairs of French gloves; and silks and satins, tobacco and cigars, are here consumed in vast quantities: the ashes being sold by the ton as manure, for killing insects, and to soap-boilers and chemical manufacturers. Nails and other pieces of iron, sifted from the ashes, are prized for their toughness in making gun-barrels; gold and silver, the remains of plate, watches and jewellery thrown into the furnace, are also found in the ashes.

Lastly, the London Docks are worked by from 1000 to 3000 hands, as the business is brisk or slack: and this is one of the few places in the metropolis where men can get employment without either character or recommendation. At the Dock-gates, at ½ past 7 in the morning "may be seen congregated swarms of men, of all grades, looks, and kinds. There are decayed and bankrupt master-butchers, master-bakers, publicans, grocers, old soldiers, old sailors, Polish refugees, broken-down gentlemen, discharged lawyer's-clerks, suspended government-clerks, almsmen, pensioners, servants, thieves—indeed, every one who wants a loaf and is willing to work for it." (*Henry Mayhew.*)

WEST INDIA DOCKS, the most extensive in the world, (Jessop engineer,) lie between Limehouse and Blackwall, and their long lines of warehouses, and lofty wall, 5 feet thick, are well seen from the railway. These Docks were commenced 1800, when William Pitt laid the first stone; and they were opened 1802. Their extent is nearly thrice that of the London Docks, their entire area (including the canal made to avoid the bend of the river at the Isle of Dogs) being 295 acres this canal is nearly three-quarters of a mile long, with lock-gates, 45 feet wide, and is used as a dock for timber-ships. The northern or Import Dock will hold 250 vessels of 300 tons each: when originally opened, it took ten hours to fill, 24 feet deep, though the water was admitted at 800 gallons per second. The southern or Export Dock will hold 195 vessels. Here the ship is seen to the greatest advantage, fresh-painted, standing-rigging up, colours flying, &c.; whereas in the Import Dock, the vessels, though more picturesque, have their rigging down and loose, the sides whitened by the sea, and contrasting with outward-bound vessels. The warehouses will contain 180,000 tons of merchandise; and there have been at one time, on the quays and in the sheds, vaults, and warehouses, colonial produce worth 20,000,000*l.* sterling; comprising 148,563 casks of sugar, 70,875 barrels and 433,648 bags of coffee, 35,158 pipes of rum and Madeira, 14,000 logs of mahogany, and 21,000 tons of logwood, &c. In the wood-sheds are enormous quantities of mahogany, ebony, rosewood, &c., logs of which 4 or 5 tons weight are lifted with locomotive cranes, by four or five men. For twenty years from their construction, these Docks were compulsorily frequented by all West India ships trading to the Port of London, when the maximum revenues amounted to 449,421*l.*, in 1813; since the expiry of this privilege, and the depreciation of the West India trade, the revenues have much declined. The Docks are now used by every kind of shipping, and belong to the East and West India Dock Company.

DOCTORS' COMMONS,

A College of Doctors of Civil Law, and for the study and practice of the Civil Law, is situated in Great Knight-Rider-street, south of St. Paul's-churchyard; in the south-west corner of which is an arched gateway, and within it the Lodge of Porters to direct strangers to "the Commons." The civilians and canonists were originally lodged in a house, subsequently the Queen's Head tavern, in Paternoster-row; whence they removed to a house purchased for them in Elizabeth's reign by D. Harvey, Dean of the Arches; here they "were living (for diet and lodging) in a collegiate manner, and *commoning* together, whence the college was named Doctors' Commons; and the doctors still dine together on every court-day. This house was destroyed by the Great Fire of 1666; when the College removed to Exeter House, Strand, till the rebuilding of the edifice in Great Knight-Rider-street, in 1672, as we now see it, with a side entrance on Bennet's-hill, nearly opposite Heralds' College. It is of brick, and consists of two quadrangles, chiefly occupied by the Doctors; a hall for the hearing of causes, &c.

In Doctors' Commons are—the Court of Arches, named from having been formerly kept in Bow Church, Cheapside, originally built upon arches (see CHURCHES, p. 142), and the supreme ecclesiastical court of the whole province; the Prerogative Court, where all contentions arising out of testamentary causes are tried; the Consistory Court of the Bishop of London; and the High Court of Admiralty: all these courts hold their sittings in the College Hall, the walls of which above the wainscot are covered with the richly-emblazoned coats of arms of all the doctors for a century or two past.

The *Court of Arches* has jurisdiction over thirteen parishes or peculiars, which form a deanery exempt from the Bishop of London, and attached to the Archbishop of Canterbury; hence the judge is named *Dean of the Arches.* The business includes, as in Chaucer's time, cases

> " Of defamation and avouterie,
>   Of church reves and of testaments,
>   Of contracts and lack of sacraments,
>   Of usury and simony also;"

besides those of sacrilege, blasphemy, apostacy from Christianity, adultery, partial or entire divorce, &c.; likewise brawling and smiting in churches or vestries: but the majority of the cases are matrimonial.

In the *Prerogative Court* wills are proved and all administrations granted, that are the prerogative of the Archbishop of Canterbury.

There are several Registries in Doctors' Commons, under the jurisdiction of the Archbishop of Canterbury and the bishops. Some of the very old documents connected with them are deposited for security in St. Paul's Cathedral and Lambeth Palace. At the Bishop of London's Registry, and the Registry for the Commission of Surrey, Wills are proved for the respective dioceses, and Marriage Licenses granted. At the *Vicar-General's Office* and the *Faculty Office*, Marriage Licenses are granted for any part of England. The Faculty Office also grant Faculties to notaries public, and dispensations to the clergy; and formerly granted privilege to eat flesh upon prohibited days. At the Vicar-General's Office, records are kept of the confirmation and consecration of bishops.

Marriage Licenses, special and general, if to be solemnised according to the law of the Established Church, are procured upon personal application to a proctor by one of the parties: a residence of fifteen days is necessary by either party in the parish or district where the marriage is to be performed. The expense of an ordinary license is 2*l.* 12*s.* 6*d.*; but if either is a minor, 10*s.* 6*d.* further charge; and the party appearing swears he has obtained the consent of the proper person having authority in law to give it: there is no necessity for either parents of minor to attend. A Special License for Marriage is issued after a fiat or consent has been obtained from the archbishop; and is granted only to persons of rank, judges, and members of parliament, the archbishop having a right to exercise his own discretion. The expense of a Special License is usually twenty-eight guineas. This gives privilege to marry at any time or place, in private residence, or at any church or chapel situate in England; but the ceremony must be performed by a priest in holy orders, and of the Established Church. With the marriages of Dissenters, including Roman Catholics, Jews, and Quakers, the Commons has nothing to do, their licenses being obtainable of the Superintendent-Registrar. *Divorce* when sought is carried through one of the courts in this profession (according to the diocese), and is conducted by a proctor; and the evidence of witnesses is taken privately before an examiner of the court, and neither the husband, wife nor any of the witnesses need appear personally in court. A suit is seldom conducted at an expense less than 200*l.*

The *High Court of Admiralty* consists of the Instance Court and the Prize Court. The Instance Court has a criminal and civil jurisdiction: to the former belong piracy and other indictable offences on the high seas, which are now tried at the Old Bailey; to the latter suits arising from ships running foul of each other, disputes about seamen's wages, bottomry, and salvage. The Prize Court applies to naval captures in war, proceeds of captured slave-vessels, &c. A silver oar is carried before the judge as the emblem of his office. The business is very onerous, as in embargoes and the provisional detention of vessels, when incautious decision might involve the country in war; the right of search is another weighty question. Lord Stowell, the judge, in one year (1806) pronounced 2206 decrees.

The Admiralty Registry is in Paul's Bakehouse-court, Doctors' Commons, where are kept records of prizes adjudicated.

The practitioners in this court are advocates (D.D.C.L.) or counsel, and proctors or solicitors. The judge and advocates wear in court if of Oxford, scarlet robes and hoods lined with taffety; and if of Cambridge, white minever and round black velvet caps. The proctors wear black robes and hoods lined with fur.

The College has a good library in civil law and history, bequeathed by an ancestor of Sir John Gibson, judge of the Prerogative Court; and every bishop at his consecration makes a present of books.

The PREROGATIVE WILL OFFICE is, however, the most interest

ing feature of Doctors' Commons. Wills are always to be found here at half an hour's notice, and generally in a few minutes. They are kept in a fire-proof "strong-room." The original wills begin with the date 1483, and the copies from 1383. The latter are on parchment, strongly bound, with brass clasps, and fill the public-room and an apartment above-stairs. In one year the searches have amounted to nearly 30,000; country commissions, 4580; and extracts from wills, 6414. Some entries of early wills, engrossed by the monks, are beautifully illuminated, the colours remaining fresh to this day.

To obtain Perusal of a Will.—On entering the office apply at the first small box or recess on the right hand, where a clerk, on receiving a shilling, and the surname of the maker of the will required, directs the applicant to the *Indexes*, which are arranged chronologically and alphabetically on the left-hand side of the room. A search must then be made through these volumes for the entry of the will; which being found, a clerk at the further end of the room, on being furnished with the exact title and date of the will, ushers the inquirer into another apartment, lit by a skylight, and furnished with a table and benches. Here two clerks are seated; and the actual will being brought to the inquirer, he may inspect it at his leisure. He must not, however, copy any thing from it, or make even a pencil memorandum; and if he attempt to do so, he will be checked by the clerks.

To obtain the Copy of a Will.—Apply to the clerks in the room, and they will state the expense per folio. The order for a copy must be left at the box at the entrance of the office, where the time will be named for the delivery of the copy within a few days, on payment of the cost. To insure correctness, the copy is read out to the applicant in the office, and compared with the original will; and the copy is moreover duly attested by certain authorities of Doctors' Commons.

If the applicant merely desires to see the copy of a Will, the clerk in the outer room, on being shewn the entry in the *Index*, will refer him by a written note to an attendant, who will at once bring the copy to him; the same rules against copying and making extracts prevail here also.

The Prerogative Office is open (except on holidays) from October till March from 9 till 3, and the remaining six months till 4.

The Wills of celebrated persons are the *Curiosities* of the place. Here is the will of Shakspeare, on three folios of paper, each with his signature, and with this interlineation in his own handwriting: " I give unto my wife my brown best bed, with the furniture." Next is the will of Milton, a nuncupative one, the great poet being blind; but which was set aside by a decree of Sir Leoline Jenkins, the judge of the Prerogative Court. Here, too, is the will of Napoleon Bonaparte, made at St. Helena, April 1821.

DOMESDAY-BOOK,

The Register of the lands of England, framed by order of William the Conqueror, the earliest existing English record, and "not only the most ancient, but beyond dispute the most noble monument of the whole of Britain" (*Spelman*), is the great treasure in the Chapter House of Westminster Abbey, where it is preserved to this day in its pristine freshness, fair and legible as when first written. It is comprised in two volumes, one a large folio, the other a quarto. The first is written on 382 double pages of vellum, in one and the same hand, in a small but plain character, each page having a double column. Some of the capital letters and principal passages are touched with red ink, and others are crossed with lines of red ink. The second volume, in quarto, is written in 450 pages of vellum, but in a single column, and in a large fair character. At the end of the second volume is the following memorial, in capital letters, of the time of its completion: " Anno Millesimo Octogesimo Sexto ab Incarnatione Domini, vigesimo vero regni Willielmi, facta est ista Descriptio, non solum per hos tres Comitatus, sed etiam per alios." From internal evidence, the same year, 1086, is assignable as the date of the first volume.

Although in early times Domesday, precious as it was alway deemed, occasionally travelled, like other records, to distant part: till 1696 it was usually kept with the King's Seal at Westminster, b the side of the Tally Court, in the Exchequer, under three locks an keys; in the charge of the auditor, the chamberlains, and deputy-cham berlains, of the Exchequer. In 1696 it was deposited among othe valuable records in the Chapter House, where it still remains. It kept "in the vaulted porch never warmed by fire. From the fir deposit of Domesday volume in the Treasury at Winchester, in th reign of the Conqueror, it certainly never felt or saw a fire, yet ever page of the vellum is bright, sound, and perfect." (*Sir F. Palgrave* In making searches or transcripts, you are not allowed to touch th text, a rule which has been kept from time immemorial, and to whic the excellent condition of the record may be partly ascribed.

It is a remarkable fact, that Domesday-Book, which is usually s minute in regard to our principal towns and cities, is deficient in respec to London. It only mentions a vineyard in Holborn, belonging to th Crown; and ten acres of land near Bishopsgate, belonging to the Dea and Chapter of St. Paul's: yet certainly, observes Sir Henry Ellis, i his Introduction to Domesday, no mutilation of the manuscript ha taken place; since the account of Middlesex is entire, and is exactl coincident with the abridged copy of the survey taken at the time, an now lodged in the office of the King's Remembrancer in the Excheque: Still, a distinct and independent survey of the City itself might hav been made at the time of the general survey, although now lost or de stroyed, if not remaining among the unexplored archives of the Crow

The parish of St. Giles-in-the-Fields possesses a Book of Recor called Domesuay-Book, which is of vellum, and was made in 1624, b direction of the then Bishop of London, as a perpetual parish record entitled "Treasure deposited in Heaven, or the Book of God's House of things worthy to be remembered in this parish of St. Giles-in-the Fields, and in the first place of the church now lately restored, som account touching the same." This book was advertised as missing i the *Examiner* newspaper, Dec. 21, 1828, and was soon afterwards foun

"DREADNOUGHT" HOSPITAL-SHIP (THE)

Is the establishment of the Seamen's Hospital Society, and is moore off Greenwich, for the reception of sick and diseased seamen of a nations in the Port of London. The hospital was originally establishe in 1821 on board the *Grampus*, a 50-gun ship; but this vessel not bein large enough, the Government exchanged her for the *Dreadnough* 104-gun ship, which was fitted up in 1831. She fought at Trafalga under Captain Conn, and captured the Spanish three-decker the *Sa Juan*, previously engaged by the *Bellerophon* and the *Defiance*.

The establishment on board the *Dreadnought* consists of a superin tendent, surgeons, apothecary, visiting physicians, chaplain, &c. Th ship is moored contiguous to the bulk of the shipping in the docks an in the river, and is the only place for the reception of sick seamen ar riving from abroad, or to whom accidents may happen between th mouth of the river and London-bridge. Sick seamen *of every natio* on presenting themselves alongside, are immediately received, withot the necessity of any recommendatory letters; and shipwrecked sailo and vagrant seamen are admitted, if deserving. Patients receive in 1851, 2242; out-patients, 1642. The Emperor of Russia, the Quee of Spain, and other foreign potentates, are subscribers. The *Drea* nought may be inspected daily, except Sundays, between 11 and 3, wit out any ticket. The patients are ranged upon the lower decks, the por holes affording ventilation; and the cabins are converted into surgerie

Patients of different nations between 1821 and 1852:—Englishmen, 38,482; Scotchmen, 7980; Irishmen, 5876; Frenchmen, 240; Germans, 872; Russians, 838; Prussians, 1291; Dutchmen, 215; Danes, 870; Swedes and Norwegians, 2146; Italians, 606; Portuguese, 497; Spaniards, 296; East Indians, 1093; West Indians, 1122; British Americans, 895; United States, 1237; South Americans, 133; Africans, 383; Turks, 16; Greeks, 58: New Zealanders, 31; Australians, 34; South-Sea Islanders, 34; Chinese, 38; born at sea, 134. Total, 65,587. Usually 200 in-patients at one time. Sooner than enter a land hospital, many a poor sailor will perish afloat; and seamen often travel from the most distant parts of the kingdom to be received in the *Dreadnought*.

DRURY-LANE,

Which extends from the north side of the Strand to Broad-street, Bloomsbury, was originally the " Via de Aldwych," still preserved in Wych-street. At the west end was the mansion of the Drurys, wherein Dr. Donne had apartments assigned him by Sir Robert Drury; and here, in 1612, Mrs. Donne died of childbirth, at the same day and hour that Dr. Donne, then at Paris, saw her in a vision pass twice before him, " with her hair hanging about her shoulders, and a dead child in her arms." William Lord Craven, the hero of Creutznach, became the next owner of Drury House, which he rebuilt in four stories,—a large square pile of brick, afterwards called Craven House, where the Earl died in 1697. This mansion was taken down in 1803, and the ground purchased by Philip Astley for the site of his Olympic Pavilion. In its latter time, the Craven mansion was a public-house with the sign of " The Queen of Bohemia,"—a reminiscence of its former occupancy by the daughter of James I., through whom the family of Brunswick succeeded to the throne of England, and who is suspected to have been secretly married to her heroic champion, Lord Craven. The present Craven-Head public-house was one of the offices of Craven House, and the adjoining stabling belonged to that mansion. Craven Buildings, erected in 1723, occupy a portion of the grounds.

On the end wall of Craven-buildings was formerly a fresco portrait of Earl Craven in armour, with a truncheon in his hand, and mounted on his white charger; on each side was an earl's and a baron's coronet, and the letters ' W. C.' This portrait was twice or thrice repainted in oil, the last time by Edward Edwards, A.R.A. (Brayley's *Londiniana*, vol. iv. p. 301.) Hayman, the painter, once lived in Craven-buildings; Mrs. Bracegirdle, the actress, had here a house, afterwards tenanted by the equally celebrated Mrs. Pritchard; and in the back parlour of No. 17 Dr. Arne composed the music of *Comus*.

The Cock and Magpie public-house (opposite Craven-buildings) evidently dates from the better days of Drury-lane. Next-door is one of the few paneled houses existing; and the east side of Little Drury-lane, leading to the church of St. Mary-le-Strand, is a range of old houses, apparently contemporary with the Cock and Magpie, or probably two centuries and a half old. Wych-street, which runs at an obtuse angle with this passage, likewise contains some houses of considerable antiquity. (Archer's *Vestiges of Old London*, part v.)

In the Coal-yard, at the Holborn end of Drury-lane, was born Nell Gwynne; and in Maypole-alley (now Little Drury-lane), she lodged when Pepys saw her looking at the dance around the Strand maypole:

" 1st May, 1667. To Westminster, in the way meeting many milkmaids with their garlands upon their pails, dancing with a fiddler before them; and saw pretty Nelly standing at her lodging-door, in Drury-lane, in her smock-sleeves and bodice, looking upon one: she seemed a mighty pretty creature."—*Diary*.

Drury-lane was nobly tenanted till late in the 17th century; but a paper by Steele in the *Tatler*, No. 46, represents the lane in its decline; and Gay's propitiatory lines,

" Oh, may thy virtue guard thee through the roads
Of Drury's mazy courts and dark abodes !"

are almost as applicable now as at the day they were written : Hogarth has made it the locality of the " Harlot's Progress." Pit-place (above Princes-street) was the site of the Cock-pit, the first Drury-lane theatre.

EARTHQUAKES IN LONDON.

From Mr. Milne's elaborate register of Earthquakes in Great Britain,* the most complete record of its class, we select the majority of the following details of shocks felt in the metropolis:—

1692, September 8, London and Flanders.

1750, February 8, London and Westminster. Motion of ground from W. to E. Several chimneys thrown down, and walls rent. A shepherd at Kensington heard the noise rush past him, and instantly he saw the ground, a dry and solid spot, wave under him like the face of the river; the tall trees of the avenue where he was, nodded their tops very sensibly, and quivered.—*Philos. Trans.* vol. xlvi.

1750, February 8, between 12 and 1 P.M., all over Westminster. " Stacks of heavy chimneys were dislodged, and the Thames became greatly agitated. The barristers were greatly alarmed, for they thought that Westminster Hall was falling down."— *Walcott.*

1750, March 8. Motion from E. to W.; houses near the Thames were most shaken. Near London there was a continued and confused lightning till within a minute or two of shock; dogs howled, fish jumped three feet out of water; sound in air preceded concussions; flashes of lightning and a ball of fire were seen just before explosion. The President of the Royal Society (Martin Folkes) stated that he did not on this occasion perceive that lifting motion which he was sensible of on 8th February, but he felt very quick shakes or tremors horizontally. A boatman on the Thames felt his boat receive a blow at the bottom, and the whole river seemed agitated. The Rev. Mr. Pickering stated, that he was lying awake in his bed, which stood N. and S. He first " heard a sound like that of a blast of wind. I then perceived myself raised in my bed, and the motion began on my right side, and inclined me towards the left." In the Temple Gardens, the noise in the air was greater than the loudest report of cannon. At the same instant, the buildings inclined over from the perpendicular several degrees. The general impression was, that the whole city was violently pushed to S.E., and then brought back again. The sound preceded the concussions, resembling the discharge of several cannon, or distant thunder in the air, and not a subterranean explosion. Flashes of lightning were observed an hour (before?), and a vast ball of fire. At Kensington, the bailiff of Mr. Fox, at a quarter past five A.M., heard (when in the open air) a noise much like thunder at a distance, which, coming from N.W., grew louder, and gave a crack over his head, and then gradually died away. The sky was clear, and he saw no fire or appearances of lightning. Immediately after the crack, the ground shook, and it moved like a quagmire. The whole lasted a minute.—*Philos. Trans.* vol. xlvi.

" At half-past five A.M. the whole city of Westminster was alarmed by another shock more severe than the former (Feb. 8), accompanied by a hollow rumbling noise; and numbers of people were awakened in amazement and fear from their sleep. Great stones were thrown from the 'new spire' of Westminster Abbey, and fish jumped half a yard above the water; and in several steeples the bells were struck by chime-hammers. An impostor pretended to foretel an earthquake on a particular day, which would lay Westminster in ruins; and when the appointed time arrived, the people ran out in crowds into the country to escape such a terrible catastrophe. The churches could scarcely contain the throngs of

* Notices of Earthquake-Shocks felt in Great Britain. By David Milne, Esq. F.R.S.E., M.W.S., F.G.S., &c. Communicated to *Jameson's Journal*, No. 61.

worshippers. The pulpits and public prints were employed in deprecating God's wrath and calling a degenerate people to repentance. But unhappily it was a devotion as shortlived only as their fear."—Walcott's *Westminster*, p. 22.

Horace Walpole writes to Sir Horace Mann, March 11, 1750,—"In the night, between Wednesday and Thursday last (exactly a month since the first shock), the earth had a shivering fit between one and two; but so slight, that if no more had followed, I don't believe it would have been noticed. I had been awake, and had scarce dozed again, when on a sudden I felt my bolster lift up my head; I thought somebody was getting from under my bed, but soon found it was a strong earthquake, that lasted near half a minute, with a violent vibration and great roaring. I rang my bell, my servant came in frightened out of his senses; in an instant we heard all the windows in the neighbourhood flung up. I got up and found people running into the streets, but saw no mischief done; there has been some,—two old houses flung down, several chimneys, and much china-ware. The bells rung in several houses. Admiral Knowles, who had lived long in Jamaica, and felt seven there, says this was more violent than any of them. Francesco prefers it to the dreadful one at Leghorn. * * * It has nowhere reached above ten miles from London. The only visible effect it has had was on the Ridotto, at which being the following night, there were but 400 people. A parson who came into White's the morning of earthquake the first, and heard bets laid on whether it was an earthquake or the blowing up of powder-mills, went away exceedingly scandalised, and said, 'I protest they are such an impious set of people, that I believe if the last trumpet was to sound, they would bet puppet-show against Judgment.'"

1756, February 18. About 8 A.M., a shock felt at Dover and London.

1761, February 8. A shock most sensibly felt along the banks of the Thames from Greenwich near to Richmond. At Limehouse and Poplar, chimneys were thrown down; and in several parts of London, the furniture was shaken, and the pewter fell to the ground: at Hampstead and Highgate, it was also very perceptible.

1761, March 8. A more violent shock, between five and six A.M., the air being very warm, and the atmosphere clear and serene; though, till within a few minutes preceding, there had been strong but confused lightning in quick succession. The violence of the motion caused many persons to start from their beds and flee to the street, under the impression that their houses were falling. In St. James's Park, and in the squares and open places about the West-end of the town, the tremulous vibration of the earth was most distinguishable; it seemed to move in a south and north direction, with a quick return towards the centre, and was accompanied with a loud noise as of rushing wind.

A crazy life-guardsman predicted a third earthquake within a month from the above, and drove thousands of persons from the metropolis; whilst another wight advertised pills "good against earthquakes."

In 1842, an absurd report gained credence among the weak-minded, that London would be destroyed by earthquake on the 17th of March, St. Patrick's Day. This rumour was founded on certain doggrel prophecies: one pretended to be pronounced in the year 1203, and contained in Harleian Collection (British Museum), 800 b. folio 319; the other by Dr. Dee, the astrologer (1598, Ms. in the British Museum). The rhymes, with these "authorities," inserted in the newspapers, actually excited some alarm, and a great number of timid persons left the metropolis before the 17th. Upon reference to the British Museum, the "prophecies" were not, however, to be found; and their forger has confessed them to have been an experiment upon public credulity.

EAST INDIA HOUSE,

Or the House of the East India Company, " the most celebrated commercial association of ancient or modern times, and which has extended its sway over the whole of the Mogul empire,"—is situated on the south side of Leadenhall-street.

The tradition of the House is, that the Company, incorporated December 31, 1600, first transacted their business in the great room of the Nag's Head inn, opposite St. Botolph's Church, Bishopsgate-street. The maps of London, soon after the Great Fire of 1666, place the India House on a part of its present site in Leadenhall-street. Here originally stood the mansion of Alderman Kerton, built in the reign of Edward VI., rebuilt on the accession of Elizabeth, enlarged by its next purchaser, Sir William Craven, lord mayor in 1610: here was born the great Lord Craven, who in 1701 leased his house and a tenement in Lime-street to the Company, at 100l. a-year. A scarce Dutch etching in the British Museum shews this house to have been half-timbered, its lofty gable surmounted with two dolphins and a figure of a mariner, or, as some say, of the first Governor; beneath are merchant-ships at sea, the royal arms, and those of the Company. This grotesque structure was taken down in 1726, and upon its site was erected " the old East India House," portions of which yet remain; although the present stone front, 200 feet long, and great part of the house, were built 1798 and 1799, and subsequently enlarged by Cockerell, R.A., and Wilkins, R.A. It has a hexastyle Ionic portico of six fluted columns, from the ancient temple of Apollo Didymæus; and in the tympanum of the pediment are sculptured, by Bacon, jun., figures emblematic of the commerce of the East, shielded by George III.: on the upper acroterium is a statue of Britannia; and on the two lower, a figure of Europe on a horse, and Asia on a camel.

The interior contains many fine statues and pictures. The new Sale-room approaches in interest the Rotunda of the Bank of England. The Court-room (Directors') is an exact cube of 30 feet; is richly gilt, and is hung with six pictures of the Cape, St. Helena, and Tellichery; and over the chimney is a large marble group of figures, supported by caryatides. The general Court-room (Proprietors') has in niches statues of Lord Clive, Warren Hastings, the Marquis Cornwallis, Sir Eyre Coote, General Lawrance, Sir George Pococke, and the Marquis Wellesley. The Finance and Home Committee-room has one wall entirely occupied by a picture of the grant of the Dewanee to the Company in 1765, the foundation of the British power in India: here also are portraits of Warren Hastings and the Marquis Cornwallis; Mirza Abul Hassan, the Persian envoy to London in 1809, &c. The Library contains, perhaps, the most splendid assemblage of Oriental Mss. in Europe, many with illuminated drawings; Tippoo Sultan's Register of Dreams (with interpretations), and his Koran; a large collection of Chinese printed books; and a Ms. Sanscrit tract on the Astrolabe, of which Chaucer's celebrated *treatise* is a literal translation, though the poet may have translated it from an Arabic or a Latin version.

Here is also a Museum, which is open gratuitously to the public on Fridays from 11 to 3; and with the Library on other days by tickets from Directors. (See MUSEUMS.)

The East India Company is now an exclusively political institution; the Act 3 & 4 Will. IV., prolonging the charter till 1854, debarring the Company from the privilege of trading. Before this reduction, nearly 400 men were employed in the warehouses, and the number of clerks was above 400. The fifteen warehouses often contained 50,000,000lbs. (above 22,000 tons) of tea; and 1,200,000lbs. have been sold in one day. (In 1668, the Company ordered "one hundred pounds weight of good teye" to be sent home on speculation!) The clerks' business was very heavy: from 1793 to 1813, the explanatory matter from the Indian Government filled 9094 large folio volumes; and from that year to 1829, 14,414; and a military despatch has been accompanied with 199 papers, containing 13,511 pages. In 1826, the patronage of each East India Director for the year was estimated at 20,000l. sterling.

The twenty-four directors receive 300l. each, and 500l. for their "chairs," being a charge on the Hindoos of 7700l. per annum. Except a few satrapies, cadies, high-priests, and leaders of hosts, the directors exercise the whole patronage of nomination to Indian office, civil, military, and clerical.

EASTCHEAP.

This ancient thoroughfare originally extended from Tower-street westward to the south end of Clement's-lane, where Cannon-street begins. It was the Eastern Cheap or Market, as distinguished from Westcheap, now Cheapside; and was crossed by Fish-Street-hill, the eastern portion being Little Eastcheap (now Eastcheap), and the western Great Eastcheap: the latter, with St. Michael's Church, Crooked-lane, disappeared in the new London Bridge approaches.

Mr. Kempe, F.S.A., considers Eastcheap to have been the principal or Prætorian gate of the Roman garrison, leading into the Roman Forum; and in 1831 there were found here a Roman roadway, two wells, the architrave of a Roman building, &c.; in Miles-lane, a piece of the Roman wall, cinerary urns, coins of Claudius and Vespasian; and in Bush-lane, remains of the Prætorium itself, in fragments of brick, with inscriptions designating them as formed under the Prætorship of Agricola.—(*Gent. Mag.* March 1842.)

Eastcheap was next the Saxon Market, celebrated from the time of Fitzstephen to the days of Lydgate for the provisions sold there:

> "Then I hyed me into Est-Chepe,
> One cryes ribbes of befe and many a pye:
> Pewter pottes they clattered on a heape."—*London Lyckpenny.*

In Great Eastcheap was the *Boar's Head Tavern*, first mentioned *temp.* Richard II.; the scene of the revels of Falstaff and Henry V., when Prince of Wales, in Shakspeare's Henry IV., Part 2. Stow relates a riot in " the cooks' dwellings" here on St. John's eve 1410, by Princes John and Thomas, for unceremoniously quelling which the mayor, aldermen, and sheriff were cited before Chief-Justice Gascoigne, but discharged honourably, the king reproving his own sons. The tavern was destroyed in the Great Fire of 1666, but was rebuilt in two years, as attested by a boar's head cut in stone, with the initials of the landlord, I. T., and the date 1668, above the first-floor window. This sign-stone is now in the Guildhall library. The house stood between Small-alley and St. Michael's-lane, and in the rear looked upon St. Michael's churchyard, where was buried a *drawer*, or waiter, at the tavern, d. 1720: in the church was interred John Rhodoway, "Vintner at the Bore's Head," 1623.

Maitland, in 1739, mentions the Boar's Head, with " This is the chief tavern in London" under the sign. Goldsmith (*Essays*), Boswell (*Life of Dr. Johnson*), and Washington Irving (*Sketch-book*), have idealised the house as the identical place which Falstaff frequented, forgetting its destruction in the Great Fire. The site of the Boar's Head is very nearly that of the statue of King William IV.

In 1834, Mr. Kempe, F.S.A., exhibited to the Society of Antiquaries a carved oak figure of Sir John Falstaff, in the costume of the 16th century. It supported an ornamental bracket over one side of the door of the Boar's Head, a figure of Prince Henry sustaining that on the other. The Falstaff was the property of Mr. Thomas Shelton, brazier, Great Eastcheap, whose ancestors had lived in the shop he then occupied ever since the Great Fire. He well remembered the last Grand Shakspearean Dinner-party at the Boar's Head, about 1784. A boar's head with silver tusks, which had been suspended in some room in the tavern, perhaps the Half-Moon or Pomgranate (see Henry IV. act ii. sc. 4), at the Great Fire fell down with the ruins of the house, and was conveyed to Whitechapel Mount, where, many years after, it was recovered and identified with its former locality. At a public-house, No. 12 Miles-lane, was long preserved a tobacco-box with a painting of the original Boar's Head tavern on the lid.

In High-street, Southwark, between Nos. 25 and 26, was formerly the *Boar's Head Inn*, part of Sir John Fastolff's benefaction to Magdalen College, Oxford. Sir John was one of the bravest generals in the French wars, under the fourth, fifth, and sixth Henries; but he is not the Falstaff of Shakspeare. The Boar's Head premises in Southwark, latterly a court of eleven tenements, were taken down for the New London Bridge approaches.

EGYPTIAN HALL, PICCADILLY.

This edifice and a smaller structure in Welbeck-street are, in single features and details, the only specimens of Egyptian architecture in London. The latter was, as originally erected, the most correct in character, but has since been almost spoiled. The Hall in Piccadilly conforms to the style in the columns and the general outline, as indicated by the inclined torus-moulding at the extremity of the front, the cornice, &c.; though the composition itself is at variance with the principles of genuine Egyptian architecture, the front being divided into two floors, with wide instead of narrow windows to both. The details are mostly from the great temple of Tentyra, with the scarabæus, winged mundus, hieroglyphics, &c. The architect's name, G. F. Robinson, is inscribed upon the façade. The entablature is supported by colossal figures of Isis and Osiris, sculptured by L. Gahagan. The Hall cost 16,000*l.*, and was built in 1812 for a museum of natural history collected by W. Bullock, F.L.S., during thirty years' travel in Central America, which was exhibited here until 1819, when it was sold in 2248 lots.*

The Egyptian Hall contains lecture-rooms, a bazaar, and a large central room, "the Waterloo Gallery." As the Hall has been a sort of Ark of Exhibitions, we enumerate the *Curiosities* which have been shewn here:

1816. *The Judgment of Brutus*, painted by Le Thiere, president of the Academy of St. Luke, at Rome.—*Water-colour Paintings of Minerals and Shells*, by Chev. de Barde.—*Napoleon's Travelling-Chariot*, built for his Russian campaign, and adapted for a bed-room, dressing-room, pantry, kitchen, &c.; captured at Waterloo: seen at the Egyptian Hall by 800,000 persons; now in the Tussaud Exhibition.

1819. Sale of Bullock's Museum: produce, 9974*l.* 13*s.*; cost, 30,000*l.*

1821. *Fac-simile of the Tomb of Psammuthis, King of Thebes*, discovered by Belzoni; constructed and painted from drawings and wax-impressions taken by him of all the original figures, hieroglyphics, emblems, &c.; the two principal chambers illuminated: first day, 1900 admissions, at 2*s.* 6*d.* each.

1822. *Laplanders and Reindeer:* 100*l.* per day taken for six weeks.—*Pair of Wapeti*, or Elks, from the Upper Missouri; and a pretended *Mermaid*, visited by 300 and 400 persons daily.†

1824. *Mexican Museum*, ancient and modern.—*Esquimaux Man and Woman.*—*Hatching Chickens by Artificial Heat.*

1825. *Rath*, or *Burmese Imperial State-Carriage*, captured by the British in 1824: the coach and the throne-seat, studded with 20,000 gems, are stated to have cost 12,500*l.* at Tavoy.—*Model of Switzerland.*

1826. *The Musical Sisters*, four and six years old, harpist and pianist.—*Altar-piece*, by Murillo.—The *Pæcilorama*, views painted by Stanfield.

1827. *The Tyrolese Minstrels*, four males and one female.

---

* Bullock's "Liverpool Museum" was opened at 22 Piccadilly, in 1805, in the room originally occupied by Astley for his *evening* performance of horsemanship; his amphitheatre not being roofed until 1780, and therefore allowing only day exhibitions.

† In *Manners and Customs of the Japanese*, published in 1841, the above "Mermaid" (the head and shoulders of a monkey neatly attached to a headless fish) is proved to have been *manufactured* in Japan, brought to Europe by an American adventurer, and valued at 1000*l.* A pretended Mermaid was also exhibited in London in 1775; and in Broad Court, Covent Garden, in 1794.

1828. *Pictures of Battles of the French Armies*, painted by General Le Jeune.—*The Death of Virginia*, painted by Le Thiere.—Haydon's *Picture of the Mock Election in the King's Bench*, bought by George IV. for 800 guineas, and sent from the Egyptian Hall to St. James's Palace.

1829. *Troubadours* (singers).—*The Siamese Twins*, two youths of eighteen, natives of Siam, united by a short band at the pit of the stomach—"two perfect bodies, bound together by an inseparable link."

1830. *Vox Bipartitus*, or two voices in one.—*Sculpture*, by Lough.—*Tableaux Vivans* (ancient pictures by living figures).—*Michael Boai*, or the chin-chopper, à la Buckhorse.

1831. *Model of the Theatre Francaise* at Paris.—A *Cobra di Capello*, the first brought alive to Europe.—*Two Orang-outangs* and a *Chimpanzee.*—A *Double-sighted Boy*, M'Kean, aged eight years.—*Scrymegour's Picture of the First Sign in Egypt.*—*Double-sighted Dog.*—The Egyptian Hall converted into a Bazaar.

1832. *Museum of Etruscan Antiquities.*—*Royal Clarence Vase*, of glass, made at Birmingham.—*The Brothers Koeller*, singers, from Switzerland.—Haydon's *Pictures of Xenophon and the* 10,000; and his *Mock Election*, lent by George IV. for exhibition; *Death of Eucles*, &c.

1835. *Views of Paris*, painted by M. Dupressoir.

1837. *A living Male Child*, with four hands, four arms, four legs, four feet, and two bodies, born at Staleybridge, Manchester.—*Masquerades.*

1838. *Le Brun's Picture of the Battle of Arbela, embossed on copper*, by Szentpetery.—Captain Siborne's *Model of the Battle of Waterloo*, with 190,000 figures; now in the Museum of the United Service Institution.

1839. *Skeleton of a Mammoth Ox.*—*Pictorial Storm at Sea*, introducing Grace Darling and the "Forfarshire Wreck."

1840. *Aubusson Carpets.*—*Ung-ka-puti* (Gibbon monkey), from Sumatra.—*Bioplulax*, or Life and Property Protector.—Haydon's large *Picture of the General Anti-Slavery Convention.*

1841. *Catlin's North-American Indian Gallery* of 310 portraits of chiefs, and 200 views of villages, religious ceremonies, dances, ball-plays, buffalo-hunts,—in all, 3000 full-length figures, with costumes and other produce, from a wigwam to a rattle, filling a room 106 feet long.—The *Missouri Leviathan* skeleton,—The *Great Pennard Cheese*, presented to the Queen.

1843. *Sir George Hayter's Great Picture of the First Reformed Parliament*, figures half-life size.—*Model of Venice.*—The *Napoleon Museum.*

1844. The *American Dwarf*, "Tom Thumb,"* whose exhibition often realised 125*l.* a-day; while, in sickening contrast, in an adjoining room, the pictures of Haydon (to whom Wordsworth wrote "High is our calling, friend") were scarcely visited by a dozen persons in a week. The "Banishment of Aristides," Haydon's last picture, was shewn here, and its failure hastened the painter to his awful end.—*Nine Ojibbeway Indians*, from Lake Huron, in their native costumes, exhibiting their war-dances and sports.—*German Dwarfs.*

1845. The *Eureka*, a machine for composing hexameter Latin verses; a practical illustration of the law of evolution.— Second Exhibition of Captain Siborne's *Model of the Battle of Waterloo.*

1846. *Prof. Faber's Euphonia*, or speaking automaton, enunciating sounds and words; played by keys.—*Mammoth Horse.*—*Polar Dog.*—*Bosjesman Family.* —The *Rock Harmonicon.*—*Curiosities from Australia.*—*Professor Kist's Poses Plastiques.*—A Dwarf dressed in a bear-skin: the "*What is it?*"; immediately detected.

1847. Second *Family of Bosjesmans* (Bushmen), from Southern Africa.— *Models of Ancient and Modern Jerusalem*, by Brunetti.—*Exhibition of Modern Paintings;* free to artists.

---

* "Tom Thumb" (Charles S. Stratton) was born at Bridgeport, Connecticut, U.S., January 11, 1832. He was, in 1845. 25 inches high, and weighed 15 pounds. He was first exhibited in New York; in 1844 he came to London, and appeared at the Princess' Theatre February 21, 1844. He was next shewn to the Queen and Queen Dowager, and received several costly presents. He then appeared in a pretty miniature chariot, drawn by two Shetland ponies, with which he visited Paris in 1845, and was shewn to Louis-Philippe. He next visited Belgium and Spain, and was present at a bull-fight with Queen Isabella. He then revisited England, and returned to New York.

.· 1848. *Pictures of Recent Political Events in Paris.—The Mysterious Lady.—* Figure of a *Russian Lady in veined marbles.—Banvard's Dioramic Picture of the Mississippi and Missouri Rivers,* 3000 miles, stated to be painted on three miles of canvass (!); sketched before the painter was of age.

1850. *Panorama of Fremont's Overland Route to California.—Bonomi's Panorama of the Nile,* 800 feet long: representing 1720 miles distance, closing with the Pyramids and Sphinx.

·. 1852. March 15, Mr. Albert Smith first gave the narrative of his *Ascent of Mont Blanc* in 1851, accompanying the exhibition of cleverly-painted moving dioramic pictures of its perils and sublimities.

The Egyptian Hall usually realises a clear net rental of 1100*l.* per annum; after paying ground-rent and rates, 413*l.*: for Tom Thumb's exhibition-room was paid 44*l.* per month. In the western wing was the Medical Hall of Dr. Reece, the champion of Joanna Southcott.

(See also MANSION HOUSE: Egyptian Hall.)

ELECTRIC TELEGRAPHS.

The Electro-telegraphic system in England has been carried out exclusively by the Electric Telegraph Company, at their Central Office in Lothbury, which has thus become the metropolis of stations. Here the whole system is most clearly exhibited; the Company having purchased all Cooke and Wheatstone's patents, and adopted their peculiar features,—the suspended conducting-wire and the Double Needle Telegraph; and, in certain cases, Mr. Bain's chemical Printing Telegraph. The Office is in Founders'-court,[*] on the north side of the Bank of England; where anciently dwelt *founders* "that cast candlesticks, chafing-dishes, spice-mortars," &c., and "turned them bright with the feet, making a loathsome noise, whence the name of Loth-*berie,* or court" (*Stow*); all which is strikingly contrasted with the wonder-working silence of the Electric Telegraph operations.

The entrance to the office is bold and picturesque: above the doorway is a balcony; and between two enriched Ionic pilasters, carrying an arched pediment, is the large transparent dial of an electric clock.

You first enter a hall 42 by 32 feet, entirely lighted from the coved roof of plate-glass in panels. At the east and west ends is a screen of two stories; the first story supported by Doric columns, the upper Corinthian; both communicate with the apartments in which are the electric-telegraph machines, and the two ends are connected by side-galleries, there being thus two railed stories or galleries throughout the hall; at each end, below, are counters, and above them the names of the various places to which messages can be sent. At the counters are clerks, who receive the messages, enter them, and pass them to another set of clerks, who transmit them to those employed at the machines above by lifts or small trays, working by cords in square tubes,—a lift and bell to each desk.

Behind the counter is the "translating office," where all messages are transferred into the abbreviated code arranged by the Company. Such messages as descriptions of persons suspected of dishonesty are not translated, but sent in full: only the lists of prices in corn, share, and other markets are so abbreviated.

The west side of the hall is devoted to the business of the towns on the North-Western and Great-Western lines; and the eastern side is for the Eastern, South-Eastern, and South-Western lines, and the Admiralty.

* Founders' Hall, now a Dissenters' meeting-house, was in 1792 nicknamed "the cauldron of sedition." Here Waithman made his first political speech, and with his fellow-orators was routed by constables sent by the Lord-Mayor, Sir James Sanderson, to disperse the meeting.

The station is connected with the Euston-square station by wires laid along Moorgate-street, Finsbury-square, the City-road, and the New-road; with the Shoreditch station by wires thence to the other system of wires at Finsbury; and from the Nine Elms, Waterloo, and London-Bridge stations, by wires laid to the latter station; and thence over London-bridge and along King-William-street to the Central Office.

Several wires are laid to each terminus, lest any of them become defective, when the connexion can be carried on by other wires, as the expense of taking up the pavement would be enormous for so slight a cause. The wires are of copper, and are covered with gutta-percha, India-rubber, or some resinous substances, which, being non-conductors, prevent the escape of the electricity.

The wires from the several railway termini are brought through iron pipes laid down under the pavement of the streets; and meeting in Founders'-court, are continued through the south wall of the basement of the station, and descending into the "test-box," are fastened there to pegs fitted into the back of the box. At the bottom run a corresponding number of "house-wires," and these go to the machines in the galleries. Connexion is maintained between the line and house-wires by small wires running perpendicularly from one to the other. All the wires are numbered at the desks to correspond from batteries to machines, and from machines to the test-box, that the electric circle may thus be complete.

In the galleries the wires are carried along the ceilings from the respective machines to the battery-chambers and the test-box; the battery-wires running east and west, and the house-wires to test-box north and south. Several long and narrow chambers are devoted to the batteries, which, when charged, are found to remain above a month in good working order. They are so numbered and arranged in reference to the wires, that any defect can be immediately rectified. Each railway has a division to itself, and thus all risk of confusion is avoided. The communications are spelt through letter by letter, and each word is verified by the receiver to the sender as the message proceeds. The average speed is somewhat more than two letters per second, being nearly at the same rate as ordinary writing.

At the Central Station, also, a sort of Telegraphic editor prepares from the morning newspapers, at an early hour, a short abstract of the most important news; the general commercial information most in request; the state of the stock and share market, and of the money-market, the state of the wind and weather at different ports of the kingdom, shipping and sporting intelligence, the rates of the markets of every description, and the leading general political news. This, when written out, is sent up to the instrument-room, from whence it is despatched to various subscription-rooms in different parts of the country, where it arrives by eight o'clock in the morning. All news of adequate importance is thus diffused over the kingdom literally with the speed of lightning. Thus, the public in Edinburgh are informed by eight o'clock in the morning of all interesting facts which appear in the London morning journals; and the provincial journals are similarly supplied.

Bain's chemical Printing Telegraph is worked by the Company on commercial lines of railway. By this telegraph 300 words per minute have been sent, and 56,000 messages per month have been transmitted on the Eastern Counties line for railway purposes alone; and for mercantile purposes, the contents of a closely-printed octavo volume have been sent out in messages, per day, from the Central Telegraph Office alone. Such is the facility afforded by the instruments now in use, that they are chiefly worked by boys taken from the London Orphan Asylum, who fully understand how to manage them after a fortnight's practice. By this telegraph the Queen's speech in 1852 (754 words) was *printed to* Manchester in twenty-five minutes.

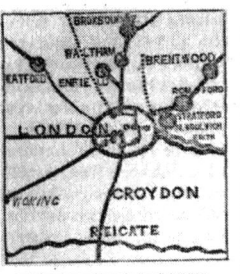

ELECTRIC TELEGRAPH LINES.

The Houses of Parliament have an Electric Telegraph of their own, communicating with the clerks' offices, committee-rooms, &c.

There are also, in communication with the Central Office in Lothbury, stations at the several Railway termini; at the General Post-Office, St. Martin's-le-Grand; No. 7 Knightsbridge-terrace; and at No. 448 West Strand, open day and night. Rate of charge for twenty words, 100 miles and under, 2s. 6d.; over 100 miles, 5s. An addition of one-half the rate for each ten words or fraction of ten words additional, or a charge of 3d. per word, at the option of the sender. The tariff of charges may be had at the office; with a map of the stations, whence the annexed woodcut is taken.

In 1851, the Admiralty Semaphores were removed, and the Electric Telegraph substituted for them. By this means, despatches can be sent off and received by night or day, and in any kind of weather; whereas, the Semaphores could only work by day, and that in fine weather: this was a great inconvenience to Government, especially the naval department, which had only one line, from the Admiralty, Whitehall, to Portsmouth; whilst now, orders can be transmitted in a moment to the Royal arsenals of Woolwich, Chatham, and Sheerness, Portsmouth, Plymouth and Devonport, Pembroke, &c. (See ADMIRALTY, page 2.) Not only is the Electric Telegraph of great importance to Government, but to our merchants and shipping interest, in the announcement of the arrivals and departures of the foreign and colonial mails, and vessels from all parts of the globe; the last prices of the markets and stocks; Parliamentary bills, and intelligence of what is passing in both Houses of Parliament during the session; courts of law, &c.

In 1851, the Needle Telegraph of Wheatstone was carried round the Great Exhibition Building in Hyde Park, and thence to the Police Station, Great Scotland-yard, Whitehall. And in 1852, the exact Greenwich time was first conveyed by the Electric Telegraph to various parts of England.

The first newspaper report by Electric Telegraph appeared in the *Morning Chronicle*, May 8, 1845, detailing a railway meeting held at Portsmouth on the preceding evening. On April 10, in the same year, a game of chess was played by Electric Telegraph, between Captain Kennedy, at the South-Western Railway terminus, and Mr. Staunton, at Gosport: the mode of playing was by numbering the squares of the chess-board and the men; and in conveying the moves, the electricity travelled backward and forward during the game upwards of 10,000 miles.

In 1845, by the Electric Telegraph then laid from Paddington to the Slough station, on the Great Western Railway, John Tawell was captured on suspicion of having murdered Sarah Hart at Salt-hill, on Jan. 1. Tawell left Slough by the railway on that evening; and at the same instant, by telegraph, his person was described, with instructions to the police to watch him on his arrival at Paddington: he was accordingly followed by a police-sergeant in an omnibus to the Bank, thence to the Jerusalem Coffee-house, over London-bridge to the Borough, then back to Scott's-yard, Cannon-street, where he was apprehended and identified. On Nov. 13, 1851, the Submarine Electric Telegraph between Dover and Calais was first worked for the public; and the opening and closing prices of the Paris Bourse were transmitted to the Stock Exchange, London, during business-hours.

ELY PLACE.

All that remains of this celebrated palace, anciently Ely House, which stood on the north side of Holborn-hill, and was the town mansion of the Bishops of Ely, is the Chapel of St. Etheldreda, already described at pp. 167 and 243. The site is otherwise occupied by two rows of houses known as Ely-place, and a knot of tenements, streets, and alleys; but the locality is fraught with the historic associations of five centuries. Its first occupier, Bishop John de Kirkby, dying in 1290, bequeathed a messuage and nine cottages on this spot to his successors in the see of Ely. William de Luda, the next bishop, annexed some lands, added to the residence, and in 1297 devised them to the see, on condition that his successor should provide for the service of St. Ethelreda's Chapel. John de Hotham, who died in 1336, planted a vineyard, kitchen-garden, orchard, &c. Thomas de Arundel, preferred to the see in 1374, re-edified the episcopal buildings and the Chapel; and erected a large gate-house towards Holborn, the stonework of which remained in Stow's time. Ely House was in part let by the see to noblemen. Here "old John of Gaunt, time-honoured Lancaster," died Feb. 13, 1399; and Shakspeare has made it the scene of Lancaster's last interview with Richard II. Following Hall and Holinshed, too, Shakspeare refers to this Place when Richard Duke of Gloucester, at the Council in the Tower, thus addresses the Bishop:

> "*D. of Glou.* My lord of Ely, when I was last in Holborn,
> I saw good strawberries in your garden there;
> I do beseech you send for some of them.
> *B. of Ely.* Marry, and will, my lord, with all my heart."
> *Richard III.* act iii. sc. 4.

At Ely House were kept divers feasts by the Sergeants-at-Law: at one in 1495, Henry VII. was present with his queen; and at another feast in 1531, on making eleven new Sergeants, Henry VIII. and Queen Katherine were banquetted here with sumptuousness wanting "little of a feast at a coronation;" and open-house was kept for five days. In 1576, at the mandatory request of Queen Elizabeth, Bishop Cox leased to Sir Christopher Hatton for twenty-one years the greater portion of the demesne, on payment at Midsummer-day of a red rose, ten loads of hay, and 10*l.* per annum; the Bishop reserving to himself and his successors the right of walking in the gardens, and gathering 20 bushels of roses yearly. Hatton largely improved the estate, and then petitioned the Queen to require the Bishop to make over the whole property; whereupon ensued the Bishop's remonstrance, and Elizabeth's undignified threat to "unfrock" him: and in 1578 the entire property was conveyed to Hatton, and Elizabeth further retaliated by keeping the see of Ely vacant for eighteen years from the death of Bishop Cox in 1591.

Aggas's map shews the vineyard, meadow, kitchen-garden, and orchard, of Ely Place to have extended northward from Holborn-hill to the present Hatton-wall and Vine-street; and east and west, from Saffron-hill to nearly the present Leather-lane: but except a cluster of houses (Ely Rents) on Holborn-hill, the surrounding ground was entirely open and unbuilt on; the names of Saffron-hill, Field lane, and Lily, Turnmill, and Vine streets, carry the mind's-eye back to this suburban appropriation. The Sutherland View, 1543, also shews the gate-house, chapel, great banquetting-hall, &c. Sir Christopher lived in great state in Hatton House, as Ely Place was now called; but Elizabeth, "which seldom gave loans, and never forgave due debts," pressed the payment of some 40,000*l.* arrears, which the Chancellor could not meet; so it went to his heart, and he died Nov. 20, 1591. He was succeeded by his nephew, whose widow, the strange Lady Hatton, in 1598 was married to Sir Edward Coke, then attorney-general, but who could not gain admission to Hatton House: she died "at her house in Holbourne," Jan. 3, 1646. The Bishops of Ely made several attempts to recover the entire property; but, during the imprisonment of Bishop Wren by the Long Parliament, most of the palatial buildings were taken down, and upon the garden were built Hatton-garden, Great and Little Kirby-streets, Charles-street, Cross-street, and Hatton-wall. During the Interregnum, Hatton House and offices were used

Crown; a town-house was built for the Bishops, No. 27 Dover-street, Piccadilly; and about 1775 the present Ely-place was built, the Chapel remaining on the west side. A remnant of the episcopal residence is preserved in, and has given name to, Mitre-court, leading from Hatton-garden to Ely-place. There, worked into the wall, as the sign of a public-house, is a mitre sculptured in stone, with the date 1546, which probably once decorated Ely Palace or its precinct gateway.

The stage-play of "Christ's Passion" was acted in the reign of James I. "at Elie House, in Holborn, when Gundomar (the Spanish Am-bassador) lay there on Good Friday at night, at which there were thou-sands present" (Prynne's *Histriomastix*, p. 117, note); this being the last performance of a Religious Mystery in England. At Ely House, also, was arranged the grand masque given by the four Inns of Court to Charles I. and Queen Henrietta-Maria, at Whitehall, on Candlemas-day, 1634, at the cost of 21,000*l.*; when the masquers, horsemen, musi-cians, dancrs, with the grand committee (including the great lawyers Whitelocke, Hyde (afterwards Lord Clarendon), and Seldon, went in procession by torchlight from Ely House, down Chancery Lane, along the Strand, to Whitehall.

EXCHANGE ALLEY,

Now 'Change-alley, between No. 24 Cornhill and No. 70 Lombard-street, is described by Strype as "a place of a very considerable con-course of merchants, seafaring men, and other traders, occasioned by the great coffee-houses that stand there. Chiefly now brokers, and such as deal in the buying and selling of stocks, frequent it." Thither Jews and Gentiles migrated in 1700: for a century it was the focus of all the monetary operations of England, and in great part of Europe; and even to this hour, the Stock Exchange bears the generic designa-tion of "the Alley." The rendezvous of the jobbers and brokers was Jonathan's Coffee-house, where gambling of all kinds was carried on; notwithstanding a formal prohibition against their assemblage issued by the City of London, which provision continued unrepealed till 1825.

Exchange-alley was the great arena of the South-Sea Bubble of 1720, and was every day blocked up by crowds who came "to venture in the Alley:"

> "There is a gulf where thousands fell,
> Here all the bold adventurers came;
> A narrow sound, though deep as hell;
> 'Change Alley is the dreadful name.
> * * *
> Meanwhile, secure on Garraway's cliffs,
> A savage race, by shipwrecks fed,
> Lie waiting for the founder'd skiffs,
> And strip the bodies of the dead."—*Swift.*

In a print called the "Bubblers' Medley" are "stock-jobbing cards, or the humours of 'Change-alley."[*]

> "The headlong fool that wants to be a swopper
> Of gold and silver coin for English copper,
> May in 'Change Alley prove himself an ass,
> And give rich metal for adulterate brass."
> *Nine of Hearts, in a Pack of Bubble Cards.*

The scene has been excellently painted by E. M. Ward, with the motley throng in 'Change-alley, beaux and ladies turned gamblers, and the accessory pawnbroker's shop, in a truly Hogarthian spirit: the picture is in the Vernon Gallery.

Defoe (1722) describes Garraway's as frequented by "people of quality who have business in the City, and the most considerable and

[*] See Mackay's *Memoirs of Extraordinary Popular Delusions* (illustrated), vol. i. p. 60. 1852.

wealthy of the citizens;" Robins's, by "the foreign banquiers, and often even foreign ministers;" and Jonathan's by "buyers and sellers of stock." 1766 was a South-Sea year in East India stock, when patriots were made or marred by jobbing: "from the Alley to the House," said Walpole, "is like a path of ants."

"The centre of the jobbing is in the kingdom of Exchange-alley and its adjacencies. The limits are easily surrounded in about a minute and a half: viz. stepping out of Jonathan's into the Alley, you turn your face full south; moving on a few paces, and then turning due east, you advance to Garraway's; from thence going out at the other door, you go on still east into Birchin-lane; and then halting a little at the Sword-blade Bank, to do much mischief in fewest words, you immediately face to the north, enter Cornhill, visit two or three petty provinces there in your way west; and thus having boxed your compass, and sailed round the whole stock-jobbing globe, you turn into Jonathan's again; and so, as most of the great follies of life oblige us to do, you end just where you began."—*The Anatomy of Exchange Alley*, 1719.

'Change Alley is a maze of thoroughfares. "With something like four or five entrances, two from Lombard-street, two from Cornhill, and one from Birchin-lane, there is great danger of losing your way either to the right or the left; you may possibly find that, instead of going as you intended through the Alley, and reaching Cornhill, you have in reality only taken another turning which leads you into Lombard-street, whence you started."—*The City*, p. 169.

EXCHANGES.

THE ROYAL EXCHANGE, at the north-western extremity of Cornhill, is the *third* Exchange built nearly on the same site, for the meeting of merchants and bankers. The first "goodely Bursse" was projected by Sir James Gresham, Lord Mayor in 1538, who submitted to Thomas Cromwell, Lord Privy-Seal, a plan taken from the Burse at Antwerp. This application failed; but the project was renewed thirty years later by Thomas Gresham, the younger son of Sir James, born in London in 1519, apprenticed to his uncle Sir John Gresham, and admitted in 1543 to the Mercers' Company; in whose hall hangs a contemporary portrait of Sir Thomas Gresham, who was royal agent at Antwerp to Henry VIII., Edward VI., and Elizabeth, and was knighted when ambassador at the court of the Duchess of Parma. Like other bankers and merchants of that day, Gresham had his shop in Lombard-street, as yet the only Exchange. The house was on the site of No. 68, the banking-house of Martin, Stone, and Co.: over the door was Gresham's crest,* a grasshopper, as a sign, which was seen by Pennant, but has disappeared by piecemeal.

On June 6, 1566, the first stone of the Burse was laid in Cornhill, by Sir Thomas Gresham and several aldermen, each of whom "laid a piece of gold, which the workmen picked up." The City had previously purchased and taken down eighty houses, and prepared the site; the whole having been conveyed to Sir Thomas Gresham, who "most frankly and lovingly" promised, that within a month after the Burse should be finished, he would present it in equal moieties to the City and the Mercers' Company; as a pledge of which Gresham, before Alderman Rivers and other citizens, gave his hand to Sir William Garrard, and *drank a carouse* to his kinsman Thomas Rowe. "How rarely do ancient documents furnish us with such a picture of ancient manners!" By November 1567, the Burse was finished. As Flemish materials, Flemish workmen, and a Flemish architect (Henryke) had been employed, so

* The letters of James Gresham, in the Paston Collection, are *sealed* with a grasshopper; sufficient refutation of a tradition accounting for the adoption of that heraldic symbol by Sir Thomas Gresham, from a grasshopper having saved his life when he was a poor famished boy, by attracting a person to the spot where he lay in a helpless condition! Still, it were almost a pity to disturb the popular legend, teaching, as it simply does, reliance upon God's providence.

the design closely imitated a Flemish building, the Great Burse of Antwerp. Two prints, date 1569, and probably engraved by Gresham's order, shew the exterior and interior: a quadrangle, with an arcade; a corridor, or *pawn** of stalls above; and in the high-pitched roof, chambers with dormer windows. On the east side of the Cornhill entrance was a lofty bell-tower, from which, at twelve at noon and at six in the evening, was rung a bell, the merchants' call to 'Change; while, on the north side, a Corinthian column rose twice the height of the building; both tower and column surmounted by a grasshopper, also placed at each corner of the quadrangle. The columns of the court were marble; the upper portion was laid out in 100 shops, the lower in *walks* and rooms for the merchants, with shops on the exterior. Thus there were the "Scotch Walk," "Hambro," and the "Irish," "East Country," "Swedish," "Norway," "American," "Jamaica," "Spanish," "Portugal," "French," "Greek," and "Dutch and Jewellers'" walks. Long after the opening of the Burse, the shops remained "in a manner empty;" when, upon a report that the Queen was about to visit it, Gresham prevailed upon the shopkeepers in the upper pawn to furnish their shops with "wares and wax-lights," on promise of "one year rent-free." The rent was then 40s. a shop, in two years raised to 4 marks, and then to 4l. 10s. a year, all the shops being let. "Then the milliners or haberdashers sold mouse-traps, bird-cages, shoeing-horns, Jews' trumps, &c.; armourers, that sold both old and new armour; apothecaries, booksellers, goldsmiths, and glass-sellers." (*Howes.*) All being prepared, on Jan. 23, 1570-1, amidst the ringing of bells in every part of the City, "the Queen's Majesty, attended with her nobility, came from her house in the Strand called Somerset House, and entered the City by Temple Bar, through Fleet-street, Cheap, and so by the north side of the Burse, through Threadneedle-street, to Sir Thomas Gresham's house in Bishopsgate-street, where she dined. After dinner, her majesty returning through Cornhill, entered the Burse on the south side" (*Stow*); and having viewed the whole, especially the Pawne, which was richly furnished with the finest wares, the Queen caused the Burse, by herald and trumpet, to be proclaimed "The Royal Exchange:"

> "Proclaim through every high street of the city,
> This place be no longer called a Burse;
> But since the building's stately, fair, and strange,
> Be it for ever called—the Royal Exchange."
> *Queen Elizabeth's Troubles, Part 2.*—A Play by Thomas Heywood, 1609.

Sir Thomas Gresham died suddenly, Nov. 21, 1579, in the evening, on his return from the Exchange; "being cut off by untymely death, having left a part of his royall monument unperformed: that is, xxx. pictures (statues) of kings and queenes of this land; and to that purpose left 30 roomes (niches) to place them in." It was then proposed that before any citizen should be elected alderman, he should be "enjoyned to pay the charge of makyng and fynishing one of the forsaid kings or queenes theire pictures, to be erected in the places aforesaid in the Exchange, not exceeding 100 nobles (66l. 6s. 8d.); the pictures to be graven on wood, covered with lead, and then gilded and paynted with oyle-cullors;" and the Court of Common Council subsequently made the erection of one such statue a part of the fine for being freed from the office of Sheriff. The building was often in danger from feather-makers, and others that kept shops in the upper pawne, using "pannes

* Corrupted from *bahn*, German for a path or walk. There is a curious tradition, not unsupported by facts, that the framework of the Exchange was constructed upon Gresham's estate at Rinxhall, near Battisford, Suffolk, formerly rich in wood; the remains of saw-pits are still discernible. The stone, slates, iron, wainscot, and glass, were brought from Antwerp.

of fyer," which were therefore forbidden by an order of the Court of Aldermen. A print by Hollar, date 1644, shews the merchants in full 'Change, with the picturesque costumes of the respective countries:

> " The new-come traveller,
> With his disguised coat and ringed ear,
> Trampling the Bourse's marble twice a day."

The statues, from Edward the Confessor to Queen Elizabeth, were thus provided; and subsequently, James I., Charles I., and Charles II. The statue of Charles I. was removed immediately after his execution, and on its pedestal was inscribed *Exit tyrannorum ultimus ;* which was in turn removed, and replaced with a new statue, after the Restoration. Here also, on May 28, 1661, the acts for establishing the Commonwealth were burned by the hands of the common hangman.

Gresham's Exchange was almost entirely destroyed in the Great Fire of 1666; " when the kings fell down upon their faces, and the greater part of the building after them, *the founder's statue* only remaining." Pepys refers to " Sir Thomas Gresham in the corner" as the only statue that was left standing. After the death of Sir Thomas Gresham, the affairs of the Royal Exchange passed under the management of the Gresham Committee, as the trustees appointed under his will, with certain members nominated by the Corporation. Thus originated the Grand or Joint Committee, under whose direction the Exchange was rebuilt after the Great Fire upon the old foundations, by Edward Jerman, one of the City Surveyors, and not by Sir Christopher Wren, as often stated; but Wren was consulted in the project of the rebuilding. Mr. Jupp, of Carpenters' Hall, possesses two large and beautiful drawings of Jerman's design for the building, executed in Indian ink upon vellum. Meanwhile, the merchants met " in the gardens or walkes of Gresham College," being the site of the great court-yard of the Excise Office; on which a temporary Exchange was erected for a similar purpose, after the burning of the second Exchange in 1838.

Among the payments for Jerman's building is one by the Committee to Sir John Denham, the poet, "His Majestie's Surveyor-General of his Workes, for his trouble from time to time in coming down to view the Exchainge and streetes adjoihing; as also in furthering theire addresses to His Majesty, and giving them full warrants for Portland-stone ;" the Committee therefore ordered provision to be made " of six or eight dishes of meate att the Sun Tavern, on Wednesday next, to intertayne him withal at his comeing downe, and to present him with thirty guinney-pieces of gold, as a toaken of theire gratitude."

Among other entries, we find that Caius Gabriel Cibber was appointed carver ; the clock was to be set up by Edward Stauton, under the direction of Dr. Hook, having chimes with four bells, playing six tunes; William Wightman was to furnish a set of sound and tuneable bells, at 6*l.* 5*s.* per cwt.; four balconies were to be made from the inner-pawn into the quadrangle, at a charge of not more than 300*l.*; and the signs to the shops in the pawns were not to be hung forth, but set over the frieze of each shop.

The celebrated Sir Robert Viner, on March 22d, 1668 (1669), proffered to give his Majesty's statue on horseback, cut in white marble, to stand upon the Royal Exchange: this offer was declined because of the "bignesse" of the statue, which Sir Robert Viner afterwards gave to be erected over the conduit at Stocks'-market ; though the royal figure was an altered John Sobieski.

On Oct. 23d, 1667, Charles II. fixed the first pillar on the west side of the north entrance to the Exchange. " The King was entertained by the City and Company with a chine of beef, grand dish of fowl, gammons of bacon, dried tongues, anchoves, caviare, etc., and plenty of several sorts of wine. He gave 20*l.* in gold to the workmen. The interteynment was in a shedd built and adorned on purpose, upon the Scotch walke." On the 31st, the Duke of York founded the corresponding pier ; and on Nov. 18th, Prince Rupert fixed the pillar on the east side of the south entrance; both princes being similarly entertained.

This *second Exchange* was opened Sept. 28, 1669; its cost, 58,962*l.*, being defrayed in equal moieties by the City and the Mercers' Company. It was quadrangular in plan, and had its arcades, pawn above, and statues in niches, like Gresham's Exchange; it had also a three-storied tower, with lantern and gilt grasshopper vane. The edifice thus remained until the extensive repairs of 1820-26 (George Smith, architect), when a stone tower, 128 feet high, was built on the south front, in place of the timber one: these repairs cost 33,000*l.*, including 6000*l.* for stone staircases and floors. The Cornhill front had a lofty archway, with four Corinthian columns; emblematic statues of the four quarters of the globe; statues of Charles I. and II. by Bushnell; statue of Gresham by E. Pierce; four busts of Queen Elizabeth; alto-relievos of Britannia, the Arts and Sciences, &c., and of Queen Elizabeth, and her heralds proclaiming the original Exchange. The area within the quadrangle was paved with "Turkey stones;" in the centre was a statue of Charles II. by Gibbons; in the arcade was a statue of Gresham by Cibber; and of Sir John Barnard, placed there in his lifetime (*temp.* George II.). The arcade and area were arranged, nominally, into distinct walks for the merchants.

> " For half an hour he feeds: and when he's done,
> In's elbow-chair he takes a nap till one;
> From thence to 'Change he hurries in a heat
> (Where knaves and fools in mighty numbers meet,
> And kindly mix the bubble with the cheat);
> There barters, buys and sells, receives and pays,
> And turns the pence a hundred several ways.
> In that great hive, where markets rise and fall,
> And swarms of muckworms round its pillars crawl,
> He, like the rest, as busy as a bee,
> Remains among the henpeck'd herd till three."
> *Wealthy Shopkeeper*, 1700.

The royal statues were, on the south side, Edward I., Edward III., Henry V., and Henry VI.; on the west, Edward IV., Edward V., Henry VII., and Henry VIII.; on the north, Edward VI., Queen Mary, Queen Elizabeth, James I., Charles I., Charles II., and James II; on the east were William and Mary, in a double niche, George I., George II., and George III. These figures were in armour and Roman costume, the Queens in the dresses of their respective times; most of them were originally gilt. George III. was sculptured by Wilton, George I. and George II. by Rysbrack, and the major part of the others by Caius Gabriel Cibber.

Originally, the offices in the upper floors were let as shops for rich and showy articles; but they were forsaken in 1739 (*Maitland*), and the galleries were subsequently occupied by the Royal Exchange Assurance Offices, Lloyd's Coffee-house, the Merchant Seamen's Office, the Gresham Lecture-room, and the Lord Mayor's Court Office: the latter a row of offices divided by glazed partitions, the name of the attorney being inscribed in large capitals upon a projecting board. The vaults beneath the Exchange were let to different bankers; and the East India Company, for stowage of pepper. Surrounding the exterior were shops, chiefly tenanted by lottery-office keepers, newspaper-offices, watch and clock makers, notaries, stock-brokers, &c. The tower contained a clock, with four dials, and chimes, and four wind-dials.*

On Jan. 10th, 1838, this Exchange was entirely burnt: the fire commenced in Lloyd's Rooms shortly after 10 P.M., and before 3 next morning the clock-tower alone remained, the dials indicating the exact

* The chimes played at 3, 6, 9, and 12 o'clock—on Sunday, the 104th Psalm; Monday, "God save the King;" Tuesday, "Waterloo March;" Wednesday, "There's nae luck about the house;" Thursday, "See the conquering hero comes;" Friday, "Life let us cherish;" Saturday, "Foot-Guards' March."

time at which the flames reached them; north at 1h. 25m.; south, 2h. 5m.: the last air played by the chimes, at 12, was, "There's nae luck about the house." The conflagration was seen twenty-four miles round London; the roar of the winds, and the rush and crackling of the flames, the falling of huge timbers, and the crash of roofs and walls, were a fearful spectacle.

At the sale of the salvage, the porter's large hand-bell, rung daily before closing the 'Change, (with the handle burnt,) fetched 3*l.* 3*s.*; City Griffins, 30*l.* and 35*l.* the pair; busts of Queen Elizabeth, 10*l.* 15*s.* and 18*l.* the pair; figures of Europe, Asia, Africa, and America, 110*l.*; the statue of—Anne, 10*l.* 5*s.*; George II., 9*l.* 5*s.*; George III. and Elizabeth, 11*l.* 15*s.* each; Charles II., 9*l.*; and the sixteen other royal statues similar sums. The copper-gilt grasshopper vane was reserved.

After an interval of nearly four years, the rebuilding of the Exchange was commenced from the designs of William Tite, F.R.S.; the site being enlarged by the removal of Bank-buildings, west of the old Exchange, and the buildings eastward, nearly to Finch-lane. In excavating for the foundations was found a deep pit full of remains of Roman London, specimens of which are preserved in the Museum at Guildhall. (See CORNHILL, p. 234.) The foundation-stone of the new Exchange was laid by Prince Albert, on Monday, Jan. 17th, 1842, in the mayoralty of Alderman Pirie; the circumstances being recorded in a Latin and English inscription upon a zinc plate, placed in the foundation-stone. The Exchange was completed within the short space of three years, for somewhat less than the architect's estimate, 137,600*l.*; or, including the sculpture, architect's commission, &c., 150,000*l.*

The new Exchange was formally opened by Her Majesty Oct. 28, 1844, when the Royal and Civic Processions joined within Temple Bar; the Aldermen in gowns and chains, and the Lord-Mayor in a crimson velvet robe, collar, and jewel,—on horseback; his Lordship bearing immediately before the Queen's state-carriage the great pearl sword presented to the City of London by Queen Elizabeth on her opening the first Exchange. The procession of 1844 was altogether the most magnificent pageant of the present reign. At the Exchange, an address was presented to the Queen, followed by a breakfast, distribution of commemorative medals, and a procession to the centre of the quadrangle, where the Queen, surrounded by her Ministers and the City authorities, said: "It is my Royal will and pleasure that this building be hereafter called 'The Royal Exchange.'" The event was commemorated with great civic festivity; and the Lord Mayor, Magnay, received a patent of baronetcy.

The Royal Exchange first opened for business Jan. 1, 1845; stands nearly due east and west; extreme length, 308 feet; west width, 119 feet; east, 175 feet. The foundation is concrete, in parts 18 feet thick; and the walls and piers are tied together by arches, the piers strengthened by beds of wrought-iron hooping. The foundation of Gresham's Exchange was laid upon piles.

The architecture is florid, and even exuberant, characteristic of commercial opulence and civic state. The leading idea of the plan is from the Pantheon at Rome. The material is the finest Portland stone.

The West front has a portico " very superior in dimensions to any in Great Britain, and not inferior to any in the world." It is 96 feet wide and 74 high, and has eight columns (the architect's Composite), 4 feet 2 inches in diameter and 41 feet high, with two intercolumniations in actual projection, and the centre also deeply recessed; the interior of the portico is strikingly magnificent, in the vastness of the columns, and the beauty of the roof of three arches, enriched after a Roman palace. Flanking the central doorway are two lofty Venetian windows, with the architect's monogram, W. T., beneath.

On the frieze of the portico is inscribed: ANNO XIII. ELIZABETHÆ R. CONDITVM. ANNO VIII. VICTORIA R. RESTAVRATVM. Over the central doorway are the Royal arms, by Carew. The key-stone has the merchant's mark of Gresham; and the key-stones of the side arches, the arms of the merchant-adventurers of his day, and the staple of Calais. North and south of the portico, and in the attic, are the City sword and mace, with the date of Queen Elizabeth's reign and 1844; and in the lower panels, mantles bearing the initials of Queen Elizabeth and Queen Victoria respectively: the imperial crown is 12 inches in relief, and 7 feet high. The tympanum of the pediment of the portico is filled with sculpture, by Richard Westmacott, R.A.; consisting of 17 figures, carved in limestone, nearly all entire and detached. The centre figure is Commerce, with her mural crown, 10 feet high, upon two dolphins and a shell; she holds the charter of the Exchange: on her right is a group of three British merchants, as lord-mayor, alderman, and common-councilman; a Hindoo and a Mahommedan, a Greek bearing a jar, and a Turkish merchant: on the left are two British merchants and a Persian, a Chinese, a Levant sailor, a negro, a British sailor, and a super-cargo: the opposite angles are filled with anchors, jars, packages, &c. Upon the pedestal of Commerce, selected by Prince Albert, is this inscription: " THE EARTH IS THE LORD'S, AND THE FULNESS THEREOF."—Psalm xxiv. 1. The ascent to the portico is by 13 granite steps.

· The *East front* has four Composite columns, which support the tower, in the first story of which is a statue of Sir Thomas Gresham, 14 feet 6 inches high, by Behnes; above are the clock-faces; and next a circular story, with Composite columns and a dome carved in leaves, surmounted by the original grasshopper vane, of copper gilt, 11 feet long; height of tower and vane, 177 feet. Beneath the tower is the great eastern entrance to an oblong open area, where are the entrances to Lloyd's and the Merchants' Area.

The *Clock*, constructed by Dent, with the assistance of the Astronomer-Royal, is true to a second of time, and has a compensation-pendulum. The *Chimes* consist of a set of fifteen bells, by Mears, cost 500*l.*; the largest being also the hour-bell of the clock. In the chime-work, by Dent, there are two hammers to several of the bells, so as to play rapid passages; and three and five hammers strike different bells simultaneously. All irregularity of force is avoided by driving the chime-barrel through wheels and pinions; there are no wheels between the weight that pulls and the hammer to be raised; the lifts on the chime-barrel are all epicycloidal curves; and there are 6000 holes pierced upon the barrel for the lifts, so as to allow the tunes to be varied: the present airs are, "God save the Queen," " The Roast Beef of Old England," " Rule Britannia," and the 104th Psalm. The bells, in substance, form, dimensions, &c., are from the Bow-bells patterns; still, they are thought to be too large for the tower. The chime-work is stated to be the first instance in England of producing harmony in bells.

The *South front* has a line of pilasters, upon ground-floor rusticated arches; the three middle spaces deeply recessed, and having richly-embellished windows, a cornice, balustrade, and attic. Above the three centre arches are the Gresham, City, and Mercers' Company arms, which are repeated on the east front entablature.

The *North front* has a projecting centre, and otherwise differs from the south: in niches are statues of Sir Hugh Myddleton, by Joseph; and Sir Richard Whittington, by Carew. Over the centre arch is Gresham's motto, *Fortun à my ;* on the dexter, the City motto, *Dne. dirige nos ;* and on the sinister, the Mercers' Company, *Honor Deo.*

The *principal or first floor* has four suites of apartments : — 1. Lloyd's, east and north ; 2. Royal Exchange Assurance, west ; 3. London Assurance Corporation, south ; 4. Offices originally intended for Gresham College, south and west.

The *ground-floor*, externally, as in the two former Exchanges, is occupied by shops and offices, each having a mezzanine and basement.

The *Interior* consists of the open Merchants' Area, resembling the *cortile* of an Italian palace; its form, as that of the building, is parallelogram, and the inner area exactly a double square.*　The ground-

* It is singular that the opportunity has not been taken of covering in the Merchants' Area, every edifice of the kind erected within the last century being so covered : as, the Royal Exchange, Dublin; the Bourse at Paris; the Exchange at Hamburg; that at New York; and the Birzha, or Exchange, at St. Petersburg.·

floor is a Doric colonnade, and rusticated arches; the upper floor has Ionic columns, with arches and windows, and an enriched parapet, pierced. The key-stones of the upper arches are sculptured with national arms, in the order determined at the Congress of Vienna. The Ambulatory, or merchants' walk, surrounding the area, has its trabeated and paneled ceiling, richly decorated and emblazoned with national arms, in encaustic, Italian and arabesque, by Sang; but the humidity of the London atmosphere has sadly dimmed their brilliancy. In the four angles are the arms of Edward the Confessor, Edward III., Queen Elizabeth, and Charles II. At the north-east angle is a statue of Elizabeth, by Watson; at the south-east, Gibbons's marble statue of Charles II., formerly in the centre of the old Exchange; nearly upon the spot where is now a marble statue of Queen Victoria, by Lough: the sovereigns in whose reigns the three Exchanges were built.

In panels of the Ambulatory are emblazoned the arms of the three mayors (Pirie, Humphery, and Magnay), and of the three Masters of the Mercers' Company, in whose years of office the Exchange was erected. The arms of the Chairman of the Gresham Committee, Mr. R. L. Jones, and of the architect, Mr. Tite, complete the heraldic illustrations. The Yorkshire pavement of the Ambulatory is panelled and bordered with black stone, and squares of red granite at the intersections. The open area is paved with the traditional "Turkey stones" from the old Exchange, in patterns, with red granite bands.

On the side-wall panels are the names of the walks, inscribed upon chocolate tablets. In each of the larger compartments are the arms of the "walk" corresponding with the merchants'. As you enter the colonnade by the west, are the arms of the British empire, with those of Austria on the right, and Bavaria on the reverse side. Then in rotation are the arms of Belgium, France, Hanover, Holland, Prussia, Sardinia, the Two Sicilies, Sweden and Norway, the United States of America, the initials of the Sultan of Turkey, Spain, Saxony, Russia, Portugal, Hanseatic Towns, Greece, and Denmark. On a marble panel in the Merchants' Area are inscribed the dates of the building and opening of the three Exchanges.

"Here are the same old-favoured spots, changed though they be in appearance; and notwithstanding we have lost the great Rothschild, Jeremiah Harman, Daniel Hardcastle (the Page No. 1 of the *Times*), the younger Rothschilds occupy a pillar on the south side of the Exchange, much in the same place as their father; and the Barings, the Bateses, the Salomons, the Doxats, the Durrants, the Crawshays, the Curries, and the Wilsons, and other influential merchants, still come and go, as in olden days."—(*City*, 2d edit.). Many sea-captains and brokers still go on 'Change; but the "Walks" are disregarded. The hour of High 'Change is from ½ past 3 to ½ past 4 P.M., the two great days being Tuesday and Friday for foreign exchanges.

Lloyd's Subscription Rooms are approached by a fine Italian staircase; the stairs are each a single block of Cragleith granite, 14 feet long. In the vestibule is a marble statue of Prince Albert, by Lough; a marble statue, by Gibson, R.A., of the late Mr. Huskisson, presented by his widow; a mural testimonial to the *Times*' exposure of a fraudulent conspiracy in 1851; and a monument to John Lydekker, Esq., who bequeathed 58,000l. to the Seamen's Hospital Society: it has figures of disabled seamen, and a scene from the Southern Whale Fishery.

Lloyd's is the rendezvous of the most eminent merchants, shipowners, underwriters, insurance, stock, and exchange brokers, &c. Here is obtained the earliest news of the arrival and sailing of vessels, losses at sea, captures, re-captures, engagements, and other shipping intelligence; and the proprietors of ships and freights are insured by the underwriters.

Lloyd's originated with a coffee-house keeper of that name, at the corner of Abchurch-lane, Lombard-street:

> "To Lloyd's Coffee-house, he never fails
> To read the letters and attend the sales."—*Wealthy Shopkeeper*, 1700.

In 1710 Steele dates from Lloyd's (*Tatler*, No. 246) his Petition on

Coffee-house Orators and Newsvenders; and Addison, in *Spectator*, April 23, 1711, speaks of the auction-pulpit at Lloyd's: but the auction business has been transferred to Garraway's Coffee-house. Lloyd's was subsequently removed to Pope's Head-alley, and in 1774 to the north-west corner of the Royal Exchange, where it remained until the fire in 1838; the subscribers then met at the South-Sea House, till they returned to their present location in the new Exchange. The rooms are in the Venetian style, with Roman enrichments. They are—1. The Subscribers' or Underwriters', the Merchants', and the Captains' Room. *The Subscribers' Room* is 100 feet long by 48 feet wide, and is opened at 10 o'clock and closed at 5: annual subscription, four guineas; if an underwriter or insurance-broker, he pays also an entrance-fee of twenty-five guineas; admission and questions determined by ballot, each underwriter having his own seat. At the entrance of the room are exhibited the Shipping Lists, received from Lloyd's agents at home and abroad, and affording particulars of departures or arrivals of vessels, wrecks, salvage, or sale of property saved, &c. To the right and left are "Lloyd's Books," two enormous ledgers: right hand, ships "spoken with," or arrived at their destined ports; left hand, records of wrecks, fires, or severe collisions, written in a fine Roman hand, in "double lines." To assist the underwriters in their calculations, at the end of the room is an Anemometer, which registers the state of the wind day and night; attached is a rain-gauge.

On the roof of the Exchange is a sort of mast, at the top of which is a fan, like that of a windmill, the object of which is to keep a plate of metal with its face presented to the wind. Attached to this plate are springs, which, joined to a rod, descend into the Underwriters' Room upon a large sheet of paper placed against the wall. To this end of the rod a lead-pencil is attached, which slowly traverses the paper horizontally, by means of clock-work. When the wind blows very hard against the plate outside, the spring, being pressed, pushes down the rod, and the pencil makes a long line down the paper vertically, which denotes a high wind. At the bottom of the sheet, another pencil moves, guided by a vane on the outside, which so directs its course horizontally that the direction of the wind is shewn. The sheet of paper is divided into squares, numbered with the hours of night and day; and the clock-work so moves the pencils, that they take exactly an hour to traverse each square: hence the strength and direction of the wind at any hour of the twenty-four are easily seen.

The subscribers number about 1900; and, with the underwriters, represent the greater part of the mercantile wealth of the country. (See *City*, 2d edit. pp. 108 to 122.) Above the Subscribers' Room is the *Chart-room*, where hangs an extensive collection of maps and charts.

The Merchants' Room is superintended by a master, who can speak several languages: here are duplicate copies of the books in the underwriters' room, and files of English and foreign newspapers: annual subscription, two guineas.

The Captains' Room is a kind of coffee-room, where merchants and ship-owners meet captains, and sales of ships, &c. take place: annual subscription, one guinea.

The members of Lloyd's have ever been distinguished by their loyalty and benevolent spirit. In 1802, they voted 2000*l.* to the Life-boat subscription. On July 20, 1803, at the invasion panic, they commenced the Patriotic Fund with 20,000*l.* 3-per-cent. consols; besides 70,312*l.* 7*s.* individual subscriptions, and 15,000*l.* additional donations. After the battle of the Nile, in 1798, they collected for the widows and wounded seamen 32,423*l.*; and after Lord Howe's victory, June 1, 1794, for similar purposes, 21,281*l.* They have also contributed 5000*l.* to the London Hospital; 1000*l.* for the suffering inhabitants of Russia in 1813; 1000*l.* for the relief of the militia in our North American colonies, 1813; and 10,000*l.* for the Waterloo subscription, in 1815. The Committee vote medals and rewards to those who distinguish themselves in saving life from shipwreck.

Lloyd's Register of British and Foreign Shipping, No. 2 White-

Lion-court, Cornhill, was originally established in 1760, and re-established in 1834, and gives the class and standing of vessels, date of building and where built, materials, &c., ascertained by careful surveys; but is a distinct body from Lloyd's Subscription Rooms.

The entrance-gates in each front of the Exchange are fine specimens of iron-casting, bronzed. The western or principal gates, cast by Grissell, are 22½ feet high, 11 feet 4 inches wide. The design is Elizabethan: on the flanks, and around the semicircle, are the shields of the twelve great City companies; in the crown of the arch, Gresham's arms, and beneath is his bust, upon a mural crown, backed by the civic mace and sword; on the panels are the arms of Elizabeth and Victoria.

In the neighbourhood of the Exchange are the finest architectural objects in the City. Northward is the Bank of England, an elaborately-enriched pile, very picturesque in parts; and beyond it are the palatial edifices of the Alliance and Sun Insurance Offices. Westward is the Mansion House, in effect a massive Italian palace. Eastward is Royal Exchange-buildings, an enriched specimen of street-architecture. Before the Exchange portico is an equestrian statue of the Duke of Wellington (the last work modelled by Chantrey), placed here by the citizens in gratitude for the Government grant of 1,000,000l. for improvements in their ancient city. From this spot radiate Moorgate and Prince's-streets; the former with Italian *palazzo* offices, less showy but of far better architectural character than Regent-street; and King William-street, highly embellished, but more interesting as leading to London-bridge, which contests with another structure across the same stream the distinction of "the finest bridge in the world."

The cost of enlarging the site, including improvements and widening of Cornhill, Freeman's-court, Broad-street, and removal of the church of St. Benet Fink, the French Protestant church, Bank-buildings, Sweeting's-alley, &c., was 223,578l. 1s. 10d. — *City Chamberlain's Return,* October 30, 1851.

"Sir Thomas Gresham left the Exchange during the life of his widow to her use; and at her death, he left his mansion in Threadneedle-street, since occupied by the Excise Office, for a college, to be called Gresham College, as a London University, the funds for its support being provided by the rents of the shops and pawnes of the Exchange. By the Great Fire, this source of income was entirely cut off; and not only so, but the two Corporations of the City of London and the Mercers' Company incurred a debt of nearly 60,000l. in rebuilding the Exchange. They, notwithstanding, out of their own resources continued the College until the year 1745, when the debt amounted to 111,000l. In 1768, the College was put an end to by an Act of Parliament, and the site let to the Commissioners of Excise. The Gresham Professors were always continued, and gave their lectures in a room in the Exchange up to the fire of 1838. The Gresham Committee have, from their own funds, rebuilt Gresham College, in Gresham-street, at an expense of upwards of 15,000l.; and the debt incurred by the two Corporations, in maintaining the Exchange and rebuilding it twice, in maintaining the Gresham Professors, and some almshouses founded also by Sir Thomas Gresham, amounts now to considerably more than 200,000l."—*W. Tite, F.R.S.*

A large medal, by Wyon, R.A., bears on the obverse Lough's statue of the Queen in profile; on the reverse is a bust in high relief of Gresham, in the cap and starched frill of his period.

COAL EXCHANGE.—Three hundred years ago, when the use of coal instead of wood had only just commenced in the metropolis, two or three ships were enough for the supply. A charter of Edward II. shews Derbyshire coal to have been then used in London, though a proclamation of Edward I. shews its introduction as a substitute for wood to have been much opposed; and in the reign of Elizabeth, the burning of stone-coal was prohibited during the sitting of Parliament, lest it should affect the health of the members.

The "Coal Exchange," up to 1807, was in the hands of private individuals; in that year it was purchased by the Corporation for 25,600l. In 1845, the coal-trade petitioned for the enlargement and rebuilding of the Exchange. This was done by the City architect, J. B. Bunning; and the new Exchange was opened with great *éclat*, by Prince Albert, accompanied by the Prince of Wales and the Princess Royal, Oct. 29, 1849; when the Lord Mayor (Duke), himself a coal-merchant, received a patent of baronetcy. The Exchange has two principal fronts of Portland stone, in the Italian style,—one in Lower Thames-street, and the other in St. Mary-at-Hill; with an entrance at the corner by a semi-circular portico, with Roman-Doric columns, and a tower 106 feet high, within which is the principal staircase. The public hall, or area for the merchants, is a rotunda 60 feet in diameter, covered by a glazed dome, 74 feet from the floor. This circular hall has three tiers of projecting galleries running round it; the stancheons, galleries, ribs of dome, &c. are iron, of which about 300 tons are used.

The floor of the rotunda is composed of 4000 pieces of inlaid woods, in the form of a mariner's compass, within a border of Greek fret; in the centre is the City shield, anchor, &c.; the dagger-blade in the arms being a piece of a mulberry-tree planted by Peter the Great, when he worked as a shipwright in Deptford dockyard.

The entrance vestibule is richly embellished with vases of fruit, arabesque foliage, terminal figures, &c. In the rotunda, between the Raphaelesque scroll supports, are panels painted with impersonations of the coal-bearing rivers of England: the Thames, Mersey, Severn, Trent, Humber, Aire, Tyne, &c.; and above them, within flower-borders, are figures of Wisdom, Fortitude, Vigilance, Temperance, Perseverance, Watchfulness, Justice, and Faith. The arabesques in the first story are views of coal-mines: Wallsend, Percy Pit-Main, Regent's Pit, &c. The second and third story panels are painted with miners at work: and the twenty-four ovals at the springing of the dome have upon a turquoise blue ground figures of fossil plants found in coal-formations. The minor ornamentation is flowers, shells, snakes, lizards, and other reptiles, and nautical subjects. The whole is in polychrome, by Sang. The gallery-fronts and other iron-work are cable pattern. The cost of the enlarged site, the building, and approaches, was 91,167*l.* 11*s.* 8*d.*

In a basement on the east side of the Exchange are the remains of a Roman bath, in excellent preservation, discovered in excavating the foundations of the new building; and there is a convenient access to this interesting relic of Roman London.

About the year 1550 one or two ships sufficed for the coal-trade of London; in 1615, about 200; in 1705, about 600; and in 1845, 2695 ships. The increase in the importation during ten years, from 1838 to 1848,—when the respective importations were 2,518,085 tons and 3,418,340 tons,—was upwards of 90 per cent. Now, by taking 2700 vessels as the actual number employed, each averaging 300 tons burden, and giving to a vessel of that size a crew of eight men, it will appear that 21,600 seamen were then employed in the carrying department of the London coal-trade.

The price of coals as given in the London markets in the daily newspapers is, the price up to the time when the coals are *whipped* from the ship to the merchant's barges. It includes: 1st, the value of the coals at the pit's mouth; 2d, the expense of transit from the pit to the ship; 3d, the freight of the ship to London; 4th, the Thames dues; and 5th, the whipping. The emptied coal-ships are ballasted to Newcastle with gravel or sand dredged up from Woolwich Reach; so that to say this is carrying the bed of the Thames to the banks of the Tyne has a per-centage of truth in it.

About 12,000 persons are engaged in mining and shipping coals for London; 22,000 in navigating the coal-ships from the North to the Thames; 2000 in whipping; and 1000 in selling the coals to the consumers in London; besides coal-bargemen upon the Thames and canals, coal-heavers at the wharfs, and coal-wagoners in the streets. The carriage of coals by railway is already very considerable.

CORN EXCHANGE (the), Mark-lane, was established in 1747, when the present system of factorage commenced. It consists of an open Doric colonnade, within which the factors have their stands; it resembles the *atrium*, or place of audience, in a Pompeian house; with its *impluvium*, the place in the centre in which the rain fell. (*W. H. Leeds*.) In 1827-8, adjoining was built a second Corn Exchange (G. Smith, architect): it has a central Grecian-Doric portico, surmounted by the imperial arms and agricultural emblems; the ends have corresponding pilasters. Here lightermen and granary-keepers have stands, as well as corn-merchants, factors, and millers; the seed-market is in another part of the building.

"This is the only metropolitan market for corn, grain, and seeds. The market-days are Monday, Wednesday, and Friday; hours, ten to three. Wheat is paid for in bills at one month, and other corn and grain in bills at two months. The Kentish "hoymen," distinguishable by their sailor's jackets, have stands free of expense, and pay less for metage and dues than others; and the Essex dealers enjoy some privileges: in both cases said to be in consideration of the men of Kent and Essex having continued to supply the city when it was ravaged by the Plague."—Knight's *London*, vol. iii. p. 365.

KING'S EXCHANGE (the), "for the receipt of bullion to be coined," was in Old Exchange, now Old 'Change, Cheapside.

"It was here that one of those ancient officers, known as the King's Ex-changer, was placed; whose duty it was to attend to the supply of the Mints with bullion, to distribute the new coinage, and to regulate the exchange of foreign coin. Of these officers there were anciently three: two in London, at the Tower and Old Exchange, and one in the city of Canterbury. Subsequently, another was appointed with an establishment in Lombard-street, the ancient rendezvous of the merchants; and it appears not improbable that Queen Eliza-beth's intention was to have removed this functionary to what was pre-eminently designated by her 'the Royal Exchange,' and hence the reason for the change of the name of this edifice by Elizabeth."—*W. Tite, F.R.S.*

No. 36 Old 'Change was formerly the "Three Morrice-Dancers" public-house, with the three figures sculptured on a stone as the sign and an ornament, *temp.* James I.: the house was taken down about 1801: there is an etching of this very characteristic sign-stone.

NEW EXCHANGE, on the south side of the Strand, was built by the Earl of Salisbury on the site of the stables of Durham House, and was opened by James I. and his queen, who named it "the Bursse of Bri-tain." It was erected partly on the plan of the Royal Exchange, with vaults beneath, over which was an open paved arcade; and above were walks of shops occupied by perfumers and publishers, milliners and sempstresses:

"The sempstress speeds to 'Change with red-tipt nose."—*Trivia*, b. ii. l. 337.

When, at the Restoration, Covent Garden rose to be a fashionable quarter, the New Exchange became very popular. It is a favourite scene with the dramatists of the reign of Charles II., and was the great resort of the gallants of that day.

At the "Three Spanish Gipsies," in the New Exchange, lived Anne Clarges, married to Thomas Ratford, who there sold wash-balls, powder, gloves, &c., and she taught girls plain work. Anne became sempstress to Colonel Monk, and used to carry him linen : "she was a woman," says Lord Clarendon, "of the lowest extraction, without either wit or beauty ;" but who contrived to captivate Monk, "old George," and was married to him at St. George's Church, Southwark, in 1652, it is believed while her first husband was living. "She became the laughing-stock of the court, and gave general disgust." (*Pepys,* iii. 75.) She died Duchess of Albemarle, leaving a son, Christopher, who succeeded to the dukedom; he is said to have been "suckled by Honour Mills, who sold apples, herbs, oysters, &c."

At the Revolution, in 1688, there sat in the New Exchange, as a sempstress, Frances Jennings, the reduced Duchess of Tyrconnel, wife to Richard Talbot, lord-deputy of Ireland under James II.: she supported herself for a few days (till she was known, and otherwise provided for) by the little trade of this place: to avoid detection, she sat in a white mask and a white dress, and was therefore known as "the white widow."*

Another romantic story is told of the place. In November 1653, a quarrel having arisen in the public walk of the Exchange between M. Gerard (at that time engaged in a plot against Cromwell) and Don Pantaleon Sa (brother to the Portuguese ambassador), the latter next day came to the Exchange, accompanied by assassins, who mistaking another person, then walking with his brother and mistress, for M. Gerard, seized upon him, and stabbed him to death with their poniards. For this crime Don Pantaleon was condemned to death; and, by a strange coincidence, he suffered on the same scaffold with M. Gerard, whose plot had been discovered.

The Exchange latterly became famous for its exhibitions of waxwork, and for a magnificent stock of English and foreign china kept for sale; but by the intrigues, assignations, and indecent licenses of the fops with the milliners, the place lost its character, was little resorted to after the death of Queen Anne, and in 1737 was taken down, and the site covered with houses; but the name is retained in Exchange-court opposite.

In the Strand, exactly opposite Ivy Bridge, (a short distance east of the New Exchange site,) Thomas Parr, the "olde olde man," had lodgings, when he came to London to be shewn as a curiosity to Charles I. The authority for this fact is a Mr. Greening, who in the year 1814, being then about 90 years of age, mentioned it to the author, saying that he perfectly well remembered, when a boy, having been shewn the house by his grandfather, then 88 years of age. The house, which stood at the commencement of the present century, had been known for more than 50 years as the "Queen's Head" public-house.—Smith's *Streets of London*, edit. 1849, p. 145.

STOCK EXCHANGE, the heart of "the Bank for the whole world" (*Rothschild*), is in Capel-court, Bartholomew-lane, facing the eastern front of the Bank of England. It has four entrances: from Capel-court; Shorter's-court and New-court, Throgmorton-street; and Hercules-court, Broad-street. The speculators in stock, who greatly increased with the National Debt, hitherto met at Jonathan's Coffee-house, Change-alley; then at a room in Threadneedle-street, admission 6*d.*; and bargains in stocks were next made in the Bank rotunda. In 1801, the present building was commenced by subscription (James Peacock, architect), in Capel-court, the site of the offices and residence of Sir William Capel, lord mayor in 1504. The inscription placed beneath the foundation-stone states, "at this era the public funded debt had accumulated in five successive reigns to £552,730,924;" adding propitiatorily, "the inviolate faith of the British nation, and the principles of the constitution, sanction and secure the property embarked in this undertaking. May the blessing of that constitution be secured to the latest posterity!" The building was opened March 1802; and in 1822 the business in the foreign funds was removed here from the Royal Exchange.

The number of members (stock-brokers, bullion, bill and discount, railway and other share brokers,) has varied from 1000 to 400; annual subscription, 10*l.* There are three branches, or houses: the English, for stocks and Exchequer-bills; the foreign, for stocks; and the railway or share market, a market for mining shares being added in 1850. In New-court are fireproof safes for

---

* This anecdote was ingeniously dramatised by Mr. Douglas Jerrold, and produced at Covent Garden Theatre, in 1840, as "The White Milliner."

keeping securities. Lists are daily published of the prices of stocks and shares, and twice a-week of bullion and foreign exchanges. The admission is by ballot, as is also the election of the Stock-Exchange Committee of 28, who have absolute power to expel, suspend, or reprimand. Every new member of the "House" must be introduced by three members, each giving 300*l.* security for two years. Each member, as well as the Committee, has to meet the probation of re-election every Lady-day. A bankrupt ceases to be a member, and cannot be re-admitted unless he pays 6*s.* 8*d.* in the pound beyond that collected from his debtors. The names of defaulters are posted on the "black board," and they are termed "lame ducks;" this rule was established in 1787, when twenty-five "lame ducks waddled out of the Alley." To avoid a libel, the notice runs thus: "Any person transacting business with A. B. is requested to communicate with C. D." Only members are allowed to transact business at the Stock Exchange, as notified at each entrance; and strangers who stray in are quickly hustled out: but a view of the Exchange can be obtained through the glass-doors in the entrance from Hercules-court. The brokers usually deal with the jobbers; and among the Exchange cries are, "Borrow money?" "What are Exchequer?" "Five with me," "Ten with me," making up a strange Babel. "A thousand pounds' consols at 96¾-96½:" ("Take 'em at 96½," is the vociferous reply of a buyer:) "Mexican at 27½-27; Portuguese fours at 32⅝-32½; Spanish fives at 21; Dutch two-and-halfs at 50½-50¼:" and so on till the hour for closing strikes. Railway companies and bankers often lend large sums, and bankers are sometimes borrowers, as are also the Bank of England and the East India Company. The charge by a broker for buying and selling English stock is 2*s.* 6*d.* per cent. The fluctuations in the rate of interest enjoin "watching the turn of the market;" for, on the same day, money has been lent at 4 per cent in the morning, and at 2 o'clock could scarcely be borrowed at 10 per cent.

The Stock Exchange has had its vocabulary of terms for more than a century—traceable to the early transactions in the stock of the East India Company.

A *Bull* is one who speculates for a rise; whereas a *Bear* is he who speculates for a fall. The *Bull* would, for instance, buy 100,000*l.* consols for the account, with the object of selling them again during the intervening time at a higher price. The *Bear*, on the contrary, would sell the 100,000*l.* stock (which, however, he does not possess,) for the same time, with the view of buying them in and balancing the transaction at a lower price than that at which he originally sold them. If Consols fall, the *Bull* finds himself on the wrong side of the hedge; and if they rise, the poor *Bear* is compelled to buy in his stock at a sacrifice.—*The City*, 2d edit.

Lord Chatham designated stock-jobbers "the cannibals of Change-alley." "To me, my lords," he once said, "whether they be miserable jobbers of Change-alley or the lofty Asiatic plunderers of Leadenhall-street, they are equally detestable."

The Stock Exchange has many startling episodes of fraud and panic, rise and ruin. Speculation often produces permanent benefit to the public: to the fever of 1807 and 1808, London owes Vauxhall and Waterloo Bridges. Late in Napoleon's career the funds varied 8 and 10 per cent within an hour; but the immediate effect of the battle of Waterloo news on the funds was only 3 per cent: the decrease of the public expenditure was two millions per month. At the panic of 1825, which more affected the public funds than did the news of Napoleon's escape from Elba, the entrance to the Stock Exchange became so choked up, that a fine of 5*l.* was imposed upon each person who stopped the way. Pigeon-expresses for the earliest intelligence are chiefly worked from May to September; the birds generally used are of the Antwerp breed, strong on the wing, and fully feathered: they are, however, likely to be superseded by the electric telegraph. Exchequer-bills let in fraud the year after their creation. The last fraud in Exchequer-bills was that committed by Beaumont Smith, chief clerk in the Audit Office, and the victim of Rapallo, an Italian jobber; and it was stated on the trial of Smith at the Old Bailey, that Rapallo provided the funds for the

Boulogne expedition of Prince Louis Napoleon against the government of Louis Philippe!

Political hoaxes, from the reported death of Queen Anne to the fraud of 1814, in which Lord Cochrane was implicated, chequer the Stock-Exchange chronicles; and victims flit about its gates—from the Goldsmids whose credit was whispered away by envy, to the poor Miss Whitehead, whose wits were turned to melancholy by the forgeries of her brother. The recollection of large loans raised here reminds one of the mighty power which reigns supreme on this very spot, once the most opulent part of Roman London.

"The warlike power of every country depends on their Three-per-Cents. If Cæsar were to re-appear on earth, Wettenhall's List would be more important than his Commentaries; Rothschild would open and shut the Temple of Janus; Thomas Baring, or Bates, would probably command the Tenth Legion; and the soldiers would march to battle with loud cries of 'Scrip and Omnium reduced!' 'Consols and Cæsar!'"—*Rev. Sydney Smith.*

The most remarkable man among the Stockbrokers of our time was the late Mr. Francis Baily, F.R.S., the astronomer, who retired from the Stock-Exchange, in 1825. In 1838, in the garden of his house, Tavistock-place, Russell-square, constructed a small observatory, wherein Mr. Baily repeated the "Cavendish experiment," the government having granted 500*l.* towards the expense of the apparatus, &c. This is the building in which the earth was weighed, and its bulk and figure calculated; the standard measure of the British nation perpetuated, and the pendulum experiments rescued from their chief source of inaccuracy. Mr. Baily died President of the Astronomical Society in 1844.

EXCHEQUER-TALLIES.

The Receipt of Exchequer at Westminster, the most ancient revenue department of the State, with all its antiquated machinery of tallies and checks, was not abolished until the year 1834; when a new office for the payment of pensions and public moneys, and the receipt of revenue, was opened at the Bank of England. By the statute of 23 Geo. III. cap. 82, however, indented check receipts were issued from the Tally Court instead of tallies, which, as instruments of loan, declined with the growth of Exchequer Bills. In the accompanying woodcut is shewn

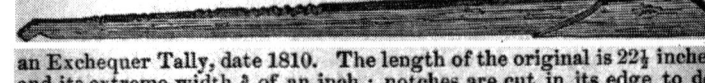

an Exchequer Tally, date 1810. The length of the original is 22½ inches, and its extreme width ⅞ of an inch : notches are cut in its edge to denote the reckoning, and from the cross-line in the lower part has been stripped off the counter-tally, cutting the date-line of the transaction written on the edge; so that identity consisted not only in the wood fitting, but in the halved date and notches corresponding, like a halved bank-note. The specimen before us is of elm, and roughly cleft.

> "From his rug the skew'r he takes,
> And on the stick ten equal notches makes;
> With just resentment flings it on the ground,
> There, take my *tally* of ten thousand pound."—*Swift.*

As one of the Exchequer apartments at Westminster was filled with the old tallies in 1834, it became advisable to destroy them; and an order was issued from the Board of Works to burn these ancient relics, although persons curious in such matters would have purchased bundles of them for museums and collections. The tallies were, accordingly, burnt in the principal stove of the House of Lords; and to the consequent overheating of the flues proceeding in every direction from the stove through the wood-work of the House, on October 16, 1834, nearly the whole of both Houses of Parliament was consumed by fire.

Pepys, in assembling his worldly wealth at the alarm at the Great Fire of

1666, got ready to carry away his bags of gold, his chief papers of accounts, and put his "*tallies* into a box by themselves."

"Under the early loan acts, tallies were delivered to the first contractors. When a sale was effected, the name of the purchaser was indorsed on the tally, and then entered into the government books, for the convenience of paying the dividends to the right person. This clumsy machinery was afterwards abolished; but though in 1717 the transfers and dividends of the National Debt were first undertaken by the Bank, it was not until 1783 that the present mode of transfer was adopted."—*Francis's Chronicles and Characters of the Stock Exchange*, p. 148.

EXETER HALL,

No. 372, on the north side of the Strand, a large proprietary establishment, was commenced in 1829 (Gandy Deering, architect), and was originally intended for religious and charitable Societies, and their meetings. It has a narrow frontage in the Strand, but the premises extend in the rear nearly from Burleigh-street to Exeter-street. The Strand entrance is Græco-Corinthian, and has two columns and pilasters, and the word ΦΙΛΑΔΕΛΦΟΝ (Loving Brothers) sculptured in the attic. A double staircase leads to the Great Hall, beneath which are a smaller one, and passages leading to the offices of several Societies.

The Great Hall, opened in 1831, is now used for the " May Meetings" of religious societies, and for the Sacred Harmonic Society's and other concerts. This Hall has been twice enlarged, is now 131 ft. 6 in. long, 76 ft. 9 in. wide, and 45 ft. high, and will accommodate upwards of 3000 persons. At the east end is an organ and orchestra, the property of the Sacred Harmonic Society; at the west end is a large gallery, extending partly along the sides; and on the floor are seats rising in part amphitheatrically; and a platform for the speakers, with a large carved chair.

In 1850 the area of the hall was lengthened nearly forty feet; the flat-panelled ceiling was also removed, and a coved one inserted, without disturbing the slating in the roof: S. W. Daukes, architect. To the principals were attached wrought-iron girders, circular on the under side, composed of plates of boiler-iron, with angle-irons and stiffners, and strips to cover the joints. These girders were raised into the roof in pieces, and supported from the tie-beams till they were fastened together with 2500 red-hot rivets, a furnace being erected in the roof. Each girder was weighted with seven tons, and thus bolted to the timber principal. The ends of the girders were supported upon sliding plates of smooth and greased iron affixed to the wall-plate, so as to allow of the spread corresponding to the deflection (1½ inch) of the arched iron, without affecting the walls: the extent of the spread being 1½ inch at each end. There are two stronger independent iron girders weighing about nine tons each, and nine smaller ones, all properly tested. The whole of the iron-work being fixed, the original tie-beams and other timbers (which had been used as scaffolding for the furnace and riveters) were cut away to the edge of the curved iron girders, and the ceiling joists and boarding were then attached to the iron flanges. Nearly eighty tons of iron have been introduced into the roof, which, with the new ceiling, is one-third less weight than the original roof.

The ceiling has gained 15 feet in height at the ends, and 12 feet in the centre; and the sound and ventilation are much improved. The *Orchestra* is on the acoustic principle successfully adopted by Mr. Costa at the Philharmonic Society; it is 76 feet wide, 11 feet more than the Birmingham Town-Hall. Every member has a view of the conductor; the organ-player sees his *baton* in a glass, among the phalanx of instrumentalists—16 double-basses, 16 violoncellos, 82 first and second violins and violas, besides the wood and brass bands and colossal drums. The band and choir number 800. The works of Handel, Haydn, and Mozart are here given with mighty effect; and Spohr and Mendelssohn have here conducted their own productions.

The *Organ*, built by Walker in 1840, is 30 feet wide and 40 feet high: it has 2187 pipes; the longest are 20 feet from the base, diameter 15 inches, weight of each 4 cwt.; in gilding one-half of each pipe 750 leaves of gold were used: there are three rows of keys, and two octaves of pedals.

From April to the end of May, various societies hold their anniversary meetings at Exeter Hall. The smaller hall holds about 1000 persons, and a third hall 250. Haydon has painted the Meeting of Anti-Slavery Delegates in the Great Hall, June 12, 1840, under the presidency of the venerable Thomas Clarkson, then in his 81st year. On June 1, 1840, Prince Albert presided in the Great Hall at the first public meeting of the Society for the Extinction of the Slave Trade, the Prince's first appearance at any public meeting in England.

Exeter Hall, with its various religious and benevolent aggregations, is one field with many encampments of distinct tribes. "Wesleyan, Church, Baptist missionary societies, all maintain a certain degree of reserve towards each other, all are jealous of the claims of rival sects, and yet all are attracted by a common sense of religious earnestness. The independent and often mutually repelling bodies who congregate in Exeter Hall are one in spirit, with all their differences. Without a pervading organisation, they are a church."—*Spectator newspaper.*

Mr. Hullah's system of popular singing was formerly illustrated here, when 2000 pupils combined their voices in the performances. The Great Hall is let for 30*l.* per night, lighting included. The rental in the year ending April 1849 was 4181*l.*

EXETER HOUSE AND EXETER 'CHANGE.

Exeter 'Change is now only kept in remembrance by a clock-dial, inscribed with its name in place of figures, upon the attic-front of the house No. 353, eastward of the 'Change site, on the north side of the Strand. Here was formerly the parsonage-house of the parish of St. Martin, with a garden, and a close for the parson's horse; till Sir Thomas Palmer (*temp.* Edward VI.) obtained it by composition, and began to build here "a magnificent house of brick and timber" (*Stow*). But upon his attainder for high treason (1 Queen Mary), the property reverted to the Crown, and so remained until Queen Elizabeth presented it to Sir William Cecil, lord treasurer, and the great Lord Burleigh (properly Burghley), who completed the mansion, with four square turrets; whence it was called Cecil House and Burleigh House, and afterwards Exeter House, from the son of the great statesman Thomas Cecil, Earl of Exeter. The mansion fronted the Strand, and extended from the garden-wall of Wimbledon House (on the site of D'Oyley's warehouse) to a green lane, the site of the present Southampton-street, westward. Queen Elizabeth visited Lord Burleigh at Exeter House; and here his obsequies were celebrated by a lying-in-state.[*] In the chapel attached, the pious John Evelyn, on Christmas-day 1657, was seized by the soldiers of the Commonwealth for having observed "the superstitious time of the Nativity," and was temporarily shut up in Exeter House. Here lived the first Earl of Shaftesbury, and here was born his grandson, who wrote the *Characteristics.* After the Great Fire of 1666, the courts of Doctors' Commons were held in Exeter House until 1672.

EXETER CHANGE was built as a sort of bazaar, by Dr. Barbon, a speculator in houses, *temp.* William and Mary, when Exeter House was taken down; and probably some of the old materials were used

---

[*] Burghley died at Theobalds, Aug. 4, 1598, where the body lay. Hentzner, however, states that when he called to see Theobalds at Cheshunt, there was "nobody to shew the palace, as the family was in town attending the funeral of their lord."

for the 'Change, including a pair of large Corinthian columns at the eastern end. (See a View, by G. Cooke.) About the same time, Exeter-street was erected. The 'Change extended from the house No. 352 to the site of the present Burleigh-street: it projected into the Strand, the northern foot-thoroughfare of which lay through the shops or stands of the lower floor, first occupied by sempsters, milliners, hosiers, &c.

The body of the poet Gay lay in state in an upper room of the 'Change: here, too, were upholsterers' shops, the offices of Law's Land Bank, auction-rooms, &c. Cutlery then became the merchandise of the lower floor, where one Clark, a cutler, accumulated a vast fortune.

Thomas Clark, "the King of Exeter 'Change," took a stall here in 1765 with 100*l.* lent him by a stranger. By parsimony and trade he grew so rich, that he once returned his income at 6000*l.* a year; and long before his death, in 1816, he had rented the whole ground-floor of the 'Change. He left nearly half a million of money, and one of his daughters married Mr. Hamlet, the celebrated jeweller.

The upper rooms of Exeter 'Change were occupied as a menagerie successively by Pidcock, Polito, and Cross; admission to Pidcock's, in 1810, 2*s.* 6*d.* The roar of the lions and tigers could be distinctly heard in the street, and often frightened horses in the roadway. During Cross's tenancy, in 1826, Chunee, the stupendous elephant shewn here since 1809, in an oak den which cost 350*l.*, was shot, and his skin sold for 50*l.*; his skeleton, sold for 100*l.*, is now at the College of Surgeons. (See MUSEUMS.) Cross's menagerie was removed in 1828 to the King's Mews, Charing-cross; and Exeter 'Change was entirely taken down in 1829.

EXCISE OFFICE (THE),

Old Broad-street, (Dance, sen., architect), occupies the site of Gresham College, which the Gresham Trustees sold, in 1768, to the Crown for a perpetual rent of 500*l.* per annum; when 18,000*l.* was also paid out of the Gresham fund to the Commissioners towards pulling down the College, and building an Excise Office! (*Burgon.*) The business was removed in 1848 to the Inland Revenue Office, Somerset House. In the court-yard of the Broad-street Excise Office, a temporary Exchange was put up for the merchants in 1838; and was used during the rebuilding of the Royal Exchange. (See GRESHAM COLLEGE, p. 209.)

The Excise system was established by the Long Parliament, in 1643, to raise funds for the war against the King! The Commissioners first sat in Haberdashers' Hall, and then at their office in Smithfield, which was taken down in 1647, the mob carrying off the materials in triumph. In 1680, the office was at Cockaigne House, formerly the mansion of Eliab, the brother of Dr. William Harvey, the discoverer of the Circulation of the Blood. Thence the Excise Office was removed to Sir John Frederick's mansion, on the site of Frederick's-place, Old Jewry; and then to Broad-street.

FASHIONS, OLD, IN DRESS.

The mutability of dress is proverbial; but Old Fashions are retained among Londoners to a far greater extent than one would at first imagine. Thus, "the whole dress of the boys of Christ's Hospital is the costume of the citizens of London at the time of the foundation of that charity by Edward VI. Blue coats were the common habit of apprentices and serving-men, and yellow stockings were very generally worn at this period. The jackets of our firemen and watermen are also of this date; the badge being made in metal and placed on the sleeve in the sixteenth century, instead of embroidered on the breast or back of the garment itself as previously."—Planché's *History of British Costume*, p. 252.

The Yeomen of the Guard, royal beef-eaters (*buffetiers*), wear the dress of private soldiers of the time of Henry VII., with some variation; but it has continued unaltered since at least the reign of Charles II., in the scarlet embroidered tunic, the red stockings, the parti-coloured shoe-bows, the stiff white ruff; and the black velvet cap with its circlet of red, blue, and white ribbon knots.

"The London charity-school girls wear the plain mob-cap and long gloves of the time of Queen Anne. In the brass badge of the cab and omnibus men we see a retention of the dress of the Elizabethan retainers; while the shoulder-knots that once decked an officer now adorn a footman. He alone carries the cane which was borne by ladies and physicians in our time. (Several canes are preserved in the College of Physicians, in Pall-Mall East; and one of the last who bore a gold-headed cane was the late Dr. Baillie.) The sailors' dress of the era of William III. is now seen amongst our fishermen. The University dress is as old as the age of the Smithfield martyrs. The linen bands of the pulpit and the bar are abridgments of the falling collar. The butchers' blue is a guild uniform."—*Notes and Queries*, No. 82.

Wilkes wore a flap-waistcoat of scarlet and gold; and Murphy, the dramatist, a good deal later, a suit of the like fashion, and a large cocked hat. The fashion of scarlet coat, flap-waistcoat, and frilled sleeves, survived into this century. The last man in London who is believed to have worn this costume was a quack-doctor, who lived in a corner-house of Salisbury-square, and who might be seen any day pacing the pavement in front of his establishment, until he took to his bed and died of extreme old age. Mr. Pitt usually wore a blue coat, buckskin breeches, and boots, round hat, with powder and pig-tail. Mr. Fox had been a beau in his youth, but lived to be Quaker-like as to dress, with plain coloured clothes, a broad round hat, and white stockings.

What will not fashion do to gratify her ever-changing conceits? she has even ransacked the tombs for a "new pattern," in the starched frill and flounce of the *shroud*, known as *pinking*: this has been sold to our belles by the furnishing undertakers of the metropolis, whose trade thus lay almost as much among the living as the dead.

The Dandy belongs to our times. The reigns of Queen Anne and the two Georges could furnish no type of him; he was unknown to Addison, Fielding, Smollett, Hogarth; unless we date him from Colly Cibber's Lord Foppington, reproduced by Sheridan.

Plant Badges.—In London, the Welsh (but chiefly the members of clubs) wear leeks on St. David's day (March 1), from the leek being assumed as a badge after the battle of Bosworth-field, won by Henry VII, who had many Welshmen, his countrymen, in his army. The Irish wear the shamrock on St. Patrick's day (March 17), in honour of that saint, who is said to have advocated the Trinity by plucking a leaf of the plant, and shewing it to contain three in one. The statue of Charles I. is no longer dressed with oak-branches on Restoration-day (May 29); but the tomb of the Pendrells in St. Giles's churchyard is so decorated on this day, the custom having been revived in 1835. Laurel is worn by the Foot-Guards on the 18th of June, in memory of Waterloo.

FETTER-LANE,

Fleet-street, eastward of St. Dunstan's Church, extending to Holborn Hill, "is so called of fewters (or idle people) lying there, as in a way leading to gardens" (*Stow*); but when he wrote "it was built through on both sides with many fair houses.", Here lived the leatherseller of the Revolution, "Praise God Barebones," and his brother, "Damned Barebones," both in the same house. In No. 16, over Fleur-de-lis court, Dryden is said to have lived; but not by his biographers. At the right-hand corner of Fleur-de-lis court, the infamous Mrs. Brownrigg murdered her apprentice in 1767; the cellar-grating, whence the poor child's cries issued, is on the side of the court. On the Rolls estate, nearly opposite, was commenced a new Record Office, by Pennethorne, in 1851. No. 32 Fetter-lane is the entrance to the Moravian Chapel, which was attacked and dismantled in the Sacheverel riots. (See DIS-SENTERS' CHAPELS, p. 174.) The Fleet-street and Holborn ends of Fetter-lane were formerly places of execution: strange labyrinths of courts and alleys lie between Chancery, Fetter, and Shoe lanes, which, in the reign of Queen Elizabeth, intersected gardens and straggling cottages. This district was the principal part of Saxon London, and was nearly all burnt A.D. 982, when the City had "most buildings from Ludgate towards Westminster, and little or none where the heart of the City now is; except in divers places was housing that stood without order." (*Stow*.)

The White Horse Inn, Fetter-lane, was formerly the great Oxford house: here Lord Eldon, when he left school and came to London, in 1776, met his brother, Lord Stowell. "He took me," says Lord Eldon, "to see the play at Drury-lane. Love played *Jobson* in the farce; and Miss Pope played *Nell*. When we came out of the house it rained hard. There were then few hackney-coaches, and we both got into one sedan-chair. Turning out of Fleet-street into Fetter-lane, there was a sort of contest between our chairman and some persons who were coming up Fleet-street, whether they should first pass Fleet-street, or we in our chair first get out of Fleet-street into Fetter-lane. In the struggle, the sedan-chair was overset, with us in it."—Lord Eldon's *Anecdote-Book*.

FIELD OF FORTY FOOTSTEPS.

The fields behind Montague House, Bloomsbury, appear to have been originally called Long Fields; and afterwards (about Strype's time) Southampton Fields. On St. John Baptist's Day, 1694, Aubrey saw at midnight twenty-three young women in the pasture behind Montague House looking for a coal, under the root of a plantain, to put under their heads that night, and they should dream who would be their husbands. The fields were the resort of depraved wretches, chiefly for fighting pitched battles, especially on the Sabbath-day: such was the state of the place up to 1800.

A legendary story of the period of the Duke of Monmouth's Rebellion relates a mortal conflict here between two brothers, on account of a lady, who sat by; the combatants fought so ferociously as to destroy each other; after which, their footsteps, imprinted on the ground in the vengeful struggle, were said to remain, with the indentations produced by their advancing and receding; nor would any grass or vegetation ever grow over these *forty footsteps*. Miss Porter and her sister, upon this fiction, founded their ingenious romance, *Coming Out, or the Field of Forty Footsteps;* but they entirely depart from the local tradition. At the Tottenham-street Theatre was produced, many years since, an effective melodrama, founded upon the same incident, entitled the *Field of Forty Footsteps*.

Southey records this strange story in his *Commonplace Book* (second Series, p. 21). After quoting a letter from a friend, recommending him to "take a view of those wonderful marks of the Lord's hatred to *duelling*, called *The Brothers' Steps*," and describing the locality, Southey thus narrates his own visit to the spot: "We sought for near half an hour in vain. We could find no steps at all within a quarter of a mile, no, nor half a mile, of Montague House. We were almost out of hope, when an honest man, who was at work, directed us to the next ground, adjoining to a pond. There we found what we sought, about three quarters of a mile north of Montague House, and 500 yards east of Tottenham-Court-road. The steps are of the size of a large human foot, about three inches deep, and lie nearly from north-east to south-west. We counted only seventy-six; but we were not exact in counting. The place where one or both the brothers are supposed to have fallen, is still bare of grass. The labourer also shewed us the bank where (the tradition is) the wretched woman sat to see the combat." Southey adds his full confidence in the tradition of the indestructibility of the steps, even after ploughing up, and of the conclusions to be drawn from the circumstance.—*Notes and Queries*, No. 12.

Joseph Moser, in one of his *Commonplace Books*, gives this account of the *footsteps*, just previous to their being built over: "June 16, 1800, Went into the fields at the back of Montague House, and there saw, for the last time, the *forty footsteps*; the building materials are there, ready to cover them from the sight of man. I counted more than *forty*, but they might be the foot-prints of the workmen."—Dobie's *St. Giles-in-the-Fields, and St. George, Bloomsbury*; and Dr. Rimbault, *in Notes and Queries*, No. 14.

FIELD-LANE,

An infamous rookery of "the dangerous classes," extended from the foot of Holborn-hill, northward, parallel with the Fleet Ditch, but has been mostly taken down since it was thus vividly painted in 1837:

"Near to the spot on which Snow-hill and Holborn meet, there opens, upon the right hand as you come out of the City, a narrow and dismal alley leading to Saffron-hill. In its filthy shops are exposed for sale huge bunches of pocket-handkerchiefs of all sizes and patterns—for here reside the traders who purchase them from pickpockets. Hundreds of these handkerchiefs hang dangling from pegs outside the windows, or flaunting from the door-posts; and the shelves within are piled with them, Confined as the limits of Field-lane are, it has its barber, its coffee-shop, its beer-shop, and its fried-fish warehouse. It is a commercial colony of itself,—the emporium of petty larceny, visited, at early morning and setting-in of dusk, by silent merchants, who traffic in dark back-parlours, and go as strangely as they come Here the clothesman, the shoe-vamper. and the rag-merchant, display their goods as sign-boards to the petty thief; and stores of old iron and bones, and heaps of mildewy fragments of woollen-stuff and linen, rust and rot in the grimy cellars."—Dickens's *Oliver Twist*.

From Field-lane, northward, runs Saffron-hill, named from the saffron which it once bore; next is Vine-street, the site of Ely-House vineyard. Strype (1720) describes this locality as "of small account both as to buildings and inhabitants, and pestered with small and ordinary alleys and courts, taken up by the meaner sort of people;" others are "nasty and inconsiderable."

In 1844 was taken down part of Old Chick-lane, which debouched into Field-lane. Here was a notorious thieves' lodging-house, formerly the Red-Lion Tavern: it had various contrivances for concealment, and the Fleet Ditch in the rear, across which the pursued often escaped by a plank into the opposite knot of courts and alleys.

FINSBURY;

Or *Fensbury*, named from its fenny ground, is a manor of high antiquity, which abuts in part upon the City, Cripplegate, and Moorgate boundaries, and was anciently named Vynesbury. A great part of the manor is held by the Corporation of London, by virtue of a lease dated 22d May, 1315, from Robert de Baildok, prebendary of Haliwell and Finsbury, in St. Paul's Cathedral, at an annual rent of 20s. The lease, which has been renewed from time to time, will expire in the year 1867. The Corporation appoints the steward and other officers of the manorial courts; but the manor is not within the jurisdiction of the City. The Finsbury court leet and baron are holden in October every year, before the senior Common Pleader, to whose office the stewardship of the manor of Finsbury is incident. (*Municipal Corporation Report*, pp. 3, 136; and Maitland's *London*, vol. ii. 1369.) Finsbury has been drained and built over, and is now a populous parliamentary borough, including the ancient district of Moorfields.

In early times, the chief magistrate of London was no more than a provost. Afterwards, the title of Mayor—that is, *Major Chief*—was given to him; but in all the olden chronicles and documents he is simply called by that name, without the prefix of Lord. When the manor of Finsbury was annexed to the City property, and the mere marsh was turned into a place of general recreation, he was, in virtue of his office, Lord of the Manor of Finsbury. Hence, in process of time, the compound title of Lord Mayor: Mayor, that is, of London, and Lord of the Manor of Finsbury.

FIRE OF LONDON (THE),

Or the GREAT FIRE of 1666, broke out about one o'clock on Sunday morning, September 2, and raged nearly four days and nights. It commenced at the house of one Farryner, the "King's Baker," in Puddinglane, near New Fish-Street-hill, and within ten houses of Lower Thames-street, into which it spread within a short time; nearly all the contiguous buildings being of lath and plaster, and the whole neighbourhood mostly close passages and narrow lanes and alleys, of wooden pitched houses. Driven by a strong east-north-east wind, the flames spread with great rapidity: however, it was proposed to the Lord Mayor (Sir Thomas Bludworth,) who came before three o'clock, to pull down some houses, to prevent their extending; but he neglected this advice, and before eight o'clock the fire had reached London Bridge.

The tremendous event is finely described by Evelyn in his *Diary*, wherein he tells us that it made the atmosphere as light as day "for ten miles round about; .. all the skie was of a fiery aspect, like the top of a burning oven, the light seen above forty miles round about. Above 10,000 houses all in one flame; the noise and cracking and thunder of the impetuous flames, ye shrieking of women and children, the hurry of people, the fall of towers, houses and churches, was like an hideous storme, and the air all about so hot and inflam'd, that at last one was not able to approach it, so that they were forc'd to stand still and let ye flames burn on, wch they did for neere two miles in length, and one in bredth. The clouds of smoke were dismall, and reached upon computation neer 50 miles in length."

On the 5th, Evelyn writes: "In this calamitous condition, I return'd with a sad heart to my house, blessing and adoring the mercy of God to me and mine, who in the midst of all this ruine, was, like Lot, in my little Zoar, safe and sound."

Pepys's account, in his *Diary*, is fully as minute as that of Evelyn, but is mingled with various personal and official circumstances. Pepys was then clerk of the Acts of the Navy: his house and office were in Seething-lane, Crutched Friars; he was called up at three in the morning, Sept. 2, by his maid Jane, and so rose and slipped on his nightgown, and went to her window; but thought the fire far enough off, and so went to bed again, and to sleep. Next morning, Jane told him that she heard above 300 houses had been burnt down by the fire they saw, and that it was then burning down all Fish-street, by London Bridge. "So," he writes, "I made myself ready presently, and walked to the Tower, and there got up upon one of the high places, and saw the houses at that end of the bridge all on fire, and an infinite great fire on this and the other side of the end of the bridge," &c. On Sept. 5, he notes: "about two in the morning my wife calls me up, and tells me of new cries of fire, it being come to Barking Church, which is at the bottom of our Lane." The fire was, however, stopped, "as well at Mark-lane end as ours; it having only burned the dyall of Barking Church, and part of the porch, and there was quenched."

The limits of the Great Fire, according to the *London Gazette*, Sept. 8, 1666, were: "at the Temple Church, near Holborn Bridge, Pye Corner, Aldersgate; Cripplegate, near the lower end of Coleman-street, at the end of Basinghall-street, by the Postern; at the upper end of Bishopsgate-street and Leadenhall-street, at the Standard in Cornhill, at the Church in Fenchurch-street, near Clothworkers' Hall, in Mincing-lane, at the middle of Mark-lane, and at the Tower Dock."

"It is observed and is true, in the late Fire of London, that the Fire burned just as many parish churches as there were hours from the beginning to the end of the Fire; and next, that there were just as many churches left standing in the rest of the City that was not burned, being, I think, thirteen in all of each; which is pretty to observe."—Pepys' *Diary*, Jan. 7, 1667-8.

The Fire consumed almost five-sixths of the whole City; and without the walls, it cleared a space nearly as extensive as the one-sixth part left unburnt within. Public edifices, churches, and dwelling-houses were alike consumed; and it may be stated that the flames extended their ravages over a space of ground equal to an oblong square of a mile and a half in length, and half a mile in breadth. In one of the inscriptions on the Monument, which was drawn up from the reports of the surveyors appointed after the Fire, it is stated that "the ruins of the City were 436 acres (viz. 373 acres within the walls, and 63 without them, but within the liberties); that, of the six-and-twenty wards, it utterly destroyed fifteen, and left eight others shattered and half-burnt; and that it consumed eighty-nine churches, four of the city gates, Guildhall, many public structures, hospitals, schools, libraries, a great number of stately edifices, 13,200 dwelling-houses, and 460 streets."

Lord Clarendon says, that "the value or estimate of what that devouring Fire consumed could never be computed in any degree." A curious pamphlet upon the *Burning of London*, first published in 1667, however, estimates the loss at 7,335,000*l.*; but it is believed to have been nearer ten millions sterling.

Whether the Great Fire were the effect of design or of accident, has been much controverted. Lord Clarendon admits the public impression to have been, "that the Fire was occasioned by conspiracy and combination;" and although he himself maintains the negative, his own account furnishes opposite testimony. "It could not be conceived," he says, "how a house that was distant a mile from any part of the Fire could suddenly be in a flame, without some particular malice; and *this case fell out every hour.*" One Robert Hubert, a French Papist, seized in Essex, confessed to have begun the Fire; and was hanged accordingly: he stated that he had been "suborned at Paris to this action;" that there "were three more combined with him to do the same thing," and that "he had set the first house on fire." Yet Lord Clarendon strangely remarks, that "neither the judges, nor any present at the trial, did believe him guilty, but that he was a poor distracted wretch weary of his life, and chose to part with it in this way." This was not credited by Howell, then recorder of London. "Tillotson believed the City was burnt on design." (*Burnet.*)

On the 26th of April, 1666, a plot was discovered for taking the Tower and firing the city, which was to have been put in execution on the 3d of September, a day regarded as peculiarly lucky to the anti-royalist faction. It is worthy of remark that the "Great Fire of London" broke out on the 2d of September in that year, the very day before that appointed by the conspirators.

An extremely impressive narrative of the progress of the conflagration, and of the distress and confusion it occasioned, has been given by the Rev. T. Vincent, a nonconformist divine, in his tract, *God's Terrible Advice to the City by Plague and Fire*, of which thirteen editions were published within five years.

The stationers and booksellers lost their stocks, which they had deposited in St. Paul's crypt: too eager to ascertain its condition, as the fire subsided, they caused an aperture to be made in the smouldering pile, when a stream of wind rushed in and consumed the whole:

> "Heavens, what a pile! whole ages perish'd there;
> And one bright blaze turn'd learning into air."

Aubrey relates that on St. Andrew's Day, (Nov. 30,) 1666, as he was riding in a coach towards Gresham College, at the corner of Holborn Bridge a cellar of coals was opened by the labourers, and "there were burning coals which burnt ever since the Great Fire; but being pent so close from air, there was very little waste."—*Nat. Hist. Wilts.*

Westminster Hall was filled with the citizens' goods and merchandise; and Pepys oddly complains that he could not "find any place in Westminster to buy a shirt or pair of gloves; Westminster Hall being full of people's goods."

A Court of Judicature was appointed by Parliament, to settle all differences arising in respect to the destroyed premises; and the judges of this Court gave such satisfaction, that their portraits were painted, at the expense of the citizens, for 60*l.* a piece, and are now in the Courts of Common Pleas and Queen's Bench, Guildhall.

Not more than six persons lost their lives in the Fire; one of whom was a watchmaker, living in Shoe-lane, behind the Globe Tavern, and who would not leave his house, which sunk him with the ruins into the cellar, where his bones, with his keys, were found.

(See Hollar's small view of London before and after the Fire; and an ingenious picture-plan by F. Whishaw, C.E., shewing the part of the City destroyed, and its altered condition in 1839.)

Whilst the city was rebuilding, temporary edifices were raised, both for divine worship and the general business. Gresham College, which had escaped the flames, was converted into an Exchange and Guildhall; and the Royal Society removed its sittings to Arundel House. The affairs of the Custom-House were transacted in Mark-lane; of the Excise Office, in Southampton-fields, near Bedford House; the General Post-Office was removed to Brydges-street, Covent Garden; Doctors' Commons to Exeter House, Strand; and the King's wardrobe was consigned from Puddle Wharf to York Buildings. The inhabitants, for a time, were mostly lodged in small huts, built in Finsbury and Moorfields, in Smithfield, and on all the open spaces in the neighbourhood of the metropolis. The whole calamity was bravely borne: Evelyn mentions that the merchants complied with their foreign correspondence as if no disaster had happened, and not one failure was heard of. Within two days after the conflagration, both Wren and Evelyn had presented to the king plans for a new city: neither of these was accepted; but London was principally rebuilt within little more than four years after its destruction.—(See MONUMENT, the.)

FIRES, MEMORABLE, IN LONDON.

Southwark burnt by William the Conqueror, about twenty years before the Domesday Survey.

962.—St. Paul's Minster burnt.

1086.—All the houses and churches from the west to the east gate burnt. (*Baker's Chronicle.*)

1087.—St. Paul's burnt.

1093.—The wooden houses and straw roofs of the London citizens again in flames, and great part of the city destroyed.

1136.—The houses burnt from near London-stone eastward as far as Aldgate; and to the shrine of St. Erkenwald, in St. Paul's Cathedral, west.

1212.—July 10. Southwark and the Church of St. Mary Overie, burnt, when the people crowding thither, and the houses of the north and south end of

London Bridge taking fire simultaneously, the crowd was between two fires, and 3000 persons were burned or drowned.

1512.—Great part of the Palace at Westminster "once again" burnt (4 Hen. viii.), and not since re-edified; only the Great Hall, with adjoining offices, kept in good repair.

1534.—Aug. 16. The Mews, Charing Cross, burnt.

1613.—June 29. The Globe Theatre burnt.

1619.—Jan. 12. The old banqueting-house, Whitehall Palace, burnt.

1621.—Dec. 9. The Fortune Theatre burnt. Dec. 20. Six Clerks' Office, Chancery-lane, burnt.

1630-31.—Feb. 20, Sunday. Alarm of fire in Westminster Hall.

1632-33.—Feb. 3. More than one-third of the houses on London Bridge burnt; the Thames almost frozen.

1666.—The GREAT FIRE. (See preceding article).

1671-2.—The King's Theatre, Drury-lane, burnt.

1676.—May 26. The Town-hall and part of Southwark (600 houses) burnt.

1686.—Jan. 19. Montague-House, Bloomsbury, burnt.

1691.—April 10. At Whitehall Palace all the buildings over the stone gallery to the water-side burnt; 150 houses, chiefly of the nobility, consumed, and 20 blown up.

1697.—Jan. 4. Whitehall Palace, except Inigo Jones's banqueting-house, burnt; all its pictures destroyed, and 12 persons perished.

1716.—In Wapping: 150 houses burnt.

1718.—The Custom-House (Wren's) destroyed.

1725—Sept. 8. At London Bridge foot, Southwark: 60 houses burnt.

1730.—Jan. 30. Bowyer's printing-office, White-Fryars, burnt; the sufferer indemnified by royal brief, and subscriptions of printers and booksellers.

1736.—At Shadwell: 50 houses burnt.

1748.—March 25. In Cornhill ward: 200 houses burnt; commenced in Change-alley, and was the largest since the Great Fire of 1666 (see CORNHILL, p. 235).

1752.—Great fire in Lincoln's-Inn.

1758.—Apr. 11. The temporary wooden London Bridge destroyed by fire, stopping all communication between the city and Southwark, except by boats. This produced the Act of Parliament which made any wilful attempt to destroy the bridge or its works punishable with death, without benefit of clergy.

1759.—Nov. 30. The Sardinian Ambassador's chapel, Duke-street, Lincoln's-Inn-Fields, burnt. In King-street, Covent-garden, several houses burnt.

1760.—April 10. Fire at an oilman's, Lower Thames-st.; 7 dwelling-houses,

all the warehouses on Fresh Wharf, and the roof of St. Magnus Church, burnt (see CHURCHES, p. 135).

1761.—Feb. 10. Fishmongers' Hall and several houses in Thames-street burnt. April 11. In East Smithfield, 28 houses burnt. April 24. In Swallow-street, 14 houses burnt. May 2. At Shadwell, 30 houses burnt.

1765.—Nov. 7. In Cornhill and Bishopsgate-street: upwards of 90 houses burnt in 12 hours (see CORNHILL, p. 235).

1775.—Sept. 28. At Wapping; 20 houses burnt.

1780.—April 30. At Horsleydown; 30 houses burnt. June 2 to 7. Several incendiary fires by the Rioters.

1783.—Sept. 23. At Gun-dock, Wapping; 14 houses burnt.

1789.—June 17. Italian Opera-house (Vanbrugh's) burnt.

1790.—April 1. At Hermitage-stairs; damage 30,000l. Oct. 4. At Rotherhithe; 20 houses burnt.

1791.—March 2. Albion Mills, Blackfriars Bridge, burnt. Sept. 14. At Rotherhithe; several vessels, and 60 houses burnt. Dec. 12. Great sugar-house, Wellclose-square, destroyed.

1792.—Jan. 4. The Pantheon, Oxford-street, burnt. July 28. Timber-yard, Moorfields; damage 10,000l.

1793.—At Hawley's-wharf, Hermitage-wharf; damage to sugar, 10,000l. Dec. 13. In Duck-lane, Wardour-st.; 13 houses burnt.

1794.—June 18. At Limehouse Hole, many houses burnt. July 22, 23. At Ratcliffe Cross; 630 houses and an East-India warehouse burnt: loss, 1,000,000l.

1795.—Aug. 17. Astley's Amphitheatre and 19 houses burnt. Sept. 12. St. Paul's Church, Covent-garden, burnt.

1799.—July 14. In the King's Bench prison; 50 apartments burnt.

1800.—Feb. 11. Three West-India warehouses, Lower Thames-st., burnt. Oct. 6. At Wapping; 30 houses, besides warehouses.

1802.—Sept. 27. Brewery burnt in Store-street, Tottenham Court Road.

1803.—Feb. 21. Hamilton's printing-office, Falcon-court, Fleet-street, destroyed. July 9. Central tower of Westminster Abbey took fire. Sept. 2. Astley's Amphitheatre and 40 houses burnt.

1805.—Aug. 12. Royal Circus Theatre, St. George's Fields, burnt.

1807.—Nov. 5. Bensley's printing-office, Bolt-court, Fleet-street, burnt.

1808.—Sept. 20. Covent Garden Theatre destroyed.

1809.—Jan. 21. Wing of St. James's Palace destroyed. Feb. 24. Drury Lane Theatre burnt. July 8. Fire in Conduit-street, at which Mr. Windham received an injury which caused his death.

1810.—Jan. 1. At Whitefriars Dock;

30,000l. worth of timber and 9 houses burnt. July 13. In Little Tichfield-street; 7 houses and Huntingdon's chapel burnt. July 29. Gillett's printing-office, Salisbury-square, burnt, 2d time; first, 1805.

1811.—June 18. Half Bury-street, St. Mary Axe, burnt.

1812.—Oct. 17. Every house in Bil-liter-lane destroyed.

1814.—Feb. 12. The Custom-House and adjoining houses destroyed. Aug. 28. Oil and mustard mills, Bankside, burnt; remains of Winchester Palace discovered in the ruins.

1815.—Oct. 30. The Eastern and southern wings of the Royal Mint burnt.

1816.—April 23. Stock Exchange Coffee-house and several adjoining houses burnt.

1819.—June 26. Bensley's printing-office, and Dr. Johnson's house, Bolt-court, Fleet-street, burnt.

1821.—Jan. 11. Smith and Co.'s sugar-refinery, Mile-End, destroyed; loss, 200,000l. Nov. 3. A West-Indiaman burnt on the Thames.

1822.—March 2. At Bagster's, Pater-noster-row; large stock of bibles burnt. Aug. 11. Plate-glass manufactory, Up. East Smithfield, burnt; loss, 100,000l.

1824.—Nov. 14. Great fire in Fleet-street, opposite St. Bride's church.

1825.—June 21. In Great Tichfield-street, Wells-street, Marylebone; 30 houses and shops burnt.

1826.—April 11. The Royalty The-atre, Wellclose-square, burnt.

1829.—May 28. Fire at Queen's Ba-zaar, (now Princess' Theatre,) Oxford-street: Diorama burnt.

1830.—Feb. 6. Argyll-Rooms, Re-gent-street, burnt. Feb. 16. English Opera-House and several houses burnt. April 18. Fire in Fetter-lane, Holborn; 7 persons burnt.

1832.—Jan. 31. Fire at 15 Oxford-st.: Wilmshurst's Great Painted Window (430 square feet,) burnt; cost 3000l. May 22. Fire at Barclay and Perkins's Brewery, Southwark. Nov. 27. In Long-acre; 14 houses burnt in three hours.

1834.—Oct. 16. Both Houses of Par-liament destroyed by a fire which was not completely extinguished for several days: the libraries and state papers pre-served. The fire originated in burning heaps of old exchequer-tallies (see page 286). In 1828 Sir John Soane, noticing the great quantity of timber used in the House of Lords, prophetically asked: "Should a fire happen, what would be-come of the Painted Chamber, the House of Commons, and Westminster Hall? where would the progress of the fire be arrested?" The latter was saved by the favourable direction of the wind; for had the flames and flakes of fire from the two Houses been wafted towards the vast timber roof of the hall, it must have been inevitably destroyed. Among the strange stories in support of the fire being the work of political incendiaries, is the statement of Mr. Cooper, an iron-monger, of Drury-lane, that he heard at Dudley, in Worcestershire (119 miles from London), a report of the conflagra-tion about three hours after it broke out.

1835.—March 2. Great fire in Silver-street, Golden-square.

1836.—Feb. 17. Christchurch steeple, Spitalfields, burnt; and clock, bells, and chimes destroyed. March 26. Western Exchange, Burlington Arcade, burnt. Aug. 30. Fenning's Wharf, London-bridge, burnt.

1837. — Dec. 28. Davies's Wharf, Tooley-street, burnt, with 5000 barrels of rough turpentine, and 800 tuns of oil.

1838.—Jan. 10. The Royal Exchange burnt within five hours; with a great amount of property, documents of cor-porations, &c. March 6. Great fire in Paper-buildings, Temple.

1841. — Feb. 7. The old church at Camberwell burnt. June 8. Astley's Amphitheatre destroyed. Oct. 30. Great fire in the Tower; the great storehouse, with 280,000 stand of arms, and the Bowyer and Butler Towers, burnt.

1843.—Aug. 17. Great fire at Top-ping's Wharf, London Bridge; Watson's telegraph tower and St. Olave's Church burnt (see CHURCHES, p. 151).

1844.—Oct. 14. New Cross Railway-Station burnt.

1845.—Aug. 18. Great fire in Alder-manbury.

1846. — Dec. 2. Fergusson's Wax-work, New Cut, Lambeth, burnt, with serpents, monkeys, &c.

1849.—March 29. The Olympic The-atre and a dozen other buildings burnt in three hours. Oct. 6. Extensive fire at London-wall; Carpenters' Hall in-jured; loss, 100,000l.

1850.—March 29. St. Anne's Church, Limehouse, destroyed. Sept. 19. Great fire in Mark-lane and Seething-lane; loss, 100,000l. In the ruins was dis-covered a tablet, inscribed: "This was rebuilt in 1792. The foundation, or 'base courts,' are the remains of the original palace where the city standard of weights and measures was formerly kept, and designated, in Saxon phrase-ology, 'Assay Thing Court,' the entrance to which was in, as is now called, 'Seething lane.'"

1851.—Feb. 19. Alderman Humphrey's warehouses, Tooley-st., burnt; and on June 23, his warehouses in Montague-close, opposite, consumed. Sept. 20. Picture-frame-maker's workshops in Mount-row, Westminster-road, fired by an aerolite.

FIRE-BRIGADE.

The earliest mechanical contrivance for the extinction of fires in London appears to have been a syringe or squirt, numbers of which were kept by the parochial authorities. In the vestry-room of St. Dionis', Back-church, Fenchurch-street, are preserved three of these squirts: each is about 2 feet 3 inches long, and when used was attached by straps to the body of a man: others were worked by three men, two holding the squirt by the handles and nozzle, while a third worked the piston within it. Such was the rudiment of our first fire-engine.

> "Now streets grow throng'd, and busy as by day:
> Some run for buckets to the hallow'd quire;
> Some cut the pipes, and some the *engines* play,
> And some, more bold, mount ladders to the fire."
> Dryden's *Annus Mirabilis* (1666).

The "engines" were the syringes, which were greatly increased after the Great Fire, but were shortly afterwards superseded by regular fire-engines. By order of the Corporation of London, a Fire Police was established in 1668; the several parishes were provided with leathern buckets, ladders, pickaxes, sledges, shovels, and *hand-squirts* of *brass*; which supply the companies, aldermen, and subsidy-men contributed; and among other provisions, was the ringing of a bell. The fire-cocks, and the "F.P." and "W.M." upon houses to denote the place of the fire-plug and water-main; and the rewards for bringing the parish-engines; date from stat. 6 Anne, cap. 31.

The Great Fire led to the establishment of Insurance Offices against losses by fire: in 1681, the Court of Common Council attempted to establish one, but unsuccessfully; the earliest was the Phœnix, at the Rainbow Coffee-house, Fleet-street, in 1682; the Friendly Society, 1684 (badge, a sheaf of arrows); and the Hand-in-Hand, established in 1696; next was the Sun, projected by one Povey, about 1706, and by the present Company in 1710; the Westminster Fire Office, 1717; each office keeping its firemen in liveries, with silver badges; and their fire-engines, which they from time to time improved. In 1676 was patented an engine with leathern pipes, for quenching fire; and about 1720, two Germans had at Bethnal-green a manufactory of water-tight seamless hose.

> "Now with thick crowds th' enlighten'd pavement swarms,
> The fireman sweats beneath his crooked arms;
> A leathern casque his vent'rous head defends,
> Boldly he climbs where thickest smoke ascends.
> Mov'd by the mother's streaming eyes and prayers,
> The helpless infant through the flame he bears,
> With no less virtue than through hostile fire
> The Dardan hero bore his aged sire.
> See forceful engines spout their leveled streams,
> To quench the blaze that runs along the beams;
> The grappling-hook plucks rafters from the walls,
> And heaps on heaps the smoky ruin falls.
>   *   *   *   *   *   *
> Hark! the drum thunders! far, ye crowds, retire:
> Behold! the ready match is tipt with fire,
> The nitrous store is laid, the smutty train
> With running blaze awakes the barrell'd grain;
> Flames sudden wrap the walls; with sullen sound
> The shatter'd pile sinks on the smoky ground."—Gay's *Trivia*, b. iii.

In 1798 was formed the Fire-watch or Fire-guard of London; the Insurance Offices still keeping their separate engine establishments. In 1808, Sir F. M. Eden, then chairman of the Globe Insurance Office, proposed to form a general fire-engine establishment, but the attempt failed. About 1825, the Sun, Union, and Royal Exchange formed a brigade, subsequently joined by the Atlas and Phœnix. The number

f engines varied from 38 to 50; and in 1815, the number of firemen
protected from impressment by the Building Act was 398. In 1832,
en of the Insurance Companies formed an alliance for assisting each
ther at fires; hence the "London Fire-Engine Establishment," which
ommenced operations in 1833, and has since been joined by all the
ther Companies, except three. By the rules, London is divided into
ive districts: 1. Eastward of Aldersgate-street and St. Paul's; 2.
Thence westward, to Tottenham-Court-road and St. Martin's-lane;
3. All westward of the second; 4. South of the river; in each of which
districts are engine-stations: besides a floating engine off Rotherhithe
and Southwark Bridge; these require more than 100 men each for
working, and throw up two tuns of water per minute. The easternmost station is at Ratcliff; the westernmost near Portman-square.
A certain number of the men or "Fire Brigade," superintended by
Mr. Braidwood, are ready at all hours of the day and night, as are also
the engines, to depart at a minute's alarm, in case of fire. The Associations award a gratuity of 10s. to a policeman who gives an alarm to the
nearest engine-station; and the director or captain of each engine pays
strangers or bystanders for aid: it requires from twenty to thirty
men to work each engine; and at a large fire, 500 strangers have been
thus employed. Sometimes the engines are summoned by electric
telegraph, and conveyed by railway to fires in the country.

The number of engines kept is 37; of the Fire Brigade, 96. The men wear a
dark grey uniform, trimmed with red, with the number of each man marked in
red on the left breast; they have black leathern waist-belts, hardened leathern
helmets, reminding one of the leathern casque and "the Dardan hero" of Gay's
Trivia. The engines are provided with scaling ladders, which may readily be
connected, and thus form a ladder of any required height; a canvass sheet, with
handles of rope round the edge, to form a fire-escape; besides lengths of 2½-inch
ropes, hose, branch-pipes, suction-pipes, a flat rose, goose-neck, dam-board, boat-
hook, saw, shovel, mattock, pole-axe, screw-wrench, crowbar, portable cistern,
two dog-tails, strips of sheep-skin, small cord, instruments for opening the fire-
plugs, and keys for turning the stop-cocks of the water-mains.

Another ingenious provision is a smoke-proof dress, consisting of a leathern
jacket and head-covering, fastened at the waist and wrist, so that the interior is
smoke-proof: two glass windows serve for the eyes to look through, and a pipe
attached to the girdle allows fresh air to be pumped into the interior of the jacket,
to support the respiration of the wearer: thus equipped, the fireman may dare
the densest smoke.

A register of all fires attended is kept; and useful statistics are thus
obtained. In five years' average, the largest number of fires occurred
in December, then in May, March, and July; on Sunday evenings, between ten and eleven o'clock. Mr. Braidwood states 5794 fires to have
occurred in ten years; in which 269 houses were totally burned down;
persons perished, 158. In five years' fires, private and lodging houses
were 45 per cent of the total number. Next in frequency were sale-
shops, public-houses, carpenters, bakers, oilmen, stables, cabinet-makers,
tinmen and braziers, booksellers, binders, estate-owners, warehouses,
hat-makers, brokers, brokers and dealers in old clothes, grocers, ships,
wine and spirit sellers, drapers and mercers. Lucifer-match makers
considerably exceed fire-work makers. Accidents from candles are
nearly 30 per cent of the causes; then flues and stoves; gas accidents,
1½ per cent; airing linen, nearly 8 per cent. There are large classes of
causes: apparel ignited on the person; children playing with fire;
incautious fumigation; intoxication; lucifer-match making; loose shav-
ings ignited; spontaneous combustion; and tobacco-smoking.

Steam-power was first applied to work a fire-engine in 1830. (See
ARGYLL ROOMS, page 19.) There is also on the Thames a steam float-
ing-engine, the machinery of which either propels the vessel, or works
the pumps, as required.

With Fire Insurance is usually combined Life Insurance. The offices are mostly buildings of architectural and sculptural decoration; some of them resembling in design highly-enriched palaces. The pawn-brokers have an insurance company of their own, from the general Companies charging them high rates.

A Parisian journalist acknowledges: "I compared our wretched little engines, dragged with difficulty over the pavement of Paris by our brave *pompiers*, already half dead with that fatigue before the real occasion for their exertion begins,—I compared these with the powerful pump-engines brought to the spot by four powerful horses at full gallop, and the firemen sitting at their ease on the engines. I thought of the wild confusion of our chains, of the cries of all the workmen, of our leathern buckets brought empty to the engines, while I saw before me the water pouring, the streets inundated, and the pipes like brilliant *jets d'eau*, lit up by countless torches, and rising above the crowd as a symbol of safety to man in the midst of dangers from fire. With us every passer-by is stopped to work the engine; here, the difficulty is to prevent the people from so doing."

Fire-escapes are stationed in various districts by the Society for the Protection of Life from Fire; each station costing about 70*l.*; and its maintenance with a conductor, about 80*l.* annually. In 1851, they saved twenty-four lives.

FLEET PRISON (THE),

Abolished and removed in 1846, after nearly eight centuries' existence, was indisputably named from the creek or stream of the Fleet, upon the eastern bank of which it was erected. This was once a busy river covered with ships and small craft; now it is a dark, hidden stream.

The prison was formerly held in conjunction with the manor of Leveland, in Kent, and with "the king's houses at Westminster;" the whole being part of the ancient possessions of the See of Canterbury, traceable in a grant from Archbishop Lanfranc, soon after the accession of William the Conqueror. The wardenship or serjeancy of the prison was anciently held by several eminent personages, who also had custody of the king's palace at Westminster.* It was "a place," in the worst sense of the phrase; for, so long ago as 1586, the persons to whom the Warden had underlet it were guilty of cruelty and extortion,—crimes, however, characteristic of the Court of Star Chamber, of which the Fleet was at this time the prison. Up to this period, its history is little better than a sealed book; the burning of the prison by the followers of Wat Tyler seeming to have been the only noticeable event.

In the reigns of Edward VI. and Mary, the Fleet was tenanted by several victims of religious bigotry. Bishop Hooper was twice committed to the Fleet, which he only quitted (1555) for the stake and the fire, at Gloucester; upon his way whither, he slept at the Angel Inn, St. Clement's: in the Fleet, his bed was "a little pad of straw, with a rotten covering;" his "chamber was vile and stinking."

The Warden's fees in the reign of Elizabeth were: an Archbishop, Duke, or Duchess, for his commitment-fee, and the first week's "dyett," 21*l.* 10*s.*; a lord, spiritual or temporal, 10*l.* 5*s.* 10*d.*; a knight, 5*l.*; an esquire, 3*l.* 6*s.* 8*d.*; and even "a poor man in the wards, that hath *a part at the box*, to pay for his fee, having no dyett, 7*s.* 4*d.*" The Warden's charge for license to a prisoner "to go abroad" was 20*d.* per diem.

From the reign of Elizabeth to the sixteenth year of King Charles I. (1641), the Star-Chamber Court was in full activity; and several bishops and other persons of distinction were imprisoned in the Fleet for their religious opinions. Thither, too, were consigned the political victims of the Star Chamber: two of the most interesting cases of this period

---

* To the Warden belonged the rents of the shops in Westminster Hall.

being those of Prynne and Lilburne. Prynne was taken out of the prison, and, after suffering pillory, branding, mutilation of the nose, and loss of ears, was remanded to the Fleet. Lilburne—" Freeborn John"—and his printer, were committed to the Fleet for libel and sedition: the former was " smartly" whipped at the cart's tail, from the prison to the pillory, placed between Westminster Hall and the Star-Chamber; and subsequently " doubly ironed" in the prison wards.

Another tenant of the Fleet at this period was James Howel, the author of the *Familiar Letters,* several of which are dated from the prison. By a letter " to the Earl of B., from the Fleet," Nov. 20, 1643, Howel was arrested " one morning betimes," by five men armed with " swords, pistols, and bils," and some days after, committed to the Fleet; " and," he adds, " as far as I see, I must lie at dead *anchor* in his *Fleet* a long time, unlesse some gentle *gale* blow thence to make me *launch* out." Then we find him consoling himself with the reflection that the English " peeple" are in effect but prisoners, as all other islanders are. Other letters, by Howel, date from the Fleet, 1645-6-7.

The prison was burnt on Sept. 4, 1666, during the Great Fire; when the prisoners were removed to Caroone or Caron House, in South Lambeth, until the Fleet was rebuilt on the original site.

After the abolition of the Star Chamber, in 1641, the Fleet became a prison for debtors only, and for contempt of the Court of Chancery, Common Pleas, and Exchequer. It appears to have been used for the confinement of debtors from the thirteenth century, at least by a petition from John Frauncey, a debtor in the Fleet, A.D. 1290.

Long after the abolition of the Star Chamber, the Wardens continued their extortionate fees, and loading debtors with iron: their cruelties were exposed in 1696. In 1727, after a parliamentary investigation, Bambridge and Huggins (Wardens) and some of their servants were tried for different murders, yet all escaped by a verdict of not guilty! Hogarth has, however, made them immortal in their infamy, in his picture of Bambridge under examination, whilst a prisoner is explaining how he has been tortured.

In " the Riots" of 1780, the Fleet was destroyed by fire, and the prisoners liberated by the mob; consequently great part of the papers and prison-records were lost, though there remain scattered books and documents of several centuries back. Mr. Eyles, then Warden, was directed by the Lord Mayor not to make any resistance to the mob, which, as an eye-witness has informed the writer, might have been easily dispersed by a few soldiers. The prison was accordingly burnt. (From *A Brief Account* published in 1843.) The mob were polite enough to send notice to the prisoners of the period of their coming, and, on being informed it would be inconvenient on account of the lateness of the hour, postponed their visit to the following day.

Immediately after " the Riots," the prison was rebuilt: it consisted chiefly of one long brick pile, parallel with Farringdon-street, and standing in an irregularly-shaped area, so as to leave open spaces before and behind, connected by passages round each other. This pile was called the Master's Side. The front in Farringdon-street had an arched opening into a room, and was technically called " the grate," from its crossed iron bars. Above was inscribed, " Pray remember the poor prisoners having no allowance;" a small box was placed at the window-sill, to receive the charity of passengers in the street, while a prisoner within shouted in suppliant tone the above prayer. This was a relic of the ancient prison, corresponding with the " begging at the grate" in some old comedies; and " having a part at the box" already mentioned. Disorderly prisoners were put in the stocks, or strong-room; and those who attempted to escape were confined in a tub at the prison-gate.

Above the entrance to the prison was the figure 9 ; so that a delicate address given by the prisoners was " No. 9 Fleet-Market."

Alack! what "strange bedfellows" did debt — a phase of misery — make men acquainted with in the Fleet ! If a prisoner was unwilling to go to the Common Side, (for which he paid nothing,) he had the choice of going down into " Bartholomew Fair," the lowest and sunken story, where he paid 1s. 3d. for the undisturbed use of a room; or up to some of the better apartments, where he paid the same rent, but was subject to chummage, i. e. a fellow-prisoner put into his room, or " chummed upon him," but who might be got rid of by a payment of 4s. 6d. per week, or more, according to the fulness of the prison. The latter prisoner would then provide himself with a common lodging, by letting which prisoners in the Fleet are known to have accumulated hundreds of pounds in the course of a few years. The prison sometimes had 1000 inmates.

It was throughout a sad scene of recreant waste, vagabondism, and ruffian recklessness: it had a skittle-shed; and a racket-ground, where Cavanagh was a noted fives-player. (See Hazlitt's life of him, Examiner, Feb. 17, 1819.) Here you might hear the roar of the great town from without, in contrast with the stagnant life within the prison-walls, above the chevaux-de-frise of which might be seen a church-spire or two.

Happily, this pest of a prison, the Fleet, by Act of Parliament, 1842, was abolished, and its few inmates were drafted to the Queen's Prison. The property, covering nearly an acre of ground, was purchased of the government by the Corporation of London for 25,000l. It was taken down, and the materials sold, in 1846; comprising nearly three millions of bricks, 50 tons of lead, 40,000 feet of paving, &c.

The liberty of the Rules and the Day-Rules of the Fleet may be traced to the time of Richard II., and their antiquity is not surprising when we find them to be matters of profit and extortion by the Wardens. However, they were confirmed by a rule of Court during the reign of James I. The Rules were enlarged in Easter Term, 1824, by rule of the Court of Common Pleas; which extension included the neighbouring parish churches, St. Bride's, and St. Martin's, Ludgate, and the adjacent streets of New Bridge-street, Blackfriars, to the Thames, Dorset-street and Salisbury-square, and part of Fleet-street, Ludgate-hill and street, to the entrance of St. Paul's Churchyard, the Old Bailey, and the various lanes, courts, &c. in the vicinity of the above; the extreme circumference of the liberty about a mile and a half. Those requiring the rules were obliged to provide sureties for their forthcoming, and duly keeping within the boundaries, and to pay a per centage on the amount of debts for which they were detained; which also entitled them to the liberty of the Day-rules, enabling them during term, or the sitting of the courts at Westminster, to go abroad during the day, to transact or arrange their affairs, &c. The Fleet and the Queen's Bench were the only prisons in the kingdom to which these privileges had for centuries been attached.

Fleet Marriages, i. e. clandestine marriages, were performed in this prison previously to the year 1754; and though not legal and regular, they were tacitly recognised as being valid and indissoluble. Many of these weddings were really performed in the chapel of the prison; though, as the practice extended, " the Fleet parsons" and tavern-keepers in the neighbourhood fitted up a room in their lodgings or houses as a chapel; and most of the taverns near the Fleet kept their own registers. In 1702, the Bishop of London interfered to prevent this scandalous practice, but with little effect ; and it was not until the Act of Parliament came into operation, March 25, 1754, that the custom was put an end to. On the day previously, (March 24,) in one register-book alone, were recorded 217 marriages, which were the last of the Fleet weddings. In 1821, a collection of these register-books, weighing more than a ton (recording Fleet marriages between 1686 and 1754), was purchased by Government, and deposited in the Registry Office of the Bishop of London, Godliman-street, Doctors' Commons. Many celebrated names figure in these registers; and although they are not now, as formerly, received in evidence on trials, they are not altogether useless as matters of record, &c. For their history, their parsons and registers, see Mr. J. Burns' volume.

Pope commemorates the Fleet Prison as a " Haunt of the Muses." Here were confined Lord Surrey, the soldier-poet; Nash, the fantastical satirist ("Pierce Penniless"); Dr. Donne, for his secret marriage; Wycherley, the peet, here for even years; Richard Savage (in "the Rules"); and Richard Lloyd, the friend of Churchill, who was married in the Fleet. Here died Sir Richard Baker, the chronicler; and Francis Sandford, the genealogist. Arthur Murphy, provoked by the satires of Churchill and Lloyd, describes them as among the poor hacks

> "On Ludgate-hill who bloody murders write,
> Or pass in Fleet-street supperless the night."

Howel's *Letters*, already mentioned, have had a parallel in our time, in Richard Oastler's *Fleet Papers*, "a weekly epistle on public matters," inscribed to Thomas Thornhill, Esq. of Fixby Hall, Yorkshire, whose steward Oastler had been, and at whose suit he was imprisoned here; he was liberated by subscription, Feb. 12, 1844.

FLEET RIVER AND FLEET DITCH.

The small, rapid stream *Fleet*, which has given name to the prison and street, and the portion of the City Wall ditch from Holborn to the Thames, has its origin in a nursery-ground on the eastern ridge of Hampstead Hill. Here it becomes a sewer, after which it issues from the side of a bank below Well Walk; and then flows down a small valley of gardens and orchards to near the reservoir of the Hampstead water-heads, to feed which the springs of the Fleet were collected in 1589, and were afterwards leased out by the City of London. From Hampstead the Fleet may be traced to the upper part of Kentish Town, after which it is diverted from its original course for the sewerage of Camden Town; but its ancient channel may be traced at the back of the Castle Tavern, Kentish Town, and next in the King's-road, near Pancras Workhouse; and about 1825, the Fleet was conspicuous all along the Bagnigge-Wells road, but is now covered over. Its further course is under the walls of the House of Correction, in Clerkenwell Fields, thence to the workhouse in Coppice-row, under Eyre-street (formerly Hockley-in-the-Hole), having here been formerly joined by "the River of the Wells," formed by Clerken, Skinners', and other wells; and thus to the bottom of Holborn. Here it received the waters of the Old Bourne, which rose near Middle-row, and the channel of which forms the sewer of Holborn Hill to this day. Thence the united streams flowed beneath what is now called Farringdon-street into the Thames.

Stow mentions, "that a Parliament being holden at Carlisle in the year 1307, the 35 Edward I., Henry Lacy Earle of Lincolne complained, that whereas (in times past) the course of water, running at London under Old-borne bridge, and Fleet bridge, into the Thames, had beene of such bredth and depth that ten or twelve ships, Navies at once, with Merchandises, were wont to come to the aforesaid bridge of Fleet, and some of them unto Old-borne Bridge," &c.

An anchor has been discovered as high as the present Bagnigge-Wells road; and even, it is said, the remains of a ship, in the bed of this ancient river, near Camden Town.

The upper supply of water being diverted, the ditch became stagnant, and into it were thrown all sorts of offal, dogs and cats, and measled hogs, which Ben Jonson has minutely described: it became also a sort of *cloaca maxima*, impassable with boats; in 1652 it was ordered to be cleansed, but the nuisance was scarcely abated.

The Fleet was anciently crossed by four bridges within the boundary of the city: the first of these, Holborn Bridge, was covered up in 1802, but the arch and part of the parapet were discovered during a repair of the ditch, in 1841. The second was Fleet-lane Bridge, near the Prison.

In the bed of the Fleet many Roman and Saxon coins have been discovered. In 1670, various Roman utensils were found between Holborn and Fleet Bridge; besides Roman coins, including silver ring-money. At Holborn Bridge were dug up two brazen *lares*; about four inches long,—'Bacchus and Ceres; also arrow-heads, scales, and seals, with the proprietors' names upon them in Saxon characters; spur-rowels, keys, and daggers; medals, crosses, crucifixes, &c.

Fleet Bridge, the third, connected Fleet-street with Ludgate Hill: it was destroyed in the Great Fire of 1666; and in its place, another, the breadth of the street (Strype), was erected, ornamented with pine-apples and the City arms: it was finally removed in 1765. A fourth bridge crossed the Fleet opposite Bridewell, formerly the site of a tower, supposed to have appertained to the Saxon kings of England.

After the Great Fire, the Fleet, or Town Ditch, between Holborn and the Thames, was cleansed and deepened by the Corporation, so that barges ascended to Holborn Bridge, as formerly: wharfs and landing-places were constructed; and Seacoal and Newcastle lanes, and large inn-yards, remaining to this day, attest the barge traffic. This "New Canal," as it was called, cost 27,777*l*., but proved unprofitable; it became choked with Thames mud, and again relapsed into a common sewer. Gay sings of its "muddy current;" and Pope points

> " To where Fleet ditch, with disemboguing streams,
> Rolls the large tribute of dead dogs to Thames;
> The king of dykes, than whom no slime of mud
> With deeper sable blots the silver flood."—*The Dunciad.*

Swift thus revels in its *deliciæ*, in his *City Shower* :

> " Now from all parts the swelling kennels flow,
> And bear their trophies with them as they go;
> Filth of all hues and odours seem to tell
> What street they sail'd from by their sight and smell.
> They, as each torrent drives its rapid force,
> From Smithfield to St. 'Pulchre's shape their course,
> And in huge confluence joined at Snowhill ridge,
> Fall from the Conduit prone to Holborn Bridge;
> Sweepings from butchers' stalls, dung, guts, and blood,
> Drown'd puppies, stinking sprats, all drench'd in mud,
> Dead cats, and turnip-tops, come tumbling down the flood."

The ditch, however, grew to be so pestilential a nuisance,[*] its slime smothering many persons who fell into it, that the space between Holborn Bridge and Fleet-street was arched over, and Stocks Market removed here, changed to Fleet Market, and opened for the sale of meat, fish, and vegetables Sept. 30, 1737; and upon the site of Stock Market was built the Mansion House. The remaining portion of the Fleet, the mouth of which Pennant describes as "a muddy and genuine ditch," continued open until 1765, at the building of Blackfriars Bridge the foul stream was then arched over, and it now enters the Thames on the west side of the bridge, and is conveyed some distance into the river by a culvert: the vaulting at this end is 12 feet high, and the channel 18 feet wide.

" Here many persons enter at low tide, armed with sticks to defend themselves from rats, as well as for sounding on their perilous way among the slimy shallows and carrying a lantern to sight the dreary passages, they wander for miles under the crowded streets, in search of such waifs as are carried there from above. A more dismal pursuit can scarcely be conceived: so near to the great concourse of London streets, that the rolling of the numerous vehicles incessantly thunder ing overhead, and even the voices of wayfarers, are heard, where, here and there, grating admits the light of day; yet so utterly cut off from all communion with the busy world above, so lonely in the very heart of the great and populous city, that of the thousands who pass along, not one is even conscious of the proximity of the wretched wanderer creeping in noisome darkness and peril beneath his very feet. A source of momentary destruction ever lurking in these gloomy regions exist

---

[*] Chamberlayne (1727), however, mentions it as " a mighty chargeable an beautiful work: the curious stone bridges over it; the many huge vaults on each side thereof, to treasure up Newcastle coals for the use of the poor."

in the gases, which generate in their confined and putrefying atmosphere, and sometimes explode with a force sufficient to blow up the very masonry; or which, taking light from the lantern, might envelope the miserable intruder in sudden flame. Many venturers may have sunk down in such a dismal pilgrimage, to be heard of no more; may have fallen suddenly choked, sunk bodily in the treacherous slime, become a prey to swarms of voracious rats, or have been overwhelmed by a sudden increase of the polluted stream."—Archer's *Vestiges of Old London*, Part III., with an interior View of the Ditch.

Since 1841, Fleet Ditch, at the back of Field-lane, has been covered over; but it may be traced in the alleys at the back of Cow-cross, whence it continues open to Ray-street, Clerkenwell; while Brookhill and Turnmill streets keep in memory the brook which ran here into the Fleet, and the mill belonging to the Knights of St. John of Jerusalem, which was turned by its waters.

In 1829 was completed a new market between the west end of Farringdon-street and Shoe-lane; whither, in Nov. 20, was removed Fleet Market, the premises of which were then taken down. At the south end of Farringdon-street is a granite obelisk, erected in 1839 to the memory of Alderman Waithman, who commenced business as a linendraper close to this spot in 1785: was Lord Mayor in 1823-24, and was returned six times to Parliament for the city of London. Opposite Waithman's obelisk is a monument which bears the name of a much less worthy man, John Wilkes, and the year of his mayoralty, 1775.

FLEET-STREET,

Named from the river Fleet, and extending from the junction of Farringdon-street and New Bridge-street, is one of the most ancient and celebrated thoroughfares in London. For many centuries it has been noted for its exhibitions and processions; its printers, stationers, and booksellers; its early coffee-houses and taverns, and banking-houses. It has leading from it thirty-four streets, lanes, and courts.

Fleet-street was noted for its signs: the counting of them, "from Temple Bar to the furthest conduit in Cheapside," &c., is quoted as a remarkable instance of Fuller's memory. (*Life*, &c., p. 76, ed. 1662.) The swinging of one of these broad signs, in a high wind, and the weight of iron on which it acted, sometimes brought the wall down; and one front-fall of this kind in Fleet-street maimed several persons, and killed "two young ladies, a cobler, and the King's jeweller."—(*The Doctor*, by R. Southey, one vol. edit. p. 237.)

Before the Great Fire, and long after, Fleet-street was badly paved; the houses, mostly of timber, overhung in all imaginable positions; and the shops were rude sheds with a penthouse, beneath which the tradesmen unceasingly called "What d' ye lack, gentles? What d' ye lack?" It was then but a suburb. Temple-bar was originally a wooden gate-house across the road to divide the city from Westminster; and often in Fleet-street might be seen men playing at football.

The street was encumbered with posts, upon which the performances at the theatres were announced; hence posting-bills. Taylor, the water-poet, relates that master Field, the player, riding up Fleet-street at a great pace, a gentleman called him, and asked him what play was to be played that day? He being angry to be stayed on so frivolous a demand, answered that he might see what play was to be played on every *post*. "I cry your mercy," said the gentleman; "I took you for a *post*, you rode so fast."

Fleet-street retains its celebrity for printing-offices in the adjoining lanes and courts, greatly increased by the newspapers of the last two centuries. It has two churches, St. Bride's and St. Dunstan's. (See pages 121 and 124.) The Great Fire of 1666 stopped three houses eastward of St. Dunstan's, and within a few doors of the Inner Temple-gate, nearly opposite.

No. 103 (now *Sunday Times* office,) was formerly Alderman Waithman's shop, whither he removed from the south end of Fleet Market. At No. 37, the sign of the Red Lion, Hardham's 37 snuff was first made and sold by John Hardham, *olim* Garrick's "numberer."

In *Bride-lane* is the ancient St. Bride's Well, over which is a pump; and here is Cogers' Hall, a tavern, where the Cogers have met since 1756.

In *Shoe-lane*, leading to Holborn-hill, was a notorious cockpit in Pepys's time: at the north end, from 1378 to 1647, was the town-house of the Bishop of Bangor; and a part of the garden, with lime-trees and a rookery, existed in 1759; the mansion was taken down in 1828. Shoe-lane is associated with four poets: in the burial-ground of St. Andrew's workhouse, now covered by Farringdon Market, was buried Chatterton; in St. Andrew's churchyard lies Henry Neele; in Gunpowder-alley, in 1658, died in abject poverty Richard Lovelace, the cavalier poet, "the most amiable and beautiful person that eyes ever beheld;"[*] in 1749, in a wretched lodging off Shoe-lane, died Richard Boyce. In Gunpowder-alley, too, lived Evans, the astrologer, the friend and instructor of Lilly, the "Sidrophel" of Hudibras.

Opposite Shoe-lane was the famous Fleet-street Conduit. (See page 125.) At No. 134, the Globe tavern, frequented by Goldsmith, and Macklin the actor, was held the Robin Hood club. *Salisbury-court*, nearly facing, was once the inn of the bishops of Salisbury; then of the Sackvilles, and was called Sackville House and Dorset House; whence Dorset-street. After the Great Fire, Wren built for Davenent "the Duke's Theatre," opened 1671, where Betterton played: it had a picturesque front to the Thames; upon its site are the city Gas-works. Salisbury or Dorset-court had also its playhouse, originally the granary of Salisbury House; it was pulled down by sectarian soldiers in 1649, rebuilt in 1660, but destroyed in the Great Fire. The court was a scene of the mug-house riots of 1716, and here was a noted mug-house. In Salisbury court (now square) Richardson wrote his *Pamela*, and printed his own novels; his printing-office being at the top of the court, now No. 76 Fleet-street: Goldsmith was once Richardson's "reader;" and here was printed Maitland's *London*, folio, 1739. Richardson was visited here by Hogarth, Dr. Johnson, Dr. Young; Secker, Archbishop of Canterbury; and Mrs. Barbauld, when a playful child.

Water-lane (now *Whitefriars-street*) leads to Whitefriars, named from a convent of white-robed Carmelites, and called Alsatia from 1608 to 1696 (see Scott's *Fortunes of Nigel*); extending from Fleet-street to the Thames, and from the western side of Water-lane to the Temple: it was a privileged sanctuary, abolished 1697: a notorious retreat for cheating creditors, had its cant Lombard-street; and had many a Cheatly, Shamwell, Hackum, and Scapeall. (See Shadwell's *Squire of Alsatia*.) At the Harrow, in Water-lane, lived Filby, Goldsmith's tailor.

No. 64 Fleet-street is the Bolt-in-Tun inn, named in a grant, 1443.

Opposite is *Bolt-court*, where, at No. 8, Dr. Johnson lived from 1776 till his death in 1784; while here, Johnson unsuccessfully applied (in 1776) to the Earl of Hertford, requesting apartments in Hampton Court Palace. Johnson's house was subsequently Bensley's printing-office, and was burnt June 26, 1819. The *Johnson's Head* tavern was not contemporary with the Doctor. (See *Notes and Queries*, No. 123.) At No. 4, Ferguson, the astronomer, died Nov. 1776. In the court, Cobbett wrote, printed, and published his *Political Register*, and sold Indian corn. No. 3 was bequeathed to the Medical Society of London by Dr. Lettsom; over the door is an emblematic bas-relief. The Society removed, in 1851, to 33 George-street, Hanover-square.

[*] George Petty, haberdasher, in Fleet-street, carried twenty shillings to Lovelace every Monday morning, from Sir —— Many, and Charles Cotton, Esq., for months, until the poet's death.

Wine-office-court : Goldsmith lodged here in 1761, when Johnson first visited him ; Goldsmith then wrote for the *Public Ledger* newspaper, and began the *Vicar of Wakefield.* Here is a good old chophouse, the *Cheshire Cheese.*

Johnson's-court : at No. 7 Samuel Johnson lived 1765 to 1776 ; the *John Bull* newspaper was commenced here, at No. 11, in 1820. Northward is *Gough-square,* where, at No. 17, Johnson compiled the greater portion of his Dictionary, 1748 to 1758.

Serjeants' Inn, on the south side of Fleet-street, was formerly an inn of court ; the handsome offices were designed by Adam. No. 13 Fleet-street, the Amicable Life Assurance office, was rebuilt in 1839 ; the Society was first chartered by Queen Anne.

CRANE-COURT. (See page 237.)

Red Lion-court : printing-offices of John Nichols (*Gentleman's Magazine*), burnt Feb. 8, 1808 ; of Messrs. Valpy(*Classics*), where *Punch* is now printed ; and of Richard Taylor, F.R.S. (*Philosophical Mag.*)

Mitre-court : Mitre tavern, the favourite rendezvous of Dr. Johnson's evening parties, including Goldsmith, Percy, Hawksworth, and Boswell ; here was planned the Tour to the Hebrides. Johnson had a strange nervous feeling, which made him uneasy if he had not touched every post between the Mitre and his own lodgings. Chamberlain Clark, who died in 1831, aged 92, was the last surviving of Dr. Johnson's Mitre friends. William Scott (Lord Stowell) also frequented this tavern. Here, in 1640, Lilly met old Will Poole, the astrologer, then living in Ram-alley ; the Royal Society Club dined at the Mitre from 1743 to 1750, the Society then meeting in Crane-court. Mitre-court was a sanctuary, abolished 1697.

FETTER-LANE. (See page 290.)

Hare-court (originally Ram-alley), opposite Fetter-lane, was formerly noted for its public-houses and cook-shops, often mentioned in the 17th-century plays; and was a sanctuary until 1697.

In Fleet-street were the earliest printing-offices and *stationery* marts for books : Wynkyn de Worde (assistant of Caxton) at the signs of the Golden Sun, Swan,* and Falcon, the latter in Falcon-court ; in the house over which (32 Fleet-street) lived John Murray, sen., the publisher. In Fleet-street, too, were the printing-houses of Richard Pynson ; Rastall (Star) ; Tottel (Hand and Star), afterwards Jaggard and Joel Stephens, in part of Dick's Coffee-house. (See Cunningham's *Hand-book,* p. 188.) Among the booksellers was Bernard Lintot (Cross Keys), "between the two Temple gates;" and against Old St. Dunstan's Church, Edmund Curll (Dial and Bible).

Here, also, are the oldest banking firms, except Stone, Martin and Co., Lombard-street, who claim to be the successors of Sir Thomas Gresham. No. 1 Fleet Street (formerly the Marygold) is the banking-house of Child and Co., who date from soon after the Restoration ; they occupy the rooms over Temple-bar for their books of accounts.

The principal of the firm is the Countess of Jersey, wife of George Child Villiers, Earl of Jersey, who assumed the name of Child upon his Countess inheriting the estates of her maternal grandfather, Robert Child, Esq., of Osterley

---

* Imprint to the " Demaundes Joyous :"
"Emprynted at London in Fletestre
te at the signe of the Swane by
me Wynkyn de Worde
In the yere of our
lorde A M
c c c c c
and XI
.*.

Park, Middlesex. "In the catalogue of a sale of prints, &c., by Mr. Hodgson, 9th June, 1834, lot 270, is an original sketch in oil by Hogarth, representing a memorable occurrence in the house of Child and Co., when they were delivered by temporary munificence of the Duchess of Marlborough."

Next is Gosling's, No. 19, sign of Three Squirrels in the iron-work of a window, originally on a lozenge shield.

Gosling, as founder of the house, is thus mentioned in the account of Secret Service Monies of Charles II. and James I.: "To Richard Bakenham, in full, for several parcells of gold and silver lace, bought of William Gostling and partners, on 2d May, 1674, by the Dutchess of Cleveland, for the wedding-clothes of the Lady Sussex and Lichfield, 640*l.* 8*s.*

Messrs. Hoares', No. 37 (Golden Bottle), dates from 1680.

Richard Hoare, Esq., the principal of the firm, succeeded Sir F. Child as Alderman of the Ward of Farringdon Without; was Sheriff in 1740-41, in which year there were three Lord Mayors. Mr. Hoare has left a manuscript journal of his shrievalty, illustrating various customs, privileges, and "treats" of the City, and concluding thus: "after being regaled with sack and walnuts, I returned to my own house in my private capacity, to my great consolation and comfort." He was Lord Mayor in 1746.

The old Fleet-street taverns and coffee-houses are mostly *up passages:* upon the site of Child's-place was the Devil tavern, sign St. Dunstan pulling the Devil's nose: here, in the Apollo chamber, over the door, were inscribed the verses by Jonson, commencing,

> "Welcome, all who lead or follow,
> To the oracle of Apollo."

Here Ben Jonson and his sons used to make their liberal meetings; the rules of Ben's Club in gold letters over the chimney. (*Tatler*, No. 79.) These are preserved in the premises, at the back of Child's bank, No. 1, with a terra-cotta bust of Apollo: the contemporary landlord was Sim Wadlow, "the king of skinkers." (*Jonson.*) The club-room, fitted with a music-gallery, was afterwards used for balls and entertainments; and the house continued to be the resort of the wits of the last century: "I dined to-day" (Oct. 12, 1710) "with Dr. Garth and Mr. Addison, at the Devil tavern, near Temple-bar; and Garth treated." (*Journal to Stella.*) Here Dr Johnson presided at a supper celebrating the publication of Mrs. Lennox's first book, when the whole night was spent in festivity: the tavern was taken down in 1788. Opposite, is Apollo-court; and next door east, is the Cock tavern, with an old carved and gilt sign-bird. (See TAVERNS.) The Horn Tavern, now Anderton's Hotel, No. 164, was famous in 1604. (See COFFEE-HOUSES Dick's, Rainbow, and Peele's, pp. 201-3-4.)

One of the *Curiosities* of Fleet-street was Mrs. Salmon's Moving Waxwork originally established at the Golden Salmon, St. Martin's, near Aldersgate (Harl Ms. 5931. Brit. Mus.): "it would have been ridiculous for the ingenious Mrs. Salmon to have lived at the sign of the Trout." (*The Spectator*, No. 28.) Thence the Waxwork was removed to No. 189 Fleet-street, since of Messrs. Praed's banking house. At the death of Mrs. Salmon, aged 90, the collection was purchased by Mr. Clarke, a surgeon, (father of Sir Charles Mansfield Clarke, M.D.) as an investment for his wife. Mrs. Clarke continued the exhibition as Mrs Salmon's, at No. 189, until 1795, when it was removed to No 17, nearly opposite, at the east corner of Inner Temple-lane; and here shewn, with a figure of Anne Siggs, on crutches, at the door, until Mrs. Clarke's death in 1812. The collection, much reduced, was then sold for 50*l*, and subsequently shewn at the west corner of Water-lane. No. 17 Fleet-street (now a hairdresser's), is advertised as "formerly the Palace of Henry VIII. and Cardinal Wolsey" Mrs. Salmon, with more probability, styled it "once the Palace of Henry Prince of Wales, son of King James I.;" but this residence is not mentioned by his biographers: the first-floor front-room, has, however, an enriched plaster ceiling, inscribed P. (triple plume H., which, with part of the carved wainscoting, denote the house to be of the time of James I.

Wax-work and nine-day wonders are still to be seen east of St. Dunstan's Church. In the bay-windowed house, Nos. 184 and 185, lived Drayton, the poet. West of St. Dunstan's is the Law Life Assurance Office, of James I. street-architecture, built by Shaw in 1834: next is the passage to Clifford's Inn. Chaucer, when a student of the Inner Temple, was fined 2s. by the Society for beating a Franciscan friar in Fleet-street; so states Speght, the illustrator of the poet. Cowley was born near Chancery-lane; his father was a grocer. Isaac Wal on lived two doors west of Chancery-lane, whither, in 1632, he removed. (See CHANCERY-LANE, p. 70.) At No. 197 was Rackstrow's Anatomical Museum, and collection of natural and artificial curiosities, natural magic, &c., exhibited from 1736 to 1798. *Bell-yard* and *Fetter-lane* were once noted for fishing-tackle shops, of which few remain.

Shire-lane (now Lower Serle's-place), hard by Temple-bar, named from its dividing the City from the Shire, was once a place of note. Here was born Sir Charles Sedley, the poet, and witty contemporary of Rochester; here lived Elias Ashmole, by turns astrologer, alchemist, and antiquary, who called "father" one Backhouse, an adept, in Fleet-street, over against St. Dunstan's Church.

In 1658, Ashmole left the astrologers and alchemists; in 1660, he was called to the bar in Middle Temple Hall; and on Jan. 26, 1679, by a fire in his chambers in the Middle Temple, he lost most of his library, a cabinet of 9000 coins, besides seals, charters, &c., and a curious collection of engraved portraits.

At the upper end of Shire-lane lived Isaac Bickerstaff, the *Tatler*, who led the deputation of "Twaddlers" down the lane, across Fleet-street, to Dick's Coffee-house. At the Trumpet (afterwards the Duke's Head) public-house, in Shire-lane, the *Tatler* met his club; and in the lane lived Christopher Katt, at whose house originated the Kit-Kat Club. (See p. 195.)

Fleet-street was the scene of the annual grand burning of the Pope (on Nov 17,) in the reign of Charles II.; the torchlight procession beginning at Moorfields, and ending at Fleet-street, where the effigies of the Pope was burnt, opposite Middle Temple-gate. These saturnalia were kept up until after the expulsion of James II.; when the anti-popish mummery was transferred to Nov. 5. (See TEMPLE and TEMPLE BAR.)

FOG OF LONDON.

This phenomenon is caused by the half million of blazing coal-fires in the metropolis contributing a vast quantity of fuliginous matter, which, mingling with the vapour, partly arising from imperfect drainage, produces that foggy darkness, which Londoners not inaptly term "awful." Sometimes it is of a bottle-green colour; but if the barometer rise, it will either totally disappear or change into a white mist. At other times it is of pea-soup yellow; in the midst of which the street gas-lights appear like the pin-head lamps of old. The latter is the genuine "London Fog."

> " First at the dawn of lingering day,
> It rises of an ashy gray;
> Then deeping with a sordid stain
> Of yellow, like a lion's mane.
> Vapour importunate and dense,
> It was at once with every sense.
> The ears escape not. All around
> Returns a dull, unwonted sound.
> Loath to stand still, afraid to stir,
> The chilled and puzzled passenger,
> Oft blundering from the pavement, fails
> To feel his way along the rails;
> Or at the crossings, in the roll

Of every carriage dreads the pole.
Scarce an eclipse with pall so dun
Blots from the face of heaven the sun.
But soon a thicker, darker cloak
Wraps all the town, behold, in smoke,
Which steam-compelling trade disgorges
From all her furnaces and forges
In pitchy clouds too dense to rise,
Descends rejected from the skies;
Till struggling day, extinguished quite,
At noon gives place to candle-light."—*Henry Lutirel.*

The fog too sensibly affects the organs of respiration: hence, a Scotch physician has asked, "if a person require half a gallon of pure air per minute, how many gallons of this foul atmosphere must be, as it were, filtered by his lungs in the course of a day?"

Sometimes the fog is caused by a very ordinary accident,—a change of wind, thus accounted for: the west wind carries the smoke of the town eastward, in a long train, extending twenty or thirty miles; as may be seen in a clear day from an eminence five or six miles from the town,— say, from Harrow-on-the-Hill. In this case, suppose the wind to change suddenly to the east, the great body of smoke will be brought back in an accumulated mass; and as this repasses the town, augmented by the clouds of smoke from every fire therein, it causes the murky darkness.

By accurate observation of the height of the fog, relatively with the higher edifices, whose elevation is known, it has been ascertained that the fogs of London never rise more than from 200 to 240 feet above the same level. Hence, the air of the more elevated environs of the metropolis is celebrated for its pure and invigorating qualities, being placed above the fogs of the plain, and removed from smoky and contaminated atmosphere. The height of the Norwood hills, for example, is 390 feet above the sea-level at low water; and thus enjoys pre-eminent salubrity.

FORTIFICATIONS.

The defence of the City of London by the wall built by our later Roman colonists has been already described. (See CITY WALL AND GATES, p. 184.) In later times, the metropolis had again to be fortified.

During the Civil Wars, in 1642, the Parliament ordered that trenches and ramparts should be made near the highways leading to the City, and in different parts about London and Westminster. These fortifications consisted of a strong earthen rampart, flanked with bastions, redoubts, &c., surrounding the whole city and its liberties, including Southwark. In Tyburn Road, in 1643, there were three forts erected, viz. a redoubt, with two flanks, near St. Giles's Pound; a small fort at the east end of the road; and a large fort with four half bulwarks, across the road opposite Wardour-street. From *The Perfect Diurnal* of this period, we gather that many thousands of men, women, and servants assisted in the works; as did also a great company of the Common Council, and other chief men of the City, and the Trained Bands, with spades, shovels, and pickaxes; also feltmakers, cappers, shoemakers, and porters, to the number of many thousands, assisted in raising the defences.

Upon the site of Mount-street was the fort of "Oliver's Mount;" and on the ground now occupied by Hamilton-place at Hyde-Park-corner was a large fort with four bastions.

"From ladies down to oyster-wenches,
    Labour'd like pioneers in trenches."—Butler's *Hudibras*, Part ii. Canto 2.

The women, and even the ladies of rank and fortune, not only encouraged the men, but worked with their own hands. Lady Middlesex, Lady Foster, Lady

Anne Walker, and Mrs. Dunch, have been particularly celebrated for their activity.—Dr. Nash's *Notes*.

FOUNDLING HOSPITAL (THE),

In Guilford-street, was established by Royal Charter, granted in 1739 to Thomas Coram (master of a trading vessel), "for the reception, maintenance, and education of exposed and deserted young children," in an hospital erected "after the example of France, Holland, and other Christian countries." This shews that Coram contemplated the indiscriminate admission of all foundlings, as is the case in the above countries; and such was the practice up to the commencement of the present century. The Governors first opened a house in Hatton-garden, on March 25, 1740-1; and any person bringing a child, rang the bell at the inner door, and waited to hear if the infant was returned from disease or at once received, no questions whatever being asked as to whom the child belonged, or whence it was brought; and when the full number of children had been taken in, a notice of " *The House is full*" was affixed over the door : often there were 100 children offered, when only twenty could be admitted; riots ensued, and thenceforth the women balloted for admission by drawing balls out of a bag.

The present Hospital was built by Jacobson; and the children, 600 in number, were removed there in 1754, when the expenses of the establishment were more than five times the amount of the income. The Governors then applied to Parliament, who voted them 10,000*l.*, and sanctioned the general admission of children, the establishment of country hospitals, &c.* A basket was hung at the gate of the hospital in London, in which the children were deposited, after ringing a bell to give notice to the officers in attendance.† On June 2d, 1756, the first day, 117 children were thus received; and between that day and December 31st, 1784, 3727 were admitted. In the year 1757 printed bills were posted in the streets apprising the public of their privilege. The consequences were lamentable : prostitution was greatly increased by this easy means of disposing of illegitimate offspring; and from the want of means of rearing so many children, the greater number died: of 14,934 children received in three years and ten months, 10,389 perished. At length, in 1760, this indiscriminate admission was discontinued by Act of Parliament, the legislature undertaking to support all the children who had been already received at its suggestion. Still, so late as 1795 the practice of admitting children without inquiry, on payment of 100*l.*, had not become extinct; but it was abolished in 1801.

Hogarth, one of the earliest " Governors and Guardians," greatly assisted his friend Captain Coram, whose full-length portrait he painted and presented to the Hospital, with other pictures. These were shewn to the public, and became very attractive; and out of this success grew the first Exhibition of the Royal Academy, in the Adelphi, in the year 1760. The painters often met at the Hospital; the exhibition of their pictures drew daily crowds of spectators, in their splendid equipages; and a visit to the Foundling became the most fashionable morning lounge of the reign of George II. The grounds in front of the Hospital were a fashionable promenade; and brocaded silks, gold-headed canes,

---

* Branch establishments were opened in the country; and at one of them (Ackworth, in Yorkshire) was made cloth, in suits of which several of the artist-patrons appeared at the Festival of 1761. Another branch hospital was at Aylesbury : of this John Wilkes (M.P. for that borough) was appointed Treasurer; but when he left the kingdom in 1764, his accounts were deficient.

† An aged banker in the north of England, received into the Hospital, being desirous of ascertaining his origin, all the information afforded by the books of the establishment was, that he was put into the basket at the gate naked.

and laced three-cornered (Egham, Staines, and Windsor) hats, formed a gay bevy in Lamb's-Conduit-fields.

The pictures represent the state of British art previously to the patronage of West by George III. In the collection is Hogarth's March to Finchley, and Moses brought to Pharaoh's Daughter; Dr. Mead, by Allan Ramsay; Handel, by Kneller; Lord Dartmouth, by Sir Joshua Reynolds; Views of the Foundling and St. George's Hospitals, by Richard Wilson; the Charter-House (Sutton's Hospital), by Gainsborough; Chelsea and Bethlem Hospitals, by Haytley; Christ's Hospital, St. Thomas's and Greenwich Hospitals, by Wale; a bas-relief by Rysbrack; and a bust of Handel, by Roubiliac.

The Chapel has an altar-piece (Christ presenting a little Child), painted by West. At the suggestion of Handel, the musical service has been a source of great profit to the Hospital funds. (See CHAPELS, p. 169.) Dr. Burney attempted to found an " Academy of Music" on this basis, just as an Academy of Arts had been raised; but the project failed. Several blind children, who had been received into the Hospital during the indiscriminate admission, were trained as a choir. Mr. Grenville, the organist: Mr. Printer, Miss Thetford, and Jenny Freer, singers, were all blind foundlings.

Coram is buried in the vaults. Here also rest several benefactors, including Lord Chief-Justice Tenterden, whose bust is at the eastern entrance to the chapel: some verses written by his Lordship are sung at the Festival of the Governors. Upon the lodges are two characteristic bas-relief medallions, nicely executed.

From 1760, the Institution ceased to be a hospital for foundlings—

" A race unknown,
At doors expos'd, whom matrons call their own."—*Dryden.*

Unfortunately, the name has been retained, and hence great misapprehension in the public mind as to the present objects and purposes of the Charity. The present practice of admitting children requires that they be illegitimate, except the father be a soldier or sailor killed in the service of his country; that the mother have borne a good character previous to her misfortune; and that she be poor and have no relations able or willing to maintain her child. There are other conditions enforced by the Governors; their benevolent object being " to hide the shame of the mother, as well as to preserve the life of the hild," and dismiss her from the Hospital with the charge to "sin no more." There are several eloquent defences of the objects of the Hospital. Sterne preached a sermon for the Charity in 1761; and the Rev. Sydney Smith was one of the appointed preachers.

There are at present 500 children supported by the Charity, from extreme infancy to the age of fifteen; the Governors have not the privilege of *presenting* children, after the manner of other establishments, the claim for admission depending upon the proven misery of the case. The general health of the children within the walls of the Hospital is remarkably good; indeed, the building occupies one of the healthiest sites in London. At an apprenticeable age, the girls are put out to domestic service, and the boys to trades.

The qualification of a Governor is a donation of 50*l.* The revenue of the Hospital is principally derived from the improved value of the Lamb's-Conduit estate (56 acres), which the Governors purchased as a site for the Hospital, in 1741, for the sum of 5500*l.*, collected by benefactions and legacies; when the Charity bought the whole estate, not because they required it, but because the Earl of Salisbury, its owner, would not sell any fractional part of it. As London increased, it approached this property; and the ground is now mostly covered with squares and streets of houses, the ground-rents producing an annual income equal to the purchase-money! The Governors have likewise established a Benevolent Fund, for the relief of aged and destitute persons who were inmates of the Hospital when infants. (See *Memoranda of the Foundling Hospital,* by John Brownlow, 1847.)

FOUNTAINS.

London has, in comparison with the Continental cities, but few decorative Fountains, of " the nature that sprinkleth or spouteth water." Early in the last century, however, the fountains were more numerous. Hatton (1708) mentions in Privy Garden, at Somerset House, Middle Temple, Lincoln's Inn, and King's Square, "the most publick ones." The court-yards and gardens of mansions had also their fountains: Montague House was celebrated for them. The courts of the Companies' Halls and City-merchants' houses boasted of their fountains, a few of which remain to this day, as in Mark-lane. The private garden of Draper's Hall has a basin, with a fountain and statue.

Old Somerset House had its geometrical water-garden and fountain.

Whitehall had its fountains; and Queen Elizabeth had a cascade made to play in her gardens, which, when touched by a distant spring, sprinkled all who approached it.

The King's (Soho) Square fountain had in the middle of the basin a stone statue of Charles II. in armour, on a pedestal enriched with crowns and foliage; on the four sides of the base were as many figures, with inscriptions, of the Thames, Severn, Tyne, and Humber rivers, spouting water. The statue of Charles remains, but the basin has been filled up, and is now a flower-garden.

St. James's-square had in its centre, in 1720, a basin with a jet of water 15 feet high; the basin was filled from York-buildings, was 6 or 7 feet deep, and 150 feet diameter, and upon it was kept a pleasure-boat: the site is now occupied by an equestrian statue of William III.

In the middle of New-square, Lincoln's Inn, was a fluted Corinthian column, and a clock with three dials near its vertex; and at each angle of the pedestal was a Cupid blowing water through a short twisted shell.

In the Benchers' Garden, Lincoln's Inn, in the centre of a basin, was the figure of a mermaid rising out of reeds, with a lofty jet of water.

The fountain was a popular ornament of our old tea-gardens: Bagnigge Wells had a curious specimen — half fountain, half grotto; and the fountain lingers among the cool delights of Vauxhall Gardens.

Kensington Gardens had a lofty sculptured fountain in the basin opposite the palace; but here, and in the Parks, the jets-d'eau are now tasteless and unornamental.

The fountain in Fountain-court, Middle Temple, rises from a marble-bordered basin, and in Hatton's time was kept " in so good order as always to force its stream to a vast and almost incredible altitude. It is fenced with timber palisades, constituting a quadrangle, wherein grow several lofty trees, and without are walks extending on every side of the quadrangle, all paved with Purbeck, very pleasant and delightful." The timber palisades have given way to iron railing; the jet is half-inch, and throws the water 10 feet height, and the effect of its sound and sparkle through the trees is very refreshing. Miss Landon has left a poem of pensive beauty, commencing thus :

> " The fountain's low singing is heard on the wind,
> Like a melody bringing sweet fancies to mind;
> Some to grieve, some to gladden: around them they cast
> The hopes of the morrow, the dreams of the past.
> Away in the distance is heard the vast sound,
> From the streets of the city that compass it round,
> Like the echo of fountains or ocean's deep call:
> Yet that fountain's low singing is heard over all."

The pair of fountains and basins in Trafalgar-square are the largest works of the kind in the metropolis. They were designed by Sir C. Barry, R.A., and executed in Peterhead granite by M'Donald and Leslie,

Aberdeen. Around each base are four dolphins' heads and fins, supporting a large flat vase and a pedestal, with a smaller vase, in the centre of which is the jet whence the water is thrown up; while a flat stream issues from each of the dolphins' mouths. The water is supplied from two Artesian wells, one in Orange-street, 300 feet deep, and the other in front of the National Gallery, 395 feet, connected at 170 feet depth by a tunnel to contain 70,000 gallons of water; the wells and tunnel at rest holding about 122,000 gallons. The wells are worked, the jets of the fountains thrown, and the water otherwise supplied, by a large Cornish pumping steam-engine, and a small inverted direct-action engine: outlay, 9000*l*.; annual rent, 500*l*.; engineers, Easton and Amos, Southwark. The contract for " spouting water" is thirteen hours per day in summer, and in winter seven hours; the height of the jets varies with the weather from 25 to 40 feet from the ground; supply, 500 gallons per minute; to the Treasury, Admiralty, Houses of Parliament, and other public offices, 100 gallons per minute. In the ornamental garden adjoining the Bank (of England) Parlour, is a stone basin, with a jet of water 20 feet high.

Fountains are useful ornaments of markets. At Billingsgate is a cast-iron fountain, with a basin about 15 feet in diameter, and a stem of rushes whence the water rises; and around the basin-lip lie twelve dolphins, which discharge water for the use of the market-people.

FREEMASONS' HALL,

In the rear of Freemasons' Tavern, 62, Great Queen-street, Lincoln's Inn Fields, was commenced May 1, 1775, from the designs of Thomas Sandby, R.A., Professor of Architecture in the Royal Academy: 5000*l*. was raised by a Tontine towards the cost; and the Hall was opened and dedicated in solemn form, May 23, 1776; Lord Petre, Grand-Master. " It is the first house built in this country with the appropriate symbols of masonry, and with the suitable apartments for the holding of lodges, the initiating, passing, raising, and exalting of brethren." (*Elmes.*) Here are held the Grand and other lodges, which hitherto assembled in the Halls of the City Companies.

Freemasons' Hall, as originally decorated, is shewn in a print of the annual procession of Freemason's Orphans, by T. Stothard, R.A., It is a finely-proportioned room, 92 feet by 43 feet, and 60 feet high; and will hold 1500 persons: it was re-decorated in 1846: the ceiling and coving are richly decorated; above the principal entrance is a large gallery, with an organ; and at the opposite end is a coved recess, flanked by a pair of fluted Ionic columns, and Egyptian doorways; the sides are decorated with fluted Ionic pilasters; and throughout the room in the frieze are masonic emblems, gilt, upon a transparent blue ground. In the intercolumniations are full-length royal and other masonic portraits, including that of the Duke of Sussex, as Grand-Master, by Sir W. Beechey, R.A. In the end recess is a marble statue of the Duke of Sussex, executed for the Grand Lodge, by E. H. Baily, R.A. The statue is 7 feet 6 inches high, and the pedestal 6 feet; the duke wears the robes of a Knight of the Garter, and the Guelphic insignia; at his side is a small altar, sculptured with masonic emblems.

The Hall is let for public dinners and meetings. Here meet the Madrigal Society, the Melodists' and other musical clubs; and the annual dinners of the Literary-Fund and Artists' Societies, and other public institutions, are given here.

St. Paul's, 604, and St. Peter's, Westminster, 605, were built by Freemasons. Gundulph, Bishop of Rochester, said to have built the White Tower, governed the Freemasons. Peter of Colechurch, architect of old London Bridge, was

Grand-Master. Henry VII., in a lodge of master Masons, founded his Chapel at Westminster Abbey. Sir Thomas Gresham, who planned the Royal Exchange, was Grand-Master; as was also Inigo Jones, who built the Banqueting-House, Whitehall; Ashburnham House, Westminster, &c. Sir Christopher Wren, Grand-Master, founded St. Paul's with his Lodge of Masons, and the trowel and mallet then used are preserved. Covent Garden Theatre was founded, 1808, by the Prince of Wales, Grand-Master; and the Grand Lodge.

"The connexion between the operative masons and a convivial society of goodfellows,—who, in the reign of Queen Anne, met at the 'Goose and Gridiron, in St. Paul his Church-yard,'—appears to have been finally dissolved about the beginning of the eighteenth century. From an inventory of the contents of the chest of the Worshipful Company of Masons and Citizens of London, it appears not long since to have contained a book wrote on parchment, or bound or stitched in parchment, containing an 113 annals of the antiquity, rise, and progress of the art and mystery of masonry. But this document is not now to be found."—Sir F. Palgrave; *Edinburgh Review*, April 1839.

FROSTS, AND FROST-FAIRS ON THE THAMES.

1281-2. " From this Christmas till the Purification of Our Lady, there was such a frost and snow, as no man living could remember the like; wherethrough, five arches of London Bridge, and all Rochester Bridge, were borne downe and carried away by the streame; and the like happened to many bridges in England. And, not long after, men passed over the Thames, between Westminster and Lambeth, dry-shod."—*Stow*, edited by Howes, 1631.

1410. " Thys yere was the grete frost and ise and the most sharpest wenter that ever man sawe, and it duryd fourteen wekes, so that men myght in dyvers places both goo and ryde over the Temse."—*Chronicle of the Grey Friars of London.*

1434-5. The Thames frozen from below London Bridge to Gravesend, from Dec. 25 to Feb. 10, when "the merchandise which came to the Thames mouth was carried to London by land."—*Stow.*

1506. " Such a sore snowe and a frost that men myght goo with carttes over the Temse and horses, and it lastyd tylle Candelmas."—*Chronicle of the Grey Friars of London.*

1515. The Thames frozen, when carriages passed over the ice from Lambeth to Westminster.

1564, Dec. 21. Stow and Holinshed state that on New-year's eve,

" People went over and alongst the Thames on the ise from London Bridge to Westminster. Some plaied at the foot-ball as boldlie there, as if it had beene on the drie land; diverse of the Court being then at Westminster, shot dailie at prickes set upon the Thames; and the people, both men and women, went on the Thames in greater numbers than in anie street of the City of London. On the third daie of January at night, it began to thaw, and on the fifth there was no ise to be seene between London Bridge and Lambeth, which sudden thaw caused great floods and high waters, that bare downe bridges and houses, and drowned manie people in England."

1608. Great frost described in Howes's continuation of Stow:

" The 8th of December began a hard frost, and continued until the 15th of the same, and then thawed; and the 22d of December it began againe to freeze violently, so as divers persons went halfe way over the Thames upon the ice; and the 30th of December, at every ebbe, many people went quite over the Thames in divers places, and so continued from that day until the 3d of January." From Jan. 10th to 15th, the ice became firm, and men, women, and children went boldly upon it; some shot at prickes, others bowled and danced, and many "set up booths and standing upon the ice, as fruitsellers, victuallers, that sold beere and wine, shoomakers, and a barber's tent;" the ice lasting until Feb. 2. There is a very rare tract, describing this frost, mentioned by Gough, in his *British Topography*, vol. i. p. 731, which has a woodcut representation of it, with London Bridge in the distance; it is entitled "Cold Doings in London, except it be at the Lottery," &c., 4to, 1608.

1609. Great frost commenced in October, and lasted four months. The Thames frozen, and heavy carriages driven over it.

1683-4. From the beginning of December until the 5th of February, frost "congealed the river Thames to that degree, that another city, as it were, was erected thereon; where, by the great number of streets and shops, with their rich furniture, it represented a great fair, with a variety of carriages, and diversions of all sorts; and near Whitehall a whole ox was roasted on the ice." *(Maitland.)* Evelyn, who was an eye-witness of the scene, thus describes it, Jan. 24, 1684:

" The frost continuing more and more severe, the Thames before London was still planted with boothes in formal streetes, all sorts of trades and shops furnished, and all full of commodities, even to a printing-presse, where the people and ladies tooke a fancy to have their names printed on the Thames; this humour tooke so universally, that 'twas estimated the printer gain'd 5*l.* a day for printing a line onely, at sixpence a name, besides what he got by ballads, &c. Coaches plied from Westminster to the Temple, and from several other staires, to and fro, as in the streetes; sheds, sliding with skeetes, and bull-baiting, horse and coach races, puppet-plays and interludes, cookes, tipling, and other lewd places; so that it seemed to be a bacchanalian triumph, or carnival on the water."

King Charles II. visited these diversions, and even had his name printed on the ice, with those of several other personages of the royal family. Mr. Upcott possessed a specimen,—a quarter of a sheet of coarse Dutch paper; within a type border, were the names of

> CHARLES, KING.
> JAMES, DUKE.
> KATHERINE, QUEEN.
> MARY, DUTCHESS.
> ANNE, PRINCESS.
> GEORGE, PRINCE.
> HANS IN KELDER.
>
> London : Printed by G. Croom, on the Ice, on
> the River of Thames, January 31, 1684.

Feb. 6, the day after the break-up of this great frost, Charles II. died.

In some curious verses, entitled " Thamasis's Advice to the Painter, from her frigid zone," &c., " printed by G. Croom, on the river of Thames," occurs :

> " To the *Print-house go,*
> Where *Men* the *Art of Printing* soon do know;
> Where, for a *Teaster,* you may have your *Name*
> Printed, hereafter for to show the same:
> And sure, in *former Ages,* ne'er was found
> . A *Press* to *print,* where men so oft were dround !"

The principal scene of this " Blanket-Fair" was opposite the Temple-stairs, as we see in a pencil and Indian-ink sketch, supposed by Thomas Wyote, dated " Munday, February the 4th, 1683-4 :" in front are various groups of figures, and a line of tents ; " Temple-street" stretches across the Thames. This drawing, with some prints, &c., illustrative of this frost, is in the Crowle Pennant, in the British Museum.—(See Thomson's *Chronicles of London Bridge,* pp. 469-717.)

1688-9. Great frost, Dec. 20 to Feb. 6: pools frozen 18 inches thick, and the Thames' ice covered with streets of shops, bull-baiting, shows, and tricks; hackney-coaches plied in the ice-roads, and a coach and six horses was driven from Whitehall almost to London Bridge; yet in two days all the ice disappeared.

1709. The Thames again frozen over, and some persons crossed it on the ice : in the Crowle Pennant (Brit. Mus.) is a coarse bill, within a woodcut border of rural subjects, containing, " Mr. John Heaton, Printed on the Thames at Westminster, Jan. the 7th, 1709."

1715. Severe frost, from the end of November until Feb. 9 follow-g, when the sports of 1683 were all renewed : in the Crowle Pennant a copperplate view, with a line of tents from Temple-stairs, and other marked "Thames-street ;" " Printed on the Thames 1715-16 ;" d above it, " Frost Fair on the River Thames."

1739-40. Dec. 25, another severe frost: the Thames floated with cks and shoals of ice ; and when they fixed, represented a snowy field, ery where rising in masses and hills of ice and snow. Several artists ade sketches ; tents and printing-presses were set up, and a complete rost Fair was again held upon the river, over which multitudes alked, though some fell victims to their rashness. It was in this fair at Doll, the pippin-woman, lost her life :

> " Doll every day had walk'd these treacherous roads ;
> Her neck grew warp'd beneath autumnal loads
> Of various fruit: she now a basket bore;
> That head, alas ! shall basket bear no more.
> Each booth she frequent past, in quest of gain,
> And boys with pleasure heard her thrilling strain.
> Ah, Doll ! all mortals must resign their breath,
> And industry itself submit to death !
> The crackling crystal yields ; she sinks, she dies,—
> Her head, chopt off, from her lost shoulders flies ;
> Pippins she cried, but death her voice confounds,
> And pip, pip, pip, along the ice resounds."—*Gay's Trivia*, b. ii.

nother remarkable character, "Tiddy Doll," died in the same place d manner. (*J. T. Smith.*) In the Crowle Pennant are several prints this Frost and Ice Fair. Some vintners in the Strand bought a rge ox in Smithfield, to be roasted whole on the ice ; and one Hodge-n, a butcher in St. James's Market, claimed the privilege of felling or nocking down the beast as a right inherent in his family, his father aving knocked down the ox roasted on the river in the Great Frost, 584; as himself did that roasted in 1715, near Hungerford Stairs : odgeson to wear a laced cambric apron, a silver-handled steel, and hat and feathers. The breaking-up of this frost was an odd scene ; he booths, shops, and huts being carried away by the swell of the aters and the ice separating.

1768. A violent frost, Jan. 1-21, when the piles of London Bridge erlings were much damaged by the ice ; on Jan. 5, a French vessel as wrecked upon a sterling, and two others were driven through the ntre arch, losing their main-masts, and carrying away the lamps from he parapet.

1789. Jan 8. The Thames frozen over, several purl-booths erected, d many thousands of persons crossed upon the ice from Tower-wharf the opposite shore. The frost had then lasted six weeks. No sooner d the Thames acquired a sufficient consistency, than booths, turn-bouts, &c., were erected; the puppet-shows, wild-beasts, &c., were ansported from every adjacent village; and the watermen broke in he ice close to the shore, and erected bridges, with toll-bars, to make very passenger pay a halfpenny for getting to the ice. A large pig as roasted on one of the roads, and a young bear hunted on the ice ear Rotherhithe ; and the printing-press was erected, as usual, to ommemorate the strange scene. Vast quantities of boiling water ere every morning poured upon the bridge water-works, to set the heels in motion, and twenty-five horses were used daily to remove he ice from around them ; while at Blackfriars the masses of ice were 8 feet thick. The sudden breaking up of the ice, with the rush of the eople to the shores, at night, was a fearful scene. A vessel lying off otherhithe, fastened by a cable and anchor to a beam of a public-house, in the night, veered about and pulled the house to the ground, killing five sleeping inmates.

1811. January: the Thames frozen over.

1813-14. Great frost, commenced Dec. 27, with a thick fog, followed by two days' heavy fall of snow. During nearly four weeks' frost, the wind blew almost uninterruptedly from the north and north-east, and the cold was intense. The river was covered with vast heaps of floating ice, bearing piles of snow, which, Jan. 26-29, were floated down, filling the space between London and Blackfriars Bridges; next day, the frost recommenced, and lasted to Feb. 5, uniting the whole into a sheet of ice. Jan. 30, persons walked over it; and Feb. 1, the unemployed watermen commenced their ice-toll, by which many of them received 6l. per day. The Frost Fair now commenced: the street of tents, called the City-road, put forth its gay flags, inviting signs, and music and dancing: a sheep was roasted whole before sixpenny spectators, and the "Lapland mutton" sold at a shilling a slice! Printing-presses were set up, and among other records was printed the following:

Frost Fair.

Amidst the Arts which on the THAMES appear,
To tell the wonders of this *icy* year,
PRINTING claims prior place, which at one view
Erects a monument of THAT and YOU.

Printed on the River Thames, February 4, in the 54th year of the reign of King George III. Anno Domini 1814.

One of the invitations ran thus:

"You that walk here, and do design to tell
Your children's children what this year befell,
Come buy this print, and then it will be seen
That such a year as this hath seldom been."

In the Fair were swings, books-stalls, dancing in a barge, suttling-booths, playing at skittles, frying sausages, &c. The ice and snow, in upheaved masses, as a foreground to St. Paul's and the city, had a striking effect; and the scene, by moonlight, was singularly picturesque. On Feb. 5, the ice cracked, and floated away with booths, printing-presses, &c.; the last document printed being a *jeu-de-mot* "to Madame Tabitha Thaw." Among the memorials is a duodecimo volume, pp. 124, now before us. It is entitled "*Frostiana; or, a History of the River Thames in a frozen state, with an Account of the late Severe Frost, &c.; to which is added the Art of Skating.* London: Printed and published on the ICE on the River *Thames, February 5, 1814, by G. Davis;*" the title-page was worked upon a large ice-island between Blackfriars and Westminster Bridges. In the *Illustrated London News*, No. 138, is an engraving of the Frost Fair of 1814, sketched near London Bridge, by Luke Clennell.

FULWOOD'S RENTS.

Vulgo, "Fuller's Rents," in Holborn, nearly opposite Chancery-lane, is a court, now meanly inhabited; but was of much better repute in the time of James I., when its possessor, Christopher Fulwood, Esq., resided here. Strype describes it as running up to Gray's Inn, "into which it has an entrance through the gate" (now closed); "a place of good resort, and taken up by coffee-houses, ale-houses, and houses of entertainment, by reason of its vicinity to Gray's Inn. On the east side is a handsome open place, with a freestone pavement, and better uilt, and inhabited by private housekeepers. At the upper end of this ourt is a passage into the Castle Tavern, a house of considerable rade, as is the Golden Griffin Tavern, on the west side." Here was ohn's, one of the earliest coffee-houses; and adjoining Gray's Inn gate, n the west side, is a deep-coloured brick house, once Squire's coffee-ouse, whence some of the *Spectators* are dated: it has been handsome nd roomy, with a wide staircase, but is now let in tenements. Within ne door of Gray's Inn was New Ward's (London Spy) punch-house, nuch frequented by the wits of the day: Ward died here in 1731. The Castle Tavern, mentioned by Strype, was many years kept by Thomas Winter, ("Tom Spring,") the pugilist, who died here, August 20, 1851.

About the centre of the east side of Fulwood's Rents is a curious abled and projecting house, *temp.* James I. Mr. Archer has engraved ground-floor room, entirely paneled with oak; the mantel-piece is vell carved in oak, with caryatides and arched niches; the ceiling eams are carved in panels; and the entire room is original, except the vindow. A larger room on the first floor contains another old mantel-iece, very florid. The front of the house is said to be covered with rnament, now concealed by plaster. (*Vestiges of Old London*, part v.)

~~~~~~~~~~~~~~~

GARDENS.

Fitzstephen states that in the time of Henry II. (1154-1189) the itizens of London had large and beautiful gardens to their villas. The oyal garden at Westminster was noted for its profusion of roses and ilies in 1276; and there is extant an order of Edward I. for pear-trees or this garden, and that at the Tower.

Sir Thomas More, in his *Utopia*, (about 1516), describes the gardens of Amaurot a model city) as lying behind all the houses: "these are large, but enclosed vith buildings that on all hands face the streets, so that every house has both a loor to the street and a back-door to the garden. They cultivate their gardens vith great care, so that they have vines, fruits, herbs, and flowers in them; and his humour of ordering their gardens so well is not kept up by the pleasure they ind in it, but also by an emulation between the inhabitants of the several streets, vho vie with each other."

"Within the compass of one age, Somerset House and the buildings were alled country-houses; and the open places about them were employed in gardens or profit; and also many parts within the City and liberties were occupied by vorking gardeners, and were sufficient to furnish the town with garden-ware: or then but a few herbs were used at the table in comparison to what are spent low."—*Stow.*

About two and a half centuries since, the citizens took their noon-ide and evening walks in their gardens. Cornhill was then an open pace, and the ground from thence to Bishopsgate-street was occupied s gardens, as were also the Minories. Goodman's Fields were an xtensive enclosure; and most of East Smithfield was an open space, partly used for bleaching. Spitalfields were entirely open. From Houndsditch, a street, but interspersed with gardens, extended nearly to Shoreditch Church, then nearly the last building in that direction. Moorfields were used for drying linen; cattle grazed and archers shot n Finsbury Fields, at the verge of which were three windmills. Gos-well-street was a lonely road; and Islington Church stood in the dis-tance, with a few houses and gardens near it. In Smithfield, horses were exercised, and on the western side was a row of trees. Clerken-well was mostly occupied by the precincts of St. John's Priory, beyond which, on the Islington-road, were a few detached houses, with gardens. From Cow Cross to Gray's-Inn-lane, the ground was either waste or n gardens; and between Shoe-lane and Fetter-lane was much open ground. At Drury-lane commenced the *village* of St. Giles: near the church were a few houses surrounded with trees. Beyond the church all was open country, the main roads being distinguished by avenues of trees. Leicester Fields and Soho were open ground. (See *Coven Garden*, p. 235.) Spring Garden was literally a garden, reaching to the site of the present Admiralty. The dwellings in the lower part of Westminster were inns and poor cottages, with small gardens. White hall Palace had its stately gardens, as had also the several noble man sions on the south side of the Strand. Isaac Walton quotes from a con temporary German poet:

> "So many gardens, dressed with curious care,
> That Thames with royal Tiber may compare."

These gardens had their water-gates; one of which, York-House gate, built by Inigo Jones, remains, with a terrace shaded by lime-trees.[*]

Leicester House, at the north-east corner of Leicester-square, had its spacious gardens, now the site of Lisle-street, built in 1791.

Holborn (Old-bourne) was famed for its gardens: Ely-place had its kitchen and flower gardens, vineyard and orchard, and the bishops were celebrated for raising choice fruit. (See ELY PLACE, p. 270.) Before the year 1597, John Gerrard, citizen and surgeon, had a large physic garden near his house in Holborn, where he raised 1100 plants and trees a proof "that our ground could produce other fruits besides hips and haws, acorns and pignuts." (*Oldys.*)

Baldwin's Gardens, between Leather-lane and Gray's-Inn-lane were, according to a stone upon a corner-house bearing the arms of Queen Elizabeth, named after Richard Baldwin, one of the royal gardeners, who began building here in 1589.

Montague House, Bloomsbury, had its spacious gardens, "after the French manner;" and the gardens of the houses in Great Russell-street were noted for their fragrance. Strype (1720) describes the north side as having gardens behind the houses, with the prospect of pleasant fields up to Hampstead and Highgate, "inasmuch as this place is esteemed the most healthful in London."

The garden of the Earl of Lincoln was highly kept, long before the mansion became an Inn of Court. The Earl's bailiff's accounts (28 Edward I.) shew it to have produced apples, pears, large nuts, and cherries sufficient for the Earl's table, and to yield by sale in one year 135*l.*, modern currency. The vegetables grown were beans, onions, garlick, leeks; hemp was grown; the cuttings of the vines much prized of pear-trees there were several varieties; the only flowers named are roses. (*T. Hudson Turner.*) The "walk under the elms," celebrated by Ben Jonson, was a favourite resort of Isaac Bickerstaff. In 1 and 2 Philip and Mary, the walk under the trees in the coney-garth[†] on cottrel-garden was made; and in 15 Car. II. A.D. 1663, the garden was enlarged, and a terrace-walk made on the left side; of which Pepys says: "to Lincoln's-Inn, to see the new garden which they are making which will be very pretty." The garden-wall in Chancery-lane is said to have been partly the labour of Ben Jonson.

> "Gray's Inn for walks, Lincoln's Inn for wall,
> The Inner Temple for a garden, and the Middle for a hall."
> (*Lincoln's Inn*; by W. H. Spilsbury, Librarian, 1850.)

---

* The entrance-gate to the terrace, "Villiers Walk," was for some years kept by Hugh Hewson, a hairdresser in St. Martin's parish, and the original of Hugh Strap, in Smollett's *Roderick Random:* Hewson died in 1809, aged 85.

† The coney-garth was "well stocked with rabbits and game," and by various ordinances of the Society, *temp* Edw. IV., Hen. VII., and Hen. VIII., penalties were imposed on the students hunting the rabbits with bows and arrows, or darts

The Inns of Court always boasted of their gardens. The Middle Temple has its gardens with an avenue of limes; the Inner Temple, a more extensive garden and promenade. In "the Temple Garden," Shakspeare has laid the scene of the origin of the red and white roses as the cognisances of the houses of York and Lancaster: Richard Plantagenet plucks a *white* rose, and the Earl of Somerset a *red* one; an alteration ensues, when the Earl of Warwick thus addresses Plantagenet:

> "In signal of my love to thee,
> Against proud Somerset and William Poole,
> Will I upon thy party wear this rose:
> And here I prophesy,—this brawl to-day,
> Grown to this faction, in the Temple Garden,
> Shall send, between the red rose and the white,
> A thousand souls to death and deadly night."
> *First Part of Henry VI.* act ii. sc. 4.

The red and white Provens rose no longer blossoms here; but both the Temple Gardens are well kept, and chrysanthemums here attain surprising perfection until mid-winter:

> "Still lone, 'mid the tumult, these gardens extend;
> The elm and the lime over flower-beds bend;
>   *   *   *   *
> The boat, and the barge, and the wave, have grown red;
> And the sunset has crimsoned the boughs over-head:
> But the lamps are now shining, the colours are gone,
> And the garden lies shadowy, silent, and lone."—L. E. L.

Both Lincoln and Gray's Inn had an uninterrupted view over fields and gardens to Hampstead and Highgate, which had then scarcely lost the rich woodland scenery of the ancient forest of Middlesex.

Gray's-Inn Gardens were laid out under the direction of Lord Bacon.

"In the 40 Eliz., at a pension of the bench, 'the summe of 7*l.* 15*s.* 4*d.* laid out for planting elm trees' in these gardens, was allowed to Mr. Bacon (afterwards Lord Verulam and Lord Chancellor). On the 14th November, in the following year, there was an order made for a supply of more young elms; and it was ordered 'that a new rayle and quickset hedges' should be set upon the upper long walk, at the discretion of Mr. Bacon and Mr. Wilbraham; the cost of which, as appeared by Bacon's account, allowed 20th April, 42 Eliz., was 60*l.* 6*s.* 8*d.* Mr. Bacon erected a summer-house on a small mount on the terrace, in which, if we may be allowed the conjecture, it is probable he frequently mused upon the subjects of those great works which have rendered his name immortal."—Pearce's *Inns of Court.*

To this day here is a *Catalpa* tree, raised from one planted by Lord Bacon, slips of which are much coveted. The walks were in high fashion in Charles II.'s time; and we read of Pepys and his wife, after church, walking "to Gray's Inne, to observe fashions of the ladies, because of my wife's making some clothes."

The City Halls, and mansions of the civic aristocracy, usually had their gardens, with terraces and lime-tree walks, fountains, and summer-houses, and decorative grottoes.

Grocers' Hall had in 1427 its pleasant garden, to which the citizens were admitted on petition to the Company: it contained "alleys, hedge-rows, and a bowling-alley," but was reduced in 1802, as we now see it. Drapers' Hall had a garden in 1551, when rents were paid for admission-keys, and it became a fashionable promenade: it is now open to the public. Merchant Tailors' Hall had its garden, with alleys and a terrace, a treasury and summer banqueting-room. Salters' Hall (Oxford-place) had its large garden, into which the infamous Empson and Dudley (*temp.* Henry VII.), living in "two faire houses" in the rear, had a dore of intercourse;" and here "they met and consulted of matters at their leasures" (*Stow*); this being originally the garden of the Priors of Tortington. Ironmongers' Hall had also its garden, for which we find charges for "cutting of the vines and roses, and knots of rosemary."

Sir Paul Pindar, contemporary with Sir Thomas Gresham, had his garden and park, with an embellished lodge in the rear of his mansion now a public-house in Bishopsgate-street; the grounds are covered with lanes, alleys, and blind courts, reaching to Finsbury-square. Gresham House had also its spacious walks and gardens.

Milton had a poetic liking for "*garden-houses*," of which there were many in his time: his house in Aldersgate-street opened into a garden; in 1651, he lived in Petty France, Westminster (York-street, No. 19) "a pretty garden-house, opening into the Park:" a cotton-willow tree is said to have been planted here by the poet's hand.

Sir John Hill's famous "physic-garden" was at Bayswater: here he cultivated medicinal plants, and prepared essences, tinctures, &c.

Goring House, which occupied the site of Buckingham Palace, had a fountain-garden, westward of which was the cherry-garden and kitchen-garden of Hugh Audley, Esq., from whom Audley-street, Grosvenor-square, is named. Here, too, was a grove of mulberry-trees planted by King James I.; afterwards "the Mulberry Garden." There was another mulberry-plantation at Chelsea.

Waller describes the wall in St. James's Park as

" All with a border of rich fruit-trees crown'd."

Brompton-Park Nursery can be traced from 1681. Evelyn describes it as a large and noble assembly of trees, evergreens, and shrubs, for planting the boscage, wilderness, or grove; with elms, limes, platans, Constantinople chestnuts, and black cherry-trees: its "potagere, melo niere, culinierie" garden; seeds, bulbs, roots, and slips, for the flowering garden; occupying about 56 acres. In 1705, its plants at 1*d.* each were valued at 40,000*l.*; and it had a wall half a mile long, covered with vines. London and Wise were the proprietors in 1694: they are praised by Addison in the *Spectator* for their laying-out of Kensington Gardens, where we see also Kent's ha-ha. The "Brompton Stock" is a memorial of the celebrity of this district, which extended to Chelsea: but the gardens are fast disappearing, and their ground built upon: the site of Trinity Church, Brompton, was in 1828 a market-garden. Chelsea Hospital, however, retains its terraces, little canals, and shady lime-walks, and gigantic plane-trees, a curious specimen of the Dutch style, *temp.* William III.; it has an octagon summer-house, built by Sir John Vanbrugh. "The Old Men's Gardens" to the south-east, including part of the site of old Ranelagh, were added in 1826, when Lord John Russell was Paymaster-General: here each pensioner has his garden the dressing of which affords society and employment.

As the eighteenth century advanced, the Botanic Garden at Chelsea, and its curator, Philip Miller, came into notice. (See BOTANIC GARDENS, p. 50.)

Buckingham-Palace Gardens comprise about forty acres, of which nearly five are a lake: upon a mount is a pavilion of Chinese design; the interior decorated in the Pompeian and Raphaelesque style, with paintings from Milton's *Comus*, and Scott's novels and poems; by Eastlake, Maclise, Ross, &c.: the grounds are secluded by majestic elms; whilst the principal front of the palace commands the landscape-garden of St. James's Park. The old palace of St. James's, and Marlborough House, have their gardens; and in the same line were the grounds of Carlton House, with conservatories and rookery, now occupied by lofty terraces of mansions; but Buckingham House, and the several Clubhouses on the south side of Pall Mall, have their gardens.

Kensington Palace has its flower-garden of quaint design. In this direction lies Holland House, with its stately cedars, oaks, and planes; its flower-garden, with evergreens clipped into fantastic forms; beds of Italian and old English character, fountains and terraces befitting the architectural garden of this Elizabethan mansion : in the " French Garden," in 1804, was first raised in England the Dahlia, from seeds sent by Lord Holland from Spain.

Campden House, Kensington, has a sheltered garden, in which the wild olive once flourished; and here a caper-tree produced fruit yearly for a century.

Vauxhall, noticed by Evelyn in 1661, as "the New Spring Garden, a pretty-contriv'd plantation," is mentioned otherwise than as a mere promenade: Monoconys, about 1663, describes its squares "inclosed with hedges of gooseberries, within which were roses, beans, and asparagus."

Hard by was Tradescant's garden at South Lambeth, well stored with rare and curious plants collected in his travels: including roses from Rose Island, near Port St. Nicholas. This garden existed in 1749, and is described in *Philos. Trans.* vol. 46. Tradescant was " king's gardener," *temp.* Charles I.; and, with his son, assembled at Lambeth the rarities which were the nucleus of the Ashmolean Museum.

In the Catalogue of their garden, published by the second Tradescant, are Hollyhocks, Southernwood, Wormwood; the classical Acanthus, Prince's Feathers; that "great Flouramour, or purple flowre gentle;" Anemones of all sorts, Dogsbane; the "Arbor Judæ, or Judas Tree, with red flowres;" the Birthworts of the south; numerous North-American plants; meadow Saffrons from Constantinople; that "Fragraria Novæ Angliæ nondam descripta," the mother of our Keens, Seedlings, and Scarlet and British Queen Strawberries; the "Hippomarathrum," or Rhubarb of the Monks; Marvels of Peru; "Paralysis fatua, foolish Cowslip, or Jack-an-apes on Horseback," probably the green monster of the common Oxlip; Pappas, or Virginian Potatoes; "Populus alba Virginiana Tradescanti," apparently one of our Tacamahacs; Musk Roses, Double Yellow Roses, and "Muscovie Roses;" Fox Grapes, from Virginia; White and Red Burlett Grapes, Currant Grape, Muscadells, "Frontinack or Musked Grape, white and red;" and other rarities, filling more than 100 pages.—*Gardener's Chronicle*, March 11, 1852.

Lambeth was formerly noted for its public gardens. Here was Cuper's garden, laid out with walks and arbours by Boydell Cuper, gardener to Thomas Earl of Arundel, who gave him some of the mutilated Arundelian marbles (statues,) which Cuper set up in his garden: it was suppressed in 1753: the site is now crossed by Waterloo-Bridge-road. Between the site of St. John's Church, and Christ Church, Blackfriars-road, was formerly occupied by gardens, through which lay the old Halfpenny Hatch footpath. (See ST. GEORGE'S FIELDS, p. 327).

Opposite the Asylum were the Apollo Gardens, opened about 1788: the old orchestra is now in Sydney Gardens, Bath. In the present Southwark-Bridge-road was Finch's Grotto and Garden, established about 1760: here Suett and Nan Cattley acted and sang: the old Grotto house was burnt in 1795, but was rebuilt, and a stone inserted with this inscription:

> " Here Herbs did grow,
> And Flowers sweet;
> But now 'tis call'd
> St. George's street."

Attached to some of the modern mansions *in the town* are pleasant landscape-gardens: from the rear of Devonshire House is a *rus-in-urbe* seemingly extending to Berkeley-square, by means of the sunken passage between the grounds of Lansdowne and Devonshire Houses.

The gardens in the centres of the several squares are refreshing as oases in the desert waste; and several of them are highly kept.

GAS-LIGHTING.

Although the Chinese have for ages employed natural coal-gas for lighting their streets and houses, only within the present century has Gas superseded in London the dim oil-lights and crystal-glass lamps of the preceding century. Dr. Johnson is said to have had a prevision of this change; when, one evening, from the window of his house in Bolt-court, he observed the parish lamp-lighter ascend a ladder to light one of the glimmering oil-lamps: he had scarcely descended the ladder half-way when the flame expired; quickly returning, he lifted the cover partially, and thrusting the end of his torch beneath it, the flame was instantly communicated to the wick by the thick vapour which issued from it. "Ah!" exclaimed the Doctor, "one of these days the streets of London will be *lighted by smoke!*" (*Notes and Queries*, No. 127.)

Coal-gas had been used for lighting by William Murdoch, in Corn-wall, Birmingham, and Manchester, when F. A. Winsor, a German, after several experiments, lighted the old Lyceum Theatre in 1803-1804; he also established a New Light and Heat Company, with 50,000*l.* for further experiments; in 1807 he lighted one side of Pall Mall, and on the King's birthday (June 4,) brilliantly illuminated the wall between Pall Mall and St. James's Park; and next exhibited gas-light in Golden-lane, August 16, 1807.

In 1809, Winsor applied to parliament for a charter, when the testimony of Accum, the chemist, was bitterly ridiculed by Mr. Brougham, F.R.S. In 1810-12 was established the Gas-Light and Coke Company, in Cannon-row, Westminster; removed to Peter-street, or Horseferry-road, then the site of a market-garden, poplars, and a tea-garden. In 1814, Westminster Bridge was lighted with gas; and the old oil-lamps removed from St. Margaret's parish, and gas lanterns substituted; and on Christmas-day, 1814, commenced the general lighting of London with gas. Yet the scheme had been so ridiculed, that Sir Humphry Davy, P.R.S., asked "if it were intended to take the dome of St. Paul's for a gasometer;" and a deputation of Fellows of the Royal Society, on visit-ing the Peter-street gas-works, speculated upon frightful consequences from the leakage and explosion of the gasometer. In 1822, St. James's Park was first lighted with gas; and the last important locality to adopt gas-lighting was Grosvenor-square in 1842. Theatres were first lighted in 1817-18; church clock-dials in 1827.

London is now lighted by fourteen gas companies, having twenty gas-making establishments in the town and its suburbs. Their invest-ment of capital is about four millions.

Coal-gas is made from coal enclosed in red-hot cast-iron or clay cylinders, or retorts; when hydro-carbon gases are evolved, and coke left behind; the gas being carried away by wide tubes, next cooled and washed with water, and then exposed to lime in close purifiers. It is then stored in sheet-iron gas-holders, miscalled gasometers: some of which hold 700,000 cubic feet of gas; and the several London Companies have storage for ten million cubic feet of gas. Thence it is driven by the weight of the gas-holders through cast-iron mains or pipes under the streets, and from them by wrought-iron service-pipes to the lamps and burners: of the gas-mains there are nearly 2000 miles.

The London Gas Company's works, Vauxhall, are the most powerful and complete in the world: from this point, their mains pass across Vauxhall Bridge to western London; and by Westminster and Waterloo Bridges to Hampstead and Highgate, seven miles distant, where they supply gas with the same precision and abundance as at Vauxhall.

Gas made from oil and resin is too costly for street-lighting, but has been used for large public establishments. Covent Garden Theatre was formerly lighted with oil-gas, made on the premises; and the London Institution, with resin gas, first made by Mr. Daniell. The Lime-ball, Bude, Boccius, and Electric lights have been exhibited experimentally 'or street-lighting, but are too expensive. Upon the patent Air-light from the vapour of hydro-carbon mixed with atmospheric air), proposed n 1838, upwards of 30,000*l.* were expended unsuccessfully.

A Journal of Gas-lighting is devoted exclusively to the records of :his wonderful "art which doth excel nature."

What has the new light of all the preachers done for the morality and order of London, compared to what has been effected by Gas-lighting! Old Murdoch alone has suppressed more vice than the Suppression Society; and has been a greater police-officer into the bargain than old Colquhoun and Sir Richard Birnie inited.—*Westminster Review,* 1829.

GATE-HOUSE (THE), WESTMINSTER,

Built *temp.* Edward III. as the principal approach to the Monastery, stood at the western entrance of Tothill-street, and consisted of two gates, the southern, leading out of Great Dean's-yard, and a receptacle or felons. On the east side was the Bishop of London's prison for clerks-convict; the rooms over the other gate adjoining, but towards the west, being a prison-house for state, ecclesiastical, and parliamentary offenders, prisoners from the Court of Conscience, as well as for debtors and felons. The latter were brought hither through Thieving-lane and Union-street, to prevent escape by entering the liberties of Sanctuary.

Among the distinguished prisoners confined here, were Nicholas Vaux, for propagating the Romish religion; he died here of cold and hunger, 1571: Lady Purbeck, for adultery, 1622; she escaped to France, disguised in a man's dress: John Selden, 1630; Sir Walter Raleigh, his last prison-house, whence he was led to the block in Old Palace-yard; Lovelace, the Cavalier-poet, who wrote here his loyal song, "To Althæa, from prison;" Sir Charles Lyttleton, whom Clarendon said was "worth his weight in gold;" in 1690, Pepys, the Diarist, charged with being affected towards the abdicated James II.; Sir Jeffrey Hudson, the court-dwarf, suspected of joining the Popish Plot, died here; in 1701, five "men of Kent," for a "scandalous, insolent, and seditious" petition to the House of Commons; in 1716, Thomas Harley, for prevarication to the House of Commons; the non-juring Jeremy Collier, 1692; and Richard Savage, the poet, committed here for the murder of Mr. Sinclair in a tavern fray. The debtors used to let down upon a pole an alms-box, to collect money from the passers in the street. The Gate-house was taken down in 1777; except one arch, which remained till 1836 in the wall of the house once inhabited by the Right Hon. Edmund Burke. (See Walcott's *Westminster,* p. 273.)

GEOLOGY OF LONDON.

The area on which the metropolis is situated, as well as the surrounding district to a distance varying from a radius of ten to twenty or thirty miles, consists of the marine tertiary *eocene* (dawn of recent) strata, which have been deposited in, and still occupy, a depression or excavation of the chalk called the London basin. Around this formation, the chalk forms a distinct boundary, on the south, west, and north rising up into chains of hills or downs, averaging 400 feet in height above the level of the Thames; but on the east the range is broken, and the tertiary basin lies open to the sea, affording a passage for the Thames and its tributary streams. (*Mantell.*)

The chalk, so prominent in the country around Gravesend, Croydon, and Epsom, passes beneath London at a depth not exceeding 150 to 250 feet. It is covered, first, by a series of beds of sand and mottled clays, 50 to 80 feet thick; and these are again overlaid by the London clay, from 100 to 400 feet thick: in the south-east corner of the county it is only 44 feet thick; while at White's Club-house, St. James's-street, it is 235 feet. This clay is usually very tough and tenacious, with the exception of a portion of its upper beds, which are mixed with sand. Mr. R. W. Mylne, F.G.S., in his "Geological and Topographical Maps," 1852, has been the first to point out the exact extent of these higher beds, upon the nature of the surface on which the pleasant character of the country of Highgate and Hampstead is dependent. But the most remarkable variety in the geological features—a variety attended by a corresponding diversity of scenery—occurs in the district between Woolwich, Greenwich, Blackheath, and Lewisham. We there find the outcrops of no less than five different groups of strata, commencing with the chalk, and ending with the London clay. Throughout a great part of London, this clay is overlaid by drift gravel, varying from 5 to 20 feet in thickness. The chalk basin, formed by the strata bending or dipping in the middle, contains pure water; into this formation the Artesian Wells of London are often carried down; but it is a question as to the quantity. (See ARTESIAN WELLS, p. 20.)

The gravel is not confined to the low grounds, but caps the highest summits of the districts: e.g. Highgate on the north, and Shooter's Hill on the south, of the Thames. To explain this distribution of the gravel by the operation of the actual rivers, we must first suppose that an uniform plane originally existed from the summit of Highgate to the Hertfordshire chalk downs, and from the top of Shooter's Hill to those of Kent, on the surface of which the river once flowed; secondly, that these rivers have subsequently washed away all that immense mass of materials which would be requisite thus to re-construct the surface; and thirdly, that having worn down that surface into nearly its present form, the rivers perpetually shifted their channels, so as to distribute the gravel equally over the whole plain of London, yet remained long enough in each channel to lodge there deposits of this gravel 20 or 30 feet thick. (*Conybeare.*)

Amongst the contents of the London basin are balls of imperfect ironstone, (*septaria,*) of which Parker's cement is made; branches and stems of trees, penetrated by the *teredo navalis,* are found here, as is also a species of resin. A fossil tree and nautili were found in digging the Primrose-Hill railway-tunnel. Remains of turtles and crocodiles, and elephants' teeth and tusks, have been dug out of the clay at Highgate and Islington.

Fossils are occasionally found on the rising slopes near Holloway, formed by the earth thrown up in 1812, when the Highgate tunnel was made. Fine specimens of *echinus marinus* (sea urchin,) have been picked up in a field contiguous to the archway, together with a fish resembling a sole; another fish, resembling a mackerel, in the brick-fields; and a narrow stratum of dusty earth abounds with mussels, pectines, and other fossil bivalves; with large quantities of iron combined with sulphur, in the form of pyrites. In a meadow behind Caen Wood is a spring highly impregnated with iron.

In 1813, Mr. Trimmer's brick-fields, at Brentford, yielded such a collection of sea-shells, sharks' teeth, bones of the elephant, hippopotamus, ox, and deer, together with fresh-water shells, as to remind one of the relics of a vast menagerie of animals from all quarters of the globe; and in 1840, in excavating 40 feet deep near Kew Bridge, were found several nautili, and smaller marine shells. For the disappearance of the British mammoths, whose remains are found here, Sir R. I. Murchison accounts by viewing England as the comparatively small island she was, when the ancient estuary of the Thames, including the plains of Hyde Park, Chelsea, Hounslow, and Uxbridge, were under water, and the country thus afforded but insufficient feeding-grounds for these stupendous quadrupeds.

ST. GEORGE'S FIELDS,

Between Lambeth and the Borough of Southwark, was an important district, occupied by the Romans, attested by the large quantities of coins, bricks, an urn-full of bones, tesselated pavements, &c. found here; the urn is preserved in the Museum of the Royal Society. St. George's Fields were also crossed by the great Roman road, Watling-street, presumed to have passed from Kent through Old Croydon, or Woodcote, (supposed to be the ancient Noviomagus,) Streatham, and Newington, to Stone-street in Southwark; and thence by a ferry over the Thames to Dowgate and the Watling-street of our day. A branch of the Ermine-street, from Chichester in Sussex, is also conjectured to have assumed the name of Stone-street on entering Surrey; and to have passed by Dorking, Woodcote, Streatham, Kennington, and Newington, across St. George's Fields, into Southwark.

St. George's Fields anciently included the whole space peninsulated by the bend of the river Thames, commencing at Greenwich, and terminating at Nine Elms. This was, probably, originally a large marshy bay, across which were several lines of transit at low water, leading from the rising grounds at Norwood, Camberwell, and Dulwich, to fords at various places across the Thames. Ptolemy (second century) mentions that the Romans had then settled south of the river, though the north bank was their original station: subsequently, the tract called St. George's Fields having been partially drained, and *causeways* (as at Newington) through the marshes constructed, forts and other buildings were erected, and a southern suburb of London gradually arose. — Brayley's *Surrey*, vol. v. p. 337.

Nearly to the present century, the Fields lay waste, and were the scene of brutalising sports, political meetings, and low places of entertainment. In their water-ditches Gerrard found plenty of water-violets: and scores of gardens existed here to our time. Here a riot was raised by the mobs who met to visit Wilkes in the King's Bench Prison, in 1768; and here Lord George Gordon's rioters met, June 2, 1780; on the 7th, the 700 prisoners in the King's Bench were liberated, and the building set on fire by the populace. Here were the Dog and Duck wells, in 1695, which grew to be a Sabbath-breaking tavern; the premises were last tenanted as the School for the Indigent Blind; the site is now included in Bethlem Hospital, and the sculptured sign-stone preserved in the boundary-wall denotes the site of the tavern-entrance. (See BETHLEM HOSPITAL, p. 42; BLIND SCHOOL, p. 49; and ST. GEORGE'S ROMAN CATHOLIC CHURCH, p. 151.)

ST. GILES'S,

Originally a village in the north-west suburbs of London: was named from an hospital for lepers, dedicated to the saint, built on the site of a small church or oratory, and nearly upon the site of the present church, about 1117, by Matilda, queen of Henry I. The gardens and precincts extended between High-street and Hog-lane (now Crown-street), and the Pound,* west of Meux's brewery. In 1213, the village was laid out in garden-plots, with cottages; it had its ancient stone cross; and about 1225 there was a blacksmith's shop at the north-west end of Drury-lane, which remained long after the suppression of the Hospital,† or about 1600, when the "verie pleasant village" was built over: "on the High-street, Holborn," says Stow, "have ye many faire houses builded, and lodgings for gentlemen, inns for travellers, and such like, up almost, for it lacketh little, to St. Giles's-in-the-Fields."

Aggas's plan shews fields and gardens from St. Giles's Hospital

---

* The exact site of St. Giles's Pound, (whence miles on the Oxford road were measured,) is an area of 30 feet of the broad space where St. Giles's, High-street, Tottenham-Court-road, and Oxford-street meet: around it was a nestling-place of crime:

"At Newgate-steps Jack Chance was found,
And bred up near St. Giles's Pound."

† The celebrated Dr. Andrew Boorde rented for many years the Master's House, *temp.* Henry VIII.

wall to Chancery-lane, eastward, with a few houses at the north en(
of Drury-lane, and opposite the present Red Lion-street, Holborn
Thence to the north side of the Strand are two or three houses ir
Covent Garden; Drury House, at the bottom of Drury-lane; and cattl
grazing on the site of Great Queen-street, Lincoln's-Inn-Fields. Earl
in the reign of Queen Anne, the whole parish of St. Giles's, except the
neighbourhood of Bedford-square and the present Bloomsbury, wa
covered with houses.

The village of St. Giles's was noted for its early inns and houses of entertain
ment. Here was Croche House (*Le Croche Hose*, or the Crossed Stockings, sign]
which belonged to the Hospital cook, anno 1300, and was opposite the north en(
of Monmouth-street. The Swan on the Hop, in Holborn, east of Drury-lane, i
mentioned 34 Edward III.; and the White Hart, corner of Holborn and Drury
lane, is shewn in Aggas's plan, 1560, and was an inn till 1720. Not far eastwar(
was the Rose, named in a deed Edward III.; with the Vine, a little east of Kings
gate-street, supposed to have been on the site of the Vineyard in Holborn
named in Domesday Book. The Vine was taken down in 1817, and the hous(
built on its site was occupied by Probert, the accomplice of the murderer Johi
Thurtell. The Maidenhead inn, in Dyot-street, flourished early in the reign o
Queen Elizabeth. The Turnstile Tavern, south-west corner of Great Turnstile
(now a butcher's shop,) was bequeathed to the parish in 1640; and the Cock an(
Pye was in the fields of that name.

About the year 1413, the gallows was removed from the Elms ii
Smithfield to the north end of the garden-wall of St. Giles's Hospital
and it is figured in an ancient plan of the district. (See p. 129.)

1416. "Thys yere the xiiij day of December Sir John Oldecastell Knyght
was drawne from the tower of London un to sent Gylles in the felde and ther
was hongyd (on a gallows new made) and brent."—*Chronicle of the Grey Friar
of London.*

The gallows was again removed westward to Tyburn; when St. Giles'
became a sort of half-way house for condemned criminals, who stoppe(
at the Hospital, and afterwards at an hostel built on its site, and wer(
there presented with a large bowl of ale. This gave a moral taint t(
St. Giles's, and made it a retreat for noisome and squalid outcasts
The Puritans made stout efforts to reform its morals; and, as the parisl
books attest, "oppressed tipplers" were fined for drinking on th(
Lord's day, and vintners for permitting them; fines were levied fo
swearing oaths, travelling and brewing on a fast-day, &c. Again, S(
Giles's was a refuge for the persecuted tipplers and ragamuffins o
London and Westminster in those days; and its blackguardism wa
increased by harsh treatment. It next became the abode of knot(
of disaffected foreigners, chiefly Frenchmen, of whom a club was hel(
in Seven Dials. Smollett speaks, in 1740, of "two tatterdemalion(
from the purlieus of St. Giles's, and between them both there was bu(
one shirt and a pair of breeches." Hogarth painted his moralities fron
St. Giles's: his "Gin-lane" has for its background St. George's Churcl
Bloomsbury, date 1751: "when," says Hogarth, "these two print(
("Gin-lane" and "Beer-street,") were designed and engraved, th(
dreadful consequences of gin-drinking appeared in every house in Gin
lane; every circumstance of its horrid effects is brought to view *in ter
rorem,*—not a house in tolerable condition but the pawnbroker's an(
the gin-shop—the coffin-maker's in the distance." Again, the scene o
Hogarth's Harlot's Progress is in Drury-lane; Tom Nero, in his Fou
Stages of Cruelty, is a St. Giles's charity-boy; and in a night-cellar her(
the idle apprentice is taken up for murder.* Here were often scene(

* A Middlesex magistrate said, in 1817: "In the early part of my life (I r(
member almost the time which Hogarth has pictured) *every house in St. Giles'*
whatever else they sold, sold gin; every chandler's shop sold gin: the situatio(
of the people was dreadful."

f bloody fray, riot, and chance-medley; for in this wretched district ere grouped herds of men but little removed from savagery. The .ound-house (Watch-house,) of St. Giles's was probably one of the ιst that remained: it stood in an angle of Kendrick-yard, and its ιck windows looked upon the burial-ground of St. Giles's Church; it ˈas built in a cylindrical form, like a modern Martello tower, though, ˈom bulging, it resembled an enormous cask set on its end: it was ˈo stories high, and had a flat roof, surmounted by a gilt vane in the ιape of a key. (See W. H. Ainsworth's *Jack Sheppard.*)

Seven Dials was built *temp.* Charles II. for wealthy tenants. ˈvelyn notes, 1694: "I went to see the building near St. Giles's, ˈhere Seven Dials make a star from a Doric pillar placed in the middle f ˈa circular area, said to be by Mr. Neale (the introducer of the late ˈtteries), in imitation of Venice, now set up here for himself twice, ιd once for the state."

> " Where famed St. Giles's ancient limits spread,
> An in-rail'd column rears its lofty head;
> Here to seven streets seven dials count their day,
> And from each other catch the circling ray:
> Here oft the peasant, with inquiring face,
> Bewilder'd trudges on from place to place;
> He dwells on every sign with stupid gaze,
> Enters the narrow alley's doubtful maze,
> Tries every winding court and street in vain,
> And doubles o'er his weary steps again."—Gay's *Trivia*, book ii.

The seven streets were Great and Little Earl, Great and Little ˈhite Lion, Great and Little St. Andrew's, and Queen; though the dial- ιone had but six faces, two of the streets opening into one angle. The ιlumn and dials were removed in June, 1773, to search for a treasure ιd to be concealed beneath the base: they were never replaced, but ˈ 1822 were purchased of a stone-mason, and the column was sur- ιounted with a ducal coronet, and set up on Weybridge Green as ˈmemorial to the late Duchess of York, who died at Oatlands in 1820. ˈhe dial-stone is now a stepping-stone at the adjoining Ship inn.

" Every body whose affairs lead him to be constantly running about London ιows the dirty labyrinth of Seven Dials; indeed, we might rather say every ιdy does not know it, for it takes a long apprenticeship in pavement-polishing ˈ become acquainted with its bearings and intricacies. The respective gin-shops ˈits corners are the only guides. In other wildernesses of natural objects, ˈstead of bricks and mortar, the sun and stars would serve to indicate points of ˈe compass, but in Seven Dials the sun and the stars are seldom visible. A ιavy tarpaulin of fog, and smoke, and reeking odours, covers the entire district, ˈutting out the heavens by a murky medium, under which increases and ˈultiplies the most unlovely race of the mammoth metropolis. They never get ˈlung-full of good air. The only innocuous atmosphere they breathe is that ˈhich sometimes surges down over the roofs of the many-peopled houses from ˈe adjacent brewery, and even that is artificial."—*Albert Smith.*

Long Acre, the Seven Dials, and Soho were Cock and Pie Fields, ιe resort of the idle and dissolute, until, *temp.* William III., Mr. Neale ιilt upon the ground. Wyld-street is named from the mansion ˈere of the Welds, the Dorset Roman Catholic family; Bainbridge ιd Buckeridge streets, from their owners, men of wealth, *temp.* ˈharles II.; and Dyott-street (now George-street), from Sir Thomas ˈyott, who died in the same reign, devising the property, since Dyott ιd other streets, upon the condition that it should be appropriated to ιe same style of building, and the same description of inhabitants ιat so long kept possession of it. Out of these very streets was ˈrmed the Rookery, removed for New Oxford-street. Here the Irish ˈst colonised London, in the reign of Queen Elizabeth; hence St. Giles's has been called Little Dublin; and in 1637, *cellars* are first mentioned in the parish-books as places of residence.

On Sept. 27, 1841, died, aged 70, in the house in which he was born, Mr. Robert Smith, 12, Great St. Andrew-street, Seven Dials, a smith, possessed of 400,000*l.* in funded, freehold, and leasehold property: he built between 150 and 200 houses in the Hampstead-road.]

Monmouth (now *Dudley*) *street*, said to be named after the unfortunate Duke (who had a mansion on the site of Bateman's-buildings, Soho-square), is noted for its sign-board painters; its dealers in amateur theatrical properties, singing-birds, old clothes, and second-hand boots and shoes; but the "laced and embroidered coats in Monmouth-street," mentioned by Lady Mary Wortley Montague, have become exchanged for the sombre suits of our fashion. Here also are public-houses noted for fancy-dog shows. Whole families and schools live in the cellars. In 1797, many horse-shoes nailed to the thresholds to hinder the power of witches, were seen in Monmouth-street; in 1813, Sir Henry Ellis counted seventeen horse-shoes; in 1841 there were six; in 1852, eleven. Jews preponderate in this street, Irish abounding most in the lanes and courts.

The modern St. Giles's is bounded north by the brewery in Bainbridge-street; south by the brewery in Castle-street; and extends from Crown-street on the west to Drury-lane on the east. The literature of St. Giles's has long fixed its abode in the Seven Dials; and in Great White-Lion-street, Mrs. Pilkington exhibited in her lodging window, "Letters written here." Printing-presses, booksellers, stationers, and circulating libraries abound here; Pitts and Catnach being the great ballad-printers. (See BALLAD-SINGING, p. 7.) One of their authors confessed to Mr. Henry Mayhew:

"The little knowledge I have, I have picked up bit by bit, so that I hardly know how I have come by it. I certainly knew my letters before I left home, and I have got the rest off the dead walls and out of the ballads and papers I have been selling. I write most of the Newgate ballads now for the printers in the Dials, and indeed, anything that turns up. I get a shilling for a 'Copy of verses written by the wretched culprit the night previous to his execution.' I wrote Courvoisier's sorrowful lamentation: I called it 'A Voice from the Gaol.' I wrote a pathetic ballad on the respite of Annette Meyers. I did the helegy, too, on Rush's execution: it was supposed, like the rest, to be written by the culprit himself, and was particularly penitent. I didn't write that to order—I knew they would want a copy of verses from the culprit. The publisher read it over, and said 'That's the thing for the street public.' I only got a shilling for Rush. Indeed, they are all the same price, no matter how popular they may be. I wrote the life of Manning in verse. Besides these, I have written the lament of Calcraft the Hangman on the decline of his trade, and many political songs."—*Morning Chronicle.*

"The Rookery" was a triangular space bounded by Bainbridge, George, and High streets: it was one dense mass of houses, through which curved narrow tortuous lanes, from which again diverged close courts—one great maze, as if the houses had originally been one block of stone, eaten by slugs into numberless small chambers and connecting passages. The lanes were thronged with loiterers; and stagnant gutters, and piles of garbage and filth infested the air. In the windows, wisps of straw, old hats, and lumps of bed-tick or brown paper, alternated with shivered panes of broken glass; the walls were the colour of bleached soot, and doors fell from their hinges and worm-eaten posts. Many of the windows announced, "Lodgings at 3*d.* a night," where the wild wanderers from town to town held their nightly revels. With such scenes the public were familiarised by Pierce Egan's *Life in London* (1820), upon our minor metropolitan stages, where they excited as much curiosity as a romance of bygone life. The Rookery has, however, almost entirely disappeared; and in its place stands a block of

Model Houses for Families," with perfect ventilation and drainage, and rents lower than the average paid for the airless, dark, and fetid rooms of the old "Rookery." Elsewhere, lanes and alleys of squalid tenements have disappeared, and their site is now occupied by the embellished lines of New Oxford-street. (See *Rookeries of London*, 1850.)

"The degraded condition of the Seven Dials (says a Report of 1848) is notorious, —vagrants, thieves, sharpers, scavengers, basket-women, char-women, army-seamstresses, and prostitutes, compose its mass: infidels, chartists, socialists, and blasphemers exist there as in head-quarters. In addition to the street traffic on the Sabbath, there are 150 shops then open in the streets. Lodging-houses of the lowest and dirtiest description afford temporary shelter to the vagrant and the criminal. In the very heart of this debased and debasing locality is situated a Ragged School; its entrance-door in the extreme angle of an irregular, three-cornered yard—so uninviting, that few respectable persons have courage to venture through it." The flagrant evil cannot be more formidably met; and the moral regeneration of the district is thus rapidly progressing.

St. Giles's has also its Parochial, National, and Infant Schools; and its Almshouses, endowed by the Earl of Southampton in 1656. It has its District Visiting Society, its Lying-in charity; a lending library; Savings Fund, to which more than 1000 poor contribute annually, induced by the premium of 1*d.* in the 1*s.*; and Ragged and Industrial schools for 300 children, established in 1852.

St. Giles's Church and the Tomb of Richard Pendrell, the preserver of Charles II. (See page 129). The monument is new, its base being the black marble slab of the old tomb. Pendrell lived in Turnstile-lane, Holborn, in 1668. It is supposed that after the Restoration he followed the King to town, and settled in St. Giles's parish, to be near the Court. Pendrell died in 1674; one of his name occurs as overseer in 1702; and a great grand-daughter of Richard Pendrell was living in 1818, in the neighbourhood of Covent Garden.—Dr. Rimbault, in *Notes and Queries*, No. 16.

GILTSPUR-STREET

Was in Stow's time also called Knight-rider's-street, "of the knights and others riding that way into Smithfield." The portion beyond the Compter prison was originally Pie-corner, "noted chiefly for cooks' shops and pigs drest there during Bartholomew Fair." (*Strype.*) Here the Great Fire of London ended; to commemorate which, was erected against a public-house ("the Fortune of War,") in Pie-corner, a carved wooden figure of a boy upon a bracket, his arms folded across his breast, and the following inscription written from under the chin downward: This boy is in memory put up for the late Fire of London, occasioned by the sin of gluttony, 1666." This is no longer legible. The whole is engraved by J. T. Smith, and in Lester's "Illustrations," 1818. The houses that escaped the Fire on this spot were taken down in 1809. On the west side of Giltspur-street is Cock-lane, the scene of "the Cock-lane ghost" imposture in 1672: "the house is still standing, and the back room, where 'scratching Fanny' lay surrounded by princes and peers, is converted into a gas-meter manufactory." (*Notes and Queries*, No. 16.) An account of the detection of the imposture was printed by Dr. Johnson; a pamphlet describing the whole affair was written by Goldsmith. Churchill, in his poem, *The Ghost*, satirised the hoax, and caricatured Johnson as a believer in it; which Boswell has disproved.

GOG AND MAGOG,

The two Giants in Guildhall," are supposed to have been originally made for carrying about in pageants, a custom not peculiar to London; for "the going of the giants at Midsummer" occurs among the ancient customs of Chester, before 1599. Puttenham (1589) speaks of "Mid-summer pageants in London, where, to make the people wonder, are set forth great and uglie gyants, marching as if they were alive," &c.

Again, "one of the gyants' stilts" that stalks before my Lord Mayor's
Pageants occurs in the old play of the *Dutch Courtezan.* (*Marston's
Works*, 1633.)   Bishop Hall, in his *Satires*, compares an angry poet to

> "The crab-tree porter of the Guildhall,
> While he his frightful Beetle elevates."

In 1415, when Henry V. entered London by Southwark, a male and
female giant stood at the entrance of London Bridge; in 1432, here a
"mighty giant" awaited Henry VI.; in 1554, at the entry of Philip
and Mary, "Corinæus and Gog-magog" stood upon London Bridge;
and when Elizabeth passed through the City the day before her coronation (Jan. 12, 1558), these two giants were placed at Temple Bar
(*W. F. Fairholt, F.S.A.*)   Jordan, in describing the Lord Mayor's
Pageant for 1672, notices as exceeding rarities, "two extreme great
giants, at least 15 feet high, that do sit and are drawn by horses in two
several chariots, talking and taking tobacco as they ride along, to the
great admiration and delight of all spectators."

Ned Ward describes the Guildhall giants in his *London Spy*, 1699;
and among the fireworks upon the Thames, at the coronation of James
II. and his queen, April 24, 1685, "were placed the statues of the two
giants of Guildhall." Bragg, in his *Observer*, Dec. 25, 1706, tells us
that when the colours taken at Ramilies were put up in Guildhall
"the very giants stared with all the eyes they had, and smiled as well
as they could." (*Malcolm.*)

"Before the present giants inhabited Guildhall, there were two giants made
only of wicker-work and pasteboard, put together with great art and ingenuity;
and those two terrible giants had the honour to grace my Lord Mayor's Show,
being carried in great triumph in the time of the pageants; and when that eminent annual service was over, remounted their old stations in Guildhall—till by
reason of their very great age, old Time, with the help of a number of City rats
and mice, had eaten up all their entrails. The dissolution of the two old weak
and feeble giants gave birth to the two present substantial and majestic giants,
who, by order, and at the City charge, were formed and fashioned," by Captain
Richard Saunders, an eminent carver, in King-street, Cheapside; and then " were
advanced to those lofty stations in Guildhall, which they have peaceably enjoyed
ever since the year 1708." We quote this from a very rare "Gigantic History of
the Two famous Giants in Guildhall, London," third Edit. 1741, published when
Guildhall, when shops were permitted there. This work also relates that "the
first honour which the two ancient wicker-work giants were promoted to in the
City, was at the Restoration of King Charles II., when, with great pomp and
majesty, they graced a triumphal arch at the end of King-street, in Cheapside."
This was before the Great Fire, which the City Giants escaped, till their infirmities
and the "City rats" rendered it necessary to supersede them; and the City accounts in the Chamberlain's Office contain a payment of 70*l.* to Saunders, the
carver, in 1707.

The "Gigantick History" supposes the Guildhall giants to represent
Corinæus and Gog-magog, in Geoffry of Monmouth's chronicle, in
Milton's *Early History of Britain*, and thus in a broadsheet of 1660:

> "And such stout *Coronæus* was, from whom
> Cornwall's first honour, and her name doth come.
> For though he sheweth not so great nor tall,
> In his dimensions set forth at *Guildhall,*
> Know 'tis a poet, only a poet can define
> A gyant's posture in a gyant's line.
> *   *   *   *   *
> And thus attended by his direful dog,
> The gyant was (God bless us) Gogmagog."
> *British Bibliogr.* iv. p. 277.

"Each of these giants," says Archdeacon Nares (*Glossary*), "measures upwards of 14 feet in height; the young one is believed to be
Corinæus, and the old one Gog-magog," whence "Gog and Magog."

The present costumes of the Giants are in *rococo* taste, as follow :

Gog.—Body-armour *à la Romaine*, with a red scarf across the shoulder; plumed lmet, with the City Dragon for a crest; a sword by his side, and in his hands alberd, and a shield ensigned with a spread-eagle.

Magog.—Body-armour and scarf as Gog; sword at side, bow and arrows over shoulder, and in his hand a "morning-star;" his hair long and flowing, and circled with a "*couronne d'honneur*."

In 1815, the giants were removed from the north side of the Hall, hen Mr. Hone examined them, and found them to be "made of wood, d hollow within ; and from the method of joining and gluing the terior, are evidently of late construction ; but they are too substan- lly built for the purpose of being either carried or drawn, or any ay exhibited in a pageant." (Hone, on *Ancient Mysteries*.) In 1837, e dresses of the giants were renewed, their armour polished, &c. his year also, copies of the giants, 14 feet high, were introduced in the ord Mayor's show : each walked by means of a man within side, who rned the giant's face, which was level with the first floor windows.

GOODMAN'S FIELDS

re described by Stow to have been, in his time, a farm belonging to e Abbey of the Nuns of St. Clare, called the Minories; "at the which rm (says Stow) I myself, in my youth, have fetched many a halfpenny- orth of milk, and never had less than three ale pints for a halfpenny in e summer, nor less than one ale quart for a halfpenny in the winter, ways hot from the kine, as the same was milked and strained." One rolop, and afterwards Goodman, were the farmers; and next Good- an's son, who let out the ground first for grazing of horses, and then r garden-plots. Strype (1720) describes the Fields covered with escod or Prescot, Ayliffe, Leman, and Maunsell streets, the initials of hich names make the word *palm;* these streets are mostly inhabited thriving Jews. Strype also mentions tenters for cloth-workers, d a roadway out of Whitechapel into Well-close. In digging the undations for houses, about 1678, were found a vast number of Roman nereal urns, some with ashes of bones in them, denoting Goodman's ields to have been originally a Roman burying-place.

Goodman's-style, Goodman's-gardens, and Rosemary-lane, denote is rural district. On the site of Leman-street was the New Wells pa, now denoted by Well-yard. (See Theatres: Goodman's Fields.)

GREY FRIARS.

In 1224, four of the Friars Minors, or Grey Friars, arrived in ondon from Italy, and were first entertained in the house of the riars Preachers, or Dominicans. Afterwards, they hired a house in ornhill, of John Travers, then sheriff, where they made some small lls, and continued until the following summer; when the devotion of e citizens enabled the Friars to purchase the site of their future resi- nce near Newgate. Their first and principal benefactor was John Iwyn, tizen and mercer, who gave them some land and houses in the parish f St. Nicholas in the Shambles, by deed 9th Henry III. Upon this they ected their original building. The first chapel, which became the oir of the church, was built at the cost of Sir William Joyner, mayor London in 1239; the nave was added by Sir Henry Waleys, mayor ring several years of the reign of Edward I.; the chapter-house by alter the potter, citizen and alderman (sheriff in 1270 and 1273), who so presented all the brazen pots for the kitchen, infirmary, &c.; the rmitory was erected by Sir Gregory de Rokesley, mayor from 1275 1282; the refectory by Bartholomew de Castro, another citizen; e infirmary by Peter de Helyland; and the studies by Bonde, king of the heralds. The convent was principally supplied with water by William, called from his trade the Taylor, and who served King Henry III. in that capacity.*

A more magnificent church was commenced in 1301, and completed 1327: first, the choir was rebuilt, chiefly at the cost of Margaret of France, the second wife of King Edward I., who assigned it for her place of interment; and the nave was added from the benefactions of John of Britany, Earl of Richmond, and his niece Mary, Countess of Pembroke: it was 300 feet long, 89 feet wide, and 64 feet high; all the columns and the pavement were of marble. In 1421, was added the library, "furnished with desks, settles, and wainscoting or ceiling," by Sir Richard Whittington, the celebrated mayor in the reign of Henry V.

On St. George's day, 1502, the Grey Friars relinquished the "London russet," which they had for some time worn, and resumed the undyed *white-grey*, which had been their original habit. On the feast of Saint Francis, July 16, 1508, the mayor and aldermen were received with grand procession as founders, which custom continued long after; but not until 1522 did the convent provide a feast for the corporation on that anniversary. In 1524, King Henry and Cardinal Wolsey personally visited the house. In 1528, in the case of a prisoner who had broken away from the sessions at Newgate, the convent asserted its right of Sanctuary, a privilege that could scarcely be often put in requisition, as the much-frequented Sanctuary of St. Martin-le-Grand was in the immediate vicinity. The Franciscans seem to have passively acquiesced in the course of events: for, November 12, 1539, their warden, and twenty-five of his brethren, signed and sealed their deed of surrender to the king, being convinced "that the perfeccion of Christian livyng dothe not consiste in doine ceremonyes, wering of a grey coatte, disgeasing our selffes after straunge fassions, dokynges, nodyngs, and bekynges, in gurding our selffes wythe a gurdle full of knots, and other like papisticall ceremonyes," &c.

After the surrender, the house of the Grey Friars was not given up to immediate destruction; but remained unoccupied in the king's hands until 1544, when, with the houses of the late Austin and Black Friars it became a receptacle for the merchandise captured at sea from the French; every part of the Grey Friars church being filled with wine it was not, however, dismantled; for in 1546 the "partitions" or screen remained; the altars, pictures, images, and pulpit; the monuments and grave-stones; the candlesticks, organs, and desks. Subsequently, by the king's gift, the church of the Grey Friars was to become the parish church of "Christ's Church within Newgate;" but the king dying in the same year and month, the altars, stalls, &c. were removed, and the church reduced in length, the nave being rented to a schoolmaster for 10s. per annum. All the tombs and grave-stones were sold for about 5l.; and Weever states there to have been buried in the church four queens,† four duchesses, four countesses, one duke, two earls, eight barons, and some thirty-five knights; in all, 663 persons of quality

* In the chapter of the Register, the main channel or pipe is traced under Newgate, through the rivulet at Holborn Bridge, up Leather-lane (Liworne-lane) and so to the Conduit-heads in the fields.

† The Queens were — the foundress of the church, Margaret, consort of Edward I.; Isabella, consort of Edward II.; Joan, queen of Scots, daughter of Edward II.; and Isabella, queen of Man. Besides these, the church had received the heart of a fifth Queen, Alianor, consort of Henry III.; and also the heart of King Edward II., deposited under the breast of his queen's effigy. The catalogue is not, however, complete; for, during some excavations on the site about 183- were found two ancient inscribed grave-stones not in the Register: they commemorate a monk of Ely, and a supposed Italian merchant, and are preserved in the burial-ground of Christchurch.

the catalogue of the monuments is preserved, and is a very valuable genealogical record.

These details are abridged principally from Mr. Nichols's Preface to the *Chronicle of the Grey Friars of London*, printed for the Camden Society (1852), from the register-book of the Fraternity. The history of the Grey Friars convent next merges into that of the establishment of Christ's Hospital, which Mr. Nichols refers to Henry's grant of the Grey Friars' house to the City, aided by their subscriptions, and not to Edward VI., who merely recognised the Hospital which the citizens themselves had set on foot.

"Moreover, Christ's Hospital was not founded as a school; its object was to rescue young children from the streets, to shelter, feed, clothe, and, *lastly*, to educate them — in short, to do exactly what in later times has been done by each individual parish for the orphan and destitute offspring of the poor."—*Nichols.*

The great picture in the hall of Christ's Hospital is commonly referred to as contemporary evidence of King Edward's share in the foundation. "This picture is usually attributed to Holbein, but in error. It is an amplification of Holbein's picture of the same subject which is at Bridewell Hospital. That picture contains only eleven figures, including the painter himself; the picture at Christ's Hospital has ninety or more, and not only is it very inferior as a work of art, but obviously of posterior date in point of costume." Mr. Nichols adds: "the picture at Christ's Hospital is derived from Holbein's, so far as the principal figures go: my own impression is that it is of the period of James I. or Charles I."

Some of the buildings of the ancient convent, including the fratry and refectory, were standing in the early part of the present century. The walls and windows of Whittington's library were to be traced in a mutilated state on the north side of the cloisters. Even now, the southern walk of the friars' cloisters remains, and its pointed arches and buttresses may be seen from the exterior. The western walk of the cloisters was under the Great Hall, which was pulled down in 1827, as was Whittington's library about the same time. The shield of Whittington, with a quatrefoil, was inserted in various parts of this building; and a stone so carved is now in the museum of Mr. E. B. Prince, F.S.A., and is etched at the end of Mr. Nichols's Preface to the *Chronicle*. (See CHRIST'S HOSPITAL, pp. 80-84.)

GRUB-STREET,

Cripplegate, is now called Milton-street, "not after the great poet, as some persons have asserted, but from a respectable builder so called, who has taken the whole street on a repairing lease." (*Elmes*, 1830.) Grub-steet was originally tenanted by bowyers, fletchers, makers of bow-strings, and of every thing relating to archery. It is the last street shewn in Aggas's map; all beyond, as far as Bishopsgate-street Without. being gardens, fields, or morass. After the Great Fire of 1666, the Goldsmiths' Company met in Grub-street temporarily, in the house of Sir Thomas Allen, grocer, and Lord Mayor in 1659. Here dwelt Fox, the martyrologist; Speed, the antiquary, like Stow, a tailor; and Henry Welby, Esq., "the Grub-street Hermit," who lived here forty-four years, during which he was only seen by his maid-servant, who died Oct. 23, 1696, and Welby, in six days after, aged 84: he owned a large estate in Lincolnshire, but betook himself to this seclusion in misanthropic resentment of an attempt made upon his life by a younger brother.

In Grub-street, Dec. 9, 1695, one Stockden, a victualler, was murdered by four men, three of whom were revealed in three successive dreams to the victualler's widow, and were tried, condemned, and hanged; the narrative attested and published "by the Curate of Cripplegate."

Here lived the authors of "anonymous treason and slander," published during the usurpation, when a prodigious number of seditious and libellous pamphlets and papers were issued. Possibly, from Grub-street being the booksellers' suburb of Aldersgate and Little Britain, it became the abode of small authors. Arbuthnot speaks of "the meridian of Grub-street;" and Gay of "Grub-street lays." In the *Tatler*, No. 41, the authors are mentioned as faithful historians of an exercise at arms of the Artillery Company. In the *Spectator*, No. 184, "one of the most eminent pens in Grub-street is employed in writing the dream of the miraculous sleeper," Nicholas Hart; and the orators of Grub-street dealt very much in plagues. (*Spectator*, No. 150.) There was also a *Grub-street Journal;* and Swift wrote a Grub-street Elegy on the pretended death of Partridge, the almanack-maker, and Advice to the Grub-street Versifiers. The halfpenny newspaper-stamp duty of 1712, however, occasioned "the fall of the leaf," and utter ruin among Grub-street authors.

"August 7: Do you know that all Grub-street is dead and gone last week? No more ghosts or murders now for love or money."—*Swift to Stella.*

The *Memoirs of the Grub-Street Society* were commenced Jan. 8, 1730 (the year before the *Gentleman's Magazine*,) and were published weekly until the close of 1737. The avowed objects of the work were to counteract the original Grubeans, who "made themselves most remarkably infamous for want of integrity, by wilfully publishing what they knew to be false;" and to repress "the exorbitances of Authors, Printers, Booksellers, and Publishers." The Society met once a week at the Pegasus, in Grub-street; and the principals of the staff were Dr. John Martyn and Dr. Richard Russel* (*Bavius* and *Mævius*), the latter being secretary until 1735. The work was then conducted by a committee, but was dropped in 1737. after a struggle of six years, eleven months, and two weeks: it was revived as the *Literary Courier of Grub-street*, of which only a few numbers were printed.

In these *Memoirs*, most of the personages of the *Dunciad* are unsparingly satirised; and the productions of Eusden, Cibber, Concanen, Curll, Dennis, Henley, Ralph, Arnall, Theobald, Welsted, &c. are treated with great severity. The *Memoirs* "meeting with encouragement," says Sir John Hawkins, "Cave projected an improvement thereon in a pamphlet of his own;" and in the following year appeared the *Gentleman's Magazine*.

Grub-street figures in the *Dunciad:*

" Not with less glory mighty Dulness crown'd,
    Shall take through Grub-street her triumphant round."

"Pope's arrows are so sharp, and his slaughter so wholesale, that the reader's sympathies are often enlisted on the side of the devoted inhabitants of Grub-street. He it was who brought the notion of a vile Grub-street before the minds of the general public; he it was who created such associations as author and rags —author and dirt—author and gin. The occupation of authorship became ignoble through his graphic descriptions of misery, and the literary profession was for a long time destroyed."—*W. M. Thackeray.*

In his notes to the *Dunciad*, Bishop Warburton describes a libeller as "nothing but a Grub-street critic run to seed." Dr. Johnson's friend, John Hoole,† received his early instruction in Grub-street, from his uncle "the metaphysical tailor," who used to draw squares and triangles on his shopboard. (Boswell's *Johnson*, vol. iv.)

Grub-street was formerly "much inhabited by writers of small histories, dictionaries, and temporary poems; whence any mean production is called Grub-street." (Johnson's *Dictionary*.) The Doctor himself "was but a Grub-street man, paid by the sheet, when Goldsmith entered Grub-street, periodical writer and reviewer." (Forster's *Life of Goldsmith*, p. 73.)

* Dr. Russel subsequently settled at Brighthelmstone, and wrote a *Treatise o Sea-Water*, advocating the practice of sea-bathing, which laid the foundation of the unexampled prosperity of Brighton.

† Father of the Rev. Samuel Hoole, who was born in a hackney-coach, which was conveying his mother to Drury-lane Theatre to witness the performance of the tragedy of *Timanthes*, written by her husband. Mr. Samuel Hoole prayed with Johnson in his last illness: he long kept as memorials the chair in which the Doctor usually sat, and the desk upon which he mostly wrote his *Rambler* Mr. Hoole died in March, 1839.

" Grub-street performances" had long been applied to "bad matter
pressed in a bad manner, false confused histories, low creeping poetry,
d grovelling prose," whether written in the Court or in the City, or
ewhere. Hence "a Grub-street author" became a term of common
proach, which, however, has passed away with the change in the
cial position of men of letters, who no longer resemble the literary
cks of the reign of George II.: but literature takes rank with other
arned professions; and those authors who neglect it as a means of
bsistence are, in a twofold sense, foremost in their abuse of it.

Grub-street, now Milton-street, is noted for its great number of
eys, courts, and backways, and old inn-yards: in Hanover-court was
house, *temp*. Charles I., traditionally the residence of General Monk.
pposite Hanover-court is a large building, once the City Chapel; in
31 opened as a theatre, and now the City of London Baths; facing
hich, in odd contiguity, are the old City Soap-Works, established 1712.

GUILDHALL (THE),

t the north end of King-street, Cheapside, is the "Town-hall" of
e City of London, where the principal Corporation business is trans-
ted, and its magnificent hospitality exercised. The first Alderman's
ry or court-hall was a low and mean building, in the street named
erefrom, Aldermanbury, which occurs in a deed of the year 1189:
he Courts of Maior and Aldermen were held here until the new
uildhall was built. I myself (says Stow) have seen the ruines of
e old court-hall in Aldermanbery-streete." Elsewhere Stow says:
Thomas Knoles, grocer, maior 1410, with his brethren the aldermen,
gan to build the Guildhall in London, and instead of an old little
ttage in Aldermanberie-street, made a faire and goodly house, more
are unto Saint Laurence Church in the Jurie." The expense of erect-
g "the Great Hall," first built, was defrayed by large benevolences
om the City companies; and fees, fines, and amercements, ordered to
so applied for ten years. In 1422-23, Sir Richard Whittington's
ecutors gave 35*l*. towards paving the Great Hall with "hard stone
Purbecke;" and they also glazed some of the windows. The
ayor's Court was founded in 1424; then the Mayor's Chamber and
e Council-Chamber; and lastly, a stately entrance-porch, "beautified
ith images of stone." In 1481, Sir W. Harryot, mayor, gave 40*l*. for
aking and glazing "two louvers." The kitchen and other offices were
ilt about 1501, by "procurement" (subscription among the City
ompanies) of Sir John Shaw, goldsmith, mayor, knighted on Bos-
orth Field, and who gave in the Guildhall the first Mayor's Feast,
therto kept in the Merchant-Tailors' and Grocers' Halls. In 1505,
r Nicholas Aldwyn, mayor in 1499, bequeathed 73*l*. 6*s*. 8*d*. "for a
nging of tapestrie" for principal days in the Hall. In 1614-15, was
ected a new Council-chamber, and Record-room over.

The Guildhall has been the scene of some of the most striking events in our
story. Here—1483, June 24— Richard III. (through the Duke of Buckingham)
empted to beguile the assembled citizens into an approval of his usurpation.
83.—Trial and condemnation of Anne Askew for heresy, before Bishop Bonner:
e was burnt at the stake in Smithfield. 1547.—Trial of the Earl of Surrey,
d his conviction of high treason. 1553, Nov. 13.—Trial and condemnation of
dy Jane Grey and her husband. 1554, April 17.—Trial and acquittal of Sir
icholas Throgmorton, for participation in Thomas Wyatt's rebellion against
een Mary. 1606, March 28. — Trial and conviction of the Jesuit Garnet.
unpowder Plot.) 1642, Jan. 5.—Charles I. attended at a Common Council,
d claimed their assistance in apprehending Hampden and other patriots, who
d taken shelter in the City to avoid arrest. During the Civil War and the
mmonwealth, the Guildhall was the arena of many a patriotic movement; and
ter the abdication of James II. the Lords Parliament assembled here, and
clared for the Prince of Orange.

In the Great Fire of 1666, all the combustible parts of the edific were consumed; but the walls are of such solidity, that the Hall stoo in the flames "in a bright shining coal, as if it had been a palace o gold, or a great building of burnished brass." After the Fire, the Hal was repaired nearly as we now see it. In 1789, the southern fron which was highly enriched, was taken down, and the present heteroge neous façade substituted by Dance; the ancient porch being left, as i to contrast with the poverty of the new design. In 1822, was take down the chapel built by Whittington on the east side of the Hall.

The figures in the porch personified Religion, Fortitude, Justice, and Ten perance; Law and Learning; there was also a figure of our Saviour. After the removal, they lay in a cellar until Alderman Boydell, by permission of the Co poration, gave them to the eminent sculptor, Thomas Banks, R.A., after whos death, in 1809, they were purchased for 100*l.* by Mr. Bankes, M.P.: they are fin works of art, and are etched in Carter's *Ancient Sculpture and Painting.*

The Great Hall is internally decorated in coarse imitation of th nave of Winchester Cathedral. The length of the Hall is 153 feet, i breadth 50 feet, and height 55 feet. The side walls (5 feet thick) a divided each into eight spaces by clustered columns and moulding reaching from the pavement nearly to the summit of the cornice; the heights having two ranges of traceried arches between panels; in t upper tier are handsome windows, now closed. At each end of t Hall is a large Gothic window occupying the whole width, the arch resting on short columns, and retaining perfect their rich tracery. T upper compartments are filled with painted glass (restored and moder of the royal arms, and stars and jewels of the Garter, Bath, Thistl and St. Patrick, in the east window; and the City arms, supporter &c. in the west window. Beneath the eastern window, under can pies, and at the back of the spot where the ancient court of husting is still holden, are statues of Edward VI., Queen Elizabeth, and Kin Charles I. from the Guildhall chapel: they are said to be sculptured b Stone. By an entry in the City records, the figure of Charles I. orig nally occupied a place in the Royal Exchange.

In the angles at the opposite end of the hall, on lofty octagon: pedestals, are the celebrated colossal figures of the giants Gog a Magog, sometimes called Gogmagog and Corinæus. (See page 332 They were placed in their present position during the alterations 1815, having formerly stood on each side of the steps leading to t upper rooms, these steps being where Beckford's monument now is; t monument then standing against the great western window.

This old entrance was very picturesque: on each side of the ste was an octangular turreted gallery, balustraded, for the hall-keeper each surrounded by iron-work palm-trees, supporting a balcony a ornamented three-dial clock, and a resplendent gilt sun underneat The flanking giants, in their singular costume, gave the whole unique character. At the sides of the steps, under the hall-keeper offices, were two dark cells, or cages, in which unruly apprentices wer occasionally confined, by order of the City Chamberlain: these wer called *Little Ease*, for a boy could not stand upright in them.

The capitals of the clustered columns, whence originally sprung t open timber-roof, now bear guideron shields, with the arms of the twelv Great Companies. After the destruction of the ancient roof, an add tional story was raised to the summit of its lofty pitch, and the eig large circular-headed windows were added on each side; the ceilin covering this is flat and square-paneled,—an anomaly effected und Sir Christopher Wren's directions. The meanness of the side windov strangely contrasts with the gorgeousness of the ends.

Three of the compartments on the north side of the hall, and one e south, contain sculptured monuments erected at the expense of the orporation—to Admiral Lord Nelson, by J. Smith, 1810, inscription by eridan; Alderman Beckford, Lord Mayor in 1762 and 1769, by Moore; e Earl of Chatham, by Bacon, 1782, inscription by Burke; the Right on. W. Pitt, by Bubb, 1813, inscription by Canning. Upon Beck- rd's monument is the speech which was long believed to have been ldressed by him to George III. on his throne.

Gifford (*Ben Jonson*, vol. vi. p. 481) denies this; and Isaac Reed asserts that Beckford did not utter one syllable of this speech. It was penned by Horne oke, and by his art put on the records of the city and on Beckford's statue, as told me, Mr. Braithwaite, Mr. Seyers, &c. at the Athenian Club." The style of these monuments (which cost 3000 and 4000 guineas each) is ill apted for a Tudor hall, and they rank low as works of art: for example, in that Nelson, the only indication of its object is a small medallion of the hero; in ckford's, the decline of the City and Commerce is represented by figures in a ooping state!—a literal allegory.

The Guildhall will contain between 6,000 and 7,000 persons. Here ve been held the Inauguration Dinners of the Lord Mayors since 1501. ere Whittington entertained Henry V. and his Queen, when he threw e king's bonds for 60,000*l.* into a fire of spice-wood. Charles I. was asted here in 1641, with a political object, which failed. Charles II. as *nine times* entertained here;* and from 1660, with only three excep- ons, our sovereign has dined at Guildhall on the Lord Mayor's Day, ter his or her accession or coronation. The exceptions were James ., who held the City Charter upon a writ of *quo warranto* at his ac- ssion; George IV., who was rendered unpopular by his quarrel with s Queen; and William IV., who apprehended political tumult. But eorge IV. (when Regent) was entertained here, June 18, 1814, with lexander, Emperor of Russia, and Frederick-William III., King of russia, when the banquet cost 25,000*l.*, and the value of the plate used as 200,000*l.*† On July 9 following, the Duke of Wellington was enter- ined in Guildhall. The banquet to George III. cost 6,898*l.*, when 200 guests dined in the Hall; that to Queen Victoria, Nov. 9, 1837, ost 6870*l.*; and an evening entertainment to her Majesty, July 9, 1851, celebrate the Great Exhibition, cost 5120*l.* 14*s.* 9*d.*, being 129*l.* 5*s.* 3*d.* ss than the sum voted: invitations, 1452.

The Guildhall is magnificently decorated for royal entertainments, hen the sovereign is seated beneath a state canopy at the east end. The ghting of the vast Hall with gas is by stars, mottoes, and devices of 000 or 7000 jets in the large windows, filled with planking, and sheet- on to prevent accident by fire: a stupendous crystal star; a Prince f Wales's plume in spun glass, nine feet high, are superb insignia; the rchitectural lines of the edifice are marked out with 5000 gas-jets; nd from the roof hang two painted chandeliers, each 12 feet diameter; he whole flood of gaslight exceeding that of 46,000 wax-candles.

* Charles II. dined with the citizens the year that Sir Robert Viner was ayor, who getting elated with continually toasting the royal family, grew a ttle fond of his majesty. "The king understood very well how to extricate imself in all kinds of difficulties, and, with an hint to the company to avoid eremony, stole off, and made towards his coach, which stood ready for him in uildhall-yard. But the mayor liked his company so well, and was grown so ntimate, that he pursued him hastily, and catching him fast by the hand, cried ut with a vehement oath and accent, 'Sir, you shall stay and take t'other ottle!' The airy monarch looked kindly at him over his shoulder, and with a mile and graceful air (for I saw him at the time, and do now) repeated this line f the old song:

'He that is drunk is as great as a king,'

nd immediately returned back and complied with his landlord."—*Spectator*, No. 462. † On the first anniversary of this festival, June 18, 1815, was fought the attle of Waterloo.

The *Dinner on Lord Mayor's Day* is a magnificent spectacle: the Lord Mayor and his distinguished guests advance to the banquet by sound of trumpet; and the superb dresses and official costumes of the company, about 1200 in number, with the display of costly plate, is very striking. The Hall is divided: at the upper, or hustings tables, the courses are served hot; at the lower tables the turtle only is hot. The baron of beef is brought in procession from the kitchen into the Hall in the morning, and being placed upon a pedestal, at night is cut up by "the City carver." The Kitchen, wherein the dinner is dressed, is a vast apartment; the principal range is 16 feet long, and 7 feet high, and a baron of beef (3 cwt.) upon the gigantic spit is turned by hand. There are 20 cooks, besides helpers; 14 tons of coals are consumed; some 40 turtles are slaughtered for 250 tureens of soup; and the serving of the dinner requires about 200 persons, and 8000 plate-changes. Next morning the fragments of the Great Feast are doled out at the kitchen-gate to the City poor.

The Crypt, under the Guildhall, and of the same age, is the finest and most extensive remaining in London. (See CRYPTS, page 241.)

North of the Hall is the *Court of Exchequer*, formerly the King's Bench Court. It was built immediately after the Great Hall (*temp.* Henry VI.) for the Mayor's Court, still held here. Some of the windows were glazed by the executors of Whittington, and emblazoned with his arms: Stow describes among the glass, "the mayor pictured sitting in habite, party-coloured, and a hood on his head; his sword before him, with an hatte or cap of maintenance; the common cleark, and other officers bare-headed, their hoodes on their shoulders." This Court had at the back of the judges' seats paintings of Prudence, Justice, Religion, and Fortitude. Here is a large picture by Alaux of Paris, presented by Louis-Philippe, representing his reception of an address from the City on his visit to England in 1844; Humphery, mayor, and many other portraits. Here also are portraits of George III. and Queen Charlotte, by Ramsay; and William III. and Queen Mary, by Van der Voort.

The Common-Council Chamber contains, in a niche behind the Mayor's chair, a marble statue of George III., by Chantrey, the inscription by Alderman Birch, in whose mayoralty, 1815, the statue was erected: on the right is a whole-length portrait of Queen Victoria, by Hayter; and left are half-lengths of Caroline, queen of George IV., and her daughter, the Princess Charlotte, both by Lonsdale; in the angles are busts—of Nelson, by Mrs. Damer; and Wellington, by Turnerelli.

North side: Portraits—Chamberlain Clarke, by Lawrence; Aldermen Waithman and Wood, by Patten; Nelson, by Beechey; Lord Denman, by Mrs. Pearson. Busts,—Granville Sharp, by Chantrey; R. Lambert Jones and Thomas Clarkson, by Behnes; and Henry Beaufoy, by Marshall. Paintings.—Defence of Gibraltar and burning of gun-boats, 1782, by Paton; Rodney's Victory, 1782, by Dodd; and Sir William Walworth killing Wat Tyler, in Smithfield, by Northcote. East side, Siege of Gibraltar, by Copley, father of Lord Lyndhurst: it covers the entire side and was painted by the artist raised on a platform. South side: Alderman Boydell, by Beechey; Lord Heathfield, by Reynolds; Murder of Rizzio, by Opie; Lord Cornwallis, by Copley; Defence and Relief of Gibraltar, by Paton; Rodney breaking the French line, 1782, by Dodd; and bust of Alderman Waithman.

Here are also three pictures of municipal ceremonies and festivities: the Civic Oath administered to Alderman Newnham, as Lord Mayor, on the Hustings in the Guildhall, Nov. 8, 1782, with 140 portraits; the Lord Mayor's Show by Water—boats by Paton, figures by Wheatley; and the Royal Entertainment in Guildhall, June 18, 1814, by Daniell, R.A.

The Court of Aldermen is profusely gilded, and painted with allegorical figures of the City of London, Prudence, Justice, Temperance, and Fortitude, by Sir James Thornhill, who was presented by the Corporation with a gold cup, value 225*l.* 7*s.* (See page 2.)

The Chamberlain's Office is on the right: he is keeper of the City
sh, regalia, and trust-money; admits, on oath, persons to the free-
m of London, and registers and enrols all apprentices, adjudicates
tween them and their masters, and has power to commit either to
idewell. The Chamberlain bears on state occasions an ancient staff,
rmounted with a jewelled crown: this sceptre is presented with the
ty keys, mace, and sword, on the entry of the sovereign by Temple Bar;
d is formally surrendered on the yearly re-election of the Chamberlain,
ovember 18. There is neither record nor tradition of a defalcation in
s office in upwards of 700 years. The Chamberlain's ancient seal is a
yal crown, lion passant, the City sword, and two keys: legend,
*gillum Cameræ Londini.**

In the office hangs the picture of the battle of Towton, painted by
lderman Boydell; and here, where the City apprentices sign their
dentures, suggestively hangs a fine set of Hogarth's prints of the
dustrious and Idle Apprentices.

In the *Chamberlain's Parlour* are duplicate copies of the freedoms
d thanks voted to distinguished personages by the City; they are fine
ecimens of penmanship, mostly by Mr. Tomkins, whose portrait, by
eynolds (and said to be his latest picture,) hangs here.

In the *Waiting Room*, among the pictures are Reynolds's portrait of
e great Lord Camden, and Opie's Murder of James I. of Scotland.

A large folding-screen, painted, it is said, by Copley, represents the Lord Mayor
ckford delivering the City sword to King George III. at Temple Bar; interest-
g for its portraits and record of the costume of the period; presented by Alder-
an Salomons to the City in 1850. Here, too, is a large picture of the battle of
incourt, painted by Sir Robert Ker Porter, when 19 years of age, assisted by
r. Mulready, now R.A., and presented to the City in 1808.

In the *Library*, rich in books, tracts, and MSS. relating to the City, and
rst opened in 1828, are portraits of several aldermen; and a Museum
relics discovered at Old London Bridge, the Royal Exchange, and
sewhere in the City. (See MUSEUMS.)

In the *Courts of Common Pleas and Queen's Bench*, built upon the
te of Guildhall chapel, by Montague, in 1823, are portraits of the
dges who adjudicated the disputed properties of the citizens after
e Great Fire of 1666. These and other pictures were formerly hung
the Guildhall: in stormy political times they were occasionally in-
red; for, in the *London Gazette* of 1681, the Lord Mayor and Court
f Aldermen advertised a reward of 500l. for the discovery of the per-
on who offered an indignity to the portrait of the Duke of York
James II.) in the Guildhall, to shew their deep resentment at that
insolent and villanous act."

HACKNEY-COACHES.

Coaches were first let for hire in London in 1625, and were hence
alled hackney-coaches; that they were named from being first em-
loyed in conveying the citizens to their villas at Hackney, is a popu-
ar error, though supported by Maitland. The term is said to be from
he French *haquenée*, a slow-paced or ambling nag; as, "he had in his
table an *hackenay*." (Chaucer's *Romaunt of the Rose*.) But *haquenée*

* Wilkes was Chamberlain from 1779 until his death in 1797: he was suc-
eeded by Alderman Richard Clark, who, when sheriff, took Dr. Johnson to a
dges' dinner at the Old Bailey; the judges being Blackstone and Eyre. Mr.
lark, when 15, was introduced to Johnson, whom he last met at the Essex Head

"does not include the idea of hiring. To hack is to offer a thing f(
common sale or hire; and a coach (along with the horses) kept for hi
is a hackney-coach." (David Booth's *Analytical Dictionary*, p. 30(
Hackney-coaches were first kept at inns, but soon got into the street
as appears from *Strafford's Letters*, April 1634:

"One Captain Bailey hath erected some four *Hackney-coaches*, put his men
livery, and appointed them to stand at the *May-Pole* in the Strand (where S
Mary's Church now is), giving them instructions at what rates to carry men in
several parts of the town, where all the day they may be had. Other hackne
men seeing this way, they flocked to the same place, and perform their journe
at the same rate. So that sometimes there is twenty of them together, whi
disperse up and down; that they and others are to be had everywhere, as wate
men are to be had by the water-side."

A successful rival, however, soon appeared; when Sir Saunde
Duncombe, upon a petition to Charles L, stated the streets to be great
encumbered with the coaches, and that in many parts beyond sea pe(
ple were much carried in chairs that are covered, whereby few coach
were used among them; and the king granted Duncombe "the sole pri\
lege to use, let, or hire a number of the said covered chairs for fourte(
years;" the fare being 1*s.* per mile. Yet the hackney-coaches had
increased in 1635, as to be considered a nuisance by the Court, and to l
limited by Star-chamber. In 1637, however, Charles granted a speci
commission to his master of the horse to license fifty hackney-coacl
men in London and Westminster, each to keep twelve horses, for abo
200 coaches, which Sir William Davenant describes as "uneasily hun
and so narrow that he took them for sedans on wheels." Their rat
were fixed by Act 14 Charles II. In 1694 they were limited to 700.

Hackney-coaches were first excluded from Hyde Park in 1695, when "sevel
persons of quality having been affronted at the Ring by some of the persons th
rode in hackney-coaches with masks, and complaint thereof being made to tl
Lord Justices, an order is made that no hackney-coaches be permitted to go in
the said Park, and that none presume to appear there in masks." (*Post-Bo*
June 8, 1695.) And the exclusion continues to this day.

By coach was the usual mode of sight-seeing: "I took (*Tatle*
June 18, 1709) three lads, who are under my guardianship, a-ramblin
in a hackney-coach, to shew them the town; as the lions, the tomb
Bedlam," &c. Gay's *Trivia* glances at this period:

"When on his box the nodding coachman snores,
And dreams of fancy'd fares."

In 1771 the number of coaches was fixed at 1000, and their far
were raised; again increased in 1799, and the office removed to Some
set House 1782; since 1833, their number has not been limited.
1814 hackney-chariots were introduced; and in 1820 *cabriolets,*
cabs. The double-seated hackney-coach was usually a cast-off carriag
often to be seen covered with the emblazoned arms of its former nob
owner; and the driver notoriously "rude, exacting, and quarrelsome
Both coaches and chariots are drawn by a pair of horses; but the c
dispenses with one horse, and the fare is thus reduced one-thir
The cab (from Paris) was at first open and chaise-like, with a pair
wheels, but very liable to accidents, which soon begat a host of "safet
improvements. The cab, or sedan-like coach-body upon four whee
often reminds one of a seventeenth-century coach, such as we s
sculptured on Thynne's tomb in Westminster Abbey.

On July 7, 1852, the number of hackney-carriages (coaches, cabs, omnibus
and other stage carriages) licensed in the Metropolitan District was 3277;
which between 1100 and 1200 were omnibuses. In the year, Sept. 1, 1650,
Sept. 1, 1851, there were 6,039 drivers; and 2152 articles found by drivers in
carriages, and deposited at the proper office; of which number, 1154 articles w

HALLS OF THE CITY COMPANIES.

Foremost in vastness and antiquity is the Guildhall of the City of
ondon, already described. (See page 337.) The latter affords the
st idea of the Companies' ancient halls, the majority of which were
stroyed in the Great Fire of 1666. They were the guild-halls, from
e *gild-hallas* of the Anglo-Saxons, wherein wares were exposed for
le, as in most towns of the Middle Ages.

The ancient Hall mostly had an open timber roof; whence the Fish-
ongers', and probably other Companies, suspended the properties of
eir pageants. In the centre of the roof was a *louvre*, or lantern; at
e sides were Gothic windows, filled with painted glass; and beneath
ng gorgeous tapestry, which, in the Merchant-Tailors' Hall, con-
ined the history of their patron, St. John the Baptist. The floor was
rewed with rushes; the tables were planks placed on tressels; a
redos, or grand screen, crossed the apartment, hiding the entrances
the buttery, larder, and kitchen; "the minstrailes" were in a gallery
oft; and there were temporary platforms or stages for players.
ther passages branched to the wine and ale cellars, and to the cham-
rs. Annexed to the buttery were the bakehouse and brewhouse;
e kitchen passage was guarded by a spiked hatch, and was well stored
ith "spittes, rakkes, and rollars." There is also named in Brewers'
all, *temp.* Henry VI. "the tresaunce," or cloister between the great
tchen and the hall; and an "almarie cupboard," for the Company's
ms (apparently broken provisions), in the great kitchen.

The Companies possessed halls from the date of their first charters,
der Edward III. The Merchant-Tailors, however, had a hall at the
ck of the Red Lion, in Basing-lane, long before they bought their
all in Threadneedle-street, in 1331. The Weavers, Bakers, Butchers,
d other ancient gilds, must also have had halls in very remote times:
ese, and other meeting-places, particularly of the Minor Companies,
ere probably, at first, but mean buildings, as the original Guildhall in
ldermanbury; and before the founding of their halls, the Companies
et at various great mansions in the City.

In their Halls the Twelve Great Companies gave grand feasts to
rious monarchs, who enrolled themselves as members. In the in-
rregnum they were the meeting-places of the Government Commis-
oners; by the Parliamentary commanders they were converted into
arracks; by the puritanical clergy into preaching-places; and by suc-
eding lord mayors into temporary mansion-houses. In Elizabeth's
d the Stuarts' reigns, every Hall was obliged to have also a granary
d an armoury; and the Company's almshouses adjoined the Hall, that
e alms-folk might be ready to join in processions and pageants.

The donations of plate to the Companies included drinking-cups,
allon-pots, basins and ewers, large silver salvers, goblets, and salts
f "sylver, sylver-guylte, parcel-gylte, or sylver-white;" and to the
ntry of the name and gift was usually attached an ejaculatory prayer
r the donor, as " Ih'u be mercyfull unto his soul;" " God send him
ng life and welfare," &c.

Liveries are not mentioned to have been worn by any of the Com-
anies before *temp.* Edward I.; the hood, evidently copied from the
onk's cowl, was an indispensable appendage; and the Company's
trade conizances" were embroidered conspicuously on the dress.

The Companies were, at first, half-ecclesiastical bodies : "This demi-religious
aracter evidenced itself in the mode of their foundation : in their choosing
atron-saints and chaplains; founding altars to such saints in the churches they
eld the advowson of, and in various other ways: none of the trades assembled

and if possible, they chose a saint who either bore a relation to their trade, or to some other analogous circumstance. The Fishmongers a~opted St. Peter, and me at St Peter's church; the Drapers chose the Virgin Mary, mother of the ' Ho Lamb,' or fleece, as the emb'em of that trade, and appropriately assembled, like manner, at St. Mary Bethlem church, Bishopsgate; the Goldsmiths' patro was St. Dunstan, reported to have been a brother artisan; the Merchant-Tailor another branch of the draping business, marked their connexion with it by selec ing St. John Baptist, who was the harbinger of the holy Lamb, so adopted by tl Drapers: and which, as being anciently cloth-dealers, still constitutes the cre of that society.

"In other cases, the Companies denominated themselves fraternities of tl particular saint in whose church or chapel they assembled, and had their alta Thus, the Grocers called themselves the fraternity of St. Anthony, because the had their altar in St. Anthony's church; the Vintners, 'the fraternity of St. Ma tin,' from the like connexion with St. Martin's Vintry church; and the Skinne and the Salters, both societies of Corpus Christi, from meeting, the one at the alt of that name in St. Laurence Poultry church; and the other at Corpus Chris chapel, in All Saints, Bread-street."—(Herbert's *Hist. of the Twelve Great Live Companies,* vol. i. p. 66-7.) Nor until after the Reformation could the fraterniti be regarded as strictly secular.

In their processions to church the Companies were joined by tl religious orders in their rich costumes, bearing wax torches and sing ing, and frequently attended by the lord mayor and great civic authc rities in state. Funerals were as religiously observed by them; and t celebrate with becoming grandeur the obsequies of deceased member almost the whole of these fraternities kept a state-pall, or hearse cloth, a few of which are preserved to this day; members of superic rank were followed to interment by the lord mayor and civic ar thorities; and it was customary to provide funeral dinners, with sun left by the deceased, or sent after death by the relatives to their Halls such sums, *temp.* Elizabeth and James, were generally not less than 20

"The great Sir Philip Sidney, who was publicly buried at St. Paul's Cathedr in 1587, was a brother of the Grocers' Company, and was attended by that live in all their formalities, who were preceded by the lord mayor. aldermen, an sheriffs, 'rydinge in purple.' The number of the Grocers' livery amounted 120, and are represented in a print of the procession by De Brie."—Nichols *Progresses of Queen Elizabeth,* ii. pp. 19-26.

At the funeral of Sir Thomas Lovell (of Shakspeare memory, at Holywe Nunnery, Shoreditch), "the gentlemen of the inns of court (Sir Thomas bui Lincoln's-Inn fine gateway), with certeyn *crafts of London*," received the corp at the convent gate, accompanied by the mayor and aldermen, who, on the bod being placed under the hearse, or canopy, encircled the ralls. and repeated tl *De profundis.* Meanwhile, "there was *a drynkynge* in all the cloister, the none halls and parlors of the said place."

The Election-feasts in the Halls, *temp.* Henry IV., were partake of by the first nobility, and even princes, besides the city dignitaries when the luxuries included the mighty "baron" or "ribbes of beef, "frumentie with venison," brawn, fat swan, boar, congor, sea-ho and other delicacies stored above *the salt;*[*] whilst "sotilties" of th Company's patron, trade, or saint, recalled the origin of the fraternity and there were "voyds of spice-bread, ypocras, and comfits," to th renewed "noise" (music) of the minstrels, or "waits," or the high merriment of the London clerks "playing some holy play."

Thus, 5th September, 1419, 17 Henry V., we have the following Election-dinn of the Brewers' Company. the "Ordinaire de la Feste," in Norman-French:

First Course.—Brawn with mustard; cabbages to the pottage; swan standar

---

* The *salt,* or salt-cellar, was a magnificent piece of plate, forming, in t Middle Ages, a division between the upper and lower part of the table. Mr. Fo broke believed one, in the Tower of London, and of silver-gilt, to belong to t Mercers' Company. To be seated above the salt was a mark of honour; and o ancestors seem often to have placed persons below it in order to mortify them.

apons roasted; great custards. (For the "fat swan" and the cygnet, the citizens had their annual "swan uppings.")

Second Course.—Venison in broth, with white mottreids; cony standard; partridges, with cocks roasted; leche lumbard, doucetts with little parneuse.

Third Course.—Pears in syrop; great birds with little ones together; fritters, paynpuffs with a cold baked meat.

The cost of another Election-feast of the Brewers, A.D. 1425, was 38*l.* 4*s.* 2*d.*, a very large sum, considering that money was then of five times its present value. Melted fat, or lard, was then used where we now use butter, then a great dainty; as was also sugar, the place of which was supplied by honey. Furmenty, the *furmentaria* of Ducange, was wheat boiled in milk, such as is eaten to this day. "Aromatising" the Hall with the precious Indian wood, sanders, and Brazil wood, by fumigation, greatly enlivened the table. Not only did widows, wives, and single women, who were members of the Company, join the feast; but from the Grocers' ordinances of 1348, "bretherene" could introduce their wives or companions, and damsels; indeed, a wife was not to be excused, unless "*malade, ou grosse danfant, et près sa deliverance.*"

The Election-ceremonies took place after the feast, when the newly-elected principals were crowned "with garlondes on their hedes." Then followed the "loving cup," as is still the custom;* and next the minstrels and players; the minstrels including harpers, who played and sang in the intervals of the others sounding their cornets, shalms, flutes, horns, and pipes. The dramas then in fashion often consisted of single subjects; and this taste continued till long after the establishment of the regular theatres. In the Guildhall library is an original license from the master of the revels, in 1662, authorising "George Bailey, musitioner, and eight servants, his company, to play for one year a play called Noah's Flood;" these eight persons personating the patriarch and his family.

The Companies' Barges also formed pageants, now greatly shorn of their splendour. Thus, at the coronation of the queen of Henry VII., she was attended "from Greenwich" by water, by "the maior, shrifes, and aldermen of the citie, and divers and many worshipfull comoners, chosen out of every crafte, in their liverays, in barges freshly furnished with banners and stremers of silke, rechely beaton with the armes and bagges of their craftes." In the same reign, among "a great and goodly nombre of barges," either fastened up, or "roweing and skym'-ying in the riv' and Thamys," was, "first for the cittie of London, the mayer's barge, the sherevys' barge, aldermens dy'rs bargs; *and then the crafts of the cytie,* having their standards and stremers, w' ther conizances right weel dekkyd, and replenyshid w' w'shipfull company of the citizens."

The earliest Triumph, Pageant, or "Riding," connected with the trades, occurred in 1298, on the return of Edward I. from his victory over the Scots, when "every citizen, according to their severall trades, *made their severall shew.*" They also joined in coronation processions, as that of Henry IV. in 1399, when Froissart states Cheapside to have had seven fountains running with red and white wine; the different Companies of London, led by their wardens, were clothed in their .

---

* "*The Loving Cup*" is a splendid feature of the Hall-feasts of the City and Inns of Court. The Cup is of silver, or silver-gilt, and is filled with spiced wine, immemorially termed "sack." Immediately after the dinner and grace, the Master and Wardens drink to their visitors a hearty welcome; the cup is then passed round the table, and each guest, after he has drunk, applies his napkin to the mouth of the cup before he passes it to his neighbour. The more formal practice is for "the person who pledges with the loving cup to stand up and bow to his neighbour, who, also standing, removes the cover with his right hand, and holds it while the other drinks; a custom said to have originated in the precaution to keep the right, or 'dagger-hand,' employed, that the person who drinks may be assured of no treachery, like that practised by Elfrida on the unsuspecting King Edward the Martyr, at Corfe Castle, who was slain while drinking. This was why the loving cup possessed a cover.—*F. W. Fairholt, F.S.A.*

proper liveries, and bore banners of their trades. Chaucer describes an idle City apprentice of his day:

> " When there any *ridings* were in Chepe,
> Out of the shoppe thider would he lepe;
> And till that he had all the sight ysein,
> And danced wel, he would not come again."

From this sketch of the early Halls of the Companies, and their ancient state and observances, we proceed to the City Halls of the present day, commencing with the

HALLS OF THE TWELVE GREAT COMPANIES,

in their order of precedency.

1. MERCERS' HALL, Cheapside, between Ironmonger-lane and Old Jewry, occupies the site of the ancient hospital of St. Thomas Acon's, whereon the Mercers first settled in London, hence called "the Mercery." On the site of the present entrance to the Hall from Cheapside stood the house of Gilbert Becket, father of Becket, archbishop of Canterbury; after whose murder was built here, by his sister Agnes and her husband, a chapel and hospital, destroyed in the Great Fire of 1666. Soon after were built upon the same site the present Hall and Chapel; the front of the latter, by Wren, now only remains: above the ornamented doorway are cherubim mantling the Virgin's head, the cognisance of the Company; the front has also figures of Faith, Hope, and Charity; the whole in stone kept in handsome repair.* The chapel is at the extremity of the ante-chapel; over which, upon Doric columns, is the hall, handsomely wainscoted and carved: here are held the Gresham Committees. Among the paintings are original portraits of Sir Thomas Gresham and Dean Colet; and a fanciful portrait of Whittington. Among the Mercers' Trust-estates are St. Paul's and Mercers' Schools. (See pp. 217 and 219.)

The Mercers' is the first of all the Twelve Companies, and of it there have been several kings, princes, and nobility; and to 1708, ninety-eight had been lord mayors, and one as early as 1214: Richard II., who granted the first charter in 1393, was a mercer; as were also Whittington and the illustrious Gresham. Among the Company's documents are a curious illustration of Whittington dying (ordinances of his college), and portraits of the first three wardens. In 1513, the Mercers possessed Conduit Mead, now covered by New Bond-street, which, had they retained, it would more than quadruple the value of all their present estates. (*Herbert.*) Among their property is the north side of Long Acre (about 8½ acres,) and the adjacent streets, including Mercer-street; in 1650, "part of the possessions of Charles Stuart, late King of England, for which the warden and company then paid to the Crown 13s. 4d. per annum. There is scarcely a single mercer in the Company at the present day." (*Herbert.*) Sir Baptist Hicks (founder of the Campden family) was a great mercer in Cheapside, who supplied the court when James I. and "his bare Scotch nobility and gentry came in:" he built the first Hicks's Hall, and was one of the first citizens that after knighthood kept their shops.

The Mercers' Company lend money to livery-men, or freemen, without interest, upon approved security. The Company also established the first insurance office for lives, in 1698. (*Hatton.*) The Golden Lectureship is in their gift.

The Mercers' Election-Cup, of early sixteenth-century work, is silver-gilt, decorated with fretwork and female busts; the feet, flasks; and on the cover is the popular legend of an unicorn yielding its horn to a maiden. The whole is enamelled with coats of arms, and these lines:

> "To elect the master of the mercerie hither am I sent,
> And by Sir Thomas Leigh for the same intent."

The Company also possess a silver-gilt Wagon and Tun, covered with arabesques and enamels, of sixteenth-century work.

* In a shop in the porch of Mercers' Chapel, Guy (founder of Guy's Hospital) was apprenticed to a bookseller in 1660; and the house rebuilt after the Great Fire was rented by Guy, then a master-bookseller.

2. GROCERS' HALL, Grocers' Hall-court, Poultry,* is the third edifice built for the Company, upon "voide grounde sum tyme the Lord Fitz-walter's halle:" the first was completed in 1428, in a large garden, and had an ancient turret, probably part of the Fitzwalter mansion, and one of the oldest buildings within the City walls. This Hall was let "for dinners, funerals, county feasts, and weddings;" in 1641, "the Grand Committee of Safety" removed its sittings from Guildhall here; Cromwell and Fairfax were feasted here by the Grocers; and at the Restoration, Gen. Monk. In the Great Fire of 1666, the roof and wood-work of the Hall only were destroyed; the old walls were then newly roofed, and in 1668-9, the parlour and dining-room were rebuilt by Sir John Cutler, four times master of the Company, who passed him "a strong vote of thanks," and his statue and picture, thus proving Cutler to have been the reverse of the miser described by Pope, whose satire, however, has reached far beyond the Grocers' gratitude. The old Hall, which had "a Gothic front and bow-windows," was renovated, in 1681, by Sir John Moore, who kept his mayoralty at Grocers' Hall, and paid the Company 200l. rent; and it was let for the same object till 1735. The Bank of England held their courts here from 1694 to 1734. The present Hall was built upon the ancient site between 1798 and 1802,† (T. Leverton, architect,) and thoroughly repaired in 1827, when the statue of Sir John Cutler, weather-beaten in the garden, was renovated, and removed into the Hall; and the garden-front was enriched with the arms of the Company on each side their crest, and a loaded camel, emblematic of the ancient conveyance of the grocer's commodities. The Hall is spacious, and has a music-gallery: here are Cutler's portrait, a fine picture; portraits of Sir John Moore and Sir John Fleet: and on the staircase are the Company's arms, painted on glass by Willement. The Grocers munificently support various free schools, almshouses, exhibitions, &c.; and the gifts for loans to poor members amount to 4670l.

The Grocers' Company, originally Pepperers, next united with the Apothe-caries, was incorporated by Edward III., in 1435, as "the Mystery of Grocers:" among other privileges, they possessed the management of the Kings' Beam, at the Weighing-house. Charles II. and William III. were masters of the Com-pany; and among the eminent Grocers were the Duke of York, afterwards James II.; George Monk, Duke of Albemarle; and Sir Philip Sidney, at whose funeral the Company rode in procession. In the reign of Henry IV., twelve aldermen were of the Grocers' Company at the same time. The fraternity also boasts of the patriotic Sir John Philpot; John Churchman, who founded the Custom House; Thomas Knolles, who began the Guildhall; Sir John Crosby, of Crosby House; Sir William Laxton, founder of Oundle School; and Laurence Shireff, of Rugby; besides the vilified Sir John Cutler. The Company sold their plate in aid of the defence of the City in the Civil Wars, and were famed for their loyal and costly pageants. In the Great Fire, they lost nearly all their property, except a few tenements in Grub-street, when they assembled in the turret-house in their garden: their hall was once seized for debt, in part from loans made to the City; but the Grocers, like the rest of the Companies, recovered their position before the Revolution of 1688; and in the year after, William became sovereign master of the Grocers. By a charter of Henry VI., confirmed by Charles I., the wardens of the Company, or their deputies, could, like modern excisemen, enter drug-gists', apothecaries', and confectioners', as well as grocers', shops, and impose fines, and even imprisonment, for deceits; always seizing the spurious articles.

The statutes of the ancient Pepperers (mentioned *temp.* Henry II., and pro-bably a guild long before,) exist among the City archives. The Grocers first existed as a sort of club. Twenty-two Pepperers in Sopers-lane, Cheapside (now

---

* Anciently "Conningshop-lane," *i. e.* cony-shop-lane, from the sign of three conies (rabbits), hanging over a poulterer's stall at the lane end.
  † The garden was then nearly severed in half for enlarging Prince's-street. For this latter slice, which cost the Grocers 31l. 17s. 8d. in 1433, the Company received from the Bank of England more than 20,000l. (*Herbert.*)

a part of Queen-street), on the 12th of June, 1345, after dinner, elected two of their number wardens, and appointed a chaplain to celebrate divine offices for their souls. Every member at the feast subscribed 1s. to pay for it, and contributions were then made towards the chaplain's salary.

The Grocers met in 1345 and 1346, at the town-mansion of the Abbot of Bury, in St. Mary Axe, now Bevis Marks; in 1347, "at the abbot's place of St. Edmund;" in 1348, "at the house of one Fulgeman, called the Ryngdehall," near Garlickhythe; where, and at the hotel of the abbot of St. Cross, they continued till 1383, when they took up their temporary residence in Bucklersbury, at the Cornets' Tower, used by Edward III. as his exchange of money and exchequer.

3. DRAPERS' HALL is in Throgmorton-street, where the Company settled in 1541, in a large mansion built *temp.* Henry VIII. "in the place of olde and small tenements, by Thomas Cromwell, Mayster of the King's Jewel-house," and afterwards Earl of Essex; upon whose attainder, the property was purchased by the Drapers and made their "Common Hall," till about the period of the Great Fire of 1666, which was here stopped in its progress northward.

Stow relates that his father had a garden adjoining Cromwell's, and close to his south pale a house, which, by the Mayster's order, was removed upon rollers, so as to gain a strip of ground, as Cromwell had taken from other neighbours. "No man," says Stow, " durst go to argue the matter, but each man lost his land, and my father payed his whole rent, which was vj². vijd. the yeare, for that halfe which was left. Thus much of mine owne knowledge have I thought good to note, that the sodaine rising of some men causeth them to forget themselves."

Cromwell's House is figured on Aggas's plan with four embattled turrets. The garden, which is well kept up to this day, became celebrated in 1551, when the country lay open in its rear nearly all the way to Hampstead and Highgate (see GARDENS, p. 321).

Although the Fire of London stopped at Drapers' Hall, it was "all consumed to ashes;" but the Company's property was saved by removing it into the garden, and "watching it ther for seaven days and nights." The Hall was rebuilt by Jarman, but nearly destroyed by fire in 1774, after which it was partly rebuilt (as we now see it) by the brothers Adam. It consists of a quadrangle surrounded by an ambulatory of arches and columns; the front in Throgmorton-street is highly enriched with stone-work, but the Drapers' arms over the gateway have for supporters lions instead of leopards. On the noble stone staircase is a marble bust of George IV. The Hall ceiling is embellished with Phaeton and the signs of the zodiac; the screen is curiously carved, and above it is a fine portrait of Lord Nelson by Beechey; and over the master's chair is a half-length on panel (in oil, and therefore not contemporary) of Fitz-Alwin, the first Mayor of London, whom the Drapers claim as of their Company, whereas Stow and other writers describe him of the Goldsmiths'. In the wainscoted gallery are full-length portraits of the English sovereigns from William III. to George IV., the last by Lawrence; with the celebrated whole-length of Mary Queen of Scots and her son James I., ascribed to Zucchero, traditionally said to have been thrown over the wall into the Drapers' garden during the Fire of London, and never afterwards owned: it has been copied by Spiridione Roma, and engraved by Bartolozzi.

There is another tradition of this picture: that Sir Anthony Babington, confidential Secretary to Queen Mary, had her portrait, which he deposited for safety either at Merchant-Tailors' Hall or Drapers' Hall, and that it had never come back to Sir Anthony or his family. It has been insinuated that Sir William Boreman, clerk to the Board of Green Cloth in the reign of Charles II., purloined this picture from one of the royal palaces. Some have suggested that it is the portrait of Lady Dulcibella Boreman, the wife of Sir William; but the style and costume are much older.—See *The Crypt.* No. 4. Oct. 10. 1827.

In the Court-room is a marble bas-relief of the Company receiving their charter. In the ladies' chamber, balls are given. In the Livery-room, among other portraits, is a three-quarter length of Sir Robert Clayton, by Kneller, 1680; and a small portrait of Thomas Bagshaw (died 1794), beadle to the Company forty years. The windows of this room look into the private garden, where are a fountain and statue.

The Drapers' Company was founded in 1332, and incorporated in 1364; they possess seven original charters, finely written, and claim to reckon more lord mayors than any other Company,—Strype states 87 years'. Their grant of arms, in 1439, is the only document of its kind of so early a date; the Heralds' College possessing none of the arms of the London Livery Companies. The Drapers' grant is kept at the British Museum, and contains illustrative historical notices of the Company; and the books continue its history for above two centuries. In the Wardens' accounts are apprentice-fees, called "Spoon Silver;" "potacions at our Lady Fair in Southwark," &c. In an entry of 1485, pippins are first mentioned; 1491, "the aldermen of the taylo's were treated with brede and wine at Drapers' halle:" 1494, "for cresset-staffs and banuers, and bread, ale, and candell, in keeping xij. days' watch after the riot at the Steel-yard," 11s. 9d.; "for a barge two times to the Shene (Richmond), to speak wth the King;" 1496, the Drapers "riding to the king at Woodstock," accompanied by "Mr. Recorder, Mr. Faoyan," and other eminent persons; 1509, 114s. "for xij. torches for the beryall of King Henry the VIIth, weying ccxx$^{lbs.}$ and 1 quart^r; 1521, the Drapers took the lead in settling the contribution required by the Government from the Great Companies towards furnishing ships of discovery under the command of Sebastian Cabot.

The Company had "the Drapers' Ell" granted to them by Edward III., for measuring the cloth sold at St. Bartholomew's and Southwark fairs; it bore the name of "the Yard," "the Company's Standard," &c. In the entries for relief "to those fallen in poverty," 1526, is ijs. and iiijd. to Sir Laurence Aylmer, one of the Drapers, two or three times Master of the Company, Sheriff 1501, and Lord Mayor 1507-8.

The Dress or Livery of this Company varied more than that of any other, and the colours were changed at almost every election until *temp.* James I., when a uniform livery was adopted; their observances consisting of election ceremonies, funerals, obits, and pageantries at state and civic triumphs. At their last public procession in 1751, their poor carried a pair of shoes and stockings, and a suit of clothes, an annual legacy.

The Drapers had a Hall in St. Swithin's-lane, Cannon-street, whither they removed from Cornhill. The St. Swithin's-lane Hall is first mentioned in 1405; when we find entered "a hammer to knock upon the table," the great parlour, the "high table" of the dining-hall (then strewed with rushes), the ladies' chamber, and the chekker chamber, all which at feasts were hung with tapestry: the kitchen had three fire-places. The ladies' chamber (an apartment which the Drapers still retain) was solely for the sisters of the fraternity, and in which they occasionally had separate dinners, instead of mixing with the company in the hall. The married ladies only, and those of the highest class, were the guests, "the chekker chamber being for maydens." A ladies' feast in 1515 included brawn and mustard, capon boiled, swan roasted, pyke, venison baked and roast, jellies, pastry, quails, sturgeon, salmon, and wafers and ipocras.

The Drapers thus early gave more splendid feasts than any other Company, their guests usually being the dignified and conventual clergy; including the abbot of Tower Hill, the prior of St. Mary Overy, Christ-church, and St. Bartholomew; the provincial and the prior of "Freres Austyn's," the masters of St. Thomas Acon's and St. Lawrence Pulteney. The sisters formed part of the usual guests, as did also the wives of members, whether enrolled amongst them or not: and visitors of high rank were personally waited on by the heads of the Company. Among the items of the Midsummer Feast, 1514-15, is perhaps the earliest mention of *players* as *companies:* "To Johan Slye and his *company*, for ij. plays on Monday and Tewsday," including "Robert Williams, the

Harp, and Henry Colet, the Lut, iiij^s." Among the rules " for the syt-tyng in ye halle" was, " No brother of the frat^rnite to presume to sytte at any table in the halle tyll the mayr and the states *have wasshed* and be sett att the hygh table, on peyne of iij^s. iiij^d."

The Drapers' Company have very large estates, and are trustees of numerous beneficent bequests, besides Almshouses. There are many females free of the Company, who invariably come on the list to par-ticipate in the charities. The Earls of Bath and Essex, the Barons Wotton, and the Dukes of Chandos, derive their descent from members of the Drapers' Company.

4. FISHMONGERS' HALL, at the north-west foot of London Bridge, was rebuilt by Roberts in 1830-3, and is the third of the Company's Halls nearly on this site.* It is raised upon a lofty basement cased with granite, and containing fireproof warehouses, which yield a large rental. The river front has a balustraded terrace, and a Grecian-Ionic hexastyle and pediment. The east or entrance front is enriched with pilasters and columns, and has in the attic the arms of the Company, and two bas-reliefs of sea-horses. The entrance-hall is separated from the great staircase by a screen of polished Aberdeen granite columns; and at the head of the stairs is a statue, carved in wood by E. Pierce, of Sir William Walworth, a Fishmonger, who carries a dagger.

In his hand was formerly a dagger, said to be the identical weapon with which he stabbed Wat Tyler, though in 1731 a publican of Islington pretended to possess the actual poniard. Beneath the statue is the inscription:

" Brave Walworth, knight, lord-mayor, y^t slew
Rebellious Tyler in his alarmes;
The King, therefore, did give in liew
The dagger to the City armes.
In the 4th year of Richard II. anno Domini 1381."

A common but erroneous belief was thus propagated; for the dagger was in the City arms long before the time of Sir William Walworth, and was intended to represent the sword of St. Paul, the patron saint of the Corporation.

The reputed dagger of Walworth, which has lost its guard, is preserved by the Company: the workmanship is of Walworth's period. The weapon now in the hand of the statue, (which is somewhat picturesque, and in our recollection was coloured *en costume*,) is modern.

The Company has numbered about fifty lord mayors, among whom was Sir William Walworth, who, in his second mayoralty, slew Wat Tyler, commemorated in a pageant in 1740 by a personation of Wal-worth, dagger in hand, and the head of Wat Tyler carried on a pole. Next among the lord mayors was Sir Stephen Foster, who rebuilt Ludgate prison; Sir Thomas Abney, the friend of Dr. Isaac Watts; and Matthew Wood, twice lord mayor, 1816 and 1817. Dogget, the comedian, was a Fishmonger; and his bequest of a coat and a silver badge is in the direction of this Company, who have added four money-prizes.

Thomas Dogget, who wrote *The Country Wake*, a comedy, 1696, was born in Castle-street, Dublin. He first appeared on the Dublin stage; and subsequently with Robert Wilks and Colley Cibber, became joint-manager of Drury-lane Theatre. He was a friend of Congreve, who wrote for him the characters o Fondlewife in the *Old Bachelor*, and Ben in *Love for Love*. Dogget's style o acting was very original, and he was an excellent *dresser*. He died in 1721, and being a staunch Whig, bequeathed a sum of money to purchase a coat and silve badge, to be rowed for on the Thames on the 1st of August annually, to com memorate the accession of the House of Hanover to the throne of Great Britain.

" Tom Dogget, the greatest sly drole in his parts,
In acting was certain a master of arts;

---

* Part of the site of the present Hall was then purchased at the rate of 630,000 per acre!.

A monument left—no herald is fuller,
His praise is sung yearly by many a sculler;
Ten thousand years hence, if the world lasts so long,
Tom Dogget will still be the theme of their song;
When old Noll, with great Lewis and Bourbon, are forgot,
And when numberless kings in oblivion shall rot."
Written on a window-pane at Lambeth, August 1, 1736.

The Garrick Club possess an original portrait of Dogget. (See page 194.)

The Court dining and drawing rooms face the river, of which they have a fine view, with the Kent and Surrey hills. The banqueting-hall is 73 feet by 38 feet, and 33 feet high, and has Sienna scagliola Corinthian pilasters, between which are suspended the arms of the benefactors and past prime-wardens of the Company; at one end of the hall are the royal arms, and opposite, those of the Goldsmiths, in stained glass; and on he front of the music-gallery are emblazoned the arms of the City and Twelve Great Companies: this introduction of heraldic insignia in a Grecian hall being novel, but very striking, and especially when lighted up by eight chandeliers. Among the *Curiosities*, besides Sir W. Walworth's dagger, is his funeral pall, of cloth-of-gold; the sides embroidered with the Saviour giving the Keys to St. Peter, and the Fishmongers' Arms; and the ends with the Deity and ministering Angels: here, too, is a plan of the show at Walworth's installation as mayor, probably the oldest representation of a lord mayor's show extant. Here also are eight curious pictures of fish, by Spiridione Roma, skilfully grouped and correctly coloured. Among the portraits are William III. and Queen, by Murray; George II. and Queen, by Shackleton; he Duke of Kent and Admiral Earl St. Vincent, by Beechey; and Queen Victoria, by Herbert Smith. In the Court dining-room is a splendid silver chandelier, weight 1350 oz. 14 dwts.

The Fishmongers' Company was formed by the junction of the two Companies of Salt Fishmongers and Stock Fishmongers, and was incorporated by Henry VIII. in 1536: yet long before either of the above dates the Fishmongers were united as a brotherhood, and, from the extent of their trade in Roman Catholic times, had obtained great sway and affluence. In 1290, they were fined 500 marks for forestalling; and in 1382, Parliament enacted that "no Fishmonger should for he future be admitted Mayor of the City," which prohibition was, however, removed next year. Before the union of the Salt and Stock Fishmongers, they had "six several Halls: in Thames-street, twain; in New Fish-street, twain; and in Old Fish-street, twain."—*Stow*.

The first Hall of the joint Company in Thames-street, in Hollar's view, 1647, has a dining-hall across the original quadrangle: the whole pile was of stone, embattled, and reaching to the water's edge; it had Tudor-shaped windows and square wing-towers, and altogether resembled a castle. In the Great Fire of 1666,

"A key of fire ran all along the shore,
And frighten'd all the river with a blaze."—Dryden's *Annus Mirabilis*.

The *hall* was entirely destroyed, but was rebuilt by Jarman in 1671: this edifice had a stately river-front, with an entrance from Thames-street, and was taken down in 1831, the Company having sold a portion of the land to the City for the new London Bridge approach. Among the Trust-estates and Charities of the Company is St. Peter's Hospital, originally erected at Newington, but taken down in 1851, and rebuilt on Wandsworth Common. (See ALMSHOUSES, page 5.)

The Stock-Fishmongers, from the earliest times, adopted St. Michael's Church, Crooked-lane (rebuilt and enlarged by their two eminent members, John Lovekyn and William Walworth,) as their general burial-place, to which they added "the Fishmongers' Chapel." St. Michael's was destroyed in the Great Fire, was rebuilt by Wren, but was taken down in 1831 for the new London Bridge approach.

5. GOLDSMITHS' HALL, Foster-lane, Cheapside, back of the General Post Office, built by Philip Hardwick, R.A., 1832-35, is the most magnificent City Hall, and the third erected for the Company on this site; its cost being defrayed without trenching on their funds for charitable purposes. The architecture is Italian, seventeenth and eighteenth centuries: the building is 180 feet in front and 100 feet in depth, completely insulated; the basement is Haytor granite, and the superstructure fine Portland stone. The west or principal façade has six attached Corinthian columns, the whole height of the front, supporting a rich Corinthian entablature and bold cornice of extraordinary beauty, continued all round the building. The east, north, and south fronts are decorated with pilasters, which also terminate the angles. The plinth is 6 feet high, and some of the blocks in the column-shafts and entablature weigh from 10 to 12 tons each. The windows of the principal story have enriched and bold pediments, supported by handsome trusses, and the centre windows have massive balustraded balconies; the echinus moulding in this story is much admired. The intercolumniations of the centre above the first floor, in place of the continuation of the windows of the second story, have the Company's arms, festal emblems, and naval and military trophies, floridly sculptured. The entrance-door is a rich specimen of cast-work: the Hall roof is entirely covered with lead.

This noble Hall is ill placed, but its sumptuous architecture is best appreciated when seen from the rear of the Post Office. The interior is correspondingly superb: from the vestibule branches right and left a grand staircase, on the balustrade of which are four marble statuettes of the Seasons by Nixon; in the central niche is a marble bust of William IV. by Chantrey; and above are portraits—of George IV. by Northcote; and George III. and his Queen, by Ramsay. The ascent is to a gallery, with screens of scagliola verde-antique columns, between which are statues of Apollo Belvidere, and Diana and the hart; from the dome hangs a magnificent chandelier: the effect of the whole is fascinating and scenic, particularly when viewed through the four piles of columns. The banqueting-hall, 80 by 40 feet, and 35 feet high, has a range of Corinthian columns along its sides, which are raised on pedestals and insulated. The five lofty and arched windows are filled with armorial bearings; and at the north end is a spacious alcove for the display of plate, lighted from above. On the sides is a large mirror, with busts of George III. and IV. by Chantrey. Between the columns are lofty portraits of Queen Adelaide, by M. A. Shee; and William IV. and Queen Victoria, by Hayter. The Court-room has an elaborate stucco ceiling; and here, beneath glass, is preserved a Roman altar, (sculptured with figures of Apollo and a dog, and a lyre,) which was found in digging the foundations of the present Hall. In the Court-room is Janssen's portrait of Sir Hugh Middleton (a Goldsmith), who brought the New River to London: the picture is in the style of Vandyke; Sir Hugh wears a black habit, his hand rests upon a shell, and near him is inscribed "Fontes Fodinæ." Next is a portrait (said by Holbein) of Sir Martin Bowes, lord mayor 1545, introducing the cup he bequeathed to the Goldsmiths' Company: here also hangs a large painting of St. Dunstan (patron of the Goldsmiths), in rich robe, and crozier in hand; in the background the saint is taking the devil by the nose, the heavenly host appearing above: the marble chimney-piece of this room was brought from Canons, and its two large terminal busts are attributed to Roubiliac. The drawing-room (crimson, white, and gold,) has immense mirrors, and a ceiling exquisitely wrought with flowers, fruits, birds, quadrupeds, and scroll-work, relieved with gay coats of arms. The Court dining-room has in the marble chimney-ece two boys holding a wreath, encircling the head of Richard II., whom the Goldsmiths' incorporation was confirmed.

In the Livery tea-room is a conversation-picture by Hudson, (Reynolds's master,) containing portraits of six lord mayors, all Goldsmiths: r H. Marshall, 1745; W. Benn, 1747; J. Blachford, 1750; R. Allsop, 52; Edmund Ironside and Sir Thomas Rawlinson, both in 1754, the rmer having died during his mayoralty.

The Goldsmiths' Company, anciently the "Gilda Aurifabrorum," as probably of foreign origin, and was fined as Adulterine, by enry II. in 1180: incorporated in 1327, first of Edward III.; the ant being confirmed by Richard II. in 1392. The Company have together fifteen charters. They purchased the site of their present all, with tenements, in 1323; their second hall was built by Sir Drew arentyne, goldsmith, and lord mayor in 1398: it was hung with emish tapestry, representing the history of St. Dunstan, whose silverlt statue stood on the reredos, or screen: Sir B. Rede, when mayor, ve in this hall a feast, with "a paled park, furnished with fruitfull ees and beasts of venery." The Hall, from 1641 till the Restoration, as the Exchequer of the Parliamentarians, wherein was stored up the oney accumulated by "sequestrations," or forfeitures of the Royalists' tates, as we read in the newspapers of that day. The Hall was nearly stroyed in the Great Fire of 1666, after which it was repaired and rtly rebuilt; but was taken down in 1829: the interior was sumptuous.

Cheapside, Old 'Change, Foster-lane, St. Martin's-le-Grand, and the avenues ar Goldsmiths' Hall, were the oldest localities of the goldsmiths' trade; there re also Gutter-lane, Seynt Marten's, Maydenyng-lane, Westminster, Southwark, ush-lane, Lombard-street, Silver-street, and other places. The moneyers, or eremoniers (such as cut out the plates to be stamped), occupied the Old 'Change d Sermon-lane. The shopkeepers, or sellers of plate, "sat in the High-street Chepe." The Goldsmiths always strove to prevent foreign workmen from setting in London,—the best artists being Italians,—from Cavalini, who made the rine of Edward the Confessor, to Torregiano, the maker of the superb brazen onument of Henry VII.; and in the fourth year of Edward IV. a trial of skill tween English goldsmiths and foreign ones took place at the Pope's-Head Tavern, ornhill (now Pope's-Head-alley), which was adjudged in favour of our workmen. arious entries shew the Company to have been both operative goldsmiths and the same time bankers.

Among the mayors of the Goldsmiths' Company were, Gregory de Rokesley ix times mayor); Nicholas de Faringdon, appointed mayor in 1308 by Edward II., as long as it pleased him;" Sir John Chace, M.P., and Bartholomew Rede; Sir artin Bowes, who lent Henry VIII. 300l.; Sir Robert Vyner; Sir John Shorter; r Francis Child, banker; and Sir Charles Duncombe.

The Goldsmiths' Pageants were formerly very costly; they maintin a splendid barge to this day, and they have a rich pall or hearseloth. St. Dunstan's image, of silver-gilt, set with gems, once adorned eir Hall; and they drank his memory from "St. Dunstan's Cup."

The Company's plate is very magnificent, and comprises a chandeer of chased gold, weighing 1000 ounces; two superb old plates f gold, having on them the arms of France quartered with those of ngland, but without those of Hanover; the cup bequeathed by Sir artin Bowes, and out of which Queen Elizabeth is said to have drunk t her coronation. At the Great Exhibition of 1851, the Company warded 1000l. to the best artists in gold and silver plate; and, as a rther commemoration, resolved to add to their treasures 5000l. worth f plate of British manufacture.

The *Assay* possessed by the Goldsmiths' Company compels every article of anufacture in gold or silver to be marked with the "Hall mark" before it leaves e workman's hands, and authorises the wardens to break whatever article is low standard. The Assay, anciently "the touch," with the marking or stamping and proving of the coin at "the Trial of the Pix," were privileges conferred on the Goldsmiths' Company before the statute 28th Edward I.; and they had an assay-office more than 500 years ago. "The same Act orders all goldsmiths' work to be stamped with the leopard's head,—that animal, before the adoption of the lion, being the armorial cognisance of England." (*Herbert.*) "The touch-warden and assay-master have large steel puncheons and marks of different sizes." The manner of making the assay is thus: "The assay-master puts a small quantity of the silver upon trial in the fire; and then taking it out again, he, with his exact scales, that will turn with the weight of the *hundredth part of a grain*, computes and reports the goodness or badness of the gold and silver."—*Touchstone for Goldsmiths' Wares.*

The *Hall mark* shews where manufactured, as the leopard's head for London. *Duty mark* is the head of the sovereign, shewing the duty is paid. *Date mark* is a letter of the alphabet, which varies every year: thus, the Goldsmiths' Company have used, from 1716 to 1755, Roman capital letters; 1756 to 1775, small Roman letters; 1776 to 1795, Old English letters; 1796 to 1815, Roman capital letters from A to U, omitting J; 1816 to 1835, small Roman letters, a to u, omitting j; from 1836, Old English letters. The *Standard mark* for gold is, England, lion passant; silver, the figure of Britannia. If under 22 carats, gold has the figure 18. The *Manufacturer's mark* is the initials of the maker.

The Company are allowed 2½ per cent, and the fees for stamping are paid in to the Inland Revenue Office.

6. SKINNERS' HALL, Dowgate-hill, rebuilt after the Great Fire of 1666, was refronted by Jupp about 1790: in the pediment are the Company's arms, and the frieze is ornamented with festoons and leopards heads. The drawing-room is lined with odoriferous cedar, carved and enriched, and has been restored by George Moore, F.R.S., who has also rebuilt the dining-hall, in Italian style with an enriched ceiling, a recess for the sideboard at the daïs end, and opposite an Ionic gallery for "minstrels." On the walls above the wainscot are panels for frescoes. Here is the portrait of Sir Andrew Judd, skinner, lord mayor 1551, and founder of the Tunbridge School, managed by the Company.

Among Judd's bequests was his "croft of pasture, called the *Sandhills*, or the backside of Holborn," in the parish of St. Pancras, which probably let for a few pounds at the time of the testator's decease, but is now covered with houses the ground-rents of which amount to several hundreds a year. At the expiration of the present leases in 1906, the rental of this estate alone will exceed 20,000*l.* a year—a vast income for a public school."—Britton's *Tunbridge Wells*, 1832.

The Skinners were incorporated in 1327, and purchased *temp.* Henry III Coped Hall, destroyed in the Great Fire. In the present Hall, the lord mayor sometimes kept his mayoralty; and the new East India Company first met here.

Budge-row, so called of Budge fur, in Watling-street, hard by, was chiefly tenanted by skinners; and Skinners' Well, Clerkenwell, was so called, says Stow, "for the skinners of London held there certain plays yearly, played of Holy Scripture."

The master and wardens of the Company are elected by a cap of maintenance fitting the intended new officers (the ceremony being attended by ten Blue-coat boys, the Company's almsmen, and trumpeters), and drinking wine out of three large silver cups in the form of cocks or fowls.

7. MERCHANT-TAILORS' HALL, Threadneedle-street, was built by Jarman soon after the Great Fire of 1666. The banquetting-room is the largest of the City Companies' Halls, and has a stately screen and music-gallery. Upon the walls are shields emblazoned with the Masters' arms, and whole-length portraits of King William and Queen Mary, and other sovereigns. The Hall has, from an early period, been frequently lent to public corporations: the "Sons of the Clergy" anniversary meeting is held here; a splendid banquet was given here in 1815 to the Duke of Wellington, when he was invested with the freedom of the Company. Among the great political feasts held here was the dinner to Sir Robert Peel, May 11, 1835, at which the Duke of Wellington and the Conservative Members of the House of Commons were present.

Among the pictures in the hall, court-room, &c., is a head of Henry VIII. by Paris Bordone; head of Charles I.; three-quarter and full-length of Charles II.; full-lengths of James II. and Queen Anne; George III. and his Queen, by Ramsay; he late Duke of York, by Lawrence; Lord Chancellor Eldon, by Briggs; the Duke of Wellington, by Wilkie; Mr. Pitt, by Hoppner. Here too are portraits f Sir Thomas White, Master of the Company 1561, founder of St. John's College, Oxford; portraits of other lord mayors, Merchant-Tailors; and a modern picture f Henry VII. presenting his Charter of Incorporation, attended by Archbishop Varham, Fox Bishop of Winchester, and Willoughby Lord Brooke.

The Merchant-Tailors, anciently "Taylors and Linen Armourers," arose from guild dedicated to St. John Baptist, originally incorporated by Edward IV. in 466, but re-incorporated in 1503 by Henry VII., one of its members. Their first hall, in Threadneedle-street, was the mansion of E. Crepin, and as called the "New Hal, or Taylers' Inne," to distinguish it from their old hall Basing-lane. This Hall was rebuilt, was hung with tapestry of St. John Baptist, nd had on the screen a silver image of St. John in a tabernacle; the windows ere painted with armorial bearings; the floor strewed with rushes; from the ceil-ig hung silk flags and streamers; and on feast-days the tables on tressels were overed with the richest damask linen and glittering plate. Among the other tall buildings was the Treasury, in the garden, for plate, money, securities, &c.; 1e King's Chamber, for the reception of royal personages, who visited the Mer-ant-Tailors oftener than any other Company; and the Summer banqueting-room, 1 the garden. The Company's armoury is first mentioned in 1600, when there ere three state-palls and eighteen banners, besides pavises and pennons. After 1e Great Fire, from among the Hall ruins was collected the Company's melted plate 200 lbs. weight of metal), which they sold to begin a fund to rebuild.

One of the most splendid festivals in the old Hall was that given to ames I. and Prince Henry in 1607, when a child "delivered a short peech containing xviii. verses, devised by Mr. Ben. Johnson;" and "in he Ship which did hang aloft in the Hall were three rare men and very kilful, who song to His Majesty." James dined in the King's chamber, here Mr. John Bull, doctor of music, and a brother of the Company, layed a pair of organs all the dinner-time. Then His Majesty came own to the Great Hall, where "the three rare men in the shippe" ing a song of farewell, which so pleased the King, that he caused the ime to be sung three times over.

The Company are possessed of, and are Trustees to, great estates for oble purposes, besides the eminent School which bears their name. (See [ERCHANT-TAILORS' SCHOOL, p. 217.) In 1664, the scholars acted in 1e old Hall Beaumont and Fletcher's comedy of "Love's Pilgrimage."

In the list of the distinguished freemen of the Company are 11 overeigns, about as many princes of the blood-royal, 13 dukes, two uchesses, nearly 30 archbishops and bishops, 15 abbots and priors, and long list of nobility.

One of the most eminent tailors (professionally so) was Sir John lawkwood, "Johannes Acutus," who "twined his needle into a sword, nd his thimble into a shield," and became "the first general of modern mes; the earliest master, however imperfect, in the science of Tu-nne and Wellington." (Hallam's *Middle Ages*.) Sir Ralph Black-ell, stated to have been a fellow-apprentice of Hawkwood, and, like im, knighted for his valour by Edward III., was also a Merchant-aylor; as were Speed and Stow, the historians, both tailors by trade. tow enjoyed an annuity from the Company, who keep in repair his onument in St. Andrew's Undershaft. (See CHURCHES, p. 118.)

In the Merchant-Tailors' records, we find this gratifying entry: "1654, l. 6s. 8d. given to Ogilby the poet, free of this Company, on his petition that he id, at much study and expense, translated Virgil into English metre, with an-otations, and likewise Æsop's Fables, both which he had presented to them fairly und."—Herbert's *Twelve Great Livery Companies*, vol. ii. p. 406.

8. HABERDASHERS' HALL, No. 8 Gresham-street West, corner of taining-lane, is a heavy brick pile, built by Wren shortly after the

Great Fire of 1666. Here are a small statue of Henry VIII.; a painting of the Wise Men's Offering; and several portraits of benefactors, including Robert Aske, who left the Company 30,000l. to build and endow alms-houses at Hoxton; also Sir George Whitmore, lord mayor in 1631, who entertained Charles I. and his Queen in his noble mansion and gardens of Baumes, or Balmes, Kingsland-road, Hoxton.

The Company's Court books extend only to the reign of Charles I. but they possess a small vellum book of ordinances, which has a good illumination of St. Katherine, the Haberdashers' patron saint.

The Haberdashers, or Hurrers of old, date their ordinances from 1372, and were incorporated by Henry VI. in 1447. They were also called Milliners, from dealing in merchandise from Milan. They were originally a branch of the mercers, and Lydgate places their stalls together in the mercery at Chepe. Here were also haberdashers of hats, as well as of small wares. In the reign of Edward VI. there were only twelve milliners' shops in all London, but in 1580 th town became full of them; and this encouragement of foreign manufacture doubt less led to the sumptuary regulations anciently issued to the Companies and City

The site of the present Haberdashers' Hall was bequeathed to th Company in 1478: the old Hall must have been very spacious, for th Parliament commissioners met in it during the Interregnum. Th charitable devises vested in the Company include alms-houses, hospi tals, and free-schools; besides legacies to poor members and loans t young ones; gifts to debtors in the City prisons, &c.; altogether be tween 3000l. and 4000l. yearly.

9. SALTERS' HALL, St. Swithin's-lane, Cannon-street, the fifth hal of the Salters' Company, was rebuilt by Henry Carr, architect 1823-27: it has a handsome Ionic portico, surmounted by the Com pany's arms. The Great Hall has a music-gallery, and is hung with banners from the ceiling. Over the doorways are busts of George III and IV., the Duke of York, Nelson, and Wellington. In the Electio Hall are portraits of Charles I.; Adrian Charpentier, painted by him self, 1760; and William III. on horseback. In the waiting-room i preserved the bill of a feast to 50 Salters in 1506,—1l. 13s. 2½d.

In the Company's books is a receipt "For to make a moost choyce Paaste Gamys to be eten at ye Feste of Chrystemasse" (17th Richard II. A.D. 1394). pie so made by the Company's cook in 1836 was found excellent. It consisted a pheasant, hare, and capon: two partridges, two pigeons, and two rabbits; all bon and put into paste in the shape of a bird, with the livers and hearts, two mutto kidneys, forced-meats, and egg-balls, seasoning, spice, catsup, and pickled musl rooms, filled up with gravy made from the various bones.

The Salters' (Dry Salters) Company was not regularly incorpo rated till 1558; a Salter attended the Mayor as chief-butler at the coro nation of Richard III., 1483, and was represented at the coronation o George IV. The original of the Salters' only printed pageant was sol in Bindley's sale, in 1818, for 20 guineas.

The Salters' first Hall was in Bread-street, next their kindre tradesmen the Fishmongers, in the Old Fish-market, Knight-Rider street. This Hall was rebuilt, the Company's third Hall being th town inn or mansion of the Priors of Tortington, purchased in 164 and afterwards "Oxford-place," from John de Vere, 16th Earl of Ox ford. It adjoined the dwellings of the infamous Empson and Dudley temp. Henry VII., who met in the garden of Oxford-place, now Salter Garden. The fourth Hall succeeded the Great Fire of 1666, and had a arcade opening into the garden; and next to it was Salters'-Hall Meet ing-house, rented of the Company, but taken down in 1821.

10. IRONMONGERS' HALL, Fenchurch-street, nearly opposite Mark lane, built by T. Holden, in 1748, has a handsome stone front, of Italia architecture, with Ionic pilasters, and a well-proportioned pedimer

which are sculptured the Company's arms, &c. From the vestibule, ivided by Tuscan columns, a large staircase leads to the banqueting-all; the decorations of which are in Louis Quatorze taste, in Jack-n's papier-mâché and carton-pierre imitative oak, aided by old carv-gs, and are economically effective. The Company's pictures consist iefly of portraits of benefactors, including Mr. Thomas Betton, a urkey merchant, who, in 1723-24, left 26,000l., half the interest of which as to be expended in ransoming British subjects, captives in Barbary r Turkey. Here, also, is a fine portrait of Admiral Lord Viscount ood, by Gainsborough, presented by his lordship in 1783, when he was dmitted to the freedom of the Company, in testimony of his distin-uished naval services. One of the hall windows contains a whole-ngth portrait, in painted glass, of Sir Christopher Draper, date 1639.

The Ironmongers* were first incorporated by Edward IV. in 1464: their first House," built upon the site of the present hall, had a gate-house, the refec-ry strewed with rushes, court-chamber hung with tapestry; and an armoury ntaining, in 1556, 17 back and breast plates. 17 pair of splints, 12 gorgets, 12 rords, and 11 daggers, to which were afterwards added corslets, skull-caps and d caps, black bills, morris pikes, white coats with red crosses, 14 sheaves of rows, &c. At the raising of the army of the Earl of Essex in 1642, the ompany lent, " to be returned or paied for," 10 russet armours, 10 pikes, 10 rords with belts, 10 head-pieces, 10 musquets with bandelores and rests, and murrions. In 1523, the Company lent Henry VIII. a large sum of money, r selling some of their plate and pawning the rest; and Elizabeth compelled e Company to lend her money, which forced the citizens to borrow of her at 7 r cent on pledges of gold and silver plate, &c.

In the list of Masters and Wardens is John London, Esq. 1727, who ave name to London-street, nearly opposite Ironmongers' Hall. ew Wardens are chosen at the end of the Election dinner, when the afers are brought in : 1671, Sept. 21, " I din'd in the city, at the Fra-rnity Feast in Ironmongers' Hall, where the four stewards chose their iccessors for the next yeare, with a solemn procession, garlands about ieir heads, and music playing before them ; so coming up to the upper ibles where the gentlemen sate, they drank to the new stewards, and we parted."—Evelyn's *Diary.*

The Company's Pageants were very costly and characteristic; one aving Vulcan and his forge, with smiths at work; and an " Estridge," Ostrich), ridden by an Indian boy, from the common belief that this ird could eat and digest *iron ;* the supporters of the Company's rms are salamanders, supposed, like *iron,* to be unhurt by fire. A east item of 1719 is "for playing on the tongs, 10s. ;" and a meat break-ast in 1542 is charged " for the cook, turnspit, and woman, for dressing, iijd." Funeral feasts were also celebrated in the Hall.

Among the Company's Charities are the handsome Almshouses in he Kingsland-road, originally founded by the will of Sir Robert effery, lord mayor in 1686.

11. VINTNERS' HALL, Upper Thames-street, near Southwark Bridge, as rebuilt by Wren, after the Great Fire of 1666 ; when were destroyed e first Hall, in a *quadrant,* given by Sir John Stodie, vintner, and lord ayor in 1357 (*Stow*) ; and the adjoining almshouses devised to the Com-iny by Guy Shuldham, in 1446. The present Hall has been refronted, id is wainscoted and richly carved. In the Court-room are whole-ngth portraits of Charles II., James II. and his queen, George Prince

* In Ironmonger-lane, Cheapside, the trade first congregated ; and many inent ironmongers were buried in the church of the adjacent parishes of St. ave Jewry, and St. Martin, Ironmonger-lane. Strype subsequently speaks of e removal of " the ironmongers of Ironmonger-lane" into Thames-street, where

of Denmark; and a picture, attributed to Vandyke, of St. Mart (tutelar of the Company) dividing his cloak with the beggar.

The Vintners were incorporated as Wine-Tunners by Henry VI. in 1437; E ward III. having granted them, in 1365, a charter for the exclusive importati of wines from Gascony: the freemen, or "free vintners," of the Company ha the privilege of retailing wine without a license. Stow tells us the Vintners we of old called "Marchants Vintners of Gascoyne," and "great Bourdeous me chants of Gascoyne and French wines;" and *temp.* Edward III. Gascoyne win were sold in London at 4*d.*, and Rhenish at 6*d.*, the gallon.

The Vintry, which gives name to the Ward, was part of the nor bank of the Thames, where Vintners' Hall and Queen-street-place a now built; it was at the south end of Three Cranes-lane, so called fro the implements with which the merchants "craned their wines out lighters and other vessels," and landed them: it was so magnificent building, that Henry Picard, vintner and mayor in 1356, entertain therein the kings of England, Scotland, France, and Cyprus, in 136 After the Great Fire, the Vintners' Almshouses were rebuilt in tl Mile-End-road. The Company keep swans on the Thames (see p. 362

12. CLOTHWORKERS' HALL, on the east side of Mincing-lane, Fei church-street, is of red brick, adorned with brick fluted pilasters. Tl Hall is richly wainscoted, and has life-sized carved figures of James and Charles I. In the windows are painted arms of benefactors, ii cluding Samuel Pepys, Master of the Company in 1677, who presente them with a silver election-cup and cover, embossed and partly gili the foot inscribed, "Samuel Pepis, Admiraliti Angliæ Secretes Societ.: Pannif: Lond. Mr. (Master) An. 1677."

The Clothworkers were originally incorporated by Edward IV. in 1482 Shermen (Shearers), and were united with the Fullers in 1528 by Henry VIII., tl conjoined fraternity being then named Clothworkers. James I. incorporated hir self into the Clothworkers, "as men dealing with the principal and noblest stap wares of all these islands, woollen cloths." Among their pageants is that of Sir Jol Robinson, lord mayor 1662-63, reviving " the true English and manlike exerci of wrestling, archery, sword, and dagger;" when at his mayoralty feast in Clotl workers' Hall, he entertained the king, queen, and queen-mother, the Duke an Duchess of York. The Hall was in part destroyed by the Great Fire: "bi strange," says Pepys, " it is to see Clothworkers' Hall on fire these three da and nights in one body of flame, it having the cellars full of oyle." The *Gazel* of Sept. 8, 1666, announces the Fire to have stopped near Clothworkers' Hal The list of the Company's charities is remarkable for its number of anniversar sermons and lectures, and for its bequests for blind persons. The Company Almshouses (now at Islington) were originally in Whitefriars, on part of a garde belonging to Margaret Countess of Kent, held by her of the prior of that friary.

Howes relates that James I. being in the open Hall, inquired who was Maste of the Company; and the Lord Mayor answering "Syr William Stone," to him tl King said, "Wilt thou make me free of the Clothworkers?" "Yea," quoth tl Master, "and think myself a happy man that I live to see this day." Then tl King said, "Stone, give me thy hand; and now I am a Clothworker."

HALLS OF THE MINOR CITY COMPANIES.

Of the 69 Minor Companies, nearly half possess Halls. Each Con pany has its position in the order of precedence, commencing with tl Dyers' and ending with the Carmen; but here the arrangement alphabetical.

APOTHECARIES' HALL, Water-lane, Blackfriars. (See page 17.)

ARMOURERS' AND BRAZIERS' HALL, Coleman-street, is a mode building, with a Doric portico, on the site of the Armourers' old Hɛ of the Company, incorporated in 1422 by Henry VI., who also becan a member. They formerly made coats of mail; and made and present queting-hall is Northcote's picture of the *Entry of Richard II. and Bolingbroke into London*, purchased by the Company from Boydell's Shakspeare Gallery in 1825. The Hall is characteristically decorated with armour.

BAKERS' HALL, No. 16 Harp-lane, Great Tower-street, is on the site of the ancient mansion of John Chichley, Chamberlain of London, and nephew of Archbishop Chichley. Among the pictures in the wainscoted banqueting-hall is one of St. Clement, patron of the Company, incorporated by Edward II. in 1307. The Hall was last repaired by James Elmes, who wrote the *Memoirs of Sir Christopher Wren*.

BARBER-SURGEONS' HALL, Monkwell-street, has its semicircular end supported on a bastion of the City Wall, and was built a few years after the Great Fire of 1666, which destroyed the original Hall: the street entrance has a shell canopy, is enriched with the Company's arms, and festoons of fruit and flowers. The Theatre of Anatomy, built by Inigo Jones, in 1636, escaped the Great Fire, through being detached.

"The room contained four degrees of cedar seats, one above another, in elliptical form, adorned with figures of the seven Liberal Sciences, the twelve signs of the Zodiac, and a bust of King Charles I. The roof was an elliptical cupola. This, as Walpole calls it, 'one of the best of Jones's works,' was repaired in the reign of George I. by the Earl of Burlington, and was pulled down in the latter end of the last century, and sold for the value of the materials. 'The designe of the Chirurgeons' Theatre,' an oval, dated 1636, is preserved in the portfolio of Jones's drawings at Worcester College, Oxford."—*Life, by P. Cunningham; printed for the Shakspeare Society.*

Originally, surgery and shaving were carried on in London by the same person. In 1512, an Act was passed to prevent any besides barbers practising surgery within the City and seven miles round, excepting such as were examined by the Bishop of London or Dean of St. Paul's, or their assistants. In 1540 they were united into one corporate body; but all persons practising shaving were forbidden to intermeddle with surgery, except to draw teeth and let blood; whence Barber-Surgeons. The Rev. John Ward, vicar of Stratford-upon-Avon 1662 to 1681, relates that when he came to London, he lodged at the Bell, in Aldersgate-street, "to be near Barber-Chirurgeons' Hall," then the only place in the metropolis where anatomical lectures were publicly delivered.

In the Court-room, which has an enriched ceiling, is Holbein's celebrated picture of King Henry VIII. presenting the Charter to the Company. This painting is 10 feet 6 inches long and 7 feet high, contains 18 figures, nearly life-size, and represents a room in the palace hung with tapestry. In the centre, on a throne, sits the King, seemingly thrusting the Charter into the hands of Master Thomas Vicay, who receives it kneeling; the King's costume and ornaments are as fine as miniature-painting. Around him are the members of the Court kneeling: Sir John Chambre, in a cap and furred gown; the famous Dr. Butts, whose conduct in the scene in the play of *Henry VIII.* of the degradation of Cranmer, while waiting at the door of the council-chamber, is so well drawn by Shakspeare. All the heads are finely executed; the flowered and embroidered robes, gold chains, jewels, and rings of the chirurgeons, their moustaches and beards, are most carefully painted. Seven of the figures are livery-men of the Company. Every part of the picture is most elaborately and delicately finished; the colouring is chaste, and the care and style of the whole admirable. Pepys tried, after the Great Fire, to buy this picture, "by the help of Mr. Pierce (a surgeon), for a little money. I did think," he adds, "to give 200*l.* for it, it being said to be worth 1000*l.*; but it is so spoiled that I have no mind to it, and is not a pleasant though a good picture."—*Diary*, 29th Aug. 1668.

Next is a whole-length of Sir Charles Scarborough, by Walker, chief physician to Charles II., James II., and William III.: he is lecturing in the doctor's scarlet cap, hood, and gown; on the left is the demonstrating surgeon, Anthony Bligh, in the livery-gown, holding up the arm of a dead subject, which lies on a table partly covered with a sheet. Next are portraits of Dr. Arris and Dr. Thomas Arris, and Dr. Nehemiah Grew. Here, too, is a curious portrait of Mr. Lisle, barber to Charles II.; and of John Paterson, clerk to the Company, and the projector of several improvements in the City of London after the Great Fire.—*Abridged from the Art-Union*, 1839.

Holbein's picture was painted in the 32d of Henry VIII., when were united the Barbers and Surgeons, formerly separate companies, which they again became in 1745; the Surgeons then removed to their Hall in the Old Bailey, and subsequently into a Royal College in Lincoln's-Inn-fields. (See COLLEGES, page 208.) Barbers, however, continued to let blood (whence the pole) and draw teeth until our time: the latest we remember of this class, and with pain, was one Middleditch, in Great Suffolk-street, Southwark, in whose window were displayed heaps of drawn teeth.

Among the Barber-Surgeons' Plate is: 1. A Silver-gilt Cup, given by Henry VIII. in 1540: it is richly embossed with the rose, fleur-de-lys, and portcullis, and lions' masks, in the style of Holbein; from the bowl hang bells, and inside are the Company's arms. 2. A Silver Cup, with Cover, given in 1678 by Charles II.; the stem and bowl an oak-tree, with four pendent acorns, and the lid the Royal crown; royal badges, the Company's arms, &c. 3. Two Chaplets, with perforated silver oak-foliage borders, the Company's arms, &c.; besides a large chased silver Punch-bowl, presented by Queen Anne; several tankards, &c.

The Barber-Surgeons are exempt, as formerly, from serving as constables or on the nightly watch, on juries, inquests, attaints, or recognisances.

BLACKSMITHS' HALL, Lambeth-hill, Doctors' Commons, is now let as a warehouse; the Company's business being transacted at Cutlers' Hall.

BREWERS' HALL, No. 19 Addle-street, Wood-street, Cheapside, is a modern edifice, and contains among other pictures a portrait of Dame Alice Owen, who narrowly escaped braining by an archer's stray arrow from Islington fields, in gratitude for which she founded a hospital. (See ALMSHOUSES, p. 5.) In the Hall windows is some old painted glass. The Brewers were incorporated in 1438. The quarterage in this Company is paid on the quantity of malt consumed by its members. In 1851, a handsome schoolhouse was built for the Company, in Trinity-square, Tower-hill.

In 1422, Whittington laid an information before his successor in the Mayoralty, Robert Childe, against the Brewers' Company, for selling *dear ale*, when they were convicted in the penalty of 20*l.*; and the Masters were ordered to be kept in prison in the Chamberlain's custody, until they paid it.

BRICKLAYERS' HALL, behind No. 53 Leadenhall-street, is now let as a Synagogue for Dutch Jews. The Bricklayers and Tilers were incorporated in 1568.

BUTCHERS' HALL, Pudding-lane, Eastcheap, was rebuilt after a fire in 1829, which destroyed the old Hall. The Butchers were fined by Henry II., in 1180, for setting up an unlicensed guild; but they were not incorporated till 1605, by James I.

CARPENTERS' HALL, on the southern side of London Wall, is one of the few City Halls which escaped the Great Fire of 1666, which surrounded it.* The Hall was originally built in 1429: the walls of old London faced it, and beyond were Moorfields, Finsbury, and open ground. The exterior possesses no traces of antiquity. The Court-rooms were built in 1664, and the principal staircase and entrance-hall by W. Jupp about 1780: the latter is richly decorated with bas-reliefs of carpentry figures and implements, with heads of Vitruvius, Palladio,

* Carpenters' Hall was also nearly destroyed in a great fire Oct. 6, 1849, when the end walls and windows were burned out, and the staircase and roof much damaged; while the burning building was only separated from Drapers' Hall by the garden and fore-court.

Inigo Jones, and Wren, designed by Bacon; and the street archway has also a fine bust of Inigo Jones, by Bacon.

The Great Hall has a rich and beautiful ceiling, put up in 1671, the supporting pillars springing from the corbels of the old arched timber roof. On the western side, surmounted by an embattled oak beam, is a series of four fresco paintings, which were discovered in 1845 by a workman in repairing the Hall. The subjects are divided by columns painted in distemper: the groundwork is laths, with a thick layer of brown earth and clay held together with straw, and a layer of lime, upon which the paintings are executed.

The subjects are: 1. Noah receiving the commands from the Almighty for the construction of the Ark: in another portion of the picture are Noah's three sons at work. 2. King Josiah ordering the repair of the Temple. (2 Kings chap. xxii., mentioning *carpenters* and builders and masons as having no reckoning of money made with them, "because they dealt faithfully.") 3. Joseph at work as a carpenter, the Saviour as a boy gathering the chips; Mary spinning with the distaff;* the figure of Joseph represents that in Albert Durer's woodcut of the same incident, executed in 1511. 4. Christ teaching in the synagogue: "Is not this the *carpenter's* son?" Each painting has a black-letter inscription, more or less perfect. The figures are of the school of Holbein: the costumes are *temp.* Henry VIII. Above the pictures, in the spandril of the arch, are painted the Company's arms, and "shreeves" and "Robard" of an inscription remain, intimating it to commemorate the benefaction of some sheriffs. The southern wall has some decorative Elizabethan work. The eastern window has carved oak mullions and *renaissance* bases, and has some armorial painted glass, date 1586. There are a few carved wooden panels, besides the series of corbels, some of good workmanship.—*F. W. Fairholt, F.S.A.*

The Carpenters' Company's earliest charter is dated 1477; their common seal and grant of arms, 1466; but a guild of carpentry is noticed in 1421-2. The earliest entry in the Company's books is dated 1438: they contain many proofs of their power over the trade. Among the pictures are portraits of William Portington, master carpenter to the Crown *temp.* Elizabeth and James I.; and John Scott, ordnance carpenter and carriage-maker *temp.* Charles II. The Company also possess four very curious caps or crowns (the oldest 1561), still used by the Master and Wardens. Among their plate are three silver-gilt *hanaps* (1611, 12, 28), which are borne in procession round the Hall on election-day. Cakes are presented to the members of the Court, on Twelfth Day, and ribbon-money to them on Lord's Mayor's Day. (See *An Historical Account of the Company*, by E. Basil Jupp, Clerk. 1849.)

COACHMAKERS' HALL, Noble-street, Foster-lane, was originally built for the Scriveners' Company, who, falling into poverty, sold it to the Coachmakers, originally incorporated by Charles II. in 1671.

Coachmakers' Hall was noted at the beginning of the war with revolutionary France as the resort of "a kind of religious Robinhood Society, which met every Sunday evening for free debate."—(Boswell's *Johnson.*) But the most memorable meeting ever held in the hall was on May 29, 1780, when the whole body of the Protestant Association, by formal resolution, undertook to attend in St. George's Fields on June 2, "to accompany Lord George Gordon to the House of Commons, on the delivery of the Protestant petition." The Association, accordingly, met; and the result was the memorable "Riots of 1780," and a week's defiance of all government. The flowers of rhetoric, however, continued long after to bloom in Coachmakers' Hall: Mr. Britton, in 1798 (*Autobiography*, . 89), joined a Debating Society held here.

COOPERS' HALL, Basinghall-street, is handsomely built, and has a large wainscoted banqueting-room. The Coopers' Company was in-

* Nash, the Elizabethan satirist, mentions the chips "which Christ in Carpenters' Hall is paynted gathering up, as Joseph his father strewes, having a piece of timber, and Mary his mother sitts spinning by."

corporated by Henry VII. in 1501; and Henry VIII. empowered them to search and gauge beer, ale, and soap vessels in the City and two miles round, at a farthing for each cask. At Coopers' Hall were formerly drawn State Lotteries; the drawing of the last Lottery, on October 18, 1826, is described in Hone's *Every-day Book*, vol. 2.

CORDWAINERS' HALL, Great Distaff-lane, Friday-street, is the third of the same Company's halls on this site, and was built in 1788 by Sylvanus Hall: the stone front, by Adam, has a sculptured medallion of a country girl spinning with a distaff, emblematic of the name of the lane, and of the thread of cordwainers or shoemakers; in the pediment are their arms. In the hall are portraits of King William and Queen Mary; and here is a sepulchral urn and tablet, by Nollekens, to John Came, a munificent benefactor to the Company.

The Cordwainers were originally incorporated by Henry IV. in 1410, as the "Cordwainers and *Cobblers*," the latter then signifying dealers in shoes and shoemakers. In the reign of Richard II., "every cordwainer that shod any man or woman on the Sunday, to pay thirtie shillings." Among the Company's plate is a piece for which Camden the antiquary left 16*l.* Their charities include Came's bequests for blind, deaf, and dumb persons, and clergymen's widows, 1000*l.* yearly; and, in 1662, the Bell inn at Edmonton was bequeathed for poor freemen of the Company.

CUTLERS' HALL is in Cloak-lane, Dowgate-hill. The Cutlers maintained a dispute with the Goldsmiths before Parliament in 1405. They were originally forgers of blades, or bladers, makers of hafts, and sheath-makers, united as cutlers by Henry VI. in 1425. In the Hall is a portrait of Mrs. Craythorne, who, in 1568, bequeathed the Belle Sauvage Inn, on Ludgate Hill, to the Cutlers, for charitable purposes. (See INNS.)

CURRIERS' HALL is on the south side of London Wall. The Curriers founded a guild in 1367 in the conventual church of Whitefriars, Fleet-street; and they were incorporated by James I. in 1605. In Curriers' Hall preached E. Calamy, jr., the nonconformist, *temp.* Chas. II.

DYERS' HALL, College-street, Upper Thames-street, was built about 1776. The Dyers were incorporated in 1472; its ancient Hall, in Upper Thames-street (upon the site of Dyers' Hall Wharf), was destroyed in the Great Fire of 1666.

The Dyers and Vintners are the only Companies who have the privilege *of keeping Swans on the Thames;* to catch and take up which, "Swan-voyages," termed *Swan-upping,* are made in August, when the cygnets are marked, and the

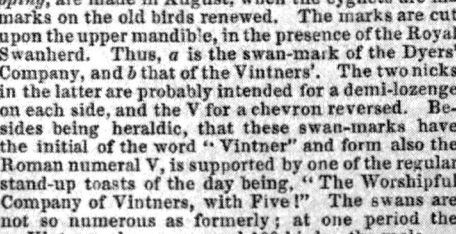

marks on the old birds renewed. The marks are cut upon the upper mandible, in the presence of the Royal Swanherd. Thus, *a* is the swan-mark of the Dyers' Company, and *b* that of the Vintners'. The two nicks in the latter are probably intended for a demi-lozenge on each side, and the V for a chevron reversed. Besides being heraldic, that these swan-marks have the initial of the word "Vintner" and form also the Roman numeral V, is supported by one of the regular stand-up toasts of the day being, "The Worshipful Company of Vintners, with Five!" The swans are not so numerous as formerly; at one period the Vintners alone possessed 500 birds: the male is called a *Cob*, the female a *Plu*. (*A. J. Kempe, F.S.A.*) The swanherds wear swan-feathers in their caps, and the *uppings* are made by the Companies in their state barges, with much festivity.

Swan-mark. Dyers' Company.

Swan-mark. Vintners' Comp

EMBROIDERERS' HALL, Gutter-lane, Cheapside, is a modern structure: the Company was incorporated by Queen Elizabeth in 1561.

FOUNDERS' HALL, Founders'-court, Lothbury, is now a Dissenters

Meeting-house. The Founders' Company was incorporated in 1614, with the power of searching all brass weights and brass and copper wares within the City, and three miles round. Founders' Hall has also been noted for its political meetings. (See p. 268, *note*.)

GIRDLERS' HALL, No. 39 Basinghall-street, was rebuilt after the Great Fire of 1666, on the site of their ancient hall. The Girdlers' or Girdle-makers' Company was incorporated by Henry VI. in 1449, and confirmed by Elizabeth, in 1658, and then united with the Pinners and Wire-drawers. The gridiron or *girdle*-iron in their arms is thought to be a rebus on the Company's name. (See Thoms's *Stow*, p. 107.) The Company possess a document, dated 1464, by which Edward IV. confirmed the privileges granted to them by Richard II. and Edward III., among which was the following :—In the girdles then worn, silver and copper were used in their fabrication and embroidery, and power was given to the Company to sieze all girdles found within the City walls with spurious metals. At the annual Election, the Clerk of the Company crowns the Master with a crown embroidered in gold on silk with the Girdlers' devices; and the Masters with three ancient caps; whereupon they pledge their subjects in a loving-cup of Rhenish wine—a picturesque ancient ceremonial.

INNHOLDERS' HALL, College-street, Upper Thames-street, was built after the Great Fire of 1666: the Company incorporated 1515.

JOINERS' HALL, Joiners'-Hall-buildings, between Nos. 79 and 80, Upper Thames-street, has a carved screen and entrance-doorway: and the piers are surmounted with the Company's crest, a demi-savage, life-size, wreathed about the head and waist with oak-leaves. The Joiners were incorporated 1567.

LEATHER-SELLERS' HALL, St. Helen's-place, Bishopsgate-street, was rebuilt about 1815, upon the site of the Company's old Hall, a portion of the hall of St. Helen's Priory, taken down in 1799: it was wainscoted, had a curiously carved Elizabethan screen, and an enriched ceiling with pendants. Beneath the present Hall is the priory crypt. (See page 242.) In the Hall yard is a pump sculptured by Caius Gabriel Cibber in 1679, in payment to the Company of his livery fine of 25*l.*: the design, a mermaid pressing her breasts, is very characteristic. The crypt, kitchen, and pump, are engraved by J. T. Smith. The Leathersellers were incorporated by Richard II. in 1442; and by a grant from Henry VII., the Wardens were empowered to inspect sheep, lamb, and calf leather throughout the kingdom.

MASONS' HALL is in Masons'-alley, between Basinghall-street and Coleman-street. The Masons, with whom are united the Marblers, were incorporated about 1410 as "the Free Masons," and received their arms in 1474; but were not incorporated as Masons until 1677.

PAINTER-STAINERS' HALL, Little Trinity-lane, Upper Thames-street, occupies the site of the old Hall, destroyed in the Great Fire of 1666. The livery hall has a richly painted ceiling. The Painter-stainers' Company was incorporated by Queen Elizabeth in 1582, but existed long before as a guild. Among their minutes are orders to compel foreign painters resident in London to pay fines for practising their art without being free of the Painter-stainers' Company. Inigo Jones and Vandyck were asked together to their dinners, as appears by an entry in the Company's books. (*Life*, by P. Cunningham : Shakspeare Society.) Camden, whose father was a Painter-stainer in the Old Bailey, bequeathed the Company 16*l.* to buy a silver cup, to be inscribed: " Gul. Camdenus, Clarencieux, filius Sampsonis, Pictoris Londinensis, dono dedit;" which cup is used at every Election-feast on

St. Luke's day. Charles Catton, one of the foundation members of the Royal Academy, was master of the Painter-stainers' Company in 1784: he was known for his heraldic painting, more especially for his emblazonment of the lord mayor's state-coach.

Amongst the Company's pictures are St. Luke writing his gospel, by Van Somer; Reason governing Strength, C. Catton, R.A.; Landscape by Lambert, with figures by Hogarth; Queen Anne (medallion), by Feilot; the Fire of London, by Waggoner; Charles I. copied from Vandyke by Stone; Charles II. and his Queen, by Huysman; Queen Anne, by Dahl; William III. by Kneller, presented by him; Camden, in his tabard, as Clarencieux. The Painter-stainers' Company assist diseased and paralysed painters in going to Bath to drink the waters.

PARISH CLERKS' HALL, No. 83 Wood-street, Cheapside, is the third hall of the Company, first incorporated in 1233, as the Fraternity of St. Nicholas; re-incorporated by James I. in 1611; and confirmed by Charles I. in 1636. The Hall contains a few portraits, and in a painted glass-window, David playing on the Harp, St. Cecilia at the Organ, &c. The first hall stood in Bishopsgate-street; the second in Broad-lane, Vintry Ward. The Parish Clerks were the actors in the old Miracle Plays, the parish clerks of our churches dating only from the commencement of the Reformation. (See CLERKENWELL, p. 186.)

The "Bills of Mortality" were commenced by the Parish Clerks' Company in 1592, who about 1625 were licensed by the Star Chamber to keep a printing-press in their Hall for printing the Bills, valuable for their warnings of the existence or progress of the Plague. The "Weekly Bill" of the Parish Clerks has, however, been superseded by the "Table of Mortality in the Metropolis" issued weekly from the Registrar-General's Office at Somerset House since July 1, 1837.

The Parish Clerks' Company neither confer the freedom of the City nor the hereditary freedom.

PEWTERERS' HALL, No. 17 Lime-street, contains a portrait of Sir William Smallwood, Master of the Company in the second year of Henry VII., and who gave them their Hall, &c. The Pewterers were incorporated in 1474: they assay pewter-ware, and use a mark, or touch, registered on a pewter plate. The Hall was formerly let for lectures; and here Macklin the actor commenced his "school of oratory and criticism," lecturing in full-dress, but to be laughed at by Foote and other wits of the day.

PINMAKERS' HALL, Pinners'-court, Old Broad-street, is on part of the Priory of St. Augustine, or Austin Friars. The Hall has been, since the reign of Charles II., let as a Dissenters' meeting-house, and is now so occupied. The Pinmakers' Company was incorporated by Charles I. in 1636.

The Corporation Commission (2d Report) states that no returns to the Pin-makers' Company appear in the Chamberlain's books within the last forty years: "it is supposed that one or two individuals belonging to the Company are yet living."

PLASTERERS' HALL, Addle-street, Wood-street, Cheapside, was built after the Great Fire of 1666: here are some rich ceilings. The Company was first incorporated by Henry VIII. in 1501.

PLUMBERS' HALL, Great Bush-lane, Cannon-street, is a modern brick building: the Company was incorporated by James I. in 1611.

PORTERS' HALL is on St. Mary's-hill, Billingsgate. The Fellow-ship was incorporated in 1646, and consists of tackle and ticket porters; with the City arms for their armorial badge, and the alderman of Billingsgate ward for their governor. They claim the exclusive privilege, under the appointment and control of the Common Council, of unloading all vessels that come to the port of London laden with corn, nalt, seeds, potatoes, fruit, salt, fish, &c., at a fixed rate of prices; vhich, being high in comparison with the rates in the Docks and at he various outports of the kingdom, were greatly reduced in 1852, to neet the Free-trade exigencies.

The Ticket-porter of our times, "Toby Veck, who waited for jobs outside the hurch-door, with wind, and frost, and snow, and a good storm of hail, his red-etter days, and was called Trotty from his pace, which meant speed if it didn't nake it"—is the best character in Charles Dickens's Christmas story, *The Chimes.*

SADDLERS' HALL, No. 143 Cheapside, is denoted by the Company's rms; azure, a chevron between three saddles, or crest, a horse bridled nd saddled; supporters, two horses bridled. The Great Hall is hand-ome, and the Company wealthy: the fraternity are mentioned *temp.* Richard I., and were incorporated by Edward I. They preserve a umptuous crimson velvet and gold funeral pall, a curious specimen of Middle-Age embroidery. In the Hall is a whole-length portrait of Frederick Prince of Wales (father of George III.), who became Master f the Company from having accepted an invitation to witness the Lord Mayor's Show from their stand.

Sir Richard Blackmore, schoolmaster, physician, and small poet, "the Cheap-ide Knight" and "the City Bard," and the general butt of the wits of his day, robably wrote some peoms recited at Saddlers' Hall; whence Sir Samuel Garth ddressed these lines "To the merry Poetaster at Saddlers' Hall, in Cheapside."

> "Unwieldy Pedant, let thy awkward Muse
> With Censures praise, with Flatteries abuse.
> To lash, and not be felt, in Thee's an Art;
> Thou ne'er mad'st any but thy School-boys smart.
> Then be advis'd, and scribble not agen;
> Thou'rt fashion'd for a Flail, and not a Pen.
> If B——l's immortal Wit thou would'st descry,
> Pretend 'tis he that writ thy Poetry.
> Thy feeble Satire ne'er can do him wrong;
> Thy Poems and thy Patients live not long."

"To Sir R—— Bl——, on the two Wooden Horses before Saddlers' Hall:

> 'Twas kindly done of the good-natured Cits,
> To place before thy door a brace of tits."—*Tom Brown.*

STATIONERS' HALL, Stationers' Hall-court, Ludgate-street, occu-ies the site of Burgaveny House, whither the Stationers' Company emoved in 1611: it was destroyed in the Great Fire of 1666;* after which the present Hall was erected; the eastern front was cased with stone about the year 1800. The Court-room has some fine carv-ngs, attributed to Gibbons; and at the extremity is West's touching icture of King Alfred dividing a loaf with St. Cuthbert the pilgrim, resented by Alderman Boydell, Master of the Company; and of whom ere is a portrait as lord mayor, with allegorical absurdities, by Gra-nam. In the Stock-room and Hall are excellent portraits of Prior and Steele, presented by John Nichols; of Samuel Richardson, the novelist, nd his wife, by Highmore (Richardson was Master of the Company in 754); of Vincent Wing, the astrologer, who died in 1668, although a heet almanac with his name is still published by the Stationers' Company; of John Bunyan, presented by Mr. Hobbs, the singer; a alf-length of Bishop Hoadley; Robert Nelson, by Kneller; Andrew Strahan and his father, William Strahan; and a bust of William Bow-er, "last of the learned printers," with a grateful inscription written y himself. The Hall has also a large window filled with painted ar-

* Hansard's *Typographia* contains a view of Bergavenny House as altered or the Hall of the Stationers, printed from the original block engraved for the ompany.

morial glass. Here was held the Music Feast on St. Cecilia's day, for which Dryden wrote his celebrated ode, last performed here in 1703. In the Hall, on Almanac-day, November 22, at three o'clock, are published the almanacs printed for the Company.

The Stationers were formed into a guild in 1403, and their first Hall was in Milk-street. They were first incorporated May 4, 1557 (3d and 4th Philip and Mary); this charter was renewed by Elizabeth in 1588; amplified by Charles II. 1684; and confirmed by William and Mary, 1690, which is the existing charter of the Company. These charters gave them inquisitorial privileges of search and seizure of obnoxious books; printers were compelled to serve their time to a member of the company; and every publication was required to be " Entered at Stationers' Hall." The first entry on the books is 1558: " To William Pekerynge, a ballett, called *A Ryse and Wake*, 4d." 1603, Oct. 29, the Company obtained a patent from James I. for the sole printing of Primers, Psalms, Almanacks, &c., employing Lilly, Partridge, and Moore; Partridge's astrological almanack is humorously ridiculed by Swift. "Lilly's hieroglyphics were stolen from old monkish manuscripts; Moore has stolen them from him." (*Aubrey*.)

The funeral feast of Thomas Sutton, of the Charter-house, was given May 28, 1612, in Stationers' Hall; the procession having started from Dr. Law's, in Paternoster-row. For this repast were provided 32 neats' tongues, 40 stone of beef, 24 marrow-bones, 1 lamb, 46 capons, 32 geese, 4 pheasants, 12 pheasants' pullets, 12 godwits, 24 rabbits, 6 hearnshaws, 48 turkey-chickens, 48 roast chickens, 18 house-pigeons, 72 field-pigeons, 36 quails, 48 ducklings, 160 eggs, 3 salmons, 4 congers, 10 turbots, 2 dories, 24 lobsters, 4 mullets, a firkin and keg of sturgeon, 3 barrels of pickled oysters, 6 gammons of bacon, 4 Westphalia gammons, 16 fried tongues, 16 chicken-pies, 16 pasties, 16 made dishes of rice, 16 neats'-tongue pies, 16 custards, 16 dishes of bait, 16 mince-pies, 16 orange-pies, 16 forst back-meats, 16 gooseberry-tarts, 8 redcare-pies, 6 dishes of whitebait, and 6 grand salads.—*Malcolm.*

In 1712, Thomas Parkhurst, master of the Company in 1683, left 37*l.* to purchase annually Bibles with Psalms, to be given to the poor: hence the present custom of giving Bibles to apprentices bound at Stationers' Hall.

The Company's astrological and other predictions in their almanacs have continued, though modified, to our times; one year they experimentally omitted from Moore's Almanac the column on the moon's influence on the parts of the human body, when most of the copies were returned upon their hands. (Baily, on the *Nautical Almanac.*) The Company retains its original character intact, being restricted to members of the bookselling, stationery, printing, bookbinding, printselling, or engraving trades. The invested capital is upwards of 40,000*l.*, divided into shares; but their only publications are almanacs and a Latin Gradus. The original entry of published books has been dispensed with; but, under the Copyright Act, the proprietor of every published work must register the same, as well as all assignments, in the books of the Stationers' Company, to substantiate his claim at law: the registry fee is 5*s.*

The Company's charities consist chiefly of pensions; and foremost among the benefactors are the respected names of Guy, Bowyer, Boydell, and Strahan. The Hall plate includes several presentation cups. The Company are distinguished in civic pageants; and they possess a superbly gilt barge, in which, on the morning of Lord Mayor's Day they visit Lambeth Palace, when the household of the Archbishop of Canterbury bring on board the barge hot spiced ale, buns and cakes and wine; the latter is served to the Stationers in small wooden bowls or sack-cups, provided by the Company, who, at a certain period of the year, present to the Archbishop of Canterbury copies of their several almanacs. In the list of masters is Sir John Key, Bart., lord mayor two successive years, 1831 and 1832.

TALLOW-CHANDLERS' HALL, Dowgate-hill, is built in the style of Wren, with a colonnade of Tuscan arches. The Company was incorporated by Edward IV. in 1460.

WATERMEN'S HALL, St. Mary-at-Hill, Billingsgate, was built in 786. The Company's old Hall in Cold-harbour faced the Thames.

The fares of the Thames watermen and wherrymen were regulated by Henry III. in 1514. Taylor the Water-poet, *temp.* Elizabeth, states the Watermen etween Windsor and Gravesend at 40,000. They were made a Company by hilip and Mary in 1555, with eight overseers and rulers, "the most wise, discreet, nd best sort of watermen," selected by the Lord Mayor and Court of Aldermen. his statute regulates the dimensions of the boats and wherries, then dangerously shallow and tickle;" the Lord Mayor and Alderman to limit the watermen's res, to be confirmed by the Privy Council. Strype was told by one of the Com- any that there were 40,000 watermen upon their rolls; that they could furnish ,000 men for the fleet; and 8000 men were then in the service. Taylor the fater-poet, with his fellow-watermen, violently opposed the introduction of coaches trade-spillers. The Company condemned the building of Westminster and lackfriars Bridges, for their injury to the ferries between Vauxhall and the emple, the profits of which were given to the poor, aged, decayed, and maimed atermen and their widows; and in both cases the Company were compensated r their losses. The substitution of steam-boats for wherries has, however, een as fatal to the watermen as railways to stage-coachmen.

WAX-CHANDLERS' HALL, No. 13 Gresham-street West, nearly op- osite Haberdashers' Hall, was taken down in 1852, to be rebuilt. The fax-Chandlers' Company was incorporated by Richard III. in 1483. he chandler of old set his mark to the several articles which he made; nt out wax-tapers for hire; and in Roman Catholic times wax was rought to the chandlers, to be made into "torches, torchettes, prykettes r perchers, chaundelle or tapers for women ayenst Candelmas."

WEAVERS' HALL is in Basinghall-street. The Weavers' Company, riginally cloth and tapestry weavers, was the first incorporated of he livery companies, and in the reign of Henry I. paid 16*l.* a year to he Crown for their immunities. Their privileges were confirmed to hem at Winchester by Henry II. in 1184, the charter being sealed by homas à Becket.

The great *Curiosity* of Weavers or Stocking-weavers' Hall is its old picture, in hich William Lee or Lea is pointing out his stocking-loom to a female knitter; eneath which is this inscription: "In the year 1589, the ingenious William Lee, faster of Arts of St. John's College, Cambridge, devised this profitable art for ockings (but being despised, went to France,) yet of iron to himself, but to us nd others of gold: in memory of whom this is here painted." By some the icture is thought to have suggested the story of Lee's having invented the achine to expedite knitting, and thus allow the girl, of whom he was ena- oured, more time to listen to his love-making; or the picture may be an illus- ation of the story. Aaron Hill gives the invention to a poor student of Oxford, supersede his wife's knitting for their family's support; but Hill wrote this in 715 upon hearsay; and Lee is named as the inventor in a petition of the Frame- ork-knitters, or Stocking-makers, to Cromwell for a charter, subsequently ranted by Charles II. in 1663. Hill's version has, however, been adopted by lmore in his very clever picture of "the Invention of the Stocking-loom," ainted in 1847.

The existing Companies are so many trusteeships for "charitable urposes" and "chartered festivals:" and their earliest object was he formation of a common stock for the relief of poor or decayed embers. Stow devotes some twenty-five folio pages of his *Survey* to harities for this purpose, and which he characterises as "the Honour f Citizens and Worthiness of Men." These charities comprise pen- ions to decayed members, almshouses, gifts of money to the poor; unds for the support of hospitals, schools, exhibitions at the universi- ies, prisoners in the City gaols; for lectures and sermons, and do- ations to distressed clergymen; loans to young beginners in busi- ess, &c.

Of the 89 Companies, 8 are practically extinct; and a ninth, the Parish Clerks, has no connexion with the municipality of London. The others are divided by the Parliamentary Commissioners into three classes. 1. Companies still controlling their trade, namely, the Goldsmiths and the Apothecaries: both these also belong to class 2. 2. Companies exercising the right of search, or making wares &c., including the Stationers,' at whose Hall all copyright books must be "entered;" the Gun-makers, who prove all the guns made in the City; the Founders, who test and mark weights; the Saddlers, who examine the workmanship of saddles; the Painters, who issue a trade price-list of some authority; and the Pewterers and Plumbers, who make assays. 3. Companies into which persons carrying on certain occupations in the City are compelled to enter: such are the Apothecaries, Brewers, Pewterers, Builders, Barbers, Bakers, Saddlers, Painter - stainers, Plumbers, Innholders, Founders,* Poulterers, Cooks,† Weavers, Scriveners, Farriers, Spectacle-makers, Clockmakers,‡ Silk-throwers, Distillers. Tobacco-pipe-makers, and Carmen; the last mentioned exclusively consisting of persons belonging to the trade. Admission to the body of freemen is obtained by birth, apprenticeship, purchase, or gift; and thence into the livery by fees.

The Needlemakers' is the only City Company not incorporated by a crowned head, they having received their Charter from Cromwell in 1656. They have no Hall, but these characteristic arms: *vert, three needles in fess argent, each ducally crowned or:* crest, a Moor's head, couped at the shoulders in profile proper, wreathed about the temples argent, and in his ear a pearl (the crest originally was an apple-tree and serpent); supporters, a man and woman (termed Adam and Eve), wreathed round the waist with leaves, all proper, in the woman's dexter hand a needle argent; motto, "they sewed fig-leaves together and made themselves aprons." Stow tells us that needles were sold in Cheapside in the reign of Queen Mary, and were then made by a Spanish negro, by a secret art; they are also said to have been made in London by a native of India, in 1545; and by one Elias Krause, a German, in 1566. Needles were first made, or rather finished, in Whitechapel, by one Mackenzie; hence the cry of "Whitechapel needles, twenty-five for a penny." The trade then removed to the borders of Warwickshire and Worcestershire; but Whitechapel labels are still used, and the fame of "Whitechapel sharps" has reached the interior of Africa.

The arms of the several Companies (some very curious) are correctly given in Moule's *English Counties:* Middlesex. Their records are ancient; for the Great Companies' title deeds mostly extend to the 13th century.

HALLS, MISCELLANEOUS.

BLACKWELL HALL, or Bakewell Hall, Basinghall-street, adjoined the south side of Guildhall chapel, was founded by the opulent family of the Basings, and was hence called Basing's Haugh, or Hall, giving

* The Fruiterers' Company have no Hall: they present the lord mayor yearly with twelve bushels of early apples, and are entertained by him.
† The Cooks' Company have no Hall. By their charter of Charles II. they claim to serve the sovereign on all civic occasions, as well as exemption from serving on juries. They also claim the right of selling beer without a license; but the Court of Excise have decided against this privilege by the Act of Parliament which exempts only members of the Vintners' Company from the wine license. The Cooks' Company, are, however, exempted from serving on juries in the City courts.
‡ The Clockmakers' Company have a lending library, rich in treatises on horology and the allied sciences; besides a cabinet of specimen watches, &c. The Company have no hall, but an office, 6 Cowper's-court, Cornhill; whence the Master-Wardens, and Court of Assistants, May 10, 1852, memorialised Her Majesty's Commissioners of Works and Buildings against the order given direct to Mr. Dent to make the great Clock for the New Palace at Westminster, instead of submitting it, as originally intended, to competition.

ame to the surrounding ward, corrupted to Bassishaw. In the 36th of
dward III., Basing's Hall was the dwelling of Thomas Bakewell; in
he next reign (20th Richard II.), it was purchased by the City, and
nade a storehouse or market-place for all woollen cloth brought into
ondon, and which was not to be sold elsewhere, under pain of for-
eiture, until it had been first lodged at Bakewell Hall; part of the
olls or *hallage* was given by Edward VI. to Christ's Hospital, whose
overnors managed the warehouses. Bakewell Hall was rebuilt in
588, burnt in the Great Fire of 1666, and re-erected about 1672; but
nally removed in 1820, for the site of the Bankruptcy Court.

BRIDEWELL HALL (see BRIDEWELL HOSPITAL, page 53).

CHARTER-HOUSE HALL (see CHARTER-HOUSE, page 72).

CHELSEA HOSPITAL HALL (see CHELSEA HOSPITAL, page 77) is an
xact parallelogram, 110 feet by 30 feet. Here are double rows of
ables, covered with cloths, as if for dinner; but the Pensioners have
ot dined here for more than sixty years, though their messes are served
t the buttery-hatch. Upon the gallery-front is an exquisitely carved
hield of the royal arms (Charles II.).

CHRIST'S HOSPITAL HALL (see CHRIST'S HOSPITAL, page 80).

COMMERCIAL HALL, Mincing-lane, for the public sale of Colonial
roduce, was built in 1811, from the designs of Joseph Woods, F.S.A.,
uthor of *Letters from an Architect:* it consists of a lofty rusticated
asement, and an Ionic upper story, ornamented with characteristic
assi-relievi by J. G. Bubb.

CROSBY HALL (see page 139).

EGYPTIAN HALL, Piccadilly (see page 266; also MANSION HOUSE).

EXETER HALL (see page 287).

FLAXMAN HALL, University College, Gower-street, is the central
partment under the cupola, designed by Professors Cockerell and
onaldson, for the reception of Flaxman's models, presented by his
ister-in-law and adopted daughter, Miss Maria Denman. The collec-
ion consists of about 140 casts in plaster from the original models,
tatues and groups of figures, and reliefs, some retouched by the great
culptor. Immediately beneath the lantern is the group of Michael and
atan; and around and above are his monumental and other *relievi*,
rranged in compartments. In a niche in the vestibule is the large
roup of Hercules and Omphale; and in adjoining rooms are the Pas-
oral Apollo, the Shield of Achilles, small models of Raphael and Mi-
hael Angelo, and other of Flaxman's works; and on a landing is a
ne statue of the sculptor by M. L. Watson. (See UNIVERSITY COL-
EGE, page 215.)

FREEMASONS' HALL (see page 314).

GERARD'S HALL (see CRYPTS, p. 241).

GRESHAM HALL (see GRESHAM COLLEGE, page 209).

HALL OF COMMERCE, Threadneedle-street, was designed and built
1840-43 by Mr. Moxhay, formerly a biscuit-baker in the same street:
occupies the site of the French Protestant Church, in clearing away
hich a fine Roman tesselated pavement was discovered, and is now in
e British Museum.

The Hall façade has a bas-relief 73 feet in length, with life-size figures, by
. L. Watson: the central figure is Commerce, with outspread wings and hands,
ncouraging the Fine Arts; the groups symbolising the intellectual and physical
dvantages of Commerce. Thus, *sinister* are Peace; Industry, agricultural and
echanical figures bringing fruits and produce, and others spinning; next is
avigation, guided by Astronomy and Geography; and Education and Civilisation,
ith Liberty freeing the Slave. *Dexter* is History; next is a group of the Arts and

Sciences; Enterprise guided by Genius, and awaiting their arrival is a group of aborigines. The sculptor died young, in 1847.

The building was opened as a mercantile club-house, but did not succeed, and is now let as offices. In the vestibule is a statue of Whittington; and right and left are two superb halls, with Corinthian columns and pilasters, picturesque friezes, and elegantly coved ceilings. The larger hall is 130 feet long, 44 feet wide, and 50 feet high: here, March 1, 1851, was given the dinner to Mr. Macready on his retirement from the stage; upwards of 500 guests. The Hall of Commerce, after Mr. Moxhay's death in 1849, was sold for 44,900*l.*; the site alone is stated to have cost him 35,000*l.*

HICKSES'S or HICKS'S HALL, in the middle of the roadway of St. John-street, Clerkenwell, opposite the Windmill Inn (as denoted by an inscription at the corner of St. John's-lane), was built by Sir Baptist Hickes in 1612, as a Shire-hall, or Sessions-house, for Middlesex; until which, the justices met at the Castle Inn, near Smithfield Bars. The old Hall was taken down after the erection of the New Sessions-house on Clerkenwell Green, which, however, was long after called "Hicks's Hall." (See CLERKENWELL, page 177.) The exterior is decorated with the county arms, and medallions of Justice and Mercy; the court is in the form of D; and here is a James I. chimney-piece from the old Hall; and a fine portrait of Sir Baptist Hickes.

HUDSON'S BAY COMPANY'S HALL, Fenchurch-street, is a handsome edifice, with an interesting collection of *Curiosities* from the countries to which the Company trade, by barter and otherwise, for rich furs, skins, &c., sold here in spring and autumn. They were incorporated by Charles II. in 1670. Their hunting-ground extends from Hudson's Bay to the Pacific, and from the United States' frontier to the Arctic Sea. In the Hall is a vast pair of horns of the Moose Deer, weighing 56 lbs.; and in another room, the picture of an Elk, the European Moose, killed in the presence of Charles XI. of Sweden: it weighed 1229lbs.

LAMBETH PALACE HALL (see LAMBETH PALACE).

ST. MARTIN'S HALL, Long Acre, was built by R. Westmacott for Mr. Hullah's singing-classes. The style is Elizabethan, with iron arched and panelled roof of immense span: the Hall will accommodate 3000 persons, and was opened Feb. 11, 1850.

ST. MATTHEW'S TOWN-HALL, Bethnal Green, was built in 1852, for holding vestry-meetings, instead of in the parish church. This Hall is of Old English design, and has a handsome Caen-stone front, a committee-room, spacious bay-windowed board-room, decorated entrance-porch, and surveyor's residence adjoining. In the same year was completed a Vestry-Hall in High-street, Kensington; in the old English style, with gables, crested roof, and central clock-turret with cupola: besides a Vestry-Hall in Lambeth, in the Roman style.

ROYAL MUSIC HALL, Adelaide-street, Strand, was formerly the Adelaide Gallery (see page 18). The Apollonicon (see page 16) was removed here in 1851: and the Hall was next fitted up as a theatre for the performances of Marionettes, or Puppets.

SOUTHWARK TOWN-HALL, St. Margaret's-hill, was built in 1793, in place of a Hall erected in 1686 upon the site of St. Margaret's Church, which, after the union of that parish with St. Saviour's, was used as a prison and court of justice, until destroyed in the fire of 1676. Here the City authorities hold courts, and the oldest alderman sits as justice of the peace; the borough of Southwark being under his almost nominal jurisdiction, as the ward of Bridge Without: the elections for members of parliament are also held opposite the Hall.

Under a pediment, in front of the former Hall, was a statue of Charles II., which, in 1793, was removed to the roof of a watch-house in Three-Crown-court, High-street. A figure of Justice, which, with one of Wisdom, had formerly supported the lord mayor's seat in the hall, was also then placed near the bar of a neighbouring coffee-house; and hence this *jeu d'esprit*, which may possibly explain why watchmen were called "Charleys:"

> "Justice and Charles have left the Hill,
> The City claimed their place;
> Justice resides at Dick West's still,
> But mark poor Charles's case:
> Justice, safe from wind and weather,
> Keeps the tavern score;
> But Charley, turned out altogether,
> Keeps the watch-house door."

UNION HALL, Union-street, Southwark, was built by subscription, upon the site of the Greyhound inn, in 1781, for the use of the justices of the peace, before which they sat at the Swan inn. They attended at Union Hall daily till the passing of the Police Act in 1793, when it was made one of the offices ; the business was next removed to a new office at Stones' End ; Union Hall was then let as warehouses, destroyed by fire Dec. 6, 1851.

UNIVERSITY HALL, Gordon-square, St. Pancras (see page 215).

WESLEYAN CENTENARY HALL and MISSION HOUSE, Bishopsgate-street, faces Threadneedle-street. The Centenary Hall was formerly the City of London Tavern. The great hall for Wesleyan meetings will hold 1200 persons. In the rear is the Mission House, built in 1842 : here is the picture by Parker of the rescue of John Wesley from the flames, when a boy. The arrangement of the warehouses, for books, clothes, implements, and other outfittings of the missionaries, illustrates the extent of the Society's transactions *geographically :* here Ashantee, there Tonga ; there Caffraria, Gambia, &c.

An interesting Sale of Thank-offerings from the Friendly and Fejee Islands to the Wesleyan Missionary Society was held in their Hall, June 19 and 20, 1851 : including temples, cloths, and mats; spears and clubs, shells and bowls; elephants' and whales' teeth; costumes, idols, and musical instruments; — all picturesquely grouped, and touching as a lesson of gratitude exemplary to the silken baron of civilisation.

WESTMINSTER GUILDHALL, on the south side of the Sanctuary, near the Abbey, was built in 1805, by Cockerell, upon the site of the market-house, built by subscription in 1568. The Guildhall is octagonal in plan, and has a Doric entrance-portico : here are held the sessions, previous to 1752 held at the Town Court-house, near Westminster Hall, at a rent upon sufferance. (Walcott's *Westminster*, p. 86.)

Halls are likewise attached to the INNS OF COURT AND CHANCERY, which see. See also WESTMINSTER HALL, WESTMINSTER SCHOOL, p. 214.

HAYMARKET (THE),

" A very spacious and public street, length 340 yards, where is a great market for hay and straw" (*Hatton*, 1708). Hay was sold here in the reign of Elizabeth ; and Aggas's plan has "the Haymarket," with hedge-rows and a few straggling houses ; and washerwomen then dried their linen upon the grass of the site of the present Opera-house. A Token in the British Museum denotes one of the earliest venders of sea-*coal* to have lived here: "Nathaniel Robins, at the Sea-coal seller, 1666." Reverse.) "Hay Markett in Pickadilla, his halfpenny." Charles II. granted the right of holding a cattle-market in the street twice a week, opened 1664: it was paved 1697, by fines on the carts: 3d. for each load of hay, and 2d. for straw. The market for hay was removed by Act of Parliament, in 1830, to Cumberland Market, Regent's Park.

The acclivity of the Haymarket at 490 feet from Piccadilly was, in 1842, 1 foot in 22: this has been ingeniously overcome in building the front of Her Majesty's Theatre, the divisions of which have been taken advantage of to lower the lines, whilst the great length of the façade has rendered the rise unnoticeable: it was designed by Novosielski, but re-fronted by Nash and Repton, 1818. Nearly opposite is the Haymarket Theatre, built by Nash in 1821, with a fine Corinthian portico: the site of Potter's "Little Theatre" is occupied by the Café de l'Europe.

Opposite Her Majesty's Theatre is *Suffolk-place*, leading to *Suffolk-street*, the site of a mansion of the Earls of Suffolk. In Strype's time the houses were handsome: Moll Davies lived here from 1667 to 1674, in a mansion richly furnished for her by Charles II., which Pepys thought "a most infinite shame:" she kept also "a mighty pretty fine coach." Here lived Sir John Coventry, who, on his way home, when at the corner of the street, had his nose cut to the bone, "for reflecting on the king," in 1669; whence dates the *Coventry* Act against cutting and maiming.

Suffolk-street has some classic house-fronts: No. 2 has four characteristic oil-jars; No. 6, next the Society of British Artists' Gallery, is from Andrea Palladio's house at Vicenza. The Gallery, No. 6½, has a Roman-Doric tetrastyle portico on three semicircular arches, by Nash: the suite of five rooms, planned by James Elmes, are lit by large ceiling lanterns, inclined from the perpendicular, and diffusing even light. No. 19 is the stage-door of the Haymarket Theatre. At the south end is the University Club-house (see p. 199).

On the east side of the Haymarket is James-street, dated 1673; with the Tennis-court of Piccadilly Hall (see TENNIS, p. 16), the last house in Faithorne's plan of 1658. Above is Panton-street, which, with Panton-square, Coventry-street, was named from Colonel Panton, the ground-landlord, who was a noted and successful gamester, and the last proprietor of Piccadilly Hall.

In 1772, Puppets were exhibited in Panton-street, and were visited by Burke and Goldsmith. "Burke praised the dexterity of one puppet in particular, who tossed a pike with military precision; 'Psha!' remarked Goldsmith with some warmth, 'I can do it better myself.'" (Forster's *Goldsmith*.) Boswell relates that Goldsmith "went home with Mr. Burke to supper, and broke his shin by attempting to exhibit to the company how much better he could jump over a stick than the puppets."

On the west is Norris-street, leading to St. James's Market, once the great western butchers' and poulterers' market, noted by Pepys in 1666 as just built by my Lord St. Albans: in a room over the market-house, Richard Baxter used to preach. Here, too, is Jermyn-street, named after the above Henry Jermyn, Earl of St. Albans: here is the One Tun Tavern, a haunt of Sheridan's.

HIPPODROME (THE),

A race-course (named from the Greek, *hippos*, a horse, and *dromos*, a course), was opened in 1838 at Notting-hill, now Kensington Park: it was an imperfect affair, and was unsuccessful as a speculation.

In 1851, a Hippodrome was built for Mr. Batty's stud in the Kensington-road, at the corner of Victoria-road: in plan an oval, 360 feet longest diameter, with covered ranges of seats for 14,000 spectators, the area being open to the sky; the stables around it, with the entrance to the course, beneath a music-gallery: the whole was completed in little more than a month: G. L. Taylor, architect. Here Batty, Ducrow's successor, exhibited horse pageants, races with camels and ostriches, and balloon ascents, and feats of equestrianism and equitation, by daylight.

The above is not the first occasion of horsemanship being exhibited in this locality; for in Cromwell Gardens, Mr. Hughes, who built the Surrey Theatre, gave his horsemanship performances in the open air.

HOLBORN,

A thoroughfare of varying widths, extends from the north end of Farringdon-street to Broad-street, Bloomsbury. It was anciently called Old-bourne, from being built upon the side of a brook or bourne, which "broke out of the ground about the place where now the bars do stand, and ran down the whole street till Old-bourne Bridge, and into the River of the Wells, or Turnemill Brook." (*Stow.*) 1502. "The deche from the Temse to Holborne-brygge new cast." (*Grey Friars' Chronicle.*) The stream now runs the same course along the common sewer; and the arch of Holborn-bridge was uncovered in 1841. Holborn was first paved in 1417, at the expense of Henry V., when the highway "was so deep and miry that many perils and hazards were thereby occasioned, as well to the king's carriages passing that way, as to those of his subjects." (Rymer's *Fœdera*, vol. ix. p. 447.) By this road criminals were conveyed from Newgate and the Tower to the gallows at St. Giles's and Tyburn; whither a ride in the cart "up the Heavy Hill" implied going to be hung, in Ben Jonson's time.

> " As clever Tom Clinch, while the rabble was bawling,
> Rode stately through Holborn to die of his calling,
> He stopt at the George for a bottle of sack,
> And promised to pay for it when he came back."—*Swift*, 1727.

"An old Counsellor in Holborn used every execution-day to turn out his clerks with this compliment: ' Go, ye young rogues, go to school and improve.' " —*Tom Brown.*

To remedy the declivities of Holborn and Snow Hill, various plans have been proposed, by viaducts crossing the valley of the Fleet, and otherwise; and the inconvenience has been modified by lowering Holborn Hill, the acclivity of which in 1842 varied from 1 in 16½ to 1 in 23. In 1838 Mr. Whishaw assumed the average annual amount of traffic between Fetter-lane and the Old Bailey at "20,000,000 pedestrians, 871,640 equestrians, 157,752 hackney-coaches, 372,470 carts and wagons, 78,876 stages, 82,258 carriages, 135,842 omnibuses, 460,110 chaises and axed carts, and 354,942 cabs."

Alderman Skinner, who built Skinner-street, proposed to construct a bridge from Snow-hill across the valley to Holborn-hill; and to lift the valley 17 feet forms part of Mr. Charles Pearson's plan.

Gerrard, the herbalist, lived in Holborn, where he had a large physic-garden (see GARDENS, p. 320); and the first edition of his *Herbal* is dated from here.* Howel dates one of his *Familiar Letters*, Holborn, Jan. 1641, "to Sir Kenelm Digby, at his house in Saint Martin's-lane." Sir Kenelm lived, before the Civil Wars, between King-street and Southampton-street; Milton in Holborn-row, in a house opening into Lincoln's-Inn-fields; and Dr. Johnson, in 1748, at the Golden Anchor, Holborn Bars. These were the City boundaries, now marked by two granite obelisks near Middle-row, at the south-east corner of which Sir James Branscomb kept a lottery-office forty years : he had been servant to the Earl of Gainsborough, and was knighted when sheriff of London and Middlesex in 1806.

---

* Gerrard had another physic-garden, in Old-street : his earliest publication was the Catalogue (in Latin) of his own garden in Holborn, printed 1596, 4to; reprinted in 4to, 1599. The first edition was dedicated to Lord Burghley, whose garden Gerrard had superintended for twenty years : the second edition was dedicated to Sir Walter Raleigh. A copy of the first edition (of extreme rarity) is in

In Holborn are Thaive's, Barnard's, Furnival's, Staple, and Gray's Inns. (See INNS OF COURT. At the corner of Furnival's Inn, and in Queen-street, Cheapside, Mr. Edward Kidder, the famous pastry-cook (who died April 1739, aged 73 years), had two schools, in which he taught nearly 6000 ladies the art of making pastry. Kidder published his receipts, engraved on copper, in a thin 8vo, with his head prefixed.

Southampton-buildings, Holborn, denotes the site of the mansion of the Wriothesleys, Earls of Southampton; and Brook-street that of the residence of Sir Fulke Greville, Lord Brooke, the friend of Sir Philip Sidney. Gate-street, and Great, Little, and New Turnstiles, lead into Lincoln's-Inn-fields; between the north side of which and the south side of Holborn is Whetstone's Park, a profligate resort of two centuries since, commemorated in the plays of Dryden, Shadwell, and Wycherley.

On the north side of High Holborn, between Nos. 110 and 77, (see boundary-marks in the pavement,) is the *Holborn Charity Estate* of St. Clement Danes parish, who purchased the same, a plot of ground and some old buildings, in 1552, for 160*l.*, when Holborn was almost a country road from the City to the village of St. Giles's. The property now produces 4000*l.* a-year, expended in schools, almshouses, and other charities. The Almshouses were first built at the east end of St. Clement's church, Strand; next, about 1790, at the back of Clement's Inn Hall; and in 1848-9 the charity was removed to forty almshouses built in Garratt-lane, Streatham: Infant Schools were erected in Milford-lane, Strand, in 1852. Upon the Holborn Estate is Day and Martin's Blacking Factory, No. 97, built at a cost of 12,000*l.*: here Mr. Day amassed great wealth, and, dying in 1836, left 100,000*l.* for the benefit of persons, like himself, deprived of sight.

In Endell-street, (formerly Old Belton-street,) High Holborn, leading to Long Acre, on the east side, is the Early English Christ Church, erected in 1845; next is the British Lying-in Hospital, a picturesque Elizabethan structure, built in 1849; and a handsome Italianised edifice for Baths and Wash-houses, built in 1852, not far from the site of "Queen Anne's Bath:" whilst, nearly in a line with Endell-street, on the north side of Holborn, are the Industrial Schools, opened in 1852; and in Bloomsbury-street, northward, side by side, are three chapels in Early Pointed, Lombardic, and *rococo* styles: six of these seven edifices of religion and philanthropy were erected within eight years.

Kingsgate-street, between 116 and 117 High Holborn, is named from the King's-gate, this being the royal road to Newmarket; and Pepys records, 3 March, 1668-9, the King and the Duke of York, and the Duke of Monmouth, leaving Whitehall at three in the morning, in their coach, which was overset at the King's-gate: "it was dark, and the torches did not, they say, light the coach as they should do." Here in 1852 was an old public-house, sign the Red Gate.

In Holborn also are FIELD-LANE, ELY-PLACE, FETTER-LANE, FULWOOD'S RENTS, CHANCERY-LANE, and DRURY-LANE, which names see. From Farringdon-street to Fetter-lane is "Holborn Hill;" Fetter-lane to Brook-street, "Holborn;" and from Brook-street to Drury-lane, "High Holborn."

HOLLAND HOUSE, KENSINGTON,

A little west of the town, and about two miles from the metropolis, is a picturesque Elizabethan pile, placed in a beautiful park about midway between the Kensington and Uxbridge roads. This mansion, which is the manor-house of Abbots Kensington, was built in 1607 for Sir Walter Cope, and descended to his son-in-law, Henry Rich, first Earl of Holland; whence it was named Holland House. The Earl was twice made prisoner here by Charles I. in 1633, for his challenging Lord Weston; and by command of the Parliament, after his attempt to restore the king, for which he was beheaded in 1649. Holland House was next occupied by Fairfax as his head-quarters:

"The Lord-General (Fairfax) is removed from Queen-street to the late Earl of Holland's House at Kensington, where he intends to reside."—*Perfect Diurnal*, 9th to 16th July, 1649.

The mansion was, however, soon restored to the Countess of Holland. During the Protectorate, "in Oliver's time," plays were privately performed here. In 1716 the estate passed to Addison the Essayist, by his marriage with Charlotte, Countess Dowager of Holland and Warwick; and here Addison died June 17, 1719: having addressed to the dissolute Earl of Warwick these solemn words: "I have sent for you that you may see how a Christian can die!" he shortly after expired:

"There taught us how to live, and—oh, too high
The price for knowledge!—taught us how to die."

The young Earl himself died in 1721. About the year 1762, the estate was sold to Henry Fox, the first Baron Holland of that name, whose second son, Charles James Fox, passed his early years at Holland House; and here lived his nephew, the late accomplished peer, at whose death, in 1840, the estate descended to his only son, the present Lord Holland, by whom the olden character of the mansion and its appurtenances is studiously maintained: the latest restorations are by Barry, R.A.

Thorpe's drawings of Holland House are preserved in the Soanean Museum. Its plan is that of half the letter H; it first consisted of the centre and turrets only, to which Henry Rich, Earl of Holland, added the wings, and their connecting arcades: the materials are deep-red brick, with stone finishings; but the exterior has lost many of its original features. Eastward is a stone gateway, designed by Inigo Jones, and carved by N. Stone; the lodges and enriched metal gates in the Kensington-road were added in 1838. The raised terrace, with an open parapet and vases of plants, was added to the south front in 1848, when also the public footpath was diverted to the east side of the Park. In the Hall is the model of Westmacott's statue of Fox, erected in Bloomsbury-square. In the Journal-room (which contains a complete set of the Journals of the Lords and Commons) is a large collection of preserved birds, reptiles, insects, shells, minerals, &c. The Great Staircase and the Gilt Room are of the time of James I.: the former has massive balustrades, carved into arches, &c. The Gilt Room is mostly by Francis Cleyn, who was much employed by James I. and Charles I.: the ceiling "in grotesque," by Cleyn, fell down during the minority of the late Lord Holland; the wainscot-panels have alternately gold fleurs-de-lis on blue, within palm-branches; and gold crosslets on red, encircled with laurel; with the arms of the Rich and Cope families, and the punning motto, *Ditior est qui se?*—who more *rich* than he? The entablature has a painted leaf enrichment, with gilt acorns between; the compartments of the two fire-places are painted with female figures and bas-reliefs from the antique fresco of the Aldobrandini Marriage, executed by Cleyn, and not unworthy of Parmegiano: among the furniture are carved and gilt shell-back chairs, also by Cleyn, and a table from the Charter-house hall. Here are marble busts of George IV. when Regent; William IV.; Henry IV. of France; the Duke of Sussex; the Duke of Cumberland of Culloden, by Rysbrack; the late Lord Holland; C. J. Fox, by Nollekens, a duplicate made for the Empress Catherine of Russia; Napoleon, by Milne; Ariosto, copied from his tomb; and Henry Fox, first Lord Holland, often declared by Bartolozzi to be "one of the finest specimens of sculpture since the days of Phidias or Praxiteles." In the bow recess are models of Henry Earl of Pembroke and Thomas Winnington, Esq. (See Richardson's *Architectural Remains of the Reigns of Elizabeth and James I.*)

In the Breakfast-room are family portraits by Lely, Kneller, Reynolds, Hoppner, &c.; and in the Great Drawing-room (40 feet by 18 feet) are some very fine pictures, including a scene by Hogarth from Dryden's *Indian Emperor*, acted by children, all portraits; a Sea-port, by Velasquez; a Holy Family, on copper, by Murillo; a Man and Boy eating Fruit, by Velasquez; and Hope nourishing Love, and half-lengths of Garrick and Sterne, by Reynolds. The Library, or Long Gallery, 102 feet by 17 feet 4 inches, forms the eastern wing of the mansion: the collection exceeds 18,000, besides MSS. and autographs, including three plays of Lope de Vega. In the other apartments are valuable pictures, miniatures, drawings, sculptures; with enriched cabinets, vases, carvings in ivory, china, filagree-work, time-pieces, &c. In the Ante-room is the celebrated collection of miniatures. Here, too, is Reynolds's celebrated picture of Lady Susan Lenox leaning from a bay-window on the north side of Holland House, to receive a dove from Lady Susan Strangeways, near whom is C. J. Fox, when a boy of 14.

This "brave old house" is charmingly placed upon high ground:

> "Thou hill, whose brow the antique structures grace."
> *Tickell, on the Death of Addison.*

the upper apartments are stated to be on a level with the stone gallery of St. Paul's Cathedral. The southern park is enclosed with noble elms. Against the house grow some curious old exotic plants. The gardens abound with architectural quaintness: of parterres in Italian scrolls and devices, and box and dwarf oaks clipped into globes; flower beds in the forms of a *fox*, (in allusion to the family name,) and the old English Ꝑ.; the effect of the flowers aided by coloured sand, and the outlines of box-edging. In a parterre near the house, upon a granite column, is a bronze bust of Buonaparte, by Canova, the pillar inscribed with a verse from Homer's *Odyssey;* and in the north garden-wall is an arbour with this distich by the late Lord Holland:

> "Here ROGERS sat—and here for ever dwell
> With me those ' Pleasures' which he sang so well."—Vᴸ. Hᵈ.

Beneath are some lines added in 1818 by Henry Luttrel.

In the French garden, in 1804, was first raised in England the Dahlia, from seeds sent to the late Lord Holland from Spain. The grounds westward, with their stately oaks and cedars, were laid out and planted in 1769 by Mr. Charles Hamilton, of Pains Hill.

Aubrey relates two supernatural appearances at Holland House: the first to "the beautiful Lady Diana Rich, daughter to the Earl of Holland, as she was walking in her father's garden at Kensington," when she "met with her own apparition, habit and every thing, as in a looking-glass. About a month after she died of the small-pox." Aubrey's second story is that the third daughter of Lord Holland, not long after her marriage with the first Earl of Breadalbane, "had some such warning of approaching dissolution."

In a meadow west of Holland House was fought, March 7, 1804, a fatal duel between the late Lord Camelford and Captain Best, R.N.: upon the spot where Lord Camelford fell is an antique Roman altar, placed there and thus inscribed by the late Lord Holland: "HOC DIS MAN. VOTO DISCORDIAM DEPRECAMUR."

The Highland and Scottish Societies' gatherings, with their characteristic sports and pastimes, have been annually held in Holland Park north, since 1849.

There is a traditional story that Addison, to escape from his termagant countess, often walked from Holland House to the White-Horse

nn, at the corner of "Lord Holland's Lane," (no longer a thorough-
are,) on the site of the present Holland-Arms Inn; and there enjoyed
'his favourite dish, a fillet of veal, his bottle, and perhaps a friend."—
Spence.) Before his marriage, Addison lived in Kensington-square.

Holland House is associated "with the courtly magnificence of Rich, with
he loves of Ormond, the councils of Cromwell, with the death of Addison." It
as been for nearly two centuries and a half the favourite resort of wits and
eauties, of painters and poets, of scholars, philosophers, and statesmen. In the
ifetime of the late Lord Holland it was the meeting-place of "the Whig Party;"
nd his liberal hospitality made it "the resort not only of the most interesting
ersons composing English society, literary, philosophical, and political, but also
o all belonging to those classes who ever visited this country from abroad."
Lord Brougham.) In this delightful circle, "every talent and every accomplish-
nent, every art and science, had its place. . . The last debate was discussed in
ne corner, and the last comedy of Scribe in another; while Wilkie gazed with
dmiration on Reynolds's Baretti; while Mackintosh turned over Thomas
Aquinas to verify a quotation; while Talleyrand related his conversations with
Barras at the Luxembourg, or his ride with Lannes over the fields of Austerlitz."
Murray's *Environs of London.*) "Holland House" (says *Macaulay*) "can
oast of a greater number of inmates distinguished in political and literary history
han any other private dwelling in England."

HORSE-FERRY (THE),

Between Westminster and Lambeth, was the only Horse-ferry permitted
on the Thames at London, and was granted by patent to the Archbishop of Canterbury; the ferry-boat station being near the palace-
gate. Here were two inns for the reception of travellers, who arriving
at night, did not choose to cross the water at such an hour, or in case
of bad weather, might prefer waiting for better. On opening Westminster Bridge, 1750, the ferry ceased, and compensation was granted
to the See. (BRIDGES, p. 68.)

The rates were, for a man and horse, 2s.; horse and chaise, 1s.;
coach and two horses, 1s. 6d.; coach and four horses, 2s.; coach and six
horses, 2s. 6d.; cart loaden, 2s. 6d.; cart or wagon, each 2s.

At the time of the Usurpation, a wooden house was built for a small guard
posted here. M. de Lauzun mentions the ferry in his account of the escape of
the Queen of James II., Dec. 9, 1688: Sir Edward Hales being in attendance with
a hackney-coach, "we drove from Whitehall to Westminster, and arrived safely
at the place called the Horse-ferry, where I had engaged a boat to wait for me."
The same author adds: "the King, attended by Sir Edward Hales, who was
waiting for him, descended the back stairs, and crossing Privy Gardens, as the
Queen had done two nights before, proceeded to the Horse-ferry, and crossed the
Thames in a little boat with a single pair of oars to Vauxhall. He threw the
Great Seal into the river by the way; but it was afterwards recovered, in a net
cast at random, by some fishermen."

"Very early one morning, the Duke of Marlborough, with his hounds, desired
to cross by the ferry; one Wharton, the waterman at hand, was subsequently
rewarded by the Duke obtaining for him a grant of the ferry-house, the present
owner of which is a descendant of Wharton."—Walcott's *Westminster*, p. 333.

HORSE-GUARDS (THE),

At Whitehall, is named from a troop of Horse-Guards being constantly
on duty here: the buildings comprise the offices of the Secretary-at-War,
the Commander-in-chief, the Adjutant-General, and Quarter-Master
General. The Horse-Guards were originally raised by Charles II.,
who had built for them stables and barracks in the tilt-yard of Whitehall, which Pennant has engraved, with "the banquetting-house, one
of the gates, the treasury in its ancient state, and the top of the cockpit in the back view." These stables and barracks were removed in
1751, and the present Horse-Guards was built of stone from a design

attributed to Kent, but "broken into complex forms, much in the picturesque style of Vanbrugh." (Weale's *London*.) It consists of a centre and two pavilion wings, with a turret and clock; the west front opening into St. James's Park, by a low and mean archway; the *entrée* for carriages is only for royal and other privileged personages. In the rear is the parade-ground, part of the ancient tilt-yard, with a guard-station for infantry; and here inspections of the troops take place. In the vestibule of the building is the boundary-line of the parishes of St. Martin's and St. Margaret's, Westminster, denoted by inscriptions. In the Audience-room, facing the Park, the Military Secretary and the Commander-in-chief hold their levees: here are portraits, by Gainsborough, of George III. and his Consort; and a bust of the late Duke of York. Attached to the Quarter-Master-General's office is a Board of Topography, with a depôt of maps, plans, and a library of military works. In the Guards' Mess-room is a portrait of Aubrey de Vere, Earl of Oxford, in armour, commander of Charles II.'s "Regiment of Horse," and after whom were named the "Oxford Blues," now the Royal Horse-Guards Blue.

In two stone alcoves, flanking the gates, facing Whitehall, is stationed a guard of two mounted cavalry soldiers from ten to four o'clock, relieved every two hours; when the doors in the rear are thrown open, and the two relieving guards enter; whilst those relieved ride out in front, describe a semicircle, meet, and ride side by side through the central gate, and so back to their stables. Orders concerning all the Guards in London are given out by the field officer on duty at the Horse-Guards. Thus, should any of them be wanted on an emergency, the Commander-in-chief communicates with him, and he arranges what regiment is to supply the detachment required. The marching and countermarching of the Guards drawn from the cavalry barracks at Knightsbridge and the Regent's Park, is a picturesque scene, as the troop passes through the Parks, on the march line of Portland-place, Regent-street, and Waterloo-place : their stately cuirassed and helmeted figures, and the splendour of their accoutrements, rendering them the most magnificent "Household troops" in Europe.

HORSE-GUARDS' CLOCK.

This accredited timekeeper has about the same popular reputation for correct time at the west end of the town, that St. Paul's clock holds in the City. The Horse Guards' Clock was originally made by Thwaites, in 1756: it is a large 30-hour clock, striking the quarters upon two bells; and shewing the time upon two dials, one facing St. James's Park, and the other Whitehall. The frame is of wrought-iron; the wheels are of yellow brass; and the pinions are iron, case-hardened. The going-part discharges the hours as well as the quarters, which is a considerable drag upon the clock, the present practice being to make the quarters discharge the hours. Originally, the clock had a common recoil escapement, and the pallets became much worn; the pendulum was 8 feet 2 inches long, and to reduce the arc of vibration it was furnished with fans (it has been preserved as a *Curiosity*) ; the train consisted of a great wheel, centre, third, and escape wheels, as usual; and the striking-parts were of the ordinary description. The work was throughout very coarsely executed.

In 1815-6, the going-part, including the dial-works and hands, and connecting rod-work, was made new by B. L. Vulliamy, F.R.A.S., clockmaker to the King, and maker of the great clock at Windsor Castle, the General Post-office clock, &c. The new going-train now consists of only three wheels: an escape, which makes one revolution in four minutes; a centre wheel, one revolution in an hour; and a great wheel and two pinions, each of 22 teeth, or leaves as they are sometimes called. The brass barrel and caps are new; and a ratchet attached to the great wheel keeps the clock going

while being wound. The wheels are of the best yellow brass, and
the escape and centre wheel arbours and pinions are steel, hardened and tempered. The pivots work in gun-metal holes in bosses,
which are held by screws (not riveted as ordinarily); this facilitates the
cleaning of the pivots and pivot-holes. The front pivot of the escape-
wheel carries a seconds-hand, which (the pendulum vibrating two
seconds) shews the seconds by the hand advancing two seconds each
vibration. The pendulum has a teak-wood rod, and a cast-iron bob
weighing 170lbs.: it is terminated by a gun-metal screw, and nut cut
into a strong thread, by which the clock is regulated. The pendulum
is hung upon an A-cock, independent of the frame of the clock, which
can be taken to pieces and the clock cleaned without disturbing the
pendulum. It is suspended by a cross screw-pin, by which it may
be set relatively to the pivot of the verge; so that, as far as possible, the pendulum and crutch have one common centre of motion.
The crutch has these advantages: the pendulum cannot become dis-
engaged from it, or have too much or too little shake in it; and the
friction by any difference in the centre of motion is reduced to the
smallest possible quantity. There is a special adjustment for setting the
clock in beat by two screws, such as are employed in the best regulators.

The escapement is the pin-wheel, but differs from Le Paute's or
any other in this respect: that if any of the pins, from defect of execution, do not stand perpendicular to the face of the wheel, still the pin
will have a flat and complete bearing upon the pallet, both during the
rest and the impulse. The escapement is exceedingly well made, and
there is, consequently, very little drop or loss of power. (It is completely described, with an engraving, in " *Etudes sur diverses Questions
d'Horologerie*," par Henri Robert. Paris, 1852.) The weight of the
maintaining power, suspended by a double line, is about 30lbs., pulley
5lbs. = 35lbs.; and the arc of vibration of the pendulum is about 3° 15'
on each side.

To indicate correctly the arc of vibration of the pendulum, a portion
of a circle divided into degrees and minutes, having for radius the length
of the pendulum, is engraved upon a brass plate placed under it, with
this inscription:

" This Clock was repaired by the order of the Right Hon. Viscount Palmerston,
Secretary-at-War, and made to shew seconds. New two-seconds pendulum with
teak-wood rod, and new suspension for the pendulum, a new escapement, new
intermediate wheel, new barrel and going-ratchet, new dial-works and rod-work,
new hands, new pulleys, new stool, new box, and new fitting-up, and this degree-
plate, were made by Vulliamy and Son, clockmakers to the King, London, A.D.
1816."

In this clock are applied, it is believed for the first time to a turret or
public clock in the metropolis, the following improvements:* a dead pin-
wheel escapement; a two-seconds pendulum, without disturbing which
the clock can be taken to pieces; the shewing of seconds, which facilitates the regulating and taking the rate of the clock; a ratchet to keep
the clock going while being wound; and a degree-plate to indicate
very correctly the arc of vibration of the pendulum.†

Being a 30-hour clock, it is necessarily wound every day,—not set
every day, as sometimes understood: this facilitates the taking of
its daily rate, which was done with little intermission from 1815 to
1851, when the clock ceased to be under Mr. Vulliamy's care. It has constantly measured time with extraordinary accuracy, altogether sufficient

* Le Paute's clock at the Hotel de Ville, Paris, has a two-seconds pendulum;
with a nine-bar compensation-rod; but this clock is without a seconds-hand.
† Communicated by Mr. B. L. Vulliamy, F.R.A.S., Clockmaker to the Queen,
and to their late Majesties George III., George IV., and William IV.

for any practical purpose not connected with astronomical observations; much of its reputation may be conventional—from the rigid punctuality with which the slightest military movement is executed. By a barometer and register-thermometer placed in the clock-room, the variations have been regularly taken with the rate of the clock. The dials are each 7 feet 5 inches diameter, and painted white, with black numerals and hands; the Whitehall dial is very effectively illuminated at night by a strong light thrown from a lamp, with a reflector, placed on the projecting roof in front of the clock-tower.

HOSPITALS.

Of the more than 500 Charitable Institutions of the Metropolis, one quarter consists of general Medical Hospitals, Medical Charities for special purposes, Dispensaries, and Societies for the preservation of life and public morals, mostly supported by donations and annual subscriptions. Of these palaces of humanity, the following are the principal.

ST. BARTHOLOMEW'S HOSPITAL, see page 31.

BETHLEM HOSPITAL, see page 42.

CHARING CROSS HOSPITAL, Agar-street, was commenced by Decimus Burton, as a portion of the West-Strand Improvements, in 1831; when the first stone was laid, Sept. 15, with Masonic solemnity, by the Duke of Sussex, Grand Master of the Freemasons. The Charity, founded in 1818, comprises a Dispensary and Casualty Hospital, being the eighth established in the Metropolis, the population of which had doubled since the seventh Hospital was instituted. The architecture is Grecian, and the circular termination of the plan well accords with the form of the site. Although upwards of 1000 in-patients and 17,000 out have been treated in one year, the annual average cost of the establishment is stated at only 2506*l*.

In the year ending July 1852 there were 17,995 patients, including 1200 in-patients: accidents admitted during the year, 2,238, of which 728 were from falls from elevations; from falling of earth and buildings, &c., 93; steam-engine, mill, and crane accidents, 78; injuries from vehicles, 168; burns, scalds, and explosions, 74; immersion in water, taking deleterious articles and noxious gases, 25; bites of animals, 42; personal violence, blows, and stabs, 278; from cutting instruments and contusions, 580; apoplexy, 65; hernia and hæmorrhages, 65.

CITY OF LONDON LYING-IN HOSPITAL, corner of Old-street, City road, was built 1770-3, and has a small unmeaning spire. It was instituted 1750, at Shaftesbury House, Aldersgate-street. This Hospital is for the reception and delivery of the pregnant wives of seamen and soldiers, mechanics, and laborious poor; the annual number of women delivered here being 550.

CITY OF LONDON HOSPITAL FOR DISEASES OF THE CHEST, Victoria Park (once Bishop Bonner's Fields), was founded by Prince Albert, June 25, 1851. The building, by Ordish, is in the Queen Anne style, and has a central campanile: the interior is warmed and ventilated by hot water, as the heating and extracting power.

CONSUMPTION HOSPITAL, Brompton, fronting the Fulham-road, was commenced 1844, June 11, when Prince Albert laid the first stone; the site was formerly a nursery-garden, and the genial, moist air of Brompton has long been recommended for consumptive patients. The Hospital is in the Tudor style, of red brick, with stone finishings; Francis, architect: it was opened in 1846. In 1850 was attached an elegant memorial chapel (see CHAPELS, p. 164); and in 1852 was added the western wing of the Hospital, towards which Mdlle. Jenny Lind, when residing at Old Brompton, in July 1848, munificently presented

,606*l.* 16*s.*, the proceeds of a concert held by her for this aid. This noble act is gracefully commemorated by Mdlle. Lind's bust being placed upon he Hospital staircase: here also is a painted window, of characteristic lesign, presented by a governor. The Hospital is ventilated by machinery, worked by a steam-engine; and is warmed by water heated by two arge Arnott stoves. In the kitchen, steam is used for boiling caldrons of beef-tea, mutton-broth, arrow-root, coffee, chocolate, &c.; and the provisions are wound up a shaft to the respective wards. The patients ake exercise in the well-ventilated passages; and the wards are tempered by warm fresh air, which enters at the floor, and escapes by valves n the ceiling. There is a library for the in-patients, and the Rose Charity Fund for convalescents. The deaths in this new Hospital have ave never exceeded one in every five in-patients, whereas in the former Iospital they were one in four.

St. George's Hospital, Hyde-Park Corner, originated with a arty of dissentient Governors of Westminster Hospital, who, in 1733, onverted Lanesborough House, Grosvenor-place, into an Infirmary.

Pennant describes the old mansion as the *country-house* of

> "The sober Lanesborow dancing, in the gout:"

ence also the quaint distich inscribed on the house-front:

> "It is my delight to be
> Both in town and country."

'he Hospital has been rebuilt; architect, Wilkins, R.A., in 1831: the rand front, facing the Green Park, is very elegant. The number of eds is 350; in the original infirmary there were but 60.

An ingenious telegraph has been devised here for the transmission of orders rough the different wards. In the hall is a column three feet high, with a dial f engraved signals, and on the walls of the different wards are corresponding ials; so that when the pointer to the hall-dial is moved to any signal, all the thers move accordingly, and a little hammer strikes a bell: by which means bout fifty signals are transmitted daily in each ward, without the possibility of rror or the least noise.

William Hunter was a surgical pupil at St. George's in 1741, when e resided with the eminent Smellie, at that time an apothecary in 'all Mall. William's brother, John Hunter, was appointed Surgeon to t. George's in 1768; and here, in 1793, he died of disease of the heart. Ie had long disputed with his colleagues a matter of right; and on the corning of the sad day, October 16, he remarked that if any dispute ccurred, it would prove fatal: he attended a meeting of the Governors, ne of whom flatly contradicted Hunter, when he retired to an adjoining oom, and there fell lifeless into the arms of Dr. Robertson, one of the Iospital Physicians. Hunter was a man of acute feeling: Lavater, a seeing his portrait, remarked, "That man thinks for himself."

General Lying-in Hospital, York-road, Lambeth, was originally stablished in 1765, by Dr. John Leake, in the Westminster-bridge-road; id was incorporated in 1830, when the present Hospital was built.

Guy's Hospital, Southwark, on the south side of St. Thomas's-reet, was built by Dance, the City architect, in 1722-4, at the sole pense of Thomas Guy, the bookseller in Lombard-street, who by inting and selling Bibles made a fortune: this he greatly increased purchasing seamen's tickets at a large discount, and afterwards vesting them in the South-Sea Company.

Guy was the son of a lighterman at Horselydown, where he was born in 1644. was apprenticed to John Clarke, bookseller and binder, in a house in the rch of Mercers' Hall, Cheapside, in 1660. In this house, rebuilt after the Great e, Guy commenced business for himself; and he subsequently removed to the house between Cornhill and Lombard-street, since known as "the Lucky Corner," and Pidding's Lottery Office, nearly on the site of the Globe Insurance Company's Offices. Guy had agreed to marry his housekeeper, who, however, displeased him, and thenceforth he devoted his immense fortune to works of charity. In 1707, he built and furnished three wards of St. Thomas's Hospital; the stately iron gate, with the large houses flanking it in High-street, Guy also built at the expense of 3000*l.* He was also a liberal benefactor to the Stationers' Company; built and endowed almshouses and a library at Tamworth, in Staffordshire, the place of his mother's birth, and which he represented in Parliament. In his 76th year, he took of the president and governors of St. Thomas's Hospital a piece of ground opposite the south side of their Hospital for 999 years, at a ground-rent of 30*l.* a-year; thereon, in the spring of 1722, Guy laid the first stone of a Hospital for the cure of sick and impotent persons; and the building was roofed in before his death, Dec. 27, 1724. The expense of erecting and finishing the Hospital was 18,792*l.* 16*s.*, and the sum left to endow it it was 219,499*l.* 0*s.* 4*d.*; the largest sum ever left by an individual for charitable purposes. His noble example has been followed by Mr. Hunt of Petersham, who, in 1829, bequeathed to the Hospital 196,115*l.*, stipulating for the addition of accommodation for 100 patients. About 10,000*l.* has also been received from other benefactors.

"The annual income is now between 25,000*l.* and 30,000*l.*, arising chiefly from estates purchased with the valuable bequests of Guy and Hunt, in the counties of Essex, Hereford, and Lincoln. The usual number of governors is 60, who are self-elective. The office cannot be constituted by any contribution, and there is no published list of them."—Low's *Charities of London,* 1850.

The Hospital consists of a centre and two wings; behind is a quadrangle, and beyond is a lunatic house for twenty-four insane patients, with a garden and airing-ground for their recreation; in 1839, one of these patients had been in the Hospital fifty-three years. In the wings are the officers' apartments, a surgery, an apothecary's shop, laboratories, medical and operating theatres, and a room for the application of electricity and galvanism. Here, too, are a museum, library, a very fine anatomical collection, models in wax by Towne, &c. Westward is the Chapel; and eastward, the Court-room. Attached to the Hospital is a botanic garden for the students. In 1852 were added two handsome wings, heated by Sylvester, and ventilated by a shaft 200 feet high, and 14 feet square inside, with an open cupola and a wind-vane, which sends down the shaft fresh air into the wards; while two lower shafts carry off the effluvia.

In the front court is a metal statue of Guy, in his livery-gown, by Scheemakers; the pedestal bears representations in relief of Christ healing an impotent man; the Good Samaritan; Guy's arms, and an inscription. In the centre of the front are two characteristic statues by John Bacon, a native of Southwark.

In the Chapel (service daily at 9 A.M.) is a fine marble statue of Guy, by Bacon, which cost 1000*l.*: he stands in his livery-gown, with one hand raising an emaciated figure from the ground, and with the other pointing to a second sufferer, as he is borne on a bier into the Hospital, at the back: on the pedestal are emblematic medallions and a glowing inscription, asserting that Guy "rivalled the endowment of kings." Here is buried Sir Astley Cooper, the distinguished surgeon, to whom there is a marble monument. In the Court-room, over the president's chair, is a portrait by Dahl, a Danish painter, of Guy, in the black gown and long flowing wig of his time: on the ceiling is painted his apotheosis.

The *Physical Society* of Guy's Hospital was founded in 1771, and is composed of the medical officers and students of St. Thomas's and Guy's Hospitals; the contributions being medical or physiological papers.

Guy's Hospital, before 1852, made up about 580 beds; average of in-patients at one time, 500; entire annual average, 50,000.

HAHNEMANN HOSPITAL, 6 Bloomsbury-square, for the treatment of patients on the Homœopathic system of Dr. Hahnemann, was opened ept. 16, 1850; in two years were treated about 450 in-patients, and upwards of 7000 out-patients.

IDIOTS' ASYLUM: Office, 29 Poultry; instituted 1847, for the maintenance, education, and general treatment of Idiots; with the motto, "We plead for those who cannot plead for themselves." The Asylum was first opened at Park House, Highgate, January 1848; and next year, in Essex Hall, Colchester.*

The number of Idiots exceeds that of Lunatics, as stated at a meeting of the Friends of the Asylum, March 19, 1851; when the Earl of Carlisle observed: "There is nothing grand or picturesque in this form of human calamity. Milton was blind, Virgil asthmatic, Horace blear-eyed—even about insanity there is a moody majesty; but the poor idiot cannot be made the Lear or Belvidera of tragedy. He is also subject to insult and contempt in real life—the butt and scarecrow of the village-green, the drudge of the domestic hearth. At best, his life is one of negatives. Dead to the noblest impulses, the uninstructed idiot is powerful for mischief, while free from responsibility. Here, then, is the want and justification of the present institution." The subscription which followed included 250 guineas from the Prince of Wales; 200 guineas from the City of London; and 200 guineas from the Drapers' Company. About the room were arranged specimens of drawing, writing, and handicraft work by the poor idiot children in the temporary Asylum; refuting the assertion of their faculties being irredeemably waste.

KING'S COLLEGE HOSPITAL, Carey-street, Lincoln's-Inn Fields, was established in 1839 for the sick poor, for affording practical instruction to the medical students of King's College, under their own professors. The building of a new Hospital, by subscription, was commenced June 18, 1852, when the first stone was laid by the Archbishop of Canterbury: the wards to be very spacious, light, and airy; with ventilation by opposite windows and open fire-places, without artificial aid; and the arrangement for teaching to include an operating theatre and chapel, dispensary, laboratory, &c.

LOCK HOSPITAL, Harrow-road; CHAPEL and ASYLUM, Westbourne Green: the Hospital established 1746, for the treatment of the peculiar disease incident to profligate women; the Asylum founded 1787 by the Bible commentator, the Rev. Thomas Scott, for the reclamation of the cured inmates into virtuous habits; and the Chapel in 1764, for the ministration to the unfortunate patients and inmates. The establishment was originally formed in Grosvenor-place, where the Chapel, by its popular preachers, became a source of income to the institution. This is the only Asylum existing in connexion with a hospital; all penitentiaries are necessarily shut against the sick and dying outcasts; and for such there is no complete refuge save "the Lock Hospital." (See Low's *Charities*, p. 99.) In 1842, the Institution was removed to its present site: in 1849, the success of an autograph appeal by the late Duke of Cambridge provided for the admission of double the number of patients. The Chapel yields a clear income of 200l. a year.

The Lock Hospital is so called from the Loke or Lock, in Kent-street, Southwark, a spital for leprous persons, of early date. The name has been referred to the old French *loques*, rags, from the linen applied to sores; "but otherwise, and with more probability, from the Saxon *lok*, shut, closed, in reference to the necessary seclusion of the leper on account of the infectious nature of his disease." (Archer's *Vestiges*, Part I.) We find Lock "an infirmary" in Bailey's Dictionary. Others trace the Southwark Hospital to the stream, or open sewer, called "the Lock," which divided the parishes of St. George and St. Mary, Newington, and is shewn in Rocque's large map of Surrey. The Hospital, known to have existed temp. Edward II., had a chapel dedicated to St. Leonard. (*Tanner.*) It came into the possession of St. Bartholomew's Hospital, whence it received patients: falling into decay, it was let in tenements, was taken down in 1809, and its site laid into the Dover-road; a portion of the site was, however, consecrated as the parish burial-ground more than a century since, and so continues.

There were other "Locks:"—2. Between Mile End and Stratford-le-Bow. 3. At Kingsland, between Shoreditch and Stoke Newington, the chapel of which, St. Bartholomew's, remained till 1840. (See CHAPELS, page 164.) A sun-dial on the premises formerly bore this inscription significant of sin and sorrow:

                  "Post voluptatem misericordia."

Prior to its alienation from the mother hospital, the house had a communication with the chapel, so contrived that the patients might take part in the service without seeing or being seen by the rest of the congregation; and there was a similar arrangement in the Lock chapel in Grosvenor-place. 4. At Knightsbridge, east of Albert-gate, was a lazar-house under the patronage of the Abbot and Convent of Westminster: the Hospital chapel (Holy Trinity) remains: it was rebuilt in 1627, by a license from Dr. Laud, then Bishop of London, as a chapel of ease to St. Martin's-in-the-Fields, within the precincts of which it was situated; but it was subsequently assigned to the parish of St. George, Hanover-square, and now forms part of Kensington.—*Notes and Queries*, No. 114.

The two largest Leper Hospitals were, however, *St. James's*, Westminster, founded before the Conquest (*Stow*), and made a royal palace by Henry VIII.; the original gateway remains. Next was *St. Giles's-in-the-Fields*, founded about 1117. (See ST. GILES'S, p. 327.)

LONDON FEVER HOSPITAL, Liverpool-road, Islington, was opened 1849; its erection cost 19,483*l.* 2*s.* 9*d.*, defrayed by the compensation-vote of 20,000*l.* paid by the Great Northern Railway Company, whose terminus now occupy the site of the old Hospital, instituted 1803.

LONDON HOSPITAL, Whitechapel-road, originally "the London Infirmary," was instituted 1740, in a large old mansion in Prescott-street, Goodman's Fields; it was incorporated in 1758, and the present Hospital built on "the Mount," Whitechapel-road. The Charity was established for the poor sick, particularly manufacturers, seamen, watermen, coal-heavers, shipwrights, labourers on the river, and children. In 1791, a *Samaritan Society*, at the suggestion of Sir W. Blizard (the first established), was appended to this Hospital, for the benefit of homeless convalescents, sending them to the sea-side, &c.

ST. LUKE'S HOSPITAL for Lunatics was first established 1751, in a house upon Windmill-hill, on the north side of Moorfields, nearly opposite the present Worship-street. In 1753, pupils were admitted to the Hospital; and Dr. Battie, the original physician, allowed medical men to observe his practice. This law fell into disuse, but was revived in 1843; and an annual course of chemical lectures established, at which pupils selected by the physicians of the different metropolitan hospitals are allowed to attend gratuitously. In 1754, incurable patients were admitted on payment to the Hospital on Windmill-hill. In 1782, was commenced the present St. Luke's, in Old-street-road, when the foundation-stone was laid by the Duke of Montague, July 30; the cost about 40,000*l.*, being defrayed by subscription; Dance, jun., architect.

"There are few buildings in the metropolis, perhaps in Europe, that, considering the poverty of the material, common English clamp-bricks, possess such harmony of proportion, with unity and appropriateness of style, as this building. It is as characteristic of its uses as that of Newgate, by the same architect."—*Elmes.*

The Hospital was incorporated 1838; the end infirmaries added in 1841; a chapel in 1842, and open fire-places set in the galleries; when also coercion was abolished, padded rooms were provided for violent patients, and an airing-ground set apart for them; wooden doors were substituted for iron gates, and unnecessary guards and bars removed from the windows. In 1843 were added reading-rooms and a library for the patients, with bagatelle and backgammon boards, &c. By Act 9 and 10 Vic., cap. 100, the Commissioners of Lunacy were added to the Hospital direction. In 1848, Sir Charles Knightley presented an organ to the chapel, and daily service was first performed. The Hospital was next lit with gas; the drainage, ventilation, and supply of water improved, by subscription at the centenary festival, June 25, 1851.

On St. Luke's Day (October 18), a large number of the patients are ntertained with dancing and singing in the great hall in the centre of he Hospital, when the officers, nurses, and attendants join the festival. 3alls are also given fortnightly.

The Hospital will accommodate 260 patients. The per-centage of recoveries ras, from 1821 to 1830, 47¼ per cent; 1831 to 1840, 56¼ ditto; 1841 to 1850, 0⅜ ditto: shewing the results of the improved treatment. But the largest per-entage of recoveries, with one exception, was 69½, in 1851. Thirty patients, in n average period of twelve weeks' treatment, increased in the aggregate 358 lbs. f solid flesh. The number of patients in the Hospital is usually 200, of whom alf are incurable.

Since the year 1684, when Bethlem Hospital admitted into its wards venty-three lunatic patients, and since the establishment of St. Luke's 1750, about 40,000 insane persons have been treated in these two in-titutions. Within the last twenty years, insanity in England has more han tripled; and within the same period three large Asylums have een built in the metropolitan counties: Hanwell, 1831; Wandsworth, 840; and Colney Hatch, 1851, with 1881 feet 6 inches frontage.

MARYLEBONE AND PADDINGTON HOSPITAL, Cambridge-place, was ommenced in 1845, when, June 28, (Coronation-day,) the first stone ras laid by Prince Albert; the site was originally a reservoir of the rand Junction Water-works. The Hospital, opened in 1850, is of ed brick, similar to Chelsea Hospital: it is warmed and ventilated by he circulation of tempered atmospheric air, and the withdrawal of the oul air from the wards; there are shafts for conveying the food from he kitchen and medicines from the laboratory, besides other novel echanical applications. Hon. architect, Mr. Hopper.

MIDDLESEX HOSPITAL, Charles-street, facing Berners-street, was tablished 1745: the present building was commenced 1755, then in larylebone Fields; and much enlarged and improved 1848; the baths, ooking apparatus, laboratory works, ventilating shaft, and laundry, re supplied with steam-power. The Cancer-ward, a special addition this Hospital, was made in 1792, upon a plan by the benevolent John loward, at the sole expense of Mr. Whitbread, M.P., who endowed he ward with 4000l., that cancer-patients might remain here for life.

In the Council-room is a large vellum Benefaction-book, wherein are beauti-ully written the names of the Benefactors to the Hospital, from its foundation. he binding is elaborately carved oak, by W. G. Rogers; and the clasps, corners, nd bosses, are rich ormoulu. This sumptuous volume is protected by an orna-ental iron stand: it is intended to supersede the large black benefaction-boards hich cover the hospital walls.

OPHTHALMIC (ophthalmos, Gr., the eye) HOSPITALS were established 1804; that in Moorfields being the first. In the same year, the Royal nfirmary, Cork-street, was founded by Sir Wathen Waller (originally hipps, the celebrated oculist) submitting to their Majesties a plan ggested by the sufferings he was then endeavouring to relieve among e soldiers and sailors who had returned from the Egyptian Expedi-on. The late Duke of Wellington was president of the Royal West-inster Ophthalmic Hospital, Chandos-street, Charing Cross, where atients are admitted without letters; since its establishment, 1816, pwards of 1700 cases have here been restored to sight by operation for taract; the important operations averaging 100 annually.

ORTHOPÆDIC (orthos, Gr., straight, and paidos, of a child) HOSPITAL, OYAL, 6 Bloomsbury-square, established 1838 for the cure of club-ot and other contractions, by dividing the tendons, &c., was founded y Dr. Little, who introduced the Stromeyerian operation of sub-taneous tenotomy into the Metropolis.

QUEEN CHARLOTTE'S LYING-IN HOSPITAL was originally established in 1752, in St. George's-row, near Tyburn Turnpike, whence it was removed to Bayswater in 1791; and in 1810, to its present location, corner of Harcourt-street, New Road, whereon a commodious and well-ventilated Hospital will be erected. This excellent charity has been patronised by Queen Charlotte, the Duke of Sussex, Queen Adelaide, and every member of the royal family. It affords an asylum for indigent females during childbirth, as well as to out-patients, especially to the wives of soldiers or sailors; penitent patients are admitted once, but in no instance a second time.

ROYAL FREE HOSPITAL, Gray's-Inn-road, affording free and instant relief to the destitute sick, was originally founded 1828, in Greville-street, Hatton Garden: in 1832, 700 cholera patients were admitted here when other Hospitals were closed against them; a demonstration of the *free* principle which led to the removal of the Hospital, in 1843, to the present extensive premises, formerly the barracks of the Light-Horse Volunteers. In 1851, there were relieved 30,929 patients; and since the foundation, 369,611. The establishment of this Hospital was prompted by its founder, Mr. Marsden, a surgeon, having seen, in the winter of 1827, a wretched young woman lying on the steps of St. Andrew's Churchyard, Holborn-hill, after midnight, perishing through disease and famine: she was a stranger in London, without a friend, and died two days afterwards unrecognised!

At the Hospital-gate, in Gray's-Inn-road, is a subscription-box, wherein have been found the following donations by stealth: Dec. 27, 1843, a bank-note for 100*l.*, labelled " A Passer-by;" June 14, 1844, 100*l.*, "Another Passer-by;" Nov. 2, 1844, 100*l.*, with " Winter is coming on. *Bis dat qui cito dat;*" Oct. 9, 1850; 50*l.*; June 21, 1851, 20*l.*; and frequently bank-notes of 10*l.* and 5*l.*

ROYAL MATERNITY CHARITY (Office, 17 Little Knight-rider-street, Doctors' Commons) provides advice and good nurses for delivering poor married women at their own homes in Eastern London; and the cases annually average nearly 3500.

This institution was originally founded as "the Lying-in Charity," in 1768. The Prince of Wales, when but five years old, being nominated president, a donation of 500*l.* was made in his name; thenceforth he contributed annually 20*l.* George IV. became president in 1818; and from the time of his Regency to his death, contributed to the Hospital fund 1800*l.*

SEAMEN'S HOSPITAL. (See DREADNOUGHT HOSPITAL-SHIP, p. 260.)

SMALL-POX AND VACCINATION HOSPITAL, instituted 1746, for those attacked with natural small-pox, and for preventing it by vaccination, was first opened at Battle Bridge, St. Pancras, 1767; but this Hospital and site being required for the terminus of the Great Northern Railway Company, the Hospital was rebuilt in a healthy and picturesque situation at the foot of Highgate Hill, at a cost of 20,000*l.*, paid out of the Railway Company's compensation.

ST. THOMAS's HOSPITAL, Wellington-street, Southwark, was originally a house of alms, founded by the Prior of Bermondseye, in 1213, adjoining the wall of that monastery. After the surrender in 1539, it was purchased by the City of London, chartered, in 1551, as one of the five royal foundations, and opened in 1552. In 1569, the funds were so low that a lease was pawned for 50*l.* The Hospital was rebuilt between 1701 and 1706, with the aid of subscriptions, to which Sir Robert Clayton, the President, contributed 600*l.*; he also bequeathed to the sick poor 2300*l.* The Hospital was enlarged in 1732: the wards Frederic and Guy are named from their founders, the latter of whom built a pair of iron gates in High-street; on the two piers were statues of cripples, which are preserved to this day. The entrance-gates and lodges with the north and south wings, have been rebuilt of stone; James Field architect. The Hospital consists of three courts, and colonnades: in

e first court is a bronze statue of Edward VI., by Scheemakers, set up
y Charles Joyce, Esq., 1737. In the second court is the chapel for
itients—service daily; the parish church, described at page 163; the
ill, and kitchen; and over the Doric colonnade is the Court-room, with
ortraits of Edward VI., William III. and Queen Mary, Sir Robert
layton, and other of the Hospital presidents. In the third court is
ie. statue of Sir Robert Clayton, robed as Lord Mayor, erected in his
e-time by the Hospital governors. In a smaller court are the cutting-
ard, surgery, bathing-rooms, theatre, and dead-house. There are
venty wards for patients, each superintended by a Sister. The in-
me averages 25,000*l.* a year: number of beds, 428; total number of
itients in 1851, 55,043.

The site of the new north wing of the Hospital, at the south end of London
idge, was purchased of the City of London for the sum of 40,850*l.*, which was
t considered an extravagant price, though at the rate of 54,885*l.* per acre. The
e of two houses adjoining the above spot was sold by the Hospital to the City at
e enormous rate of 69,935*l.* per acre!

UNIVERSITY COLLEGE HOSPITAL, Upper Gower-street, was founded
33, under the presidency of Lord Brougham, in connexion with Uni-
rsity College, which the Hospital building faces.

WESTMINSTER HOSPITAL originated from an infirmary "for reliev-
g the sick and needy," and is the oldest subscription hospital in the
etropolis. It was first established in Petty France, next in Chapel-
reet, then in James-street; and the present noble Hospital was built
the Broad Sanctuary, opposite Westminster Abbey, upon a piece of
ound purchased of the government for 6000*l.*, originally part of the
e of the ancient Sanctuary cruciform church, and subsequently of
estminster Market. The Hospital foundation is 6 feet depth of con-
ete; the design, by the Inwoods, is Elizabethan, with windows *temp.*
enry VII.; the central and end oriels, and the embattled porch, are
e; the whole frontage is 200 feet, and the windows number 260; the
of, nearly half an acre, is an airing-walk for the patients. The build-
g is embattled throughout; the materials are white Suffolk bricks,
ith stone finishings; and among the enrichments are bosses of the
estminster portcullis arms.

In our larger Hospitals, each ward is presided over by a *Sister*, who
rries into effect the medical instructions, administers medicines, re-
orts changes of symptoms in patients, and orders their diet, and su-
rintends the *Nurses*. Institutions have been formed for training
sters and Nurses, akin to the "ministering angels" of monastic life.

The Medical Students of the various Hospitals have long been noted for their
egularities; and in 1851, Mr. Henry, a Bow-street magistrate, described them
"the most disorderly class with whom the police and magistrates have to
al." To this unqualified stigma has, however, been opposed the assertion, that
lmost every idle dissolute young man who, in a fit of drunken folly, is guilty
some crime, will, if he wears a decent garb, arrogate to himself a respectability
which he has no right, by claiming the title of a medical student." Mr. Albert
ith, himself a "Middlesex man," was the first to sketch the Medical Student's
in London.—(See *Punch*, vol. ii.)

General Hospitals: two founded before 1500, five between 1718 and 1745, and
e between 1818 and 1850=12: annual incomes, 142,906*l.*, including voluntary
tributions 31,265*l.*; Beds, 3,326; In and Out Patients (1848-9), 329,608. —
w's *Charities*, p. 4.

DISPENSARIES were first established in 1770, when the *Royal Dis-
sary* was founded in Shaftesbury House, Aldersgate-street. There
upwards of forty Dispensaries in London.

"Medicine and every other relief under the calamity of bodily diseases, no
than the daily necessaries of life, are natural provisions which God has made
our present indigent state, and which He has granted in common to the

children of men, whether they be rich or poor: to the rich by inheritance and
acquisition; and by their hands, to the disabled poor. Nor can there be any
doubt that Public Dispensaries are the most effectual means of administering
sick relief."—*Bishop Butler.*

HOUNDSDITCH

Extends from opposite St. Botolph's Church, Bishopsgate-street, to St
Botolph's, Aldgate. Beaumont and Fletcher call it Dogsditch.

"From Aldgate north-west to Bishopsgate lieth the ditch of the City, called
Houndsditch, for that in old time, when the same lay open, much filth (conveyed
from the City), especially dead dogs, were there laid or cast."—*Stow.*

Into this filthy ditch, by command of King Canute, was thrown Edie, the
Saxon, the murderer of his master, Edmund Ironside, after having been drawn by
his heels from Baynard's Castle, and tormented to death by burning torches
The ditch was subsequently enclosed with a mud wall, against which was a "far
field," with cottages for poor bed-rid people, and where devout people walked
(especially on Fridays) to relieve the bed-ridden, who lay on the ground-floor, a
the window, with a clean linen cloth, and a pair of beads, to shew to charitable
passengers that "there lay a bed-rid body unable but to pray only."

Houndsditch was first paved 1503. Late in the reign of Henry VIII
a foundry for casting brass ordnance was established here, which drove
the poor bed-rid people out of their cottages; and upon their site were
built houses and shops for "brokers, joyners, braziers, and such as
deal in old clothes, linen, and upholstery." (*Strype.*) Braziers abound
here to the present day. Here lived Tench, the joiner, to whom it was
sworn on the trial of Hugh Peters, in 1660, that his orders were given
on the scaffold to prepare the block for the beheading of Charles I.
and in Rosemary-lane lived Ralph Jones, the ragman, who assisted
Brandon, the common hangman in the execution. Anthony Munday
speaks indignantly of the "unconscionable broking usurers, a base kind
of vermin, who had crept into Houndsditch;" which, with Long-lane
were the Rag Fairs of two centuries since; and Houndsditch is to this
day the centre of the Jews' quarter.

Houndsditch was the general name of the different parts of the City
ditch. In a chantulary of St. Giles's Hospital, beginning of fifteenth
century, *Houndesdic* and *Houndesdich* are part of the ditch in the
parish of St. Sepulchre. Howell's *Londinopolis* shews, by the same
name, parts of the fosse between Ludgate and Newgate; and by
Barbican.

HOUSES OF OLD LONDON.

Anterior to the reign of Stephen, Houses in London were built
much as they had been in the earlier Saxon times, almost wholly of
wood, roofed with straw and reeds: thus a carpenter is described a
"making houses and bowls." Hence the frequent fires; and especiall
the great conflagration of 1097, which spread from London Bridge to
the church of St. Clement Danes in the Strand. By an assize (1s
year of Richard L) all houses in London were hereafter to be built of
stone, with party-walls of the same: but this mandate was rarely com
plied with; and it was not until the reign of Edward IV., when bric
was made from the clay of Moorfields, that it occasionally took th
place of the timber which had hitherto been used for houses; reeds wer
then replaced by tiles and slates. In two centuries, to gain ground
many stone houses were taken down, and others of timber built i
their place; and it is distinctly stated that London, to the period of th
Great Fire of 1666, was chiefly built of chestnut, filled up with plaster
After the Great Fire, the houses were rebuilt with brick; but betwee
1618 and 1636 several fine brick houses were erected in Aldersgate
street, Great Queen-street, Lincoln's-Inn-fields, and Covent Garden
Still, the general form of roof was the high-pitched gable, whole row

: which have disappeared in our time, with several specimens of florid plaster and carved wood fronts. A few specimens, however, remain.*

Aldgate High-street, No. 76, with central bay-windows, enriched brackets, and a projecting penthouse-shop, has panels decorated with the Prince of Wales' feathers, the fleur-de-lis of France, the Thistle of Scotland, portcullis of Westminster, and other armorial bearings. Of this period also is the house No. 17 Fleet-street, already described at page 308.

Ashburnham House, Westminster, one of Inigo Jones's finest mansions, is described at page 23.

Bagnio, the, in Bath-street, Newgate-street, was built by Turkey merchants, and first opened in 1679 (*Aubrey*), for sweating, rubbing, shaving, hot-bathing, and cupping, after the Turkish model. The cupola-roof and walls neatly set with Dutch tiles, described by Hatton 1708, exist to this day and is now a cold bath. (See BATHS, p. 32.)

Bangor House, Shoe-lane, south of St. Andrew's church, is described the palace of the Bishops of Bangor in a roll of 48 Edward III. being deserted as an episcopal residence, some mean dwellings were built upon the grounds; yet a garden with lime-trees, and a rookery, remained about ninety years ago. The last of the mansion, octangular and two-storied, was removed in 1828; but is kept in memory by Bentley's Printing-office, named "Bangor House;" and by Bangor-court, opposite which are some remains of "Oldborne Hall," in Stow's time letten out in divers tenements."

Baumes, or *Balmes* (from two Spanish merchants so named), stood west of the Kingsland-road, Hoxton, and was taken down in 1852. It was built by the Balmeses, about 1540; Sir George Whitmore resided here occasionally when lord mayor, 1631; and on this spot Sir W. Acton, lord mayor, with the aldermen, &c., waited the arrival of Charles I. on his return from Scotland, Nov. 25, 1641; when the royal coaches were conducted, by a road formed for the occasion, through Balmes's grounds to Hoxton, and thence to Moorgate, into the City, the road between Kingsland and Shoreditch being then impassable by the depth and foulness of it." Baumes-march was long a favourite archery and artillery exercise;† but the ground attached to the house is now the site of De Beauvoir Town, named from the De Beauvoir family, its owners since 1696. A print of 1580 shews Baumes, with its gate-house, farmery, spacious gardens and grounds, avenues of fruit-trees and stately elms; and the Italianised brick mansion with its two-storied roof, moated and approached by a drawbridge; the house and moat were supplied from the ancient well in Canonbury Field. The interior of Balmes was rich in carved ceilings, paneling and staircase, armorial glass and tapestry.

Brookes's Menagerie (subsequently Herring's), taken down in 1851, was an old wooden house at the western corner of Brook-street, New-road: it was standing when Tottenhall Fair was in its glory; and almost the only house between St. Giles's Pound and Primrose-hill was Tot-

---

* The remains of Roman London consist chiefly of portions of the City wall, foundations of buildings; tesselated pavements, often of so much beauty as to denote a corresponding style in the superstructure; baths, sewers, bronzes, and various ornaments admirable as works of art. A Roman bath, nearly complete, still exists in Strand-lane; and a Roman hypocaust is preserved beneath the Coal Exchange (see p. 282). The remains of the *superstructures* of Roman London which have yet been discovered, are, however, unimportant.

† The Robin Hood public-house (now refronted) originally looked over Finsbury-fields, and was much frequented by the metropolitan archers; the sign, Robin Hood and Little John, in Lincoln-green, formerly swung from a tree before the door. A few dealers in archery implements, and preservers of animals, have lingered in the City-road to our day—the last relics of the chivalry of Hogsden.

tenhall, a house of entertainment in 1615, on the site of which is the "Adam and Eve tavern."

Bulk Shops have only disappeared in our time. In 1846 was taken down an old house south-west of Temple Bar, which is engraved in Archer's *Vestiges*, part i. A view in 1795, in the Crowle Pennant, presents one tall gable to the street; but the pitch of the roof had been diminished by adding two imperfect side gables. The heavy pents originally traversed over each of the three courses of windows; it was a mere timber frame filled up with lath and plaster, the beams being of deal with short oak joints: it presented a capital example of the old London bulk-shop (sixteenth century), with a heavy canopy projecting over the pathway, and turned up at the rim to carry off the rain end-wise. This shop had long been held by a succession of fishmongers, among whom was the noted Crockford, who quitted it for "play" in St. James's (see CLUB-HOUSES, p. 193). Crockford would not permit this house-front to be altered in his lifetime.

Burnet's (Bishop) House, St. John's-square, Clerkenwell, is now let in tenements, and has an arched thoroughfare to a court of houses built on the site of the garden. In this house Burnet died 1715, and was buried in St. James's church, when the rabble threw dirt and stones at his funeral procession. The Bishop's house and tomb are engraved from original drawings in the *Mirror*, 1837, No. 836.

Campden House, Kensington, originally approached from the town by an avenue of elms, was built about 1612 by Sir Baptist Hicks, afterwards Viscount Campden, who purchased the property of Sir Walter Cope; or, traditionally, won it of him "at some sort of game." The house is of red brick, with stone finishings, and has a central porch, bay-window once fitted with armorial glass, and flanking turrets with cupolas. The great dining-room, in which Charles II. supped with Lord Campden, has a rich armorial ceiling in stucco, floridly carved wainscot, and a tabernacle mantelpiece, with Corinthian columns and caryatidal figures, finely sculptured. The State Apartments on the first floor include Queen Anne's bed-chamber; and the Globe room, originally a chapel, and communicating with the garden terrace: all the other rooms have richly stuccoed ceilings and marble mantelpieces. During the Protectorate, the Sequestration Committee sat here. Queen Anne, when Princess of Denmark, resided five years at Campden House, with her son the Duke of Gloucester, who kept a regiment of boy-soldiers here, and had a puppet-theatre built. Lord Lechmere, the lawyer and staunch Whig, lived here when he had his quarrel with Sir John Guise, ridiculed in Swift's ballad of "Duke upon Duke:"

> " Back in the dark, by Brompton Park,
> He turn'd up thro' the Gore,
> And slunk to Campden-house so high,
> All in his coach and four.
> The Duke in wrath call'd for his steeds,
> And fiercely drove them on :
> Lord ! Lord ! how rattled then thy stones,
> O kingly Kensington!"

The gardens, in which the wild olive and the caper-tree once flourished, have been much reduced; but the house retains its original front. Among the relics are two dogs (supporters of the Campden arms) which formerly surmounted the gateway-piers, and are cleverly sculptured. Westward is *Little Campden House*, built during the Princess Anne's residence at Campden House: it has an outer arcaded gallery, and was once occupied by the Rt. Hon. William Pitt.

Canonbury Place, Islington, was originally the country-house of the Priors of St. Bartholomew. (See CANONBURY TOWER, p. 63.)

: "Canonbury House internally is one of the richest specimens of the archi- cture of James I. in the neighbourhood of London. The house, or rather the mains, form at the present time several large dwelling-houses; including a ortion of the old great chamber, with a rich ceiling, date 1599, a quaintly carved k fireplace with statuettes of Mars and Venus draped, and a doorway with bust an old English gentleman and dame, the Roman mouldings and enriched frieze ry fine; several other rooms are sumptuously carved, and the parlour retains s original decoration."—*C. J. Richardson, F.S.A.*

Carey-street, Chancery-lane, corner of Bell-yard, is an Italianised ouse, with columns, pilasters, and panels, and has an interesting interior.

Carlisle House, Carlisle-street, Soho-square, formerly the mansion f the Dowager Lady Carlisle, was built *temp.* James II.: it has a mar- le-floored hall and grand decorated staircase; the rooms are large and fty, and have enriched ceilings. The mansion originally stood in the idst of a garden, a portion of which remains in the rear; the "cherry- arden" is built upon. The lower walls of Carlisle House are of old nglish bond, of brilliant red brick; the leadwork of the cisterns is ated 1669, the year of the creation of the Earldom of Carlisle. The ansion was long tenanted by Angelo, the fencing-master, and is now ccupied by W. Gibbs Rogers, the carver: in the ball-room the Col- ge of the Freemasons of the Church hold their monthly meetings.

"*Caxton's House*," Westminster, and other old houses in the lmonry, are described at p. 4.

Crosby Hall, Bishopsgate-street, the finest specimen of olden omestic architecture in the metropolis, is described at p. 238.

Drury-lane (see page 261) has the *Cock and Magpie*, a low public- ouse of the seventeenth century, with a paneled house next door, and range of tenements in Little Drury-lane of the same date. These ere then the only houses in the eastern part of Drury-lane, except the ansion of the Drurys. Hither the youths and maidens who on May- ay danced round the May-pole in the Strand, were accustomed to esort for cakes and ale: Pope has named it as the scene of "the high eroic games devised by dulness to gladden her sons."

"*Dyot's House*," Dyot-street, now George-street, St. Giles's, was he mansion of Richard Dyot, Esq., a vestryman of St. Giles's parish *mp.* Charles II., and was inhabited till our time by his descendant, hilip Dyot, Esq.

Elizabethan Houses. Among the earliest examples of the Eliza- ethan period was a house in Grub-street, engraved in Smith's *Anti- uities*, in which the mouldings, quatrefoil, and other Gothic orna- ents, were combined with the Italianised panels and brackets of a later ate. Some brackets remain in Milton-street. Malcolm, in his *Anec- otes*, has engraved two Elizabethan houses in Goswell-road, built bout 1550, and standing in 1807; with bay-windows, overhanging pper story, and gable: next door, for contrast, is a house built about 00, three floors of the former being scarcely equal to two of the latter.

"The roofs (ceilings) of your houses are so low, that I presume your ancestors ere very mannerly, and stood bare to their wives, for I cannot discern how they uld wear their high-crowned hats."—*Sir W. Davenant.*

Fowler's House, Islington, fronts Cross-street: a ceiling bears the ate 1595: at the extremity of the garden is a lodge, probably built as summer-house by Sir Thomas Fowler the younger, whose arms and e date 1655 are in the wall. Sir Thomas Fowler the elder, who died 24, was a juryman on Sir Walter Raleigh's trial. (See INNS, p. 400.)

Fulwood's Rents, Holborn, has a house *temp.* James I. (See p. 319.)

Gray's-Inn-lane, east side, north end, has three Elizabethan houses, iginally one, and probably a hostelry on the road to Theobalds: its ree stories project over each other upward, the top one being of.

weather-board plastered inside, and the roof having four pointed gables: at the ends of the first and second stories are carved brackets, one 1559.

Grub-street. In Sweedon's passage, Grub-street, was an ancient timber-built house, traditionally the residence of Sir Richard Whittington, *temp.* Henry IV.; and of Sir Thomas Gresham, *temp.* Elizabeth. The massive timbers were oak and chestnut, the ground-floor chimneys being of stone: it had a boldly projecting staircase, which, with the house, was taken down in 1805, and three small houses were built upon its site, one inscribed " Gresham House, once the residence of Sir Richard Whittington, Lord Mayor 1406, rebuilt 1805." (See Smith's *Ancient Topography,* p. 41.)

Holborn. In the volume of MS. drawings by John Thorpe, preserved in Sir John Soane's Museum, is a sketch of a wooden house described as standing in Thorpe's time at the "water end of Holborn."

" From the garden you ascend by five steps the enclosed terrace in front of the building; this has, as Thorpe expresses it, a ' terrace overhead:' a small porch leads into the great hall. The kitchen is on the right; the larder is the small square room leading out of it. The small room in front, on the same side as the kitchen, is the buttery, with cellar under, the small steps conducting down to it. Above the hall is ' the great chamber,' the staircase leading to which opens into a gallery communicating to the rooms of the rest of the building. The square compartments at the back of the house, represented in plan as staircase and larder, are carried up above the roof as turrets ; a small prospect tower is placed in front of the building."—*C. J. Richardson, F.S.A.*

Holland House is described at pp. 374-377.

Hoxton. A few years since there stood in Hoxton Old Town the reputed " oldest house in the metropolis," in taking down which was found a brick dated above 150 years back ; but most of the bricks were of a much earlier period, being deep-red and highly glazed: the door was beautifully carved with the oak and vine, &c. The Parliamentary Survey, No. 78, as reported in Sir H. Ellis's *History of Shoreditch,* of which Hoxton is one of the divisions, states that about this spot, during the Interregnum, a house was in the possession of Charles Stuart, some time King of England, in 1653, which was valued at 4*l.* per annum.

Kennington Manor-house, a portion of the royal lodging built of brick upon part of the site of the old palace near Kennington-cross, exists to this day. Its last royal tenant was Charles I. when Prince of Wales, Kennington having been an occasional residence of the Kings of England prior to the Conquest. The manor was annexed to the Duchy of Cornwall, *temp.* Edward III., and was tenanted by the Black Prince. John of Gaunt took refuge here in 1377 from the exasperated Londoners. Henry VII. and Katherine of Arragon resided here; and James I. settled the manor on Henry Prince of Wales, his eldest son; and after his decease, 1612, on Prince Charles, afterwards Charles I. The stables of the earlier palace, built of flint and stone, and known as the *Long Barn,* remained till 1795 ; and fragments of flint, chalk, and rubble-stone walls of the ancient palace are traceable in houses in Park-place.

Kensington House, nearly opposite the palace-gates, was the residence of the Duchess of Portsmouth, the French mistress of Charles II. Here Elphinstone, the friend of Jortin, Franklin, and Johnson, kept a school from 1776 till 1788: he is unsparingly ridiculed in Smollett's *Roderick Random.* The mansion was next a Roman Catholic Boarding-house, where Mrs. Inchbald, the player and novelist, died in 1821. *Colby House,* facing the Palace-road gates, was built about 1720, for Sir Thomas Colby: it has a painted grand staircase with Herculaneum ceiling, and a small chapel. *Kensington National Schools,* a stately pile of brickwork, west of the church, were built by Sir John Vanbrugh, who " is singularly fortunate in this design, his lines presenting a re-

trained degree of civil architecture, in the middle class of uprights"
(*John Carter*). Here are costumed figures of a charity boy and girl
of the last century.

Hale House, Earl's Court, traditionally the residence of Oliver
Cromwell, is dilapidated and desolate; but a few seventeenth-century
decorations remain. Near the West London Cemetery is *Coleherne
House, temp.* Charles I., the property of Sir William Lister; next of
Gen. Lambert, the first President of Cromwell's Council; and in 1820,
of the widow of Major-Gen. Sir W. Ponsonby, who fell at Waterloo.

Lindsey House, Chelsea, west of the old church, was built by Bertie,
Earl of Lindsey, upon the site of the mansion of Sir Theodore Mayerne,
physician to James I. and Charles I. In 1751 Lindsey House was
purchased by the United Brethren, or Moravians, whose Bishop, Count
Zinzendorf, died here in 1760: in the rear of the house is a burial-
ground for the Brethren, with a small chapel; but their only place of
worship in London is the chapel in Fetter-lane (see page 174). Lindsey House is now five residences: the central one has been tenanted
by Sir I. K. Brunel and son, and Bramah, the engineers: it is now
inhabited by John Martin, K.H., the epic painter, who in a summer-
house in the garden has executed a fine fresco.

Lindsey House, on the centre of the west side of Lincoln's-Inn-fields,
was built by Inigo Jones for the above Bertie, Earl of Lindsey, and
was for some time the residence of the proud Duke of Somerset: it has
a handsome stone façade, and had formerly vases upon the open balustrade. At the south-west angle of Lincoln's-Inn-fields is *Portsmouth
House*, built in Inigo Jones's rich style for the Earl of Portsmouth,
but now let in chambers. It gives name to Portsmouth-street, where
is the Black-Jack public-house, frequented by Joe Miller, and long
known as "the Jump," from Jack Sheppard's leaping from one of its
first-floor windows, to escape his pursuers.

Little Moorfields, No. 23 is the King's Arms public-house, with a
plaster front richly wrought with flowers, and a pair of large scrolls
surmounted with the Ionic volute. In London Wall was until lately
a house-front *temp.* Charles I., enriched with groups of foliage and
figures, and engraved in Lester's *Illustrations*, 1818.

Long-lane, Smithfield, has a few houses remaining of Elizabethan
date; and *Cloth Fair* has relics of this and a later period.

Marylebone Manor-house, attached to the Royal Park, was built
temp. Henry VIII., and was a palace of Mary and Elizabeth. Here,
about 1703, was established a school of great repute; the interior had
a beautiful saloon and gallery, in which private concerts were given.
The house, which stood at the top of High-street, nearly opposite the
old church, was taken down in 1791. South of the Manor-house site was
Oxford House, built specially for the Library and MSS. (Harleian) of
the Earl of Oxford, now in the British Museum.

Milborn's Almshouses, Crutched Friars, were built of brick and
timber, in 1535, by Sir John Milborn, lord mayor in 1521, for thirteen
aged poor men and their wives, of the Drapers' Company. Over the
Tudor gateway is sculptured in stone the Assumption, the Virgin supported by six angels in a cloud of glory, with inscription beneath.

Newcastle House, at the north-west angle of Lincoln's-Inn-fields,
has beneath its south wing an arcade over the southern footway of
Great Queen-street. It was originally Powis House, built for the
Marquis of Powis, about 1686, by Captain William Winde, a scholar of
Webbe, a pupil of Inigo Jones. It was bought by Holles, Duke of
Newcastle, and inherited by his nephew, who led the Pelham adminis-
tration under George II.

"*Old City of London Workhouse*," Bishopsgate-street Without, the first workhouse built in London, dates from 1680: in the court-room is a portrait of Sir Robert Clayton, the first governor. The house was originally partitioned into the steward's side, for poor children; and the keeper's side, for "rogues and vagabonds."

Post-office, Lombard-street, formerly the General Post-office, was originally built by "the great banquer," Sir Robert Viner, on the site of a noted tavern destroyed in the Great Fire of 1666. Here Sir Robert kept his mayoralty in 1675. Strype describes it as a very large and curious dwelling, with a handsome paved court, and behind it "a yard for stabling and coaches."

Queen-street, Lincoln's-Inn-fields, has on the south side some early brick houses, built by Inigo Jones and his pupil Webbe; those on the south being charged with the fleur-de-lys, in compliment to Queen Henrietta-Maria, daughter of Henry IV. of France, after whom the street was named: it is said to have been designed for a square, and built at the charge of the Jesuits, on the site of the common path which anciently separated Aldewych Close from the northern division of Aldewych, extending to Holborn. The street was originally entered from the west by "the Devil's Gap," a narrow passage; altered 1765.

"In the last century Queen-street was the residence of many people of rank. Among others was Conway House, the residence of the noble family of that name; Paulet House, belonging to the Marquis of Winchester; and the house in which Lord Herbert of Cherbury finished his romantic career. The fronts of certain houses, possibly of those or others of the nobility, are distinguished by brick pilasters and rich capitals."—*Pennant.*

Howel writes to Lord Herbert, 13th July, 1646: "God send you joy of your new habitation, for I understand your Lordship is removed from the *King's*-street to the *Queen's.*"—*Familiar Letters.*

Here lived Sir Thomas Fairfax, the Parliamentary general, when he took possession of Holland House, Kensington (see page 375). Also, Sir Godfrey Kneller; Hudson, Sir Joshua Reynolds's master; and Sir Robert Strange, the engraver. Lord Herbert's house is near the east corner of Wild-street. One of Howel's *Familiar Letters* is addressed "To the R. H. the Earl Rivers, at his house in Queen-street."

"May 26th, 1671. The Earl of Bristol's House, in Queen-street, Lincoln's-Inn-fields, was taken for the Commissioners of Trade and Plantations, and furnished with rich hangings of the King's. It consisted of seven rooms on a floor, with a long gallery, gardens, &c."—*Evelyn's Diary.*

Schomberg House, Pall Mall, Nos. 81 and 82, south side, was built about 1650, when Pall Mall was planted with elm-trees, "standing in a very regular and decent manner on both sides of the walk;" and the house is described as "a fair mansion inclosed with a gar-den." In 1660, at the Restoration, it was occupied by several Court favourites; and subsequently by Edward Griffin, Treasurer of the Chamber, and ancestor of the present Lord Braybrooke. In 1670 Schomberg House and the adjoining mansions had gardens which ex-tended to St. James's Park, and had earthen mounds or terraces, which looked over the green walks to the Palace.

Next door, on the site of the present No. 79, (tenanted by the Society for the Propagation of the Gospel in Foreign Parts,) lived Nell Gwyn, after her removal from a house at the east end of the north side of Pall Mall. Evelyn records a walk made March 2, 1671, in which he attended Charles II. through St. James's Park, where he both saw and heard "a familiar discourse between the King and Mrs. Nellie, as they called an impudent comedian, she looking out of her garden on a terrace at the top of the wall, and the King standing on the green walk under it." Part of the terrace or mound on which Nelly stood may still be seen under the park wall of Marlborough House; and among Mr. Robert Cole's Nell Gwyn papers (bills sent to Nelly for payment) there is a charge for this very mound. (Cunningham's *Story of Nell Gwyn*, p. 119.) This scene has been admirably painted by E. M. Ward, A.R.A.

Here lived the Duke of Schomberg, who was killed at the Battle of the Boyne, 1690, and after whom the house is named. It was beautified for Frederick, third and last Duke of Schomberg, for whom Peter Berchett painted the grand staircase with landscapes in lunettes. In 1699, the house had nigh been demolished by a mob of disbanded soldiers; and in the Gordon riots of 1780, attempts were made to sack and burn it. William Duke of Cumberland, "the hero of Culloden," died here in 1760. John Astley, the painter and "the Beau," who lived here many years, partitioned the mansion into three, and placed the bas-relief of Painting above the middle doorway. Astley also built on the roof a large painting-room, his "country-house," looking over the Park, to which and some other apartments he had a private staircase. After Astley's death, Cosway the portrait-painter tenanted the centre. Gainsborough occupied the west wing from 1777 to 1788, when he died in a second-floor room: he sent for Sir Joshua Reynolds, and was reconciled to him; then exclaiming, "We are all going to heaven, and Vandyke is of the company," he immediately expired. Part of the house was subsequently occupied by Robert Bowyer for his "Historic Gallery;" and by Dr. Graham, the empiric, for his "Celestial Bed" and other impostures, advertised by two gigantic porters stationed at the entrance, in gold-laced cocked hats and liveries. The house is a good specimen of the red-brick seventeenth-century mansion. It was partly occupied by Payne and Foss, with their valuable stock of old books, until 1850. Another portion is tenanted by Harding and Co., silk-mercers, who have rebuilt the eastern wing in elegant Italian style.

Shaftesbury House, originally Thanet House, on the east side of Aldersgate-street, was built by Inigo Jones for the Tuftons, Earls of Thanet; whence it passed into the family of Anthony Ashley Cooper, Earl of Shaftesbury. In 1708 it returned to the Thanet family; in 1720, became an inn; in 1734, a tavern; 1750, a Lying-in Hospital; and in 1849, a Dispensary. The façade is of red brick, decorated with eight pilasters, but painted stone-colour. Nearly opposite was *London House*, originally Peter House, of handsome brick: it was the town-mansion of the Bishop of London after the Great Fire of 1666.

Southwark retained in High-street some of its olden house-fronts, almost to the rebuilding of London Bridge. In 1830 were removed two houses with enriched plaster decoration and armorial ensigns of the 16th century; and the writer remembers, about 1809, the demolition of a long range of wood and plaster and gable-fronted houses on the west side of High-street.

" *The Spanish Ambassador's House*," eastward of Houndsditch, in Gravel-lane, was taken down in 1844. This was one of the "garden-houses," which Stow describes as built amidst "fair hedgerows of elm-trees, with bridges and easie stiles to pass over into the pleasant fields." More than a century later Strype adds: "There was a house on the west side, a good way in the lane, which, when I was a boy, was commonly called *the Spanish Ambassador's House*, who, in King James's reign, dwelt here; and he, I think, was the famous Count Gondemar." The house was built *temp.* James I., in a courtyard, with a ine gateway, upon a flight of steps, approached by "Seven-Step Alley:" t had three stories, with pilasters between the windows, the lower rooms were oak paneled, and had richly-carved fireplaces and stucco ceilings; and on the first floor was a large chamber, with an elaborately-traceried ceiling in Italian taste, charged with Latin mottoes and the arms of the founder, Robert Shaw, and those of the Vintners' Company, of which he was master: here, too, was a superb fireplace, of coloured marbles and carved oak (see Archer's *Vestiges*, part v.).

Staple Inn, Holborn, has three overhanging stories, the upper one with four pointed gables; the ground-floor has modern shop-fronts, but the central arched entrance to the Inn has the original therm pilasters of the Jacobean style.

Star-Chamber and Exchequer Buildings, the, stood on the eastern side of New Palace-yard; and adjoining northward was an arched gateway(Henry III.), communicating by stairs with the Thames. These buildings, bay-windowed and gabled, were taken down between 1807 and 1836 : the last remaining were the offices for trials of the Pix, and printing Exchequer bills. In an apartment here the Court of Star Chamber sat from *temp*. Elizabeth until its abolition, 1641 : over a doorway was the date 1602, E. R. and an open rose on a star. It had a richly-carved Tudor-Gothic oak ceiling, with moulded compartments, roses, pomegranates, portcullises, and fleurs-de-lis; and it had been gilt and coloured, though it had not a trace of gilt stars. The mantel-piece was decorated with fluted columns, and the chimney-opening was a Tudor arch. Drawings of the whole were made in 1836. Behind the Elizabethan paneling were found three Tudor-arched doorways, and under the staircase a Gothic wood-hole entrance, its spandrels ornamented with roses; proving this to have been the original *Camera Stellata*, newly fitted *temp*. Elizabeth. The Chamber has been restored at Leasowes Castle, Shropshire.

The Strand retains a few old house-fronts : as west of the Adelphi Theatre; and immediately east of Strand-lane are three houses of the reign of Charles I. retaining a few of their classic mouldings, cornices, and window pediments. No. 273 has a fine old dormer-window.

Tradescant's House, South-Lambeth-road, a large brick edifice, nearly opposite Spring-lane, was the residence of the Tradescants, father and son ; and of Elias Ashmole, who "added a noble room to it, and adorned the chimney with his arms, impaling those of Sir William Dugdale, whose daughter was his third wife." The house, with its Museum, was called "Tradescant's Ark." (See GARDENS, p. 323.)

Warwick House, Cloth Fair, Smithfield, built *temp*. Elizabeth, was bought with the Priory of St. Bartholomew, and the right to hold the Fair, by Sir Robert Rich, in 1544, and devolved to his descendants, the Earls of Warwick and *Holland;* whence that "uproarious rabblement," called *Lady Holland's Mob*, which assembled on the eve of St. Bartholomew to proclaim the Fair (see p. 30).

Weather-boarded house-fronts, in part plastered, are of old date: there was, until 1853, a row of these wood tenements on the east side of Milford-lane, Strand; and up a passage in Bell-yard, Fleet-street, a little north-west of a house *temp*. Charles I., is a square court entirely of weather-board and plaster, bespeaking the inflammable nature of London before the Great Fire of 1666. Other buildings of this kind, but of earlier date, may be seen near St Giles's Church, Cripplegate. Several examples of Old London Houses are engraved and described in the *Builder*, Nos. 486, 489, and 494, and 515.

INNS OF OLD LONDON.

Of Olden Inns, up gateways, and consisting of rooms for refection below, and long projecting balustraded galleries above, leading to the chambers—time and change have spared a few interesting specimens.

Angel, Islington, (actually in St. James's, Clerkenwell,) once a busy resort of travellers on the Great North Road, is reputed to have been established upwards of 200 years: it was rebuilt in 1819. The old inn-yard was nearly quadrangular, with double galleries, supported by plain columns, and pilasters carved with caryatid and other figures. (See Pugin's *Views in Islington and Pentonville*, 1819.) A coloured drawing of this old inn-yard hangs in the present coffee-room.

Angel, St. Clement's, Strand, retains its gables and portions of covered galleries, with an old lattice-fronted attic passage. Data of three centuries since also attest its antiquity: Bishop Hooper, the venerated martyr of the Reformation, upon his second committal to the Fleet Prison in 1553, refusing to recant his opinions, was condemned to be burnt in January 1555. It was expected that he would have accompanied Rogers, a prebendary of St. Paul's, to the stake; but Hooper was led back to his cell, to be carried down to Gloucester, to suffer among his own people. Next morning he was roused at four o'clock, and being committed to the care of six of Queen Mary's Guard, they took him, before it was light, to the Angel Inn, St. Clement's, *then standing in the fields;* and thence he was taken to Gloucester, and there burnt with dreadful torments on the 9th of February.

In the *Public Advertiser*, March 28, 1769, is the following advertisement:
"To be sold, a Black Girl, the property of J. B——, eleven years of age, who is extremely handy, works at her needle tolerably, and speaks English perfectly well; is of an excellent temper and willing disposition. Inquire of Mr. Owen, at the Angel Inn, behind St. Clement's Church in the Strand."

Ape, Philip-lane, London Wall: here were formerly two galleried inns, the *Ape* and the *Cock*, of great antiquity: the sign of the former is preserved on the house No. 14.

Baptist's Head public-house, east side of St. John's-lane, Clerkenwell, just without the Priory-gate, is a fragment of an Elizabethan mansion, and until its renovation had an overhanging front grotesquely carved, and lit by large bay-windows, with painted glass: some of the interior scroll-paneling remains. This house was the residence of Sir Thomas Forster, Knt., one of the judges of the Court of Common Pleas; he died in 1612, and his arms, sculptured upon the chimney-piece of the present tap-room, have been collated in Cromwell's *Clerkenwell*. The sign may have been chosen in compliment to Sir Baptist Hicks; and the public-house is said to have been frequented by Samuel Johnson and Oliver Goldsmith in their transactions at Cave's printing-office over St. John's Gate, which see.

Bell, Great Carter-lane, Doctors' Commons: hence, Oct. 25, 1598, Richard Quiney addressed to his "loveing good ffrend and countryman, Mr. Wm. Schackespere," (then living in Southwark, near the Bear-garden,) for a loan of thirty pounds; which letter we have seen in the possession of Mr. R. Bell Wheler, at Stratford-upon-Avon: it is believed to be the only existing letter addressed to Shakspere. The *Bell* inn has disappeared, but has given name to Bell-yard.

Bell, Warwick-lane, Newgate-street: here Archbishop Leighton, the steady advocate of peace and forbearance, died 1684.

"He often used to say, that if he were to choose a place to die in, it should be an inn; it looking like a pilgrim's going home, to whom this world was all as an inn, and who was weary of the noise and confusion in it. * * * And he obtained what he desired."—Burnet's *Own Times.*

Bell Savage, or *Belle Sauvage*, Ludgate-hill, is a specimen of the players' inn-yard before our regular theatres were built. The landlord's token, issued between 1648 and 1672, bears an Indian woman holding a bow and arrow. The sign is thus traced:

"As for the Bell Savage, which is the sign of a savage man standing by a bell, I was formerly very much puzzled upon the conceit of it, till I accidentally fell into the reading of an old romance translated out of the French, which gives an account of a very beautiful woman who was found in a wilderness, and is called in the French 'la Belle Sauvage,' and is every where translated by our countrymen the Bell Savage."—*Spectator*, No. 28.

The sign, however, was originally a bell hung within a hoop, as proved by a grant *temp.* Henry VI., wherein John French gives to Joan French, widow, his mother, "all that tenement or inn called

Savage's Inn, otherwise called the Bell on the Hoop." In the *London Gazette*, 1676, it is termed *"* an antient inn." Stow affirms it to have been given to the Cutlers' Company by one Isabella Savage; but their records state by Mrs. Craythorne (see CUTLERS' HALL, p. 362). Here Sir Thomas Wyat's rebellion was stopped.

"And he (Wyet) himself came in at Te(mple Bar, and) soo downe alle Fletstrete, and soo un-to the Belle Savage. And then was his trayne (attacked at) the commandment of the erle of Pembroke, and sartayne of hys men slayne. And whan (he saw) that Ludgatte was shutt agayne hym, he departed, saynge, ' I have kepte towche,' and soo went (back) agayne; and by the Tempulle barre he was tane, and soo brought by watter unto the (Tower) of London."—*Chronicle of the Grey Friars of London.*

Fuller, in his *Church History*, states that after Wyat's adherents had forsaken him, he flung himself on a bench opposite the Bell Savage, and began to repent the rashness of his enterprise, and lament his folly. He was summoned by an herald to submit, which he agreed to do, but would yield only to a gentleman;—and afterwards surrendered to Sir Maurice Berkeley.

In Bell-Savage-yard lived Grinling Gibbons, "where he carved a pot of flowers which shook surprisingly with the motion of the coaches that passed by."— *Walpole.*

Blossoms, Lawrence-lane, Cheapside, " corruptly Bosoms Inn," hath to sign ' St. Laurence the Deacon,' in a border of blossoms or flowers," which, says the legend, sprung up " on the spot of his cruel martyrdom." This was one of the inns hired for the retinue of Charles V. on his visit to London in 1522, when " xx. beddes and a stable for ix. horses" were ordered here.

Bolt-in-Tun, Fleet-street, No. 64, in a grant to the White Friars in 1443, is termed "Hospitium vocatum Le Boltenton." In Whitefriars-street, No. 10, is the *Black Lion*, a small inn-yard with exterior wooden balustraded gallery, &c.

Bull, Bishopsgate, in its galleried yard, accommodated audiences for our early actors, before the building of licensed theatres. Tarlton frequently played here.

Bull and Mouth, St. Martin's-le-Grand, now the Queen's Hotel, was rebuilt in 1830: the centre is of stone, and has boldly sculptured a Bull and Mouth, above which are the bust of Edward VI. and the arms of Christ's Hospital, to which the ground belongs. The old inn was in Bull-and-Mouth-street; and the sign is corrupted from Boulogne Mouth, in commemoration of the destruction of the French flotilla at the mouth of Boulogne harbour, by Henry VIII, in 1544.

Clerkenwell. In St. John-street is the *Cross Keys*, where the carrier of Daintree lodged in 1637; Hatton mentions the *Three Cups*, near Hicks's Hall. Here also are the *Golden Lion* and the *Windmill*; and in Woodbridge-street was the *Red Bull* inn, the yard once the pit of the Red Bull Theatre. (See CLERKENWELL, p. 187.)

Coach and Horses, at the entrance to Bartholomew Close, is a portion of the ancient priory, probably the *hospitium*, at the end of the north cloister: the first floor has an arched roof and 16th-century cornice; the tap-room has an Early-English window; and the beer-cellar, a crypt, has a 12th-century clustered column. Of St. Bartholomew's, also, exist the prior's house, (see p. 240,) and the hall, with an ancient timbered roof, now used as a tobacco-manufactory. Close by is the monastery kitchen, from which a subterranean passage, in our time, communicated with the church: it has two paneled rooms, one with a vaulted roof and carved mantel-piece. (See Archer's *Vestiges of Old London*, part v.)

Cock, in Tothill-street, is probably the most ancient domestic edifice in Westminster: it is built entirely of timber, and at the back is a long inn-yard, with heavy timber sheds. The upper part of the ouse consists of one story, in which are several rooms on different vels, one of which remains in its original state, a curious specimen of a early timbered room, being entirely of chestnut-wood : the ascent to ese rooms is by a narrow twisted staircase.   The exterior is very picresque, although plastered and painted.   The house is entered by a escent of three steps : in the parlour is a massive oak carving of the doration of the Magi, of Flemish work, well executed and painted the life.   Another piece of carved work, more in the high German anner, an alto-relievo of Abraham offering up Isaac, is preserved in an ljoining room.   The *Cock* is said to have been frequented by the ilders of Henry VII.'s Chapel ; and there is a further tradition that it as the pay-table of the workmen at the building of the Abbey, *temp.* lenry III.   In 1845, Mr. Archer found in the kitchen the old sign of e Royal Arms, now placed upon the front of the house; and which, ith the Flemish carving and ancient bedchamber, are engraved in the *estiges of Old London*, part vi.   From this house started the first xford coach ; and a portrait of its original driver is shewn here.

Cross Keys, Gracechurch-street : here Banks exhibited his wonderl horse, Marocco ; the spectators being mostly in the galleries.   This gn, and the *Cross Keys* in Wood-street, are derived from the adjoing churches of St. Peter.

Elephant and Castle, Newington Butts, was a noted stage-coach use until the railway times ; and was originally a low-built roadside inn, ith outer gallery, a drawing of which hangs in the present tavern. djoining was a large sectarian chapel, inscribed in gigantic capitals, ΓHE HOUSE OF GOD !' held by the dupes of Joanna Southcott, whose eams and visions were painted upon the walls.

Four Swans, Bishopsgate-street Without, is perhaps the most perct old London inn, its galleries being entire.   Hobson, the Camidge carrier, put up here.

"This memorable man stands drawn in fresco at an inn (which he used) in shopsgate-street, with an hundred-pound bag under his arm, with this inscripn upon the said bag :

'The fruitful mother of a hundred more.' "—*Spectator*, No. 509.

George and Blue Boar, Holborn, is associated with a great event in r history : here was intercepted Charles I.'s letter, by which Ireton scovered it to be the King's intention to destroy him and Cromwell, hich discovery brought about Charles's execution.   Nearly opposite e *George and Blue Boar* was the *Red Lion*, the largest inn in Holrn ; and where the bodies of Cromwell, Ireton, and Bradshawe were rried from Westminster Abbey, and next day dragged on sledges to burn—a retributive coincidence worthy of note.   In old St. Giles's urch was " a red lyon painted in glasse, given by the inneholder of Red Lyon." (*Aubrey*).

George, Snowhill, is a relic of the time when this hill was the only ghway from Holborn-bridge eastward ; the house appears to have en an extensive inn for carriers at a very early date, and

" St. George that swing'd the dragon,
And sits on his horseback at mine hoste's door,"

ough much dilapidated, is a good specimen of a carved-stone sign.

Gerard's Hall, Basing-lane and Bread-street, Cheapside, replaced ancient Hall of the Gisors, the fine Norman crypt of which remained a wine-cellar ; but, with the superstructure, was removed in 1852, orming New Cannon-street. (See CRYPTS, p. 241.)

Green Man, Oxford-street, was formerly the Farthing Pye-house, the top of Portland-row, kept by Price, the noted rolling-pin and salt-box player: it was then a low public-house, much frequented by company from masquerades at the Pantheon.

Half-way House, Kensington-road, opposite the site of the building for the Great Exhibition of 1851, and near the Prince of Wales's Gate, Hyde Park, was removed in 1846 at an expense of 3050*l.*, in addition to the purchase of the fee.

Holborn Hill. The *Rose* has disappeared within our recollection: from this inn, Taylor the Water-poet started in the Southampton coach for the Isle of Wight, 19th October, 1647, while Charles I. was there:

> " We took one coach, two coachmen, and four horses,
> And merrily from London made our courses,
> We wheel'd the top of the heavy hill call'd Holborn,
> (Up which hath been full many a sinful soul borne,)
> And so along we jolted past St. Giles's,
> Which place from Brentford six or seven miles is."
> Taylor's *Travels from London to the Isle of Wight*, 1647.

The *Old Bell*, Holborn, bears the arms of Fowler, of Islington, viz. azure, on a chevron, argent, between three herons, as many crosses formée gules. These arms also occur on a building supposed to have been the lodge of Fowler's house in Islington, of which remains exist.

King's Arms, Leadenhall-street, No. 122: in the reign of William III., Sir John Fenwick and others met here to plan the restoration of James II.

Oxford Arms, Warwick-lane, Newgate-street, was the inn of Edward Bartlet, Oxford carrier, who removed here, after the Great Fire of 1666, from the *Swan* at Holborn-bridge.

Paul Pindar's Head, corner of Half-moon-alley, No. 160 Bishopsgate-street Without, was the mansion of Sir Paul Pindar, the wealthy merchant, contemporary with Sir Thomas Gresham. The house was built towards the end of the 16th century, with a wood-framed front and caryatid brackets, and the principal windows bayed, their lower fronts enriched with panels of carved work. In the first-floor front room is a fine original ceiling in stucco, in which are the arms of Sir Paul Pindar. In the rear of these premises, within a garden, was formerly a lodge, of corresponding date, decorated with four medallions, containing figures in Italian taste. (See p. 322.)

Piccadilly Inns. At the east end were formerly the *Black Bear* and *White Bear* (originally the *Fleece*), nearly opposite each other. The *Black Bear* was taken down 1820. The *White Bear* remains; it occurs in St. Martin's parish-books 1685: here Chatelain and Sullivan, the engravers, died; and Benjamin West, the painter, lodged the first night after his arrival from America. Strype mentions the *White Horse Cellar* in 1720; and the booking-office of the *New White-Horse Cellar* is to this day in " the cellar." The *Three Kings* stables gateway, No. 75, has two Corinthian pilasters, stated by D'Israeli to have belonged to Clarendon House: "the stable-yard at the back presents the features of an old galleried inn-yard, and it is noted as the place from which General Palmer started the first Bath mail-coach." (J. W. Archer: *Vestiges*, part vi.) The *Hercules' Pillars* (a sign which meant that no habitation was to be found beyond it) stood a few yards west of Hamilton-place, and is mentioned as one extremity of London by Wycherly, in 1676. Here Squire Western "placed his horses" when he arrived in London with the fair Sophia (see *Tom Jones*); here "the horses of many of the quality stood;" and it became the scene of fashionable dinner-parties of officers of the army, often headed by the Marquis of Granby. The *Hercules' Pillars*, and another roadside inn the *Triumphant Car*, were standing about 1797, and were mostly frequented by soldiers. Two other Piccadilly inns, the *White Horse* and *Half-moon*, have given names to streets.

Pied Bull, Church-row, Islington, traditionally the residence of Sir Walter Raleigh, and in the Elizabethan style, was taken down in 1826-7. The late front was modern; but the parlour (the original dining-room) had an elaborately-carved chimney-piece, with figures of Faith, Hope, and Charity; and a stuccoed ceiling, with personifications of the Five Senses. In a window were painted the arms of Sir John Miller, who lived here 1634; and a bunch of green leaves above the shield was popularly regarded as the tobacco-plant introduced by Raleigh.

Queen's Head, Lower-street, Islington, was a still more perfect Elizabethan house than the above. The walls were strong timber framework, filled in with laths and plaster; the three stories projected, and the windows were supported by carved brackets; the entrance-porch being ornamented by caryatides and Ionic scrolls. The interior had paneled wainscot, and stuccoed ceilings of rich design. The house has been rebuilt, and portions of the woodwork are preserved.

Pindar of Wakefield, Gray's-Inn-road, was a roadside inn in Aubrey's time, 1685, who mentions the yellow-flowered Neapolitan bankcresses growing there, as well as on the ruins of London, after the Great Fire of 1666. This plant is the London Rocket mentioned at p. 57.

Rose of Normandy, on the east side of High-street, Marylebone, built in the 17th century, is the oldest house in the parish, and has the original exterior, staircase, and balusters. In the rear was formerly a bowling-green, enclosed with walls set with fruit-trees and quickset hedges, " indented like town-walls."

Saracen's Head, Snow-hill (actually in Skinner-street), and of old " without Newgate," was in Stow's time "a fair and large inn for the receipt of travellers."

Saracen's Head, Friday-street, Cheapside, adjoined St. Matthew's Church, and No. 5, said to have been the dwelling-house of Sir Christopher Wren. The inn consisted of three floors with open galleried fronts, besides the ground-floor: it was taken down in 1844; and upon its site, extending nearly to Old Change, large Manchester warehouses were erected. There was also a *Saracen's Head,* No. 5 Aldgate: it was once a common London sign; which Selden thus illustrates:

" When our countrymen came home from fighting with the Saracens, and were beaten by them, they pictured them with huge, big, terrible faces (as you still see the sign of the Saracen's head is), when in truth they were like other men. But this they did to save their own credit."—*Table-Talk.*

Southwark Inns. — Stow enumerates here " many fair inns for receipt of travellers, by these signs: the Spurr, Christopher, Bull, Queene's Head, Tabarde, George, Hart, King's Head," &c. Of these the most ancient is the *Tabard* (now *Talbot*), No. 75 High-street, opposite the Townhall. The tabard is a jacket or sleeveless coat, worn in times past by noblemen, with their arms embroidered on it, but now only by heralds, as their coat of arms in service. " This was the hostelry where Chaucer and the other pilgrims met together, and with Henry Baily, their hoste, accorded about the manner of their journey to Canterbury." (*Speght,* 1598.)

> " Befell that in that season, on a day
> At Southwark at the Tabard as I lay,
> Readie to wander on my Pilgrimage
> To Canterburie with devout courage,
> At night was come into that hosterie
> Well nine-and-twenty in a companie,
> Of sundrie folke, by adventure yfall
> In fellowship, and pilgrimes were they all,
> That toward Canterburie wouden ride:
> The chambers and the stables weren wide,
> And well we weren eased at the best." &c.—*Chaucer*

Within the *Tabard* was also the lodging of the Abbot of Hide, by Winchester, which, with the inn, was repaired, and the latter enlarged by Master J. Preston. Upon the brestsummer beam of the gateway facing the street was formerly inscribed: "This is the inne where Sir Jeffry Chaucer and the nine-and-twenty pilgrims lay in their journey to Canterbury, anno 1383." This was painted out in 1831, and was originally inscribed upon a beam across the road, whence swung the sign, removed in 1763, when the inscription was transferred to the gateway. The sign was changed about 1676, when, says Aubrey, "the ignorant landlord or tenant, instead of the ancient sign of the Tabard, put up the Talbot, or dog!" The buildings of Chaucer's time have disappeared, but were standing in 1602: the oldest remaining is of the age of Elizabeth; and the most interesting portion is a stone-coloured wooden gallery, in the front of which is a picture of the Canterbury Pilgrimage, said to be painted by Blake: immediately behind is "the Pilgrims' Room" of tradition, but only a portion of the ancient hall. The gallery formerly extended throughout the inn buildings; the inn facing the street was burnt in the Great Fire of Southwark: "this house," says Aubrey, "*remaining before the fire of* 1676, was an old timber house, probably coeval with Chaucer's time;" it is shewn in the oldest view of the Tabard extant, in Urry's *Chaucer*, 1720.[*]

The other inns named by Stow remain, except the Christopher; but they have mostly lost their galleries and other olden features. The *King's Head* sign was within our recollection a well-painted half-length of Henry VIII. At the *Hart* lodged Jack Cade on his arrival in Southwark, July 1, 1450; "for," says Fabyan, "he might not be suffered to enter the Citie:" again, of Cade's rebels, "at the Whyt Harte in Southwarke one Hawaydine of Sent Martyns was beheddyd." (*Chronicle of the Grey Friars of London.*)

Spread Eagle, Gracechurch-street, is mentioned by Taylor the Water-poet in his *Carrier's Cosmographie*, 1637.

Swan with Two Necks, Lad-lane, now Gresham-street, was long the head coach-inn and booking-office for the north. The sign has been referred to a corruption of two *nicks*, or the Vintners' Company's swan-marks on the bill; but this popular notion is discountenanced by Mr. Kempe, F.S.A.: are the two necks an heraldic monstrosity?

"The carriers of Manchester doe lodge at the Two-Neck'd Swan in Lad-lane," (Taylor's *Carrier's Cosmographie*, 1637), originally Lady's-lane.

Three Cups, Aldersgate-street, is mentioned by Hatton; with the same sign in St. John-street, near Hicks's Hall; in Bread-street, near the middle. Beaumont and Fletcher have "the Three Cups in St. Giles's;" and Winstanley mentions Richard Head at the same sign in Holborn, making verses over a glass of Rhenish.

White Hart Tavern, Bishopsgate-street, taken down in 1829, bore on the front the date 1480: it was three-storied, with overhanging upper floor, and occupied the site of "a faire inne for receipt of travellours, next unto the parish church of St. Buttolph" (*Stow*).

White Hart, corner of Welbeck-street, was long a detached public-house, where travellers customarily stopped for refreshment, and to examine their fire-arms, before crossing the fields to Lisson-green. The land westward to the bourn (whence the parish, now Marylebone, was named) was a deep marshy valley: here was Fenning's Folly, *upon the top of which* has been built a fishmonger's; the shop, now level with the street, having been the Folly upper story.

White Horse, Fetter-lane, was formerly the great Oxford house. (See FETTER-LANE, page 291.)

[*] Taylor the Water-poet mentions another *Tabard* inn, "neere the Conduit" in Gracechurch-street.

Whitefriars Inns. Among the lands and tenements in St. Dunstan's occur the *Bore's Hede*, rented at 4*l.*; *le Bolte and Tonne*, 4*l.*; and *le Blake Swanne*, 4*l.*; all in Fleet-street.

Yorkshire Stingo, New-road, has been celebrated for a century and a quarter, and appears in a plan dated 1757: here was held annually, on May 1, a fair, until suppressed as a nuisance.

INNS OF COURT AND CHANCERY.

The hostels or abodes of the practisers and students of the law before the reign of Edward II. were called *Inns of Court*, because their inhabitants belonged to the *King's Court*, first noticed on the Placita Rolls, 10th Richard I. One of these, Johnson's Inn, is said to have been at Dowgate; another in Fewter's (Fetter) lane; and a third in Paternoster-row. The Serjeants and Apprentices (of the Law) then each had his pillar in St. Paul's church, where he heard his client's case:

> " A serjeant of the law both ware and wise,
> That often had yben at the *Perwyse*."—Chaucer's *Canterbury Tales.*

And in the reign of Charles I., upon the making of serjeants, they went to St. Paul's in their formalities, and *chose their pillars.*

Sir John Fortescue, Chief-Justice to Henry VI., enumerates four Inns of Court—the Inner Temple, the Middle Temple, Lincoln's Inn, and Gray's Inn—and ten Inns of Chancery: the former frequented by the sons of nobility and wealthy gentry; and the latter by merchants and others, who had not the means of paying the greater expenses (about 20 marks per annum) of the Inns of Court. The first were called *apprenticii nobiliores*, the latter *apprenticii* only. On the working-days they applied themselves to the study of law; on the holydays to holy Scripture. They also learned singing and all kinds of harmony, dancing, and other noblemen's pastimes. The only punishment for misdeeds was expulsion (as is the case now), which was greatly dreaded.

In 1634, the four Inns of Court gave a grand masque to Charles I. and Queen Henrietta-Maria at Whitehall. (See page 272, where, for Seldon, read Selden.)

The Court of Star Chamber, however, took care of their morals by desiring the principals of the Inns of Court and Chancery not to suffer the students to be out of their houses after six o'clock at night, " without very great and necessary causes, nor to wear any kind of weapon;" and the Court records prove the Star Chamber to have committed to the Tower the Earl of Surrey, Sir Thomas Wyatt, and young Pickering, for breaking windows, and eating flesh in Lent.

In the reign of Philip and Mary it was ordained by all the four Inns of Court, " that none except knights and benchers should wear in their doublets or hose any light colours, save scarlet and crimson; nor wear any upper velvet cap, or any scarf or wings in their gowns, white jerkins, buskins, or velvet shoes, double cuffs in their shirts, feathers or ribbons in their caps; and that none should wear their study gowns in the City any farther than Fleet-bridge or Holborn-bridge; nor, while in Commons, wear Spanish cloak, sword and buckler, or rapier, or gowns and hats, or gowns girded with a dagger on the back." —Dugdale's *Origines Judiciales.*

The students in the reign of Henry VI. were: 4 Inns of Court, each 200 = 800; 10 Inns of Chancery, each 100 = 1000: total, 1800. In 1850 there were in the four Inns of Court upwards of 4000.

The Temple and other Inns of Court are closed on Holy Thursday, to prevent the parochial processions passing through, which might establish a public thoroughfare. The two Temples and Gray's Inn are extra-parochial, *i. e.* pay no poor-rates and maintain their own poor; but Lincoln's Inn has not entirely that exemption.

THE TEMPLE lies between Fleet-street and the Thames, north and south; and Whitefriars and Essex-street, east and west; divided by Middle Temple-lane into the Inner and Middle Temple, each having its hall, library, and garden, quadrangles, courts, &c. Originally there was also the Outer Temple, comprising Essex House and gardens.

The ancient hostels existed until 1346 (20th Edward III.), when the Knights Hospitallers of St. John of Jerusalem (to whom the forfeited estates of the rival brotherhood of the Templars had been granted by the Pope) demised the magnificent buildings, church, gardens, "and all the appurtenances that belonged to the Templars in London," to certain students said to have removed thither from Thaive's Inn, Holborn, in which part of the town the Knights Templars themselves had resided before the erection of their superb palaces on the Thames. In this New Temple, "out of the City and the noise thereof, and in the suburbs," between the King's Court at Westminster and the City of London, the studious lawyers lived in quiet, increasing in number and importance; so that, although the mob of Wat Tyler's rebellion plundered the students, and destroyed almost all their books and records ("To the Inns of Court! down with them all!" *Jack Cade*), it became necessary to divide the Inn into two separate bodies, the Hon. Societies of the Inner and Middle Temple; having separate halls, but using the same church, and holding their houses as tenants of the Knights Hospitallers until the Dissolution by Henry VIII., and thenceforth of the Crown by lease. In the sixth year of James I. the two Temples were granted by letters patent to the then Chancellor of the Exchequer, the Recorder of London, and others, the bankers and treasurers of the Inner and Middle Temple, which, by virtue of this grant, are held to this day by an incorporated society of the "students and practisers of the laws of England."

The INNER TEMPLE is entered from Fleet-street by a gateway, built 5th James I., beneath No. 17 Fleet-street (see p. 308), by Inner Temple-lane: at No. 1 lived Dr. Johnson from 1760 to 1765; the door-case is inscribed, "Dr. Johnson's Staircase." At the foot of the lane is the magnificent western doorway of the church (described at pp. 161-3); and westward are the cloisters, built by Wren after the fire of 1678, which fire Titus Oates pretended to the Council was "a contrivance."

"Some gentlemen of the Inner Temple would not endeavour to preserve the goods which were in the lodgings of absent persons, nor suffer others to do it, 'because,' they said, 'it was against the law to break up any man's chamber!'."—Lord Clarendon's *Own Life*, p. 355.

Upon the broad terrace facing the garden are the Library (containing Bacon's *History of the Alienation Office*, in MS.), and the Parliament Chamber in the Tudor style, completed by Smirke, R.A. in 1835; adjoining is the Hall, built upon the site of a structure of the age of Edward III. Here are full-length portraits of Coke and Littleton; and an emblematic Pegasus, by Sir James Thornhill. Here dinner is served to the members of the Inn daily during term-time; the masters of the bench dining on the *state* or *dais*, and the barristers and students at long tables extending down the hall to the carved screen at the western end. On grand days are present the judges, who dine in succession with each of the four Inns of Court.

"At the Inner Temple, on certain grand occasions, it is customary to pass huge silver goblets (loving cups) down the table, filled with a delicious composition immemorially termed 'sack,' consisting of sweetened and exquisitely flavoured white wine: the butler attends its progress to replenish it, and each student is restricted to a *sip*. Yet it chanced not long since at the Temple, that, though the number present fell short of seventy, thirty-six quarts of the liquid were consumed!"—*Quarterly Review*, 1836, No. 110.

The gentlemen of the Inner Temple were of old famed for their plays, masques, and revels, and sumptuous entertainments. Christmas, Halloween, Candlemas, and Ascension-day, were anciently kept with great splendour in the Hall. In 1661 Charles II. dined here, and was received with *twenty violins*, dinner being served by fifty gentlemen of the society in their gowns. Next year the Duke of York and Prince Rupert were admitted members. For these feasts, the master of the revels arranged the dancing and music: after the play, a barrister sang a *song* to the judges and serjeants; and dancing was commenced by the judges and benchers round the sea-coal fire. This dance is satirised in Buckingham's witty play of the *Rehearsal;* and the revels have been ridiculed by Dr. Donne in his *Satires,* Prior in his *Alma,* and Pope in the *Dunciad:*

"The judge to dance, his brother serjeant calls."

Sir Christopher Hatton, with four other students of the Inner Temple, wrote the play of *Tancred and Gismund,* which, in 1568, was acted by that Society before the Queen. Sir Christopher wrote the fourth act, signed "*Composuit Mr. Hatton:*" it was first printed in 1592, and there is a copy among the Garrick plays in the British Museum.

The last revel in any of the Inns of Court was that held Feb. 2, 1733, in the Inner Temple Hall, in honour of Mr. Talbot, a bencher, having the Great Seal delivered to him. A large gallery built over the screen was filled with ladies; and music in the little gallery at the upper end of the Hall played all dinner-time. After dinner, began the play *Love for Love,* and the farce of *The Devil to Pay,* by actors from the Haymarket. After the play, the Lord Chancellor, the Master, Judges, and Benchers retired into their Parliament Chamber; in half an hour they returned to the Hall, and led by the Master of the Revels, formed a ring, and danced, or rather walked, round the fire-place, according to the old ceremony, three times; the ancient song, accompanied with music, being sung by one Tony Aston, dressed in a bar-gown. This was followed by dancing, in which the ladies from the gallery joined; then a collation was served, and the company returned to dancing. The Prince of Wales was present.

Among the eminent members were Audley, Lord Chancellor to Henry VIII.; Nicholas Hare (who built Hare-court), Master of the Rolls to Queen Mary; Littleton and Coke (in the reign of James I. the Temple was nicknamed "my Lord Coke's shop"); Sir Christopher Hatton, Selden, Heneage Finch, Judge Jeffreys, and Sir William Follett; and the poets Beaumont and Cowper. Speght's statement that Chaucer studied here is much disputed. Among the Readers was "the judicious Hooker," of whom, in 1851, a memorial bust was placed at the south-west angle of the choir of the Temple Church.

"The view from the Temple Gardens, when, on the opposite side of the river, the eye ranged over the green marshes and gradually rising round to the Surrey hills, and the rich oak and beech woods that clothed them, must have been beautiful." (Pearce's *Inns of Court.*) The public are admitted to the Inner Temple Garden, about 3 acres, in summer evenings from 6 to 9: it is already described at p. 321. Towards its south-eastern corner are the New Paper Buildings, of red brick and stone, erected 1848, by Sydney Smirke, A.R.A., with overhanging oriels and angle turrets, assimilating to Continental examples of the Tudor style.

The MIDDLE TEMPLE, west of the lane, is entered from Fleet-street by a red-brick and stone-fronted gate-house, built by Wren, 1684, "in the style of Inigo Jones, and very far from inelegant" (*Ralph*). It occupies the site of the gate-house erected by Sir Amias Paulet, as a fine imposed by Wolsey, whose prisoner he was; and which he garnished with cardinal's hats and arms to appease "his old unkind displeasure." Abutting on the garden (see page 321) is Middle Temple Hall, built 1562-72, in the treasurership of Plowden, the jurist:

it is 100 feet long, 40 feet wide, and upwards of 60 feet in height, and has a fine open timber roof, which omits the principal arched rib, and multiplies the pendants and smaller curves; it is very scientifically constructed, and contains a vast quantity of timber. There is also a Renaissance carved screen and music-gallery, dight with Elizabethan armour and weapons; on the side windows are emblazoned the arms of eminent members, as also on the great bay-windows, on the dais or state; above hang portraits of Charles I. and II.; James II. when Duke of York; William III., Queen Anne, and George II.: the central portrait, by Vandyke, of Charles I. on horse-back, is claimed as an original, as are also the same portraits in Windsor and Warwick Castles. Around are imitative bronze busts of the twelve Cæsars; and on the dais, marble busts of Lords Eldon and Stowell, by Behnes. The oaken tables extend from end to end: " they cut their meat on wooden trenchers, and drink out of green earthen pots" (*Hatton*, 1708). In this noble hall was performed Shakspeare's *Twelfth Night*, as recorded in the table-book of John Manningham, a student of the Middle Temple: " Feb. 2, 1601(2). At our feast we had a play called 'Twelfth Night, or what you will.'"— " It is yet pleasant to know that there is one locality remaining where a play of Shakspere was listened to by his contemporaries, and that play *Twelfth Night*." (Charles Knight: *Pictorial Edit. Shakspere*.) The Middle Temple feasts were sumptuous: Evelyn describes that of 1688 " so very extravagant and great, as the like had not been seen at any time;" he condemns the revels as " an old but riotous custom." Aubrey was admitted 1646; here and at Trinity College, Oxford, he " enjoyed the greatest felicity" of his life. Among his " Accidents:" " St. John's Night, 1673, in danger of being run through with a sword by a young templar, at Burges' chamber in the Middle Temple." (Britton's *Memoir of Aubrey*, pp. 14, 19.) Ashmole was called to the bar in the Middle Temple, in 1660. (See page 309.)

Among the eminent members were Plowden, the jurist; Sir Walter Raleigh; Sir Thomas Overbury; John Ford, the dramatist; Sir Edward Bramston, who had for his chamber-fellow Mr. Edward Hyde (afterwards Lord Chancellor Clarendon); Bulstrode Whitelocke; Lord Keeper Guildford; Lord Chancellor Somers; Wycherley and Congreve; Shadwell and Southerne; Sir William Blackstone; Dunning, Lord Ashburton; Lord Chancellor Eldon and Lord Stowell; Edmund Burke; Richard Brinsley Sheridan; and the poets Cowper and Moore. Oliver Goldsmith had chambers in Garden-court, at the window of which he loved to sit and watch the rooks in Temple Garden; Goldsmith also lived in Brick-court, No. 2, second floor, over the chambers of Blackstone, then finishing vol. 4 of his *Commentaries*.

Sun-dials.—There remain three dials, with mottoes: Temple-lane, " Pereunt et imputantur;" Essex-court, " Vestigia nulla retrorsum;" Brick-court, " Time and tide tarry for no man:" in Pump-court and Garden-court are two dials without mottoes; and in each Temple Garden is a pillar dial. Upon the old brick house at the east end of Inner Temple-terrace, removed in 1828, was another dial, with this quaint inscription: " Begone about your business."

LINCOLN'S INN, on the west side of Chancery-lane, occupies the site of the palace of Ralph Neville, Bishop of Chichester, and Lord High Chancellor to Henry III.; and of the ancient monastery of Black Friars in Holborn, granted to Henry de Lacy, Earl of Lincoln, who built thereon his town-house, or *inn*: soon after whose death, in 1312, it became an Inn of Court, named from him Lincoln's Inn; when also the greater part of the estate of the see of Chichester was leased to students of the law. (See CHANCERY-LANE, p. 70.) The Earl of Lincoln's garden, with a pond or vivary for pike, is noticed at p. 320.

The precincts of Lincoln's Inn comprise the old buildings, about 500 feet frontage in Chancery-lane, erected between the reigns of Henry VII. and James I. The Gatehouse, a fine specimen of Tudor brick-work, was built mostly at the expense of Sir Thomas Lovell, "double reader," and treasurer of the Society. The entrance is an obtusely-pointed arch, originally vaulted, between two four-storied square towers. The bricks and tiles used in the Gatehouse and Hall were made from clay dug from a piece of ground on the west side of the Inn, and called the Coneygarth, "well stocked with rabbits and game."

Over the Gatehouse arch are painted and gilt the royal arms of King Henry VIII. within the garter, and crowned, having on the dexter side the arms of Henry Lacy, Earl of Lincoln; [and on the sinister side the arms and quarterings of Sir Thomas Lovell, K.G.; beneath, on a riband, Anno Dom. 1518. Lower down is a tablet denoting an early repair, inscribed: "Insignia hæc refecta et decorata Johanne Hawles Armig. Solicitat. General. Thesaurario 1695." The original doors of oak, put up 6 Eliz. 1564, still remain. In the court on the west is the ancient Hall (the oldest structure in the Inn), and the old kitchen, now chambers; on the north is the Chapel (described at p. 170); and in the centre are the two Vice-Chancellors' Courts, built 1841.—Spilsbury's *Lincoln's Inn*.

This and the three other courts of chambers were chiefly built *temp.* James I. At No. 13, from 1645 to 1650, lived John Thurloe, Secretary of Oliver Cromwell. In these chambers, it is said, was discussed early in 1659, by Cromwell and Thurloe, Sir Richard Willis's plot for seizing Charles II: in the same room sat Thurloe's assistant, young Morland, at his desk, apparently asleep, and whom Cromwell would have dispatched with his sword, had not Thurloe assured him that Morland had sat up two nights, and was certainly fast asleep: he, however, divulged the plot to the king, and thus saved Charles's life. The narrative is given by Birch in his Life of Thurloe, but rests upon questionable evidence. Here was discovered in the reign of William III. a collection of papers, concealed in a false ceiling of the apartment: they form the principal part of Dr. Birch's "Thurloe State-Papers." There is a tradition that Cromwell had chambers in or near the Gatehouse, but his name is not in the registers of the Society: his son Richard was admitted a student 23 Charles II.

Sun-dials.—On two of the old gables are, 1. A southern dial, restored in 1840, which shews the hours by its gnomon from 6 A.M. to 4 P.M., and is inscribed, "Ex hoc momento pendet æternitas." 2. A western dial, restored in 1794, the Right Hon. William Pitt Treasurer, and again [restored in 1848, from the different situation of its plane, only shews the hours from noon till night; inscription, "Qua redit, nescitis horam."

The Old Hall, rebuilt 22 Henry VII. 1506, occupies the site of the original Hall, and has a louvre on the roof, date 1552, and an embattled parapet; opposite the entrance, at the south end, is the old kitchen. The "goodly hall" is about 71 feet in length and 32 in breadth; height about equal to the breadth. It has on each side three large three-light windows, with arched and cusped heads; and a great oriel, transomed, with arched head and cusps: at each end the room was lengthened 10 feet in 1819, when the open oak roof was removed, and the present incongruous coved plaster ceiling substituted. At the lower end is a massive screen, erected in 1565, grotesquely carved, and emblazoned with the full achievements of King Charles II., James Duke of York, Prince Rupert, the Earl of Manchester, Lord Henry Howard, and Lord Newport, date Feb. 29, 1671: at the end of the Hall, in panels, are the arms of distinguished members of the Society, including Lords Mansfield, Loughborough, Ellenborough, Brougham, &c. On the dais is the seat of the Lord Chancellor. The *commons* of the Society were held here until the building of the New Hall.

Among the earliest distinguished members of Lincoln's Inn were,

Sir John Fortescue, *temp.* Henry VI.; Sir Thomas More, who removed here from New Inn; Lambard and Spelman, the antiquaries; the learned John Selden; Noy, Attorney-General to Charles I.; Lenthall, the Cromwellian Speaker; and the great Lord Chancellor Egerton.

In this ancient Hall were held all the revels of the Society, their masques and christmasings; when the benchers laid aside their dignity, and dancing was enjoined for the students, as conducive " to the making of gentlemen more fit for their books at other times" (Dugdale's *Origines*); and by an order 7th of James I. "the under-barristers were, by decimation, put out of commons, for example's sake, because they had not danced on the Candlemas-day preceding, when the judges were present." Of Christmas 1661 Pepys writes: "The king (Charles II.) visited Lincoln's Inn to see the revells there; there being, according to an old custome, a prince and all his nobles, and other matters of sport and charge." Here were present Clarendon, Ormond, and Shaftesbury, at the revels of Hale, Ley, and Denham the poet; and the gloomy Prynne standing by. At these entertainments the Hall cupboard was set out with the Society's olden plate, which includes silver basins and ewers, silver cups and covers, a silver college-pot for festivals, and a large silver punch-bowl with two handles.

In 1671 Charles II. made a second visit, with his brother the Duke of York, Prince Rupert, and the Duke of Monmouth, who were entertained in the Hall, and admitted members of the Society, and entered their names in the admittance-book, which contains also the signatures of all members from the reign of Elizabeth to the present time. Sir Matthew Hale entered here student in 1629: he bequeathed a large collection of Mss. to the Library.

Not many years ago it was the custom at Lincoln's Inn for one of the servants, attired in his usual robes, to go to the threshold of the outer door about twelve or one o'clock, and exclaim three times, "*Venez manger!*"—when neither bread nor salt was upon the table.

New Square, southward of the ancient buildings, was completed in 1697, by Mr. Henry Serle, a bencher of the Inn: in the centre was formerly a Corinthian column, with a vertical sun-dial; and at the base were four Triton *jets-d'eau*: the area was enclosed and planted in 1845. In the reign of Charles II. this was open ground, known as Little Lincoln's Inn Fields, or Fickett's Fields: it is not part of the Inn.

The Stone Buildings, at the north-east extremity of the Inn, was partly built by Sir Robert Taylor, and was completed by Hardwick in 1845: the architecture is beautiful Corinthian. This is only part of a design, in 1780, for rebuilding the whole Inn; the drawings for which, in the possession of the Society, are by Sir John Leach (Master of the Rolls), originally a pupil of Sir Robert Taylor.

The Gardens were much curtailed by the building of the New Hall and Library; when disappeared " the walks under the elms," celebrated by Ben Jonson. The garden was enlarged, and the terrace-walk on the west was made, in 1663:

" To Lincoln's Inn, to see the new garden which they are making, which will be very pretty,—and to the walk under the chapel by agreement."—Pepys's *Diary.*

Into Lincoln's Inn walks Isaac Bickerstaff sometimes went instead of the tavern (*Tatler*, No. 13); and a solitary walk in the garden of Lincoln's Inn was a favour indulged in by several of the benchers, Isaac's intimate friends, and grown old with him in this neighbourhood (*Tatler*, No. 100).

The ruined gamester (*Tatler*, No. 13) in the morning borrows half-a-crown of the maid who cleans his shoes, "and is now gaming in Lincoln's-Inn Fields among the boys for farthings and oranges, until he has made up three pieces; and then he returns to White's, into the best company in town."

Among the officers of the Society is a " Master of the Walks." (See GARDENS, page 320.) And, in 1662, was revived the ancient custom of electing a Lord-Lieutenant, and Prince of the Grange.

On the western side of the garden, almost on the site of the Coney-garth, are the *New Hall* and *Library*, a picturesque group, finely situated for architectural effect, in the late Tudor style (*temp.* Henry VIII.), having a corresponding entrance-gate from Lincoln's-Inn Fields; architect, Philip Hardwick, R.A. The foundation-stone was

l April 20, 1843: the hall is arranged north and south, and the
rary east and west; the two buildings being connected by a vesti-
e, flanked by a drawing-room and council-room. The materials are
l bricks, intersected with black bricks in patterns, and stone dress-
s. The south end has a lofty gable, inscribed, in dark bricks, " P. H."
ilip Hardwick), and the date 1843; flanked on each side by a square
ver, battlemented; beneath are shields, charged with lions and
rines, the badges of the Society: between the towers is the great
ndow of the Hall, of seven lights, transomed, and the four-centred
h filled with beautiful tracery. On the apex of the gable, beneath a
opied pinnacle, is a statue of Queen Victoria; Thomas, sculptor.
e side buttresses are surmounted by octagonal pinnacles. The
f is leaded, and in its centre is an elegant louvre, surrounded by
der pinnacles bearing vanes; the capping has crockets and gurgoyles,
l is surmounted by a vane with direction-points in gilded metal-
rk — the whole very tasteful. The entrance to the Hall is at the
th-east tower, by a double flight of steps to the porch, above which
the arms of the Inn. Above is the clock, of novel and beautiful
ign, with an enriched pedimental canopy in metal-work.
The central building, the entrance to the Library and Great Hall, has
l oriels, and an octagonal embattled crown or lantern, filled with
nted glass, and reminding one of the octagon of Ely Cathedral.
om the esplanade is the entrance by flights of steps to a porch, the
le bearing the lion of the Earl of Lincoln holding a banner; and at
apex of the great gable of the library roof is a circular shaft, sur-
unted by an heraldic animal supporting a staff and banner. The
rary has large end oriels, of beautiful design, and five bay-windows
the north side; the lights being separated by stone compartments,
h boldly sculptured with heraldic achievements of King Charles II.
nes Duke of York, K.G., Queen Victoria, Prince Albert, K.G. (all
tors of the Society), and Albert Edward Prince of Wales. The
tresses dividing the bays are terminated by pillars, surmounted by
aldic animals. At the north-west angle of this front is an octagonal
l-turret. On the western front, towards Lincoln's-Inn Fields, the
stered chimneys have a beautiful effect: they are of moulded red
ck, resembling those at Eton College and Hampton Court Palace.
e bosses, gurgoyles, and armorial grotesque and foliated ornaments
oughout the building are finely sculptured.
Entering by the southern tower, the corridor is arranged on the
n of the college halls of the Universities, and has a buttery-hatch,
l stairs leading to the vaulted kitchen, 45 feet square and 25 feet high,
h one of the largest fire-places in England; adjoining are cellars for
hundred pipes of wine.
From the corridor, through a carved oak screen, you enter the
ll: length, 120 feet; width, 45 feet; height to the apex of roof, 62
. In size it exceeds the halls of the Middle Temple, Hampton
rt Palace, and Christ-church, Oxford; but is exceeded in length
he hall of Christ's Hospital, which is 187 feet. The upper part of
screen serves as the front of the gallery, between the arches of
ch, upon pedestals, in canopied niches, are costumed life-size figures
hese eminent members of the Society: Lord Chief-Justice Sir
tthew Hale; Archbishop Tillotson, one of the preachers of Lincoln's
; Lord Chief-Justice Mansfield; Lord Chancellor Hardwicke;
hop Warburton, one of the preachers; and Sir William Grant,
ter of the Rolls. The sides of the Hall are panelled with oak, and
cornice is enriched with gilding and colours. The five large stained-
s windows on either side contain, in the upper lights, the arms,
ts, and mottoes of distinguished members of the Society, chrono-

logically arranged, from 1450 to 1843; and the lower divisions are diapered with the initials " L. I." and the milrine. Above the windows is a cornice enriched with colour and gilding.

The roof is wholly of oak, and is divided into seven compartments by trusses, each large arch springing from stone corbels, and having two carved pendants (as in Wolsey's Hall at Hampton Court) at the termination of an inner arch, that springs from hammer-beams projecting from the walls. These pendants are illuminated blue and red, and gilt, and they each carry a chandelier to correspond. Between the wall trusses is a machicolated cornice, paneled and coloured.

On the northern wall, above the dais paneling, is the picture of Paul before Felix, painted in 1750 by Hogarth, and removed from a similar position in the Old Hall.* Mrs. Jameson describes this picture as curiously characteristic, not of the scene or of the chief personage, but of the painter. St. Paul, loaded with chains, and his accuser Tertullus, stand in front; and Felix, with his wife Drusilla, is seated on a raised tribunal in the background; near Felix is the high-priest Ananias. The composition is good; the heads are full of vivid expression—wrath, terror, doubt, attention; but the conception of character most ignoble and commonplace. (*Poetry of Sacred Art.*) At the opposite end of the hall is a noble marble statue, by Westmacott, of Lord Erskine, Chancellor in 1806.

On either side of the dais, in the oriel, is a sideboard for the upper or benchers' table; the other tables, ranged in gradation, two crosswise and five along the hall, are for the barristers and students, who dine here every day during term: the average number is 200; and of those who dine on one day or other during the term, " keeping commons," is about 500.

The western oriel window contains, in the upper lights, the armorial bearings of Ralph Neville, Bishop of Chichester; Henry Lacy, Earl of Lincoln; William de Haverhyll, Treasurer to King Henry III.; Edward Sulyard, Esq., by whom the inheritance of the premises of Lincoln's Inn was transferred to the Society in 1580; whose arms are also here—motto: " Longa professio est pacis jus." In the middle of the window are the arms of King Charles II. within the garter, and surmounted by the crown, with the supporters and motto; also the arms of James Duke of York and of Prince Rupert. On the other side, the quarrels of the whole window are diapered, like the other windows of the hall, with the milrine and L. I. The oriel window, on the eastern side, contains all the stained glass removed from the old hall, consisting of the armorial insignia of noblemen, legal dignitaries, &c. All the heraldic decorations, with the exception of the eastern oriel, are by Mr. Willement.—Spilsbury's *Lincoln's Inn*, pp. 104-5.

From the dais of the Hall large folding-doors open into the vestibule, east of which is the Council-chamber; and west, the Drawing-room: the stone chimney-pieces are finely sculptured. In the Drawing-room are portraits of Justice Glanville, 1598; Sir John Granville, Speaker of the House of Commons, 1640; Sir Matthew Hale, 1671, by M. Wright (acquired by the Society, with his collection of Mss.); Sir Richard Ransford, Lord Chief-Justice, K.B. 1676, by Gerard Soest; Lord Chancellor Hardwicke, 1737, after Ramsay; Lord Chancellor Bathurst, 1771, by Sir N. Dance; Sir John Skynner, Lord Chief Baron, 1771, by Gainsborough; Sir William Grant, Master of the Rolls, by Harlow; Francis Hargreave, Treasurer in 1813, by Sir Joshua Reynolds; and Sir H. Addington, Speaker of the House of Commons.

In the Council-room is a portrait of Sir John Franklin, of Mavourn,

---

* By the will of Lord Wyndham, Baron of Finglass, and Lord High Chancellor of Ireland, the sum of 200*l.* was bequeathed to the Society, to be expended in adorning the Chapel or Hall, as the benchers should think fit. At the recommendation of Lord Mansfield, Hogarth was engaged to paint the picture, which was at first designed for the chapel.—Spilsbury's *Lincoln's Inn*, p. 103.

eds, Knight, a master in chancery 33 years; ob. 1707. Here are also several copies from the old masters; and a Lady with a Guitar, by William Etty, R.A. The walls of both Council and Drawing-rooms re also hung with a valuable collection of engraved portraits of legal ignitaries, eminent prelates, &c.

The Library, 80 feet long, 40 feet wide, and 44 feet high, has an pen oak roof, of much originality. The projecting book-cases form eparate apartments for study, and have an iron balcony running round nem about midway, and another gallery over them against each wall. lach of the oriel windows displays arms of the present benchers; as lso the five northern windows, except the lower lights of the central ne, which are filled with the arms of Queen Victoria, of brilliant olour and broad treatment. The glass of the windows consists of nall circular panes, termed beryl glazing, of remarkable brilliancy.

The Society's valuable collection of Mss., mostly bequeathed by Sir Matthew Hale, are deposited in two rooms opening from the Library. The books and Mss. exceed 25,000: the collection of law books is the most complete in this country, and here are many important works on istory and antiquities. The Library, founded in 1497, is older than any ow existing in the metropolis; and many of the volumes still retain on rings, by which they were secured by rods to the shelves. The arly Year-books are chiefly in their original *oak* binding; and four f them belonged to William Rastell, nephew of Sir Thomas More. Among the other rarities are, Le Mirror de Justices per Andrew Horne, in a hand of the reign of James I.; Placita of the whole reign f Edward II. on vellum, written in the fourteenth century; two olumes of statutes on vellum, Edward III. and Henry V.; a MS. year-ook, Edward III.; the fourth volume of Prynne's Records, bought r 335l. by the Society at the Stowe sale, in 1849 (it was published the year of the Great Fire, when most of the copies were burnt); everal MSS. in the handwriting of Sir Matthew Hale, Archbishop Usher, and the learned Selden; a beautiful copy of the works of King Charles I., which had belonged to King Charles II.; Baron Maseres's opy of his "Scriptores Logarithmici," six vols. 4to; Charles Butler's ne copy of "Tractatus Universi Juris," with index, 28 vols. folio, &c. See Spilsbury's *Lincoln's Inn*, specially devoted to the Library; to hich carefully-written work we are much indebted.)

The New Hall and Library were inaugurated October 30, 1845, by Queen Victoria and Prince Albert, when Her Majesty held a levee in he Library, at which the Treasurer of the Inn, J. A. F. Simpkinson, as knighted; the Prince became a member of the Society, and with he Queen signed his name in the Admittance-book. Her Majesty and rince Albert then partook of an early banquet in the Great Hall; this eing the first visit of a sovereign to the Inn for nearly two centuries.

Lincoln's Inn is exempted from poor-rates as extra-parochial. The round on which the New Hall is built belonged, at the time of building, the parish of St. Giles in the Fields; but was, by agreement, subsenently severed from that parish, and annexed to the vill or township Lincoln's Inn, the Society paying annually a compensation to the arish for the rates.

GRAY'S INN, on the north side of Holborn, and west of Gray's-Inn-ne, appears to have been "a goodly house since Edward III.'s time" Stow). It was originally the residence of the noble family of Gray of Wilton, who, in 1505, sold to Hugh Denny, Esq. "the manor of Port-pole (one of the prebends belonging to St. Paul's Cathedral), otherwise alled Gray's Inn, four messuages, four gardens, the site of a windmill, ght acres of land, ten shillings of free rent, and the advowson of the antry of Portpoole." The manor was next sold to the prior and convent of East Sheen, in Surrey, who leased "the mansion of Portpoole" to "certain students of the law," at the annual rent of 6l. 13s. 4d.; and after the Dissolution by Henry VIII. the benchers of Gray's Inn were entered in the king's books as the fee-farm tenants of the Crown, at the same rent as paid to the monks of Sheen.

The principal entrance to Gray's Inn is from Holborn, by a gateway erected 1592, a fine specimen of early brickwork, leading to South-square (formerly Holborn-court), separated by the hall, chapel, and library from Gray's-Inn-square. Westward is Field-court, with a gate, now blocked up, to Fulwood's Rents (see page 318); and opposite is the lofty gate of the gardens; Verulam-buildings east, Raymond-buildings west; the northern boundary-wall being in King's-road.

The Hall was completed in 1560. It has an open oak roof, divided into seven bays by Gothic arched ribs, the spandrels and pendants richly carved; in the centre is an open louvre, pinnacled externally. The interior is wainscoted, and has an oaken screen, decorated with Tuscan columns, caryatides, &c. The windows are richly emblazoned with arms. The men of Gray's Inn had their masques and revels, and were "practisers" of gorgeous interludes and plenteous Christmasings: a comedy acted here Christmas 1527, written by John Roos, a student of the Inn, and afterwards serjeant-at-law, so offended Wolsey, that its author was degraded and imprisoned. Adjoining is the Chapel, probably on the site of the "chantry of Portpoole," wherein masses were daily sung for the soul of John, the son of Reginald de Gray, for which lands were granted to the prior and convent of St. Bartholomew, Smithfield: at their expense divine service was subsequently performed here on behalf of the society; and after the Dissolution, the chaplain's salary was paid out of the Augmentation Court. At the Reformation, the Popish utensils, with a pair of organs, were sold, but were restored by Mary; and by command of Henry VIII. was taken out a window, "wherein the image of St. Thomas à Becket was *gloriously* painted." Richard Sibbs, author of *the Bruised Reed*, was one of the preachers.

In 29 Elizabeth, for the better relief of the poor in Gray's-Inn-lane, alms were distributed thrice by the week at Gray's Inn gate.

James I. signified by the judges that none but *gentlemen of descent* should be admitted of Gray's Inn. The Readers had liberal allowances of wine and venison; vid. and viiid. was paid for each mess; and eggs and green sauce were the breakfast on Lenten-day; and beer did not exceed 6s. per barrel. Caps were compulsorily worn at dinner and supper; and hats, boots, and spurs, and standing with the back to the fire, in the hall, were forbidden under penalty. Dice and cards were only allowed at Christmas. Lodging double was customary in the old inn; and at a pension, 9 July, 21 Henry VIII., Sir Thomas Nevile accepted Mr. Attorney-General (Sir Christopher Hales) to be his bedfellow in his chamber here.

Gray's Inn has been noted for its exercises, called by Stow "Boltas Mootes," and putting of cases." Bailey defines "Bolting (in Gray's Inn), a kind of exercise, or arguing cases among the students." (*Dict.* 3d edit. 1737.) "Bolting is a term of art used in Gray's Inn, and applied to the bolting or arguing of *moot* cases" (Cowell's *Law Dict.*); and he argues the bolting of cases to be analogous to the *boulting* or sifting of meal through a bag. Judge Hale has, "beats and bolts out the truth." Danby Pickering, Esq. of Gray's Inn was the last who voluntarily resumed these mootings.

The Garden (Gray's-Inn-walks) was first planted about 1600, when Mr. Francis Bacon, after Lord Verulam, was treasurer. (See GARDENS, p. 321.) Howel, in a letter from Venice, June 5, 1621, speaks of Gray's-Inn-walks as the pleasantest place about London, with the choicest society; and they were in high fashion as a promenade and place of assignation in Charles II.'s time, when from Bacon's summer-house, on a mount, there was a charming view towards Highgate and Hampstead. The Garden was formerly open to the public, like those of the Inner Temple and Lincoln's Inn.

Hall the chronicler, and Gascoigne the poet, studied at Gray's
[In]n: Gascoigne and his fellow-student Kinwelmersh translated the
[J]ocasta of Euripides, which was acted in Gray's-Inn-hall 1566. Brad-
[sh]aw, president at the trial of Charles I., was a bencher. Sir Thomas
[H]olt was treasurer of Gray's Inn; and his son, Lord Chief-Justice
[H]olt, was entered upon the Society's books before he was ten years
[ol]d: he is Verus the magistrate, in the *Tatler*, No. 14.

Lord Burghley entered at Gray's Inn in 1541, and made genealogy
[hi]s special study. Sir Nicholas Bacon kept his terms here, was
[ca]lled to the bar in the Society, and was elected treasurer 1552; and his
[so]n Francis, Lord Verulam, was admitted here, and made an antient in
[15]76: here he sketched his great work the *Organon*, though law was
[hi]s principal study. In 1582, he was called to the bar; in 1586, made a
[be]ncher; in 1588, appointed Reader to the Inn; and in 1600, the Lent
[do]uble Reader: in the interval he wrote his *Essays*, dedicated "from
[m]y chamber at Graie's Inn, this 30 of Januarie, 1597." In 1583, he
[st]ood among the barristers at Temple Bar to welcome Queen Elizabeth
[in]to the City. Bacon had chambers in Gray's Inn when Lord Chancel-
[lo]r; and here he received the suitors' bribes, by which his name became
[ta]rnished with infamy. After his downfall and distress, when he had
[pa]rted with York House, he resided, during his visits to London, at his
[ol]d chambers in Gray's Inn; whence, in 1626, on a severe day, he went
[in] his coach to Highgate, took cold in stuffing a fowl with snow as an
[an]ti-putrescent, became too ill to return to Gray's Inn, and was carried
[to] the Earl of Arundel's house at Highgate, where he died within a
[w]eek. Lord Bacon is traditionally said to have lived in the large house
[fa]cing Gray's Inn garden-gates, where Fulke Greville, Lord Brooke,
[fr]equently sent him home-brewed beer from his house in Holborn.
[B]asil Montagu,* however, fixes Bacon's chambers on the site of No. 1
[G]ray's-Inn-square, first floor; the house was burnt Feb. 17, 1679, with
[8] other chambers. (*Historian's Guide*, 3d edit. 1688.) Lord Campbell
[sp]eculatively states that Bacon's chambers "remain in the same state
[as] when he occupied them, and are still visited by those who worship
[hi]s memory." (*Lives of the Lord Chancellors*, vol. ii. p. 274.) The
[as]sociation with Bacon is recorded in "Verulam-buildings:"

> " Whene'er through Gray's Inn porch I stray,
> I meet a spirit by the way;
>   *   *   *   *
> He tells me truly what I am—
> I walk with mighty Verulam."—*Town Lyrics*, by C. Mackay, 1848.

[Da]vid Jones, the patriotic Welsh judge, *temp.* Charles I., was of Gray's
[In]n; Romilly was also a member; and Southey was entered here on
[lea]ving Oxford. The students were formerly often refractory. Pepys
[wr]ites in May 1667: "Great talk of how the barristers and students
[of] Gray's Inn rose in rebellion against the benchers the other day, who
[ou]tlawed them, and a great deal to do; now they are at peace again."

Within Gray's-Inn-gate, next Gray's-Inn-lane, lived Jacob Tonson,
[wh]o published here Dryden's *Spanish Friar*, 1681, said to be the first
[wo]rk published by the Tonsons: Jacob was the second son of a barber-
[su]rgeon in Holborn. At Gray's-Inn-gate, also, lived Thomas Os-
[bo]rne, the bookseller, who gave 13,000*l.* for the *books* from the Harleian
[li]brary, for the binding of a portion of which Lord Oxford is stated by
[Ma]bdin to have paid 18,000*l.*

The *Gray's-Inn Journal*, in the style of the *Spectator*, was started

* Mr. Montagu, who died in 1852, possessed a glass and silver-handled fork,
[wit]h a shifting silver spoon-bowl, which once belonged to Lord Bacon, whose
[cre]st, a boar, modelled in gold, surmounts the fork-handle.

by Arthur Murphy in 1752, and continued weekly two years. Murphy studied the law, was refused admission to the societies of the Temple and of Gray's Inn because he had been an actor, but was admitted of Lincoln's Inn.

In Gray's Inn lived Dr. Rawlinson ("Tom Folio" of the *Tatler*, No. 158), who stuffed four chambers so full with books, that he slept in the passage. In Holborn-court (now South-square) were the chambers of Joseph Ritson, the literary antiquary and rigid Pythagorean: the site is now occupied by the libraries, between the hall and chapel, built by Wigg and Pownall, in 1841; style, elegant Italian.

Admission to the Inns, and Call to the Bar.—The four Inns of Court, viz. the two Temples, Lincoln's Inn, and Gray's Inn, have exclusively the power of conferring the degree of Barrister-at-Law, requisite for practising as an advocate or counsel in the Superior Courts. Lincoln's Inn is generally preferred for students who contemplate the Equity Bar; it being the locality of Equity Counsel and Conveyancers, and of Equity Courts or Courts of Chancery. If the student design to practise the common law, either immediately as an advocate at Westminster, the assizes, and sessions, or as a special pleader (a learned person who, having kept his terms, is allowed to draw legal forms and pleadings, though not actually at the bar), his choice lies usually between the Inner Temple, the Middle Temple, and Gray's Inn, though he may adopt Lincoln's Inn. The Inner Temple, from its formerly insisting on a classical examination before admission, became more exclusive than the Middle Temple or Gray's Inn. Gray's Inn is numerously attended by Irish students, and has produced some of the greatest luminaries at the Irish Bar, including Daniel O'Connell.

To procure admission to either of these Inns, the student must obtain the certificate of two barristers, coupled in the Middle Temple with that of a bencher, to the effect that the applicant is a fit person to be received into the Inn for the purpose of being called to the Bar. Once admitted, the student has the use of the Library, and is entitled to a seat in the church or chapel of the Inn, and to have his name set down for chambers. He is then required to keep *commons*, by dining in the hall for twelve terms (four terms occur in each year); on commencing which, he must deposit with the treasurer 100*l.*, to be retained with interest until he is *called;* but members of the Universities are exempt from this deposit. The student must also sign a bond with sureties for the payment of his commons and term-fees. In all the Inns no person can be called unless he is above twenty-one years of age and three years' standing as a student. The *call* is made by the benchers in council; after which the student becomes a barrister, and takes the usual oath at Westminster. In certain Inns, however, the student must, before his call, attend certain lectures, which are a revival of the old readings, without their festivities.

A Hall Dinner is a formal scene. At five or half-past five o'clock, the barristers, students, and other members in their gowns, having assembled in the hall, the benchers enter in procession to the dais; the steward strikes the table three times, grace is said by the treasurer or senior bencher present, and the dinner commences: the benchers observe somewhat more style at their table than the other, members do at theirs: the general repast is a tureen of soup, a joint of meat, a tart, and cheese, to each mess consisting of four persons; each mess is also allowed a bottle of port-wine. The dinner over, the benchers, after grace, retire to their own apartment. At the Inner Temple, on May 29, a gold cup of "sack" is handed to each member, who drinks to the happy restoration of Charles II. At Gray's Inn a similar custom prevails, but the toast is the memory of Queen Elizabeth. The Inner Temple Hall waiters are called *panniers*, from the *panarii* who attended the Knights Templars. At both Temples the form of the dinner resembles the repasts of the military monks: the benchers on the dais representing the Knights; the barristers, the *Frères*, or Brethren; and the students, the Novices. The Middle Temple still bears the arms of the Knights Templars, viz. the figure of the Holy Lamb.

The entrance expenses at the Inner Temple (the average of the costs at other Inns) are 40*l.* 11*s.* 5*d.*, of which 25*l.* 1*s.* 3*d.* is for the stamp; on call, 82*l.* 12*s.*, of which 52*l.* 2*s.* 6*d.* is for the stamp: total, 123*l.* 3*s.* The commons bill is about 12*l.* annually.

Arms of Temple, Inner: Az. a pegasus salient, or. *Temple, Middle:* Arg. or a cross gu. a paschal lamb or, carrying a banner of the first, charged with a cross of the second. *Lincoln's Inn:* Or, a lion rampant purp. These were the arms of Lacy Earl of Lincoln. *Gray's Inn:* Sa. a griffin segreant, or.

INNS OF CHANCERY.

These Inns were formerly the nurseries of our great lawyers; but they are at present attached only by name to the parent Inns of Court: the Inner Temple has three, *Clement's*, *Clifford's*, and *Lyon's Inns*; the Middle Temple one, *New Inn*; Lincoln's Inn one, *Thavie's*; and Gray's Inn two, *Barnard's* and *Staple Inns*.

BARNARD'S INN, Holborn, anciently Mackworth's, from having belonged to Dr. John Mackworth, Dean of Lincoln, *temp.* Henry VI., was next occupied by one Barnard, when it was converted into an Inn of Chancery; the arms of the house are those of Mackworth, viz. party per pale, indented ermine and sables, a chevron, gules, fretted or. The ancient Hall, maintained in the olden taste, is the smallest in the London Inns: it is 36 feet long, 22 feet wide, and 30 feet high.

In Barnard's Inn, No. 2, second-floor chambers, lived the chemist, Mr. Peter Woulfe, F.R.S., *a believer in alchemy.* Among his contributions to the *Phil. Trans.* are " Experiments to shew the nature of Aurum Mosaicum." Woulfe was a tall, thin man; he died in Barnard's Inn in 1805, and his last moments were remarkable. By his desire, his laundress shut up his chambers, and left him, but returned at midnight, when Woulfe was still alive: next morning, however, she found him dead; his countenance was calm and serene, and, apparently, he had not moved from the position in which she had last seen him.

Westward, in Holborn, in Dyers'-buildings, (the site of some almshouses of the Dyers' Company,) lived William Roscoe when he published his edition of Pope's works, with notes and a life of the poet, 10 vols. 8vo, 1824.

CLEMENT'S INN, Strand, is named from being near the church of St. Clement Danes, and St. Clement's Well. It was a house for students of the law in the reign of Edward IV. The Elizabethan iron gate, erected in 1852, bears the device of St. Clement, an anchor without a stock, with a C couchant upon it; as also does the Hall, built in 1715. In the small garden is a kneeling figure supporting a sun-dial; it is painted black, and has hence been called a blackamoor.

Shakspeare has left us a picture from this Inn at his period:

Shallow. I was once of Clement's Inn, where, I think, they will talk of mad Shallow yet.

Silence. You were called lusty Shallow, then, cousin.

Shallow. By the mass, I was called any thing; and I would have done any thing indeed, and roundly too. There was I, and little John Doit of Staffordshire, and Black George Barnes of Staffordshire, and Francis Pickbone, and Will Squele, a Cotswold man; you had not four such swinge-bucklers in all the Inns of Court again.

Then Shallow tells of Sir John Falstaff breaking " Skogan's head at the courtgate when he was a crack not thus high; and the very same day did I fight with one Sampson Stockfish, a fruiterer, behind Gray's Inn."

Shallow. Oh, Sir John, do you remember since we lay all night in the Windmill in St. George's Fields?

Falstaff. We have heard the chimes at midnight, Master Shallow.

Shallow. I remember at Mile-End Green (when I lay at Clement's Inn), I was then " Sir Dagonet" in Arthur's Show.

Then Falstaff says of Shallow: I do remember him at Clement's Inn, like a man made after supper of a cheese-paring.—*Henry IV.* Part II. act iii. sc. 2.

St. Clement's Well, on the east of the Inn, and lower end of Clement's-lane, is mentioned by Fitzstephen: it is now covered, and has a pump placed in it. Lord Chief-Justice Saunders (1681) was originally a poor boy, who used to beg scraps at Clement's Inn, where an attorney's clerk taught him to earn some pence by hackney writing.

CLIFFORD'S INN, behind St. Dunstan's Church, Fleet-street, is named from Robert Clifford, to whom the property was granted by Edward II., and by his widow was let to students of the law. The arms are those of the Lords Clifford, viz. checky, or and azure, a fe and bondure gules, besante sable. Sir Edward Coke was admitted this Inn, 1571; and Selden, 1602. Harrison, the regicide, was an atto ney's clerk here: in the same office with him was John Bramsto cousin of Sir John Bramston, who records: "When the warr began his fellow-clerke, Harrison, perswaded him to take armes (this is the famous rogue Harrison, one of the King's judges,) which he did, th he might get to the King, which he soon did." (*Autobiography.*)

The Hall is modern Gothic, but has some old armorial glass. He is an oaken case, in which are the Society's rules written on vellu with illuminated initials and the arms of England, *temp.* Henry VI In this Hall Sir Matthew Hale and the judges sat after the Great Fi of 1666, to adjudicate in disputes between landlords and tenants, & The most authentic record of any settling of the Law Societies in t reign of Edward III. is a demise, in the 18th year, from Lady Cliffo *apprenticiis de Banco,* "of that house near Fleet-street called Cli ford's Inn."

FURNIVAL'S INN, between Brook-street and Leather-lane, was or ginally the town mansion of the Lords Furnival, and was an Inn Chancery in the 9th of Henry IV.; was held under lease *temp.* E ward VI., and the inheritance in the then Lord Shrewsbury was so early in Elizabeth's reign to the benchers of Lincoln's Inn, wl leased the property to the Society of Furnival's Inn. Sir Thom More was Reader here for three years. The original buildings we mostly taken down in Charles I.'s time, and then re-edified with a loft street-front of fine brickwork, decorated with pilasters. The o Gothic Hall remained until 1818, when the entire Inn was taken dow and rebuilt of brick by Peto in modern style, with stone columns ar other accessories. Thomas Fiddall, attorney of this Inn in 1654, wro a Conveyancing Guide, published with his portrait. Furnival's Inn let in chambers, but is no longer an Inn of Court or Chancery.

"In the 32d of Henry VI., a tumult betwixt the gentlemen of innes of co and chancery and the citizens of London hapening in Fleet-street, in whi some mischief was done, the principals of Clifford's Inne, Furnivalle's Int and Barnard's Inne, were sent prisoners to Hartford castle."—Stow's *Annals.*

LYON'S INN, Strand, between Holywell-street and Wych-stree was originally a hostelry with the sign of the Lyon, converted to Inn of Chancery *temp.* Henry VIII. The Hall bears the date 1700, a a lion sculptured in its pediment. The Inn formerly had its sun-di and a few trees. Sir Edward Coke was Reader at Lyon's Inn in 15

NEW INN, Wych-street, adjoins Clement's Inn: the Hall and oth buildings are modern. On the site, about 1485, was a guest inn, hostelry, with the sign of the Virgin Mary, and thence called O Lady's Inn. It was purchased or hired by Sir John Fineux, Chi Justice of the King's Bench, in the reign of Edward IV., at 6*l.* p annum, for the law-students of St. George's Inn, in St. George's-la Little Old Bailey; here also the students of the Strand Inn nestle after they were routed from thence in the reign of Edward VI. by t Duke of Somerset. The armorial ensigns of New Inn are, vert, flower-pot argent. Sir Thomas More studied here in the reign Henry VII., before he entered himself of Lincoln's Inn; and in afte life he spoke of "New Inn fare, wherewith many an honest man is w contented." Against the Hall is a large vertical sun-dial; motto, "Ti and tide tarry for no man."

SCROOPE'S INN, Holborn-hill, adjoining Ely-place, was an inn f Serjeants-at-law in the reign of Richard III.; and was originally t town-house of one of the Lords Scroope, of Bolton. The Serjea left it about 1500; its site is Union-court, formerly Scroope's-court, between Nos. 96 and 97 Holborn-hill.

. SERJEANTS' INN, Chancery-lane, was originally the inn of John Skarle, and "Faryngdon's Inn," the estate of the Bishops of Ely; let to the Judges and Serjeants-at-law at 4*l.* rent per annum in 1411, and first called "Serjeants' Inn" about 1484. In 1837-8, the Inn was rebuilt by Sir Robert Smirke, R.A.;* except the old dining-hall of the Society, which was then fitted up as a court for Exchequer equity sittings: the windows have some old armorial glass.

. SERJEANTS' INN, Fleet-street, was the residence of the Serjeants-at-law in the reign of Henry VI.; was destroyed in the Great Fire of 1666; rebuilt in 1670, with chapel, hall, &c.; and again rebuilt, as we now see it, with a handsome stone-fronted edifice designed for the Amicable Society by Adam. The Inn has long been left by the Serjeants.

. "The degree of Serjeant-at-law is the highest in the profession of the common law, on receiving which the Serjeants formerly gave costly entertainments resembling coronation-feasts; and to this day the custom is retained of giving gold rings to the queen, lord-chancellor, and other persons. Upon the removal of the newly-created serjeant from the Inn of Court of which he had been a member to Serjeants' Inn, he receives a purse of ten guineas as a retaining fee from the Society of which he takes leave. Certain privileges of the degree of Serjeant-at-law have lately been abolished; and in a few years this ancient order will be all but extinct."—*G. Bowyer,* 1847.

. STAPLE INN, Holborn, nearly opposite Gray's-Inn-lane, is traditionally named from having been the inn or hostel of the Merchants of the (Wool) Staple, whither it was removed from Westminster by Richard II. in 1378. It became an Inn of Chancery *temp.* Henry V.; and the inheritance of it was granted 20th Henry VIII. to the Society of Gray's Inn. The Holborn front is of the time of James I., and one of the oldest existing specimens of our metropolitan street-architecture. The Hall is of a later date, has a clock-turret, and had originally an open timber roof: some of the armorial window-glass is of date 1500; there are a few portraits, and at the upper end is the wool-sack, the arms of the Inn; and upon brackets are casts of the Twelve Cæsars. In the garden adjoining is a luxuriant fig-tree which nearly covers the south side of the hall. Upon a terrace opposite are the offices of the Taxing Masters in Chancery, completed in 1843, Wigg and Pownall architects; in the purest style of the reign of James I., with frontispiece, arched entrances, and semicircular oriels, finely effective: the open-work parapet of the terrace, and the lodge and gate leading to Southampton-buildings, are very picturesque.

. Dr. Johnson lived in Staple Inn in 1759: in a note to Miss Porter, dated March 23, he informs her that "he had on that day removed from Gough-square, where he had resided ten years, into chambers at Staple Inn;" here he wrote his *Idler,* seated in a three-legged chair, so scantily were his chambers furnished. In 1760, Johnson removed to Gray's Inn. Isaac Reed lived at No. 11 Staple Inn.

STRAND INN, or CHESTER INN from its being near the Bishop of Chester's house, was taken down, *temp.* Edward VI., by the Duke of Somerset for building his palace; it occupied part of the site of the present Somerset House. Occleve, the pupil of Chaucer, in the reign of Henry V., is said to have studied the law at "Chestre's Inn."

. SYMOND'S INN, Chancery-lane, though named from a gentleman of the parish who died in 1621, is stated to be the only portion retained by the Bishops of Chichester of their property in Chancery-lane, where

. * Nearly opposite Serjeants' Inn, Chancery-lane, were two houses, date 1611, taken down in 1853. The richly-carved and picturesque house at the south-west corner, in Fleet-street (often engraved), was taken down for widening the lane in 1799.

they formerly had a palace; and here are Bishop's-court and Chichester-rents. (See page 70.)

THAVIE'S INN, between Nos. 56 and 57 Holborn-hill, was originally the dwelling of John Thavie, of the Armourers' Company, who let the house *temp.* Edward III. to apprentices to the law, and was subsequently purchased as an Inn of Chancery by the benchers of Lincoln's Inn, by whom it was sold in 1771; destroyed by fire, and rebuilt as a private court. In the adjoining church of St. Andrew is a monument to John Thavie, who, in 1348, "left a considerable estate towards the support of this fabrick for ever," from which property the parish now derive an annual income of 1300*l.*

ISLE OF DOGS (THE),

A part of Poplar Marsh, lying within the bold curve of the Thames between Blackwall and Limehouse, was originally a peninsula; but in 1799-1800, a canal was cut through the isthmus by the Corporation of London, to save ships the long passage round the Isle; but since sold to the West India Dock Company, and now a timber-dock. (See page 256.) Here Togodumnus, brother of Caractacus, is said to have been killed in a battle with the Romans under Plautius, A.D. 46. Traditionally, it was named from the hounds of Edward III. being kept there, for contiguity to Waltham and other royal forests in Essex. Again, *Isle of Dogs* is held to be corrupted from *Isle of Ducks*, from the wildfowl upon it. Here (says Lysons) stood the chapel of St. Mary, mentioned in a will of the 15th century, "perhaps an hermitage founded for saying masses for the souls of mariners." Pepys speaks of it as "the unlucky Isle of Doggs." The ground is very rich, and in Strype's time oxen fed here sold for 34*l.* a piece: the grass was long prized for distempered cattle. The island is a pleistocene drift or diluvial deposit, in which has been found a subterranean forest of elm, oak, and fir trees, eight feet below the grass, and lying from south-east to northwest; some of the elms were three feet four inches in diameter, accompanied by human bones and recent shells, but no metals or traces of civilisation: the marsh is now inclosed by a pile and brick embankment. Here Captain Brown, R.N., established his works for the manufacture of iron suspension-bridges and iron cables: in 1813, he built here a suspension-bridge for foot-passengers, weighing only 38 cwt., but carts and carriages passed safely over it; the span was 100 feet. Captain Brown also constructed the Chain Pier at Brighton, in 1822-3. About this time the Isle of Dogs began to be thickly inhabited: here is St. Edmund's Roman Catholic Chapel. The Isle is now covered with stone-wharves, iron ship-building and chemical works, &c. (See BLACK-WALL, p. 49.) Adjoining are the dockyards of the Wigrams and Greens, formerly Perry's, mentioned by Pepys in 1660-61: the picturesque old masting-house is 120 feet high. Near the principal entrance to the West India Docks is a bronze statue (by Westmacott) of Mr. Milligan, by whom the Docks were begun and principally completed.

ISLINGTON,

Called also Iseldon, Yseldon, Eyseldon, Isendune, and Isondon, and of all the villages near London alone bearing a British name, was originally two miles distant north of the town, to which it is now united. *Iseldon* is conjectured to signify the lower fort, or station; and as there was undoubtedly a Roman camp at Highbury, this name may have been given to the camp which a few years since was visible in the field beside Barnsbury Park. Iseldon, in Domesday Book, possesses nearly 1000 acres of arable land alone; and so well cleared was the property, that there only remained "pannage for 60 hogs" (woodlands) adjoining Hornsey.

The great benefactor of Islington was Richard de Cloudesley, who by will, dated 1517, among other bequests to the parish, left to poor men gowns with the names of *Jesu* and *Maria* upon them; also 40s. for repairing and amending the causeway between his house and Islington Church; and a load of straw to be laid upon his grave: but superstition would not let Cloudesley's "bodie rest until certain exorcises, at dede of night," had quieted him with "diners diuine exercises at torchlight." The name of this benefactor is preserved in Cloudesley Square and Terrace. Algernon Percy, Earl of Northumberland, is said to have resided at Newington Green, where Henry VIII. was a frequent visitor, probably on his hawking excursions; and one of his proclamations, in 1516, commands that "the games of hare, partridge, pheasant, and heron, be preserved for his owne disport and pastime; that is to saye, from his palace of Westminster to St. Gyles in the Fields, and from thence to Islington, to our Lady of the Oke, to Highgate, to Hornsey Parke, to Hamsted Heath," &c.

Islington retained a few of its Elizabethan houses to our time, and its rich dairies are of like antiquity: in the entertainment given to Queen Elizabeth at Kenilworth Castle, in 1575, the Squier Minstrel of Middlesex glorifies Islington with the motto, "*Lac caseus infans;*" and it is still noted for its cow-keepers. (See DAIRIES, p. 250.) It was once as famous for its cheese-cakes as Chelsea for its buns; and among its other notabilities were custards and stewed "pruans," its mineral spa, and its ducking-ponds, Ball's Pond dating from the time of Charles I. At the lower end of Islington, in 1611, were eight inns, principally supported by summer visitors:

> "Hogsdone, *Islington,* and Tothnam Court,
> For cakes and creame had then no small resort."
> Wither's *Britain's Remembrancer,* 1628.

Islington parish includes Upper and Lower Holloway, three sides of Newington Green, and part of Kingsland; the southern portion of the village being in the parish of St. James, Clerkenwell. Besides St. Mary's, the mother-church (described at page 144), here are a large church in Lower Holloway; St. John's, Upper Holloway; St. Paul's, Ball's Pond; and Trinity, Cloudesley-square—all three built by Barry, R.A., 1828-9, who also built St. Peter's, in 1835; and Christchurch, Highbury, by Allom, in 1849, with a picturesque tower and spire, and interior of novel plan. There are also other district churches; St. John the Evangelist's (Roman-Catholic), with lofty gable and flanking towers; besides numerous chapels for every shade of dissent: Claremont Chapel, built in 1820, was named in memory of the lamented Princess Charlotte.

Among the celebrated *old houses* of Islington is Sir Thomas Fowler's, No. 41 Cross-street, with the Royal arms, E. R., and the date 1595, fleurs-de-lys, medallions, and $\frac{F}{TI}$ (Thomas and Jane Fowler): attached is a garden-lodge.

Canonbury, about half a mile north-east of the old church, was once the country-house of the Prior of the Canons of St. Bartholomew: the tower is described at page 63. At the entrance of the village from Clerkenwell was a *hermitage,* in the fields adjoining which Dame Alice Owen, in the reign of Queen Mary, escaped "braining" by a stray arrow, denoted by arrows upon the top of the school and almshouses which she built upon the spot. (See ALMSHOUSES, p. 5.)

Among the *old inns and public-houses* was, near the church, the *Pied Bull,* popularly a villa of Sir Walter Raleigh's; in Lower-street, the *Crown,* apparently of the reign of Henry VII., and the *Queen's Head,* a half-timbered Elizabethan house; near the Green, the *Duke's Head,* kept by Topham, "the Strong Man of Islington;" in Frog-lane, the *Barley-mow,* where George Morland painted; at the *Old Parr's Head,* in Upper-street, Henderson the tragedian first acted; *White Conduit House* has been twice rebuilt within our recollection; and *Highbury Barn,* though now a showy tavern, nominally recals its rural origin; the *Three Hats,* near the turnpike, was taken down in 1839; and the *Angel* was originally a galleried inn. Timber gables and rudely-carved brackets are occasionally to be seen in house-fronts; also here and there an old "house of entertainment," which, with the little remaining of "the Green," remind one of Islington *village.*

Islington abounds in chalybeate springs, resembling the Tunbridge Wells water; one of which was rediscovered in 1683, in the garden of Sadler's music-house, subsequently Sadler's Wells Theatre; and at the *Sir Hugh Middleton's Head* tavern was formerly a conversation-picture with twenty-eight portraits of the Sadler's Wells Club. In Spa Fields, about fifty years ago, was held "Gooseberry Fair," where the stalls of Gooseberry-fool vied with the "threepenny tea-booths" and the beer at "my Lord Cobham's Head."

The New River enters Islington by Stoke Newington, and passing onward, beneath Highbury, to the east of Islington, ingulfs itself under the road, in a subterraneous channel of 300 yards; again rises in Colebrook-row, and still coasting the southern side of Islington, reaches its termination at the New River Head, Sadler's Wells. From this vast circular basin the water is conveyed by sluices into large brick cisterns, and thence by mains and riders to all parts of London. (See NEW RIVER.)

The centre of Islington is perforated by the *Regent's Canal* brick tunnel, commencing westward of White Conduit House, and terminating below Colebrook-row. The tunnel is 17 feet wide, 900 yards long, 18 feet high (including 7 feet 6 inches depth of water).

Highbury was originally a summer camp of the Romans, and adjoined the Herman-street. The manor was given to the Priory of St. John of Jerusalem between 1271 and 1286, and was the Lord Prior's country residence, destroyed by Jack Straw in 1371. The site is now occupied by Highbury House, where is a lofty observatory, partly built by John Smeaton, F.R.S.

Holloway was once famous for its cheese-cakes, which, within recollection, were cried through London streets by a man on horseback. Du Val's lane was traditionally the scene of the exploits of Du Val, the highwayman, executed at Tyburn Jan. 21, 1669, "to the great grief of the women." Within memory, the lane was so infested with highwaymen, that few people would venture to peep into it, even in midday: in 1831 it was lighted with gas. (*J. T. Smith.*) At *Lower Holloway* Mrs. Foster, grand-daughter of Milton, kept a chandler's-shop for several years; she died in poverty at Islington, May 9, 1754, when the family of Milton became extinct.

Between Islington and Hoxton was built, in 1786, a curious windmill for grinding white-lead, worked by five flyers, at right angles to which projected a beam with smaller shafts. In 1853 was built at the Rosemary Branch Gardens a Circus, to seat 5000 persons. At Hoxton were the "Ivy Gardens" of Fairchild, who, dying rich, left to the parish of St. Leonard, Shoreditch, 50*l.* (increased to 100*l.* by the parishioners), the interest to be devoted to a lecture on Whit-Tuesday in the parish-church, "On the goodness of God as displayed in the vegetable creation." In Fairchild's employ was William Bartlett, "a simpler," who died at the age of 102 years; and his son James, "a simpler," aged 80.

In the Lower-road is "the Islington Cattle-Market," originated with a view to the removal of the cattle-market from Smithfield, and established by Act of Parliament in 1835; but it failed as a market, and has since been only used for the lairage of cattle: it occupies fifteen acres of land, walled in.

Among the more eminent inhabitants of Islington were John Bagford, the antiquary and book and print collector; William Collins, whilst under mental infirmity, was visited here by Dr. Johnson; Alexander Cruden, compiler of the

Concordance, died here in 1770; Oliver Goldsmith, and Ephraim Chambers the cyclopedist, lodged in Canonbury tower; Quick, the comedian, in Hornsey-row; John Nichols, F.S.A., editor of the *Gentleman's Magazine*, lived in Highbury-place; where Richard Percival, F.S.A., formed a matchless collection of drawings and prints of Islington; William Knight, F.S.A., of Canonbury, a collection of angling-books and missals (he greatly assisted John Rennie in his design for London Bridge); William Upcott, F.S.A., the bibliographer and autograph-collector, died here in 1845; and Charles Lamb retired from his clerkship in the India House to a cottage in Colebrook-row, in 1825: "the New River (rather elderly by this time) runs (if a moderate walking pace can be so termed) close to the foot of the house" (*C. Lamb*). Hard by was "Starvation Farm," where the owner, a foreign baron, kept his emaciated stock.

JAMES-STREET, WESTMINSTER,

Facing St. James's Park and Buckingham Gate, has been the abode of two distinguished *literati*. At No. 11 lived the poet Glover, whose song of "Hosier's Ghost" roused the nation to a Spanish war, and will be read and remembered long after his "Leonidas" is forgotten. At No. 6 died, December 31, 1826, William Gifford, editor of the *Quarterly Review* from its commencement in 1809 to 1824; and working editor of the *Anti-Jacobin Review*, writing the refutations and corrections of "the Lies," "Mistakes," and "Corrections." Gifford also translated Juvenal, wrote the satires of the *Baviad* and *Mæviad*, and edited Massinger, Ben Jonson, Ford, and Shirley.

On the west side of James-street stood Tart Hall, partly built in 1638, by N. Stone, for Alathæa Countess of Arundel; after whose death it became the property of her second son William, the amiable Viscount Stafford, beheaded on Tower-hill Dec. 29, 1680, upon "the perjured suborned evidence of the ever-infamous Oates, Dugdale, and Tuberville." The gateway of Tart Hall was not opened after Lord Stafford had passed under it for the last time. The second share of the Arundel Marbles was deposited here, and produced at a sale in 1720, 8851*l.* 19*s.* 11¾*d.* (*Minutes, Soc. Antiquaries.*) Dr. Mead bought a bronze head of Homer for 136*l.*; it is now in the British Museum, catalogued as a head of Pindar. The Hall was taken down soon after the sale: Walpole told Pennant it was very large and venerable. According to Strype, it was part in the parish of St. Martin's-in-the-Fields, and part in St. James's; on the garden-wall, a boy was whipt annually to remember the parish bounds; upon the site of the wall was built Stafford-row: in one of the adjoining passages, Mrs. Abington, the actress, had an *incognito* lodging, for card-parties.

ST. JAMES'S.

Although the Hospital dedicated to St. James is believed to have been founded prior to the Norman Conquest, and was rebuilt as a palace in 1532, not two centuries have elapsed since St. James's formed part of the parish of St. Martin's-in-the-Fields, and occupied the furthest extremity of the western boundaries of Westminster. "The Court of St. James's" dates from after the burning of Whitehall in the reign of William III., when St. James's became the royal residence; the church was consecrated in 1685, in honour of the reigning monarch, to St. James. (See CHURCHES, page 131.)

Hatton (1708) describes the parish as "all the houses and grounds comprehended in a place heretofore called St. James's Fields, and the confines thereof, containing about 3600 houses, and divided into seven wards." In the reign of Queen Anne it had acquired the distinction of the Court quarter.

"The inhabitants of St. James's, notwithstanding they live under the same laws and speak the same language, are a distinct people from those of Cheapside;

who are likewise removed from those of the Temple on the one side, and those of Smithfield on the other, by several climates and degrees in their way of thinking and conversing together."—Addison; *Spectator*, No. 403, 1712.

St. James's-street, in 1670, was called "the Long Street," and is described by Strype as beginning at the Palace of St. James's, and running up to the road against Albemarle-buildings; the best houses, at the upper end, having a terrace-walk before them. Waller, the poet, lived on the west side from 1660 till 1687, when he died at Beaconsfield; Pope lodged "next door to ye Golden Ball, on ye second terras." Gibbon, the historian, died Jan. 16, 1794, at No. 76, then Elmsley the bookseller's, who would not enter upon "the perilous adventure of publishing the 'Decline and Fall,'" by which the publishers have profited ten times the amount paid to the author for his copyright.

Horace Walpole relates: "I was told a droll story of Gibbon the other day. One of those booksellers in Paternoster-row, who publish things in numbers, went to Gibbon's lodgings in St. James's-street, sent up his name, and was admitted. 'Sir,' said he, 'I am now publishing a *History of England*, done by several good hands; I understand you have a knack at them there things, and should be glad to give you every reasonable encouragement.' As soon as Gibbon had recovered the use of his legs and tongue, which were petrified with surprise, he ran to the bell, and desired his servant to shew this encourager of learning downstairs."

Sir Christopher Wren had a house in St. James's-street, where he died, Feb. 25, 1723. Lord Byron lodged at No. 8 in 1811; Gillray, the caricaturist, lodged at No. 29, Humphrey the printseller's, when, in 1815, he threw himself from an upstairs window, and died in consequence.

Humphrey was the publisher of Gillray's caricatures, the copperplates of which were estimated, in 1815, to be worth 7000*l.* After Humphrey's death, his widow could raise only 1000*l.* upon the plates; subsequently, when offered by auction, they were bought in at 500*l.*; and upon the widow's death, her executors, unable to dispose of the plates as engravings, sold them to Mr. H. G. Bohn, the publisher, as *old copper*, for as many pence as they were originally said to be worth pounds; and sets are now to be bought at one-fifth of the first cost. (See the *Account*, &c. by Wright and Evans, 1851.)

About 1708, Peyrault's, or Pero's "Bagnio," now Fenton's Hotel, was in high fashion. At the south-west end was the St. James's Coffeehouse (Whig), taken down in 1806; it was the Foreign and Domestic News-house of the *Tatler*, and the "fountain-head" of the *Spectator*. (See Coffee-houses, p. 202.) Here, too, was the Tory house, Ozinda's; and the Cocoa-tree, to which belonged Gibbon and Lord Byron.

In St. James's-street are the following Club-houses, already described: Albion, Arthur's, Boodle's, Brookes's, Conservative, late Crockford's, the Dilettanti Society, and White's. (See pp. 190 to 199.)

At White's is a pair of views by Canaletti: one, London Bridge, with the houses, from Old Somerset House Gardens; and Westminster Bridge (just built), taken from the water, off Cuper's Gardens.

Next to Brookes's Club, in 1781, lived C. J. Fox. At No. 62 was Betty's fruit-shop, famous in Horace Walpole's time. The Thatched House Tavern in part remains next the Conservative Club; it is noted for the Public School Dinners given here. Sheridan called St. James's-street the Campus Martius of the beaux' cavalry.

Facing St. James's-street, upon the site of Albemarle-street, was Clarendon House, on the road whither, on Dec. 6, 1670, between six and seven in the evening, the great Duke of Ormond was dragged from his carriage by Blood and his accomplices, tied to one of them on horseback, and carried along Piccadilly towards Tyburn, there to hang the duke; but the alarm being given at Clarendon House, the servants followed and recovered his grace from a struggle in the mud with the man he was tied to, and who, on regaining his horse, fired a pistol at the duke and escaped. In the *Historian's Guide*, third edit. 1688, are stated to have been "six ruffians mounted and armed;" the duke's six footmen, who usually walked beside his carriage, were absent when the attack was made.

Bury (properly *Berry*) *street*, on the east, is named from the ground-landlord, a half-pay officer *temp.* Charles I.: he died Nov. 1733, aged above 100 years. Swift and Steele, Crabbe and Thomas Moore, occasionally lodged in this street.

Jermyn-street, on the east side of St. James's-street, was named from Henry Jermyn, Earl of St. Albans. Here, in 1765-81, lived the Duke of Marlborough, when Colonel Churchill, at the west end, south side. Gray, the poet, lodged here, at the east end. Sir Isaac Newton lived in this street before he removed to St. Martin-street, Leicester-square; as did also William and John Hunter. East of St. James's Church is the entrance-front of the Museum of Practical Geology, a lofty Italian building by Pennethorne; completed in 1850.- (See MUSEUMS.)

In Jermyn-street, near St. James's Church, about 1713, lived Mrs. Howe and her husband, who was absent from her seventeen years, as she supposed in Holland; though, in fact, living disguised in a mean lodging in Westminster. From Jermyn-street, Mrs. Howe removed to Brewer-street, Golden-square; Mr. Howe often visited at an opposite house, whence he saw his wife in her dining-room receiving company; and for seven years he went every Sunday to St. James's Church, and there had a view of his wife, but was not recognised by her. (See Dr. King's *Anecdotes*.)

King-street, leading to St. James's-square, has at the south-east corner the St. James's Bazaar, described at page 36. Here is the St. James's Theatre, designed by Beazley for Braham the singer; it occupies the site of Nerot's Hotel, No. 19, which cost Braham 8000*l.* (See THEATRES.) Nerot's was of the time of Charles II., and had a carved staircase, and panels painted with the story of Apollo and Daphne. Next are Willis's Rooms (see ALMACK'S, p. 3); and opposite are Christie and Manson's (late Christie's) auction-rooms, celebrated for sales of pictures and articles of *vertu*. There are four streets in this neighbourhood named from *King, Charles,* and the *Duke* of *York*.

In King-street, St. James's, was born, May 4, 1749, Charlotte Smith, the poet and novelist; and here she mostly resided with her father, Mr. N. Turner, from her twelfth to her fifteenth year, when she married Mr. Richard Smith, a West India merchant, aged 21.

St. James's-place, west side of St. James's-street, was built about 1694. Addison lodged here in 1712. Here also lived Parnell, the poet; Mr. Secretary Craggs; Bishop Kennett, the antiquary, who died here 1728; John Wilkes lived here in 1756 "in very elegant lodgings;" and Mrs. Robinson, the charming actress, lodged in No. 13. Lady Hervey lived in a house built for her by Flitcroft, afterwards occupied by the Earl of Moira (Marquis of Hastings). Spencer House, facing the Green Park, was designed by Vardy; the figures on the pediment by M. H. Spong, a Dane. At No. 25 lived Lord Guildford, who had the library lined with snake-wood from Ceylon, of which island he was Governor: the next tenant was Sir Francis Burdett, who expired here Jan. 23, 1844, of grief for the loss of his wife, who died thirteen days previously. At No. 22, built by James Wyatt, R.A., has lived, since 1808, Samuel Rogers, the poet: here Sheridan, Lord Byron, Sir James Mackintosh, "Conversation" Sharp, and Thomas Moore, were often guests.

Mr. Rogers' choice collection of pictures, sculpture, Etruscan vases, antique bronzes, and literary curiosities, may be seen through the introduction of any accredited artist or connoisseur. The paintings include these gems from the Orleans Gallery: Christ bearing the Cross (A. Sacchi); "Noli me tangere" ("mellow and glorious union of landscape and poetry"), (Titian); Holy Family (Correggio); large Landscape (Claude); Christ on the Mount of Olives (Raphael). Also, Christ disputing with the Doctors (Mazzolina di Ferrara), and the Coronation of the Virgin (A. Caracci), from the Aldobrandini Palace; Triumphal Procession

(Rubens), after Andrea Mantegna; St. Joseph and the Infant Saviour (Murillo); Landscapes by Rubens and Domenichino, Gainsborough, and R. Wilson. Virgin and Child (Raphael); Knight in Armour (Giorgione); Allegory, and Forest Scene, sunset (Rembrandt); Virgin and Child, with six Saints (L. Caracci); a Mill, a small octagon (Claude); Head of Christ crowned with thorns (Guido); Virgin and Child (Van Eyck); two large compositions (N. Poussin); Sketch for Mary Magdalen anointing the feet of the Saviour (P. Veronese); Sketch for the Miracle of St. Mark (Tintoretto); Study for the Apotheosis of Charles V. (Titian); Portrait of Himself (Rembrandt); Infant Don Balthazar on horseback (Velasquez); the Evils of War (Rubens); Virgin and Child, a small miniature (Hemmelinck); three original Drawings (Raphael); black chalk Study (Michael Angelo); Puck, the Strawberry Girl, the Sleeping Girl, Girl with Bird, Cupid and Psyche, and the Painter's House at Richmond (Sir Joshua Reynolds); Napoleon upon a rock at St. Helena (Haydon); and twelve Elizabethan miniatures. The paintings are lighted by lamps with reflectors. Among the sculpture are: Cupid pouting and Psyche couching, and Michael Angelo and Raphael, statuettes by Flaxman. Here also are seven pictures by Stothard (including a copy of the Canterbury Pilgrims), and a cabinet with his designs. Among the autographs is the original assignment of Dryden's *Virgil* to Tonson, witnessed by Congreve. Milton's agreement with Symons for *Paradise Lost*, long possessed by Mr. Rogers, was presented by him to the British Museum in 1852.

(See also PALACES, St. James's; and SQUARES, St. James's.)

JEWS IN LONDON.

The Jews were settled in England in the Saxon period, A.D. 750. In 1189, great numbers were massacred on the coronation-day of Richard I., when they lived in the Jewries, extending along both sides of the present Gresham-street to Basinghall-street, and Old Jewry on the east; the first synagogue in the metropolis being at the north-west corner of Old Jewry, which Stow describes as "a street so called of Jews some time dwelling there and near adjoining." The only burial-place appointed them in all England was the Jews' Garden, Red-cross-street, Cripplegate; until 1177, the 24th Henry II., when a special place was assigned to them in every quarter where they dwelt. (*Stow.*) The site of the present Jewin-street, Aldersgate-street, anciently "Leyrestowe," was granted them as a burial-place by Edward I. In 1262 there were slain in London 700 Jews, from one of them having forced a Christian to pay more than 2s. per week as interest upon a loan of 20s. (*Stow.*) Finally, in the reign of Edward I. (1287), 15,600 Jews were apprehended in one day, and all were banished from the kingdom. The Jews made no effort to return to England till the protectorship of Oliver Cromwell, when they proposed to pay 500,000l. for certain privileges, including the use of St. Paul's Cathedral as a synagogue; but 800,000l. was demanded, and the negotiation was unsuccessful. They next applied to Charles II., then in exile at Bruges, when the king proposed they should assist him with money, arms, or ammunition, to be repaid; and Dean Tucker remarks, that the restoration of the Stuarts was attended with the return of the Jews into Great Britain. The Jews themselves aver that they received a private assent to their re-admission; and Bishop Burnet asserts that Cromwell brought a company of Jews over to England, and gave them leave to build a synagogue. Dr. Tovey, however, in the Jewish registers, finds that, by their own account, until the year 1663 the whole number of Jews in England did not exceed twelve; so that the date of their return must be referred to the reign of Charles II. The first synagogue was built by Portuguese Jews, in King-street, Duke's-place, in 1656; and a school was founded by them in 1664, called "the Tree of Life." The first German synagogue was built in Duke's-place in 1691, and occupied till 1790, when the present edifice was erected. (See p. 179.)

The principal Jewish Cemeteries are two on the north side of the Mile-End-road belonging to the Portuguese Jews, and a third to the

German Jews. The old Portuguese ground was first used 1657 : some of the tombs bear bas-reliefs from Scripture; as the story of Joseph and his brethren, Jacob wrestling with the angel, &c. Near Queen's Elm, Fulham-road, is "the burying-ground of the Westminster Congregation of Jews," established 1816.

The number of Jews in London is 18,000, of whom 12,000 live in the City. The Jewish quarter is bounded north by High-street, Spitalfields; east by Middlesex-street (Petticoat-lane); south by Leadenhallstreet, Aldgate, and Whitechapel; and west by Bishopsgate-street.

"Within this area, but especially about Bevis Marks, Houndsditch, St. Mary Axe, and Petticoat-lane, you might readily imagine yourself transported to Frankfort, Warsaw, or any place enjoying a superabundant Jewish population. Here every face is of the shape, and somewhat of the complexion, of a turkey-egg; every brow pencilled in an arch of exact ellipse; every nose modelled after the proboscis of a toucan; locks as bushy and black as those of Absalom abound, and beards of the patriarchal ages. Here, and hereabouts, Isaac kills beef and mutton according to the old dispensation; Jacob receives accidental silver spoons, and consigns gold watches to the crucible, kept always at white-heat in his little dark cellar, and no questions asked. Here, at the corners, Rebecca disposes of fried liver and 'tatoes, smoking hot, on little bright burnished copper platters. Solomon negotiates in the matter of rags; Esther rejoices in a brisk little business of flat fish fried in oil—a species of dainty in which the Jews alone excel. Moses and Aaron keep separate marine stores, where every earthly thing furtively acquired, from a chain-cable to a Cardigan, finds a ready sale. Rachel, albeit a widow, dispenses from behind the bar to the thirsty tribes. Ruth deals wholesale in oranges and other foreign fruits. Melchizedec dabbleth in Hebrew books and tracts. Absalom sells opium and Turkey rhubarb. Mordecai is a 'crimp,' the vulture of seafaring men. Nothing is to be seen above, below, around, but Jewish physiognomies, Jewish houses, and Jewish occupations."— *John Fisher Murray.*

The Clothes' Exchange of Cutler-street, Houndsditch, is popularly known as *Rag Fair;* through which must pass, at one stage or another, half the second-hand habiliments of the empire. The trade in renovated clothes, too, is very great, so as to make the epithet " worn-out" a popular error. But factitious arts make up the mighty business of Rag Fair; and Bevis Marks has long been the Oporto of London, noted for its manufacture of " cheap port-wine."

Saturday in the Hebrew quarter is a day of devotion and rest : every shop is shut ; and striking is the contrast between the almost conventual silence on that day of Bevis Marks, Houndsditch, and St. Mary Axe, and the bustle of Whitechapel, Bishopsgate, and Leadenhall. How the Christian Sabbath is kept is denoted by such a notice as this : "Business will commence at this Exchange on Sunday morning at 10 o'clock. By order of the managers, Moses Abrahams." Again, from 8 to 12 o'clock on Sunday morning, Duke's-place is the great market for the supply of *oranges* to the itinerant Jews.

The wealth of the leading Jews in London is very great, and their influence on the money-market is overwhelming. Their shipping trade is very extensive. The largest clothing-establishments are carried on by Jews. The trade in old silver goods, pictures, old furniture, china, and curiosities, is chiefly carried on by Hebrew dealers.

Jews are admissible to all public offices and dignities, except to a seat in Parliament. In 1828 baptised Jews were allowed to purchase the freedom of the City of London, a privilege forbidden by the Court of Aldermen in 1785. Mr. David Salomons (1835) and Sir Moses Montefiore (1837) have served as sheriffs of London, these being the first Jews who filled that office; and Sir Moses is the first Jew ever knighted in Britain. Mr. Salomons was elected Alderman for Cordwainers' Ward in 1847, and is the first Jew who ever sat in the Court.

The Jews take care of their own poor; and their schools, hospitals, and asylums are numerous. You may see many poor Jews, but never a Jewish beggar. In 1852, the amount of offerings during the sacred festivals of the New Year, Day of Atonement, &c., for the relief of the poor at the principal metropolitan Synagogues, were:—Great Synagogue, Duke's-place, 800*l.*; Sephardim, ditto; Bevis Marks, 500*l.*; New, ditto; Great St. Helen's, 600*l.*; Hamburgh, ditto; Fenchurch-street, 150*l.*; West London, ditto; Margaret-street, 70*l.*—total, 2120*l.* The Western Synagogue, St. Alban's-place, has abolished offerings, substituting in lieu thereof a charge on the seats. In 1852 there were distributed in Passover week to the poor of the Synagogues and the itinerant poor, 55,000 pounds of Passover cakes, costing 916*l.* 13*s.* 4*d.*

The Rabbinical College, or Beth Hamedrash, Smith's-buildings, Leadenhall-street, contains one of the most splendid Jewish libraries in Europe, and is open to the public by tickets: here lectures are delivered gratuitously to the public, on Friday evenings, by learned Jews.

Jew's-row, at Chelsea, has been made by Wilkie the background of his picture of "the Chelsea Pensioners reading the Gazette of the Battle of Waterloo," now in Apsley House.

"Jews'-row has a Teniers-like line of mean public-houses, lodging-houses, rag-shops, and huckster-shops, on the right-hand, as you approach Chelsea College. It is the Pall Mall of the pensioners; and its projecting gables, breaks, and other picturesque attributes were admirably suited, in the artist's opinion, for the localities of the picture."—*Mrs. A. T. Thomson.*

ST. JOHN'S GATE, CLERKENWELL,

Is nearly all that remains of the magnificent monastery of the Knights of St. John of Jerusalem, that chivralous order which for seven centuries "was the sword and buckler of Christendom in the Paynim war." The priory was founded in 1100, and was almost of palatial extent. King John resided here in 1212; and our sovereigns occasionally held councils here. Three acres of ground lying without the walls, between the land of the Abbot of Westminster and of the Prior of St. John of Jerusalem, was called *No-man's Land.* In November 1326, Anthony d'Espagne, a wealthy merchant, who collected a burdensome duty of 2*s.* a tun on wine, was dragged barefoot out of the City, and beheaded by the populace on *No-man's Land*—a fitting name for the site of such an atrocity! In 1382 the whole commandery was burnt by Wat Tyler's mob; and the grand prior was beheaded in the courtyard, the site of St. John's-square, at the southern entrance of which stands the gateway. Late in the 15th century, the rebuilding of the monastery was commenced by Prior Docwra, who, according to Camden, "increased it to the size of a palace," and completed this entrance about 1504, "as appeareth by the inscription over the gate-house yet remaining" (*Stow*).

In a Chapter held here 11th Jan. 1514, Sir T. Docwra prior, a lease was granted to Cardinal Wolsey of the manor of Hampton, which the most eminent physicians of England and learned doctors from Padua had selected as the healthiest spot within twenty miles of London for the site of a palace for the cardinal. In this curious document (*Cotton. Mss.* British Museum) is a grant of four loads of timber annually for piles for the Hampton Weir, to be cut "in and fro Seynt John's Woode, Midd." The grant is printed in the *Gentleman's Magazine*, January 1834.

Docwra was grand-prior from 1502 to 1520, and was the immediate predecessor of the last superior of the house, who died of grief on Ascension-day, 1540, when the priory was suppressed. Five years subsequently, the site and precinct were granted to John Lord Lisle, for his service as high-admiral; the church becoming a kind of store-house "for the king's toyles and tents for hunting, and for the warres." It was, however, undermined and blown up with gun-

powder, and the materials were employed by the Lord Protector to
King Edward VI. in building Somerset Place; the Gate also would
probably have been destroyed, but from its serving to define the property. The Priory was partly restored upon the accession of Mary,
but again suppressed by Elizabeth. In 1604 the Gate was granted to
Sir Roger Wilbraham for his life. Hollar's etchings shew the castellated hospital, with the Gatehouse, flanked by strong walls, 1661.

At this time Clerkenwell was inhabited by people of condition.
(See CLERKENWELL, page 186.) Forty years later, fashion had travelled westward; and the Gate became the printing-office of Edward
Cave, who, in 1731, published here the first number of the *Gentleman's
Magazine*, which to this day bears the Gate for its vignette. Dr. Johnson was first engaged upon the magazine here by Cave in 1737: " his
practice was to shut himself up in a room assigned to him at St. John's
Gate, to which he would not suffer any one to approach, except the
compositor or Cave's boy for matter, which, as fast as he composed, he
tumbled out at the door." (*Hawkins.*) At the Gate Johnson first
met Richard Savage; and here in Cave's room, when visitors called, he
ate his plate of victuals behind the screen, his dress being "so shabby
that he durst not make his appearance." One day, while thus concealed, Johnson heard Walter Harte, the poet and historian, highly
praise the *Life of Savage*. Garrick, when he first came to London,
frequently called upon Johnson at the Gate; and at Cave's request, in
the room over the great arch, and with the assistance of a few journey-
man-printers to read the other parts, Garrick represented the principal
character in Fielding's farce of the *Mock Doctor*. Goldsmith was also
a visitor here. When Cave grew rich, he had St. John's Gate painted,
instead of his arms, on his carriage, and engraven on his plate. After
Cave's death in 1754, the premises became the "Jerusalem" public-
house, and the "Jerusalem Tavern."

The latter name was assumed from the Jerusalem Tavern, Red Lion-street,
in whose dank and cobwebbed vaults John Britton served an apprenticeship to a
wine-merchant; and in reading at intervals by candle-light, first evinced that love
of literature which has characterised his long life of industry and integrity. He
remembers Clerkenwell in 1787, with St John's Priory-church and cloisters;
when Spa-fields were pasturage for cows; the old garden-mansions of the aristocracy remained in Clerkenwell-close; and Sadler's Wells, Islington Spa, Merlin's
Cave, and Bagnigge Wells, were nightly crowded with gay company.

In 1845, under the new Metropolitan Buildings' Act, a survey of
St. John's Gate was made, and a notice given to the then owner to
repair it; and by the aid of " the freemasons of the church," and Mr.
W. P. Griffith, architect, the north and south fronts have been restored.

The gateway is a good specimen of groining of the 15th century,
with moulded ribs, and bosses ornamented with shields of the arms of
the Priory, Prior Docwra, &c. The south or principal front has a
double projection; has numerous small windows; and a principal
window over the crown of the arch in each front, in the wide and
obtusely-pointed style. The south front bears the arms of France and
England, and the north or inner front those of the Priory and Docwra.
In the west side of the gateway is an ancient carved oak door-
head, discovered in 1813, when that part of the building (now a coal-
shed) was converted into a watch-house for St. John's parish. In the
spandrels are the monastery arms, as also in a low door-case of the
west tower from the north side of the Gate; these spandrels also bear
a cock and a hawk, and a hen and a lion. This was the entrance to
Cave's printing-office. The east basement is the tavern bar, with a
beautifully moulded ceiling. The stairs are Elizabethan. The principal room over the arch has been despoiled of its window-mullions

and groined roof. The foundation-wall of the Gate face is 10 feet 7 inches thick, and the upper walls are nearly 4 feet, hard red brick, stone-cased: the view from the top of the staircase-turret is extensive. In excavating there have been discovered the original pavement, 3 feet below the Gate; and the Priory walls, north, south, and west.

St. John's Church, in St. John's-square, is built upon the chancel and side aisles of the old Priory-church, and upon its crypt; the capitals of the columns, ribbed mouldings, lancet windows, are fine; from the key-stone of each arch hangs an iron lamp-ring: in 1849, the crypt was found by excavation to have extended much further westward. The turret-clock belonged to old St. James's Church, as did also the silver head of the beadle's staff (James II. 1685). Here, too, is a portable baptismal bowl, with a scriptural inscription, and " Deo est sacris :" it was formerly used as the church font. (See *Ye History of ye Priory and Gate of St. John*. By B. Foster, 1851.)

ST. KATHERINE'S HOSPITAL,

Or "St. Katherine's at the Tower," was originally founded in 1148, by Maud, wife of King Stephen; when the site, with a mill, was purchased for 6*l.* a year: its custody was conferred on the prior of the Holy Trinity, Maud reserving to herself and the succeeding queens of England the nomination of the master of the Hospital. In 1273 it was dissolved,* and refounded by Queen Eleanor, widow of Henry III, for a master, three brothers, chaplains, and three sisters, ten poor bedeswomen, and six poor scholars, to lodge within the building; the nomination being reserved as heretofore.

Queen Eleanor's charter states the object of her foundation to be "for the health of the soul of her late husband, and of the souls of the preceding and succeeding kings and queens." One of the priests was daily required to sing a mass; another to "celebrate daily divine service, solemnly and devoutly, for the foresaid souls;" and on Edmund the Confessor's day, Nov. 15, the day of the death of her husband King Henry, there should be bestowed one halfpenny, in form aforesaid, upon one thousand poor men.

The Hospital was enlarged by Philippa, Queen of Edward III., who liberally aided the rebuilding of the church in 1340, and founded chantries; Richard II. also founded a chantry; and Henry VI. rebuilt the church, and granted to the Hospital the tolls of a twenty-one days' fair annually on Tower-hill, besides other privileges, which a fraudulent master sold to the City in 1560 for 456*l.* 13*s.* 4*d.* At the Dissolution, Anne Boleyne claimed the Hospital as part of her dowry, and the peculiar property of the queens consort of England; it was saved from spoliation: the annual revenues were then 315*l.* 14*s.* 2*d.*, a great income. The foundation was not a monastery; for the brothers were secular priests, and the sisters made no vows, but were permitted to go abroad, provided they returned "by curfew."

In 1442, the district of the Hospital was made a royal precinct; and no one could be arrested here for debt, except by an order from the Board of Green Cloth. Within the walls was born Verstegan, the antiquary; and here Lilly, the alchemist, wrote his celebrated *Testament.*

The precinct possessed both a spiritual and temporal court: the former a royal jurisdiction for all ecclesiastical causes, probate of wills, &c.; in the temporal court the high-steward of the jurisdiction of St. Katherine's presided; and the court had its high-bailiff, prothonotary, and prison.

* Had not the original Hospital been dissolved, St. Katherine's would now be the most ancient ecclesiastical community in the kingdom; and it is still the fourth in point of antiquity, coming after Peter House, Cambridge; and Merton and Balliol Colleges, Oxford.

In 1698, the Lord Chancellor Somers, as visitor, drew up rules and orders for the government of the Hospital. In 1705, a school was established for the children of the precinct, at the charge of the Hospital. In 1824, by royal assent, the Hospital-site was disposed of for St. Katherine's Docks. (See page 254.) The church, wherein service was last performed Oct. 30, 1825 (see Hone's *Every-day Book*, vol. i.), had lofty windows, the whole height of the structure: it is engraved by Hollar, 1660; and described by Dr. Ducarel, the antiquary, who was buried here. The church, cloisters, and monastic houses were removed in 1825-6, with a great number of tenements, described by Stow as "homely cottages, having inhabitants, English and strangers, more in number than in some cities in England." The compensation then made to the Hospital, under the direction of Lord Chancellor Eldon, amounted to 125,000*l.*, as the value of the precinct estate; 6,000*l.* for building a new hospital; 2000*l.* for the purchase of a site; and smaller sums to those whose interests suffered by the removal.

Meanwhile, the Hospital was rebuilt on the eastern side of the Regent's Park, by Poynter, in the ancient ecclesiastical and domestic style: it consists of a chapel and chapter-house (see page 134), dwellings for the brethren and sisters, lodgers, &c.; and opposite, a handsome residence for the master. In the courtyard is a conduit; and upon the several buildings are the royal and collegiate arms, and inscriptions: "Elianora fundavit;" "Fundavit Mathilda, 1148;" "In hoc tu restit. 1828," &c.

In the church, removed from the ancient edifice, is the tomb of John Holland, Duke of Exeter, and his two wives; the setting up and restoration of which cost nearly a thousand pounds: here also is the curious octagonal wooden pulpit, carved with views of the ancient Hospital and its gates;* and beneath each compartment, EZRA THE SCRIBE—STOOD UPON A—PULPIT OF WOOD—WHICH HE HAD—MADE FOR THE—PREACHIN *Neh*—*e* chap. viii. 4. This pulpit was given to the church by Sir Julius Cæsar, appointed Master of the Hospital by Queen Elizabeth in 1596.

Speed, Dugdale, Ducarel, Ellis, and other antiquaries, are of opinion that the Queens Consort or Dowager, having once possessed the right of the Hospital appointments, the death of the King does not alienate it, it having existed in the person of the Consort during his life; that they nominate, *pleno jure*, the master, brothers, and chaplains; that they may increase or lessen the number, or remove them altogether, alter any statute, or make new ones at pleasure; and that when there is no Queen Consort, the Queen Dowager has the right of appointing; that when there is neither Queen Consort nor Dowager, the reigning sovereign has the power of nomination. In 1840, on the death of the master, General Sir Herbert Taylor (successively private secretary to George III. and Queen Charlotte, and the Duke of York), there being no Queen Consort, the patronage fell to the Queen Dowager Adelaide, who appointed the Vice-Chamberlain of her Household, the Hon. W. Ashley, the present Master.

The School, now attached, consists of thirty boys and twenty girls, who are educated, clothed, and apprenticed: they dine at the Hospital every Sunday. The colour of the boys' clothes is green; but the statute of Queen Philippa ordains, that the brethren shall not wear "green cloaths, as tending to dissoluteness." The affairs of the Hospital are managed by the chapter of brethren (in orders) and sisters (unmarried or widows).

The bedesmen and women are appointed by the chapter, are non-resident, and receive 10*l.* per annum for life. The appointment of the master and brethren and sisters is held by her Majesty the Queen, the thirty-second royal patroness. The Hospital income is about 6000*l.* per annum; expenditure, about 5000*l.* Master's income, 1200*l.* a year;

* The site of the principal gate "by the Tower" is still called "Iron Gate."

brother, 300*l.*; sister, 200*l.* The real alms-people are non-resident; and sisters have let their residences in the Hospital at 90*l.* a year each.

KENNINGTON,

A manor of Lambeth, is named from the Saxon Lynenze and tun, the place or town of the king; and was occasionally a royal residence until the reign of Charles I. (see KENNINGTON MANOR-HOUSE, p. 392). Camden says, though erroneously, "of this retreat of our ancient kings neither the name nor ruins are now to be found." At Kennington Green, in 1852, was built a large Vestry Hall, in semi-classic style, for the district of Lambeth. In Kennington-lane is the School of the Friendly Society of Licensed Victuallers, built 1836. Kennington Common (about 20 acres) was formerly noted for its cricket-matches, pugilism, and itinerant preachers, and as the exercise-ground of volunteer regiments. It was the common place of execution for Surrey, before the erection of the County Gaol, Horsemonger-lane; and *on the site of St. Mark's Church*, south of the Common, some of the rebels of 1745, tried by special commission in Southwark, were hanged, drawn, and quartered: among them was "Jemmy Dawson," the hero of Shenstone's touching ballad; and of another ditty, set to music by Dr. Arne, and sung about the streets. On Kennington Common was held, April 10, 1848, the great revolutionary meeting of "Chartists," brought to a ridiculous issue by the unity and resolution of the Metropolis, backed by the judicious measures of the Government, and the masterly military precautions of the late Duke of Wellington. (*S. Warren,* F.R.S.) In 1852, the Common, with the site of the Pound of the Manor of Kennington, were granted by Act of Parliament, on behalf of the Prince of Wales, as part of the Duchy of Cornwall estate, to be enclosed and laid out as "Pleasure-grounds for the recreation of the public; but if it cease to be so maintained, it shall revert to the Duchy." They comprise twelve acres, disposed in grass-plots, and planted with shrub sand evergreens; and at the main entrance have been reconstructed the model cottages originally built at the expense of Prince Albert for the Great Exhibition of 1851: the walls are built with hollow and glazed brick, and the floors are brick and stucco; the whole being fireproof.

KENSAL GREEN,

Harrow-road, formerly a hamlet of "unlettered fame," has become celebrated as the seat of the first cemetery established for London, whose many hundred tombs whiten the high ground in the prospect. (See CEMETERIES, page 68.) A twin-towered church has been built here; and the busy railway runs close to the walls of the silent burial-ground: here is another novelty of our age, the works of the Western Gas Company, for manufacturing gas from Cannel Coal. In the hamlet was the Plough public-house, reputed to have been built as early as 1500: it was a haunt of George Morland, who, with all his dissipation, painted 4000 pictures during a lifetime of 40 years.

KENSINGTON, BROMPTON, AND KNIGHTSBRIDGE.

KENSINGTON, a mile and a half west of Hyde-Park-corner, contains the hamlets of Brompton, Earl's Court, the Gravelpits, and part of Little Chelsea, now West Brompton; but the royal palace, and about twenty other houses north of the road, are in the parish of St. Margaret, Westminster. On the south side, the parish of Kensington extends beyond the Gore, anciently Kyng's Gore, the principal houses between which and Knightsbridge are also in St. Margaret's. The old church (St. Mary Abbot's) is described at page 141. The village contains several teresting houses of "kingly Kensington" (see page 392), which mostly ate from the enlargement of the royal palace. The mineral spring which once possessed may have contributed to the celebrity of Kensington. Iolland House is described at page 374. Nearly opposite, in the Kensington-road, is the Adam and Eve public-house, where Sheridan, on his ray to or from Holland House, regularly stopped for a dram; and there e ran up a long bill, which Lord Holland had to pay. (Moore's *Diary*.) Kensington Palace Gardens lead from the High-street of Kensington to he Bayswater-road, and contain several costly mansions; including one f German-Gothic design, built for the Earl of Harrington in 1852. On ampden Hill is the observatory of Sir James South, one of the founders f the Royal Astronomical Society : among the working instruments is 7-feet transit instrument, a 4-feet transit circle, and one of the equato- als with which, between 1821 and 1823, Sir James South (at Blackman- reet, Southwark) and Sir John Herschel made a catalogue of 380 ouble stars. In Little Chelsea was born, in 1674, Charles Boyle, fourth arl of Orrery, patron of Graham who first constructed an orrery.

In Orbell's-buildings, Kensington, lodged Sir Isaac Newton from January 25 until his death, March 20, 1727, in his 85th year. His body, on March 28, y in state in the Jerusalem Chamber, and was thence buried in Westminster bbey.

t Kensington Gore, in 1808, Mr. Wilberforce had a cheerful house, the ostliness of which made him uneasy, lest it should curtail his charities. ore House was tenanted by the Countess of Blessington, whose Cu- osities were sold here in 1849. The house was opened by Soyer as *restaurant* (" Symposium") during the Exhibition of 1851.

In 1852, the Gore House estate, 21½ acres, was purchased for 60,000*l*. as a site r a new National Gallery; and the Baron de Villars's estate, adjoining, 48 res, fronting the Brompton-road, was bought for 153,500*l*. as a site for a Mu- um of Manufactures : these localities being recommended for the dryness of e soil, and as the only ground safe for future years amidst the growth of the etropolis.—*Second Report of the Commissioners for the Exhibition of* 1851.

The yellow gravel of Hyde Park and Kensington, so often found covering the ondon clay, is, comparatively speaking, of very modern date, and consists of ightly rolled, and, for the most part, angular fragments, in which portions of e white opaque coating of the original chalk-flint remain uncovered.—*Sir harles Lyell, F.G.S.*

The eastern extremity of the Gore, now the site of Ennismore ardens, is the highest point of ground between Hyde-Park-corner nd Windsor Castle. (Faulkner's *Kensington*.) Kingston, next Ennis- ore, and now Listowel, House, was the residence of the Duchess of ingston, "the notified Bet Cheatley, Duchess of Knightsbridge," who ied here in 1788. Here in 1842 died the Marquis Wellesley; in the orridor is a large window, a garden-scene, painted by John Martin hen he was a pupil of Muss. At Old Brompton, upon the site of lorida Tea-gardens, was Orford Lodge, built for the late Duchess of loucester, and subsequently tenanted by the Princess Sophia of Glou- ester; and the Right Hon. George Canning, who was here visited by ueen Caroline. The house was afterwards called " Gloucester Lodge," nd was taken down in 1852. Here also was Hale or " Cromwell" Iouse (see page 393), taken down in 1853. The large space of ground etween the Kensington and Brompton roads included the Brompton ark nursery (see GARDENS, page 322); and here (in 1853) were re- ains of the wall of Brompton Park. Brompton Hall, mostly modern, as a noble Elizabethan room, wherein Lord Burghley is said to have eceived Queen Elizabeth.

BROMPTON has long been frequented by invalids for its genial air. See CONSUMPTION HOSPITAL, page 380, and HOLY TRINITY CHURCH, age 130.) At No. 7 Amelia-place died in 1817 the Right Hon. J.

P. Curran. In Brompton-square, at No. 13, died Charles Incledon, the singer, 1826 ; and in the same year, at No. 22, George Colman the younger. At the Grange, taken down in 1842, lived Braham, the singer; at No. 45 Brompton-row, Count Rumford, the heat-philosopher; Rev. W. Beloe, the "Sexagenarian;" and Sir Richard Phillips, when writing his *Million of Facts.* At No. 14 Queen's-row Arthur Murphy died in 1805, aged 77.

KNIGHTSBRIDGE lies in the parishes of Chelsea, Kensington, and St. Margaret, Westminster. It was anciently written Knyghtbrigg; and in 1362, all oxen, hogs, &c. were ordered to be killed here and at Stratford, and not within the City. The name is traceable to the manor of Neate, and a stone bridge near Hyde-Park-corner, mentioned by Norden in 1593. Here is a district Chapel, formerly attached to a lazar-house (see p. 384). Westward is Albert-gate, Hyde Park, opened 1846 : the stags upon the piers were formerly at the Ranger's Lodge, Green Park, and were modelled from a pair of prints by Bartolozzi. The ground, with the site of the large and lofty houses east and west, was purchased by the Crown from the Dean and Chapter of Westminster, when the Cannon Brewery was removed : the house east was bought for 15,000*l.* by Mr. Hudson, once "the Railway King."

Immediately west of St. George's Hospital (see page 381), at No. 14, John Liston, the comedian, lived several years, and here he died, March 22, 1846. Liston was born in Norris-street, Haymarket, in 1776, and was educated in Archbishop Tenison's school : he first appeared on the stage, at the Haymarket Theatre, in 1805 ; and retired at the Olympic Theatre in 1837 : he died worth 40,000*l.*

In 1842, opposite the Conduit in Hyde Park (see page 230), was built the St. George's Gallery, for the exhibition of Mr. Dunn's Chinese Collection; subsequently occupied by Mr. Gordon Cumming's African Exhibition, and Bartlett and Beverly's Diorama of the Holy Land.

The original entrance was copied from a Chinese summer-house, inscribed "Ten thousand Chinese things." The collection, formed by Mr. Nathan Dunn in twelve years, and first exhibited in Philadelphia, consisted of a vast assemblage from China of its idols, temples, pagodas, and bridges ; arts and sciences manufactures and trades; parlours and drawing-rooms; clothes, finery, and orna ments; weapons of war, vessels, dwellings, &c. Here were life-size groups of temple of idols, a council of mandarins, and Chinese priests, soldiers, men of letters, ladies of rank, tragedians, barbers, shoemakers, blacksmiths, boat-women servants, &c., amidst set scenes and furnished dwellings. Here was a two storied house from Canton, besides shops from its streets; here were persons of rank in sumptuous costumes, artisans in their working-clothes, and altogether such a picture of Chinese social life as the European world had never before seen. Part of the collection was subsequently exhibited in 1851, in a gay pavilion built for the occasion west of Albert Gate; the site of which is now occupied by handsome five-storied mansion.

Westward is St. Paul's Church (see page 155) ; on the Kensington road are the Cavalry Barracks ; nearly opposite is the Phœnix Floor cloth Manufactory, "founded by Nathan Smith, 1754, being the first ever established ; burnt down 1794 ; restored 1795; rebuilt 1824." I the rear of Ennismore-place, opposite the site of the Crystal Palace in Hyde Park, is All Saints' Church, in the Lombardic style, by Vull nny, consecrated 1849; incumbent, Rev. W. Harness, A.M., one of the editors of Shakspeare.

At Rutland Gate (on the site of a mansion of the Dukes of Rutland) is the house of John Sheepshanks, Esq., and his collection of 228 pictures (with two exceptions), by modern British artists: including 6 works by A. Callcott, R.A. W. Collins, R.A., 7; John Constable, R.A., 5; C. W. Cope, R.A., 7; W. Etty R.A., 2; Edwin Landseer, R.A., 9; C. Leslie, R.A., 9; W. Mulready, R.A., 1; W. Redgrave, R.A., 6; C. Stanfield, R.A., 3; J. M. W. Turner, R.A., 5; Uwins, R.A., 4; T. Webster, R.A., 5. The collection can only be seen by letter of introduction.

Knightsbridge was formerly a noted "Spring Garden," with several taverns of gay and questionable character; and late in the last century, the road thence to Kensington was infested by footpads.

In the trial of a highwayman for robbery in 1752, the principal witness deposed, "the chaise to the Devizes having been robbed two or three times, as the post-boy told him, near the Half-way House between Knightsbridge and Kensington, he, the witness, set out in the chaise, was stopped near the house by the prisoner on foot, who was taken; the postboy having just before stated, that if they did not meet the highwayman between Knightsbridge and Kensington they should not see him at all"—proving the frequency of such occurrences in that neighbourhood.

Again, within the memory of man, at Kensington a bell used to be rung at intervals, to muster the people returning to town. As soon as a band was assembled sufficiently numerous to insure mutual protection, it set off; and so on.

Kensington and Chelsea contain the largest unrepresented town population in the kingdom: Kensington, 119,990; Chelsea, 56,543.

KENSINGTON GARDENS.

These delightful gardens, which include an area of above 350 acres, did not, when purchased by William III., soon after his accession, exceed 26 acres. In 1691 they were described by the Rev. Dr. Hamilton, to the Society of Antiquaries, as "not great, nor abounding with fine plants. The orange, lemon, myrtle, and what other trees they had there in summer, were all removed to London or Mr. Wise's greenhouse at Brompton Park, a little mile from there." Queen Anne added 30 acres. Evelyn notes: "Sept. 2d, 1701. I went to Kensington and saw the houses, plantations, and gardens, the work of Mr. Wise, who was there to receive me." (*Diary*, vol. ii. p. 75.) Bowack, in 1705, described the gardens as "beautified with all the elegances of art (statues and fountains excepted). There is a noble collection of foreign plants, and fine neat greens, which makes it pleasant all the year; the whole, with the house, not being above 26 acres. Her Majesty has pleased lately to plant near 30 acres more towards the north, separated from the rest only by a stately greenhouse, not yet finished." Thus, previous to 1705 Kensington Gardens did not extend farther north than the conservatory; and the eastern boundary was nearly in the line of the broad walk which crosses before the east front of the palace. The kitchen-gardens, which formerly extended northward towards the gravel-pits, and the 30 acres north of the conservatory, added by Queen Anne to the pleasure-gardens, may have been the 55 acres "detached and severed from the park, lying in the north-west corner thereof," granted in the 16th of Charles II. to Hamilton, Ranger of the Park, and Birch, Auditor of Excise, the same to be walled and planted with "pippins and red-streaks," on condition of their furnishing apples or cider for the King's use. At the end of the avenue leading from the south front of the palace to the wall on the Kensington-road, is a large and lofty architectural alcove, built by Queen Anne's orders; so that Kensington Palace, in her reign, seems to have stood in the midst of fruit and pleasure gardens, with pleasant alcoves on the west and south, and a stately conservatory on the east, the whole confined between the Kensington and Uxbridge roads, the west side of Palace Green, and the broad walk before the east front of the palace. Addison, in the *Spectator*, No. 477, dignifies Wise and London as the heroic poets of gardening, and is enraptured with their treatment of the upper garden at Kensington, which was at first nothing but a gravel-pit; the hollow basin and its little plantations, and a circular mount of trees, as if scooped out of the hollow, greatly delighting the essayist. Tickell opens his elegant eclogue with a glance at the morning promenade of his day; where—

" The dames of Britain oft in crowds repair
To gravel walks and unpolluted air:
Here, while the town in damps and darkness lies,
They breathe in sunshine, and see azure skies;
Each walks with robes of various dyes bespread,
Seems from afar a moving tulip-bed,
Where rich brocades and glossy damasks glow,
And chintz, the rival of the showery bow."

Caroline, queen of George II. added to the Gardens nearly 300 acres from Hyde Park, and had a canal formed at the cost of 6000l.; whilst with the soil dug was raised a mount to the south-east, with a revolving prospect-house. The Gardens were planted and laid out by Bridgeman, who banished verdant sculpture, but adhered to straight walks and clipped hedges, varied with a wilderness and open groves.

A plan of 1762 shews the formal Dutch style on the north of the palace. On the north-east, a fosse and low wall reaching from the Uxbridge-road to the Serpentine at once shut in the Gardens, and conducted the eye along their central vista, over the Serpentine (formed between 1730 and 1733), to its extremity; and across the Park to the east of Queen Anne's gardens, immediately in front of the palace, a reservoir was formed into " the round pond;" thence long vistas were carried through the wood that encircled it, to the head of the Serpentine, to the fosse and Bridgeman's ha-ha wall, affording a view of the Park; and to the mount already mentioned, which, with its evergreens and temple, has disappeared within recollection.

After King William took up his abode in the palace, a court end of the town gathered round it. The large gardens laid out by Queen Caroline were opened to the public on Saturdays, when the king and court went to Richmond; all visitors were then required to appear in full-dress. When the Court ceased to reside at Kensington, the Gardens were thrown open in the spring and summer; and next open throughout the year. On stated days in the London season, military bands perform.

Of late years Kensington Gardens have been greatly improved by drainage, relaying out, and the removal of walls and substitution of open iron railing. Viewed from near the palace, eastward are three avenues through dense masses of ancient trees. Immediately in front of the palace is a quaintly-designed flower-garden, between which and Kensington are some stately old elm-trees. The broad walk, 50 feet in breadth, was once the fashionable promenade. On the southern margin of the Gardens is a walk, bordered by the newer and rarer kind of shrubs, each labelled with its Latin and English name, and its country. The most picturesque portion of the Gardens, however, is at the entrance from near the bridge over the Serpentine, where is a delightful walk east of the water, beneath some noble old Spanish chestnut-trees. The elegant stone bridge across the west end of the Serpentine was designed by Sir John Rennie in 1826, and cost 36,500l. A pair of magnificent Coalbrook-dale iron gates (from the Great Exhibition of 1851) has been erected adjoining the southern lodge; and several of the double seats (dos-à-dos) from the Exhibition building are placed here.

Queen Anne's Banqueting-house, north of the palace, completed in 1705, is a fine specimen of brickwork: the south front has rusticated columns supporting a Doric pediment, and the ends have semicircular recesses. The interior, decorated with Corinthian columns, was fitted up as a drawing-room, music-room, and ball-room; and thither the queen was conveyed in her chair from the western end of the palace. Here were given full-dress fêtes à la Watteau, with a profusion of " brocaded robes, hoops, fly-caps, and fans," songs by the court lyrist, &c. But when the court left Kensington, Queen Anne's building was converted into an orangery and greenhouse. (See PALACES.)

KENT-STREET, SOUTHWARK,

Originally "Kentish-street," is a wretched and profligate part of St. George's parish. In 1633 it was described as "very long and ill-built, chiefly inhabited by broom-men and mumpers;" and for ages it has been noted for its turners' shops, and broom and heath yards. Evelyn tells of one Burton, a broom-man, and his wife, who sold kitchen-stuff in Kent-street, whom God so blessed that Burton became a very rich and a very honest man, and Sheriff of Surrey. At the east end of Kent-street, in 1847, was unearthed a pointed arched bridge of the 15th century, probably erected by the monks of Bermondsey Abbey, lords of the manor. In Rocque's Map, 1750, (when the Kent-road was lined with hedge-rows,) this arch, called Lock's-bridge, from being near the Lock Hospital, carries the road over a stream which runs from Newing-ton-fields to Bermondsey. Yet, what long lines of conquest and devotion, of turmoil and rebellion, of victory, gorgeous pageantry, and grim death, have poured through this narrow inlet of old London! The Roman invader came along the rich marshy ground now supporting Kent-street (says Bagford, in a letter to his brother-antiquary Hearne); thousands of pious and weary pilgrims have passed along this causeway to St. Thomas of Canterbury; here the Black Prince rode with his royal captive from Poictiers, and the victor of Agincourt was carried in kingly state to his last earthly bourne. By this route Cade advanced with his 20,000 insurgents from Blackheath to Southwark; and the ill-fated Wyat marched to discomfiture and death. And to the formation of the Dover-road, in our time, Kent-street continued part of the great way from Dover and the Continent to the Metropolis.

KENTISH TOWN,

A hamlet of St. Pancras, and a prebendal manor of St. Paul's, was formerly written Kaunteloe, and is the property of the Camden family. Here was the Castle tavern, which had a Perpendicular stone chimney-piece; the house was taken down in 1849: close to its southern wall was a sycamore planted by Lord Nelson, when a boy, at the entrance to his uncle's cottage; the tree has been spared. Opposite were the old Assembly-rooms, taken down in 1852: here was a table with an inscription by an invalid, who recovered his health by walking to this spot every morning to take his breakfast in front of the house. Kentish Town Chapel, originally built by Wyatt in 1784, has been enlarged and altered to the Early Decorated style: here is buried Grignion, the engraver. (See page 170.) In 1848 was built here a large Congregational Nonconformist Chapel in ecclesiastical style. (See p. 174.) In Gospel-terrace is the Roman Catholic Chapel of St. Alexis, established 1847. In 1848 were erected the National Infant and Sunday Schools, by Hakewill, upon the plan of the Committee of Privy Council on Education; the site is part of an estate bequeathed by the witty divine, Dr. South, to Christ Church, Oxford. Near Highgate Rise is the *Grove*, where Charles Mathews the elder made his collection of paintings, prints, and other memorials of theatrical history, now at the Garrick Club-house. (See p. 194.) Nearly opposite was "a miniature Wanstead House," the villa of Mr. Philip Hurd, of the Inner Temple, who collected here a costly library, including the celebrated *Breviarium Romanum*, purchased by him, in 1827, from Mr. Dent's library for 378*l.*: it consists of more than 500 leaves of vellum, illuminated by Flemish painters in Spain, of the 15th century, with miniatures and borders of flowers, fruit, and grotesque figures, upon a gold ground. (See Dibdin's *Bibliographical Decameron*, vol. i. pp. 163-7.) The villa was taken down in 1851. The river Fleet, which runs in the rear of the hamlet, has its source from springs on the south side of the hill between Hampstead and Highgate. In July 1846 were sold 27 acres of building-ground in Gospel-Oak and Five-Acre Fields, between Kentish Town and Hampstead, for nearly 400*l.* an acre. Beneath the Gospel Oak preached some of our earliest Reformers, and Whitefield the Methodist.

In the last century, the road between the metropolis and Kentish-Town was beset with highwaymen. In the *Morning Chronicle and London Advertiser*, Jan. 9, 1773, appears: "Thursday night some villains robbed the Kentish Town stage, and stripped the passengers of their money, watches, and buckles. In the hurry they spared the pockets of Mr. Corbyn, the druggist; but he, content to have neighbour's fare, called out to one of the rogues, ' Stop, friend, you have forgot to take my money!'"—*Notes and Queries*, No. 62.

Camden Town, begun 1791, built on the estate of the Marquis of Camden; and *Somers Town*, begun 1786, on the estate of Earl Somers,—are also hamlets of Pancras parish, and both are now united with London.

The original "Mother Red Cap," Kentish Town, was a place of terror to travellers, and is believed to have been the "Mother Damnable" of Kentish Town in early days; at this house "Moll Cutpurse," the highwayman of the time of Oliver Cromwell, dismounted and frequently lodged.—Smith's *Book for a Rainy Day*, p. 20.

KILBURN,

A hamlet about two and a half miles north-west from London, at the south-western extremity of the parish of Hampstead, is named from Cold-bourne, a stream which rises near West End, and passes through Kilburn to Bayswater; and after supplying the Serpentine reservoir in Hyde Park, flows into the Thames at Ranelagh. Kilburn has its station upon the London and North-Western Railway. In the last century, the place was famed for its mineral spring (Kilburn Wells), which rises about 12 feet below the surface, and is inclosed in a brick reservoir, the door-arch of which bears on its keystone 1714. The water is more strongly impregnated with carbonic acid gas than any other known spring in England. In 1837 was taken down a cottage at Kilburn in which Oliver Goldsmith had resided.

Kilburn originated from Godwyn, a hermit, who, *temp.* Henry II. built a cell near the little rivulet called *Cuneburna, Keelebourne, Coldbourne*, and *Kilbourne*, on a site surrounded with wood. Between 1128 and 1134, Godwyn granted his hermitage and adjoining lands to the conventual church of St. Peter at Westminster, who soon after assigned the property to Emma, Gunilda, and Cristina, maids-of-honour to Maud (queen of Henry I.), herself a Benedictine nun; and hence the cell of the anchorite became a nunnery: Godwin being appointed its master or warden, and guardian of the maidens, for his life. Certain estates were granted to the nuns in Southwark and Knightsbridge (which manor still belongs to Westminster), the latter property in the place called Gara, probably Kensington Gore. Provisions, kitchen-fare, wine, mead, and beer were also assigned; and in return the vestals prayed for St. Edward the Confessor, and the church at Westminster.

At the Dissolution, in 1536, the "Nonne of Kilbourne" was surrendered; when the inventory shews the chamber furniture to have included "bedsteddes, standing bedd w*t* 4 postes, fetherbedds, matteres, cov'lettes, wollen blankettes, bolsters, pillowes of downe, sheetes," &c. The name of the last prioress was Anne Browne. Soon after, the king assigned the priory estate, with other lands, to Weston, prior of the Hospital of St. John of Jerusalem, in exchange for Paris Garden in Surrey, &c. The church was dedicated to St. Mary and St. John the Baptist; the latter, in his camel-hair garment, is portrayed on the priory seal. The Abbey Farm at Kilburn includes the site of the priory: the only view known of the conventual buildings is an etching, date 1722.

Several relics, including pieces of pottery, a few coins, and a bronze vessel, all mediæval, were found on the Priory site in the autumn of 1852, and shewn to the Archæological Institute.

LAMBETH,

Also called *Lambhith, Lambhyde,* and *Lambhei,* is probably derived from *lam,* dirt, and *hyd* or *hythe,* a haven; or from *lamb* and *hythe.* It was anciently a village of Surrey, but is now united with Southwark; and is one of the metropolitan boroughs, returning two members to Parliament under the Reform Act of 1832. The parish ranges along the south bank of the Thames from Vauxhall towards Southwark, and extends to Norwood, Streatham, and Croydon; in Aubrey's time it included part of the forest of oaks called Norwood, belonging to the see of Canterbury, wherein was the Vicar's Oak (cut down in 1679), at which point four parishes meet. Hardyknute, the last of the Danish kings of England, died suddenly in June 1041 at Lambeth. In 1062, King Edward gave Lambeth to the monastery of Waltham, in Essex; and Harold placed the crown on his head, with his own hands, at Lambythe. (*William of Malmesbury.*) King John granted Lambeth a market and fair, long since discontinued. The Archbishops of Canterbury have resided here since the twelfth century. (See LAMBETH PALACE.)

The mother church (St. Mary's) adjoins the Palace, and is described at page 144. Beneath its walls, Mary, queen of James II., found shelter with her infant son, having crossed the river by the horse-ferry from Westminster : here the queen remained a whole hour in the rain on the night of December 9, 1688, until a coach arrived from the next inn and conveyed her to Gravesend, whence she sailed for France. St. Mary's Church was rebuilt in 1851-2, save the tower, in the same style as formerly, except the open timber roof. Memorial and other windows are filled with stained glass; "the Pedlar and his Dog" has been replaced, and the tombs and monumental brasses restored. The district churches have little that is noteworthy.

The site of *St. John's,* Waterloo-road, was a swamp and horse-pond: the church (built 1823-4) has a peal of eight bells, tenor 1900 lbs. weight : in a vault is buried Robert William Elliston, the comedian (d. 1831). The district commences at the middle of Westminster Bridge, whence an imaginary boundary-line passes through the middle of the river Thames and Waterloo Bridge.

On the south side of Church-street was Norfolk House, the mansion of the Earl of Norfolk *temp.* Edward I. : here resided the celebrated Earl of Surrey when under the tuition of John Leland, the antiquary. The house has long been demolished, and its site and grounds occupied by Norfolk-row and Hodges's distillery. The Dukes of Norfolk also had in Lambeth, on the bank of the Thames, a garden, which was let to Boydell Cuper, who opened it as Cuper's Garden, and decorated it with some fragments of the Arundelian marbles, given him by the Earl of Arundel, whose gardener he had been. Other fragments of the sculptures were set up in a piece of ground adjoining, and afterwards were buried with rubbish from the ruins of St. Paul's Cathedral, then rebuilding by Wren; but the sculptures were subsequently disinterred, and the site was let to Messrs. Beaufoy for their Vinegar-works, removed to South Lambeth on the erection of Waterloo Bridge.

Carlisle Street, Lane, and Chapel, keep in memory Carlisle House, the palace of the Bishops of Rochester from the thirteenth to the sixteenth century, when Henry VIII. granted it to the see of Carlisle. Here in 1531 Richard Roose or Rose, a cook, poisoned seventeen persons; for which he was attainted of treason and boiled to death in Smithfield, by an *ex post facto* law passed for the purpose, but repealed in the next reign. On the grounds of Carlisle House was subsequently built a pottery, which existed *temp.* George II. The house then became a tavern, brothel, dancing-school, and academy; and was taken down 1827.

Lambeth has long been celebrated for its places of public amusement.

Vauxhall Gardens are mentioned by Evelyn, in his *Diary*, July 2, 1661: "I went to see the New Spring Garden, at Lambeth, a pretty contrived plantation;" and the place is to this day licensed annually as "the Spring Garden, Vauxhall." *Belvidere House and Gardens** adjoined *Cuper's Garden* in Queen Ann's reign; and still further west were *Cumberland Tea-Gardens* (named after the great Duke), which existed until 1813, their site being now crossed by Vauxhall Bridge-road. The *Dog and Duck* dates from 1617, the year upon the sign-stone in the garden-wall of Bethlem Hospital (see page 42): here is preserved a drawing of the old tavern and its grounds. The *Hercules Inn and Gardens* occupied the site of the Asylum for Female Orphans, opened in 1758; and opposite were the *Apollo Gardens* and the *Temple of Flora*, Mountrow, opened 1788. A century earlier there existed, in King William's reign, *Lambeth Wells*, in Three Coney Walk, now Lambeth Walk; it was reputed for its mineral waters, sold at a penny a quart, "the same price paid by St. Thomas's Hospital." About 1750 a musical society was held here, and lectures and experiments were given on natural philosophy by Erasmus King, who had been coachman to Dr. Desaguliers. In Stangate-lane, Carlisle-street, is the *Bower Saloon*, with its theatre and music-room, a pleasure-haunt of our own time.

Astley's Amphitheatre originated with Philip Astley, who in 1763 commenced horsemanship in an open field near Glover's "Halfpenny Hatch" at Lambeth. Thence Astley removed to the site of the present theatre, near Westminster Bridge, when his ground-landlord had a preserve or breed of pheasants near the spot: the theatre was burnt in 1794, 1803, and 1841. The *Victoria Theatre*, formerly the *Coburg*, opened in 1818, is built on ground held of the manor of Lambeth: the site was a swampy open field; and part of the stone materials of the old Savoy Palace, Strand, then being cleared away, was used for the theatre foundation. The *Royal Circus*, St. George's Fields, was built in 1781, by Dibdin and Hughes, to compete with Astley; the Circus was burnt in 1805, and rebuilt in 1806.

The Asylum for Female Orphans, just mentioned, was established chiefly through Sir John Fielding, the police-magistrate, whose portrait, attributed to Hogarth, is preserved here; with a head of George III. and his youngest son, the Duke of Cambridge, who was long president of the institution: in the chapel is a tablet to his memory. The site cost the charity 16,000*l*.; premises rebuilt 1826.

In Oakley-street, at the Oakley Arms, November 16, 1802, Colonel Edward Marcus Despard and thirty-two other persons were apprehended on a charge of high treason: and in February following, the Colonel, with nine associates, were tried by a special commission at the Surrey Sessions House; and being all found guilty, seven, including Despard, were executed February 21 on the top of Horsemonger-lane Gaol.

Lambeth has been noted as the residence of astrologers. At Tradescant's house, in South Lambeth-road, lived Elias Ashmole, who won Aubrey over to astrology (see pp. 309 and 396). Simon Forman's burial is entered in the Lambeth parish-register: he died on the day he had prognosticated. Lilly says, Forman wrote in a book left behind him: "this I made the devil write with his own hand in Lambeth Fields, 1569, in June or July, as I now remember." Captain Bubb, contemporary with Forman, dwelt in Lambeth Marsh, and "resolved horary questions astrologically," a ladder which raised him to the pillory. At the north corner of Calcot-alley lived Francis Moore,

---

* Dr. Rawlinson, in his additions to Aubrey's *Surrey* (written in 1719), imagines Belvidere Gardens to have been the site of a *saw-mill* erected in Cromwell's time, and which he protected by Act of Parliament.

astrologer, physician, and schoolmaster, and the original author of
' Moore's Almanack." Next to Tradescant's house lived the learned
Dr. Ducarel, one of the earliest Fellows of the Society of Antiquaries,
and librarian at Lambeth Palace.

At South Lambeth, upon the site of Sir Noell Caron's mansion and
deer-park, are *Beaufoy's Vinegar and Wine Works.* Here were a vessel
of sweet wine containing 59,109 gallons, and another of vinegar of 56,799
gallons; the lesser of which exceeded the famous Heidelberg tun by 40
barrels. Mr. Beaufoy, F.R.S. was an eminent mathematician, and a
munificent patron of education; and his bust is placed in the Council
Chamber, Guildhall (see p. 340).

In Lambeth Walk, close upon the South-Western Railway, are the
Lambeth Ragged Schools, founded in 1851 by Mr. Beaufoy, at the expense of 10,000l., and 4000l. endowment, as a memorial of the benevolent Mrs. Beaufoy, the wife of the founder.

On part of the site of Belvidere House and Gardens were established, in 1785, the *Lambeth Water-works,* first taking their water
from the borders of the Thames; then from its centre, near Hungerford Bridge, by a cast-iron conduit-pipe 42 inches in diameter;
whence, in 1852, the works were removed to Seething Wells, Ditton,
23 miles by the river course from London Bridge. Thence the water
is supplied to the Company's reservoirs at Brixton, 10¾ miles, by steam
pumping-engines, at the rate of 10,000,000 gallons daily; from these reservoirs, 100 feet above the Thames, the water flows by its own gravity
through the mains; but at Norwood it is lifted by steam-power 350
feet, or the height of St. Paul's Cathedral, above the supplying river.

In *Belvidere-road* is *Goding's Ale Brewery,* built in 1836: the upper
floor is an immense tank for water, supplying the floor below, where
the boiled liquor is cooled; it then descends into fermenting tuns in
the story beneath; next to the floor for fining; and lastly to the cellar
or store-vats.

Lambeth Marsh, by Hollar's map, extended from near Stangate to
Broadwall; and was bounded by the river on the north-west, and the
ancient way or road called Lambeth Marsh on the south-east. The
names of Narrow-wall and Broad-wall were derived from the embank-
ments subsequently made.

In cutting for the railway and lines of sewerage at the great terminus near
York-road (a space in size equal to Grosvenor-square), there was found a large
deposit from the inundations of the Thames, containing gravel-stones and dark
wet clay, or pressed river-mud, imbedding fragments of twigs, bones, pieces of
Roman tile, &c.

Narrow Wall, Vine-street, and Cornwall-road are delineated in
views of these suburbs in Queen Elizabeth's reign: Vine-street is from
8 to 10 feet below the level of the adjacent streets.

Plate-glass for mirrors and coach-windows was first made, in 1670, by
Venetian artists, with Rosetti at their head, under the patronage of the
second Duke of Buckingham, at Fox-hall (Vauxhall), with great success,
" so as to excel the Venetians, or any other nation, in blown plate-
glass." But about 1780 the establishment was broken up, and a
descendant of Rosetti's left in extreme poverty. (*Hist. of Lambeth,*
1786.) Some of the finest " Vauxhall plates" are to be seen in the
Speaker's state-coach. The *Falcon Glass-house,* Holland-street, Blackfriars-road, occupies the site of the tide-mill of the old manor of Paris
Garden, and has existed more than a century; here is made about a
fortieth part of the flint-glass manufactured in England.*

* Mr. Apsley Pellatt, the proprietor of the Falcon Works, elected M.P. for
Southwark in 1852, has published *Curiosities of Glass-making* (1849); the expe-
riences of a lifetime unceasingly devoted to the study and practice of the art.

Lambeth has long been famed for its stone-ware. The *Vauxhall Pottery*, established two centuries since, by two Dutchmen, for the manufacture of old Delft ware, is probably the origin of all our existing potteries. Two other Potteries at Lambeth were commenced in 1730 and 1741. The potters procure the clay from Devon and Dorset, and the flint, already ground, from Staffordshire. Salt-glazed stone-ware is made in Lambeth of the yearly value of 100,000*l.*, of which more than one-half is paid for labour; at Green's manufactory are made chemical vessels for holding from 300 to 400 gallons.

In *Hunt's Chemical Works*, High-street, are combined the crushing of bones and the grinding of mustard with the manufacture of colours, soap, and bone brushes; and stearine, glue, hartshorn, and phosphate of lime are obtained by steam-power from the refuse of slaughtered cattle. *Hawes's Soap and Candle Works*, at the Old Royal Barge House, have existed for 80 years.

Above Vauxhall Bridge are *Price's Stearine Candle Company's Works* (established 1842): covering two acres; employing 900 workpeople, and immense hydraulic and steam power; and making 100 tons (7000*l.* worth) of candles weekly, from cocoa-nut-oil brought from the Company's plantations in Ceylon, and palm-oil from the coast of Africa, landed from barges at the wharf at Vauxhall. The oil being converted by chemical processes into stearine, is freed from oleic acid by enormous pressure; is liquefied by steam, and then conveyed into the moulding machinery, by which 800 miles of wicks are continually being converted into candles. The buildings are of corrugated iron, and include the auxiliaries of a laboratory, engineers', carpenters', tinmen's, coppersmiths', and weavers' shops; forges, a cooperage, a sealing-wax manufactory, and steam printing-machine; the several furnaces consuming their own smoke. This is the most colossal establishment in the world in this branch of chemical manufacture; the annual profits are from 40,000*l.* to 50,000*l.*

Shot is made in the lofty towers immediately above and below Waterloo Bridge. The height of the quadrangular tower is 150 feet: the upper floor is a room wherein the alloy of arsenic and lead is melted by a furnace; the fluid metal is then ladled into a kind of cullender, through the holes of which it falls *like rain* for about 130 feet into water at the lower floor of the building. An iron staircase leads from the bottom to the top of the tower: on Jan. 5, 1826, the upper floor was destroyed by fire, which happening at night, presented a magnificent effect.

The circular shot-tower, 100 feet high, is strikingly beautiful. Mr. Hosking, the architect, considers this structure to rival the Monument: "they are both," he observes, "of cylindrical form; but the one is crowned by a square abacus, and the other by a bold cornice, which follows its own outline (*i.e.* of the tower): the greater simplicity and consequent beauty of the latter is such as to strike the most unobservant."

Maudslay and Field's Works, in the Westminster-road, commenced in 1810 with 150 men and one steam-engine, now employ 1000 men, besides steam-power for the heavy labour. In Duke-street, Stamford-street, is *Clowes's Printing-Office and Foundry*, the largest in the world, commenced by Applegath the eminent engineer; here two steam-engines put in motion 26 printing-machines.

The "New Cut," from Westminster to Blackfriars Road, has become a street within the recollection of the writer, who remembers low-lying fields, with a large windmill, east of the raised roadway. *Pedlar's Acre* (for the name see page 145), a portion of the Marsh, by old admeasurement contains 1 acre·17 poles, with a frontage on the Thames. In 1504 by the churchwardens' accounts, it was an osier-bed, and in 1623, Church Osiers; the name of *Pedlar's Acre* does not occur until 1690, probably from its being the squatting-place of pedlars, as were the New Cut fields within memory.

In 1504-5, the annual rent of this estate was 2s. 8d.; in 1506, 4s.; 1520, 6s.; 1556, 6s. 8d.; in 1564, 13s. 4d.; in 1581, 1l. 6s. 8d.; and in 1651, 4l., at about hich sum it continued until the commencement of the last century. After the raining of Lambeth Marsh, and the erection of Westminster and Blackfriars ridges, Pedlar's Acre, in 1752, was held on a long lease at a yearly rent of 100l. ad 800l. fine. In 1813, when it had been much built upon, it was let by auction r twenty-one years, in three lots, at 78l. per annum, and 6000l. premium. The nts and proceeds are applied to parochial purposes, under the Act 7 Geo. IV. p. 46.

At Narrow Wall flourished for nearly 60 years Coade's Manu- ctory of burnt Artificial Stone (a revival of *terra-cotta*), invented y the elder Bacon, the sculptor, and first established by Mrs. Coade, om Lyme Regis, in 1769. Of this material are the bas-relief in e pediment over the western portico at Greenwich Hospital, re- resenting the Death of Nelson, designed by West, and executed by acon and Panzetta; and the rood-screen or loft at St. George's Chapel, indsor. The manufacture (now Austin and Seeley's) has been removed the New-road.

Lambeth, a few years since a feverish marsh, has been greatly im- roved by drainage : in 1810, Maudslay's Foundry was raised on pillars om the swamp, where at times a boat might have floated ; it is now, drainage, firm and dry at all seasons. Lett's Timber Wharf, from e time of Queen Elizabeth until the beginning of this century, lay idst ponds and marsh-streams, but is now dry and healthy.

Lambeth early in the present century contained 1400 houses ; in 20 they had increased to 5000; in 1841, to 18,000 ; in 1851, to 20,520. cross this thickly-peopled district extends the South-Western Rail- ay from its terminus in the Waterloo Bridge road to Nine Elms, miles 50 yards, executed at a cost of 800,000l.

LAMBETH PALACE,

ambeth House of old, has been for six and a half centuries the ansion of the Archbishops of Canterbury, who had resided at Lam- eth seventy years previously; and in 1197 obtained the entire manor, y exchange with the Bishop of Rochester for certain lands in Kent. ence the present palace is the manor-house; and, with the gardens d grounds, forms an extra-parochial district.

The oldest part of Lambeth Palace is the *Chapel*, and a *Crypt*, sup- osed to be a portion of the ancient manor-house, built by Archbishop ubert Walter about 1190. Archbishops Langton, Boniface, Arun- el, Chicheley, Stafford, Morton, Warham, Cranmer, Pole, Parker, and ancroft, expended great sums on the palace, as have succeeding arch- ishops. Cranmer's additions included " the Steward's Parlour," and a summer-house in the garden, of exquisite workmanship;" both hich have disappeared. In Wat Tyler's rebellion, " the commons om Essex" plundered the palace, and beheaded the archbishop, Sud- ry, on Tower Hill. In 1642, the Parliamentary soldiers dismantled e Chapel, broke the painted windows, which it was alleged Arch- shop Laud had restored " by their like in the mass-book;" while ud's " books and goods were seized on, and even his very diary ken by force out of his pocket." The palace was then used as a ison for the Royalists; and after its sale by the Parliament for 73l., the Chapel was converted into a dancing-room, and the Great ll demolished. The latter was rebuilt by Archbishop Juxon, at the arge of 10,500l. The palace was attacked by the rioters of 1780, when was protected by a detachment of Guards, and subsequently by a litia regiment as a garrison for some weeks. Between 1828 and 1848 rchbishop Howley rebuilt the habitable portion of the palace, and restored other parts, at a cost of 60,000*l*. The garden front is of Tudor character; and with its bays and enriched windows, battlements, gables, towers, and clustered chimney-shafts, is very picturesque.

The Gate-house, built by Archbishop Morton about 1490, consists of an embattled centre and two immense square towers, of fine red brick with stone dressings, and a spacious Tudor arched gateway and postern. The towers are ascended by spiral stone staircases, leading to the *Record-room* containing many of the archives of the see of Canterbury. Adjoining the archway is a small prison-room, with high and narrow windows, and thick stone walls to which are fastened three strong iron rings; and in the wall are cuttings, including John Grafton, and a cross and other figures near it. The walls and towers of the gate-house, and the ancient brick wall on the Thames side, are chequered with crosses in glazed bricks.

At this gate the *dole* immemorially given to the poor by the Archbishops of Canterbury is constantly distributed. It consists of fifteen quartern loaves, nine stone of beef, and five shillings worth of halfpence, divided into three equal portions, and distributed every Sunday, Tuesday, and Thursday among thirty poor parishioners of Lambeth; the beef being made into broth and served in pitchers.

The Lollards' Tower, on the left of the outer court, is embattled, and chiefly of dark-red brick, faced with stone on its outer sides. It was built (1434-5) by Archbishop Chicheley, whose arms are sculptured on the outer wall on the Thames side; beneath them is a Gothic niche, wherein formerly stood the image of St. Thomas à Becket. In this tower is the *Post-room*, with a flat and panelled ceiling, carved with angels and scrolls, and a head resembling that of Henry VIII. On the east side is an entrance to the Chapel; and through a small door you ascend by a steep spiral staircase to the *Lollards' Prison* (in an adjoining square tower on the north side), entering by a narrow, low, pointed archway of stone, with an oaken inner and outer door, each 3½ inches thick, closely studded with iron rivets and fastenings. The chamber is nearly 15 feet in length, by 11 feet in width, and 8 feet high; and has two narrow windows, and a small fireplace and chimney. About breast-high are fixed in the walls eight large iron rings; and upon the oaken wainscoting are incisions of initials, names, short sentences, crosses,

(Incisions upon the wall of Lollards' Tower.)

cubes, &c. cut by the unhappy captives. It is no longer considered that they were exclusively Lollards, nor is there positive evidence that these followers of Wicliffe were imprisoned here; although the registers of the see of Canterbury record several proceedings against the sect, and Wicliffe himself is said to have been examined in the Chapel at Lambeth. Archbishop Arundel was the fiercest persecutor of the Lollards, and his successor, Chicheley, built "the Lollards' Tower," possibly on the site of other prisons here, which the registers of the see prove the archbishops to have possessed. To Lambeth House the Popish prelates, Tunstall and Thirlby, were committed by Queen Elizabeth: and here were confined the Earl of Essex; the Earls of Chesterfield and Derby; Sir Thomas Armstrong, afterwards executed for participation in the Duke of Monmouth's rebellion; Dr. Allestry, the eminent divine; and Richard Lovelace, the poet.

In the three stories above the Post-room are apartments for the archbishop's chaplains and librarian. The view of the river and the metropolis from the roof of the tower is singularly fine; and the new Palace at Westminster is there seen to great advantage.

The Chapel, entered from the Post-room, is divided by an elaborately carved screen; but the arched roof is concealed by flat paneling, bearing the arms of Laud, Juxon, and Cornwallis. At the east end are five long lancet-shaped lights, filled with diapered modern glass; and at each side are three triplicated windows, resembling those of the Temple Church. Here are the archbishop's stall, seats for the officers of his household, and below for the male servants; the females being seated in the outer chapel, in a small gallery, where was formerly an organ. In front of the altar is buried Archbishop Parker, beneath a marble slab, inscribed, " Corpus Matthæi archiepiscopi tandem hic qviescit."* The tomb, which Parker " erected while he was yet alive," near the spot where he " used to pray," was demolished by Col. Scot in 1642, and the Archbishop's corpse thrown into a dung-heap; but it was recovered and reinterred after the Restoration. Archbishop Bancroft has narrated these facts in an epitaph of elegant Latin, inscribed on a tomb raised by him to Parker's memory. In the Chapel have been consecrated upwards of 150 bishops: Dr. Howley's consecration as Bishop of London (1813) was witnessed by Queen Charlotte, when 70 years of age: as Archbishop of Canterbury, he crowned three sovereigns. Here the present Archbishop (Sumner) held his first ordination, June 18, 1848. The *Crypt* beneath the chapel has been already noticed at page 242.

The Library (Juxon's Hall) and the *Great Dining-room* (on the site of the Guard-chamber) form the west side of the inner court. On the north are the new buildings of the palace, by E. Blore; the entrance is between two octagonal towers, 84 feet high. In the private library is a portrait on board of Archbishop Warham, consecrated 1504; this was painted by Holbein, and presented by him to the archbishop, with a head of his friend Erasmus: the latter is missing. In the ante-room is a whole-length portrait of Charles I., ascribed to Vandyke; and a picture on panel of St. Ambrose, St. Jerome, St. Augustine, and St. Gregory, with the Holy Spirit: both pictures belonged to Cardinal Pole.

The Guard-chamber is mentioned in 1424 as the " *Camera Armigerorum*," from the arms being kept here for the defence of the palace; but they were carried off in the plunder of 1642, and were never replaced. In this chamber Archbishop Laud kept his *state*, Sept. 19, 1633, the day of his consecration. The apartment is 58 feet long and 27 feet 6 inches wide; it has a very elegant oak roof, with the lofty two-centred and bold tracery of Early Perpendicular work; it was long plastered over, but was restored by Blore about 1832, when it was under-propped, and the walls were rebuilt. The roof is paneled, and supported by bold arches springing from octangular corbels; the spandrels of the arches being filled by quatrefoils in circles, and trefoil mouldings. On the gabled sides of the roof similarly enriched arches stretch between the great roof arches; on the walls also arches span from corbel to corbel, and support an embattled frieze; and the fireplace is turreted.

In this room, besides smaller portraits, is a series of half and three-quarter lengths of all the Archbishops of Canterbury since 1633: including Laud, by Vandyke; Juxon (who attended Charles I. on the scaffold), from an original at Long-

* In this Chapel Archbishop Parker was consecrated, Dec. 5, 1559, according to the " duly appointed ordinal of the Church of England," as recorded in Parker's Register at Lambeth, and in the library of Corpus Christi College at Cambridge; thus falsifying the absurd calumny promulgated by the Romanists, of Archbishop Parker having been irregularly consecrated at the Nag's Head Tavern, at the east end of Friday-street, Cheapside, by one bishop only.

leat; Herring, by Hogarth; Secker, by Reynolds; Sutton, by Beechey; Howley, by Shee. These portraits shew the gradual change in the clerical dress, in bands and wigs, and the large ruff in place of the band: Tillotson's being the first wig, unpowdered, and not unlike the natural hair. Here also are smaller heads of the earlier archbishops: Arundel, from a curious portrait at Penshurst; Chicheley, Cranmer, and Grindal; and Cardinal Pole, from an original in the Barberini Palace at Rome. Pole maintained great hospitality at Lambeth: in the Ms. Library is his patent (4 Philip and Mary) for retaining one hundred servants. The body of the Cardinal lay in great state at Lambeth during forty days, prior to its interment at Canterbury.

In the *Picture Gallery*, built by Pole, among other paintings are: Archbishop Potter when six years old (1680), holding a Greek Testament, which he is said then nearly to have read; Martin Luther, from Nuremburg; Cardinal Pole (curious, on board, and probably a genuine likeness); Queen Catherine Parr, original, on board; Luther and his Wife (?), attributed to Holbein, and copied on enamel by Bone; Henry Prince of Wales, eldest son of James I. (full-length, curious costume); Bishop Burnet, as Chancellor of the Garter; an old view of Canterbury Cathedral; Archbishop Juxon, after his decease; Bishop Hoadley, painted by his second wife; Archbishop Parker,* painted in 1572 by Richard Lyne, who practised painting and engraving in the palace; Archbishop Tillotson, by Mrs. Beale.

In this Hall are given annually, on "public days," a certain number of state entertainments, termed "Lambeth Palace dinners," to the bishops and leading clergy. The Rev. Sydney Smith facetiously asks: "Is it necessary that the Archbishop of Canterbury should give feasts to aristocratic London; and that the domestics of the Prelacy should stand with swords and bag-wigs, round pig and turkey and venison, to defend, as it were, the orthodox gastronomer from the fierce Unitarian, the fell Baptist, and the famished children of Dissent?"— *Second Letter on Church Reform.*

The Great Hall is built of dark-red brick, with strong buttresses and stone finishings. In the centre of the roof is a two-storied hexagonal lantern, surmounted by a large vane, in which are the arms of the see of Canterbury, impaled with those of Juxon (a cross between four negroes' heads), surmounted by the archiepiscopal mitre. The interior was converted into a library for the printed books belonging to the see, between 1830 and 1834; when a new entrance-gateway to the inner court was built, with a fireproof room over it, in which are kept the MSS. The library is 93 feet by 38 feet, and upwards of 50 feet high from the ground-floor: the large north-west bay-window is richly ornamented stained and painted glass; in the top division is a very large coat of the arms of the see and Archbishop Juxon; and underneath are the arms of the see and Archbishop Howley, 1829. Around are smaller coats of the arms of about twenty-four archbishops, each impaled with the arms of the see. Here are also the arms of Philip II. king of Spain; but the most curious piece of painted glass is an ancient portrait of Archbishop Chicheley.

The roof is of oak, and a fine specimen of olden carpentry: it consists of eight main ribs, with longitudinal braces, springing from corbel brackets, and enriched with carved spandrels, pendants, enwreathed mitres, and the arms of Juxon and the see of Canterbury several times repeated. Above the two fireplaces are painted the arms of the see, impaling those of Bancroft, the founder of the library; and of Secker, a liberal contributor. The books, over-estimated by Ducarel at 25,000 volumes, are kept in wall and projecting oak cases; the earliest printed works being in the south-west bay-window recess. Until Bancroft bequeathed his books in 1610, each archbishop brought his own private collection. Bancroft's books remained at Lambeth till 1646, two years after the execution of Laud, when being seized by the Parliament, the use of them was granted to Dr. Wincocke. They were subsequently

* This portrait strongly resembles the small print of the Archbishop engraved by R. Berg (Remigius Hogenberg), which Vertue considered to be the first portrait engraved in England.

given to Sion College, and many began to get into private hands; when Selden suggested to the University of Cambridge a right to them, and they were delivered, pursuant to an ordinance of Parliament, dated Feb. 1647, into their possession. After the Restoration, and repeated demands by Juxon and Sheldon, the books were collected, including those in private hands, and in the possession of John Thurloe and Hugh Peters. Evelyn writes to Pepys, in 1689, that the library was then "replenished with excellent books, but that it ebbs and flows, like the Thames running by it, at every prelate's accession or translation." The books left by Archbishops Bancroft, Abbot, Laud, Sheldon, and Tenison, bear their arms. There is only one volume in the collection known to have belonged to Archbishop Parker, which is a volume of Calvin's writing: his arms are on the outside, and within is written in red lead, " J. Parker," who was the archbishop's son.

The first complete Catalogue made of the printed books was drawn up by Bishop Gibson when librarian. In 1718 it was fairly copied by Dr. Wilkins, in three volumes folio; and it has been continued by his successors to the present time. The library consists of rare and curious editions of the Scriptures, commentaries of the early fathers, scarce controversial divinity, records of ecclesiastical affairs, English history and topography; many fine copies, splendidly embellished.

The early printed books (see the Rev. Dr. Maitland's two Catalogues) include, Caxton's *Chronicles of England* and *Description of Britain*, both " fynsshed" in 1480, the finest copies extant; Lyndewode's *Constitutiones Provinciales*, printed by Wynkin de Worde in 1499; *The Golden Legend*, emprynted at London in Fletestrete. in the Sygne of the George, by Richard Pynson, in 1507, and another edition of the same work by Wynkin de Worde in 1527; Gower's *Confessio Amantis*, a splendid copy by Caxton, 1483; *Dives and Pauper*, by Pynson, 1493; *Chaucer's Works*, folio, by John Reynes, in 1452, and Islip, in 1598. Here, too, is a small folio, executed at Paris, on vellum, about 1500, intituled, *La Dance Macabre* (the Dance of Death), printed with old Gothic types and beautifully illuminated. Here also, in volumes, is Bancroft's collection of black-letter tracts, pamphlets, and sermons; remarkable for St. Paul's Cross sermons, Mar-Prelate tracts, and the writings of the Brownists and other Elizabethan separatists. Here, too, is a copy of Archbishop Parker's Antiquities, printed by Dayes in 1572 (only two complete copies extant): it contains the very rare portrait of Parker, taken just before his death, by Berg.

Among the Manuscripts are, the ancient French version and exposition of the Apocalypse, with miniature paintings, No. 75; the Latin copy of the Apocalypse, No. 209 (thirteenth century), with 78 brilliant illuminations; and No. 200, a copy of the treatise *De Virginitate*, in praise of celibacy, by Aldhelm, Abbot of Malmesbury, eighth century. Among the sacred Mss. are Greek Testaments; the Old Testament in Armenian; the whole Bible, Wicliffe's translation; and Latin Psalters, beautifully written and illuminated. Here, too, are Scripture expositions of Bede; Anglo-Saxon sermons (tenth century) and Saxon homilies (twelfth century). Among the Missals is a very beautiful Salisbury missal, folio, on vellum, emblazoned with Archbishop Chicheley's arms. The Mss. of Greek and Latin classics are extremely valuable. Here are the Lambeth Registers, 40 vols. folio, on vellum; containing homages, popes' bulls; letters to and from popes, cardinals, kings, and princes; commissions and proxies, marriages and divorces, &c. 1279 to 1747 (except 1644 to 1660): the registers of the primates subsequent to Potter, 1747, are kept at Doctors' Commons. Also two large folio volumes of papal bulls; ancient charters of the see, 13 vols.; accurate transcripts of the parliamentary surveys of the property of bishops, deans, and chapters, made during the Commonwealth, 21 vols.

The collection is stored with Mss. of English history, civil and ecclesiastical, including chronicles and collections of histories; and important documents, particularly of the relations of France with England (*temp.* Hen. V. and VI.). Among the Mss. on Heraldry and Genealogy are many written or corrected by Lord Burghley. Here are stores of old English poetry and romances: including Lydgate's Works, and Gawen Douglas's Translation of Virgil's *Æneid;* and the metrical legend of Libeaus Disconus.

Among the *Letters* are those of Lord Verulam, published by Dr. Birch; those of his brother, Anthony Bacon, 16 vols.; the letters of the Earl of Shrewsbury, and of other persons, *temp.* Henry VIII. to James I.

But the most curious and beautifully written of the miscellaneous Mss. (between 1200 and 1300 in number) is Lord Rivers's translation from the French of " the Notable Wise Sayings of Philosophers," with a very fine illumination of Earl Rivers presenting Caxton the printer to King Edward IV., in presence of his queen and infant son, afterwards Edward V. (*Londiniana, vol.* iii. p. 316.)

Here is an original copy of Aggas's map of London, *temp.* Elizabeth; and here are laid up the service-books which have been used at the coronations of different sovereigns. The coronation-chairs claimed by the archbishops have descended to their respective families.

Among the *Curiosities* is the *habit of a priest*, consisting of a stole, manuple, chasuble, cord, two bands marked P., and the corporal; also, a crucifix of base metal, a string of beads, and a box of relics. Here is kept the shell of the tortoise, believed to have lived in the palace-garden from the time of Laud (1633) to 1753, when it perished by the negligence of the gardener: the shell is 10 inches in length, and 6½ inches in breadth.

The *Gardens and grounds* extend to eighteen acres. Here were formerly two fine white Marseilles fig-trees, traditionally planted by Cardinal Pole against that part of the palace which he founded: these trees were more than 50 feet in height and 40 in breadth; their circumferences 28 and 21 inches. They were removed during the late rebuilding, but some cuttings from the trees are growing between the buttresses of the Library. The Terrace is named Clarendon Walk, from having been the scene of the conference between the great and wise Earl of Clarendon and the ill-fated Laud.

A superb feature in the Archbishop's *state* was formerly a river barge, in which he went to Parliament; but this custom has been discontinued a century, or since Archbishop Wake's primacy.

The Stationers' Company's Barge calling at Lambeth Palace on Lord Mayor's Day (see p. 366) thus originated: when Tenison possessed the see, a near relation of his who was master of the Stationers' Company thought it a compliment to call at the Palace in his stately barge on the morning of Lord Mayor's Day, when the archbishop sent out a pint of wine for each liveryman, with bread and cheese and ale for the watermen and attendants; and this grew into a settled custom. The Stationers' Company in return present to the archbishop a copy of the several almanacks which they publish.

Lambeth House has at various times proved an asylum for learned foreigners who have been compelled to flee from the intolerant spirit of their own countrymen. Here the early reformers, Martyr and Bucer, found a safe retreat; and the learned Antonio, Archbishop of Spalatre, was entertained by Archbishop Abbot. The archbishops have frequently been honoured by visits from their respective sovereigns. Henry VII., just before his coronation, visited Archbishop Bourchier. Henry VIII. was a guest of Warham, in 1513; and one evening in 1543 he crossed the Thames to Lambeth, to acquaint Cranmer (whom he called into his barge) of the plot against him instigated by Bishop Gardiner. Queen Mary is said to have refurnished Lambeth House, at her own expense, for the reception of Cardinal Pole, whom she several times visited here during his short primacy. Elizabeth often visited Archbishop Parker; his successor, Grindal, was out of favour; but Whitgift, the next archbishop, was visited fifteen times by Elizabeth, who occasionally stayed two or three days. James also visited Whitgift. Mary, Queen of William III. had a conference here in 1694 with Archbishop Tillotson, who was honoured with a visit from Peter the Great, to witness the ceremony of an ordination.

LAW COURTS.

For nearly eight centuries, existing record proves Law Courts to have been held at Westminster, within the palace of the sovereign: one of the earliest notices being in the *Annals of Waverley*, 1069, when Elfric, Abbot of Peterborough, was tried before the king *in curia*. But it was not until 1225 (9 Hen. III.) that the Law Courts, hitherto held wherever the king was temporarily resident, were permanently fixed at Westminster. Here the Courts were frequently held before the monarch in person; and the phrase of summons, "in *banco reginæ*," still is, "before the queen herself."

The old Law Courts in Westminster Hall were thus arranged. At the entry, on the right hand, were settled the Common Pleas, for civil matters; at the upper end, in the south-east corner, was the King's Bench, for pleas of the Crown; and in the south-west angle sat the Lord Chancellor, the Master of the Rolls, and eleven men learned in the civil law, called Masters of the Chancery, deriving its name from the lattice-work, "cancelli," which separated this Court (in the last century shutting it out of sight) from the lower part of the Hall. (The screen was removed before the coronation of King George IV.) Near the King's Bench, going to the large chamber (White Hall) was the Court of Wards and Liveries, instituted by Henry VIII.; in this chamber, then called the Treasury, were kept valuable state-papers. Adjoining, but inferior to the Chancery, was the Equity Court of Requests, or Conscience, for trying suits made by way of petition to the sovereign; and sometimes called the Poor Man's Court, because he could there have right without paying money. It began its sittings in 1493, and was remodelled in 1517; the Lord Privy Seal sitting as judge.—Walcott's *Westminster*, p. 252, abridged.

The Old Court of Requests, just mentioned, was, at the Union, fitted up as the King's Robing-room and the House of Lords; and after the great fire in 1834, this Court was newly roofed, and fitted up as the House of Commons; the old Painted Chamber being similarly provided as the House of Lords.

ADMIRALTY COURT (see page 258).

AUGMENTATIONS' COURT (the) was remodelled by Henry VIII. under the Lord Chancellor, for surveying and governing all forfeited ecclesiastical property secularised to the use of the king: all deeds and resignations of abbeys, priories, and lands, and their valuations, were kept here. This Court was dissolved by Queen Mary; but its Tudor building was not removed until 1793.

CENTRAL CRIMINAL COURT (the) forms part of the Sessions House, formerly "the Justice Hall," divided by a broad yard from the prison of Newgate, in the Old Bailey. The Court, established 1834, sits monthly; so that a prisoner has been apprehended one day, committed by a magistrate on the second, and tried, convicted, and sentenced on the third or fourth day. The judges are, the Lord Mayor (who opens the Court), the Sheriffs, the Lord Chancellor (such is the order of the Act), the Judges, the Aldermen, Recorder, Common Serjeant of London, judge of the Sheriffs' Court, or City Commissioner, and any others whom the crown may appoint as assistants. Of these, the Recorder and Common Serjeant are in reality the presiding judges; a judge of the law only assisting when unusual points of the law are involved, or when conviction affects the life of the prisoner. Here are tried crimes of every kind, from treason to the pettiest larceny, and even offences committed on the high seas. The jurisdiction comprises the whole of the metropolis as now defined; together with the remainder of Middlesex; the parishes of Richmond and Mortlake in Surrey; and great part of Essex.

The Court-house, built in 1773, was destroyed in the Riots of 1780, but was rebuilt and enlarged 1809, by the addition of the site of Surgeons' Hall. The Old Court is a square hall, with a gallery for visitors; below is a dock for the prisoners, with stairs descending to the covered passage by which they are conveyed to and from Newgate; opposite is the bench, with the chief seat, above it a gilded sheathed sword upon the crimson wall; and a canopy overhead, surmounted with the royal arms. To the left of the dock is the witness-box, and further left is the jury-box; which arrangement enables the jury to see, without turning, the faces of the witnesses and prisoners; the witnesses to identify the prisoner; and lastly, the judges on the bench, and the counsel in the centre of the Court below; keeping jury, witnesses, and prisoners all at once within nearly the same line of view. The Court formerly sat at 7 A.M.; the present hour is 10. Upon the front of the dock is placed rue, to prevent infection. In 1750, when the jail-fever raged in Newgate, the effluvia entering the Court, caused the death of Baron Clarke, Sir Thomas Abney, the judge of the Common Pleas; and Pennant's "respected kinsman," Sir Samuel Pennant, Lord Mayor; besides members of the bar and of the jury, and other persons: this disease was also fatal to several persons in 1772. In the New Court, adjoining, are tried the lighter offences.

In 1841, both Courts were ventilated upon Dr. Reid's plan, from chambers beneath the floors, filled with air filtered from an apartment outside the building; the air being drawn into them by an enormous discharge upon the highest part of the edifice, or propelled into them by a fanner. From the entire building the vitiated air is received in a large chamber in the roof of the Old Court, whence it is discharged by a gigantic iron cowl, 15 feet in diameter, weighing two tons, and the point of the arrow of the guiding-vane 150 lbs. The subterranean air-tunnels pass through a portion of the old City wall.

Above the Old Court is a stately dining-room, wherein, during the Old Bailey sittings, the dinners are given by the sheriffs to the judges and aldermen, the Recorder, Common Serjeant, city pleaders, and a few visitors. Marrow-puddings and rump-steaks are invariably provided. Two dinners, exact duplicates, are served each day, at 3 and 5 o'clock; the judges relieve each other, but aldermen have eaten both dinners; and a chaplain, who invariably presided at the lower end of the table, thus ate two dinners a-day for ten years. Theodore Hook admirably describes a Judges' Dinner in his *Gilbert Gurney*. In 1807-8, the dinners for three sessions, nineteen days, cost Sheriff Phillips 35*l.* per day = 665*l.*; 145 dozen of wine, consumed at the above dinners, 450*l.*: total 1115*l.* The amount is now considerably greater, as the sessions are held monthly.

"The Press Yard," between the Court-house and Newgate, recals the horrors of the old criminal law, in the *peine fort et dure* (the strong and hard pain); a torture applied to persons refusing to plead, who were stripped and put in low dark chambers, with as much weight of iron placed upon them as they could bear, *and more*, there to lie until they were dead; which barbarous custom of *pressing to death* continued until 1734.

Memorable Trials at the Old Bailey and Central Criminal Court: Major Strangwayes, the assassin, 1657; Col. Turner and his family, for burglary in Lime-street, 1663; the Regicides, 1660; Green, Berry, and Hill, for the murder of Sir Edmundberry Godfrey, 1678; Count Koningsmark and three others, for the assassination of Mr. Thynne, 1681; Lord William Russell, William Hone, and two others, for high treason, 1683; Rowland Walters and others, for the murder of Sir Charles Pym, bart. 1688; Harrison, for the murder of Dr. Clenche, 1692; Beau Fielding, for bigamy, 1706; Richard Thornhill, Esq., for killing Sir Cholmeley Deering in a duel, 1711; the Marquis di Paleotti, for the murder of his servant in Lisle-street, 1718; Major Oneby, for killing in a duel, 1718 and 1726; Jack Sheppard, the house-breaker, 1724; Jonathan Wild, the thief-taker (who lived nearly opposite the Court-house), 1725;* Catherine Hayes, murder of her husband, 1726; Richard Savage, the poet, for murder, 1727; the infamous Col. Charteris, 1730; Sarah Malcolm, for murder, 1733; Elizabeth Canning, an inexplicable mystery, 1753; Ann Brownrigg, for murder, 1767; Baretti, for stabbing, 1769; the two Perraus, for forgery, 1776; the Rev. Dr. Dodd, for forgery, 1777; the Rev. Mr. Hackman, for shooting Miss Reay, 1779; Ryland, the engraver, for forgery, 1783; Barrington, the pickpocket, 1790; Renwick Williams, for stabbing, 1790; Theodore Gardelle, for murder, 1790; Hatfield, for shooting at George III., 1800; Capt. Macnamara, for killing Col. Montgomery in a duel, 1803; Aslett, the Bank clerk (forgery on the Bank, 320,000l.), 1803; old Patch, for murder, 1806; Holloway and Haggerty, for murder, 1807; Governor Wall, for murder by flogging, 1812; Bellingham, the assassin of Perceval, 1812; Eliza Fenning, for poisoning, 1815; Cashman, the seaman, for riot on Snow-hill (where he was hanged), 1817; Richard Carlile, for blasphemy, 1819 and 1831; Cato-street conspirators, 1820; Fauntleroy, for forgery, 1824; St. John Long, the "counter-irritation" surgeon, for manslaughter, 1830 and 1831; Bishop and Williams, for murder by "burking," 1831; Greenacre, for murder, 1837; E. Oxford, for shooting at the Queen, 1840; Courvoisier, for the murder of Lord William Russell, 1840; Blakesley, for murder in Eastcheap, 1841; Beaumont Smith, for forgery of Exchequer Bills, 1841; J. Francis, for attempt to shoot the Queen, 1842; Mac Naughten, for assassination, 1384; Dalmas, for murder on Battersea Bridge, 1844; Barber, Fletcher, &c. for Will-forgeries, 1844; Manning and his wife, for murder, 1849.

CLERKENWELL SESSIONS HOUSE (see page 187).

COURT OF ARCHES (see DOCTORS' COMMONS, page 257).

COURTS OF EQUITY (the),—namely, those of the Lord Chancellor, the Master of the Rolls, and the Vice-Chancellor of England,—sit at Westminster in term-time; but in the intervals the Lord Chancellor and Vice-Chancellor sit at Lincoln's Inn, and the Master of the Rolls at the Rolls House, in Chancery-lane: the two additional Vice-Chancellors, appointed in 1841, also sit at Lincoln's Inn. The Lord High Chancellor was originally a sort of confidential chaplain, or before the Reformation, confessor, to the king, and keeper of the king's conscience. As chief secretary, he advised his master in matters temporal; prepared royal mandates, grants, and charters; and when seals came in, affixed the same: hence the appointment to the office takes place by the delivery of the Great Seal. His Court has exclusive cognisance of trusts, and the suitors' property exceeds 40,000,000l.

COURT OF CHANCERY. The present Law Courts, on the west side of the Great Hall at Westminster, were built by Soane, 1820-25, upon the site of the old Exchequer Chamber, &c. There is little to interest the visitor, except in the Lord Chancellor's Court, where his lordship sits in state, with the mace and an embroidered bag before him; in this bag the seal is deposited when the Chancellor receives it from the Sovereign, and when, upon his retirement from office, he delivers it into the royal hands: formerly, the Great Seal was worn by the Chancellor on his left side.

The Great Seal itself is a silver pair of dies, which are closed to receive the melted wax, poured, when an impression is to be taken, through an orifice left in the top. As each impression is attached to a document by a ribbon or slip of parchment, its ends are put into the seal before the wax is poured in; so that when the hard wax is taken from the dies, the ribbon or parchment is affixed to it. The impression of the seal is six inches in diameter, and three-quarters of an inch thick. On every accession to the throne, a new seal is struck, and the old one is cut into four pieces and deposited in the Tower of

* Amongst the old manuscript documents in the Town Clerk's Office at Guildhall is a petition from Jonathan Wild to the Court of Aldermen, dated 1724, praying to be free of the City, for apprehending and convicting divers felons returned from transportation, since October 1720. In 1839, the skeleton of Jonathan was in the possession of a surgeon at Windsor.

London. Formerly, the seal was broken "by the king's command," and the fragments were given to the poor of religious houses.

The present Great Seal was executed by Benjamin Wyon, R.A. in 1839. *Obverse:* The Queen wearing a flowing and sumptuous robe and regal diadem, bearing a sceptre. and riding a charger richly caparisoned with plumes and trappings, while a page, bonnet in hand, gracefully restrains the steed. The legend in the exergue, " Victoria Dei Gratia Britanniarum Regina, Fidei Defensor," is engraved in Gothic letters; the interspaces of the words being filled with heraldic roses; a crown above, and a trident-head and oak-branches beneath. *Reverse:* The Queen royally robed and crowned, holding the sceptre and orb, and seated upon a throne beneath a Gothic canopy : on either side is a figure of Justice and Religion; and beneath are the royal arms and crown; the whole encircled by a border of oak and roses.

The Seal-bag is about twelve inches square, of crimson silk embroidered in gold, with the royal arms on each side, fringed with gold bullion; to the bag is attached a stout silken cord, by which it is carried; within is placed the Seal, in a leather pouch, enclosed in a silk purse.

The Chancellor's Mace is silver-gilt, and about five feet long. The staff and its massive bands are deeply chased with the rose, shamrock, and thistle; the upper portion consists of a large and richly chased crown, surmounted with the orb and cross, and encircled with crosses-patées and fleurs-de-lis; and supported on a bold circlet, ornamented in high relief with the emblems of the United Kingdom.

The mace and seal-bag are laid before the Chancellor when seated upon the woolsack as Speaker of the House of Lords; and they are placed upon the table in the Court of Chancery, accompanied by a large nosegay of flowers, conjectured to be the representative of the judge's bough or wand.

COURT OF EXCHEQUER (the) was formed by William I. in 1079, as a superior Court of Record, in the place of a similar court in his Duchy of Normandy : it included the Common Pleas until 16 John, 1215; it was remodelled into its present form by Edward I. The name of Exchequer is from the parti-coloured carpet of a table before the Barons, on which the sums of certain of the king's accounts were reckoned by counters: the Chancellor of the Exchequer is the treasurer; he presides only when the Court sits as a Court of Equity.

The Great Roll of the Exchequer ("the Pipe Roll") contains an account of the Crown revenue from 5 Stephen to the present time. To this document nearly every ancient pedigree is indebted; it has a perfect list of the Sheriffs of the different counties, and almost every name in English history.

The Court of Exchequer regulates the election of Sheriffs. Thus, on the morrow of St. Martin, Nov. 12, a Privy Council is held in the Exchequer Court, to receive the report of the Judges of the persons eligible in the several counties to serve as Sheriff. On the bench sits the Chancellor of the Exchequer, in his figured silk gown, trimmed with gold; next are Members of the Privy Council, the Lord Chancellor, and Judges of the Queen's Bench and Common Pleas; below sit the Judges and Chief Baron of the Exchequer, and on the left the Remembrancer of the Court. At this meeting the Judges report the names of *three* persons eligible for Sheriff in each county, when excuses for exemption are pleaded. The list is again considered by the Privy Council, and the names finally determined on the approval of Her Majesty in Council, which is done by the Sovereign pricking through the name approved on a long sheet of paper called the Sheriffs' Roll.

The Sheriffs of London and Middlesex are, however, chosen by the Livery; but are presented, on the morrow of the Feast of St. Michael, in the Court of Exchequer, accompanied by the Lord Mayor and aldermen, when the Recorder introduces the Sheriffs and details their family history, and the Cursitor Baron signifies the sovereign's approval; the writs and appearances are read, recorded, and filed, and the Sheriffs and senior under-sheriff take the oaths; and the late Sheriffs present their accounts. The Crier of the court then makes proclamation for one who does homage for the Sheriffs of London to "stand forth and do his duty;" when the senior Alderman below the chair rises, the usher of the court hands him a bill-hook, and holds in both hands a small bundle of sticks, which the Alderman cuts asunder, and then cuts another bundle with a hatchet. Similar proclamation is then made for the Sheriff of Middlesex, when the Alderman counts six horse-shoes lying upon the table, and sixty-one hob-nails handed in a tray; and the numbers are declared twice. The sticks are thin peeled twigs, tied in a bundle at each end with red tape; the horse-shoes are of large size, and very old; the hob-nails are supplied fresh every year. By the first ceremony the Alderman does suit and service for the tenants of a manor in Shropshire, the chopping of sticks betokening the custom of the tenants supplying their lord with fuel. The counting of the horse-shoes and nails is another suit and service of the owners of a forge in St. Clement Danes, Strand, which formerly belonged to the City, but no longer exists. Sheriff Hoare, in his MS. journal of his shrievalty, 1740-41, says, where the tenements and lands are situated "no one knows, nor doth the City receive any rents or profits thereby."

On Nov. 9 the oath is administered in the Court of Exchequer to the Lord Mayor elect; the late Lord Mayor renders his accounts; and the Recorder invites the barons to the inauguration-banquet at Guildhall.

The Court of Exchequer has *two seals:* the *Great Seal,* used not more than ten or twelve times a year, except on Seal Days, in passing the accounts in court. The other, a small *Initial Seal,* which formerly contained the Chancellor's initials, but now bears the letters C. E., is affixed to writs, "is in daily use, and seldom idle during official hours."—*Notes, by F. S. Thomas, Record Office.*

The Courts of Exchequer, Queen's Bench, and Common Pleas are also held at Guildhall on certain days, four in each term.

Into the *Exchequer Chamber* are adjourned "Crown Reserved Cases," writs of error from other Courts, before the whole of the Judges, who upon such occasions wear their scarlet robes.

INSOLVENT DEBTORS' COURT, Portugal-street, Lincoln's-Inn-fields:

"A temple dedicated to the genius of seediness," and "the place of daily refuge of all the shabby-genteel people in London. There are more suits of old clothes in it at one time than will be offered for sale in all Houndsditch in a twelvemonth; and more unwashed skins and grisly beards than all the pumps and shaving-shops between Tyburn and Whitechapel could render decent between sunrise and sunset. There is not a messenger or process-server attached to the Court who wears a coat that was made for him; the very barristers' wigs are ill-powdered, and their curls lack crispness. But the attorneys, who sit below the commissioners, are, after all, the greatest curiosities. The professional establishment of the more opulent of these gentlemen consists of a blue bag and a boy. They have no fixed offices, their legal business being transacted in the parlours of public-houses or the yards of prisons, whither they repair in crowds, and canvas for customers after the manner of omnibus-cads. They are of a greasy and mildewed appearance; and if they can be said to have any vices, perhaps drinking and cheating are most conspicuous among them."—*Pickwick Papers.*

MARSHALSEA and PALACE COURT was an appendage to the royal house at Westminster: anciently it had exclusive jurisdiction in matters connected with the royal household, and was presided over by the Earl Marshal. It next became a minor court of record for actions for debt, &c. within Westminster and twelve miles round it, except the City of London; its prison being in High-street, Southwark, until consolidated with the Queen's Bench and Fleet in 1842. The Court, with the Knight-Marshal for judge, existed until Dec. 28, 1849, when it was formally adjourned for the last time, and rose never to resume its sittings; the suits being transferred to the Common Pleas and County Courts, and the records to the charge of the Master of the Rolls. The Marshalsea Court sat in Southwark until 1801, and subsequently in Great Scotland-yard, Whitehall; but it was probably first held in the "Court of Requests," part of the Norman palace at Westminster. Littleton, the eminent lawyer, was appointed by Henry VI. Steward or Judge of the Marshalsea Court.

MAYOR'S COURT (the) has jurisdiction over all personal and mixed actions within the City, and is held at Guildhall, nominally before the Lord Mayor and aldermen, but really before the Recorder. The office of the Court was formerly in a long gallery at the west end of the Royal Exchange (see p. 276). The records of the Court were saved from the great fire at the Royal Exchange in 1838, and have been arranged in a strong fire-proof closet in a record-room at Guildhall by the town-clerk; with other records of the reigns of Edward I. Edward III. Richard II. Henry IV. V. and VI.; books of precedents, James I.; records from Elizabeth to George I. Francis Bancroft was an officer of this Court, and despised for his mercenary conduct, which he atoned for by bequeathing his ill-gotten wealth to build almshouses and a school. (See ALMSHOUSES, p. 6, and CHURCHES, p. 130.)

PRIVY COUNCIL. The Judicial Committee hold their sittings at the Council Office, Whitehall, in a spacious chamber nearly the whole height of the edifice: it is ornamented with Ionic columns of Sienna scagliola shafts and white capitals, and has a rich coved ceiling, with an elegant lantern.

ROLLS COURT. In vacation the Master sits at the Rolls House, in the Liberty of the Rolls, between Chancery-lane and Fetter-lane: it is exempt from the power of the Sheriff of Middlesex, and of every other officer, except with leave of the Master. The Court adjoins the Master's House and the Chapel, described at page 172. The House, designed by Colin Campbell, was built 1717, when Sir Joseph Jekyll was Master. A great portion of the estate was formerly laid out in gardens, upon which has been built the central portion of a new Record Office. Opposite the Rolls Chapel was Herflet Inn, belonging to the priors of Nocton Park, and occupied by the Six Clerks in the Court of Chancery, who subsequently removed to the west side of the north end of Chancery-lane: they were abolished 1842.

When Sir William Grant was Master of the Rolls, the court sat in the evening from 6 to 10, and Sir William dined after the court rose: his servant, when he went to bed, left two bottles of wine on the table, which he always found empty in the morning. Sir William lived on the ground-floor of the Rolls House, and when shewing it to his successor in the Mastership, he said: "Here are two or three good rooms; this is my dining-room; my library and bed-room are beyond; and I am told there are some good rooms upstairs, but I was never there."

SHERIFF'S COURTS (the) are held by each of the Sheriffs of London, near Guildhall, before a judge appointed by him.

STAR CHAMBER (the) was the ancient council-chamber of the palace at Westminster, wherein the king sat in extraordinary causes. The last-existing Star-Chamber buildings are described at page 396.

LEADENHALL-STREET,

(Extending from Cornhill to Aldgate) and the adjoining Market, are named from the manor-house of Leadenhall, which belonged to Sir Hugh Neville in 1309; in 1419 Simon Eyre erected upon its site a granary, which he gave to the Corporation; and adjoining he built a chapel in the Perpendicular style, for the market-people, Leadenhall having then become a market. In this Hall were kept the artillery and other arms of the city; doles were distributed from here; in Stow's boyhood, the common beams for weighing wool, and the scales to weigh meal, were kept here; and in the lofts above were painted devices for pageants. Chamberlayne describes it, in 1726, as "a noble ancient building, where are great markets for hides and leather, for flesh, poultry, and other sorts of edibles." In 1730 the market-place was partly rebuilt; and the leather-market in 1814, when the Chapel and other ancient portions were removed. The "Green Yard" was a portion of the garden of the Nevilles; and the Chapel, in Ram-alley, was inscribed "Dextra Domini exaltavit me."

Leadenhall was formerly the great meat-market. Don Pedro de Ronquillo, on visiting it, said to Charles II., that he believed there to be more meat sold in that market alone, than in all the kingdom of Spain in a year; and "he was a very good judge."

Beneath No. 71 Leadenhall-street is the ancient chapel of St. Michael, Aldgate (see CRYPTS, p. 243). No. 153 has an Early English crypt. Here, too, at "the Two Fans," Peter Motteux, the translator of Rabelais and Don Quixote, kept an India House for "China and Japan wares, fans, tea, muslins, pictures, arreck, and other Indian goods;" rich brocades, Dutch atlases, and other foreign silks, fine Flanders lace and linens. (*Spectator*, Nos. 288 and 552, by Steele). Motteux wrote a poem upon Tea: he was found dead (murdered) on his birthday, Feb. 19, 1717-18, in a house of ill-fame in Star-court, Butcher-row, Temple Bar.

In Leadenhall-street, opposite the East India House portico, in 1803, was found *the most magnificent Roman tesselated pavement yet discovered in London.* It lay at only 9½ feet below the street, but a third side had been cut away for a sewer; it appeared to have been the floor of a room more than twenty feet square. In the centre was Bacchus upon a tiger, encircled with three borders (inflexions of serpents, cornucopiæ, and squares diagonally concave), and drinking-cups and plants at the angles. Surrounding the whole was a square border of a bandeau of oak, and lozenge figures and true-lovers' knots, and a five-feet outer margin of plain red tiles. The pavement was broken in taking up, but the pieces are preserved in the library of the East India Company; a fragment of an urn and a jaw-bone were found beneath one corner. "In this beautiful specimen of Roman mosaic," says Mr. Fisher, who published a coloured print of it, "the drawing, colouring, and shadows are all effected by about twenty separate tints, composed of tessellæ of different materials, the major part of which are baked earths; but the more brilliant colours of green and purple, which form the drapery, are of glass. These tessellæ are of different sizes and figures, adapted to the situations they occupy in the design."

In Leadenhall-street are the churches of St. Andrew's Undershaft (see page 117) and St. Catherine Cree (page 122). On the wall of the latter is a large sun-dial; and at the east end a curious gateway, built 1631. The churchyard was noted for performances of miracle-plays, the earliest known of which relates to St. Catherine. (See also EAST INDIA HOUSE, page 263.)

LEICESTER SQUARE,

Within memory, was called Leicester Fields, from the mansion at its north-east corner, built for Robert Sydney, Earl of Leicester, who died 1677. It was let to Elizabeth Queen of Bohemia, daughter of James I.: she died here 1661. Colbert and Prince Eugene also resided here. Pennant well calls it "the pouting place of princes;" because George II., when Prince of Wales, having quarrelled with his father, retired to Leicester House; and his son Frederick, Prince of Wales, did the same thing, for the very same reason. The Prince died here in 1751: his eldest son occasionally resided here until his accession to the throne as George III., when in the front of the mansion he was here hailed as king.

The last royal tenant of Leicester House was the Duke of Gloucester, grandson of George II. It was then let to Sir Ashton Lever, whose collection (the Leverian Museum) was exhibited here about 1778. In 1788, the Museum was won by lottery by Mr. Parkinson, and removed to the Blackfriars-road, where it was dispersed by auction in 1806. In 1791, New Lisle-street was built upon the gardens of Leicester House.

Dryden dedicates from Gerrard-street (No. 43) his *Don Sebastian* to Lord Leicester, and calls himself "a poor inhabitant of his Lordship's suburbs, whose best prospect is on the garden of Leicester House."

The *Leverian Museum* consisted of ancient guns and other weapons, and horse-shoes; Curiosities from New Zealand and the Pacific islands; the Sandwich-room, collected in Cook's last voyage; a magnificent specimen of Raphael-ware, from the Medicean collection; specimens of rare plants, zoophytes, minerals, and fossils; a Brazilian natural magnet, 184 lbs. weight; costumes; amphibia in spirits; and preserved birds, quadrupeds, and fish. (See Dr. Shaw's *Catalogue*, coloured plates, 1792-6.)

Westward, adjoining Leicester House, was the residence of the Earl of Aylesbury; where the Marquis of Caermarthen, in 1698, entertained Peter the Great. The mansion was named Savile House, from its belonging to the Savile family; and here resided Sir George Savile, M.P., in 1780, when the rioters stripped his house of its valuable furniture, books, and paintings, which they burnt in the Fields.

Miss Linwood's Needlework was exhibited at Savile House from the commencement of the present century until the year after her death in 1845, in her 90th year. She worked her first picture when 13 years old, and the last piece when 78 years. The designs were executed with fine crewels dyed expressly for her, on a thick tammy, and were entirely drawn and embroidered by herself. In 1785, the pictures were exhibited to the Royal Family at Windsor; next at the Pantheon, Oxford-street; removed in 1798 to the Hanover-square Rooms; and then to Leicester-square. The Collection consisted of 64 pictures, including a portrait of Miss Linwood, at 19, from a crayon painting by Russell; her first piece, Head of St. Peter (Guido); Salvator Mundi (Carlo Dolci), for which 3000 guineas had been refused (this picture was bequeathed by Miss Linwood to Her Majesty); Woodman in a Storm (Gainsborough); Jephtha's Rash Vow (Opie). The pictures were sold by auction, by Christie and Manson, at Savile House, April 23, 1846, when the Judgment upon Cain, which occupied ten years' working, brought 64*l.* 1*s.*; the price of neither of the other pictures exceeding 40*l.* The original Hubert and Arthur, by Northcote, sold for 38*l.* 17*s.* The entire sale did not realise 1000*l.*

At Savile House the National Political Union held its Reform meetings; and here was exhibited, in 1849, an extensive moving Panorama of the Mississippi River, &c. The place has since been a very *Noah's Ark* of exhibitions, of greater variety than delicacy.

Leicester Square was built between 1630 and 1671. In 1677, rows of elm-trees extended in the Fields nearly half the width of the present Square, which was enclosed about 1738. In the centre, upon a sculptured stone pedestal, is an equestrian metal statue of George I., modelled by C. Buchard for the Duke of Chandos, and brought from Canons in 1747, when it was purchased by the inhabitants of the square; it was "finely gilt," and within memory was regilt:* over the statue has been built Wyld's colossal Model of the Earth.

At No. 47, west side, Sir Joshua Reynolds lived from 1761 till his death in 1792. Here he built a gallery for his works, and set up a gay coach, upon the panels of which were painted the four Seasons. Here were given those famous dinner-parties, the first great example in this country " of a cordial intercourse between persons of distinguished pretensions of all kinds; poets, physicians, lawyers, deans, historians, actors, temporal and spiritual peers, House of Commons men, men of science, men of letters, painters, philosophers, and lovers of the arts, meeting on a ground of hearty ease, good humour, and pleasantry, which exalt my respect for the memory of Reynolds. It was no prim fine table he set them down to. Often was the dinner-board prepared for seven or eight required to accommodate itself to fifteen or sixteen; for often, on the very eve of dinner, would Sir Joshua tempt afternoon visitors with intimation that Johnson, or Garrick, or Goldsmith, was to dine there."—Forster's *Life of Goldsmith*, p. 523.

Sir Joshua painted in an octagonal room; the sticks of his brushes were 18 inches long; he held his pallettes by handle; one of mahogany, 11 by 7 inches, is possessed by Mr. Cribb, King-street, Covent Garden, whose father received it from Sir Joshua's niece, the Marchioness of Thomond. Here, in 1790, the good-natured P.R.A. painted for two schoolboys a flag bearing the Royal arms, which was borne at the next breaking-up of King's Academy, Chapel-street,

---

* This statue has also been described as that of the Duke of Cumberland, the hero of Culloden, which may have arisen from the Duke's birth at Leicester House in 1721.

Soho. Sir Joshua died here Feb. 28, 1792; his remains were interred in the crypt of St. Paul's Cathedral. The house was afterwards the Western Literary and Scientific Institution, when was added a theatre for lectures.

On the opposite side of the Square, in the house now the northern wing of the Sabloniere Hotel, lived William Hogarth from 1753; his name upon a brass-plate on the door, and the sign of the Golden Head over it: he usually took his evening walk within the enclosure in a scarlet rocquelare and cocked hat: here he published, by subscription, the Harlot's and Rake's Progresses, and other prints: he died here suddenly Oct. 25, 1764. Next door lived John Hunter from 1783: in the rear he built rooms for his anatomical collection, lectures, dissection, Sunday-evening medical levees, &c.; and from here, in 1793, Hunter was buried in St. Martin's church. To No. 28, also east, was removed the National Repository (on the plan of the *Arts et Métiers* at Paris) from the King's Mews, taken down in 1830; and here was housed, in 1836, the Museum of the Zoological Society.

In the centre of the east side of the Square is the *Panopticon of Science and Art,* erected 1852-3, by a chartered company for a polytechnic exhibition: it has a pair of minarets nearly 100 feet high, a domed roof, and other eastern features. The interior has a hall 97 feet in diameter, lecture-theatres, laboratory, colossal machinery for experiments; an electrifying-machine, plate eight feet diameter, &c.

In the centre of the Square is the *Model of the Earth,* just mentioned. The ground was leased, in 1851, for ten years, for 3000*l.*, to Mr. Wyld, the geographer, for whom has been erected here (H. R. Abraham, architect,) a circular building 90 feet across, enclosing a Globe 60 feet 4 inches in diameter, and lighted by day from the centre of the dome (as at the Pantheon at Rome), and by gas at night. The frame of the Globe consists of horizontal ribs, battened to receive the plaster modelling, thus to figure the earth's surface on the inside instead of the outside of a sphere, and to shew at one view the physical features of the world. The visitor passes into the interior of the Globe, and by a winding staircase proceeds round it, viewing every part of the model at four feet distance from the eye. The scale is ten miles to an inch horizontal, and one mile to an inch vertical, so as effectively to exhibit the details of hill and valley, lake and river: the great oceans occupying nearly 150,000,000 square miles; and the old and new continents, and all the islands, only 60,000,000 square miles; the gigantic model being made up of some thousand castings in plaster. The Circumpolar Regions are similarly illustrated; and by these ingenious means has "the desert of Leicester-square been converted into a great geographical school."

In *Cranbourne-alley,* now *street,* lived Ellis Gamble, silversmith, to whom Hogarth was apprenticed to learn silver-plate engraving, and engraving on copper; and from 1718 till 1724 he earned his livelihood by engraving arms, crests, ciphers, shop-bills, &c. An impression of Hogarth's allegorical shop-card, dated 1720, has been sold for 25*l.*!

Burford's Panorama, at the north-east angle of Leicester Square, has been established nearly 70 years; the building having been erected in 1783, by a number of patrons of the arts, who were repaid their capital by Robert Barker, the inventor of the Panorama, succeeded by Henry Aston Barker, and John and Robert Burford. (See PANORAMAS.)

In *Leicester-place,* Charles Dibdin, the song-writer, built in 1796 the *Sans Souci* theatre for his musical entertainment: the premises, No. 2, now an hotel, occupy the site of the Feathers public-house, frequented by "Athenian Stuart;" Scott, the marine painter; Luke Sullivan, the miniature-painter, who engraved Hogarth's March to Finchley; Capt. Grose and Mr. Hearne, the antiquaries; Henderson, the actor; John Ireland, editor of *Hogarth Moralised,* &c. In *Lisle-street* is the Royal Society of Musicians, founded in 1738 for the benefit of the families of indigent musicians: it originated in the two orphan sons of Kaitch, the oboist, being seen driving milch-asses down the Haymarket. In Lisle-street lived Henry Bone, R.A., the enamel-painter, who received for an enamel, 18 by 16 inches, 2200 guineas: he died 1834, aged 80, leaving a long series of Elizabethan portraits.

Leicester-street is described, in 1720, as " ordinarily built and inhabited, except the west side, towards the fields, where there is a very good house and curious garden which fronts the fields."

In *St. Martin-street*, next the chapel, is the last town residence of Sir Isaac Newton, who removed here, in 1710, from Jermyn-street: upon the roof is a small observatory, built by a subsequent tenant, a Frenchman, but long shewn as Newton's. In a scarce pamphlet, *A List of the Royal Society, &c.*, in 1718, we find: "Sir Isaac Newton, St. Martinstreet, Leicester-fields." The house was subsequently tenanted by Dr. Burney, when writing his *History of Music*: and his daughter, Fanny, wrote here her novel of *Evelina*. Mr. Bewley, "the philosopher of Massingham," died here, during a visit to Dr. Burney, who, in an anecdote related to Boswell (*Life of Johnson*), erroneously states Newton to have died here: he died at Kensington (see page 431).

Fanny Burney (Madame D'Arblay), writes from here in 1779 and 1780 (*Diary and Letters*, vol. i.); and Mr. Thrale, writing to Miss Burney, styles the inmates of the house in St. Martin's-street, "dear *Newtonians*."

In *Green-street*, at now No. 11, lived William Woollett, the landscape and historical engraver, known by his masterly plates of Wilson's pictures and his battle-pieces: his portrait, by Stuart, hangs in the Vernon Gallery. He died 1785, and is buried at St. Pancras (see p. 152); his grave-stones were restored by the Graphic Society in 1846.

In *Orange-court*, Leicester-fields, lodged Opie, the painter; and here was born, Dec. 10, 1745, Thomas Holcroft, his father a shoemaker.

"Cradled in poverty, with no education save what he could pick up for himself, amid incessant struggles for bare existence—by turns a pedlar, a stable-boy, a shoemaker, and a strolling-player—he yet contrived to surmount the most untoward circumstances, and at last took his place among the most distinguished writers of his age as a novelist, a dramatist, and a translator."—*Preface to Holcroft's Life*, by William Hazlitt.

Leicester-square has long been the resort and habitat of foreigners; and Maitland (1739) describes the parish (St. Anne's) so greatly abounding with French, "that it is an easy matter for a stranger to imagine himself in France."

LEVELS.

The data for the following Levels, from actual surveys and private documents, adopting the standard of Trinity High Water Mark at London Bridge, have been communicated through the courtesy of Mr. Wyld, the geographer.

	Feet.		Feet.
Berkeley-square	57	Hampstead Heath	424
British Museum	72	(84 feet higher than the cross of St. Paul's Cathedral.)	
Brompton-square	12		
Caledonian-road: Great Northern Railway	112	Hampstead Vale (Waterworks)	207
Camden Town: Brecknock Arms	150	(5 feet higher than the top of the Monument.)	
Camden Town: London and North-Western Railway Station	100	Haverstock Hill: Orphan School	258
		(28 feet higher than the steeple of St. Bride's Church, Fleet-st.)	
Clapham Common (S.W.)	93	Highbury Barn	132
Drury-lane, opposite Great Queen-street	66	(12 feet higher than the towers of St. Michael's Church, Cornhill, and St. Dunstan's, Fleet-st.)	
Farringdon-street	11		
Gloucester-road, Kensington	18	Highgate Archway (top)	317
Guildhall, King-street	37	,, ,, Tavern	179

	Feet.
ighgate Chapel	412
olloway: New City Prison (surface)	112
ornsey Wood House Tavern	147
yde-park: site of Great Exhibition Building	52
lington: Angel Inn . . .	99
,, Ball's Pond-road .	59
,, Green	115
ansion House	32
ew Oxford-street, opposite Charlotte-st., Bloomsbury .	72
ew River: Stoke Newington Reservoir	87
ew-road: Gower-street . .	76
otting-hill (by St. John's Wood).	85
otting-hill Reservoir . . .	123
unhead Cemetery Hill . .	189
(14 feet higher than the spire of St. Giles's Church.)	
ark-lane, halfway	69
entonville Prison (surface) .	120
egent's-park: York and Albany	99
(The houses in Circus-road, St. John's Wood, are level with the summit of Primrose Hill.)	
erpentine (surface)	38
hooter's-hill	412
horeditch Workhouse, Kingsland-road.	51
mithfield: St. Bartholomew's Hospital	45
tamford-hill	97
trand, average	20

Westbourne - terrace, Hyde-park - gardens (ground-floor); 70 feet above high-water mark, and on a level with the attics of Eaton and Belgrave squares.

Westminster: the further we proceed from the river, the lower the ground becomes, thus :—

	Above high-water mark.	
	ft.	in.
St. Margaret's-street, near Canning's statue	5	2½
Millbank-street	4	4½
West end of Tothill-street . .	9	
Broad-way	9	
New-way		6½
Old Pye-street		5½

	Below high-water.
New Tothill-street	3½
Road in front of Mr. Elliot's dwelling-house	11½
Palmer's Village	12½

Mr. Bardwell, the Architect.

The architect of the New Prison was compelled to raise the ground 7 feet; the ground has also been much raised around the New Palace, over and above that which was made when the Bird-cage Walk was carried over the site of Rosamond's Pond.

Again, the sill of a door in Park-street is somewhat more than 8 feet higher than the sill of a door in Tothill-street, Dartmouth-street only intervening.

The highest ground in London is about the middle of Pannier-alley, etween Newgate-street and Paternoster-row ; the spot being denoted y a boy sitting upon a pannier, upon a pedestal, all of stone; the latter scribed, "WHEN YE HAVE SOVGHT THE CITTY ROVND, YET STILL THIS THE RIGHT GROVND. AVGVST THE 27, 1688."

The made ground and accumulated débris occurring in the City, and ciently populated parts adjacent, varies from 8 to 18 feet in thickness; Westminster, from 6 to 12 feet.

LIBRARIES.

"The greatest city in the world is destitute of a public library," rote Gibbon towards the close of the last century; since which riod little has been done to afford the masses facilities for mental ture by an *open public library* from which books may be taken out.

"There is no library in London, public or private, which contains every work m which one authoritative statement on matters of science might be made."— f. De Morgan, *Compan. Almanac,* 1843.

AGRICULTURAL SOCIETY OF ENGLAND (ROYAL), 12 Hanover-square : ary of the Board of Agriculture, increased by purchases, &c.

ANTIQUARIES, SOCIETY OF, Somerset House : valuable collections of red Broadsides and Ballads; rare Prints, illustrating Ancient London; the Book of St. Albans, fol. St. Albans, 1486, finest state. Among the Mss. are, 1. Cartulary of the Abbey of Peterborough. 2. Original Ms. of Weever's *Funeral Monuments.* 3. Indentures for Coining Money in England and Ireland, from Edward I. to Elizabeth. 4. The "Winton Domesday," on 33 leaves of vellum, and in the original stamped cuir-bouilli covers: this MS. (*temp.* Edward I.) contains an exact account of every tenement in Winchester at that period. 5. Original Letters of Antiquaries and Literary Men (18th century). 6. Letters of Eminent Englishmen (17th century). Autograph of John Bunyan, doubtful. The Society's Transactions, *Archæologia,* commenced 1710.

ARTILLERY GROUND, or Military Yard, behind Leicester House.
Near Leicester-fields, upon the site of Gerrard-street, was a piece of ground walled in by Prince Henry, eldest son of James I., for the exercise of arms: where were an armoury, and a well-furnished library of books relating to feats of arms, chivalry, military affairs, encamping, fortification, in all languages, and kept by a learned librarian. It was called the Artillery Ground; and after the Restoration of Charles II. it was bought by Lord Gerard, and let for building about 1677.

ASIATIC SOCIETY (ROYAL), 5 New Burlington-street: scarce books and Mss., including a collection of Sanscrit Mss., formed by Colonel Tod in Rajasthan. Here is a Chinese Library, of which see the Catalogue, by the Rev. S. Kidd, 1838.

ASTRONOMICAL SOCIETY, ROYAL, Somerset House: valuable collection of astronomical works, including Peter Apian's *Opus Cæsareum* printed at Ingolstadt in 1540; and the library of the Mathematical Society. (See page 463.)

BANK OF ENGLAND LIBRARY, instituted by the Directors for the use of the clerks, was opened May 1850; the Court having voted 500*l.* for the purchase of books.

BARBER-SURGEONS' HALL, Monkwell-street: a curious collection of books on olden Anatomy.

BEAUMONT INSTITUTION, Mile-end, built and endowed with 13,000*l.* by Mr. Barber Beaumont, has a library of 4000 volumes, a music-hall and museum of natural history.

BIBLE SOCIETY, BRITISH AND FOREIGN, 10 Earl-street, Blackfriars: collection of versions of the Scriptures, in various languages or dialects.
Since its foundation, the Bible Society has issued upwards of 25,402,300 copies of the Scriptures, and has aided other Societies in the distribution of about 18,000,000 more. In Ireland, since 1806, 2,700,000 Bibles and Testaments have been dispersed. In France, since 1818, 3,000,000 have been circulated. In 1849, 27,000 were introduced into Italy.

BOTANICAL SOCIETY, 20 Bedford-street, Covent Garden, has a library of works on botany for reference and circulation; besides British and general herbaria for the exchange of specimens.

BRITISH MUSEUM. See MUSEUMS.

CHARTER-HOUSE, Aldersgate: a collection presented by booksellers and others for the reading of the Brotherhood. In 1851 Queen Victoria presented the *Quarterly Review,* 86 vols.

CHELSEA HOSPITAL: History, Voyages, and Travels, and Military Memoirs, Newspapers, and Periodicals for the pensioners' reading.

CHRIST'S HOSPITAL, Newgate-street, "formerly the Grey Friars, hath a neat library for the use of the masters and scholars; besides collection of mathematical instruments, globes, ships, with all the rigging, for the instruction of the lads designed for the sea." (*H. L.-moine,* 1790.) To the library of Mss., Whittington was a great benefactor.

CHURCH MISSIONARY SOCIETY, Salisbury-square, Fleet-street: miscellaneous collection, rich in voyages and travels.

CITY OF LONDON INSTITUTION, Aldersgate-street, commenced in 1825, contained upwards of 7000 volumes for reference and circulation; dispersed in 1852, when the Institution was dissolved.

CIVIL ENGINEERS (INSTITUTION OF), 25 Great George-street, Westminster: upwards of 3000 volumes, and 1500 tracts, upon bridges, canals, railways, roads, docks, navigation, ports, rivers, and water; Transactions of Societies, Parliamentary Reports, &c. Here are some volumes of MS. observations by Telford in his early engineering career. This library has the advantage of a printed catalogue, admirably arranged by C. Manby, Secretary to the Institution.)

CLOCKMAKERS' COMPANY, London Tavern, Bishopsgate-street: a sounding library of valuable English and foreign works on Horology and the allied sciences, with a printed catalogue.

CLUB-HOUSES (the) have extensive general libraries.

COLLEGE OF PHYSICIANS, Pall Mall East. (See page 227.) In this collection are the libraries of Selden and the Marquis of Dorchester; and Sir Theodore Mayerne, physician to James I.

COLLEGE OF SURGEONS, Lincoln's-Inn-fields: library commenced by John Hunter's donation of his published works on Anatomy and Surgery in 1786, the unique autograph letter accompanying which is possessed by Mr. Stone, the present Librarian. Sir Charles Blicke bequeathed his medical library, and 300l.; and the collection now numbers 30,000 volumes (cost 23,000l.); mostly works on the history, science, and practice of medicine and the collateral sciences: its collection of Transactions and Journals is very perfect.

Among the *Curiosities* is " Approved Medicines and Cordiall Receiptes," dated 1580: it bears in several places the signature and initials of Shakspeare; *but* it was bought at the sale of the forger Ireland's effects. Among the early books are the *Compendium Medicinæ nondum Medicis sed Cyrurgis utilissimum*, 1510, by Albertus Anglicus, circ. 1230; the works of *John of Gaddesden*, or *Johannes Anglicus*, circ. 1320. *Herbarium Germanicæ*, 1485, beautifully illuminated, and bound in oak, brass ornaments, dated 1549; a collection of engraved portraits of medical men, formerly possessed by Fauntleroy, the banker, and presented by him to William Wadd, the facete surgeon. The library, designed by Barry, extends the entire length of the College façade; above the bookcases are a gallery and portraits of Harvey, Cheselden, Nesbitt, Nourse, Blizard, Hunter, Pott, &c.; and adjoining is a room with a collection of Voyages and Travels, works on Natural History and Science. Members of the College can introduce a visitor.

CORPORATION OF LONDON LIBRARY, Guildhall: rich in works relating to the Cities of London and Westminster, and the Borough of Southwark; rare tracts preceding, accompanying, and following, the Commonwealth; and several volumes of original proclamations, *temp.* 1638 to 1698. Here are *Domesday Survey* and the *Monasticon*; in history, Ven. Bede, Matthew Paris, Decem Scriptores, and other old English chroniclers; in foreign history, Kempfer, Pontoppidan, Wormius, Duhalde, D'Herbelet, Mezeray, &c.; Hackluyt's *Voyages*, first edit. black letter, and Evans's very brilliant edit. 5 vols. 4to; Lysons's *Environs of London*, with drawings, prints, and armorial bearings, 3 thick volumes, perhaps the most elaborately illustrated work extant. Among the recent additions are: the great French work on Egypt, 14 vols. atlas folio, and 9 vols. folio letterpress; *Il Vaticano*, by Erasmus Pistolesi, 8 vols. folio; M'Kenney's *History of the Indian Tribes of North America* (superb coloured engravings), 3 vols. folio. Portfolios of Maps, Views, and Plans of London, of various dates.

Book Rarities:—Nuremburg Chronicle, 1493, with MS. Notes, 16th century; and Lists of Bailiffs, Mayors, and Sheriffs of London, 1st Rich. I. to 4 Hen.

VIII., with marginal notes of events; woodcuts, mostly coloured. *Complaint of Roderick Mars*, sometime a Gray Fryare (Geneva), said by Kennett to have been written by Henry Brincklow, a London merchant. Bonner's *Profitable and Necessary Doctrine*, bl. l. 1555. Declaration of Bonner's Articles, bl. l. 1561. A Boke made by John Fryth, Prysoner in the Tower of London, bl. l. 1546. *The Actes of English Votaryes*, by Johan Bale, bl. l. 1546. *The Castel of Helth* (by Sir Jo. Elyot), bl. l. 1541. *The Burnynge of Paule's Church*, &c. (written against Popery, by Pilkington, Bishop of Durham), bl. l. 1591. *Legenda Sanctorum*, fol. bl. l. n. d.* A collection of early printed Plays and Pageants.

Among the autographic *Curiosities* is the Charter granted by William the Conqueror to the City of London in 1067. It is beautifully written in Saxon characters, in about four lines, upon a slip of parchment six inches long and one broad.

Also, in a glass-case, is the signature of Shakspeare, purchased in 1843, by the Corporation of London, for 145*l.* : it is affixed to a deed of bargain and sale of "all that messuage or tente with the app'tennes lyeing and being in the blackfryers in London, neare the Wardrobe," by Henry Walker to William Shakspeare, dated March 10, 1612; and has the seals attached, and the names of the attesting witnesses on the back. The house is described as "abutting upon a streete leading down to Pudle wharffe" (now St. Andrew's Hill), and was in Ireland-yard, named after the tenant, William Ireland, about the time of the above sale: it was bequeathed by Shakspeare in his will to his daughter Susannah Hall. Here, too, is the sign-stone of the Boar's Head Tavern (See EASTCHEAP, page 265.)

COTTONIAN LIBRARY (the), now in the British Museum, was collected by Sir Robert Bruce Cotton, the learned antiquary, who greatly profited by the dissolution of monasteries half a century before, by which the records, charters, and instruments were thrown into private hands. Sir Robert Cotton was the friend of Camden, and greatly assisted him in his *Britannia*. The library was kept in Cotton House, at the west end of Westminster Hall, and was greatly increased by Sir Robert's son and grandson; in 1700 it was purchased by Act of Parliament, and in 1706 Cotton House was sold to the Crown for 4500*l.* but the mansion falling into decay, in 1712 the library was removed to Essex House, Strand; and thence, in 1730, to Ashburnham House, Westminster (see page 22). Here, Oct. 23, 1731, a fire broke out, by which 111 MSS. were lost, burnt, or entirely defaced, and 99 rendered imperfect. What remained were removed into the new dormitory of Westminster School. In 1738 was bequeathed to the collection Major Arthur Edwards's library of 2000 printed volumes; and in 1757 the whole were transferred to the British Museum. The Cottonian collection originally contained 958 volumes of original Charters, Royal Letters, Foreign State Correspondence, Ancient Registers: it was kept in cases, upon which were the heads of the 12 Cæsars; and the Mss. are distinguished by the press-marks of the Cæsars. Humphrey Wanley published a catalogue of the Cottonian Library, which is minutely noticed by Chamberlayne, *Magnæ Britanniæ Notitia*, 1726. Above the bookcases were portraits of the three Cottons, Judge Dodderidge, Spelman, Camden, Dugdale, Lambard, Speed, &c. An extended catalogue was printed in 1802.

Besides Mss., the Cottonian collection contained Saxon and old English coins and Roman and English antiquities, all now in the British Museum. Sir Robert Cotton aided Speed in his *History of England*, and Knolles in his *Turkish History*, Sir Walter Raleigh, Selden, and Lord Bacon drew materials from the Cottonian Library; and, in our time, Lingard's and Sharon Turner's *Histories of England*, and numerous other works, have proved its treasures unexhausted.

---

* From notes obligingly communicated by Mr. W. T. Alchin, Librarian,

DEPARTMENT OF PRACTICAL ART, Marlborough House, Pall Mall: collection of works of reference for Manufactures and Ornamental t, originally formed for the Schools of Design. About 1500 volumes architecture, sculpture, painted glass, general antiquities, and deco- ion; prints and drawings, including Raphael's Arabesques, coloured; ginal Sketches of the Cathedral of Messina, and the Church of Ambrose, Milan; and many elementary and practical works on art d ornamental design.

DOCTORS' COMMONS (College of Advocates), Great Knight Rider- eet. See page 258.

DULWICH COLLEGE LIBRARY. See page 209.

DUTCH CHURCH, Austin Friars: for the use of foreign Protestants d their clergy: containing Mss. and Letters of Calvin, Peter Martyr, d others, foreign Reformers; the Ten Commandments, believed to in the handwriting of Rubens.

EAST INDIA COMPANY, Leadenhall-street, north-east wing of the dia House: printed books and tracts relating to the history and geo- aphy of the Eastern hemisphere; the history, commerce, and adminis- ition of the East India Company, printed in Europe or India; books, awings, and prints of the people, scenery, and antiquities of Asiatic untries; Mss. on palm-leaves in Sanscrit, Burmese, and other lan- ages of the Archipelago, and Sanscrit Mss. in 3000 bound volumes; inese printed works; Tibetan Cyclopædia in 300 large oblong lumes, printed with wooden blocks; Arabic and Persian Mss.; mi- ture copies of the Koran; another Koran, in old Cufic characters, ritten out by the Khalif Othman (d. A.D. 655), and other volumes of library of Tippoo Sultan; his autograph "Register of Dreams," . Open to students recommended. (See EAST INDIA HOUSE, page 264.)

GEOGRAPHICAL SOCIETY (ROYAL), 3 Waterloo-place, Pall Mall: up- rds of 4000 volumes, mostly geographical; 150 Atlases; more than 00 pamphlets; 10,000 maps and charts: available as a circulating rary by the Fellows.

GEOLOGICAL SOCIETY'S LIBRARY, Somerset House, contains seve- l rare and curious treatises, &c., chiefly of the 17th century, and re- ting to the cosmogonical and hypothetical notions about the earth and structure, the origin and nature of minerals and fossils, natural story, early chemistry, &c.

GRESHAM COLLEGE, Basinghall-street, has a small library of mo- rn books for the use of the lecturers. The College does not appear have originally possessed a library, but to have used that of the oyal Society, the removal of which to Crane-court in 1710 proved a eat disadvantage to the Gresham Professors. (Ward's Lives, p. 175.) ee GRESHAM COLLEGE, p. 209.) The books subsequently possessed the College were burnt in the Royal Exchange, Jan. 10, 1838.

HALLS OF THE CITY COMPANIES (THE) often contain collections of rly treatises upon their arts and mysteries.

HARLEIAN LIBRARY and Mss. (See MUSEUMS: British.)

HEBREW LIBRARY, Duke's-place, Aldgate.

The Jews, in Bevis Marks, had a valuable library in their Synagogue, relating their ceremonials and Talmudical worship; but some narrow minds among m conceiving that if they should get into the hands of Christians, they would disgraced by shameful translations, agreed among themselves to cause them be burnt; for which purpose they employed some of their scribes, or tephilim ters, to examine into the correctness of the copies; and receiving a report eeable to their wishes, they had them conveyed to Mile End, where they were all destroyed in a kiln; for it is contrary to their maxim ever to make waste paper of the sacred language.—H. Lemoine; *Gentleman's Magazine*, July 1790.

HERALDS' COLLEGE (College of Arms), see page 211. Here is a curious collection of works on Heraldry, Arms, Ceremonies, Coronations, Marriages, Funerals, Christenings, and Visitations; an ancient Nennius on vellum, and Robert of Gloucester's Chronicle.

HORTICULTURAL SOCIETY, 21 Regent-street: the largest collection of horticultural works in the kingdom, and an assemblage of drawings of fruits and ornamental plants.

HOSPITALS, the several, possess medical libraries.

INCORPORATED LAW SOCIETY, Chancery-lane: the law and literature connected with the profession; Votes, Reports, Acts, Journals, and other proceedings of Parliament; County and Local Histories; topographical, genealogical, and antiquarian works, &c.

INNS OF COURT. The INNER and MIDDLE TEMPLE each possesses a good library, with valuable Mss. The INNER TEMPLE Mss., principally collected by William Petyt, Esq., Keeper of the Tower Records, were presented by his trustees in 1707: they exceed 400 Mss., parliamentary statutes and common law, ecclesiastical records, year-books, Hoveden, Higden, and other English historians, letters and papers, with signs-manual of kings and queens of England. The MIDDLE TEMPLE LIBRARY, adjoining the Hall in Garden-court, was founded under a bequest from Robert Ashley, Esq., in 1641: the Mss. include Placita records, Edward I.; Parliament Rolls, Edward II. to Henry VI.; Parliamentary Journals, &c. See LINCOLN'S INN, page 411; (also Spilsbury's *Lincoln's Inn and its Library*); GRAY'S INN, law and history. Most of the INNS OF CHANCERY have also libraries.

KING'S COLLEGE, Somerset House, has large medical and general libraries; including the Marsden Library, 3000 volumes on Philosophy and Oriental Literature, presented in 1835 by William Marsden, F.R.S. The Medical Library contains about 2000 volumes.

LAMBETH PALACE LIBRARY. See page 445.

LINNÆAN SOCIETY, 32 Soho-square: the Library and Herbarium of Linnæus, purchased by Sir James Smith for 1000*l.* In the Society's house Sir Joseph Banks collected his valuable library of works on Natural History, now in the Banksian department of the British Museum: the catalogue fills five octavo volumes, and is very rare.

LITERARY FUND (ROYAL), 73 Great Russell-street, Bloomsbury: a collection of books, mostly modern, and presents. Here is also the Ms. of Thorlaksin's Icelandic version of *Paradise Lost*, sent to the Institution by himself, through the Danish government. Here is the dagger with which Colonel Blood stabbed Edwards, keeper of the Regalia in the Tower of London, when Blood attempted to carry off the crown; also a dagger taken from Parrot, Blood's accomplice. Both weapons are of French manufacture, and very curious: they were bequeathed to the Institution by Mr. Thomas Newton, who believing himself to be the last descendant of Sir Isaac Newton, left his entire estate to the Literary Fund.

LONDON INSTITUTION, Finsbury-circus, commenced in 1806 with part of the library of the first Marquis of Lansdowne, contains about 30,000 volumes: rich in English Antiquities and Topography; scarce collections of Foreign Laws; several thousand Tracts; Bibliography, including rare editions from the early presses of Germany, Italy, and France; and fine specimens of the printing of the celebrated Antoine Verard, the Wechels, the Stephani, Claude Morel, Christopher Plantin, Johann Froben, Guarinus, Hieronymus Commelin, Henricus Petrus, the ldi, the Sessæ, Gabriel Giolito, and the Giunti; with some from the nglish printers, Julian Notary, Peter Treveris, Richard Grafton, Thoas Marshe, John Cawood, &c. The first librarians were Professor orson and William Upcott; one of the present librarians is Richard homson, author of the *Chronicles of London Bridge*, 1827. This llection is valued at 40,000*l.*

LONDON LIBRARY, 12 St. James's-square (the house tenanted by ord Amherst when Commander-in-chief), was established in May 41 at 57 Pall Mall, and removed to St. James's-square in 1844. It upon the subscription and lending plan, and the collection admirable.

ST. MARTIN'S, 42 Castle-street, Leicester-square: about 4000 voimes, bequeathed by Archbishop Tenison in 1685, then Rector of St. [artin's: here is a fine copy of Chaucer. The Library is described as a noble structure, extremely well contrived for the placing of the ooks and lights, and furnished with the best modern books in most culties: the best of its kind in England."—*H. Lemoine*, 1790.

MATHEMATICAL SOCIETY, Crispin-street, Spitalfields, established 1717, had a library, of which a catalogue was published in 1821; but e books and archives were removed to Somerset House in 1845, when e Mathematical Society merged into the Royal Astronomical Society.

MECHANICS' INSTITUTE, Southampton-buildings, Holborn, founded y Dr. Birkbeck in 1823; who also, in 1825, advanced a large sum for uilding the fine theatre of the Institution. The library has 6000 vols.

MEDICAL AND CHIRURGICAL SOCIETY, 53 Berners-street, Oxfordreet: about 20,000 volumes on Medicine, Surgery, &c.

MEDICAL SOCIETY OF LONDON, 33 George-street, Hanover-square, as a collection of books, including the library bequeathed by Dr. Lettm, with a house in Bolt-court, Fleet-street. (See page 306.)

MERCHANT-TAYLORS' SCHOOL LIBRARY, Suffolk-lane, Cannonreet, contains a fair collection of Hebrew and other Oriental works f reference; some good copies of the Fathers; nearly all the standard assical and other Lexicons; and the best writers in English Theology. he Merchant-Taylors' Company devote thirty guineas per annum to e increase and keeping up of this library; and frequent presents have een made to it by Members of the Court.

MICROSCOPICAL SOCIETY, 21 Regent-street: a library of standard orks on the Microscope; the perfection of which valuable instrument the object of the Institution.

MUSEUM OF PRACTICAL GEOLOGY, Jermyn-street, St. James's: are edition of the works of Aldrovandus; collection of alchemical eatises and histories; Kircher's works; olden Topography, Voyages nd Travels; collection of Surveys, &c.

NEW COLLEGE, St. John's Wood (see page 212), possesses a library f 20,000 volumes, including the theological collections from Coward, omerton, and Highbury Colleges; and is otherwise rich in works for the Congregational denomination."

PARLIAMENT (HOUSES OF) possess large and valuable libraries.

ST. PAUL'S CATHEDRAL Library, in the gallery over the southern isle, was collected by Bishop Compton: 7000 volumes, with Mss. elating to Old St. Paul's. (See page 92.)

ST. PAUL'S SCHOOL, St. Paul's Churchyard, contains the library of ean Colet, the munificent founder. The original statutes of this hool were accidentally picked up at a bookseller's by the late Mr. amper of Birmingham, and by him presented to the British Museum.

PHARMACEUTICAL SOCIETY (THE), 17 Bloomsbury-square, has a library, museum, and laboratory.

ROYAL ACADEMY OF ARTS, Trafalgar-square: all the best works on Art; besides Prints, including a valuable collection of engravings from the Italian School, from the earliest period, collected by George Cumberland. The former library-room, at Somerset House, has a ceiling painted by Angelica Kauffman, Sir Joshua Reynolds, and other Academicians. The office of Librarian is usually given to an Academician: Wilson, Fuseli, and Stothard were librarians.

ROYAL ACADEMY OF MUSIC, 4 Tenterden-street, Hanover-square, has a library of music, practical, for the use of the students. Here is preserved the original deed, dated 1719, signed by several noblemen, subscribers to a Royal Academy of Music, from which was formed the first Italian Opera in England.

ROYAL INSTITUTE OF ARCHITECTS, 16 Grosvenor-street: about 2000 volumes on Architecture and its attendant sciences; including the Prussian Government's educational works; that by Lepsius on Egypt; and large and expensive books of curiosity and reference, such as Piranesi and Canina. The Mss. and original Drawings comprise Stuart's commencement of a Dictionary of Architecture; Weennick's *Lives of Flemish Architects;* and about 2000 drawings of antiquities, modern edifices, and designs by English, French, Italian, and German architects of the 17th, 18th, and 19th centuries.

ROYAL INSTITUTION, Albemarle-street: about 27,000 volumes, including the curious library of Astle, the antiquary; topographical, antiquarian, classical, and scientific works; parliamentary history, &c.

ROYAL LIBRARY (THE), ST. JAMES'S PALACE, was originally founded by Edward VI., who appointed Bartholomew Trahuon keeper, with a salary of 20*l*.: the first books mostly collected by Leland, at the dissolution; and here were deposited his "Collections," presented by him to King Edward, but subsequently dispersed. James I. refounded the library, and added the collection of the learned Isaac Casaubon. The entire collection was presented to the British Museum, in 1757, by George II.; and to the gift was annexed the privilege, which the Royal Library had acquired in the reign of Queen Anne, of being supplied with a copy of every new publication entered at Stationers' Hall. In St. James's Palace was also the *Queen's Library,* built by Kent, for Caroline, consort of George II., in the Stable-yard: here were two fine marble busts of George II. and Queen Caroline, by Rysbrack, both now in Windsor Castle.

ROYAL SOCIETY, Somerset House: the Library occupies five rooms extremely rich in the best editions of scientific treatises, besides rare and valuable theological historical works, lent to Fellows of the Society. The catalogue of books, Mss., and letters, 1841, fills 2 volumes 8vo ("The collection is very poor in some departments."—*A. De Morgan.* The Society also possess upwards of 5000 maps, charts, engravings, drawings, &c. The library of Arundel House, presented to the Royal Society by Mr. Henry Howard, 1666-7, forms the nucleus of the present collection, each book being inscribed *Ex dono Henrici Howard, Norfolciensis:* "it consists of 3287 printed books, chiefly first editions, soon after the invention of printing; and Hebrew, Greek, Latin, Turkish, and other rare Mss., 544 volumes." (*Maitland.*) In 1830, the Arundel Mss. (excepting the Hebrew and Oriental) were sold to the British Museum for 3559*l*., which was expended in purchasing scientific works for the Royal Society's Library, now exceeding 42,000 volumes.

'Here are Chaucer's *Canterburie. Tales,* fol. 1480 (Caxton); 'Copernicus's *Iistory of Astronomy,* first edition; original Ms. of the *Principia,* written by Sir saac Newton; and documents in the *Commercium Epistolicum* (invention of 'luxions); Ms. of Aubrey's *Natural History of Wiltshire.*

ROYAL SOCIETY OF LITERATURE, 4 St. Martin's-place, Trafalgar-quare: a valuable library, greatly enriched by the lexicographical and ntiquarian works presented by the Rev. H. J. Todd, editor and en-irger of Johnson's *Dictionary;* also papers by the most eminent rriters on history, philology, poetry, philosophy, and the arts. The ociety's House was built by the leading members upon Crown-land ranted in 1826 by George IV., who contributed 1100 guineas a-year.

It is true that George IV. was committed to this large annual subscription by misconception of Dr. Burgess, Bishop of Salisbury: the king intending a dona-on of 1000 guineas, and an annual subscription of 100 guineas: but his majesty ot only cheerfully acquiesced, but amused himself with the incident.

RUSSELL INSTITUTION, Great Coram-street: about 15,000 volumes; lowed to be taken out by proprietors or subscribers. Here is Hay-on's grand heroic picture of "Xenophon and the Ten Thousand:" was disposed of by lottery for 800 guineas in 1836, when it was won y John, Duke of Bedford, and presented by him to the Institution.

SION COLLEGE Library, London Wall (see page 214), though uunded for the clergy of the City and suburbs of London, is now ccessible daily upon the same conditions as the British Museum Library. he Sion collection was increased by the bequest of the library of Dr. Villiam Harris: here are many curious black-letter theological works, id scarce tracts of the Puritan times.

SIR JOHN SOANE'S MUSEUM: Architecture and the Fine Arts ge-erally, by English, Italian, French, German, and Russian artists and terati; original Drawings and Mss. by Thorpe, Jones, Vanbrugh, Vren, and Chambers; Pennant's *London,* illustrated with 2000 draw-gs, prints, &c. (Fauntleroy's); Tasso's MS. *Gerusalemme Liberata;* rst, second, third, and fourth folio editions of Shakspeare, from J. P. .emble's library.

SOCIETIES, LITERARY AND SCIENTIFIC, in Islington, Marylebone outhwark, and Westminster, contain modern libraries.

SOCIETY OF ARTS, John-street, Adelphi, has a collection of technical orks, which is very far from complete, but was intended to contain copies f all special treatises on the arts and manufactures. The most inte-sting and important part of the library is the MS. correspondence and urnal-books. Amongst the rejected communications and condemned ventions are many since the subjects of patents; and these volumes e the most remarkable registers in the country of the inventions of e last century. The books are lent to the members.

STATISTICAL SOCIETY, 12 St. James's-square: a large collection of atistical Returns, imperfectly catalogued.

UNITED SERVICE INSTITUTION, Middle Scotland-yard, White-ll: an admirable library of reference (10,000 volumes), especially va-able in its practical utility to soldiers; pamphlets on the services; gineering papers; rich in old Italian military literature; a French an of fortification in MS., corrected in the handwriting of Vauban.

UNIVERSITY COLLEGE, Gower-street: about 43,000 volumes, and 00 pamphlets, general, legal, and medical; including the Chinese li-ary, 10,000 volumes, left by Dr. Morrison; the Ricardo library (poli-al economy) left by David Ricardo; and a large collection bequeathed Dr. Holmes of Manchester. The marble statue of Locke, in the incipal library, is by Sir Richard Westmacott, R.A. (See page 215.'

H H

WESTMINSTER ABBEY Library (Chapter House) was once the monks' "parlour," or "parleying" place, but made a "public library" by Lord Keeper Williams, whilst Dean of Westminster. The books were burnt in 1664, and but one MS. saved out of 320: they are catalogued in the Harleian MSS. Chamberlayne (1726) describes "a fair publick library, free for all strangers in term time:" about 11,000 volumes. In each boarding-house of Westminster School is also a library; and there is a small school collection of old editions of the classics.

WILLIAMS's LIBRARY, Redcross-street, Cripplegate: 20,000 volumes, collected by the Rev. Dr. Daniel Williams, the nonconformist, and Dr. Bates; and bequeathed by the former, with provisions for a building; opened 1729. This library has been increased by gifts, and by a small income from estates left by Dr. Williams: it is rich in controversial divinity, is open to the public by a Trustee's order, and books are allowed to be taken out. Here are some manuscripts of the early history of the Reformation. Dr. Williams purchased most of the books of the heirs of one Baker, of Highgate: by negligence many of the Mss. were burnt, including the pompous and curious Book of the Ceremonies of the Coronation of the Kings of England.—*H. Lemoine*, 1790.

. Also, *The Salisbury Liturgy*, finely illuminated; *The Hours of the Virgin*, Paris, 1498; Illuminated Bible; miniature copy of the Head of Christ, from a painting in the Vatican; the glass baptismal basin of Queen Elizabeth.

Here is a very interesting collection of portraits of Dissenting Ministers.

ZOOLOGICAL SOCIETY, 11 Hanover-square: Transactions of Learned Societies, and scientific zoological works of modern date.

CIRCULATING LIBRARIES date from 1740, when one Wright, at No. 132 Strand, established the first. Dr. Franklin writes in 1725, lodging in Little Britain: "Circulating libraries were not then in use." Among Wright's earliest rivals were the Nobles, in Holborn and St. Martin's-court; Samuel Bathoe, Strand; and Thomas Lowndes, Fleet-street. Another early Circulating Library was in Crane-court, Fleet-street, where the Society of Arts met in 1754 and 1755. In 1770 there were but four Circulating Libraries in the metropolis.

FREE LIBRARIES: the first established in Marylebone, 1853.

LINCOLN'S INN FIELDS,

The fine square west of Lincoln's Inn, date from 1618, when "the grounds were much planted round with dwellings and lodgings of noblemen and gentlemen of quality, but at the same time were deformed by cottages and mean buildings, — encroachments on the fields, and nuisances to the neighbourhood." To reform these grievances, a commission was appointed by the Crown "to plant and reduce to uniformity Lincoln's-Inn-Fields, as it shall be drawn by way of map or ground-plot by Inigo Jones." A view, painted in oil, of Inigo's plan is preserved at Wilton House: it is taken from the south, and the principal feature is Lindsey House, on the centre of the west side (see page 393). It still remains, but has lost the handsome vases which originally surmounted the open balustrade at the top. (*Life of Inigo Jones*, by P. Cunningham. Shakspeare Society, 1848.)

The proportions of the square were long stated to be those of the Great Pyramid of Egypt; which, says Walpole, "would have been admired in those ages when the keep of Kenilworth Castle was erected in the form of a horse-fetter, and the Escurial in the shape of St. Lawrence's gridiron." But the fact is otherwise: the base of the Great Pyramid measures 764 feet on each side, whereas Lincoln's Inn Fields, although 821 feet on one side, is only 625 feet 6 inches on the other.

and *the area of the Pyramid* is greater by many thousand square feet. (Colonel Howard Vyse, *On the Pyramids*.) The west side only was completed by Inigo Jones.

Lincoln's-Inn-Fields have been used as a place of execution. Here, Sept. 20 and 21, 1586, Babington and his accomplices were "hanged, bowelled, and quartered, on a stage or scaffold of timber strongly made for that purpose, even in the place where they used to meet and to conferre of their traitorous purposes." And here in the middle of the square, July 21, 1683, was beheaded the patriotic Lord William Russell. (See CHANCERY-LANE, p. 70.)

Burnet thus describes the sad scene: "Tillotson and I went with him in the coach to the place of execution. Some of the crowd that filled the streets wept, while others insulted. He was singing psalms a great part of the way, and said he hoped to sing better soon. As he observed the great crowd of people all the way, he said to us, 'I hope I shall quickly see a much better assembly.' When he came to the scaffold, he walked about it four or five times. Then he turned to the sheriffs and delivered his paper. . . He prayed by himself, then Tillotson prayed with him. After that he prayed again by himself, and then undressed himself, and laid his head on the block without the least change of countenance, and it was cut off at two strokes."

The Fields continued to be the resort of idle and vicious vagrants : such were "Lincoln's-Inn-Fields Mumpers;" and "Scarecrow, the beggar in Lincoln's Inn Fields, who disabled himself in his right leg, and asks alms all day, to get himself a warm supper and a trull at night." (*Spectator*, No. 6.) Boys gambled for farthings and oranges ; and a favourite game here was "the Wheel of Fortune," played with a movable hand pointing to a circle of figures, such as we remember in Moorfields, the prizes being gingerbread-nuts the size of farthings. Gay, in his *Trivia*, cautions the pedestrian :

" Where Lincoln Inn's wide space is rail'd around,
Cross not with vent'rous step; there oft is found
The lurking thief, who, while the daylight shone,
Made the walls echo with his begging tone:
That wretch, which late compassion moved, shall wound
Thy bleeding head, and fell thee to the ground."

Lincoln's-Inn-Fields *Rufflers* were wretches who assumed the characters of maimed soldiers, and begged from the claims of Naseby, Edgehill, Newbury, and Marston Moor; their prey was people of fashion, whose coaches they attacked, and if refused relief, they told their owners, "'Tis a sad thing that an old crippled cavalier should be suffered to beg for a maintenance, and a young cavalier, that never heard the whistle of a bullet, should ride in his coach."

The Fields were not, however, inclosed with iron railing until after 1735, in consequence of Sir Joseph Jekyll, then Master of the Rolls, being ridden over ; "before which time it was a receptacle for rude fellows to air horses, and many robberies were committed in it." (*Gentleman's Magazine*, Aug. 1773.) But Ireland states that Jekyll was attacked and thrown down by the mob, in consequence of his aid in the passing of the Act of Parliament to raise the price of gin.

In "the Fields" was often set up, until its final abolition, the Pillory, handy for the rabble of Clare Market.

On the north side is SIR JOHN SOANE'S MUSEUM (see MUSEUMS); south, the COLLEGE OF SURGEONS (see page 208) ; east, LINCOLN'S INN NEW HALL (see page 408) ; west, through Inigo Jones's archway, in Duke-street, is the SARDINIAN ROMAN CATHOLIC CHAPEL (see page 482); opposite which, over an Italian warehouse, lodged Dr. Franklin, when a compositor at Watts's printing-office.

Great and *Little Turnstile* are named from the turning stiles which, two centuries since, stood at their ends next Lincoln's Inn Fields, to prevent the straying of cattle therefrom. Sir Edward Sandys's curious *Europæ Speculum*, 4to, 1637, was "sold by George Hutton, at the *Turning Stile* in Holborne." The English translation of Bishop Peter Camus's *Admirable Events*, 4to, 1639, was also "sold in Holborne, in *Turnstile Lane*." In 1685 was built *New Turnstile*.

. *Turnstile-alley*, leading to Holborn, was first designed as a change for selling Welsh friezes, flannels, &c. Here Cartwright, the book-seller, kept shop: he was an excellent player, and bequeathed his plays and pictures to Dulwich College.

The concentration of the Law Courts in Lincoln's Inn Fields has been proposed; and in 1841 Mr. Barry designed a large building, of Grecian character, containing a Great Hall (nearly equal to the area of Westminster Hall), surrounded by 12 courts; the whole occupying one-third of the area within the rails, to be belted with plantations. Funds were wanting, and the blocking up of the open space was objected to: persons had considered this area as their "country walk," and that "they had been *in the country* when they had been round Lincoln's Inn Fields." (*Evidence before Parliament.*)

LITERARY FUND (ROYAL),

73 Great Russell-street, Bloomsbury, administers assistance to authors in distressed circumstances, " or deprived, by enfeebled faculties or declining life, of the power of literary exertion;" such assistance being extended, at the death of an author, to his widow and children. A by-law enacts that the applicant, to be entitled to assistance, *must have published a book.*

. " With equal promptitude and delicacy, its committee are ever ready to administer to the necessities of the unfortunate scholar, who can satisfy them that his misery is not the just punishment of immoral habits. Some of the brightest names in contemporary literature have been beholden to the bounty of this Institution, and in numerous instances its interference has shielded friendless merit from utter ruin."—*Quarterly Review.*

The Society was established by subscription, in 1790, by Mr. David Williams, who has detailed its objects in a work entitled *The Claims of Literature.* It was first proposed by Williams in 1773, to a club which met at the Prince of Wales's Tavern, Conduit-street, Hanover-square; Dr. Franklin presided, but discouraged Williams by observing, " the event will require so much time, perseverance, and patience, that the anvil may wear out the hammer." The first anniversary dinner was held in 1793: in 1794 an ode was recited; and this practice was continued until 1830. Among the writers of these poems were Captain Morris, Mr. Fitzgerald, Mr. Disraeli, Mr. George Dyer, Mr. Boscawen, the Rev. Henry Kett, the Rev. Dr. Charles Symmons, the Rev. George Crabbe, the Rev. Thomas Maurice, Mr. Henry Neele, and Mr. Allan Cunningham. The first patron of the Fund, the Prince Regent, contributed 5455*l.*; and the Dukes of Kent, Sussex, York, and Cambridge presided at its dinners; and, in 1842, Prince Albert. In the Society's armorial bearings are the imperial crown and the Prince of Wales's plume. The first house of the Fund was 36 Gerrard-street, Soho, where Williams died in 1816: he was buried in St. Ann's church, and his gravestone bears, " DAVID WILLIAMS, ESQ., AGED 78 YEARS, FOUNDER OF THE LITERARY FUND." Yet Canning, in political spite, once classed Williams amongst " creeping creatures, venomous and low!" The Fund was incorporated 1818: the average number of authors relieved annually is 40, among whom poets and tale-writers predominate; annual grants about 1400*l.* The Reserve Fund was in 1853 nearly 40,000*l.* (See LIBRARIES, page 462.)

LITTLE BRITAIN,

Anciently Breton or Britain-street, west of Aldersgate-street, is named from the Earls of Britons, who had here a magnificent town-mansion, to which adjoined Montagu House and other noble residences.

Little Britain was as remarkable for its booksellers through the reigns of Charles I. and II., James II., and William and Mary, as Paternoster-row is at present. This location of booksellers may have been influenced by John Day, the eminent printer, living over Aldersgate; and from Grub-street being the abode of authors. (See GRUB-STREET, pp. 335-7.) "Bartholomew-close printers" are also mentioned by Dryden.

Roger North, in his *Life of the Hon. and Rev. Dr. John North*, speaking of the booksellers in the reign of Charles II., says: "Little Britain was a plentiful and perpetual emporium of learned authors, and men went thither as to a market. This drew to the place a mighty trade, the rather because the shops were spacious, and the learned gladly resorted to them, where they seldom failed to meet with agreeable conversation; and the booksellers themselves were knowing and conversible men, with whom, for the sake of bookish knowledge, the greatest wits were pleased to converse; and we may judge the time as well spent there as (in latter days) either in tavern or coffee-house. But now this emporium has vanished, and the trade contracted into the hands of two or three persons."

Robert Scott appears to have been a principal dealer in Little Britain. A newspaper of 1644 states 460 pamphlets to have been published here in four years. Richard Chiswell, of Little Britain, buried in St. Botolph's Church, Aldersgate, in 1711, is described as "the metropolitan bookseller of England." At the Dolphin, in Little Britain, lived Samuel Buckley, publisher of the *Spectator*, commenced March 1, 1711. In 1725, Benjamin Franklin, when working at Palmer's printing-office in Bartholomew-close, lodged in Little Britain, next door to Wilcox the bookseller, who lent Franklin books "for a reasonable retribution."

Milton, after he had left Jewin-street, lodged for a time in Little Britain with Millington, the book-auctioneer, who was accustomed to lead his venerable inmate by the hand when he walked in the street, as mentioned by Richardson, on the testimony of an acquaintance of Milton. (Symmons's *Life of Milton*, 2d edition, p. 501.) Richardson also relates, that in Little Britain the Earl of Dorset, when beating about for books to his taste, "met with *Paradise Lost*, and was so struck with some of its passages that he bought it, the bookseller begging him to speak in its favour if he liked it, for that they (the copies in his shop, not the impression, as Malone states) lay on his hands as waste paper. The Earl read the poem, and sent it to Dryden, who returned it with the memorable opinion: 'This man cuts us all out, and the ancients too.'"

"The race of booksellers in Little Britain is now almost extinct; honest Ballard, well known for his curious divinity catalogues, being their only genuine representative" (*Gentleman's Magazine*, No. 1, 1731). He died Jan. 2, 1796, aged 88, in the house wherein he was born.

Duke-street, formerly Duck-lane, leading into Smithfield, was once celebrated for refuse book-shops:

"And so may'st thou, perchance, pass up and down,
And please awhile th' admiring court and town.
Who after all shall in Duck-lane shops be thrown."
Oldham's *Satires*, circ. 1680.

Washington Irving describes the locality as "a cluster of narrow streets and courts of very venerable and debilitated houses, several ready to tumble down, the fronts of which are magnificently enriched with old oaken carvings of hideous faces, unknown birds, beasts, and fishes, and fruits and flowers, which it would perplex a naturalist to classify" (*Sketch-book*). Most of this grotesque ornamentation has, however, long disappeared.

LOMBARD-STREET,

"A certain street of the greatest credit in Europe," (*Addison*,) is proved by Stow to have borne that name before the reign of Edward II., and is so called of the Longobards, the first of whom were the Caursini family, a rich race of bankers who settled here, and their countrymen soon grouped around them. They were also the goldsmiths, who took pledges in plate, jewels, &c.; and the badge of the Lombards (the three golden pills of the Medici family) has descended as the sign of the pawnbrokers.* The black-letter ballad in the Pepys collection makes the husband of Jane Shore a goldsmith here:

> " In Lombard-street I once did dwelle,
> As London yet can witnesse welle;
> Where many gallants did beholde
> My beauty in a shop of golde.
> *   *   *   *
> I penance did in Lombard-streete
> In shameful manner in a sheete."

Here the merchants assembled twice daily in all weathers. In 1537, Sir Richard Gresham proposed to Cromwell (then Lord Privy Seal) "to make a goodely Bursse in Lombert-strette, for marchaunts to repayer unto." Hence originated the Exchange built by Sir Richard's son, Sir Thomas Gresham, who was then living in Lombard-street, described by Hentzner as the handsomest street in London.

Here, like other bankers, Gresham kept a shop on the site of the banking-house (No. 68) of Martin, Stone, and Martins, who in Pennant's time possessed the large gilt grasshopper (Gresham's crest) which was placed over his door as a sign. It existed entire until 1795, when the present house was built, and the sign disappeared piecemeal.

Hentzner, in 1593, saw in Lombard-street "all sorts of gold and silver vessels exposed to sale, as well as ancient and modern coins, in such quantities as must surprise a man the first time he sees and considers them." At Gresham's death, much of his wealth consisted of gold chains. Lombard-street has retained its character as well as its name for at least five centuries and a half; and within the last thirty years several gold and silver lacemen lived there.—Burgon's *Life and Times of Sir Thomas Gresham*, vol. i. p. 281: 1839.

The Pope's merchants also chaffered here for their *wafer-cakes* and *pardons*. Sir Simon Eye built here a large tavern, "the Cardinal's Hat;" and Pope's Head Alley, leading from Lombard-street to Cornhill, is named from "the Pope's Head Tavern," which existed in 1464: it had a finely painted room in Pepys's time. The Alley was once famous for its printsellers, for toys, turnery, and cutlery; and stalls of fine fruit. The poet Pope was born in Lombard-street, May 22, 1688, "at the house which is now Mr. Morgan's, an apothecary" (Spence's *Anecdotes*); a name long since forgotten, although J. T. Smith took much pains to discover it. Pope's father was a linen-draper, and a Roman Catholic, and the poet was partly educated by the family priest. Pope apostrophises John Moore, "author of the celebrated worm-powder,"

> " O learned friend of *Abchurch-lane.*"

Lombard-street had also its booksellers. The imprint to Howel's Familiar Letters, 5th edition, is : "London, printed for *Thomas Guy*, at the Corner-shop of little *Lombard-street* and *Cornhill*, near *Woolchurch* Market, 1678." And 1696, Sept. 17, *Lloyd's News* was first "printed for Edward Lloyd (Coffee-man) in Lombard-street." Towards Birchin (anciently Birchover's)-lane stood the house of William de la Pole, created in France, by Edward III., Knight Banneret; he was King's Merchant, and from him sprang a numerous race of nobility.

Sir Martin Bowes, the wealthy goldsmith, lived upon the site of No. 67, now Glyn's banking-house.

In *George-yard* was the George hostelry, the London lodging of Earl Ferrers, whose brother, in 1175, was slain here in the night, and thrown into the dirty street, which led to the setting of night-watches.

Lombard-street highway passes over the site of Roman houses, and has been

---

* By others the sign is traced to the three pieces of gold, which are the emblem of the charitable St. Nicholas. (See Mrs. Jameson's *Sacred and Legendary Art.*)

the field of three great *finds* of Roman remains, in 1730, 1774, and 1785-6; the latter, in its stratum of wood ashes, supposed to indicate the burning of London by Boadicea. Ten feet below the street-level was found a wall of the smaller-sized Roman bricks, pierced by flues or chimneys; likewise tile and brick pavements; in Birchin-lane, a tesselated pavement of elegant design, heaps of Roman coins, glass bottles, keys, and beads; vessels and fragments of earthenware; and a large vessel of red Samian ware, richly embellished, and reminding us that "Rome did not want its Wedgwood." The causeway, which Wren considered the northern boundary of the Roman station, was then also discovered in Birchin-lane.

In Lombard-street are sixteen banking-houses, and fire and life insurance-offices; mostly handsome buildings. The *Pelican Life Office* was built by Sir Robert Taylor; and the emblematic group, designed by Lady Diana Beauclerk, was executed by Coade, at Lambeth.

The General Post-Office was removed to Lombard-street early in the last century (see p. 394), and thence to St. Martin's-le-Grand in 1829.

Here are the churches of Allhallows (see page 116); St. Edmund (p. 126); and St. Mary Woolnoth (p. 148).

LONDON INSTITUTION,

Finsbury Circus, was established by a proprietary, 1805, "for the advancement of literature and the diffusion of useful knowledge:" upon its first committee were Mr. Angerstein and Mr. Richard Sharp (" Conversation Sharp"). The Institution was temporarily located at 8 Old Jewry (the fine brick mansion of Sir Robert Clayton, *temp.* Charles II.), and opened with a library of 10,000 volumes; incorporated in 1807: the sun in splendour, a terrestrial globe, open book, and air-pump, among the armorial ensigns of the common seal, characterising the objects of the Institution. In 1812 it was removed to King's Arms'-yard, Coleman-street; and thence, in 1819, to the present mansion, built on the north side of Moorfields (Brooks, architect); the first stone laid November 4, 1815, by the Lord Mayor, Birch: the façade is of Portland stone, and has a Corinthian portico, modified from the Temple of Vesta at Tivoli; cost of the building, 31,124*l.* The Library is 97 by 42 feet, and 28 in height, and has a gallery throughout: the collection of books is " one of the most useful and accessible in Britain " (see LIBRARIES, page 462). In the rear of the mansion is the Lecture-room, or Theatre, for 700 auditors; and adjoining are the Apparatus-room and Laboratory; the latter designed by W. H. Pepys, F.R.S., and engraved in Parkes's *Chemical Catechism*, 13th edition, 1834. The apparatus in pneumatics, hydrostatics, electricity, and magnetism, is very perfect; but the great battery of 2000 double plates, and another with a pair of plates 200 feet square, with which Sir Humphry Davy experimented, have long been destroyed.

LONDON STONE,

Cannon-street, is a fragment of the *Lapis Milliaris* (mile-stone) of the Romans, " a pillar set up by them in the centre of the forum of Agricola's station, the *gnoma* or *umbilicus castri Londinensis.*" (*A. J. Kempe, F.S.A.*) Stow describes it on the *south* side of the street, near the channel of Walbrook, "pitched upright, a great stone, called London Stone, fixed in the ground very deep, fastened with bars of iron, and so strongly set, that if carts do run against it through negligence, the wheels be broken, and the stone itself be unshaken." There is evidence to the belief that it was placed here a thousand years ago; and Camden considers it to have been the great central mile-stone, from which the British high-roads radiated, and the distances on them were reckoned, similar to that in the Forum at Rome.*

* A like stone, of the time of Hadrian (2d century), was found on the side of the Roman Foss-way, near Leicester, in 1771; and is preserved in the Museum of the Leicester Literary and Philosophical Society.

London Stone is referred to as a local mark of immemorial antiquity in Saxon charters. Stow found it mentioned as a landmark in a list of rents belonging to Christ's Church, in Canterbury, at the end of "a fair-written gospel-book," given to that foundation by the West-Saxon King Athelstane, who reigned from 925 to 941. Of later time we read, that in the year 1135, the 1st of King Stephen, a fire, which began in the house of one Ailward, near unto London Stone, consumed all east to Aldgate. Henry Fitz-Alwyn, "the draper of London Stone," was the first Mayor of London, 1189. Lydgate, about 1430, sings:

> " Then I went forth by London Stone
> Throughout all Canwick Street."—*London Lackpenny.*

Holinshed mentions the Stone in describing the insurrection of Jack Cade, who, when he had forced his way into the capital, struck his sword upon London Stone, exclaiming, "Now is Mortimer lord of this city." Shakspeare has introduced this dramatic incident in the Second Part of Henry IV. act iv. sc. 1. In " Pasquill and Marforius," 1589, we read: " Set up this bill at London Stone. Let it be doone solemnly, with drom and trumpet; and looke you advance my cullour on the top of the steeple right over against it." Also, "if it please them these dark winter nights, to sticke uppe their papers uppon London Stone." Here it is presumed to have been customary to affix official papers.

Luther's *Table-Talk*, English translation, was first "printed by William Du Gard, dwelling in Suffolk-lane, near London-stone."

Watling-street, of which Cannon-street is a continuation, is supposed to have been the principal street of Roman London; but it may have been a British road before the arrival of the Romans, to which earlier period Strype refers London Stone. After the Great Fire of 1666, the ground in Cannon-street was much disturbed, and the "large foundations" of London Stone led Wren to consider it to have been some more considerable monument than even the Roman milliarium; for adjoining " were discovered some tesselated pavements, and other extensive remains of Roman workmanship and buildings. Probably, this might, in some degree, have imitated the *Miliarium Aureum* at Constantinople, which was not in the form of a pillar at Rome, but an eminent building," containing many statues. The Stone, before the Great Fire, was " much worn away, and as it were but a stump remaining." (*Strype.*) It was then cased over by Wren with a new stone, handsomely wrought and cut hollow, something like a Roman altar or pedestal, admitting the ancient fragment, " now not much larger than a bomb-shell," to be seen through a large aperture near the top. The Stone, in its old position on the *south* side of the street, being complained of as a nuisance, was removed to the *north* side in 1742, close to the kerb: here again it proved an obstruction; and in 1798, when the church was about to be repaired, the venerable Stone was by some of the parishioners doomed to destruction; but Mr. Thomas Maiden, of Sherborne-lane, printer, prevailed on the parish-officers to have it placed against the south wall of the church, where it now remains.

LONDON WALL,

Moorfields, is a street named from its north side occupying the site of that portion of the City Wall which divided the City Liberty from the manor of Finsbury, and against which was built Bethlem Hospital, taken down 1817-8; when also the Wall was removed: "found uncommonly thick, and the bricks double the size of those now used; the centre filled in with large loose stones, &c." (Hughson's *Walks*, 1817.) The level of the street has been in part raised two feet within the last

30 years. Over *Helmet Court* entrance is a helmet, boldly sculptured in stone. Here is *Sion College*, described at page 214.

The Wall, believed to be the work of the later Roman period, when London was often exposed to hostile attacks, extended from the Tower, through the Minories to Aldgate, Houndsditch, Bishopsgate, *along London Wall* to Fore-street, through Cripplegate and Castle-street to Aldersgate, and so through Christ's Hospital by Newgate and Ludgate towards the Thames. (See CITY WALL AND GATES, pp. 184-5.)

LONG ACRE,

The main street between Covent Garden and St. Giles's, and extending from Drury-lane west to St. Martin's-lane, was (*temp.* Henry VIII.) an open field, called the Elms, from a line of those trees growing upon it, is shewn in Aggas's plan. It was next called Seven Acres; and *temp.* Charles I., when it was first laid out, it was changed to Long Acre, from the length of the slip of ground first made a pathway. In Phœnix-alley, now Hanover-court, on the south, John Taylor, the water-poet, and a contemporary of Shakspeare, kept an ale-house, first with the sign of "The Mourning Crown," for which, at the Commonwealth, he sub-tituted his own head, with this motto:

> "There's many a head stands for a sign;
> Then, gentle reader, why not mine?"

Taylor, as a Thames waterman, stoutly assailed coaches, among the builders of which he died, in Phœnix-alley, in 1653.

It is related of Prior, the poet, that after spending the evening with Oxford, Bolingbroke, Pope, and Swift, he would go and smoke a pipe, and drink a bottle of ale with a common soldier and his wife in Long Acre, before he went to bed. This woman (also said to have been a cobbler's and an alehouse-keeper's wife) was the beautiful Chloe of Prior's poems: "he used to bury himself for whole days and nights together with this poor mean creature" (*Pope*).

Defoe (*Journey through England*, 1722) describes "the Mug-house Club, in Long Acre, where, every Wednesday and Saturday, a mixture of gentlemen, law-yers, and tradesmen, meet in a great room, and are seldom under a hundred. They have a grave old gentleman, in his own grey hairs, now within a few months of ninety years old, who is their president, and sits in an arm'd chair some steps higher than the rest of the company, to keep the whole room in order. A harp plays all the time at the lower end of the room, and every now and then one or other of the company rises and entertains the rest with a song, and (by the by) some are good masters. Here is nothing drunk but ale, and every gentleman hath his separate mug, which he chalks on the table where he sits as it is brought in; and every one retires as he pleases, as from a coffee-house. The room is always so diverted with songs, and drinking from one table to another to one another's healths, that there is no room for politicks, or any thing that can sour conversation. One must be there by seven to get room, and after ten the com-pany are for the most part gone."

Long Acre was at first inhabited by persons of note, and some of the houses are handsomely built; but coachmakers, and the subordinate trades of coach-trimmers, colourmen, and varnish-makers, have probably lived in Long Acre since the general introduction of coaches, *circ.* 1630. John Locke (in his *Diary*, 1679) recommends "Mr. Cox, of Long Acre, for all sorts of dioptical glasses." A few old signs, includ-ing the goldbeater's gilded arm and hammer, remain upon the house-fronts; but the coachmakers have of late years followed fashion west-ward. The chapel on the north side of Long Acre was the private pro-perty of the Rev. John Warner, D.D., an eloquent preacher (d. 1800). In conjunction with Dr. Lettsom and Mr. Nichols, Dr. Warner origi-nated the erection of the statue of John Howard in St. Paul's Cathedral. Among the *nostrums* of Long Acre were Dr. Gardner's Worm-destroying Medicines, &c.; and Burchell's Anodyne Necklaces, strongly recommended for teeth-cutting, by Dr. Turner, the inventor; and Dr. Chamberlain, who possessed the secret.

In *Rose-street*, the notorious Edward Curll, the bookseller, kept shop, with Pope's Head for his sign. In this street Dryden was cudgelled on his way home from Will's Coffee-house to Long Acre.

Endell-street, on the south, leads to Holborn (see p. 374). *St. Martin's Hall* was built in 1849, beween Charles and Wilson streets (see p. 370); and in Castle-street, in 1850, the *St. Martin's Northern Schools* (Wyld, architect). The style is Byzantine, with two tiers of pointed arches; the top story being a covered playground, 100 feet long, opening to the front by a colonnade,—a novel contrivance for keeping the children from the evil ways of the street.

LORD MAYOR'S STATE.

The salary and allowances paid to the Lord Mayor from the City funds during his year of office, with sums from other sources, amount to about 7900*l*. He resides in the Mansion House, which is sumptuously furnished, and provided with plate and jewelled ornaments said to be worth from 20,000*l*. to 30,000*l*.: his household consists of 20 gentlemen, including the Sword-bearer, the Common Hunt, the Common Crier, and the Water-bailiff, all of whom have the title of esquires. He has a splendid retinue of servants, and keeps three tables; he is provided with a gorgeous state-coach, but not with horses; and he finds the dress-carriage and horses for the Lady Mayoress. (See STATE COACHES.) He is expected to give a certain number of state banquets during the year, in addition to bearing half of the expense of the inauguration-dinner at Guildhall on the 9th of November. The Lord Mayor's dinners are provided by contract, but the wines are supplied from the Mansion-House cellars. The mayoralty expenses, unless "cool was his kitchen," generally exceed by 4000*l*. the City allowance. The state liveries usually cost 500*l*.

The Fool was formerly one of the Lord Mayor's household; and he was bound by his office to leap, clothes and all, into a large bowl of custard, at the Lord Mayor's inauguration dinner:

> "He may, perchance, in tail of a Sheriff's dinner,
> Skip with a rime o' the table, from new nothing,
> And take his almain leap into a custard,
> Shall make my Lady Mayoress and her sisters
> Laugh all their hods over their shoulders."—*Ben Jonson.*

Custard was " a food much used in City feasts." (Johnson's *Dict.*)

> " Now may'rs and shrieves all hush'd and satiate lay;
> Yet eat, in dreams, the custard of the day."—*Pope.*

Costume and Jewels.—On ordinary state occasions the Lord Mayor wears a massive black silk robe richly embroidered, and his collar and jewel. In the courts and civic meetings he has a violet silk robe, furred, and barred with black velvet; and on the bench at the Mansion House, and in the Central Criminal Court, he wears a scarlet robe, furred, and bordered with black velvet. In conducting the Sovereign through the City, the Lord Mayor wears a rich crimson velvet robe. Beneath the robe is worn a rich court suit, with point-lace; and the velvet hood of old has been superseded by a three-cornered dress hat, trimmed with black ostrich-feathers.

The *wear of robes* of various colours upon certain days was fixed by a regulation in 1562, and, with the customs and orders for meeting, was printed in a tract by John Day, now very scarce. But the present authority for the customs is a pamphlet printed by direction of the Common Council in 1789.

The Collar is of pure gold, composed of a series of links, each formed

)f a letter S; a united York and Lancaster, or Henry VII. rose; and a
nassive knolt. The ends of the chain are joined by the portcullis, from
.he points of which, suspended by a ring of diamonds, hangs the Jewel.
The entire Collar contains 28 SS, 14 roses, and 13 knolts, and measures
$4 inches. The Jewel contains in the centre the City arms, cut in
:ameo, of a delicate blue, on an olive ground. Surrounding this, a
garter, of bright blue, edged with white and gold, bearing the City
notto, "Domine dirige nos," in gold letters. The whole is encircled
with a costly border of gold SS, alternating with rosettes of diamonds,
iet in silver. The Jewel is suspended from the collar by a portcullis;
)ut when worn without the Collar, is suspended by a broad blue ribbon.
The investiture is by a massive gold chain; and when the Mayor is re-
ilected, by two chains.

Mace and Swords.—The Mace is silver-gilt, is 5 feet 3 inches in
ength, and bears on the lower part W. R.; it is surmounted with a
'egal crown and the imperial arms, and has the handle and staff richly
:hased. The "Pearl Sword," presented by Queen Elizabeth upon open-
ng the Royal Exchange, has a crimson velvet sheath thickly set with
)earls; and the handle, of gold, is richly chased in devices of Justice
ind Mercy. There are a Sunday sword for church; a common sword
'or the Sessions: and a black sword for the 30th of January, and Sept.
!d, the anniversary of the Great Fire of 1666.

Seals.—The Corporate Seal is circular. *Obverse:* St. Paul, bearing a sword,
ind a flag ensigned with three lions passant-gardant, standing in a city, over the
;ate of which is a key; legend, SIGILLVM: BARONVM: LONDONIARVM. *Reverse:*
he City Arms, with mantlings, &c.; legend, LONDONI: DEFENDE: TVOS: DEVS
)PTIME: CIVES. The second Seal, made 4 Richard II., bears the effigies of SS.
Peter and Paul, canopied. Beneath are the present arms of the City: a cross
with a dagger in the dexter quarter, supported by two lions. It appears to have
)een surmounted with a low-pointed arch. The centre compartment is flanked
with two canopied niches; in each a demi-figure, a sergeant-at-arms, bearing a
nace, and wearing a triangular cap. The pedestals of the canopies sustain kneel-
ng figures paying adoration to the Virgin Mary, whose effigy (much effaced) ap-
)ears in the centre niche at the top of the seal. Legend, SIGILLVM OFFICII:
MAJORATVS: CIVITATIS: LONDINI: very indistinct from wear.

The Mayor has been chief butler to the Sovereign at coronation feasts
since the reign of Richard III., receiving for his fee a gold cup and cover.[*]

The most memorable name in the civic annals is that of Sir Richard
Whittington, "thrice Lord Mayor," 1398, 1407, 1420.

Whittington was the son of Sir William Whittington, Knight, and his early
destitution rests but upon the nursery tale. His prosperity is referred to the
:oal-carrying *cat* of Newcastle; but a scarce print, by Elstrucke, of Whittington
n his mayoralty robes, has a cat beside the figure, shewing the version of the
nursery tale to have been then popular: in the early impressions of this plate a
skull appears in place of the cat, which has rendered the original print a rarity of
great price among collectors. Whittington's wealth rebuilt Newgate, and St.
Michael's Church, Paternoster Royal; built part of St. Bartholomew's Hospital,
ind the library of Christ's Hospital, and added to the Guildhall. He also bequeathed his house at "College-hill" for a college and almshouse, which have
)een taken down, and the institution removed to a handsome collegiate building
near Highgate Archway, not far from the stone marking the spot whereon tradi-
;ion states Whittington to have rested when a poor boy and listened to the bells of
Bow; the original stone (removed in 1821) is said to have been set up by desire of
Whittington, to assist horsemen to mount at the foot of the hill. Whittington
was buried in St. Michael's Church, beneath a costly marble tomb; but his remains
were twice disturbed before the church was destroyed by fire, and now there is
10 olden memorial of Whittington to be traced; his statue has been placed in

[*] There is current a piece of City gossip, of a Silver Cradle being custo-
narily presented at the accouchement of a Lady Mayoress; but in 1835 and 1843,
uch an event was merely signalised by a congratulatory vote of the Court of
Common Council.

the Royal Exchange. Whittington was of the Mercers' Company, "flos mercatorum:" his will at Mercers' Hall bears a curious illumination of Whittington on his death-bed, his three executors, a priest, &c. Whittington is also said to have lived in Sweedon's-passage, Grub-street (see page 392); and in a court in Hart-street, Mark-lane, was formerly a building termed in old leases "Whittington's Palace."

Sir Geoffry Bullen, Lord Mayor in 1453, was grandfather to Thomas Earl of Wiltshire, father to Anne Bullen, and grandfather to Queen Elizabeth; the highest genealogical honour the City can boast of.

"The ennobled families of Cornwallis, Capel, Coventry, Legge, Cowper, Thynne, Ward, Craven, Marsham, Pulteney, Hill, Holles, Osborne, Cavendish, Bennet, and others, have sprung either directly or collaterally from those who have been either Mayors, Sheriffs, or Aldermen of London; and a very large portion of the peerage of the United Kingdom is related, either by descent or intermarriage, to the citizens of the metropolis."—*Thomas Moule.*

It was at the table of the Lord Mayor, in 1497, that Erasmus first met Sir Thomas More, whence sprung one of the most interesting friendships in literary history.

LUDGATE, LUDGATE HILL AND STREET.

Ludgate, one of the principal gates of the City, was situated at the western extremity of Bowyer's-row, now Ludgate-hill, between the London Coffee-house and St. Martin's Church. Geoffrey of Monmouth states the gate to have been built by the British King Lud, 66 B.C.: hence its traditional name; but more probably from the Flood, or Flud, which ran into Fleet river. We find no further mention of it until 1215, when it was fortified or rebuilt by the barons leagued against King John, and who employed as materials the remains of the stone houses of opulent Jews, which had been destroyed, as proved by a stone discovered in 1586, inscribed in Hebrew, "This is the ward of Rabbi Moses, the son of the honourable Rabbi Isaac." In 1260 the gate was again repaired, and ornamented on the east side with statues of Lud and his two sons; and subsequently the statue of Queen Elizabeth was placed in the west front. Ludgate was much injured in the Great Fire of 1666, and is shewn in Greffier's picture, engraved by Birch. The gate is described by Chamberlayne (1726) as a prison "only for debtors who are freemen of London." In the *Spectator*, No. 82, is "a voice bawling for charity at the grate;" just as in our time the prisoners of the Fleet loudly called upon those who passed the grate, "*Pray* remember the poor debtors," as the board above stated, "having no allowance." Pennant describes Ludgate, within his memory, "a wretched prison for debtors." It was taken down, 1760-62, when the statue of Elizabeth was placed at the east end of St. Dunstan's Church, Fleet-street (see page 125), and the other statues were disposed of as described at page 184. By a plan preserved in St. Martin's vestry-room, the great arch and postern of Ludgate was 37 ft. 6 in. wide in front, and 39 ft. deep. Ludgate was made a free prison in 1378 (1st Richard II.); but its privileges were soon violated, and it became a place of great oppression. Rowley's comedy of *A Woman never vext, or the Widow of Cornhill*, is founded upon the tradition of the handsome Stephen Foster, Lord Mayor in 1454, *begging at the grate* of Ludgate, and attracting the sympathy of a rich widow, who paid the debt for which he was confined, and afterwards married him:

"*Mrs. S. Foster.* But why remove the prisoners from Ludgate?
Stephen Foster. To take the prison down and build it new,
With leads to walk on, chambers large and fair;
For when myself lay there, the noxious air
Choked up my spirits. None but captives, wife,
Can know what captives feel."—Act v. sc. 1.

etween 1454 and 1463 the prison was much enlarged, and a chapel
uilt by Dame Agnes Foster and the executors of Stephen her hus-
and, as thus recorded on a copperplate upon the walls:

> "Deout soules that passe this way,
>   for *Stephen Foster*, late Maior, heartily pray,
>   And Dame Agnes, his spouse, to God consecrate,
>   that of pitie this house made of Londoners in *Ludgate*,
>   So that for *lodging and water* prisoners here nought pay,
>   as their keepers shall all answere at dreadful doomes day."

At the rebuilding of Ludgate in 1586, "the verse being unhappily turned inward
the wall," Stow tells us he had the like "graven outward in prose, declaring
m (Foster) to be a fishmonger, because some upon a light occasion (as a maiden's
ead in a glass window) had fabled him to be a mercer, and to have begged there
Ludgate," &c.

A quarto tract, *Prison Thoughts*, by Thomas Browning, a prisoner
Ludgate, "where poore citizens are confined and starved amidst
pies of their freedom," was published in that prison by the author
1682, and is supposed to have suggested Dr. Dodd's *Prison Thoughts*.

Ludgate-hill extends from Fleet-street to St. Martin's Church (see
age 140); and Ludgate-*street* from thence to St. Paul's. On the hill,
pposite the gate, stopped the rebellion of Sir Thomas Wyat (see p. 398).
elow is the Bell Savage Inn, described at p. 397. Ludgate-street
d hill was famous for mercers in Stow's time. At the north-east
rner (St. Paul's Churchyard), No. 65, lived John Newbery, for whom
oldsmith wrote *Goody Two-shoes*, a pamphlet on the Cock-lane Ghost,
d a *History of England*, and edited the *Public Ledger* newspaper.
o Newbery succeeded John Harris, and next Grant and Griffith. At
the Dunciad," in Ludgate-street, D. Griffiths published the *Monthly
eview*, No. 1, May 1749.

On the north is Ave-Maria-lane, leading to Amen-corner and
aternoster-row; and Stationers' Hall-court, leading to the hall of the
tationers' Company (see p. 365). On the south is Creed-lane.

In 1792 was discovered a barbican, or watch-tower, between Ludgate and the
leet-ditch, forming part of the extension of the City wall in 1276; a fine fragment
which exists in St. Martin's-court, opposite the Old Bailey. In a bastion of the
all, in 1800, was found a sepulchral monument, in the rear of No. 24, the London
ffee-house, where it is now preserved: it is dedicated to Claudina Martina, by
r husband Anencletus, a provincial Roman soldier. Here are also a fragment
a statue of Hercules, and a female head.

At No. 32, north side, was the picturesque old shop-front of Rundell
d Bridge, goldsmiths and diamond-jewellers to the Crown, with the
gn of the Golden Salmon. Here was executed Flaxman's Shield of
chilles, in silver-gilt: and here was fitted up the imperial crown for
e coronation of George IV. in 1821; and a silver wine-cooler, which
cupied two years in chasing. Mrs. Rundell wrote *The Art of Cookery
Domestic Cookery*), for which she ultimately received 2000 guineas.
t No. 45, William Hone published his political satires, with woodcuts
Cruikshank; and his *Every-day Book, Ancient Mysteries, &c.*

Through Ludgate hill and street there have passed, in twelve hours,
52 vehicles, 13,025 horses, and 105,352 persons.

MAGDALEN HOSPITAL,

. George's Fields, for the relief and reformation of unfortunate
omen and penitent prostitutes, was projected by Robert Dingley,
nas Hanway, and a few others, in 1758;* and opened at a house in
rescot-street, Goodman's Fields, when eight unhappy objects were

* A plan of the kind was suggested in the *Gentleman's Magazine* for April
51; and the *Rambler*, No. 107.

admitted; and from thence to Feb. 26, 1761; there were received into "Magdalen-house" 281 : of 100 inmates, not a seventh were 15 years old.

Among the names of the earliest benefactors occurs that of Omychund, the black merchant of Calcutta. He bequeathed between this and the Foundling Hospital 37,500 current rupees, to be equally divided. Unfortunately, however, " a portion only of this munificent legacy could be extracted from the grasp of Hurzorimal, his executor, notwithstanding the zealous interference of the governor-general (Warren Hastings) and other eminent functionaries."—*Brownlow.*

Another early promoter was the Rev. William Dodd, who, in 1759, preached a sermon for the benefit of the charity; and again in 1760, before Prince Edward, Duke of York : both sermons are eloquent compositions, were printed, and large editions sold.* The Magdalens wore a grey uniform dress, high in the neck, long black mittens, mob-cap, and a broad black chip hat. In the list of contributors we find " A Lady unknown, a Lottery Ticket, No. 34987, in the Lottery 1758, a Prize of 500*l.*;" Lord Chesterfield, 21*l.* per annum; "Will's Coffee-house, Lincoln's Inn, 16*l.* 16*s.*;" and the " Charity Boxes," in one year, received 458*l.* 10*s.*; and the women's needlework produced 282*l.* 11*s.* 3*d.*: there being about 100 in the house.

Among their employments was making their own clothes, spinning the thread and making the cloth; to knit their stockings; to make bone-lace, black lace, artificial flowers, children's toys, winding silk, embroidery, millinery, making women's and children's shoes, mantuas, stays, coats, cauls for wigs, weaving hair for perukes, making leathern and silken gloves and garters, drawing patterns, making soldiers' clothes and seamen's slops, making carpets after the Turkey manner, &c.

In 1769, the charity was incorporated, and the institution declared extra-parochial: the present Hospital was commenced, 6½ acres of St. George's common fields having been purchased by the governors. Attached to the Hospital is a Chapel, rendered attractive by the singing of the Magdalens, screened from the congregation; and the donations at the chapel doors are very productive to the Hospital funds : formerly, the admission on Sunday evenings was by ticket. Queen Charlotte patronised this charity 56 years. Queen Victoria became patroness in 1841.

Fit objects for the Magdalen charity are admitted without any recommendation, on their own application and petition, on the first Thursday in every month. Nearly 8000 have been received since the Hospital was established; more than two-thirds have been permanently reclaimed, and many have married and become respectable members of society: all who have behaved well are discharged with some provision for their future maintenance.

MANSION-HOUSE (THE)

Of the Lord Mayor, and his residence during his year of office, occupies the site of Stocks' Market, nearly facing the area of the Royal Exchange. The foundation of the Mansion House was laid in 1739, by Lord Mayor Perry; but the building was not finished until 1753, in the mayoralty of Sir Crisp Gascoigne, the first Lord Mayor who resided in it. The architect was the elder Mr. Dance; the style is that of Palladio; and the building, which is entirely insulated, is of Portland-stone, and resembles a massive Italian palace. The principal front has a very fine Corinthian portico, with six fluted columns, supporting a pediment, in the tympanum of which is a group of allegorical sculpture by Sir Robert Taylor. In the centre is a female impersonation of the City of London, trampling on her enemies; on her right is the Roman lictor, and a boy bearing the cap of liberty; and beyond them is Neptune and nautical insignia. To the left of the centre is another female attended by two

* Account of the Magdalen Charity; with the above Sermons, Advice to the Magdalens, Prayers, Rules, &c. Printed in 1761.

boys, and bearing an olive-branch and cornucopia; the extreme angles being filled with casks, bales, and other emblems of commerce. On each side a flight of steps, balustraded, ascends to the entrance beneath the portico; and in the rusticated basement is the entrance to the offices. On the west side is a Roman-Doric porch. A long narrow attic, called the Mare's (Mayor's) Nest, has been removed from the roof.

The interior of the block of buildings was an open court of elaborate character, similar to that part of an Italian palace; but the central area is now filled with the saloon, which is of wood. This grand banquet-room was designed by the Earl of Burlington, and is called the Egyptian Hall, from its accordance with the Egyptian Hall described by Vitruvius. It has two side screens of lofty scagliola Sienna columns, supporting a vaulted roof, and lit by a large western window: it can dine 400 guests, and here the Lord Mayor gives his state-banquets. In the side walls are sixteen niches, to be hereafter filled with sculptured groups or figures.

There are other dining-rooms; as the Venetian Parlour, Wilkes's Parlour, &c. The drawing-rooms and ball-room are superbly decorated; above the latter is the Justice-room (constructed in 1849), where the Lord Mayor sits daily. In a contiguous apartment was the State Bed. There are a few gallery portraits and other pictures. The kitchen and wine-cellars have a cryptal spaciousness.

MANSIONS.

APSLEY HOUSE, (Duke of Wellington), Hyde-Park-corner, Piccadilly, and happily called by a foreigner "No. 1 London," was built about 1785-6, by the Adams, for Henry Bathurst Baron Apsley, Earl Bathurst, and Lord Chancellor, who died in 1794. Here resided the Marquis Wellesley, elder brother of the great Duke of Wellington, who purchased the house in 1820. It was then a plain brick mansion, but was cased with Bath-stone in 1828, by B. Wyatt, who designed the tetrastyle Corinthian portico and pediment upon a rusticated entrance arcade; built a gallery and suite of rooms on the west or Hyde-Park side, and enlarged the garden by a strip of ground from the Park. These additions and repairs are stated to have cost 130,000*l.*

The bullet-proof iron Venetian blinds (the first of the kind) were put up by the late Duke of Wellington, after his windows had been broken by the Reform Bill mobs; and these blinds were not removed during the Duke's life-time. "They shall stay where they are," was his remark, "as a monument of the gullibility of a mob, and the worthlessness of that sort of popularity for which they who give it can assign no good reason. I don't blame the men that broke my windows; they only did what they were instigated to do by others who ought to have known better. But if any one be disposed to grow giddy with popular applause, I think that a glance towards these iron shutters will soon sober him."

The courtyard is inclosed by richly bronzed metal gates (in which the Grecian honeysuckle is finely cast); and the stone piers have curious chapiters. The hall-door and knocker belonged to the original house. In the waiting-room is Steell's bust of "the Duke;" Castlereagh, by Chantrey; Pitt, by Nollekens; and a reduced copy of Rauch's statue of Blucher; busts of Mr. Perceval, Colonel Gurwood, Mr. Ponsonby, &c. At the foot of the grand staircase is Canova's colossal marble statue of Napoleon, holding a bronze figure of Victory in his right hand: it is Canova's noblest and most antique-looking work; it is 11 feet high, and, except the left arm, was cut from one block of marble.

The pictures in the first drawing-room include the Card-players, by Caravaggio, fine in expression, and marvellous in colour, light, and shade; the great Duke of Marlborough on horseback (from White Knights), probably by Vandermeulen; "Chelsea Pensioners reading the

Gazette of the Battle of Waterloo," a commission to Wilkie from the Duke, for which he paid 1200 guineas in bank-notes; and the companion-picture, "Greenwich Pensioners," by Burnet, and bought from him by the Duke for 500 guineas; Van Amburg in the Den with Lions and Tigers, painted by Sir E. Landseer, R.A., after the instructions of the Duke, who, with the Bible in his hand, pointed out the passage (Gen. i. 26) in which dominion is given to Adam over the earth and animals: "he caused the text to be inscribed on the frame as the authority which conferred on him a privilege of power, and gave to himself 'the great commission' which he carried out on the fields of battle and chase." (*Quarterly Review*, No. clxxxiv.) Next are large copies by Bonnemaison, after the four celebrated pictures by Raphael at Madrid; the Melton Hunt, by Grant, R.A.; Napoleon studying the Map of Europe, a small full-length; Mr. Pitt, by Hoppner; the Highland Whisky-still, by Landseer, R.A.; and portraits of Marshal Soult, Lord Beresford, Lord Lynedoch, and Lord Anglesey, by Sir Thomas Lawrence; Lord Nelson, by Sir William Beechey; Sir George Murray, Sir Thomas Picton; and Sarah the first Lady Lyndhurst, by Wilkie: the canvas was pierced by a stone during a Reform Bill riot, but it has been cleverly repaired. Here also are George IV. and William IV. (whole-lengths), by Sir D. Wilkie. There are at least six portraits of Napoleon; and full-lengths of the Emperor Alexander; and Kings of Prussia, France, and the Netherlands. Still, there is no faithful or worthy representation of the Duke in the collection; nor of statesmen of his generation—not even Peel. There is but one battle-scene—Waterloo, taken from Napoleon's head-quarters, by Sir W. Allan; of this picture the Duke observed, "Good, very good—not too much smoke."

Among the furniture are two magnificent Roman mosaic tables; a splendid pair of Sèvres vases, the gift of Louis XVIII.; a malachite vase, from Alexander Emperor of Russia; a service of Sèvres china, from Louis XVIII., &c.

In the Picture-gallery, in the western wing, the Waterloo Banquet was held annually on June 18, until 1852. Over the fireplace hangs a copy of the "Windsor" Charles I. on horseback. Here is the gem of the collection, "Christ on the Mount of Olives," by Correggio, on panel, the most celebrated specimen of the master in this country: the light proceeds from the Saviour. This picture was captured in Spain, in the carriage of Joseph Buonaparte, and restored by the captor to Ferdinand VII., but was presented to the Duke by that sovereign. Next in excellence are the examples of Velasquez, chiefly portraits, and "the Water-seller;" a Female holding a wreath, by Titian; specimens of Claude, Teniers, and Jan Steen; the Signing of the peace of Westphalia, by Terburg, from the Talleyrand collection. Here is also a repetition of the Madonna della Leda of Raphael, by Giulio Romano; and a marble bust of Pauline Buonaparte, by Canova. In the centre are two majestic candelabra of Russian porphyry, 12 feet high, presented by Alexander Emperor of Russia; and two fine vases of Swedish porphyry, from the King of Sweden. The Gallery and the Waterloo Banquet are well seen in Salter's large picture, engraved by Greatbatch; and the Duke receiving his guests has been painted by J. P. Knight, R.A.

In the China-room, on the ground-floor, are a magnificent Dresden dessert-service, presented by the King of Saxony, painted with the Duke's victories in India, the Peninsula, and at Waterloo; other services of china presented by the Emperor of Austria, the King of Prussia, and Louis XVIII.; the silver plateau 30 ft. long and 3½ ft. wide, and lighted by 106 wax-tapers, the gift of the King of Portugal; three silver-gilt candelabra (a foot-soldier, life-size), presented by the Corporation of London; the superb Waterloo Vase, from the City merchants and bankers; and *the Wellington Shield*, designed by T. Stothard, R.A., and in general treatment resembling Flaxman's Shield of Achilles. It is silver-gilt.

ircular, about 3 ft. 8 in. diameter. In the centre is the Duke of Wellington on orseback, the head of his charger forming the boss of the shield; around him are is illustrious officers; above is Fame crowning the Duke with a wreath of laurel; nd at his feet are prostrate figures of Anarchy, Discord, and Tyranny. The onder of this central group is the management of the horses within the circle (of ak-branches), the evolutions of the charges emanating from the centre,—in itself a ost original conception. The border of the shield is in ten compartments, each earing a bas-relief of the principal events in the Duke's military life, to the peace f 1814, and are as follow: Assaye, Vimiera, the Douro, Torres Vedras, Badajoz, alamanca, Vittoria, the Pyrenees, Toulouse, and the Duke receiving his coronet om the Prince Regent. Stothard's designs are large drawings in sepia: he made is own models for the chaser, etched the designs the same size as the originals, nd received his own demand, 150 guineas. The columns, by Smirke, stand one n each side of the shield, about 4 ft. 3 in. high, surmounted with figures of Fame nd Victory: each column consists of a palm-tree, with a capital of leaves; round the base are emblematic figures, and military trophies and weapons at he angles. The cost of this superb national gift, completed in 1822, was 7000l.

In the China-room, also, are bronze busts, of great spirit and finish, of lenri Quatre, the Prince of Condé, Louis XIV., Marshal Turenne, and he Marquis Wellesley. Beyond is the Secretary's-room, the Great)uke's Private-room, and lastly his Bed-room, which, early in 1853, he public were permitted to inspect, precisely arranged as they were ast used by his Grace in September 1852: the library he con-ulted, the books he kept beside him for reference, the mass of papers, aaps, and documents, even to the latest magazine, were undisturbed. he Duke's room was lined with bookcases and despatch-boxes, and had red morocco reading-chair, a second chair, a desk to stand and write at; circular-topped writing-table; two engravings of the Duke, one when oung, the other (by Count D'Orsay) when old; a small drawing of the. ountess of Jersey, by Cosway, between medallions of the present)uchess of Wellington and Jenny Lind. In the Secretary's-room was a ough unpainted box, which accompanied the Duke through all his wars; a which he stowed away his private documents, and whereon he wrote aany of his despatches, and traced the orders for military manœuvres.

A short passage to the east leads to "the Duke's Bed-room," rhich is narrow, shapeless, and ill-lighted; the bedstead small, provided rith only a mattress and bolster, and scantily curtained with green ilk; the only ornaments of the room being an unfinished sketch of the resent Duchess of Wellington, two cheap prints of military men, and small portrait in oil. Yet here slept the great Duke, whose "eightieth ear was by." In the grounds and shrubbery he took daily walking ex-rcise; where, with the garden-engine, he was wont to enjoy exertion.* astly, "in fine afternoons, the sun casts the shadow of the Duke's eques-rian statue full upon Apsley House, and the sombre image may be seen liding spirit-like over the front." (Quarterly Review, No. clxxxiv.) The house and pictures can only be seen by special permission. A atalogue raisonnée is published by Mitchell, Old Bond-street.

Part of the site of Apsley House was a piece of ground given by George II. an old soldier, Allen, whom the king recognised as having served in the battle Dettingen. Upon this spot Allen built a small tenement, in place of the apple-ll kept by his wife; and on the erection of Apsley House, in 1784, the ground as sold for a considerable sum by Allen's successors to Apsley, Lord Bathurst. he apple-stall is shewn in a print dated 1766.

ARGYLL HOUSE, Argyll-street, centre of the east side, is a plain ansion, with a front court-yard, and was formerly the residence of e Duke of Argyll, by whom it was sold, about 1820, to the Earl of berdeen: here "the Aberdeen Ministry" was formed in 1852.

* Jan. 2, 1820. General Bonaparte was "amusing himself with the pipe of a fire-engine, spouting water on the trees and flowers in his favourite garden." ournal of Capt. Nicholls; Captivity of Napoleon at St. Helena; Sir Hudson we's Letters and Journals, 1853.

I I

BARING, Mr. T., No. 41 Upper Grosvenor-street, has a fine collection of pictures; Dutch and Flemish from the cabinet of the Baron Verstolk, at the Hague; Italian, formerly Sir Thomas Baring's; English pictures, mostly from the exhibitions of the Royal Academy. Among the Spanish pictures are four specimens by Murillo, including the Madonna on the Crescent. Here, also, is St. Jerome in his Study, an authentic picture by J. Van Eyck; with works of N. and G. Poussin, Parmegiano, L. Caracci, C. Dolci, Salvator Rosa, Morales, &c. The collection can be seen only through introduction of Mr. Baring's friends.

BATH HOUSE (Lord Ashburton), No. 82 Piccadilly, built by the first Lord Ashburton upon the site of the old mansion of Sir William Pulteney, Bart. The entrance is from Bolton-street: the hall occupies the centre of the mansion to the roof, of embossed glass; and the principal apartments open into its gallery, which has a richly-gilt balustrade. This hall has a parqueted oak floor, and the walls are painted with Pompeian subjects: here are antique busts and modern statues; including Thorwaldsen's Hebe, and Mercury as the Slayer of Argus. The principal apartments command a view over the Green Park and St. James's Park, with Buckingham Palace; Piccadilly being masked by the terrace-wall: all the floors are oak, and every door is mahogany.

The Ashburton collection is pre-eminent for its Dutch and Flemish pictures, from the cabinet of Talleyrand. Here are: Portraits of Jansen, and the writing-master Lieven van Coppenhol, by Rembrandt; Moses before the Burning Bush, Domenichino; Alehouse, and Playing at Nine Pins, Jan Steen; La Ferme au Colombier, Wouvermans; Rape of the Sabines, and Reconciliation of Romans and Sabines, small, but cost 1000l.; St. Thomas of Villeneuva dividing his Cloak with Beggar-boys, and the Virgin attended by Angels, Murillo; Water-mill, Karl du Jardin; fine specimens of Cuyp, Wouvermans, Teniers, Ostade, and Paul Potter; Hay-harvest, A. Vandervelde; Lobster-catchers, and Le Fagot, N. Berghem; the Infant Christ asleep in the arms of the Virgin, an Angel lifting the quilt, Leonardo da Vinci (belonged to the Prior of the Escurial); St. Peter, St. Margaret, St. Mary Magdalene, and Andrew of Padua, Correggio; Daughter of Herodias with the head of St. John, Titian; Christ on the Mount of Olives, P. Veronese; Stag-hunt, Velasquez; Wolf-hunt, Rubens; Virgin and Child, and Charles I. and Henrietta-Maria (full-lengths), Vandyke; Hermit praying, G. Douw; Boy blowing Bubbles, Netscher; Street in Utrecht (sunshine), De Hooghe; Head of Ariadne, Sir Joshua Reynolds; Head, Holbein; works of Wynants, Ruysdael, Hobbema, &c.

In the dining-room of Bath House were wont to meet Thomas Moore, J. W. Croker, Sydney Smith, and J. G. Lockhart; Dr. Coplestone, Bishop of Llandaff; Rogers, Hallam, Chantrey, Wilkie, and Theodore Hook.

BEAUFORT HOUSE (Duke of Beaufort), No. 22 Arlington-street, Piccadilly, is superbly painted in fresco by Latilla, chiefly in the style of Herculaneum and Pompeii: the banquetting-room is chaste bacchanalian; and the drawing-room is gold and silver, *temp.* Henry IV., with panels of the story of Mary Queen of Scots.

BEDFORD, DUKE OF, No. 6 Belgrave Square: the mansion contains a small but very choice collection of Dutch pictures, &c.

Here are: Herodias with the Head of John the Baptist, by Giorgione; study of Two Dogs, by Titian; Twelfth Night, by Jan Steen; Interior, by Bassen and Polemberg; the Nativity, by A. Werf; Travellers, by I. Ostade; Landscape, by Ruysdael; Moses treading on Pharaoh's Crown, by N. Poussin; Gulliver amongst the Houyounims, by Gilpin; 4 Cuyps, small but excellent; Dutch Courtship, by A. Brouwer; Little Girl, by Rembrandt; the Pont Neuf at Paris, by P. Wouvermans; Pair of Landscapes, by Salvator Rosa; the Death of Hippolytus, study by Rubens; River View, by Van der Capella; Sabine Mountain City, by G. Poussin; the Tribute Money, by Sir G. Hayter; Village Fête, by Teniers (portraits); Going out Hawking, and Landscape and Cattle, by Paul Potter; Landscape, by A. and S. Both; Heads in *grisaille*, by Vandyke; Dead Christ, by Guercino; Sunset, Claude

BRIDGEWATER HOUSE (Earl of Ellesmere), on the east side of the Green Park, adjoins Spencer House, and has its south or entrance front in Cleveland-row, named from that "beautiful fury," Barbara Duchess of Cleveland, to whom Charles II. presented Berkshire House, which formerly stood here. The new mansion, designed by Sir Charles Barry, R.A., is almost a square: south front 142 feet 6 inches; west 122 feet. The elevations and details are mostly from palaces of Rome and Venice; the chimney-shafts form architectural features; the main cornice is richly carved with flowers, and the second-floor string-course, a folded ribbon, is very picturesque. The fenestration is very characteristic: the principal windows have arched pediments, each filled with arabesque foliage, and a shield with the monogram of E E entwined, dos-à-dos; in the panel beneath is the Bridgewater motto "Sic donec;" the first-floor window-dressings have elegant festoons of fruit and foliage; and the balustrade is surmounted with sculpture. The entrance-porch on the south is inscribed, "Restauratum 1849;" and the keystone of the arched doorway bears a lion rampant, the crest of the Earl of Ellesmere. The Picture-gallery, on the north side, is the height of the two floors, 110 feet long, and has a separate entrance for the public: it is lighted by glazed panels in the coved ceiling, at night from burners outside.

This renowned collection was formed principally from the gallery of the Duke of Orleans, by the Duke of Bridgewater; whence it is called the Bridgewater Gallery; and being left by the duke to his nephew, the Marquis of Stafford, it is likewise frequently called the Stafford Gallery. It has been much enlarged by the present possessor, the Marquis's second son, now Earl of Ellesmere. It is the finest private collection in England: from the time of Raphael, the series is unequalled; and in the Caracci school it is without rival. Among the 305 pictures are 4 by Raphael, 5 by Titian, 7 by A. Caracci, 5 by L. Caracci, 5 Domenichino, 4 Claude, 8 N. Poussin, 8 Teniers, 5 Berghem, 6 Cuyp, 6 A. Ostade, 5 Rembrandt, 7 Vandervelde, 2 Paul Veronese, 3 Velasquez, 2 Guido, 3 Rubens, 1 Vandyke, 3 G. Douw, 3 Hobbema, &c. The great Assumption of the Virgin, by Guido, has the chief honour of the gallery; the Vierge au Palmier is one of the purest Raphaels in England; the Seven Sacraments of N. Poussin, and Moses striking the Rock, are very fine; Cuyp's Landing of Prince Maurice looks as if the painter had dipped his pencil in sunlight. Here, also, are Turner's Gale at Sea, nearly equal to the finest Vandervelde in the collection; De la Roche's large picture of Charles I. in the Guard-room; a Wilson equal to Niobe; and the Chandos Portrait of Shakspeare, purchased by Lord Ellesmere at Stowe, in 1848, for 355 guineas: it is presumed to have been painted by Burbage, the actor; was left by Taylor, the Poet's Hamlet, to Sir W. Davenant; was possessed by Betterton the actor, and Mrs. Barry the actress; and must be regarded as the most authentic likeness of Shakspeare.* The collection is valued at nearly 250,000l. : it vies with the Esterhazy and Lichtenstein galleries, at Vienna; the Manfrini gallery, at Venice; the Zambeccari collection, at Bologna; and the Borghese, Colonna, Sciarra, and Doria collections, at Rome.

BURLINGTON HOUSE (Hon. C. C. Cavendish), No. 49 Piccadilly, was originally built for Richard Boyle, second Earl of Burlington, by Sir John Denham, Surveyor-general to Charles I. A view by Kip shews the house in 1700, devoid of ornament, with its quaint gardens, and beyond them the country; and the Piccadilly front is planted with large trees. The mansion was fronted by the celebrated amateur-architect, Lord Burlington, with Portland stone, and a classic Doric colonnade, borrowed from a palace by Palladio at Vicenza; the wall was rebuilt, and an arched gateway added: in the Vitruvius Britannicus the colonnade and gateway are attributed to Colin Campbell, and this in Lord Burlington's lifetime. Horace Walpole was in Italy when these embellishments were completed; and going to a ball at Burlington House at night, did not perceive their beauty; next morning, at sun-

* A presumed contemporary portrait of Shakspeare is at Ely House, Dover-street: it bears no name, but cleaning has revealed, "Æt. 39, 1603," which agrees with the age of Shakspeare in that year.

rise, looking out of the window, Walpole was surprised with the vision of the colonnade: "it seemed one of those edifices in fairy tales that are raised by genii in a night-time."

> "Burlington's fair palace still remains;
> Beauty within, without proportion reigns:
> Beneath his eye declining art revives,
> The wall with animated pictures lives!"

Thus far Gay (*Trivia*), who often met there Pope and Arbuthnot. Marco Ricco painted the hall staircase and some ceilings; "the interior," says Pennant, "built on the models of Palladio, and adapted more to the climate of Lombardy, and to the banks of the Adige or the Brenta, than to the Thames, is gloomy and destitute of gaiety and cheerfulness." Kent, the architect and landscape-gardener, was greatly patronised by Lord Burlington, and had apartments in this mansion; he died here in 1748. The Earl converted "Ten-Acres Field," at the back of his gardens, into a little town, bounded by Bond-street and Swallow-street; and in 1719 he sold a piece of ground in Boyle-street for a school-house, which he designed for the trustees. Lord Burlington died in 1753, when the mansion fell to the Devonshire family, conditionally that it should not be demolished. On the expiry of the lease in 1809, it was proposed to take down the mansion, and erect a street upon the site; but a renewal was secured by Lord George Cavendish (created Earl of Burlington 1831), who restored the house, raised the Venetian windows in the south front, and thus saved "one of the finest pieces of architecture in Europe." (*Sir W. Chambers.*) The Duke of Portland, Prime Minister to George III., died at Burlington House in 1809, a few days after he had resigned the seals of office. In the western wing were deposited the Elgin Marbles, before they were removed to the British Museum. In 1814 a grand ball was given here to the Allied Sovereigns by White's Club. (See page 199.) In 1819 was built upon a slip of the grounds the Burlington Arcade.

The archway has a lofty pediment, flanked by the supporters of the Burlington arms, and supported by four rusticated columns, coupled. It is commemorated by Hogarth in a *caricatura* print (1731) inscribed, "The Man of Taste, containing a View of Burlington Gate:" on the summit is Kent (served by Lord Burlington as a labourer) flourishing his palette and pencils over Michael Angelo and Raphael; lower down is Pope whitewashing the front, and bespattering the Duke of Chandos in the street. Ralph refers to the front as "the most expensive wall in England: the height wonderfully proportioned to the length, and the decorations both simple and magnificent; the grand entrance is elegant and beautiful, and by covering the house entirely from the eye, gives pleasure and surprise, at the opening of the whole front with the area before it at once." Any passenger who has seen the mansion through the great gateway from the footpath may appreciate the above effect.

CAMBRIDGE HOUSE, No. 94 Piccadilly, was previously Cholmondeley House. Here died, July 8, 1850, Adolphus, Duke of Cambridge, youngest son of George III., born 1774.

CHESTERFIELD HOUSE (the Earl of Chesterfield), South Audley-street, was built by Ware, 1749, for Philip, fourth Earl, who describes the boudoir as "the gayest and most cheerful room in England," and the library "the finest room in London;" and they remain unsurpassed. The columns of the screen facing the court-yard, and the superb marble staircase (each step a single block twenty feet long), are from Canons (Duke of Chandos's); and the gilt hall-lantern, for eighteen lights, from Houghton (Sir Robert Walpole's). In the library, above the bookcases, are portraits of eminent authors contemporary with the fourth Earl of Chesterfield, who wrote here his celebrated *Letters to is Son.* Under the cornice of the room, extending all round in capi-als twelve inches high, are these lines from Horace:

NUNC'VETERUM'LIBRIS'NUNC'SOMNO'ET'INERTIBUS'HORIS.
DUCERE'SOLICITÆ'JUCUNDA'OBLIVIA'VITÆ.

Throughout the room are busts of ancient orators, besides vases and bronzes and modern statuettes. The windows look upon the finest private garden in London, and in the lofty trees are a few rooks.

CLARENCE HOUSE (Duchess of Kent), on the east side of Stable-ard, St. James's Palace, was built for the Duke of Clarence, after-wards King William IV.: it has a handsome portico in two stories, the lower Doric, and the upper Corinthian.

DE GREY, EARL, No. 4 St. James's-square, possesses a choice gallery of pictures, including portraits, mostly whole-lengths, by Vandyke; "Ti-ian's Daughter" holding a casket; a pair of landscapes by Claude; a ine picture by Salvator Rosa; and a few examples of the Dutch school.

DEVONSHIRE HOUSE (Duke of Devonshire), Piccadilly, occupies the ite of Berkeley House, formerly "Hay Hill Farm:" it was built by William Kent for the third Duke of Devonshire, at the cost of 20,000*l.*, ncluding 1000*l.* for the design. It was also called Stratton House.

Berkeley House was built about 1665 for Lord John Berkeley, and is stated by Evelyn to have cost "neere 30,000*l.*:" it was remarkable for its great number of chimneys, noble state-rooms, cedar staircase, the walls painted by Laguerre, and gardens, "incomparable by reason of the inequalities of the ground, and a pretty piscina," and holly-hedges on the terrace, advised by Evelyn. The Princess Anne, afterwards Queen Anne, resided here, from her leaving Whitehall, until 1697: in he *Postman,* No. 94 (1695), is advertised a silver cistern, valued at 750*l.*, stolen out of Berkeley House. The first Duke of Devonshire purchased the mansion in 1697; and March 31, he entertained King William III. at dinner there. The duke died here in 1701: it was destroyed, October 16, 1733, by fire, through the boiling over of a glue-pot while the workmen were at breakfast; the house was entirely consumed, but the library, pictures, medals, and other curiosities were saved. "Lord Pembroke (Shakspeare's Lord Pembroke), Donne, Waller, Denham, and Dryden read their verses here. Devonshire House, towards the close of the last century, was famous as the head-quarters of Whig politics, and for the fascina-ions of its beautiful Duchess, whose verses on William Tell produced a burst of admiration from Coleridge:

'Oh, lady, nurs'd in pomp and pleasure,
Where learnt you that heroic measure?'

She learnt it from her race (the Spencers); from their family tutor, Sir William Jones; and from her own cordial nature."—*Leigh Hunt.*

Devonshire House has an unpretending exterior, with an ill-matched portico: the old entrance, by a double flight of steps, was removed in 1840; and in the rear of the house has been erected a state staircase, with white scagliola walls, marble stairs, gilt-brass balustrades, and glass hand-rail. The whole interior has been refitted by the present Duke; except a small room, blue and silver, designed by the celebrated Duchess. The Grand Saloon, originally the vestibule, is superbly deco-rated and painted in the rich style of Le Brun, and hung with Lyons brocade-silk; portraits over the doors, &c. The Ball-room, white and gold, is hung with French silk brocatelle, blue and gold, and a few magnificent pictures. In this superb room took place the first amateur performance of Sir Edward Bulwer Lytton's comedy of *Not so Bad as we Seem,* for the benefit of the Guild of Literature and Art, before Her Majesty and Prince Albert, May 16, 1851. The grounds of Devon-shire House are a fine specimen of town landscape-gardening. (See GARDENS, page 323.) Upon the gate-piers in Piccadilly are garlanded vases, gracefully sculptured. Among the pictures are Dobson's por-rait of Sir Thomas Browne; Lord Burlington, the architect, by

Kneller; and Lord Richard Cavendish, by Reynolds. In a glass-case are "the Devonshire Gems," 564 cut stones and medals. Here is the renowned *Libro di Verita*, in which Claude Lorraine made drawings of all the pictures he ever executed: they number about 200, and on the back of each is Claude's monogram, the place for which the picture was painted, usually the person ordering it, and the year, the "Claudio fecit" never wanting. By reference to this volume, the authenticity of reputed Claudes may be tested; hence it is called "the Book of Truth:" it is well known by Earlom's engravings. Upon the back of the first drawing is inscribed, in Claude's own handwriting:

" Audi 10 dagosto 1677. Ce livre Aupartien a moy que je faict durant ma vie. Claudio Gillee, dit le Loraine. A Roma ce 23 Aos. 1680."

Among the bibliographical rarities are "the Kemble Plays," and other old English plays, the richest collection in the world, annotated by the Duke of Devonshire; also, a large collection of playbills; early editions of Shakspeare; designs, by Inigo Jones, for buildings, sketches from pictures, costumes for characters in masques, scenery, &c.

DORCHESTER HOUSE (Mr. R. S. Holford), Park-lane, built by Lewis Vulliamy, 1851-3: a parallelogram, nearly as large as Bridgewater House, faced with Portland-stone; the principal cornice and frieze richly carved by C. H. Smith; the chief projecting stones are each 8 feet 4 inches square; the external walls are 3 feet 10 inches thick. The grand staircase is of marble. The mansion occupies the site of old Dorchester House, in which died the Marquis of Hertford, 1842.

While this mansion was building, Mr. Holford's fine collection of pictures was temporarily placed in the house No. 65 (formerly Sir Thomas Lawrence's) in Russell-square. The collection includes portraits by Velasquez, Vandyke, Dosso Dossi, Bellini, S. del Piombo, Titian, and Tintoretto; two of the famous Caracci series (by Agostino and Ludovico), from the Giustiniani Palace; among the Dutch pictures is a long view of Dort,.and a large Hobbema; here are exquisite small pictures by Murillo, Greuze, and others; and fine works by Teniers, Wouvermans, Paul Potter, C. Du Jardin, W. Vandervelde; Giorgione, Bonifazio, Fra Bartolomeo;.Holy Family and Saints, by Andrea del Sarto; Holy Family and St. John, by Gaudenzio di Ferrara; Evening, by Claude; Rubens' masterly sketches of his Entry of Henry IV. (Luxembourg); and the Assumption of the Virgin (Antwerp). The collection may be seen by recommendation of known artists or amateurs.

DOVER HOUSE (Lady Dover), Whitehall, opposite the Banquetting House, has a very tasteful and classical façade, and was built by Payne for Sir Matthew Featherstonhaugh; and has been the residence of Viscount Melbourne, and the Duke of York, for whom Holland added the domed hall and picturesque Ionic portico.

DUDLEY HOUSE (Lord Ward), Park-lane, contains a fine collection of 130 pictures, tracing the Italian and Flemish schools to their source.

Here are the Crucifixion, one of Raphael's earliest works, and the Last Judgment, by Fiesole, both from Cardinal Fesch's Gallery; small figures of Saints, by Raphael, in tempera; the Virgin and Child, and the Virgin, Infant Christ, and Joseph, by Francia; Sta. Caterina, by Lo Spagna: two figures of Saints, in penand-ink and tempera, by Perugino; Virgin and Child, enthroned, by A. Dasisi; altar-piece of Saints and Infant Christ, by Pierino del Vaga; altar-piece, Adoration of the Shepherds, by B. Peruzzi; the Death of Abel, by Guido; Head of the Magdalen, by Carlo Dolce; four Illuminations by Andrea Mantegna; Christ bearing his Cross, by L. Caracci; a seated Cardinal, by Guercino; curious specimens of the Venetian School, by Carlo Crivelli; two Colossal Heads, by Correggio, and a reputed *replica* of his Magdalen; the three Marys, and Dead Christ, by Albert Durer; Celebration of the Mass, by Van Eyck; St. Peter, by Spagnoletto; the Burgomaster, by Rembrandt (half-length), from the Stowe Collection; the Mocking of Christ, by Teniers; Landscape, by Gaspar Poussin; Venetian View, very fine, by Canaletti; Shipwreck, by Vernet, &c. Here are also several pieces of antique Sculpture; and a seated Venus, by Canova; and a duplicate of the Greek Slave, by Hiram Powers.

FORD, Mr. Richard (author of the excellent *Handbook of Spain*), 23 Park-street, Grosvenor-square, has some fine Spanish pictures; and several classical examples of Richard Wilson.

GARVAGH, LORD, No. 26 Portman-square : here is Raphael's masterpiece, the Virgin Mary holding the infant Christ, who is presenting pink to the youthful St. John.

GLOUCESTER HOUSE (Duchess of Gloucester), Piccadilly, corner of Park-lane, was previously the Earl of Elgin's, and here were deposited the Elgin Marbles. Lord Byron calls Elgin House "a stone-shop," and

> "General mart
> For all the mutilated blocks of art."—*E. Bards and S. Reviewers.*

The Marbles were next removed to Burlington House, and to the British Museum in 1816. Gloucester House was purchased by the late Duke of Gloucester, on his marriage with the Princess Mary. In the late drawing-room is a needlework carpet, presented to the Duchess of Gloucester upon her birth-day, by 84 ladies of the aristocracy, each having worked a compartment.

GROSVENOR HOUSE (Marquis of Westminster), Upper Grosvenor-street, has a magnificent open stone colonnade or screen, Romanesque : it is 110 feet long, and has two carriage-ways, with pediments sculptured with the Grosvenor arms, and panels of the four Seasons above the foot-entrances; between the columns are massive candelabra, which, with the metal gates, are composed of demi-figures, rich foliage, fruit and flowers, and armorial designs. The whole screen is picturesque and elegant, and was completed in 1842 by T. Cundy, the architect of the western wing of the mansion (the Picture-gallery) in Park-lane : the latter consists of a Corinthian colonnade, with six statues and an attic, after the manner of Trajan's Forum at Rome ; on the acroteria are vases and a balustrade, and between the columns are rich festoons of fruit and flowers ; the whole is grand and architectural.

Here is the celebrated "Grosvenor Gallery," commenced by Richard, first Earl Grosvenor, by the purchase of Mr. Agar's pictures for 30,000 guineas ; increased to 200 paintings, including :

Raphael, 5; Murillo, 3; Velasquez, 2; Titian, 3; Paul Veronese, 3; Guido, 5; Salvator Rosa, 4; Claude, 10; N. and G. Poussin, 7; Rembrandt, 7; Rubens, 11; Vandyke, 2; Hobbema, 2; Cuyp, 4; Snyders, 2; Teniers, 3; West, 5; Hogarth, 3; Gainsborough, 3; with specimens of Lebrun, Paul Potter, Gerard Douw, Van Huysum, Vandervelde, Wouvermans, Sir Joshua Reynolds, and Wilson; Perugino, Bellini, Giulio Romano, and Sasso Ferrato; Correggio, Parmegiano, L. da Vinci, &c. Among the most celebrated are the four colossal pictures by Rubens, painted in Spain in 1629,—the Israelites gathering Manna, Abraham and Melchisedek, the Four Evangelists, and the Fathers of the Church,—from the convent of Leches, near Madrid, purchased for 10,000*l.*; Cattle and Landscape, by Paul Potter, a miracle of art; Gentleman holding a Hawk, and Lady with a Fan, by Rembrandt, two of the finest portraits ever painted; Mrs. Siddons as the Tragic Muse, Sir Joshua Reynolds's masterpiece, cost 1760*l.* In the ante-room is a very large painting, by Canaletti, of a grand Bull-fight in St. Mark's Place, Venice, in 1740, with many thousand figures.

Among the rarities is a triptych panel-picture by Memmelinck, 15th century : the central compartment contains our Saviour, the Virgin Mary, and St. John the Evangelist; the *volets*, St. John the Baptist, and Mary, the sister of Martha and Lazarus, with the pot of ointment: of most elaborate execution; bought by the Marquis of Westminster in 1845.

"No private gallery in this country exceeds the Grosvenor Gallery in point of variety. The number of pictures in the Bridgewater collection is more than double, the series more complete, and some of them exceed any here in value and variety; but the fascination of the Claudes, the imposing splendour of the Rubenses, and the interest attached to a number of the English pictures ('Mrs. Siddons,' 'the Blue Boy,' and 'General Wolfe,' for instance), long contributed to render the Grosvenor Gallery quite as popular as a resort for the mere amateur, and not less attractive and improving to the student and enthusiast."—Mrs. Jameson's *Private Galleries of Art.*

Among the sculpture is Susanna, life-size, by Pozzi; Cupid and Psyche, by Sir R. Westmacott, R.A.; a Faun (antique); and busts of Mercury, Apollo, Homer, Paris and Helen, Charles I. and Cromwell, &c. The vases are fine; and the superb plate includes antique salvers, and a profusion of race-cups, won by the Marquis of Westminster's celebrated stud. The pictures are to be seen only, on a specific day, by admissions obtainable by personal acquaintances of, or introduction to, Lord Westminster.

HARCOURT HOUSE (Duke of Portland), on the west side of Cavendish-square, originally built for Mr. Bingley, and altered from Archer's design, is described by Ralph, in 1734, as "one of the most singular pieces of architecture about town; rather like a convent than the residence of a man of quality," resembling a copy of some of Poussin's landscape ornaments: and so it remains to this day. The third Duke of Portland died here in 1809.

HERTFORD HOUSE (Marquis of Hertford), No. 105 Piccadilly, was formerly the Pulteney Hotel, where Alexander, Emperor of Russia, and his sister the Duchess of Oldenburg, sojourned in 1814. The original façade, rich Italian, was by Novosielski, with a Grecian-Doric porch added by Sir Robert Smirke. The mansion was designed for the Earl of Barrymore, but was unfinished at his death; was first let as an hotel, and then to the late Marquis of Hertford. It was taken down and re-built mostly with the same Portland stone, in 1851, when the house was heightened from 57 to 71 feet. The drawing-rooms have a vista of 114 feet, and the picture-gallery 50 feet.

The collection contains *chef-d'œuvres* from the gallery of the King of Holland: Water-mill, Hobbema; Holy Family, Rubens (cost 2478*l.*); Alchemist, Teniers; la Vierge de Pade, A. del Sarto; Vandyke, by himself; Oxen in a Meadow, Paul Potter; several pictures by Cuyp; the Annunciation, by Murillo; Landscape with Herdsman, Claude; his own Portrait, by Rembrandt; Christ giving the Keys to St. Peter, Rubens: and, from the Stowe collection, the Sibyl, by Domenichino; and the Unmerciful Servant, by Rembrandt. The Marquis also possesses a fine collection of china, and costly objects of art and *vertu.*

HOLDERNESSE HOUSE (Marquis of Londonderry), No. 16 Park-lane, contains a magnificent Sculpture-gallery, wherein are several works by Canova and other great sculptors; Theseus and the Minotaur, from the Fries Gallery at Florence; the Kneeling Cupid, &c.; full-length portraits of British and Foreign Monarchs of the present century, by Sir Thomas Lawrence; life-size model of Thomas's Statue of Lord Castlereagh, the celebrated minister, placed in Westminster Abbey; and presented to the same, a colossal Sèvres Vase, by Louis XVIII., and a valuable diamond-hilted sword; besides cuirasses, helmets, and other trophies, captured by the soldier-Marquis in the Peninsular War.

HOPE HOUSE (Mr. H. T. Hope), south-east corner of Down-street, Piccadilly, was built in 1849, under the joint superintendence of M. Dusillion, a French artist, and Professor Donaldson. The fronts are Caen stone, and have panels of decorative marbles in the piers between the windows: the arrangement of which is novel, especially in the attic-story. The total height from the street-level to the balustrade (surmounted with superbly-carved vases) is 62 feet. The entrance-porch in Down-street is very rich; in the principal window-pediments are sculptured the armorial bearings of Mr. Hope, repeated with the initial H. in the very handsome iron railing, cast by André in Paris. The details throughout shew very careful and elegant drawing; and the carving, wholly by French artists, is beautifully executed. The grand staircase

nd hall occupy the centre of the building; the upper hall is paved
vith coloured marbles in patterns. The walls are plaster-of-Paris
olished, scagliola panels, and marble plinths; the floors, fire-proof, are
f cast-iron girders and tile arches. The ceilings are paneled and en-
iched; the principal doors are of oak, carved with the initial H. in
hields; some of the chimney-pieces are of *pierre-de-tonnerre*, paneled
vith French marbles; others are of bronzed metal, with caryatid figures.
'he kitchen department has a "lift" to each floor, speaking-tubes, &c.;
he mansion is lighted with gas, except in the drawing-rooms; and
here is an apparatus for warming the vestibule, staircase, and passages.
'he stables (for 12 horses) and coach-houses are in the rear of the
iansion. W. Cubitt and Co. builders; ornamental work (wainscot
oors, ceilings, stone carvings, mahogany casements) by French artists;
ost, exclusive of final decorations, 30,000*l*. There are few pictures here,
Ir. Hope's collections having been removed to Deepdene, in Surrey.
mong the antiques are Sir W. Hamilton's second collection, made at
[aples. The mansion may be seen on Mondays, from April to July, by
ards obtainable by introduction to the owner.

The collection was formed at the celebrated mansion in Duchess-street, Port-
nd-place, in the decoration of which the late Mr. Hope, the author of *Anas-*
sius, exemplified the classic principles illustrated in his large work on "House-
old Furniture and Internal Decorations," 1805. Thus, the suite of apartments
cluded the *Egyptian or Black Room,* with ornaments from scrolls of papyrus and
ummy-cases; the furniture and ornaments were pale, yellow and bluish-green,
lieved by masses of black and gold. *The Blue or Indian Room,* in costly Oriental
yle. *The Star Room:* emblems of Night below; and above, Aurora visiting Ce-
halus on Mount Ida, by Flaxman; furniture, wreathed figures of the Hours.
he Closet or Boudoir, hung with tent-like drapery; the mantel-piece an Egyp-
an portico; Egyptian, Hindoo, and Chinese idols and curiosities. *Picture Gal-*
ry: Ionic columns, entablature, and pediment from the Temple of Erectheus at
thens; car of Apollo, classic tables, pedestals, &c. In four separate apartments
ere arranged 200 Greek vases, including two copies of the Barberini or Port-
nd Vase; the furniture partly from Pompeian models. *The New Gallery,* for
)0 pictures of the Flemish school, antique bronzes and vases; furniture of ele-
nt Grecian design. Mr. Hope died at Duchess-street in 1831: he will ever be
membered for his taste and munificence as the early patron of Chantrey, Flax-
an, Canova, and Thorwaldsen.

LANSDOWNE HOUSE (Marquis of Lansdowne), which, with its gar-
en, occupies the south side of Berkeley-square, was commenced by
.obert Adam for the Marquis of Bute, but was sold unfinished to Lord
helburne, created Marquis of Lansdowne in 1784. The purchase-money
·as 22,000*l.,* but the mansion cost Lord Bute 25,000*l.*

The Marquis, in 1804, acknowledged the possession of the secret of the author-
ip of Junius's Letters, which he promised to publish; but his lordship died in
e following week. The "Letters" are believed by some to have been the joint
roduction of Lord Shelburne, Colonel Barré, and Dunning, Lord Ashburton;
id their three portraits, painted in one picture by Sir Joshua Reynolds, in 1784-5,
ave been regarded as evidence of the joint authorship. Possibly, therefore,
inius's Letters were written in Lansdowne, then Shelburne, House. It is better
tablished that oxygen was discovered here, Aug. 1, 1774, by Dr. Priestley, then
rarian to Lord Shelburne.

The reception-room contains a fine collection of sculpture, including
)out fifty statues, as many busts, besides bassi relievi: it was com-
enced by Gavin Hamilton, who first excavated the site of Adrian's
illa. At the foot of the staircase is a noble statue of Diana launching
1 arrow; in the great dining-room are nine antique statues in niches,
cluding Germanicus, Claudius, Trajan, and Cicero; also the Sleeping
ymph, the last work of Canova; in the front drawing-room his
enus quitting the Bath; and a statue by Rauch, of Berlin, of a Child
)lding an alms-dish. In the gallery, 100 feet in length, at the east

end are life-size statues of Hercules, Marcus Aurelius, Mercury, Diomede, Theseus, Juno, an Amazon, Juno standing, Hercules when a youth, Jason, &c.; and here are two Egyptian black marble statues, found at Tivoli. On the sides of the gallery are the busts, reliefs, &c.

The collection of pictures, formed by Lord Lansdowne since 1809, is famed for its portraits, including Rembrandt holding a palette, by himself; a Lady (1642), Rembrandt; Velasquez, by himself; Pope Innocent X., Velasquez; A. del Sarto, by himself; a Gentleman, by Titian; Count Frederigo Bozzola, by Seb. del Piombo; Queen Henrietta-Maria, Vandyke; Sausovino, the Venetian architect, by Giorgione; a Cardinal and Andrea Doria, Tintoretto; a Burgomaster and Lady in a Ruff, Rembrandt; Charles V. in his cradle, by Velasquez; Kitty Fisher and Laurence Sterne, by Sir Joshua Reynolds; Alexander Pope, Jervas; Dr. Franklin, Gainsborough; Sir Humphry Davy, by Linnell; Francis Horner, Raeburn; the Marquis of Lansdowne, by Sir Thomas Lawrence; Ladies Ilchester, Mary Cole, and Elizabeth Fielding, by Reynolds; Peg Woffington, by Hogarth: Flaxman the sculptor, by John Jackson, R.A.; Sir Robert Walpole and his first Wife, Catherine Shorter, by Eckhart, (elaborate black and gold frame by Gibbons,) from the blue bed-chamber of Strawberry Hill. Also, here are twelve pictures by Sir Joshua Reynolds, including the Strawberry Girl and the Sleeping Girl.

MANCHESTER HOUSE, Manchester-square, was commenced for the Duke of Manchester in 1776, but was not completed until 1788. At the Duke's death, in 17—, the house became the residence of the Spanish Ambassador, who built the Roman Catholic chapel in Spanish-place. Manchester House was next the town mansion of the Marquis of Hertford, a *bon-vivant* companion of the Prince Regent. The French Embassy was next located here; with Talleyrand, Guizot, and Sebastiani, successive representatives.

MARLBOROUGH HOUSE, Pall Mall, was built by Wren, in 1709-10, for the great Duke of Marlborough, upon part of the site of the pheasantry of St. James's Palace, and of the garden of Mr. Secretary Boyle, the latter taken out of St. James's Park. The ground was leased by Queen Anne to Sarah Duchess of Marlborough, who states the Duke to have paid for the building between 40,000*l.* and 50,000*l.*, "though many people have been made to believe otherwise." The house is a fine specimen of red brickwork, Wren being employed as architect, to mortify Vanbrugh. The great Duke died here in 1722. The Duchess loved to talk of "neighbour George," the King, at St. James's Palace; and here, Jan. 1, 1741, she received the Lord Mayor and Sheriffs, to thank her for a present of venison: "she received us," says Sheriff Hoare, "in her usual manner, sitting up in her bed; . . . and after an hour's conversation upon indifferent matters, we retired." The Duchess intended to have improved the entrance to the court-yard: an archway was opened in the wall, but was blocked up; for her Grace was frustrated by Sir Robert Walpole, who, to annoy her, bought the requisite houses in Pall Mall. The court-yard is dull, but the front towards St. James's Park has a cheerful aspect, and a garden. The vestibule is stately, and is painted with the battles of Hochstet and Blenheim, and the taking of Marshal Tallard prisoner; upon the ceiling are allegories of the Arts and Sciences. In 1817, Marlborough House was purchased by the Crown for the Princess Charlotte and Prince Leopold; it was the Prince's town-house for several years; and after the death of William IV. the residence of the Dowager-Queen Adelaide. In 1850, the mansion was settled upon the Prince of Wales, on his attaining his eighteenth year. In the meantime, the Vernon collection of pictures, and others of the English school, have been removed to the lower apartments of Marlborough House; and the upper rooms have been granted to the Department of Practical Art, for a library, museum of manufactures, the ornamental casts of the School of Design, a lecture-room, &c. Here was designed, in 1852, the Duke of Wellingn's Funeral Car, which was subsequently exhibited to the public in a mporary building in the courtyard, 1853.

The Vernon Collection is open gratis on the first four days of each week, ex-¦t a month in autumn. Here are 162 pictures, 6 busts, and 1 group of figures ¦ marble, presented by Mr. Vernon; and other English pictures from the ¦tional Gallery. Among the latter are 9 works by Reynolds; 6 by Hogarth ¦arriage à la Mode); 2 by R. Wilson; 2 by Wilkie; and others by Lawrence, ¦nsborough, Constable, &c. The Vernon Collection comprises 11 works of ¦ty, 9 of Calcott; 5 by Wilkie; 4 by R. Wilson; 7 by Landseer; 4 by Gains-¦rough. Here are, Youth at the Prow, and Pleasure at the Helm, and the ¦thers, by W. Etty, R.A.; and William III. Landing at Torbay, a Landscape, ¦ 2 Views in Venice, by J. M. W. Turner, R.A. An authenticated Catalogue, ¦ce 2d., is sold in the vestibule.

George IV. (while Regent) proposed to connect Carlton House with Marl-¦rough House and St. James's Palace by a gallery of the Portraits of the Sove-¦gns and other historic personages of England; but, unfortunately, Mr. Nash's ¦culation of buying Carlton House and Gardens, and overlaying St. James's ¦rk with terraces, prevailed, and the design of a truly National Gallery was ¦ndoned: although the Crown of England possesses materials for an Historical ¦lection which would be infinitely superior to that of Versailles.

MONTAGUE HOUSE, Bloomsbury. (See MUSEUM, BRITISH.)

MONTAGUE HOUSE (Duke of Buccleuch), Whitehall, was built for ¦lph, third Lord Montague, created in 1689 Duke of Montague and ¦scount Monthermer. It has a spacious marble floored and pillared ¦ll; and a large collection of full-length portraits of the Montagues ¦d their connexions, by Vandyke, Lely, and Reynolds; sketches en ¦saille by Vandyke; a fine assemblage of English miniatures; and ¦ew of Whitehall, by Canaletti. The furniture is in the old French ¦le, richly carved and gilt; and cabinets in buhl or ebony; tables of ¦rble, mosaic, or inlaid wood; hangings of dark velvet, damask, or ¦tin. In the dining-room and library are portraits of the British ¦hool; a few Gainsboroughs and Wilsons in the boudoir; and both ¦awing-rooms are hung with very fine old tapestry, representing hunt-¦g scenes in the forest of Fontainebleau. The mansion is screened ¦m the street by trees and a garden; and between it and the Thames ¦ a terraced garden, with venerable trees, fountains, and statues, and ¦ open pavilion commanding a fine view of the Thames.

Montague House is one of the mansions built after the Court had abandoned ¦itehall, when various noble families obtained leases of parts of the Privy ¦rdens. The Dukes of Richmond for a hundred years occupied here a stately ¦nsion surrounded with pleasure-grounds, on part of which is built Richmond-¦rrace. Pembroke House was erected under like circumstances; between which ¦d the site of Richmond House stands the mansion inherited from the Montague ¦ily by the Duke of Buccleuch.

MONTAGUE HOUSE, the elegant detached mansion at the north-west ¦gle of Portman-square, was built for the celebrated Mrs. Elizabeth ¦ntague, who resided here many years; and who annually, on the 1st ¦May, on the front lawn, regaled the chimney-sweepers of the metro-¦lis, "so that they might enjoy one happy day in the year."*

MUNRO, Mr. H. A. J., No. 6 Hamilton-place, Piccadilly, possesses a fine ¦lection of pictures of the ancient foreign schools, including Raphael's ¦a Vierge aux Candelabres," and "La Vierge à la Legende," formerly ¦he gallery of Charles I.; a grand landscape by Claude; St. Anthony ¦ding the infant Saviour, by Murillo; the Toilet of Venus, by A. ¦racci; Les Deux Petites Marquises, by A. Watteau. Among the ¦glish pictures are about a dozen of the finest landscapes and com-¦itions of J. M. W. Turner, R.A.; and examples of Richard Wilson, ¦nington, Etty, &c.

¦ There was a fourth Montague House, viz. the mansion built by Viscount ¦ntague, or his son, upon part of the site of the priory of St. Mary Overey, in ¦thwark close, 1545; the precinct being named Montague close.

NORFOLK HOUSE (Duke of Norfolk), No. 21 St. James's-square, occupies the site of the residence of Henry Jermyn, Earl of St. Albans (temp. Charles II.); the first tenant of the Norfolk family being the seventh Duke, who died here 1701. The old mansion extended to the site of Waterloo-place eastward: here King George III. was born, May 24, 1738 (O. S.); and Edward Augustus Duke of York, March 24, 1739: the room still remains, with a ceiling painted by Sir James Thornhill; and the state-bed is preserved at Worksop. The present Norfolk House was commenced by Brettingham, in 1742, for Thomas Duke of Norfolk, and completed for his brother Edward in 1762: the portico was added in 1842. The rooms are gorgeously carved and gilt in the Queen Anne style, and contain a collection of pictures of the Italian, Spanish, and Flemish schools; and conspicuous among the plate displayed at state-banquets, are the coronation-cups received in various reigns by the Dukes of Norfolk as hereditary Earls Marshal: here Queen Victoria and Prince Albert were sumptuously entertained June 19, 1849.

In the old mansion are deposited the records of the Howard, Fitzalan, and Mowbray families. Among the pictures is a portrait of the first Duke of Norfolk by Holbein; shield presented to the chivalrous soldier-poet, Henry Howard, Earl of Surrey, at a tournament in 1537; the family of Thomas Earl of Arundel, who collected the " Marbles;" portrait of his wife, by Rubens.

Here expired, Dec. 16, 1815, Charles, eleventh Duke of Norfolk: a few hours before he died, by his desire, a servant was sent to a bookseller's in Pall Mall to procure Drelincourt's Book of Consolations against the Fear of Death, which was read to the penitent Duke in his last moments.

NORMANTON, LORD, No. 3 Seamore-place, May Fair: here are some important pictures by Holbein; Holy Family, by Parmegiano; and works of the English school.

NORTHUMBERLAND HOUSE (Duke of Northumberland), Strand, occupies the site of the hospital of St. Mary Rounceval, founded temp. Henry III.; its large conventual chapel reaching to the Thames in the Sutherland View of London, 1543. The present mansion was built about 1605, for Henry Howard, Earl of Northampton, son of the poet Lord Surrey. The architects were Bernard Jansen and Gerard Christmas; and it was then called Northampton House. The Earl of Northampton died here in 1614, having bequeathed the mansion to his nephew Thomas Howard, Earl of Suffolk, when the name was changed to Suffolk House: a drawing by Hollar shews it to have been quadrangular in plan, with a lofty dome-crowned tower at each angle, in the Dutch style. It originally had three sides, the fourth remaining open to the gardens and the Thames; when the quadrangle was completed by the addition of the state-rooms, attributed, but erroneously, to Inigo Jones. Since the marriage of Elizabeth, daughter of Theophilus, second Earl of Suffolk, with Algernon Percy, tenth Earl of Northumberland, in 1642, the mansion has been called Northumberland House. In 1660 General Monk was invited to this house by Earl Algernon; and here, with other leading men of the nation, he proposed and planned the restoration of Charles II. On the death of Joscelyne Percy, the son of Algernon, in 1670, without male issue, his only daughter, Elizabeth, became heiress of the Percy estates. She married, in 1682, Charles Seymour, "the proud Duke of Somerset," who resided at Northumberland House in great state. On the death of the Duke in 1748, he was succeeded by his eldest son, Algernon Earl of Hertford, and seventh Duke of Somerset, created Earl of Northumberland in 1749, with remainder, failing issue male, to his son-in-law, Sir Hugh Smithson, who assumed the name and arms of Percy, and was created Duke of Northumberland in 1766, and was the grandfather of the present Duke, and his immediate predecessor. Of the old mansion, little more than the

entral stone gateway, facing the Strand, remains; this being part of
ie original work of Gerard Christmas, and, with its characteristic
ulpture, a curious example of the Jacobean style. It is surmounted
y a lion passant, the crest of the Percys, cast in lead: it is inscribed
ith the family motto, " Espérance en Dieu." Along the façade was a
order of capital letters, in place of the present ugly parapet : one of
iese letters (S) fell down at the funeral of Anne of Denmark, 1619, and
illed a spectator. The date 1749 denotes a year of repairs; and the initials
.S.P.N., Algernon Somerset, Princeps Northumbriæ. In 1766, great
art of the northern front was rebuilt; as also after the fire in 1780,
rhich consumed most of the upper rooms. The court-yard is of plain
talian character; and the living apartments are the southern or garden
ide of the quadrangle. The glory of the interior is the double state-stair-
ase, with marble steps; rich *ormolu* balustrade, chandelier, and lamps;
nd carved marble podium. The principal drawing-room has medallions
y Angelica Kauffman, and a Raphaelesque ceiling. Beyond is a small
oom hung with tapestry, designed by Zuccarelli, and worked in Soho-
quare, in 1758. The state-gallery, or ball-room, is 106 feet long, and
7 wide; it is gorgeously gilt with groups in relief, of eagles, boys, and
oliage, and is decorated in compartments with paintings after the Ro-
an school; the chimney-pieces are supported by Phrygian captives in
iarble : the noble room will accommodate 800 guests. Upon the walls
re admirable copies, original size, of the School of Athens, of Raphael,
y Mengs; the Presentation, and Marriage of Cupid and Psyche, both
lso after Raphael, by Pompeio Battoni; and copies of A. Caracci's
lacchus and Ariadne, by Constansi; and Guido's Aurora, by Massaccio.
Iere are two cabinets of marbles and gems, once the property of Louis
LIV., and valued at 1000*l.* each. In the centre is a Sèvres china vase,
ine feet high, exquisitely painted with Diana and her Nymphs disarm-
ig Cupid. This was presented by Charles X. to Hugh, second Duke
f Northumberland, when Ambassador to France.

The most important original picture in the Northumberland collection is the
ortrait-group of the "Cornaro Family" (Evelyn called it "yᵉ Venetian Sena-
rs"), by Titian, which was bought by Algernon Earl of Northumberland, *temp.*
harles I. from Vandyke, for 1000 guineas. Among the other pictures are St.
ebastian, bound on the ground, and two angels in the air, by Guercino, with
gures life-size; a small "Adoration of the Shepherds," by G. Bassano; "a
retty Girl with a Candle, before which she holds her hands, by G. Schalken, of
emarkable clearness, and good impasto" (*Waagen*); Alnwick Castle, and West-
iinster Bridge, building and completed, by Canaletti; a curious portrait of Ed-
ard VI., with a long inscription, by Mabuse; a Fox-hunt and Deer-hunt, by F.
nyders; Christ crowned with Thorns, by Caravaggio; portrait of Napoleon
hen First Consul, by Philips (a fine likeness); several family portraits, including
ercy, Earl of Northumberland, one of Vandyke's finest portraits. Also, carvings
i ivory, after pictures by Teniers and others; and sumptuous ormolu articles.
he mansion can only be seen by special permission; in the Great Exhibition
eason, 1851, the public were admitted by tickets, 10,000 a-week.

In the Strand front, west of the central gateway, by an ingenious contrivance,
portion of the wall is opened for the egress of carriages upon state-occasions.

Hugh, second duke, who died at Alnwick Castle, was interred from North-
mberland House, with great state, in Westminster Abbey, Feb. 22, 1847; the
ineral pageant reaching from Charing Cross to the western door of the Abbey.

OVERSTONE, LORD, No. 22 Norfolk-street, Park-lane : a valuable
ollection of Italian, Flemish, and Dutch masters, the latter including
camples from the cabinet of Baron Verstolk, at the Hague.

PEEL, LADY, No. 4 Privy Gardens, Whitehall: the mansion contains
portion of the choice collection of pictures formed by the late Sir
obert Peel; including Rubens's celebrated Chapeau de Paille, for
hich Sir Robert gave 3500 guineas; also, 3 by Cuyp; 4 Coast-scenes

by Collins; the Poulterer's Shop, by G. Douw; 4 by Hobbema; 2 by Isaac Ostade; Landscape and Castle, by Paul Potter, 1654; 2 by Ruysdael; 7 by D. Teniers; Genoese Senator and his Wife, by Vandyke; 4 by A. Vandervelde; 7 by W. Vandervelde; 6 by Wouvermans; 2 by Wynants. The Portraits, by Reynolds and Lawrence, have been removed to Drayton Manor. In the dining-room of the above mansion Sir Robert Peel was placed immediately after his fatal accident; and in this room he expired, July 2, 1850. Between the doors hangs Wilkie's fine picture of John Knox preaching.

RUTLAND HOUSE, No. 16 Arlington-street, Piccadilly: here, Jan. 5, 1827, died the Duke of York, second son of George III.

SPENCER HOUSE (Earl Spencer), St. James's-place, was built by Vardy, a pupil of Kent, for the first Earl Spencer, father of the collector of the *Bibliotheca Spenceriana.* The mansion fronts the Green Park, and has a pediment, upon which are three graceful figures by Spong, a Danish sculptor.

STAFFORD HOUSE (Duke of Sutherland), on the west side of Stable-yard, St. James's Palace, occupies part of the site of the Queen's Library, built by Kent for Caroline, consort of George II.: in Pennant's time it was a lumber-room. The Stafford mansion was commenced in 1825, by B. Wyatt, for the Duke of York, second son of George III.; who dying before the building was completed, the Crown lease was sold by Act 4 & 5 Vict. c. 27, to the first Duke of Sutherland, for 72,000*l.*, subject to an annual ground-rent of 758*l.* The mansion is entirely of hewn stone; the north front in Stable-yard has a Corinthian portico of eight columns, beneath which is the entrance. The garden-fence is curiously made of slate.

The interior was planned by Barry, by whom were added the second and third stories, the latter concealed by a balustrade. The grandest feature is the hall, or tribune, and state-staircase, opening through all the stories, and lighted by a lantern filled with engraved glass, and supported by eighteen palm-trees; the ceiling contains Guercino's celebrated apotheosis of St. Grisogno; and beside the fireplace are Murillo's Prodigal Son's Return, and Abraham and the Angels, from the Soult Gallery. The walls are imitative Giallo antico, divided by white marble Corinthian columns and pilasters; and in compartments are copies, by Lorenzi, of Paul Veronese's colossal pictures. The whole interior strikingly reminded Dr. Waagen of many of the palaces of Genoa: it is a square of 80 feet, rising in the centre to 120, the roof richly painted and gilt, the floor a sea of red and white marble; and when lighted by scores of candelabra, the effect is truly gorgeous. On the first landing is a marble statue of a Sibyl, by Ronaldi. Thence two flights of stairs diverge upwards to a corridor, decorated with marble columns and balustrades, round three sides of the hall; the fourth being the gallery, 120 feet long, with a fretted gold roof, and lighted by Roman candelabra in gilt-bronze; the walls are hung with paintings of the Italian, Flemish, Spanish, and modern English schools.

Among the pictures in the gallery are, Vandyke's portrait of Thomas Howard, Earl of Arundel; Morone's portrait of a Jesuit (Titian's Schoolmaster); Correggio's Mule-driver, reputed to have been painted for a tavern-sign; Christ before Pilate, Honthorst's finest work, from the Lucca collection; Christ at Emmaus, by Paul Veronese; Christ bearing his Cross, by Raphael; Don Francis Borgia entering the Jesuits' College, several life-size figures, by Velasquez; and three works of Zurbaran, from the Soult collection; Lord Strafford on his way to the Scaffold, receiving Laud's blessing, by Delaroche; and Winterhalter's portrait of the Duchess of Sutherland.

The other three sides consist of eight state-rooms: three towards

he Green Park are drawing-rooms hung with Gobelin tapestry, de-
igned by Delaroche. Northward is the great dining-room, 70 feet by
0 feet, where is a statue of Ganymede, by Thorwaldsen; and on the
hird side are two saloons hung with a long series of paintings of the
ld Italian schools above the bookshelves.

In the dining-room, on the ground-floor, are assembled all the por-
raits of the Orleans Gallery: the royal and historical personages
uring the reign of Louis XIV., the Orleans regency, the reign of
ouis XV., and the happy part of the life of Louis XVI. and Marie
ntoinette. The adjoining rooms are dedicated solely to modern
ritish art: including *chef-d'œuvres* of Reynolds, Lawrence, Opie,
Vilkie, Turner, Landseer, Calcott, &c.; busts by Chantrey, and elegant
roups by Westmacott, senior and junior; and in her Grace's drawing-
oom the chimney-piece supports are statues of her two lovely daugh-
ers, exquisitely sculptured by the younger Westmacott. Other marble
himney-pieces are adorned with small bronzes and elegant vessels,
fter the antique; busts, and bas-reliefs.

Among the pictures on the ground-floor are, Winterhalter's Scene from the
ecameron; a River Scene, by J. Van Goyen, his finest work; St. Justina and
t. Rufina, half-lengths, by Murillo, very fine; the Marriage of St. Catherine, by
ubens; Festival before the Flood (17 figures), by W. Etty, R.A.; Scene from
he *Spectator*, by T. Stothard, R.A.; the Breakfast Table, by Wilkie, R.A.; Cas-
andra foretelling Hector's Death, by B. R. Haydon; the Passage of the Red Sea
y the Israelites, by F. Danby, A.R.A.; the Assuaging of the Waters, by John
artin; Death of the Virgin, by Albert Durer; Head of a Young Man, by Par-
egiano; Lady Gower (now Duchess of Sutherland) and her Daughter (now
uchess of Argyle), by Sir Thomas Lawrence; the Day after the Battle of Chevy
hace, by E. Bird, R.A. Also a drawing, by Prince Albert, of his son, the Prince
f Wales; and a life-size bronze statue of the Marquis of Stafford, by Feucheres.
mong the historic memorials is a bronze cast taken from the face of Napoleon,
fter death.

The collection of pictures can only be seen by special invitation or
ermission of the family.

TOMLINE'S (Mr. G.), No. 1 Carlton-House-terrace, contains a few
rst-class pictures; including the Pool of Bethesda, or Christ healing
he Paralytic, by Murillo, purchased by Mr. Tomline from the Soult
ollection for 7500*l.* Here also is the picture of Christ and the Woman
f Samaria, by Annibal Caracci; and the identical portrait of Charles V.,
o paint which Titian journeyed to Bologna.

UXBRIDGE HOUSE (Marquis of Anglesey), Burlington Gardens,
uilt by Vardy in 1792, occupies the site of Queensbury House (Leoni,
rchitect, 1726), where died the poet Gay, Dec. 4, 1732.

MARKETS.

Few of the Market-buildings of the metropolis are of tasteful design,
ich as we are accustomed to admire in the ancient and modern market-
laces of the continent. The early history and location of the London
arkets are, however, curious.

> " Shall the large mutton smoke upon your boards?
> Such Newgate's copious market best affords.
> Wouldst thou wish mighty beef augment thy meal?
> Seek Leadenhall: St. James's sends thee veal;
> Thames-street gives cheeses, Covent Garden fruits;
> Moorfields old books, and Monmouth-street old suits."
>   Gay's *Trivia*, book ii.

BILLINGSGATE is described at pp. 45 and 46. It was once a landing-
ace for other merchandise than fish: "1550. There came a sheppe of
ges and shurtes and smockes oute of France to Byllyngesgatte."
rey Friars' Chron.) The Market has been rebuilt and enlarged, 1849-

·53,.by the City architect, J. B. Bunning: it has a river. frontage of Italian design, with a central clock and bell tower, and arcade of red brick and Portland stone; it is ventilated, supplied with water, cleansèd, and drained by Bessemer's centrifugal pumping machinery; and a cast-iron fountain discharges from rushes and dolphins water into a basin 15 feet in diameter, for the use of the market-people.

BOROUGH MARKET, Southwark, for provisions, occupies the site of a mansion of the see of Rochester; and the ground is held of the Bishop by the parish of St. Saviour, at an annual rent of 14*l*. 13*s*. 6*d*.

CLARE MARKET, at the south-west angle of Lincoln's Inn Fields, for butcher's-meat, fish, and vegetables, was built by William Hollés, Baron Houghton and Earl of Clare, in Clement's Inn Fields, about the year 1660, and was first called *New Market*.

The City and Lord Clare had a long lawsuit concerning this estate; the City yielded; "and from the success of this noble lord, they have got several charters for the erecting of several other markets since the year 1660: as that of St. James, by the Earl of St. Alban's; Bloomsbury, by the Earl of Southampton; Brook Market, by the Lord Brook; Hungerford Market; Newport Market; besides the Haymarket, New Charing-cross, and that at Petty France at Westminster, with their Mayfair in the fields behind Piccadilly."—*Harl. MS.* 5900.

Here was a chapel for the use of the butchers, whither Orator Henley removed from Newport Market, and preached in a tub covered with velvet and gold; the altar being inscribed, "The Primitive Eucharist." Henley, "preacher at once, and zany of the age," lectured "at the Oratory" upon theology, "skits of the fashions," "the beau monde from before Noah's flood," and "bobs at the times;" but straying into sedition, he was cited before the Privy Council, who dismissed him as an impudent fellow. He lectured here for nearly 20 years; the admission was 1*s.*, and he had medals struck as tickets. In Gibbon's-court, Clare Market, was a theatre, where Killigrew's company performed some time. "Nov. 20th, 1660. Mr. Shepley and I to the new playhouse near Lincoln's Inn Fields (which was formerly Gibbon's Tennis-court), where the play of 'Beggar's Bush' was newly begun: it is the finest playhouse, I believe, that ever was in England." (*Pepys*.) Its remains were long used as a carpenter's shop, slaughter-houses, &c.

Clare Market lying between the two great theatres, its butchers were the arbiters of the galleries, the leaders of theatrical rows, the musicians at actresses' marriages, the chief mourners at players' funerals. In and around the market were the signs of the Sun; the Bull and Butcher, afterwards Spiller's Head; the Grange; the Bull's Head, where met "the Shepherd and his Flock Club," and where Dr. Radcliffe was carousing when he received news of the loss of his 5000*l.* venture; here is the Black Jack in Portsmouth-street, the haunt of Joe Miller, the comedian, and where he uttered his time-honoured "Jests:" the house remains, but the sign has disappeared. Miller died in 1738, and was buried in St. Clement's upper ground, in Portugal-street, where his gravestone was inscribed with the following epitaph, written by Stephen Duck: "Here lie the remains of honest Joe Miller, who was a tender husband, a sincere friend, a facetious companion, and an excellent comedian. He departed this life the 15th day of August, 1738, aged 54 years.

> "If humour, wit, and honesty could save
> The humorous, witty, honest, from the grave,
> This grave had not so soon its tenant found,
> With honesty, and wit, and humour crown'd.
> Or could esteem and love preserve our health,
> And guard us longer from the stroke of Death,
> The stroke of Death on him had later fell,
> Whom all mankind esteem'd and loved so well."

he stone was restored by the parish grave-digger at the close of the
1st century; and in 1816 a new stone was set up by Mr. Jarvis Buck,
hurchwarden, who added "S. Duck" to the epitaph. At the Black
ack (also called "the Jump," see page 393), a club known as "the
lonourable Society of Jackers" met until 1816. (See "Jo: Miller, a
iography," by W. H. Wills, prefixed to *The Family Jo : Miller*, 1848.)
t the old tavern, next Miller's burial-place, meet the "Noviomagians,"
club founded by the late A. J. Kempe, F.S.A., on the discovery of the
uins of Noviomagus (a Roman station at Old Croydon, or Woodcote,
urrey): the members are Fellows of the Society of Antiquaries, who
ine together once a month during the season.

CORN MARKET, Mark-lane. (See CORN EXCHANGE, page 282.)

COVENT-GARDEN MARKET was established towards the end of
harles II.'s reign (see page 235), on the site of the garden of the
onvent at Westminster; and in Chamberlayne's *Notitia*, 1726, it is
rinted Convent Garden. Strype describes it, in 1698, as held for
uits, herbs, roots, and flowers, "beneath a small grotto of trees," on
uesdays, Thursdays, and Saturdays, the present market-days. In 1704,
hen Tavistock-row was built, the market-people were compelled to
ssemble in the square, and here their stalls increased to dwellings.

Steele (*Tatler*, No. 454, Aug. 11, 1712), in his boat-voyage from Richmond,
soon fell in with a fleet of gardeners, bound for the several market-ports of
ondon. * * It was very easy to observe by their sailing, and the countenances
f the ruddy virgins who were supercargoes, the part of the town to which they
ere bound. There was an air in the purveyors for Covent Garden, who fre-
uently converse with morning rakes, very unlike the seeming sobriety of those
ound for Stocks Market. * * I landed, with ten sail of apricot boats, at Strand
ridge, after having put in at Nine Elms and taken in melons, consigned by Mr.
uffe, of that place, to Sarah Sewell and Co., at their stall in Covent Garden."

Still the market was a strange assemblage of shed and penthouse,
de stall and crazy tenement, coffee-house and gin-shop, intersected
y narrow and ill-lit footways, until the site was cleared for a new
arket in 1829. The present market-buildings were designed by Fow-
r, and are perfectly fitted for their various uses ; evince considerable
rchitectural skill, and are so characteristic of the purpose for which the
arket has been erected, that it cannot be mistaken for any thing else
ut what it is; unless the inscription, "JOHN, DUKE OF BEDFORD,
rected MDCCCXXX.," over the east end, lead posterity to regard this
s a patriotic act ; whereas the Bedford family derive a large rental
rom the market, stated at 5000*l.* per annum. The area is 3 acres. The
ent of some of the shops is from 400*l.* to 500*l.* per annum.

Alack, how changed is Covent Garden ! "the convent becomes a
layhouse ; monks and nuns turn actors and actresses. The garden, for-
al and quiet, where a salad was cut for a lady-abbess, and flowers
ere gathered to adorn images, becomes a market, noisy and full of
fe, distributing thousands of fruits and flowers to a social metropolis."
—W. S. Landor's *Imaginary Conversations*.

The plan consists of a quadrangle, with two exterior colonnades on
e north and south sides, in front of shops; and in the central building
n "avenue" open to the roof, with shops on each side for forced
rticles, the choice fruits, vegetables, &c. At the east end is a quad-
ple colonnade, with a terrace over, and two large conservatories, a
andsome fountain of Devonshire marble, and an emblematical group
f figures on the pediment of a screen between the conservatories. At
e west end is a colonnade with a conservatory over; and below is an
on projection of tasteful design, beneath which is held "the Flower
arket." There are store-cellars almost throughout the area; and
ater is supplied from an Artesian well sunk beneath the central path,

K K

280 feet deep, and affording 1600 gallons per hour: it is distributed by a steam-engine; and the conservatories are heated by steam and hot water. The buildings are of brick, with stone facings; the columns are single pieces of Scotch and Devon granite: the colonnade terraces are composed of large slabs of stone, resting upon hollow cast-iron beams, into which is drained the water; and these are supported upon iron and stone columns. The whole is admirably built by Cubitt.

The supplies of fruit and vegetables sent to this market, in variety, excellence, and quantity, surpass those of all other countries. There is more certainty of being able to purchase a pine-apple here, every day in the year, than in Jamaica and Calcutta, where pines are indigenous. Forced asparagus, potatoes, sea-kale, rhubarb-stalks, mushrooms, French beans, and early cucumbers, are to be had in January and February; in March, forced cherries, strawberries, and spring spinach; in April, grapes, peaches, and melons, with early peas; in May, all forced articles in abundance. The supply of forced flowers, of greenhouse plants, and in summer of hardy flowers and shrubs, is equally varied and abundant; and of curious herbs for domestic medicines, distilleries, &c., upwards of 500 species may be procured at the shop of one herbalist.

Beneath the arcade, at the early market hour, are stationed hawkers of account-books, dog-collars, whips, chains, curry-combs, pastry, money-bags, tissue-paper for the tops of strawberry-pottles, and horse-chestnut leaves for garnishing fruit-stalls; coffee-stalls, and stalls of pea-soup and pickled eels; basket-makers; women making up nosegays: and girls splitting huge bundles of water-cresses into little bunches. Here are fruits and vegetables from all parts of the world: peas, and asparagus, and new potatoes, from the south of France, Belgium, Holland, Portugal, and the Bermudas, are brought in steam-vessels. Besides Deptford onions, Battersea cabbages, Mortlake asparagus, Chelsea celery, and Charlton peas, immense quantities are brought by railway from Cornwall and Devonshire, the Isle of Man, Guernsey and Jersey, the Kentish and Essex banks of the Thames, the banks of the Humber, the Mersey, the Orwell, the Trent, and the Ouse. The Scilly Isles send early articles by steamer to Southampton, and thence to Covent Garden by railway. Strawberries are sent from gardens about Bath. The money paid annually for fruits and vegetables sold in this market is estimated at three millions sterling: for 6 or 700,000 pottles of strawberries; 40,000,000 cabbages; 2,000,000 cauliflowers; 300,000 bushels of peas; 750,000 lettuces; and 500,000 bushels of onions. In Centre-row, hothouse grapes are sold at 25s. per pound, British Queen and Black Prince strawberries at 1s. per ounce, slender French beans at 3s. per hundred, peas at a guinea a quart, and new potatoes at 4s. 6d. per lb.; a moss-rose for half-a-crown, and bouquets of flowers from one shilling to two guineas each. (Household Words, No. 175.) Green peas have been sold here at Christmas at 2l..the quart, and asparagus and rhubarb at 15s. the bundle.

The foreign green-fruit trade of Covent Garden is very extensive in pineapples, melons, cherries, apples and pears. The cheap West India pineapple trade dates from 1844, when pines were first cried in the streets " a penny a slice." Of the 250,000,000 oranges imported annually into England, comparatively few are sold in Covent Garden.

Mr. Cuthill, the gardener, of Camberwell, states the ground under cultivation for the supply of the London markets to be about 12,000 acres occupied by vegetables, and about 5000 by fruit-trees. These lie chiefly in Middlesex, Essex, Hertford, and Bedford, north of the Thames, and Kent and Surrey south; some 35,000 persons are employed on them. From distant counties are sent up the produce of acres of turnip-tops, cabbages, and peas; while hundreds of acres in Cornwall and Devon grow early potatoes, brocoli, peas, &c., which reach London by railway.

The quantity of water-cresses annually sold in the principal wholesale markets of London (above one-third of which are retailed in the streets) is as follows:— Covent Garden, 1,578,000 bunches; Farringdon, 12,960,000: Borough, 180,000; Spitalfields, 180,000; Portman, 60,000; total, 14,958,000. The amount realised by the sale is 13,949l.—Henry Mayhew's London Labour.

FARRINGDON MARKET, between the west end of Shoe-lane and Farringdon-street, covers 1½ acres of ground, and was built by William Montague, the City architect; it was opened in 1829, on the removal of

leet Market. It is well placed for drainage, parallel with Holborn-
ll; the site and buildings (including a clock-tower of Italian design)
)st about 250,000*l.*; but the Market is little frequented.

HUNGERFORD MARKET, West Strand, occupies the site of a market-
lace built in 1680 by Sir Edward Hungerford, from his town-house and
rounds, extending to the Thames. In 1685, Sir Stephen Fox and Sir
hristopher Wren were proprietors of the market-estate; in the centre
as a lofty hall, with a bust of one of the Hungerfords, and an inscrip-
on stating the market-place to have been erected "*utilitati publicæ;*"
at Strype, in 1720, describes it as "baulk'd at first," and turned to
ttle account. The old hall and a colonnade remained until 1830, when
ie present buildings, adapted from a Roman market, were commenced
r a Company by Fowler, architect of Covent-Garden Market. The
ungerford buildings consist of two quadrangles, with stone Tuscan
)lumns, and a large central hall; with a handsome river front, a tho-
)ughfare to the suspension-bridge. Here is the great focus of the
)per Thames steam-navigation, where are a million of embarcations
id landings annually. The estate comprises about 3¼ acres; the
wer quadrangle is the fish-market, and the upper for vegetables,
uit, meat, &c. The market was publicly opened July 2, 1833; but
is been alike unprofitable with the original Hungerford scheme. The
rge exhibition-hall and bazaar-gallery beneath were built in 1851;
hen M. Bouton produced here his dioramas of Fribourg and Venice.

LEADENHALL MARKET, Gracechurch-street, which is described at
ige 453, is now the great poultry and game market, where 4,000,000
rds, &c. have been sold in one year. In 1533 the beef sold here was
ot to exceed a halfpenny a pound, and mutton a halfpenny half-farthing.

In severe winters here are large supplies of wild ducks, principally from Hol-
nd; woodcocks, &c.; snipes from Ireland; pigeons from France; rabbits from
stend; blackcocks from Scotland. "Sometimes, after a grand *battue*, there is a
ut of hares and pheasants in Leadenhall Market." (*Macculloch.*) The returns
r poultry, game, and rabbits in one year equal half a million of money. A few
ars since Ostend rabbits were hardly saleable in London; now, from 50 to 100
ns are imported weekly by steamers, and 1000 persons are employed in this
bbit trade. On Christmas Eve here are displayed 100,000 geese and turkeys,
cluding importations from France, Belgium, Holland, and Ireland. Here, also,
a market for live animals,—fancy dogs and rabbits, cage-birds, &c.

NEWGATE MARKET, between Paternoster-row and Newgate-street,
as formerly kept in the latter street, and was a market for meal.
1548. This yere before Alhalloutyd was sett up the howse for the
arkyt folke in Newgate Market for to waye melle in." (*Grey Friars'
hron.*) It is now the great Meat Market. In the old College of
hysicians, Warwick-lane, is held another meat-market.

Butcher-Hall-lane (now King Edward-street), Newgate-street, was originally
amed from the great number of *butchers* living here; and there is extant a pe-
tion to Parliament, dated 1380, praying that they might be restrained from
rowing the blood and entrails of slaughtered animals into the river Fleet, and
at they might be compelled to "kill" at "Knyghtsbrigg," or elsewhere out of
ondon; and this seems to have been done for several reigns.

The markets of Newgate and Leadenhall are places disgraceful to any large
ty at the present day. They are in fact great slaughtering places as well as
arkets; in which the cattle are killed and flayed in dark, confined, and filthy
llars, in some of which from fifty to a hundred sheep together will be confined
the closest possible space, until the working butchers shall have successively
espatched the whole of them.—*Proceedings of the Statistical Society,* 1847.

In the time of the Commonwealth, when the Established Church had
st its authority, banns of marriage were published on market-days in
ewgate Market; and the couples were afterwards married "at the
lace of meeting called *the church.*"—*Register of St. Andrew's.*

NEWPORT MARKET, Soho, named from the town-house of the Earl of Newport in the neighbourhood, is a meat-market, with its butchers, slaughtermen, and drovers. Here Orator Henley held his mock preaching. The father of John Horne Tooke was a poulterer in Newport market,—as he told his schoolfellows, "a Turkey merchant."

OXFORD MARKET, north of Oxford-street, was built for Edward, Earl of Oxford, in 1731. Barry, the painter, who lived in Castle-street, describes it as "the most classic London market—that of Oxford."

SMITHFIELD, or West Smithfield (so called to distinguish it from East Smithfield, east of Tower Hill), is the only "live" market, and the oldest in the metropolis. The name signifies a smooth plain; 'smith' being corrupted from the Saxon *smeth*, smooth. Fitzstephen calls it "a certain *plain* field (*planus campus*), both in reality and name, situated without one of the City gates, even in the very suburbs:" horses and cattle were sold here in 1150, horse-racing was common, and the horse-market is to this day called "Smithfield races." The original extent of Smithfield was about three acres; the market-place was paved, drained, and railed in, 1685; subsequently enlarged to 4½ acres, and since 1834 to 6¼ acres. Yet this enlargement proved disproportionate to the requirements: in 1731 there were only 8304 head of cattle sold in Smithfield; in 1846, 210,757 head of cattle, and 1,518,510 sheep. This over-crowding has led to dreadful cruelties to the poor animals by drovers and others; whilst the market is surrounded by slaughter-houses and knackers' yards, tallow-melting, bone-boiling, tripe-washing, and other offensive trades; and over-peopled and ill-drained alleys, yards, and lanes,—a pestilential nuisance to the City, producing to the Corporation by its tolls less than 4000*l.* per annum. The old City laws for its regulation are called the "statutes of Smithfield." Here may be shewn 4000 beasts and about 30,000 sheep, the latter in 1509 pens: and there are 50 pens for pigs. The market-days are, Monday and Friday for cattle and sheep; Tuesday, Thursday, and Saturday for hay and straw; Friday for calves and milch cows, and from two o'clock till dusk for horses and asses, mules, dogs, and goats: the horses sold are mostly spavined, lame, and blind, and are bought up by the knackers; here is a market for old harness, barrows, costermongers' carts, donkeys, and donkey-carts. Altogether, Smithfield is the largest live market in the world, and its sales amount to 7,000,000*l.* annually.

"It was market morning. The ground was covered nearly ankle-deep with filth and mire; and a thick steam perpetually rising from the reeking bodies of the cattle, and mingling with the fog, which seemed to rest upon the chimney-tops, hung heavily above. All the pens in the centre of the large area, and as many temporary ones as could be crowded into the vacant space, were filled with sheep; and tied up to posts by the gutter-side were long lines of beasts and oxen three or four deep. Countrymen, butchers, drovers, hawkers, boys, thieves, idlers, and vagabonds of every low grade, were mingled together in a dense mass: the whistling of drovers, the barking of dogs, the bellowing and plunging of beasts, the bleating of sheep, and grunting and squeaking of pigs; the cries of hawkers, the shouts, oaths, and quarrelling on all sides, the ringing of bells, and the roar of voices that issued from every public-house; the crowding, pushing, driving, beating, whooping, and yelling: the hideous and discordant din that resounded from every corner of the market; and the unwashed, unshaven, squalid, and dirty figures constantly running to and fro, and bursting in and out of the throng, rendered it a stunning and bewildering scene which quite confused the senses."—Charles Dickens's *Oliver Twist.*

The market, with its attendant nuisances of knackers' yards, tainted sausage-makers, slaughter-houses, tripe-dressers, cat's-meat boilers, catgut-spinners, bone-houses, and other noxious trades, in the very heart of London, was, however, in 1852, condemned by law to be removed into Copenhagen Fields, Islington. (See also SMITHFIELD.)

STOCKS MARKET, for fish and flesh, was established in 1282, on the site of the present Mansion House, and was named from a pair of stocks placed there for punishing offenders. After the Great Fire it became a fine market for fruit, roots, and herbs, " surpassing all the other fruit-markets in London" (*Strype*) : "where is such a garden in Europe as the Stocks Market?" (*Shadwell*, 1689.) At the north end was the Conduit; and the equestrian statue of John Sobieski, set up by Sir Robert Viner, with a new head, as Charles II.; and removed for the Mansion House site in 1779. A few dealers in costly fruit kept shops hard by until our time.

STREET MARKETS.—The phantasmagoria of London presents few more striking lights than in its street markets, mostly held in great thoroughfares by costermongers, those wandering stall-keepers, who sell about the town fish, fruit, and vegetables, in donkey-carts, hand-barrows, baskets, and trays.

"The scene in these parts has more of the character of a fair than of a market. There are hundreds of stalls, and every stall has its one or two lights; either it is illuminated by the intense white light of the new self-generating gas-lamp, or else is brightened up by the red smoky flame of the old-fashioned grease-lamps. One man shews off his yellow haddock with a candle stuck in a bundle of firewood; his neighbour makes his candlestick of a huge turnip, and the tallow gutters over its sides; while the boy shouting ' E-eight a penny, pears !' has rolled his dip in a thick coat of brown paper, that flares away with the candle. Some stalls are crimson with a fire shining through the holes beneath the baked-chestnut stove; others have handsome octohedral lamps; while a few have a candle shining through a sieve. These, with the sparkling ground-glass globes of the tea-dealers' shops, and the butchers' gas-lights streaming and fluttering in the wind like flags of flame, pour forth such a flood of light, that, at a distance, the atmosphere imme-diately above the spot is as lurid as if the street was on fire."—*Henry Mayhew.*

MARTIN'S (ST.), LANE,

extending northward from Charing Cross and the east side of Tra-falgar-square, to the junction of Long Acre with Cranbourn-street, appears in Aggas's plan (early in Elizabeth's reign) as a *green lane,* with only a few houses beyond St. Martin's Church, abutting into Covent Garden, which extended into Drury-lane. St. Martin's-lane was mostly built about 1613, and was first named "West Church-lane." A few of the houses are spacious and have noble staircases, those on the west side being the largest; some exteriors on the east side are good spe-cimens of brickwork. Among the early tenants was Sir Theodore May-erne, physician to James I.; Daniel Mytens, the painter; Sir John Suck-ling, the poet. Sir Hugh Platt, the most ingenious husbandman of his age, had a garden in St. Martin's-lane in 1606. Howell sends a maiden copy of his poem " to Sir Kenelm Digby, at his house in St. Martin's-lane," in 1641. (*Familiar Letters,* 5th edit. 1678, p. 393.) Here also lived the great Earl of Shaftesbury; Dr. Tenison, when vicar of St. Martin's; and Ambrose Philips, the Whig poet. Here too dwelt, early opposite May's-buildings, Sir Joshua Reynolds, when he first came to London; Sir James Thornhill, who, at the back of his house, established an artists' school, from which arose the Royal Academy; Roubiliac, who commenced practice in St. Peter's-court, a favourite haunt of artists; Fuseli, at No. 100 (first floor and staircase good). Old Slaughter's Coffee-house was once the great evening resort of artists, and Hogarth was a constant visitor. At No. 101 was built and exhibited the Apollonicon (see page 16). No. 112 was the picture premises of Mr. Samuel Woodburn, the eminent English dealer in art, who died in 1853, leaving a valuable collection of the Italian, Ger-man, and Flemish old masters: among the English pictures was Ho-garth's Midnight Modern Conversation, painted for Rich, of Covent Garden Theatre. No. 31 has a classically decorated exterior, in the style of Inigo Jones, and is engraved in Hakewill's *Architecture of the Seventeenth Century*, 1853. The first floor has an enriched ceiling.

A labyrinth of courts and alleys about St. Martin's church was removed in 1829: including the Bermudas, Carribbee or Cribbee Islands; and Porridge Island, noted for its cook-shops. Another knot, on the west side of St. Martin's-lane, was cleared away for Trafalgar-square, including Duke's-court, where lived Roger Payne, the celebrated bookbinder (died 1797): his *chef-d'œuvre*, Æschylus, in Lord Spencer's library, cost fifteen guineas binding.

MARTIN'S (ST.) LE GRAND,

A College founded by Withred King of Kent, in 700, and rebuilt and endowed about 1056 by the Saxon brothers Ingelric and Girard, was dedicated to St. Martin, to which was added *le Grand*, from its privileges, granted by monarchs who occasionally resided here. The church and collegiate buildings covered the insulated ground now occupied by the General Post-Office; and the Sutherland View, 1543, shews the lofty spire and tower, wherein curfew was rung. Among the deans was William of Wykeham, who rebuilt the church: the advowsons were given by Henry VII. to the Abbots of Westminster. St. Martin's-le-Grand was a noted Sanctuary; and after the demolition of the College, the site was built upon and occupied by non-freemen, to avoid the City jurisdiction. French, Germans, Dutch, and Scotch abounded here; their trades being shoemakers, tailors, makers of buttons and button-moulds, goldsmiths, &c.; and here are said to have first settled in England silk-throwsters. Among its counterfeit finery was its copper "St. Martin's-lace." Each trade had its quarter; hence Mould-makers'-row, removed in our time; and Shoemakers'-row, now the west side of St. Martin's-le-Grand; while Dean's, Bell, and Angel alleys denote the old ecclesiastical locality. In 1818, when the site was cleared for the Post-Office, a crypt by William of Wykeham was destroyed. (See CRYPTS, page 243.) Lower down were found remains of the Roman times: coins, beads, glass, and pottery; amphoræ, Samian ware, funereal urns, lachrymatories, &c.: denoting this to have been an important site of Roman London. (See Kempe's *St. Martin's-le-Grand*.)

Among the distinguished residents of Aldersgate-street, in a line with St. Martin's-le-Grand, was Mr., afterwards Sir William, Watson; at whose house, in 1746, were exhibited the effects of the Leyden phials, then newly invented: and here the Duke of Cumberland, recently returned from Scotland, took the shock with the point of the sword with which he had fought the battle of Culloden.— *The Gold-headed Cane*, p. 115.

In St. Martin's-le-Grand was the *Taborer's Inn*, of the time of Edward II.; and the *Crown Tavern*, at the end of Duck-lane, which, in 1709, had a noble room painted with classical subjects. Between Aldersgate and St. Anne's-lane end; was the *Mourning Bush*; the owner having painted black his carved sign (a bush), after the beheading of Charles I.: its vaulted cellars, with regular courses of Roman brick, form the foundation of the present *New Post-office Coffee House.* Adjoining these massive remains runs a portion of the City wall.

MARYLEBONE,

A manor of the hundred of Ossulston, in Middlesex, and the largest parish of London (more than twice the extent of the City, and population greater), was, at the commencement of the last century, a small village, about a mile N. W. from the nearest part of the metropolis. It was originally called Tyburn, or Tybourne, from its being on the *bourne*, or brook, which runs from Hampstead into the Thames; and its church being dedicated to St. Mary, the parish was named St. Mary-at-the-bourne, Mary-le-bone, or Marybone. In a record of Henry VIII.

it is called Tyborne, alias Maryborne, alias Marybourne (*Lysons*). It extends northward to Primrose Hill, west to Kilburn turnpike, and south to Oxford-street, inclusive: it is 8¼ miles in circumference, and contains about 1700 acres of land; of which, till about 1760, two-thirds were chiefly pasture-fields.

The Manor of Tybourn, valued at 52 shillings in Domesday-book, and in K. Edward's time at 100 shillings, was exchanged by the then lord, in 1544, with Henry VIII. for certain church lands; it was leased by Queen Elizabeth, in 1583 and 1595, at the yearly rent of 16*l*. 11*s*. 8*d*.; in 1611 it was sold by James I. (*excepting the park*) for 829*l*. 3*s*. 4*d*.; in 1710 it was sold for 17,500*l*., the rental being then 900*l*. per annum; and about 1813 the manor passed from the second Duke of Portland to the Crown, by an exchange of land valued at 40,000*l*. The manor-house was taken down in 1791. (See page 393.)

Marylebone Park was a hunting-ground in the reign of Queen Elizabeth: in 1600 the ambassadors from Russia and their retinue rode through the City to hunt in Marylebone Park; and here Sir Charles Blount (afterwards Earl of Devonshire), one of the challengers in the Field of Cloth-of-Gold, had a tilt with the Earl of Essex, and wounded him. The park, reserved by James I., was assigned by Charles I. as a security for debt; but was sold by Cromwell for 13,215*l*. 6*s*. 8*d*., including deer, and timber, except that marked for the navy. At the Restoration the park was re-assigned, till the debt was discharged. The site had been previously disparked, and was never afterwards stocked; but was let on leases, upon the expiry of which the ground was relaid out, by Nash, and named the Regent's Park.

Bowling-greens were also among the celebrities of Marylebone: where, says the grave John Locke (*Diary*, 1679), a curious stranger 'may see several persons of quality bowling, two or three times a-week, all the summer." The bowling-green of the Rose Tavern and gaming-house in High-street is referred to in Lady Mary Wortley Montague's memorable line (see page 8); and it is one of the scenes of Capt. Macheath's debaucheries, in Gay's *Beggar's Opera*. This and an adjoining bowling-green were incorporated in *Marylebone Gardens,* open gratis to all classes; but the company becoming more select, one shilling entrance-money was charged, an equivalent being allowed in viands. Here were given balls and concerts; and Handel's music was played, under Dr. Arne's direction, followed by fireworks, and in 1772, a model-picture of Mount Etna in eruption. Burlettas from Shakspeare were recited in the theatre here in 1774; and in 1776 was exhibited a representation of the Boulevards at Paris, Egyptian Pyramids, &c.: but the gardens were suppressed in 1777-8, and the site was let to builders.

A deed of assignment made by Thomas Lowe, the singer, conveying his property in Marylebone Gardens, to trustees, for the benefit of his creditors, in 1769, was in the possession of the late Mr. Sampson Hodgkinson, who was familiar with the parochial history of Marylebone. From this deed we learn that the premises of Rysbrack, the statuary, were formerly part of the *Great* (Marylebone) *Garden.* (See Smith's *St. Marylebone*, 1833.)

Prize-fighting was a pastime of this period, and Marylebone a place at which " to learn valour" (*Beggar's Opera*). Here was the boarded house of Figg, "the Atlas of the Sword," whose portrait is in the second plate of Hogarth's Rake's Progress. Near Figg's was Broughton's Amphitheatre, often crowded with amateurs of high rank. (See page 8.)

In the *Evening Post,* March 16, 1715. we find: " On Wednesday last, four gentlemen were robbed and stripped in the fields between London and Mary-le-bon."

Between 1718 and 1729 was built the north side of Tyburn-road, now Oxford-street; and the squares and streets northward were then commenced: still, much of the ground between the new buildings and the village of Marylebone was pasture-fields; and Maitland, in his *History of London*, 1739, states there to have been then only 577 houses in the parish, and 35 persons who kept coaches. In 1795 there were 6200 houses; in 1851, 16,669 houses.

In 1841 the Vestry of St. Marylebone accepted tenders from certain contractors to the amount of 4150*l*. for permission to cart away the ashes (breeze) from the several houses in this vast parish.

Marylebone is a parliamentary borough, containing the three parishes of St. Marylebone, Paddington, and St. Pancras.

(See CHURCHES, St. Marylebone, p. 142; and ALMSHOUSES, p. 6.)

MAY FAIR,

The district north of Piccadilly, and between Park-lane and Berkeley-square, was originally Brookfield; but received its present name from a *fair* being held there by grant of James II., after the suppression of St. James's Fair, to commence on *May* 1, and continue 15 days, where multitudes of the booths were "not for trade and merchandize, but for musick, showes, drinking, gaming, raffling, lotteries, stage-plays, and drolls." It was frequented "by all the nobility in town;" but was suppressed in 1708, when the downfal of May Fair quite sunk the price of Pinkethman's tame elephant, and sent his ingenious company of strollers to Greenwich. (See *Tatler*, Nos. 4 and 20.) The fair was, however, revived; and John Carter describes its "booths for jugglers; prize-fighters, both at cudgels and back-sword; boxing-matches, and wild beasts. The sports not under cover were mountebanks, fire-eaters, ass-racing, sausage-tables, dice ditto, up-and-downs, merry-go-rounds, bull-baiting, grinning for a hat, running for a shift, hasty-pudding-eaters, eel-divers," &c. The site of the Fair is now occupied by Hertford-street, Curzon-street, Shepherd's Market, &c.; but the old wooden public-house, "The Dog and Duck," with its willow-shaded pond for duck-hunting, is remembered: at fair-time, the second story of the market-house was let for the playhouse. The Fair was not finally abolished until late in the reign of George III. In Curzon-street was "the Rev. Alexander Keith's Chapel," with an entrance like a country church-porch, where marriages at a minute's notice were almost as notorious as at the Fleet—6000 in one year. The chapel was much frequented during May Fair: here the Duke of Kingston was married to Miss Chudleigh; the Baroness Clinton to the Hon. Mr. Shirley; and James, fourth Duke of Hamilton, in 1752, to the youngest of the two beautiful Miss Gunnings, with a bed-curtain ring, half an hour after midnight. The registers of the May-Fair marriages, in three folio volumes, closely and clearly written, are kept with the parish-books of St. George's, Hanover-square. Keith's charge was one guinea, with a license on a five-shilling stamp and certificate.

MEWS, ROYAL.

Upon the site of the National Gallery, on the north side of Charing Cross, when falconry was a royal pastime, were kept the king's hawks, in a building called *the Mews*. In 1319 (13 Edward II.) John De la Becke had the custody of the King's Mews ("*de mutis apud Charryng juxta Westmonasterium*"). In the reign of Richard II., Sir Simon Burley was Keeper of the King's Falcons; and Chaucer was Clerk of the King's Works, and of the Mews at Charing. In 1534, the royal stables at Lomsbery (since Bloomsbury) were burnt; after which the hawks were removed from Charing Cross, and the premises rebuilt for the stabling of the king's horses, in the reigns of Edward VI. and Queen

Mary; the building retaining the name of *Mews*, and public stables assuming the same Here Colonel Joyce was imprisoned by order of Oliver Cromwell; being carried away by musqueteers and put into the Dutch prison, and removed thence to another chamber in the Mews. It was a gamblers' resort: Gay, in his *Trivia*, says of "careful observers":

> "Untempted, they contemn the juggler's feats,
> Pass by the Meuse, nor try the thimble's cheats."

In 1732 the façade was rebuilt from the design of Kent, with three stone cupolas. Mac Owen Swiney was made Keeper of the Mews; he had been manager of Drury Lane and the Queen's Theatres, and died in 1754, leaving his fortune to Peg Woffington. At the Mews were kept the royal stud, the gilt state-coach, and the other royal carriages, until their removal to the new Mews at Pimlico, in 1824. The building at Charing Cross was occupied, in 1828, as the exhibition-rooms of the National Repository, and by Cross's Menagerie from Exeter Change; and here were temporarily housed a portion of the Public Records. The premises were taken down in 1830, for the site of the National Gallery. The last of the original Mews was occupied as a barrack: it was built of red Tudor brick, with buttresses, and crenellated; stone window-cases and dressings.

At the Mews-gate lived for more than 40 years "honest Tom Payne" (d. 1799), the bookseller; whose little shop, in the shape of an L., was the first named a literary coffee-house, from its knot of literary frequenters.

THE QUEEN'S MEWS, at the rear of Buckingham Palace, Queen's-row, Pimlico, was built in 1824, and consists of two quadrangles, entered by a Doric archway beneath a clock-tower. Visitors are admitted by a ticket from the Master of the Horse. In the first quadrangle are the coach-houses, and in the second the horses. Here are usually 40 carriages, besides Her Majesty's state-coach: the dress-carriages are fine specimens of coach-building. The horses include road-teams, saddle-horses, and hacks; and the dun and black Hanoverian state-horses (generally from 12 to 14 of each) for the state-coach; and here are usually kept the foreign horses presented to the sovereign. In the harness-room is the red morocco state-harness for eight horses, with massive silver-gilt furniture, the harness for each horse weighing 1 cwt.; besides the purple morocco state-harness made when George IV. was Regent.

The Mews Clock has stone dials (6 feet 10 inches in diameter), with the figures sunk (as in the Egyptian monuments), and a sunk centre for the hour-hand to traverse, so as to bring the minute-hand close to the figures, and thus avoid nearly all error from parallax—an improvement by Vulliamy.

The Riding-House belonged to Buckingham House: here, in 1771, were publicly exhibited the Queen's elephants, from one of which Lindley Murray, the grammarian, had a narrow escape.

ROYAL MEWS, Prince's-street, Westminster, was built by Decimus Burton, upon a space formerly occupied by a nursery of 200 trees, planted upon the site of the markets and narrow streets on the north side of Westminster Abbey, and removed between 1804 and 1808. At this Mews are kept the carriages and horses of official personages; and here may be seen the Speaker's state-coach. (See STATE-COACHES.)

MINORIES (THE),

Leading from Aldgate High-street to Tower-hill, is named from the "Sorores Minores," "Minoresses," or nuns of the order of St. Clare, founded 1293, whose convent stood in this street: upon its site, on the east side, is built the church of the Holy Trinity. The parish was formerly the convent close, and is without the walls of London, although in the Liberty of the Tower of London; therefore its inhabitants have no vote in the Common Council. In Haydon-square is a spring of pure water, which was the convent fountain; and here lived Sir Isaac Newton when warden and master-worker of the Mint: the house was taken down in 1852. On May 24, 1853, during excavations on the west side of Haydon-square, was found a stone sarcophagus of the late Roman period, sculptured with a basket of fruit, a medallic bust, and foliage, and containing a leaden coffin with the remains of a child: the sarcophagus is now in the British Museum. In the Minories neighbourhood have been found sculptured sepulchral stones and urns, and a third brass coin of Valens. In the churchyard are deposited some bones taken from the field of Culloden in 1745; and in the church is preserved a head, though from what body is unknown.

The parish of Holy Trinity is minutely described in the *Archæologia*, in 1803, by the Rev. Dr. Fly, F.S.A., 63 years incumbent of the parish; and the account was reprinted in 1851 (with additions), by the Rev. T. Hill, incumbent. After the dissolution of the convent, there were built here "storehouses for armour and habiliments of war, with divers work-houses serving to the same purpose" (*Stow*):

> "The Mulcibers who in the Minories sweat."—*Congreve.*

The street has been noted for its gunsmiths to our time: and in 1816 their shops were plundered by the Spa Fields rioters on their way to "summon the Tower!" From the Minories station the Blackwall Railway crosses the street by an unsightly enclosed viaduct.

MINT (THE ROYAL),

London, has been the chief seat of the Mint from the remotest period. Some of the Roman emperors are presumed to have coined money here; but "the silver penny of Alfred," says Ruding, "is the first authentic coin yet discovered which can with certainty be appropriated to the London Mint." The Mint in the Tower dates from the erection of that fortress; and it has been worked in almost every reign from the Conquest to our own times. The Mint buildings—"houses, mills, and engines"—used for coining were between the outer and inner ward or ballium, thence named *Mint-street.*

In the 35th Henry III. the warden's salary was 2s. a-day. The constitution of superior officers, established in the reign of Edward II., continued with few alterations until 1815. In 1287, 600 Jews were confined within the Tower at one time for clipping and adulterating the coin of the realm. In 1546, one William Foxley, a pot-maker for the Mint, fell asleep in the Tower, and could not be waked for fourteen days and fifteen nights. Some of the Mint officers are buried in the church of St. Peter in the Tower, the chaplain and rector of which, by grant of Edward III., received 10s. from the clerk of the Mint, 13s. 4d. from the master of the Mint, and 1d. per week from the wages of each workman and teller of coins.

Lully, the alchemist, worked "in the chamber of St. Katherine" in the Tower, and was believed to supply the Mint with gold; and Edward III., Henry VI., and Edward IV. had faith in being able by alchemy to furnish the Mint with cheap gold and silver.

In the reign of Edward III. the masters of the Mint were empowered by letters patent to take goldsmiths, smiths, and others, for the works of the Mint in the Tower; and to imprison any rebellious within the said Tower, until the king should determine their punishment; and this power was not discontinued in the reign of Elizabeth.

Before the Reformation, ecclesiastics were sometimes comptrollers: "Should we," says Latimer, "have ministers of the Church to be comptrollers of the Mint? . . . . I would fain know who comptrolleth the devil at home at his parish, while he comptrolleth the Mint ?" (*Sermon*, 1548.) During the re-casting of the corrupt coin in the reign of Elizabeth, the queen publicly coined at the Tower several pieces with her own hand, and distributed them among her suite.

In 1695, Mr., afterwards Sir Isaac Newton, was appointed warden of the Mint; and in 1699 he was promoted to the mastership, which post he held until his death: his mathematical and chemical knowledge was of great service in this office; he wrote an official report on the coinage, and drew up a table of assays of foreign coins. Newton lived some time in Haydon-square, Minories. In 1851 were sold several Mint *Curiosities*, once possessed by Stanesby Alchorne, king's assaymaster: including the standard troy pound, determined by the Mint officers in 1758; also Crocker's Register-book of Drawings for Medals, certified by officers of the Mint, and containing thirty autographs of Sir Isaac Newton,—purchased by the British Museum.

The establishment formerly consisted of a master and worker, deputy-master, comptroller, king's assay-master, king's clerk, and superintendent of machinery and dies; the master assayer, probationer assayer, weigher and teller, surveyor of meltings, surveyor of money-presses, chief and second engraver, medallist, &c.; besides the company of moneyers, who had coined the public money from a very early period, with exclusive corporate rights. The office of warden was abolished in 1817. A new constitution was introduced in 1815, and was changed in 1851: it is now vested in the master and his deputy, subject to the Treasury. The mastership was formerly a political office: it was last so filled by Richard Lalor Shiel; in 1851 was appointed the present master and worker, Sir John F. W. Herschel, Bart., the astronomer; a worthy successor to the office once filled by the illustrious Newton. The operative branch of the Mint consists of the assayer, the melter, and refiner. The moneyers have been abolished, and Government now coins for the public on its own account, the master being the executive head of the establishment.

The present Mint, upon Little Tower-hill, is a handsome stone structure of mixed Grecian and Roman architecture, commenced by Mr. Johnson, and completed by Sir Robert Smirke, between 1806 and 1811: the cost, including the machinery, was a quarter of a million of money. It was formerly supplied with water through a tunnel from the Tower ditch, and it was one of the earliest public offices lighted with gas. Upon the site was "sometime a monastery, called New Abbey, founded by King Edward III. in 1359" (*Stow*). After the Suppression, was built here the Victualling Office, subsequently tobacco-warehouses.

At the Mint is executed the coinage of the three kingdoms, and of many of our colonies; and such is the completeness of the steam machinery by Boulton and Watt, Maudslay and Co., and John and George Rennie, that fifty thousand pounds worth of gold received one morning in bullion may be returned the next in coin, strangely contrasting with the old method of striking every piece by hand, and carrying on the whole process in a single room. The present stupendous machinery is unequalled in the mint of any other country. The furnaces have long been supplied with smoke-consuming apparatus. The gold and silver being alloyed, are cast into small bars, are passed through powerful rollers, and by the draw-bench brought to the exact thickness required. The circular disks or blanks are then punched out of the sheets of metal by other machines; and are then separately weighed, sounded, have the protecting rim raised, and are blanched and annealed. The blanks are then taken to the coining-room, and placed in the screw-presses, each of which by the same stroke stamps on both sides, and mills at the edge, thus making a perfect coin: each press will coin between four and five thousand pieces per hour, and feeds itself with the blanks. For the dies a matrix is cut by the Mint engraver in soft steel, which being hardened furnishes many dies. .The newly-coined money is now ready for the Trial of the Pix, when one of each coin is placed in a pix or casket, sealed with three seals, and secured with three locks; and the coins are then compared with the trial-plates at Westminster (see page 99) by a jury from the Goldsmiths' Company, the Lord Chancellor, or the Chancellor of the Exchequer, presiding. The early matrices, and the collection of coins and medals, at the Mint, are among its *Curiosities.*

The following are the best Mint engravers from the reign of Charles I. to the present time: Briot, Simon, Rawlins, Roettier (3), Croker or Crocker, Tanner, Dassier, Yeo, Natter, Pingo (2), Pistrucci, and the Wyons (3).

Applications to view the Mint must be made in writing to the Master or Deputy-master; the party of visitors not to exceed six, for whom the applicant is responsible: the order available only for the day specified, and not transferable.

MINT (THE), SOUTHWARK,

A large section of the parish of St. George the Martyr, and so called from "a mint of coinage" having been kept here by Henry VIII. It was originally named Suffolk Manor; and opposite St. George's church, upon the site of the premises of Messrs. Pigeon, the distillers, was Suffolk Place, the magnificent mansion of Charles Brandon, Duke of Suffolk, brother-in-law of Henry VIII. This house the duke gave to the king in exchange for a palace of the Bishop of Norwich in the parish of St. Martin's-in-the-Fields: it was then called Southwark Place and Duke's Place. In the Sutherland View of London, 1543, it is shewn as "ye Mint."

In the fourth year of Edward VI. (1550) Sir Edward Peckham, Knight, was appointed high-treasurer, and Sir John Yorke under-treasurer, of this Mint; and in 1551 were issued crowns, half-crowns, shillings, and sixpences, with the mint-mark Y for Sir John Yorke.

In 1549 Edward VI. came from Hampton Court to visit the Mint, when it was spoken of as "the capital messuage, gardens, and park in Southwark." Southwark had also its Saxon and Norman Mint, A.D. 978 to 1135; and coins of Ethelred II., Canute, Harold, Edward the Confessor, William I. and II., Henry I. and Stephen, with the Southwark mint-mark, are known to collectors. The old Saxon spelling of Southwark was ZVÐLUERE, *Suthgwere;* and on Saxon coins we find it abbreviated ZVÐ, ZVÐL, ZVÐLE, ZVÐLEU. With the reign of Stephen ceased the power of coining money, granted by the Tower Mint to smaller mints near London, as Southwark, Stepney, &c. The site of the original Mint in Southwark is unknown; but it was, probably, within the ancient town of Southwark (now the Guildable Manor), which extended only from St. Mary Overie's Dock, by St. Saviour's Church, to Hays-lane, and southward to the back of the present Town Hall. It is conjectured that the Saxon Mint may have been attached to the original Town Hall, nearly opposite the church of St. Olave; or, the Southwark Mint may have been under the direction of the early bishops of Winchester, at or near their manor of the Clink, and who may have been moneyers here, as well as at the Winchester Mint. Of Henry, Bishop of Winton, and the illegitimate brother of King Stephen, there exists a silver penny (the only specimen known), which was bought at the Pembroke sale for 20l. 10s., and is now in the British Museum. We cannot suppose the original Southwark Mint to have occupied the site of the Mint in St. George's parish, which was not within the ancient town; and was not "the King's Manor" until after Henry VIII. had obtained it from Cranmer, Archbishop of Canterbury.

Queen Mary gave the Mint property to Nicholas Heath, Archbishop of York, in recompense for York House, Whitehall, which had been taken from Cardinal Wolsey by Henry VIII. Archbishop Heath sold the Mint in 1557, when a great number of mean dwellings were erected upon the estate; but the mansion was not entirely taken down, or it must have been rebuilt, before 1637, when Alderman Bromfield, Lord Mayor of London, resided at Suffolk Place, which he possessed until 1650.

The Mint is described by Strype as consisting of several streets and alleys; the chief entrance being from opposite St. George's church by Mint-street, "running into Lombart-street, thence into Suffolk-street, and so into George street;" each entrance having its gate. It became early an asylum for debtors, coiners, and vagabonds; and of the "traitors, felons, fugitives, outlaws, condemned persons, convict persons, felons defamed, those put in exigent of outlawry, felons of themselves, and such as refuse the law of the land," who in the time of Edward VI. herded in St. George's parish. The Mint at length became such a pest, that statutes 8 & 9 William III., and 9 & 11 Geo. I., ordered the abolition of its *privileges*. One of these statutes (9 Geo. I. 1723) relieved all those debtors under 50l. who had taken sanctuary in the Mint from their creditors; and the *Weekly Journal* of Saturday, July 20, 1723, thus describes their exodus:

" On Tuesday last, some thousands of the Minters went out of the land of bondage, alias the Mint, to be cleared at the quarter sessions at Guildford, according to the late act of parliament. The road was covered with them, insomuch that they looked like one of the Jewish tribes going out of Egypt; the cavalcade consisting of caravans, carts, and wagons, besides numbers on horses, asses, and on foot. The drawer of the two fighting-cocks was seen to lead an ass loaded with geneva, to support the spirits of the ladies upon the journey. 'Tis said that several heathen bailiffs lay in ambuscade in ditches upon the road, to surprise some of them, if possible, on their march, if they should straggle from the main body; but they proceeded with so much order and discipline, that they did not lose a man upon this expedition."

The Mint was the retreat of poor poets:

" Then from the Mint walks forth the man of rhyme."—*Pope.*

And one of the offences with which Pope reproached his needy antagonists was their " habitation in the Mint." " Poor Nahum Tate" (once poet laureate) died in the Mint in 1715, where he had sought shelter from his rapacious creditors. The place is a scene of Gay's *Beggar's Opera;* and " Mat of the Mint" figures in Macheath's gang. It was also one of the haunts of Jack Sheppard; and Jonathan Wild kept his horses at the Duke's Head in Red Cross-street, within the precincts of the Mint. Illicit marriages were also performed here, as in the Fleet Prison, May Fair Chapel, &c. Officers of justice sent here to serve processes were commonly pumped upon almost to suffocation, and even thrown into " the Black Ditch" of mud and filth. Here is said to have occurred the first case of Asiatic cholera in London in 1832. Much of the district still consists of streets and alleys, of wretched tenements inhabited by an indigent and profligate population; also " lodgings for travellers:" few of the old houses remain.

MONUMENT (THE),

On the east side of Fish-Street-hill, occupies part of the site of St. Margaret's Church, destroyed in the Great Fire of 1666. It was erected by Sir Christopher Wren, between 1671 and 1677 (pursuant to 19 Charles II. c. 3, s. 29), to commemorate the Great Fire and rebuilding of the City: the expense was about 14,500l., defrayed out of the Orphans' Fund. The Monument is of the Italo-Vitruvian-Doric order, and is of Portland stone, of which it contains 21,126 solid feet. It consists of a pedestal about 21 feet square, with a plinth 27 feet, and a fluted shaft 15 feet at the base; on the abacus is a balcony encompassing a moulded cylinder, which supports a flaming vase of gilt bronze, indicative of its commemoration of the Great Fire; though some repudiating Roman-Catholics assert this termination to be intended for the civic cap of maintenance! Defoe quaintly describes the Monument as "built in the form of a candle," the top making "a handsome gilt flame like that of a candle." Its entire height is 202 feet, stated in one of the inscriptions to be equal to its distance eastward from the house where the fire broke out, at the king's baker's, in Pudding-lane.

On the front of the house, on the east side of Pudding-lane, was a stone with this inscription: "Here, by the Permission of Heaven, Hell broke loose upon this Protestant City, from the malicious Hearts of barbarous Papists, by the Hand of their agent *Hubert*, who confessed, and on the Ruins of this Place declared the Fact, for which he was hanged, viz. That here begun that dreadful Fire which is described and perpetuated on and by the Neighbouring Pillar. Erected Anno 1681, in the Mayoralty of Sir Patience Ward, Kt."—*Hatton*, 1708.

The Monument is loftier than the pillars of Trajan and Antoninus at Rome, or that of Theodosius at Constantinople; and it is not only the loftiest, but also the finest isolated, column in the world. Within is a staircase of 345 black marble steps, opening to the balcony, whence the view of the metropolis, especially of its Port, is very interesting. It was at first used by the members of the Royal Society for astronomical purposes, but was abandoned on account of its vibration being too great for the nicety required in their observations. Hence the report that the Monument is unsafe, which has been revived in our time; "but," says Elmes, "its scientific construction may bid defiance to the attacks of all but earthquakes for centuries to come." Wren proposed a more characteristic pillar, with flames blazing from the loopholes of the shaft, and figured in brass-work gilt; a phœnix was on the top rising from her ashes, in brass-gilt likewise. This, however, was rejected; and Wren then designed a statue of Charles II., 15 feet high;[*] but the king preferred a large ball of metal, gilt; and the present vase of flames, 42 feet high, was adopted: when last triply regilt, it cost 120*l*. On June 15, 1825, the Monument was illuminated with portable gas, in commemoration of the laying of the first stone of London Bridge: a lamp was placed at each of the loopholes of the column, to give the idea of its being wreathed with flame; whilst two other series were placed on the edges of the gallery, to which the public were admitted during the evening. The west face or front of the pedestal is rudely sculptured by Caius Gabriel Cibber, in alto and bas-relief: Charles II., bewigged and be-Romanised, is attended by Liberty, Genius, and Science; in the background are labourers at work and newly-built houses; and at the king's feet is Envy peering from an arched cell, and blowing flames to rekindle the mischief. The scaffolding, ladders, and hodmen are more admired for their fidelity than the monarch and his architect. The north and south sides bear Latin inscriptions by Dr. Thomas Gab, afterwards Dean of York; that on the north recording the desolation of the city; the south its restoration and improvement, and the means employed; while the east is inscribed with the years in which it was begun and finished, and the names of the Lord Mayors during its erec-

* A large print of the Monument represents the statue of Charles so placed, for comparative effect, beside a sectional view of the apex, as constructed. Wren's autograph report on the designs for the summit were added to the MSS. in the British Museum in 1852. A model, scale ⅛ inch to the foot, of the scaffolding used in building the Monument, is preserved. It formerly belonged to Sir William Chambers, and was presented by Heathcote Russell, C.E., to the late Sir Isambart Brunel, who left it to his son, Mr. I. K. Brunel: the ladders were of the rude construction of Wren's time, two uprights, with nailed treads or rounds on the face.

tion. Around the base of the pedestal was also the following inscription, beginning at the west:

(w.) "THIS PILLAR WAS SET VP IN PERFETVALL REMEMBRANCE OF THAT MOST DREADFUL BURNING OF THIS PROTESTANT (S.) CITY, BEGUN AND CARRYED ON BY Yᵉ TREACHERY AND MALICE OF Yᵉ POPISH FACTIO, IN Yᵉ BEGINNING OF SEPTEM IN Yᵉ YEAR OF (E.) OUR LORD 1666, IN ORDER TO Yᵉ CARRYING ON THEIR HORRID PLOTT FOR EXTIRPATING (N.) THE PROTESTANT RELIGION AND OLD ENGLISH LIBERTY, AND THE INTRODUCING POPERY AND SLAVERY."

And the north inscription concluded with:

"SED FUROR PAPISTICUS QVI TAMDIRA PATRAVIT NONDUM RESTINGVITVR."

These offensive legends are not mentioned by Wren, but were added in 1681, by order of the Court of Aldermen, amid the horror of the Papists spread by the Titus Oates plot. They were obliterated in the reign of James II., but recut deeper still in the reign of William III., and excited Pope's indignant couplet:

"Where London's column, pointing at the skies,
Like a tall bully, lifts the head and lies."

The legends were ultimately erased (by an Act of Common Council) Jan. 26, 1831. On the cap of the pedestal, at the angles, are four dragons, the supporters of the City arms: these cost 200*l*., and were the work of Edward Pierce, jun. Six persons have committed suicide by throwing themselves from the Monument gallery: 1. John Cradock, a baker, July 7, 1788; 2. Lyon Levi, a Jew diamond-merchant, Jan. 18, 1810; 3. same year, Leander, a baker; 4. Margaret Moyes, daughter of a baker in Heminge's-row, Sept. 11, 1839; 5. Hawes, a boy, Oct. 18, 1839; 6. Jane Cooper, a servant-girl, Aug. 19, 1842. To prevent similar deaths, the gallery has been encaged with iron-work, as we now see it. William Green, a weaver, is erroneously recorded as a suicide, June 25, 1750; for, in reaching over the railing, to look at a live eagle kept there in a wooden cage, he accidentally lost his balance, and fell over against the top of the pedestal, thence into the street, and was dashed to pieces. The fall is exactly 175 feet. In 1732, a sailor slid down a rope from the gallery to the Three-Tuns Tavern, Gracechurch-street; as did also, next day, a waterman's boy. In the *Times* newspaper of August 22, 1827, there appeared the following burlesque advertisement:

"Incredible as it may appear, a person will attend at the Monument, and will, for the sum of 2500*l*., undertake to JUMP clear off the said Monument, and in coming down will drink some beer and eat a cake, act some trades, shorten and make sail, and bring ship safe to anchor. As soon as the sum stated is collected, the performance will take place; and if not performed, the money subscribed to be returned to the subscribers."

Admittance to the gallery of the Monument from 9 till dusk; charge reduced, in 1851, from 6*d*. to 3*d*. each person. In the reign of George I. the charge was 2*d*.

MOORFIELDS

is first mentioned by Fitzstephen (*temp*. Henry II.) as "the great fen or moor which watereth the walls of the City on the north side," and stretched "from the wall betwixt Bishopsgate and Cripplesgate to Fensbury and to Holywell" (*Stow*). When the moor was frozen, Fitzstephen tells us the young Londoners, by placing the leg-bones of animals under their feet, and tying them round their ankles, by aid of an iron-shod pole, pushed themselves with great velocity along the ice; and one of these *bone-skates*, found in digging Moorfields, is in the Museum of Mr. C. Roach Smith, F.S.A., 5 Liverpool-street. In the reign of Edward II., Moorfields was let for four marks a-year; in 1415,

the Mayor made a breach in the wall, and built the Moorgate pos
tern. Bricks are stated to have been made here, before any othe
part of London, in the 17th Edward IV., for repairing the City wal
between Aldgate and Aldersgate; when "Moorfields was searched fo
clay, and bricks were made and burnt there." Facing the wall was
black ditch; hence "the melancholy of Moorditch." (Shakspeare, Henr
IV. Part I.) In 1497, the gardens in Moorfields were made plain; th
Moor was drained in 1527, and laid out in walks and planted in 1606.

In a blind alley about Moorfields met the *Calves'-Head Club*, where an ax
hung up in the Club-room, and was reverenced as a principal symbol in this dia
bolical sacrament. Their great Feast of Calves' heads was held the 30th of Janu
ary (the anniversary of the martyrdom of King Charles I.), the Club being erecte
"by an impudent set of people, in derision of the day, and defiance of monarchy.'
Their bill of fare was a large dish of calves' heads, dressed several ways; a larg
pike, with a small one in his mouth, as an emblem of tyranny; and a large cod'
head, to represent the person of the king (Charles I.) singly, as by the calve'
heads before they had done him together with all them that suffered in his cause
and a boar's head, with an apple in its mouth, to represent the king by this a
bestial, as by the others they had done foolish and tyrannical. After the repas
the *Eikon Basilike* was burnt, anthems were sung, and the oath was sworn upon
Milton's *Defensio Populi Anglicani*. The company consisted of Independent
and Anabaptists; Jerry White, formerly chaplain to Oliver Cromwell, said grace
and the table-cloth being removed, the Anniversary Anthem, as they impiously
called it, was sung, and a calf's skull filled with wine or other liquor, and then
brimmer went about to the pious memory of those worthy patriots that had kille
the tyrant, &c. (See the *Secret History of the Calves'-Head Club*, 6th edit. 1706.)

Evelyn, recording the Great Fire of 1666, says the houseless peopl
took refuge about Moorfields, under tents and miserable huts an
hovels; and Pepys found Moorfields full of people, and "poor wretche
carrying their goods there;" next year the fields were built upo
and paved. On the south side was erected Bethlehem Hospital i
1675-6 (see page 42), which has disappeared in our time, with the lon
line of furniture-dealers' shops from the north side.

> "Through fam'd Moorfields extends a spacious seat,
> Where mortals of exalted wit retreat;
> Where, wrapp'd in contemplation and in straw,
> The wiser few from the mad world withdraw."
> *Gay to Mr. Thomas Snow, Goldsmith, near Temple Bar.*

Under Bethlehem wall, in 1753-4, Elizabeth Canning, by her own tes
timony, was seized, robbed, and gagged; thence dragged to Mother
Wells's at Enfield Wash, and there nearly starved to death.

The Moor reached from London Wall to Hoxton; and a thousand
cartloads of human bones brought from St. Paul's charnel-house in
1549, and soon after covered with street-dirt, became so elevated, that
three windmills were built upon it. (Aggas's plan shews three windmills on the site of Finsbury-square: hence Windmill hill, now street.
The ground on the south side being also much raised, it was named
Upper Moorfields. On the north of the fields stood the Dogge-house,
where the Lord Mayor's hounds were kept by the Common Hunt:
hence "Dog-house Bar," City-road. Eastward the Moor was bounded
by the ancient hospital and priory of Bethlehem, separated by a deep
ditch, now covered by Blomfield-street. The lower part of the fields
was paled into four squares, each planted with elm-trees, round a grass-
plat, and intersected by broad gravel-walks; a favourite promenade in
evenings and fine weather, and called "the City Mall;" where beaux
wore their hats diagonally over their left or right eye, hence called "the
Moorfields cock." Here was the Foundry at which, previous to the
year 1706, the brass ordnance for the British Government was cast.
Near the Foundry Whitefield built his Tabernacle (see page 176).

Moorfields was, till near Pennant's time, the haunt of low gamblers, the great gymnasium of our capital, the resort of wrestlers, boxers, and football-players. Here mountebanks erected their stages, and dispensed infallible medicines to the gaping gulls. Here, too, field-preachers set up their itinerant pulpits, beneath the shade of the trees; and here the pious, well-meaning Whitefield preached so winningly, as to gain from a neighbouring charlatan the greater number of his admirers.

Moorgate was erected opposite Albion Chapel, at the south west angle of the fields, and was rebuilt in 1672; the central gateway higher than usual, for the City Trained Bands to march through it with their pikes erected. The fields are now covered by Finsbury-square and Circus, and adjoining streets: the name survives in "Little Moorfields."

In Finsbury-place was " the Temple of the Muses," built by James Lackington, the celebrated bookseller, who came to London in 1773 with only half-a-crown in his pocket. In 1792 he cleared 5000l. by his business; and in 1798 retired with a large fortune, amassed by dealing in old books, and reprinting them at a cheap rate. He was succeeded by his cousin George Lackington, Allen, Hughes, Mavor (a son of the Rev. Dr. Mavor), Harding, and Co. ; and next by Jones and Co., the publishers of *London in the Nineteenth Century.* Lackington's " Temple," which was a vast building, was destroyed by fire in 1841.

MUSEUM, THE BRITISH,

Great Russell-street, Bloomsbury, occupies the site of Montague House, built for Ralph Montague, first Baron Montague, of Boughton, by Robert Hooke, the celebrated mathematician and horologist. Evelyn describes it, in 1679, as " Mr. Mountague's new palace neere Bloomsbery, built somewhat after the French pavilion way," with ceilings painted by Verrio. On Jan. 19, 1686, it was burnt to the ground, through the carelessness of a servant " airing some goods by the fire ;" the house being at the time let by Lord Montague to the Earl of Devonshire. Lady Rachel Russell, in one of her letters, describes the sparks and flames covering Southampton House and filling the court. The loss is stated at 40,000l., besides 6000l. in plate ; and Lord Devonshire's pictures, hangings, and furniture. The mansion was rebuilt upon the foundations and burnt walls of the former one, the architect being Peter Puget. La Fosse painted the ceilings, Rousseau the landscapes and architecture, and Jean Baptiste Monoyer the flowers. Lord Montague, who in 1705 was created Marquis of Monthermer and Duke of Montague, died here in 1709; his son resided here until his mansion was completed at Whitehall. Montague House was built on the plan of a first-class French hotel, of red brick, with stone dressings, lofty domed centre, and pavilion-like wings. In front was a spacious court, inclosed with a high wall, within which was an Ionic colonnade, the principal entrance being in the centre, by the " Montague Great Gate," beneath a picturesque octangular lantern, with clock and cupola; and at each extremity of the wall was a square lantern. The old mansion was removed between 1845 and 1852, when portions of the painted walls and ceilings, La Fosse's deities, and Baptiste's flowers, were preserved.

Montague House and gardens occupied seven acres. In the latter, in 1780, were encamped the troops stationed to quell the Gordon riots ; and a print of that period shews the gardens in the rear of the mansion, laid out in grass terraces, flower-borders, grass-plots, and gravel-walks, where the gay world resorted on a summer's evening: the back being open to the fields, extending west to Lisson-green and Paddington; north to Primrose Hill, Chalk Farm, Hampstead, and Highgate; and east to Battlebridge, Islington, St. Pancras, &c. On the side of the garden next Bedford-square was a fine grove of elm-trees; and the gardens of Bedford House, in Bloomsbury-square, reached to those of the British Museum, before that house was taken down, and Russell-square and the adjacent streets were built on its site. (See FIELD OF FORTY FOOTSTEPS, page 291.)

The *British Museum* has been the growth of a century, between the

, first purchase for the collection in 1753, and the near completion of the new buildings in 1853. The Museum originated in a suggestion in the will of Sir Hans Sloane (d. 1753), offering his collection to parliament for 20,000*l.*, it having cost him 50,000*l.* The offer was accepted; and by an Act (26th George II.) were purchased all Sir Hans Sloane's "library of books, drawings, manuscripts, prints, medals, seals, cameos and intaglios, precious stones, agates, jaspers, vessels of agate and jasper, crystals, mathematical instruments, pictures," &c. By the same Act was bought, for 10,000*l.*, the Harleian Library of Mss. (about 7600 volumes of rolls, charters, &c.); to which were added the Cottonian Library of Mss., and the library of Major Arthur Edwards. (See LIBRARIES, page 460) By the same Act also was raised by lottery 100,000*l.*, out of which the Sloane and Harleian collections were paid for; 10,250*l.* to Lord Halifax for Montague House, and 12,873*l.* for its repairs; a fund being set apart for the payment of taxes and salaries of officers. Trustees were elected from persons of rank, station, and literary attainments; and the institution was named the BRITISH MUSEUM. There had also been offered Buckingham House, with the gardens and field, for 30,000*l.*; and at one time it was proposed to deposit the Museum in Old Palace-yard, in the place designed by Kent for new Houses of Parliament. To Montague House were removed the Harleian collection of Mss. in 1755; other collections in 1756; and the Museum was opened to the public January 15, 1759.

The new Museum, courtyard, and grounds, occupy seven acres. The buildings were commenced in 1823 from the designs of Sir Robert Smirke, R.A., succeeded in 1846 by his brother Mr. Sydney Smirke, A.R.A.; old Montague House being removed piecemeal as the new buildings progressed, so that the Museum was not closed for the re-building. The plan consists of a courtyard, flanked east and west with the official apartments. The main buildings form a quadrangle, inclosing the ground of the gardens of Montague House; and with its Ionic porticoes and stately windows, having a solemn air in the midst of the busy hive of London. The architecture throughout the exterior is Grecian-Ionic. The southern façade consists of the great entrance portico, eight columns in width, and two intercolumniations in projection; on either side is an advancing wing: entire front 370 feet, surrounded by a colonnade of 44 columns, 5 feet at their lower diameter, and 45 feet high; height of colonnade from the pavement 64½ feet. At the foot of the portico are 12 stone steps, 120 feet in width, terminating with pedestals for colossal groups of sculpture. "Since the days of Trajan or Hadrian, no such stones have been used as those recently employed at the British Museum, where 800 stones, from 5 to 9 tons weight, form the front. Even St. Paul's contains no approach to these magnitudes." (*Prof. Cockerell's Lectures*, 1850.) The tympanum of the pediment is enriched with a group allegorical of the "Progress of Civilisation," and thus described by the sculptor, Sir Richard Westmacott, R.A.:

"Commencing at the western end or angle of the pediment, Man is represented emerging from a rude savage state through the influence of Religion. He is next personified as a hunter and tiller of the earth, and labouring for his subsistence. Patriarchal simplicity then becomes invaded, and the worship of the true God defiled. Paganism prevails, and becomes diffused by means of the Arts. The worship of the heavenly bodies, and their supposed influence, led the Egyptians, Chaldeans, and other nations to study astronomy, typified by the centre statue—the key-stone to the composition. Civilisation is now presumed to have made considerable progress. Descending towards the eastern angle of the pediment is Mathematics, in allusion to Science being now pursued on known sound principles. The Drama, Poetry, and Music balance the group of the Fine Arts on the western side, the whole composition terminating with Natural History, in which such objects or specimens only are represented as could be made most effective in sculpture." The crocodile is emblematic of the cruelty of man in savage life, the tortoise of his slow progress to civilisation. The figure of Astronomy is 12 feet high, and weighs between 7 and 8 tons. The several figures are executed in Portland-stone, and the decorative accessories are gilt.

The ornamental gates and railing inclosing the courtyard were commenced in model by Lovati, who died before he had made much progress; they were completed by Mr. Thomas and Messrs. Collmann and Davis. The railing—spears painted dark copper, with the heads gilt, and with an ornamented band—is raised upon a granite curb. In the centre of the railing is a grand set of carriage-gates and foot-entrances, strengthened by fluted columns with composite capitals, richly gilt, surmounted by vases. The frieze is wholly of hammered iron : the remainder of the iron-work is cast from metal moulds, and was chiefly piece-moulded, in order to obtain relief. The carriage-gates are moved by a windlass, both sides opening simultaneously. Each half of these gates weighs upwards of five tons. The height of the iron-work is 9 feet to the top rail : the length of the whole palisade is about 800 feet. The metal-work was contracted for by Walker, of York, and cost nearly 8000l. Upon the granite gate-piers are to be placed sitting statues of Bacon and Newton, and upon the two end piers Milton and Shakspeare; the four statues by Sir Richard Westmacott, R.A. The buildings have cost upwards of 800,000l.

As you stand beneath the portico, the effect is truly majestic, and you are impressed with the feeling that this is a noble institution of a great country. The principal entrance is by a carved oak door, 9 feet 6 inches in width, and 24 feet in height. The hall is Grecian-Doric. The ceiling, trabeated and deeply coffered, is enriched with Greek frets and other ornaments in various colours, painted in encaustic. Here are three marble statues: the Hon. Mrs. Damer, holding a small figure of the Genius of the Thames; Shakspeare, by Roubiliac; and Sir Joseph Banks, Bart., by Chantrey. The statue of Shakspeare was bequeathed by Garrick to the Museum after the death of his widow; the statue of Sir Joseph Banks was presented by his personal friends.

East of the hall is the Manuscripts Department; west, the principal staircase (with carved vases of Huddlestone stone), and a gallery which forms the approach to the Collection of Antiquities.

At the top of this staircase commence the Natural History Rooms, which occupy the upper eastern portion of the south front, and the whole of the eastern and northern sides of the quadrangle. In the remainder of the upper floor are the smaller Egyptian Antiquities; Greek Vases and Bronzes; the Ethnographical Collection; and the Coins and Medals.

On the lower floor, the eastern portion of the south front, and part of the east wing, is the Library of Manuscripts. The remainder of the east side, and the whole of the northern side of the quadrangle, are occupied by the Printed Books.

In the ground-floor of all the buildings to the west of the quadrangle are the more massive Egyptian Antiquities; the Greek and Roman Marbles, including the Towneley, Elgin, and Phigaleian; the Assyrian Sculptures; the Lycian Antiquities; and the Canning Marbles.

In the basement of the north-west corner is the general Collection of Insects; and in the apartments above are Prints and Drawings.

All that we shall attempt here will be to describe the leading *Curiosities* of the several collections.

ZOOLOGICAL COLLECTIONS, only second to that in the Museum at Paris, are contained in three galleries : the beasts, birds, reptiles, and fishes, in the wall-cases; shells, corals, sea-eggs, star-fish, crustacea, and insects, in the table-cases.

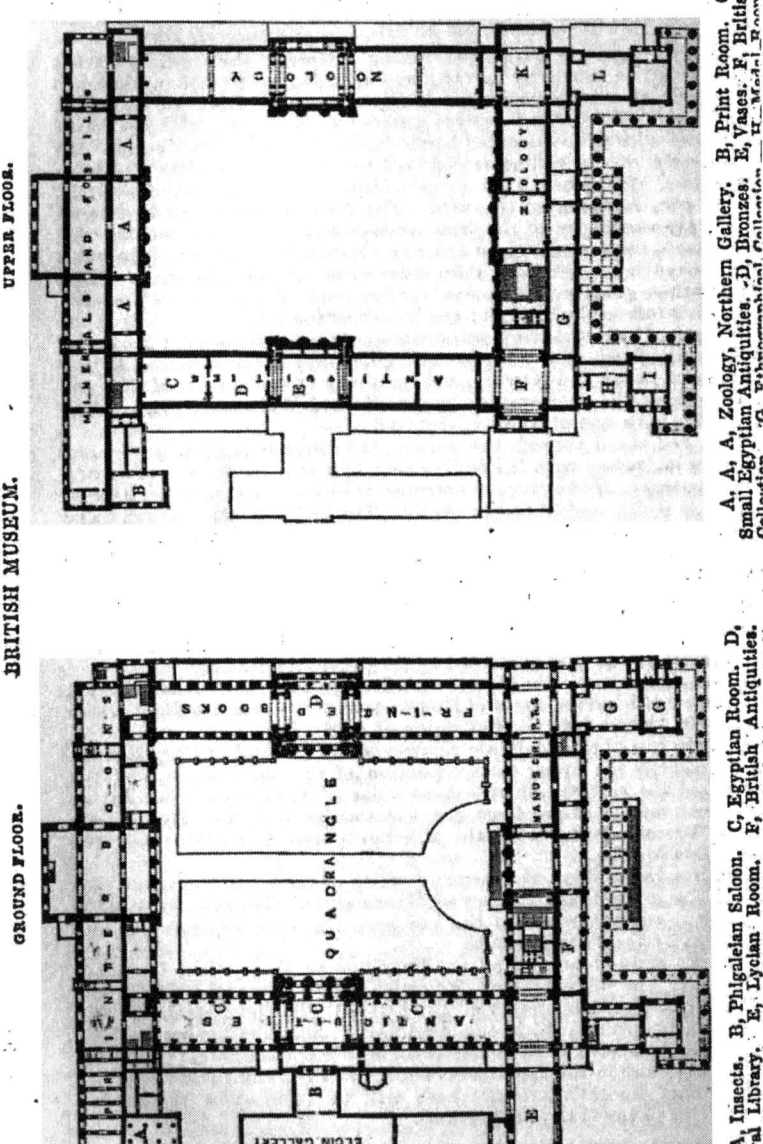

BRITISH MUSEUM.

UPPER FLOOR.

GROUND FLOOR.

A, A, A, Zoology, Northern Gallery. B, Print Room. C, Small Egyptian Antiquities. D, Bronzes. E, Vases. F, British Collection. G, Ethnographical Collection. H, Model Room. ...

A, Insects. B, Phigaleian Saloon. C, Egyptian Room. D, Royal Library. E, Lycian Room. F, British Antiquities.

Central Saloon—Antelopes, goats, and sheep; horns of oxen; on the floor are giraffes from North and South Africa, the African rhinoceros, Manilla buffalo, and the walrus.

Southern Zoological Gallery—Oxen, deer, camels, llamas, horses, swine, armadillos, manises, and sloths; horns of antelopes; elephants, rhinoceroses, hippopotami, and wild oxen. The aurochs, or shaggy-maned Lithuanian bison, presented by the Emperor of Russia, is said to be the finest specimen of stuffing in the Museum. Above the bison of the prairies is the ornithorhyncus, with a bird-like bill,—the water-mole of Australia.

Mammalia Saloon—Old World monkeys, including the chimpanzee, closely resembling man; New World monkeys, including the howlers; lemurs; feræ, a black leopard, which killed its keeper; the bear tribe; a Mexican lapdog, very minute; marsupials, or pouched animals, from Australia; cete, or whale-like animals. Corals in the table-cases; above are the sword-fish, sturgeon, and conger.

Eastern Zoological Gallery, 300 feet long and 50 feet wide, contains a magnificent collection of stuffed birds in the wall-cases, and their eggs in table-cases; horns of deer, and a fine collection of shells. Here is a Reeves's Chinese pheasant (tail-feathers 5 ft. 6 in. long); and next the ostriches are a Dutch painting of the extinct dodo, a foot of the bird supposed to be more than two and a half centuries old, and a cast of the head; also, a specimen of the rare apteryx, or wingless bird of New Zealand.

Above the wall-cases are 116 portraits of sovereigns, statesmen, heroes, travellers, and men of science,—a few from the Sloanean and Cottonian collections: including two portraits of Oliver Cromwell (one a copy from an original possessed by a great-grandson of Cromwell; the other an original presented by Cromwell himself to Nath. Rich, a colonel in the parliamentary army, and bequeathed to the Museum, in 1784, by Sir Robert Rich, Bart.); three portraits of Mary Queen of Scots; Richard II., Edward III., Henry V., Edward VI., Queen Elizabeth, James I., Charles I. and II., &c.; three portraits of Sir Hans Sloane; Peter I. of Russia, Stanislaus Augustus I. of Poland, Charles XII. of Sweden, and Louis XIV. of France; Lord Bacon; the poets Pope and Prior; Dr. John Ray, the first great English naturalist; George Buchanan, 1581, on panel; Sir Francis Drake and Captain Dampier; Martin Luther, 1546, on panel; Guttenberg, the inventor of printing; Richard Baxter, the Nonconformist; Vesalius, by Sir Antonio More; Mary Davis, 1688, "ætatis 74," with a horn-like wen on her head; Sir Robert Cotton, Dr. Birch, Humphrey Wanley, Sir H. Spelman, and Sir H. Dugdale; Camden, on panel; Thomas Britton, the musical small-coal-man; Andrew Marvell, said to be the only portrait extant of him; &c. This is, probably, the largest collection of portraits in the kingdom: many are ill-painted, others very curious, and some unique; the majority of them had long lain in the lumber-lofts of the old Museum, when they were hung up, chiefly at the suggestion of the late Mr. William Smith, print-collector, of Lisle-street. A very interesting *catalogue raisonnée* of these pictures appeared in the *Times*, Nov. 27 and Dec. 8, 1838.

Northern Zoological Gallery contains five rooms. 1. Bats, and nests of birds and insects; annulose animals; and shells. 2. Lizards, snakes and serpents, tortoises and turtles, crocodiles and amphisbænas, batrachian animals, sea-eggs, star-fish, &c. 3. The British zoological collection. 4. Exotic bony fish, insects, and crustacea (to be seen every Tuesday and Friday): here are the praying-mantis, walking-leaf, and a Brazilian wasp's-nest. 5. Sharks, torpedoes, rays, sponges, &c. The Collection of Insects is as extensive as the entomological collection at Paris. Over the wall-cases are the Herschel pike-fish, from the Cape of Good Hope; the sudia, from Berbice; and the bony pike, from North America.

MINERALOGY AND GEOLOGY.—*North Gallery*—General collection of *Minerals* (mostly on Berzelius's system), in four rooms: mass of meteoric iron (1400lbs.) from Buenos Ayres; native silver from Konsberg; trunk of a tree converted into semi-opal; large mass of Websterite from Newhaven; tortoise sculptured in nephrite, or jade, from the banks of the Jumna; Esquimaux knife and harpoon, of meteoric iron; a large collection of meteoric stones chronologically arranged. Here, also, are diamonds of various forms, and models of celebrated diamonds. The collection is superior to any in Europe, and includes a splendid cabinet of minerals from the Harz Mountains, formerly preserved in the Observatory at Richmond.

Fossils, in six rooms: 1. Vegetables; ferns and palmæ, fossil wood and sandstone, with supposed footmarks of animals when the stone was in a semi-fluid state. 2. The megatherium from Buenos Ayres, gigantic tortoise, and bones of extinct dinornis. 3. Frog, tortoise, and crocodile fossils: gigantic salamander, mistaken for a human skeleton; remains of iguanodon, 70 feet long, from Tilgate Forest, Sussex; of the hylæosaurus, or wealden lizard; and the plesiosaurus. 4. Large specimens of ichthyosaurus; hyena remains from the Torquay and Kirkdale caverns; phlascotherium Bucklandi, from the great oolite, Stonesfield, Oxon. 5. Fossil fishes, arranged after Agassiz; skull of the sivatherium; teeth of rhinoceros, found in Essex; complete skeleton of the large extinct Irish elk. 6. Remains of dinotherium (18 feet high), mastodon, and elephant; cast of the skeleton of the megatherium Americanum, found in Buenos Ayres; fossil human skeleton from Guadaloupe, &c. In Saurian Fossils the Museum is eminently rich; as well as in gigantic osseous remains, and impressions of vegetables, fruit, and fish.

THE BOTANICAL OR BANKSIAN DEPARTMENT contains the Herbaria of Sir Hans Sloane (336 volumes bound in 262); the Herbaria of Plukenet and Petiver; collections from those of Merret, Cunningham, Hermann, Bobart, Bernard de Jussieu, Tournefort, Scheuchzer, Kamel, Vaillant, Kœmpfer, Catesby, Houston, and Boerhaave; the plants presented to the Royal Society by the Company of Apothecaries from 1722 to 1796, as rent paid by the Company for the Botanic Garden at Chelsea. Also the Herbarium of the Baron de Moll; the Herbarium of Sir Joseph Banks, mostly in cabinets, nearly 30,000 species, including Sir Joseph's collections upon his voyage with Captain Cook, and the plants collected in subsequent voyages of discovery; Loureiro's plants from Cochin China; an extensive series presented by the East India Company; Egyptian plants, presented by Wilkinson, &c. The flowers and fruits preserved in spirits, and the dried seeds and fruits, are fine.

GALLERY OF ANTIQUITIES.—*Assyrian Sculptures,* collected by Layard: fragments of the disinterred Assyrian palaces of Nimroud (Nineveh) and Kouyunjik; cuneiform (arrow-headed) and other writing; gypsum or alabaster bas-reliefs that lined the interior walls; detached sculptures; ivories and other ornaments; winged lions, weighing 15 tons each; winged bulls, each 14 feet high; sculptured slabs of battle-pieces and sieges, combats, treaties and triumphs, lion and bull hunts, armies crossing rivers; winged and eagle-headed human figures; religious ceremonies; sculptured obelisks; inscription on a bull, connecting the Assyrian dynasty of Sennacherib with Hezekiah of the Bible; fragments of a temple built by Sardanapalus; and a basalt Assyrian statue, closely resembling the Egyptian style; costumes, field-sports, and domestic life of 2000 years since. Here also are a few stones with cuneiform inscriptions, excavated by Mr. Rich from the presumed site of Nineveh, near Mosul; but previous to Mr. Layard's researches, " a case scarcely three feet square enclosed all that remained not only of the great city Nineveh, but of Babylon itself!" (See Layard's *Nineveh and its Remains, Monuments, &c.*)

Phigaleian Saloon—Bas-reliefs of the battle of the Centaurs and Lapithæ, and the combat of the Greeks and Amazons, from among the ruins of the Temple of Apollo Epicurius, near Phigaleia; built by Ictinus, contemporary with Phidias, and architect of the Parthenon, (*Pausanias*). Their historical value, representing the art of the Praxitelian period, is scarcely less than that of the Parthenon marbles. In two model pediments from the eastern and western ends of the Temple of Jupiter Parhellenius, in the island of Ægina, are, west, 10 original statues, representing Greeks and Trojans contesting for the body of Patroclus; east, 5 figures, expedition of Hercules and Telamon against Troy, these statues being the only illustration extant of the armour of the heroic ages. In this saloon, also, are the *Canning Marbles*, or *Bodroum Sculptures*, from Bodroum, in Asia Minor, the site of Halicarnassus; 11 bas-reliefs (combat of Amazons and Greek warriors), formerly part of the celebrated Mausoleum erected in honour of Mausolus, King of Caria, by his wife Artemisia, B.C. 353: it was one of the Seven Wonders of the World. These, and other sculptures from Bodroum, were presented by the Sultan to Sir Stratford Canning (whence their name), and by him to the British Museum.

British and Anglo-Roman Remains—Tesselated pavements, Roman altars, sarcophagi, Roman pigs of lead; tesselated pavements from the Bank of England and Threadneedle-street and other parts; Roman mill fragments from Trinity-House-square, and a sarcophagus from Haydon-square.

Greek and Roman Sculptures—Statues and bas-reliefs by Greek artists, or from Greek originals; busts of mythological, poetical, and historical personages; statues and busts of Roman emperors; architectural and decorative sculptures and bas-reliefs; sepulchral monuments, Etruscan, Greek, and Roman; Roman altars; pavement from Carthage; bas-relief of Jupiter and Leda; the group of Mithra; the Rondini Fawn; torso of Venus, from Richmond House; bas-relief of the Apotheosis of Homer, cost 1000*l.*; Persepolitan marbles, presented by Sir Gore Ouseley and the Earl of Aberdeen; a Venus of the Capitol; and other high-class marbles from the collections of Sir W. Hamilton, R. Payne Knight, and Edmund Burke, including, from the latter, the copy of the Cupid of Praxiteles, presented by the painter Barry to Burke. Here also are a sarcophagus from Sidon, sculptured with combats of Greeks, Amazons, and Centaurs; and a magnificent marble tazza 4 feet 3½ inches high, and 3 feet 7 inches diameter.

The Towneley Collection of bas-reliefs, vases, statues and groups, heads and busts, includes 88 terra-cottas: the famed Discobulus, or Quoit-thrower, in marble, from the bronze of the sculptor Myron; Venus, or Dione, the finest Greek statue seen by Canova in England; Venus Victrix, of the highest style of art; busts of Pallas, Hercules, Minerva, and Homer; bust of "Clytie rising from a sunflower;" and busts of Greek poets and philosophers. The Bacchus is finest—so beautiful, self-possessed, and severe; Bacchus, the mighty conqueror of India—not a drunken boy—but the *power*, not the *victim* of wine.

These stores of Greek and Roman art were collected by Mr. Charles Towneley, chiefly at Rome, between 1765 and 1772; and were arranged by him at No. 7 Park-street, Westminster, with accompaniments so classically correct, that the house resembled the interior of a Roman villa. The dining-room had walls of scagliola porphyry; and here were placed the largest and most valuable statues, lighted by lamps almost to animation. Mr. Towneley died in 1805; and his collection of marbles and terra-cottas was purchased by the British Museum for

20,000*l.*, and first exhibited in a gallery built for their reception in 1808. Mr. Towneley's bronzes, coins, gems, drawings, &c., chiefly illustrating the sculptures, were subsequently purchased by the Museum for 8200*l.* A bust of Mr. Towneley, by Nollekens, is placed near the entrance to the Central Saloon.

Elgin Saloon.—The Elgin marbles, brought from the Parthenon at Athens by the Earl of Elgin: some are the work of Phidias himself. (See in this room two models of the Parthenon, each 12 feet long, made by R. C. Lucas, described in *Remarks on the Parthenon* by R. C. Lucas, Sculptor; Salisbury, 1844: 1. The temple after the bombardment in 1687; 2. The Parthenon restored.) The Metopes from the Frieze (15 originals and 1 cast), representing the battle of the Centaurs and Lapithæ, in alto-relievo: for the original the English government agent bid 1000*l.* at the sale of the collection of the Count de Choiseul Gouffier; but he was outbid by the Director of the French Museum, where the metope now is. The Panathenaic Frieze, 524 feet in length, is probably the largest piece of sculpture ever attempted in Greece: its men, women, and children, in all costumes and attitudes; horsemen, charioteers; oxen and other victims for sacrifice; images of the gods; sacred flagons, baskets, &c.—have an astonishing air of reality. Of the 110 horses, no two are in the same attitude: "they appear," says Flaxman, "to live and move; to roll their eyes, to gallop, prance, and curvet; the veins of their faces and legs seem distended with circulation." Here are about 326 feet of the Frieze; 76 feet casts, and about 250 feet of the genuine marble which Phidias put up.

"The British Museum," says Professor Welcker, "possesses in the works of Phidias a treasure with which nothing can be compared in the whole range of ancient art." Flaxman said that these sculptures were 'as perfect representations of nature as it is possible to put into the compass of the marble in which they are executed—and nature, too, in its most beautiful form.' Chantrey spoke enthusiastically of 'the exquisite judgment with which the artists of these sculptures had modified the style of working the marble, according to the kind and degree of light which would fall on them when in their places.' Lawrence said that, 'after looking at the finest sculptures in Italy, he found the Elgin marbles superior to any of them.' Canova said, in reply to an application made to him respecting their repair or restoration, that 'it would be sacrilege in him or any man, to presume to touch them with a chisel.'"

Pedimental sculptures, placed upon raised stages: East, the birth of Minerva; Hyperion, and heads of two of his horses; Theseus, ideal beauty of the first order, the finest figure in the collection, of which more drawings have been made than all the other Athenian marbles put together: "the back of the Theseus is the finest thing in the world." Head of a horse from the chariot of Night, valued at 250*l.*, the finest possible workmanship. West pediment: Contest between Athena and Poseidon for the naming of Athens; the recumbent statue of the river god Ilissus, pronounced by Canova and Visconti equal to the Theseus; torso, supposed of Cecrops, grand in outline; fragment of the head and statue of Minerva. Also, a capital and part of a shaft of a Doric column of the Parthenon; piece of the ceiling, and Ionic shaft, from the Temple of Erechtheus at Athens; imperfect statue of a youth; piece of a frieze from the tomb of Agamemnon, exceedingly ancient; circular altars from Delos; bronze sepulchral urn, very richly wrought; casts from the Temples of Theseus, the best preserved of all the ancient Athenian monuments; the Wingless Victory and the Choragic monument of Lysicrates; from the Choragic monument of Thrasyllus, a colossal statue of Bacchus, inferior only to the Phidian sculptures; Eros (Cupid), discovered by Lord Elgin within the Acropolis (headless), has in the limbs the grace and elegance of the age of Praxiteles; the Sigean inscription, most ancient Grecian, in the *Boustrophedon* style: *i. e.* the lines read as an ox passes from one furrow to another.

To Haydon must be conceded the genius of instantly appreciating the beauty of the Elgin Marbles; yet they were utterly neglected until Canova, on seeing them, declared, "Sans doute, la vérité est telle, les accidents de la chair et les formes sont si vraies et si belles, que ces statues produiront un grand changement dans les arts. Ils renverseront le système mathématique des autres antiques." Haydon soon roused the public interest in the sculptures, and they were purchased by Parliament for 35,000*l.* "You have saved the marbles," Lawrence said to Haydon, "but it will ruin you."—Haydon's *Autobiography*, 1853.

Tuesdays and Thursdays in every week, and the whole month of September in every year (when daylight is usually the steadiest and strongest), are exclusively devoted to artists and students in the Elgin and Towneley Galleries.

Lycian Saloon — Reliefs, tombs, and sarcophagi discovered and brought to England by Sir Charles Fellows, principally from the ruins of Xanthus, S. W. Asia Minor; dating from the earliest Greek period to that of the Byzantine empire, and earlier than the Parthenon. Model of the Harpy Tomb, with its actual white marble reliefs, presumed to represent the daughters of Pandarus carried off by Harpies: the tomb itself was a square shaft, 80 tons weight. Model of an Ionic peristyle building, with 14 columns and statues; the friezes representing the conquest of Lycia by the Persians, and the siege of Xanthus. Tomb of Paiafa: roof resembling an inverted boat, and an early Gothic arch; the sides sculptured with combats of warriors on horseback and foot; a chariot, sphinxes, &c. Casts from the sculptured Rock-tomb at Myra, with bilingual (Greek and Lycian) inscription.

British and Mediæval Room, containing antiquities found in Great Britain and Ireland, and extending from the earliest period to the Norman Conquest; also, Mediæval objects, English and foreign; including

Celts; stone knives, arrow-heads, and hammers; models of Celtic cromlechs, or sepulchres; paintings of Plas Newydd and Stonehenge; bronze celts, swords, daggers, spear-heads, helmet, and buckler; half-baked pottery from British barrows; fragments of Roman buildings; Kimmeridge coal-money; a Coway stake from the Thames; Roman service of plate; Roman glass; Saxon brooches. *Mediæval*: personal ornaments and weapons; ivory chessmen and draughtsmen; paintings from St. Stephen's Chapel, Westminster; Dr. Dee's crystal ball and wax cakes; and (from Strawberry Hill) the Show-stone (cannel coal) into which Dee "used to call his spirits." Here also are tenure and state swords; Limoges enamels; Venetian glass; Alhambra tiles; Bow porcelain; Wedgwood copy of the Portland Vase, and two superb Chelsea porcelain vases, valued at 300 guineas, presented by Wedgwood.

Egyptian Galleries.—On the west side of the Museum the Egyptian Sculptures (from Thebes, Karnac, Luxor, and Memphis, and 800 in number) are placed in chronological order, from north to south: in the vestibule, early period; northern gallery, 18th dynasty; central saloon, monuments of Rameses II.; and in the southern gallery, those posterior to that monarch, descending to the latest times of the Roman empire. The Egyptian, Assyrian, and Greek Antiquities are thus exhibited in three parallel lines; a fourth, or transverse line, along the southern extremity of the others, being appropriated to Roman remains. Among the sculptures from Egypt are, the celebrated head of Memnon, from Thebes, of first-class Egyptian art. The head and arm of a king, a statue originally 26 feet high. Amenoph III. seated on his throne—the great Memnon in miniature. Two colossal red granite lions, couchant, from Upper Nubia; fine specimens of early Egyptian art in animal forms. Breccia sarcophagus, supposed tomb of Alexander the Great, carved with 21,700 characters. The Rosetta Stone, black basalt, the most valuable existing relic of Egyptian history, inscribed in hieroglyphics, the ancient spoken language of Egypt, and in Greek, with the services of Ptolemy V. Epiphanes; the deciphering of which has afforded a key to Champollion, Wilkinson, &c. The Tablet of Abydos, giving a chronological succession of the monarchy. Sepulchral tablets and fragments of tombs; Egyptian frescoes, painted perhaps 3000 years ago, yet fresh in colour. Arragonite vases from the fourth dynasty. Plaster casts taken in Egypt, and coloured after the originals.

Egyptian Rooms (two), upstairs, contain divinities, and royal personages, and sacred animals; sepulchral remains; and miscellaneous objects, specially illustrative of the domestic manners of the Egyptians: mostly from the collections of Salt, Sams, and Wilkinson. Here are mummies and mummy-cases, wooden figures from tombs, bronze offerings, and porcelain figures; painted, gilt, stone, bronze, silver, and porcelain deities; figures of the jackal, hippopotamus, baboon, lion, cat, ram, &c.; a coffin and body from the third pyramid; model of an Egyptian house, granary, and yard; furniture, as tables, stools, chairs, and head-rests, couches and pillows, keys, locks, hinges, bolts, and handles; from the toilet, the black wig and box, caps, aprons, tunics, sandals, shoes, combs, pins, studs, and cases for eye-lid paint; vases and lamps, bowls and cups, agricultural implements, warlike weapons, writing and painting implements, working tools, and weaving looms, toys, and musical instruments. A stand, with a cooked duck and bread-cakes, from a tomb; sepulchral tablets, scarabæi, and amulets; rings, necklaces, and bracelets, and mummy ornaments. Above the wall-cases are casts of battle-scenes, triumphs, and court ceremonies, coloured after the originals, from temples in Nubia.

Bronze Room—Figures of divinities, furniture, mirrors, tripods, candelabra, lamps and vases, armour, personal ornaments, &c.; including copper-bronze lions, bronze remains of a throne, fragments of glass vessels and of armour, discovered by Mr. Layard in Assyria. A large collection of bronze objects from Greece Proper, from Rome and of the Roman period; and from the sepulchres of ancient Etruria, and the excavations at Pompeii and Herculaneum. These include fragments of statues; spear-heads, daggers, helmets, and Roman eagles; steelyards, amphoræ, and tripods; candelabra, vases, votive figures, and statuettes; mirrors and their cases; the exquisite 798 bronzes bequeathed by R. Payne Knight; and the celebrated bronzes of Siris, from the south of Italy. Miscellaneous Greek and Roman objects, including astragali of crystal, cornelian, and ivory; dice, anciently loaded; tickets for the games; hair-pins and ivory busts; ancient glass vases and pateræ; fragments of cornelian, onyx, and jasper cups, and a crystal vessel holding gold; animals in bronze; styli for writing; keys, plates, enamel-work; Etruscan and Roman fibulæ and finger-rings. Above the wall-cases are fac-simile paintings of Games, from tombs at Vida.

Vase Rooms (two) contain Etruscan and Græco-Italian vases, painted from the myths or popular poetry of the day: classified into Early Italian, Black Etruscan, and Red Etruscan ware; varnished ware, mostly early; Italian vases, of Archaic Greek style; vases of Transition style, finest Greek, and the Basilicata and latest period. (*Vaux's Handbook*.) Here are the ancient fictile vases purchased of Sir William Hamilton in 1772; and then the largest collection known.

The Hamilton Vase, on being examined in 1839 by M. Gerhard, was found to bear the name of each personage depicted on it; from which it appears that the myth, or story, is totally distinct from that assigned to it by M. D'Haaearville, in his schedules of the Vases of the Hamilton collection; thus overturning his theory, and reading a strange lesson to virtuosi and antiquaries.

Here also are Greek and Roman terra-cottas, of various epochs and styles. Above the wall-cases are painted fac-similes, by Campanari, of entertainments from Etruscan tombs.

The Barberini or Portland Vase, the property of the Duke of Portland, has been deposited in the Museum since 1810.

The Portland Vase was found about 1560, in a sarcophagus in a sepulchre under the Monte del Grano, 2½ miles from Rome. It was deposited in the palace of the Barberini family until 1770, when it was purchased by Byres, the antiquary; and sold by him to Sir William Hamilton, of whom it was bought, for 1800 guineas, by the Duchess of Portland, at the sale of whose property it was bought in by the family for 1029*l.* The vase is 9¾ inches high and 7¼ inches in diameter, and has two handles. It is of glass; yet Breval considered it calcedony; Bartoli, sardonyx; Count Tetzi, amethyst; and De la Chausse, agate. It is ornamented with white opaque figures upon a dark-blue semi-transparent ground; the whole having been originally covered with white enamel, out of which the figures have been cut, like a cameo. The glass foot is distinct, and is thought to have been cemented on after bones or ashes had been placed in the vase. The seven figures, each 5 inches high, are said by some to illustrate the fable of Thaddeus and Theseus; by Bertoli, Proserpine and Pluto; by Winckelmann, the nuptials of Thetis and Peleus; Darwin, an allegory of Life and Immortality; others, Orpheus and Eurydice; Fosbroke, a marriage, death, and second marriage; Tetzi, the birth of Alexander Severus, whose cinerary urn the vase is thought to be; while Mr. Windus, F.S.A., in a work published 1845, considers the scene as a love-sick lady consulting Galen. The vase was engraved by Cipriani and Bartolozzi in 1786; copies of it were executed by Wedgwood, and sold at 50 guineas each, the model for which cost 500 guineas: there is a copy in the British and Mediæval Room.

The Portland Vase was exhibited in a small room of the old Museum buildings until Feb. 7, 1845, when it was wantonly dashed to pieces with a stone by one William Lloyd; but the pieces being gathered up, the Vase has been restored by Mr. Doubleday so beautifully, that a blemish can scarcely be detected. The Vase is now kept in the Medal Room. A drawing of the fractured pieces is preserved.

The Ethnographical Room contains objects illustrating the religion, arts, and industry of various countries: including the model of a movable Indian temple; a Chinese bell, captured from a Buddhist temple near Ningpo in 1844; model of Nelson's ship, the Victory, and a piece of its actual timber with a 40lb. shot in it from the battle of Trafalgar; a plaster cast of the Shield of Achilles, modelled by Flaxman from the 17th book of Homer's *Iliad;* a colossal gilt figure of the Burmese idol Gaudma; Chinese figures of deities, beggars, mandarins, and trinkets; Hindoo deities, measures, vessels, and arms; Chinese and Japanese matchlocks, bows and arrows, shoes, mirrors, screens, and musical instruments; richly-decorated cloth from Central Africa; a Foulah cloak from Sierra Leone; an Ashantee loom, umbrellas, tobacco-pipes, flyflappers, and sandals; terra-cotta Mexican figures (mostly from Bullock's Museum); Aztec vases, idols, and armaments; Peruvian mummies and silver images; musical instruments, weapons, tools, ornaments, and costumes, from Guiana, the Marquesas and Sandwich Islands, Tahiti and the Friendly Isles, New Zealand and Australia, Borneo, New Guinea, the Pelew Islands, Siam, &c.; and a tortoise-shell bonnet from the Navigators' Islands.

The Medal Room contains a collection of Coins and Medals superior to that of Vienna and Florence, if not Paris. The nucleus of the British Museum collection was Sir Hans Sloane's coins, worth 7000*l.* as bullion, to which were added Sir Robert Cotton's coins; 6000 medals from the Hamilton collection; the Cracherode coins and medals, valued at 6000*l.*; coins from the Conquest to George III. (Roberts's), purchased for 4000 guineas; a series of Papal medals, and a collection of Greek coins; the Towneley Greek and Roman coins; a vast collection of foreign coins, presented by Miss Banks; Payne Knight's Greek coins; Rich's early Arabian, Parthian, and Sassanian coins; medals and coins attached to the library of George III.; Marsden's Oriental coins; Burnes's Bactrian coins; and contributions and purchases of *finds* of Anglo-Saxon, Anglo-Gallic, and early English coins. The collection is arranged in, 1. Ancient coins—Greek in geographical order, and Roman chronologically. 2. Modern coins—Anglo-Saxon, English, Anglo-Gallic, Scotch, and Irish, and the coins of foreign nations, arranged according to countries: the Anglo-Saxon and English series is complete from Ethelbert I. Of Queen Anne's farthings here are seven varieties, one only of which circulated, the others being pattern-pieces.* 3. Medals, including an almost perfect series of British medals, besides the Papal and Napoleonic medals. Here is kept a gold snuff-box set with diamonds, and a miniature portrait of Napoleon, who presented it to the late Hon. Mrs. Damer, by whom it was bequeathed to the Museum, on condition that the portrait should never be copied. Also a gold snuff-box with a cameo lid, presented by Pope Pius VI. to Napoleon, and by him bequeathed to Lady Holland, with a card in Napoleon's handwriting. Here are the engraved gems, antique pastes and glass, and gold trinkets, including the breastplate of a British chieftain.

LIBRARIES.—The Royal Library and general collection of Printed Books occupy the east and north sides of the ground-floor of the Museum buildings. The *King's Library*, collected by George III., and presented to the nation in 1823 by George IV., is deposited in a magnificent hall 300 feet long and 65 feet wide in the centre, where are four Corinthian columns of polished Peterhead granite 25 feet high, with Derbyshire alabaster capitals: the door-cases are marble, and the doors oak inlaid with bronze. This library, the finest and most complete ever formed by a single individual, is exceedingly rich in early editions of the classics, books from Caxton's press, history of the states of Europe in their respective languages, in Transactions of Academies, and grand geographical collection,—80,000 volumes, exclusive of pamphlets: among the Jesuits' books, purchased in 1768, was the Florence Homer of 1488. Here is one of the most extensive and interesting collections of maps in Europe. The collection cost 130,000*l.*; catalogue, 5 vols. folio.

The Grenville Library, 20,240 volumes, cost 54,000*l.*, was bequeathed to the Museum by the Right Hon. Thomas Grenville, whose bust is placed here. Among its rarities are a Mazarine Latin Bible on vellum, the earliest printed Bible, and the earliest printed book known (supposed Gutenberg and Fust, Mentz, 1455); also the first Psalter, the first book with a date, and earliest printed in colours.

The General Library, 510,110 volumes (July 1853), ranks with the public libraries of Vienna and Berlin, and is inferior only to those of Munich and Paris. The collection occupies twelve or thirteen rooms, and, with the manuscripts and charters, fills upwards of thirteen miles of shelves. Among the rarities is Coverdale's Bible, 1535, the first complete edition of the Scriptures in English; "The Game and Playe of the Chesse," the first book printed in English, from Caxton's press, 1474; the first edition of Chaucer's "Tales of Canterburye," only two perfect copies known, &c.; pamphlets and periodicals of the Civil Wars of Charles I.; the musical libraries of Sir John Hawkins and Dr. Burney; Garrick's old Plays; Tracts of the Revolutionary History of France. Books of Divinity are bound in blue, History in red, Poetry in yellow, and Biography in olive-coloured, leather. The catalogues of the several collections are in themselves a library, of 632 volumes. The catalogue, 7 vols. 1813-19, has been expanded, by interleaving and ma-

---

* The real Queen Anne's Farthing, with the figure of Britannia on the reverse, and below it, in the exergue, the date 1714, brings from 7*s.* to a guinea; but at Baron Bolland's sale, in 1841, a pattern piece fetched 9*l. 9s.* The idea that there is but one Queen Anne's farthing in existence, and that only three were struck, is a popular error, several hundreds having been struck. This erroneous belief has caused the British Museum authorities almost as many annoyances as the rarity of a "tortoise-shell tom-cat."

nuscript entries, into 67 folio volumes. About 2000*l.* is expended annually in adding old and foreign works to the library; and, under the Copyright Act, 5 and 6 Vic. cap. 48, a copy of every book, pamphlet, sheet of letterpress, sheet of music, chart, or plan, published within her Majesty's dominions, must be delivered to the British Museum.

The Newspapers are the largest collection in England. It was commenced by Sir Hans Sloane; and to it, in 1813, was added Dr. Burney's collection, purchased for 1000*l.*; since which the Commissioners of Stamps have transferred to the Museum copies of all the stamped newspapers. The oldest in the collection is a Venetian Gazette of the year 1570. Dr. Birch's Historical Collections, No. 4106, contain "The English Mercurie" of July 23, 1588, long believed "the earliest English newspaper," now proved to be a forgery. In Dr. Burney's library is "Newes out of Holland," May 16, 1619, the earliest newspaper printed in England; and "The News of the Present Week," the first weekly newspaper.

The Reading Room (two of the largest apartments of the library of printed books) contains mostly dictionaries, magazines, encyclopedias, topographical works, and other books of reference: entrance from Montague-place.

The Reading Room is open every day, except on Sundays, on Ash Wednesdays, Good Fridays, Christmas-day, and on any Fast or Thanksgiving days ordered by authority; except also between the 1st and 7th of May, the 1st and 7th of September, and the 1st and 7th of January, inclusive. The hours are from 9 till 7 during May, June, July, and August (except on Saturdays, at 5), and from 9 till 4 during the rest of the year. To obtain admission, persons are to send their applications in writing, specifying their Christian and surnames, rank or profession, and places of abode, to the principal Librarian; or, in his absence, to the Secretary; or, in his absence, to the senior under-librarian; who will either immediately admit such persons, or lay their applications before the next meeting of the Trustees. Every person applying is to produce a recommendation satisfactory to a Trustee or an officer of the establishment. Applications defective in this respect will not be attended to. Permission will in general be granted for six months, and at the expiration of this term fresh application is to be made for a renewal. The tickets given to readers are not transferable, and no person can be admitted without a ticket. Persons under 18 years of age are not admissible.

The Reader having ascertained from the Catalogue the book he requires, transcribes literally into a printed form the press-mark, title of the work wanted, size, place, and date, and signs the same. Readers, before leaving the room, are to return the books or Mss. they have received to an attendant, and are to obtain the corresponding ticket, the reader being responsible for such books or Mss. so long as the ticket remains uncancelled. Readers are allowed to make one or more extracts from any printed book or Ms.; but no whole or greater part of a Ms. is to be transcribed without a particular permission from the Trustees. The transcribers are not to lay the papers on which they write on any part of the book or Ms. they are using, nor are any tracings allowed without special leave of the Trustees. No person is, on any pretence whatever, to write on any part of a printed book or Ms. belonging to the Museum.

The persons whose recommendations are accepted are Peers of the realm, Members of Parliament, Judges, Queen's Counsel, Masters in Chancery or any of the great law-officers of the Crown, any one of the 48 Trustees of the British Museum, the Lord Mayor and Aldermen of London, rectors of parishes in the metropolis, principals or heads of colleges, eminent physicians and surgeons, and Royal Academicians, or any gentleman in superior post to an ordinary clerk in any of the public offices.

MANUSCRIPTS ROOM.—The Manuscripts are mostly bound in volumes, and deposited in cases round the room, but some are kept in table-cases; and each collection is catalogued. The *Cottonian Collection* is especially rich in historical documents from the Saxons to James I.; registries of English monasteries; the charters of the Saxon Edgar and King Henry I. to Hyde Abbey, near Winchester, written in golden letters; and "the Durham Book," a copy of the Gospels in Latin, written about 800, splendidly illuminated in the style of the Anglo-Saxons by the monks of Lindisfarne, and believed once to have belonged to the Venerable Bede. The collection is rich also in royal and other original letters. (See LIBRARIES, page 460.) *The Harleian Collection* abounds in geographical and heraldic Mss.; in visitations of counties, and English topography; legal and parliamentary proceedings; abbey registers; Mss. of the classics, including one of the earliest known of the *Odyssey* of Homer; in missals, antiphonaries, and other service-books of the Romish Church; and in old English poetry. Also two very early copies of the Latin Gospels, written in golden letters; splendidly illuminated Mss.; an extensive mass of Correspondence; nearly 300 Bibles and biblical books, in the Chaldaic, Hebrew, Greek, Arabic, and Latin, in manuscript; nearly 200 volumes of the writings of the Fathers of the Church; and works on the arts and sciences. Here is the oldest specimen of a Miracle-Play in English, of the earlier part of the reign of Edward III. *The Sloanean Collection* consists chiefly of Mss. on natural history, voyages, travels, and the arts, and also on medicine. It comprises the chief of Kœmpfer's Mss., with the voluminous medical collection of Sir Theodore Mayerne, and the annals of his practice at the Court of England from 1611 to 1649; also scientific and medical Correspondence, and historical Mss. The drawings of animals are beautifully rich and accurate: two volumes on vellum, by Madame Merian, contain the insects of Surinam. *The Royal Mss.* contain the collection by our kings, from Richard II. to George II.; including the *Codex Alexandrinus*, in 4 quarto volumes of fine vellum, written, probably, between A.D. 300 and A.D. 500, and presumed to be the most ancient Mss. of the Greek Bible now extant in uncial character: it was a present from Cyril, patriarch of Constantinople, to King Charles I. This and other Mss. came into the royal possession at the destruction of the monasteries. Old scholastic divinity abounds in the collection; and many of the volumes are superbly illuminated in a succession of periods to the 16th century. Here also are several of the domestic music-books of Henry VIII.; and the *Basilicon Doron* of James I. in his own handwriting. *The Lansdowne Collection*, purchased in 1807 for 4925l., consists of the Burghley and Cæsar papers; the Mss. of Bishop Kennett; numerous valuable historical documents; and about 200 Chinese drawings. Here are Hardyng's Chronicle, presented by the chronicler to King Henry VI.; a copy of the very rare French version of the Bible, upon vellum, translated by Raoul de Prede for Charles V. of France; also five volumes of Saxon homilies, transcribed by Mr. Elstob and his sister; and a fac-simile of the Vatican *Virgil*, made by Bartoli in 1642. *The Hargreave Mss.*, added in 1813, contain, besides early Law Reports, an abridgment of equity practice, in 45 volumes, by Sir Thomas Sewell, Master of the Rolls. *The Burney Mss.*, collected by the Rev. Charles Burney, and purchased in 1818, consist chiefly of the Greek and Latin classics, including the Towneley *Homer*, a Ms. of the *Iliad* similar to that of the *Odyssey* in the Harleian collection (cost 600 guineas); also two early Mss. of Greek rhetoricians; a volume of the mathematical tracts of Pappus; and a magnificent Greek Ms. of Ptolemy's Geography, enriched with maps of the 15th century. The *Oriental Mss.* include the valuable collection made by Mr. Rich while consul at Bagdad, and comprising several Syriac copies of the Scriptures; also Arabic and Peruvian Mss. of great value, bequeathed by Mr. J. F. Hull in 1827. Here also are *Mss. of French History and Literature*, bequeathed by the Earl of Bridgewater in 1829. *The Howard-Arundel Mss.*, acquired from the Royal Society in 1831, more than 500 volumes in every branch of learning.

The Ancient Rolls and Charters of the Museum, many thousands in number, partly from the Cottonian, Harleian, and Sloanean collections, illustrative of English history, monastic and other property, are separately catalogued.

Magna Charta, if not the original, a copy made when King John's seal was affixed to it, was acquired by the British Museum with the Cottonian Library. It was nearly destroyed in the fire at Westminster in 1731; the parchment is much shrivelled and mutilated, and the seal is reduced to an almost shapeless mass of wax. The Ms. was carefully lined and mounted; and in 1733 an excellent *fac-simile* of it was published by John Pine, surrounded by inaccurate representations of the armorial ensigns of the 25 barons appointed as securities for the due performance of Magna Charta. An impression of this *fac-simile,* printed on vellum, with the arms carved and gilded, is placed opposite the Cottonian original of the Great Charter, which is now secured under glass. It is about 2 feet square, is written in Latin, and is quite illegible. It is traditionally stated to have been bought for fourpence, by Sir Robert Cotton, of a tailor, who was about to cut up the parchment into measures! But this anecdote, if true, may refer to another copy of the Charter preserved at the British Museum, in a portfolio of royal and ecclesiastical instruments, marked Augustus II. art. 106.; and the original Charter is believed to have been presented to Sir Robert Cotton by Sir Edward Dering, Lieut.-Governor of Dover Castle; and to be that referred to in a letter dated May 10, 1630, extant in the Museum Library, in the volume of Correspondence, Julius C. III. fol. 191.

The Commissioners on the Public Records regarded the original of Magna Charta preserved at Lincoln to be of superior authority to either of those in the British Museum, on account of several words and sentences being inserted in the body of that Charter, which in the latter are added at the foot, with reference-marks to the four places where they were to be added. These notes, however, possibly may prove that one of the Museum Charters was really the first written, to which those important additions were made immediately previous to the sealing on Runnemede, and therefore the actual original whence the more perfect transcripts were taken.—Richard Thomson, Author of *An Historical Essay on the Magna Charta of King John, &c.* 1829.

In the Museum, also, is the original Bull, in Latin, of Pope Innocent III. receiving the kingdoms of England and Ireland under his protection, and granting them in fee to King John and his successors, dated 1214, and reciting King John's charter of fealty to the Church of Rome, dated 1213. Also, the original Bull, in Latin, of Pope Leo X. conferring the title of Defender of the Faith upon Henry VIII.

The Donation Manuscripts include Madox's collection for his *History of the Exchequer;* Rymer's materials for his *Fœdera,* used and unused; the historical and biographical Mss. of Dr. Birch; the Decisions of the Judges upon the Claims after the Great Fire of London in 1666; also Sir William Musgrave's *Obituary;* Cole's collection for a history of Cambridge and Cambridgeshire, and an Athenæ Cantabrigienses: besides many Coptic and other ancient Mss. taken from the French in Egypt; Ducarel's abstract of the Archiepiscopal Registers at Lambeth Palace; and a long series of calendars of the original rolls from the 1st of Henry VIII. to the 2d of James I. Also Linacre's translation of Galen's *Methodus Medendi,* on spotless vellum; the presentation copies of Henry VIII. and Cardinal Wolsey: the former illuminated with the Royal arms, the latter with the Cardinal's hat.

Here is the Bible written by Alcuin for Charlemagne, large folio, 449 leaves of vellum, said to have occupied 20 years in transcribing, and illuminated. Psalters of Henry VI. and Henry VIII.; and Prayer-books of Lady Jane Grey and Queen Elizabeth. The Breviary of Isabella of Castile, 1496-97; a profusely adorned specimen of Flemish and Spanish art. The Bedford Missal, a Book of Hours, written and sumptuously illuminated in France for the Regent, John Duke of Bedford, and his Duchess, Anne of Burgundy, between 1423 and 1430. Ms. of Valerius Maximus, splendidly illuminated. Original Letters of all the great Reformers; the English Kings; and Poets and Philosophers. The Ms. of "paper-sparing" Pope's *Homer*, written on the backs and covers of letters. Three original assignments: Milton's *Paradise Lost* to Symmons; Dryden's *Virgil* to Tonson; and Goldsmith's *History of Em'nent Persons* to Dodsley. Selections from the Rupert and Fairfax correspondence, 1640-49, including letters of Charles I., Charles II., Fairfax, and Hyde (Lord Clarendon). The original marriage-contract of Charles I. when Prince of Wales. The pocket-book taken from the Duke of Monmouth after the battle of Sedgmoor, certified in the handwriting of James II.

Papyri.—In the Egyptian Room is a framed specimen of this style of writing; and among the. Mss. is a Greek papyrus, probably of B.C. 135, containing the translation of a deed of sale; and a book of sheets of papyrus sewn together, brought from Egypt, and bearing a copy in Greek of part of the Psalms of David. Several Egyptian papyri, written in the hieroglyphical, hieratical, enchorial, or demotic character, framed and glazed, are arranged in the passage leading to the Print Room.

THE PRINT ROOM has only been an independent department since 1837. In 1836 was purchased from the Messrs. Smith, the Dutch and Flemish portions of Mr. Sheepshanks's collection for 5000*l.* Valuable additions have since been made, and the Print Room now contains the most perfect collection known of the works of the Engravers of the early Italian, German, Dutch, and Flemish Schools. Among the *Curiosities* are, in the *Early Italian School,* an engraved silver plate (a Roman Catholic Pax), by Maso Finiguerra, 3½ inches high by 2½ inches wide, sold in 1824 for 300 guineas. An impression in sulphur, a similar subject, the first step in the discovery of this branch of printing, cost 250 guineas. Another similar subject, printed on paper, probably the earliest exemplar known, cost 300 guineas. Specimens of this description are much more numerous in the British Museum than in all other collections combined. *Early German School:* works of F. Van Bocholt (1466), Martin Schoengauer, Israel Van Meeken, Albert Durer (a beautiful series, including some unfinished plates), Lucas Van Leyden, &c. *Dutch and Flemish Schools:* works of Rembrandt, worth probably from 15,000*l.* to 20,000*l.*; the large portrait of the Dutch writing-master Coppenal is valued at 500 guineas. *French School:* an admirable series of etchings by the hand of Claude. *English School:* works of Sir Robert Strange and Woollett; prints after the pictures of Sir Joshua Reynolds, West, and Sir Thomas Lawrence; 4000 prints after Stothard.

The Print Room also contains an excellent representative series illustrative of Mezzotint Engraving: specimens by the inventor, Count Siegen, and by its earliest practisers, Prince Rupert, the Canon Fustenberg, &c., are remarkably fine and numerous. Also, an extensive series of British Portraits and British Topography. Some thousand drawings and prints collected and bequeathed by Mr. Crowle, cost upwards of 7000*l.*, including some of Turner's earliest drawings. *Original Drawings* by Raphael, Albert Durer, Holbein, Rembrandt, Vandyke; and some beautiful designs by Claude, a portion of his *Liber Veritatis.* Here are the finest specimens in the world of Ostade and Backhuysen; cost 200 guineas each. In an adjoining room is a small selection of the most capital drawings, framed and glazed. In the Print Room, also, is a carving in hone-stone (Birth of John the Baptist) by Albert Durer, dated 1510, a wonderful cutting in high relief, which cost 500 guineas; also, a beautifully chased silver Cup, attributed to Benvenuto Cellini. The whole contents of the Print Room are worth considerably more than 100,000*l.* They can only be seen by very few persons at a time, and by particular permission.

The first Keeper of the Prints was Mr. Alexander, so well known for his Views and Costumes of China. He was succeeded by Mr. J. T. Smith, the eminent topographer, and author of the amusing *Life and Times of Nollekens.* Mr. Young Ottley, the eminent collector, and author of the *Early History of Engraving,* was his successor; and he was followed by Mr. Henry Jozi, to whose energy a large amount of the present prosperity of this department is due. On his decease in 1845, the post was given to Mr. Carpenter, F.S.A., the present Keeper, to whose attainments and kindness all visitors to the Print Room will bear ample testimony.

Here are a few small portraits: viz. Geoffrey Chaucer, 1400, a small whole-length on panel; a limning of Frederic III. of Saxony, by L. Cranach; Molière; Corneille; and an unknown head by Dobson, all on panel; with the portrait of a Pope or Cardinal.

The public are admitted to the collections of Zoology, Minerals, and Antiquities on Mondays, Wednesdays, and Fridays, between the hours of 10 and 4 during November, December, January, and February; from 10 till 5 during September, October, March, and April; and from 10 till 6 from the 7th of May to the 1st of September.

The Museum is closed from the 1st to the 7th of January, the 1st to the 7th of May, and the 1st to the 7th of September inclusive; on Ash-Wednesday, Good Friday, and Christmas-day; and also on any special fast or thanksgiving days.

A list of Descriptive Catalogues, &c. published by the British Museum is appended to the Synopsis; with a list of the prices of casts from ancient marbles, bronzes, &c. in the Museum.

A list of objects added to the several collections in each year is printed in the Parliamentary Return, usually in April or May.

MUSEUMS.

ADELAIDE GALLERY OF PRACTICAL SCIENCE (the), Agar-street, Strand, was built by Jacob Perkins, the engineer, and opened by a Society in 1832, for the exhibition of Models of Inventions, works of Art, and specimens of Novel Manufacture. Here, in a canal, 70 feet long, and containing 6000 gallons of water, were shewn steamboat models, with clock-work machinery; experimental steam-paddles; lighthouse models, &c. Next were exhibited the combustion of the hardest steel; the compression of water; a mouse in a diving-bell; steam sugar-mill and gas-cooking apparatus; a model of the Liverpool and Manchester Railway; electro-magnets; a mechanical trumpet; a magic bust; models, from the Temples of Egypt to the Thames Tunnel; looms at work; mummy-cloth 2000 years old; and Carey's Oxy-hydrogen Microscope, shewn on a disc 17 feet diameter; automatic ship and sea, &c.

Here *Perkins's Steam-gun* was exhibited, propelling balls with four times greater force than that of gunpowder, the steam being raised to from 300 to 500 lbs. to the square inch; and the balls, on reaching the cast-iron target, fired at a distance of 100 feet, were reduced to the substance of tin-foil. It was possible to propel 420 balls in a minute, or 25,200 balls in an hour; and the gun was promised to mow down a regiment in less than ten minutes! The Duke of Wellington predicted its failure in warfare.

A living Electrical Eel (Gymnotus) was brought here from South America in 1838; its length was 40 inches, and it resembled in appearance dark puce and brown plush. Professor Faraday obtained from it a most intense electric spark; and by one shock not only was the needle of a galvanometer deflected, but chemical action and magnetic induction were obtained. The eel died March 14, 1842.

In 1776, a living Gymnotus was exhibited in London, 5*s.* each visitor.

ANATOMICAL MUSEUMS, mostly from the Continent, are often exhibited in London; of which Dr. Kahn's collection, shewn at the Portland

M M

Gallery in 1853, may be taken as a specimen. It was arranged in three apartments, one exclusively for medical and scientific men. The other rooms contained physiological subjects, beginning with the development of the human form, and shewing the growth of the bones, the process of dentition, &c. The five senses were delineated by dissections; comparative anatomy in specimens of brain, human and animal; the temperaments were exhibited by heads moulded and coloured, so as to represent the sanguineous, phlegmatic, bilious, &c. A long range of heads exhibited all the known varieties of countenance and frontal development of the different races of humanity. Here were also microscopic specimens of embryology; diseases of distortion and of anomalous growth represented,—the most remarkable being that of Madame Dimanche, who, at the age of 80, had a horn 10 inches long extracted from her forehead, and lived seven years after.

ANTIQUARIES, SOCIETY'S MUSEUM, Somerset House, contains Egyptian, Greek, and Etruscan antiquities; Roman antiquities, mostly found in Britain; British and Anglo-Roman remains; hair of Edward IV., and fragment of his queen's (Elizabeth) coffin; dagger, &c. found near the site of Sir W. Walworth's residence; stone-shot from the Tower moat; brass-gilt spur from Towton battle-field; reputed sword of Cromwell; Bohemian astronomical clock, 1525; presumed Caxton woodcut-block; matrices of medieval seals; decorative tiles found in London; coins, medals, and provincial tokens; Worcester Clothiers' Company's pall, and human skin from the doors of Worcester Cathedral; West Indian antiquities and curiosities; geological specimens (elephant's fossil teeth from Pall Mall); Porter's map of London (Charles I.).

Among the old pictures are, a "Greek Paynting on wood;" portraits of Henry V., Edward IV., Henry VII.; folding picture of Preaching at Paul's Cross, and Procession of James I., 1616; the Fire of London, from near the Temple; 26 ancient pictures (Kerrick's); portraits of Edward IV., Richard III., Henry VI. VII. and VIII., Mary I., &c. Drawings of ancient mural paintings in St. Stephen's Chapel, Westminster (see Catalogue, by A. Way, F.S.A.); portraits of distinguished Antiquaries; the very curious prescriptions ordered for Charles II. on his deathbed, signed by 16 doctors (*Medicorum Chorus*), the names, according to court etiquette, being written at full-length, and not, as ordinarily indicated, by initials only. Among "the Milton Papers" preserved here is the signature of John Bunyan to a memorial to Cromwell and the Council of the Army, dated 1658; a collection of Antiquities from Ithaca; and a valuable Regulator, presented by B. L. Vulliamy, and made by his great-grandfather and grandfather, the former clockmaker to King George II.

The Society of Antiquaries was founded in 1707, by Wanley, Bagford, and others, at the Bear Tavern, Strand; removed to the Young Devil Tavern, Fleet-street; and next to the Fountain, where their plan was drawn out by Humphrey Wanley; refounded 1717; removed successively to Gray's Inn; the Temple; the Mitre, Fleet-street; and their house, Chancery-lane, whence they removed to apartments in Somerset Place, granted them by George III., 1781. The Society's gilt-iron mace was presented by Vertue, 1735-6. Charter granted by George II. 1751. The College of Antiquaries, founded in 1572, by Archbishop Parker and Sir Robert Cotton, was dissolved by James I. in 1604.

ANTIQUITIES, LONDON, 5 Liverpool-street, City.—This extensive collection of Roman and Mediæval relics has been made, within the last fifteen years, by Mr. C. Roach Smith, F.S.A. It consists chiefly of objects illustrative of the domestic and social life and customs of the inhabitants of London in the time of the Romans and during the middle ages. In the first of these divisions are a bronze shield and weapons from the Thames; remarkably fine bronze statuettes of Apollo and Mercury; a bronze hand of colossal size; a pair of forceps elaborately decorated with busts of gods and goddesses, and with heads of animals; an extensive series of fictile vessels, among which are embossed red bowls and vases of great beauty and rarity; wall-paintings from houses, and tiles for conducting the heated air to the apartments; flat glass, such as the Romans, or their predecessors, used for windows; also other Roman glass. Some of the tiles used in the buildings are stamped PR. BRIT. LON., and are remarkable as presenting, perhaps, the earliest example extant of an abbreviation of the word Londinium, now London. The leather sandals are rare and curious specimens of Roman costume. Steel styli for writing, personal ornaments, and many examples of coloured and ornamented glass, are also worthy of reference; while the coins, chiefly from the Thames, include rare types. Of the later antiquities, the Saxon knives, swords, and spears present some uncommon examples. There is also a rival to the celebrated Alfred Jewel in the Ashmolean Museum at Oxford, in an ouche, or brooch, of gold filagree-work, set with pearls and enclosing a portrait of a regal personage. or possibly a saint, exquisitely worked in opaque, coloured, vitreous pastes. This valuable relic, and some Norman bowls in bronze, preserved in this collection, have been engraved in the *Archæologia.* Bone skates curiously illustrate Fitzstephen's account of an old City pastime, as practised on the ice on the site of Moorfields; and the *cuir bouilli,* or stamped leather, shows how artistically this useful material was worked in the middle ages. The shoes of the time of Edward III. and Richard II. are elegant in their ornamentation; and one is covered with mottoes in Latin and in Norman French, and with designs of groups of figures. The Pilgrims' Signs, in lead, form an almost unique series, illustrative of an old religious observance; and there are some fine early leaden Tokens of London tradesmen. A few of the objects have been engraved in the *Collectanea Antiqua;* and an illustrated Catalogue of the whole has been printed. Mr. Roach Smith grants full and free access to his collections, under the easy condition of appointment.

The Private Museum of Mr. W. Chaffers, F.S.A., 20 Old Bond-street, contains more than 1000 specimens discovered in London excavations. Here is a bronze archer with silver eyes, found in Queen-street, Cheapside, in 1842, and described in the *Archæologia,* vol. xxx. pp. 543-4. In this collection, also, are Roman amphoræ; funeral urns and bones; vases and Samian drinking-cups, with Roman designs; Roman tiles and pavement, and frescoes; fibulæ, rings, pins, beads, and buckles; strigils, spoons, keys, spear-heads; bronze Penates; terra-cotta lamps; Roman glass, and Saxon and early English drinking-vessels; coins, medals, &c. (See also Mr. SAULL's MUSEUM, page 542.)

ARCHÆOLOGICAL ASSOCIATION AND INSTITUTE. (See page 18.) Neither of these Societies possesses a Museum of noteworthy specimens. The Institute has presented its principal articles to the British Museum, for the room of British Antiquities. Each Society, however, assembles a Museum from the city or town wherein is held its annual meeting.

At the Rooms of the Archæological Institute, 26 Suffolk-street, in 1853, was exhibited the *Fejeveray Museum,* illustrative of the history of Art, and consisting of Egyptian remains, purely artistic; Etruscan remains, principally in bronze; engraved gems; Egyptian, Assyrian, Babylonian, ancient Persian, Etruscan, Greek, and Roman remains. The collection comprises also a noble set of Majolica ware, twenty-five pieces in number, two painted by Georgio, two others by Sante, and several after designs by F. Francia; a very curious case of niello-work, one piece of which belonged to Luigi Sforza, Duke of Milan; many curious terra-cottas; some striking Byzantine objects; artistic antiquities illustrative of art in Hindostan, China, Persia, &c. &c.; a mass of Celtic objects; and a rare assemblage of Hungarian, Transylvanian, and Sclavic coins.

ARCHITECTS, BRITISH, ROYAL INSTITUTE MUSEUM, 16 Lower

Grosvenor-street, contains a series of busts and portraits of architects; and an original statuette in terra-cotta of Inigo Jones, by Rysbrack; medals, &c. of Schadow and Perrier; examples of Continental marbles; two flutes of the Parthenon; "growing stone" from Hieropolis; auriferous quartz from California; building-stones, including 117 specimens whence was chosen the stone for the New Palace at Westminster; casts of ornaments from ancient and mediæval buildings; models of public buildings, roofs, and scaffoldings; and apparatus for painting the dome of St. Paul's Cathedral, &c.

ARCHITECTURAL MUSEUM (the), Canon-row, Westminster, originated by Mr. G. G. Scott, F.S.A., was opened in 1853, as an exhibition and study for workmen sketching and modelling, in connexion with a School of Art for Architectural Workmen. The leading objects of this Museum are plaster casts of foliage, figures, &c.; casts or impressions of ancient seals or gems; tracings of stained glass, wall decorations, ornamental pavements, &c.; rubbings of brasses and incised stones; specimens or casts of ancient metal-work and pottery; photographs, or other faithful drawings; architectural books, prints, &c. Here are casts from effigies in our Cathedrals, Westminster Abbey, and a beautiful selection from the Chapter House; panels from the Baptistery gates at Florence; figures and details from the French Cathedrals, casts from Venice, &c. The Museum is supported by architects, builders, and sculptors; and small subscriptions from students, carvers, and other artist-workmen.

ASIATIC SOCIETY (ROYAL), 5 New Burlington-street. This Museum contains oriental coins and medals, marbles and inscriptions; armour and weapons, including Malay and Ceylonese spears, and an entire suit of Persian armour; Ceylonese jingals, and Hindoo statues. The public are admitted on Tuesday, Wednesday, or Thursday, by Members' tickets.

AUTOGRAPHS.—The collections in the metropolis are too numerous for us to detail. Mr. Robert Cole, 52 Upper Norton-street, Portland-place, has assembled nearly 200 volumes of Mss. and Original Letters, which may be seen by previous introduction and arrangement. These include *Queen Caroline*: Her Letters to Lady Anne Hamilton; the draft of the Queen's Letter to George IV., claiming the right to be crowned with him : the Narrative of her sojourn on the Continent, from her leaving England to her return as Queen, the whole autograph, continued by Lady Anne Hamilton to the Queen's death in 1821. Also, a mass of Letters and Poetry inscribed to the Queen; and many of the original Addresses presented at Brandenburgh House, with drafts of the replies, in Dr. Robert Fellowes's handwriting. Several hundred Letters from "the Princess Olive of Cumberland." *Nell Gwyn*: Treasury order for payment of Annuity to Nell; her signature E. G. to receipts; her power of attorney to Fraser, signed E. G., and witnessed by Thomas Otway, the poet. Nell's apothecary's bill, and many accounts for silks and satins, hay and corn, ale, spirits, &c. supplied to her. *Lewis Paul*: his papers and Cotton-manufacture Patents, granted many years before Arkwright's; proving that Paul was the original inventor of Cotton-spinning Machinery. *Regalia of Charles II.*: Papers relating to those made for his coronation. *Flora Macdonald* : her only known letter. *Nelson*: the introduction letter; the gunner's expense-book at the battle of St. Vincent, signed by Nelson. The original *Jubilee Address* of the Royal Academy to George III., signed by all the Members. Also, Letters, &c. of James Watt and John Rennie, James Barry, &c.*

BOTANICAL SOCIETY, 20 Bedford-street, Covent Garden, has an extensive herbarium, open to members and other botanists, on Friday

* Among the Dealers in Autographs are Waller and Son, 188 Fleet-street.

evening, to facilitate the exchange of British and foreign specimens in forming herbaria.

BROOKES's MUSEUM, Blenheim-street, in the rear of 13 Great Marlborough-street (late Colburn the publisher's), was a fine anatomical collection of more than 6000 preparations, models, and casts, made by Joshua Brookes, F.R.S., during thirty years. The greater part was sold in 1828. Brookes was for more than forty years a distinguished teacher of anatomy, and had 7000 pupils; yet he died in comparative poverty, and in despondency at the dispersion of his museum.

BULLOCK's MUSEUM. (See EGYPTIAN HALL, page 266.)

CIVIL ENGINEERS, INSTITUTION OF (THE), 24 Great George-street, Westminster, formerly possessed a museum of models and specimens, which, on the extension of the library and theatre, were distributed among other scientific societies; but at the annual Conversazione of the President of the Institution is assembled a large collection of working models of new machinery, works of art, and specimens of manufacture. In the theatre are portraits of Thomas Telford and of succeeding presidents of the Institution. (See LIBRARIES, page 459.)

The Institution of Civil Engineers first met at the King's Head Tavern, Poultry, Jan. 2, 1818; and was incorporated 1828. Telford bequeathed to the Society a large portion of his library, professional papers, and drawings; and a considerable sum of money, the interest to be expended in annual premiums. Mr. Charles Manby, F.R.S., Secretary, Resident Librarian, and Curator.

COLLEGE OF PHYSICIANS' (ROYAL) MUSEUM, Pall Mall East, contains the very curious preparations which Harvey either made at Padua, or procured from that celebrated school of medicine. They consist of six tables or boards, upon which are spread the different nerves and blood-vessels, carefully dissected out of the body: in one of them are the semilunar valves of the aorta, which, placed at the origin of the arteries, must, together with the valves of the veins, have furnished Harvey with the most conclusive arguments in support of his novel doctrines of the Circulation of the Blood. Of the lectures which he read to the College in 1616, the original Mss. are preserved in the British Museum. The above preparations were presented to the College, in 1823, by the late Earl of Winchilsea, the direct descendant of Lord Chancellor Nottingham, who married Harvey's niece, and possessed his property. Here also is Dr. Matthew Baillie's entire collection of anatomical preparations, mostly put up by his own hands, and from which his great work on anatomy is illustrated. Like Harvey, Baillie gave this collection in his lifetime (1819). The latter were restored in 1851 by Mr. G. E. Blenkins, whom the College presented with a silver inkstand and a purse of fifty guineas. Here also is a gold-headed cane, which had been successively carried by Drs. Radcliffe, Mead, Askew, Pitcairn, and Baillie, whose arms are engraved on the head: presented by Mrs. Baillie. Among the Mss. is *Bustorum aliquot Reliquiæ*, Baldwin Harvey's account of his contemporaries, and the amount of their fees; and in the library are Harvey's Ms. notes and criticisms upon Aristophanes. Admission by a Physician's order.

COLLEGE OF SURGEONS' (ROYAL) MUSEUM, Lincoln's Inn Fields, was commenced with the collection of John Hunter, of specimens in natural history, comparative anatomy, physiology, and pathology, purchased by the Corporation of Surgeons, and first opened in 1813; greatly enlarged in 1836, and again in 1853. The total number of specimens is 23,000, of which 10,000 belonged to Hunter's original museum, the remainder having since been added. There are elaborate catalogues of the whole: arranged in " the Physiological Department, or Normal Structures;" and " the Pathological Department, or Abnormal Structures." Besides the anatomical preparations are the following *Curiosities:* fossil shell of a gigantic extinct armadillo; fossil skeleton of the mylodon, a large extinct sloth from Buenos Ayres; skeleton of a hippopotamus; bones of the pelvis, tail, and left hind-leg of the mighty megatherium; skeleton (8 ft. high) of Charles O'Brian, the Irish giant, who died in 1783, aged twenty-two; skeleton (20 in. high) of Caroline Crachami, the Sicilian dwarf, who died in 1824, aged ten years; plaster casts of hand of Patrick Cotter, another Irish giant, 8 ft. 7 in. high; and hand of M. Louis, a French giant, 7 ft. 4 in. high; glove of O'Brian; plaster casts of bones of the extinct bird, the *dinornis giganteus* of New Zealand, which must have stood 10 ft. high; skeleton of the gigantic extinct deer, exhumed from beneath a peat-bog near Limerick (span of antlers, 8 ft.; length of antler, 7 ft. 3 in.; height of skull, 7 ft. 6 in.); great penguin from the southernmost point touched by Sir James Ross; skeleton of the giraffe; skeleton of the Indian elephant Chunee, purchased for 900 guineas, in 1810, to appear in processions on Covent Garden Theatre stage, and subsequently sold to Mr. Cross at Exeter Change, where it was shot in 1826, during an annual paroxysm, aggravated by inflammation of one of the tusks, but not killed until it had received more than 100 bullets (see Hone's *Every-day Book*, vol. i.): the skeleton was sold for 100 guineas: the head is 13 ft. from the ground; the bones weighed 876 lbs., the skin 17 cwt. Plaster cast of a young negro, and a bust of John Hunter, by Flaxman; skeleton of a man who died from water on the brain, skull 48 in. in circumference; skulls of a double-headed child, born in Bengal, who lived to be four years old, when it was killed by the bite of a cobra di capello: the skulls are united by their crowns, the upper head being inverted; it had four eyes, which moved in different directions at the same time, and the superior eyelids never thoroughly closed, even when the child was asleep. Skeleton, whose joints are anchylosed, or rendered immovable, by unnatural splints of bone growing out in all directions. "The shaft case:" the chest of a man impaled by the shaft of a chaise, the first tug-hook also penetrating the chest, and wounding the left lung; the patient recovered, and survived the injury eleven years: the preparation of the chest is side by side with the shaft. Iron pivot of a try-sail, which, in the London Docks, Feb. 26, 1831, was driven through the body of John Taylor, a seaman, and passed obliquely through the heart and left lung, pinning him to the deck; the try-sail mast 39 ft. long, and 600 lbs. weight: Taylor was carried to the London Hospital, where he recovered in five months, so as to walk from the hospital to the College and back again, and he ultimately returned to his duties as a seaman. Wax cast of the band uniting the bodies of the Siamese twins. Among the mummies is the first wife of the late Martin van Butchell; and a female who died of consumption in 1775, the vessels and viscera injected with camphor and turpentine. Also a sitting mummy, supposed of a Peruvian nobleman, who immolated himself with his wife and child some centuries ago. Since 1835, Professor Owen, F.R.S., has been Conservator of the Museum, and the catalogues have been prepared by him. Here are:

Twelve wax models of the anatomy of the Cramp-fish (*Torpedo galvanii*), presented by Professor Owen.

Fossil Bones of the Dinornis, or extinct gigantic wingless Bird of New Zealand (tibia 3 feet in length).

Coloured casts of the Eggs of the gigantic extinct Bird of Madagascar (*Æpyornis*), supposed the original *Roc* of Arabian romance. One egg contains the matter of 12 ostrich-eggs, 140 hen's-eggs, and 10,000 humming-bird's eggs.

Skeleton of the Skulls of the great Chimpanzee (*Trologdytes gorilla*). This animal is upwards of 5 feet high, of prodigious muscular strength, and much dreaded by the Negroes of the West coast of Tropical Africa.

- A Series of prepared Skulls of different classes of Animals, illustrative of Professor Owen's "Archetype of the Vertebrate Skeleton."
 Skeleton of male Boschman (diminutive Hottentot); and plaster casts of the male and female, from life.

- Here, too, are some preparations similar to those of Harvey in the College of Physicians; they originally belonged to the Museum of the Royal Society, kept at Gresham College, and were the gift of John Evelyn, who bought them at Padua, where he saw them taken out of the body of a man, and very curiously spread upon four large tables: they were the work of Fabritius Bartoletus, then Veslingius's assistant.

- The Museum is open to Fellows and Members of the College, and to visitors introduced by them, or by written orders (not transferable), on Mondays, Tuesdays, Wednesdays, and Thursdays, from twelve to four o'clock; on Fridays it is open only for the purposes of study. The arrangements for the admission of learned and scientific foreigners, state-officers, church and law dignitaries, and members of scientific bodies, are liberal and judicious.

CORPORATION MUSEUM, Guildhall, contains the relics of Roman London discovered in excavating for the foundation of the Royal Exchange, arranged by Mr. Tite, F.R.S.: 1. Pottery and glass: moulded articles, bricks and tiles; jars, urns, vases, amphoræ; terra-cotta lamps; Samian ware; potters' marks; glass. 2. Writing materials: tablets, and styles in iron, brass, bone, and wood. 3. Miscellaneous: domestic articles; artificers' tools; leather manufactures. 4. Coins, of copper, yellow brass, silver, and silver-plated brass, of Augustus, Tiberius, Claudius, Nero, Vespasian, Domitian, &c.; Henry IV. of England, Elizabeth, &c.; foreign, Flemish, German, Prussian, Danish, Dutch. 5. Horns, shells, bones, and vegetable remains. 6. Antiquities and articles of later date. The Catalogue, printed for the Corporation in 1846, is scarce. Here, also, is the City charter (William I.): the Shakspeare deed of sale,* &c. (See LIBRARIES, page 460.)

- Here is a Cabinet of the *London Traders', Tavern, and Coffee-house Tokens* current in the 17th century, presented to the Corporation Library by Henry Benjamin Hanbury Beaufoy, citizen and distiller. They consist of Tokens of iron, lead, tin, brass, copper, and leather, and 9 Royal (Copper) Farthing Tokens; in all 1174. The Leaden Tokens were issued anterior to 1649, and the others from 1649 till 1672, by traders of the City, as small change and advertisement; each Token generally bearing the name, residence, and sign of the house; the index of them being a record of the olden topography and history of London, and a Key to streets and localities long lost. Here is the Token struck by Farr, of the Rainbow Coffee-house, Fleet-street, which escaped the Great Fire of 1666; and the Tokens of the Turk's Head, in Change-alley; and the Boar's Head Tavern, Eastcheap.

 A Descriptive Catalogue of these Tokens, with historical notes, edited by Jacob Henry Burn, was printed for the Corporation in 1853.

* The most important fact of the town property of Shakspeare is that first pointed out by Mr. Halliwell in his 8vo Life of the Poet; viz. that the house purchased by him of Henry Walker, in March 1612-13, and the counterpart of the conveyance of which is preserved in the Guildhall Library, with Shakspeare's signature attached, and which is described there as "abutting upon a streete leading doune to Pudle Wharfe (Blackfriers) in the east part right against the Kinges Majesties Wardrobe," is still identified, or rather sheltered, in the churchyard of St. Andrew's there. The *very house* was, most probably, destroyed in the Great Fire of 1666; but the house stands on its proper spot; and until within these few years, it had been tenanted by the Robinson family, to whom Shakspeare leased it. Close behind this house, in Great Carter-lane, stood the Old Bell Inn, mentioned in a letter addressed to Shakspeare (see page 396); and the poet was probably often in this house, the site of which was noted, after the destruction of the original building, by a richly-sculptured *bell*, dated 1687, and still affixed to the front of a house in Great Carter-lane, on the north side.

COTTINGHAM MUSEUM, 43 Waterloo-bridge-road, Lambeth, collected by the late S. N. Cottingham, the architect, contained about 31,000 specimens of Domestic and Ecclesiastical Architecture, Sculpture, and Furniture; a complete series of studies from the Norman period to the close of the reign of Elizabeth. Here was an Elizabethan ante-room and parlour, with a pair of enameled fire-dogs, once Sir Thomas More's; a ceiling from Bishop Bonner's palace, Lambeth; busts of Elizabeth, Mary Queen of Scots, Raleigh, and Burghley; ebony table from Norwich; Queen Anne Boleyn's sofa, from the Tower; a gallery had a ceiling from the council-chamber of Crosby Place, temp. Richard II. (see page 239); perforated Spanish brass lantern-chandelier, temp. Henry VII.; Spanish pattern lantern, date 1600; fireplace from the Star-chamber, Westminster; figures of saints and bishops, and busts of English monarchs; Flemish oak screen (1490), carved with the history of our Lord, and figures in niches, richly painted and gilt; a reliquary, sixteenth century, painted and carved; cabinet with ceiling (Henry VII.), and decorated window painted with Henry VII. and his queen; models and casts of tombs of the children of Edward III., William of Windsor, and Blanche de la Tour; a gallery with ceiling, Henry VI.; oak panelling from the palace of Layer Marney, Essex; facsimile of doorway, Rochester Cathedral; altar and altar-piece, with canopied figures; ancient stall-seats (thirteenth century); throne, and figures; grand figures of the Virgin, Mary Magdalen, &c.; splendid facsimiles of lofty tombs, with recumbent effigies; seven rooms filled with models and casts; branches, with prickets for candles, temp. Henry V.; supposed canopy of Chaucer's tomb; marble keystone mask from Pompeii; cast from the Stratford bust of Shakspeare; fragments from Hever Castle, St. Katherine's-at-the-Tower, the palace and abbey at Westminster, &c.; processional cross from Glastonbury Abbey, &c. The collection, sold by auction in 2205 lots, Nov. 1851, produced but 2009l. 13s. 6d., being depreciated at least fifty per cent by this dispersion. The collection is described in an illustrated Catalogue, by Henry Shaw, F.S.A.

CUMINGIAN MUSEUM, 80, Gower-street, Bedford-square, collected by Mr. Hugh Cuming, contains upwards of 124,000 species and varieties, including 68,000 specimens of Shells; besides Genera in spirits, with the animals carefully preserved; from Patagonia, Chili, Peru, Columbia, Central America, the Gallapagos Islands, Sumatra, the Malayan Peninsula, Java, the Philippines, and the South Pacific Islands.

In the luxuriant forests, on the arid plains, the mountain-sides, the sheltered bays and rocky shores of these countries, and by exploring the floor of the ocean, species of Mollusca, hitherto imperfectly known, were found in abundance, and numerous forms were discovered entirely new to science; entitling Mr. Cuming to rank with Sloane, Hunter, and Montague. The collection may be seen by persons interested in Conchology, and by scientific men generally, on application.

EAST INDIA COMPANY'S MUSEUM, India House, Leadenhall-street, contains the Babylonian inscriptions, in the Persepolitan character, collected by Sir Harford Jones at Bagdad; and a fragment of jasper, two feet long, inscribed with characters. Here is also a collection of Hindoo and other idols, oriental arms and ornaments, and relics and curiosities of the Topes of Affghanistan; models of Chinese villas; Indian, Malay, Javanese, and Abyssinian dresses, arms, and ornaments; models of boats, various instruments, the city of Lahore, and figures characteristic of the people of India and other Asiatic nations. The trophies taken from Tippoo Saib—standards, pieces of armour, helmets, and the golden footstool of his throne; his mantle, rendered invulnerable by dipping in the well at Mecca; "Tippoo's tiger," a piece of mechanism tearing to pieces an English siphai, and imitating the cries of the man and the growl of the tiger—a toy found in Tippoo's palace at

Seringapatam; also, Tippoo's silver elephant-howdah and bird-canopy, with gems for the eyes. Copies of the paintings on the roofs and walls of the rock temples of the Ajunta Pass, painted about the beginning of the Christian era, and illustrating Buddhism and Saiva Brahminism. An apartment is devoted to specimens of the animals and birds of India and the Archipelago, and Abyssinian and Javanese entomology: of the mammalia there is a printed catalogue. Upon the basement story are Hindoo sculptures; a state palankeen and elephant-seat from Bhurtpore; Chinese lanterns; models of the car of Jagannath, and of a large well of Hindostan; and the cases of an Egyptian mummy. Here is also a large collection of fossil remains from the Himalaya, principally of the genera elephas and mastodon; the sivatherium, an extinct rhinoceros, and a gigantic tortoise; Eastern mammalia and Indian fishes; also, five gold and silver medals of the orders of honour and merit among the native officers of British India. Among the pictures is David's portrait of Napoleon, the most accurate likeness of him extant.

Admission daily by tickets from members of the Court, or other authorities; or without tickets on Friday; closed during September.

ENTOMOLOGICAL SOCIETY'S MUSEUM, 17 Old Bond-street: a collection of insects, commenced with Mr. Kirby's specimens, from which the first of monographs ever published was formed. (Kirby and Spence's *Introduction*.) Here is also a library of reference on Entomology.

GEOLOGY, PRACTICAL, MUSEUM OF, No. 28 to 32 Jermyn-street, originated in a suggestion by Sir H. De la Beche, C.B., in 1835; for the collection of geological and mineralogical specimens during the progress of the Geological Survey of the United Kingdom. The collections were first exhibited in a house in Craig's Court, Charing Cross; but becoming too extensive for this accommodation, the present handsome edifice was erected, with entrance in Jermyn-street, and frontage in Piccadilly: Pennethorne architect; style, Italian palazzo.

In the lower hall is a collection of British building and ornamental stones—sandstones, oolites, limestones, granites, and porphyries, in six-inch cubes. The entrance is lined with Derbyshire alabaster; and the hall has pilasters of granite from Scotland, serpentine from Ireland, and limestones from Devonshire, Derbyshire, &c. On one side is an elaborate screen, with Cornish serpentine pilasters and cornice; and Irish serpentine panels, framed with Derbyshire productions. Here is a large copy of an Etruscan vase cut in Aberdeen granite; and on the floors are a very fine tesselated pavement of Cornish clay, and examples of encaustic tiles; pedestals of British marbles support vases, and statuettes of artificial stone, cement, &c.

The principal floor has an apartment 95 feet by 55 feet, with an iron roof, glazed with rough plate-glass. Around run two light galleries. Here are specimens of iron, copper, tin, lead, manganese, antimony, cobalt, &c. of the United Kingdom and the colonies; also a good collection of similar ores from the most important metalliferous countries of the world. The processes of raising these from the mines are illustrated by an extensive series of models, with the modes of dressing the ores for the market, and the final production of the metal; mining tools, safety-lamps, &c.; including models of Taylor's Cornish pumping-engine, the water-pressure engine, the turbine and other wheels, and a beautiful set of valves. The models of mines can be dissected, and the mode of working shewn; with the machines for lowering and raising the miners, models of stamping and crushing engines, and iron-smelting by the hot and cold blast. Here, also, are tools of the Cornish, German, Russian, and Mexican miners.

The history of the metals may also be read in a collection of bronzes

and brasses, and gold and silver ornaments; examples of metal casting and steel manufacture are shewn; as are also metal statuettes,
electrotype deposits, and illustrations of electro-plating and gilding,
and photographic processes. Here is also a large and valuable collection of ancient glass, in beads, bottles, jugs, &c. historically arranged:
the old Venetian glass is exceedingly curious. The processes of ena-
melling are illustrated; and here are specimens of fine Limoges, modern
works, and Chinese enamels.

Next is a collection of Roman pottery. The China clays, China stone,
and other raw materials of earthenware and porcelain, are shewn; and
here is a complete series of the wares of the Staffordshire potteries;
also, specimens of those of Derby, Worcester, Swansea, Chelsea, Bow,
and other districts, in comparison with the earthenware of the ancients,
the ceramic manufactures of Italy, Germany, France, and the Orientals.

In the galleries round the large room is a very complete collection
of British fossils, arranged in the order of their occurrence and labelled,
so that a collector may compare and identify any specimen he may find.

Attached to the Museum is the Mining Records Office, in which are
collected plans and sections of existing and abandoned mines. Here
also are a Library, and a Lecture-theatre with 580 sittings. Lastly are
well-fitted Laboratories, communicating by a hydraulic lift with a fire-
proof room in the basement-story, containing an assay-furnace. The
collections are open to the public gratuitously on the first three days
of the week; and on the other three days to the students.

GEOLOGICAL SOCIETY'S MUSEUM, Somerset House, is rich in the original types of fossils described in the *Geological Transactions.* The
collection contains a series of British fossils and rocks, arranged stra-
tegraphically; likewise, an assemblage of selected minerals, and a foreign
collection geographically arranged. The Society possesses also a fine
library of works upon geological science.

GEOLOGICAL: MR. J. S. BOWERBANK'S Collection, 3 Highbury-
grove, Islington, consists more especially of British fossils strate-
graphically arranged; and is particularly rich in the crag, London clay,
and chalk formations; the whole occupying 400 drawers. Also the most
extensive collection of British and foreign Sponges in Europe, consisting of many hundred species from Australia, Africa, the West Indies,
&c. Mr. Bowerbank receives British or foreign scientific visitors, with
suitable introductions, on Monday evenings, at eight o'clock, from May
to November, inclusive. (See also MR. SAULL'S MUSEUM, page 542.)

GUIANA EXHIBITION, 209 Regent-street (Cosmorama), was a Museum of objects illustrative of the ethnography and natural history of
British Guiana, collected by Mr. (now Sir) H.Robert Schomburgk, and
exhibited in 1840. The saloon was fitted up as a Guianese hut; and here
were three living natives, part of Schomburgk's boat's crew, in their
picturesque costumes. Besides collections of mammalia, birds, reptiles,
fishes, mollusca, and insects, specimens in osteology, geology, &c., here
was a painting of the Victoria Regia lily; Guianese furniture, clothing, and other manufactures; poisoned arrows and blowpipe; a native
hammock and bark shirt; the boa, puma, and ant-eater; splendid rock
manakins and humming-birds, &c. The three natives, wearing only
waistcloths, and jaguar-skin cloaks, and teeth necklaces, and feather-
caps, and their skins painted and tattooed, exhibited their blowpipe
shooting and dances, which were very attractive.

At the Cosmorama was revived, in 1839, the "Invisible Girl," of some thirty
years previously, the invention of M. Charles, and detailed by Sir David Brewster
in his *Natural Magic.* The poet Moore inscribed, with exquisite fancy, "Lines
to the Invisible Girl." The invention "consisted of an apparatus with trumpets,

communicating by a pipe beneath the floor of the room to an apartment in which sat a lady, who, through a small hole in the partition, saw what was going on in the exhibition-room, and answered through the tube accordingly; the sound losing so much of its force in its passage, as to appear like the voice of a girl."

HOSPITALS, the principal, possess Anatomical Museums.

HUDSON'S BAY COMPANY'S HOUSE, Fenchurch-street, possessed many years since a Museum of stuffed Birds, and other objects of natural history from Rupert's Land; the greater portion of which has ʼeen presented to the British Museum and the Zoological Society.

HUNTER'S (WILLIAM) MUSEUM was collected at his large house on the east side of Great Windmill-street, Haymarket. Hunter employed many years in the anatomical preparations and in the dissections; besides making additions by purchase from the museums of Sandys, Falconar, Blackall, and others. Here was a sumptuous library of Greek and Latin classics; and a very rare cabinet of ancient medals, besides coins, purchased at 20,000*l.* expense. Minerals, shells, and other specimens of natural history were gradually added to this museum, which hence became one of the Curiosities of Europe. The cost of the whole exceeded 70,000*l.*; and was bequeathed by Hunter to the University of Glasgow, with 8000*l.* to support and augment the whole.

KING'S COLLEGE MUSEUM, Strand, consists of the collection formed at the Kew Observatory by King George III., and of a cabinet of natural history specimens from Kew Palace; presented to the College in 1843, and known as " George the Third's Museum." Here are the celebrated " Boyle models," and " forty-one brass plates, engraved with astronomical, astrological, and mathematical delineations;" a large orrery, date 1733; an armillary sphere, 1731; apparatus made for Desaguliers's lectures; a rude model of Watt's steam-engine; Attwood's large arch of polished brass voussoirs, &c. There have been added Wheatstone's speaking-machine; a model, fifteen feet long, of the celebrated Schauffhausen timber bridge; a bust of Queen Victoria, by Weekes; and a statuette of George III., by Turnerelli. The collection also includes small philosophical apparatus, entomological specimens, fossils, minerals, &c. Here also is a portion of Mr. Babbage's Calculating Machine, which has succeeded in printing mathematical and astronomical tables. At the College is likewise an Anatomical Museum, a Cabinet of Natural History, and a chemical theatre, with a Daniell constant battery of great power.

The College possesses a beautifully-illuminated Ms. containing the Statutes of the Order of the Garter; a drawing of the House of Lords, *temp.* Edward I.; and the Statutes in more elegant Latin, corrected in the handwriting of King Edward VI., superbly emblazoned with arms, &c. The Museum can be seen by the Curator's order.

LEVERIAN MUSEUM: described at page 453.

LINNÆAN SOCIETY, 32 Soho-square (the house of Sir Joseph Banks, and bequeathed by him to the Society), contains in its Museum the herbarium of Linnæus, purchased, with the library, by the late Sir J. E. Smith, for 1000*l.* The herbarium is kept in three small cases, and is a curious botanical antiquity, of great value in ascertaining with certainty the synonyms of the writings of Linnæus. The museum is very rich in the botanical department, containing the herbaria of Linnæus, Smith, Pulteney, Woodward, Winch, &c.; besides a valuable herbarium presented by the East India Company in 1833. The entomological collections are extensive; the zoology is rich in Australian marsupials, birds, and reptiles; and the shells are fine.

Here is a collection of paintings, including a portrait of Linnæus, from the original by Roslin at Stockholm, described as the most striking likeness ever executed. This copy was painted for Archbishop Von Troil, by whom it was presented to Sir Joseph Banks.

In this house Sir Joseph Banks gave public breakfasts on Thursdays, and *conversazioni* on Sunday evenings, to the Fellows of the Royal Society, during his long presidency. He left an annuity of 200*l.*, his library, and botanical collections, for life, to his librarian, Mr. Robert Brown, F.R.S., afterwards to come to the British Museum; but by arrangement the library and collections have been transferred to the Museum.

MEAD'S (DR.) MUSEUM was in the garden of No. 49 Great Ormond-street, where was also a library of 10,000 volumes. The collection included prints and drawings, coins and medals; marble statues of Greek philosophers and Roman emperors; bronzes, gems, intaglios, Etruscan vases, &c.; marble busts of Shakspeare, Milton, and Pope, by Scheemakers; statues of Hygæia and Antinous; a celebrated bronze head of Homer; and an iron cabinet (once Queen Elizabeth's) full of coins, among which was a medal with Oliver Cromwell's head in profile, legend, " the Lord of Hosts, the word at Dunbar, Sept. 1650;" on the reverse, the parliament sitting. After Dr. Mead's death, in 1754, the sale of his library, pictures, statues, &c. realised between 15,000*l.* and 16,000*l.* Mead, when not engaged at home, generally spent his evenings at Batson's coffee-house; and in the forenoons, apothecaries came to him at Tom's, Covent Garden, with written or verbal reports of cases, for which he prescribed without seeing the patient, and took half-guinea fees. Dr. Mead's gay *conversazioni*, in Ormond-street, were the first meetings of the kind.

MISSIONARY MUSEUM (the), 8 Blomfield-street, Finsbury, contributed chiefly by the missionaries of the London Missionary Society, and travellers generally, is remarkable for its great number of idols and objects of superstitious regard, costumes, domestic utensils, implements of war, music, &c. from islands in the Pacific Ocean, China, and ultra-Ganges India, including the three Presidencies; Africa and Madagascar; North and South America; " especially the idols given up by their former worshippers, from a full conviction of the folly and sin of idolatry." Here also is an assemblage of natural history specimens, principally Polynesian: its Tahitian collection rivals Capt. Cook's, in the British Museum.

Some of the idols are 12 feet high. Among the rarities are 18 model pictures of Japanese costumes, obtained at great risk; and six coloured etchings by a Chinese artist, the Progress of the Opium-smoker, a counterpart to Hogarth's " Rake's Progress." Admission by Director's or officer's tickets, on Tuesday, Thursday, and Saturday.

MANUFACTURES AND ORNAMENTAL ART MUSEUM, Marlborough House, Pall Mall, was opened temporarily in 1852, with purchases from the Great Exhibition, with 5000*l.* voted by Parliament; including gorgeous scarfs and shawls from Cashmere and Lahore; the French shawl of Duché ainé et Cie, the most perfect specimen of shawl-weaving ever produced; glittering swords, yatagans, and pistols from Tunis and Constantinople; the famous " La Gloire" vase from the Sèvres manufacture; Marcel Frères' hunting-knife of St. Hubert; Changarnier's sword, from the workshop of Froment Meurice; Vecte's splendid shield; a fac-simile of the celebrated Cellini cup; and other art-illustrations of the highest order. To these have been added purchases; and the articles are grouped into six classes: woven fabrics, metal works, pottery, furniture, and miscellanies. The metal-work department consists also of the rich and splendid manufacture of the East, with a few rude specimens illustrative of the innate taste of their workmen; the silver and bronze materials of France, cups of English and brooches of Irish manufacture, and Elkington's electrotypes. The division of pottery was enriched by the Queen's Sèvres collection, and by valuable works from

Baring, Minton, Copeland, Webb, and Farrar: the royal collection, though of forty-two pieces only, being worth 12,000*l.* The casts of ornamental art have been removed here from Somerset House; and the collection includes ancient Greek and Roman, mediæval or Roman-esque, Saracenic or Gothic, Renaissance, figures, busts, masks, animals, &c.; the Renaissance (A.D. 1400 to 1600) arranged chronologically.

There is a collection of 3489 specimens of enrichment, British and foreign examples, for the guidance as to style of the carvers employed in the New Houses of Parliament; and another collection of 3283 casts, from models prepared for stone and wood carvings, deposited in the Government Works at Thames Bank, and at the New Houses of Parliament. These examples cost 7000*l.*, and are intended to form part of a National Museum of Mediæval Art.— *First Report Dep. Practical Art*, 1853.

On Monday and Tuesday the admission is free; on Wednesday, Thursday, and Friday, by an entrance-fee of sixpence; and on Saturday the Museum is closed.

NATIONAL REPOSITORY (the) was formed in 1828, in the upper gallery of the south-west side of the King's Mews, Charing Cross; and 35 adjoining rooms were reserved for the reception of products from the chief manufacturing towns. Here were silk-looms to work at certain hours, English Mechlin lace, crystallo-ceramic ornamental glass; models of steam-engines, steam-boat paddles, suspension-bridges, and public buildings; new kaleidoscopes, rain-gauges, musical glasses, Indian corn-mills, life-buoys, &c. The collection was removed to Leicester-square (see page 455), and there merged into the "Museum of National Manufactures and the Mechanical Arts."

NAVAL MUSEUM ("The Model Room"), Somerset House, may be seen by order of the Surveyor-general of the Navy. Here are models of the science and trade of ship-building, with sections of interior and exterior construction, from the "Great Harry" and the "Sovereign of the Seas" to our own time. In the central room is a large model of the "Victoria," 110 guns, laid down in 1839; and above hangs a model of the "Victory," built 1735, and lost in 1744, with an admiral and its entire crew. Here also are models of the "Bucentaur;" a Chinese Junk; a Burmese War-boat; the "Queen," 110 guns; and the "Agamemnon" steam-screw war-ship, 91 guns.

PHARMACEUTICAL SOCIETY (the), 17 Bloomsbury-square, incorporated 1842, possesses the most extensive and complete Museum of the kind in existence; comprising rare specimens of the animal, vegetable, and mineral kingdoms; and substances and products used in Medicine and Pharmacy. Also, groups and series of authenticated specimens, valuable for identifying, comparing, and tracing, the origin and natural history of products. Here is the valuable Museum of the late Dr. Pereira, including collections of Cinchona barks by eminent foreign naturalists. The collection may be seen daily, except Saturdays, by Member's order, or on application to the Curator.

ROYAL SOCIETY'S MUSEUM, Somerset House, was commenced in 1665; then was "the collecting a repository, the setting up a chemical laboratory, a mechanical operatory, an astronomical observatory, and an optick chamber:" next year Evelyn presented the table of veins, arteries, and nerves, which he had made 'out of the natural human bodies,' in Italy." Sir R. Moray presented "the stones taken out of Lord Balcarras's heart, in a silver box;" and "a bottle full of stag's tears." Hooke gave "a petrified fish, the skin of an antelope which died in St. James's Park, a petrified fœtus," and other rarities. In 1681, when Dr. Grew published his curious catalogue, the Museum contained several thousand specimens of zoological subjects and foreign curiosities: among the eighty-three contributors are Prince Rupert, the Duke of Norfolk, Boyle, Evelyn, Hooke, Pepys, &c. (Weld's *History* *of the Royal Society*, vol. ii. p. 278.)* Ned Ward (*London Spy*, part iii.) satirically describes this Museum of Wiseacres' Hall, or Gresham College. The account of its rarities in Hatton's *London*, 1708, fills 20 pages.

Relics of Sir Isaac Newton.—An autograph note. from the Mint Office; one. of the solar dials made by Newton when a boy; his richly-chased gold watch, with a medallion of Newton, and inscribed: " Mrs. Catherine Conduit to Sir Isaac Newton. Jan. 4, 1708." " The first reflecting telescope, invented by Sir Isaac Newton, and made with his own hands," 1761; the mask of his face, from the cast taken after death, which belonged to Roubiliac; a small lock of Newton's silver-white hair; and three portraits of him in oil, painted by Jervas, Marchand, and Vanderbank. Here likewise is the original model of the safety-lamp, made by Sir Humphry Davy's own hands in 1815.

SALTERO'S (DON) MUSEUM was first established at a coffee-house, now the Swan Tavern, in Cheyne-walk, Chelsea, in 1695, by one Salter, a barber, who assembled there a collection of Curiosities, which remained in the coffee-room till August 1799, when they were dispersed by public auction; previous to which printed Catalogues were sold, with the names of the principal benefactors to the collection. In Dr. Franklin's Life we read : " Some gentlemen from the country went by water to see the College, and Don Saltero's Curiosities," at Chelsea.

SAULL'S MUSEUM, 15 Aldersgate-street, is a private collection, which the proprietor liberally allows to be inspected on Thursdays, from 11 A.M. The *Antiquities*, principally excavated in the metropolis, consist of early British vases, Roman lamps and urns, amphoræ, and dishes, tiles, bricks, and pavements, and fragments of Samian ware; also, a few Egyptian antiquities : and a cabinet of Greek, Roman, and early British coins. The *Geological Department* contains the collection of the late Mr. Sowerby, with additions by Mr. Saull, F.G.S.; together exceeding 20,000 specimens, arranged according to the probable order of the earth's structure. Every article bears a descriptive label : and the localisation of the antiquities, some of which were dug up almost on the spot, renders these relics so many medals of our metropolitan civilisation.

SLOANE MUSEUM (the), collected by Sir Hans Sloane, at Chelsea, consisted of natural and artificial Curiosities, which cost Sir Hans 50,000*l*; after his death in 1753, they were sold to Parliament for 20,000*l*., and formed the nucleus of the British Museum. The collection consisted of a library of 50,000 volumes; Mss. upon natural history, voyages and travels, and the arts, especially medicine; 23,000 medals and coins; anatomical preparations; natural history specimens; and an herbarium of 336 volumes. The Catalogue of the collection extended to 38 vols., folio, and 8 vols. 4to. (See BRITISH MUSEUM.)

SOANE MUSEUM (the), 13 Lincoln's Inn Fields (north side), was founded and endowed by Sir John Soane, the architect; at whose death, in 1837, the trustees appointed by Parliament took charge of the " Museum, Library, Books, Prints, Manuscripts, Drawings, Maps, Models, Plans, and Works of Art, and the House and Offices;" providing for the free admission of amateurs and students in painting, sculpture, and architecture; and general visitors.

The Museum is open to general visitors on Thursdays and Fridays during April, May, and June in each year; and likewise on Tuesdays, from the first in February to the last in August, for the accommodation of foreigners and persons making but a short stay in London; also artists, and those prevented by special circumstances from visiting the museum in the months first specified.

---

* From the Charter-book Mr. Weld has collected into a volume fac-similes of 300 of the Fellows (from the period of the institution of the Royal Society to the present time), an illustrious set of autographs.

Admission is obtained by cards, to be applied for a day or two previously, either to a Trustee, by letter to the Curator, or personally at the Museum, where the applicant is expected to leave the name and address of the party desiring admission, and the number of persons proposed to be introduced; when, unless there appears to the Curator some reason to the contrary, a card of admission for the next open day is forwarded by post.

Access to the books, drawings, Mss., or permission to copy pictures or other works of art, is granted on special application to the Trustees or the Curator, Mr. George Bailey, who resides at the Museum.

A general description of the collection, abridged from that printed by Sir John Soane in 1835, may be had at the Museum. The larger work (only 150 copies printed) is interspersed with poetic illustrations by Mrs. Hofland.

The house, built by Mr. Soane in 1792, was in 1812 faced with a stone screen, in which are introduced Gothic corbels, 12th century; and terra-cotta canephoræ, copied from the caryatides of the Temple of Pandrosus at Athens. The entrance-hall is decorated with medallion reliefs after the antique. The dining-room and library ceiling are painted by H. Howard, R.A. Here are a large collection of drawings of buildings by Sir John Soane;* plaster models of ancient Greek and Roman edifices, restored; a cork model of Pompeii; fictile vases, alabaster urns, and antique bronzes; windows filled with old stained glass; busts of Homer, Shakspeare, Ben Jonson, Camden, and Inigo Jones; Greek and Etruscan vases, and Wedgewood's imitations; Sir Joshua Reynolds's Snake in the Grass, purchased for 510 guineas by Soane, at the Marchioness of Thomond's sale; and a portrait of Soane, almost the last picture painted by Lawrence, 1829. Here also is a walnut-tree and marble table, formerly Sir Robert Walpole's; and over the bookcases are busts after the antique. The Little Study contains marble fragments of Greek and Roman sculpture, antique bronzes, and some natural Curiosities. In the Monks' Yard are Gothic fragments of the ancient palace at Westminster, picturesquely arranged to resemble a ruined cloister. In the Corridor are casts from Westminster Hall; and Banks's model of a Sleeping Girl, at Ashbourne; also two engravings, the Laughing Audience, and the Chorus, by Hogarth; and a drawing by Canaletti. The Monks' Parlour has its walls covered with fragments and casts of mediæval buildings. The Monument Court contains architectural groups of various nations. The Picture-room has movable planes, which serve as double walls, on each side of which are hung the pictures: here are Hogarth's Rake's Progress, eight paintings, purchased for 570 guineas; and Hogarth's Election, 4 paintings, for 1650 guineas; also, 3 pictures by Canaletti, one, the Grand Canal of Venice, his chef-d'œuvre; Van Tromp's Barges entering the Texel, by J. M. W. Turner, R.A.; the Study of a Head, from one of Raphael's Cartoons,—a relic saved from the wreck of the lost Cartoons, which remained in the possession of the family of the weaver who originally worked them in tapestry; also copies of two other heads from the same, by Flaxman; pictures by Watteau, Fuseli, Bird, Westall, Turner, Calcott, Hilton, &c.

In the Catacombs are ancient marble cinerary urns and vases. In the Sepulchral Chamber is the sarcophagus discovered in 1817, by Belzoni, in a royal tomb near Gournou, Thebes: it is 9 feet 4 inches long and 2 feet 8 inches deep, and is formed out of a mass of arragonite, or alabaster; it is transparent when a light is placed inside it, and is sculptured within and without with several hundred figures 2 inches in

* Sir John Soane, the son of a Berkshire bricklayer, designed a greater number of public edifices than any contemporary: from the Bank of England in the City, to Chelsea Hospital at the western extremity; from Walworth in the southern, to the Regent's Park in the north-western suburbs. His last work (1833), the State Paper Office, in St. James's Park, is very unlike any other of his designs. He died at his house in Lincoln's Inn Fields, Jan. 20, 1837.

height, and supposed by Belzoni to represent funeral processions and ceremonies; within is a full-length figure of Isis, the guardian of the dead. Dr. Young considered it to be the tomb of Psammis;-and the hieroglyphics in the cartouche to indicate Osirei-menephtha, the father of Rameses II.: although Sir Gardner Wilkinson considers it was not that monarch's sarcophagus, but his cenotaph. It was purchased by Sir John Soane of Mr. Salt, in 1824, for 2000*l*.

In the Crypt are several cork models of ancient tombs and sepulchral chambers discovered in Sicily, the walls decorated with painting and sculpture; and in the centre the remains of the deceased, amidst vases and other funereal accompaniments.

In various apartments are a plaster cast of the Apollo Belvidere, taken by Lord Burlington about 1718; a marble bust of Sir John Soane, presented by the sculptor, Chantrey; a richly-mounted pistol, taken by Peter the Great from the Turkish Bey at Azof, 1696, and presented by Alexander Emperor of Russia to the Emperor Napoleon at Tilsit in 1807, and given by him to a French officer at St. Helena; also, a portrait of Napoleon in his 28th year, by a Venetian artist; and a miniature of Napoleon, painted at Elba, in 1814, by Isabey; statuettes of Michael Angelo and Raphael, cast from the model, by Flaxman, in Mr. Rogers's collection; marble bust of Sir William Chambers; bust of R. B. Sheridan, by Garrard; carved and gilt ivory table and chairs, formerly Tippoo Saib's; the watch, measuring-rods, and compasses used by Sir Christopher Wren; a large collection of ancient gems and intaglios; and a set of the Napoleon Medals, once the Empress Josephine's. (See LIBRARIES, p. 465.)

The *Sculpture, Marbles, Casts*, and *Models*, contain 40 specimens of Flaxman, including a plaster cast of his "Shield of Achilles;" 10 works of Banks; and specimens of Michael Angelo, John de Bologna, Donatello, Rysbrack, Westmacott, Chantrey, Gibson, Baily, Rossi, &c.

The *Architectural* department includes drawings, models of buildings, and details. Among the drawings are those of all Sir John Soane's works, and others by Piranesi, Zucchi, Bibiena, Campanella, Thornhill, Chambers, Kent, and Smirke; and a volume of drawings by Thorpe, the Elizabethan architect. There are busts of Palladio, Wren, Chambers, Dance, &c.

The nine Etruscan Vases exhibit the variety of shapes to be found in much larger collections: one (the Englefield) is of extreme rarity; and the Cawdor vase is of extraordinary size, and elegantly enriched. Among the Roman antiquities are real specimens and casts from the temple of Jupiter Stator at Rome, and of the Sibyl or Vesta at Tivoli, &c.

The *Antiquities* and *Curiosities* are as useful to artists and pattern-drawers as the new rooms in the Louvre at Paris. The entire collection cost Sir John Soane upwards of 50,000*l*.

SOCIETY OF ARTS, 18 John-street, Adelphi (the house built by the brothers Adam, in 1772-74), has Barry's celebrated pictures upon the walls of the Council-room, and a few portraits, &c.; to be seen gratis, between 10 and 4 daily, except Wednesday and Sunday.

The Model Repository, 42 feet by 35 feet, on the ground-floor, contains one of the most extensive collections of models in Europe.

Here are "hands for the one-handed, and other instruments for those who have lost both; clothes of all sorts of materials from all countries; medals of Charles I.'s reign, and the last new stove of Victoria's; fire-escape ladders to run down from windows and scaffolds, rising telescope-fashion out of a box, to mount roofs; beehives and turnip-slicers, ploughs and instruments to restrain vicious bulls, pans to preserve butter in hot countries, safety-lamps; models of massive cranes, and of little tips for umbrellas; life-buoys and maroon-locks; diving-bells and expanding keys; safety-coaches and traps; clocks, and tail-pieces for violoncellos; instruments to draw spirits and to draw teeth; samples of tea, sugar, cinnamon, and nutmegs, in different stages of growth; models of Tuscan pavement; beds for invalids; methods to teach the blind how to write" (Knight's *London*); also, the first piece of Gutta Percha seen in Europe, and presented to the Society 1843.

In the Ante-room, upstairs, are Nollekens's medallion of Jephtha's Vow, Barry's picture of Eve tempting Adam, &c. The large pictures in the Council-room were presented gratuitously by Barry, between 1777 and 1783, and were commenced when he had but sixteen shillings in his pocket. They are, 1. Orpheus Civilising the Inhabitants of Thrace. 2. A Grecian Harvest-home. 3. Crowning the Victors at Olympia. 4. Commerce, or the Triumph of the Thames. 5. The Distribution of Premiums in the Society of Arts. 6. Elysium, or the State of Final Retribution. Barry has published etchings of these pictures, and has minutely described the subjects in his published Works, vol. ii. p. 323, edit. 1809. They were exhibited, and produced Barry 500*l.*, to which the Society added 200*l.* The Victors at Olympia is the finest work of the series: Canova declared the sight of it to be worth a voyage to England. In the Distribution picture are introduced portraits of Shipley, Arthur Young, the Prince of Wales, Mrs. Montagu, Sir George Savile, Bishop Hurd, Soame Jenyns, the two beautiful Duchesses of Rutland and Devonshire, the Duke of Richmond, Lord Folkestone, William Lock, Edmund Burke, and Dr. Johnson. The Retribution contains great and good men of all ages and times. Each of the latter pictures is 42 feet long. Barry died in 1806, and his remains lay in state in the room which the grandeur of his genius had so magnificently adorned. In the ante-room is a portrait of Barry; and in the large room are portraits of Lord Folkestone, by Gainsborough; Lord Romney, by Sir Joshua Reynolds; a marble statue of Dr. Ward, by Carlini; busts of Dr. Franklin and Barry; and casts of Venus, Mars, and Narcissus, by John Bacon.

The Society have held in the Great Room annual Exhibitions of Decorative Manufactures, and Ancient and Mediæval Art; and the collected works of Mulready and Etty.

TRADESCANTS' MUSEUM, at South Lambeth (see page 145), contained not only stuffed animals and dried plants, but also minerals; implements of war and domestic use, of various nations; and a collection of coins and medals. In the Catalogue, entitled *Museum Tradescantium*, 1656, we find, "Two feathers of the phœnix tayle;" "a natural dragon;" and a stuffed specimen of the Dodo, believed to have been exhibited alive in London in 1638, the head and foot of which are preserved in the Ashmolean Museum at Oxford, of which the Tradescants' collection formed the nucleus.

TRINITY HOUSE MUSEUM, Tower Hill, contains various models of lighthouses, floating-lights, life-boats, and a noble model of the "Royal William," 150 years old. Among the naval Curiosities is the flag taken by Sir Francis Drake, in 1588, from the Spaniards; pen-and-ink plans of sea-fights, *temp.* Charles II.: Chinese map; pair of colossal globes, &c.; besides a large picture, by Gainsborough, of the elder Trinity brethren, and numerous portraits and busts. To be seen by Secretary's order.

UNITED SERVICE INSTITUTION MUSEUM, Whitehall-yard, contains an Armoury, Chinese cabinet and model gallery, antiquities, and an ethnological collection; a lecture-theatre and library. Among the Curiosities are a stirrup cross-bow (*temp.* Henry VIII.); a group of ancient swords; Cromwell's basket-handled cut-and-thrust sword, used by him at the siege of Drogheda, 1649; General Wolfe's sword, Quebec, 1759; an Australian Bomarang; the stone upon which Capt. Cook fell dead at Owhyee; war implements from all parts of the world; a piece of the deck of the Victory, from the spot on which Nelson fell; Napoleon Bonaparte's fusil, razor and shaving-brush, and fragment of his coffin; articles found on the field of Waterloo; relics of the Royal George, sunk 1760, and the Mary Rose, 1545; chronological series of fire-arms' (James II. to William IV.); skeleton of the horse Marengo, rode by

Napoleon at Waterloo; Chinese trophies and chain-shot; Polar bear and wolf shot by Sir George Back; wooden Chinese cage for human prisoner; first uniform worn in the British navy; hat of Lord Nelson; Chinese magic mirror; models of ships of all nations; fortification models; great model of Linz and its camp: and pictures of battles. Also, Capt. Siborne's Model of the Battle of Waterloo; scale, 9 feet to a mile, area 440 square feet; shewing the entire field, and the British, French, and Prussian armies, by 190,000 metal figures; with the villages, houses, farmyards, and clumps of trees: cost Captain Siborne, 4000*l.*; purchased for the Institution by subscription.

The United Service Institution, established 1830, is supported by entrance-fees, 1*l.*; annual subscription, 10*s.* The public are admitted daily, free, by members' orders; for three days at Easter and Christmas, and on the anniversaries of the Battles of Waterloo (June 18) and Trafalgar (Oct. 21), the Museum is open.

UNIVERSITY COLLEGE, Gower-street. The Anatomical Museum, based upon the collection of Sir Charles Bell, consists of 4066 specimens in catalogue, and large additions. Also, the models in wax by Tuson, including the celebrated case of Icthyosis cornea; 700 coloured drawings by Sir R. Carswell, and 200 by Armstrong; the heart and throat of Ramo Samee (the sword-swallowing Indian juggler), ob. 24 July, 1849; a Skull from the Wreck of the Royal George; bones and a Skull from ancient Greek graves; a Head from the Catacombs in Paris; an Elephant's Heart; reputed fragments of bones of the Good Duke Humphrey and Robert Bruce; and a cast from Hervey Leach (Hervio Nano), ob. March 1847. Here, also, is the Skeleton of Jeremy Bentham, dressed in the clothes which he usually wore, and with a wax face modelled by Dr. Talrych; also a portion of skin from the body of the first person obtained under the New Anatomical Act (Lady Barrington). A Museum of Comparative Anatomy, and a fine Materia Medica collection. The Natural Philosophy Models are good. In the Drawing School are three marble figures in relief of the Hindoo Trinity, Brahma, Vishnu, and Siva, dug up from the ruins of a city in a forest 50 miles east of Baroda. In the School, also, is a collection of Casts, including the Apollo made in Rome for Flaxman, the Laocoon, &c.

University College site, 7 acres, cost 30,000*l.* The Library of General Literature contains 38,718 volumes of printed books, besides 6460 pamphlets, and about 10,000 Chinese works, the donation of the late Rev. Robert Morrison, D.D.: containing a Chinese Encyclopædia and 3 Dictionaries; prints of ancient vessels and costumes; a tabular Index to the Twenty-four Historians, &c. The Medical Library consists of 3790 volumes, and 1191 pamphlets. The Books are lent to the Students, on a deposit. See also LIBRARIES, p. 465.

WATERLOO MUSEUM, see PALL MALL.

WEEKS's MUSEUM, 3 Tichborne-street, established about 1810, was famed for its mechanical Curiosities. The grand room, by Wyatt, had a ceiling painted by Rebecca and Singleton. Here were two temples, 7 feet high, supported by 16 elephants, and embellished with 1700 pieces of jewellery. Among the automata were the tarantula spider and bird of paradise. Weeks's Museum has long been dispersed; the premises were subsequently the show-rooms of the Rockingham Works, where, in 1837, was exhibited a splendid porcelain dessert-service, made for William IV.: 200 pieces, painted with 760 subjects, occupied 5 years, and cost 3000*l.* In 1851 the place was refitted by Robin, the conjuror.

ZOOLOGICAL SOCIETY'S MUSEUM (the) was originally commenced in Bruton-street, then removed to No. 26 Leicester-square; and is now contained in a building erected for it in the Society's Garden, Regent's Park, about 1843. This Museum was projected upon an extensive scale: during the earlier years of its formation, it was, scientifically, the great collection of this country; but it soon became eclipsed by the rapid accumulation with which Dr. Gray enriched the galleries of the British Museum; and as the national collection gradually assumed the important place which it now occupies among the great public institutions of Europe, the Council of the Zoological Society withdrew from the competition, and concentrated their efforts towards their Vivarium. Their Museum is arranged to convey an idea of the Generic Forms of the Vertebrate Division of the Animal Kingdom; including about 1500 species of Mammalia, and 7000 species of Birds. By this method, most of the essential differences of form are well illustrated in a reduced number of specimens, so as to impress a casual observer with the distinctive features of each family. Among the animals preserved are many of the rarest and most curious known to exist, and selected from the original collection, commenced with the gifts of Sir Thomas Stamford Raffles, the first President of the Zoological Society; and Mr. N. A. Vigors, its first Secretary.

In the original Prospectus, dated 1824, it was proposed, "that the Society shall have a Museum, as well as a Library of all Books connected with the subject."

PRIVATE COLLECTIONS.—The following can only be seen by private introduction to their proprietors.

Auldjo, Mr. John, Noel House, Kensington: an extensive assemblage of Antique and Mediæval Articles of Vertu; including a portion of a Greek glass vase, of similar execution to the Portland Vase: it is ornamented with foliage and birds, and was found at Pompeii in 1833.

Bernal, Mr. R., No. 93 Eaton-square: Pictures, Arms, and Articles of Vertu (sixteenth and seventeenth centuries). The pictures are portraits, and representations of public processions or historic events; curious, and by celebrated painters. Armour, remarkable for the artistic elaboration of its details. An extensive series of examples of Raphael-ware, Flemish and French pottery and china, form a Ceramic Museum. Also fine specimens of early metal-work; and a valuable collection of ancient watches, of extremely curious design and construction.

Gwilt, Mr. George, No. 8 Union-street, Southwark; and *Gwilt, Mr. Joseph, 20 Abingdon-street, Westminster:* Collections of Architectural Antiquities; the former especially rich in Southwark relics (some Roman), Old London Bridge, &c.

Londesborough, Lord, No. 8 Carlton-House-terrace, possesses a collection of Antiquities ranging from the earliest English period. Saxon remains, urns, arms, and articles of personal decoration, principally excavated by his lordship from tumuli in Kent. Also Irish gold antiques, valuable and curious; and mediæval gold and silver work in jewels, cups, &c. Arms and armour, artistically wrought and richly decorated (but chiefly preserved at Grimstone, in Yorkshire). Lady Londesborough has also collected a series of many hundred antique rings, ranging from the early Egyptian times to the seventeenth century. These collections are shown at *conversazioni* given by Lord and Lady Londesborough during the London season. There is a privately printed Catalogue, by Mr. T. Crofton Croker, F.S.A.

Magniac, Mr. H., No. 87 Jermyn-street, St. James's: a collection chiefly remarkable for its fine Ecclesiastical Works—crosiers, reliquaries, pyxes, &c. Also fine examples of Ancient Carved Furniture, and other specimens of mediæval art.

Marryatt, Mr. P., author of a *History of Pottery,* has a large collection of Ceramic Works, particularly Flemish and German, but exhibiting generally the varied forms and peculiarities of the entire manufacture: formerly at Richmond-terrace, Whitehall; removed to the Ynescedwyn Iron-works, Swansea.

Morgan, Mr. Octavius, Pall Mall, possesses a very valuable series of

Ancient Clocks and Watches; particularly remarkable for its historic illustration of the gradual improvement in watches, from the earliest period to that of Quare and Tompion.

— *Rothschild, the Baron Lionel de, No. 148 Piccadilly,* has a costly collection of Mediæval Art. Also Antique Pottery, including a candlestick formed of white clay, rare Henry II. ware (French), which cost the Baron 220*l.*: not more than 27 articles of this ware are known to exist.

Sainsbury, Mr., No. 13 Upper Ranelagh-street, Pimlico : Historical Mss. and Autographs, 1473 to 1848; enamels, miniatures, medals, and coins; books, drawings, and prints; Shakspeare relics (including the Garrick cup); Napoleon Collection exhibited at the "Napoleon Museum," at the Egyptian Hall, Piccadilly (see page 266).

Slade, Mr. Felix, Walcot-place, Lambeth, possesses a collection of Pottery and Glass of the middle ages; unmatched in fine examples of Venetian workmanship.

Windus, Mr. T., Stamford Hill, possesses, in a building of style 1550, carvings in ivory, mother-of-pearl, and wood; crystals, antique gems, and rings; mosaics, cameos, medals, and coins; Grecian pottery; drawings by Rubens, Rembrandt, and Vandyke; facsimile of the sarcophagus in which the Portland Vase was found.

NATIONAL GALLERY (THE),

On the north side of Trafalgar-square, was built between 1832 and 1838, from the design of Professor Wilkins, R.A., and was his latest work. Its length is 461 feet, and the greatest width 56 feet; and it is built partly with the materials of the King's Mews, the site of which it occupies. The best feature is the centre, the Corinthian columns of which are from the portico of Carlton House, and are adapted from the Temple of Jupiter Stator at Rome.* This portico has interior columns, the only example in the metropolis; and the view commands the broad vista of Parliament-street and Whitehall, and the picturesque towers of the Palace at Westminster. But the Gallery central dome is ill-proportioned and puny; and the corresponding cupolas upon the wings are poor imitations of Vanbrugh's embellishment of private mansions. Through the western wing is a passage leading to a barrack parade; and in the eastern wing is a thoroughfare to Duke's-court, claimed by the inhabitants as *a right of way* long enjoyed by them through the King's Mews. The vestibule is divided, by screens of scagliola columns (with scenic effect), into two halls; and from each is a staircase leading to the upper floors, each a suite of five rooms. The eastern wing is appropriated to the ROYAL ACADEMY OF ARTS, which see. The western wing is occupied by the national collection of pictures, but is ill adapted for large gallery pictures. The ground-floor is mostly official apartments, but was originally intended as a depository for public records: here was temporarily exhibited the Vernon Collection, previous to its removal to Marlborough House. (See page 490.)

In the vestibule is the stupendous Waterloo Vase, sculptured by Sir Richard Westmacott, R.A., from Carrara marble captured from the French, who intended it for a vase to commemorate Napoleon's triumphs: the principal relief celebrates the battle of Waterloo. In the hall is S. Joseph's marble statue of David Wilkie, R.A., with his palette inserted beneath glass in the pedestal. Here also is a fine alto-relievo, in marble, by T. Banks, R.A., of Thetis and her Nymphs rising from the Sea to condole with Achilles on the loss of Patroclus.

* A complete set of casts from these fine specimens of ancient art exists in the Museum of Mr. Joseph Gwilt, F.S.A., Abingdon-street, Westminster.

The National Gallery was founded in 1824, by the purchase of Mr. Angerstein's collection of pictures for 57,000*l.*: it is said, upon the suggestion of George 1V.; but it originated equally in Sir George Beaumont's offer, in 1823, to the Trustees of the British Museum, to present his collection to the public. The Angerstein pictures (38) were first exhibited in the house of Mr. Angerstein, 100 Pall Mall, May 10, 1824; whither Sir George Beaumont's 16 pictures were transferred in 1826. In 1831, 35 pictures were bequeathed by the Rev. W. Holwell Carr; in 1836, 6 pictures were presented by William IV.; 17 bequeathed in 1837 by Lieut.-Col. Ollney; 15 bequeathed in 1838 by Lord Farnborough; 14 bequeathed in 1846 by R. Simmons: and the Gallery has since been increased, by donations, bequests, and comparatively few Government purchases, to about 200 pictures; independently of Mr. Vernon's works of the English School, presented in 1847, and since removed, with the other English pictures, to Marlborough House.

The first Catalogue of the National Gallery, by W. Young Ottley, has long been out of print: the fullest extant is by R. N. Wornum. Among the more notable pictures are two Groups of Saints, by Taddeo Gaddi, painted in tempera, bright colour upon a gold background; curious specimens of middle-age art.

Italian School: The Virgin and Child, with Saints, and a Dead Christ (lunette) from an altar-piece, by Frances o Franc a, early Bolognese School. Virgin and Child, with St. John, by P. Perugino; divinely holy in character and expression. The Raising of Lazarus, by Sebastian del Piombo; the figure of Lazarus by Michael Angelo. St. Catherine of Alexandria, the Vision of a Knight, portrait of Pope Julius II., and fragment of a Cartoon of the Murder of the Innocents, by Raphael. Three of Correggio's greatest works: Mercury instructing Cupid in the presence of Venus; the Ecce Homo; and the Holy Family (La Vierge au Panier): the three pictures cost 14,400*l.* A Holy Family, and Bacchus and Ariadne, by Titian. Susannah and the Elders, by Ludovico Caracci. Eight works of Annibale Caracci: Silenus gathering Grapes; Pan (or Silenus) teaching Apollo to play on the Reed; and Christ appearing to St. Peter. Eight works of Guido, including Susannah and the Elders; and Andromeda. Ten works of Claude (Landscapes and Seaports), including the Chigi and Bouillon Claudes, the latter the Embarkation of the Queen of Sheba. A fine Landscape (Mercury and the Woodman) by Salvator Rosa.

Spanish School: Philip of Spain hunting the Wild Boar, by Velasquez. The Holy Family, St. John with the Lamb, and the Spanish Peasant-boy, by Murillo.

Flemish School: Portraits of a Flemish Gentleman and Lady, in a bedchamber; under the mirror is written, "Johannes de Eyck fait hic, 1434." Nine works of Rubens: including the Sabine Women; Peace and War, presented to Charles I. by Rubens, in 1630; the Brazen Serpent; St. Bavon, harmonious and picturesque; Rubens's own Chateau; the Judgment of Paris, from the Orleans Collection; and the Apotheosis of James 1., sketched for the Whitehall ceiling. Vandyke's magnificent St. Ambrosius and the Emperor Theodosius; and the same painter's "Gevartius," or Vander Geest, a portrait scarcely equalled in the world,—but by some attributed to Rubens. The Woman taken in Adultery, one of Rembrandt's finest early works; his Christ taken down from the Cross; his Adoration of the Shepherds; a Woman Bathing; and three of his marvellous portraits. A sunny Landscape, with cattle and figures, by Cuyp. The Misers, or Money-changers, by David Teniers.

French School: Eight works of Nicolas Poussin, including two Bacchanalian Festivals, and the Plague, of Ashdod, very fine. Also, six works of Gaspar Poussin, including his masterpiece, a Landscape with Abraham and Isaac; and his fine classical picture of Dido and Æneas in a storm.

The National Gallery is open to the public on Mondays, Tuesdays, Wednesdays, and Thursdays; and on Fridays and Saturdays to students only. It is open from 10 to 5, from October until April 30, inclusive; and from 10 to 6, from May 1, inclusive, until the middle of September, when it is wholly closed until the end of October. The expenses of the Gallery (exclusive of purchases) are about 1000*l.* per annum; and it has been visited in one year by more than half a million persons.

The design and inadequacy of the Gallery building have been universally condemned; but it should be remembered that it scarcely cost more than the marble arch for Buckingham Palace.

NEW RIVER,

A fine artificial stream yielding almost half the water-supply of London, or nearly the whole of the City and a large portion of the metropolis northward of the Thames. New River rises from Chadwell Springs, and springs at Amwell, between Hertford and Ware, 21 miles from London, and is fed by the river Lea and wells sunk in the chalk. To preserve a level, it takes a winding course, and was originally conveyed across valleys in immense wooden troughs or aqueducts; but it now flows through raised mounds of earth, at the rate of two miles an hour, and averages 18 feet wide and 5 deep, falling 3 inches in each mile. Having reached Stoke Newington, it passes onward by a subterraneous channel of 300 yards, beneath Highbury, to the east of Islington; rising again in Colebrooke-row, and reaching its termination at the New River Head, Clerkenwell: its entire length is 38¾ miles 16 poles. It has 43 sluices, 215 bridges, and nearly 60 culverts, including the Islington Tunnel. At Stoke Newington are two immense store reservoirs, covering 38 acres of land, where the water remains about seven days for subsidence; whence it passes to the Clerkenwell reservoir, about 5 acres, 85 feet above the mid-tide level of the Thames. Thence the water flows by its own gravity into the mains (of iron, substituted for wooden pipes between 1810 and 1820) supplying the lower district; while two steam-engines pump the water into another reservoir 30 feet higher, in Claremont-square, for the high services. The northern district, including the hills of Hampstead, Highgate, &c., is supplied from the Stoke Newington reservoirs, by steam-power; and at Highgate are two other reservoirs, 320 and 430 feet above the Thames. In the Hampstead-road is a reservoir, supplied by steam-power from a well sunk into the chalk, 230 feet deep. The entire supply of New River water is about 18,000,000 gallons per day.

The New River was projected by Hugh Myddleton, a native of Denbigh, and "citizen and goldsmith," who proposed to the City to bring to London a supply of water at his own cost. His offer was accepted; and April 20, 1608, was commenced the work, with very imperfect mechanical resources. Myddleton embarked the whole of his fortune in the undertaking: the original number of shares was only 36; the labourers received half-a-crown a-day. The works were stopped at Enfield for want of funds; Myddleton applied to the citizens for aid, which they refused; he then solicited James I., who, on May 2, 1612, agreed to pay half the expense and become a partner, and advanced 6,437l. 11s. 10½d., for which 19 additional shares were created. The works were now resumed; and on the 29th of September, 1613, five years and five months from the commencement of the undertaking, and the day on which Sir Thomas Myddleton, Hugh's brother, was elected lord-mayor, the water was let into the basin at Clerkenwell, with great ceremony, before the lord-mayor, aldermen, and principal citizens: a troop of labourers "wearing green Monmouth caps, and carrying spades, shovels, and pickaxes," marched after drums round the cistern; and one man delivered 48 lines in verse, ending:

> "Now for the fruits, then. Flow forth, precious spring,
> So long and dearly sought for, and now bring
> Comfort to all that love thee; loudly sing,
> And with thy crystal murmurs struck together,
> Bid all thy true well-wishers welcome hither."

"When the floodgates flew open, the stream ran gallantly into the cisterne, drummes and trumpets sounding in triumphall manner, and a brave peal of chambers (guns) gave full issue to the intended entertainment." The work cost about 500,000l. Myddleton was created a baronet in 1622. The proprietors were incorporated in 1619 as the New River Company, Sir Hugh being appointed the first governor, and this being the first water-company; although Ben Jonson, in 1598, says, "We have water-companies now, instead of water-carriers." (*Every Man in his Humour.*)

No dividend was made by the Company till 1633, when 11*l.* 9*s.* 1*d.* was divided upon each share. The second dividend amounted to only 3*l.* 4*s.* 2*d.*, and more money was required; when Charles I., rather than advance it, in 1636 re-conveyed to Sir Hugh Myddleton the whole of King James's shares for an annual rent of 500*l.*, and the royal moiety was divided into 36 "King's Shares," from which the above rent is paid to this day into the Exchequer; the other moiety being 36 "Adventurers' Shares:" these 72 shares were in 1756 worth 5000*l.* per share; they have since been subdivided, and a whole thirty-sixth share of the King's has been sold for 10,600*l.* Sir Hugh Myddleton died in 1633, holding shares in the Company, and others in mines in Wales, and was not so poor as usually represented. He bequeathed to the Goldsmiths' Company one New River share, which formerly produced 314*l.* per annum, but now does not reach 200*l.*: it is distributed half-yearly among the poor of the Company, especially to men of Myddleton's name or kindred. There is a fine portrait of Sir Hugh, by Janssen, at Goldsmiths' Hall. (See page 352.) Yet his family fell into decay: Lady Myddleton, the mother of the last Sir Hugh, received from the Goldsmiths' Company a pension of 20*l.* per annum, which was afterwards continued to her son, with whom the baronetcy became extinct. (*Gentleman's Magazine*, vol. liv. p. 805.) Some of the family have since sought relief from the New River Company.

The New River Head is a vast circular basin enclosed by a brick wall, whence the water is conveyed by sluices into large brick cisterns, and thence by mains and riders, named according to the districts which they supply. Here is the Company's house, originally built in 1613: the board-room, over one of the cisterns, is wainscoted, and has a fine specimen of Gibbons's carving; on the ceiling are a portrait of William III., and the arms of Myddleton and Green.

North of the New River Head, the stream was formerly let into a tank or reservoir under the stage of Sadler's Wells Theatre, which was drawn up by machinery for "real water" scenes, the water being sufficiently deep for men to swim in. Formerly, in the fields behind the British Museum, the New River pipes were propped up 6 and 8 feet, so that persons walked under them to gather watercresses.

The 72 New River Shares are stated to yield an annual profit of 43,200*l.*, or 600*l.* a share; and a single share has been sold for 14,000*l.* On Jan. 28, 1852, three-sevenths of a quarter of a King's New River Share sold for 1600*l.*; the dividend on this share of a share producing about 90*l.* per annum. The entire works have cost about a million and a half of money; and the gross income of the Company is about 140,000*l.* per annum.

NEW-ROAD (THE),

From the Angel Inn, Islington, to the Yorkshire Stingo, Lisson Green, was formed in 1757, "to avoid the stones:" and among advantages promised by the Act of Parliament, was the avoidance of "driving cattle from the western road through the streets to Smithfield Market;" and in times of threatened invasion, "this New-road will form a complete line of circumvallation, and his Majesty's forces may easily and expeditiously march this way into Essex, to defend our coasts, without passing through the cities of London and Westminster." Yet the road was formidably opposed by the Duke of Bedford, lest the dust might annoy him in his house half a mile off, and buildings might be erected;

which would intercept his prospect; "but," said Walpole, "if he (the Duke) is in town, he is too short-sighted to see the prospect." Within half a century, Bedford House was levelled to the ground, and the fields beyond it are now covered with houses, enlarging by many thousands the income of the Bedford family, with a reversionary interest in a city of itself. The New-road is the great omnibus route from Paddington to the City; whereas in 1798 only one coach ran from Paddington to the Bank, and the proprietor was nearly ruined by the speculation! Shillibeer, the first omnibus-proprietor, fared no better in 1829. In 1853, Parliament sanctioned a railway to run beneath the New-road, from Paddington to Battle-bridge.

NEWGATE-STREET,

Named from the City-gate at its east end, has on the south side the end of Newgate Prison, and extends eastward to Cheapside, with lanes and courts on the south leading to Paternoster-row. On the north side is the front of the great hall of Christ's Hospital (see page 80), built upon the site of Grey Friars' monastery; the principal gates have characteristic casts and sculpture. Nearly opposite is *Warwick-lane*, with a bas-relief of Guy Earl of Warwick, dated 1668; the old College of Physicians (see page 207); and the old inns, the *Bell* and *Oxford Arms*. Next is *Ivy-lane*, "so called of ivy growing on the walls of the Prebend-house." (*Stow.*) Here Dr. Johnson, in 1748, with Hawkesworth and Hawkins, formed a Club for literary discussion. Here also have lived publishers for two centuries.

"I was at Rayston's shop, in Ivie Lane, Febr. the 8, 1661. Hee printed the Marquis of Winchester's conference with the King: hee printed most of the Royalists' works, as Hamond's, Taylor's pieces, and others."—*Diary of Rev. John Ward.*

On the north side, up a passage, is Christ Church, described at page 123. Next is *King Edward-street* (see page 499). Above *Bull-Head-court* is a stone bas-relief of William Evans, 7 feet 6 inches high, porter to Charles I.; and Jeffrey Hudson, the king's dwarf, 3 feet 9 inches high. *Bath-street*, first Pincock or Pentecost lane, and next Bagnio-court, was named from there being here the first Bagnio in the town, after the Turkish fashion; now hot and cold baths. Nearly opposite is *Pannier-alley*, on the east wall of which is the sculptured stone described at page 457: it is stated by Stow to have been a sign. In Ben Jonson's *Bartholomew Fair* we hear of the stinking tripe of Panyer-alley. In *Queen's-Head-passage* is a Queen Anne tavern, now *Dolly's Chop-house*: Gainsborough is said to have painted Dolly.

NEWINGTON, OR NEWINGTON BUTTS,

A large parish in Surrey, adjoining St. George, Southwark, north and east; Camberwell, south; and Lambeth, west. In Domesday Book (11th century), the only inhabited part of this parish was Walworth, where, according to the Norman survey, was a church, upon the rebuilding of which on a new site it probably became "surrounded with houses, which obtained the name of *Neweton*, as it is called in the most ancient records; it was afterwards spelt Newenton and Newington." (Lysons's *Environs*, vol. i. p. 389.) Here were *butts* for archery practice: the earliest record of *Newington Butts* is in the register of Archbishop Pole at Lambeth, date 1558. In the reign of Henry VIII. (1546), three men were condemned as Anabaptists, and "brent in the highway beyond Southwark, towards Newenton." (Stow's *Chronicle*, p. 964.) The only manor in the parish is *Walworth*, given by King Edmund Ironside to Hitard, his jester, who, in the reign of Edward the Confessor, gave the vill of Walworth to the monks of Christ Church at

Canterbury. They received from Edward II. a grant of free-warren here; and in the reign of Edward III. and Richard II., and subsequently, the manor is said to have been held by persons of a family named from this place: thus, Margaret de Walworth, lady of the manor in 1396, was the widow of the famous Sir William Walworth; and at Walworth is a modern sign of his killing Wat Tyler in Smithfield. In the museum of the Society of Antiquaries is a dagger which was found on the supposed site of Sir William's house at Walworth. (See FISHMONGERS' HALL, page 350.) Sir George Walworth died seized of the manor in 1474. In the valuation of Church property, 26 Henry VIII., it is rated at 37l. 8s. In the reign of Henry III., the queen's goldsmith held of the king, in capite, one acre of land in Neweton, by the service of rendering one gallon of honey. The old church (St. Mary's) is described at page 146. There are district churches and various sectarian chapels. South of Newington Causeway (the first road across the swampy fields) is Horsemonger-lane, opposite wh'ch was formerly a hay-market. In the lane is the County Gaol and Surrey Sessions-house, built upon the site of a market-garden, three and a half acres, by George Gwilt, 1798-9. At Walworth, upon a demesne once attached to the manor-house, are the Surrey Zoological Gardens, where Cross removed his menagerie from the King's Mews in 1831.

Maitland notes: west of the Fishmongers' Almshouses (see page 5) "is a moorish ground, with a small watercourse denominated the river Tygris, which is part of Cnut's trench; the outflux of which is on the east side of Rotherhithe parish, where the Great Wet Dock is situate." In 1823, when the road between the almshouses and Newington church was dug up for a new sewer, some piles and posts were discovered, with rings for mooring barges; also a pot of coins of Charles II. and William III. A parishioner named Farns, who died, aged 109 years, early in the present century, remembered when boats came up this "river" as far as the church at Newington. (Brayley's Surrey, vol. iii. p. 405.) The old Elephant and Castle is noticed at page 399.

NEWINGTON GREEN,

In the parishes of Stoke Newington and Islington, had, within the present century, several ancient houses, one of which, on the south side, was traditionally a palace of Henry VIII.; and a path leading from the Green to Ball's Pond turnpike has been, time out of mind, called King Henry's Walk: the house was, however, evidently built in the reign of James I. At the north-west corner of the Green was "Bishop's Place," where Henry Algernon, Earl of Percy, is said to have written his memorable letter disclaiming matrimonial contract with Queen Anne Boleyn, dated "at Newington Greene," the 13th of May, 28th Henry VIII. Here lived several of the ejected ministers, towards the close of the 17th century. (See DISSENTERS' CHAPELS, page 175.) Adjoining Bishop's Place was a porch-house, wherein was born, in 1762, Samuel Rogers, the poet.

"His boyish enthusiasm led Rogers to sigh for an interview with Dr. Johnson; and to attain this, he twice presented himself at the door of Johnson's well-known house in Bolt-court, Fleet-street. On the first occasion, the great moralist was not at home; and the second time, after he had rung the bell, the heart of the young aspirant misgave him, and he retreated without waiting for the servant. Rogers was then in his fourteenth year."—R. Carruthers.

NEWINGTON, OR STOKE NEWINGTON,

In Domesday, Newtone, and Stoke Neweton as early as 1391, is named from the Saxon stoc, wood, it having been part of the ancient forest of Middlesex; and in 1649 here were upwards of 77 acres of woodland in demesne. It is separated from Hackney and Ossulston by the great road, anciently the Ermen-street. Tradesmen's tokens were issued from here in the 17th century : one exists with " Laurence Short, Adam and Eve" (in the field between Islington church and the City-road) ; and another, " John Ball, at the Boarded House, neere Newing-ton Greene," who kept a low house for bull-baiting, duck-hunting, &c. at Ball's Pond, long since filled up, but it gives name to a little hamlet. At Stoke Newington lived Fleetwood, the Parliamentary general; Daniel Defoe and Thomas Day (*Sandford and Merton*) were educated here; John Howard, the philanthropist, lodged here, and married his land-lady ; Hannah Snell, the soldier, lived in Church-street ; here died Mrs. Barbauld, in 1825, in her 82d year. The mansion of Sir Thomas Abney, where Dr. Watts resided with his pious friend, existed until 1844, the fine grounds now being the Abney Park Cemetery. (See page 69.)

NEWSPAPERS.

The earliest printed London newspaper is preserved in the British Museum, and is the *Weekly Newes*, May 23, 1622, by Nathaniel But-ter, whose invention was ridiculed in Ben Jonson's *Staple of News*, 1625 ; and a few months after, in Fletcher's *Fair Maid of the Inn*: it was sold " at the Exchange, and in Pope's-head Pallace." In 1696 there were nine newspapers published in London, all weekly. In 1709 the newspapers had increased to eighteen : in this year appeared the *Daily Courant*, the first morning paper; and to the reign of Queen Anne the first publication of " regular newspapers" must be referred. In 1724 there were three daily, six three times a-week, seven three times a-week, three halfpenny posts, and the *London Gazette* twice a-week; in 1792, thirteen daily, and twenty semi-weekly and weekly papers.

The oldest existing London papers are, the *English Chronicle, or Whitehall Evening Post*, started 1747;[*] the *Public Ledger*, commenced Jan. 12, 1760, by Newbery, the bookseller, and in which appeared Goldsmith's *Citizen of the World*; the *St. James's Chronicle*, 1761; and the *Morning Chronicle*, 1769.

The *Morning Chronicle* was conducted by William Woodfall till 1789, when he was succeeded by James Perry, who introduced the present system of reporting the debates in Parliament. Mr. (Serjeant) Spankie was long editor of the *Chronicle*; Lord Campbell commenced on it his London career, and was its theatrical critic in 1810. Cole-ridge and Campbell were contributors. Sheridan names the *Chronicle* in his *Critic*; Canning, in a poem; Byron addressed to it a familiar letter; Hazlitt was its theatrical critic; and here first appeared *Sketches by Boz* (Charles Dickens), who resides in Tavistock House, where Mr. Perry lived many years. After Perry's death (1821), the *Chronicle* was purchased for 42,000*l*. by Mr. Clement, who, in 1834, sold it to Sir John Easthope, Bart. Until 1822, the *Chronicle* was printed at 143 Strand : and in the same office was subsequently printed, by John Limbird, the *Mirror*, the first of the cheap illustrated periodicals.

The *Morning Post*, established in 1772, circulated in 1795 only 350 a-day. Coleridge, in his *Table-Talk*, states that he raised the sale in one year to 7000; in 1803 it was 4500 :

"Coleridge, long before his flighty pen ·
Let to the *Morning Post* its aristocracy."—Byron's *Don Juan*.

Sir James Mackintosh and Charles Lamb were also contributors; and Mackworth Praed, the poet, was some time editor.

The *Morning Herald* was commenced Nov. 1, 1780, by Mr. Bate, afterwards Sir Henry Bate Dudley, who seceded from the *Morning Post*.

* There had previously been a *London Chronicle*, which was regularly read by George III., whose copy of it may be seen in the British Museum.—Hunt's *Fourth Estate*, vol. ii. p. 99.

The Times was commenced by John Walter, in Printing-House-square, Blackfriars, previously the site of the King's Printing-House.* The first number, Jan. 1, 1788 (that in the British Museum has no stamp), was a continuation of the *Daily Universal Register*, No. 939, which, with the *Times*, was " printed logographically," *i. e.* with stereotyped words and metal letters. In 1803, the late John Walter, son of the above, became joint-proprietor and exclusive manager of the *Times*, whence, by priority of its intelligence, it has risen to be " the leading journal of Europe.'' The *Times* of Nov. 29, 1814, was the first newspaper printed by steam, from two machines made by Kœnig, which produced 1800 per hour, until 1827, when they were superseded by Applegath and Cowper's four-cylindered machine, yielding 5000 impressions per hour : and in 1848 was erected Applegath's vertical machine, producing 8000 copies in an hour. Mr. Walter died in Printing-House-square in 1847, bequeathing a large personal estate, and having erected and endowed a handsome church at Bearwood, Berks. He devised his interest in the *Times* to his son, Mr. John Walter, M.P. for Nottingham, the present proprietor ; the journal being thus still in the hands of the family of its founder, and in this respect standing alone amongst the morning papers. (Hunt's *Fourth Estate*, vol. ii. p. 153.) Amongst the many valuable services rendered by the *Times* to the commercial world, was the detection and exposure of the Bogle conspiracy in 1841 ; in indemnification of which, 2625*l.*—the *Times* Testimonial—was subscribed by the London merchants and bankers, but was declined ; and the amount was invested in scholarships at Christ's Hospital and the City of London School, where and in the Royal Exchange are commemorative tablets, as also upon the façade of the *Times* Office.

The Times Printing Machinery may be inspected, by previously obtained cards, at 11 a.m., when the second edition of the paper is being printed. In a large room is a circular gallery, about 25 feet in diameter and 6 from the ground, surmounting 8 large fabrics radiating from a central tower or drum, each fabric being attached to one of the 8 printing-cylinders. In the gallery are 8 men feeding the 8 mouths of the machine, each at the rate of 1 sheet in 4 seconds : under these 8 men are 8 others, who take off the printed sheets thrown out of the machine. On the face of the drum are the four forms of type, in contact with which are brought the 8 printing-cylinders, their bearings being carried by the framing which supports the central drum, so that they all revolve in perfect correspondence. Between the forms of type on the drum are inking-tables, which communicate the ink to upright rollers placed between the several printing-cylinders, the rollers in their turn inking the type. In fact, the machine is composed of the parts in ordinary use, but made circular, and placed in a vertical instead of a horizontal position. The ingenious mode of feeding the printing-cylinders with sheets of paper, and shifting their positions, is the great problem of the invention. (See Weale's *London*, page 76.)

The *Times* has quintupled its circulation since 1838. Its average sale in the year 1855 was 59,000 per diem. The Paper and Supplement, 72 columns, are made up of more than a million of pieces of type. In 1846, the profit on each copy was stated to be ⅜ of a penny, out of which were to be defrayed all the expenses of the journal, except paper and stamp : the annual amount of stamp-duty was then 60,000*l.* The large issues of the *Times* were, Oct. 29, 1844 (opening of the New Royal Exchange), 50,000. Jan. 28, 1846 (Sir R. Peel's speech on the

* Beneath the *Times* office is a fragment of the Roman wall, upon which is a Norman or Early English reparation ; and upon that are the remains of a passage and window, which probably belonged to the Blackfriars monastery.—*National Miscellany*, October 1853.

·Corn Laws and the Tariff), 52,000, when the usual number was between 27 and 28,000. March 1, 1848 (French Revolution), 48,000. April 11, 1848 (Chartist Meeting), 46,000. May 2, 1851 (opening of the Great Exhibition), 55,000. Sept. 15 and 16, 1852 (Death of the Duke of Wellington), 2 days, each 53,000. Nov. 19, 1852 (Funeral of the Duke), 70,000. The advertisements during June 1853 averaged 1500 each day; and in one day in June there were 2250 inserted! the greatest number that ever appeared in one paper. It has been stated, that in printing one of the above large issues were used 7 tons of paper; surface printed, 30 acres; weight of type, 7 tons.

Among the literary *collaborateurs* of the *Times*, the names of Barnes, Sterling, and Twiss are prominent. Mr. Justice Talfourd and Baron Alderson were once upon its staff. The editorship was offered to Southey, with a salary of 2000l. per annum, but was declined; and a similar offer was made to the poet Moore, with a like result.

The Morning Advertiser was established in 1795, as the organ of the interests and charities of Licensed Victuallers.

The Daily News dates from 1846, and is the only successful attempt (save one, the *Advertiser*) to establish a morning paper since the *Times*.

The Star, the first daily evening newspaper, established in 1788 by Peter Stuart, was long conducted by Dr. Tilloch, editor of the *Philosophical Magazine.*

Johnson's Sunday Monitor, the first newspaper published on the Sabbath, appeared in 1778. The oldest weekly newspaper is the *Observer*, established 1792. *Bell's Weekly Messenger* dates from 1796.

The Illustrated London News, projected by Herbert Ingram, and commenced May 14, 1842, enjoys the largest sale of the weekly papers; in 1855 its usual weekly sale exceeded 140,000. Its largest issue was 230,000, double number (Funeral of the Duke of Wellington).

Newspapers are filed at Peele's Coffee-House, Nos. 177 and 178 Fleet-street (see page 203); at Deacon's, No. 3 Walbrook (see page 201); and at the British Museum (see page 525).

OLD BAILEY,

The street extending from Ludgate-hill to Newgate-street; "outside of Ludgate, parallel with the walls as far as Newgate." Hence the name—from the *ballium*, or outer space, near Ludgate,* its relative position in regard to the ancient wall of the City; the remains of which may be traced in some massive stone-work in Seacoal-lane, at the bottom of Breakneck-steps, west of the Old Bailey; and opposite its entrance from Ludgate-hill, in St. Martin's-court. (See page 447.) Maitland, however, refers Old Bailey to Bail-hill; an eminence whereon was situated the *bail*, or bailiff's house, wherein he held a court for the trial of malefactors: and the place of security where the Sheriff keeps the prisoners during the session is still named the *Bail-dock*. Stow states the Chamberlain of London to have kept his court here in the reign of Edward III. In Pennant's time, here stood Sydney House (then occupied by a coachmaker), the mansion of the Sydneys till they removed to Leicester-fields. (See page 453.) The Old-Bailey Sessions-house is described at pp. 447-448.

"By a sort of second-sight, the Surgeons' Theatre was built near this court of conviction and Newgate, the concluding stage of the lives forfeited to the justice of their country, several years before the fatal tree was removed from Tyburn to

* The church of St. Peter in the Bailey, at Oxford, derives its appellation from having formerly stood within the outer ballium of Oxford Castle.

present site. It is a handsome building, ornamented with Ionic pilasters, and with a double flight of steps to the first floor. Beneath is a door for the admission of the bodies of murderers and other felons, who, noxious in their lives, make a sort of reparation to their fellow-creatures by becoming useful after death."—*Pennant.*

After the execution of Lord Ferrers, at Tyburn, in 1760, the body was conveyed in his own landau and six to Surgeons' Hall, to undergo the remainder of the sentence. A large incision having been made from the neck to the bottom of the breast, and another across the throat, the lower part of the belly was laid open, and the bowels were taken away. The body was afterwards publicly exposed to view in a first-floor room; and a print of the time shows the corpse "as it lay in the Surgeons' Hall." Here sat the Court of Examiners, by whom Oliver Goldsmith was rejected 21st December, 1758; and in the books of the College of Surgeons, amidst a long list of candidates who passed, occur: *James Bernard, mate to an hospital. Oliver Goldsmith, found not qualified for ditto.*" "A rumour of this rejection long existed; and on a hint from Maton, the king's physician, Mr. Prior succeeded in discovering it." (Forster's *Life and Adventures of Oliver Goldsmith,* page 140.) Surgeons' Hall was taken down in 1809, and upon its site was built the New Sessions-house; whence the prison of Newgate extends on the east side of the street, widened at the north end by the removal of the houses of the Little Old Bailey. Here the place of execution was changed from Tyburn in 1783, and the first culprit executed Dec. 9. The gallows was built with three cross-beams, for as many rows of sufferers; and between February and December 1785, ninety-six persons suffered by "the new drop," substituted for the cart. About 1786, here was the last execution followed by burning the body; when a woman was hung upon a low gibbet, and life being extinct, fagots were piled around her and over her head, fire was set to the pile, and the corpse burnt to ashes. On one occasion the old mode of execution was renewed: a triangular gallows was set up in the road opposite Green-Arbour-court, and the cart was drawn from under the criminals' feet.*

Memorable Executions in the Old Bailey.—Mrs. Phepoe, murderess, Dec. 11, 1797. Governor Wall, murder, Jan. 28, 1802. Holloway and Haggerty, murder, Feb. 22, 1807 (30 spectators trodden to death). Bellingham, assassin of Mr. Perceval, May 18, 1812. Eliza Fenning, poisoning, July 26, 1815. Arthur Thistlewood and 4 others (Cato-street gang, see page 67), murder and treason, May 1, 1820 (their bodies were decapitated by a surgeon on the scaffold). Fauntleroy, the banker, forgery, Nov. 30, 1824. Joseph Hunton (Quaker), forgery, Dec. 8, 1828. Bishop and Williams, murder (burkers), Dec. 5, 1831. John Pegsworth, murder, March 7, 1837. James Greenacre, murder, May 2, 1837. Courvoisier, murder of Lord William Russell, July 6, 1840.

In Green-Arbour-court, No. 12, at the corner of Breakneck-steps, in Seacoal-lane, leading from Farringdon-street, lodged Oliver Goldsmith from 1758 to 1760, when he wrote for the *Monthly Review;* and the editor, Griffiths, became security for the suit of clothes in which Goldsmith offered himself for examination at Surgeons' Hall. In this miserable lodging he was writing his *Polite Learning Enquiry,* when Dr. Percy called upon him, and the fellow-lodger's poor ragged girl came to borrow "a chamberpotful of coals." The house was taken down twenty years since, and stables now occupy its site.

* It was formerly the usage to execute the criminal near the scene of his guilt. Those who were punished capitally for the Riots of 1780 suffered in such parts of the town as they were detected; and in 1790 two incendiaries were hanged in Aldersgate-street, at the eastern end of Long-lane, opposite the site of the house they had set fire to. Since that period there have been few executions in London, except in front of Newgate. The last deviation from the regular course was in the case of the sailor Cashman, who was hung, in 1817, in Skinner-street, opposite the shop of Mr. Beckwith, the gunsmith, which he had plundered.

Peter Bales, the celebrated penman, in Queen Elizabeth's reign, kept a writing-school, in 1590, at the upper end of the Old Bailey, and published here his *Writing School-Master :* in a writing trial he won a golden pen, value 20*l.* ; and the "*arms of caligraphy,* viz. azure, a pen or, were given to Bales as a prize." (*Sir George Buck.*) Prynne's *Histrio-Mastix* was printed "for Michael Sparke, and sold at the Blue Bible, in Little Old Bayly, 1633."

William Camden, "the nourrice of antiquitie," was born in the Old Bailey, where his father was a painter-stainer. In Ship-court, on the west side, was born William Hogarth, the painter; and at the corner of Ship-court, No. 67, three doors from Ludgate-hill, William Hone kept a little shop, where he published his noted "Parodies" in 1817, for which he was three times tried and acquitted.* Next door, at No. 68, lived the infamous Jonathan Wild.

OLD JEWRY,

A street leading from the Poultry to Cateaton-street; and "so called" of Jews some time dwelling there and near adjoining" (*Stow*), first brought here by William Duke of Normandy. They had here, at the north-west corner, a synagogue, suppressed in 1291; it was next the church of the Friars of the Sack : here Robert Large kept his mayoralty in 1439; Hugh Clopton in 1492; and in Stow's time it was the Windmill Tavern, mentioned in Ben Jonson's *Every Man in his Humour :* its site is denoted by Windmill-court. "In the reign of Henry VI., at the north end was one of the king's palaces" (*Hatton*); in the reign of Richard III. it was called the Prince's Wardrobe; and in 1548, end Edward VI., it was sold to Sir Anthony Cope. On the west side, about 40 yards from Cheapside, was built in 1670 the Mercers' Chapel Grammar School, removed in 1787, when Old Jewry was widened.

On the eastern side is the Lord Mayor's Court-office (see p. 452). In a courtyard here is the stately mansion built by Sir Robert Clayton for keeping his shrievalty in 1671. It stands upon a stone balustraded terrace. The house is of ornamental brickwork: the staircase was painted with the story of Hercules and Omphale, by Sir James Thornhill, in chiaro-oscuro ; besides a copy of the Rape of Deïanira, after Guido. John Evelyn, who had a great feast here, describes in his *Diary*, Sept. 26th, 1672, the mansion as "built indeede for a greate magistrate, at excessive cost. The cedar dining-room is painted with the history of the Gyants' War, incomparably done by Mr. Streeter ; but the figures are too near the eye." Mr. Bray, the editor of the *Diary*, adds (1818), "These paintings have long since been removed to the seat of the Clayton family at Marden, near Godstone, in Surrey."

In 1679-80, March 9, Charles II. and the Duke of York supped at the mansion in the Old Jewry, with Sir Robert Clayton, then Lord Mayor : the balconies of the houses in the streets were illuminated with flambeaux ; and the king and the duke had a passage made for them by the Trained Bands upon the guard, from Cheapside. The mansion was subsequently tenanted by several eminent citizens; then by Samuel Sharp, the celebrated surgeon; in 1806 it was opened as the temporary

---

* At the same time, Hone kept shop at 55 Fleet-street: here he published the *Life of Eliza Fenning,* who was hung, in 1815, for administering poison to the family of Turner, a law-stationer, in Chancery-lane. Hone's account of Eliza Fenning shews her to have been guiltless; and Turner's house had to be protected from the fury of the populace. In 1833 it was stated in the *Times* newspaper, that Turner's brother, upon his deathbed, had confessed that he had administered the poison, for which crime Eliza Fenning had suffered innocently. In Fleet-street Hone published the first of his political satires, illustrated by George Cruikshank. No. 62 was the shop of Richard Carlile, the freethinking publisher.

house of the London Institution (see page 471); next as the Museum of the London Missionary Society; and it is now divided into offices.

In Ben Jonson's *Every Man in his Humour,* Master Stephen dwells at Hogsden, the dwellers of which have a long suburb to pass before they reach London. "I am sent for this morning by a friend in the Old Jewry to come to him: it is but crossing over the fields to Moorgate." In the Old Jewry dwelt Cob the waterman, by the wall at the bottom of Coleman-street, "at the sign of the Water Tankard, hard by the Green Lattice."—C. Knight's *London,* vol. i. p. 368.

OLD-STREET,

Or *Eald-street,* is part of a Roman military way, which anciently led from the eastern to the western parts of the kingdom. Old-street extends from opposite the north-eastern corner of Charter-house garden to St. Luke's church (see page 164); whence to Shoreditch church (see page 134) the continuation is *Old-Street-road,* where are St. Luke's (see page 384) and the London Lying-in Hospitals. St. Leonard's, Shoreditch, was anciently a village upon the Eald-street, at some distance north of London; Hoxton, or Hocheston, was originally a small village, and had a market; and the manor of Finsbury, in the reign of Henry VIII., consisted chiefly of fields, orchards, and gardens. Old-street was also famous for its nursery-grounds; and here are several almshouses, mostly built when this suburb was open, healthful ground. *Pesthouse-lane* (now Bath-street) is named from a pesthouse established here during the Great Plague of 1665, and removed in 1737. In *Brick-lane* is one of the three earliest stations established by the first Gas Light Company in the metropolis, incorporated in 1812.

Picthatch, a profligate resort, named in the plays of Shakspeare, Ben Jonson, and Middleton, was supposed to have been in Turnmill-street, Clerkenwell, until Mr. Cunningham identified Picthatch with "Pickax-yard," in Old-street, near the Charter-house. (See *Handbook,* 2d edit. p. 400.)

At the corner of Old-street, in the City-road, are Vinegar-works, formerly the property of Mr. James Calvert, who won the first 20,000*l.* prize ever drawn in an English lottery, and in a subsequent lottery gained 5000*l.*; yet he died in extreme poverty, Feb. 26, 1799.

OMNIBUS (THE),

A hackney carriage for twelve or more passengers inside, is stated to have been tried about the year 1800, with four horses and six wheels, but unsuccessfully. We remember a long-bodied East Grinstead coach in 1808; and a like conveyance between Hemel Hempstead, Herts, and the metropolis. The Greenwich stages were mostly of this build; and a character in the farce of *Too Late for Dinner,* produced in 1820, talks of "the great green Greenwich coach," the omnibus of that period. Still, its invention is claimed for M. Baudry, of Nantes. It has been extended to all parts of the world: even in the sandy environs of Cairo you are whisked to your hotel in an Oriental omnibus.

Mr. Shillibeer, in his evidence before the Board of Health, states that on July 4, 1829, he started the first pair of omnibuses in the metropolis—from the Bank to the Yorkshire Stingo, New-road; copied from Paris, where M. Lafitte, the banker, had previously established omnibuses in 1819. Each of Shillibeer's vehicles carried 22 passengers inside, but only the driver outside; and each omnibus was drawn by three horses abreast: the fare was 1*s.* for the whole journey, and 6*d.* for half the distance; and for some time the passengers were provided with periodicals to read on the journey. Shillibeer's first "conductors" were the two sons of British naval officers, who were succeeded by young men in velvet liveries. The first omnibuses were called "Shillibeers," and the name is common to this day in New York. Omnibuses ruined the elder branch of the Bourbons in 1830: the accidental upset of an omnibus suggested the first idea of a barricade, and thus changed the whole science of revolutions.

Each London omnibus costs about 120*l.*, and 10 horses for the same 200*l.*; harness, 20*l.*; stable utensils, 5*l.*; annual repairs, 52*l.*; wear and tear of horses, 20*s* per week for each omnibus; rent of stabling, 20*l.* The salaries of drivers, conductors, stable-men, time-keepers, clerks, smiths, &c. (upwards of 11,000), average 28*s.* each man. Each omnibus pays about 108*l.* yearly duty. There are nearly 3000 omnibuses, stated to have cost 1,020,000*l.*, and to require a further annual outlay of 2,700,000*l.* to maintain on the streets. The 30,000 horses cost annually two millions of money for hay, straw, and corn, and shoeing. Each omnibus has about 300 fares daily, or 2000 per week; and the whole number of omnibuses 6,000,000 per week, or 300,000,000 a-year. Each omnibus averages between 40 and 50 miles a-day. Annual amount of fares three millions sterling.

OXFORD-STREET,

Originally *Tyburn-road*, and next *Oxford-road* (the highway to Oxford), extends from the site of the village pound of St. Giles's (where High-street and Tottenham-Court-road meet), westward to Hyde Park Corner, 1½ mile in length, containing upwards of 400 houses. Hatton, in 1708, described it "between St. Giles's Pound east, and the lane leading to the gallows west." It follows the ancient military road (*Via Trinovantica*, Stukeley), which crossed the Watling-street at Hyde Park Corner, and was continued thence to Old-street (Eald-street), north of London. During the Civil War, in 1643, a redoubt was erected near St. Giles's Pound, and a large fort with half bulwarks across the road opposite Wardour-street. In a map of 1707, on the south side. King-street, Golden-square, is perfect to Oxford-road, between which and Berwick-street are fields; hence to St. Giles's is covered with buildings, but westward not a house is seen; the north side contains a few scattered buildings, but no semblance of streets west of Tottenham-Court-road. A plan of 1708 shews, at the south end of Mill-hill Field, the Lord Mayor's Banquetting-house, at the north-east corner of the bridge arcross Tyburn brook (over which is built the west side of Stratford-place). In the above plan is also shewn the Adam and Eve, a detached roadside public-house in the "Dung-field," near the present Adam-and-Eve-court, almost opposite Poland-street; and in an adjoining field is represented the boarded house of Figg the prize-fighter. "The row of houses on the north side of Tyburn-road was completed in 1729, and it was then called Oxford-*street*" (Lysons's *Environs*); but a stone upon a house on the north side is inscribed, "Rath bone-place, Oxford-street, 1718:" it was built by Captain Rathbone. In this year were commenced Hanover-square, and "round about, so many other edifices, that a whole magnificent city seems to be risen out of the ground. On the opposite side of the way, towards Marylebone is marked out a square, and many streets to form avenues to it.' (*Weekly Medley*, 1718.) Vere street Chapel and Oxford Market were built about 1724; five years later were begun most of the streets leading to Cavendish-square.

A map of 1742 shews the little church of St. Marylebone, in the fields, with two zigzag ways leading to it: one near Vere-street, then the western limit of the new buildings; and the second from Tottenham-Court-road. Rows of houses with their backs to the fields, extend from St. Giles's Pound to Oxford Market but Tottenham-Court-road has only one cluster on the west side, and the spring water house. Thus, Oxford-street, from Oxford Market to Vere-street, south and west, Marylebone-street north, and the site of Tichfield-street east, form the limit of the new buildings; the zigzag way from Vere-street (now Mary lebone-lane) leading from the high-road to the village.

Pennant remembered Oxford-street "a deep hollow road, and full of sloughs; with here and there a ragged house, the lurking-place of cut-throats:" insomuch that he "never was taken that way by night," in a hackney-coach, to his uncle's in George-street, but he "went in dread the whole way."

Cumberland-place, begun about 1774, was named from the hero of Culloden, of whom there is a portrait-sign at a public-house in Great Cumberland-street. At the western extremity of Oxford-street, in the first house in Edgware-road, immediately opposite to Tyburn turnpike, lived for many years the Corsican General Paoli, who was godfather to the Emperor Napoleon. (*Notes and Queries.*)

Stratford-place was built 1787-90, upon the site of Conduit-Mead. At the north end is Aldborough House (erected for Edward Stratford, Earl of Aldborough), with a handsome Ionic stone front and a Doric colonnade. Here, until 1805, stood a naval trophied Corinthian column with a statue of George III., set up in 1797 by Lieut.-Gen. Strode.

No. 315, Oxford-street, is the façade of the Laboratories of the COLLEGE OF CHEMISTRY. (See page 206.)

Portland-place was built by the architects Adam, about 1778: it is 126 feet wide, and in 1817 was terminated at the north end by an open railing looking over the fields towards the New-road; when "the ample width of the foot-pavement, the purity of the air, and the prospect of the rich and elevated villages of Hampstead and Highgate, rendered Portland-place a most agreeable summer promenade." (Hughson's *London.*) Here lived Robert Farquhar, the *millionaire,* who purchased Fonthill; at No. 43, Sir Felix Booth, from whom Sir John Ross named Boothia Felix; Lord Chief-Justice Denman at No. 38. In Park-crescent long resided the Count de Surveilliers (Joseph Bonaparte); and in the garden, facing Portland-place, is a bronze statue (height 7 feet 2 inches), by Gahagan, of the Duke of Kent, father of Queen Victoria.

The Crystal Palace in Hyde Park was nearly the length of Portland Place. I walked out one evening," says Sir Charles Fox, " and there setting out the 848 feet upon the pavement, found it the same length within a few yards; and then considered that the Great Exhibition Building would be three times the width of that fine street, and the nave as high as the houses on either side."

Newman-street and *Berners-street,* built between 1750 and 1770, were from the first inhabited by artists of celebrity. In the former lived Banks and Bacon, the sculptors; and West and Stothard, the painters: in the latter, Sir William Chambers, the architect; and Fuseli and Opie, the painters. Facing is the Middlesex Hospital, described at page 385.

The *Pantheon,* on the south side of Oxford-street, was originally built by James Wyatt, in 1768-71; was burnt down in 1792, but was rebuilt; taken down in 1812, and again reconstructed. (See PANTHEON.)

Nearly opposite is the *Princess' Theatre,* No. 73, formerly the Queen's Bazaar, opened in 1840. (See THEATRES.)

Wardour-street, built 1686, and named from Lord Arundel of Wardour, is noted for its Curiosity-shops. (See page 246).

Hanway-street bears a stone dated 1721, and was originally a zigzag lane to Tottenham-Court-road: it was called Hanway-yard to our time, and is noted for its china-dealers and Curiosity-shops, as it was in the reign of hoops, high-heeled shoes, and stiff brocade.

No. 54, corner of Berners-street, has a *Rénaissance* or Elizabethan shop-front and mezzanine floor; a picturesque composition of pedestals, consoles, and semi-caryatid figures. No. 76 has a Byzantine façade. No. 86 has a front of studied design. At No. 15 was exhibited, in 1830-2, a large painted window of the Tournament of the Field of Cloth-of-Gold, by Wilmshurst; destroyed by fire in 1832.

o o

At the east end of Oxford-street, in 1838, were laid experimental specimens of the various roadway Wood Pavements.

NEW OXFORD-STREET, extending the houses from 441 to 552, and occupying part of the site of St. Giles's "Rookery," was opened in 1847: the house-fronts are of Ionic, Corinthian, domestic Tudor, and Louis XIV. character, including a glass-roofed Arcade of shops. (See ST. GILES'S, page 330.)

PADDINGTON,

Named from the Saxon *Pædingas* and *tun*, the town of the Pædings, (Kemble's *Saxons in England*), was, in the last century, a pleasant little rural village, scarcely a mile north of Tyburn turnpike, upon the Harrow-road. Paddington is not mentioned in Domesday Book; and the charters professedly granting lands here by Edgar to the monks of Westminster are discredited as forgeries. The district would rather appear to have been cleared, soon after the Norman Conquest, from the vast forest of Middlesex, (with pasture for the cattle of the villagers, and the fruits of the wood for their hogs,) and to have lain between the two Roman roads (now the Edgeware and Uxbridge roads) and the West bourn, or brook, the ancient Tybourn. In the first authentic document (31 Hen. II.), Richard and William of Paddington transfer their "tenement" to the Abbot and Convent of Westminster; and from the close of the thirteenth century, the whole of the temporalities of Paddington (rent of land, and young of animals, valued at 8*l*. 16*s*. 4*d*., were devoted to charity. Tanner speaks of Paddington as a parish *temp.* Richard II.; and by the Valor Ecclesiasticus of Henry VIII., the rectory yielded, like the manor, a separate revenue to the Abbey. Upon the dissolution of the Bishopric of Westminster, the manor and rectory were given by Edward VI. to Ridley, Bishop of London, and his successors for ever; they were then let at 41*l*. 6*s*. 8*d*., besides 20*s*. for the farm of "Paddington Wood," 30 acres.

The population of Paddington, by the Subsidy Roll of Henry VIII scarcely exceeded 100; in Charles II.'s reign it was about 300; 50 years ago, it contained 324 houses, and a population of 1881 souls; from 1833 to 1841, it increased 1000 per annum; from 1841 to 1851, above 2000 annually; and it now has nearly 7000 houses, and 50,000 souls Thus, from the forest village has risen a large town, and one of the three parishes forming the Parliamentary borough of Marylebone.

"A city of palaces has sprung up within twenty years. A road of iron, with steeds of steam, brings into the centre of this city, and takes from it in one year a greater number of living beings than could be found in all England a few years ago; while the whole of London can be traversed in half the time it took to reach Holborn Bars at the beginning of this century, when the road was in the hands of Mr. Miles, his pair-horse coach, and his redoubtable Boy,"[*] long the only appointed agents of communication between Paddington and the City. The fares were 2*s*. and 3*s*.; the journey took more than three hours; and to beguile the time at resting-places, "Miles's Boy" told tales and played upon the fiddle.

In the middle of the last century, nearly the whole of Paddington had become grazing-land, upwards of 1100 acres; and the occupiers of the Bishop's Estate kept here hundreds of cows. At the beginning of the last century, next to the rurality of Paddington, the gallows and the gibbet were its principal attractions. About 1790 were built nearly 100 small wooden cottages, tenanted by a colony of 600 journeymen artificers; but these dwellings have given way to Connaught-terrace.

[*] Paddington, Past and Present, by William Robins, 1853: an able contribution to our local histories.

Paddington consists chiefly of two hills, Maida-hill and Craven-hill; the north-eastern slope of Notting-hill; and a valley through which runs the Tybourn, a favourite resort of anglers early in the present century, but now a covered sewer. From this brook, the newly-built district, mostly of palatial mansions, is named *Tyburnia*.

Paddington Green, now a russet spot, was the green of the villagers, shown in all its rural beauty in prints of 1750 and 1783. Upon a portion of it were built the Almshouses, in 1714; but their neat little flower-gardens have disappeared. South of the green is the new Vestry-Hall.

At *Dudley Grove* was modelled and cast, by Matthew Cotes Wyatt, the colossal bronze statue of the Duke of Wellington, now upon the Green Park Arch: it is 30 feet high, and was conveyed from the foundry, upon a car, Sept. 29, 1846, to Hyde Park Corner.

Westbourne Green has been cut up by the Great Western Railway; and Westbourne-place, built by Ware, with the materials of old Chesterfield House, May Fair, has disappeared. Close by is the Terminus of the *Great Western Railway*, with a magnificent Hotel, designed in the Louis Quatorze taste, by P. Hardwick, R.A.: the allegorical sculpture of the pediment is by Thomas: the rooms exceed 130.

At *Craven Hill* was the Pest-house Field, exchanged for the ground in Carnaby-street, given by Lord Craven as a burial-place if London should ever be again visited by the Plague: but the field is now the site of a handsome square of houses named Craven Gardens.

Bayswater, a hamlet of Paddington, is described at page 85.

Knotting, or *Notting Hill*, seems but to have been a corruption of *Nutting*; the wood on and around the hill of that name having for centuries been appropriately so named.

Kensell, or *Kensale*, is "the Green-lane" and Kingsfelde Green in a Harleian Ms. of Mary's reign. (See page 430.)

Maida Hill and *Maida Vale* were named from the famous battle of Maida, fought in 1806.

The Grand Junction Waterworks were established in 1812; and on Camden Hill is a storing reservoir containing 6,000,000 gallons. At Paddington the basin of the *Grand Junction Canal* joins the Regent's Canal, which passes under Maida Hill by a tunnel 370 yards long. On the banks of the canal, the immense heaps of dust and ashes, once towering above the house-tops, are said to have been worth 10,000*l*. a heap.

"*The Bishop's Estate*" (Bishop's-road, Blomfield-terrace, &c.) produces 30,000*l*. a-year to the Bishop of London and the lay lessees.

Among the parochial *Charities*, the aniversary festival of an Abbot of Westminster is thought to explain "the Bread and Cheese Lands;" and until 1838, in accordance with a bequest, bread and cheese were thrown from the steeple of St. Mary's church, to be scrambled for in the churchyard. (See LOCK HOSPITAL, p. 383; ST. MARY'S, p. 385.)

Oxford and Cambridge Squares and Terraces will long keep in memory the munificence of the Lady Margaret, Countess of Richmond, to the Universities of Oxford and Cambridge.

Paddington possessed a church before the district was assigned to the monks of Westminster, in 1222. An "old and ruinous church" was taken down about 1678, and was thought, from its painted window, to have been dedicated to *St. Katherine*. Next, *St. James's Church* was built by the Sheldons, *temp.* Charles I.: here Hogarth was married to Sir James Thornhill's daughter, in 1729. This church was taken down, and *St. Mary's* built upon the Green, 1788-91, "finely embosomed in venerable elms:" near it were the village stocks, and in the churchyard were an ancient yew-tree and a double-leaved elder. Here is the tombstone of John Hubbard, who died in 1665, "aged 111 years." Near the grave of Mrs. Siddons lies Haydon, the ill-fated painter, who devoted "forty-two years to the improvement of the taste of the English people in high art:" he lived many years at 1 Burwood-place, Edgeware-road; and here, June 22, 1846, with his own hand, he terminated the fitful fever of his existence. *St. Mary's Church* is described at page 146. Next was built *Bayswater Chapel*, by Mr. Orme, the printseller, in 1818; *Connaught Chapel*, in 1826, now St. John's; and at the western extremity of the Grand-Junction-road, *St. James's*, which in 1845 became the parish church. In 1844-6 was built *Holy Trinity Church*, Bishop's-road (see page 130): cost 18,458*l*., towards which the Rev. Mr. Miles gave 4000*l*. In 1847 was erected, in Cambridge-place, *All Saints Church*, upon a portion of the site of the old Grand Junction Water-works' reservoir, at the end of Star-street. *St. John's*, in Southwick-crescent, has a fine stained window. The erection of Dissenters' places of worship was long restricted in Paddington by the Bishops of London; but there are several chapels, including one for the Canal boatmen, constructed out of a stable and coach-house. At the western extremity of the parish is a large Roman-Catholic church.

Paddington has long been noted for its *old public-houses*. The "White Lion," Edgeware-road, dates 1524, the year when hops were first imported. At the "Red Lion," near the Harrow-road, tradition says, Shakspeare acted; and another "Red Lion," formerly near the Harrow-road bridge over the bourn, is described in an inquisition of Edward VI. In this road is also an ancient "Pack-horse;" and the "Wheatsheaf," Edgeware-road, was a favourite resort of Ben Jonson. (See Robins's *Paddington, Past and Present*.)

Paddington and Marylebone appear to have been favoured by religious enthusiasts. At No. 26 Manchester-street died, in 1814, the notorious Joanna Southcott, after having imposed upon six medical men with the absurd story of her being about to give birth to the young "Shiloh.' Richard Brothers, the self-styled "Nephew of God," lodged at No. 5 Paddington-street, and died in Upper Baker-street, in 1824. Spence the disciple of Emanuel Swedenborg, lived in Great Marylebone-street he was known as "Dr. Spence," when he was the only surgeon in the *village* of Marylebone.

PAINTED CHAMBER (THE),

Represented to have been the bed-chamber and death-place of Edward the Confessor, in the old Palace at Westminster, existed in its foundation-walls until the great fire in 1834. It was also called St. Edward' Chamber; and assumed its second name after it had been *painted* by order of Henry III. In the ceremonial of the marriage of Richard Duke of York, in 1477, the Painted Chamber is called St. Edward' Chamber; and Sir Edward Coke, in his Fourth Institutes, states that the causes of Parliament were in ancient time shown in *La Chambr Depeint*, or St. Edward's Chamber. Before the fire of 1834, this apart ment had two floors, one tesselated, and the other boarded: it was 8 feet 6 in. in length, 26 feet wide, and its height from the upper floo was 31 feet. The ceiling, *temp*. Henry III., was dight with gilded an painted tracery, including small wainscot paterae, variously ornamented It was hung with tapestries, chiefly representing the Siege of Troy probably put up *temp*. Charles II. Sandford, in his *Coronation o James II.*, mentions these tapestries as "Five pieces of the Siege of Troy, and one piece of Gardens and Fountains." In 1800, these hang ings and the wainscoting were removed,* when the walls and window jambs were found covered with paintings of the battles of the Macca bees; the Seven Brethren; St. John, habited as a pilgrim, presenting ring to King Edward the Confessor; the canonisation of King Edward with seraphim, &c.; and black-letter Scripture texts. The painting are noticed in the MS. Itinerary of Simon Simeon, and Hugo the Illu

* About the year 1820, the tapestry was sold to Mr. Charles Yarnold, of Gre St. Helen's, for 10*l*.

minator (Franciscan friars), in 1322; who name "that well-known chamber, on whose walls all the histories of the wars of the whole Bible are painted beyond description:" and an Exchequer Roll, 20 Edw. I. anno 1292, headed, " p'ma op'ac'o picture," or first work of Painting, contains an account of the disbursements of Master Walter, the painter, for the emendation of the pictures in the King's *Great Chamber*, as the Painted Chamber was then called.* Specimens of these paintings are given by J. T. Smith in his *Antiquities of Westminster;* and in the *Vetusta Monumenta*, vol. vi.; and in 1835, drawings of the pictures were exhibited to the Society of Antiquaries. . ·'

In the Painted Chamber, Parliaments were opened, before the Lords sat in the Court of Requests. Here Conferences of both Houses were held; here sat in private the High Court of Justice for bringing Charles I. to trial; and here the death-warrant of the unhappy King was signed. After the great fire of 1834, the walls of the Chamber were roofed, and the interior was fitted up as a temporary House of Lords. The building was taken down in 1852, when the brick and stone work of the north side, and the ends of the Chamber, including several Gothic stone window-cases, were sold for 50*l*.

PAINTED GLASS.

The finest specimens are described under WINDOWS, PAINTED.

PALACES, ROYAL.

The three royal metropolitan palaces are, Buckingham Palace, the residence of the Sovereign and the Court; St. James's Palace, used exclusively for State purposes; and Kensington Palace, no longer the abode of royalty.

Hatton (in 1708) says: " Of *Courts of our Kings and Queens* there were heretofore many in London and Westminster: as the *Tower of London*, where some believe Julius Cæsar lodged, and William the Conqueror; in the *Old Jewry*, where Henry VI.; *Baynard's Castle*, where Henry VII.; *Bridewell*, where King John and Henry VIII.; *Tower Royal*, where Richard II. and King Stephen; *Wardrobe*, in Great Carter-lane, where Richard III.; also at *Somerset House*, kept by Queen Elizabeth; and at *Westminster*, near the Hall, where Edward the Confessor and several other kings kept their Courts. But of later times, the place for the Court, when in town, was mostly *Whitehall;* a very pleasant and commodious situation, looking into St. James's Park, the canal, &c. west, and the noble river of Thames east; Privy Gardens, with fountains, statues, &c., and an open prospect to the statue at Charing Cross, north. This palace being, in January 1697, demolished by fire, except the Banqueting House (built by Inigo Jones, temp. James I.), there has since been no reception for the Court in town but *St. James's* Palace, which is pleasantly situated by the Park; and *Whitehall* will doubtless be rebuilt in a short time, being designed one of the most famous palaces in Christendom."

" Her Majesty has also these noble palaces for the Court to reside in at pleasure: *Kensington House* (so near, that it may be said to be in town), *Campden House, Windsor Castle, Hampton Court, Winchester House;* all which palaces, for pleasant situation, nobleness of building, delightful gardens and walks, externally; and for commodious, magnificent rooms, rich furniture, and curious painting, internally,—cannot be matched in number and quality by any one prince on earth."

BUCKINGHAM PALACE, the town residence of the Sovereign, on the west side of St. James's Park, was built by Nash and Blore, between 1825 and 1837, upon the site of Buckingham House, of which the ground-floor alone remains. The northern side of the site was a portion of the Mulberry-garden, planted by James I. in 1609, which in the next two reigns became a public garden. Evelyn describes it in

* There are also entries in the Close Rolls, 12 Hen. III. (1228), for painting the Great Exchequer Chamber; and 1236, for the King's Great Chamber; proving that oil-painting was practised in England nearly two centuries before its presumed discovery by John ab Eyck, in 1410.

1654 as "ye only place of refreshment about ye towne for persons of ye best quality to be exceedingly cheated at;" and Pepys refers to it as "a silly place," but with "a wilderness somewhat pretty." It is a favourite locality in the gay comedies of Charles II.'s reign.

Dryden frequented the Mulberry Gardens; and according to a contemporary, the poet ate tarts there with Mrs. Anne Reeve, his mistress. The company sat in arbours, and were regaled with cheesecakes, syllabubs, and sweetened wine; wine-and-water at dinner, and a dish of tea afterwards. Sometimes the ladies wore masks. "The country ladys, for the first month, take up their places in the Mulberry Gardens as early as a citizen's wife at a new play."—Sir C. Sedley's *Mulberry Garden*, 1668.

> " A princely palace on that space does rise,
> Where Sedley's noble muse found mulberries."—*Dr. King.*

Upon the above part of the garden site was built *Goring House,* let to the Earl of Arlington in 1666, and thence named *Arlington House:* in this year the Earl brought from Holland, for 60s., the first pound of tea received in England; so that, in all probability, *the first cup of tea made in England was drunk upon the site of Buckingham Palace.* There is a rare print of Arlington House, by Sutton Nichols, and a copy by John Seago. In 1698 the property was sold to Sheffield, Duke of Buckingham, for whom the house was rebuilt in 1703, in the heavy Dutch style, of red brick, with stone finishings. Some vignettes of the mansion, then *Buckingham House,* are engraved at the heads of chapters, and in illuminated capitals, of the second volume of the collected poems of Buckingham, "the Muses' friend, himself a Muse." On the four sides he inscribed, in gold, four pedantic mottoes: " Sic siti lætantur Lares;" " Rus in urbe ;" "Spectator fastidiosus sibi molestus ;" and "Lente incœpit, cito perfecit." The house was surmounted with lead figures of Mercury, Secresy, Equity, Liberty, Truth, and Apollo ; and the Four Seasons. Defoe describes it as "one of the great beauties of London, both by reason of its situation and its building :" its fine garden, noble terrace (with prospect of open country), a little park with a pretty canal; and the basin of water, and Neptune and Tritons fountain in the front court. The Duke of Buckingham, in a letter to the Duke of Shrewsbury, minutely describes the mansion : its hall painted in the school of Raphael; its parlour by Ricci; its staircase with the story of Dido ; its ceiling with gods and goddesses ; and its grand saloon by Gentileschi. The flat leaded roof was balustraded for a promenade ; and here was a cistern holding 50 tuns of water, driven up by an engine from the Thames.

To his third wife, a natural daughter of James II. by Catherine Sedley, the Duke was tenderly attached, and studied her convenience in planning Buckingham House: "the highest story of the private apartments," he tells us, "is fitted for the women and children, with the floors so contrived as to prevent all noise over my wife's head during the mysteries of Lucina."

Buckingham House was purchased by George III. for 21,000l. in 1761, shortly after the birth of the Prince of Wales at St. James's Palace: their Majesties soon removed here, and all their succeeding children were born here. In 1775 the property was settled on Queen Charlotte (in exchange for Somerset House), and thenceforth Buckingham House was called "the Queen's House." Here the King collected his magnificent library, now in the British Museum (see p. 524). Dr. Johnson, by permission of the librarian, frequently consulted books; and here he held his memorable conversation with George III.

"It is curious that the royal collector (George III.) and his venerable librarian (Mr. Barnard) should have survived almost sixty years after commencing the formation of this, the most complete private library in Europe, steadily appropriating 2000l. per annum to this object, and adhering with scrupulous attention to the instructions of Dr. Johnson, contained in the admirable letter printed by order of the House of Commons."—*Quarterly Review,* June 1826.

In 1766 the Cartoons of Raphael were removed here, to an octagonal apartment at the south-east angle; but they were transferred to Windsor Castle in 1788. The Saloon was superbly fitted as the Throne-room, and here Queen Charlotte held her public drawing-rooms; and in the Crimson, Blue Velvet, and other rooms, was a fine collection of pictures. Thus the mansion remained until 1825, externally "dull, dowdy, and decent; nothing more than a large, substantial, and respectable-looking red brick house."

The Palace, as reconstructed by Nash, consisted of three sides of a square, Roman-Corinthian, raised upon a Doric basement, with pediments at the ends; the fourth side, enclosed by iron palisades, with a central entrance arch of white marble, adapted from that of Constantine at Rome. Mr. Nash was succeeded by Mr. Blore, who raised the building a story; and the palace was opened for public inspection in 1831. William IV. and Queen Adelaide did not remove here; but on July 13, 1837, Queen Victoria took up her residence here. In 1846 the erection of the east side was commenced; and in 1851 the marble arch was removed to the north-east corner of Hyde Park. There have since been added a spacious Ball-room, &c. on the south side of the Palace.

The east front of Buckingham Palace is German, of the last century: its extent is 360 feet, height 77 feet; extreme height of centre 90 feet; frontage 70 feet in advance of the former wings. The four central gate-piers are capped by an heraldic lion and unicorn, and dolphins; and the state entrances have golden grilles of rich design. The wings are surmounted by statues of Morning, Noon (Apollo), and Night; the Hours, and the Seasons; and upon turrets flanking the central shield (bearing " V. R. 1847") are colossal figures of Britannia and St. George; besides groups of trophies, festoons of flowers, &c. The inner front has a central double portico; the tympanum is filled with sculpture, and the pediment crowned with statues of Neptune, Commerce, and Navigation in the centre. Around the entire building is a scroll frieze of the rose, shamrock, and thistle. The garden or western front, architecturally the principal one, has five Corinthian towers, and a balustraded terrace; the upper portion having statues, trophies, and bas-reliefs, by Flaxman and other sculptors.

The Marble Hall and Sculpture Gallery have mosaic bordered floors, and ranges of Carrara columns with mosaic gold bases and capitals. The sculpture consists chiefly of busts of the Royal Family and eminent statesmen. Beyond the Sculpture Gallery is the *Library*.

The Grand Staircase is marble, with ormolu acanthus balustrades: the ceiling has frescoes by Townsend, of Morning, Evening, Noon, and Night, on a gold ground; besides wreaths of flowers, imitative marbles, &c., in the Italian manner. The brief pageant of the Queen leaving the Palace to proceed in state to open Parliament may be witnessed by Tickets of admission to the Hall, issued by the Lord Great Chamberlain. Upon such occasions, the Yeomen of the Guard, Yeomen Porters, and other official persons, in their rich costumes, while the Sovereign proceeds to the State-carriage, presents a magnificent scene.

The Vestibule is richly decorated in vermilion and gold: here are a marble statue of the Queen, by Gibson, R.A.; and of Prince Albert, by Wyatt; and bas-reliefs of Peace and War, by Thomas. The looking-glass and ormolu doors cost 300 guineas a-pair, and each mosaic gold capital and base 30 guineas.

The principal *State Apartments* are: the *Green Drawing-room*, in the centre of the east front, and opening upon the upper portico: for state balls, Tippoo Saib's Tent is added to this room, upon the portico, and is lighted by a gorgeous "Indian sun," 8 feet in diameter. Next is the *Throne Room*, which is 64 feet in length: the walls are hung with crimson satin; and the coved ceiling is emblazoned with arms, and gilded in the boldest Italian style of the fifteenth century. Beneath is a white marble frieze, sculptured by Baily, with the Wars of the Roses, Stothard's last great design.* On the north side of the apartment is an alcove, with crimson velvet hangings, gilding, and emblazonry, and a fascia of massive gilt wreaths and figures. In this recess is placed the royal throne, or chair of state; seated in which, surrounded by her ministers, great officers of state, and the court, her Majesty receives addresses. In this room also are held Privy Councils.

The Picture Gallery, in the centre of the palace, is about 180 feet in length by 26 feet in breadth, and has a semi-Gothic roof, with a triple row of ground-glass lights, bearing the stars of all the orders of knighthood in Europe; but Von Raumer considers the light false and insufficient, and broken by the architectural decorations. Occasionally, this gallery is used as a ball-room, and for state banquets. The door-cases have colossal caryatidal figures, and are gorgeously gilt; and the marble chimney-pieces are sculptured with medallion portraits of great painters.

The collection of pictures formed by George IV. is pre-eminently rich in Dutch and Flemish art. The chief exceptions are Reynolds's Death of Dido, his Cymon and Iphigenia, and Sir Joshua's portrait in spectacles; the Penny Wedding, and Blind Man's Buff, by Wilkie; a Landscape by Gainsborough, and a few recent English works; and 4 pictures by Watteau. In the collection are an Altar-piece by Albert Durer; 7 pictures by Rembrandt, including the Shipbuilder and his Wife, for which George IV., when Prince of Wales, gave 5000 guineas; Rubens, 7; Marriage of St. Catherine, and 4 others, by Vandyke; Vandervelde, 7; younger Vandervelde, 4; G. Dow, 8; Paul Potter, 4; A. Ostade, 9; younger Teniers, 14; Vandermeulen, 13; Wouvermans, 9; Cuyp, 9. In the State Rooms are royal portraits, by Kneller, Lely, A. Ramsay, N. Dance, Copley, Gainsborough, Wright, Lawrence, Wilkie, Winterhalter, &c.

In the western front is the Grand (central) Saloon, north of which is the Yellow Drawing-room, communicating with the Private Apartments of her Majesty, which extend along the north front of the palace. The Grand Saloon has a semicircular bay, and scagliola lapis-lazuli columns with mosaic gold capitals, supporting a rich architrave, and bas-reliefs of children with emblems of music; the domed ceilings are richly gilt with roses, shamrocks, and thistles, and acanthus-leaves, and the royal arms in the spandrels. The State Ball-room, north of the Grand Saloon, has scagliola porphyry Corinthian columns, with gilded capitals, carrying an entablature and coved ceiling, elaborately gilt: here are Winterhalter's portraits of the Queen and Prince Albert; and Vandyke's Charles I. and Henrietta-Maria. South of the Ball-room is the State Dining-room, which has an elegantly wrought ceiling, and circular panels bearing the regal crown and the monogram V. R.; the whole in stone-tint: here are Lawrence's whole-length of George IV. in his coronation robes, and other royal portraits.

The merit of the architectural sculptures is their nationality. The friezes and reliefs of scenes in British history are mostly by Baily, R.A.: those of Alfred expelling the Danes, and delivering the Laws, on the garden-front, and the Progress of Navigation on the main front, are fine compositions; as are also Stothard's Wars of the Roses, in the Throne-room; and the eastern frieze of the rose, shamrock, and thistle. But the marble chimney-pieces and door-cases, sculptured with caryatides, fruit and flowers, and architectural ornament, often present a strange mixture of fragments of Egypt, Greece, Etruria, Rome, and the Middle Ages, in the same apartment.

* The venerable Stothard was between seventy and eighty years old when he designed this frieze; yet it possesses all the vigour and imagination which had distinguished his best days. The drawings were sold at Christie's, on the decease of the painter; Mr. Samuel Rogers became the purchaser.

In the garden were formerly two Ionic Conservatories; the southern-most of which is now the *Palace Chapel*, consecrated by the Arch-bishop of Canterbury, March 25, 1843. The aisles are formed by rows of Composite cast-iron columns; and at the west end, facing the altar, is the Queen's closet, supported upon Ionic columns from the screen of Carlton House.

The *Pleasure-grounds* comprise about 40 acres, including the lake of 5 acres; at the verge of which, upon a lofty artificial mound, is a pic-turesque pavilion, or garden-house, with a minaret roof. In the centre is an octagonal room, with figures of Midnight and Dawn; and 8 lu-nettes, painted in fresco, from Milton's *Comus*, by Eastlake, Maclise, Landseer, Dyce, Stanfield, Uwins, Leslie, and Ross; besides relief ara-besques, medallions, figures and groups, from Milton's poems. On the right is a room decorated in the Pompeian style, copied from existing remains. The apartment on the left is embellished in the romantic style, from the novels and poems of Sir Walter Scott. (See Gruner's *Illus-trations*, described by Mrs. Jameson).

Buckingham Palace has been the scene of two superb Costume Balls—in 1842 and 1845: the first in the style of the reign of Ed-ward III.; and the fête in 1845 in the taste of George II.'s reign.

The *Royal Mews* is described at page 505.

Immediately under the Palace passes "the King's Scholars' Pond Sewer," the main drain of one of the principal divisions of the Westminster connexion of sewers, occupying the whole channel of a rivulet formerly known as Tye Brook, having its source at Hampstead, and draining an area of 2000 acres, 1500 of which are covered with houses. A large portion of the sewer arches was recon-structed, under densely-populated neighbourhoods, without any suspicion on the part of the inhabitants of what was going on a few feet below the foundations of their houses. In its present complete state, this is, perhaps, the most remarkable and extensive piece of sewerage ever executed in this or any other country.

St. JAMES'S PALACE, Westminster, on the north side of St. James's Park, and at the western end of Pall Mall, occupies the site of a hospital, founded by some pious citizens prior to the Norman Conquest, for four-teen leprous females, to whom eight brethren were added to perform divine service. The good work was dedicated to St. James, and was en-dowed by the citizens with lands; and in 1290, Edward I. granted to the foundation the privilege of an annual Fair, to be held on the eve of St. James and six following days. The house was rebuilt by Berkynge, abbot of Westminster, in Henry III.'s reign; and in 1450 its perpetual custody was granted by Henry VI. to Eton College. In 1532, Henry VIII. obtained in exchange for Chattisham and other lands in Suffolk: he then dismissed the inmates, pensioned the sisterhood; and having pulled down the ancient structure, he "purchased all the mea-dows about St. James's, and there made a faire mansion and a parke for his greater commoditie and pleasure" (*Holinshed*): the Sutherland View of 1543 shows the palace far away in the fields. "The Manor House," as it was then called, is believed to have been planned by Holbein, and built under the direction of Cromwell, Earl of Essex. Henry's gate-house and turrets face St. James's Street: the original hospital, to judge from the many remains of stone mullions, labels, and other ma-sonry, found in 1838, on taking down some parts of the Chapel Royal, was of the Norman period. It was occasionally occupied by Henry as a semi-rural residence, down to the period when Wolsey surrendered Whitehall to the Crown. Edward and Elizabeth rarely resided at St. James's: but Mary made it the place of her gloomy retirement during the absence of her husband, Philip of Spain; and here she expired. The Manor House, with all its appurtenances, except the park and the stables or the mews, were granted by James I. to his son Henry in

1610; at whose death, in 1612, they reverted to the Crown. Charles I. enlarged the palace, and most of his children (including Charles II.) were born in it: here he deposited the gallery of antique statues principally collected for him by Sir Kenelm Digby. In this reign was fitted up the chapel of the hospital, on the west side, as the *Chapel Royal*, described at page 165. Here Charles I. attended divine service on the morning of his execution: " from hence the king walked through the Park, guarded with a regiment of foot and partisans, to Whitehall." (Whitelocke's *Memorials*, p. 374.) The *Queen's Chapel*, now the *German Chapel*, was built for Catherine of Braganza, in the friary of the conventual establishment founded here by her majesty, under the direction of Cardinal Howard.

The Queen first heard mass there on Sunday, September 21, 1662, when Lady Castlemaine, though a Protestant, and the King's avowed mistress, attended her as one of her maids of honour. Pepys describes " the fine altar ornaments, the fryers in their habits, and the priests with their fine crosses, and many other fine things."—*Diary*, vol. i. p. 312.

At " St. James's House " Monk resided while planning the Restoration. In the old bed-chamber, now the ante-chamber to the levee-room, was born James (the old Pretender), the son of James II. by Mary of Modena: the bed stood close to the back stairs, and favoured the scandal of the child being conveyed in a warming-pan to the Queen's bed. In this reign Verrio, the painter, was keeper of the palace-gardens. During the Civil Wars, St. James's became the prison-house, for nearly three years, of the Duke of York and Duke of Gloucester, and the Princess Elizabeth: on April 20, 1648, the Duke of York escaped from the palace-garden into the Park, through the Spring Garden, to a hackney-coach in waiting for him; and, in female disguise, he reached a Dutch vessel below Gravesend. After the Restoration, the Duke occupied St. James's; and one of its rooms was hung with portraits of the Court Beauties, by Sir Peter Lely. Here the Duke slept the night before his coronation, and next morning proceeded to Whitehall.

On December 18, 1688, William Prince of Orange came to St. James's, where, three days afterwards, the peers assembled, and the household and other officers of the abdicated sovereign laid down their badges. Evelyn says: " All the world goes to see the Prince at St. James's, where there is a greate court. There I saw him: he is very stately, serious, and reserved." (*Diary*, vol. i. p. 680.) King William occasionally held councils here; but it was not until after the burning of Whitehall, in 1697, that this Palace became used for state ceremonies, whence dates *the Court of St. James's*. William and Mary, however, resided chiefly at Kensington; and St. James's was next fitted up for George Prince of Denmark, and the Princess Anne, who, on her accession to the throne, considerably enlarged the edifice. George I. lived here like a private gentleman: in 1727 he gave a banquet here to the entire Court of Common Council. The fourth plate of Hogarth's " Rake's Progress " shows St. James's Palace gateway in 1735, with the quaint carriages and chairs arriving on the birthday of Caroline, George II.'s consort: her Majesty died at St. James's in 1737. The wing facing Cleveland-row was built for Frederick Prince of Wales, on his marriage in 1736. The State Rooms were enlarged on the accession of George III., whose marriage was celebrated here September 6, 1761. George IV. was born here August 12, 1762; and shortly afterwards the Queen's bed was removed to the Great Drawing-room, and company were admitted to see the infant prince on drawing-room days. The Court was held here during the reign of George III., though his domestic residence was at Buckingham House. St. James's was refitted on the marriage of the Prince of Wales, April 8, 1795, in the

Chapel Royal. On January 21, 1809, the east wing of the palace, in-cluding their majesties' private apartments and those of the Duke of Cambridge, was destroyed by fire, and has not been rebuilt. In 1814 the State Apartments were fitted up for the Emperor of Russia and the King of Prussia, when also Marshal Blucher was an inmate of the palace. In 1822 a magnificent banqueting-hall was added to the state-rooms. In January 1827 the remains of the Duke of York lay in state in the palace. William IV. and Queen Adelaide resided here; but since the accession of her present Majesty, St. James's has only been used for levees and drawing-rooms.

The lofty brick gatehouse bears upon its roof the bell of the *Great Clock*, dated A.D. 1731, and inscribed with the name of Clay, clockmaker to George II. It strikes the hours and quarters upon three bells, re-quires to be wound every day, and originally had only one hand. A print of the court-yard, with the meeting of Mary de Medicis and her daughter Henrietta-Maria, in 1638, shows a dial which must have be-longed to a previous clock. The present clock has been under the care of the Vulliamys, the royal clockmakers, since 1743.

When the gatehouse was repaired in 1831, the clock was removed, and not put up again, on account of the roof being reported unsafe to carry the weight. The inhabitants of the neighbourhood then memorialised William IV. for the replacement of the timekeeper: the King, having ascertained its weight, shrewdly inquired how, if the palace roof was not strong enough to carry the clock, it was safe for the number of persons occasionally seen upon it to witness processions, &c. The clock was forthwith replaced, and a minute-hand was added, with new dials: the original dials were of wainscot, in a great number of very small pieces, curiously dovetailed together.

The gatehouse enters the quadrangle, named the *Colour Court*, from the colours of the military guard of honour being placed here : in this court one of the three regiments of Foot Guards is relieved alternately every morning at eleven o'clock, when the keys of the garrison are de-livered and the regimental standard exchanged, during the performance of the bands of music. Westward is the *Ambassadors' Court*, where are the apartments of certain branches of the Royal Family; and beyond it the *Stable-Yard*, anciently the stable-yard of the palace, and where was the Queen's Library, upon the site of Stafford House. (See p. 494.) On the east side is the Lord Chamberlain's office, where permission may be obtained to view the palace. Eastward of the gatehouse is the *Office of the Board of Green Cloth ;* and still further, the office of the Lord Steward of Her Majesty's Household. Beyond are the gates leading to the quadrangle known of old as "*the Chair Court.*" The *State Apartments,* in the south front of the palace, front the garden and St. James's Park. The sovereign enters by the garden gate ; and it was here, on the 2d of August 1796, that Margaret Nicholson attempted to assassinate George III. as he was alighting from his carriage. The *State Apartments* are reached by the Great Staircase, the *Entrée Gal-lery,* the *Guard Chamber* (its walls covered with weapons in fanciful devices), and a similar apartment. Here are stationed the Yeomen of the Queen's Guard; and the honours of the Guard Chamber are paid to distinguished personages on levee and drawing-room days.

Yeomen of the Guard were first instituted in 1485, by Henry VII., upon the model of a somewhat similar band retained by Louis XI. of France. They were at first archers; but on the death of William III. all took the partisan, as now carried. The dress has continued unaltered since the reign of Charles II. *The Corps of Gentlemen-at-Arms* (changed from Pensioners by William IV.) was instituted by Henry VIII., disbanded during the Civil Wars, but re-constructed at the Restoration, and at the Revolution of 1688. In 1745, when George II. raised his standard on Finchley Common, these "Gentlemen" were ordered to provide themselves with horses and equipment to attend his majesty to the field. Their present uniform is scarlet and gold ; and the corps carry on parade small battle-axes covered with crimson velvet. On April 10, 1848, on the apprehension of a Chartist outbreak, St. James's Palace was garrisoned and guarded by these ancient bodies.

Beyond the Guard Chambers is the *Tapestry Room*, hung with gorgeous tapestry, made for Charles II., and representing the amours of Venus and Mars. The stone Tudor arch of the fireplace is sculptured with the letters H. A. (Henry and Anne Boleyn), united by a true lovers' knot, surmounted by a regal crown; also the lily of France, the portcullis of Westminster, and the rose of Lancaster. Here the sovereigns of the House of Brunswick, on the death of their predecessors, are received by the Privy Council, and from the capacious bay-window proclaimed and presented to the people assembled in the outer court, where are the sergeants-at-arms and band of household trumpeters. The proclamation of her present Majesty, on June 21, 1837, was a touching spectacle. Next the Tapestry Room is *Queen Anne's Room*, the first of the four great state apartments. In this room the remains of Frederick Duke of York lay in state in January 1827. This apartment opens to the *Ante-Drawing-Room*, leading by three doors into the *Presence Chamber* or *Throne Room*, beyond which is the *Queen's Closet*. The throne, at the upper end of the Presence Chamber, is large and stately, and emblazoned with arms: the window-draperies here and in the Queen's Closet are of splendid *tissue-de-verre*. The entire suite is gorgeously gilt, hung with crimson Spitalfields damasks, brocades, and velvets, embroidered with gold; and the Wilton carpets bear the royal arms.

The public are admitted to the corridor by tickets to see the company upon Drawing-room days; and upon certain occasions, when bulletins of the health of the sovereign are issued, they are shown to the public as they pass through the state-rooms.

Pictures in the State Apartments.—Large paintings of the Siege of Tournay, and the Siege of Lisle, by the Duke of Marlborough. Portraits of Charles II., George I., George II., and Queen Anne; George III., the Prince of Wales, and the Duke of York, by Sir Joshua Reynolds; George IV. and the Duke of York, by Sir Thomas Lawrence. Count La Lippe, and the Marquis of Granby, by Sir Joshua Reynolds. Beauties of the Court of Charles II., copied from Hampton Court. Lord Nelson, Earl St. Vincent, and Lord Rodney, by Hoppner. The Battles of Vittoria and Waterloo, by G. Jones, R.A. In the Entrée Gallery are whole-length portraits of Henry VIII., reputed by Holbein; Queen Mary; Queen Elizabeth, by Zucchero; James I.; Charles I., after Vandyke; Charles II., James II., and William and Mary.

The curious pictures which were here in Pennant's time have been removed: including a Child, 3 years 6 months old, in the robes of a Knight of the Garter, the second son of James I.; also Geoffrey Hudson, the Dwarf; and Mabuse's Adam and Eve, painted with navels.

Here George IV. formed a fine collection of pictures, to which was added, in 1828, Haydon's "Mock Election," which the King purchased of the painter for 500 guineas, erroneously stated 800 guineas at page 267.

KENSINGTON PALACE, about two miles west of the metropolis, is named from the adjoining town, although it is situated in the parish of St. Margaret, Westminster:

　　　　" High o'er the neighbouring lands,
　　'Midst greens and sweets, a regal fabric stands."—*Tickell.*

The original mansion was purchased (with the grounds, six acres) by King William III., in 1691, of Daniel Finch, second Earl of Nottingham. Evelyn notes:

" Feb. 25, 1690-1.—I went to Kensington, which King William had bought of Lord Nottingham, and altered, but was yet a patched-up building; but with the gardens, however, it is a very neat villa."—*Memoirs*, vol. ii.

In the following November the house was nearly destroyed by fire, and the king narrowly escaped being burned in his bed. The premises had been possessed by the Finch family about half a century; and after Sir Heneage Finch's advancement to the peerage, the mansion was called "Nottingham House." William III. employed Wren and Hawksmoor, who built the King's Gallery and the south front; the eastern front was added by George I., from the designs of Kent; the north wing is part of old Nottingham House. The entire palace is of crimson brick, with stone finishings; and consists of the Clock Court, Prince's Court, and Princess' Court. King William held councils in this palace; its decoration was the favourite amusement of Queen Mary; and it was next fitted up as the residence of Queen Anne and Prince George of Denmark: for her luxurious Majesty was built the Banqueting-House, described at page 434. The principal additions made by Kent, for George I., were the Cupola Room and the Great Staircase; the latter painted with groups of portraits from the Court, Yeomen of the Guard, pages, a Quaker, two Turks in the suite of George I., and Peter the Wild Boy. George II. and Queen Caroline passed most of their time here; and during the King's absence on the Continent, the Queen held at Kensington a court every Sunday. In this palace died Queen Mary and King William; Queen Anne and the Prince Consort; and George II.

The *Great Staircase*, of black and white marble, and graceful ironwork (the walls painted by Kent with mythological subjects in chiaroscuro, and architectural and sculptural decoration), leads to the suite of twelve State Apartments, some of which are hung with tapestry and have painted ceilings. The *Presence Chamber* has a chimney-piece richly sculptured by Gibbons with flowers, fruits, and heads; the ceiling is diapered red, blue, and gold upon a white field, copied by Kent from Herculaneum; and the pier-glass is wreathed with flowers by Jean Baptiste Monnoyer. The *King's Gallery*, in the south front, has an elaborately painted allegorical ceiling; and a circular fresco of a Madonna, after Raphael. The *Cube Room* is forty feet in height, and contains gilded statues and busts; and a marble bas-relief of a Roman marriage, by Rysbrack. The *King's Great Drawing-room* was hung with the then new paper, in imitation of the old velvet flock. The *Queen's Gallery* in the rear of the eastern front, continued northwards, has above the doorway the monogram of William and Mary; and the pediment is enriched with fruits and flowers in high relief and wholly detached, probably carved by Gibbons. The *Green Closet* was the private closet of William III., and contained his writing-table and escritoire; and the *Patchwork Closet* had its walls and chairs covered with tapestry worked by Queen Mary.

During the reign of George III. the palace was forsaken by the sovereign; towards its close, a suite of rooms was fitted up for the Princess of Wales, and her aged mother the Duchess of Brunswick. The lower south-eastern apartments beneath the King's Gallery were occupied by the late Duke of Kent: here, May 24, 1819, was born Queen Victoria; christened here on June 24th following; and on June 20, 1837, her Majesty held here her first Council, which has been admirably painted by Wilkie. The south wing of the older part of the palace was occupied by the late Duke of Sussex, who died here April 21, 1843.

Here the Duke of Sussex, during 25 years, collected the celebrated *Bibliotheca Sussexiana*, numbering nearly 50,000 printed books and Mss., purchased volume by volume, at the sacrifice of many an object of princely luxury and indulgence. The collection included nearly 300 Theological Mss. of the tenth, twelfth, thirteenth, fourteenth, and fifteenth centuries; besides about 500 early printed books relating to the Holy Scriptures. Among the rarities were 48 Hebrew Mss., some rolled; a richly illuminated Hebrew and Chaldaic Pentateuch, thirteenth century; a Greek New Testament, thirteenth century, illuminated; 16 copies of the Vulgate, on vellum, two with 100 miniatures in gold and colours; a splendidly illuminated Psalter, tenth century; missals, breviaries, hours, offices, &c.; *La Bible Moralizée* (fifteenth century); *Historia del Vecchio Testamento*, with 519 miniatures of the school of Giotto; several copies of the Koran, including that found by the conquerors of Seringapatam in the library of Tippoo Sultan, with his spectacles between the leaves, as if the perusal of it had been one of the latest acts of Tippo's life; Armenian copy of the Gospels, thirteenth century; Mss. in the Pali, Burmann, Cingalese, &c. In the printed books were all the celebrated Polyglots, in fine condition; 74 editions of the Hebrew Bible; 17 Hebrew-Samaritan and Hebrew Pentateuchs (Bomberg editions), and the Great Rabbinical Bible, magnificent specimens of Hebrew printing; Greek Bibles, of precious value; Latin Bible, 200 editions; Bibles in other languages, 1200 editions. In the Divinity classes were, the first Armenian, the first Irish, the first Sclavonic, the first German, and the first Reformed, editions of Luther; the first English Bible, by Coverdale; the first Great Bible, or Cranmer's, &c.; besides Classics, Lexicography, Chronicles, Law, and Parliamentary Histories, of immense extent. The theological collection filled an apartment 100 feet in length; and here, seated in a curtained chair, the Duke passed the life of a toil-worn student. In these rooms he gave his *conversazioni* as President of the Royal Society.

In Kensington Palace was formerly deposited the greater part of the royal collection of paintings, commenced by Henry VIII.; and, removed here by William III., as appears from a Catalogue taken in 1700, and now in the British Museum. The collection was much augmented by Queen Caroline; but after the death of George II., several of the finest pictures were removed to Windsor and elsewhere. In 1818, however, here were more than 600 pictures, which were catalogued by B. West, P.R.A. Few now remain; but in the southern apartments (still retained, though not tenanted, by the Duchess of Kent,) is a collection of Byzantine, early Italian, German, and Flemish paintings, formerly the property of Prince Louis D'Ottingen Wallerstein. Admission by permission, of Prince Albert, to be applied for through the keeper of the collection, Mr. L. Gruner, 13 Fitzroy-square. The majority of these 103 pictures are curious specimens of sacred art,—triptychs, altar-pieces, and other works of primitive design and elaborate antiquity.

The *Green*, westward of the Palace, and called in ancient records "the Moor," was the military parade when the Court resided here, and the royal standard was hoisted daily. Here are barracks for foot-soldiers, who mount guard at the Palace. Northward of the Palace were the kitchen-gardens, about 20 acres, now Queen's-road, with two lines of elegant villas. (See KENSINGTON GARDENS,* pp. 433-434.)

PALL MALL,

" A fine spacious street between the Haymarket N. E., and St. James's-street S. W." (*Hatton*, 1708), and one-third of a mile in length,. is named from the French game of *paille-maille* having been played there. The space between St. James's House and Charing Cross, about 1560, appears to have been fields, with three or four houses at the east end of the present Pall Mall, and opposite a small church, the name of which Pennant could not discover. Down this road came Sir Thomas Wyatt, " on foot, hard by the Court-gate of St. James's, with four or five auncients, his men marching in good way," and thus proceeded to Charing Cross and Whitehall.

At the east end of Pall Mall, in the reign of Henry VI., stood a group of monastic buildings called " the Rookery," belonging to the monks of Westminster: here resided Erasmus, by favour of Henry VIII. and the interest of Anne Boleyn. When these buildings were demolished at the Reformation, tradition relates

* " The gravel of Kensington is of European repute. At the gardens of Versailles, and Caserta, near Naples, the walks have been supplied from the Kensington gravel-pits."—*Quarterly Review*, No. cxxxix. p. 237.

there was found a secret smithy; which had been erected by order of Henry VI. for the practice of alchemy. The premises were subsequently used as an inn, and upon the site was built the first Carlton House. (See page 64.)

In the reign of Charles II. Pall Mall was occasionally called Catherine-street. Faithorne's Plan, 1658, shows a row of trees on the north side. Pepys mentions, in 1660, an old tavern, "Wood's at the Pell Mell." In 1662 was fought here the duel between Mr. Jermyn and Capt. Thomas Howard, the latter wearing mail under his dress. The *London Gazette* of 1685 has an advertisement address, "the Sugar-loaf in the Pall Mall." Dr. Sydenham died here, in 1689, at his house next "the Golden Pestle and Mortar;" which sign remained to our day, on the north side of the street. Another olden sign, "the Golden Ball," has lasted to our time; but "the Golden Door" and "the Barber's Pole" have disappeared. Nell Gwyn's houses* here are mentioned at page 394; where also is described *Schomberg House*, on the south side, built about 1650.

"Nelly at first had only a lease of the house, which as soon as she discovered, she returned the conveyance to the king, with a remark characteristic of her wit, and of the monarch to whom it was addressed. The king enjoyed the joke, and perhaps admitted its truth; so the house in Pall Mall was conveyed *free* to Nell and her representatives for ever. The truth of the story is confirmed by the fact, that the house which occupies the site of the one in which she lived, now No. 79, is the only freehold on the south or Park side of Pall Mall."—Cunningham's *Nell Gwyn*, p. 115. Mr. Cunningham adds: "No entry of the grant is to be found in the Land Revenue Record Office."

Eastward of Nell Gwyn's lived Sir William Temple, and the Hon. Robert Boyle, and Bubb Doddington. In the Mall, in 1689, resided "the Lady Griffin, who was seized for having treasonable letters put into false bottoms of two large brandy-bottles, in the first year of his majesty's reign." Defoe characterises Pall Mall, in 1703, as "the ordinary residence of all strangers, because of its vicinity to the Queen's palace, the park, the parliament-house, the theatres, and the chocolate and coffee houses, where the best company frequent." Gay thus celebrates the modish street in his time:

> "O bear me to the paths of fair Pall Mall!
> Safe are thy pavements, grateful is thy smell!
> At distance rolls the gilded coach,
> Nor sturdy carmen on thy walks encroach;
> No lets would bar thy ways were chairs deny'd,
> The soft supports of laziness and pride;
> Shops breathe perfumes, through sashes ribbons glow,
> The mutual arms of ladies and the beau."—*Trivia*, book ii.

Marlborough House, next St. James's Palace, was built in 1709-10. (See page 490.) In front lived Sir Robert Walpole. Strype describes Pall Mall as "a fine long street," with garden-houses on the south side, many with raised mounts, and prospects of the King's garden and St. James's Park.

In gay bachelor's chambers in Pall Mall lived Beau Fielding, Steele's "Orlando the Fair;" here he was married to a supposed lady of fortune, brought to him in a mourning-coach and widow's weeds, which led to his trial for bigamy. Fielding's namesake places Nightingale and Tom Jones in Pall Mall, when they leave the lodgings of Mrs. Miller in Bond-street.

Lætitia Pilkington, for a short time, kept here a pamphlet and print shop. At the sign of "Tully's Head," Robert Dodsley, formerly

---

* A relic of Nell Gwyn, her looking-glass, is preserved in the Visitors' Dining-room of the Army and Navy Club-house, in Pall Mall. The glass was bought with the house of Lord De Mauley, which was taken down for the Club-house site.

a footman, with the profits of a volume of his poems and a comedy (published through the kindness of Pope), opened a shop in 1735; and here he published his *Annual Register, Economy of Human Life*, and Sterne's *Tristram Shandy*. Dodsley retired in 1759; but his brother James, his partner, continued the business until his death in 1797 : he is buried in St. James's Church, Piccadilly. " Tully's Head" was the resort of Pope, Chesterfield, Lyttleton, Shenstone, Johnson, and Glover; Horace Walpole, the Wartons, and Edmund Burke.

At the corner of St. Alban's-street lived Gilray the caricaturist, when assistant to Holland, the printseller. In a house opposite Market-lane, the " Royal Academy of Art" met, from the time of their obtaining the patronage of George III. until their removal to Somerset House, in 1771.

Among the coffee-houses of Pall-Mall was the Smyrna, of the days of the *Tatler* and *Spectator;* where subscriptions were taken in by Thomson for publishing his *Seasons*, &c.

At the Star and Garter Tavern, at a meeting of the Nottingham-shire Club, Jan. 26, 1765, arose the dispute between Lord Byron and his relation and neighbour Mr. Chaworth, as to which had the most game on his estates: they fought with swords across the dining-table, by the light of one tallow candle, when Mr. Chaworth was run through the body, and died next day. Lord Byron was tried before his peers in Westminster Hall, and found guilty of manslaughter; but claiming the benefit of the statute of Edward VI., he was discharged on payment of his fees. In the same house (the Star and Garter), Winsor made his gas-lighting experiments; he lighted the street wall in 1807. (See GAS-LIGHTING, p. 324.)

At the Queen's Arms Tavern, Lord Mohun supped with his second on the two nights preceding his fatal duel with the Duke of Hamilton, in Hyde Park. At the King's Arms met the Liberty or Rump-steak Club of Peers, in opposition to Sir Robert Walpole.

Nearly opposite the south-west corner of the Opera-house, " Thomas Thynne, Esq., on Sunday (Feb. 12, 1681), was most barbarously shot with a musketoon in his coach, and died next day." The instigator was Count Koningsmark, in hopes of gaining Lady Elizabeth Ogle, the rich heiress, to whom Thynne was either married or contracted. Three of Thynne's ruffians were tried at the Old Bailey, found guilty, and hanged at the spot whereon the murder was committed. Borosky, " who did the murther," was hung in chains beyond Mile End Town: the Count was tried as an accessory, but was acquitted. The assassination is sculptured upon Thynne's monument in Westminster Abbey.

Pall Mall had early its notable sights and amusements. In 1701 were shown here Models of William the Third's Palaces at Loo and Hunstaerdike, " brought over by outlandish men," with Curiosities disposed of " on public raffling-days." In 1733, " a holland smock, a cap, checked stockings, and laced shoes," were run for by four women in the afternoon, in Pall Mall; and one of its residents, the High Constable of Westminster, gave a prize laced hat to be run for by five men, which created so much riot and mischief, that the magistrates " issued precepts to prevent future runs to the very man most active in promoting them." Here lodged George Psalmanazar, when he passed for an islander of Formosa, and invented a language which baffled the best philologists in Europe. Here lived Joseph Clark, the posture-master, celebrated for personating deformities: now deceiving, by feigned dislocated vertebræ, the great surgeon, Moulins; then perplexing a tailor's measure with counterfeit humps and high shoulders.

At the Chinese Gallery was exhibited, in 1825, " *the Living Skeleton*" (Anatomie Vivante), Claude Ambroise Seurat, a native of Troyes, in

Champaigne, 23 years old. His health was good, but his skin resembled parchment, and his ribs could be counted and handled like pieces of cane: he was shown nude, except about the loins; the arm, from the shoulder to the elbow, was like an ivory German flute; the legs were straight, and the feet well formed. (See Hone's *Every-day Book*.)

In the old Star and Garter house, westward of Carlton House, was exhibited, in 1815, the *Waterloo Museum* of portraits and battle-scenes, cuirasses, helmets, sabres, and fire-arms, state-swords, truncheons, rich costumes, and trophies of Waterloo; besides a large picture of the battle, painted by a Flemish artist. At No. 59 Salter spent five years in painting his great picture of the Waterloo Banquet at Apsley House, engraved for Alderman Moon. At No. 121 Campanari exhibited his Etruscan and Greek Antiquities, in rooms fitted up as the Chambers of Tombs. In apartments at No. 120 Captain Marryat wrote his *Poor Jack*. At Nos. 67 and 68 lived B. L. Vulliamy, the scientific horologist, whose family have been clockmakers to the Sovereign in five reigns.

The Society for the Propagation of the Gospel in Foreign Parts, at No. 79, has been founded 150 years; and its operations have been extended from North America to the West Indies, South Africa, India, Ceylon, Borneo, Australia, and New Zealand. When the Society was first established, there were not 12 clergymen of the Church of England in these lands; there are now nearly 3000. The Society's expenditure in 1850 was 84,000*l*.

At No. 90 died, in 1849, Mr. W. J. Denison, in his 80th year, bequeathing 2½ millions sterling : he sat in Parliament 31 years for Surrey. No. 91, Buckingham House, was built by Soane for the Marquis of Buckingham, 1790-4. At No. 100 lived Mr. Angerstein, whose pictures were bought for the nation, and were shown here before their removal to the National Gallery; and at No. 50 died Mr. Robert Vernon, who bequeathed to the country his pictures of the English School, which were for a short time exhibited here.

No. 50 was built by Alderman Boydell as the *Shakspeare Gallery*, for his pictures illustrative of Shakspeare, painted by West, Reynolds, Northcote, and others, and which were dispersed by lottery after being engraved. In 1806 the gallery was purchased by a committee of noblemen and gentlemen, by whom was established here the *British Institution*: here are exhibited the works of Living Artists in the spring, and Old Masters in the autumn. Here was exhibited West's large picture (9 ft. by 14 ft.) of Christ healing the Sick in the Temple; bought by the British Institution for 3000 guineas, and presented to the National Gallery. Upon the house-front is a large bas-relief of Shakspeare attended by Poetry and Painting, for which Alderman Boydell paid Banks, the sculptor, 500 guineas; and in the hall is Banks's colossal Mourning Achilles, a noble work of pathos and heroic beauty. No. 53 is the Exhibition-room of the *New Society of Painters in Water-colours*.

No. 86, the *Ordnance Office* (Correspondence), was originally built for Edward Duke of York, brother of George III., and was subsequently a Subscription Club-house, called the Albion Hotel; this being the first modern club-mansion in Pall Mall, which, however, had its "houses for clubbing" in Pepys's time. After the removal of Carlton House, in 1827, the erection of the present splendid club-houses in Pall Mall was commenced with the Senior United Service and the Athenæum; the precise site of Carlton House being the roadway between these two club-houses, which, with others in Pall Mall, are described at pp. 190, 192, 195, 196, 198. Of Carlton House, the Riding-house, a substantial stone building, remains; and here (Carlton Ride) is deposited a portion of the Public Records. Thence a flight of steps leads to Warwick-street: here stood Warwick House, whence the

Princess Charlotte, in 1814, escaped in a hackney-coach to the house of her mother, as vividly described by Lord Brougham in the *Edinburgh Review*. In Warwick-street is a public-house with the old sign of "The Two Chairmen," recalling the sedans of Pall Mall:

> "Who the footman's arrogance can quell,
> Whose flambeau gilds the sashes of Pall Mall,
> When in long rank a train of torches flame,
> To light the midnight visits of the dame."—Gay's *Trivia*, book iii.

Here, in 1731, were found, in digging the great sewer of Pall Mall, the fossil teeth of an elephant, 28 feet underground: they are preserved in the Museum of the Society of Antiquaries, Somerset House.

Gray, the poet, relates: "In the year 1688, my Lord Peterborough had a great mind to be well with Lady Sandwich, Mrs. Bonfoy's old friend. There was a woman who kept a great coffee-house in Pall Mall, and she had a miraculous canary-bird that piped twenty tunes. Lady Sandwich was fond of such things, had heard of and seen the bird. Lord Peterborough came to the woman, and offered her a large sum of money for it; but she was rich, and proud of it, and would not part with it for love or money. However, he watched the bird narrowly, observed all its marks and features, went and bought just such another, sauntered into the coffee-room, took his opportunity when no one was by, slipped the wrong bird into the cage and the right into his pocket, and went off undiscovered to make my Lady Sandwich happy. This was just about the time of the Revolution; and, a good while after, going into the same coffee-house again, he saw his bird there, and said, 'Well, I reckon you would give your ears now that you had taken my money.' 'Money!' says the woman, 'no, nor ten times that money now, dear little creature! for, if your lordship will believe me (as I am a Christian, it is true), it has moped and moped, and never once opened its pretty lips since the day that the poor king went away!'"—*Correspondence of Gray and Mason, edited by Mitford*, 1853.

Dr. Graham's "Goddess of Health" (see *Schomberg House*, p. 395) was a lady named Prescott. Mr. Cosway, R.A., the next tenant of Schomberg House, was the fashionable miniature-painter of his day; and here his accomplished wife, Maria Cosway (also a painter), gave her musical parties, the Prince of Wales being a frequent visitor. Mrs. Cosway made a pilgrimage to Loretto, which she had vowed to do if blessed with a living child.—*Notes and Queries*, No. 147.

In Pall Mall was *Almack's Gaming Club*, where the play was only for rouleaus of 50*l.* each, and generally there was 10,000*l.* in specie on the table. The gamesters "began by pulling off their embroidered clothes, and put on frieze greatcoats, or turned their coats inside outwards for luck. They put on pieces of leather (such as are worn by footmen when they clean the knives) to save their laced ruffles; and to guard their eyes from the light and to prevent tumbling their hair, wore high-crowned straw hats with broad brims, and adorned with flowers and ribbons; masks to conceal their emotions when they played at quinze. Each gamester had a small neat stand by him, to hold his tea; or a wooden bowl with an edge of ormolu, to hold the rouleaus." (*Memoir and Correspondence of Charles James Fox, edited by Lord John Russell*, 1853.) Of this club, Fox and Gibbon the historian were members; the latter dates several letters from here.

At Marlborough House, in February 1850, were sold the furniture and personal effects of the late Queen Dowager; the public being admitted by tickets, and the price affixed to each article.

PALL MALL EAST, on the north side of Cockspur-street, contains the University Club-house, described at page 199; and the College of Physicians, described at page 206. Here also is M. C. Wyatt's equestrian statue of George III. (see STATUES.) At No. 4 (Harding, Lepard, and Co.) were exhibited, in 1831, the exquisite water-colour copies made by Hilton and Derby for Lodge's *Portraits of Illus-*

trious Personages, from pictures by Titian, Holbein, Vandyke, Mark Gerard, Zucchero, Jansen, Retel, Walker, Van Somer, Honthorst, Lely, Ant. More, Mytens, Kneller, Reynolds, Dahl, Jarvis, Riley, Rubens, Fleck, Juan de Pantoxa, Mirevelt, and P. Oliver. No. 5 is the *Gallery of the Society of Painters in Water-colours*. At No. 1 Dorset-place lived John Thelwall, the classic elocutionist and dramatic lecturer, who late in life left political agitation for the calm pursuits of literature. He was worthily characterised by Coleridge as "intrepid, eloquent, and honest; perhaps the only acting democrat that is honest." Between Whitcombe-street and Charing Cross was formerly Hedge-lane, 300 yards in length; in the days of Charles I. a lane through the fields, and bordered with hedges.

At a low tavern in Suffolk-street, on Jan. 30, 1735, "several young gentlemen of distinction" happening to meet in a drunken frolic, had a bonfire lit in the street before the tavern-door, and drank loyal and popular healths to the mob out of the windows, which led to a riot; and the incident became engrafted upon the history of "the Calves' Head Club."

PANCRAS, ST.,

Originally a solitary village "in the fields," north of London, and one mile from Holborn Bars, is the most extensive parish in Middlesex, being 18 miles in circumference. It is a prebendal manor, and was included in the land granted by Ethelbert to St. Paul's Cathedral about 603; it was a parish before the Conquest, and is called St. Pancras in Domesday. The history of its church, which Norden thought "not to yield in antiquitie to Paules in London," is narrated at page 152. The prebendary of St. Pancras was anciently confessor to the Bishop of London: in the list are Lancelot Andrewes, Bishop of Winchester; Dr. Sherlock, and Archdeacon Paley. Lysons supposes it to have included the prebendal manor of Kentish Town, or Cantelows,* which now constitutes a stall in St. Paul's Cathedral. The church has about 70 acres of land attached to it, which were demised in 1641 at 10*l.* reserved rent; and being subsequently leased to Mr. William Agar, are now the site of *Agar Town*. In Domesday, Walter, a canon of St. Paul's, holds one hide at Pancras, which is supposed to form the freehold estate of Lord Somers, on which *Somers Town* is built.

St. Pancras' parish contained, in 1251, only 40 houses; in 1503 the church stood "all alone," and in 1745 only 3 houses had been built near it. In 1765 the population was not 600; in 1801, 36,000;

	Houses.	Inhabitants.
1821	9,405	71,838
1841	15,658	129,969
1851	19,825	167,198

being the most populous parish in the metropolis. It includes one-third of the hamlet of Highgate, with the hamlets of Kentish-town, Battle-bridge, Camden Town, Somers Town, to the foot of Gray's-Inn-lane; also "part of a house in Queen-square" (*Lysons*), all Tottenham-Court-road, and the streets west to Cleveland-street and Rathbone-place.

Stukeley affirmed the site of the old church to have been occupied by a Roman encampment (Cæsar's), of which he has published a plan *Itinerarium Curiosum*, 1758); and the neighbouring *Brill* of Somers Town Stukeley traces to a contraction of Bury or Burgh Hill, a Saxon name for a fortified place on an elevated site; following Camden in his illustration of the village of Brill in Buckinghamshire.

At *Battle-bridge*, in 1842, was discovered a Roman inscription at-

* Anciently Kentesstoune, where William Bruges, Garter King-at-arms in the reign of Henry V., had a country-house, at which he entertained the Emperor Sigismund.

testing the great battle between the Britons under Boadicea, and the Romans under Suetonius Paulinus, to have been fought on this spot.

The inscription bears distinctly the letters LEG. XX. (the twentieth legion), one of the four which came into Britain in the reign of Claudius; and the vexillation of which was in the army of Suetonius Paulinus, when he made that victorious stand in a fortified pass, with a forest in his rear, against the insurgent Britons. The position is described by Tacitus. On the high ground above Battle-bridge are vestiges of Roman works; and the tract of land to the north was formerly a forest. The veracity of the following passage of the historian is therefore fully confirmed: "Deligitque locum artis faucibus, et a tergo silvâ clausum satis cognito, nihil hostium nisi in fronte, et apertam planitiem esse, sine metu insidiarum." He further tells us, that the force of Suetonius was composed o "quartadecima legio, cum vexilariis vicesimariis, et e proximis auxiliares." (*Tacit. Annal.* lib. xiv.) So that, almost to the letter, the place of this memorable engagement seems, by the discovery of the above inscription, to be ascertained.

In Ben Jonson's play, the *Tale of a Tub*, the characters move about in the fields near Pancridge (St. Pancras); Totten-court is a mansion in the fields; a robbery is pretended to be committed "in the way over the country" between Kentish Town and Hampstead Heath; and a warrant is granted by a "Marribone" justice.

St. Pancras had formerly its mineral springs, which were much resorted to. Near the old churchyard, in the yard of a house, is the once-celebrated St. Pancras' Well, slightly cathartic. St. Chad's Well in Gray's-Inn-road, has a similar property; and the Hampstead waters and walks were given in 1698 to "trustees, for the benefit of the poor."

The parish contains 24 churches, the three principal of which are described at pages 152, 153. The vicarage was valued at 28*l.* in 1650 it is rated in the King's books at 9*l.*; and at this time is stated at 1700*l.* Under the belfry of the old church was interred privately, in a grave 14 feet deep, the body of Earl Ferrers, executed at Tyburn in 1760.

The foundation of the excellent Female Charity School, next to St. James's Chapel, in the Hampstead-road, dates from 1776.

In St. Pancras are the Termini of the two largest Railways in England: the North-Western, Euston-square; and the Great Northern, at Battle-bridge, 45 acres. (See RAILWAYS.) In a house in Montgomery's nursery-gardens, the site of the north side of Euston-square, lived Dr. Wolcot (*Peter Pindar*), the satirist.

The Cemetery for St. Pancras, 87 acres (being the first extra-mural burial-ground for the metropolis, by Act 15 and 16 Victoria, cap. 85) was commenced in 1853, on "Horse-shoe Farm," in the Finchley-road about 4½ miles from St. Pancras Workhouse, and 2 miles from the extreme northern boundary of the parish: the first stone of the church was laid Nov. 24, 1853. *St. Pancras Workhouse* often contains upwards of 1200 persons, equal to the population of a large village.

PANORAMAS.

The panorama (from the Greek *pan*, all, and *orama*, a view), a circular painting having no apparent beginning nor end, was first devised by Robert Barker, an artist, who, whilst seated on the Calton-hill, Edinburgh, put up an umbrella to protect himself from the sun, when he noticed the greater effect it gave to the whole circle of the horizon. This he sought to turn to account in a pictorial contrivance, where the spectators should be placed in the middle of the picture-circle, covered overhead to give additional effect to the painting itself, which is a deviation from the ordinary flat surface to that of a curve, so as to allow of representing the whole view surrounding any spot, with entirely new rules of perspective for the purpose. Sir Joshua Reynolds foretold the failure of the novelty, and was equally surprised and delighted on witnessing its success in a small circle painted by Mr. Barker, at 28 Castle street, Leicester-square. . Larger premises were then erected at the north-east corner of Leicester-square, by the subscription of a party of noblemen and gentlemen; and here the first Panorama was produced by Mr. Barker in 1794, the success of which soon enabled the painter to repay his patrons their capital with interest. The first picture was a view of London, taken by Thomas Girtin, from the Albion Mills, at the south end of Blackfriars Bridge. Next was painted the Fleet under Lord Howe at anchor at Spithead; followed by Elba, Athens, and the Bay of Naples: the two latter were highly commended by Stothard. Among the early pictures were the battles of the Nile, Trafalgar, Badajoz, Vittoria, and Waterloo. Robert Barker was succeeded by his son, Henry Aston Barker; on whose retirement, John Burford, his pupil, became painter and proprietor; and was succeeded in 1823 by his son, Robert Burford, the present proprietor. The paintings are exhibited in one large and two smaller circles at Leicester-square: the large circle is 90 ft. in diameter, and 40 ft. in height.

The Panoramas are painted in oil by Mr. Burford, mostly from his own sketches; but the latter have been, in some instances, taken by artistic travellers. The extreme accuracy of the views, as well as their pictorial character, have gained for the exhibition reputation as ubiquitous as its subjects. The most attractive pictures have been, the Battle of Waterloo, and Jerusalem, both painted twice. The following pictures have been exhibited since 1823: .

1823. Coronation of George IV. Lausanne. Pompeii.
1824. Pompeii (second view).
1825. Edinburgh. Mexico.
1826. Madrid.
1827. Rio de Janeiro. Geneva.
1828. Navarino. Genoa.
1829. Sydney. Pandemonium. Constantinople.
1830. Calcutta. Amsterdam. Quebec.
1831. Hobart Town. Bombay. Florence.
1832. Milan. Stirling, N.B.
1833. Siege of Antwerp. Falls of Niagara.
1834. Boothia (North Pole). New York. Père-la-Chaise.
1835. Jerusalem. Thebes.
1836. Lima. Lago Maggiore.
1837. Mont Blanc. Dublin.
1838. New Zealand. Canton.
1839. Rome. The Coliseum. Malta.
1840. Versailles. Benares. Macao.
1841. Damascus. St. Jean d'Acre. Jerusalem.
1842. Battle of Waterloo. Cabool.
1843. Edinburgh. Baden-Baden. Coblentz. Treport.
1844. Hong-Kong. Baalbec. Naples.
1845. Nankin. Athens. Rouen.
1846. Constantinople. Sobraon.
1847. Cairo. Himalaya.
1848. Vienna. Paris.
1849. Pompeii. Switzerland, from the Righi. Cashmere.
1850. Arctic Regions. Lakes of Killarney. Lake of Lucerne.
1851. Niagara. Jerusalem. Lucerne.
1852. Salzburg. Battle of Waterloo.
1853. Granada and the Alhambra. Mexico. The Bernese Alps. Constantinople.

Other Panoramas were painted by Mr. Thomas Barker and Mr. Reinagle, and were exhibited on the premises now the Strand Theatre: the last picture, a view of Constantinople, was shown in 1831.

One of the earliest Panoramic paintings was that of the *Storming and Capture of Seringapatam*, painted by Sir Robert Ker Porter, when only 19, in the short space of six weeks; its length being upwards of 200 feet. West called it "a wonder of the world." Porter also painted the *Battle of Agincourt*, which he presented to the City of London; and several years afterwards it was found in one of the vaulted chambers under Guildhall, and announced to be of unknown antiquity, "before the Great Fire of London," and worth 15,000l. !

Another celebrated exhibition of this class was the *Eidophusikon*, at a theatre in Panton-street, Haymarket. The pictures were painted by De Loutherbourg, and were patronised by Sir Joshua Reynolds and Gainsborough. The views were London, from One-Tree Hill, Greenwich Park; a Storm at Sea, with the Loss of the Halsewell Indiaman; an Italian Sea-port; Satan and Pandemonium, &c.; exhibited with startling atmospheric effects, conflagrations, &c. To the exhibition were added a Learned Dog, Musical Glasses, and a Monologue by John Britton (see his *Autobiography*, p. 97): the theatre and its scenery were destroyed by fire in 1800.

In 1849 was exhibited at Saville House, Leicester-square, a Panorama of the Mississippi, advertised to be 4 miles in length! Now only ten widths of the picture (each 20 feet) were passed before the spectator in 15 minutes, and the exhibition lasted one hour and a half; 20 by 10 by 6 gives 1200 feet as the real length, or less than a quarter of a mile. Had the picture been of the pretended length (4 miles), the canvas must, during exhibition, have travelled across the stage nearly at the rate of 3 miles an hour, which would hardly allow the painting to be seen at all!

Several Panoramic and Dioramic pictures have been exhibited at the Egyptian Hall, Piccadilly. (See pp. 266-268.) Banvard's picture was taken to Windsor Castle, and exhibited to the Queen in St. George's Hall. The most popular exhibition of this class, and most deservedly so, is " The Ascent of Mont Blanc," painted by Beverley, to illustrate Mr. Albert Smith's lecture. In two seasons, this entertainment was represented at the Egyptian Hall 528 times, and once privately to Prince Albert; when the number of persons who paid for admission was 192,929; admission-money upwards of 17,000*l.*, of which only a crown-piece was counterfeit; largest audience, 471. Upon the same floor were first exhibited, Jan. 23, 1854, Dioramic Views of *Constantinople*, sketched by T. Allom, and painted by Desvignes, Gordon, and Beverley; the accompanying lecture written by Albert Smith and Shirley Brooks; and delivered by Charles Kenney, son of the clever dramatist. (See Dioramas, p. 252; and Egyptian Hall, p. 268.)

PANTHEON, OXFORD-STREET,

About one-third of a mile on the left from St. Giles's, was originally built by James Wyatt for musical promenades, and was opened Jan. 27, 1772, when 2000 persons of rank and fashion were present. It contained 14 rooms, exclusive of the rotunda: the latter had double colonnades, ornamented with Grecian reliefs; and in niches at the base of the dome were statues of the heathen deities, Britannia, and George III. and Queen Charlotte. Walpole described it as "the new winter Ranelagh," with pillars of artificial *giallo antico*, and with ceilings and panels painted from Raphael's *loggias* in the Vatican. In the first winter here were assemblies without music or dancing; and the building was exhibited at 5*s.* each person! In 1783, Delpini, the clown, got up a masquerade here, to celebrate the Prince of Wales's attaining his majority; tickets three guineas each. Next year Garrick was present at a masquerade here as King of the Gipsies. Gibbon was also a frequenter of its gay bachelors' masque fêtes. In 1784, also, the " Commemoration of Handel" was performed here, when the King, Queen, and Royal Family were present. The Pantheon was next converted into a theatre for the Italian Opera company in 1791, the orchestra including Giardini, La Motte, Cramer, Fischer, Crosdil, and Cervetto.

The Pantheon was burnt down Jan. 14, 1792: Turner painted the conflagration, which he exhibited at the Royal Academy two years after he became an exhibitor. The loss by the fire was stated at 80,000*l.* The Pantheon was rebuilt in 1795, Wyatt's entrance-front in Oxford-street and in Poland-street being retained. It was then let as a theatre and for exhibitions, lectures, and music. The theatre was reconstructed in 1812, when Miss Stephens (subsequently Countess of Essex) first appeared in London here as a concert-singer; and first appeared on the stage, at Covent Garden Theatre, in 1813. In 1814 a patent was sought from Parliament to open the Pantheon with the regular drama; but the application failed. In 1832 the property was sold for 16,000*l.*: the premises are freehold, except the Oxford-street front, which is leasehold. In 1835 the premises were remodelled by Sydney Smirke, A.R.A., and opened as a Bazaar. (See page 36.)

PARKS.

The Parks have been well denominated by an amiable statesman (Wyndham), "the lungs of London;" for they are essential to the healthful respiration of its inhabitants. Westward lie Hyde Park, St. James's and the Green Parks; eastward, Victoria Park; and southward, Kennington and Battersea Parks; and for the north of London it is proposed to form

ALBERT, or FINSBURY PARK, equidistant from Regent and Victoria Parks; and to commence at Highbury Crescent, passing along the right side of Holloway and Hornsey roads to the Seven Sisters'-road, and including all the space of fields to the west of Newington Green; afterwards inclining towards the New River, which it is proposed to cross north of the Horse-shoe, excluding the Birmingham Junction Railway, and extending to the bottom of Highbury Grove, completing the enclosure of 300 acres.

BATTERSEA PARK, upon the south bank of the Thames, opposite Chelsea Hospital, was in the course of formation in 1854.

GREEN PARK (THE), 71 acres in extent, adjoins St. James's Park on the north, and extends westward to Hyde Park Corner, the line of communication being by the fine road *Constitution-Hill.* It was formerly called Little St. James's Park, and was reduced in 1767, by George III., to add to the gardens of Buckingham House. At the Peace Commemoration, in 1814, here was erected a vast Temple of Concord, with allegorical paintings and illuminations and fireworks. In 1840-41 the entire Park was drained, and the surface relaid and planted; and the Deputy Ranger's Lodge, towards the north-west corner, has been removed. At the north-east corner is the Chelsea Waterworks Reservoir, reconstructed in 1829, 44 feet above Trinity high-water mark of the Thames, and containing 1,500,000 gallons. This high ground commands fine views of the Norwood and Wimbledon hills, and of the roof of the Crystal Palace at Sydenham.

On the east side of the Park is a row of noble mansions, including Stafford House (see p. 494); Bridgewater House (p. 483); and Spencer House (p. 494), with its finial statues, commended by Sir William Chambers. The gardens of the several houses are leased of the Crown.

Dr. King relates, that Charles II. having taken two or three turns one morning in St. James's Park, attended only by the Duke of Leeds and Lord Cromarty, walked up Constitution Hill; and as the king was crossing the road into Hyde Park, met the Duke of York in his coach, returning from hunting. The duke alighted to pay his respects to the king, and expressed his surprise to meet his majesty with such a small attendance, adding that he thought the king exposed himself to some danger. "No kind of danger, James; for I am sure no man in England will take away my life to make you king," was Charles's reply.

In Constitution-Hill-road, near the Palace, three diabolical attempts have been made to shoot Queen Victoria: by a lunatic named Oxford, June 10, 1840; by Francis, another lunatic, May 30, 1842; and by an idiot named Hamilton, May 19, 1849. On June 29, 1850, at the upper end of the road, Sir Robert Peel was thrown from his horse, and died at his house in Whitehall Gardens, on July 2.

The Arch at the entrance of the road from Hyde Park Corner is a poor adaptation from the Arch of Titus at Rome, and was originally designed as an entrance to Buckingham Palace Gardens.

HYDE PARK extends from Piccadilly westward to Kensington Gardens, and lies between the great western and Bayswater roads. It is the site of the ancient manor of Hyde, which belonged to the monastery of St. Peter, Westminster, until it was conveyed to Henry VIII. in 1536, soon after which a keeper of the park is mentioned. In 1550 the French ambassador hunted here; and in 1578 the Duke Casimir shot a doe from amongst 300 other deer in Hyde Park. In 1652 it was sold by order of Parliament, for about 17,000*l.*; the deer being valued, in addition, at 765*l.* 6*s.* 2*d.* The Park then contained 620 acres, and extended eastward to Park-lane, and on the west almost to the front of Kensington Palace: it is described in the indenture of sale as "that impaled ground called Hyde Park;" but, with the exception of Tyburn meadow, the enclosure for the deer, the old lodge at Hyde Park Corner, and the Banqueting House, the Park was left in a state of nature; and De Grammont describes it as a barn-field in the time of Charles II. Ben Jonson mentions its great spring show of coaches; and Brome names its races, horse and foot; and in Shirley's play of *Hyde Park*, 1637, is the scene of a race in the Park between an Irish and English footman.[*] After the sale by Parliament, tolls were levied.

"11th April, 1653. I went to take the aire in Hide Park, when every coach was made to pay a shilling, and every horse sixpence, by the sordid fellow (Anthony Deane, of St. Martin's-in-the-Fields, Esq.) who had purchas'd it of the State, as they were call'd."—*Evelyn.*

The Park does not appear to have been thrown open to the public until the time of Charles I., and then not indiscriminately.

In the *Character of England*, 1659, it is described as "a field near the town, which they call Hyde Park; the place not unpleasant, and which they use as our course; but with nothing of that order, equipage, and splendour; being such an assembly of wretched jades and hackney-coaches, as, next a regiment of carrmen, there is nothing approaches the resemblance. This parke was, it seems, used by the late king and nobility for the freshness of the air and the goodly prospect; but it is that which now (besides all other exercises) they pay for here in England, though to be free in all the world besides; every coach and horse which enters buying his mouthful and permission of the publicane who has purchased it, for which the entrance is guarded with porters and long staves."

At the Restoration, Mr. Hamilton was appointed Ranger of the Park, which he let in farms until 1670, when it was enclosed with a walk, and re-stocked with deer. Refreshments were thus early sold; for 25th April, 1669, Pepys carried his pretty wife to the lodge, and there in their coach ate a cheesecake, and drank a tankard of milk. De Grammont describes the promenade as "the rendezvous of fashion and beauty. Every one, therefore, who had either sparkling eyes or a splendid equipage, constantly repaired thither; and the king (Charles II.) seemed pleased with the place." *Maying* was a favourite custom here: May 1, 1661, Evelyn "went to Hide Park to take the air; where was his Majesty and an innumerable appearance of gallants and rich coaches, being now the time of universal festivity and joy." Even in the Puritan times, May (1654) "was more observed by people going a-maying than for divers years past; and, indeed, much sin committed by wicked meetings, with fiddlers, drunkenness, ribaldry, and the like. Great resort came to Hyde Park, many hundreds of coaches, and gallants in attire; but most shameful powdered-hair men, and painted and spotted women." A few days after, the Lord Protector and many of his Privy Council

[*] In Charles-street, May Fair, is a public-house with the sign of a Footman, beneath whose figure are the words, "I am the only Running Footman."

witnessed in Hyde Park "a bowling of a great ball by 50 Cornish gentlemen of one side, and fifty of the other; one party playing in red caps, and the other in white. The ball they played withal was silver, and designed for that party which did win the goal." Evelyn, in May 1658, "went to see a coach-race in Hyde Park;" and Pepys, August 1660, "To Hyde Park by coach, and saw a fine foot-race three times round the park." Here a strange accident happened to Cromwell in 1654:

"The Duke of Holstein made him (Cromwell) a present of a set of gay Friesland coach-horses; with which, taking the air in the park, attended only with his secretary, Thurloe, and a guard of Janizaries, he would needs take the place of the coachman, and not content with their ordinary pace, he lashed them very furiously. But they, unaccustomed to such a rough driver, ran away in a rage, and stopped not till they had thrown him out of the box, with which fall his pistol fired in his pocket, though without any hurt to himself; by which he might have been instructed how dangerous it was to meddle with those things wherein he had no experience."—*Ludlow.*

Cromwell was partial to Hyde Park: here Syndercombe and Cecill lay wait to assassinate him, when "the hinges of Hyde Park gate were filed off, in order to their escape." *The Ring* was, from all time previous to the Restoration till far in the reigns of the Georges, the fashionable haunt. It was situated to the north of the present Serpentine, and part of the Ranger's grounds cover its site; some of the old trees remain, with a few of the oaks traditionally said to have been planted by Charles II. Near the Ring was the Lodge called the " Grave Prince Maurice's Head," and in later times the " Lake House:" a slight stream ran before it; and the house, approached by planks, presented a very picturesque appearance: it is engraved in the *Gentleman's Magazine* for 1801.

Reviews have, for nearly two centuries, been favourite spectacles in Hyde Park. At the Restoration, during a splendid show, the Lord Mayor received notice that " Colonel John Lambert was carried by the park a prisoner unto Whitehall."

Pepys " did stand" at another review in 1664, when Charles II. was present, while "the horse and foot march by and discharge their guns, to show a French marquisse (for whom this muster was caused) the goodnesse of our firemen; which, indeed, was very good, though not without a slip now and then; and one broadside close to our coach as we had going out of the parke, even to the nearenesse to be ready to burn our hairs. *Yet methought all these gay men are not the soldiers that must do the king's business, it being such as these that lost the old king all he had, and were beat by the most ordinary fellows that could be.*"

The Militia review by George II. in 1759, the Volunteers by George III., and the encampment of the troops after Lord George Gordon's Riots in 1780, also belong to the military shows of Hyde Park. Here George III. inspected the Volunteers on his birth-day, June 4th, for several years: in 1800 they numbered 15,000. In August, 1814, was held in this park the Regent's Fête and Fair, when a mimic sea-fight was exhibited on the Serpentine, and fireworks from the wall of Kensington Gardens; and here have been held in the present century three " Coronation Fairs," and firework displays. Of sterner quality was the rendezvous of the Commonwealth troops in the park during the Civil War. Essex and Lambert encamped their forces here; and Cromwell reviewed his terrible Ironsides. In 1642 the citizens threw up a strong fort, with four bastions, at the south-east corner of the Park; and one of its strongest works, " Oliver's Mount," faced Mount-street, in Park-lane. (See FORTIFICATIONS, page 310.)

Hyde Park continued with little alteration, till, in 1705, nearly 30 acres were added to Kensington Gardens by Queen Anne; and nearly 300 acres by Caroline, Queen of George II. (see KENSINGTON GARDENS, page 433), by whose order also, in 1730-3, was formed the Serpentine River. It has also been reduced by grants of land, between

Hyde Park Corner and Park-lane, for building; and according to a survey taken in 1790, its extent was 394 acres 2 roods 38 poles.

In 1766, John Gwynne, the architect, proposed to build in Hyde Park a royal palace for George III.; and in 1825, a Member of Parliament published a magnificent design for a palace near Stanhope Gate.

Permission to "vend victuals" in Hyde Park was granted by George II. to a pilot who saved him from wreck in one of his voyages from visiting his Hanoverian dominions; and it is stated that the pilot's descendants to this day exercise the privilege. At the same time the king gave his deliverer a silver-gilt ring, which bears the arms of Poland impaled with those of Lithuania, surmounted by a regal crown. This ring was exhibited to the British Archæological Association, Feb. 9, 1853.

The *Conduits* of Hyde Park are described at p. 230. Upon the east side, 70 feet above Trinity high-water mark of the Thames, is the Chelsea Waterworks Reservoir, which contains about 1,500,000 gallons: the iron railing and dwarf wall were added to prevent suicides, which were formerly frequent here. Upon the east side was *Walnut-tree Walk*, shaded by two rows of noble walnut-trees, extended to a large circle: these trees were cut down about 1800, and the wood was used by Government for the stocks of soldiers' muskets.

The colossal statue near the south-east corner of the park, cast by Sir R. Westmacott, R.A., from twelve 24-pounders, weighing upwards of 30 tons, is about 18 feet high, and occupies a granite pedestal, bearing this inscription: "To Arthur Duke of Wellington, and his brave companions in arms, this statue of Achilles, cast from cannon taken in the battles of Salamanca, Vittoria, Toulouse, and Waterloo, is inscribed by their countrywomen." On the base is inscribed: "Placed on this spot on the 18th day of June, 1822, by command of his Majesty George IV." The figure is copied from one of the antique statues on the Monte Cavallo at Rome, and is improperly called Achilles: it has never received its sword! The cost of this monument, 10,000*l.*, was subscribed by ladies.

Gates.—The principal entrance is at Hyde Park Corner, through a triple-arched and colonnaded screen, designed by Decimus Burton, and described at page 19: eastward is Apsley House, nearly upon the site of which stood the old lodge of the park. In Park-lane is Stanhope-gate, opened about 1750; and Grosvenor-gate, in 1724, by subscription of the neighbouring inhabitants. Cumberland-gate, at the west end of Oxford-street, was opened about 1744-5, at the expense of the inhabitants of Cumberland-place and the neighbourhood: it was a mean brick arch, with side entrances: here took place a disgraceful contest between the people and the soldiery at the funeral of Queen Caroline, August 15, 1821, when two persons were killed by shots from the Horse-guards on duty. In 1822, the unsightly brick and wooden gate was removed; and handsome iron gates were substituted, at the cost of nearly 2000*l.*, by Mr. Henry Philip Hope, of Norfolk-street, Park-lane. In 1851 these gates were removed for the marble arch from Buckingham Palace, and placed on each side of it; the cost of removing the arch and rebuilding it being 4340*l.* (See ARCHES, pages 18, 19.) In the Bayswater-road is Victoria-gate: nearly opposite is the handsome terrace, Hyde-Park Gardens. Upon the south side of the park is the Kensington gate; the Prince of Wales's gate, near the site of the Half-way House; and Albert-gate, Knightsbridge.

Rotten Row, on the south side of the park, extends about 1½ mile from the lodge at Hyde Park Corner to the Kensington gate: it is for saddle-horses, who can gallop over its fine loose gravel without danger from falling; and it is crowded with equestrians between 5 and 7 P.M.

during the high London season. The name *Rotten* is traced to *rotteran*, to muster; which military origin may refer to the park during the Civil War. Between Rotten-row and the Queen's Drive was erected the Building for the Great Exhibition of 1851 :

> " But yesterday a naked sod,
>   The dandies sneered from Rotten-row,
>   And sauntered o'er it to and fro,
>   And see 'tis done!
> As though 'twere by a wizard's rod,
>   A blazing arch of lucid glass
> Leaps like a fountain from the grass,
>   To meet the sun!
> A quiet green but few days since,
>   With cattle browsing in the shade,
> And lo! long lines of bright arcade
>   In order raised;
> A palace as for fairy Prince,
>   A rare pavilion, such as man
> Saw never since mankind began,
>   And built and glazed!"
>
>   *May-day Ode*, by W. M. Thackeray : *Times*, May 1, 1851.

The Crystal Palace, as the building was appropriately named, from its roof and sides being of glass, was designed by Mr. (now Sir Joseph) Paxton, and was constructed by Mr. (now Sir Charles) Fox, and Mr. Henderson. The ground was broken July 30, 1850; the first column was placed Sept. 26; and the building was opened May 1, 1851. It was a vast expansion of a conservatory design, built at Chatsworth by Mr. Paxton, for the flowering of the Victoria Lily. The Crystal Palace was cruciform in plan, with a transept, nave, and side aisles; consisting of a framework of wrought and cast iron, firmly braced together, and based upon a foundation of concrete. It was built without a single scaffold-pole, a pair of shears and the Derick crane being the only machinery used in hoisting the materials. In the plan, every measurement was a multiple of 8. Thus the columns were all 24 feet high, and 24 feet apart; and the centre aisle or nave was 72 feet, or 9 times 8. Again, one single area, bounded by 4 columns and their crowning girders, was the type of the whole building, which was a simple aggregation of so many cubes, in extreme length 1851 feet, corresponding with the year of the Exhibition. Width 408 feet; with an additional projection on the north side, 936 feet long by 48 wide. The great avenues ran east and west; very near the centre crossed the transept, 72 feet high, and 108 wide. Its roof was semicircular, designed by Mr. (now Sir Charles) Barry, so as to preserve three fine old elms. The other roofs, designed by Mr. Paxton, were flat.

The entire area of the building was 772,784 square feet, or about 19 acres, nearly seven times as much as St. Paul's Cathedral. " The Alhambra and the Tuileries would not have filled up the eastern and western nave; the National Gallery would have stood beneath the transept; the palace of Versailles (the largest in the world) would have extended but a little way beyond the transept; and a dozen metropolitan churches would have stood erect under its roof of glass."—*Athenæum*, No. 1227.

The entire ground area was divided into a central nave, four side aisles, and several courts and avenues; and a gallery ran throughout the building. There were about 3000 columns, nearly 3500 girders, and altogether about 4000 tons of iron built into the structure.

The iron skeleton progressed with the framing and glazing, requiring 200 miles of wooden sash-bars, and 20 miles of Paxton gutters for the roof, which required 17 acres of glass; besides which, there

,were 1500 vertical glazed sashes. Flooring 1,000,000 square feet; total wood-work, 600,000 cubic feet. The hollow cast-iron columns conveyed the rain-fall from the roof. The ventilation was by louvre-boards.

The decoration of the interior, devised by Owen Jones, consisted of the application of the primitive colours, red, blue, and yellow, upon narrow surfaces: it was charmingly artistic, and was rapidly executed by 500 painters. During the months of December and January, upwards of 2000 workmen were employed throughout the building.

The vast Palace was filled with the World's Industry: in the western portion were the productions of the United Kingdom, India, and the Colonies; and the eastern, those of Foreign Countries. The value of the whole (except the Koh-i-noor diamond) was 1,781,929*l.* 11*s.* 4*d.*

The opening of the Exhibition, on May 1, 1851, was proclaimed by Queen Victoria, accompanied by Prince Albert, the Prince of Wales, and the Princess Royal. Between May 1 and Oct. 11 the number of visits paid was 6,063,986; mean daily average, 43,536. On three successive days there entered 107,815, 109,915, 109,760 persons, who paid respectively 5175*l.*, 5231*l.*, and 5283*l.* There were counted in the Palace 93,000 persons at one time. Cost of the building, 176,030*l.* 13*s.* 8*d.* Oct. 15, Jury Awards and closing ceremonial. The whole building was removed before the close of 1852; and, on Nov. 7, 1853, it was proposed to place upon the site a memorial of the Exhibition, to include a statue of Prince Albert, the originator of this display of the Industry of all Nations.

"But for Prince Albert, say what people will of others' part in the affair, we should never have had the Great Exhibition. In like manner, but for Sir Joseph Paxton we should never have had the Crystal Palace; and but for Sir Charles Fox, it is more than questionable whether that structure could have been undertaken and completed so promptly, so speedily, so securely, and with so much that is admirable and beautiful in its construction and details."—*Times,* Oct. 25, 1851.

Hyde Park being for the most part high and dry, is perhaps the most airy and healthy spot in London. The north-west or deer park, verging upon Kensington Gardens, is even of a rural character: the trees are picturesque, and deer are occasionally here. The Serpentine has upon its margin some lofty elms; but from other positions of the park many fine old timber-trees have disappeared, and the famous Ring of Charles II.'s days can be but imperfectly traced. The drives and walks have been greatly extended and improved: for the brick wall has been substituted iron railing; and the opening of three gates (Victoria, Albert, and Prince of Wales), and the Queen's Drive south of the Serpentine, denominate the improvements in the present reign.

From this high ground the artistic eye enjoys the *sylvan* scenery of the park: the old trees fringing the Serpentine, and its water gleaming through their branches; backed by the rich woods of Kensington Gardens; and the bold beauty of the Surrey hills.

The Serpentine (so called in distinction from the previous straight canals) is a pool of water covering 50 acres, formed from natural springs, and originally fed at the Bayswater extremity by a stream from West-End, near Hampstead, and the overplus of certain reservoirs, one of which occupied the site of Trinity Church. In 1834 the stream, or rather sewer, at Bayswater was cut off, and the deficiency was made up from the Chelsea Waterworks. At the eastern end the Serpentine imperfectly supplies an artificial cascade, formed in 1817; and descending into the "leg of mutton" pond, the stream leaves Hyde Park at Albert Gate, divides the parish of Chelsea from that of St. George's Hanover-square, and falls into the Thames at Chelsea. The Serpentine supplies the Knightsbridge Barracks and the Horse-guards, the lake in Buckingham Palace Gardens, and the ornamental water in St. James's Park. The depth in Hyde Park varies from 1 to 40 feet, of which Sir John Rennie found, in 1849, in the deepest parts, from 10 to 15 feet of inky, putrid mud,—"a laboratory of epidemic miasma." The Serpentine is deepest near the bridge, described at page 434 : the whole sheet has been deepened, at a cost of from 10,000*l.* to 20,000*l.* Here 200,000 persons, on an average, bathe annually, sometimes 12,000 on a Sunday morning; and in severe winters the ice is the great metropolitan skating-field. In 1847, pleasure-boats for hire were introduced upon the Serpentine : the boat-houses are picturesque.

On the north margin the *Royal Humane Society,* in 1794, built their principal receiving-house, upon ground presented by George III. In 1834 the house was rebuilt, from the design of J. B. Bunning ; the first stone being laid by the late Duke of Wellington : over the Ionic entrance is sculptured the obverse of the Society's medal,—a boy striving to rekindle an almost extinct torch by blowing it; legend, *Lateat scintillvla forsan*—" Perchance a spark may be concealed." In the rear are kept boats, ladders, ropes and poles, wicker-boats, life-preserving apparatus, &c. The Royal Humane Society was founded in 1774, by Drs. Goldsmith, Heberden, Towers, Lettsom, Hawes, and Cogan. Its receiving-houses in the parks cost 3000*l.* a-year. In odd contiguity to the Society's House in Hyde Park is the Government Magazine, containing stores of ammunition and gunpowder.

Duels fought in Hyde Park.—*Temp.* Henry VIII., the Duke of B. and Lord B., "near the first tree behind the Lodge;" both killed.—1712. The Duke of Hamilton and Lord Mohun, the former killed.—1763. Wilkes and Mr. S. Martin, the hero of Churchill's *Duellist.*—1770. Baddeley, the comedian, and George Garrick. — 1773. Mr. Whately and Mr. Temple.—1780. The Earl of Shelburne and Col. Fullarton.—1780. Rev. Mr. Bate and Mr. R., both of the *Morning Post.* —1782. Rev. Mr. Allen and Mr. Dulany.—1783. Lieut.-Col. Thomas and Col. Gordon, the former killed.—1787. Sir John Macpherson and Major Browne.— 1792. Messrs. Frizell and Clarke, law students, the former killed.—1796. Mr. Carpenter and Mr. Pride (Americans), the former killed.—1797. Col. King and Col. Fitzgerald, the latter killed.—Lieut. W. and Capt. I., the latter killed.— 1822. The Duke of Bedford and the Duke of Buckingham.

Near the site of the Humane Society's Receiving-house formerly stood a cottage, presented by George III. to Mrs. Sims, in consideration of her having lost six sons in war; the last fell with Abercrombie at Alexandria. This cottage has been painted by Nasmyth, and engraved in the *Art Journal,* No. 59, N.S.

St. James's Park is in plan an irregular triangle, 83 acres in extent. It was originally a swampy field attached to St. James's Hospital: the ground was drained and enclosed by Henry VIII., who thus made it the pleasure-ground both of the Hospital, which he had converted into St. James's Palace, and of Whitehall, whose tilt-yard, cockpit, tennis-court, and bowling-green were on the eastern verge of the Park; but during the reigns of Elizabeth and the first two Stuarts, it was little more than a nursery for deer, and an appendage to the tilt-yard. A procession of 15,000 citizens, "besides wifflers and other awayters," on May 8, 1539, passed "rounde about the Parke of St. James." In the reign of Charles I. a sort of royal menagerie took the place of the deer with which the "inward park" was stocked in the days of Henry and Elizabeth. Charles, as he walked through the Park to Whitehall on the fatal January 30, 1648-9, is said to have pointed to a tree which had been planted by his brother, Prince Henry, near Spring Gardens. Here Cromwell, as he walked with Whitelocke, asked him, "What if a man should take upon him to be king?" to which the memorialist replied : " I think that remedy would be worse than the disease." Evelyn, in his *Sylva,* mentions the branchy walk of elms in the Park, "intermingling their reverend tresses:"

"That living gallery of aged trees was once proposed to the late Council of State (as they called it) to be cut down and sold, that, with the rest of his Majesty's houses already demolished and marked out for destruction, his trees might likewise undergo the same destiny, and no footsteps of monarchy remain unviolated."

Charles II. added 36 acres to the Park, extended the wall towards Pall Mall, and had it planted by Le Nôtre, and, it is believed, by Dr. Morison, formerly employed by the Duke of Orleans. The original account for " workes and services" is signed by Charles himself. Pepys and Evelyn record the progress of the works :

" 16 Sept. 1660. To the Park, where I saw how far they had proceeded. in the Pell Mell, and in making a river through the Park." " 11 Oct. 1660. To walk in St. James's Park, where we observed the several engines at work to draw up water." " 4 Aug. 1661. Walked into St. James's Park, and there found great and very noble alterations." " 27 July, 1662. I to walke in the Parke, which is now every day more and more pleasant by the new works upon it." " 1 Dec. 1662. Over the Parke, where I first in my life, it being a great frost, did see people sliding with their skeates, which is a very pretty art." " 15 Dec. 1662. To the Duke (of York), and followed him into the Parke, where, though the ice was broken and dangerous, yet he would go slide upon his scates, which I did not like; but he slides very well." " 11 Aug. 1664. This day, for a wager, before the king, my lords of Castlehaven and Arran, a son of my Lord of Ormond's, they two alone did run down and kill a stout buck in St. James's Park."—*Pepys.* " 19 Feb. 1666-7. In the afternoon I saw a wrestling match for 100*l.* in St. James's Park, before his Ma'ty, a world of lords, and other spectators, 'twixt the Western and Northern men, Mr. Secretary Morice and Le Gerard being the judges. The Western men won. Many great sums were betted."—*Evelyn.*

The courtly Waller thus commemorates the Park, "as lately improved by his Majesty," 1661 :

> " For future shade, young trees upon the banks
> Of the new stream appear, in even ranks;
> The voice of Orpheus, or Amphion's hand,
> In better order could not make them stand.
>   *   *   *
> All that can, living, feed the greedy eye,
> Or dead the palate, here you may descry;
> The choicest things that furnish'd Noah's ark,
> Or Peter's sheet, inhabiting this Park:
> All with a border of rich fruit-trees crown'd,
> Whose lofty branches hide the lofty mound.
> Such various ways the spacious valleys lead,
> My doubtful Muse knows not what path to tread.
> Yonder the harvest of cold months laid up,
> Gives a fresh coolness to the royal cup:
> There ice, like crystal, firm and never lost,
> Tempers hot July with December's frost;
>   *   *   *
> Here a well-polish'd Mall gives us the joy,
> To see our Prince his matchless force employ."

Faithorne's plan, taken soon after the Restoration, shows the north half of the parade occupied by a square enclosure, surrounded by twenty-one trees, with one tree in the centre; and in the lower part of the parade broad running water, with a bridge of two arches in the middle. Later views show the Park with long rows of young elm and lime trees, fenced with palings, and occasionally relieved by some fine old trees.

The Mall, on the north side, a vista half a mile in length, was named from the game of "pale maille" played here, and was a smooth hollow walk planted on each side, and having an iron hoop suspended from the arm of a high pole, through which ring the ball was struck by a *maille,* or mallet. (See a drawing, *temp.* Charles II., engraved in Smith's *Antiquities of Westminster,* and a plate in Carter's *Westminster.*) Here Charles and his courtiers often played : the earth was mixed with powdered cockle-shells to make it bind; " which, however," says Pepys, "in dry weather turns to dust, and deads the ball."

"2 April, 1661. To St. James's Park, where I saw the Duke of York playing t pall-mall, the first time that I ever saw the sport."—*Pepys.*

Cibber tells us that here he had often seen Charles playing with his dogs and feeding his ducks, which made the common people adore him.

The Bird-cage Walk, on the south side of the Park, nearly in the same line as the road which still retains the name, had in Charles II.'s time the cages of an aviary disposed among the trees which bordered t. The keeper of the Volary, or Aviary, was Edward Storey, from whom or his house is named *Storey's Gate.* The carriage-road between his and Buckingham Gate was, until 1828, only open to the Royal Family, and the Hereditary Grand Falconer, the Duke of St. Albans.

In the "inward park" was made a formal *Canal,* 2800 feet in length and 100 feet broad, running from the Parade to Buckingham House. On the south of this canal, near its east end, was the *Decoy,* a triangular nexus of smaller canals, where water-fowl were kept. Within the channels of the Decoy was *Duck Island,* of which Sir John Flock and St. Evremond were, in succession, appointed governors (with a salary) by Charles II.; and Queen Caroline is said to have given the sinecure to the thresher-poet, Stephen Duck: "the island itself," says Pennant, "is lost in the late improvements."

The Park, as well as the Palace, sheltered persons from arrest; for, in 1632, John Perkins, a constable, was imprisoned for serving the Lord Chief-Justice's warrant upon John Beard in St. James's Park. To draw a sword in the Park was also a very serious offence. Congreve, in his *Old Bachelor,* makes Bluffe say, "My blood rises at that fellow. I can't stay where he is; and *I must not draw in the Park.*" Traitorous expressions, when uttered in St. James's Park, were punished more severely. Francis Heat was whipped, in 1717, from Charing Cross to the upper end of the Haymarket, fined ten groats, and ordered a month's imprisonment, for saying aloud in St. James's Park, "God save King James III., and send him a long and prosperous reign !" and, in 1718, a soldier was whipped in the Park for drinking a health to the Duke of Ormond and Dr. Sacheverel, and for saying "he hoped soon to wear his right master's cloth." The Duke of Wharton, too, was seized by the guard in St. James's Park for singing the Jacobite air, "The king shall have his own again." See Cunningham's *Handbook,* p. 260 ; where are printed, from the Letter-book of the Lord Steward's Office, two letters, dated 1677, sent with two lunatics to Bethlehem : Deborah Lyddal, for offering to throw a stone at the queen ; and Richard Harris, for throwing an orange at the king, in St. James's Park.

"Dec. 1, 1662. Having seene the strange and wonderful dexterity of the sliders on the new canal in St. James's Park, performed before their Majesties by divers gentlemen and others, with scheets after the manner of the Hollanders, with what swiftness as they pass, how suddainly they stop in full career upon the ice, I went home."—*Evelyn.*

Some of the cavaliers had, probably, acquired the art when seeking to while away a Dutch winter; and but for the temporary overthrow of the monarchy, we should not thus early have had skating in England. The Park soon became a resort for all classes, since, in 1683, the Duke of York records, Dec. 4 (a very hard frost), "this morning the boys began to slide upon the canal in the Park."

Evelyn, in 1664, went to "the Physique Garden in St. James's," where he first saw "orange-trees and other fine trees." He enumerates in the menagerie, "an ornocratylus, or pelican, a fowle between a storke and a swan; a melancholy water-fowl, brought from Astracan by the Russian ambassador ; a milk-white raven; two Balearian cranes," one of which had a wooden leg "made by a soulder :" there were also "deere of severall countries, white, spotted like leopards; antelopes, an elk, red deer, roebucks, staggs, Guinea goates, Arabian sheepe," &c. There were "withy-potts, or nests, for the wild fowle to lay their eggs in, a little above ye surface of ye water."

"25 Feb. 1664. This night I walk'd into St. James his Parke, where I saw many strange creatures, as divers sorts of outlandish deer, Guiny sheep, a white raven, a great parrot, a storke. . . . Here are very stately walkes set with lime-trees on both sides, and a fine pallmall."—*Journal of Mr. E. Browne, son of Sir Thomas Browne.*

Evelyn, on March 2, 1671, attended Charles through St. James's Park, where he saw and heard "a familiar discourse between the King and Mrs. Nelly, as they called an impudent comedian; she looking out of her garden on a terrace at the top, and the King standing on the green walk under it." (See page 394.) "Of the mount, or raised terrace on which Nelly stood, a portion may still be seen under the park-wall of Marlborough House." (Cunningham's *Nell Gwyn*, p. 118.) In the royal garden where Charles stood, and which was then the northern boundary of the Park, we find Master Pepys, in his *Diary*, stealing apples like a schoolboy. Pepys also portrays a court cavalcade in the Park, all flaunting with feathers, in which Charles appears between the Countess of Castlemaine and the Queen, and Mrs. Stewart.

While Charles was walking in the Mall, he first received intimation of Titus Oates's pretended Popish plot. On Aug. 12, 1678, Kirby, the chemist, accosted the King as he walked in the Park: "Sir," said he, "keep within the company: your enemies have a design upon your life, and you may be shot in this very walk." Charles was an early riser and a fast walker. Burnet complained that the King walked so fast he could not keep up with him. When Prince George of Denmark said that he was growing too fat, "Walk with me," said Charles, "and hunt with my brother, and you will not long be distressed with growing fat."

Aubrey relates that Avise Evans had a fungous nose; and it being told to him that the King's hand would cure him, he awaited Charles in the Park, kissed the royal hand, and rubbed his nose with it, which disturbed the King, but cured Evans.

Succeeding kings allowed the people the privilege of walking in the Mall; and the passage from Spring Gardens was opened in 1699 by permission of King William. Queen Caroline, however, talked of shutting up the Park, and converting it into a noble garden for St. James's Palace: she asked Walpole what it might probably cost; who replied, "Only three *crowns.*"

Dean Swift, who often walked here with the poets Prior and Rowe, writes of skating as a novelty to Stella, in 1711: "Delicious walking weather," says he; "and the Canal and Rosamond's Pond full of rabble sliding, and with skaitts, if you know what it is."

This Park was a favourite resort of Goldsmith:

"If a man be splenetic, he may every day meet companions on the seats in St. James's Park, with whose groans he may mix his own, and pathetically talk of the weather." (*Essays.*) The strolling player takes a walk in St. James's Park "about the hour at which company leave it to go to dinner. There were but few in the walks; and those who stayed, seemed by their looks rather more willing to forget that they had an appetite, than gain one." (*Essays.*) And dinnerless, Jack Spindle mends his appetite by a walk in the Park.

On the south-west side of the Park, connected with the Canal by a sluice, was the gloomy *Rosamond's Pond*, of oblong shape, and overhung by the trees of the Long Avenue: it is mentioned in a grant of Henry VIII. It occurs as a place of assignation in the comedies of Otway, Congreve, Farquhar, Southerne, and Colley Cibber; and Pope calls it "Rosamonda's Lake." Its name is referred to the frequency of love-suicides committed here. The Pond was filled up in 1770, when the gate into Petty France was opened for bringing in the soil to fill up the Pond and the upper part of the Canal.

About 1740, Hogarth painted a large view of Rosamond's Pond, now in the collection of Mr. H. R. Willett, at Merly House, Dorset. This picture has been engraved, but the impressions (100) have not been published; it was copied by George Cruikshank, in 1842, in his illustrations of Ainsworth's *Miser's Daughter*. Hogarth also painted a cabinet view of Rosamond's Pond, likewise in the possession of Mr. Willett, who has the receipt for 1*l*. 7*s*. (the sum charged by the painter) in the handwriting of Mrs. Hogarth. The Pond has been engraved by J. T. Smith and W. H. Toms.

In a house belonging to the Crown, at the south-east corner of Rosamond's Pond, was born George Colman the Younger, who describes the snow-white tents of the Guards, who were encamped in the Park during the Riots of 1780.

The trees have been thinned by various means. Dryden records, by a violent wind, February 7, 1698-9: "The great trees in St. James's Park are many of them torn up from the roots, as they were before Oliver Cromwell's death, and the late queen's." In 1833 were thus lost two fine trees, said to have been planted by Charles II. with acorns from Boscobel.* The uniformity of Bird-cage Walk has been spoiled by the new road.† Samouelle, in his *Compendium of Entomology*, figures a destructive moth "found in July, in St. James's Park, against trees."

After the death of Charles II., St. James's Park ceased to be the favourite haunt of the sovereign, but it continued to be the promenade of the people; and here, in the summer, till early in the present century, gay company walked for one or two hours *after dinner;* but the evening dinner has robbed the Park of this charm, and the Mall is principally a thoroughfare for busy passengers.

"My spirits sunk, and a tear started into my eyes, as I brought to mind those crowds of beauty, rank, and fashion, which, till within these few years, used to be displayed in the centre Mall of this Park on Sunday evenings during the spring and summer. How often in my youth had I been a delighted spectator of the enchanted and enchanting assemblage! Here used to promenade, for one or two hours after dinner, the whole British world of gaiety, beauty, and splendour. Here could be seen in one moving mass, extending the whole length of the Mall, 5000 of the most lovely women in this country of female beauty, all splendidly attired, and accompanied by as many well-dressed men. What a change, I exclaimed, has a few years wrought in these once happy and cheerful personages! How many of those who on this very spot then delighted my eyes, are now mouldering in the silent grave!"—Sir R. Phillips's *Walk to Kew*, 1817.

For the Peace Commemoration Fête, on August 1, 1814, the Mall and Bird-cage Walk were lighted with Chinese lanterns; a Chinese bridge and seven-storied pagoda were erected across the canal: they were illuminated with lamps, and fireworks were discharged from them, which set fire to the pagoda, and burnt its three upper stories, when two persons lost their lives.

Canova, when asked what struck him most forcibly during his visit to England, is said to have replied, "that the trumpery Chinese bridge in St. James's Park should be the production of the government, whilst that of Waterloo was the work of a private company."—*Quarterly Rev.*

The hints for supplanting the forest-trees which skirt the Park, by flowering shrubs, and dressing the ground in a gayer style, so as to

* The two old railed-in oaks on the north side of the Serpentine, in Hyde Park, where the road turns to Kensington Gardens, are said to have been planted by Charles II. from acorns of the Boscobel Oak. (See HYDE PARK: at page 585, or "Lake House" read "Cake House.")

† Here were elms planted by the late Mr. Rench, of Fulham, from trees reared in his own nursery. He married two wives, had 35 children, and died in 1783, aged 101 years, in the room wherein he was born.

convert even the gloomy alleys of St. James's Park into a lively and agreeable promenade, were first published in "A Letter to the Rt. Hon. Sir Charles Long," &c. 1825.

In 1827 was commenced the relaying out of the inner park. The straight canal was altered and extended to a winding lake, with islands of evergreens; at the west end is a fountain. The borders of the principal walk are planted with evergreens, which are scientifically labelled; some of the fine old elms remain. The glimpses of grand architectural objects from this Park are very striking, and include the towers of Westminster Abbey and the new Houses of Parliament; the extensive front of Buckingham Palace; the York Column, rising from between terraces of mansions; and the Horse Guards, terminating the picturesque vista of the lake. Upon the eastern island is the Swiss cottage of the Ornithological Society, built in 1841 with a grant of 300l. from the Lords of the Treasury: the design is by J. B. Watson, and contains a council-room, keeper's apartments, steam-hatching apparatus; contiguous are feeding-places and decoys; and the aquatic fowl breed on the island, making their own nests among the shrubs and grasses. In 1849 an experimental crop of Forty-day Maize (from the Pyrenees) was successfully grown and ripened in this Park. For the privilege of farming the chairs, 25l. is paid annually to the office of Woods and Forests.

The fine old trees of the grounds of Carlton House formerly overhung the road by the Park-wall, now the site of the Pæstum-Doric substructure of Carlton-House-terrace; the opening in which to the York Column (see page 226) was formed by command of William IV., as had been the Spring-Garden gate by William III. *Milk Fair*, leftward of this gate, is described at page 251. The vista of the Mall, which consists of elms, limes, and planes, is terminated by the grand front of Buckingham Palace.

In 1854 were found in the roof of the house of the late Mr. B. L. Vulliamy, No. 68 Pall Mall, a box containing four pairs of the mailes, or mallets, and one ball, such as were formerly used for playing the game of pall-mall upon the site of the above house, or in the Mall of St. James's Park. Each maile is 4 feet in length, and is made of lance-wood; the head is slightly curved, and measures outwardly 5½ inches, the inner curve being 4½ inches; the diameter of the maile-ends is 2½ inches, each shod with a thin iron hoop; the handle, which is very elastic, is bound with white leather to the breadth of two hands, and terminated with a collar of jagged leather. The ball is of box-wood, 2½ inches in diameter. The pair of mailes and a ball, here engraved, have been presented to the British Museum by Mr. George Vulliamy. The game was played by striking the ball (*palla*, Ital.) with the mallet or maile (*maglia*, Ital.) through a ring of iron upon a lofty pole at each end of the alley as described at page 590.

PALL AND MAILES.

The Wellington Barracks, built near the site of Rosamond's Pond, were first occupied by troops on March 1, 1814: the Military Chapel was opened May 1, 1838. Eastward was the residence of Lord Milford, fitted up in 1820 as *Her Majesty's Stationery Office*, for supplying the public departments of the Government with Stationery.

St. James's Park was not lighted with gas until 1822; although

Pall-Mall, adjoining, was the first thoroughfare in London so lighted, and that as early as 1807.

On the north side of the Parade is a piece of Turkish ordnance, of great length: it was taken by the British at Alexandria, and is mounted upon an English-built carriage. Opposite is the immense mortar cast at Seville by order of Napoleon, employed by Marshal Soult at the siege of Cadiz in 1812, and abandoned by the French army in their retreat from Salamanca: it was presented by the Spanish Cortes to the Prince Regent. The gun-metal bed and carriage were cast at Woolwich in 1814, and consist of a crouching dragon, with upraised wings and scorpion-tail, involving the trunnions; it is allegorical of the monster Geryon, destroyed by Hercules. The mortar itself is 8 feet long, 12 inches diameter in bore, and has thrown shells 3¼ miles: it weighs about 5 tons. On the pedestal are inscriptions in Latin and English. When Soult was in England, in 1838, he good-humouredly recognised his lost gun. Here was also formerly a small piece of artillery which had been taken from Bonaparte at Waterloo.

The State-Paper Office, further south, occupying part of the site of the house of Lord Chancellor Jefferies, was built by Sir John Soane in 1833: it was his latest work, and resembles an Italian palazzo. At No. 17 Duke-street, died in 1849, aged 81, Sir Marc Isambard Brunel, the engineer of the Thames Tunnel.

Upon the south side of the Park is Milton's garden-house, in Petty France. Hazlitt lived in this house in 1813, when Haydon was one of a christening-party of " Charles Lamb and his poor sister, and all sorts of odd clever people, in a large room, wainscoted and ancient, where Milton had meditated." (Haydon's *Autobiography*, vol. i. p. 211.) In the garden-wall is a doorway, now blocked up, but which once opened into the Park, and was probably that used by Milton in passing from his house to Whitehall. In Queen-Square-place, and looking upon the garden-ground of Milton's house, was the house of Jeremy Bentham, who died here in 1832.

Upon the Parade was marshalled the State Funeral Procession of the great Duke of Wellington, November 18, 1852. The body was removed from Chelsea Hospital on the previous midnight, and deposited in the Audience Chamber at the Horse-Guards. Beneath a tent upon the Parade-ground was stationed the Funeral Car, whereon the coffin being placed, and the command given, the *cortége*, in slow and solemn splendour, moved down the Mall past Buckingham Palace, whence the procession was seen by Her Majesty and the Royal Family.

The Funeral Car, chiefly designed by Mr. Redgrave, the Art-Superintendent at Marlborough House, consists of the bier, covered with a black velvet pall, diapered with the Duke's crest and field-marshals' batons, fringed with laurel-leaves in silver, and inscribed: " Blessed are the dead which die in the Lord." Upon the bier was placed the coffin, upon which lay the Duke's hat and sword, beneath a canopy of rich tissue, supported by halberts, hung with chaplets of real laurel. The platform of the car is gilt, and bears the names of the Duke's great victories; and in the centre part of the sides were groups of modern arms, helmets, guns, flags and drums, furnished by the Board of Ordnance. The carriage, 20 feet by 12, is ornamented in bronze with laurels and figures of Fame; the 12 wheels have massive lions' heads as bosses: and in front were the Duke's arms, superbly emblazoned. The car was drawn by 12 horses, in black velvet housings, decorated with trophies and heraldic achievements; and on each side were borne five superb bannerols. The Car is to be seen at Marlborough House, Pall Mall.

KENNINGTON PARK, formed from Kennington Common in 1852-3, is described at page 430: it comprises 12 acres, enclosed with iron palisading, and laid out in grass-plots, and planted with shrubs and evergreens; and Prince Albert's Model Lodging-house at the principal entrance. Old men remember when the Common was the gallows-ground: in 1848 it was the scene of Chartist mob-agitation.

PRIMROSE HILL PARK, about 50 acres at the foot of Primrose Hill, is enclosed and laid out for cricket, and planted with trees and shrubs, by the Commissioners of Woods and Forests.

REGENT'S PARK (the), 403 acres, lies between the south foot of Primrose-Hill and the New-road, and includes part of Marylebone Park. (See p. 503.) The relaying out of the estate was proposed in 1793, and a large premium offered for the best design; but it was not until 1812 that any plan was adopted—the plan of John Nash, architect, who proposed to connect this new part of the town with Carlton House and St. James's: this has been effected in Regent-street, which, with the Park, is named from their having been projected and laid out during the Regency of George IV. The Park is nearly circular in plan, and is comprised within a ride, or drive, of nearly two miles. The south side is parallel to the New-road; the east side extends northward to Gloucester-gate; the west side to Hanover-gate; and the northern curve nearly corresponds with the sweep of the Regent's Canal, at the north-western side of which are Macclesfield-bridge and gate. In the south-west portion of the Park is a sheet of water, in outline resembling the three legs on an Isle-of-Man halfpenny: it is crossed by wire suspension-bridges, and has some picturesque islets, large weeping-willows, shrubs, &c. Near the southernmost point is the rustic cottage of the Toxopholite Society (see page 7). In the southern half of the Park are two circles: the Inner Circle, formerly Jenkins's nursery-ground, was reserved by Nash as the site for a palace for George IV.: it is now the garden of the Botanic Society (see page 52). On the eastern slope, at the north end of the Park, is the garden of the Zoological Society. On the east side, a little south of Gloucester-gate, are the enclosed villa and grounds of the Master of St. Katherine's Hospital, the church and domestic buildings of which are opposite. Among the detached villas in the Park are the Holme, in the centre, built by William Burton, architect; St. John's Lodge (Sir Isaac Lyon Goldsmid's), adjoining the Inner Circle; St. Dunstan's Villa (Marquis of Hertford's), and Holford House (Mr. Holford's), on the Outer Road; and near Hanover-gate is Hanover Lodge, formerly the Earl of Dundonald's. The portico of St. Dunstan's Villa is adapted from the Temple of the Winds at Athens; the roof is Venetian; and in a recess near the entrance are the two gigantic wooden figures, with clubs and bells, from old St. Dunstan's Church, Fleet-street (see page 225): they were purchased by the late Marquis of Hertford for 200l. At the south-east corner of the Park is the Diorama building (see p. 252), converted into a Baptist chapel in 1854; beyond is the Colosseum, described at pp. 221-4. On the south, east, and north-west sides of the Park are highly-embellished terraces of houses, in which the Doric and Ionic, the Corinthian, and even the Tuscan, orders have been employed with ornate effect, aided by architectural sculpture.

In the Inner Circle, adjoining South Villa, is the *Observatory*, erected in 1837 by Mr. George Bishop, F.R.S., F.R.A.S. It consists of a circular equatorial room, with a dome roof; and an arm containing the altitude and azimuth instrument, micrometers, &c. The equatorial telescope, by Dollond, with magnifying powers up to 1200, is driven by clockwork motion; and in the room is a revolving chair. The longitude of the Observatory is 0' 37½" W., the latitude 51° 31' 29·8" N. Since 1844 Mr. J. R. Hind, F.R.A.S., has been attached to the Observatory; and his search for new comets and planets, and his study of the variable stars, have been very successful. The *Observations* of twelve years, 1839-1851, day and night, at this Observatory, are published.

VICTORIA PARK, Bethnal Green, is 290 acres in extent, or equal to the entire area of Kensington Gardens; it is bounded on the west by

he Regent's Canal, and on the south by Sir George Duckett's Canal.
The land was mostly purchased, in 1842, of the trustees of Guy's Hospital and Sir John Cass' Charity; and towards the cost of formation
was appropriated 72,000*l.*, received for the remainder of the Crown
ease of York House, St. James's. (See STAFFORD HOUSE, page 494.)
The chief entrance is at " Bonner's Field," where was a hall tradition-
lly tenanted by Bishop Bonner: the forester's lodge is of Elizabethan
haracter, by Pennethorne, and has a lofty tower and porch. The Park
s planted with an arboretum; it has two pieces of ornamental water,
or bathing, boating, and water-fowl; and upon an island is a two-
toried Chinese pagoda. Here are a gymnasium, cricket and archery
grounds, and flower, pigeon, and canary shows. The Park has often
0,000 visitors in a single day; Wednesday afternoon is the children's
ay. In the neighbourhood has been swept away a wretched village of
ovels, formerly known as Botany Bay, from so many of its inhabi-
ants being sent to the *real place.*

PARLIAMENT HOUSES (THE),

tyled also " New Westminster Palace," occupy the site of the Royal
'alace of the monarchs of England, from Edward the Confessor to
Queen Elizabeth.

Westminster Palace is first named in a charter of Edward the Con-
essor, "made" soon after 1052: here the Confessor died, Jan. 14, 1066.
In the Easter succeeding, King Harold came here from York. William
he Norman held councils here; and in 1069, Elfric, Abbot of Peterbo-
ough, was tried before the king *in curiâ* at Westminster,—this being
me of the first records of the holding of a *law-court* on this spot.
William Rufus added the *Great Hall,* wherein he held his court in
099; as did also Henry I. Stephen founded the palace chapel, which
vas dedicated to St. Stephen. In the reign of Henry II., Fitzstephen
ecords: " on the west, and on the bank of the river, the Royal Palace
xalts its head, and stretches wide, an incomparable structure, fur-
ished with bastions and a breastwork, at the distance of two miles
rom the City." The Close Rolls, in the Tower of London, contain
nany curious entries concerning the palace in the time of King John
nd Henry III.: here, in a great council, Henry confirmed the
Magna Charta and the Charta de Foresta: in this reign, also, the gib-
et was removed from the palace. In 1238 the whole palace was
looded by the Thames, and boats were afloat in the Great Hall.
There are numerous records in this reign of painting and decorating the
palace, storing its cellars with wine, &c. (See PAINTED CHAMBER,
. 565.) Of the repairs of the mews, the new butlery and kitchen, and
he rebuilding and painting of *St. Stephen's Chapel,* in the reign of
Edward I., there are minute accounts. In 1298 the palace was nearly
lestroyed by fire, but was restored by Edward II. St. Stephen's
Chapel was completed by Edward III. The poet Chaucer was clerk of
he palace works in the reign of Richard II., who rebuilt Westminster
Hall nearly as we now see it. In 1512 a great part of the palace was
once again burnt, since which time it has not been re-edified: only
he Great Hall, with the offices near adjoining, are kept in good repairs;
nd it serveth, as before it did, for feasts at coronations, arraignments
f great persons charged with treasons, keeping of the courts of jus-
ice, &c.; but the princes have been lodged in other palaces about the
City, as at Baynard's Castle, at Bridewell, and Whitehall (sometimes
alled York Place), and sometimes at St. James's " (Strype's Stow's
London, vol. ii. p. 628, edit. 1755.) Some buildings were added by
Henry VIII., who is supposed to have built the Star Chamber; a por-

tion of which, however, bore the date 1602. (See page 396.) Parliaments were held in Westminster Hall *temp.* Henry III., and thenceforth in the Painted Chamber and White Chamber. After the Suppression, the Commons sat in St. Stephen's Chapel, until its destruction by fire Oct. 16, 1834, with the House of Lords, and the surrounding Parliamentary buildings.*

The demesne of the Old Palace was bounded on the east by the river Thames; on the north by the Woolstaple, now Bridge-street; on the west by the precincts of St. Margaret's Church and Westminster Abbey, behind Abingdon-street; and on the south by the line of the present College-street, where formerly ran a stream, called the Great Ditch (now a sewer), outside the palace garden-wall.

Among the more ancient buildings which existed to our time, was the *Painted Chamber,* described at page 564. Next was the *Old House of Lords* (the old Parliament Chamber), rebuilt by Henry II. on the foundations of Edward the Confessor's reign; the walls were nearly seven feet thick, and the vaults (Guy Fawkes' cellar) had been the kitchen of the Old Palace: this building was taken down about 1823, prior to the erection of the Royal Gallery and Entrance, by Soane, R.A. Southward was the *Prince's Chamber* (then also demolished), with foundations of Edward the Confessor's time, and a superstructure with lancet-windows, *temp.* Henry III.: the walls were painted in oil with scriptural figures, and hung with tapestry representing the birth of Queen Elizabeth. Next was the *Old Court of Requests,* supposed to have been the Great Hall of the Confessor's palace: this was, until 1834, the House of Lords, and was hung with tapestry representing the defeat of the Spanish Armada in 1588: it was destroyed in the great fire, after which the interior was refitted for the House of Commons.

The Armada Tapestry was woven by Spiering, from the designs of Henry Cornelius Vroom, at Haarlem, for Lord Howard of Effingham, Lord High Admiral of the English fleet which engaged the Armada; and was sold by him to James I. It consisted originally of ten compartments, with borders containing portraits of the officers of the English fleet. The hangings were engraved by Hine in 1739.

St. Stephen's Chapel had its beautiful architecture and sumptuous decoration hidden until the enlargement of the interior in 1800, when its painting, gilding, and sculpture, its traceried and brilliant windows, were discovered. Among the mural paintings were the histories of Jonah, Daniel, Jeremiah, Job, Tobit, Judith, Susannah, and of Bel and the Dragon; the Ascension of Christ, and the Miracles and Martyrdom of the Apostles; and in the windows were the stories of Adam and Eve, and of Noah and his Family, of Abraham, Joseph, and the Israelites; and of the Life of the Saviour, from his baptism to his crucifixion and death. Among the decorations were figures of angels and armed knights, Edward III. and his family, and heraldic shields; the jewels, vestments, and furniture of the chapel were very superb. The *Cloisters* were first built in 1356, south of the chapel, on the spot subsequently called Cotton Garden.† The *Crypt,* or under-chapel of St. Stephen's, is described at page 244.

On the south side, probably, was the small chapel of *St. Mary de la Rewe,* or Our Lady of the Rew; wherein Richard II. offered to the Virgin, previously to meeting the insurgents under Wat Tyler in Smithfield, in 1381. *Westminster Hall* will be described hereafter.

* The scene of the conflagration was painted by J. M. W. Turner, R.A., bought by Mr. Chambers Hall, and sold to Mr. Colls.

† Sir Robert Cotton had a House and Garden abutting against the Painted Chamber; and it was there that his collection of Mss., now in the British Museum, was originally stored. In Cotton House, in 1820, were lodged the Italian witnesses against Queen Caroline.

Upon its western side were built the new Law Courts, by Soane, R.A., upon the site of the old Exchequer Court, &c. On the east side of New Palace-yard was an arch; *temp.*. Henry III., leading to the Thames; and the old Exchequer buildings and the Star Chamber, described at page 396. On the northern side of New Palace-yard, directly fronting the entrance-porch of the Great Hall, on a spot now hidden by the houses on the terrace, stood the famous *Clock-tower*, built and furnished with a clock, *temp.* Edward I., with a fine of 800 marks levied on Chief-Justice Sir Ralph de Hingham for altering a record: the keepers of this clock-tower were appointed by the sovereign, and were paid 6*d.* a day at the Exchequer. The tower was taken down about 1707; and its bell, " Great Tom of Westminster," was re-cast (with additional metal) for the great bell of St. Paul's Cathedral.

Hatton describes the House of Commons, altered by Sir Christopher Wren, in 1706, as " a commodious building, accommodated with several ranks of seats, covered with green cloth (baize ?), and matted under foot, for 513 gentlemen. On three sides of this house are beautiful wainscot galleries, sustained by cantaleevers, enriched with fruit and other carved curiosities."

Of the House of Lords, in 1778, we have a portion in Copley's fine picture of the fall of the great Earl of Chatham. Of the several *Gates* to the old palace, the only one of which we have any record is that begun by Richard III. in 1484, at the east end of Union-street, and taken down in 1706; but a century later, in a fragment of this gate built into a partition-wall, was found a capital, sculptured with William Rufus granting a charter to Gislebertus, Abbot of Westminster: this capital was sold by Mr. Capon to Sir Gregory Page Turner, Bart., for 100 guineas. A plan of the old palace, measured 1793-1823. is engraved in *Vetusta Monumenta,* vol. v.; in J. T. Smith's *Antiquities of Westminster;* and in Brayley and Britton's *Westminster Palace,* from drawings by R. W. Billings.

In 1836 was selected from 97 sets the design of Charles Barry, R.A. The coffer-dam for the river-front was commenced late in 1837; the river-wall early in 1839; and, on April 27, 1840, was laid the first stone, at the north end of the Speaker's house. The exterior material is fine magnesian limestone, from Anston, in Yorkshire, and Caen stone for the interior; the river-terrace is of Aberdeen granite; the whole building stands on a bed of concrete 12 feet thick. The vast pile covers about eight acres, and has four principal fronts, the eastern or river being 940 feet in length. The plan contains 11 open quadrangles or courts, which, besides 500 apartments and 18 official residences, flank the royal state-apartments and the Houses of Lords and Commons, and the great Central Hall. The interior walls are fine brick; the bearers of the floors are cast-iron, with brick arches turned from girder to girder; the entire roofs are of wrought-iron covered with cast-iron plates galvanised; so that timber has not been used in the carcases of the entire building.

The New Palace is the largest public edifice which has been erected for several centuries in England; and in the arrangement of its apartments for the transaction of public business, in its lighting, ventilation, fire-proof construction, supply of water, &c. it is the most perfect building in Europe. The style is Tudor (Henry VIII.), with picturesque portions of the town-halls of the Low Countries, and three grand features: a *Clock Tower* at the northern extremity, 40 feet square and 320 feet high, resembling that of the Town-house at Brussels; a great *Central Dome,* with an open stone lantern and spire, nearly 300 feet high; and the *Royal* or *Victoria Tower,* at the south-west angle, 80 feet square and 340 feet high.

The vast edifice covers at least twice the site of the old Palace of Westminster, about half the new ground occupied being taken from the Thames. *The East* or *River Front* has at the ends projecting wings, each 120 feet in length, with towers of beautiful design, leaving between them a terrace 700 feet long and 33 feet wide. The wing-towers have crested roofs and open-worked pinnacles, which, with those of the bays, carry gilded vanes. Between the principal and one-pair floors is a rich band of sculpture, composed of the royal arms of England in each reign, from William I. to Queen Victoria. The band below the principal floor is inscribed with the date of each sovereign's accession and decease; and the panels on each side of the coats-of-arms have sceptres and labels, with badges and inscriptions. In the parapet of each bay is a niched figure of an angel bearing a shield. The carved panels of the six oriel windows have the arms of Queen Victoria, to indicate that the building was erected in her reign. The wing-towers, with their octagonal stone pinnacles and perforated iron orna-ments at their angles and crests, remind one of the picturesque roofs of the chateaux and belfry-towers of the Low Countries.

The North Front has bays and buttresses similar to those of the river front; the bands are sculptured with the quarterings of the kings of England between the Heptarchy and the Conquest, inscriptions and dates of accession, &c.; while the niches between the windows in each bay contain effigies of the sovereigns whose arms are below. This front terminates at the west with the *Clock Tower* and turreted lantern spire. The Clock, by Dent, according to the parliamentary conditions, is to " strike the hours on a bell from eight to ten tons, and, if practicable, chime the quarters upon eight bells, and show the time upon four dials about thirty feet in diameter," or nearly twice the size of the clock-face of St. Paul's Cathedral.

The South Front resembles the north, has similar decorations chro-nologically arranged, and terminates with the *Victoria Tower*.

This will be, when completed, the largest and loftiest square tower in the world: in 1853 it had scarcely reached half its altitude. In the lower western face is an archway 50 feet high, through which the royal state-carriage is driven under the tower to the foot of the staircase. The portal is flanked by colossal lions of England bearing the national standard; and the walls and groined roof are heraldically sculptured. Within the porch, over the archway, in niches, are statues of St. George, St. Andrew, and St. Patrick; and over the archway to the royal staircase, on the north side, is a colossal statue of Queen Victoria, be-tween allegorical figures of Justice and Mercy. Again, in the exterior of the tower, above the great entrance, are statues of the Queen, the Duke and Duchess of Kent, and other members of the Royal Family. Above these are lofty windows divided by delicate arcade-work.

Saxon Kings and Queens at the South Front, commencing at the wing tower, and proceeding from base to summit in each bay:—Agatha, Harold II., Editha, Edward III., Hardicanute, Harold, Emma, Canute, Elgiva, Edmund, Emma, Ethelred, Edward II., Elfleda, Edgar, Edwin, Edred, Elgina, Edmund, Athelstan, Elfleda, Edward I., Elwitha, Alfred, Ethelred, Ethelbert, Ethelbald, Judith, Egbert, Ethelwolf; two kings of Mercia, Northumberland, East Anglia, Wessex, Essex, Kent, and Sussex; sculptured by John Thomas.

The West Front, towards New Palace-yard, is composed of bays divided by bold buttresses, the niches in which will contain statues of eminent commoners. The only other portion of this front complete to the commencement of 1854, is that opposite Henry the Seventh's Chapel, called St. Margaret's Porch; and the gable of Westminster Hall, which has been advanced southward, the great window replaced, and thus forms St. Stephen's Porch, with much of the varied and piquant character of the Town-hall of Louvain. The turrets contain statuettes of Edward III. and Queen Philippa, St. George and St. An-drew, Henry VII. and Elizabeth of York, St. Patrick and St. Stephen.

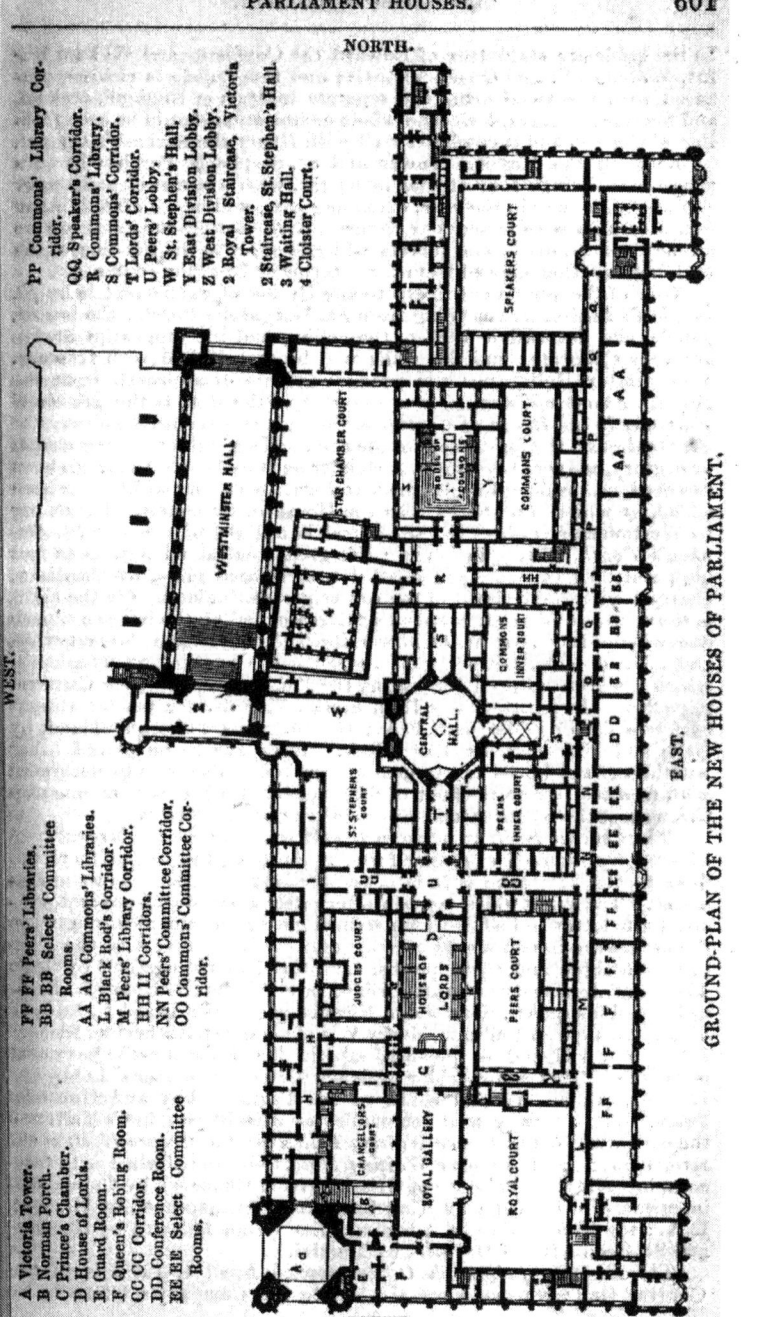

NORTH.

WEST.

EAST.

SOUTH.

A Victoria Tower.
B Norman Porch.
C Prince's Chamber.
D House of Lords.
E Guard Room.
F Queen's Robing Room.
CC CC Corridor.
DD Conference Room.
EE EE Select Committee Rooms.

FF FF Peers' Libraries.
BB BB Select Committee Rooms.
AA AA Commons' Libraries.
L Black Rod's Corridor.
M Peers' Library Corridor.
HH II Corridors.
NN Peers' Committee Corridor.
OO Commons' Committee Corridor.

PP Commons' Library Corridor.
QQ Speaker's Corridor.
R Commons' Library.
S Commons' Corridor.
T Lords' Corridor.
U Peers' Lobby.
W St. Stephen's Hall.
Y East Division Lobby.
Z West Division Lobby.
2 Royal Staircase, Victoria Tower.
3 Staircase, St. Stephen's Hall.
3 Waiting Hall.
4 Cloister Court.

GROUND-PLAN OF THE NEW HOUSES OF PARLIAMENT.

In the gable are statuettes of Edward the Confessor and William Rufus, William IV. and Queen Victoria; and this façade is richly sculptured with the royal arms, the separate insignia of England, Ireland, and Scotland, badges, &c. The whole composition should be seen from Poets' Corner, and it combines well with Henry the Seventh's Chapel.

Between the Victoria Tower and St. Stephen's Porch will be a range of buildings four stories in height, with a central clock-tower 120 feet high; and in the rear, extending east, will be a *Painted Chamber*, decorated with frescoes by Herbert, R.A. Besides the great towers, already named, oriels and turrets will add effect to the sky-line of the building, whether viewed from the exterior or from the courts.

One of the public entrances to the Houses of Parliament is by *St. Stephen's Staircase*, ascending from St. Margaret's Porch: the bosses, panels, and decorative work of the ceiling and the supporting arches are very elaborate; and the walls will be embellished with frescoes. Westminster Hall forms the grand vestibule of approach from the north. About midway, on the east side of the Hall, is the *Members' Entrance to the House of Commons*, through the restored *Cloisters of St. Stephen's:* the fan-tracery of the roof, and a small projecting chapel or oratory, are very beautiful. A cloister built by Henry VIII. has been restored, as a relic of English mediæval art. An upper cloister has been added, by which is a staircase to the House of Commons. Returning to Westminster Hall, at the south end is a flight of steps to *St. Stephen's Porch*, 65 feet in height: the great central window is 48 feet high and 25 feet wide, and is filled with stained glass, by Hardman, charged with the insignia of the sovereigns of England. On the right is the entrance from St. Stephen's Staircase, and on the left is a superb doorway leading into *St. Stephen's Hall*, 95 feet long by 30 feet wide, and 56 feet high, reared upon the ancient Crypt of St. Stephen's, which has been restored for use as the Palace Chapel. (See CRYPTS, page 244.) In St. Stephen's Hall, upon pedestals, are marble statues of Clarendon, by Marshall, R.A.; Hampden, by Foley; Falkland, by Bell; and Mansfield, by Baily, R.A. Here are to be placed other worthies of the Lords and Commons; and the walls are to be decorated with frescoes. From the floor of St. Stephen's Hall there is no one step throughout the whole extent,—*all is of one level.* Next is

The Central Hall, an octagon 70 feet square, with the largest span of stone Gothic roof, of similar form, in Europe: the height from the floor to the key-stone is 75 feet, and the bosses measure 4 feet in diameter. The eight sides contain alternately great doorways and windows, the latter to be filled with stained glass; and the niches between the arches are to contain 60 portrait and costume statues of the English sovereigns and their queens, sculptured in Caen stone by John Thomas. Amongst the most striking are William I., Henry I., Richard I. and his queen, King John, Eleanor queen of Edward I., Edward III. and his queen Philippa, Henry V. and his queen Katherine, Richard III., Henry VII. and his queen Elizabeth. The encaustic-tile pavement is very fine. Thence a corridor leads north to the Commons' Lobby and House of Commons, and south to the Peers' Lobby and House of Peers. The archway west communicates with St. Stephen's Hall: and the east leads to the *Lower Waiting Hall;* the *Conference Hall*, in the river front; and the *Upper Waiting Hall*, to be embellished with frescoes, including the Patience of Griselda (from Chaucer), by Cope; Disinheritance of Cordelia by King Lear (from Shakspeare), by Herbert, R.A.; the Temptation of Adam and Eve (from Milton), by Horsley; and St. Cecilia (from Dryden), by Tenniel.

The Electric Telegraph Office (opened April 1, 1853) is in the Central Hall; whence wires are laid to the Company's Office in St.

James's-street, and the metropolitan stations. Here is also an instrument in direct communication with the Hague, for the transmission of messages to the Continent. During the sitting of Parliament, a half-hourly report of the proceedings is telegraphed to the St. James's-street office, where it is printed, and immediately dispatched to the principal Clubs; thus enabling Members to ascertain the probability of divisions. Here is likewise an instrument in connection with the Royal Italian Opera-house, Covent Garden, whither reports of the proceedings of Parliament are transmitted. The Telegraph is extensively used by Parliamentary agents, and persons interested in Bills before Committees.

THE ROYAL ENTRANCE is by the Victoria Tower, already described. At the summit of the Royal Staircase is the *Norman Porch*, named from its statues of kings of the Norman line, and frescoes of scenes from Anglo-Norman history; its beautifully groined roof and clustered columns, rich bosses and ribs, are of the same period. To the right is the *Queen's Robing-room*, painted by Dyce, R.A., with frescoes allegorical of chivalry fostering generous and religious feelings. Next is the *Victoria* or *Royal Gallery*, 110 feet in length by 45 feet in width, and 45 feet high; to be decorated with frescoes from English history, an armorial band beneath the stained-glass windows, and a panelled and superbly enriched ceiling. To this gallery the public are admitted, by tickets (to be obtained of the Lord Great Chamberlain), to view the procession of her Majesty to open and prorogue Parliament.

The Prince's Chamber, a kind of ante-room to the House of Lords, has the entrance-doorway richly decorated with the national arms, armorial roses and quatrefoils; and opposite, on the north side, is an arch for a statue of Queen Victoria, by Gibson, R.A. Upon the walls will be 12 bas-reliefs, carved in oak, of memorable events in Tudor history; and over these panels, 28 portraits of the same period, painted on a gold ground. The frieze is enriched with oak-leaves and acorns, and armorial shields and labels; the windows are painted with the rose, thistle, and shamrock, and regal crowns; and the armorial ceiling and Tudor fire-places are dight with colour, gilding, and sculpture.

THE HOUSE OF LORDS is extremely rich in gilding, polychromy, wrought metal, and carved work: its dimensions are, length in the clear, 91 feet, breadth 45 feet, and height 45 feet, so that it is a double cube. The walls are 3 feet 1 inch thick.

East and west are 12 lofty windows, six on either side, filled with painted-glass whole-length portraits of the Kings and Queens, consort and regnant, of the United Kingdom: six containing figures of the royal line of England before the union of the crowns; three, of the royal line of Scotland from Bruce to James VI.; and three, of the sovereigns of Great Britain from the reign of Charles I. The style of colouring in these windows is that of 1450-1500.

At each end of the House are three archways, within which are the following wall-frescoes:

Over the Throne: Edward III. conferring the Order of the Garter on the Black Prince; C. W. Cope, R.A. The Baptism of St. Ethelbert; W. Dyce, R.A. Prince Henry acknowledging the authority of Judge Gascoigne; C. W. Cope, R.A.
Over the 'Strangers' Gallery: The Spirit of Justice; D. Maclise, R.A. The Spirit of Religion; J. C. Horsley. The Spirit of Chivalry; D. Maclise, R.A.

Between the windows, archways, and in the corners, are canopied niches, with pedestals supported by angels bearing shields charged with the arms of the eighteen barons who obtained Magna Charta from King John, and whose bronze effigies occupy the niches. Above these niches are segments of arches, which, as trusses, support the main arches of the ceiling, and are elaborately pierced and carved.

The ceiling is flat, and divided into compartments containing lozenges charged with devices and symbols: the royal monogram, the monograms of the Prince of Wales and Prince Albert; the cognisances of the white hart of Richard II.; the sun of the House of York; the crown in a bush, Henry VII.; the falcon, dragon, and greyhound; the lion passant of England, the lion rampant of Scotland, and the harp of Ireland; sceptres, orbs, and crowns; the scales of Justice; mitres and crosiers, and swords of mercy; coronets, and the triple plume of the Prince of Wales. Among the devices are the rose of England and the pomegranate of Castile; the portcullis of Beaufort, the lily of France, and the lion of England; and the armorial shields of the Saxon Heptarchy. The massive beams appear like solid gold: they are inscribed on the sides with religious and loyal mottoes.

Beneath the windows, the walls are covered with oak paneling and carved busts of the sovereigns of England; and above is the inscription " God save the Queen," in Tudor characters. Thence springs a coving, in the southern division emblazoned with the arms of lord chancellors and their sovereigns, and northward with the bishops' arms. This coving supports a gallery with wrought-metal railing, richly-carved paneling, and pillars which support a brattishing.

The centre of the southern end of the House is occupied by the Throne, on either side of which is a doorway leading to the Prince's Chamber. At the northern end of the House, over the principal doorway, is the Strangers' Gallery, behind the Reporters' Gallery, upon the front of which are painted the badges of the sovereigns of England; and over the archways are painted on shields the coat-armour of the Saxon, Norman, Plantagenet, Tudor, Stuart, and Hanoverian Houses; the arms of the archiepiscopal sees, and some of the bishoprics; and in front of the gallery is a clock with an exquisitely carved case and dial enameled in colours. On the right of the Bar is the seat of the Usher of the Black Rod. The peers' seats (accommodating 235) are ranged longitudinally from north to south. At the south end is the clerks' table; and beyond it are the woolsacks, covered with crimson cloth. At the north end is *The Bar*, a dwarf screen, at which appear the Members of the House of Commons, and at which counsel plead. At the four angles of the area is a superb brass candelabrum, by Hardman, 17 feet high, and weighing 11½ cwt. The carpet is gold-colour Norman roses upon a deep-blue ground.

THE ROYAL THRONE, at the south end, is elevated on steps (the centre three, and the sides two), which are covered with a carpet of bright scarlet, powdered with white roses and lions, and fringed with gold-colour. The canopy to the throne is in three compartments: the central one, much loftier than the others, for her Majesty; that on the right hand for the Prince of Wales, and that on the left for Prince Albert. The back of the central compartment is paneled with lions passant, carved and gilded, on a red ground; and above are the royal arms of England, elaborately emblazoned, surmounted by the royal monogram and " Dieu et mon droit," in perforated letters; and a brattishing of Greek crosses and fleur-de-lis crests. Above are the crests of England, Scotland, Ireland, and Wales, richly carved; the ceiling bears the monogram V. R. within an exquisite border, and the flat surfaces painted with stars. The spandrels of the canopy, and the octagonal pillars with coronal capitals, are beautifully carved. In front of the canopy, above a brattishing of perforated Tudor flowers, are five traceried ogee arches: in the central one is the figure of St. George and the Dragon; and in the two sides are knights of the Garter and Bath, the Thistle and St. Patrick. The angle-buttresses of this canopy have coronal pendants; on the fronts and sides are animals, on the summits open-worked royal crowns. On the sides likewise are shields of the arms of England, Scotland, Ireland, and Wales, beautifully carved, painted, and gilded; and upon pedestals are sitting figures of winged angels holding shields enameled with the arms of England. The side compartments of the canopy have, the one the heraldic symbols of the Prince of Wales, and the other those of Prince Albert, blended with the architectural features: they have covings, gilded, and pedestals supporting a lion and unicorn holding shields of arms; the angle-buttresses have coronal pendants, and the shafts are surmounted by crowns. On either hand is a dwarf wing with pedestal, on which are seated the royal supporters, the lion and unicorn, holding standards enameled with the arms of England.

The Queen's Chair of State, or Throne, in general outline resembles "the coronation chair;" the legs rest upon four lions couchant; the base has quatrefoil panels, with crowns and V. R., and sprays of roses, shamrocks, and thistles, and a broad bar of roses and leaves: in the panels beneath the arms of the chair are lions passant and treillage; upon the back pinnacles are a lion and unicorn, seated, holding scrolls and flanking the gable, within which is a circle of exquisitely quatre-foiled ornament, inclosing the monogram V. R.; the exterior ridge is carved with roses, and the apex surmounted with a richly decorated crown. The back of the chair is bordered with large egg-shaped pieces of crystal, within which are the royal arms of England, embroidered on velvet. The *Footstool* has carved sides, and a crimson velvet top, gor-geously embroidered with roses in a border of fleurs-de-lis.

The State Chairs for the Prince of Wales and Prince Albert are curule-shaped, have circular-headed backs, embroidered on velvet with the ostrich triple-plume and the shield of arms. The throne and foot-stool, and the two princes' chairs, are gilded throughout.

The House of Peers was first occupied by their lordships April 15, 1847.

The Peers' Lobby is 38 feet square and 33 feet high, and has on either side a lofty arch, above which are painted, within arches, the arms of the Saxon, Norman, Plantagenet, Tudor, Stuart, and Hano-verian royal lines, each surmounted by a royal crown. The north door-way opens into the House of Commons corridor, the south doorway opens into the House of Lords: the arch is boldly sculptured with Tudor roses, royally crowned; the inner arch is enriched with gilded oak-leaves. The space over is filled with the royal arms, roses, thistles, and shamrocks, coloured and gilded. The gates are of massive brass, by Hardman, and of richly floriated design, the frames studded with Norman roses. These gates weigh 1½ tons, are 11 feet high, and 6 feet wide; and are of a material not used in England for such a pur-pose for nearly 400 years. The side-wall compartments of the Lobby are filled with ogee arches; and the upper stories are windows, painted by Hardman, and Ballantyne, and Allan, with the arms of the early families of the aristocracy of England. The roof is painted with roses, thistles, and shamrocks, in squares, on a blue ground, and relieved with gilding. The pavement is encaustic tiles, by Minton; alleys of black marble, including "Dieu et mon droit" in tiles, V. R., the lions of England, &c.; and in the centre is a Tudor rose of Derbyshire marbles, bordered with engraved brass. At each corner of the lobby is a magnificent gas-standard, about 12 feet high.

THE HOUSE OF COMMONS is 75 feet long, 45 feet wide, and 41 feet high; the size being as small as possible for speaking and hearing with-out effort during the average attendance of Members, about 300. The twelve side windows are painted with the arms of boroughs, by Hard-man; and at each end is a stone screen filled with brass tracery. The ceiling has the sides and ends inclined, and the centre flat: it is divided by massive ribs into compartments, which are filled with ground-glass tinted with the rose, portcullis, and floriated circles; behind are placed the gas-lights, with Faraday's patent ventilation, cutting off connection between the gas and the air of the apartment, the vitiated air being conveyed away by tubes into a chamber above the ceiling. The floor of the House is of perforated cast-iron, covered with matting, through which hot and cold air are admitted by machinery below. It is impossible to burn the House down: you might set fire to and destroy the furniture and fittings; but the flooring, walls, and roof would remain intact. The walls are paneled with oak two-thirds up, carved with the linen-pattern, armorial shields, pendants, foliated mouldings, and brattishings. Upon three sides are galleries for Members and Strangers; the *Reporters' Gallery* being at the north end, over the *Speaker's Chair*, a sort of canopied throne elaborately carved with the royal arms, &c. Behind the brass tracery above the Reporters' Gallery is a gallery for ladies. At the northern end of the House is *The Bar*, temporarily formed by sliding rods of brass; and here is the special seat of the Sergeant-at-arms. The Ministerial seats are on the front bench to the right of the Speaker, the leaders of the Opposition occupying the front bench opposite. Below the Speaker's Chair is the *Clerks' Table*, whereon, during the business of the House, is placed the *Speaker's Mace;* not, as generally supposed, "the fool's bauble" which Cromwell ordered to be taken away, but the mace made at the Restoration. Along both sides of the House are the Division Lobbies, "Ayes" west, and "Noes" east; these being oak-paneled corridors, with stained-glass windows: the chandeliers are of chased brass.

The Commons first assembled in their new House February 3, 1852; eight days after which (February 11), Mr. Barry received knighthood.

The Commons' Lobby is a rich apartment 45 feet square, and has on each side an archway; carved open screens inscribed "Domine salvam fac Reginam;" and windows painted with the arms of parliamentary boroughs: the brass gas-standards, by Hardman, are elaborately chased. The doorways lead to the Library, the Post-office, Vote-paper Office, Central Hall, &c.

The Libraries are fitted with dark oak; and in the Peers' Libraries, above the book-shelves, in panels, are emblazoned the arms of the Chief-justices of England.

The Refreshment Rooms for the Peers and Commons are similarly arranged, and respectively are divided by a carved oak screen.

In the whole building there are niches for receiving Statues as follows: in Westminster Hall, 12; Royal Gallery, 106; Queen's Porch, 4; House of Lords, 18; St. Stephen's Hall, 12; Central Hall, 68; making 220 niches, 7 feet high. The building and its quadrangles can accommodate 270 isolated monuments or statues, and 400 mural monuments or tablets; or, in the whole, 670 monuments of various kinds.

The public are admitted to view both Houses of Parliament, and all the public portion of the New Palace of Westminster, every Saturday between 10 and 4 o'clock, during the session, by tickets; which are obtainable on Saturdays, between 11 and 4 o'clock, at the Office of the Lord Great Chamberlain, near the Victoria Tower.

Admission to hear the Debates: *Lords*—A Peer's order; *Commons*—Any Member's, or the Speaker's, order. The House of Lords is open to the public, without ticket, during the hearing of Appeals.

PATERNOSTER-ROW,

Between the north side of St. Paul's Churchyard and the south of Newgate-street, is one of a knot of monastic localities; and is named from the turners of rosaries, or Pater Nosters (or tenth-beads), dwelling there, with stationers or text-writers, who wrote and sold A B C, with the Pater Noster, Ave, Creed, Graces, &c., in the reign of Henry IV. Hatton describes it "between Cheapside Conduit east, and Amen-corner west; and the name, as also those of Ave-Maria-lane (at its west end), Creed-lane (in Ludgate-street, opposite), and Amen-corner, given by reason of the religious houses formerly of Black and Gray Fryars, between which these streets are situated." Paternoster-row was next "taken up" by mercers, silkmen, and lacemen: we read of Pepys, in 1660, buying here "moyre for a morning waistcoat;" and the street was ofttimes blocked up with the coaches of the nobility and gentry. After the Great Fire, the mercers mostly migrated westward, as to Holywell-street and Covent Garden; but in a periodical of 1707 we read of "the sempstresses of Paternoster-row;" and Strype, in 1720, enumerates among its inhabitants tire-women, mercers, and silkmen. Here lived Alderman Thomas, the mercer, whose shop bore the motto of Sir William Turner, "Keep your shop, and your shop will keep you." (Spectator, No. 509.) Strype also mentions, "at the upper end, some stationers and large warehouses for booksellers;" but we find, as early as 1564, that Henry Denham, bookseller, lived at the Star, in Paternoster-row, with the motto, Os homini sublime dedit. In the reign of Queen Anne the booksellers removed here from Little Britain; and, from about 1774, the trade became changed to publishing books in "Paternoster-row numbers." Among their publishers were Harrison, Cooke, and the Hoggs; to the latter succeeded their shopman, Thomas Kelly, Alderman of Farringdon Within, and Lord Mayor, 1836-7.

Here was the printing-office of Henry Sampson Woodfall, the printer of the Public Advertiser, wherein appeared Junius's Letters. Here, in 1823, was established "the Paternoster-row Press," by T. C. Hansard, author of the elaborate Typographia, 1824.

At "the Bible and Crown" (the sign carved in wood, coloured and gilt), lived the Rivingtons, the High-Church publishers, from 1710 to 1853: here they continued the Annual Register, originally Dodsley's, with Edmund Burke as a contributor; and here, in 1791, the Rivingtons commenced the British Critic: but "the old shop," where Horsley and Tomline, Warburton and Hurd, used to meet, was, in 1854, altered to a "shawl emporium."

At No. 47 lived Robert Baldwin, publisher of the London Magazine, commenced 1732. In Paternoster-row the Robinsons established themselves about 1763; the head of the firm was "King of the Booksellers:" here they published the Annual Register, with a sale of 7000 copies each volume; and the unsatisfactory Biographical Dictionary, by Alexander Chalmers. At No. 39 have lived more than a century and a quarter the Longmans: the imprint of Thomas Longman, with Thomas and John Osborne, at the sign of "the Ship and Black Swan," is dated 1726. Here was commenced the original Cyclopædia, by Ephraim Chambers, upon which was based the New Cyclopædia of Dr. Rees: for several years the firm gave here dinners and soirées to authors and artists; and they have acquired world-wide repute as the publishers of the works of Scott, Mackintosh, Southey, Sydney Smith, Moore, and Macaulay. Messrs. Longman's own sale of books has amounted to five millions of volumes in the year.

No. 56 is the Depôt of the Religious Tract Society, erected in 1844, at a cost of 12,000l.: the handsome stone frontage, of 120 feet, is in the Italian style. The Society commenced operations, in 1799, with a small handbill: its annual distribution of books and tracts in 1853 was nearly 26 millions, and its gross income 9,497l.

No. 50, the Chapter Coffee-house, noticed at page 201, was closed in December 1853; having been for a century and more the resort of authors, actors, and booksellers and politicians: the house is often referred to in the correspondence of Chatterton.

"A contemporary anecdote exhibits Goldsmith paymaster, at the Chapter Coffee-house, for Churchill's friend, Charles Lloyd, who, in his careless way, without a shilling to pay for the entertainment, had invited him to sup with some friends of Grub-street."—Forster's *Life of Goldsmith*, p. 232.

Between Paternoster-row and Newgate-street is Newgate Market here, in 1709 (*Tatler*, No. 44), was exhibited the Groaning Board:

"At the sign of the Woolsack, in Newgate Market, is to be seen a strange and wonderful elm-board; which being touched with a hot iron, doth express itself as if it were a man dying with groans, &c. It hath been presented to the king and his nobles, and hath given great satisfaction."—*Advertisement*.

Panier-alley, named from its having been the standing of bakers boys with their paniers, when bread was only sold in markets, and not in shops or houses, is described at pp. 457 and 552.

At "the sign of the Castle," in Paternoster-row, Tarlton, Queen Elizabeth's favourite stage-clown, kept an ordinary, stated to have been on the site of Dolly's chop-house. "The Castle," of which a token exists, was destroyed in the Great Fire, but was rebuilt; and here "the Castle Society of Music" gave their performances. The premises were subsequently the Oxford Bible Warehouse, destroyed by fire in 1822, and rebuilt.

There is likewise a *Paternoster-row* and *Little Paternoster-row* in Spitalfields, where was formerly the Priory of St. Mary Spittle.

PAVEMENT.

Archæologists have, by their excavations upon the site of the walled London of the Romans, succeeded in reaching the very streets on which they walked, and the floors of the houses in which they lived. The general level of Roman London ranges from above fifteen to seventeen feet under the present surface; thus showing an accumulation of about a foot in a century, gradually arising out of the mere occupancy and traffic of a crowded population. But there is no direct evidence of the state of our metropolitan streets until the 11th century. We have a kind of negative proof that in 1090 Cheapside had a soft earthen roadway; for the chroniclers relate that when St. Mary-le-bow was unroofed by a violent storm of wind, four beams, each 26 feet in length, sank so deeply into the ground, that scarcely 4 feet appeared above the surface.

The first toll for mending the highways is recorded to have been imposed in the reign of Edward III., for repairing the road between St. Giles's and Temple Bar; and in 1315 writs were issued for the repair of the *pavement* between Temple Bar and the Palace at Westminster. In 1353 John de Bedeford was appointed commissioner for the paving of this road; and it was ordained that the foot-pavement *pavagium*, adjoining to the dwellings on the line, should be newly laid at the expense of the owners of the nearest houses.

The lower part of Holborn was paved in 1417, at the expense of Henry V.; but Stow records this street as ill-paved a century later; and High Oldburn, leading from the bars towards St. Giles's and Shoe lane, Fetter-lane, and New-street or Chancery-lane, as also the way from Aldgate to Whitechapel Church, were paved by the grant of St. John Baptist, 1542, as had been paved "the cawsey or highway leading from Strand Bridge to Charing Cross." (*Stow*.) Other parts were first paved in 1571 and 1605; and the great cattle-market of Smithfield was first paved in 1614.

Gay, in his *Trivia,* thus describes the paving a century later:

" To pave thy realm, and smooth the broken ways,
Earth from her womb a flinty tribute pays;
For thee the sturdy pavior thumps the ground,
Whilst every stroke his labouring lungs resound.
*　　　　*　　　　*　　　　*
Does not each walker know the warning sign,
When wisps of straw depend upon the twine
'Cross the close street; that then the paver's art
Reviews the ways, denied to coach and cart ?"

In 1762 was passed the Westminster Paving Act, when the footpaths were widened and paved with broad flat stones; but about this time Goldsmith wrote, " in the midst of the pavements a great lazy puddle moves muddily along."

Stone tramways for the wheels of heavy carriages to work on are laid in the Commercial, East-India Dock, and Whitechapel roads. Little change has been made in the foot-pavements, broad flags being still generally used; but the questionable relative merits of dressed granite, macadamisation, bitumen, and wood, have led to a most heterogeneous assemblage of road-pavements. Wood pavement was first experimentally laid down by Finlayson, at Ayr, in 1800 ; and in 1835, Bradwell, the machinist of Covent Garden Theatre, submitted to the City Paving Commissioners a system of wood pavement, which was rejected. In 1839 the hexagonal blocks were first laid in London, by Stead, upon the St. Petersburg plan ; since which the varieties of pavement baffle enumeration : their slipperiness in wet weather appears insuperable.

Macadamised road (layers of small stones, so angular as to lock together in a dry, hard, and compact mass,) has been much used, but is costly. In 1827, macadamising the roadways of Regent-street, Whitehall, and Palace-yard cost 6000*l.*, besides the value of the old pavement taken up broken for that purpose, nearly 7000*l.*; the repairing, scraping, and watering in one year cost 4632*l.* In Marylebone the cost of macadamised road has been 2*s.* 4*d.* per square yard per annum; yearly rental of wood, 2*s.* 3*d.* per yard ; and 60 miles of pavement have cost the parish 15,000*l.* per mile. In the evidence before the House of Lords on the Westminster Improvement Bill, a paved road is stated to have cost 10*s.* 10*d.* per yard in ten years, and a broken stone road 2*l.* 10*s.* per yard in the same time.

Bitumen, or asphaltum, was first introduced for roads in 1837 ; and in 1838 the east end of Oxford-street was laid with experimental pavement of wood, in comparison with stone and bitumen, which led to the adoption of wood, often tested by the traffic of 7000 vehicles in 18 hours.

In certain streets we have adopted the Roman road as found at Pompeii, of three distinct layers: lowest, stones mixed with cement ; middle, gravel or small stones; to prepare an unyielding surface for the upper large masses accurately fitted together. But we have improved upon the Roman system by dressing each stone, like the voussoir of an arch, so that the tier of stones spans the street like a bridge.

Foreign materials are sometimes used. Thus, the first mile of road from Shoreditch towards Newington has been kept in substantial repair by a supply of that " best of all road materials," the black porphyry-stone, brought from China as ballast in the tea-ships; and the next half-mile has been repaired with granite from Bombay.

PENTONVILLE,

A district of St. James's parish, Clerkenwell, west of Islington, and originally a field of the Clerkenwell Nunnery. It was in part the estate of Henry Penton, Esq.; and when the New-road was formed through it, White Conduit House, and the house attached to Dobney's Bowling-green, were almost the only buildings here. One of the earliest was Hermes houses (in Hermes-street), built by Dr. de Valangin (a pupil of Boerhaave), who lived to see Penton's *ville* or town rising around him. Here lived William Huntington, S.S., when he married the widow of Sir James Sanderson, Bart. (Lady Huntingdon). Upon the north side of the New-road (Pentonville-hill) is St. James's Chapel, built 1788: it has a clever altar-picture of Christ raising the damsel Tabitha. Below the chapel is the London Female Penitentiary, established 1807. In Regent-terrace died the popular sporting writer, Pierce Egan, in 1849, at the full age of 77: and in Penton-place lived Grimaldi, " Old Joe," born in Stanhope-street, Clare Market, in 1778, the year preceding that in which Garrick died.

PICCADILLY,

A leading street, 110 yards less than a mile in length, extends, in a line with Coventry-street, from the north end of the Haymarket westward to Hyde Park Corner. The name is derived from the ruffs, called "pickadils" or " peccadilloes," worn by the gallants of James I. and Charles I.; and the stiffened points of which resembled spear-heads, or picardills, a diminutive of *pica*, Spanish and Italian. Blount, in his *Glossographia* (1656), interprets it as the round hem about the edge or skirt of a garment, and a stiff collar or band for the neck and shoulders; whence the wooden peccadilloes (the pillory) in Hudibras. Hence the first house built in the road may have been named " from its being the utmost or skirt house of the suburbs that way." Others say it took name from this: "that one Higgins, a tailor, who built it, got most of his estate by piccadillas." But the name occurs many years earlier than the mention of the first house, or Piccadilly House: thus Gerard, in his *Herbal* (1596), states that " the small wild bu-glosse growes upon the drie ditch-bankes about Pickadilla." The road is referred to, in Stow's narrative of Sir Thomas Wyatt's rebellion in 1554, as " the highway on the hill over against St. James's;" and in Aggas's Map (1560) it is lettered, " The Waye to Redinge." The upper part of the Haymarket, and the fields adjoining north and west, were the Pickadilly of the Restoration. Evelyn quotes the Commissioners' orders, July 13, 1662, to pave " the Haymarket about Pigudello ;" and tradesmen's tokens of this date bear " Pickadilla" and " Pickadilly."

Piccadilly Hall appears to have been built by one Robert Baker, in " the fields behind the Mews," leased to him by St. Martin's parish, and sold by his widow to Colonel Panton, who built Panton-square and Panton-street. Lord Clarendon, in his *History of the Rebellion*, speaks of " Mr. Hyde going to a house called Piccadilly for entertainment and gaming:" this house, with its gravel-walks and bowling-greens, extended from the corner of Windmill-street and the site of Panton-square, as shown in Porter and Faithorne's Map, 1658. Mr. Cunning-ham found (see *Handbook*, 2d edit. p. 396), in the parish accounts of St. Martin's, " Robte Backer, of Pickadilley Halle ;" and the receipts for Lammas money paid for the premises as late as 1670. Sir John Suckling, the poet, was one of the frequenters; and Aubrey remembered Suckling's " sisters coming to the Peccadillo bowling-green, crying, for the feare he should lose all their portions." The house was taken down about 1685: a tennis-court in the rear remained to our time, upon the site of the Argyll Rooms, Great Windmill-street. The Society of Antiquaries possess a printed proclamation (*temp.* Charles II. 1671) against the increase of buildings in Windmill-fields and the fields adjoining Soho; and in the Plan of 1658, Great Windmill-street consists of strag-

gling houses, and a windmill in a field on the west side. The spacious
house upon the east side was built for Dr. William Hunter in 1770: it
had an amphitheatre and a magnificent museum (see page 539). He
died here March 30, 1783. At the north-east end of the Haymarket
stood the gaming-house built by the barber of the Earl of Pembroke,
and hence called *Shaver's Hall:* it is described by Garrard, in a letter
to Lord Strafford in 1635, as "a new Spring Gardens, erected in the
fields beyond the Mews:" its tennis-court remains in James-street.

From Piccadilly being applied to the Hall and the buildings in the
fields north and west of the Haymarket (in "Dogs-fields, Windmill-
fields, and the fields adjoining Soho,") early maps show it to have been
extended to the line of street to Swallow-street, where begins Portugal-
street, named after Catherine of Braganza, queen of Charles II.: in
an Act 3 James II. is named "the mansion-house of the Earl of Burlington, fronting Portugal-street;" but that it was considered a subordinate street, is shown by Wren having made the principal front of St.
James's Church face Jermyn-street, with its handsome Ionic door. The
name of Piccadilly, however, became gradually extended to the whole
line. Hatton, 1708, describes Piccadilly as between Coventry-street and
the end of the Haymarket, and Portugal-street. Until 1721 the road
was mostly unpaved, and coaches were often overturned in the hollow.
The line from Devonshire House westward was, until the year 1740,
chiefly occupied by the figure-yards of statuaries, where also "numberless wretched figures were manufactured in lead for gardens."* About
this time an adjoining field was bought by a brewer for his empty butts
at 30*l.*, and sold in 1764 for 2500*l.* (*Malcolm.*) In 1757 a tract of ground
was leased to James Hamilton, Esq., who built thereon *Hamilton-
place.* Westward was "the Hercules Pillars," which, with other Piccadilly inns, is described at p. 400. In one of these petty taverns, at Hyde
Park Corner, Sir Richard Steele and the poet Savage dined together, after
having written a pamphlet, which Savage sold for two guineas, to enable
them to pay the reckoning. Among the straggling houses here was the
school kept by a Roman-Catholic convert named Deane, where Pope
spent nearly two years of his boyhood; and got up a play out of Homer,
the part of Ajax being performed by the gardener.

"Towards Hide Park" was Winstanley's mathematical water-theatre,
mentioned in the *Tatler*, No. 74 (Sept. 29, 1709): it had a windmill at
the top; and the quantity of water used in the exhibition was from
200 to 300 tuns, "with which curious effects produced by hydraulic
pressure were exhibited in the evening." Evelyn speaks of Winstanley, who built the first Eddystone Lighthouse; and of another mechanical genius, Sir Samuel Moreland, who writes from his "hut near Hyde
Park Gate."

NORTH SIDE.—APSLEY HOUSE, east of Hyde Park Gate, is described
at pp. 479-481. At No. 148, the Baron Lionel de Rothschild's, is a
valuable collection of Mediæval Art and antique Pottery (see p. 548).
Next door lived William Beckford, the author of *Vathek:* No. 1 Hamilton-place was built by Lord Chancellor Eldon; and at No. 4 was collected the Grenville Library, now in the British Museum. No. 140
Piccadilly was the last house which Lord Byron tenanted in England.

"Nobody needs to be told what a great wit and fine poet he (Lord Byron) was;
but every body does not know that he was by nature a genial and generous man,
spoiled by the most untoward circumstances in early life."—*Leigh Hunt.*

* East of Hertford House, "near the Queen's Mead House, in Hyde-Park-
road," was the leaden figure-yard established by John Van Nost, who came to
England with King William III. A favourite garden-figure was an African kneeling with a sun-dial on his head, such as we see to this day in the garden of
Clement's Inn, but commonly said to have been brought from Italy by Lord Clare.

At No. 138 lived the Duke of Queensbury, "Old Q," the voluptuary and millionaire, who died at the age of 86: by aid of the hackney-coach stand opposite the mansion, prurient idlers used to witness the nude orgies in the duke's saloons. No. 137, GLOUCESTER HOUSE, is described at page 487. Next is *Park-lane*, formerly Tyburn-lane.

Opposite, in the Green Park, was the Deputy-Ranger's Lodge, built by Robert Adam, 1768, taken down 1841: the pair of graceful stags upon the gate-piers, placed there by Lord William Gordon when deputy-ranger, were removed to the piers of Albert Gate, Hyde Park. Opposite, at the corner of Down-street (leading to MAY FAIR, see page 504), is the mansion of Mr. H. T. Hope, described at page 488; and further east, No. 106, COVENTRY HOUSE (see p. 193), closed as a club March 1854; No. 105, HERTFORD HOUSE, page 488; No. 94, CAMBRIDGE HOUSE, page 484; No. 82, BATH HOUSE, page 482; DEVONSHIRE HOUSE, page 485.*

Half-moon-street was built in 1730, and was named from the Half-moon ale-house at the corner.

Clarges-street was built 1717-8, and named from Sir Walter Clarges. At the south-west corner is the mansion of the Duke of Grafton, designed by Sir Robert Taylor: here is the magnificent Louvre portrait of Charles I. on his horse, by Vandyke. At No. 12 Clarges-street lived for eight years Edmund Kean, the tragedian, who kept in the house a tame puma. Next door, at No. 11, lived Lady Hamilton at the time of Lord Nelson's death.†

Bolton-street was in 1708 "the most westerly street in London, between the road to Knightsbridge south, and the fields north" (*Hatton*). Here lived the Earl of Peterborough, who, in his autobiography (fortunately never printed), confesses having committed three capital crimes before he was 20 years of age.

No. 80 Piccadilly was the house from which Sir Francis Burdett was taken into custody, April 6, 1810, by the Sergeant-at-Arms, after a resistance of four days:

"The lady she sate and she played on her lute,
  And she sung, 'Will you come to the bower?'
The serjeant-at-arms had stood hitherto mute,
And now he advanced, like an impudent brute,
  And said, 'Will you come to the Tower?'"

In the riot which ensued, the Life Guards charged the mob, whence they were nicknamed "Piccadilly Butchers."

Stratton-street was named from the Stratton line of the Berkeleys; on whose estate it was built. No. 1 was the mansion of Mrs. Coutts, the widow of the rich banker, and afterwards Duchess of St. Albans, "who brought back the dukedom to the point from which it set out—the stage" (*Leigh Hunt*). By her the mansion was bequeathed, with her immense wealth, to Miss Angela Burdett Coutts, youngest daughter of Sir Francis Burdett, Bart.

---

* The ticket of admission to the performances of the *Guild of Literature and Art* (first given at Devonshire House 1851), was designed by E. M. Ward, A.R.A. On the left is Richard Wilson, the painter, with a picture under his arm, entering a pawnbroker's shop. On the right is Daniel Defoe coming out of Edmund Curll's shop, with the manuscript of *Robinson Crusoe* in his hand: his wife is inquiring as to his success in selling the manuscript, and her little girl is standing in front. In the centre foreground are grouped a palette, brushes, and books; and at the top is a kneeling child smelling a rose, and another pouring water into a rose-bud.

† In 1855 were added to the Mss. in the British Museum 63 autograph letters of Lord Nelson, addressed to Lady Hamilton, from 1798 to 1805; including the last letter Nelson ever wrote, found in his cabin, after the battle of Trafalgar, 21st October, 1805.

Berkeley-street, built in 1642, and then the extremity of Piccadilly, was named from Berkeley House, on the site of Devonshire House.

Dover-street was built about 1688, upon the estate of Henry Jermyn, Lord Dover, who resided on the east side; as did John Evelyn, who had been "oftentimes so cheerful, and sometimes so sad, with Chancellor Hyde" on that very ground. On the west side lived Dr. John Arbuthnot, physician to Queen Anne, "Martinus Scriblerus," and the friend of Pope, Swift, Gay, and Prior. No. 37, sculptured with a mitre, is the town-house of the Bishop of Ely. At No. 38 lived Lord King, who wrote a life of his profound kinsman, John Locke; published 1829.

Albemarle-street was built by Sir Thomas Bond on part of the site of Clarendon House. In 1708 it was "a street of excellent new buildings, inhabited by persons of quality, between the fields and Portugal-street."

"The earliest date now to be found upon the site of Clarendon House is cut in stone, and let into the south wall of a public-house, the sign of 'The Duke of Albemarle,' in Dover-street, thus: 'This is Stafford-street, 1686.' In a plan of London etched by Hollar, in 1686, it is evident that the centre of Clarendon House must have occupied the whole of the site of Stafford-street."—*Smith's Streets.*

Clarendon House was commenced by Lord Chancellor Clarendon in 1664, "encouraged thereto by the royal grant of land, by the opportunity of purchasing the stones which had been designed for the repairs of St. Paul's, and by that passion for building to which he was naturally too much inclined." (*Evelyn.*) About the same time, Lord Berkeley began to build Berkeley House on the west; and Sir John Denham, Burlington House on the east. During the war and the plague year, Clarendon employed about 300 workmen, which raised a great outcry against him: "some called it 'Dunkirk House,' intimating that it was built by his share of the price of Dunkirk: others called it 'Holland House,' because he was believed to be no friend to the war; so it was given out that he had the money from the Dutch. It was visible that in a time of public calamity he was building a very noble palace." (*Burnet.*) Pepys records that some rude people, in 1667, "had been at my Lord Chancellor's, where they cut down the trees before his house and broke his windows; and a gibbet either set up before or painted upon his gate, and these words writ: 'Three sights to be seen—Dunkirk, Tangier, and a barren queen.'" He was lampooned also in one of the "State Poems," entitled "Clarendon's House-warming." The day before his lordship's flight, Evelyn "found him in his garden at his new-built palace, sitting in his gowt wheele-chayre, and seeing the gates setting up towards the north and the fields. He looked and spake very disconsolately. Next morning I heard he was gone." Evelyn, dining at Clarendon House with the Lord Chancellor's eldest son, Lord Cornbury, after his father's flight, describes the mansion as "now bravely furnished, especially with the pictures of most of our English and modern wits, poets, philosophers, famous and learned Englishmen;" most of these pictures have been brought from Cornbury, a seat of the Earls of Clarendon, Oxon, to the Grove, Watford, Herts.

Clarendon House was subsequently let to the great Duke of Ormond. After Lord Clarendon's death in exile, it was sold, in 1675, for 26,000*l.* to the young Duke of Albemarle, who soon parted with it to Sir Thomas Bond, by whom the mansion was taken down, and *Bond-street* and *Albemarle-buildings* (now *street*) and *Stafford-street* were built upon the site. A map in the Crowle Pennant shows the entrance-gate to the courtyard to have been in Piccadilly, directly opposite St. James's-street; and the grounds to have extended to the site of Bruton-street. Two Corinthian pilasters at the Three Kings inn gateway, No. 75, in Piccadilly, are believed to have belonged to Clarendon House;

and the name is preserved in the *Clarendon Hotel*, built upon a portion of the gardens between Albemarle and Bond streets.

"All the waste ground at the upper end of Albemarle and Dover streets is purchased by the Duke of Grafton and the Earl of Grantham, for gardening; and the road there leading to May Fair is ordered to be turned."—The *British Journal*, March 30, 1723. (This purchase is commemorated in *Grafton*-street.)

In Albemarle-street, at an apothecary's, lodged Dr. Berkeley when he was made Dean of Derry. Richard Glover, the merchant-poet, who wrote "Leonidas" and "Admiral Hosier's Ghost," died here in 1785. On the east side is the *Royal Institution*; the columnar façade by L. Vulliamy, 1838, adapted from the remains of Mars Ultor and Jupiter Stator, and the Pantheon at Rome. No. 23 is the ALFRED CLUB-HOUSE (see p. 189). At No. 50, since 1812, have lived John Murray, father and son, publishers; the former, "the friend and publisher of Lord Byron," died 1843. Opposite is Grillion's Hotel, where Louis XVIII. sojourned in 1814: here and at the Clarendon were held the Roxburghe Club Dinners.

Bond-street was commenced in 1686 by Sir Thomas Bond, Bart. Comptroller of the Household to Queen Henrietta-Maria. "Bond-street loungers, who pass from 2 till 5 o'clock," are mentioned in the *Weekly Journal*, June 1, 1717. At No. 41, "at the Silk-Bag Shop," died, March 18, 1786, Laurence Sterne, broken-hearted, neglected, and in debt. Some of the most touching scenes in *Tom Jones* are laid at Mr. Allworthy's lodgings in Bond-street. Here lodged James Boswell when he gave a dinner to Johnson, Goldsmith, Reynolds, and Garrick. No. 27, Ebers, the librarian, who in seven years lost 44,080*l.* by the Italian Opera-house, Haymarket. No. 10 has a large billiard-room, painted 1850 in encaustic by E. F. Lambert, with panels bordered with arabesques; the principal subjects being Bacchus and Ariadne, Hebe, "Willie brew'd a peck o' maut," "Let me the cannikin clink," and the "Wassail bowl." The tasteful house-front, No. 21, was designed by the Inwoods, architects of St. Pancras' Church, New-road.

Burlington Gardens, originally "Ten-Acres Fields," extend from Bond-street to Swallow-street: here is UXBRIDGE HOUSE, noticed at page 495: here died, April 29, 1854, Field-Marshal the Marquis of Anglesey, K. G., aged 86. In *Cork-street* the Earl of Burlington built for Field-Marshal Wade a house with a beautiful front, ill-contrived inside to suit a large cartoon by Rubens, but in vain: "Lord Chesterfield said that to be sure he (the marshal) could not live in it, but intended to take the house over against it, to look at it" (*Walpole*).

At the south-east corner of *Grafton-street* was the book-shop of Benjamin Tabart, who published so many pretty picture-books for children. At the corner of *Clifford-street* was the Clifford-street Club (see page 201).

New Bond-street site was in 1700 an open field called Conduit-mead, from the Conduit there: hence Conduit-street. In New Bond-street, at No. 141, Lord Nelson lodged in 1797. At No. 21 was exhibited, in 1831, "Napoleon at St. Helena," painted by Haydon for Sir Robert Peel, and upon which Wordsworth wrote his memorable sonnet.

In Piccadilly, east of Old Bond-street, is the BURLINGTON ARCADE (see p. 17), and BURLINGTON HOUSE* (see p. 483). No. 52, adjoining, is the *Albany Chambers*, let in suites to single gentlemen. The centre, designed by Sir William Chambers, was sold in 1770, by Lord Holland, to the first Viscount Melbourne, who exchanged it with the Duke of York for Melbourne now Dover House, Whitehall. In 1804 the mansion in Piccadilly was altered and enlarged, and first let in chambers, named *Albany* from the second title of the Duke of York.

* Purchased by Government, in 1854, for 140,000*l.*

The ceilings of the mansion were painted for Lord Melbourne by Cipriani, Wheatley, and Rebecca. In chambers here have lived George Canning, M. G. (Monk) Lewis, Lord Byron, Sir E. L. Bulwer, Mr. Macaulay, and Lord John Manners. Upon the site were originally the houses of the Earl of Sunderland, Sir John Clarges, and Lady Stanhope, with gardens reaching to Vigo-lane.

Sackville-street is the longest street in London without a turning: at the corner house, east, opposite St. James's Church, died Sir William Petty, the earliest writer on the science of political economy in England, and ancestor of the Lansdowne family: a letter from Sir William Petty to Pepys is dated Piccadilly, September 1687. The Dilettanti Club met at "The Prince," in this street, in 1783.

Swallow-street is named from "Swallow Close," part of the crown lands granted to Lord Chancellor Clarendon: here is the oldest Scottish Episcopal church in the metropolis. Swallow-street originally extended northward to Tyburn-road, from the centre of the present line of Regent-street.

Ayr or *Air street* was in 1659 the most westerly street.

SOUTH SIDE.—Hyde Park Corner turnpike-gate was removed in 1825. The long dead wall of the Park (now open railing) was hung with ballads; here robberies after dark were frequent.

Arlington-street, "a very graceful and pleasant street" (*Hatton*, 1708), was built upon the property of Henry Bennet, Earl of Arlington, about 1689: hence, also, *Bennet-street*. In Arlington-street lived the Duchess of Cleveland, after the death of Charles II.; Lady Mary Wortley Montague, before her marriage; William Pulteney, Earl of Bath, on the west side, next door to Sir Robert Walpole, where was born Horace Walpole, who wrote in 1768, "From my earliest memory, Arlington-street has been the ministerial street;" in 1750 he records a highwayman attacking a postchaise in Piccadilly, at 11 o'clock on a Sunday night, and escaping. Upon the site of Walpole's house Kent built No. 17, for Pelham the minister, the house now the Earl of Yarborough's. Lord Nelson lodged in this street in 1800-1, when Lady Nelson separated from him. At No. 16 (the Duke of Rutland's) the Duke of York, second son of George III., lay sick, from August 26, 1826, to his death, Jan. 5, 1827, as touchingly narrated by Sir Herbert Taylor. No. 26, BEAUFORT HOUSE, is described at page 482; in 1854 the mansion was sold to the Duke of Hamilton. The houses on the west side of the street command a charming view of the Green Park.

ST. JAMES'S-STREET is described at page 423.

No. 160 Piccadilly is the entrance to the Wellington Dining House (late Crockford's Club). The EGYPTIAN HALL is described at pp. 266-8.

At No. 169, Wright, the publisher of the *Anti-Jacobin*, kept shop, which was the resort of the friends of the Ministry, as Debrett's was of the Opposition. In a first-floor met the editors of the *Anti-Jacobin*, including Canning, Frere, and Pitt; with Gifford as working editor, and Upcott (Wright's assistant) as amanuensis. (See *Notes and Queries;* and *Poetry of the Anti-Jacobin*, new edition, 1854.) In Wright's shop, Peter Pindar (Wolcot) was castigated by Gifford. No. 177 was the shop of William Pickering, the eminent publisher, whose title-pages bear the Aldine anchor: his valuable stock of old books, rare works on angling, modern copyrights and reprints, was dispersed in 1854. No. 182 (Fortnum and Mason's) is designed from a mansion at Padua. ST. JAMES'S CHURCH is described at page 131; the MUSEUM OF PRACTICAL GEOLOGY at page 537. In the Inventory of Rich's Theatrical Properties (*Tatler*, July 16, 1709) is "Aurungzebe's scymitar, made by Will. Brown in Piccadilly." *Regent Circus* (see REGENT-STREET).

PIMLICO,

A name of gardens of public entertainment, often mentioned by our early dramatists, and in this respect resembling "Spring Garden." In a rare tract, *Newes from Hogsdon*, 1598: " Have at thee, then, my merrie boys, and hey for old Ben Pimlico's nut-browne!" and the place, in or near Hoxton, was afterwards named from him. Ben Jonson has,

> " A second Hogsden,
> In days of Pimlico and eye-bright."—*The Alchemist.*

" Pimlico-path" is a gay resort of his *Bartholomew Fair;* and Meer-craft, in *The Devil is an Ass,* says:

> " I'll have thee, Captain Gilthead, and march up
> And take in Pimlico, and kill the bush
> At every tavern."

In 1609 was printed a tract entitled *Pimlyco,* or *Prince Red Cap, 'tis a Mad World at Hogsden.* Sir Lionel Rash, in Greene's *Tu Quoque,* sends his daughter " as far as Pimlico for a draught of Derby ale, that it may bring colour into her cheeks." Massinger mentions,

> " Eating pudding-pies on a Sunday,
> At Pimlico or Islington."—*City Madam.*

Aubrey, in his *Surrey,* speaks of " a Pimlico Garden on Bankside."

PIMLICO, the district between Knightsbridge and the Thames, and St. James's Park and Chelsea, was noted for its public gardens: as the Mulberry Garden, now part of the site of Buckingham Palace; the Dwarf Tavern and Gardens, afterwards Spring Gardens, between Ebury-street and Belgrave-terrace; the Star and Garter, at the end of Five-Fields-row, famous for its equestrianism, fireworks, and dancing; and the Orange, upon the site of St. Barnabas' church. Here, too, were Ranelagh and New Ranelagh. But the largest garden in Pimlico was Jenny's Whim, to the left of the road over Ebury (late the Wooden) Bridge, formerly Jenny's Whim Bridge. The site is now covered by St. George's-row, but a portion of the tavern remains; it was opened *temp.* George 1. for fireworks, and in its grounds were a pond for duck-hunting, garden-plots, alcoves, and grotesque figures: it was a summer resort of the upper classes; and a tract of 1755 is entitled " Jenny's Whim, or a sure Guide to the Nobility, Gentry," &c. In later years it was frequented by crowds from bull-baiting in the adjoining fields. Among the existing old signs are, the Bag o' Nails, Arabella-row, from Ben Jonson's " Bacchanals;" the Compasses, of Cromwell's time (near Grosvenor-row); and the Gun Tavern and Tea-gardens, Queen's-row, with its arbours and costume figures. Pimlico is still noted for its ale-breweries.

Upon the verge of St. James's Park were Tart Hall (see page 421), and Arlington and Buckingham House (see page 566).

So late as 1763, Buckingham House enjoyed an uninterrupted prospect south and west to the river, there being only a few scattered cottages, and the Stag Brewery, between it and the Thames.—*W. Bardwell.*

Pimlico contains the *Belgrave* district, including Belgrave, Eaton, and Chester Squares (see page 37), and the *Grosvenor-road;* beyond which the *Eccleston* sub-district of new squares, terraces, and streets, extends to the Thames. Here are two churches in the Early Decorated style: Holy Trinity, close to Vauxhall Bridge (see p. 130); and St. Gabriel's, Warwick-square, with a spire 160 feet high; consecrated 1853.

Ebury Street and Square are named from Ebury Farm, 430 acres (lammas land), leased by Queen Elizabeth at 21*l.* per annum. The

Chelsea Water-works were first constructed in 1724, at Pimlico, by a canal being dug from the Thames near Ranelagh.

In Lower Belgrave-place, corner of Eccleston-street, Sir Francis Chantrey, R.A., lived 27 years, and executed his finest busts, statues, and monuments: he died here Nov. 25, 1841. Next door but one, at No 27, lived Allan Cunningham, the poet, and foreman to Chantrey.

In Stafford-row died, in 1796, Richard Yates, the celebrated comedian, and teacher of acting, aged 89. He was found dead through disappointment of a dinner of hash, which he ordered of his housekeeper, but which she failed to provide.

Pimlico is also the name of a place near Clitheroe, in Lancashire; Lord Orrery (in his *Letters*) mentions " Pemlicoe, Dublin ;" and " Pemlico" is the name of a bird of Barbadoes, " which presageth storms."—*Notes and Queries*, Nos. 29, 31, and 125.

PLAGUE (THE GREAT).

London has frequently suffered from the ravages of pestilence; and thousands and tens of thousands of the inhabitants have been swept by its virulence into one common grave. But at no period of its history was the mortality so devastating as in the year 1665, the "last great visitation," as it is emphatically entitled by De Foe in his *Journal of the Plague Year.* This work was originally published in 1722: now as De Foe was only two years of age when the Great Pestilence occurred, his *Journal* was long considered as much a work of imagination as his *Robinson Crusoe;* but there is abundant evidence of his having compiled the *Journal* from contemporary sources, (as the Collection of all the Bills of Mortality for 1665, published as *London's Dreadful Visitation;* the *Loimologia* of Dr. Hodges; and *God's Terrible Voice in the City,* by the Rev. Thomas Vincent, 1667); and many of the events which De Foe records derive collateral support from the respective Diaries of Pepys, Evelyn, and Lord Clarendon,—works which were not published until very long after Defoe's decease, and the manuscripts of which he could never have perused. De Foe is believed to have been familiar with the manuscript Account of the Great Plague by William Boghurst, a medical practitioner, formerly in the Sloane Collection, and now preserved in the British Museum: it is a thin quarto manuscript of 170 pages, from which only a few extracts have been published. Boghurst was an apothecary in St. Giles's-in-the-Fields; and he states that he was the only person who had then (1666) written on the late Plague from experience and observation. Rapin and Hume have recorded the event in little more than a single sentence; but Dr. Lingard has grouped the details of De Foe's *Journal* into a terrific picture, which has been compared to the celebrated delineation of the Plague of Athens by Thucydides.

The Great Plague was imported, in December 1664, by goods from Holland, where, in Amsterdam alone, 20,000 persons had been carried off by the same infection within a short time. The infected goods were opened at a house in St. Giles's parish, near the upper end of Drury-lane, wherein died four persons; and the parish books record of this period the appointment of searchers, shutting up of infected houses, and contributions by assessment and subscription. A Frenchman, who lived near the infected house in Drury-lane, removed into Bear-binder-lane (leading to St. Swithin's-lane), where he died, and thus spread the distemper in the City. Between December and the ensuing April the deaths without the walls of the City greatly increased, and in May every street in St. Giles's was infected. In July, in August, and September the deaths ranged from 1000 to 7000 per week; and 4000 are stated to have died in one fatal night! In the latter month fires were burnt in the streets three nights and days, "to purge and purify the air."

"St. James's Park was quite locked up;" and, July 22: "I by coach home, not meeting with but two coaches and but two carts, from White Hall to my own house, that I could observe; and the streets mighty thin of people."—*Pepys.*

"June 7th.—The hottest day that ever I felt in my life. This day, much against my will, I did in Drury-lane see two or three houses marked with a red cross upon the doors, and 'Lord have mercy upon us!' writ there."—*Pepys.*

"Sept. 7.—I went all along the City and suburbs, from Kent-street to St. James's,—a dismal passage, and dangerous, to see so many coffins exposed in the streets, now thin of people; the shops shut up, and all in *mournful silence*, as not knowing whose turn it might be next."—*Evelyn.*

> "Within the walls,
> The most frequented once and noisy parts
> Of town, now midnight silence reigns e'en there:
> A midnight silence at the noon of day!
> And grass, untrodden, springs beneath the feet."—*Dryden.*

The Court removed from Whitehall to Hampton Court, and thence to Salisbury and Oxford; and the Londoners leaving their city, carried the infection into the country; so that it spread, towards the end of this and the following year, over a great part of England. The Plague gradually abated in the metropolis; but it was not until Nov. 20, 1666, that public thanksgivings were offered up to God for assuaging the pestilence in London, Westminster, and within the bills of mortality. There were reported dead of the Plague in 1664-5, 68,596; probably, less by one-third than the actual number.

Among the Plague medicines were Pill Rufus and Venice treacle. Another antidote was sack. Tobacco was used as a prophylactic; and amulets were worn against infection. Among many touching episodes of the Plague, is that of a blind Highland bagpiper, who having fallen asleep upon the steps of St. Andrew's Church, Holborn-hill, was conveyed away in the dead-cart; and but for the howling of his faithful dog, which waked him from his trance, he would have been buried as a corpse. Of the piper and his dog a group was sculptured by Caius Gabriel Cibber: it was long after purchased by John the great Duke of Argyll, subsequently to whose death it for many years occupied a site in a garden in the front of No. 178 Tottenham-Court-road, whence it disappeared about 1825. (See *London Magazine*, April 1820.)

Another episode is that of a grocer in Wood-street, Cheapside, who shut himself up with his family, with a store of provisions, his only communication being by a wicket made in the door, and a rope and pulley to draw up or let any thing down into the street; and thus they escaped infection.

In the *Intelligencer*, No. 51, appeared the following advertisement:

"This is to notify that the master of the Cock and Bottle, commonly called the Cock Alehouse, at Temple Bar, hath dismissed his servants and shut up his house for this long vacation, intending (God willing) to return at Michaelmas next; so that all persons whatsoever who have any accompts with the said master, or *farthings belonging to the said house*, are desired to repair thither before the 8th of this instant July, and they shall receive satisfaction." One of these farthings is still preserved at the Cock tavern.

"No one can take up the book (Defoe's) without believing that it is the saddler of Whitechapel who is telling his own story; that he was an eye-witness to all he relates: that he actually saw the blazing star which portended the calamity; that he witnessed the grass growing in the streets, read the inscriptions upon the doors of the infected houses; heard the bellman crying, '*Bring out your dead!*' saw the dead-carts conveying people to their graves, and was present at the digging of the pits in which they were deposited."—Wilson's *Life and Times of Defoe.*

Forty years before, Evelyn records 1625 as "the year in which the pestilence was so epidemical, that there dy'd in London 5000 a week." In another great Plague year, 1603, there died 30,561:

"London now smokes with vapors that arise
From his foule sweat, himselfe he so bestirres:
'Cast out your dead !' the carcase-carrier cries,
Which he by heapes in groundlesse graves interres.
  *   *   *   *

The London lanes (thereby themselves to save)
Did vomit out their undigested dead,
Who by cart-loads are carried to the grave;
For all these lanes with folke were overfed.
  *   *   *   *

Time never knew, since he begunne his houres
(For aught we reade), a plague so long remaine
In any citie as this plague of ours;
For now six yeares in London it hath laine."
    The Triumph of Death, by John Davies, 1609.

POLICE.

The original Police of the metropolis (which, until the commencement of the last century, comprised only the "City and liberties," with Westminster) consisted of the aldermen, deputy-aldermen, common-councilmen, ward-clerk, ward-bedell, inquestmen or leet jury, and constables of the several wards, who were formerly themselves the night-watchmen by rotation, of Englishmen,—for no stranger was allowed to discharge so responsible an office: the ward, with its precincts, being no other than the highest development of the Anglo-Saxon hundred with its tithings. We find this form of Police to have existed from the earliest settlement of the valley of the Thames by a northern nation; and to have continued in use, as the type and model for the rest of the realm, until the institution of the present Police.

The few officers of central police in the City,—the upper-marshal, the under-marshal, and the marshalmen,—under whom was organised, at a very modern date, a subordinate force of sixty-eight men, were in like manner the type of the Bow-street and other police attached to the several magistrates' offices established in the outlying portions of the metropolis so recently as the close of the last century.

In the metropolitan parishes without the City, the watch was chiefly under local acts; the establishment in each consisting of a beadle, constables, and generally headboroughs, street-keepers, and watchmen, as in the several wards of the City, but working to a result much worse: the petty constables being served by deputies, in many instances characters of the worst and lowest description; having no salary, but living by extortion, and countenancing all species of vice.

To abolish such a system, Sir Robert Peel's Metropolitan Police Act of the 10th of George IV. c. 44, was passed, superseding the Bow-street foot-patrol, and the whole of the parochial police and watch outside the City, by one force both for day and night duty; in the sole appointment, order, and superintendence of two Commissioners, acting under the responsibility of the Secretary of State for the Home Department.*

"This great living machine keeps guard over our metropolis, with its ten millions of rateable property, and watches at night in order that two

* The late Vincent George Dowling claimed to be the originator of the plan on which this new police system was organised: even the names of the officers—inspector, sergeant, &c.—were published in *Bell's Life in London* (of which newspaper Dowling was editor) nearly two years before the system was proposed by Sir Robert Peel. Mr. T. Duffus Hardy contributed, from documents in the Record Office, important information to Sir Robert Peel on the ancient police arrangements of London.

millions and a half of people may sleep in safety; although six thousand professional thieves are constantly on the watch for opportunities to plunder. It consists, besides the two Commissioners, of 1 chief superintendent, 18 superintendents, 127 inspectors, 613 sergeants, and 4812 constables, in all 5571 persons. About 3700 men are on duty all night, and about 1800 all day. During the night they never cease patrolling the whole time they are on duty, being forbidden even to sit down. The Police District is mapped out into divisions, the divisions into subdivisions, the sub-divisions into sections, and the sections into beats, all being numbered, and the limits carefully defined. To every beat certain constables are specifically assigned; and they are provided with little maps called beat-cards. So thoroughly has this arrangement been carried into effect, that every street, road, lane, alley, and court within the metropolitan district,—that is, the whole of the metropolis (except that small part the City of London), the county of Middlesex, and all the parishes, 218 in number, in the counties of Surrey, Kent, Essex, and Hertfordshire, which are not more than 15 miles from Charing Cross, comprising an area of about 700 square miles, 90 miles in circumference, and with a population of 2.500,000,—is visited constantly day and night by some of the police. Within a circle of six miles from St. Paul's, the beats are ordinarily traversed in periods varying from 70 to 25 minutes; and there are points which, in fact, are never free from inspection. Nor must it be supposed that this system places the wealthier localities at a disadvantage; for it is an axiom in police, that you guard St. James's by watching St. Giles's.

"The district is divided into 18 divisions, containing, including the Thames, upwards of 121 police stands or stations. Intelligence is conveyed from one constable to the other till it reaches the station-house; thence, by an admirable arrangement of routes and messengers, it passes to the Central Office at Whitehall, thence along radiating lines to each division, and from the divisional station-house to every constable in the district. In a case of emergency, the Commissioner could communicate intelligence to every man in the force, and collect the whole 5571 men in one place, in two hours. The power of rapid concentration has worked so effectually, that since the establishment of the Metropolitan Police, it has never been found necessary to call the military into actual operation in aid of the civil force. Nor can clearer proof be given of perfect discipline, than the fact that 5000 men in the prime and vigour of life, with moderate wages,—2s. 5d. to 3s. per day, —exposed in an unusual degree to the worst temptations of London, and discharging, for the most part during the night, a very laborious duty, always irksome and often dangerous, are kept in complete control without any extraordinary coercive power."—*Edinburgh Review*.

Each police-constable has to walk 20 miles every day in his rounds, besides attending the police-offices, equal to 5 miles more. During two months out of three, each constable is on duty nine hours each night.

In one year (1839) the number of persons taken into custody by the Metropolitan Police has equalled the whole population of one of our largest towns; or, 65,965 persons, nearly equal to the population of Sheffield.

The cost of the Metropolitan Police Force in 1853 was 373,968l. 11s. 10d., raised from the parishes in the district and the Consolidated Fund. The charges for "truncheons, rattles, belts, and swords," was 29l. 9s. 3d. The expenses of the Police Courts during the year was 45,050l. 8s. 8d.; including the salary of one magistrate at 1200l. per annum, and 22 other magistrates at 1000l. per annum each.

The Corporation are allowed to have their own Police and their own Commissioner in the heart of the metropolis. The ordering of the force is vested in the Commissioner, subject to the approbation of the mayor and aldermen, or any three of them, and also of the Secretary of State for the Home Department. The number of men is about 600.

The *Horse Patrol* was added in 1836; and the *Thames Police*, with the *Westminster Constabulary* and the *Police-office Agency*, in 1838, when the old detective force was superseded.

Before the establishment of the Thames Police, by Mr. R. Colquhoun, the annual loss by robberies alone upon the river was half a million sterling; the depredators being termed river-pirates, light and heavy horsemen, mud-larks, rope-men, scuffle-hunters. They were frequently known to weigh a ship's anchor, hoist it with the cable into a boat, and when discovered, to hail the captain, tell him of his loss, and row away. They also cut craft and lighters adrift, ran them ashore, and cleared them. Many of the light-horsemen cleared five guineas a night; and an apprentice to a game-waterman often kept his country-house and saddle-horse. In 1797, the first year of the Police, the saving to the West India merchants alone was computed at 100,000*l.*; and 2200 culprits were convicted of misdemeanours on the river during the same period.

POPULATION.

Taperell and Innes's Map of London and Westminster in the early part of the reign of Queen Elizabeth (1560), based upon Vertue's Map, 1737, shows on the east the Tower, standing separated from London, and Finsbury and Spitalfields with their trees and hedge-rows; while on the west of Temple Bar, the villages of Charing, St. Giles's, and other scattered hamlets are aggregated, and Westminster is a distinct city. The intervening north bank of the river Thames, or the Strand, has a line of seats and gardens of the nobility. At the date of this map London contained about 145,000 inhabitants. In the narrative of the visit of the Duke de Nayera to the Court of Henry VIII. in 1543, London is described as one of the largest cities in Christendom, "its extent being near a league."

Sir William Petty, in his *Political Arithmetic*, printed in 1683, after much study of statistical returns and bills of mortality, demonstrates that the growth of the metropolis must stop of its own accord before the year of grace 1800; at which period the population would, by his computation, have arrived at exactly 5,359,000. Nay more, were it not for this halt, he shows that the increase would double in forty years, with a slightly accelerating increment, as he gives the amount of human beings in the city for 1840 at 10,718,880! The identical year 1800, the commencement of a truly important century, found London still enlarging: brick-fields and scaffolding were invading all its outskirts; but the inhabitants, who had increased in a reasonably rapid ratio, numbered only 830,000.

"There are no accurate accounts of the population of London previously to the Census of 1801. The population of the City was estimated by Graunt, in his famous *Treatise on Bills of Mortality*, at 384,000 in 1661; and adding one-fifth to this for the population of Westminster, Lambeth, Stepney, and other outlying parishes, he estimated the entire population at about 460,000. (*Observations*, &c. 5th ed. pp. 82, 105). In 1696 the population of the City and the out-parishes was carefully estimated, by the celebrated Gregory King, at 527,560; and considering the great additions that had been made to the metropolis between the Restoration and the Revolution, this increase does not seem to be greater than we should have been led to infer from Graunt's estimate. The population advanced slowly during the first half of the last century; indeed, it fell off between 1740 and 1750. In his tract on the population of England, published in 1782, Dr. Price estimated the population of London in 1777 at only 543,420 (p. 5). But there can be no doubt that this estimate, like that which he gave of the population of the kingdom, was very decidedly under the mark; and the probability seems to be, that in 1777 London had from 640,000 to 650,000 inhabitants."—Macculloch's *Geographical Dictionary*.

In 1801 the population was 958,863; 1811, 1,050,000; 1821, 1,274,800; 1831, 1,471,941; 1841, 1,873,676.

The Census of 1851 was taken in Craig's-court, Charing Cross, the premises formerly the Museum of Economic Geology. The following are the general results: London, comprised in an area of 115 square miles, or 73,715 statute acres, containing 176 parishes. Population, 2,361,640 inhabitants—1,103,730 males; 1,257,910 females. Houses, 329,428 — 307,722 inhabited; 16,889 uninhabited; 4,817 building. 20,536 persons, on an average, are located on a square mile, occupying 2,676 houses, or 151 square yards to each person. North side of the river Thames,—area, 49 square miles; inhabitants, 1,745,095. South side of the river Thames,—area, 66 square miles; inhabitants, 616,545.

"A conception of this vast mass of people might be formed by the fact, that if the metropolis was surrounded by a wall, having a north gate, a south gate, an east gate, and a west gate, and each of the four gates was of sufficient width to allow a column of persons to pass out freely four abreast, and a peremptory necessity required the immediate evacuation of the city, it could not be accomplished under 24 hours, by the expiration of which time the head of each of the four columns would have advanced no less a distance than 75 miles from their respective gates, all the people being in close file, four deep."—Cheshire's *Results of the Census.*

The females exceeded the males by 154,000; being an addition of nearly 30,000 over the males within 10 years (1841-51). This increase in London is the more extraordinary, as the whole of England and Wales within that period did not exceed 39,000. The marriages solemnised in London during 1850 were 24,361; increase of inhabitants in the same period, about 46,000. In 1851, nine centenarians died in London, the oldest being 106 years.

Since 1801 London has increased from 958,863 to 2,361,640, the numbers growing at each decennial period in the following order:— 1801, 958,863; 1811, 1,138,815; 1821, 1,378,947; 1831, 1,654,994; 1841, 1,948,369; 1851, 2,361,640: the rate of increase at each interval being 18, 21, 20, 17, 21 per cent; during the whole half-century above 14½ per cent; and annually at the rate of 1·81.

This external London now contains three single parishes, each of them having a population greater than that of the whole City, east, west, and within the walls, taken together, viz.: St. Pancras, 167,198; Marylebone, 157,679; Lambeth, 139,209: while a very near approach to the City numbers (127,869) is made by—Kensington, 119,990; Stepney, 110,669; Shoreditch, 109,209.

The smallest parish in London is that of St. Christopher-le-Stock which is returned as a single house, now part of the Bank of England.

London, upon its 115 square miles, contains, within 508,548, as many persons as all Scotland; or nearly equal to the population of the entire kingdom of Denmark; equal to about one-half of Sweden and Norway, of Portugal, of Belgium, of Holland, and of Bavaria; and exceeding the population of the kingdom of Hanover, of Wurtemberg, of Saxony, of Tuscany, of Baden, and some other Continental States.*

The present population of London is supposed to represent the number of inhabitants living in England and Wales four centuries and a half ago, in the reign of Edward III.

The entire county of Lancashire contains 297,727 less inhabitants than London, requiring another Liverpool to make up the difference. The inhabitants of Yorkshire about equal two-thirds of London. Wales, with its 12 counties, reckons not more than one-half of the population of London; where the people are 10,000 times as numerous

* A Summary of the Population, with a Statistical Chart of Marriages, Births and Deaths, &c. By C. Cooke. Longman and Co, 1853.

as in Bellingham, Northumberland, which contains only 18 persons to the square mile.

Each day 130 persons are added to the population. About 124 persons are daily married in London, 198 children daily born, and 156 persons die. In every 7 minutes of the day, a child is born in London; and in every 9 minutes, one of its inhabitants dies.

Mr. R. J. Jopling estimates, that "if the population continue to increase in the same ratio as in 1851, 1·515 per cent per annum, it will amount at the close of the century to 4,816,062. To accommodate this number of people, there will be required 160,535 acres of ground, containing 650,819 houses, being an increase of more than double the present area of London."—*Proceedings of the Statistical Society.*

PORT OF LONDON.

Sir John Herschel felicitously observes: "It is a fact not a little interesting to Englishmen, and, combined with our insular situation in the great highway of nations, the Atlantic, not a little explanatory of our commercial eminence, that London occupies nearly the centre of the terrestrial hemisphere."—*Treatise on Astronomy.*

Tacitus describes London, in the year 61, as not dignified with the name of a colony, but very celebrated for the number of its merchants and commerce. In 211 it was styled " a great and wealthy city ;" and in 359 there were engaged 800 vessels in the import and export of corn to and from Londinium alone.

The Port of London, legally speaking, extends 6½ miles below London Bridge, to Bugsby's Hole, beyond Blackwall. The actual Port reaches to Limehouse, and consists of the Upper Pool, the first bend or *reach* of the river, from London Bridge to near the Thames Tunnel and Execution Dock; and the Lower Pool, thence to Cuckold's Point. In the latter space colliers mostly lie in tiers; a fair way of 300 feet being left for shipping and steamers passing up and down. The depth of the river insures London considerable advantage as a shipping port. Even at ebb-tide there are 12 or 13 feet of water in the fair way of the river above Greenwich; the mean range of the tide at London Bridge is about 17 feet; of the highest spring tides about 22 feet. To Woolwich the river is navigable for ships of any burden; to Blackwall for those of 1400 tons; and to St. Katherine's Docks for vessels of 800 tons.

In one day, after heavy gales, 244 vessels have entered the port.

Emigration from the port: on one day, in 1854, there were 73 ships on the berth for the Australian colonies.

The several DOCKS are described at pp. 254-257; the CUSTOM HOUSE at p. 246; and BILLINGSGATE at p. 45.

" *In one day* (Sept. 17, 1849) there arrived in the Port 121 ships, navigated by 1387 seamen, with a registered tonnage of 29,699 tons: 106 British, 15 foreign; 52 cargoes from our colonies, 69 from foreign states—from the inhabitants of the whole circuit of the globe. The day's cargoes included 32,280 packages of sugar, from the West Indies, Brazil, the East Indies, Penang, Manilla, and Rotterdam; 317 oxen and calves, and 2734 sheep, principally from Belgium and Holland; 3967 quarters of wheat, 13,314 quarters of oats, from Archangel or the Baltic; potatoes, from Rotterdam; 1200 packages of onions, from Oporto; 16,000 chests of tea, from China; 7400 packages of coffee, from Ceylon, Brazil, and India; 532 bags of cocoa, from Grenada; 1460 bags of rice from India, and 350 bags of tapioca from Brazil; bacon and pork from Hamburg, and 8000 packages of butter and 50,000 cheeses from Holland; 767 packages of eggs (900,000); of wool, 4458 bales, from the Cape and Australia; 15,000 hides, 100,000 horns, and 3600 packages of tallow, from South America and India; hoofs of animals, 13 tons, from Port Philip, and 440 elephants' teeth from the Cape: 1250 tons of granite from Guernsey, copper ore from Adelaide, and cork from Spain; 40,000 mats from Archangel, and 400 tons of brimstone from Sicily; cod-liver oil, and 3800 sealskins, from Newfoundland; 110 bales of bark from Arica, and 1100 casks of oil from the Mediterranean; lard, oil-cake, and turpentine, from America; hemp from Russia, and potash from Canada; 246 bales of rags, from Italy; staves for casks, timber for our houses, deals for packing-cases; rosewood, 876 pieces; teak for ships, logwood for dye, lignum vitæ for ships' blocks, and ebony for cabinets; cotton from Bombay, zinc from Stettin, 1000 bundles of whisks from Trieste, yeast from Rotterdam, and apples from Belgium; of silk, 900 bales from China, finer sorts from Piedmont and Tuscany, and 200 packages from China, Germany, and France; Cashmere shawls from Bombay; wine, 1800 packages, from France and Portugal; rum from the East and West Indies, and scheidam from Holland; nutmegs and cloves from Penang, cinnamon from Ceylon, 840 packages of pepper from Bombay, and 1790 of ginger from Calcutta; 100 barrels of anchovies from Leghorn, a cargo of pine-apples from Nassau, and 50 fine live turtles; 54 blocks of marble from Leghorn; tobacco from America; 219 packages of treasure—Spanish dollars, Sycee silver from China, rupees from Hindostan, and English sovereigns."—*A Day's Business in the Port of London,* by T. Howell, Esq.

"Again, in one day's consumption, we find corahs, or silk handkerchiefs, from India; whale-fins and sperm-oil from our deep-sea fisheries; from India, shell-lac, indigo, and lac-dye; saltpetre for gunpowder, and hemp and jute for cordage; quicksilver from the mines in Spain; isinglass and bristles from Russia; Iceland moss, honey, and leeches, from Hamburg; manna from Palermo, camphor from Calcutta, maccaroni from Naples, sugar-candy from Holland, and lemon-oil from Messina; 81,000 lbs. of currants from the Ionian Islands, 5760 bars of iron from Sweden, and bees'-wax from the coast of Africa; tea, sugar, coffee, pepper, tobacco, spirits, and wine; watches, clocks, gloves, and glass-ware; needlework, ladies' shoes, bonnets, and feathers; toys, lace, and slate-pencils; zaffery and stavesacre from Hamburg; and inkle from France."—*Ibid.*

The river is protected by an admirable system of police, established in 1798, and merged into the Metropolitan Police in 1839.

Execution Dock, at Wapping, the name of one of the outlets of the river, preserves the memory of many a tale of murder and piracy on the high seas; for here used to be executed all pirates and sailors found guilty of any of the greater crimes committed on ship-board. Opposite Blackwall we remember to have seen the gibbets, on which the bodies were left to decay.

The loss of life upon the Thames, by collision of vessels and other accidents, is of frightful amount; 500 persons being annually drowned in the river, and one-third of the number in the Pool.

PORTUGAL-STREET,

In the rear of the south side of Lincoln's-Inn-fields (formerly Portugal-row), has been the site of three theatres, upon the north side of the street. The first theatre (named the *Duke's Theatre,* from the Duke of York, its great patron; and the *Opera,* from its musical performances), was originally a tennis-court, and was altered for Sir William Davenant, and opened in 1662 with his operatic *Siege of Rhodes,* when regular scenery was first introduced upon our stage. In the same year was produced here Cowley's *Cutter of Coleman-street.* Here Pepys saw, March 1st, 1662, *Romeo and Juliet,* "the first time it was ever acted;" and May 28, "*Hamlet* done, giving us fresh reason never to think enough of Betterton." "Nov. 5. To the Duke's house to see *Macbeth,* a pretty good play, but admirably acted." Pepys describes "a mighty company of citizens, ordinary prentices, and mean people in the pit;" where he first saw Nell Gwyn, April 3, 1665, during the performance of Lord Orrery's *Mustapha,* when the king and my Lady Castlemaine were there; Pepys sat in the pit next to "pretty witty Nell" and Rebecca Marshall, of the King's house. Etherege's *Love in a Tub* was so attractive here, that 1000*l.* was received in one month, then a great sum. Here female characters were first sustained by women; for which purpose Davenant engaged Elizabeth Davenport, the first Roxalana in the *Siege of Rhodes;* Mary Saunderson, famous as Queen Katherine and Juliet, and afterwards the wife of Betterton ; Mary or Moll Davis,* excellent in singing and dancing, afterwards the mistress of Charles II.; Mrs. Long, the mistress of the Duke of Richmond, celebrated in male cha- racters ; Mrs. Norris, mother of Jubilee Dicky ; Mrs. Johnson, noted as a dancer, and as Carolina in Shadwell's comedy of *Epsom Wells.* The famous Mrs. Barry was brought out here after Davenant's death.

Among the actors at the Duke's were Thomas Betterton, the rival of Burbage and Garrick, and the last survivor of the old school of actors; Joseph Harris, famous for acting Romeo, Wolsey, and Sir Andrew Aguecheek; William Smith, a barris- ter of Gray's Inn, celebrated as Zanga in Lord Orrery's *Mustapha;* Samuel Sandford, called by King Charles II. the best representative of a villain in the world; James Nokes, famous for his bawling fops; and Cave Underhill, clever as Cutter in Cowley's comedy, and as the grave-digger in *Hamlet.*—Abridged from Cunningham's *Story of Nell Gwyn.*

From 1665 (the Plague) until after the Great Fire, the theatre was closed. Davenant usually resided here.

"April 9th, 1668. I up and down to the Duke of York's playhouse, there to see, which I did, Sir W. Davenant's corpse carried out towards Westminster, there to be buried. Here were many coaches and six horses, and many hacknies, that made it look, methought, as if it were the buriall of a poor poet."—*Pepys.*

In 1671-2, in Lord Orrery's play of *Henry V.*, at the Duke's Theatre, the actors Harris, Betterton, and Smith wore the coronation suits of King Charles, the Duke of York, and Lord Oxford. This year the company removed to Dorset Gardens; and the King's company, burnt out from Drury-lane, played at the Duke's Theatre till 1673-4, when they left it, and it again became a tennis-court. It was refitted and re- opened in 1695, with (first time) Congreve's comedy of *Love for Love.* This second theatre was taken down, and a new house built for Chris- topher Rich, and opened by John Rich, in 1714, with Farquhar's comedy of the *Recruiting Officer;* when also Rich introduced the first panto- mime, Rich himself playing harlequin. Here Quin played his best parts; and from a fracas in which he was embroiled, originated the sergeant's guard at the Theatres Royal. The first English opera was performed here in 1717-18; here was originally used the stage motto, *Veluti in speculum;* and here in 1727-8 the *Beggar's Opera* was produced, and played 62 nights the first season, making " Gay rich and Rich gay." In 1732, Rich having built a theatre in Covent Garden, removed there; and the Portugal-street house was by turns let for Italian operas, ora- torios, for balls, concerts, and exhibitions; to Giffard, of Goodman's- fields, in 1756; next as a barrack and auction-room; and Spode and Copeland's China Repository, until 1848, when the premises were sold to the College of Surgeons August 28, and were taken down for enlarging their Museum. Of the theatre little remained, save the outer walls, built upon an arched cellar : there was a large Queen Anne staircase, a saloon upon the first floor ; and the attic, lighted by windows in the roof, was probably the scene-painting loft.

Upon this site the College of Surgeons completed in 1854 a third Hall for their Museum, by aid of a Parliamentary grant of 15,000*l.* Among the skeletons here is that of Chunee, the elephant shot at Exeter Change in 1826; also, skele- tons of rare whales; a large horned Indian rhinoceros; the racer, Eclipse; Su- matran tapir; walrus; narwhal; and several thousand osteological and patho- logical specimens. The Museum is open four days in the week, Monday to Thursday, from 12 to 4 p.m. (See p. 534.)

In Carey-street, nearly opposite, was a public-house and stable- yard, described in Sir William Davenant's *Playhouse to be Let* as " our

* In the part of Celania, in the *Rivals,* altered by Davenant from Beaumont and Fletcher's *Two Noble Kinsmen,* Moll Davis sang " My lodging is on the cold ground" " so charmingly, that not long after it raised her from her bed on the cold ground to a bed royal."—Downes's *Roscius Anglicanus,* p. 24, ed. 1708.

house inn, the Grange;" it was taken down in 1853 for the site of King's College Hospital. At the north-east corner of Portugal-street is one of its olden resorts, *Will's Coffee-house;* but "the Bell and Dragon ordinary," opposite the theatre, has disappeared. Portugal-street was the last locality in London where *stocks* lingered; those of St. Clement Danes parish being removed from here 1820-26. The burial-ground, with Jo Miller's grave, and the theatrical taverns of Clare Market, are noticed at page 496: Miller's grave and stone are now inclosed in King's College Hospital. The *Court for the Relief of Insolvent Debtors,* built by Soane, is described at page 451.

POST-OFFICE.

The General Post-office has had five locations since the Postmaster to Charles I. fixed his receiving-house in Sherborne-lane, in 1635, whence dates "the settling of the letter-office of England and Scotland." It was next removed to Cloak-lane, Dowgate: and then to the Black Swan, Bishopsgate-street. After the Great Fire, the office was shifted to the Black Pillars, in Brydges-street, Covent-garden; thence, early in the last century, to the mansion of Sir Robert Viner (close to Sherborne-lane), in Lombard-street, described at page 394; and to St. Martin's-le-Grand in 1829.

The General Post-office occupies the site of the College of St. Martin's-le-Grand, at the junction with Newgate-street. It was designed by Sir R. Smirke, R.A., and was built between 1825 and 1829: it is insulated, and is externally of Portland stone; 400 feet long, 130 wide, and 64 high. It stands in the three parishes of St. Anne and St. Agnes, St. Leonard, and St. Michael-le-quern; and 131 houses and nearly 1000 inhabitants were displaced to make room for this single edifice. Several Roman remains were found during the progress of the works (see page 502). The St. Martin's-le-Grand façade has three Ionic porticoes: one at each end, tetrastyle, of four fluted columns; and one in the centre, hexastyle, of six columns (from the temple of Minerva Polias, at Athens): it is surmounted by a pediment, in the tympanum of which are sculptured the imperial arms of the United Kingdom; and on the frieze is inscribed, "GEORGIO QUARTO REGE, MDCCCXXIX." Beneath are entrances to the Grand Public Hall, 80 feet long by about 60 wide, divided by Ionic columns into a centre and two aisles; and in the vaulted basement are the warm-air apparatus and gasometers. North of the Hall are the offices for newspapers, inland letters, and foreign letters; south are the offices of the London local post; the communication being by a tunnel and railway under the Hall floor. In the middle story north are the offices for dead, missent, and returned letters; south, secretary's offices, board-rooms, &c. The clock, over the principal entrance, was made by Vulliamy; the bob of the pendulum weighs 448 lbs., the object being to counteract the effect of wind on the hands of the dial. In the eastern front, facing Foster-lane, the letter-bags are received. The mechanical contrivances for the dispatch of the business of the office display great ingenuity: steam-power is variously employed: two endless chains, worked by a steam-engine, carry, in rapid succession, a series of shelves, each holding four or five men and their letter-bags, which are thus raised to various parts of the building.

The Mails were originally conveyed on horseback and in light carts, until 1784, when mail-coaches were substituted by Mr. Palmer. The first mail-coach left the Three Kings yard, Piccadilly, for Bristol, Aug. 24th, 1784; in 1839 the coaches were displaced by railways. The annual procession of the mail-coaches on the king's birthday was a metropolitan sight. The letters are now conveyed to the railways in omnibuses, nine of which are sometimes filled by one night's mail at one railway. In 1839 was invented the travelling post-office, in which clerks sort the letters during the railway journey, and the guard ties up and exchanges the letter-bags, without stopping the train. Four miles an hour was the common rate of the first mail-carts; a railway mail-train now averages 24 miles an hour; while, between certain stations on certain lines, a speed of 50 miles an hour is attained.

The Rates of Postage varied according to distance until Dec. 5th, 1839, when the uniform rate of 4*d*. was tried; and Jan. 10th, 1840, was commenced the uniform rate of 1*d*. per letter of half an ounce weight, &c. The Government received 2000 plans for a new system, and adopted that of Mr. Rowland Hill; but not until the change had been some years *agitated* by a *Post Magazine* established for the purpose. The stamped postage-covers came into use May 6, 1840; but the idea of a prepaid envelope is as old as the time of Louis XIV. A pictorial envelope was designed by W. Mulready, R.A., but little used. The postage label-stamps were first used in 1841; perforated, 1854.

Number of Letters.—The greatest number of letters, under the old system, ever known to pass through the General Post-office in one day, was received there on July 15, 1839, viz. 90,000; the amount of postage being 4050*l*., a sum greater by 530*l*. than any hitherto collected in one day. In the third week of February the number of letters is usually highest. The ordinary daily average is 400,000 letters; on 19th August, 1853, it reached 630,000. The number of letters which pass through the Post-office in a year is nearly 400,000,000. The number of miles which mails travel over railways in a year is about 7,000,000. The length of the English ocean mail-lines is 55,000 miles. The English ocean mail-packets traverse 1,600,000 miles annually.

The Post-Office Net Revenue for the year ending Jan. 5, 1838, amounted to 1,652,424*l*. 7*s*. 7¾*d*.; while that of the year ending the same date in 1853 was 1,090,419*l*. 13*s*. 5¼*d*.; cost of management, 1,400,000*l*. The gross amount of income for the year 1839 was 2,346,278*l*.; and for 1853, 2,434,326*l*. In 1851 London contributed to the Post-office revenue 953,663*l*. 17*s*. 10*d*.; Liverpool, 75,926*l*. 6*s*. 4*d*.; Manchester, 60,070*l*. 13*s*. 9*d*. The number of letters delivered in the London district is at this time (1854) as great as that which, under the old system, was delivered in the whole United Kingdom.

"It is estimated that there lies, from time to time, in the Dead-Letter Office, undergoing the process of finding owners, some 11,000*l* annually, in cash alone. In July 1847, for instance—only a two months' accumulation—the post-haste of 4658 letters, all containing property, was arrested by the bad superscriptions of the writers. They were consigned—after a searching inquest upon each by that efficient coroner, the "blind clerk"—to the post-office *Morgue*. There were bank-notes of the value of 1010*l*., and money-orders for 407*l*. 12*s*. But most of these ill-directed letters contained coin in small sums, amounting to 31*l*. 9*s*. 7*d*. On the 17th of July, 1847, there were lying in the Dead-Letter Office bills of exchange for the immense sum of 40,410*l*. 5*s*. 7*d*." (Dickens's *Household Words*, No. 1.) The value of property contained in missing letters, during twelve months, is about 200,000*l*.

There are employed in the General Post-office, including the London District letter-carriers, but exclusive of the receivers, 2500 persons, in different offices:—Secretary's, Accountant's, Receiver's, Dead-Letter, Money-Order, Inland, and London District Offices. For more than half a century there were only two secretaries to the Post-office, Sir Francis Freeling and Colonel Maberly. Sir Francis was brought up in the Post-office, had performed the humblest as well as the highest duties of the department, and was a *protégé* of Mr. Palmer, the great Post-office reformer. He was succeeded by Lieut.-Col. Maberly, M.P., who retired in 1854, when Mr. Rowland Hill, the originator of the penny-post, was appointed secretary, his services having been rewarded in 1846 by a public testimonial of 13,360*l.* It is singular that all postal reformers have been unacquainted with the department which they have revolutionised.

THE PENNY POST was originally projected by Robert Murray, a milliner, of the Company of Clothworkers; and William Dockwra, a sub-searcher in the Customs. It was commenced as a foot-post, in 1680, with four deliveries a-day. These projectors, however, quarrelled: Murray set up his office at Hall's Coffee-house, in Wood-street; and Dockwra, at the Penny Post-house in Lime-street, formerly the mansion of Sir Robert Abdy. But this was considered an infringement on the right of the Duke of York, on whom the Post-office revenue had been settled; and in a suit to try the question, a verdict was given against Dockwra. He was compensated by a pension, and appointed Comptroller of the Penny Post, but was dismissed in 1698. The first office was in Cornhill, near the 'Change: parcels were received. In 1708, one Povey set up the "Halfpenny Carriage" private post, which was soon suppressed by the Post-office authorities. They continued to convey parcels down to 1765, when the weight was limited to four ounces. The postage was paid in advance down to 1794. In 1801 the Penny Post became a Twopenny Post; and the postage was advanced to threepence beyond the limits of London, Southwark, and Westminster; but in 1840 they were consolidated with the Penny General Post.

The Money-Order Office, a distinct branch of the Post-office, is a handsome new edifice on the west side of St. Martin's-le-Grand. The number of money-orders issued yearly is 5,000,000; amount of money-orders issued annually, nearly 10,000,000*l.*; yearly revenue from commission on money-orders, 80,000*l.*

POULTRY,

The street extending from the east end of Cheapside to Mansion-house-street, was anciently occupied by the poulterers' stalls of Stocks Market, who in Stow's time had "but lately departed from thence into other streets" (Gracechurch-street and Newgate Market). In Scalding-alley (now St. Mildred's-court) was a large house where the poulterers scalded their poultry for sale. It was also called Coney-hope, or Conning-shop, or Cony-shop, lane, from the sign of three coneys (rabbits) hanging over a poulterer's stall at the lane end. Here was built the chapel of St. Mildred, called in old records, *Ecclesia Mildredæ super Walbrooke, vel in Pulletria; una cum capella beatæ Mariæ de Conyhop eidem annexa:* the site is now occupied by the church of *St. Mildred in the Poultry.* (See p. 151.)

On the same side, between Nos. 31 and 32, was the *Poultry Compter,* a Sheriffs' prison, taken down in 1817, and *Poultry Chapel* built upon the site. To the Compter were sent persons committed by the lord mayor; and to the prisoners was given the broken victuals from the Mansion-house tables. "Doctor Lamb," the conjuror, died in this prison, Jan. 13, 1628, after being chased and pelted by the mob across Moorfields; for which outrage the City was fined 6000*l.* Here died six Separatists who had been committed by Bishop Bonner for hearing the Scriptures read in their own houses. John Dunton, the bookseller, in 1688, on the day the Prince of Orange entered London, transferred himself and his sign of the Black Raven opposite the Poultry Compter, where he prospered for ten years. The prison was, in 1806, in a ruinous condition; but the court was cheerful, "having water continually running:" it was the only prison in England that had a ward exclusively for Jews; there were "the Bell," and two other rooms, "very strong, studded with nails," for felons. The debtors were allowed to walk upon the leads with the gaoler.

Hatton (1708) calls the Poultry "a broad street of very tall buildings."

At No. 22 lived the booksellers Dilly, famed for their hospitality to literary men: here Dr. Johnson first met Wilkes; and Boswell, Cumberland, Knox, and Isaac Reed often met. Dilly was the first publisher of Boswell's *Life of Johnson:* the firm was also noted for the works of Doddridge, Watts, Lardner, &c.

At No. 31 lived Vernor and Hood, the publishers of Bloomfield's poems; and the *Beauties of England and Wales,* an unequal and unsatisfactory work. Hood was the father of Thomas Hood, the wit and humorist, who was born in the Poultry in 1798: "there was a dash of ink in my blood (writes Tom); my father wrote two novels, and my brother was decidedly of a literary turn."

> "Time was when I sat upon a lofty stool,
> At lofty desk, and with a clerkly pen,
> Began each morning at the stroke of ten
> To write in Bell and Co.'s commercial school,
> In Warnford-court, a shady nook and cool,
> The favourite retreat of merchant men.
> Yet would my quill turn vagrant even then,
> And take stray dips in the Castalian pool:
> Now double-entry,—now a flowery trope,—
> Mingling poetic honey with trade wax;
> Blogg, Brothers,—Milton—Grote and Prescott—Pope—
> Bristles and Hogg—Glyn, Mills, and Halifax—
> Rogers and Towgood—Hemp—the Bard of Hope—
> Barilla—Byron—Tallow—Burns and Flax."—*Hood.*

No. 25 Poultry is the old King's Head Tavern, where Charles II. stopped, on the day of his restoration, to salute the landlady. In the Beaufoy Collection, in the Corporation Library, are Tokens of the Rose Tavern, in the Poultry, mentioned by Ned Ward (*London Spy,* 1709) as famous for its wine; the Three Cranes, destroyed in the Great Fire, but rebuilt; and the Exchange Tavern, 1671, with, on the obverse, a view of the Royal Exchange quadrangle. At the Three Cranes met "the Mendicants' Convivial Club," subsequently removed to Dyot-street, St. Giles's.

PRIMROSE-HILL

Was named from the primroses that formerly grew here in great plenty, when it was comparatively an untrodden hillock, in the fields between Tottenham Court and Hampstead. It has also been called *Green-Berry-Hill,* from the names of three persons executed for the murder of Sir Edmondsbury Godfrey, whose body was found here, Oct. 17, 1678. On the south side of the hill, during a summer drought, may be traced a green line, which was once a ditch, extending from east to the ground westward now occupied by the New-River Reservoir. In that ditch, near the site of the Water-works steam-engine chimney-shaft, was found Godfrey's body, as thus described in a letter written in 1681:

"As to the place, it was in a ditch on the south side of Primrose Hill, surrounded with divers closes, fenced in with high mounds and ditches; no roads near, only some deep, dirty lanes, made only for the conveniency of driving cows in and out of the ground; and those very lanes not coming near five hundred yards of the place, and impassable for any man on horseback with a dead corpse before him at midnight to approach, unless gaps were made in the mounds, as the constable and his assistants found by experience when they came on horseback thither."

At the trial, before the Lord Chief-Justice Scroggs, Feb. 10, 1679, the infamous witnesses, Oates, Prance, and Bedloe, declared that the un-

fortunate magistrate, Godfrey, "was waylaid and inveigled into the
Palace (Somerset House), under the pretence of keeping the peace between two servants who were fighting in the yard; that he was there
strangled, his neck broke, and his own sword run through his body;
that he was kept four days before they ventured to remove him; at
length his corpse was first carried in a sedan-chair to Soho, and then
on a horse to Primrose Hill," as represented on one of the several
medals struck as memorials of the mysterious murder. The body was
carried to "the White House," then the farm-house of the estate of
Chalcotts, abbreviated to Chalc's, and then corrupted to Chalk Farm,
which became a tavern, removed in 1853. The summit of the hill is
206 feet above the Trinity high-water mark of the Thames. (See
PRIMROSE-HILL PARK, page 596.)

Primrose Hill is a portion of the land bequeathed by "sundry
devout men of London" to St. James's Hospital, but granted by Henry
VI. to Eton College, surrendered to Henry VIII., but again returned
to the College, who, a few years since, transferred it to the Government in exchange for a piece of crown-land near Windsor; which was
done principally through the exertions of Mr. Hume, M.P., and an
Association of persons formed for securing the ground to the public.
In 1845 it was surveyed as a site for a grand Industrial Exposition,
suggested by the success of the Anti-Corn-Law League Bazaar, in
Covent Garden Theatre. In the ridge adjoining is the Primrose-Hill
Tunnel of the London and North-Western Railway; its extent is 3493
feet, or more than five-eighths of a mile: in tunnelling near the base of
the hill, fossil nautili were discovered.

The View from Primrose Hill comprises not only London, with its masses of
houses and hundreds of spires, but also the once rural retreats of Hampstead
and Highgate, now almost become portions of the great town itself. Opposite is
St. John's Wood, and in the rear of St. John's Wood the graceful spire of Harrow-
on-the-Hill; and nearer the spectator are the close streets of Portland Town,
and the elegant domain of Regent's Park. The eye, after resting upon St. Paul's
as the nucleus of the vast city, glances over Islington and Holloway to the undulating hills of Kent and Surrey; and upon a clear day may be descried the
bright roofs of the Crystal Palace at Sydenham.

PRISONS.

Upwards of 30,000 criminals and other persons (exclusive of debtors) are stated to pass through the metropolitan gaols, houses of
correction, bridewells, and penitentiaries, every year. The number of
prisons was in 1854 smaller than half a century since; but the prisons
themselves were of much larger extent. In 1796 there were eighteen
prisons in London, which in 1854 had been reduced one-third.

"Access to the national prisons, such as Millbank, Pentonville, and the Queen's
Prison, may be obtained by a warrant from the Home Secretary of State; and the
city or county prisons—Newgate and Giltspur-street Compter, or Coldbath-
fields and Horsemonger-lane—by an order from a magistrate of city or county
who happens to be for a time a visiting justice; and for every distinct visit a distinct warrant must be presented. All the great London gaols are provided with
stands of arms, by which men could be armed in a few minutes; besides signal-
rockets, which would instantly convey intelligence to the Horse Guards, and to the
barracks in St James's and Hyde Parks, of any attack; so that 2000 or 3000 men
could be concentrated at any prison in half an hour."—Dixon on *London Prisons.*

BOROUGH COMPTER, Mill-lane, Tooley-street (solely for debtors
from the borough of Southwark), was originally part of the church of
St. Margaret, at St. Margaret's Hill, where the prison site is denoted
by Counter (Compter) street.

BRIDEWELL, Bridge-street, Blackfriars, is described at page 53.

CITY PRISON, Camden-road, Holloway, is built upon land originally purchased by the Corporation for a cemetery, during the raging of the cholera in 1832. The extent is 10 acres within the boundary-wall, 18 feet high. The prison, designed by Bunning, is built in the castellated style, has fortified gateways, and is embattled throughout the six radiating wings; the number of cells is 436; the building is fire-proof; the ventilation is by a shaft 146 feet high; the water-supply from an Artesian well, 319 feet deep. The prisoners are variously employed; and the discipline is neither entire separation nor association, but the middle course. The prison was first opened Oct. 6, 1852. Cost, about 100,000*l.*

CLERKENWELL PRISON, St. James's Walk, was established by patent granted by James I., and was erected, in 1616, upon the site of "the Cage:" it was mostly rebuilt in 1820; but being ill planned, was taken down in 1846, and an enlarged gaol erected upon its site. (See MIDDLESEX HOUSE OF DETENTION.) In the old prison was confined Jack Sheppard, whose fetters, of double the usual weight, are shown.

CLINK (the), Bankside, was named from being the prison of the "Clink Liberty," in Southwark, belonging to the Bishops of Winchester; and was used in old time "for such as would brabble, frey, or break the peace on the said bank, or in the brothel-houses." (*Stow.*) About 1745, the old prison, at the corner of Maid-lane, was abandoned, and a dwelling on the Bankside appropriated in its stead; this was burnt in the riots of 1780, and no other prison has since been established for the liberty.

The palace of the Bishops of Winchester, at Bankside, was made a prison during the Civil Wars: Sir Kenelm Digby, while confined here as a Royalist, wrote his refutation of Browne's *Religio Medici.*

COLDBATH-FIELDS' HOUSE OF CORRECTION, for prisoners from Middlesex, incloses nine acres of ground; and with an average of from 1200 to 1400 occupants, is one of the healthiest prisons in the metropolis: in April 1854 there were 1595 prisoners. The oldest portion was built in 1794. It formerly had a reputation for severity:

> " As he went through Coldbath-fields, he saw
> A solitary cell;
> And the devil was pleased, for it gave him a hint
> For improving his prisons in hell."—*The Devil's Walk.*

In 1820 the Cato-street conspirators were lodged here before being sent to the Tower. The prison uniform is coarse woollen blue cloth for misdemeanants, and dark grey for felons: each prisoner is known only by the number on his back; and a star upon the arm denotes good conduct. The workshop is an interesting scene; but the oakum-picking-room, with its 400 felon faces, is a painful sight; and the tread-wheel, employing 320 prisoners at a time, is another repulsive feature. Carpenters, tinmen, blacksmiths, and other handicraftsmen work here; and in the ground is the upper part of a vessel, with masts and rigging, for teaching boys the sea-service; there are also schools and reformatory visits. (See Dixon's *London Prisons*, 1850.)

FLEET PRISON is described at pp. 300-303.

GILTSPUR-STREET COMPTER is also the City House of Correction: it was built by George Dance, in 1791, to supersede the wretched prison in Wood-street, whence the prisoners were removed in 1791: it was then only used for debtors, but subsequently for remands and committals for trial, and minor offenders. The rear of the prison abuts on Christ's Hospital, and its towers are visible from the yard: the happy shouts of the boys at play are heard by the prisoners, and the balls often fall within the prison-yards, as if to remind the fallen inmates how much innocence they had outlived! In 1808 Sheriff Phillips described Giltspur-street, with its corner, entitled "Ludgate," (for citizen debtors, clergymen, proctors, and attorneys,) and the whole prison, as greatly overcrowded by the removal to it of the Poultry Compter debtors. The solitary confinement was in front of the building, where, however, the prisoners could see the busy street, and the crowds to witness executions in front of Newgate. About 6000 prisoners were annually committed to Giltspur-street; but it was one of the worst managed and least secure of the metropolitan prisons, and the escapes from it have been the most frequent. As a proof of the lenity of its management, it is related that, on the death of Mr. Teague, the humane governor of Giltspur-street Compter, in 1841, nearly every prisoner wore a black crape hat-band!

HORSEMONGER-LANE GAOL, on the south side of Newington Causeway, was built upon the plan of John Howard, in 1791-9 (George Gwilt, architect), upon the site of a market-garden. It is a common gaol for the county of Surrey, under the Sheriff, Court of Quarter Sessions, and Magistrates, and is for debtors and criminals.

Among the several benefactions enjoyed by the debtors is a donation made to the old White Lion Prison, in Southwark (mentioned by Stow), by Mrs. Margaret Symcott, or Eleanor Gwyn, of 65 penny loaves every eight weeks, issuing from the Chamberlain's Office.

The employments are knitting, netting, oakum-picking, lime-washing, and cleansing the gaol: it will contain about 400 prisoners.

Upon the roof of the north lodge were executed, on Feb. 21, 1803, Colonel Edward Marcus Despard and six associates, who had been tried and found guilty, by a special commission, of high treason; Richard Patch for murder, April 8, 1806; and Nov. 13, 1849, the Mannings, husband and wife, for murder. Leigh Hunt was imprisoned here for a libel on the Prince Regent, in 1813; and here he was first introduced to Lord Byron. (See Leigh Hunt's *Autobiography*, vol. ii.) In June 1849 three burglars escaped from their cells in this prison by means of a key which they made from a pewter pot; but they were recaptured in scaling the 20-feet wall.

LUDGATE PRISON is described at page 476.

MARSHALSEA PRISON, "so called as pertaining to the Marshalles of England" (*Stow*), stood in High-street, Southwark. Here were confined persons guilty of piracies and other offences on the high seas. (See page 451.) In 1377 it was broken into by a mob of sailors, who murdered a gentleman confined in it for killing one of their comrades, but who had been pardoned. During the rebellion of Wat Tyler, in 1381, the marshal of this prison, and the governor of the King's Bench, Sir John Imworth, was seized and beheaded.

"To the Marshalsea Bishop Bonner was sent, on losing his see of London for adherence to Rome. A man meeting him, cried, 'Good morrow, bishop quondam;' to which Bonner replied, 'Farewell, knave semper.' He lived ten years in the Marshalsea, and died there Sept. 5, 1569; he was buried at midnight, with other prisoners, in St. George's, Southwark. In the reigns of Henry VIII., Mary, and Elizabeth, the Marshalsea was the second prison in importance in London, being inferior only to the Tower. Christopher Brooke, the poet, was confined in the Marshalsea for being concerned in the wedding of Dr. Donne. George Wither was committed here for writing the satire, *Abuses Stript and Whipt;* but he procured his release by his *Satire to the King.*"—Dixon, *London Prisons*, abridged.

The Marshalsea escaped the riots of 1780. The old prison occupied the site of the house, No. 119 High-street; it was then removed to other premises nearer St. George's Church; and these were taken down in 1842, when the prisoners were drafted to the Queen's Bench.

Tymms (*Family Topographer*, 1832) describes "the inside of the palace court very elegant."

In the Southwark prisons were confined the Nonconformist confessors. In the Marshalsea died John Udall, the Puritan martyr; and in the Queen's Bench John Penry wrote his last affecting letters. Barrowe and Greenwood, Francis Johnson and Henry Jacob, were imprisoned in the Clink.

MIDDLESEX HOUSE OF DETENTION (the), Clerkenwell, was constructed, in 1846, for the reception of prisoners before trial, the accused only; and was the first built upon that plan in England, modified from the separate system at Pentonville. There are 286 cells.

MILLBANK PRISON, Westminster, near the foot of Vauxhall Bridge, is the largest penal establishment in England. The site was purchased, in 1799, of the Marquis of Salisbury, for 12,000*l.*; but the building was not commenced until 1812, when a contract was entered into by the Government with Jeremy Bentham; and the edifice is a modification of his "Panopticon, or Inspection House." It was next changed into a regular Government prison for criminals, adult and juvenile, and became the general depôt for transports waiting to be drafted to other prisons, or placed on shipboard for dockyard labour; and here are sent the most reckless and hardened criminals from all parts of the country. The soil of the site is a deep peat, and the buildings are laid on a solid and expensive concrete; but the situation is low and unhealthy. The prison cost half a million of money, or about 500*l.* for each cell! The only entrance is in the Thames' front. The ground-plan consists of six pentagonal buildings, radiating from a circle, wherein is the governor's house; and each line terminates in a tower in the outer octagonal wall, which incloses about 16 acres; 7 covered with buildings, including 12 chapels and airing-yards, and 9 laid out as gardens. The corridors are upwards of 3 miles long; there are about 1550 cells; and from 4000 to 5000 persons pass through the prison yearly. There are 40 staircases, making in all 3 miles distance. In 1843 the name of the Penitentiary was changed, by Act of Parliament, to the Millbank Prison. From the general resemblance of its conical-roofed towers to those of the Bastile du Temple at Paris, as well as from the severity of its system, the Penitentiary has been stigmatised as "the English Bastile."

"The dark cells, 20 steps below the ground-floor, are small, ill-ventilated, and doubly barred; and no glimpse of day ever enters this fearful place, where the offender is locked up for three days, fed upon bread and water, and has only a board to sleep on."—*Dixon.*

NEWGATE, on the east side of the Old Bailey, is now used as a gaol of detention for persons about to be tried at the adjacent Central Criminal Court; here are also confined prisoners convicted of assaults or offences on the high seas, and those who are under sentence of death. Until 1815, when Whitecross-street prison was built, Newgate was used for debtors as well as felons: hence its "Debtors' Door."

Sheriff Hoare, 1740-1, tells us how the names of the prisoners in each gaol were read over to him and his colleague; the keepers acknowledged them, one by one, to be in their custody; and then tendered the keys, which were delivered back to them again; and after having executed the indentures, the Sheriffs partook of sack and walnuts, provided by the keepers of the prison, at a tavern adjoining Guildhall. Formerly the Sheriffs attended the Lord Mayor, on Easter-eve, "through the streets, to collect charity for the prisoners in the City prisons."

Old Newgate prison was over and about the City gate "so called, as built after the four principal gates were reckoned old." It was merely a tower or appendage to the gate, which stretched across the west end of Newgate-street; still, from the time of King John to that of Charles II., it was sufficient prison-room for the city and county. It was originally "Chamberlain Gate," and was rebuilt by the executors of Sir Richard Whittington, whose statue, with the traditional cat, was placed in a niche upon the wall. Here were also statues of Concord, Mercy, Justice and Truth, Peace and Plenty, &c.

"In the Beaufoy Collection, at Guildhall, is a Newgate Prison Token, No. 715. *Obv.* Belonging to ye cellor on the masters side at —— 1669. *Rev.* Newgate—View of Newgate and the Debtors' Prison. This token was struck as a monetary medium among the prisoners, and is of the utmost rarity and interest, from the delineation of the prison it affords."—Burn's *Descriptive Catalogue*, page 138.

Newgate was restored by Wren in 1672, after the Great Fire; but it was burnt to the ground in the riots of 1780, when the rioters stole the keys, which were found some time after in the basin of water in St. James'-square. Dr. Johnson and Dr. Scott (Lord Stowell) saw Newgate in ruins, "with the fire yet glowing:" the iron bars were eaten through, and the stones vitrified by the intense heat.

Maitland describes the prisoners crowded together in dark dungeons, where the foul air caused the "gaol distemper," of which they died by dozens in a day; and in 1750 the effluvia created a pestilence in the Sessions House, by which sixty persons died. (See OLD BAILEY, page 556.) The prison was then cleansed, and a ventilating machine, with sails like a windmill, was placed on the roof.

Memorable Imprisonments.—Newgate was used as a state-prison long before the Tower. Robert Baldock, chancellor to Edward III., died here. Here were imprisoned John Bradford, of Manchester, the friend of Ridley; the intrepid John Rough; John Field and Thomas Wilcox, in 1572, for writing the celebrated *Admonition to Parliament for the Reformation of Church Discipline;* and here, in prison, they maintained the Whitgift controversy. Dr. Leighton (ten years), for writing his *Appeal to Parliament.* George Wither, the poet, for writing the *Vox Vulgi.* George Sackville, poet, rake, and Earl of Dorset, occupied a cell in Newgate. In 1672, Penn, the founder of Pennsylvania, was confined here six months, for street-preaching; Titus Oates and Dangerfield were sent here, and Dangerfield died in the prison. At the Revolution, Bishops Ellis and Leyburn were confined here, and were visited by Burnet. Defoe was committed to Newgate for writing his *Shortest Way with Dissenters;* and here he wrote *An Ode to the Pillory,* and commenced his *Review.* Major Bernardi, suspected of plotting with Rookwood against King William, died in Newgate, after seven years' confinement. Richard Akerman, Boswell's friend, was gaoler. (Abridged from Dixon on the *London Prisons.*) Dr. Dodd, while imprisoned here, finished a comedy (*Sir Roger de Coverley*): and after conviction, wrote his *Prison Thoughts.* Jack Sheppard escaped from "the Castle in Newgate;" and from "the Middle Stone Room," after his being retaken in Drury-lane. His portrait was painted in the prison by Sir James Thornhill. The *Beggar's Opera* was first called *A Newgate Pastoral.* The Trials are reported in the *Newgate Calendar;* and in the *Annals of Newgate,* by the Rev. Mr. Villette, Ordinary.

The present "prison of Newgate" was designed, in 1770, by George Dance, R.A., and is one of his finest works: the architecture bespeaks the purposes of the structure, and its solidity and security at once impress the spectator. The first stone was laid, 23d May, 1770, by Lord Mayor Beckford, this being his last public act. John Howard objected to the plan, but was overruled. While yet unfinished, in 1780, Newgate was attacked by Lord George Gordon's rioters, who broke open the doors of the tenanted portion, and set 300 prisoners at large; they then set fire to the building, which was reduced to a shell: it was repaired and completed in 1782. The plan consists of a centre (the keeper's house); two lodges, stamped with gloomy grandeur and severity; and two wings of yards right and left, but not suited for the classification or reformation of the prisoners. The façades are 297 feet and 115 feet long, and are externally a good specimen of prison architecture. The outer walls are three feet thick. Early in the present century nearly 800 prisoners were confined here at one time, when a contagious fever raged. In 1808, Sheriff Phillips states, the women in Newgate usually numbered from 100 to 130; and each had only 18 inches breadth of sleeping-room, packed like slaves in the hold of a slave-ship! Mrs. Fry describes them as "swearing, gaming, fighting, singing, dancing, drinking, and dressing up in men's clothes;" and in 1838, gambling, card-playing, and draughts were common among the male prisoners. The chapel has galleries for the male and female prisoners: below, and in the centre of the floor, is placed a chair for the condemned culprit; but the public are no longer admitted to hear the "condemned sermons" on Sundays before executions: the criminal's coffin was also placed at his feet during the service! Formerly 60 persons have been seen on one Sunday in "the condemned pew," the woodwork of which was cut with the name of many a hardened wretch.

In the lower room, on the south side of the prison, died Lord George Gordon, of the gaol distemper, after several years' imprisonment, for libelling the Queen of France. The culprit in the furthest cell on the ground-floor is within a yard of the busy passers-by in the street. In the hall is a collection of ropes; also casts taken from the heads of the principal criminals who have been executed in the front of the prison.

The kitchen was formerly the hall in which debtors were received; it opens by "the Debtors' Door," through which criminals pass to the scaffold in the street, a passage being made through the kitchen by black curtains. The place of execution was changed to this spot in December 1783, at the suggestion of John Howard.

Within the walls is a cemetery, where, since 1820, have been buried the bodies of executed criminals: the first deposited there were Thistlewood and the other Cato-street conspirators. The bodies are buried, without service, at eight in the evening of the day of their execution, and at each grave is a tall stone with the rudely-inscribed name.

The Press-yard, between Newgate and the Old Bailey Courts, is described at page 556. It was formerly customary for the Lord Mayor and Sheriffs, when proceeding to proclaim Bartholomew Fair, on Sept. 2, to stop at Newgate, and drink "a cool tankard" to the health of the Governor of Newgate; but this practice was discontinued in the second mayoralty of Alderman Wood, in 1821. Two watchmen are stationed on the roof of the prison during the night.

One of the last persons confined in Newgate for a political offence was Mr. Hobhouse (now Lord Broughton), for publishing his pamphlet, *The Trifling Mistake;* when Lord Byron's prediction, that Hobhouse "having foamed himself into a reformer, he would subside into Newgate," literally came to pass: and great was the enthusiasm of the people in the street at seeing Mr. Hobhouse's hat above the prison parapet, as he walked upon the roof for exercise!

The cost of maintaining the prisoners in Newgate is 37*l.* a-head annually. The old associated system is pursued here; the silent system at Millbank, in Coldbath-fields, and Tothill-fields; and the separate system at Pentonville, Millbank, and the House of Detention; yet Newgate has the advantage, as seven out of eight of its prisoners never return to it. Nevertheless, says an official authority:

"Newgate prison is a complete quarry of stone, without any order or possibility of order in it. There are a vast number of rooms in it, over which there is no inspection whatever; and nothing as a prison can remedy it. It has a most imposing exterior, which is perhaps its greatest use as a deterrer from crime, and the worst possible interior."—Captain Williams, Prisons Inspector.

PENTONVILLE PRISON, in the road from the foot of Pentonville-hill to Holloway, and over against Barnsbury, was commenced April 10, 1840, and completed in 1842, at a cost of nearly 100,000*l.*, upon the plan of Lieut.-Col. Jebb, R.E. The area within the lofty walls is 6¾ acres, besides a curtain-wall, with massive posterns in front, where is a frowning entrance-gateway, its arched heads filled with portcullis-work:

and from the main building rises a lofty Italian clock-tower. From the inspection or central hall radiate five wings or galleries, on the sides of four of which are the 520 cells, in three stories.

Each cell is 13½ feet long by 7½ feet broad, and 9 feet high: it has an iron water-closet, pail, and wash-basin supplied with water; a three-legged stool, table, and shaded gas-burner, and a slung hammock, with mattress and blankets; in the door is an eyelet hole, that the officer may inspect from outside; and the meals are conveyed through a spring trap-door.

The heating is from stoves in the basement; and the ventilation is by an immense shaft from the roof of each wing. The chapel is fitted up with separate stalls or sittings for the prisoners, of whom the officers have the entire surveillance. The organ is by Gray. The exercising-yards, between and in front of the wings, are radiated, so that an officer may watch the prisoners, each in a walled yard. The discipline is the separate system and the silent system modified; and here were formerly sent convicts for probation, prior to transportation to the penal colonies, the plan being an adaptation from the Philadelphian system. Each cell cost 180l.; victualling and management nearly 36l. a-head; and the prisoners' labour is unproductive. The building was first named "the Model Prison," as the plan was proposed for the several gaols in the kingdom; but, from its partial success, the name has been changed to the Pentonville Prison, although it is in the parish of Islington.

POULTRY COMPTER (the) is described at page 628.

QUEEN'S PRISON, Southwark, formerly the Queen's Bench and King's Bench, was situated here in the reign of Richard II., when the Kentish rebels, under Wat Tyler, "brake down the houses of the Marshalsey and King's Bench, in Southwarke." (*Stow.*) To this prison the Prince of Wales, afterwards Henry V., was committed by Chief Justice Gascoigne, for endeavouring to rescue a convicted prisoner, one of his personal attendants (Stow's *Chronicle*); and the room in which he was confined was known as the Prince of Wales's Chamber down to the time of Oldys. In 1579 the prisoners daily dined and supped in a little low parlour adjoining the street. In this year, through "the sickness of the house," the prisoners petitioned the Queen's Privy Council for the enlargement of the prison and the erection of a chapel. During the Commonwealth it was called the Upper Bench Prison. Rushworth, author of the *Historical Collection*, was confined here for six years; and Baxter, the Nonconformist, was imprisoned here eighteen months, under a sentence passed by the infamous Judge Jefferies. The original King's Bench was built on the east side of the High-street, on the site of Layton's-buildings, adjoining the Marshalsea and White Lion prisons. Defoe describes the prison-house "not near so good as the Fleet." The present prison is situated at the lower end of the Borough-road: Wilkes was one of the early prisoners here; and the building was set on fire, and the prisoners were liberated, by the mob in the riots of 1780. (See ST. GEORGE'S FIELDS, p. 327.) By the Act 5 Victoria, c. 22, the Queen's Bench, Fleet, and Marshalsea were consolidated as the Queen's Prison, for debtors, prisoners committed for libel, assault, courts-martial, &c., under the control of the Home Secretary of State. The dietary and other expenses, 1500l. a-year, are paid by the Welsh and English counties.

The prison is inclosed by a wall 35 feet high, surmounted by *chevaux-de-frise*: it contains 224 rooms and a chapel. The wall is well adapted for rackets, much played here. Defoe said, "to a man who had money, the Bench was only the name of a prison;" but the present classification of the prisoners has abated its license and riotous living.

In the King's Bench died John Tull, the inventor of post-chaises. Lord Cochrane was imprisoned here, in 1815, for his Stock Exchange affair; he escaped, and went immediately to the House of Commons, whence the Marshal conducted him back to prison. A printer's joiner constructed here a working model of a printing-machine about 1817. Haydon painted his "Mock Election" and "Chairing Members" from a burlesque election in the prison when he was confined there; and thence he petitioned Government, and trumpeted his own distresses. (See Haydon's *Autobiography*.) The King's Bench has been called "Tenterden Priory," after Lord Chief-Justice Tenterden; and its motley life is the staple of *Scenes and Stories of a Clergyman in Debt*, by F. W. N. Bayley.

The Rules (privileges for prisoners to live within three miles round the prison, and to go out on "day-rules") are said to have been first granted in time of plague. For these rules large sums were paid to the Marshal, who, in 1813, received 2823*l.* from the rules and "liberty tickets," and 872*l.* from the sale of beer! These malversations are now abolished. Kit Smart, the translator of Horace, died within the rules; here Smollet wrote his *Sir Launcelot Greaves*, and William Combe his *Dr. Syntax*. Shadwell, in his comedy of *Epsom Wells*, 1676, says the rules extend to the East Indies; which Lord Ellenborough quoted when he was applied to to extend the rules.

Public Advertiser, Oct. 4, 1764: "A gentleman, a prisoner in the rules of the King's Bench, a branch of the family of the Hydes, Earls of Clarendon and Rochester, has a most remarkable coffin by him, against his interment. It was made out of a fine solid oak which grew on his estate in Kent, and hollowed out with a chisel. The said gentleman often lies down and sleeps in his coffin, with the greatest composure and serenity." Oct. 6 it was added: the coffin "weighs 500 lbs., and was not long since filled with punch, when it held 41 gallons 2 quarts 1½ pint."

TOTHILL-FIELDS' BRIDEWELL was first built, in 1618, as a house of correction, adjoining the east end of Green-coat Hospital.

"Over the gate is this inscription: 'Here is several sorts of work for the poor of this parish of St. Margaret's, Westminster; as also correction according to law for such as will beg and live idly in this City of Westminster. Anno 1655.'"—*Hatton*.

In the reign of Queen Anne it was converted into a gaol for criminals. "Howard describes it as being remarkably well managed in his day; and holds up its enlightened and careful keeper, one George Smith, as a model to other governors." (Dixon's *London Prisons*.) Here Colonel Despard, the traitor, was imprisoned in 1803.

Upon a site adjoining was commenced, in 1830, the erection of a new prison, from the design of Robert Abraham: it was first occupied in June 1834, when the old Bridewell was deserted and taken down, and the stone bearing the above inscription was built into the present garden-wall. The new prison, seen from Victoria-street, resembles a substantial fortress: the entrance-porch, on the Vauxhall side, is formed of massive granite blocks, iron gates, portcullis, &c. It is built on the panopticon plan, and contains a gaol for untried male prisoners, a house of correction for male convicts, and a prison for women; 8 wards, 2 schools, and 8 airing-yards; 42 day-rooms and 348 sleeping-apartments; besides 120 dark cells in the basement, all ranged round a well-kept garden; while in front is the governor's house, over which is built the chapel; these forming the keep-like mass which is seen from Pimlico and Piccadilly, and is one of the finest specimens of brickwork in the metropolis. The prison will hold upwards of 800 prisoners: the only labour is oakum-picking and the tread-wheel.

SAVOY PRISON, the west end of the ancient Palace of the Savoy, on the south side of the Strand, was used as a military prison for deserters, impressed men, convict soldiers, and offenders from the Guards: at one period their allowance was only fourpence a-day. The gateway bore the arms of Henry VII., and the badges of the rose, fleur-de-lis, and portcullis. The premises were taken down in 1819, to form the approach to Waterloo Bridge, after which deserters were imprisoned on board a vessel moored off Somerset House; but the Savoy may be said to have been first used as a prison when John King of France was confined here after the battle of Poictiers, in 1356.

TOWER (the), used as a state-prison from about 1457 to our own time, is described with the general history of that palace, prison, arsenal, and fortress.

WESTMINSTER GATEHOUSE (the), used as a prison for state, ecclesiastical, and parliamentary offenders, as well as for debtors and felons, is described at page 325.

WHITECROSS-STREET, Cripplegate, is entirely a debtors' prison: the first stone was laid by Alderman Matthew Wood, in July 1813, and the building was completed in 1815. It will hold 500 persons, and is divided into six wards—Middlesex, Poultry and Giltspur-street, Ludgate, Dietary, Remand, and Female Wards,—the inmates of which have no intercommunication. A part is also set aside for commitments under the Small Debts Act. Here are no private apartments, but a modern instance of the wise saw, " Misery acquaints a man with strange bedfellows." Opposite the Debtors' Door, in Whitecross-street, is the City Green-yard, established in 1771: here is kept the Lord Mayor's State-Coach, to be seen for a trifling gratuity.

QUEENHITHE,

Upper Thames-street, was originally the *hithe* (wharf or landing-place) of Edred the Saxon, and thence called Edred's-hithe; but falling into the hands of King Stephen, it was given by him to Will. de Ypre, who gave it to the Convent of the Holy Trinity within Aldgate: however, it came again to the crown, and it is said to have been given by King John to his mother, Eleanor, queen of Henry II.; whence it was called *Ripa Reginæ*, the queen's bank, or queen's hithe, it being a portion of her majesty's dowry. It is described by Stow as "the very chief and principal watergate of this city," " equal with, and of old time far exceeding, Belinsgate." In the reign of Henry III., ships and boats laden with corn and fish for sale were compelled to pass *beyond* London Bridge, "to the Queen's-hithe only," a drawbridge being pulled up to admit the passage of large vessels. In 1463, the market at Queenhithe was " hindered by reason of the slackness of drawing up London Bridge." Stow enumerates the customs and dues exacted from the ships and boats, and specifies " salt, wheat, rye, or other corn, from beyond the seas; or other grains, garlic, onions, herrings, sprats, eels, whiting, plaice, cods, mackarel, &c.:" but corn was the principal trade, whence the quay was sometimes called *Cornhithe*. Stow describes here a cornmill placed between two barges or lighters, which " ground corn, as water-mills in other places, to the wonder of many that had not seen the like." The charge of Queenhithe was subsequently delivered to the sheriffs; but Fabian states, that in his time it was not worth above 20 marks a year. Its trade in fish must, however, have been considerable when Old Fish-street northward was the great fish-market of London, before Billingsgate, in 1699, became " a free and open market." Beaumont and Fletcher speak of "a Queenhithe cold;" and the locality is often mentioned by our old dramatists. It is now frequented by West-country barges laden with corn and flour; the adjoining warehouses, with high-pitched gables, were built long since for stowage of corn; and the opposite church of St. Michael, with its vane in the form of a ship, the hull of which will contain a bushel of grain, is emblematic of the olden traffic in corn at the Hithe.

Tom Hill was originally a drysalter at Queenhithe; and here he assembled a fine library, described by Southey as one of the most copious collections of English poetry in existence: it was valued at 6000*l.* when, through a ruinous speculation in indigo, Hill retired upon the remains of his property to the Adelphi. (See page 1.) Hill was the patron of the almost friendless poets, Bloomfield and Kirke White.

At Queenhithe, No. 17, lived Alderman Venables, lord mayor 1826-7; at Nos. 20-21, Alderman Hooper, lord mayor 1847-8.

Queenhithe gives name to the ward, wherein were seven churches in Stow's time. Westward is *Broken Wharf*, "so called of being broken and fallen down into the Thames." Here was the mansion of the Bigods and Mowbrays, Earls and Dukes of Norfolk; and sold in 1540 to Sir Richard Gresham, father of Sir Thomas Gresham. Within the gate of this house was built, in 1594-5, an engine, by Bevis Bulmer, for supplying the middle and west of the City with Thames water.

In 1809 or 1810 was found in the bed of the river, opposite Queenhithe, a massive silver seal, with a motto denoting it to have been the official seal of the Port of London, *temp.* Edward I. It is engraved with Laing's Plan of the Custom House.

RAILWAY TERMINI.

London is girdled with Railways, except at the south-western corner; but few of the termini present grand or noticeable features.

BLACKWALL, Fenchurch-street, to the Brunswick Wharf, Blackwall, 3¾ miles, saves four miles by the river, besides the difficulty of navigating the Pool. The line of railway is carried nearly throughout on an arched viaduct of brickwork. Originally the carriages were drawn by stationary engines, two at each end of the line; which, by means of ropes, dragged the up and down trains alternately. This mode of working (by George Stephenson and G. R. Bidder) was ridiculed in Parliament as visionary and impracticable: the rope cost upwards of 1200*l.*, and the stationary engines 30,000*l.* each; but locomotive engines are now used. The terminus at Brunswick Wharf, Blackwall, is an elegant design, by W. Tite, F.R.S.

EAST AND WEST INDIA DOCKS AND BIRMINGHAM JUNCTION RAILWAY extends from the Camden Depôt, through Islington, Kingsland, Hackney, Old Ford, and Bow, to the Stepney station of the Blackwall Railway, traversing the north and north-eastern suburbs, and connecting the North-Western line with the Thames.

EASTERN AND NORTH-EASTERN COUNTIES, Shoreditch.—This line is carried upon arches through Spitalfields and Bethnal-Green.

GREAT NORTHERN, King's Cross.—This terminus occupies 45 acres of land. For the site of the Passenger Station, the Small-pox Hospital and Fever Hospital were cleared away. The front towards Pancras-road has two main arches, each 71 feet span, separated by a clock-tower 120 feet high; the clock has dials 9 feet in diameter, and the principal bell weighs 29 cwt. Each shed is 800 feet long, 105 feet wide, and 71 feet high to the crown of the semicircular roof, without a tie; the roof is formed of laminated ribs 20 feet apart, and of inch-and-a-half planks screwed to each other. The granary has six stories, and will hold 60,000 sacks of corn; on the last story are water-tanks, holding 150,000 gallons; and the grain is hoisted by hydraulic apparatus. The Goods Shed is 600 feet in length, and 80 feet wide; and the roof is glazed with cast-glass in sheets, 8 feet by 2 feet 6 inches. Under the goods platform is stabling for 300 horses. The shed adjoins the Regent's Canal, which, from thence, enters the Thames at Limehouse. The coal stores will contain 15,200 tons. The buildings are by Lewis and Joseph Cubitt. The railway passes under the Regent's Canal and Maiden-lane, beneath Copenhagen-fields, over the Holloway-road, through tunnels at Hornsey and elsewhere, and over a viaduct at Welwyn, with 42 arches, 30 feet wide and 97 feet high.

GREAT WESTERN, Paddington.—This terminus is close to and below the level of the terminal wharf of the Grand Junction Canal. The design is by Mr. Brunel, engineer to the Company; and adjoining is a magnificent hotel, in the style of Louis XIV., by P. Hardwick, R.A. The façade has two lofty towers with cupolas; four colossal termini support the balcony; and the large central pediment is filled with allegorical figures by John Thomas. The coffee-room, 2 stories in height, is enriched with columns, terminal figures, and a deeply-coffered ceiling.

NORTH-WESTERN. — This terminus, for passengers at Euston-square, and for goods at Camden Town, cost 800,000*l.* The Euston terminus, by P. Hardwick, R.A., occupies 12 acres. The *Propylæum*, or architectural gateway, is pure Grecian-Doric; its length exceeds 300 feet; its cost was 35,000*l.*; and it contains 80,000 cubic feet of Bramley Fall stone. The columns are higher than those of any other building in London, and measure 44 feet 2 inches, and 8 feet 6 inches diameter at the base, or only 3 feet 1 inch less than that of the York column. The height, to the summit of the acroterium, is 72 feet; a winding staircase in one angle leads to an apartment within the roof, used as the Company's printing-office; the rich bronze gates are by Bramah.

This propylæum is unprecedented in our modern Greek architecture, and "exhibits itself to most advantage when viewed obliquely, so as to show its line of roof and depth, especially as the cornice is of unusually bold and new design, being not only ornamented with projecting lion-heads, but crowned by a series of deep antefixæ; while, when beheld from a greater distance, the large stone slabs are also seen that cover the roof."—*Companion to the Almanac*, 1839.

The paved platforms within the gateway contain nearly 16,000 superficial feet of Yorkshire stone, some of the stones being from 70 to 80 square feet each; and each shaft of the granite Doric colonnade, 200 feet long, is a single stone. The Great Hall, designed by P. C. Hardwick, is in length 125 feet 6 inches, width 61 feet 4 inches, and height 60 feet; or very nearly two cubes. The ceiling is paneled, deeply recessed, and fully enriched, and is connected with the walls by large ornamented consoles. The walls are splashed as granite; and the Ionic columns are painted like red granite, with white caps and bases. The sculpture, by John Thomas, are a group, Britannia supported by Science and Industry; and beneath the ceiling, 8 panels in *alto-relievo*, symbolic figures of London, Birmingham, Manchester, Chester, Northampton, Carlisle, Lancaster, and Liverpool. The hall is warmed by some miles of hot-water pipes, on Perkins's system. Here was placed, April 10, 1854, Baily's colossal marble statue of George Stephenson, the originator of the railway system: this statue was purchased by the subscriptions of 3150 working-men, at 2*s.*; and 178 private friends, at 14*l.* each. The trains are received and dispatched beneath a vast shed, which has 8979 square yards of plate-glass in the skylights only. The trains are drawn up to the Camden-Town Depôt by an endless rope, 3744 yards long, and 7 inches in circumference; weight 235 cwt.; cost 480*l.* The Goods Station, engine-houses, shops for repairs, and coke-ovens (yielding 360 tons per day), are upon a vast scale; the Passenger-train locomotive sheds are 400 feet long, by 90 feet span. Pickford's goods and parcels shed* is 300 feet by 217 feet, and allows the movement of 850 tons per day by steam-machinery, which also raises water from a well in the chalk 350 feet deep. One of the engine-houses covers nearly three-quarters of an acre; the Camden-Town Depôt upwards of 30 acres, and its two chimney-shafts are each 132 feet high. In 1851, the traffic receipts of this railway for 22 weeks (Great Exhibition) were 1,314,482*l*.

SOUTH-EASTERN (the), Duke-street, Southwark side of London Bridge; provides for the Greenwich, Croydon, Brighton, Dover, South-Coast, and North-Kent lines. The Greenwich Railway, opened Dec. 14, 1836, was the first completed line from the metropolis: the rails are laid upon upwards of 1000 arches, in building which more than 70 millions of bricks were used. The line was projected by Lieut.-Col. Landmann, who became the engineer-in-chief.

The Croydon Railway presents a remarkable adaptation of one great improvement to the purposes of another; the Company having purchased the Croydon Canal (nine miles from the Thames at Deptford to Croydon), and in its bed laid the rails for a considerable distance.

SOUTH-WESTERN RAILWAY, Waterloo-Bridge-road. (See p. 441.)

THAMES JUNCTION RAILWAY (the) has a most remarkable work at Wormwood Scrubbs, where a tunnel passes under the Paddington Canal at the point where it is crossed by an iron suspension-bridge; thereby affording three different kinds of traffic, one above the other, at as many different levels.

RANELAGH,

A public garden, opened in 1742, on the site of the gardens of Ranelagh House, eastward of Chelsea Hospital; and originally projected by Lacy, the patentee of Drury-lane Theatre, as a sort of winter Vauxhall. The Rotunda, 185 feet in diameter, had a Doric portico, an arcade, and gallery outside. There was also a Venetian pavilion in the centre of a lake, upon which the company were rowed in boats; and a print of 1751 shows the grounds planted with trees and *allées verts*. The several buildings were designed by Capon, the eminent scene-painter. The interior was fitted with boxes for refreshments, and in each was a painting: in the centre was an ingenious heating apparatus, concealed by arches, porticoes and niches, paintings, &c.; and supporting the ceiling, which was decorated with celestial figures, festoons of flowers, and arabesques, and lighted by circles of chandeliers. The Rotunda was opened with a public breakfast, April 5, 1742. Walpole describes the high fashion of Ranelagh: "The prince, princess, duke, much nobility, and much mob besides, were there." "My Lord Chesterfield is so fond of it, that he says he has ordered all his letters to be directed thither." The admission was one shilling; but the ridottos, with supper and music, were one guinea. Concerts were also given here: Dr. Arne composed the music, Tenducci and Mara sang; and here were first publicly performed the compositions of the Catch Club. Fireworks and a mimic Etna were next introduced; and lastly masquerades, described in Fielding's *Amelia*, and satirised in the *Connoisseur*, No. 66, May 1, 1755; wherein the Sunday-evening's tea-drinkings at Ranelagh being laid aside, it is proposed to exhibit the story of the

* "More than 2000 parcels per day are booked at the North-Western Railway Station. In Christmas week, 5000 barrels of oysters have been sent off within 24 hours, each barrel containing 100 oysters=half a million."—Lardner's *Railway Economy*, p. 130.

T T

Fall of Man in a masquerade! Dr. Johnson said there was more of Ranelagh than of the Pantheon; or rather, indeed, the whole Rotunda appeared at once, and it was better lighted: "the *coup d'œil* was the finest thing he had ever seen."—Boswell's *Life*, vols ii. and iii.

But the promenade of the Rotunda to the music of the orchestra and organ soon declined: "There's your famous Ranelagh, that you make such a fuss about; why, what a dull place is that!" (Miss Burney's *Evelina*.) In 1802, the Installation Ball of the Knights of the Bath was given here; and the Pic-nic Society gave here a breakfast to 2000 persons, when Garnerin ascended in his balloon. Of the Peace Fête which took place here in 1803, and for which allegorical scenes were painted by Capon, Bloomfield sings in homely rhyme:

> "A thousand feet rustled on mats,
>   A carpet that once had been green;
> Men bow'd with their outlandish hats,
>   With corners so fearfully keen.
> Fair maids, who at home, in their haste,
>   Had left all clothing else but a train,
> Swept the floor clean, as slowly they pac'd,
>   And then—walk'd round and swept it again."

Ranelagh was now deserted, and in 1804 the buildings were taken down. In 1813, the foundation-walls of the Rotunda, the arches of some cellars, and the site of the orchestra, could be traced: part of the ground is now included in "the Old Men's Gardens" of Chelsea Hospital; and the name is attached to the Sewers District, and to a long street leading from Pimlico to the site of Ranelagh.

Ranelagh House was built about 1691, by Jones, first Earl of Ranelagh and third Viscount, who was a great favourite of Charles II. The ground was granted to the Earl by William III.; and the mansion is shown in a view of the Thames-bank painted by Canaletti in 1752.

In 1854, a large house built upon part of the site of Ranelagh, with some of its materials, and another mansion, Clarence House, were cleared away, to form the new road from Sloane-street to the Suspension-bridge and Battersea Park.

RECORDS, PUBLIC.

"The Records of this country have no equal in the civilised world, in antiquity, continuity, variety, extent, or amplitude of facts and details. From Domesday they contain the whole materials for the history of this country, civil, religious, political, social, moral, or material, from the Norman Conquest to the present day. (Of the decisions of the Law Courts a series is extant from the beginning of the reign of Richard I.) With the Public Records are now united the State Papers and Government Archives, and by their aid may be written the real history of the Courts of Common Law and Equity; the statistics of the kingdom in revenue, expenditure, population, trade, commerce, or agriculture, can from the above sources be accurately investigated. The Admiralty documents are important to naval history; and others afford untouched mines of information relating to the private history of families."—*Sir Francis Palgrave, Deputy-keeper of the Records.*

They include the official Records of the Courts of Common Law, of Parliament, of Chancery, of the Admiralty, the Audit Office, the Registrar-General's Office, the Commissariat, the Treasury Books, the Customs' Books, the Privy Signet Office, the Welsh and County Palatinate Courts, &c. These were deposited in more than sixty places, until the passing of the Public Records Act, 1 & 2 Victoria, cap. 94, the great object of which was the consolidation of all the Records in one depository; which is about to be attained by the erection of a building, now in progress, on the Rolls Estate, between Fetter-lane and Chancery-lane. The architect is Mr. Pennethorne; and the plan is to provide sufficient space not merely for all the Records now in the custody of the Master of the Rolls, but for all such as may be expected to accrue for fifty years to come. The building is to consist of a north front and two wings; the three portions to contain 228 rooms, 200 of which would receive nearly half a million cubic feet of Records. The front, already completed, faces the north: the style is late Gothic, or Tudoresque, somewhat of German character; the outer walls are supported by massive buttresses, between which are the windows, which are Decorated. The materials are Kentish rag-stone, with dressings of Anstone-stone. The floors are formed with wrought-iron girders and flat brick arches, laid on the top with white Suffolk tiles. The sashes and door-frames are of metal, the doors of slate, the roof iron. The hall, entered from the south side of the building, has a panelled ceiling, formed in zinc and emblazoned. Two windows are provided for each room, which is fifteen feet high, divided by a gallery or iron floor: hence the windows are unusually lofty, to light both floors, and to throw the light twenty-five feet down the passages between the Records; accordingly the front is a mass of window. As in the same architect's Museum of Practical Geology, in Piccadilly, there is no entrance in the principal façade.

In the first consignment of documents to the New Repository were, among the papers of the Solicitor to the Treasury, the Solicitor's proceedings against Bishop Atterbury and others; with an important mass of papers respecting the Rebellion of 1745-6; and " very numerous documents relating to prosecutions brought by the Crown against authors or publishers of pamphlets or newspapers." The charge and superintendence of the Public Records is vested in the Master of the Rolls, to whose custody the accumulating Records above twenty years old are delivered. Searches may be made at any of the departments of the Record Office by payment of the fees, and extracts taken; but the Deputy-keeper is authorised to grant any *literary* inquirer permission to search, and make notes, extracts, or copies, in pencil, without payment of fees, on the Deputy-keeper being satisfied that the application is for a *bonâ fide* literary purpose. To show the value of this privilege to literary inquirers, it may be stated that in 1852 one applicant consulted nearly 7000 documents, principally at the Rolls Chapel, for compiling the history of a single township. A large portion of the Records consulted by literary inquirers is the Rolls of early date, deposited in the Stone Tower, adjoining Westminster Hall, which, being the most valuable of their class, are placed in that fireproof structure. Until their removal to the New Repository, Domesday Book, the Star-Chamber proceedings, Treaties, &c., will be kept at the Chapter-house, Westminster. The early Records of the Court of Chancery are deposited in the Tower—the later in the Rolls Chapel.* The Queen's Bench, Common Pleas, and Exchequer Records are kept at Carlton Ride.

See a short Directory for searching the Public Records in the metropolis, *Companion to the Almanack* for 1838. *A Handbook of the Public Records*, 1853. *A brief Account of National Records*, in an *Essay on Topographical Literature*, by John Britton, F.S.A. (only 50 copies). The Parliamentary Report of 1800 contains the best account of the contents of our Record Offices. See also the Deputy-keeper's Reports, and Regulations issued by the Master of the Rolls to the various offices.

* William Lambarde, the eminent lawyer and antiquary, was, in 1597, appointed Keeper of the Rolls and House of Rolls, in Chancery Lane; and in 1600, Keeper of the Records in the Tower.

REGENT-STREET,

1730 yards in length (30 yards less than a mile), was designed by John Nash, in 1813, and was named from his patron the Prince Regent; although in 1766 Gwynne had proposed a great street to lead nearly in the same line. It commences at *Waterloo-place*, opposite the site of Carlton House, and proceeds northward, crossing Piccadilly, by a Circus, to the County Fire-Office, designed by Abraham, with a rustic arcade, like that at Somerset House. The roadway is probably the finest specimen of macadamisation in the metropolis. On the *East* side are the *Junior United Service Club* (see p. 199); *Gallery of Illustration* (p. 253); the *Parthenon Club* (p. 196). On the *West* are *St. Philip's Chapel* (p. 171) and *Club Chambers* (p. 192).

At No. 5 Waterloo-place, in the collection of Thomas Walesby, in 1854, was George IV. and the Duke of Wellington on the Field of Waterloo, painted by B. R. Haydon; Gore House, Kensington, with portraits of the Duke of Wellington, Lady Blessington, Count D'Orsay (the painter of the picture), &c.; also, Sir Joshua Reynolds's sitters' chair, subsequently in the possession of Sir Thomas Lawrence and Sir M. A. Shee.

From the County Fire-Office, the street trends north-west by a quadrant, so as to avoid a commonplace elbow: it exhibits Nash's genius in overcoming difficulties, for by no other contrivance could this sweep of the street have been made so ornamental; its geometrical fitness can only be fully appreciated in the view from the balcony of the York Column. The *Quadrant* had originally two Doric colonnades, projecting the extent of the foot-pavement; the columns of cast-iron, from the Carron Foundry, each 16 feet 2 inches high, exclusive of the granite plinth, supported a balustraded roof. This was a most scenic piece of street-architecture; the continuous rows of columns swept in charming perspective, and the effect was very picturesque. The colonnades were removed in November 1848, and a balcony was added to the principal floor. The property has been much improved by this change; but the public unwillingly parted with the grand street ornamentation, which reminded one of a classic city of antiquity. The 270 columns were sold at 7*l.* 5*s.* and 7*l.* 10*s.* each.

No. 45, the junction of Regent Circus with the Quadrant, has a superb shop-front, designed, in 1839, by F. Hering, in the Revival style; with fluted Ionic columns, Italianised arches, enriched pediment-heads, spandrels, escocheons, cognisances, and panels; the ornaments being of composition laid upon wood. Each plate of glass in the windows, 140 inches by 82 inches, cost 160*l.*; the plate-glass in the façade and interior 1000*l.*; and the entire design nearly 4000*l.*

From the Quadrant the vista is very fine: the blocks or groups of houses are by Nash, Soane, Repton, Abraham, Decimus Burton, &c.

East—Archbishop Tenison's Chapel, between Nos. 172 and 174, is described at page 172. *Faubert's Passage*, between Nos. 206 and 208, is named from Monsieur or Major Faubert, who, in 1681, established here a riding-academy, on premises formerly the mansion of the Countess of Bristol. Evelyn, in his *Diary*, mentions that Faubert's project was recommended by the Council of the Royal Society.

"18th Dec. 1684.—I went with Lord Cornwallis to see the young gallants do their exercise, M. Faubert having newly railed in a menage, and fitted it for the academy. Here were the Dukes of Norfolk and Northumberland, Lord Newburgh, and a nephew of (Duras) Earle of Feversham. The exercises were 1. Running at the ring; 2. Flinging a javelin at a Moor's head; 3. Discharging a pistol at a mark; and lastly, taking up a gauntlet with the point of a sword all these perform'd in full speede."

When Swallow-street was removed, the riding-school premises, then livery-stables, were taken down, except one house. The *Argyll Rooms* built for musical entertainments, at the corner of Little Argyll-street, were destroyed by fire in 1830. (See page 19.)

West—Nos. 207 and 209, the *Cosmorama* (see p. 235). *Hanover Chapel*, built 1823, by Cockerell (see p. 169). The line crosses Oxford-street by *Regent Circus*, and extends thence to the tower and spire of *All Souls' Church* (see p. 116). The street then sweeps past the mansion and garden of Sir James Langham, to *Langham-place*, built upon part of the site of Foley House, which was bought by Nash, with the grounds, for 70,000*l.*

No. 309 Regent-street, the *Polytechnic Institution*, erected by Thompson in 1838, and enlarged in 1848, contains a Hall of Manufactures, with machines worked by steam-power, and several other apartments filled with models, &c.; Cosmoramic Rooms; and Theatres for lectures and optical exhibitions. The Catalogue comprises upwards of 2000 articles. *The Diving-Bell* is the paramount attraction: it is of cast-iron, and weighs 3 tons; 5 feet in height, and 4 feet 8 inches in diameter at the mouth. Within is affixed a knocker, under which is painted:

> " More air, knock once;
> Less air, knock twice;
> Pull up, knock three times."

The Bell is about one-third open at the bottom, has a seat all round for the divers, and is lit by 12 openings of thick plate-glass. It is suspended by a massive chain to a large swing-crane, with a powerful crab; the chain having compensation-weights, and working into a well beneath. The air is supplied from two powerful air-pumps, of 8-inch cylinder, conveyed by the leather hose to any depth: the divers being seated in the Bell, it is moved over the water, and directly let down within two feet of the bottom of the tank, and then drawn up; the whole occupying only two minutes and a half. The tank and the adjoining canals hold 10,000 gallons of water, and can, if requisite, be emptied in less than one minute! Each person pays a fee for the descent, which has produced 1000*l.* in one year. The cost of the Bell was about 400*l.*

Adjoining is a school in which Photography is taught; and in the rear of the premises, at No. 5 Cavendish-square, then the *St. George's Chess Club*, was played, 27th May, 1851, the Chess Tournament, by the first general meeting of players from different parts of the world; among whom were, Szen, Horwitz, Kieseritzky, Löwenthal, Staunton, and Anderssen.—See the Games, with notes, by H. Staunton.

Next the Polytechnic Institution is a Theatre for the exhibition of Dioramic Pictures. Opposite is No. 316, the *Portland Gallery*, where the National Institution of Fine Arts exhibits paintings annually.

ROMAN LONDON.

Although Londinium was in the power of Rome for more than 400 years, or nearly one-fourth of its existence in history, the aspect of Roman London is but matter of conjecture; and tesselated pavements, incised stones, and sepulchral urns, found upon its site, are but fragmentary evidences that *wherever the Roman conquers he inhabits*. London was, however, previously a settlement of some importance, and of British origin, as we read in Llyn-dun, the hill-fortress on the lake; or Llong-dinas, the city of ships, from its maritime character; whence the Roman designation, Londinium. It is not mentioned by Cæsar, though he entered the Thames; nor was it occupied as a Roman station so early as Colchester and Verulam. The Romans are supposed to have possessed themselves of London in the reign of Claudius, about 105 years after Cæsar's invasion. Londinium is first mentioned by Tacitus (*Ann.* xix. 33) as not then dignified with the name of a *colonia*, but still as a place much frequented by merchants, and as a great depôt of merchandise. It was subsequently made a *colonia* under the name of Augusta (*Amm. Marcell.* xxvii. 8).

The Romans found the place a narrow strip of firm ground lying between the great fen (Moorfields) almost parallel to the river. At right angles to both ran the Walbrook, and on the east the Langbourne; habitations ranged closely from Finsbury to Dowgate, whence to the Tower, villas studded the bank of the Thames. The finding of sepulchral remains outside these natural boundaries proves the Romans to have there had their burial-grounds, as it was their custom always to inter their dead without their cities. That Southwark, on the opposite bank of the Thames, was also a Roman settlement, is proved by relics of the reign of Nero; outside which are likewise evidences of Roman interment.

London was inwalled A.D. 306 (see CITY WALL AND GATES, page 184). On the Thames bank, at distances of 58, 86, and 103 feet, within the range of the existing wharfs, have been found three several lines of wooden embankment, the work of the Romans, who thus reclaimed from the Thames the ground on which the present Custom House and the warehouses of Thames-street are built.

" Within the space of a century, towers belonging to the Roman wall of London were in existence; portions of the wall yet remain; and in the space which it bounded, many vestiges have, from time to time, exhibited tokens of nearly six centuries of Roman occupation."—Archer's *Vestiges of Old London.*

The main road through the City was the Watling-street, from the vicinity of the modern Ludgate, along the present Watling-street and Budge-row, to the Walbrook, which it crossed by a bridge at the junction of Cannon-street and Budge-row; and then branching off at London Stone, in Cannon-street, it ran along the Langbourne to Aldgate. Another road ran from the ferry at Dowgate (the principal Watergate) in the direction of Cripplegate.

" Roman London thus enlarged itself from the Thames towards Moorfields, and the line of wall east and south. The sepulchral deposits confirm its growth; others, at more remote distances, indicate subsequent enlargements; while interments discovered at Holborn, Finsbury, Whitechapel, and the extensive burial-places in Spitalfields and Goodman's-fields, denote that those localities were fixed on when Londinium, in process of time, had spread over the extensive space inclosed by the wall."—*C. R. Smith, F.S.A.*

After the Great Fire, the excavations brought to light much of the antiquarian wealth of " the Roman stratum" of tesselated pavements, foundations of buildings, and sculptural remains; coins, urns, pottery, and utensils, tools, and ornaments. Whenever excavations are made within the limits of the City of London, the workmen come to the floors of Roman houses at a depth of from 12 to 18 or 20 feet under the present level. (T. Wright, F.S.A. *The Celt, the Roman, and the Saxon*, p. 123.) These floors are often covered with fragments of the broken fresco paintings of the walls, of which Mr. Roach Smith has a large variety of patterns, such as foliage, animals, arabesque, &c.; and pieces of *window-glass* have often been found among these remains. —T. Wright, F.S.A., *Archæological Album.*

Collections of Roman Remains.—The Tradescant Museum, in 1656, contained only 6 Roman articles, besides coins: it was increased by Ashmole; and as it was not removed to Oxford until 1682, he probably added many specimens of London antiquities discovered after the Great

Fire. From this time their importance became appreciated: one of the first collectors was John Conyers, an apothecary of Fleet-street, who assembled most of the Roman articles which subsequently formed the museum of Dr. Woodward, dispersed after his death in 1728.

The following are the principal localities in which remains of Roman London have been, from time to time, discovered:

Aldgate, 1753.—Stone and brick tower of the Roman wall, discovered by Maitland, south of Aldgate; the bricks sound, as newly laid.

Barbican.—A Roman *specula*, or watch-tower (the *Castrum Exploratum* of Stukeley's Itinerary), stood without London, near the north-west angle of the walls, and was called in the Saxon times the *Burghkenning*, or *Barbican*, which gave name to the present street leading from Aldersgate-street to Whitecross-street.—Brayley's *Londiniana*, vol. i. p. 40.

Billingsgate, 1774.—In the parish of St. Mary-at-Hill were found human bones, fragments of Roman bricks, and coins of Domitian of the middle brass; and in 1824 urns and pavements were discovered near St. Dunstan's church, north of Billingsgate. In 1848, portions of an apartment and a hypocaust were laid open in digging the foundation of the new Coal Exchange, nearly opposite Billingsgate. The apartment is paved with common red tesseræ; the outer wall, 3 feet thick, is built of tile-like bricks and Kentish rag-stone, the mortar containing pounded brick, an unfailing evidence of Roman work. The hypocaust, or hollow floor for receiving heated air when wood was burnt in the furnace, and thus to warm the apartment above (probably a bath), agrees to half an inch in the dimensions with those given by Vitruvius in his instructions for the *hypocaustum*. The bottom is formed of concrete; and piers support the covering tiles, also covered with concrete. Pipes were also found, which, opening into the hypocaust, were inserted in the walls, and conducted the warm air throughout the building. The whole has been preserved.

Bishopsgate, 1707.—A tesselated pavement, urns with ashes and burnt bones, a blue glass lachrymatory, and remains of the Roman wall, found at the west end of Camomile-street, Bishopsgate, by Dr. Woodward. In rebuilding Bishopsgate church in 1725, several urns, pateræ, and other remains were discovered, with a vault arched with equilateral Roman bricks; and Dr. Stukeley saw there, in 1726, a Roman grave, constructed with large tiles, which kept the earth from the body. In 1836 a pavement of red, white, and grey tesseræ, in a guilloche pattern, was discovered under a house at the south-west angle of Crosby-square, Bishopsgate; supposed very early Anglo-Roman. (*Archæologia*, vol. xxvii. p. 397.) Maitland describes a similar pavement found on the north side of Little St. Helen's gateway in 1712; the site of St. Helen's Priory was probably occupied by an extensive Roman building; and remains of floors prove Crosby Hall to be on the site of a magnificent Roman edifice.

Broad-street, Old, 1854.—On taking down the Excise Office, at about 15 feet lower than the foundations of Gresham House (on the site of which the Excise Office was built), was found a pavement, 28 feet square.

It is a geometrical pattern of broad blue lines, forming intersections of octagon and lozenge compartments. The octagon figures are bordered with a cable pattern, shaded with grey, and interlaced with a square border, shaded with red and yellow. In the centres, within a ring, are expanded flowers, shaded in red, yellow, and grey; the double row of leaves radiating from a figure called a truelove knot, alternately with a figure something like the tiger-lily. Between the octagon figures are square compartments bearing various devices: in the centre of the pavement is Ariadne, or a Bacchante, reclining on the back of a panther; but only the fore-paws, one of the hind-paws, and the tail, remain. Over the head of the figure floats a light drapery, forming an arch. Another square contains a two-handled vase. In the demi-octagons, at the sides of the pattern, are lunettes: one contains a fan ornament; another, a bowl crowned with flowers. The lozenge intersections are variously embellished with leaves, shells, truelove-knots, chequers, and an ornament shaped like a dice-box. At the corners of the pattern are truelove-knots. Surrounding this pattern is a broad cable-like border, broad bands of blue and white alternately; then a floral scroll; and beyond this an edge of demi-lozenges, in alternate blue and white. An outer border, composed of plain red tesseræ, surrounds the whole. The ground of the pavement is white, and the other colours are a scale of full red, yellow, and a bluish grey. This pavement is of late workmanship. Various Roman and mediæval articles were turned up in the same excavation : among these are a silver denarius of Hadrian, several copper coins of Constantine, and a small copper coin bearing on the reverse the figures of Romulus and Remus suckled by the traditionary wolf; several Roman and mediæval tiles and fragments of pottery; a small glass of a fine blue colour, and coins and tradesmen's tokens.

Cannon-street, 1852.—Tesselated pavement, fragments of Samian ware, earthen urns and lamp, and other Roman vessels, found from 12 to 20 feet deep, near Basing-lane, New Cannon-street, upon the supposed site of Tower Royal. 1850.—Among the ruins of a Roman edifice, at 11 feet deep, was found in Nicholas-lane, near Cannon-street, a large slab, inscribed, " NVM PROV BRITA" (Numini Cæsaris Provincia Britannia).

Cheapside, 1595.—A vault and pavement found at the depth of 17 feet, at the north-west corner of Bread-street ; and near it a tree cut into steps, on the supposed edge of a brook that had run towards Walbrook. In 1671 Sir Christopher Wren, in digging for the foundation of the church of St. Mary-le-bow, at 18 feet deep, reached a Roman causeway, of bricks and rubble firmly cemented, which, it is supposed, formed, at the time it was constructed, the northern boundary of the colony; and upon this was laid the foundation of the church-tower. Wren mistook the crypt of the ancient Norman church for Roman, from a number of Roman bricks being used in the arches. (See Godwin's *Churches of London*, 1839.)

Crutched Friars, 1842.—A group of three deified females or matrons, sedent, bearing baskets of fruit, discovered in excavating for a sewer in Hart-street : it is now at Guildhall.—C. R. Smith and T. Wright: *Journ. Brit. Arch. Assoc.*

Dowgate.—The discovery of a large building and tesselated pavement here has suggested that Dowgate was the palace of the Roman prefect, and the basilica or court of justice.

Finsbury.—Opposite the Circus, at 19 feet deep, has been discovered a well-turned Roman arch, at the entrance of which, on the Finsbury side, were iron bars, apparently to restrain sedge and weeds from choking the water-passage.

Foster-lane, 1830.—In excavating for the new Goldsmiths' Hall, was found, 15 feet below the level of the street, in a stratum of clay, a stone altar of Diana, 23 inches high, sculptured in front with a figure closely resembling the Diana Venatrix of the Louvre. The sides each contain the type of a tree; on the back are the remains of an inscription, below which are a tripod, a sacrificial vessel, and a hare. The finding of this altar supports the inference that the ground was the site of the Temple of Diana, referred by some antiquaries to the spot where St. Paul's now stands. The altar is preserved in Goldsmiths' Hall. (See *Archæologia*, vol. xxix. p. 145.)

St. George's-in-the-East, 1715.—Many sepulchral remains found in digging the foundations of St. George's church, near Goodman's Fields; and in 1787, fragments of urns and lachrymatories, and an inscribed Roman stone, were dug up in the Tenter-ground.

Grey Friars, 1836.—A fluted pillar, supposed Roman, found in the fragment of a wall of the Grey Friars' Monastery : it is almost the only specimen of the kind noticed.

Houndsditch, 1845.—The torso of a white marble statue of a slinger discovered, 17 feet deep, in Petticoat-lane.

Islington.—In the fields, about midway between White Conduit House and Copenhagen House, near Islington, were, until built over, considerable remains of Reedmont (or Redmont) Field ; a camp said to have been occupied by Suetonius Paulinus, A.D. 61, whose contest with Boadicea at Battle-bridge has been confirmed by a Roman inscription discovered in 1842. Highbury, the summer camp of the Romans, is noticed at page 420. In 1825, arrow-heads and figured pavement were found at Reedmont.—Hone's *Every-day Book*, vol. ii. p. 1566.

King-William-street, Lothbury, and Princes-street, 1834, 1835, 1836. —Various remains found in forming the new thoroughfare across the heart of the City, from London Bridge to the line of the old wall at Moorgate. Evidences of Roman habitations, at the depth of 14 and 20 feet, on either side of the line of King-William-street. Near St. Clement's church, pavement, earthenware lamps, Samian ware, and coins. Along the line of Princes-street, brass scales, fibulæ, styli, needles in brass and bone, coins, a sharpening steel, several knives, and vessels of Samian ware. In Lothbury, at 10 or 12 feet deep, chisels, crowbars, hammers, &c.; a leathern sandal, red and black pottery, &c.; a coin of Antoninus Pius, with Britannia on the reverse. From Lothbury to London Wall, brass coins of Claudius, Vespasian, and Trajan ; spatulæ, styli, needles, a gold ring, brass tweezers, a hair-pin, and pottery. Near the Swan's Nest, in Coleman-street, a pit of earthen vessels, a coin of Allectus (296), a boat-hook, and a bucket-handle. At Honey-lane, under some Saxon remains, a few Roman coins. In Bread-street, richly figured Samian vases, circular earthen cooking-pans; and wall designs, fresh in colour, and resembling those of modern paper-hangings. (C. R. Smith, F.S.A. *Archæologia*, vol. xxvii.) At the corner of St. Swithin's-lane have been found several skeletons, fragments of pottery ; and coins, in second-brass, of Antonia, Claudius, Nero, and Vespasian.

Leadenhall-street, 1576.—A pavement found at the Leadenhall-street end of Lime-street, at 12 feet deep; and between Billiter-lane and Lime-street, a stone wall and arched gate, which Stow supposes to have belonged to a Roman house destroyed by fire in the reign of Stephen. 1803.—A magnificent pavement discovered in front of the India House, Leadenhall-street, described at page 453.

Lombard-street, 1786. — At about 13 feet deep were found brick ruins, upon three inches thick of wood ashes, beneath which was Roman pavement, common and tesselated (Sir John Henniker, *Archæologia*, vol. viii.). Also, near Sherbourn-lane, at 12 feet deep, a pavement running across Lombard-street, between which and the Post-office, but along the north side, ran a wall 10 feet below the street-level, built of "the smaller-sized Roman bricks," and pierced by perpendicular flues, the chimneys of a mansion. Other fragments of walls and pavements were found; and in Birchin-lane were uncovered a tesselated pavement of elegant design; and great quantities of Roman coins, fragments of pottery and glass bottles, keys and beads, a large vessel of figured Samian ware, &c.

London Stone, removed in 1742 from the south to the north side of Cannon-street, was, in 1798, placed against St. Swithin's church, where it now stands. This unique memorial of Roman London is described at pp. 471-472. According to Camden, the "London stone" was placed as the Milliarium, or milestone, on the Watling-street, a British road, forest, lane, or trackway, before the Romans arrived in England; attested by the discovery of early British remains on the line.

Lothbury, 1805.—Tesselated pavement: now in the British Museum.

Ludgate.—Upon the site of the present church of St. Martin, Wren found a small sepulchral stone monument to Vivianus Marcianus, a soldier of the second legion, erected by his wife, and sculptured with his effigies and a dedicatory inscription: this monument is now among the Arundel Marbles at Oxford. 1792.—Barbican or watch-tower of the City Wall discovered between Ludgate and the Fleet-ditch. 1800. —Sepulchral monument found in the rear of the London Coffee-house, Ludgate-hill (see page 477).

St. Martin's-lane, 1722.—In digging the foundations of the new church of St. Martin-in-the-Fields, were found, at 14 feet deep, a Roman brick arch; and "buffalo-heads," according to Gibbs, the architect. In Sir Hans Sloane's Museum was a glass vase containing ashes, which was found in a stone coffin upon the site of St. Martin's portico.

St. Martin's-le-Grand, 1819. — Roman vaultings, discovered in digging for the foundations of the General Post-office (see page 502).

Moorfields.—An inscribed stone, in memory of Grata, the daughter of Dagobitus, has been discovered at London Wall. Mr. C. R. Smith is of opinion that the London of the Britons was situated in Moorfields; and on this aboriginal establishment the Romans afterwards enlarged. In 1818 a large portion of the wall on both sides of Moorgate was demolished.

St. Pancras, 1758.—"Cæsar's Camp," near St. Pancras church, discovered by Dr. Stukeley (see page 579).

Pavements discovered in Bush-lane, Cannon-street, in 1666; near St. Andrew's church, Holborn, in 1681; at Crutched Friars in 1787; behind the Old Navy Pay-Office in Broad-street; in Northumberland-alley, Fenchurch-street; and in Long-lane, Smithfield,—about the commencement of the present century; near the church of St. Dunstan's-in-the-East, in 1824; in East Cheap in 1831; at St. Clement's church, and in Lothbury, opposite Founders'-court, in 1834; in Crosby-square in 1836; behind Winchester House, Bankside, in 1850; and in various places on both sides of High-street, Southwark, between 1818 and 1831. (G. L. Craik, in Knight's *London*, vol. i.) Some stamped *tiles* bear the earliest abbreviation of the name Londinium: they read PBR LON and P-B-LON, supposed *Probatum Londinii*, proved of the proper quality at London; or *Prima* (cohors) BR*itonum* LO*Ndinii*, the first (cohort) of the Britons at London. (*C. R. Smith, F.S.A.*) Or, Mr. Wright interprets P. PR. BR. upon another tile, as *Proprætor Britanniæ Londinii*, the Proprætor of Britain at Londinium; showing that Roman London was the seat of the government of the province. See a list of potter's stamps on pottery found in different metropolitan localities, in the *Antiquarian and Architectural Year-book* for 1844.

St. Paul's Churchyard.—In 1675 Wren, in excavating for the foundations of the present St. Paul's Cathedral, discovered many Saxon and British graves; and 18 feet or more deep, Roman urns intermixed,

"belonging to the colony, when the Romans and Britons lived and died together. The more remarkable Roman urns, lamps, and lachrymatories, fragments of sacrificing vessels, &c. were found deep in the ground, about a claypit (under the north-east-angle of the present choir) which had been dug by the Roman potters, 'in a stratum of close and hard pot-earth, that extends beneath the whole site of St. Paul's.' here 'the urns. broken vessels, and pottery-ware' were met with in great abundance.'—Wren's *Parentalia*.

Wren "rummaged" the ground, but failed to discover any traces of the Roman Temple of Diana or Apollo reputed to have been built here. Dr. Woodward, however, possessed sacrificing vessels, bearing representations of Diana, dug up at St. Paul's; besides a brass figure of Diana, found between the Deanery and Blackfriars, and believed Roman.*

Royal Exchange, 1841.—In excavating for the foundations was opened an ancient gravel-pit, filled with various Roman relics, described at page 234; many of which are preserved in the Corporation Museum (see page 535). Remains of buildings covered the whole site of the present Exchange, denoting it to have been one of the most magnificent portions of Roman London.

Shadwell, 1615.—Two coffins (stone and lead), with bones, lachrymatories, and two ivory sceptres, found in Sun Tavern Fields.

Southwark.—Discoveries of tesselated pavements on and about the site of St. Saviour's church, and other remains of buildings, pottery, lamps, glass vessels, &c. throughout the line of High-street, denote this to have been within Roman London; and a burial-ground of the period has been discovered on the site of that now attached to the Dissenters' chapel, Deverill-street, New Kent-road.—*C. R. Smith, F.S.A.*

Spitalfields.—Urns, with ashes and burnt human bones, coins (Claudius, Nero, Vespasian, and Antoninus Pius), lachrymatories, lamps, and Samian ware, found in the Lottesworth or Spitalfield.

Strand.—"The Old Roman Spring Bath" in Strand-lane, between Nos. 162 and 163, is of accredited antiquity. The bath itself is Roman: the walls being layers of brick and thin layers of stucco; and the pavement of similar brick covered with stucco, and resting upon a mass of stucco and rubble: the bricks are $9\frac{1}{2}$ inches long, $4\frac{1}{2}$ inches broad, and $1\frac{1}{2}$ inches thick, and resemble the bricks in the City Wall. The property can be traced to the Danvers (or D'Anvers) family, of Swithland Hall, Leicestershire, whose mansion stood upon the spot.

Threadneedle-street, 1840-1841.—Tesselated pavements found beneath the old French Protestant Church in Threadneedle-street, at about 12 or 14 feet deep: they are preserved in the British Museum. In 1854 was found a large deposit of Roman *débris*, in excavating the site of the church of St. Benet's Fink; consisting of Roman tiles, flue-tiles, fragments of black, pale, and red Samian pottery; glass, &c.

Thames River.—A silver Harpocrates found in 1825 in the bed of the Thames, and now in the British Museum. 1837.—Bronzes found in ballast-heaving in the Thames, near London Bridge, including Mercury, Apollo, and Atys; probably the penates of some opulent Roman family.—*C. R. Smith, F.S.A., Archæologia*, vol. xxvii.

Upper Thames-street, 1839.—Opposite Vintners' Hall, at 10 feet from the surface, were found remains of the Wall parallel with the Thames; and about the middle of Queen-street, 19 feet from the surface, was unearthed a fine tesselated pavement.

Tower, 1777.—In digging the foundations of a new office for the Board of Ordnance, within the Tower, at a great depth, were discovered remains of ancient buildings; a silver ingot impressed "Ex OFFIC. HONORII," and three gold coins of Honorius and Arcadius; a small glass crown, and an inscribed stone; thus indicating that the Romans had a fortress upon the Tower site.

Tower Hill, 1852.—Fragments of a Roman building found at the northern portion of the City Wall, including the supposed volute of a capital, and other enriched remains; besides a Roman sarcophagus nearly entire: now in the British Museum.

* In excavating, in 1853, for Cook's colossal warehouse (built in 90 days), on the south side of St. Paul's Churchyard, there was found at twenty feet deep a Danish gravestone, inscribed in Runic—KINA caused this stone to be laid over, or in memory of, TUKI. The date of this relic is about A.D. 1000; and it is said to be the only Runic monument known to have been discovered in London.—*Proc. Royal Society of Northern Antiquaries.*

Walbrook, 1774.—Wood-ashes found, 22 feet deep, in making a sewer from Dowgate through Walbrook.

Whitechapel, 1776.—Monumental stone to a soldier of the 24th legion, found in a burial-ground at the lower end of Whitechapel-lane.

In Mr. Charles Roach Smith's Museum of London Antiquities (see p. 530) are 528 Roman items, collected in the metropolis during street-improvements, sewerage, and the deepening of the bed of the Thames. These objects include Roman sculpture, bronzes, pottery, terra-cotta lamps, red glazed pottery, potters' stamps, glass; tiles, pavements, and wall-paintings; personal ornaments, sandals in leather, utensils and implements, and coins. The Museum contains the same number of Anglo-Saxon and Norman, and Mediæval remains. (See the Catalogue, with illustrations by F. W. Fairholt, F.S.A., printed for the Subscribers only, 1854.) In Mr. Saull's Museum (see p. 542) are also several Roman relics. The collection of Mr. George Gwilt, Union-street, is rich in Southwark remains.

ROTHERHITHE,

A manor and parish between Deptford and Bermondsey, on the Surrey bank of the Thames, was anciently called *Retherhith*, probably from the Saxon *redhra*, a mariner, and *hyth*, a haven, *i. e.* the sailor's harbour. (Brayley's *Surrey*.) It is vulgarly *Redriff.* At the time of Domesday, it was included in the royal manor of Bermondsey; but it was not surrendered until the reign of Charles I. A fleet was fitted out at Rotherhithe in the reign of Edward III., by order of the Black Prince and John of Gaunt. Lambarde states that Henry IV. lodged in an "old stone house here whiles he was cured of a leprosie;" and two of Henry's charters are dated here, July 1412. The mother-church of St. Mary is described at page 146 : Gataker, the erudite Latin critic, was rector from 1611 to 1654; he was imprisoned in the Fleet by Laud, and is buried here. In the churchyard lies Prince Le Boo. The registers, commencing 1556, contain many entries of ages from 90 to 99 years, and one of 120 years. Admiral Sir Charles Wager possessed the manor between 1740 and 1750. The brave Admiral Sir John Leake was born here June 1656; but Admiral Benbow, stated by Manning and Bray to have been born at Rotherhithe, was a native of Coton-hill, Shrewsbury. (See *Gent. Mag.* Dec. 1809.) George Lillo, the dramatist, who wrote *George Barnwell*, *Arden of Feversham*, and *Fatal Curiosity*, was a jeweller living at Rotherhithe in 1735. Swift's Captain Lemuel Gulliver was a native of the place :

> " In five long years I took no second spouse;
> What Redriff wife so long hath kept her vows!"
> *Gay's Epistle—Mary Gulliver to the Captain.*

A fire, June 1, 1765, destroyed here 206 houses, and property worth 100,000*l.* In 1804, a tunnel from Rotherhithe, beneath the Thames, to Limehouse, was commenced by Vasey and Trevethick, but failed. The "Thames Tunnel," by Brunel, commences at a short distance east of St. Mary's church. The Docks at Rotherhithe are described at page 254.

ROYAL ACADEMY OF ARTS (THE)

Occupies the east wing of the National Gallery in Trafalgar-square. The entire building is described at p. 548. The Academy originated in a Society of Artists in Peter's-court, St. Martin's-lane.* With its apparatus Hogarth established the Society of Incorporated Artists, who held their first Exhibition at the house of the Society of Arts, in the

* This Society (according to Edwards) was formed from a "Life School," or Living Model Academy, which was established in the house of Peter Hyde, a painter, in Greyhound-court, between Milford-lane and Arundel-street, Strand, under the direction of Mr. Morer, afterwards the first keeper of the Royal Academy. The School removed to Peter's-court about 1739. The houses in Greyhound-court were taken down between 1851 and 1854.

Adelphi, April 21, 1760; next in Spring Gardens. In 1768 certain artists seceded from the Society, were constituted a "Royal Academy," removed to Pall Mall, and elected Reynolds president (at the first exhibition, in 1769, there were 136 pictures, and only three sold); and George III. granted them, in 1771, apartments in Old Somerset House.

The Foundation consists of 40 Royal Academicians; 20 Associates, from whom the members are chosen to fill up vacancies; and six Associate Engravers. The Academicians elect from among themselves annually the President; they also appoint a Secretary and Keeper. The Council of eight members elect among the body Professors of Painting, Sculpture, and Architecture; and appoint a Professor of Anatomy, who must be a surgeon. Dr. Johnson was first Professor of Ancient Literature; and Dr. Goldsmith, Professor in Ancient History, was succeeded by Edward Gibbon. Lectures are delivered to the students and exhibiting artists, free of expense: and prize medals are awarded biennially and annually. Students are also sent to Rome at the expense of the Academy. The members are under the superintendence and control of the Queen, who confirms and signs all appointments.

Among the Foundation Members of the Academy were Sir Joshua Reynolds (*President*); Sir William Chambers, the architect of Somerset House; Gainsborough and Wilson, the eminent landscape-painters; Benjamin West (*the second President*); Joseph Wilton, the sculptor; F. Bartolozzi, the engraver; Charles Catton, Master of the Painter-Stainers' Company; and Angelica Kauffman and Mary Moser. (See Zoffany's *Picture of the Royal Academicians*, 1773.)

Upon the rebuilding of Somerset House, apartments in the western wing were given to the Academicians; and the first Exhibition here was opened May 1780.

The *Library* ceiling was painted by Sir Joshua Reynolds and Cipriani: the centre, by Reynolds, represents "the Theory of Painting," a majestic female, holding compasses and a label inscribed, "Theory is the knowledge of what is truly nature." The four compartments, by Cipriani, were personifications of Nature, History, Allegory, and Fable. The *Council-room* was painted by West: centre, the Graces unveiling Nature, surrounded by figures of the Four Elements; oval pictures of Invention, Composition, Design, and Colouring, by Angelica Kauffman; medallions of Apelles, Phidias, Apollodorus, and Archimedes; and a circle of chiaroscuro medallions of Palladio, Bernini, Michael Angelo, Fiamingo, Raffaelle, Dominichino, Titian, and Rubens, painted by Rebecca.

In 1838 the Academy removed to the National Gallery. They possess a library of prints, and books on art (see page 464), which is open to students. Here are also several pictures by old masters. The School for Drawing from the Antique is held in the Sculpture-room; the School for Painting in the West Room; and the School for Drawing from the Life-model is held in the interior of the dome of the edifice. In the Hall of Casts (mostly presented by George IV., and procured through the intervention of Canova) are a beautiful group of Niobe and her Daughters; the graceful Mercury of the Vatican; Fauns with their Cymbals; the Egyptian Jupiter, and the Olympian; Apollo and the Muses; the Laocoon; the Fighting and Dying Warrior; a mutilated remnant of a statue of Theseus, &c. Upon the ceiling of the Council-room are the paintings, by Sir Joshua Reynolds and other Academicians, transferred from the Library and Council-room at Somerset House.

The *Diploma Pictures and Sculptures* (each member presenting a work of art upon his election) are placed in the Council-room, and include Sir Joshua Reynolds's full-length portrait of George III.; Fuseli's "Thor battering the Serpent of Midgard in the boat of Hymer the Giant;" a Rustic Girl, by Lawrence; the Tribute-Money, by Copley; Charity, by Stothard; Jael and Sisera, by Northcote; the Falling Giant, by Banks; and Apollo and Marpessa, and a cast of the Shield of Achilles, by Flaxman; Christ blessing little Children, by West;

Boys digging for a Rat, by Wilkie; Opie's Infancy and Age; portrait of Gainsborough, by himself; Sir William Chambers, by Reynolds; and Sir Joshua in his doctor's robes, by himself. Cupid and Psyche, by Nollekens; bust of Flaxman, by Baily; West, by Chantrey, &c.

There are, also, a celebrated copy, size of the original, of the Last Supper, by Leonarda da Vinci, made by his pupil, Marco d'Oggione; copies of the Descent from the Cross, and the two Volets, by Rubens, made by Guy Head; and copies of the Cartoons of Raffaelle, by Thornhill,—the size of the originals. Also, small copies in oil of the frescoes by Raffaelle in the Vatican; two fine Cartoons (the Holy Family and St. Anna, and Leda,) by L. da Vinci; bas-relief in marble of the Holy Family, by Michael Angelo, presented by Sir George Beaumont, &c. Among the memorials preserved by the Academy are two palettes of Reynolds and Hogarth. The Diploma Pictures, &c. may be seen by application in writing to the Keeper of the Gallery.

The Exhibition is opened annually on the first Monday in May; admission 1s., catalogue 1s.: it closes the last week in July. All works sent for exhibition are submitted to the Council, whose decision is final. The number of works in the year's Exhibition averages 1500; and the receipts during the season average 6000l.

The qualifications for becoming a Student of the Royal Academy are, an approved drawing or model by the applicant, and testimony of his moral character; and next, an approved drawing or model of an antique figure in the Academy, accompanied by outline drawings of an anatomical figure and skeleton, not less than two feet high, with list, references, &c. A similar rule applies to Architectural Students.

The Annual Dinner is given by the Academicians on Saturday previous to the opening of the Exhibition, in the West Room, where hung the massive chandelier presented to the Academy by George IV.

ROYAL EXCHANGE.

See EXCHANGES, pp. 273-286.

ROYAL INSTITUTION (THE),

21 Albemarle-street, Piccadilly, was founded in 1799, "for diffusing the knowledge, and facilitating the general introduction, of useful mechanical inventions and improvements; and for teaching, by courses of philosophical lectures and experiments, the application of science to the common purposes of life:" hence the motto of the Institution, *Illustrans commoda vitæ*. It was incorporated in 1800. The Institution has been worthily designated as "the workshop of the Royal Society;" for within its laboratory Sir Humphry Davy made those brilliant discoveries which were published through the medium of the *Transactions* of the Royal Society; and the example of Davy has been followed by Faraday. Sir Joseph Banks, Count Rumford, and Mr. Cavendish were among the founders of the Royal Institution. In the basement was an experimental kitchen, with Rumford stoves, roasters, and boilers; apparatus for heating water by steam, &c.; a workshop for coppersmiths and braziers. Above are a laboratory, lecture-theatre, museum, library (see page 464), and model repository. Here Davy gave his first lecture, April 25, 1801; and in 1807 discovered by galvanism the composition of the fixed alkalis, and their metallic bases, potassium and sodium: his great voltaic battery consisted of 2000 double plates of copper and zinc, of 4 inches square, the whole surface being 128,000 square inches. Davy was succeeded by Brande; and Faraday fills a second chair of Chemistry, the Fullerian, founded by John Fuller, Esq., whose bequests have amounted to 10,000l. The mineralogical collection in the museum was commenced by Davy.

The history of chemical science dates one of its principal epochs from the foundation of the laboratory of the Royal Institution. Here the researches of Davy and Faraday extended over nearly half a century : including the laws of electro-chemical decomposition, the decomposition of the fixed alkalis, the establishment of the nature of chlorine, the philosophy of flame, the condensibility of many gases, the science of magneto-electricity, the twofold magnetism of matter, and the magnetism of gases. Here Coleridge gave his celebrated Lectures on Poetry. Among the Mss. in the Library are fifty-six volumes of Letters, &c. respecting the American War; Papers of Lord Stanhope; and the Laboratory Note-Books of Sir Humphry Davy.

Terms of admission : election by ballot; entrance-fee, five guineas; annually, five guineas. Meetings on Friday evenings; lectures weekly.

The Institution building, originally five houses, received its present architectural front, by L. Vulliamy, in 1839.

ROYAL SOCIETY (THE),

Somerset House, is the oldest society of its kind in Europe, except the Lyncean Academy at Rome, of which Galileo was a member. The Royal Society originated in London, about 1645 in the weekly meetings of " divers worthy persons inquisitive into natural philosophy, and other parts of human learning; and particularly the new philosophy, or experimental philosophy ;" these meetings being first suggested by Theodore Haak, a German of the Palatinate, then resident in the metropolis. This is supposed to be the club which Mr. Boyle, in 1646, designated " the Invisible or Philosophical Society." They met at Dr. Goddard's lodgings in Wood-street; at the Bull-head Tavern, Cheapside; and at Gresham College. About 1648-9, some of the members, including Dr. (afterwards Bishop) Williams, removed to Oxford, and were joined by Seth Smith, Ralph Bathurst, Sir William Petty, and the Hon. Robert Boyle, who met at Petty's lodgings in an apothecary's house, " because of the convenience of inspecting drugs." The members in London continued also to meet, until, in 1658, they were ejected from Gresham College, which was required for barracks. Evelyn, Cowley, and Sir William Petty proposed separate plans for a " philosophical college :" Sprat says that Cowley's proposition accelerated the foundation of the Royal Society, in praise of which he subsequently wrote an ode. At the Restoration, in 1660, the meetings were revived; and April 22, 1663, the Society was incorporated by royal charter, by Charles II., who bestowed upon it a mace. From this session date the *Philosophical Transactions*, wherein the proceedings and discoveries of the Society are registered. This year the Society exercised their privilege of claiming the bodies of criminals executed at Tyburn, which were to be dissected in Gresham College. In 1664, the King signed himself in the charter-book as the founder ; and his brother, the Duke of York, signed as a fellow.* In 1667 Chelsea College was granted to the Society, for their meetings, laboratory, repository, and library ; but the building was too dilapidated, "the annoyance of Prince Rupert's glass-house" adjoined it, and the property was purchased back for the King's use for 1300*l*. The Society then resumed their meetings in Gresham College, until they were dispersed by the Great Plague and Fire, after which they met in Arundel House. The Fellows now (1667) numbered 200, and their subscription 1*s*. per week; from the payment of which Newton, who joined the Society in 1674, was excused, on account

* The first charter (in Latin) has ornamented initials, and a finely executed portrait of Charles II. in Indian ink. The charter empowers the President *to wear his hat while in the chair;* and the Fellows addressed the President bare-headed, till he made a sign for them to put on their hats : customs now obsolete.

of his narrow finances: in this year he made his first communication to the *Transactions* of discoveries by him in 1666.

In 1674 the Society returned to Gresham College. They were fiercely attacked: a Warwick physician accused them of attempting to undermine the Universities, to bring in popery and absurd novelties; but a severer satire was *The Elephant in the Moon*, by Butler. Among their early practices was the fellows gathering May-dew, and experimenting with the divining-rod; and the Hon. Robert Boyle believed in the efficacy of the touch of Greatrix the Stroker for the evil. In 1686 Newton presented his *Principia* to the Society, whose clerk, Halley the astronomer, printed the work: the Ms., entirely in Newton's hand, is preserved in the library. In 1703 Newton was elected president. In 1710 the Society removed to a house in Crane-court, "being in the middle of the town, and out of noise:" here they first met Nov. 8th, and established their library and museum, described at page 541. In 1782 they removed to Somerset House, and transferred most of their olden *Curiosities* to the British Museum; but in Crane-court the meeting-room is preserved in the same condition as when Newton sat in the presidential chair. (See page 237.)

The Society's apartments are in the east wing of the north front of Somerset House. The meeting-room has one of Chambers's enriched ceilings: the president's seat is carved with the Society's arms; and upon the table are placed, during meetings, three crowns and the mace.

The Mace is silver-gilt, about 4 feet in length, and weighs 190 oz. avoirdupois; its stem is chased with the thistle, and has an urn-shaped head, surmounted by a crown, ball, and cross. Upon the head are embossed figures of a rose, harp, thistle, and fleur-de-lis, and the initials C. R. four times repeated. Under the crown are chased the royal arms; and at the other extremity of the stem are two shields, one bearing the Society's arms, the other a Latin inscription denoting the mace to have been presented to the Society by Charles II. in 1663. It was long believed by numberless visitors to be the "bauble" mace turned out of the House of Commons by Cromwell, when he dissolved the Long Parliament; but Mr. Weld, the assistant-secretary and librarian, in a communication to the Society, April 30, 1846, proved this to be a popular error, by showing the warrant for making this mace and delivering it to Lord Brouncker, the first President of the Society. Again, the "bauble" was altogether different in form from the Society's mace, and was nearly destitute of ornament, and without the crown and cross, as described in Whitelock's *Memorials*, and represented accordingly in West's picture of the Dissolution of the Long Parliament.

The Society possess marble busts of Charles II. and George III., by Nollekens; Sir Joseph Banks, by Chantrey; John Dollond, by Garland; Davies Gilbert, by Westmacott; Sir Isaac Newton, by Roubiliac; Laplace; Mrs. Somerville, by Chantrey; James Watt, after Chantrey; and Cuvier, in bronze.

Among the pictures are, three portraits of Sir Isaac Newton, P.R.S., by Jervas, Marchand, and Vanderbank; Viscount Brouncker (first president), by Sir P. Lely; Sir Humphry Davy, P.R.S., by Sir T. Lawrence; John Evelyn, Secretary, by Kerseboom; two portraits of Flamsteed, by T. Gibson; Martin Folkes, P.R.S., by Hogarth; Benjamin Franklin, LL.D.; Davies Gilbert, P.R.S., by Phillips; two portraits of Halley, Secretary, by Murray and Dahl; two of Hobbes, by Dobson, one a copy; Marquis of Northampton, P.R.S., by Phillips; Pepys, by Kneller; Sir John Pringle, P.R.S., by Reynolds; and the Presidents, Sir Hans Sloane, Lord Somers, Sir R. Southwell, Sir J. Williamson, and Sir Christopher Wren, by Kneller; and Dr. Wollaston, by Jackson; Dr. Thomas Young, by Briggs; Dr. Dalton, by Faulkner; the Duke of Sussex, P.R.S., by Phillips; Dr. Birch, by Wills. (See List in Weld's *History*.) The Society's relics of Newton are described at page 542. Here also is one of the earliest of Count Rumford's fire-grates; and to the Society's collection of scientific and mechanical instruments was added, in 1850, the original model of Davy's safety-lamp, made by Sir Humphry's own hands, and described by him to the Society in 1816. Here likewise is a very delicate balance, constructed by Ramsden, and formerly belonging to Sir Joseph Banks. Upon his decease, the secretaries wrote to his widow, apprising her that this balance was lying in the apartments of the Society, and requesting to know her wishes respecting it. "Pay it into Coutts's," was Lady Banks's reply.—Weld's *Hist. Royal Society*, vol. ii. p. 116.

Here also is the Exchequer standard yard set off upon the Society's yard: it is of brass, and is of great value since the destruction of the parliamentary standard. In the Hall is the Society's standard baro-meter; also the water-barometer, made by Professor Daniell, whose last official service was the refilling of this instrument, in 1844.

The presidents have given *conversazioni* at their private residences since the presidency of Sir Joseph Banks. In the rooms are displayed working models of new inventions, beautiful specimens of the arts, &c. The Duke of Sussex received the fellows at Kensington Palace. The Earl of Rosse was elected president in 1849. The affairs are managed by the council; and committees of Mathematics, Astronomy, Physics, Chemistry, Zoology, Botany, and Mineralogy. The meetings are held on Thursday evenings, from November to June inclusive. The anniversary is St. Andrew's day, Nov. 30th. The subscription is 4l. annually; admission-fee, 10l. The Society distributes four gold medals annually,—the Rumford, two Royal (value 50 guineas each), and the Copley; and from the donation-fund men of science are assisted in special researches.

The *Charter-book* is bound in crimson velvet, with gold clasps and corners, and inscription-plates,—1. The Shield of the Society; 2. Crest: an eagle *or*, holding shield with the arms of England. The leaves are fine vellum, and bear, superbly emblazoned, the arms of England and the Society; next, the third charter and statutes (60 pages). Autographs (1st page): ornamented scroll-border and royal shield, above the signatures, "CHARLES R., Founder" (written Jan. 9th, 1664-5); JAMES, Fellow;" and "GEORGE RUPERT, Fellow." In the next page are the autographs of various foreign ambassadors; and the third and succeeding pages contain the signatures of the fellows beneath the obligation which holds each leaf: Clarendon, Boyle, Wallis, Wren, Hooke, Evelyn, Pepys, Norfolk, Flam-steed, and Newton, are here (the name beneath that of Newton is nearly obliterated by the sad habit of touching). Seventy-one pages are occupied by the autographs of the fellows (including those on the foreign list). Here are the autographs of the successive kings and queens of England, and many sovereigns of foreign countries who have visited England. Queen Victoria has signed her name as patron of the Society; and on the same richly illuminated page are the signatures of Prince Albert and the kings of Prussia and Saxony.—Weld's *History of the Royal Society*, vol. i. p. 177 (abridged).

The *Royal Society Club* was originally formed in 1743, as "the Club of the Royal Philosophers:" they meet on Thursday at dinner; and in the minute-book are entries of presents of venison, salmon, tur-bot, and roasting-beef. The Club first met at the Mitre Tavern, Fleet-street; next, in 1780, at the Crown and Anchor Tavern, Strand; on which becoming a club-house, they removed to Freemasons' Tavern, Great Queen-street. In 1847 was formed a similar association of eminent fellows, as "the Philosophical Club."

ROYAL SOCIETY OF LITERATURE, see page 465.
ROYAL SOCIETY OF MUSICIANS, see page 455.

SAVOY (THE).

On the spot which still bears this name, but is now partly occupied by the northern approach to Waterloo Bridge and the buildings of Lancaster-place, the powerful Simon de Montford, Earl of Leicester, possessed a palace, the site of which was granted by Henry III. to Peter Earl of Savoy. This palace was bestowed by the Earl on the fraternity of Mountjoy, of whom it was purchased by Queen Eleanor for her second son, Edmund Earl of Lancaster. It was magnificently rebuilt by Henry, first Duke of Lancaster. Here was confined John King of France, taken prisoner by Edward the Black Prince, at Poictiers, in 1356; "and thyder came to se hym the kyng and the quene often tymes, and made hym gret feest and cheere:" he was released in 1360; but returning to captivity, died in the Savoy, "his antient prison," in 1364. The demesnes descended to John of Gaunt: here the poet Chaucer was his frequent guest; some of his poems were written in the Savoy; and Chaucer's *Dream* allegorises his own marriage with Philippa, a lady of the duchess' household. But Gaunt, a Wickliffite, had his palace attacked by the Londoners in 1377. In 1381 it was burnt by Wat Tyler's rebels: the costly plate and furniture were destroyed or thrown into the Thames, and the great hall and several houses were blown up. Shakespeare lays a scene of his *Richard II.* in a room of the Savoy, which, however, was then in ruins: thus it lay until 1505, when Henry VII. commenced building here an Hospital of St. John the Baptist, "to receive and lodge nightly one hundred poor folks;" and the buildings were completed by Henry VIII. In 1553 the hospital was surrendered to Edward VI., who bestowed its bedding and revenues on the newly-erected Bridewell and Christ's Hospital. The Savoy was re-endowed and refurnished by Queen Mary, and maintained by Elizabeth; but the buildings and revenues were shamefully perverted, and it became "a nursery of rogues and masterless men." Here, in 1658, the Independents met, and agreed upon their well-known Declaration of Faith; three years later was held here the "Savoy Conference" for the revision of the Liturgy; and Charles II. established here "the French Church in the Savoy."* The Mastership of the Savoy was promised to the poet Cowley by Charles I., and afterwards by Charles II., who, however, gave the office to Dr. Killigrew; upon which Cowley wrote his poem of *The Complaint*; and in the State Poems of the time he is taunted as "Savoy-missing Cowley." In this reign also, during the Dutch war, the sick and wounded were lodged in the Hospital; and great part of it was dilapidated by fire. On the demo-

* The first five churches in London appropriated to the Protestants of France were the old Temple in Threadneedle-street, and those of the Savoy, Marylebone, and Castle-street; and a church in Spitalfields, added upon the application of the consistory to James II. To these were successively added twenty-six others, mostly founded during the reigns of William III., Queen Anne, and George I. :—That of Leicester-fields, founded in 1688, of which Saurin was minister; that of Spring-gardens, whose first pastor was Francis Flahaut; that of Glasshouse-square, formed in 1688; Swallow-street, Piccadilly, 1692; Berwick-street, 1689; Charen-ton, in Newport-market, 1701; West-street, Seven Dials, which the refugees called the Pyramid, or the Tremblade; the Carré, Westminster, 1689; the Taber-nacle, 1696; Hungerford, 1689, which subsisted until 1832; the Temple of Soho, or the Patent, erected in 1689; Ryder's-court, 1700; Martin's-lane, City, 1686; St. James's, 1701; the Artillery, Bishopsgate, 1691; Hoxton, 1748; St. John, Shore-ditch, 1687; the Patent, in Spitalfields, or the New Patent, 1689; Crispin-street, 1693; Peart-street, 1697; Bell-lane, Spitalfields, 1718; Swanfields, 1721; Wheeler-street, Spitalfields, 1703; Petticoat-lane, Spitalfields, 1694; Wapping, 1711; Blackfriars. 1716. Several of these churches ultimately adopted the Anglican ritual.—*Weiss's Hist. French Protestant Refugees,* 1854.

lition of the old church of St. Mary-le-Strand, by the Protector Somerset, the Hospital church was allotted to that parish; and it was changed from St. John Baptist's to St. Mary's Church, which is described at page 147. Here is a tablet to the memory of Richard Lander, the traveller in Africa; and in the burial-ground is the tomb of Hilton, the historical painter.

Contemporary with the Fleet and May-fair marriages, the priest at the Savoy Chapel carried on a like traffic; and in the *Public Advertiser*, Jan. 2, 1754, marriages are advertised, by authority, to be performed here "with the utmost privacy, decency, and regularity;" also, registers from the time of the Reformation were kept here; and "there are five private ways by land to this chapel, and two by water." The chapel also possessed the privilege of sanctuary; and in July 1696, a creditor going into the Savoy to demand a debt of a person who had taken sanctuary there, was seized by the mob, "according to their usual custom" (says the *Postman*, No. 180), and was tarred and feathered, and carried in a wheelbarrow to the Strand, and there bound fast to the Maypole, until rescued by constables. The Hospital was finally dissolved 1702.

Strype describes the Savoy House, in 1720, as very ruinous, but the precinct containing "divers good houses:" and here were the King's printing-presses, for proclamations, acts of parliament, gazettes, &c.; next, a prison; thirdly, a parish church, and churches for the French, Dutch, High Germans, and Lutherans, and for Protestant Dissenters. (The German-Lutheran Church has been rebuilt.) A scarce etching, by Hollar, shows the river front of the Savoy in 1650; and it is seen in Canaletti's views on the Thames. The demesne was surveyed by Vertue for the *Vetusta Monumenta*, 1736: it was a massive brick, stone, and flint, fortress-like building, embattled throughout; the outer walls abutted upon the Thames, where was a flight of steps to the water; the Strand front had large pointed windows, and parapets lozenged with flints. Vertue's ground-plan shows the Middle Savoy Gate, where Savoy-street now is; and the Little Savoy Gate, where now are Savoy-steps (a triple flight); also Nutt's printing-office; and the warehouse of Vaillant, the Strand bookseller. Pennant describes the building in the form of a cross, with the walls entire to his time. Until its demolition, on the erection of Waterloo Bridge in 1816, the Savoy was principally used as barracks for soldiers, and a prison for deserters (see page 697). Wellington-street and Lancaster-place cover the entire site of the old Duchy-lane, as well as most of the Hospital.

The first manufactory of flint-glass in England was established in the Savoy House, in 1552.

SEWERS.

The passenger who rolls smoothly over the well-paved roadway of the metropolis, or elbows his way through the dense mass of human beings which throng the foot-pavement, rarely thinks of the vast reticulation of subterranean channels by which are removed the liquid refuse of the millions inhabiting the banks of the Thames. Yet during dry weather, the aggregate liquid refuse of the metropolitan population, contributed by hundreds of thousands of inlets and smaller drains, amounting to about 14,000,000 cubic feet, or 87,000,000 gallons daily, is discharged by sewers. Their utility in times of rain is more striking. The area of the metropolis is about 112 square miles—the more closely-populated portion may, perhaps, be taken at about 60 square miles; and if we assume a rain of about half an inch in depth equally over the whole of the latter area in 24 hours (a rate of fall not unusual), then, during a considerable portion of the time, in addition to the sewage from the houses, a quantity of water of about 18,000,000 gallons per hour is discharged by the London sewers. Hence it has been said: "although, considering the immense progress made of late years in hydrodynamical engineering, our system of sewerage is rude and incomplete, the sewers of London are as far superior to those of any other city in modern Europe, as those of Rome were to any city in the ancient world."—Weale's *London*, page 820.

The population of the London district, increased in 1853 to 2,468,362 inhabitants, lives in a density varying from 2 persons to an acre at Lewisham, to 284 in St. Botolph and Cripplegate; and to an elevation varying from 2 feet below high-water mark at Newington, to 350 feet above it at Hampstead. Yet the health of Londoners,

> "in populous city pent,
> Where houses thick and sewers annoy the air" (*Milton*),

contrasts favourably with the health of some of the large towns in England.

Sewers were partially provided for by statutes of Henry III., VI., VII., and VIII.; but the first general measure was the "Bill of Sewers," in 1531; superseded, in 1848, by the "Metropolitan Commission of Sewers," whose jurisdiction extends 12 miles round St. Paul's, and for whom a new block plan of the metropolis has been prepared by the Ordnance Office. By this map, the sewerage amounted to upwards of 7 millions of cubic feet on the north side of the Thames, and nearly 2½ millions on the south side. The great receptacle is the Thames; and of the new system, from 1848 to 1854, there were constructed 80 miles of brick sewers, and 346 miles of pipe-drainage.

The oldest and largest sewer is the Fleet Sewer, which drains, by many hundred collateral sewers, an area six or seven times the size of the City of London: at one point, the flow is from 18,000 to 20,000 gallons per minute, in dry weather; when increased by slight rain, no man can stand against it: in repairs, labourers often work with two-thirds of their bodies in the sewer-water, and amidst its deafening roar, in an uncertain light. This vast arterial drain is, in fact, a covered river. (See FLEET, page 304; also the *King's Scholars' Pond Sewer*, page 569.) The new Victoria-street Sewer, from Pimlico to Scotland-yard, discharges itself by cast-iron pipes into the Thames at low-water mark.

SHERIFFS.

That London had its sheriff prior to the Norman Conquest, is attested by William the Conqueror's second charter being addressed to William the Bishop and Sweyn the Sheriff. The union of the sheriffwick of London and Middlesex took place in the reign of Henry I., of whom the citizens purchased the power of electing the sheriff of Middlesex, "to farm for 300*l.*:"[*] the mayor and citizens now hold the office in fee, and appoint two sheriffs for London, which by charters is both a city and a county, though they make but one sheriff jointly for the county of Middlesex. The third charter of King John, and the first charter of Henry III., minutely describe the sheriff's office and duties. Any citizen is eligible, unless he swear himself not worth 15.000*l.*; and no alderman can be chosen lord-mayor unless he has served as sheriff. A list of citizens is nominated on Midsummer-day, when two are elected by the Livery in Common Hall; they are obliged to serve, under a penalty of 400*l.* and 20 marks; and the fines paid within the present century have exceeded 70,000*l.* In 1734 there were fined 35

* This fee-farm rent has long since been given away by the Crown, is now private property, and is paid half-yearly by the sheriff. In the charters granted to the City of London by Henry II., Richard I., and in the first charter of King John, no mention whatever is made of the sheriffwick. There are many City ordinances for the office of sheriff, disobedience to which is in some cases marked by dismissal. A History of the Sheriffdom was published in 1723.

persons, and 11 excused. But the election is sometimes contested, as in 1830, when there were six candidates. The sheriffs-elect are presented for approbation to the Cursitor Baron of Exchequer, as the representative of the sovereign, and are sworn, on the morrow of St. Michael, as described at pp. 450-1. The numerous trusts of the sheriffs are mostly performed by the under-sheriffs, but the state-duties by the sheriffs themselves. They receive from the City about 1000*l.* during their year of office; but the state and hospitality they are expected to maintain usually cost each sheriff upwards of 2000 guineas: for state-chariot, horses, and state-liveries; the inauguration dinner; a fourth of the Guildhall dinner on Nov. 9th; the Old Bailey dinners (see page 556); and meat at the City prisons, which the sheriffs superintend. There is annually subscribed, for the relief of discharged prisoners and their families, a Sheriffs' Fund, humanely founded by Sheriff Phillips in 1807-8, who also wrote and published a volume upon the duties of the office.* The first Jew sheriff was Mr. David (now Alderman) Salomons, 1835; and the first Roman-Catholic sheriff was Mr. Rd. Swift, M.P., 1851: the latter was attended in state by a Romish priest as his chaplain. A factious sheriff (Slingsby Bethel) is thus commemorated, as *Shimei,* by Dryden:

> " No Rechabite more shunn'd the fumes of wine ;
> Chaste were his cellars, and his shrivel board
> The grossness of a City feast abhorr'd :
> His cooks, with long disuse, their trade forgot—
> Cool was his kitchen, though his brains were hot."
> *Absalom and Achitophel.*

One of the oldest shrievalty customs was that of the lord-mayor drinking to persons for nomination to the office: it was revived in 1682, at the request of Charles II., with a factious object; when Sheriffs Shute and Pilkington were committed by the King to the Tower, upon a false charge of riot.

Sheriff Hoare has left a journal of his shrievalty, in 1740-41, in his own handwriting: describing his investiture in his scarlet gown, by the gold chain taken off the former sheriff and put on him; the delivery of the prisoners and prison-keys, and the keeper's treat of sack and walnuts, Sept. 28th; how the sheriffs, April 6th, entertained the Exchequer officers with 52 calves'-heads, dressed in different manners; how, Sept 2d (anniversary of the Fire of London), the sheriffs went to St. Paul's, in their "black gowns, and no chains, and heard a sermon;" how, Sept. 8th, they went with the lord-mayor to proclaim Southwark Fair ; the Christ's Hospital treat of *sweet cakes and burnt wine,* on St. Matthew's day (Sept. 21st); and sack and walnuts on Sept. 28th, when the Sheriff returned home, to his " great consolation and comfort."

SHOREDITCH,

An ancient manor and parish extending from Norton Folgate to Old-street, and from part of Finsbury to Bethnal Green. It was originally a village on the Roman military highway, called by the Saxons Eald (*i. e.* Old) Street. Stow declares it to have been called Soersditch more than 400 years before his time ; and Weever states it to have been named from Sir John de Soerdich, lord of the manor *temp.* Edward III.,† and who was with that king in his wars with France. The legend of its being called after Jane Shore dying in a *ditch* in its neighbourhood, is a popular error, traceable to a black-letter ballad in the Pepys Col-

* A Letter to the Livery of London, on the Office of Sheriff. By Sir Richard Phillips, Knt., one of the Sheriffs of London and Middlesex. 1808.
† The same family of Soerdich, or Shordich, it is believed, possessed the manor Ickenham, near Uxbridge, and resided at Ickenham Hall, from the reign of Edward III. to our own time.

lection, entitled, *The Woful Lamentation of Jane Shore, a Goldsmith's Wife in London, some time King Edward IV. his Concubine :*

> "I could not get one bit of bread,
> Whereby my hunger might be fed;
> Nor drink, but such as channels yield,
> Or stinking ditches in the field.
> Thus, weary of my life at lengthe,
> I yielded up my vital strength
> Within a ditch of loathsome scent,
> Where carrion dogs did much frequent:
> The which now, since my dying daye,
> Is Shoreditch call'd, as writers saye."

But this ballad is not older than the middle of the 17th century; and no mention is made of Jane so dying in a ballad by Th. Churchyard, dated 1587. Dr. Percy erroneously refers *Shoreditch* to "its being a common sewer, vulgarly *shore*, or drain." It is sometimes called *Sorditch;* which is the most correct, according to the above explanation. An archer of this parish, named Barlo, was styled "Duke of Shoreditch" by Henry VIII, for having outshot his competitors in a shooting-match at Windsor; and the Captain of the Company of Archers of London was long after styled "Duke of Shoreditch." In the Beaufoy Collection are four Shoreditch tokens, one with figures of Edward IV. and his mistress; and the sign of "Jane Shore" is extant in the High-street.

St. Leonard's church, at the north end of Shoreditch, is described at page 134. Near the altar is a tablet to the memory of a descendant of the royal house of Hungary; and in the crypt is the noble altar-tomb of a descendant of the great John Corvinus Huniades, whose son was elected King of Hungary. In the belfry are recorded several feats of bell-ringing, including, 16 March, 1777, when "the College Youths" performed 11,000 changes in 8 hours; adding that their names would be handed down to posterity, "insaturated with glory." In the church-yard is buried Gardner, the worm-destroying doctor of Long Acre: his tomb-stone inscribed, "Dr. John Gardner's (intended) last and best bed-room." In 1811, a writ of arrest was served by a sheriff's officer upon a dead body, as it was being conveyed to this churchyard; which occasioned Lord Ellenborough to declare the process altogether illegal.

Holywell Lane and *Mount* ("heightening of the ground for garden-plots," *Stow*), and *Holywell Row*, in Shoreditch, are named from a holy well there, and a house of Benedictine nuns of that name, founded by a Bishop of London, and rebuilt by Sir Thomas Lovel, of Lincoln's Inn: in St. Leonard's church is some painted glass from one of the Priory windows. "Neare thereunto are builded two publique houses for the acting and shewe of comedies, tragedies, and histories, for recreation. Whereof one is called the Courtein, the other the Theatre; both standing on the south-west side towards the field." (*Stow*, 1st edit. page 349.) Hence the Curtain Theatre, built in Holywell-lane, and *Curtain-road:* here, at the Blue Last public-house, porter was first sold about 1730. In 1854 were erected Almshouses in Brunswick-street, Hackney-road, for 20 aged women of Shoreditch: the architecture is Jacobean. Shore-ditch is one of the Tower Hamlets, and in 1851 contained 109,209 souls.

SKINNER-STREET AND SNOW-HILL.

Skinner-street, extending from Newgate-street to Holborn-hill, was built about 1802, to avoid the circuit of *Snow-hill*, also called Snor, Snore, and Sore Hill: the projector of the improvement was Alder-man Skinner. Upon the site of Commercial-place was a large seven-storied house, burnt down in 1813, valued at 25,000*l*. At No. 41, William Godwin, author of *Caleb Williams*, kept a bookseller's shop, and published his juvenile works under the name of Edward Baldwin: here is an artificial stone relief of Æsop narrating his fables to children. Opposite No. 58, in 1817, was hung Cashman the sailor, who had joined a mob in plundering the gunsmith's shop at the above house.

In a shop-window on Snow-hill, Vandyke saw the picture by Dobson, which led him to seek out the painter in a garret, and recommend him to the king. At the sign of the Star, on Snow-hill, at the house of his friend Mr. Strudwick, a grocer, died, 12th August, 1688, John Bunyan, author of the *Pilgrim's Progress*, and was buried in that friend's vault in Bunhill-fields burial-ground. At No. 37 King-street, Snow-hill, was formerly the Ladies' Charity School, which was established in 1702, and remained in the parish 145 years. Mrs. Thrale and Dr. Johnson were subscribers to this school; and Johnson drew from it his story of Betty Broom, in the *Idler*. In the school minutes, 1763, the ladies of the committee censured the schoolmistress for listening to the story of the Cock-lane Ghost, and "desired her to keep her belief in the article to herself." The School-house is now No. 30 John-street, Bedford-row.

SMITHFIELD,

Anciently just outside the City wall, was the great public walk of the citizens, their race-course, and live market (see page 500). It was a great field for quintain-matches, and was called "Ruffians' Hall," for its frays and common fighting with sword and buckler, superseded by the deadly fight of rapier and dagger. Ben Jonson, in his *Bartholomew Fair*, speaks of "the sword and buckler age in Smithfield" having but recently passed away; and in the *Two Angry Women of Abingdon*, 1599, complaint is made that "the sword and buckler fight begins to grow out of use." The town-green had its clump of trees, "the Elms," which was the place of public execution until the middle of the 13th century, when it was removed to Tyburn. At the Elms suffered William Fitzosbert (Longbeard); here "Mortimer was executed, and let hang two days and two nights, to be seen of the people;" and here perished the patriot Wallace, on St. Bartholomew's even, 1305: the place of blood was in Cow-lane, close to the end of St. John's-court. Upon this field, on Saturday, June 15th, 1381, Richard II. met Wat Tyler and his "shoeless ribalds," the King towards the east, near St. Bartholomew's Priory, and the Commons towards the west; when Tyler, seizing the boy-king's horse, was stabbed by Walworth, mayor of London; and a few days after, Jack Straw, the second rebel in command, was hanged at the Elms. But Smithfield has its sunnier epoch of jousts, tournaments, and feats of arms. Here Edward III. commemorated the brilliant realities of Cressy and Poictiers; and here the doting monarch feasted Alice Pierce ("the lady of the sun") with seven days' chivalric sports. Richard II. held "a great justing here" in 1390, when was "given first the badge of the White Hart, with golden chains and crowns;" and here, in 1396, the king celebrated his marriage by three days' tournament. In 1393 "certain lords of Scotland came into England, to get worship by force of arms in Smithfield" (*Froissart*). This was likewise the scene of ordeal combats, when the place of battle was strewed with rushes: here was fought the whimsical combat of Horner and Peter, as told by Holinshed, and dramatised by Shakespeare (*King Henry VI.*, Part II.)

The reality is thus recorded in the *Grey Friars' Chronicle*, Hen. VI.: "xxvᵒ Aᵒ· Thys yere was a fyghtynge in Smythfelde betwene ane armerar of fletstret and his servant, for worddes agenst the kynge, whereof hys servant asseld hym; and the servant slew the master in the felde."

In the same play (*Henry VI.*) is the king's sentence:
." The witch in Smithfield shall be burn'd to ashes."

The martyrology of Smithfield forms a still more terrible page of its history. Here were burnt the martyrs, from John Rogers, " the proto-martyr of the Marian persecution," in 1555, to Bartholomew Leggatt, in 1611, the last martyr who suffered at the stake in England. Of the 277 persons burnt for heresy in the reign of Mary, the great majority suffered in Smithfield: a large gas-light (in the middle of the pens) de-notes the reputed spot; but the discovery in 1849 of some blackened stones, ashes, and charred human bones, at three feet from the surface, opposite the gateway of St. Bartholomew's church, induces the belief that here was the great *hearth* of the bigot fires. Charred human bones and ashes were also discovered, at five feet from the surface, at the west end of Long-lane, in July 1854.

In Smithfield, also, poisoners were "boiled to death" by statute, in the reign of Henry VIII.

" xiij° A°· Thys yere was a man soddyne in a cautherne (boiled in a cauldron) in Smythfelde, and lett up and downe dyvers tymes tyll he was dede, for because he wold a poyssynd dyvers persons."

" xxij° A°· This yere was a coke boylyd in a cauderne in Smythfeld, for he wolde a powsynd the byshoppe of Rochester, Fycher, with dyvers of hys ser-vanttes; and he was lockyd in a chayne, and pullyd up and downe with a gyb-byt, at dyvers tymes, tyll he was dede."

"xxxiij° A°· The x day of March was a mayde boyllyd in Smythfelde, for poysyng of dyvers persons."—*Chronicle of the Grey Friars of London,* edited by J. Gough Nichols, F.S.A. Printed for the Camden Society, 1852.

From this *Chronicle* we learn that the gallows was " set up at sent Bartylmewys gate." The entries of burnings for " errysee" are also very numerous. Burning for other crimes was, however, continued: Evelyn records, " 1652, May 10.—Passing by Smithfield, I saw a miser-able creature burning who had murdered her husband."

In Stow's time, the encroachments by " divers fair inns, and other buildings," had left but a small portion of Smithfield for the old uses. After the Great Fire, the houseless people were sheltered here in huts.

Over against Pie-corner is *Cock-lane:* Goldsmith's pamphlet re-specting the Cock-lane ghost was first included in his collected Works edited by Peter Cunningham, F.S.A., 1854.

BARTHOLOMEW FAIR, held in Smithfield from the reign of Henry I. to our own time, is described at page 30. The Fair was finally abolished in 1853. The Priory Church of St. Bartholomew is noticed at p. 119. SMITHFIELD MARKET, see page 500.

SMITHFIELD, EAST,

Between Little Tower-hill and Ratcliffe-highway, was, according to Stow, before the reign of King Stephen, made a vineyard by the Con-stables of the Tower, being forcibly taken by them from the Priory of the Holy Trinity, within Aldgate. Here Edward III. founded New Abbey, in 1359, called the White Order, and named Eastminster. Spenser the poet is said to have been born in East Smithfield; and here, 24th July, 1629, Charles I. killed a stag, which he had hunted from Wanstead, in Essex. (*Stow.*) A plan of East Smithfield in Elizabeth's reign shows the site of an ancient stone cross, and the stocks and cage.

SOCIETY OF ANTIQUARIES.

The early history of this Society, from 1707, when the few members first met, " upon pain of forfeiture of sixpence," is noted at page 530: the plan was drawn up by Humphrey Wanley; and the minutes date from Jan. 1, 1718, when the members brought to the weekly meetings, coins, medals, seals, intaglios, cameos, manuscripts, records, rolls, genealogies, pictures, drawings, &c. The first president was Martin Folkes, 1751. The Society occupy apartments in Somerset House, adjoining those of the Royal Society; and the meetings of "the Royals" succeed those of "the Antiquaries," on the same evenings; the sessions of the two Societies beginning with the third Thursday in November, and ending with the third Thursday in June. The Antiquaries' anniversary is held on April 23, but the annual dinner was discontinued in 1854. The president is Viscount Mahon, the accomplished historian. Terms of admission reduced in 1853 from 8 to 5 guineas entrance-fee; and from 4 to 2 guineas annual subscription. The strict form of admission is by the president or presiding officer placing upon his head a cocked-hat; in one hand he holds the Society's iron-gilt mace, and with the other hand he welcomes the new Fellow, saying: "By the authority and in the name of the Society of Antiquaries of London, I admit you a Fellow thereof." To the names of the members are usually appended F.S.A. The Obligation Book contains the signatures of the leading antiquaries, Fellows of the Society. The Society possess a LIBRARY, noticed at page 458; and a MUSEUM, see page 530. A synopsis of the contents of the Museum is presented to the Fellows. The old paintings and memorials in the Meeting-room and Library are curious.

The Society's Transactions (*Archæologia*), published annually, date from 1770. Among their other publications are *Vetusta Monumenta*, vol. vi., illustrating the Baieux tapestry; Folkes's Tables of English Silver and Gold Coins; Wardrobe-book of Edward I.; Ordinances and Regulations of the Royal Households, from Edward III. to William and Mary; Roy's Military Antiquities of the Romans in Britain; Account of the Collegiate Chapel of St. Stephen, at Westminster; Accounts of the Cathedrals of Exeter, Durham, and Gloucester, and of Bath and St. Albans Abbey Churches; Cædmon's Metrical Paraphrase of the Holy Scriptures in Anglo-Saxon. The Society have also published large historical prints of the Field of the Cloth-of-Gold, 1520; Francis I.'s attempt to invade England, 1545; the Procession of King Edward VI. from the Tower to Westminster; Aggas's Plan of London, &c.

SOCIETY OF ARTS.

"The Society for the Encouragement of Arts, Manufactures, and Commerce," originated with William Shipley, a drawing-master, and brother to the Dean of St. Asaph. With the concurrence of Jacob Viscount Folkestone, Robert Lord Romney, and Dr. Maddox, Bishop of Worcester, the Society first met, March 29, 1754, at Rawthmell's Coffee-house, Henrietta-street, Covent Garden: Shipley acting as Secretary; and the plan of the Society being drawn up by William Baker, the microscopist. Oliver Goldsmith took great interest in the early proceedings of the Society, in a magazine published by Newbery; and the Doctor was a candidate for the secretaryship. Much attention was then bestowed upon "the polite arts:" among the first objects was the offer of premiums for drawings by girls and boys under 16 years of age. The Society next met, 1754-5, in apartments over a circulating-library in Crane-court, Fleet-street; next in Craig's-court, Charing Cross; at the corner of Castle-court, Strand; in 1759 they removed to a house (afterwards Dibdin's Sans Souci) opposite Beaufort-buildings; and next to their new house in John-street, Adelphi, in 1774. Presidents: Viscount Folkestone, 1755-1761; Lord Rodney, 1761-1793; the Duke of Norfolk, 1793-1815; the Duke of Sussex, 1815-1843; when was elected the present President, Prince Albert.

Early Awards of the Society.—The first prize to Richard Cosway, then 15. In 1758, Bacon, the sculptor, for a small figure of Peace; and he gained 9 other high prizes: 1761, Nollekens, for an alto-relievo of Jephtha's Vow, and in 1771 for a more important piece of sculpture; in 1768, Flaxman, and in 1771 the Society's Gold Medal. Lawrence, when 13, received a silver-gilt palette and 5 guineas for his crayon-drawing of the Transfiguration. In 1807, to Sir William Ross, then 12, a silver-gilt palette for a drawing of Wat Tyler; in 1810, a similar reward to Sir Edwin Landseer for an etching; and to B. Wyon, in 1818, the Gold Medal for a medal die. Among the other recipients of prizes may be named Allan Cunningham, Mulready, and Millais.

The first public Exhibition of the works of British Artists was held at the Society's house in the Strand, in 1760: hence originated the Royal Academy, who, in 1776, with Sir Joshua Reynolds at their head, refusing to paint the Society's Great Council-room at the Adelphi, next year Barry, who had signed the refusal with the rest, volunteered to decorate the room without any remuneration at all: the pictures are described at page 545: the room is 47 feet in length, 42 feet in breadth, and 40 in height. Among the prime objects of the Society were the application of art to the improvement of design in Manufactures, now developed in "Art Manufactures;" the improvement of Agriculture and Horticulture; and in 1783 a reward was offered for a reaping-machine. The Society has distributed more than 100,000l. in premiums and bounties. The growth of forest-trees was one of its early objects of encouragement; and among the recipients of its Gold Medal (designed by Flaxman) were the Dukes of Bedford and Beaufort, the Earls of Winterton, Upper Ossory, and Mansfield; and Dr. Watson, Bishop of Llandaff. Then came Agriculture, Chemistry, Manufactures, and Mechanics; including tapestry and the imitation of Turkey carpets, Marseilles and India quilting, spinning and lace-making, improved paper, catgut for musical instruments; straw-bonnets, and artificial flowers. Among the Society's colonial objects were the manufacture of potash and pearlash, the culture of the vine, the growth of silk-worms, indigo, and vegetable oils. Very many rewards have been given by the Society to poor Bethnal-green and Spitalfields weavers, for useful inventions in their manufacture.

The Society's LIBRARY is described at page 465; and its MUSEUM of Models, and the Pictures and Sculpture, at pp. 544-5. Dr. Johnson says of Barry's paintings, "There is a grasp of mind there which you will find nowhere else." The Society held the first regular Exhibition of Useful Inventions in 1761, when a Mr. Bailey explained the several articles to the visitors. The Premiums are annually presented in the Great Room, where have been held Exhibitions of Decorative Art, unequalled in this country. The Society greatly prepared the public mind for the Great Exhibition of 1851; and here Mr. Paxton first developed his plan of its stupendous building, Nov. 13, 1850. Annual Subscription to the Society, Two Guineas. Among the Special Prizes is the bequest of Dr. Swiney of 100 guineas, in a Silver Cup of the same value, to be given every fifth year for the best treatise on Jurisprudence; the Cup, designed by D. Maclise, R.A., is surmounted by figures of Justice, Vengeance, and Mercy; in the centre is a niello of a hall of justice; and at the base are four kneeling slaves. The Centenary of the Society was celebrated July 1854, by a banquet in the Crystal Palace, Sydenham.

For many years the office of Secretary was filled by Arthur Aikin, eldest son of Dr. Aikin, the friend of John Howard, and brother of Lucy Aikin; and who published a *Manual of Mineralogy, Arts and Manufactures*, and a *Chemical Dictionary*. He died in 1854, aged 80. Among the Society's Vice-Presidents was Thomas Hope, author of some tasteful works on costume, furniture, and decoration; and whose house in Duchess-street was a model of artistic design (described at page 489): here was a piece of carved furniture, which, many years after it was executed, was specially noticed by Sir Francis Chantrey: on being asked the reason, he replied, "That was my first work."

SOHO;

A district north-east of Piccadilly, extending to Oxford-street. Mr. Cunningham has found the name "Soho" in the rate-books of St. Martin's as early as the year 1632; thus invalidating the tradition by Pegge and Pennant, that Soho* being the watchword at the battle of Sedgemoor, in 1685, it was given to King-square, in memory of the Duke of Monmouth, whose mansion was upon the south side. The boundaries of Soho are Oxford-street, north; Crown-street, east; King-street south; and Wardour-street and Princes'-street, west. Soho-square and the adjoining fields passed by royal grants to the Earl of St. Alban, the Duke and Duchess of Monmouth, and the Earl of Portland; and the streets are named from this appropriation, or from their builders. The houses in Soho-square and the streets adjoining are remarkably well built, and were tenanted by nobility and gentry until our time. *Carlisle House* and *Street*, named from having been the residence of the Earls of Carlisle, is described at page 391 : here lived Bâch and Abel, the musical composers. *Greek-street* and *Church-street* are named from the Greek Church in Crown-street. In Greek-street the elder Wedgewood had ware-rooms before he removed to St. James's; and Mr. (after Sir Thomas) Lawrence, R.A., was living here in 1806. In *Wardour-street* (Old Soho) French Protestants were early settlers, and probably brought the trade in foreign art (see page 246). *Berwick-street* is described by Hatton (1708) as "a kind of a row; the fronts of the houses resting on columns, make a small piazza." In *Dean-street* lived Sir James Thornhill, at No. 75, which has the staircase-walls of his painting; and at No. 33 died young, in 1819, Harlowe, the painter of the Trial of Queen Katherine. *Gerard-street* is named from Gerard, Earl of Macclesfield, the owner of the site, formerly "the Military Garden" of Henry Prince of Wales, eldest son of James I. (see page 458); and *Prince's-street* is built upon part of the ground: here, in 1718, lived Halley the astronomer. The landlord's title is also preserved in *Macclesfield-street* adjoining. In Gerard House lived the rake Lord Mohun. At No. 43 John Dryden resided with his wife, Lady Elizabeth Howard: his study was the front parlour. Dryden died here in 1700; and here took place the disgraceful interference with the poet's funeral procession by a party of drunken mohocks, headed by Lord Jeffries. In Gerard-street lived Edmund Burke at the time of Warren Hastings' trial; and at the Turk's Head, in Gerard-street (removed from Greek-street, where met the Loyal Association of 1745), Johnson, Sir Joshua Reynolds, and Burke founded the Literary Club in 1764 (see page 195). Here a Society of Artists met in 1753; and another Society, including West, Wilson, Wilton, Chambers, Sandby, &c., who, from the Turk's Head, petitioned George III. to patronise a Royal Academy of Art. In Gerard-street was formerly the chief receiving-house of the Twopenny Post. *Compton-street* was built in the reign of Charles II., by Sir Francis Compton; and *New Compton-street* was first named *Stiddolph-street*, after Sir Richard Stiddolph, the owner of the land.—Dr. Rimbault, in *Notes and Queries*, No. 15. (See SQUARES: *Soho*.)

The Lion Brewery, in Soho, was formerly the property of the uncle of Sir Richard Phillips, who was brought up in this establishment, to which he was

---

* "Soho is the same as 'pray stop'" (Booth's *Analytical Dict.*): hence it may have been applied, in the above instance, to the extension of building in this direction, more especially as it was prohibited by a proclamation in 1671.

heir. This prospective fortune did not, however, overcome his distaste for the business of a brewer; and a passion for literature, and particularly for mathematics and experimental philosophy, led him, at the age of 17, to detach himself from his family connexions, and seek his own chance of life.

SOMERSET HOUSE, OLD,

Or SOMERSET PLACE, on the south side of the Strand, was commenced about 1547, by the Protector Somerset, maternal uncle of Edward VI. To obtain space and building materials, he demolished Strand or Chester's Inn, and the episcopal houses of Lichfield, Coventry, Worcester, and Llandaff, besides the church and tower of St. John of Jerusalem: for the stone, also, he pulled down the great north cloister of St. Paul's; St. Mary's church was also taken down, and the site became part of the garden. The duke's cofferer's account shows the building, in 1551, to have cost 10,091l. (present money, 50,000l.) The architect was John of Padua, contemporary with Holbein; and there is a plan of the house among Thorpe's drawings in the Soane Museum: it was the first building of Italian architecture erected in England. Stow describes it, in 1603, as " a large and beautiful house, but yet unfinished." The Protector did not inhabit the palace; for he was imprisoned in the Tower in 1549, and beheaded in 1552. Somerset Place then devolved to the Crown, and was assigned by Edward VI. to his sister the Princess Elizabeth.

" Feb. 1566-7, Cornelius de la Noye, an alchymist, wrought in Somerset House, and abused many in promising to convert any metall into gold."—*Lord Burghley's Notes.*

In 1570, Queen Elizabeth went to the Royal Exchange, " from her house at the Strand, called Somerset House;" it also occurs as " Somerset Place, beyond Strand Bridge." The queen lent the mansion to her kinsman, Lord Hunsdon, whose guest she occasionally became. At her death, the palace was settled as a jointure-house of the queen-consort; and passed to Anne of Denmark, queen of James I., by whose command it was called *Denmark House.* Inigo Jones erected " new buildings and enlargements." Here the remains of Anne and James I. lay in state. For Henrietta Maria, queen of Charles I., Inigo Jones built a chapel, with a rustic arcade and Corinthian columns, facing the Thames; and here the queen established a convent of Capuchin friars: in the passage leading from east to west, under the quadrangle of the present Somerset House, are five tombstones of the queen's attendants.

From a manuscript inventory in the library of Mr. Gough, " the *chappel goods* at Somerset House" were numerous and costly. Of the goods and furniture appraised in 1649, the *arras* hangings and tapestry were of great value; the state-beds, pavilions, canopies, cloths-of-state, carpets, mantles, table-linen, &c. were very rich : one of the beds of embroidered French satin was valued at 1000l. Among the pictures was the Madonna by Raphael, valued at 2000l. ; a Sleeping Venus by Correggio, at 1000l.; and many by Titian, And. del Sarto, Julio Romano, Guido, Correggio, Giorgione, Vandyke, &c.

Of the tenements " belonging unto Somerset House" (20 inns), the Red Lion, nearly opposite, is the only remaining one among the signs in the list: the sculptured sign-stone is built into the house No. 342.

Inigo Jones died here in 1652. During the Protectorate, the altar and chapel were ordered to be burnt; and in 1659 the palace was about to be sold for 10,000l.; but after the Restoration, the Queen-mother Henrietta returned to Somerset House, which she repaired: hence she exclaims, in Cowley's courtly verse :

"Before my gate a street's broad channel goes,
Which still 7 ith waves of crowding people flows;

> And every day there passes by my side,
> Up to its western reach, the London tide.
> The spring-tides of the term. My front looks down
> On all the pride and business of the town."

Waller's adulatory incense rises still higher :

> " But what new mine this work supplies ?
> Can such a pile from ruin rise ?
> This like the first creation shows,
> As if at your command it rose."
> *Upon Her Majesty's New Buildings at Somerset House.*

Here was introduced into England the inlaying of floors with coloured woods. Pepys gossips of " the queen-mother's court at Somerset House, above our own queen's; mass in the chapel; the garden; and the new buildings, mighty magnificent and costly," " stately and nobly furnished;" and " the great stone stairs in the garden, with the brave echo." The queen-mother died abroad in 1669. In 1669-70 the remains of Monk, Duke of Albemarle, "lay for many weeks in royal state" at Somerset House; and thence he was buried with every honour short of regality. Thither the remains of Oliver Cromwell were removed from Whitehall, in 1658, and were laid in state in the great hall of Somerset House, "and represented in effigie, standing on a bed of crimson velvet :" he was buried from hence with great pomp and pageantry, which provoked the people to throw dirt, in the night, on his escutcheon that was placed over the great gate of Somerset House: his pompous funeral cost 28,000*l.* On the death of Charles II. in 1685, the palace became the sole residence of the queen dowager, Catherine of Braganza; and in 1678 three of her household were charged with the murder of Sir Edmondbury Godfrey, by decoying him into Somerset House, and there strangling him. (See PRIMROSE HILL, page 629.) The queen had here a small establishment of Capuchins, who inhabited "the New Friary," as did the Capuchins in Henrietta-Maria's time, " the Old Friary :" both are shown in a plan, 1706.

Strype describes the palace about 1720: its front with stone pillars its spacious square court, great hall or guard-room, large staircase and rooms of state, larger courts, and "most pleasant garden;" the watergate, with figures of Thames and Isis; and the water-garden, with fountain and statues. Early in the last century, court masquerades were given here; Addison, in the *Freeholder*, mentions one in 1716: and in 1763 a splendid fête was given here by Government to the Venetian Ambassadors. In 1771, the Royal Academy had apartments in the palace, granted them by George III. In 1775, Parliament settled upon Queen Charlotte Buckingham House, in which she then resided, in lieu of Old Somerset House, which was given up to be demolished, for the erection upon the site of certain public offices; the produce of the sale of Ely House being applied towards the expenses. The chapel, which had been opened for the Protestant service, by order of Queen Anne, in 1711, was not closed until 1777. The venerable court-way from the Strand, and the dark and winding steps which led down to the garden beneath the shade of ancient and lofty trees, were the last lingering features of Somerset Place, and were characteristic of the gloomy lives and fortunes of its royal and noble inmates.

SOMERSET HOUSE

Occupies the site of the *old palace*, an area of 800 feet by 500, or a few feet less than the area of Russell-square. It is the finest work of Sir William Chambers : the first stone was laid in 1776 ; and the Strand front, 7 stories high, was nearly completed in 1780.* It consists of a rustic arcade basement of 9 arches, supporting Corinthian columns, and an attic in the centre, with a balustrade at each extremity; the whole in Portland stone. The key-stones of the arches are colossal masks of Ocean, and the eight great rivers of England—the Thames, Humber, Mersey, Medway, Dee, Tweed, Tyne, and Severn—sculptured by Carlini and Wilton. In the frieze of the three middle windows are medallions of George III., his queen, and the Prince of Wales. In the attic are statues of Justice, Truth, Valour, and Temperance; the summit being surmounted by the British Arms, supported by Fame and the Genius of England. The vaultings of the vestibule are enriched with sculptures from the antique, and are supported by two ranges of coupled Doric columns. On the east side are the entrances to the apartments of the Royal Society, the Society of Antiquaries, the Royal Astronomical Society, and the Geological Society; and on the west were those of the Royal Academy, subsequently of the School of Design, next of the University of London Board. Over the central doorway, east, is a bust of Newton; west, of Michael Angelo; by Wilton, R.A.

Facing the vestibule is a massive bronze group of George III. leaning upon a rudder, backed by the prow of a Roman (!) vessel, and a couchant lion; and at the monarch's feet is a figure of the Thames, with an urn and cornucopia: the work of John Bacon, R.A.; cost 2000l.

The inner side of the Strand front has in the attic statues of the four quarters of the globe; and over the centre are the British Arms, supported by marine deities holding a festoon of netting filled with fish, &c. Ornaments of antique altars and sphinxes screen the chimneys; and on the key-stones are sculptured masks of tutelar deities.

The east, west, and south sides of the edifice are Government Offices, which occupy; besides the superstructure, two stories below the general level of the quadrangle, the passages to which are skilfully contrived. The centre of the south side is enriched with Corinthian columns and pilasters, and a pediment with a bas-relief of the arms of the navy of Great Britain, a sea-nymph, sea-horses, and tritons; trophies, vases, &c.

The Thames front, 800 feet in length, is in the Venetian style, and is enriched with columns, pilasters, pediments, &c.: at each extremity is an archway opening to Somerset-place on the west, and King's College on the east; the latter built by Sir Robert Smirke, in 1829, in accordance with Chambers' design. In each end a portico stands on the summit of a semicircular arch, the bases of two out of its four columns resting on the hollow part, giving an air of insecurity intolerable in architecture.

The Terrace is 50 feet in width, and raised 50 feet above the bed of the river, upon a massive rustic arcade, which has a central water-gate surmounted with a colossal mask of the river Thames. The side arches are flanked by rustic columns, and surmounted by stone couchant lions, between 8 and 9 feet in length. The terrace is skirted with a balustrade; and here again is a colossal figure of the Thames. The walk was formerly open to the public on Sundays: the prospect includes the river, with its magnificent bridges and picturesque craft; the city, with its domes, towers, and spires; the forest of masts; and the Surrey hills on the south: recalling Cowley's lines:

> " My other fair and more majestick face
> (Who can the fair to more advantage place?)
> For ever gazes on itself below,
> In the best mirrour that the world can show;

---

* Upon a brick in the wall of the western terrace, or Somerset-place, is cut R. * S. 1780.

And here behold, in a long bending row,
How two joynt cities make one glorious bow;
The midst, the noblest place, possessed by me;
Best to be seen by all, and all o'ersee.
Which way soe'er I turn my joyful eye,
Here the great Court, there the rich Town I spy.
On either side dwells safety and delight;
Wealth on the left, and Power on the right."

In the quadrangle are the Admiralty Offices, where are the Model Room (see p. 541); the Audit Office, the Legacy Duty Office, and Inland Revenue Office (Stamps, Taxes, and Excise). The mechanical stamping is executed in the basement: the presses for stamping postage envelopes, by Edwin Hill, are the perfection of automatic machinery. In Somerset-place, west, is the office of the Tithe Commission and of the Registrar-General :- to the latter are transmitted registers of a million births, deaths, and marriages in a year.

Over the entrance to the Stamps and Taxes Office, on the south side, is a watch-face, popularly believed to be *the watch* of a bricklayer, and placed there as a memorial of his life having been saved in his fall, when the wall was building, by his watch-chain catching in some portion of the scaffold. Such is the traditional story; but the watch-face was really put up some forty years since as a meridian-mark for a transit instrument in a window of the Royal Society's ante-room, in the inner face of the north front.

Telford, the engineer, when he came to London in 1782, got employed on the quadrangle.

Somerset House is almost the only public building which distinguishes the reign of George III.: it cost half a million of money by the extant accounts. The style is Italian, "refined to a degree scarcely excelled by Palladio himself." (*Elmes*.) The exterior is the perfection of masonry. The Ionic, Composite, and Corinthian capitals throughout the building were copied from models executed at Rome, by Chambers, from antique originals: the sculptors employed in the decorations were Carlini, Wilton, Geracci, Nollekens, Bacon, Banks, and Flaxman.

The west wing, left incomplete by Sir W. Chambers, was resumed in 1852 (for the Inland Revenue Office), Pennethorne architect: this wing, 300 feet in length, will face Wellington-street; its south end was completed in 1853: the details are copied from the main building; but the ornamental sculpture is very inferior.

SOUTH-SEA HOUSE (THE),

Threadneedle-street and Old Broad-street, is the office of the South-Sea Company, originated by Harley, Earl of Oxford, and Sir John Blunt ("much-injured Blunt"), in 1711, for the discharge of nearly 10 millions of public debt; for which they were granted, in 1720, the monopoly of the trade to the South Seas and the mines of Spanish America. In April 1720 the Company's stock rose to 319*l.* per cent; and early in June it had risen to 890*l.* per cent. The Directors then opened fresh books for a subscription of 4,000,000*l.* at 1000*l.* per cent. Before the expiration of the month, the subscription was at 200*l.* per cent premium, and the stock at nearly 1100*l.* Newton, on being asked as to the continuance of the rising of the South-Sea stock, answered, that "he could not calculate on the madness of the people." Prior writes: "I am tired of politics, and lost in the South Sea. The roaring of the waves and the madness of the people were justly put together." A journal of Aug. 5 says: "Our South-Sea equipage increases every day; the city ladies buy South-Sea jewels, hire South-Sea coaches, and buy South-Sea estates." With the connivance of the Government, the scheme reached this climax, when the frauds of the Directors transpired; within three months the stock fell to 86*l.* per cent, and "the South Sea-Bubble" burst. (See EXCHANGE ALLEY, page 272.)

The South-Sea scheme was lampooned by Swift, and satirised by Pope:

> "Statesmen and patriots plied alike the stocks,
> Peeress and butler shared alike the box;
> And judges jobbed, and bishops bit the town,
> And mighty dukes packed cards for half-a-crown:
> Britain was sunk in lucre's sordid charms."

Among the victims was the poor maniac, "Tom of Ten Thousand" (Eustace Budgell), who lost his whole fortune and his reason. The Duke of Chandos lost 300,000*l.* Gay, the poet, possessed 20,000*l.* South-Sea Stock, which he neglected to sell, and thus lost profit and principal. (See Mackay's *Popular Delusions*.)

The Company has long ceased to be a trading body; and in 1853-4 the South-Sea stock, to the amount of 10 millions, was converted or paid off. The original office (formerly the Excise Office) was in Old Broad-street, and was known as "the Old South-Sea House." The new building in Threadneedle-street has a Doric portico, and incloses a quadrangle, with a Tuscan colonnade and a fountain; but it has "few or no traces of goers-in or comers-out—a desolation something like Balclutha's." (*C. Lamb.*) The great hall for sales and the dining-room are hung with portraits of governors and sub-governors, huge charts, &c. Underneath are vaulted cellars, wherein were once deposited dollars and pieces of eight; but the place is now an uncheery void.

SOUTHWARK.

Of the etymology of this ancient suburb, Mr. Ralph Lindsay, F.S.A., has collected *ninety-seven authorities*, commencing with Suðpepke, during the Saxon Heptarchy: but there is abundant proof that it was an extensive station and cemetery of the Romans during an early period of their dominion in Britain, attested by the fictile vases and pavements (portions of Roman houses) found in Southwark (see page 651). It was embanked, contemporaneously with the three great Roman roads shown to have terminated in St. George's Fields, and to have communicated with the City by a *trajectus*, or ferry, over the Thames to Dowgate, from Stoney-street, Bankside; and another to the Tower, or *Arx Palatina*, from Stoney-lane, Tooley-street. To its fortification may be traced the Saxon name, *Sudwerche*, the south work of London. It is called *Surder-virke* in a Danish account of a battle fought here by King Olaf in 1008; and *Suth-weorce* in the narrative of Earl Godwin's attack in 1052, when here was a wooden bridge. Southwark was burnt by William the Conqueror. In Domesday-book the Bishop of Baieux hath here one monastery (Bermondsey), and one haven (St. Saviour's dock). On coins of William I. we find *Svethewer,* or *Svetherk;* on pennies of William II., *Svthevk, Svthewi,* and *Svthewr;* and about 1086, the annual revenue derived from it was only 16*l.* In 1327, upon the complaint that Southwark was the refuge of felons and thieves, Edward III. sold the vill or town to the citizens of London,—the king still being lord of the manor, and appointing the bailiff. Edward IV. granted the citizens an annual fair; by charter of Edward VI., the full control of Southwark was vested in the citizens; and by Act of Common Council, 1550, it was constituted a ward of the City, by the name of Bridge Without,—the first alderman of which was Sir John Ayliffe, 1551. Southwark has sent members to parliament since *temp.* Edward I. It was formerly famous for its artists in glass, who, *temp.* Henry VIII., glazed the windows of King's College chapel, Cambridge.

On July 1, 1450, Jack Cade arrived in Southwark (see page 402);

and on Feb. 3, 1554, Sir Thomas Wyat and the Kentyshemen appeared here; both, probably, in St. George's Fields.

"At this time was Wyat entered into Kent-street, and so by Sainct George's Church into Southwarke. Himselfe and part of his companie cam in goode array down Barmesey-strete."—*The Chronicle of Queen Jane, Queen Mary,* &c.

In 1642, Southwark was defended by a fort with four half bulwarks, at the Dog and Duck, St. George's Fields; a large fort with four bulwarks, near the end of Blackman-street; and a redoubt with four flanks, near the Lock Hospital, Kent-street.

The ancient town, however, was but a small portion of what we know as *the Borough,* and was the Guildable Manor, extending from St. Mary Overy's Dock westward, to Hays-lane, Tooley-street, eastward; south as far as the Town-hall, thence to Counter-street and St. Mary Overy's Dock. The other portions, viz. the King's Manor and the Great Liberty Manor, were not part of the Borough until they were purchased by the Corporation of London from King Edward VI.; the Corporation being the lords.

Southwark was first called *the Borough* in the eighteenth century; it occupies an area nearly equal to that of the City of London itself. The principal street, from the south end of Old London Bridge to St. Margaret's Hill, was formerly called *Long Southwark* (Howell's *Londinopolis*), afterwards High-street, but is now *Wellington street;* thence *St. Margaret's Hill;* and next, *High-street, Blackman-street, and Newington Causeway.*

At No. 6 Blackman-street, Sir James South (eldest son of a dispensing chemist in the High-street) made several valuable astronomical observations. (See KENSINGTON, page 43L.)

At No. 104, High-street, sign of the Golden Key (of which a Token exists), lived Mr. Elliotson, chemist and druggist, father of John Elliotson, M.D., F.R.S.

The old High-street had many picturesque gabled houses in the present century, the last of which were removed for the approach to New London Bridge (see page 57). On the east side remain several old inns (see page 401): one of the taverns on the west side was "the Tumble-down Dick," in our time painted as a drunken toper, but originally a caricature of the downfal of Richard Cromwell, "the New Protector." Nearly opposite the east end of St. Saviour's Church and tower, and the Lady-chapel, was built in 1854 a Clock-tower, resembling a market-cross, of Gothic design, with a canopied niche for a statue of the great Duke of Wellington. Adjoining the *Railway Stations* (see page 641) was *St. Olave's School,* taken down in 1849 (see page 218). Here also is ST. THOMAS'S HOSPITAL, described at page 286; and ST. THOMAS'S CHURCH, at page 163.

Tooley-street (eastward of London Bridge) is corrupted from St. Olave's, or St. Olaff's, street. Here were the *Bridge House and Yard,* for the stowage of materials for the repairs of London Bridge; besides corn granaries, public ovens, and a public brew-house: the site is now Cotton's Wharf and Hays's Wharf.

The *Borough Compter,* a prison, in Mill-lane, occupies the site of the Inn of the Abbot of Battle, its mill, &c.

Southwark possessed two *Mints for coinage,* described at pages 508 and 509: the ancient mint is thought to have stood upon the site of the house of the Prior of Lewes, in Carter-lane, nearly opposite St. Olave's Church, in Tooley-street. (See CRYPTS, page 242.) Here too was "the Abbot's Inn of St. Augustine" (deed 1280), afterwards belonging to the St. Leger family: and thence called Sellinger (*i. e.* St. Leger's), now Chamberlain's, Wharf. Next was the Bridge-house; and then, eastward, the Inn of the Abbot of Battle; and Battle-bridge, over a water-course pertaining to the Abbey. The Manor of the Maze, Sir John Burcettor's, *temp.* Henry VI., is kept in memory by Maze-lane and Maze-pond; and upon the site of "St. Thomas's Tents" the Protestant refugees of the Palatinate in Germany "pitched their tents" in the reign of Queen Anne. The Maze was built upon in Aubrey's time.

Horselydown extends from Tooley-street to Dockhead: it was, *temp.* Elizabeth, a grazing-field (Horseydowne). Here has been rebuilt, upon a handsome scale, St. Olave's Grammar School for 600 boys (see p. 218).

"This street, Horselydown, (as I was told by a sober counsellor-at-law, and who said he had it from an old record,) was so called, for that the water, formerly overflowing it, was so effectually drawn off, that the place became a plain green field, where *horses* and other cattle used to pasture and *lye* down, before the street was built."—*Hatton,* 1708.

On May 11, 1854, Mr. G. R. Corner, F.S.A., communicated to the Society of Antiquaries Notices of a Drawing in the Society's possession, being a copy of a picture at Hatfield House, representing a *fête* on Horselydown; and of a plan of Horselydown in 1544, belonging to the governors of St. Olave's and St. John's Grammar-School. The picture shows a view of the Tower of London in the distance. The foreground is occupied by holiday groups; cooks are preparing a large repast at a kitchen; and in the mid-distance are the stocks, with a solitary tenant. Underneath a tree are two figures, supposed to represent Ben Jonson and Shakspeare, who are not unlikely to have been present at this *fête.*

The Priory of St. Mary Overie, and *Church of St. Saviour,* are described at pages 156-159: in the Cotton Collection is a book which formerly belonged to a Prior.

Montague-close, adjoining St. Saviour's Church, was the cloister of the monastery; and, after the Dissolution, appertained to the mansion built by Sir Anthony Brown (Viscount Montague), who obtained a grant of the site of the Priory of St. Mary Overie, and the messuages, wharfs, shops, &c.; and in St. Mary Overy's Dock was the Priory mill.

Bankside, "the Bank" (Thames-bank in Domesday-book), extends from near St. Saviour's Church to Blackfriars Bridge. Here were two "Beare-gardens, places wherein were kept beares, bulls, and other beasts, to be bayted; as also mastives, in several kenles, nourished to bayt them" (*Stow*). Here Edward Alleyn, the founder of Dulwich College, kept the Bear-garden, *temp.* Elizabeth and James I.; but "His Majesty's Bear-garden" was removed to Hockley-in-the-Hole, Clerkenwell, in 1686-7: the site of the old Bear-garden is now occupied by the Eagle Foundry, adjacent to Bear-garden Wharf. Here also were the Globe, the Rose, the Hope, and the Swan Theatres (see Theatres). Between the Bear-gardens and the Clinke Prison were the Stew-houses, regulated by parliament as remotely as 1162 (8th Henry I.): they were held by Walworth, mayor, as lessee under the Bishop of Winchester, and were spoiled and plundered by Wat Tyler: the allowed stew-houses had their signs painted on their walls towards the Thames; as a Boar's Head, the Cross Keys, the Cardinal's Hat, &c. The stews were put down by sound of trumpet, by Henry VIII. Before the Restoration the theatres had disappeared, and Bankside became the abode of dyers, "for the conveniency of the water." Here are *Cardinal's Cap Alley* and *Pike Garden;* also *Rose Alley* and *Globe Alley,* from the old theatres. Pike Garden is named in a parliamentary survey of 1649 as "late parcel of the possessions of Charles Stuart, late king of England;" and in another survey, made in 1652, occurs "the late king's barge-house, on the Bankside."

Winchester House, or Palace, founded about 1107, by Bishop Walter Giffard, with its courts, offices, and water-stairs, occupied great part of "the Bank;" and had on the south gardens, statues, fountains, and a spacious park : hence *Park-street*. The decaying palace was let as warehouses and wharfs ; and the venerable remains of its great hall, with a grand circular gable-window, of rare tracery, were laid open by a fire in August 1814. The Vinegar-works of Messrs. Pott are upon part of the park site, and are held of the see of Winchester. Adjoining was *Rochester House*, the residence of the Bishops of Rochester : it stood on the north side of the Borough Market-place, part of which was Rochester-yard; and Rochester-street still exists. This estate, anciently called Grimes Croft, was granted by William, second Earl of Warren, to the monks of Rochester, by placing his knife upon the altar of St. Andrew. Rochester House was taken down in 1604.

Deadman's-place, west of the market, is said to be corrupted from Desmond-place, where dwelt the Earl of Desmond : here are the College founded by Thomas Cure, saddler to Edward VI., Mary, and Elizabeth; almshouses built by Edward Alleyn, 1616, and other almshouses.

Southwark Tokens.—In the Beaufoy Collection, at Guildhall, are "the Bore's Head," 1649 (between Nos. 25 and 26 High-street) : it was last leased to the family of the author of the present volume, and was sublet in tenements, as "Boar's-Head-court," taken down in 1830. Next also is a "Dogg and Dvcke" token, 1651 (St. George's Fields) ; "the Greene Man," 1651 (which remains in Blackman-street) ; "ye Bull Head Taverne," 1667, mentioned by Edward Alleyn, founder of Dulwich College, as one of his resorts; "Duke of Suffolk's Head," 1669; and the "Swan with Two Necks."

Southwark and the adjacent districts are noted for their manufactures : as rope-walks and tan-pits at Bermondsey; barge and boat builders, sawyers and timber-merchants, at Rotherhithe; also, hat-making, brewing, vinegar-yards, and distilleries, glass-houses, potteries, and soap and candle works.

The Southwark Arms are, Arg., a rose displayed. The Bridge-house mark is usually, but erroneously, used to designate Southwark because the manors form part of the Bridge-house estates. That mark is, azure, an annulet ensigned with a cross patée, or, interlaced with a saltire conjoined in base, of the second. The City jurisdiction, according to the inscription upon the boundary-stone at the western extremity of Bethlehem Hospital wall, and other parts of the liberties, extends northward to the Thames, and eastward to St. Thomas-a-Watering in the Kent-road ; comprehending the parishes of St. George, St. Saviour (exclusive of the Clink Liberty), St. Thomas, St. Olave, and St. John. (See BERMONDSEY, p. 40. ROTHERHITHE, p. 652.)

SOUTHWARK FAIR,

anciently called "Our Lady Faire in Southwark," was granted by Edward VI., in 1550, when the sum of 647*l*. 2*s*. 1*d*. was paid to the King by the Corporation of London for the two manors and divers lands and tenements. The Fair, held on September 7th, 8th, and 9th, was opened by the lord mayor and sheriffs riding to St. Magnus' Church after dinner, at two o'clock in the afternoon : the former vested with his collar of SS., without his hood; and all dressed in their scarlet gowns, lined, without their cloaks. They were attended by the Sword-bearer, wearing his embroidered cap, and carrying "the pearl sword;" and at the church were met by the aldermen, all of whom, after evening prayer, rode over the bridge in procession, passed through the Fair, and continued either to St. George's Church, Newington Bridge, or to the stones pointing out the City liberties ; St. Thomas-a-Watering. They then returned over the bridge, : to the Bridge House, where a banquet was provided, when the aldermen took leave of the lord mayor; and all parties being returned home, the bridge-masters gave a supper to the lord mayor's officers. Sheriff Hoare thus describes the ceremony in 1741: On the 8th of September the sheriffs waited on the lord mayor in procession, "the City music going before, to proclaim *Southwark Fair*, as it is commonly called; although the ceremony is no more than our going in our coaches through the Borough, and, turning round by St. George's Church, back again to the Bridge House; and this is to signify the license to begin the Fair." "On this day the Sword-bearer wears a fine *embroidered cap*, said to have been worked and presented to the City by a monastery." Evelyn and Pepys describe the Fair. Jacob Hall was one of its famous rope-dancers; and early in the last century, Crawley's puppet-show of the Creation, " with the addition of Noah's Flood," Squire and Sir John Spendall; Dancing Dogs, and " the Ball of Little Dogs," danced before Queen Anne; were Sovthwark Fair sights. Hogarth, in his plate of the Fair, shows Figg the prize-fighter, and Cadman the rope-flyer. In 1743 the Fair continued fourteen days, and extended to the Mint; an attempt was then made to put down the shows, but the Fair was not finally suppressed until 1763: the booth-keepers used to collect money at their stalls for Marshalsea prisoners.

SPITALFIELDS

Includes large portions of Bethnal-green, Shoreditch, Whitechapel, and Mile-end New-town. Part of the site was anciently *Lolesworth*, a cemetery of Roman London, in breaking up which, "for clay to make brick," about 1576, were found several urns full of ashes and burnt bones, and copper coins of Claudius, Vespasian, Nero, Antoninus Pius, Trajan, &c.; also fragments of Roman pottery and glass. (See *Stow*, p. 64.) At the same time were found some stone coffins (British or Saxon), which are preserved in the vaults of Christchurch.

Spitalfields is named from its having been the site and property of the Priory and Hospital of St. Mary Spittle without Bishopsgate, founded in 1197, by Walter Brune, citizen of London, and Rosia his wife, for Augustine canons; at the Dissolution in 1534 it had 180 beds for the receipt of the poor of charity. Bagford, in Leland's *Collectanea*, mentions the priory, then standing, strongly built of timber, with a turret at one angle: its ruins were discovered early in the last century north of Spital-square. In one of the houses built here lived the celebrated Lord Bolingbroke. At the north-east corner of Spital-square was placed the Pulpit-cross, whence were preached, in the open air, the Spital Sermons* (see p. 123): the pulpit was destroyed in the Civil Wars. In the map executed in the reign of Elizabeth, the Spittle *fields* are at the north-east extremity of London, with only a few houses on the site of the Spital. The map of a century later shows a square field bounded with houses, with the old Artillery Ground on the west, which had been let by the last prior to the Artillery Company, and is now the site of Artillery-street. "A Faire in Spittle-fields" is described in a scarce pamphlet in the British Museum, whereat William Lilly announces his astrological wares for sale; and Nicholas Culpepper, the herbalist, says:

"Bid money, tho' but little ;
For night comes on, and we must leave the Spittle."

Culpepper occupied a house then in the fields, and subsequently a public-house at the corner of Red-Lion-court. Hard by the priory

* Hatton relates of a Spital-sermon: "In 1632, three brothers, named Wincope, were called from remote places, and preached on the three sermon-days, agreeing so nicely in their subject, that the second continued what the first began, and the third brought it to a conclusion."

site is Paternoster-row, where, and not in Paternoster-row, St. Paul's (see p. 608), some antiquaries maintain, Tarlton, the player at the Curtain Theatre, "kept an ordinary in these pleasant fields." Bethnal-green and Spitalfields were grassy open spaces in the last century; but Spital-square, at the south-east corner, has been the heart of the silk district since "the poor Protestant strangers, Walloons and French," driven from France by the revocation of the Edict of Nantes, settled here, and thus founded the silk-manufacture in England; introducing the weaving of lustrings, alamodes, brocades, satins, paduasoys, du-capes, and black velvets: in 1713 it was stated that silks, gold and silver stuffs, and ribbons, were made here as good as those of French fabric; and that black silk for hoods and scarfs was made annually worth 300,000*l.* During the reigns of Anne, George I. and II., the Spitalfields weavers greatly increased: in 1832, 50,000 persons were entirely dependent on the silk-manufacture; and the looms varied from 14,000 to 17,000. Of these, great numbers are often unemployed; and the distribution of funds raised for their relief has attracted to Spitalfields a great number of poor persons, and thus pauperised the district. The earnings of weavers in 1854 did not exceed 10*s.* per week, working from 14 to 16 hours a-day: the weaving is either the richest or the thinnest and poorest. The weavers are principally English, and of English origin; but the manufacturers or masters are of French extraction; and the Guillebauds, the Desormeaux, the Cha-bots, and the Turquands, the Mercerons and the Chauvets, trace their connexion with the refugees of 1685. Many translated their names into English, by which the old families may still be known: thus, the Lemaitres called themselves Masters; the Leroys, King; the Tonne-liers, Cooper; the Lejeunes, Young; the Leblancs, White; the Le-noirs, Black; the Loiseaus, Bird.

The weavers' houses, built in narrow streets, have wide latticed win-dows in the upper stories, which light the work-room. Upon the roofs are bird-traps and other bird-catching contrivances; for the weavers supply London with singing-birds, as linnets, woodlarks, goldfinches, greenfinches, and chaffinches; and many, in October and March, get their livelihood by systematic bird-catching: matches of singing or "jerking" call-birds are determined by the burning of an inch of candle. Spitalfields weavers have extremely small heads, 6½, 6⅝, and 6¾ inches being the prevailing widths; and the same fact is observable in Coventry: the medium size of the male head in England is 7 inches. The weavers' practice of *singing at their looms* was doubtless brought with them from the Continent, as was the custom of woollen-weavers.

"I would I were a weaver, I could sing all manner of songs."—*Falstaff*, in *Henry IV.* Part I. act ii.

"He got his cold with sitting up late, and singing catches with clothworkers."—*Cubbard*, in Ben Jonson's *Silent Woman*, act iii. sc. 4.

Spitalfields was a hamlet of Stepney until 1729, when it was made a distinct parish, and Christchurch was consecrated (see p. 123). Among the parochial charities is "cat and dog money," an eccentric bequest to be paid on the death of certain pet cats and dogs.

Philanthropy is at work in the Ragged School and the Artisans' Home (or club-house). In *Crispin-street* is the Government School of Design, where are awarded prizes for designs for fabrics, draw-ing and painting from nature, crayon-drawing, &c. Spitalfields Mar-ket is mentioned by Hatton, in 1708, as fine "for flesh, fowl, and roots." In the district is VICTORIA PARK (see pp. 596-7), and the *City Consumption Hospital.*

In Crispin-street, until 1845, the *Mathematical Society* occupied large apart-ments, for their philosophical instruments and library of 3000 volumes. The

Society, which also cultivated electricity, was established in 1717, and met at the Monmouth's Head, in Monmouth-street, until 1725, when they removed to the White Horse Tavern, in Wheeler-street; from thence, in 1735, to Ben Jonson's Head, in Pelham-street; and next to Crispin-street. The members were chiefly tradesmen and artisans; among those of higher rank were Canton, Dollond, Thomas Simpson, and Crossley. The Society lent their instruments (airpumps, reflecting telescopes, reflecting microscopes, electrical machines, surveying instruments, &c.), with books for the use of them, on the borrowers giving a note of hand for the value thereof. The number of members was not to exceed the square of seven, except such as were abroad or in the country; but this was increased to the squares of eight and nine. The members met on Saturday evenings: each present was to employ himself in some mathematical exercise, or forfeit one penny; and if he refused to answer a question asked by another in mathematics, he was to forfeit twopence. The Society long cherished a taste for exact science; but in 1845, when on the point of dissolution, the few remaining members made over their books, records, and memorials to the Royal Astronomical Society, of which these members were elected fellows.—Abridged from Weld's *History of the Royal Society*, vol. i. pp. 467-8. At Bethnal-green, in 1648, Sir Balthazar Gerbier established "The Academy for Foreign Languages, and all Noble Sciences and Exercises."

SPRING GARDEN,

Originally an appurtenance to the palace of Whitehall, and situate on the north-western verge of St. James's Park, is named from its waterspring or fountain, set playing by the spectator treading upon its hidden machinery—an eccentricity of the Elizabethan garden. Spring Garden, by a patent which is extant, in 1630 was made a bowling-green by command of Charles I. "There was kept in it an ordinary of six shillings a meal (when the king's proclamation allows but two elsewhere); continual bibbing and drinking wine all day under the trees; two or three quarrels every week. It was grown scandalous and insufferable: besides, my Lord Digby being reprehended for striking in the king's garden, he said he took it for a common bowling-place, where all paid money for their coming in."—*Mr. Garrard to Lord Strafford.*

In 1634 Spring Garden was put down by the king's command, and ordered to be hereafter no common bowling-place. This led to the opening of "a New Spring Garden" (Shaver's Hall), by a gentleman-barber, a servant of the lord chamberlain's. The old garden was, however, re-opened; for 13th June, 1649, says Evelyn, "I treated divers ladies of my relations in Spring Gardens:" but 10th May, 1654, he records that Cromwell and his partisans had shut up and seized on Spring Gardens, "wch till now had been ye usual rendezvous for the ladys and gallants at this season."

Spring Garden was, however, once more re-opened; for, in *A Character of England*, 1659, it is described as

"The inclosure not disagreeable, for the solemnness of the grove, the warbling of the birds, and as it opens into the spacious walks at St. James's. * * * It is usual to find some of the young company here till midnight; and the thickets of the garden seem to be contrived to all advantages of gallantry, after they have refreshed with the collation, which is here seldom omitted, at a certain cabaret in the middle of this paradise, where the forbidden fruits are certain trifling tarts, neat's tongues, salacious meats, and bad Rhenish."

"The New Spring Garden"* at Lambeth (afterwards Vauxhall) was flourishing in 1661-3; when the ground at Charing Cross was built upon, as "Inner Spring Garden" and "Outer Spring Garden." Buck-

* Named from the Garden at Charing Cross, as we do not trace any "waterspring" at Vauxhall. Sir John Hawkins says: "Sir Samuel Morland having planted the large garden with stately trees, and laid it out in shady walks, it obtained the name of Spring Gardens. There was likewise a 'New Spring Garden' at Pimlico, the name having been applied to a public garden generally."

ingham-court is named from the Duke of Buckingham, one of the rakish frequenters of Spring Garden; and upon the site of Drummond's banking-house was "Locket's Ordinary, a house of entertainment much frequented by gentry," and a relic of the Spring Garden gaiety:

"For Locket's stands where gardens once did spring."

Dr. King's *Art of Cookery*, 1709.

In Spring Garden lived Prince Rupert, from 1674 to his death:

"1682, Nov. 29. Died of a fever and pleurisy, at his house in the Spring Garden, Rupert, Prince Palatine of the Rhine, &c., in the 63d year of his age."
—*Historian's Guide*, 3d edit. 1688.

Milton, when first appointed Latin secretary, lodged at one Thomson's, at Charing Cross, opening into the Spring Garden. Here the witty and beautiful dramatist, Mrs. Centlivre, died, December 1, 1723, at the house of her third husband, Joseph Centlivre, "Yeoman of the Mouth" (head cook) to Queen Anne. Colley Cibber lived "near the Bull-head Tavern, in Old Spring Garden," from 1711 to 1714. Hatton, in 1708, describes: "Spring Garden, near Charing Cross backward, and S.W. from it, between the Red Lion inn (near the S.E. end of the Haymarket) and Wallingford House, near the Horse Guards."

Spring Garden was formerly noted for its sights: the Incorporated Society of Artists exhibited here; here, in 1806, at Wigley's Rooms, were shown Serres's Panorama of Boulogne; foreign cities and sea-pieces; also Maillardet's automatic figures, including a harpsichord-player, a rope-dancer, and a singing-bird. Here also was exhibited Marshall's *Peristrephic* Panorama of the Battle of Waterloo, which the spectators viewed turning round.

SQUARES.

The garden-spaces or planted Squares are the most recreative features of our metropolis; in comparison with which the *piazze*, *plazas*, and *places* of continental cities are wayworn and dusty areas, with none of the refreshing beauty of a garden or green field:

"Fountains and trees our wearied pride do please,
Even in the midst of gilded palaces;
And in our towns the prospect gives delight,
Which opens round the country to our sight."

Spratt, quoted in Wren's *Parentalia*.

Yet the majority of the London Squares are the growth of the last century; and few of the western squares existed before 1770; their sites being then mostly sheep-walks, paddocks, and kitchen-gardens. It was at first attempted to name squares "quadrates:" in 1732 Maitland wrote, "the stately quadrate denominated King-square, but vulgarly Soho-square;" and the phrase is retained in his edition of 1756.

BEDFORD SQUARE, built 1800-6, was formerly "St. Giles's ruins." At No. 6 lived Lord Chancellor Eldon.

BELGRAVE, CHESTER, and EATON SQUARES, named from their ground-landlord, the Marquis of Westminster, are noticed at page 37: the centres of the first and third were nursery-grounds. At No. 19 Chester-square died, in 1852, Dr. Mantell, F.R.S., the geologist.

BERKELEY SQUARE, built 1698, is named from Berkeley House, which occupied the site of Devonshire House. On the east side of this square is Lansdowne House (see page 489): the beehive upon the gate-piers is one of the family crests. At No. 11 died Horace Walpole in 1797. No 44, built by Kent, has a noble staircase and saloon. At No. 45 the great Lord Clive destroyed himself in 1774. A few link-extinguishers remain flanking doorways: the trees in the centre are old and picturesque: here was formerly an equestrian statue of George III., by Wilton.

BLOOMSBURY, first named SOUTHAMPTON, SQUARE, from Southampton House upon its north side, was built by the Earl of Southampton, whose daughter, Lady Rachel Russell, dates her *Letters* from here. Evelyn, in 1665, notes it as "a noble square or piazza, a little towne," with "good aire;" and the Grand Duke Cosmo was taken to see Bloomsbury as one of the wonders of England. Baxter, the nonconformist divine, lived here when he was persecuted by Judge Jefferies. The Earls-of Chesterfield had a mansion here. Sir Hans Sloane lived on the south side; and here Dr. Franklin came to see Sloane's Curiosities, "for which," says Franklin, "he paid me handsomely." Dr. Radcliffe lived here when he gave 520*l.* to the poor nonjuring clergy. Lord Mansfield's house was at the north-east corner, when it was burnt to the walls by the rioters of 1780, and his books, papers, and furniture made into a bonfire in the square. On the north side is a bronze sitting statue of Charles James Fox, by Westmacott. Ralph describes this side as "one of the finest situations in Europe for a palace," with gardens and view of the country.

BRIDGEWATER SQUARE, Barbican, was once the site of the mansion and gardens of the Earl of Bridgewater. "The middle is neatly enclosed with palisado pales and set round with trees, which renders the place very delightful."—*Strype.*

BRUNSWICK and MECKLENBURGH SQUARES, with the Foundling Hospital and grounds between them, form an airy group;. northward is TORRINGTON SQUARE.

BRYANSTONE and MONTAGUE SQUARES were built on Ward's Field, and the site of Apple Village, by David Porter, who was once chimney-sweeper to the village of Marylebone. At St. Mary's church, Bryanstone-square, June 7, 1838, Miss Landon (L. E. L.) was privately married, by her brother, to Geo. Maclean, governor of Cape Coast Castle.

CAVENDISH SQUARE (between two and three acres), named from the Lady Henrietta Cavendish Holles, the wife of Harley, Earl of Oxford, was planned on the north side of Tyburn-road in 1715, when the locality was infested by footpads, who often robbed and stripped persons in the fields between London and Marybone. Margaret-street Chapel about seventy years since was an isolated building in Marylebone-fields: a shady "Lover's Walk" passed close by the chapel to Manchester-square; another walk led through the fields to Paddington. The square was laid out about 1717; the whole of the north side being taken by "the Grand Duke" of Chandos, who proposed to build here a palatial residence, and to purchase all the property between Cavendish-square and his palace of Canons at Edgeware, so that he might ride from town to the country *through his own estate.* In the British Museum is a view of the mansion, designed by John Price: the wings only were built; one being the large mansion at the corner of Harley-street, which has been occupied by the Princess Amelia, aunt to George III.; by the Earl of Hopetown, and the Hopes of Amsterdam; next by George Watson Taylor, Esq., who assembled here a very valuable collection of paintings. The other wing of the Duke's plan is the corresponding mansion at the corner of Chandos-street. The centre is principally occupied by two splendid mansions, with Corinthian columns, designed by James of Greenwich. At this period Harcourt House on the west side was the only other house here: "it presents, with its high court-walls and *porte-cochère*, more of the appearance of a Parisian mansion than any other house in London." (*S. Angell.*) The ground was first sold at 2s. 6d. per foot. In the centre of the square is an equestrian metal statue of William Duke of Cumberland; and on the south side a colossal standing bronze statue of Lord George Bentinck, third son of the Duke of Portland. Southward is *Holles-street*, where, at No. 24, Lord Byron was born.

CHARTERHOUSE SQUARE is described by Hatton (1708) as "a pleasant place of good (and many new) buildings, the whole in the form of a pentagon." Here was Rutland House, in which the Venetian ambassadors lodged. Baxter the nonconformist died in this square in 1691. On the north side is the CHARTERHOUSE (see p. 71).

COVENT GARDEN, see page 235.

DEVONSHIRE SQUARE, Bishopsgate Without, "a pretty though very small square. inhabited by gentry and other merchants" (*Hatton*, 1708), was named from the Earls of Devonshire having lived there in a mansion previously possessed by the Earl of Oxford: "the queen's majesty Elizabeth hath lodged there" (*Stow*). The mansion was built in the midst of gardens and bowling-alleys, by Jasper Fisher, one of the six Clerks in Chancery, who thereby outrunning his income, the house was mockingly called "Fisher's Folly." It next became a conventicle; hence "Fisher's Folly congregation" (*Hudibras*). Here Murray and Dockwra set up the Penny Post in 1680. Murray also introduced the Club of Commerce (one of a trade); and at Devonshire House he opened a Bank of Credit, where money-bills were advanced upon goods deposited.

EUSTON SQUARE, St. Pancras, is named from the ground-landlords, the Dukes of Grafton and Earls of Euston. Upon the site of the north side of the square, then a nursery-garden, Dr. Wolcot, the political satirist (Peter Pindar), ended his misspent life in blindness.

FINSBURY SQUARE was built in 1789, by George Dance, R.A., on the north side of Moorfields. At the south-east corner lived the estimable Dr. Birkbeck, the founder of Mechanics' Institutions: he died here December 1, 1841, the eighteenth anniversary of the establishment of the first Mechanics' Institution in London.

FITZROY SQUARE is named from Charles Fitzroy, second Duke of Grafton: the E. and S. sides were commenced by W. and J. Adam in 1790.

GOLDEN SQUARE, Westminster, "not exactly in any body's way, to or from any where," was "so called from the first builder, a very new and pleasant square" (*Hatton*, 1708); contemporary evidence, more reasonable than Pennant's hearsay anecdote that the name was Gelding, altered from the sign of a neighbouring inn. One of its earliest inhabitants was Lord Bolingbroke, when secretary-at-war, 1704-8. In the centre of the square is an equestrian statue of George II., formerly at Canons, near Edgeware. Golden-square is a locality of Smollett's *Humphrey Clinker*, and of Dickens's *Nicholas Nickleby*.

HAYDON SQUARE, Minories, is named from Alderman Haydon, the ground-landlord. Close by were found, in 1852, sculptured gravestones and urns; and in 1853 a sacrophagus; all of Roman work. In Haydon-square lived Sir Isaac Newton when Master of the Mint: the house was taken down about 1852. Here is Allsopp's Burton Ale Depôt, occupying 20,000 square feet; cargoes of ale are sent here from Burton, by railway (140 miles), in an afternoon; and the platforms and wagons are lowered by hydraulic cranes into the vast cellars. Here also is a spring of pure water, which formerly supplied the priory of the Holy Trinity upon this spot.

GORDON SQUARE, New-road, has at the south-west angle the Catholic Apostolic Church: cathedral-like Early English exterior, and Decorated interior, with a triforium in the aisle-roof; the ceilings are highly enriched, and some of the windows are filled with stained glass; the northern doorway and porch, and the southern wheel-window, equal old examples; and gothic houses, with projections and gables, pointed-headed windows, and traceried balconies, group around the church: architects, Brandon and Ritchie.

GOUGH SQUARE, between Fetter-lane and Shoe-lane, contains the house, No. 17, wherein Dr. Johnson compiled most of his Dictionary; his amanuenses working in the garret.

GROSVENOR SQUARE, 6 acres, is named from Sir Richard Grosvenor, who died in 1732. The houses, some of rubbed bricks with stone finishings, are spacious. The centre landscape-garden was laid out by Kent, and the stone pedestal in the centre once bore an equestrian statue of George I.; the line of fortification during the Civil War ran across the space now the square. It is a place of high fashion; and Dr. Johnson once desired to be " Grosvenor of that ilk." Here lived Lord North and John Wilkes; and at No. 39 (the Earl of Harrowby's) His Majesty's Ministers were to have dined on the evening the Cato-street conspirators had planned to assassinate them (see page 67). A few iron link-extinguishers remain in front of the houses.

HANOVER SQUARE, built about 1718, was named in honour of George I., when it was proposed to change the place of execution from Tyburn elsewhere, lest the procession of malefactors might annoy the inhabitants of the new square. Here lived Field-Marshal Lord Cobham, the owner of princely Stowe. Admiral Lord Rodney died here in 1792. On the east side are the *Hanover Square Rooms*: the great room is 90 ft. by 35 ft., and will hold 800 persons; the ceiling was painted by Cipriani. No. 11 is the *Zoological Society;* No. 12, the *Royal Agricultural Society;* and on the west side is the *Oriental Club* (see page 196). In Tenterden-street is the *Royal Academy of Music*, founded in 1822, incorporated 1830. Upon the south side of Hanover-square is a colossal bronze statue of William Pitt, by Chantrey.

" This square, in connexion with George-street, has always struck me as one of the most scenic architectural displays that London presents : the street expanding towards the square, the unique and elegant style of the surrounding mansions, the judicious mixture of red brick and stone, Chantrey's statue, and the successful ecclesiastical work of James (St. George's), altogether produce the most agreeable effect."—*S. Angell.*

ST. JAMES'S SQUARE, between Pall Mall and Jermyn-street, is built on part of St. James's Fields; and Godfrey's print, from a drawing by Hollar, has a stone conduit near the centre of the present square. Mr. Cunningham found several of its tenants rated in the parish-books of St. Martin's-in-the-Fields in 1676; and among them, on the west side, Madame Churchill, mistress of the Duke of York; and Madame Davis (Moll Davis), mistress of Charles II. On the north side was Romney House, where, in 1695 and 1697, King William III. visited the Earl of Romney, to witness fireworks in the square; and in the latter year the Dutch Ambassador made before his house a bonfire of 140 pitch-barrels, and wine was "kept continually running among the common people." On the north side also was Ormond House, the mansion of the great Duke of Ormond; the duchess died here in 1684: in 1698 the house was let to Count Tallard, the French Ambassador, for 600*l.* per annum, then a large rent. In the rear of the present houses is *Ormond-yard,* now a mews. *Appletree-yard*, opposite, keeps in memory the apple-orchards of St. James's Fields. Hatton describes St. James's-square, in 1708, " very pleasant, large, and beautiful; all very fine spacious buildings (except that side towards Pall Mall), mostly inhabited by the prime quality." Sutton Nicholls's print, 1720, shows a fountain in the centre of the square, with a basin, "filled by contract, in 1727, with water from York-buildings." (*Malcolm.*) A pedestal for an equestrian statue of William III. was erected in the centre of the square in 1732; but the statue, cast in brass by the younger Bacon, was not set up until 1808: the bequest in 1724 for the cost having been forgotten, until the money was found in the list of unclaimed dividends. The Earl of Radnor (d. 1723) had on the north side a mansion, painted by Vanson, over doors and chimney-pieces; the staircase by Laguerre; and the apartments hung with pictures by Edema, Wyck, Roestraten, Danckers, old Griffier, young Vandervelde, and Sybricht. Next, No. 7, lived Josiah Wedgewood, and here his stock of classic pottery was dispersed by auction. No. 2 is Lord Falmouth's: the street-posts are cannon captured by his ancestor, Admiral Boscawen, off Cape Finisterre. No. 4, Earl de Grey (see page 485), who receives here the Royal Institute of British Architects. No. 6, Marquis of Bristol. No. 11, William Wyndham; Lord Chief Justice Ellenborough in 1814; John Duke of Roxburghe; now the *Wyndham Club* (see page 199). No. 12, *London Library* (see page 463): here lived Lord Amherst when Commander-in-chief. No. 13, *Lichfield House*, was built by Athenian Stuart for Lord Anson: "from the balcony, on June 20, 1815, the Prince Regent displayed the trophies just received from Waterloo to the delighted populace." No. 15 (Sir Philip Francis's) was lent by Lady Francis to Queen Caroline, in 1820, who delighted to show herself at the drawing-room windows, and proceeded from thence daily, in state, to her trial in the House of Lords; at this time No. 16 was Lord Castlereagh's. No. 17, the Duke of Cleveland's: here is Lely's fine whole-length portrait of the Duchess of Cleveland. No. 19, the Bishop of Winchester. No. 21, *Norfolk House* (see page 402), occupies the site of the mansion of Henry Jermyn, Earl of St. Albans, who died here in 1683. No. 22 is *London House*, rebuilt in 1820 for the Bishops of London. Upon the lower or Pall Mall side lived the father of H. R. Morland, and grandfather of George Morland, all painters.

LEICESTER SQUARE (see page 453).

LOWNDES SQUARE, Belgravia, was built 1837-39, and named from the ground-landlord, W. Selby Lowndes, Esq. The seven houses at the south end, by Lewis Cubitt, resemble an Italian palace, with embellished chimney-shafts, Tuscan cornice, and Venetian balconies. The site of this square was once a coppice, which supplied the Abbot and Convent of Westminster with wood for fuel.

MANCHESTER SQUARE was begun in 1776, by the building of Manchester House upon the north side (see page 490). At the north-west corner of the square is Manchester-street, where died, in 1814, the impostor Joanna Southcott, after imposing upon six medical men with the story of her being *enceinte* with the young "Shiloh."

MYDDLETON SQUARE, Islington, near the New River Head, is named from its originator, Sir Hugh Myddleton.

PORTMAN SQUARE, upon the estate of W. H. Portman, Esq., and once the property of the Knights of St. John of Jerusalem, was begun about 1764, but not completed until 1784; it is 500 ft. by 400. The centre is laid out as a shrubbery wilderness; and here is a movable kiosk constructed for the Turkish Ambassador about 1808, when he resided at No. 18: his Excellency customarily took the air and smoked here, surrounded by a party of his retinue. At the north-west angle is Montague House (see page 491): here were the feather-hangings sung by Cowper; here Miss Burney was welcomed, and Dr. Johnson grew tame.

Prince's Square. "As St. Giles's parish contains the largest square (Lincoln's Inn Fields), so it also *may boast* of the smallest, which is situated near it, namely, Prince's-square, containing only one house" (*Dobie*), between Little Queen-street and Gate-street: a stone tablet is inscribed, "Prince's-square, 1736."

Prince's Square, Ratcliffe Highway. Here is the Swedish Church, in which is interred Emanuel Swedenborg: in the vestry-room are a few portraits, including that of Dr. Serenius, Bishop of Stregnas. About the year 1816 the cranium of Swedenborg was taken from the coffin by a Swedish captain, but was replaced after his death.

Queen Square, Bloomsbury, built in the reign of Queen Anne, has a railed garden for the north side. Jonathan Richardson, the painter, died here in 1745. At the north-west corner Dr. John Campbell, editor of the *Biographia Britannia*, gave his Sunday-evening conversation-parties, at which Dr. Johnson used to meet "shoals of Scotchmen." On the south-west side is the church of St. George-the-Martyr, of which Dr. Stukeley was rector (see page 127): he lived in the square. No. 12 is a Convent of Sisters of Compassion; No. 32, of Sisters of the Holy Child; No. 26, the Industrial Home for Gentlewomen.

Queen Square, Westminster, contains a statue of Queen Anne, mentioned in 1708. Here was born, in 1684, Admiral Vernon, the hero of Portobello; in 1729 the Rev. C. M. Cracherode, who bequeathed his books, medals, and drawings to the British Museum. In this square died, in 1784, Dr. Thomas Franklin, the erudite Greek scholar. (Queen Square Chapel, see p. 171.) In 1832 died, aged 85, Jeremy Bentham, in Queen Square-place, where he had resided for nearly half a century.

Red Lion Square, "a pleasant square of good buildings, between High Holborn south and the fields north" (*Hatton*, 1708), was named from the Red Lion Inn. Here lived the philanthropic Jonas Hanway, to whom we are mainly indebted for the Marine Society, the Magdalen Charity, and Sunday Schools. Hanway died here in 1786, and was honoured with a public funeral. In the centre of the square was "a clumsy obelisk, lately vanished."—*Pennant.*

Russell Square, north of Bedford-square, occupies part of Southampton Fields (1720), subsequently Long Fields. Its dimensions are 665 ft. 6 in. north side; 665 ft. 3 in. south; 672 ft. 7 in. west; and 667 ft. 1 in. east—2661·5 ft. square, or about 140 ft. less than Lincoln's Inn Fields. In 1800 Long Fields lay waste and useless, with nursery-grounds northwards; the Toxophilite Society's ground north-west; and Bedford House, with its lawn and magnificent lime-trees, south. At the north-east end of Upper Montague-street was "the Field of Forty Footsteps" (see page 291). The east side of the square was the house and gardens of the dissolute Lord Baltimore: the mansion is now two residences. At No. 65 died Sir Thomas Lawrence, P.R.A. At No. 67 lived the amiable Sir T. N. Talfourd. On the north side is the bronze sitting statue of Francis Duke of Bedford, by Westmacott.

Salisbury Square (see Fleet Street, page 306): at the north-west corner was the printing-office of Richardson, the novelist.

Soho Square, originally King's-square, was begun in the reign of Charles II.; the south side consisting of Monmouth House, built by Wren for the Duke of Monmouth, and after his death purchased by Lord Bateman: in 1717 it was an auction-room; part of the site is now occupied by Bateman's buildings. Shadwell, in his plays (1691), mentions "Soho-square;" but Maitland, in 1739, "King's-square." It was then a sort of Court quarter: Evelyn wintered "at Soho, in the great square," in 1690. Bishop Burnet, the historian, lived here before he removed to Clerkenwell; and here his Curiosities included the supposed "original Magna Charta," with part of the Great Seal remaining. Here the shipwrecked remains of Sir Cloudesley Shovel lay in state in 1707. Here lived Alderman Beckford; and thither came the partisan City procession, who prevailed upon Beckford to serve his second mayoralty, in commemoration of which he feasted the poor of St. Ann's, Soho. At the east corner of Sutton-street was Carlisle House, where Mrs. Cornelys gave her concerts, balls, and masquerades; the present Roman Catholic chapel in Sutton-street having been Mrs. Cornleys's banquetting-room (connected with the house by "the Chinese bridge"), and the gateway (now a wheelwright's) was the entrance for sedan-chairs. In 1772 the "furniture, decorations, china, &c." of Carlisle House were sold by auction; but it was re-opened in 1774; Mrs. Cornelys returned here in 1776; and it was next an exhibition-place of "Monstrosities," a "School of Eloquence," and an "Infant School of Genius;" it was closed in 1797, and taken down in 1803 or 1804: some of its curious paintings were preserved; and an account of Mrs. Cornelys's entertainments has been privately printed by Mr. T. Mackinlay. (*Dr. Rimbault; Notes and Queries*, No. 28.) No. 20, D'Almaine's, with a banquetting-room ceiling, said to have been painted by Angelica Kauffmann, was built for Earl Tilney by Colin Campbell, architect of Wanstead House. No. 32 was Sir Joseph Banks's, P.R.S., now the house of the Linnæan Society (see page 539), exempted from the poor-rate in 1854 on account of its being used for the purposes of science. (*Court of Queen's Bench Rep.* May 30.) At a house in Soho-square, Richard Payne Knight, the classic antiquary (died 1824), assembled his collection of ancient bronzes and Greek coins, value 50,000l., which he bequeathed to the British Museum. At the corner of Bateman's-buildings, left, lived George Colman the elder; and right, Samuel Beazley, the dramatist, and architect of the Lyceum and St. James's theatres. The Soho Bazaar (north-west corner) is described at page 35. In the centre of the square is a pedestrian statue of Charles II. (See FOUNTAINS, page 313.) In *Frith-street*, on the east side of the square, died of cholera, in 1830, William Hazlitt, the eloquent essayist: he was buried in St. Anne's churchyard, where is "a stone raised by one whose heart is with him in his grave."

TAVISTOCK SQUARE, New-road, is named from the ground-landlord, the Duke of Bedford, and Marquis of Tavistock.

Southward is *Tavistock-place*. At No. 31 lived Mary Ann Clarke, mistress of the Duke of York; at No. 32, Francis Douce, the illustrator of Shakspeare, and in the same house John Galt when editor of the *Courier;* at No. 37, Francis Baily, F.R.S., who, in an observatory in the garden, weighed the earth, and calculated its bulk and figure (see page 286); at No. 19, Sir Harris Nicolas, K.C.M.G.; the peerage antiquary; and at No. 10, John Britton, before he removed to No. 17 Burton-street.

TRAFALGAR SQUARE, Charing Cross, formed by the removal of the lower end of St. Martin's-lane, a knot of courts and alleys, the Golden Cross inn,* and low buildings adjoining, was planned by Barry, and is named from the last victory of Nelson, to whom a column is erected on the south side. (See page 224.) The whole is paved with granite, has two large tanks with fountains (see page 313), and has on the north side a terrace, which imparts elevation to the National Gallery façade. At the north-east and north-west angles are granite pedestals; the former occupied by Chantrey's bronze equestrian statue of George IV., intended for the top of the marble arch at Buckingham Palace. The granite capstan posts in the area are characteristic; but the square has

* April 23, 1643, it was ordered by Parliament that the sign of the Golden Cross, at Charing-cross, be taken down, as superstitious and idolatrous!

been condemned as " an artificial stone-quarry." The massive lanterns at the angles were originally designed by Barry for Bude-lights.

In 1831, upon the ground cleared for Trafalgar-square, was exhibited in a pavilion the entire skeleton of a Greenland Whale, taken off the coast of Belgium in 1827 : total length, 95 feet ; breadth, 18 feet ; width of tail, 22½ feet ; length of head, 22 feet ; height of cranium, 4½ feet ; length of fins, 12½ feet ; weight of animal, 249 tons, or 480,000lb. ; weight of skeleton, 35 tons, or 70,000lb. ; oil extracted, 4000 gallons. The skeleton was raised upon iron supports, and visitors ascended within the ribs by a flight of steps. It had been previously exhibited at Paris, where Cuvier and others estimated the age of this whale at from 900 to 1000 years. (See *Mirror*, August 13, 1831.)

VINCENT SQUARE, Westminster, a portion of Tothill Fields, is named after Dr. Vincent, then Dean of Westminster. Here is the church of St. Mary the Virgin, consecrated 1837 : style, Early Pointed, with lancet windows ; architect, E. Blore.

WELLCLOSE SQUARE was originally called Marine-square, from its being a favourite residence of naval officers. " It is very near a geometrical square, whose area is about 2¾ acres ; it is situate between Knockfergus north and Ratcliff Highway south." (*Hatton*, 1708.) Here is the Danish (now Sailors') Church, described at page 164. In Wellstreet, adjoining, was the Royalty Theatre, burnt down 11 April, 1826 ; upon the site was built the Brunswick Theatre ; it was performed in only three nights, and fell to the ground Feb. 28, 1828 ; within six months of which was built upon the same site the Sailors' Home.

WOBURN SQUARE, St. Pancras, named from a seat of the Duke of Bedford, has in the centre a Pointed church, by L. Vulliamy, built in 1834 : the spire is 150 feet high.

STATE COACHES.

The " glistering coach" (*Shakspeare*) dates from the reign of Queen Elizabeth, who, April 2, 1571, at the meeting of Parliament, rode for the first time in a coach, drawn by two palfreys, covered with crimson velvet housings, richly embroidered : but this was the only carriage in the procession ; the Lord Keeper, and the Lords spiritual and temporal, all attending on horseback. In 1588 the Queen went from Somerset Place to St. Paul's Cross, to return thanks after the destruction of the Spanish Armada, in a coach presented to her by Henry Earl of Arundel, and called by Stow " a chariot-throne." In a print in the Crowle Pennant, in the British Museum, representing Queen Henrietta-Maria doing penance beneath the gallows at Tyburn, Charles I. is seated in a large and ornamented coach ; but this print is apocryphal.

The Coach of Queen Anne had its panels painted by Sir James Thornhill ; and a friend of J. T. Smith possessed a portion of a panel. This coach was used by George I. and II., and by George III. when he first opened Parliament, and also at his marriage ; after which it was broken up, and the State Carriage now used by the sovereign was built.

THE QUEEN'S STATE COACH was designed by Sir William Chambers, R.A., who recommended Joseph Wilton, R.A., and Mr. Pugello, to conduct the building of the carriage on premises in Queen-Anne-street East. The model was executed from Chambers' design by Laurence Anderson Holme, a Dane.

The carriage is composed of four Tritons, who support the body by cables : the two placed on the front bear the driver on their shoulders, and are sounding shells ; and those on the back part carry the imperial fasces, topped with tridents. The driver's footboard is a large scallop-shell, supported by marine plants. The pole resembles a bundle of lances; and the wheels are in imitation of those of ancient triumphal chariots. The body of the coach is composed of eight palm-trees, which, branching out at the top, sustain the roof: at each angle are trophies of British victories. On the centre of the roof stand boy-genii of England, Scotland, and Ireland, supporting the imperial crown, and holding the sceptre, the sword of state, and ensigns of knighthood; from their bodies festoons of laurel fall thence to the four corners of the roof. The intervals between the palm-trees, which form the body of the coach, are filled in the upper part with plate-glass, and the panels below with paintings as follow:

Front Panel.—Britannia on a throne, holding a staff of liberty, attended by Religion, Justice, Wisdom, Valour, Fortitude, Commerce, Plenty, and Victory, presenting her with a garland of laurel; background, St. Paul's and the Thames.

Right Door.—Industry and Ingenuity giving a cornucopia to the Genius of England. *Side Panels.*—History recording the reports of Fame, and Peace burning the implements of War.

Back Panel.—Neptune and Amphitrite in a car drawn by sea-horses, attended by the Winds, Rivers, Tritons, Naiads, &c., bringing the tribute of the world to Britain.

Upper Part of Back Panel.—The Royal Arms, ornamented with the order of St. George, the Golden Fleece, the rose, shamrock, and thistle entwined.

Left Door. — Mars, Minerva, and Mercury supporting the imperial crown. *Side Panels.*—The Arts and Sciences protected.

The body is lined with scarlet embossed velvet, superbly laced and embroidered with the star, encircled by the collar of the order of the Garter, and surmounted by the imperial crown, pendant the George and Dragon; in the corners, the rose, shamrock, and thistle entwined. The badges of St. Michael, St. George, the Guelph and Bath, St. Andrew, and St. Patrick are also among the embroidery. The hammer-cloth is of scarlet velvet, with gold badges, ropes, and tassels. The length of the carriage and body is 24 feet; width, 8 feet 3 inches; height, 12 feet; length of pole, 12 feet 4 inches; weight, 4 tons. The carving was mostly executed by Nicholas Collett, a little man, whom Waldron the actor (originally a carver in wood) delighted to call " a Garrick of a carver." The panels were painted by Cipriani, who received for the same 800*l.* The chasing was executed by Coit, the coachwork by Butler, the embroidery by Barrett, the gilding (triple throughout) by Rujolas, the varnishing by Ausel, and the harness by Ringstead. The whole cost was as follows:

	£	s.	d.
Coachmaker (including Wheelwright and Smith)	1637	15	0
Carver	2500	0	0
Gilder	935	14	0
Painter	315	0	0
Laceman	737	10	7
Chaser	665	4	6
Harnessmaker	385	15	0
Mercer	202	5	10½
Beltmaker	99	6	6
Milliner	31	3	4
Sadler	10	16	6
Woollendraper	4	3	6
Covermaker	3	9	6
	£7528	4	3½

The bill was 8000*l.*; but being taxed, was reduced as above, the odd pence arising from the ribbon-weaver's bill. The superb hammer-cloth, of scarlet silk Genoa velvet, with gold badges, fringes, ropes, and tassels, was renewed in 1838. The Royal State Coach was first used Nov. 16, 1762. Walpole writes to Sir Horace Mann:

" There is come forth a new state coach, which has cost 8000*l.* It is a beautiful object, though crowded with improprieties. Its supports are Tritons, not very, well adapted to land-carriage; and formed of palm-trees, which are as little aquatic as Tritons are terrestrial. The crowd to see it, on the opening of the Parliament, was greater than at the coronation, and much more mischief done."

The Coach was kept in a mean shed at the King's Mews, Charing Cross; upon the taking down of which, it was removed to the Royal Mews, Pimlico, where also is kept the State Harness for the eight horses by which the carriage is drawn when used by the sovereign. The Coach and Harness may be inspected upon application. (See MEWS, ROYAL, p. 505.)

THE LORD MAYOR'S STATE COACH is kept at the City Green-yard, Whitecross-street, Cripplegate, opposite the Debtors' Door: the coach may be here inspected. It was built in 1757, by a subscription of 60l. from each of the junior aldermen, or such as had not passed the civic chair. Subsequently, each alderman, when sworn into office, contributed 60l. towards keeping the coach in repair; for which purpose also each Lord Mayor gave 100l. In a few years, the whole expense fell upon the Lord Mayor, and in one year it exceeded 300l. The coach was then transferred to the Corporation, and it has since been kept in repair by the Committee of General Purposes. Twenty years after its construction, the repairs in one year cost 335l.; and the average of seven years' repairs in the present century was 115l. The design of the coach is more magnificent than graceful: the carriage consists of a pair of grotesque marine figures, who support the seat of the driver, with a large escalop-shell as a foot-board; at the hind-standard are two children bearing the City arms, beneath which is a large pelican; the perch is double, and terminates in dolphins' heads; and the four wheels are richly carved and gilt, and resemble those of ancient triumphal chariots. The body is not hung upon springs, but upon four thick red leather straps, fastened with large gilt-brass buckles of spirited design, each bearing the City arms. The roof was originally ornamented with eight gilt vases; in the centre is a leafy crown, bearing the City arms, and from which small gilt flowers trail over the remainder of the roof, painted red: originally, a group of four boys supporting baskets of fruit and flowers occupied the centre. The upper intervals of the body, save at the back, are filled with plate-glass; and the several lower panels are painted as follow:

Front Panel.—Faith supporting a decrepit figure beside a flaming altar; Hope pointing to St. Paul's Cathedral.

Back.—Charity; a wrecked sailor, with a ship in the offing, and two females casting money and fruits into his lap.

Upper Back.—The City, attended by Neptune; Commerce introducing the Arab with his horse, and other traders with the camel, elephant, &c.

Right Door.—Fame, with her wreath, presenting a Lord Mayor to the City, who bears the sword and sceptre, the mace, &c., at her feet. In the very small panel beneath are fruit and flowers. *Side Panels.*—Beauty with her mirror; female with bridled horse, &c.

Left Door.—The City seated, and Britannia pointing with her spear to a shield inscribed with "Henri Fitz-Alwin, 1189" (the first Mayor). In the very small panels beneath are the scales of justice and sword of mercy, grouped. *Side Panels.*—Justice with her scales and sword; Prudence, &c.

The original heraldic paintings were executed by Catton, one of the foundation members of the Royal Academy. In shields at the lower angles of each door, and of the back and front panels, are emblazoned the arms of the Lord Mayor for the time being. The framework is richly carved and gilt: over each door is an escallop-shell; and at the lower angles of the body are dwarf figures emblematic of the four quarters of the globe. The smaller enrichments about the panels, as shells, fruits, and flowers, are admirably carved and grouped: over the upper back panel is an exquisite *bit*—a serpent and dove. The perch and wheels are painted

ed, picked out with gold; and massive gilt bosses cover the wheel-
boxes; the wheels were renewed in 1828. The coach is lined with
crimson corded silk and lace; and in the centre is a seat for the mace
and sword bearers. The hammercloth is crimson cloth, but the original
one was of gold lace.

This coach was repaired, new-lined, and re-gilt in 1812, at an expense of 600l., when also a new seat-cloth was furnished for 90l.; and
in 1821 the re-lining cost 206l. In 1812, Messrs. Houlditch agreed to
keep the coach in fair wear-and-tear for ten years, at 48l. per annum.
The total weight of the coach is 3 tons 16 cwt.: it is drawn by six
horses, for whom a superb state harness was made in 1833, that for each
horse weighing 106 lbs.

It is not positively known by whom this Coach was carved, nor
by whom the panels were painted. Cipriani is stated by some to
be the painter; but others assert that after the present Royal State
Coach was built in 1762, the old Royal State Coach was purchased by
the City of London, and the panels repainted by Dance: such is the
statement of Smith, in *Nollekens and his Times*; but in the Report
of the Municipal Corporation Commissioners, the City Coach is stated
to have been built in 1757. The Lord Mayor rode in state upon horseback until 1712, when a state carriage, drawn by four horses, was first
used. In 1741 the horses were increased to six. This State Coach is
represented in Hogarth's print of the Industrious Apprentice, date 1747;
it is somewhat plain, but has ornamental vases upon the roof. (See
LORD MAYOR'S STATE, page 474.)

"Our Lord Mayor and his golden coach, and his gold-covered footmen and
coachman, and his golden chain, and his chaplain, and his great sword of state,
please the people, and particularly the women and girls, and when they are
pleased the men and boys are pleased; and many a young fellow has been more
industrious and attentive from his hope of one day riding in that golden coach."
—*Cobbett*.

THE SPEAKER'S STATE COACH is traditionally said to have been
Oliver Cromwell's; but it is more probably of the time of William the
Third. It is elaborately carved and heavily gilt. Figures of naval and
military prowess, Plenty, &c., support the body; the box is held by two
larger figures of Plenty; the hammercloth is of crimson velvet, trimmed
with silver fringe; and the footboard is borne by two lions, and surmounted with a large grotesque mask. The hind-standard is richly
carved with figures and devices of antique and modern design. The
framework of the panels is finely carved; and the roof has a pierced parapet or border. The upper, side, and front panels are filled with splendid
Vauxhall plates of glass. The lower panels are painted with emblematic
subjects: the door-panel has a seated figure of Britannia, to whom female
figures are bringing fruits, the horn of plenty, &c. The opposite door
has also a seated figure, and another presenting the Bill of Rights, with
Liberty, Fame, and Justice. Beneath each door and panel are sculptured maces, surmounted with a cap, emblematic of the Speaker's authority. In the four side panels are emblematic figures of Literature,
Architecture, Science, and Plenty. The back panel has a better composition of Britannia, wearing a mural crown; St. Paul's Cathedral,
shipping, &c., in the distance. The front panel also bears several
allegorical figures. In the lower part of the pictures in the principal
panels are emblazoned the Speaker's arms, and in the side-panel pictures his crest. The coach is lined and trimmed with dark crimson
velvet; it has two seats, and a centre one: on the latter sit the Speaker's
Mace-bearer and Sword-bearer; and his Chaplain and Train-bearer sit
facing the Speaker. This coach is used by the Speaker on opening
Parliament, presenting addresses to the sovereign, attending levees, &c.,

Y Y

-when it is drawn by a pair of horses in state harness. The coach was removed in 1854 from Prince's-street, to the New Palace, Westminster.

STATUES.

The following are the principal *out-door* Statues in the metropolis :

STATUES.	SITES.	SCULPTORS.	SEE P.
"Achilles"	Hyde Park	Westmacott.	586

This group is strangely miscalled " Achilles;" it being copied from one of the statues on Monte Cavallo, at Rome, which are called Castor and Pollux by the Italian antiquaries Venuti and Vasi, and by Flaxman named Bellerophon.

Albert, Prince . . .	Lloyd's, Royal Exchange .	Lough.	279
Alfred, King . . .	Trinity-square, Newington.		
Anne, Queen of Jas. I.	Temple Bar	Bushnell.	704
Anne, Queen . . .	Queen-square, Bloomsbury.		684
Anne, Queen . . .	Queen-square, Westminster.		684
Anne, Queen . . .	St. Paul's Churchyard . .	F. Bird.	95
Aske, Robert . . .	Haberd. Almsh., Hoxton.		
Bedford, Duke of . .	Russell-square	Westmacott.	684
Bentinck,Lord George	Cavendish-square	Campbell.	681
Canning, George .	New Palace-yard	Westmacott.	
Cartwright, Major .	Burton-crescent	Clarke.	
Charles I.	Charing Cross	Le Sœur.	71

" This noble equestrian statue," says Walpole, " in which the commanding grace of the figure and the exquisite form of the horse are striking to the most unpractised eye, was cast in 1633, on a spot of ground near the church in Covent Garden; and not being erected before the commencement of the Civil War, it was sold by the Parliament to John Rivet, a brazier, living at the Dial, near Holborn Conduit, with strict orders to break it in pieces. But the man produced some fragments of old brass, and concealed the statue and horse underground till the Restoration." M. d'Archenholz relates "that he cast a vast number of handles of knives and forks in brass, which he sold as made of the broken statue. They were bought with eagerness by the Royalists, from affection to their monarch—by the rebels as a mark of triumph over their murdered sovereign." Walpole adds that " they had been made at the expense of the family of Howard-Arundel;" but Mr. Cunningham refers to a memorandum in the State-Paper Office, from which he concludes this statue to have been ordered by the Lord Treasurer Weston, afterwards Earl of Portland, of Hubert Le Sœur, " for the casting of a horse in brasse, bigger than a great horse by a foot; and the figure of his Majesty King Charles proportionable, full six foot;" to be set up in the Lord Treasurer's gardens at Rochampton, in Surrey (see *Handbook of London*, 2d edit. p. 106). At the Restoration,* an order of replevin was issued by the House of Lords, upon the information of the Earl of Portland (son of the Lord Treasurer), for the recovery of the statue from Rivet ; but it was not set up until 1674, when Waller wrote his courtly lines " On the Statue of King Charles I. at Charing Cross." There is an idle story that Le Sœur, having finished the statue, defied any one to point out a defect in the work ; when, on a person denoting the absence of the girth, the sculptor, in a fit of indignation, destroyed himself. The assertion of the horse not having a girth is quoted by Malcolm from *The Medley* for August 1719; but there is a girth, which passes over a very strong rein on the right. In 1810, the sword, buckles, and straps fell from the statue; and about the coronation of Queen Victoria, in 1838, when seats were erected round the group, the sword (a rapier of Charles's period), was stolen. The George pendent from the ribbon has also been taken away, as denoted by the vacant hole in the metal where the George should hang.

The stone pedestal, sculptured with the royal arms, trophies, &c., was long admired as the work of Gibbons; but a written account proves it to be by Joshua

---

* In this year a statue of the King was restored in the City: "May 7, 1660, Charles the First his Statue set up again in Guildhall-yard."—*Histor. Guide*, 1688.

Marshall, Master Mason to the Crown. On the 29th of May (Restoration Day) this statue was formerly decorated with boughs of oak. In the spring of 1853 a cast of the statue and pedestal was taken by Brucciani, for the Crystal Palace at Sydenham : for the moulds and casts, 37 tons of plaster and 15 tons of iron were used. The following measurements were also then taken: *Pedestal*, 13 ft. 8 in. high; 9 ft. 11 in. long; 5 ft. 7 in. wide. *Statue:* height from foot to top of horse's head, 7 ft. 8 in.; plinth to top of figure, 9 ft. 2½ in.; plinth to neck of horse, 6 ft.; plinth to top of hind-quarters, 5 ft. 10 in.; length from head to tail, 7 ft. 9 in.; circumference of horse from back of saddle-cloth, 8 ft. 2 in.; round chest and hind-quarters, 16 ft. The metal casting around the left fore-foot of the horse bears HVBER(T) LE SVEVR (FE)CIT ✱ 1633.

"Although taken soon after Charles's accession, and at a time when sorrow could hardly have been put upon him, yet the character of melancholy is deeply impressed on the countenance. The horse is superb: the action is that which is taught in the *ménage*, the motion of the legs showing the spirit of the animal; yet the action is not that of progressing,—it is a movement that would not communicate motion to the body, but leaves the rider perfectly undisturbed; the bridle falls almost loose upon the neck; nor does the well-taught steed disturb the reverie of thought expressed in the countenance of its master."—*Times*, Sept. 1, 1838.

STATUES.	SITES.	SCULPTORS.	SEE P.
Charles I.	Temple Bar	Bushnell.	704
Charles II.	Temple Bar	Bushnell.	704
Charles II.	Soho-square.		685
Charles II.	Chelsea Hospital	Gibbons.	78
Comedy	Covent-garden Theatre	Flaxman.	
Clayton, Sir Robert	St. Thomas's Hospital.		387
Crosby, Sir John	Crosby Hall (front)	S. Nixon.	240
Cumberland, Duke of	Cavendish-square	Chew.	681
Elizabeth, Queen	St. Dunstan's, Fleet-street.		126
Edward VI.	Christ's Hospital.		
Edward VI.	St. Bartholomew's Hospital.		
Edward VI.	St. Thomas's Hospital	Scheemakers.	387
Eldon, Earl of	School, Wandsworth-road.		
C. J. Fox	Bloomsbury-square	Westmacott.	
George I.	St. George's Ch. Bloomsbury.		127
George III.	Somerset House	Bacon.	670
George III.	Cockspur-street	M. C. Wyatt.	578
George IV.	Trafalgar-square	Chantrey.	685

In modelling the horse standing still on all four legs, Chantrey has given the sanction of his name to a bold and judicious innovation on the old custom of representing horses in statues either curvetting or ambling.

Guy, Thomas	Guy's Hospital	Scheemakers.	382
Handel, G. F.	Sacred Harmonic Society	Roubiliac.	
Henry VIII.	St. Bartholomew's Hospital.		31
Huskisson, William	Lloyd's, Royal Exchange	Lough.	279
James I.	Temple Bar	Bushnell.	704
James II.	Whitehall	Gibbons.	

The doubt which long prevailed respecting the artist of this statue has been cleared up by the following passage in the *Autobiography of Sir John Bramston*, printed by the Camden Society. "On New Year's day, 1686, a statue in brass was to be seen (placed the day before) in the yard at Whitehall, made by Gibbons, at the charge of Toby Rustick, of the present king, James II." Thus, Walpole had a correct impression of the truth when he wrote, "I am the rather inclined to attribute the statue at Whitehall to Gibbons, because I know no other artist of that time capable of it." The likeness is extremely fine, as is the easy attitude of the figure. Many verses were made on this statue at the time of its erection. The figure looking towards the river, which was then open, was said to prognosticate the king's flight; this, however, is not more probable than that he is pointing to the spot where his father was executed, which has long been proved a vulgar error. At the accession of William the statue was not removed.

STATUES.	SITES.	SCULPTORS.	SEE P.
Kent, Duke of . .	Portland-place	Gahagan.	561
Millingan, Robert*	West India Docks.		256
Moore, Sir John .	Christ's Hospital.		81
Nelson, Lord . .	Trafalgar-square . . .	Baily.	225
Peel, Sir Robert .	Mansion House	Behnes.	
Pitt, W.	Hanover-square. . . .	Chantrey.	682
Sloane, Sir Hans .	Botanic Gardens, Chelsea	Rysbrach.	51
Tragedy	Covent-garden Theatre .	Flaxman.	
Victoria, Queen .	Royal Exchange . . .	Lough.	279
Watts, Dr. Isaac .	Abney Park Cemetery .	Baily.	69
Wellington, Duke of .	Green Park Arch	M. C. Wyatt.	19

This stupendous statue was modelled by Matthew Cotes Wyatt, and his son James Wyatt, at Dudley-grove House, Harrow-road; and was commenced in 1840, and occupied three years, and took more than 100 tons of plaster. It represents the Duke of Wellington upon his horse "Copenhagen," at the field of Waterloo: the Duke sat for the portrait, and the head and likeness are fine. The group is cast in about eight pieces, which are fastened with screws and fused together, 30 men being often employed at one time upon the bronze. It was conveyed upon an immense car, drawn by 40 horses, to the Green Park Arch, Sept. 28, 1846, and was raised by crabs. The entire group weighs 40 tons: is nearly 30 feet high; and within half of the horse eight persons have dined. The girth of the horse is 22 ft. 8 in.; nose to tail 26 feet; length of head 5 feet; length of each ear 2 ft. 4 in. The erection of this group, which cost about 30,000*l.*, originated from the close contest for the execution of the Wellington statue in the City; and the execution of both statues emanated from a suggestion of Mr. T. B. Simpson, of the Court of Common Council, Lime-street Ward.

Wellington, Duke of .	Royal Exchange	Chantrey.	281
William III.	St. James's-square . . .	Bacon, jun.	633
William IV.	King-William-street . . .	S. Nixon.	265

The several Statues in the East India House, Guildhall, British Museum, Parliament House, St. Paul's Cathedral, Westminster Abbey, Royal Exchange, and other public buildings, are described under their respective names.

At Newgate Prison, in exterior niches, are statues of Concord and Liberty, Mercy and Truth, Peace and Plenty,—from the old Gate.

STOCK EXCHANGE (THE).

The general history of the Stock Exchange has already been narrated (see EXCHANGES, page 284). A new building was completed early in 1854, by W. Cubitt and Co., from the design of Thomas Allason; and opened on March 2. It occupies the centre of a block of buildings; the principal entrance being from Bartholomew-lane, through Capel-court; there are also three entrances from Throgmorton-street, and one from Threadneedle-street. The area of the new house is about 75 squares; and it would contain 1100 or 1200 members; there are, however, seldom more than half that number present. For the cupola, laminated ribs are used. The vault, which covers the centre of the building, 39 feet in span, is of timber and iron; the whole, with the dome, &c., is covered with lead. Besides the "house," or large room, there are strong-rooms, committee-rooms, reading and refreshment rooms, &c. In the ventilation, the vitiated air is got rid of by an extracting-chamber on the apex of the dome, heated by a sun-burner with 500 jets: during the day the sun-burner is concealed from view by a perforated sliding metal screen, which may be withdrawn to light up the house without further burners. The floor, ceiling, and sides of the *Strong Room* are formed of iron girders and bars, fitted in with bricks

* Projector of these Docks: he died at Rosslyn House, Hampstead, May 1809

and pure cement; and the walls are lined with case-hardened steel, and fitted up with wrought-iron boxes. The number of members of the Stock Exchange, in February 1854, was 1026; of privileged clerks, about 700. To the name of Francis Baily, F.R.S., mentioned at p. 286, may be added David Ricardo, and several of his descendants; Charles Stokes, F.R.S.; Horace Smith, the novelist: and the authors of *The Last of the Plantagenets*, and the play of *The Templar*, 1853. It is an established fact, that, abroad and at home, all parties having large financial operations approach the London Stock Exchange with more confidence than any other money-market in the world.—*The Builder*, No. 574.

STRAND (THE)

Extends from Charing Cross to Temple Bar (1369 yards, or ¾ of a mile 49 yards), and was "probably so called as being at the brink of the Thames, before the space now built on was gained by raising the ground" (*Hatton*), which is in some places 20 feet deep. In early ages this was the great thoroughfare between the court and City, and the Inns of Court and Westminster. The site of St. Clement's Danes is recognised in tradition as "the Danes' churchyard," the burial-place of the son of Canute the Great, Harald Harefoot. Here, close by the Thames, and outside the City walls, dwelt together as fellow-countrymen the Danish merchants and mariners; and their church, like that at Aarhns in Jutland, and Trondjeun in Norway, was dedicated to St. Clement, the seaman's patron-saint. (*J. J. A. Worsae, For. F.S.A.*) Another early building was the Hermitage of St. Catherine at Charing, and adjoining or opposite, the Hospital of St. Mary Rounceval (*temp.* Henry III.); the palace of the Savoy, and the first church of St. Mary, were built before the 14th century. A petition to Edward II. (1315) describes the footway interrupted by thickets and bushes; and in 1383 tolls were granted for paving the Strand from the Savoy to Temple Bar. The south side was occupied by the mansions of the nobility and prelates, with gardens, terraces, and water-stairs down to the Thames; but the spaces between the mansions showed the river: whilst on the north side were the gardens of the Convent of Westminster, bounded by lanes and open ground; the village of St. Giles, and the church of St. Martin *in the fields*; and Charing Cross, without a house near it. The Sutherland View (Van der Wyngrerde's), 1543, shows straggling lines of houses from *the bar* (now Temple Bar) to the Savoy, and beyond it on the south side; but the north is open to Convent Garden; and in the roadway are St. Clement's and St. Mary's churches, and the Maypole, near upon the site of the Strand Cross, where "the justices itinerants sate without London" (*Stow*). Of the Thames-bank palaces are shown Somerset Place, the Savoy, and Durham House. At this time the Strand was crossed by three water-courses running from the north to the Thames, over which were bridges: the sites of two are denoted by Ivy-bridge-lane and Strand-bridge-lane; and the remains of a third bridge were unearthed in 1802, a little eastward of St. Clement's church. The Ivy-bridge stream formed the boundary between the Liberty and Duchy of Lancaster and the City of Westminster.

STRAND: SOUTH SIDE.—*Northumberland House* is described at page 492. Next door, upon the site of No. 1 Strand, was the official residence of the Secretary of State, where Sir Harry Vane the elder lived, in the reign of Charles I.

Northumberland-court was once known as "Lieutenants' Lodgings:" here Nelson lodged.

Northumberland-street, formerly *Hartshorne-lane*: here, with his mother and step-father, a bricklayer, lived Ben Jonson when he went to "a private school in St. Martin's Church," and next to Westminster School, under Camden, then junior master.

Craven-street: at No. 7 lived Dr. Benjamin Franklin, in 1771: the house is now occupied by the Society for the Relief of Persons Imprisoned for Small Debts. At No. 27 died, in 1839, James Smith, one of the authors of the *Rejected Addresses*.

At No. 18 Strand was born, 1776, Charles Mathews, the comedian: his father was a bookseller; and his shop was the resort of Dr. Adam Clarke, Rowland Hill, and other Dissenting ministers.

Hungerford-street: *Hungerford Market* is described at page 499. Hungerford Hall and its panoramic pictures were burnt March 31, 1854.

No. 31 Strand occupies part of the site of York House, originally the inn of the Bishop of Norwich; and being obtained in exchange for Suffolk House, Southwark, by Heath, Archbishop of York, *temp.* Queen Mary, the name was changed to York House. It was let to the Lord Keepers of the Great Seal: here lived Sir Nicholas Bacon; and here was born his son, Lord Chancellor Bacon, 22d Jan. 1560-1: when a boy, he used to go to play in St. James's Fields, where the echo of a brick conduit led him to seek out the cause. At York House he kept his 60th birthday. Here the Great Seal was taken from him: when importuned by the Duke of Lennox to part with the mansion, Lord Bacon replied, "For this you will pardon me: York House is the house where my father died, and where I first breathed; and there will I yield my last breath, if so please God and the king." He did not, however, return to York House after his release from the Tower, being forbidden to come within the verge of the court. The house was next lent to Villiers, Duke of Buckingham, who, in 1624, obtained the estate by grant from James I. The mansion was then taken down, and a temporary house built for state receptions, and sumptuously fitted with "huge panes of glass" (mirrors), of the manufacture of which in England Buckingham was an early patron. Near the middle of a long embattled wall, fronting the Thames, he caused to be erected, in 1626, a rustic Water-gate. After the duke's death, in 1628, York House was leased to the Earl of Northumberland. Here was a fine collection of pictures, among which is supposed to have been the lost portrait of Prince Charles, by Velasquez. Here also was the collection of sculptures which belonged to Rubens; and in the garden was John de Bologna's Cain and Abel. The "superstitious pictures" were sold by order of Parliament in 1645; and the house was given by Cromwell to General Fairfax, by the marriage of whose daughter and heiress with George, second Duke of Buckingham, it was re-conveyed to the Villiers family. The duke resided here subsequent to the Restoration; but in 1672 sold the estate for 30,000*l.*, when the mansion was pulled down, and upon the grounds and gardens were erected houses named from the last possessor of the mansion: *George*-street (now York-buildings), *Villiers*-street, *Duke*-street, *Of*-alley, *Buckingham*-street. The whole estate was called *York Buildings*.

The York Buildings Waterworks Company, for supplying the Westend of London with water, was one of the bubbles of 1720. For this purpose, however, a veritable steam-engine was constructed, which is thus described in the *Foreigner's Guide to London*, 1720:

"Here you see a high wooden tower and a water-engine of a new invention, that draws out of the Thames above three tons of water in one minute, by means of the steam arising from water boiling in a great copper, a continual fire being kept to that purpose; the steam being compressed and condensed, moves by its evaporation, and strikes a counterpoise, which counterpoise striking another, at last moves a great beam, which, by its motion of going up and down, draws the water from the river, which mounts through great iron pipes to the height of the tower, discharging itself there into a deep leaden cistern; and thence falling through other large iron pipes, fills them that are laid along the streets, and so continuing to run through wooden pipes as far as Mar-bone fields, falls there into a large pond or reservoir, from whence the new buildings near Hanover-square, and many thousand houses, are supplied with water. This machine is certainly a great curiosity; and though it be not so large as that of Marly in France, yet, considering its smallness in comparison with that, and the little charge it was built and is kept with, and the quantity of water it draws, its use and benefit is much beyond that."

The Company ceased to work this "fire-engine" in 1731; but it was shown for several years as a Curiosity. In *All Alive and Merry, or the London Daily Post,* April 18, 1741, it is stated that the charge of working the machine, "and some other reasons concurring, made its proprietors, the York Buildings Company, lay aside the design; and no doubt but the inhabitants in this neighbourhood are very glad of it; for its working, which was by sea-coal, was attended with so much smoke, that it not only must pollute the air thereabouts, but spoil the furniture." The failure is the subject of an amusing *jeu d'esprit,* entitled "The York Buildings Dragons," reprinted in Wright's *England under the House of Hanover,* vol. i. Appendix. Many of the wooden water-pipes have been taken up in excavations in Brook-street, Grosvenor-square, and in other places along the line. In Buckingham-street, in 1818, were "the Sea-water Baths," which were supplied by a vessel with water from below Southend.

Evelyn notes: "17th Nov. 1683.—I tooke a house in Villiers-streete, York-buildings, for the winter, having many important concerns to dispatch, and for the education of my daughters."—*Diary.*

Buckingham-street : at the last house on the west side (since rebuilt) lived Samuel Pepys from 1684 to 1700; and No. 15, on the east side opposite, was hired for Peter the Great in 1698: the house has some noble rooms facing the river: here the Institution of Civil Engineers once met. At No. 14, in the top chambers, lived William Etty, R.A., the painter, from 1826 to 1849. At the south end of Buckingham-street remains the Water-gate built for York House, which stood a short distance westward.

The Gate is of Portland-stone: on the northern or street side are three arches, flanked with pilasters, supporting an entablature and four balls; above the keystones of the arches are shields, those at the sides sculptured with anchors, and that in the centre with the arms of Villiers impaling those of the family of Manners. Upon the frieze is the Villiers motto: FIDEI COTICULA CRUX (the Cross is the Touchstone of Faith). The southern or river front has a large archway, opening upon steps to the water; on each side is an aperture, divided by a small column, and partly closed by balustrades. Four rusticated columns support an entablature, ornamented with escallops, and crowned with an arched pediment, and two couchant lions holding shields, on which are sculptured anchors. In the pediment, within a scroll, are the arms of Villiers, viz. on a cross, five escallops, encircled by a garter, and surmounted by a ducal coronet; at the sides are pendent festoons. This Gate has been ascribed to Inigo Jones: but in the library of the Soane Museum, in an "Account Book of Workes done by Nicholas Stone, sen. Master-mason to King James I. and King Charles," the ninth article in the list is, "The Water-gate at Yorke House hee *deesined and built,* and ye right-hand Lion hee did, fronting ye Thames. Mr. Kearne, a Jarman, his brother by marrying his sister, did ye Shee Lion."

The Gate is approached by an inclosed terrace-walk, planted with lime-trees: the stone-work was repaired, and the iron-work renewed, and the gate roofed, in 1823, at a cost of 300*l.,* defrayed by a rate levied upon the inhabitants of York-buildings; but the whole was in 1854 in a ruinous state.

The Adelphi, east of York-buildings, is described at page 1. *John-street* occupies the site of Durham House, which extended from the river to the Strand. It was built by Thomas Hatfielde, Bishop of Durham, 1345-1381, and continued to be inhabited by the see until

Bishop Tunstall exchanged the house for Coldharborough, in Thames-street. Durham Place was used as a mint by the Seymours. Edward VI. granted the place to his sister Elizabeth. It next became the resi-dence of Dudley, Earl of Northumberland; and here was celebrated his son's marriage with Lady Jane Grey, who, on assuming the crown, was lodged in Durham Place, and thence escorted to the Tower. The estate was restored by Queen Mary to Bishop Tunstall; but Elizabeth, on her accession, claimed Durham Place as one of the royal palaces, and granted it to Sir Walter Raleigh, who possessed it for 20 years, but surrendered it in 1603 to the then Bishop of Durham. Aubrey well remembered Raleigh's "study, which was on a little turret that looked into and over the Thames, and had the prospect, which is as pleasant, perhaps, as any in the world." The stables fronting the Strand were next taken down, and upon the ground was built the New Exchange (see page 283), demolished in 1737: the site is now occupied by the houses Nos. 54 to 64 inclusive, the banking-house of Coutts and Co. being the centre: the name survives in *Durham-street.* At Coutts's (No. 59), formerly in St. Martin's-lane, the sovereign and the royal family have banked (kept cash), commencing with Queen Anne: the series of accounts is preserved entire.

Beaufort-buildings occupy the site of a mansion named from its successive owners, *Carlisle House* (Bishops of Carlisle); *Bedford* and *Russell House* (Earls of Bedford); *Worcester House,* from its next oc-cupant, the Marquis of Worcester, who wrote the *Century of Inven-tions;* and from the marquis's eldest son, created Duke of Beaufort, *Beaufort House.* Lord Clarendon lived here while his house was building at the top of St. James's-street; and here, in 1660, was married Anne Hyde, the Chancellor's daughter, to the Duke of York, according to the Protestant rites. The mansion was taken down, and a smaller house built; which being burnt down, with some others, in 1695, upon the ground were erected the present Beaufort-buildings. In a house on the site was born Aaron Hill, 1685. At the east corner, upon the site of No. 96 Strand, lived Charles Lillie, who sold snuffs, perfumes, &c.; and took in letters for the *Tatler, Spectator,* &c., di-rected to him at the desire of Steele.

Nos. 101 and 102 Strand, *Ries's Divan,* a large decorated room for cigars, chess, and coffee, occupies the site of the Fountain Tavern, noted for its political club, and described by Strype; of a drawing-academy, at which Conway and Wheatley were pupils; and of the lecture-room of John Thelwall, the political elocutionist. At No. 101 lived Rudolph Ackermann, the printseller, who introduced lithography and "the Annuals" from Germany: here he illuminated his gallery with Kennel coal, when gas-lighting was a novelty.

Adam-street presents a handsome specimen of the embellished street-architecture introduced by the brothers Adam.

Salisbury-street and *Cecil-street* are built upon the site of Salisbury House, erected in 1602 by Sir Robert Cecil, Lord High Treasurer to James I., and created Earl of Salisbury in 1605. His successor divided the mansion into Great Salisbury House and Little Salisbury House: part of the latter was taken down, and upon the site was erected Salisbury-street, rebuilt as we now see it by Paine the architect; another portion was converted into the Middle Exchange, with shops and stalls, and a flight of steps to the river; the latter was taken down in 1696, with Great Salisbury House, and upon their site was erected Cecil-street. In Little Salisbury House lived the third Earl of Devon-shire, the pupil and patron of Hobbes, who, when standing at the gate, a few days after Restoration-day, was kindly recognised by Charles II. as he was passing in his coach through the Strand. In Cecil-street, and at the Globe in Salisbury-street, lived Partridge, cobbler, astrologer, and almanack-maker, whom Swift humorously killed in 1708, though he actually lived till 1715: but Partridge's Almanack (*Merlinus Liberatus*) continued to be published; and in 1723 advertised " Dr. Partridge's night-drops, night-pills, &c., sold as before, by his widow, at the Blue Ball in Salisbury-street."

Opposite *Southampton-street* lived the Vaillants, foreign booksellers, from 1686 until late in the last century.

Fountain-court is named from the above tavern : here is the *Coal Hole*, a tavern haunt of Edmund Kean. At No. 3 in this court died, Aug. 27, 1827, Blake, the epic painter, whose love of religion supported him through a life of uniform poverty, and cheered his death-bed.

Savoy-steps and *Savoy-street*, see SAVOY, page 658.

At No. 132 Strand (site of Wellington-street) was established in 1740 the first circulating library in London, by Wright, who had for his rivals Samuel Bathoe and John Bell.

Upon the site of No. 141 lived Jacob Tonson, the bookseller, " at Shakspeare's Head, over against Catherine-street, in the Strand." The house was successively occupied by the publishers, Andrew Millar, Alderman Thomas Cadell, and Cadell and Davies: Millar, being a Scotchman, adopted the sign of Buchanan's Head, a painting of which continued in one of the window-panes to our day.

No 142 occupies the site of the *Turk's Head Coffee-house*, which Dr. Johnson encouraged ; " for the mistress of it is a good civil woman, and has not much business." No. 143, site of the first office of the *Morning Chronicle* (see NEWSPAPERS, page 554). At No. 147 was published the *Sphynx*; and Jan. 2, 1828, No. 1 of the *Athenæum*, by James Silk Buckingham, the traveller in the East.

At No. 149, long known to the collectors of shells, minerals, and fossils, John Mawe kept shop : here have been sold shells at 5*l*., 10*l*., and 20*l*. each, now to be bought for a few shillings. Mr. Mawe published his *Travels in the Diamond District of Brazil*, 1812 ; *A Treatise on Diamonds;* and several elementary works on Mineralogy, Conchology, &c. His widow was succeeded by James Tennant, F.G.S., Professor of Mineralogy and Geology in King's College, London.

❦ SOMERSET HOUSE (see page 668). KING'S COLLEGE GATEWAY (see page 211).

No. 162 Strand, *Somerset Hotel* : at the bar, letters were left for the author of *Junius*. No. 165, *Inglis's Warehouse for Scot's Pills :* " Dr. Anderson's pills, sold by J. Inglis, now living at the Golden Unicorn, over against the Maypole in the Strand."—*Advertisement*, 1699.

Strand-lane, leading to the Roman Bath (see pp. 32 and 651), is the site of Strand Bridge, "and under is a lane or way down to the landing-place on the bank of the Thames" (*Stow*). Eastward were Chester's Inn, Strand Inn, and the Inn of the Bishop of Llandaff.

No. 169, *Strand Theatre*, formerly Barker's Panorama (see p. 580).

Arundel House, eastward, originally the town-house of the Bishops of Bath, was wrested from them in the reign of Edward VI. by Lord Thomas Seymour, High Admiral. After his execution, the house, with messuages, tenements, and lands adjoining, was purchased by Henry Fitz-Alan, Earl of Arundel, according to Strype, for 41*l*. 6*s*. 8*d*.; hence it was called Arundel Palace. Here died, 25 Feb. 1603, the Countess of Nottingham, after her interview with Queen Elizabeth to implore forgiveness for having withheld from her Essex's ring. Here Thomas Earl of Arundel began to assemble the celebrated Arundelian Marbles: the statues and busts in the gallery of the mansion ; the inscribed marbles inserted in the garden-walls; and the statues placed in the garden : altogether, 37 statues, 128 busts, and 250 inscribed marbles ; besides sarcophagi, altars, and fragments, and the inestimable gems.

The sculpture and picture galleries are seen in the backgrounds of Van Somer's portraits of the Earl and his Countess.

To the Earl's "liberal charges and magnificence this angle of the world oweth the first sight of Greek and Roman statues, with whose admired presence he began to honour the gardens and galleries of Arundel House, and hath ever since continued to transplant old Greece into England."—*Compleat Gentleman.*

"March 1, 1664.—I went to Arundel House, where I saw a great number of old Roman and Grecian statues, many as big again as the life, and divers Greek inscriptions upon stones in the gardens. * * * March 2.—I went to Mr. Foxe's chamber in Arundel House, where I saw a great many pretty pictures and things cast in brasse, some limmings, divers pretious stones, and one diamond valued at eleven hundred pound."—*Journal of Mr. E. Browne:* Ms. Sloan. 1906.

To Arundel House the Earl brought Hollar, who here engraved some of his finest plates. Thomas Parr ("Old Parr") was conveyed here from Shropshire by the Earl, to be shown to Charles I.: becoming domesticated in the family of the Earl of Arundel, his mode of living was changed; he fed high, drank wine, and died Nov. 14, 1635; after he had out-lived nine sovereigns, and during the reign of the tenth, at the age of 152 years and nine months: his body, by the king's command, was dissected by Harvey, who attributed Parr's death to peripneumony, brought on by the impurity of a London atmosphere and sudden change in diet.—*Philosophical Transactions,* 1669 *

Arundel House and Marbles were given back at the Restoration, in 1660, to the grandson of the earl, Mr. Henry Howard, who, at the recommendation of Selden and Evelyn, gave the inscribed marbles to the University of Oxford; and the library to the Royal Society, who met at Arundel House 9 Jan. 1666-7. Evelyn records "how exceedingly the corrosive air of London impaired" the marbles. The mansion was taken down 1678; and upon its site were erected Arundel, Surrey, Howard, and Norfolk streets. Hollar's print† shows the courtyard of Arundel House, with the great hall, and gabled buildings with dormer windows, but mostly low and mean. Sully was lodged here at the accession of James I.

Surrey-street : here, on the east side, in a large garden-house fronting the Thames, lived the Hon. Charles Howard, the eminent chemist, who discovered the sugar-refining process *in vacuo.* In Surrey-street died William Congreve, the dramatist, Jan. 19, 1728-9.

Norfolk-street : here, in a house near the water-side, lodged Peter the Great in 1698, and was visited by King William; and thence he went in a hackney-coach to dine with his majesty at Kensington Palace. At the south-west corner lived William Penn, the quaker; and subsequently, in the same house, Dr. Birch, the historian of the Royal Society. At No. 8, Samuel Ireland, originally a Spitalfields silk-merchant, whose son, William Henry Ireland, then eighteen, forged the Shakspeare Papers in 1795: here Dr. Parr and Dr. Warton fell upon their knees and kissed the Mss., — "great and impudent forgery," as Parr subsequently called it. In Norfolk-street also lived Mountfort, the player; and in Howard-street lodged Mrs. Bracegirdle, the fascinating actress, out of an attempt to carry off whom arose a bloody duel between Mountfort and Lord Mohun, when the former was killed.

Between *Arundel* and *Norfolk streets,* in 1698, lived Sir Thomas Lyttleton, Speaker of the House of Commons; and next door, the

* The evidence of Parr's extreme age is not, however, documentary; and the birth dates back to a period before Parish Registers were instituted by Cromwell. —*Census Report,* 1851.

† Hollar's View of London from the roof of Arundel House is very rare: an impression at Sir Mark Masterman Sykes's sale, in 1824, sold for 11*l.* In a Household Book of Lord William Howard (Belted Will) are "his expenses whilst living at Arundel House; and amongst them a payment to Mr. 'Shakspeare,' the parish scavenger."—*Athenæum,* No. 1403.

father of Bishop Burnet; and the house within memory was Burnet's, the bookseller, a collateral descendant of the bishop.

Arundel-street, " a pleasant and considerable street" (*Hatton*, 1708) :

> " Behold that narrow street which steep descends,
> Whose building to the shining shore extends ;
> Here Arundel's fam'd structure rear'd its frame,—
> The street alone retains an empty name :
> Where Titian's glowing paint the canvas warm'd,
> And Raphael's fair design the judgment charm'd,
> Now hangs the bellman's song, and pasted here,
> The coloured prints of Overton appear;
> Where statues breath'd, the work of Phidias' hands,
> A wooden pump or lonely watch-house stands."—Gay's *Trivia.*

On the east side was the *Crown and Anchor Tavern,* now the WHIT-TINGTON CLUB (see p. 199) : the sign was, probably, in part taken from the anchor of St. Clement's, opposite. Strype mentions it as " a large and curious house." Here was instituted the Academy of Ancient Music, in 1710. The great room is 84 ft. by 35 ft. 6 in : here, on Fox's birthday in 1798, took place a banquet to 2000 guests. Dr. Johnson and Boswell occasionally supped here; and the Royal Society dinners were held here. The very handsome Italian-fronted houses at the east and west corners of Arundel-street were designed by H. R. Abraham.

No. 191 Strand was the shop of William Godwin, bookseller, and author of *Caleb Williams,* the *Life of Chaucer,* &c.

Milford-lane is named from a *ford* over the Thames at the extremity, and a wind-*mill* in the Strand, near the site of St. Mary's Church, and shown in a print *temp.* James I. (See *Chron. London Bridge,* p. 395) : there is also a token of " the Windmill, withovt Temple Barr." Sir Richard Baker, the chronicler, lived in Milford-lane, 1632-9. (Cunningham's *Handbook,* p. 337.) The picturesque tenements on the east side, Strand end of the lane, principally of wood, with bay-windows, are described in a deed, date 1694: they were taken down in 1852, and the site is now occupied by "Milford House."

Essex-street and *Devereux-court,* formerly the Outer Temple, are named from Robert Devereux, Earl of Essex, Queen Elizabeth's last favourite. The ground was leased by the Knights of St. John of Jerusalem to the Bishops of Exeter, who built here a town-house, in which they lived till the Reformation, when it passed to William Lord Paget; next to Thomas Howard, Duke of Norfolk, son of the poetic Earl of Surrey ; to Dudley, Earl of Leicester ; and then to his step-son, the Earl of Essex : hence it was successively called Exeter House, Paget House, Norfolk House, Leicester House, and Essex House. But the chief memory of the place is associated with Essex and his abortive project for the overthrow of Elizabeth's government : he fortified the house, but was hemmed in on all sides, artillery being planted against the mansion, and a gun mounted upon the tower of St. Clement's, when Essex and his followers surrendered. Here was born and married his luckless son, whose infamous countess was implicated in the poisoning of Sir Thomas Overbury. Pepys describes Essex House as " large but ugly :" it was tenanted by persons of rank till after the Restoration, when it was subdivided and let. The Cottonian Library was kept here from 1712 to 1730, in the portion of the house upon the site of the present Essex-street Chapel (see page 174). At the Essex Head tavern, now No. 40, Dr. Johnson established, the year before he died, a club called " Sam's," from the landlord, Samuel Greaves, who had been servant to Mr. Thrale. In this street was held the Robin Hood Society, a debating club, the scene of Burke's earliest eloquence ; Goldsmith was also a member.

No. 213 Strand was *George's Coffee-house* (see page 202).
Devereux-court : here was the Grecian Coffee-house (see page 202).
No. 217 Strand was the house of Snow, the wealthy goldsmith :

> " Disdain not, Snow, my humble verse to hear ;
> Stick thy black pen awhile behind thy ear.
> * * * * *
>
> O thou, whose penetrative wisdom found
> The South-sea rocks and shelves, where thousands drown'd !
> When credit sunk, and commerce gasping lay,
> Thou stood'st, nor sent one bill unpaid away.
> When not a guinea chink'd on Martin's boards,
> And Atwell's self was drain'd of all his hoards,
> Thou stood'st (an Indian king in size and hue) :
> Thy unexhausted shop was our Peru."—*Gay.*

Palsgrave-place was the site of the Palsgrave Head tavern, set up,
in compliment to the Palsgrave Frederic, afterwards King of Bohemia,
affianced to the Princess Elizabeth in the old banqueting-house at
Whitehall, Dec. 27, 1612. Hard by was Heycock's Ordinary, much
frequented by Parliament-men and gallants.—Burn's *Catalogue*, &c.

TEMPLE BAR is described at page 704. The west side, until numbered with the Strand, was called on tokens, " Without Temple Barr."

STRAND : NORTH SIDE.—No. 238 was the last of the " Bulk-shops,"
kept by Crockford, the fishmonger ; removed in 1846 (see page 390).

Ship-yard was the site of the Ship inn, mentioned in a grant to Sir
Christopher Hatton in 1571. There is a token of this tavern, date
1649 ; and it was standing in 1756. John Reynolds, a cook, issued a
token (a fox stealing a goose) in Ship-yard in 1666. A few of the old
houses remain : one, engraved in Wilkinson's *Londina Illustrata*, is
stated to have been the residence of Elias Ashmole, the antiquary.
Faithorne published his *Art of Graving and Etching* " at his shop
next to ye signe of the Drake, without Temple barr, 1662."

In *Shire-lane* was the sign of " the Bible," a house of call for
printers. In the Strand, besides the Ship, were the Swan, the Crown,
the Robin Hood, the White Hart, the Bear and Harrow, the Holy
Lamb, and the Angel, the latter taken down in 1854. Sir John Denham, the poet, when a student at Lincoln's Inn, in 1635, in a drunken
frolic, with a pot of ink and a plasterer's brush, blotted out all the signs
between Temple Bar and Charing Cross, which cost Denham and his
comrades " some monies."—*J. H. Burn.*

The Sutherland View of London (1543) shows a " loosely-built" line
of gabled houses on the north side, from Temple Bar to St. Mary's.

From opposite Ship-yard extended an obtuse-angled triangle of
buildings, the eastern line formed by the vestry-room and almshouses
of St. Clement's, and the sides by shops ; the whole called *Butcher-row*,
from a flesh-market granted here 21 Edward I., at first shambles, but
subsequently houses of wood and plaster ; one of these, a five-storied
house, *temp.* James I., was inhabited by Count Beaumont, the French
court ambassador : here the Duc de Sully was lodged for one night
in 1603, until " the palace of Arundel" could be prepared for him.
Beaumont's house-front bore roses and crowns and fleurs-de-lis, and
the date 1581. From a Bear and Harrow orgy, Nat Lee, the dramatic
poet, was returning to Duke-street, when he fell, " overtaken with
wine," in Clare Market, and died. Here also was Clifton's eating-
house, a dining-place of Dr. Johnson. Butcher-row was removed in
1802, when were built the opposite crescent-like houses, named
Pickett-street from the projector of the improvement, Alderman
Pickett. During the sewers' works, eastward of the church, at

several feet depth, was discovered an ancient stone bridge of one arch. The almshouses were removed in 1790: here is a well 191 feet deep.

In a house in Butcher-row, east of Clement's Inn, by the confession of Winter, he, with Catesby, Wright, and Guy Fawkes, met, and there administered the oath of secresy to the conspirators, and afterwards received the sacrament in the next room.—*The Gunpowder Treason,* reprinted 1679.

The Foregate leads to CLEMENT'S INN (see page 415) and *Clement's-lane,* where lived Sir John Trevor, cousin to Lord Chancellor Jeffries, and twice Speaker of the House of Commons. *Boswell-court* occupies the site of a mansion of a Mr. Boswell: here lived Lady Raleigh, the widow of Sir Walter; Lord Chief-Justice Lyttleton, and Sir Richard and Lady Fanshawe. In *New-court* was the Independents' chapel of Burgess, Bradbury, and Winter: it was burnt in the Sacheverel riots.

St. Clement's Vestry-hall, Pickett-street, contains the altar-piece (St. Cecilia) painted by Kent for St. Clement's Church, whence it was removed, in 1725, by order of Bishop Gibson, on the supposition that the picture contained portraits of the Pretender's wife and children: it was first removed to the Crown and Anchor tavern, and next to the old vestry-room. St. Clement's was the church most frequented by Dr. Johnson: here, upon a column adjoining his pew (No. 18) in the north gallery, is a brass tablet, with the following inscription by the Rev. Dr. Croly:

" In this pew, and beside this pillar, for many years attended divine service the celebrated Dr. Samuel Johnson, the philosopher, the poet, the great lexicographer, the profound moralist, and chief writer of his time. Born 1709; died 1784. In the remembrance and honour of noble faculties nobly employed, some inhabitants of the parish of St. Clement Danes have placed this slight memorial, A.D. 1851."

Wych-street, leading to Drury-lane (see page 261): the south side retains some picturesque house-fronts. Opposite is NEW INN (p. 416).

Holywell-street is named from one of the holy springs which Fitz-Stephen described as "sweete, wholesome, and cleere; and much frequented by schollers and youth of the citie in summer evenings, when they walk forth to take the aire." The "holy well" is stated to be that under the Old Dog tavern, No. 24. Here is the old entrance to Lyon's Inn (now blocked up); and the passage opposite, sculptured with a lion's head, was formerly the inn-entrance from the Strand. Holy-well-street was, in Strype's time, inhabited by "divers salesmen and piece-brokers," who have nearly deserted it: two of their signs remain; the Indian queen, said to have been painted by Catton, R.A.; and a boldly-carved and gilt crescent moon. The street is now tenanted by dealers in old clothes, keepers of book-stalls, and publishers and vendors of cheap and low books: a few lofty gabled and bayed house-fronts remain.

Newcastle-street (formerly Magpye-alley) was named from the ground-landlord, John Holles, Duke of Newcastle.

No. 313 Strand, One Bell livery-stables: the tavern and buildings are let in tenements. The *Tatler,* March 9, 1710, announced a stage-coach "twice a week from the One Bell in the Strand to Dorchester, the proper time for writing pastorals now drawing near."

No. 317 occupies the site of the forge of a blacksmith, the father of Nan Clarges, afterwards Duchess of Albemarle: "the shop," says Aubrey (*Life of Monk,* 1680), "is still of that trade; the corner shop, the first turning on ye right hand as you come out of the Strand into Drury-lane; the house is now built of brick:" it is at the east corner of Maypole-alley,

" Where Drury-lane descends into the Strand."

Opposite was "the Maypole in the Strand," raised by the farrier to commemorate his daughter's good fortune.

The Maypole set up at the Restoration was conveyed to this spot, April 14, 1561, with great ceremony, a streamer flourishing before it, and drums and trumpets, and the acclamations of the people. This maypole, 134 feet high, was in two pieces, which being joined together and hooped with iron, the crown and vane, and the king's arms, richly gilded. were placed on the head of it; and a large top, like a balcony, about the middle of it. It was raised by twelve seamen, "by cables, pullies, and other tacklins, with six great anchors;" and "in four hours' space it was advanced upright, as near hand as they could guess where the former one stood; but far more glorious, bigger, and higher than ever any one that stood before it." It was, however, broken by a high wind about 1672; and the remaining portion, being grown old and decayed, was taken down in 1713.

Several traders' and tavern tokens bear on the reverse this Maypole, with a small building at the foot. Here was the first stand for hackney coaches, erected in 1634, and abolished March 1853.

No. 332, *Morning Chronicle Office*, was formerly the White Swan tavern. Here, in a lodging, to be near his patron, the Earl of Clarendon, in Somerset House, lived Dr. William King, who wrote the *Art of Cookery*, a poem, &c. He was the friend of Swift. King was luxurious and improvident, and died in poverty in 1712, in the above house.

Catherine-street : on the west is New Exeter 'Change, designed by Sydney Smirke, with house-fronts *temp.* James I. *Brydges-street*, Drury-lane Theatre (see COVENT GARDEN, page 235, and THEATRES).

No. 346 Strand, Doily's Warehouse, rebuilt in fanciful Italian style, by Beazley, in 1838, occupies the site of Wimbledon House, built by Sir Edward Cecil, and burnt down in 1628. Dryden names "Doily petticoats;" Steele had "a Doily suit" (*Guardian*, No. 102); and Gay a "Doily habit" (*Trivia*, book i.); and Doily introduced the small wine-glass napkin which bears his name.

Wellington-street North : on the west side is the Lyceum Theatre, rebuilt by Beazley. In *Exeter-street*, at a staymaker's, was the first London lodging of Dr. Johnson (1737), where he lived upon 4½d. per day. When Dr. Johnson first came to London with his pupil Garrick, they borrowed five pounds, on their joint note, of Mr. Wilcocks, the bookseller, Strand.* "Near the Savoy in the Strand," east of Exeter 'Change, was the Canary House, probably also Cary House, noted for its sack "with the abricot flavour" (Dryden's *Wild Gallant*, 1669); and Pepys mentions "Cary House, a house of entertainment."

At No. 352 Strand was born, Jan. 29, 1798, Henry Neele, the poet, the son of the able map and heraldic engraver. Westward was EXETER 'CHANGE, described at page 288.

"On the demolition of the building in 1830, the writer saw, cut in the stone architrave above the window at the east end, ' EXETER CHANGE. 1670,' a date much earlier in its adaptation than is generally supposed."—*J. H. Burn.*

In one of the offices abutting on the 'Change was published the *Literary Gazette*, No. 1, Jan. 25, 1817.

Exeter-street and *Burleigh-street* are named from their being parts of the site of Burleigh and Exeter House.

No. 372 Strand, EXETER HALL (see page 287).

Southampton-street was named in compliment to Lady Rachel, daughter of Thomas Wriothesley, Earl of Southampton, and wife of William Lord Russell. Near the foot of the street stood Bedford House, the town mansion of the Earl of Bedford: it was principally

---

* The following were Dr. Johnson's places of residence in and near London: 1. Exeter-street, off Catherine-street, Strand (1737). 2. Greenwich (1737). 3. Woodstock-street, near Hanover-square (1737). 4. Castle-street, Cavendish-square, No. 6 (1738). 5. Strand. 6. Boswell-court. 7. Strand again. 8. Bow-street. 9. Holborn. 10. Fetter-lane. 11. Holborn again (at the Golden Anchor, Holborn Bars, 1748). 12. Gough-square, No. 17 (1748). 13. Staple Inn (1758). 14. Gray's Inn. 15. Inner-Temple-lane, No. 1 (1760). 16. Johnson's-court, Fleet-street, No. 7 (1765). 17. Bolt-court, Fleet-street, No. 8 (1776).

built of wood, and remained till 1704; the garden extended northward, its wall bounding Covent Garden Market. In Southampton-street is a bar-gate; the Duke of Bedford having power to erect walls and gates at the end of every thoroughfare on his estate. *Bedford-street* occupies part of the site. Between these streets, east and west, is *Maiden-lane*, where, in a second floor, lodged Andrew Marvell, M.P. for Hull, when he refused a treasury-order for 1000*l.* brought to him by Lord Danby from the king. At the sign of the White Peruke lodged Voltaire.

At No. 26 Maiden-lane, corner of Hand-court, was born, in 1773, J. W. M. Turner, R.A., the landscape-painter. His father was a hair-dresser; and the painter, when a boy, coloured prints for John R. Smith, of Maiden-lane, a mezzotinto engraver. Turner removed to apartments in Hand-court, and during his residence here he exhibited at the Royal Academy fifty-nine pictures.

Opposite is the Cyder Cellar, opened about 1730: a curious tract, *Adventures underground*, 1750, contains strange notices of this "midnight concert-room" (*Notes and Queries*, No. 28): it was a haunt of Professor Porson's.

At No. 405 Strand, the Queen's Head public-house, lodged Thomas Parr, when he was brought to London to be shown to Charles 1.; as stated to J. T. Smith, in 1814, by a person then aged 90, to whom the house was pointed out by his grandfather, then 88.—Smith's *Streets*.

No. 411 Strand, the *Adelphi Theatre*, Beazley architect (see THEATRES). Westward are a few old house-fronts. No. 429, built for the Westminster Fire and Life Insurance Office, by Cockerell, R.A., has a façade of great originality: the figures (*aquarii*) over the principal windows are beautifully characteristic.

No. 430, *West Strand* commences: *King-William-street* denotes the reign in which the improvements were made (see CHARING CROSS HOSPITAL, page 380).

No. 437, LOWTHER ARCADE. (See page 17.)

No. 448, *Electric Telegraph Office*. Upon the roof is the *Electric Time Signal Ball*, completed in 1852; and in the roadway opposite is an *Illuminated Clock*. The signal consists of a zinc ball, 6 feet in diameter, supported by a rod, which passes down the centre of the column, and carries at its base a piston, which, in its descent, plunges into a cast-iron air-cylinder; the escape of the air being regulated so as at pleasure to check the momentum of the ball, and prevent concussion. The raising of the ball half-mast high takes place daily at 10 minutes to 1; at 5 minutes to 1 it is raised to its full height; and at 1 precisely, and simultaneously with the fall of the ball at Greenwich, it is liberated by the galvanic current sent from the Observatory through a wire laid for that purpose. The same galvanic current which liberates the ball in the Strand, moves a needle upon the transit-clock at the Observatory: the time occupied by the transmission being about 1-3000th part of a second; and by the unloosing of the machinery which supports the ball, less than one-fifth part of a second. The true moment of 1 o'clock is, therefore, indicated by the first appearance of the line of light between the dark cross over the ball and the body of the ball itself. In the event of accidental failure at 1 o'clock, the ball is raised half-mast high, and dropped at 2 o'clock. When fully raised, the ball is 129 feet above the level of the Thames, and falls 10 feet. The Clock in the roadway is moved by a voltaic current from a regulator in the office, which is daily set right by the fall of the ball.

No. 452, the *Golden Cross Hotel*: the old inn stood further west.

"I often," says Charles Lamb, "shed tears in the motley Strand, for fulness of joy at so much life" (*Letters*, vol. i.).

TATTERSALL'S,

The celebrated sporting rendezvous, technically "the Corner" (*i. e.* at Hyde Park Corner), lies in the rear of St. George's Hospital, and is approached from Grosvenor-place. Richard Tattersall, who was training-groom to the second and last Duke of Kingston, in 1779, bought of Lord Bolingbroke the race-horse "Highflyer," and had previously established "Tattersall's." It consists of a court-yard, with a small circular temple over a pump, surmounted by the figure of a fox, the dome bearing a bust of George IV. in his eighteenth year. Here is a well-designed subscription-room, by George Tattersall; and a counting-house, wherein hang the regulations, dated 1780. Here also are stables and covered alleys, the characteristic of the place being neatness and well-ordered system. The great public horse-auction is on Monday throughout the year, and Thursday in the height of the season, when also Sunday is the great day at Tattersall's for the sporting aristocracy. Here horses of 10,000*l.* value are sometimes sold in a day; and the foreign trade in thorough-bred horses is extensive. On show and sale days the display of horses is often very fine. The "Book-making" before the Derby or St. Leger is crowded with peers and plebeians, butchers and brokers, betting-list keepers, insurers, guardsmen and prize-fighters, Manchester manufacturers, Yorkshire farmers, sham captains, *ci-devant* gentlemen, &c. The subscription to "the Room," which is regulated by the Jockey Club, is 2*l.* 2*s.* per annum. Here is a cartoon of the race-horse "Eclipse." We have seen a clever painting, by Alken, of the horse-auction at Tattersall's.

TEMPLE (THE), (See p. 404.)

TEMPLE BAR,

Between the east end of the Strand and the west end of Fleet-street, divides the City of London from the liberty of Westminster; or rather, "it opens not immediately into the City itself (which terminated at Ludgate), but into the liberty or freedom thereof" (*Hatton*, 1708). The original division from the county (hence Shire-lane) was by posts and rails, a chain, and a *bar* (as at Holborn, Smithfield, and Whitechapel bars) placed across the street, and named from its immediate vicinity to the *Temple*. At the coronation of Queen Mary, "the Temple-barre was newly painted and hanged" (*Stow*). The bar gave place to "a house of timber" raised across the street, with a narrow gateway underneath, and an entrance on the south side under the house above. This was burned down in the Great Fire of 1666; after which the present bar-gate was built by Sir Christopher Wren, of Portland-stone. The basement is rusticated, and has a large flattened arch in the centre for the carriage-way, and a smaller semicircular arch on each side for foot-passengers. Each façade has four Corinthian pilasters, an entablature, and arched pediment. On the west, in two niches, are statues of Charles I. and Charles II. in Roman costume; and over the keystone of the centre arch were the royal arms: on the east, in similar niches, are statues of James I. and his queen, Anne of Denmark (often described as Elizabeth); and over the keystone were the City arms. Inscription:

"Erected in the year 1670, Sir Samuel Starling Mayor; continued in the year 1671, Sir Richard Ford Lord Mayor; and finished in the year 1672, Sir George Waterman Lord Mayor."

The upper portion has two bold cartouches, or scrolls, as supporters; but the fruit and flowers sculptured in the pediment, and the supporters of the royal arms, which were placed over the extremities of the posterns (now widened), have disappeared; the inscription is scarcely legible; and the stone-work of the whole is weather-worn: in 1852 the Common Council refused to spend 1500*l.* to restore the bar as Wren left it. The statues are by John Bushnell, who died in 1701; that of Charles I. has lost the baton. In the centre of each façade is a semicircular-headed window, lighting an apartment now held of the City, at an annual rent of 50*l.*, by Messrs. Child, the bankers, as a depository for their account-books. Above the centre of the pediment, upon iron spikes, were formerly placed the head and limbs of persons executed for treason. The first of these revolting displays was one of the quarters of Sir Thomas Armstrong, implicated in the Rye-House Plot; and next the quarters of Sir William Perkins and Sir John Friend, and Perkins's head, who had conspired to assassinate William III.

"April 10, 1696.—A dismal sight, which many pitied. I think there never was such a Temple Bar till now, except in the time of King Charles II., viz. Sir Thomas Armstrong."—Evelyn's *Diary.*

After the Rebellions of 1715 and 1745, the heads of some of the victims were placed upon the bar; and in 1723, the head of Counsellor Layer, who had conspired for the restoration of the Pretender: Layer's head remained here 30 years, till blown down in a gale of wind, when it was picked up in the street by an attorney. But the heads last set up here were those of Townley and Fletcher, the rebels, in 1746. Walpole writes, Aug. 16, 1746: "I have been this morning at the Tower, and passed under the new heads at Temple Bar, where people make a trade of letting spying-glasses at a halfpenny a look;" and in 1825, a person, aged 87, remembered the above heads being seen with a telescope from Leicester Fields, the ground between which and Temple Bar being then thinly built over. (*J. T. Smith.*) In 1766 a man was detected discharging musket-balls, from a steel crossbow, at these two heads; which, however, remained there until March 31, 1772, when one of the heads fell down; and shortly after, the remaining one was swept down by the wind.* The last of the iron poles, or spikes, was not removed from the Bar until the commencement of the present century.

The old gates of Temple Bar remain: they are of oak, paneled, and are surmounted by a rudely-carved festoon of fruit and flowers. These gates were originally shut at night, and guarded by watchmen; and in our time they have been closed in cases of apprehended tumult. Upon the visit of the Sovereign to the City, or upon the proclamation of a new Sovereign or of Peace, it was formerly customary to keep the gates closed, until admission was formally demanded; the gates were then opened; and upon the Royal visit, the Lord Mayor surrendered the City sword to the Sovereign, who re-delivered it to the Mayor.

At Temple Bar the above ceremony was observed when Queen Elizabeth proceeded to St. Paul's to return thanks for the defeat of the Spanish Armada; when Fairfax and Cromwell and the Parliament went in state to dine with the City; when Queen Anne went to St. Paul's to return thanks for the Duke of Marlborough's victories; when Queen Victoria dined at Guildhall in the year of her accession, 1837; and when Her Majesty went to open the New Royal Exchange in 1844; but on the Queen's visit in 1851, the ceremony at Temple Bar was dispensed with. The custom at the Proclamation of Peace, or the Accession of the Sovereign, has been for a herald, attended by trumpeters, to knock with his baton at the closed gate, when the City Marshal inquired, "Who comes there?" and the herald having replied, is admitted, and conducted to the Lord Mayor, who directed that the whole of the cavalcade should be admitted; and the proclamation was read opposite Chancery-lane. Such was the observance upon the

---

* See *Temple Bar, the City Golgotha,* by a Member of the Middle Temple, sm. 4to, 1853, for a narrative of these occurrences, in illustration of the revolting effects of capital punishments and public executions.

accession of George IV., William IV., and Queen Victoria In '1844 the ceremony consisted merely of closing the gates just before the royal procession reached
the bar, and re-opening them upon the announcement of the Queen's arrival.

At the funeral of the Duke of Wellington, Nov. 18, 1852, Temple
Bar was entirely covered with draperies of black cloth and velvet, and
cloth-of-gold; decorated with the armorial bearings and orders of the
Duke in proper colours; silvered cornices, fringe, urns, and a circle of
flambeaux upon the pediment; the whole presenting an impressive
effect of solemn triumph and gloomy grandeur.

The removal of Temple Bar has been a favourite subject o⁻agitation,
hitherto successfully resisted. A scarce print shows the Bar and the
adjoining gabled houses at the commencement of the 18th century; and
the Bar was painted by Rooker in 1772.

THAMES RIVER (THE).

The situation of London upon the banks of the Thames, although
occupying little more than one-thirtieth of its entire course, renders it
the most important commercial river in the world. The name is inferred to be of British origin: Cæsar writes it Tamesis, evidently Tames
or Thames with a Latin termination. The river rises in the south-
eastern slopes of the Coteswold Hills; for a short distance it divides
Gloucestershire from Wiltshire; next Berkshire from Oxfordshire, and
then from Buckinghamshire; it then divides Surrey and Middlesex, separating the cities of Westminster and London from Lambeth, Southwark, Bermondsey, and Rotherhithe; thence to its mouth, it divides
Kent and Essex, and falls into the sea at the Nore, about 110 miles
nearly due east from the source, and about twice that distance measured
along the windings of the river. From having no sand-bar at its mouth,
it is navigable for sea-vessels to London Bridge, about 45 miles from the
Nore, or nearly one-fourth of its entire length! In its course through
the metropolis, it varies from 800 to 1500 feet in breadth; gradually expanding, as it approaches the Nore, to seven miles broad.*

Drayton describes, as renowned for "ships and swans, Queen Thames."
Cowley thus refers to Old London Bridge impeding the prospect:

> " Stopp'd by the houses of that wondrous street,
> Which rides o'er the broad river like a fleet."

Embankment.—To the Romans we are indebted for the first embankment of the Thames; and, according to Tacitus, they pressed the
Britons into the work. The maintenance and repair of these embank-
ments have been traced to the reign of Edward I.; but the encroachments of wharfs and other buildings have materially contracted the
water-way immediately through the centre of the metropolis; so that
the only relic of the old line is to be seen adjoining Waterloo Bridge.
For example: the distance of the river front from Westminster Hall, in
an old plan, is 100 feet; it is now 300 feet. Several plans have been
proposed for the embankment of the Thames; some including railways,
arcades, terraces, &c. The only portions yet embanked are the terraces
of the Custom House, Somerset House, the Adelphi, the New Houses of
Parliament, Thames Bank; although, more than a century and a half
since, Wren designed "a commodious quay on the whole bank of the river,
from Blackfriars to the Tower." A showy architectural plan has been
published by Colonel Trench; and in 1845, John Martin, the painter,
designed a railway along both sides of the Thames, with an open walk

* There is likewise the Thames, the largest river of the plain of Upper Canada;
upon whose banks is fast rising the City of London; reminding one, otherwise
than by name, of the glories of the metropolis of the mother-country.

from Hungerford to the Tower, and from Vauxhall to Deptford. The embankment of the river above Vauxhall Bridge is in progress; it is to be continued to Battersea Bridge.*

"London with Westminster, by reason of the turning of the river, much resembles the shape (including Southwark) of *a great whale:* Westminster being the under jaw; St. James's Park the mouth; the Pall Mall, &c. northward, the upper jaw; Cock and Pye Fields, or the meeting of the seven streets, the eye; the rest of the City and Southwark to East Smithfield, the body; and thence eastward to Limehouse, the tail: and 'tis, probably, in as great a proportion the largest of towns, as that is of fishes."—*Hatton,* 1708.

The very bold reach made by the Thames adds greatly to the effect of the prospect; and by this means, before the addition of the present front of Buckingham Palace, the Sovereign, when seated upon her throne, commanded a view of the dome of St. Paul's, and the spires and towers of the City churches.

The Tide ascends about 15 miles above London Bridge to Teddington (Tide-end-town): here an immense volume of fresh water, derived from the arc of the drainage of the Thames, (calculated at 800,000,000 gallons a-day, or about 16 square miles, 90 feet deep), flows over Teddington Lock, and mixes with the water below. Even at ebb-tide there are 12 or 13 feet of water in the fair way of the river above Greenwich; the mean range of the tides at London Bridge is about 17 feet; of the highest spring-tides about 22 feet. Up to Woolwich the river is navigable for ships of any burden; to Blackwall for those of 1400 tons.

Thames Sports and Pageants.—Fitzstephen chronicles the water tournament and quintain (see page 16). Richard II. was rowed in his tapestried barge, probably the first royal barge upon the Thames: and here the king, seeing the poet Gower, called him on board, and commanded him "to make a book after his best," which was the origin of the *Confessio Amantis.* In the 15th and 16th centuries, and onward to very recent days, each palace on the north bank of the Thames had its water-gate, and its retinue of barge and wherries. The Thames was the royal road from Westminster and Whitehall to the Tower, and from thence to Greenwich. State prisoners were conveyed by the Thames to the Traitor's Gate at the Tower, and the Star-Chamber victims to a similar gate at the Fleet. The landing-places on the Thames appear to have been even less changed than the thoroughfare itself; for in the account of the penance of Eleanor Cobham, Duchess of Gloucester, in 1440, we find named Temple-bridge (stairs), the Old Swan, and Queenhithe; and in early maps of London, are Broken Wharf, Paul's Wharf, Essex Stairs, and Whitehall Stairs; all which exist by the same names to the present day. Cardinal Wolsey, when he delivered up York Place, "took his barge at his privy stairs, and so went by water to Putney," on his way to Asher. Sir Thomas More kept his great barge at Chelsea, which he gave to Sir Thomas Audley, his successor in the chancellorship, with whom he placed his eight watermen. In the "Aqua Triumphalis," in 1662, the City welcomed Charles II. from Hampton Court to Whitehall, the barges of the twelve companies being carried as far as Chelsea; and mostly all ended with a pageant. James II., 1688, embarked at Whitehall: "I saw him take barge," says Evelyn; "a sad sight." The last primate who kept his state barge at Lambeth was Archbishop Wake, who died 1737 (see page 446). Early in the 17th century, Howel numbers among the river glories, "forests of masts which are perpetually upon her;" the variety of smaller wooden bottoms playing up and down;" and Stow computes that there were in his time 2000. In 1630, the river had its own laureat, John Taylor "the Water-poet":

* In a river-side cottage, between the old church at Chelsea and Battersea-bridge, died, Dec. 19, 1851, J. M. W. Turner, R.A., the landscape-painter.

> " But, noble Thames, whilst I can hold a pen,
> I will divulge thy glory unto men :
> Thou, in the morning, when my corn is scant,
> Before the evening doth supply my want."

Taylor knew Ben Jonson ; and the water-poet " probably had the good fortune to ferry Shakspere from Whitehall to Paris Garden."—*Knight.*

The existing sports on the Thames consist of rowing, boat-racing, and yachting, or sailing, throughout the summer and autumn ; by clubs, numbering several members of the Universities of Oxford, Cambridge, and London ; the scholars of Westminster, St. Paul's, and other academic foundations. The match for Dogget's coat and silver badge is rowed for every 1st of August (see page 350). The proprietors of Vauxhall Gardens, and Astley the rider, gave wherries to be rowed for ; as did also Edmund Kean, the tragedian. In July 1776 a man safely crossed the Thames in a butcher's tray, from Somerset Stairs, for a wager ; upon which feat depended 14,000*l.*

The *Thames Watermen* formerly had their cant dialect, of which Ned Ward and Tom Brown give specimens ; and the " Thames ribaldry" (*Spectator*) has lasted to our time, in which watermen's disputes have been settled by Joe Hatch, " the Thames Chancellor."

State Barges.—The first water pageant of the City of London dates from 1454, when John Norman, the mayor, was rowed to Westminster in his barge ; but the companies had their barges for water processions half a century before this ; and the grocers' accounts, *temp.* Henry VI., mention the hiring of barges to attend the sheriffs' show by water. Hall chronicles the mayor and citizens accompanying Anne Boleyn at her coronation, in 1533, from Greenwich to the Tower, in their barges. The barge is retained in the Lord Mayor's state, which includes the water-bailiff, one of his lordship's esquires, with a salary of 500*l.* a year, a shallop, and eight men ; and in the suite are a barge-master, and thirty-two city watermen. The Lord Mayor's barge is richly carved and gilt, and cost in 1807, 2579*l.* A few of the City companies maintain their state barges " to attend my Lord Mayor:" as the Fishmongers, Vintners, and Dyers, Stationers, Skinners, and Watermen. The Goldsmiths Company sold their barge in 1850, and have not replaced it. The swan-upping excursions of the Dyers and Vintners are described at page 362. A capacious barge is kept for civic feasts : the present barge, built in 1816, was named " the Maria Wood" (from the then Lord Mayor's eldest daughter), and cost 5000*l.* The Queen maintains her river state ; and one of the royal barges, built nearly a century and a quarter since, is a curious craft : the rowers wear scarlet state liveries. The Lords of the Admiralty have likewise their state barge.

State Funerals by the Thames are rare : the remains of Anne of Bohemia, and Henry VII., who died at Richmond, were conveyed with great pomp by the river to Westminster ; and the body of Queen Elizabeth was " brought by water to Whitehall." The remains of Lord Nelson, after lying in state in the Painted Hall of Greenwich Hospital, were conveyed by the Thames* to the Admiralty, Jan. 8, 1806, and next day were buried in St. Paul's Cathedral.

THE PORT OF LONDON is described at pages 623-24.

The Bridges across the Thames at the metropolis are described at pages 54 to 63. A new iron suspension-bridge from Chelsea to Battersea Park was commenced in 1853. The erection of a new iron bridge at Westminster, very near the site of the old bridge, was begun in

---

* The Author of this volume, born August 17, 1801, has a distinct recollection of having seen this Funeral Procession upon the Thames from a back window of a house at the south foot of London Bridge.

1854: the new bridge to be of Gothic design, with seven arches, the centre one to have only 20 feet headway; the entire width 85 feet. These new bridges are designed by Thomas Page, C.E.

The two Churches immediately below London Bridge attest the occupation of London by the Danes and Northmen: St. Olave's Southwark, originally dedicated to the Norwegian king, Olaf the Saint; and St. Magnus the Martyr, from St. Magnus, a Norwegian jarl, killed in the 12th century in Orkney, where the cathedral in Kirkwall is also dedicated to him.

THE DOCKS (which have cost more than 8,000,000*l.* in the present century) are described at pages 254-57.

Thames Water has been supplied to London since 1580, when Peter Morrys, by means of a wheel and force-pumps, carried the water over the steeple of St. Magnus's Church to "the Standard in Cornhill." But the Thames water, once limpid and clear, has grown turbid with the increase of population upon the river banks: it is now a huge sewer, which, long before it reaches London, receives the refuse of a hundred towns and villages, and the surface drainage of 6600 acres. In the meantime fish have disappeared from between Putney Bridge and Greenwich. But the adulterating matters are, in some measure, decomposed by the vegetation at the bottom and sides of the river.

Sir Jonas More (or Moore), F.R.S., surveyor of the Ordnance *temp.* Charles II., says: "The Thames water, taken up about Greenwich, at low water, where it is free from all brackishness of the sea, and has in it all the fat and sullage from the great city of London, makes very strong drink;" and, again, for sea-stores, "it will of itself alone, being carried to sea, ferment wonderfully; and after its due purgations, and three times stinking (after which it continues sweet), it will be so strong that several sea commanders have told me it would burn, and has often fuddled their mariners."—*England's Interest*, 12mo, 1703.

The Chelsea Water-works were first established in 1723, when a canal was dug from the Thames, near Ranelagh, to Pimlico; thence the Company removed near to the site of Ranelagh Gardens, where the water is filtered in reservoirs, several acres in extent.

The Conservancy of the Thames by the Corporation of London dates from 1st Edward IV.; the Mayor acting as bailiff over the waters (in preserving its fisheries and channels), and as meter of marketable commodities—fruit, garden-stuff, salt, and oysters, corn and coal—from Staines to Yantlett Creek (80 miles). The Admiralty also claims a certain jurisdiction; and the Corporation of the Trinity House has authority to remove shoals, to regulate lastage and ballastage, to provide lighthouses and beacons, to license pilots, mariners, &c. The River Police was first established in 1798.

Fish.—Fitzstephen describes the Thames, at London, as "a fishful river;" and its fishermen were accustomed to present their tithe of *salmon* at the high altar of St. Peter, and claim on that occasion the right to sit at the Prior of Westminster's own table. At this period the river, even below the site of the present London Bridge, abounded with fish. In 1376-77, a law was passed in parliament for the saving of salmon and other fry of fish; and, in 1381-82, "swannes" that came through the bridge, or beneath the bridge, were the fees of the Constable of the Tower. Howel says:—"When the idler was tired of bowls, he had nothing to do but to step down to Queenhithe or the Temple," and have an afternoon of angling. "Go to the river: what a pleasure it is to go thereon in the summer time, in boat or barge, or to go a-floundering among the fishermen!" In the regulations, too, of the "Committee of Free Fishermen" is a provision that fishermen were not to come nearer London than the Old Swan, on the north bank of the river, and St. Mary Overies, on the south. Formerly, Blackfriars and Westminster bridges were anglers' stations; but the fish have now disappeared from the

Thames at London. Blackwall is, however, still famed for its white-bait (see page 49), and fish are taken in the docks below London Bridge. Salmon has not been taken in the Thames for thirty years. Strange fish have strayed here. In 1391, a dolphin, "ten feet in length," played himself in the Thames at London to the bridge. Evelyn tells of a whale, fifty-eight feet in length, killed between Deptford and Greenwich in 1658; and nearer the mouth of the river (at Grays) a whale of the above length was taken in 1809, and another in 1849. "In 1783, a two-toothed cachalot, 21 ft. long, was taken above London Bridge."—*Pennant.*

The Steam Navigation of the Thames exceeds that of any other river in the world. The first steam-boat left the Thames, for Richmond, in 1814; the next, for Gravesend, in 1815; and in the same year for Margate. The Gravesend steamers soon superseded the sailing-boats with decks, which, in 1737, had displaced the tilt-boats mentioned *temp.* Richard II. The Margate steamers, in like manner, superseded the sailing "hoy."

FROSTS AND FROST FAIRS ON THE THAMES, see pp. 315-19.

THE ISLE OF DOGS, the horse-shoe curve between Limehouse and Blackwall, is described at page 49. It has a population of 5000. Here are the building-works (twenty-five acres) of Alderman Cubitt, at whose expense was built the Early English church at the south-east extremity of the island. (See *Account of Millwall,* &c., by H. B. Cowper, 1854.)

The Folly on the Thames was a floating "musical summer-house," usually moored between Somerset-stairs and the Savoy. It was called "The Royal Diversion," from the queen of William III. having once visited it; "the *Folly,* perhaps, from the foolish things there sometimes acted." (*Hatton.*) At length it became "a confused scene of folly, madness, and debauchery," and the building fell into decay.

THAMES-STREET,

In Stow's time *Stockfishmonger's Row,* extends from Puddle Dock, Blackfriars, to the Tower. The line abounds with archæological interest.

UPPER THAMES-STREET:—*Puddle Dock* was the wharf of one Puddle, and next Puddle Water, from horses watered there. Ben Jonson calls it "our Abydos." Shadwell, in his comedy of *Epsom Wells,* 1676, has "the Countess of Pudde Dock;" and Hogarth, in 1732, met "the Duke of Puddle Dock," at the Dark-house, Billingsgate. Upon the site of old Puddle Dock is built the *City Flour Mill,* by far the largest flour-mill in the world, and a gigantic example of mechanical skill. It is constructed entirely upon piles, and occupies rather more than an acre, or 250 feet long by 60 feet wide. The mill consists of eight stories: two steam-engines, of the consecutive power of 300 horses, drive 60 pairs of enormous mill-stones, and work the Archimedean screws and buckets by which the flour is conducted through the different processes. This mill has stowage for 40,000 quarters of grain; can prepare 4000 quarters per week, and requires only one-sixth of the number of hands employed by the old system.

Castle Baynard Wharf denotes the site of Baynard's Castle, described at page 4. Nearly opposite is *Adel* or *Addle Hill,* where stood the palace of the Anglo-Saxon kings, erected by Athelstan.

Boss-court is so called (says Stow) from a spring-water *boss,* or mouth, put up by the executors of Sir Richard Whittington.

From *Lambeth-hill* to Queenhithe have been excavated portions of the river-wall mentioned by Fitzstephen.

QUEENHITHE, see p. 638. *Garlick-hill* was of old the garlick *hithe.* *Dowgate,* or *Downegate,* was named from its steep descent to the river; or from its being the *Dowr* or *Water* gate to Watling-street

(*Maitland*); near the church of St. Mary Bothaw (destroyed in the Great Fire, and not rebuilt), was the mansion of Sir Francis Drake.

The Steelyard is named from its being the place where the King's steelyard, or beam, was set up for weighing goods imported into London (*T. Hudson Turner*). The site is mostly covered with iron-wharfs.

Coldharbour-lane denotes the site of *Coldharbour*, a magnificent mansion, 13 Edward II. (Rymer's *Fœdera*). It was next the property of Sir John Poultney; in 1397, John Holland, Duke of Exeter, entertained here Richard II.; Henry V. possessed it when Prince of Wales; Richard III., in 1485, granted it to the College of Heralds; Henry VIII. exchanged it for Durham House, Strand: it is shown in ruins, in Hollar's View of London after the Great Fire of 1666. The etymology of Coldharbour is a *quæstio . vexata*. Sir John Poultney received for his mansion, yearly, a rose at midsummer, whence, or from the wars of York and Lancaster, the estate was named "the Manor of the Rose." Upon Laurence Pountney Hill are two elaborately carved doorways; and some of the houses have stone-groined vaults. Upon Laurence Pountney Hill lived Dr. William Harvey, with his brothers Daniel and Eliab, merchants: here Harvey discovered the circulation of the blood.

In *Suffolk-lane* is MERCHANT TAYLORS' SCHOOL (see page 217).

Old Swan Stairs was a Thames landing-place in the 15th century. Here were the Old Wine Shades, beneath the terrace of the former Fishmonger's Hall; the present Shades is the house built for Lord Mayor Garratt, who laid the first stone of London Bridge in 1825.

Old Swan House, facing the river, is remarkable for a mercantile concern, three successive heads of which have served the offices of Sheriff and Lord Mayor. It was founded by Alderman Sir William Stephenson, who was succeeded by Alderman Sir John Sawbridge, M.P., who, in 1795, was succeeded by Alderman George Scholey. No such succession in the list of magistrates is to be found in any other parish in the city.—Wilson's *St. Laurence Pountney*, p. 6.

At the upper end of *St. Martin's-lane*, Cannon-street East, has been built a Rectory-house, with a handsome campanile, 110 feet high. Thames-street has long been noted for its cheese-factors' warehouses: " Thames-street gives cheeses."—Gay's *Trivia*.

The south side of Upper Thames Street is mostly occupied by wharfs, once the site of river-side palaces. In the lanes, upon the north side, are several merchants' mansions, "which, if not exactly equal to the palaces of stately Venice, might at least vie with many of the hotels of old Paris. Some of these, though the great majority have been broken up into chambers and counting-houses, still remain intact."—B. *D'Israeli, jun.*

Upper Thames-street retains some old signs: as, a bas-relief of a Gardener with a spade, 1670; the Doublet (upon iron, once gilt), at Crawshay's iron-wharf, No. 36 (originally the "Sir John Anvil" of the *Spectator*, No. 299). Upon Lambeth-hill, over Crane-court, is a crane carved in stone.

. LOWER THAMES-STREET: Fish-street Hill; THE MONUMENT (see page 509). Here was the entrance to *Crooked-lane*, noted for its old fishing-tackle shops, handy for the anglers at London Bridge.

Pudding-lane (from butchers scalding hog's puddings there) commenced the GREAT FIRE of 1666 (see page 293).

Next is BILLINGSGATE (pp. 45 and 495.) (COAL EXCHANGE, p. 281.)

In *Water-lane* remains part of the Old Trinity House, built by Wren; and at the lower end of the lane is the finely-carved door-headway of the Ship Tavern. THE CUSTOM HOUSE is described at page 246.

At the east end of the street, in Stow's time, were the remains of a stone mansion, said to have been the lodging of the Princes of Wales; hence this part of the street was called Petty Wales. It was also called *Galley Quay*, from the galleys formerly lading and landing there. Tradesmen's tokens in the seventeenth century were struck here, and were hence called, *vulgo*, " Galley-quay halfpence."

THAMES TUNNEL (THE),

A brick arched double roadway, under the Thames, between Wapping and Rotherhithe, one of the grandest achievements of engineering skill.

In 1799 an attempt was made to construct an archway under the Thames, from Gravesend to Tilbury, by Ralph Dodd, engineer; and in 1804 the "Thames Archway Company" commenced a similar work from Rotherhithe to Limehouse, under the direction of Vasey and Trevethick, two Cornish miners; and the horizontal excavation had reached 1040 feet, when the ground broke in, under the pressure of high tides, and the work was abandoned; 54 engineers declaring it to be impracticable to make a tunnel under the Thames of any useful size for commercial progression.

The present Tunnel was planned by I. K. Brunel, in 1823: among the earliest subscribers to the scheme were the late Duke of Wellington and Dr. Wollaston; and in 1824 the "Thames Tunnel Company" was formed to execute the work. A brickwork cylinder, 50 feet in diameter, 42 feet high, and 3 feet thick, was first commenced by Mr. Brunel at 150 feet from the Rotherhithe side of the river; and on March 2, 1825, a stone with a brass inscription-plate was laid in the brickwork, Upon this cylinder, computed to weigh 1000 tons, was set a powerful steam-engine, by which the earth was raised, and the water was drained from within it; the shaft was then sunk into the ground *en masse*, and completed to the depth of 65 feet; and at the depth of 63 feet the horizontal roadway was commenced, with an excavation larger than the interior of the old House of Commons. The plan of operation had been suggested to Brunel, in 1814, by the bore of the sea-worm, *Teredo navalis*, in the keel of a ship; showing how, when the perforation was made by the worm, the sides were secured, and rendered impervious to water, by the insect lining the passage with a calcareous secretion. With the auger-formed head of the worm in view, Brunel employed a cast-iron "Shield," containing 36 frames or cells, in each of which was a miner who cut down the earth; and a bricklayer simultaneously built up from the back of the cell the brick arch, which was pressed forward by strong screws. Thus were completed, from Jan. 1, 1826, to April 27, 1827, 540 feet of the Tunnel. On May 18 the river burst into the works; but the opening was soon filled up with bags of clay, the water pumped out of the Tunnel, and the work resumed. At the length of 600 feet, the river again broke in; six men were drowned; and the rush of the water carried Mr. Brunel, jun. up the shaft.

> "Other great speculations have been nursed,
> Till want of proceeds laid them on the shelf:
> But thy concern was at the worst,
> When it began to *liquidate* itself."
> *Ode to M. Brunel, by T. Hood.*

The Tunnel was again emptied; but the work was now discontinued, for want of funds, for seven years.

> "Well! Monsieur Brunel,
> How prospers now thy mighty undertaking,
> To join by a hollow way the Bankside friends
> Of Rotherhithe and Wapping?
> Never be stopping;
> But poking, groping, in the dark keep making
> An archway, underneath the dabs and gudgeons,
> For coll ermen and pitchy old curmudgeons,
> To cross the water in inverse proportion.
> Walk under steam-boats, under the keel's ridge,
> To keep down all extortion,
> And without sculls to diddle London Bridge!

> In a fresh hunt, a new great Bore to worry,
> Thou didst to earth thy human terriers follow;
> Hopeful at last, from Middlesex to Surrey ,
>   To give us the 'view hollow.'"—*T. Hood.*

Scores of plans were now proposed for its completion, and above 5000*l.* were raised by public subscription. By aid of a loan sanctioned by Parliament (mainly through the influence of the Duke of Wellington), the work was resumed, and a new shield constructed, March 1836, in which year were completed 117 feet; in 1837, only 29 feet; in 1838, 80 feet; in 1839, 194 feet; in 1840 (two months), 76 feet; and by November 1841 the remaining 60 feet, reaching to the shaft which had been sunk at Wapping. On March 24 Brunel was knighted by Queen Victoria; on August 12 he passed through the Tunnel from shore to shore; and March 25, 1843, it was opened as a public thoroughfare. It is lighted with gas, and is open to passengers, day and night, at one penny toll. In each passage is a carriage-road and a footway; but the approaches for carriages have not yet been made.

The Tunnel has cost about 454,000*l.*; to complete the carriage-descents would require 180,000*l.*; total, 634,000*l.* The dangers of the work were many: sometimes portions of the shield broke with the noise of a cannon-shot; then alarming cries told of some irruption of earth or water: but the excavators were much more inconvenienced by fire than water; gas explosions frequently wrapping the place in a sheet of flame, strangely mingling with the water, and rendering the workmen insensible. Yet, with all these perils, but seven lives were lost in making the Thames Tunnel; whereas nearly 40 men were killed during the building of new London Bridge. In 1833 Mr. Brunel submitted to William IV., at St. James's Palace, "An Exposition of the Facts and Circumstances relating to the Tunnel;" and Brunel has left a minute record of his great work. It is well described and illustrated in Weale's *Quarterly Papers on Engineering.* A Visitors' Book is kept at the Tunnel, wherein are the signatures of the many illustrious persons who have inspected the works. It was visited by Queen Victoria July 26, 1843. In 1838 the number of visitors was 23,000; in 1839, 34,000. A fine medal was struck at the completion of the work: *obv.* head of Brunel; *rev.* interior and longitudinal section of the Tunnel. A Fancy Fair is held annually in the Tunnel, on Mar. 25, the anniversary of the opening-day: here are permanently shops, and exhibitions of works of art.

Width of the Tunnel, 35 feet; height, 20 feet; each archway and footpath, clear width, about 14 feet; thickness of earth between the crown of the Tunnel and the bed of the river, about 15 feet. At full-tide, the foot of the Tunnel is 75 feet below the surface of the water.

The Tunnel has been paralleled, as an engineering triumph, by Stephenson's tubular railway-bridge.

THEATRES.

ADELPHI THEATRE, No. 411 Strand, was commenced in 1802 by John Scott, a colourman, and opened 27 Nov. 1806, as the *Sans Pareil,* with musical entertainments, and next year with dramas. In 1820-1 Scott sold the theatre to Rodwell and Jones, who named it the *Adelphi;* in 1825 it was sold to Terry and Yates; and after Terry's secession, Yates was joined by Charles Mathews the elder, who gave here his latter "At Homes." The present compo' front of the theatre was designed by Beazley, in 1840. Yates was succeeded by Webster, with Madame Celeste as directress. Its great attraction was John Reeve, the low comedian, d. 1838.

ARGYLL ROOMS (the), Regent-street (see page 19), were originally opened for the performance of opera and French plays.

ASTLEY'S AMPHITHEATRE, Bridge-road, Lambeth, is the fourth theatre erected upon this site. The first was one of the 19 theatres built by Philip Astley, and was opened in 1773, burnt in 1794; rebuilt 1795, burnt 1803; rebuilt 1804, burnt June 8, 1841, within two hours, from the house being principally constructed with old ship-timber. It was rebuilt, and opened April 17, 1843, and has since been enlarged. It is the only theatre in London for equestrianism; and the stud of trained horses numbers from 50 to 60.

Philip Astley, originally a cavalry soldier, commenced horsemanship in 1763, in an open field at Lambeth: he built his first theatre partly with 60*l.*, the produce of an unowned diamond ring which he found on Westminster Bridge. Andrew Ducrow, subsequently proprietor of the Amphitheatre, was born at the Nag's Head, Borough, in 1793, when his father, Peter Ducrow, a native of Bruges, was "the Flemish Hercules" at Astley's. The fire in 1841 arose from ignited wadding, such as caused the destruction of the old Globe Theatre in 1613, and Covent Garden Theatre in 1808. Andrew Ducrow died Jan. 26, 1842, of mental derangement and paralysis, produced by the above catastrophe.

BANKSIDE THEATRES. The earliest was the Circus built for bull-baiting and bear-baiting, about 1520, in *Paris Garden*, named from Robert de Paris, *temp.* Richard II., and now the site of Christchurch parish. In this theatre, plays were also performed *temp.* James I., when Henslowe and Alleyn were lessees. Nash, in his *Strange Newes*, 1590, mentions the performance of puppets there; and Dekker asserts that Ben Jonson had acted there (*Satiromastix*). Aggas's Map, drawn about 1560, shows two *circi* lower down on "the Bank;" but still lower were the *Globe*, the *Hope*, and the *Rose*. The *Globe* was built by agreement, dated Dec. 22, 1593, for Richard Burbage, the famous actor. In 1603 James I. granted a license to Shakspeare and others to act "at their now usuall house, called the Globe." It was of wood, hexagonal in exterior form, and was occupied by Shakspeare as a summer theatre. At Dulwich College, in a paper, occurs "Mr. Shaksper," in a list of "Inhabitants of Sowtherk, Jully, 1596;" he was assessed in the liberty of the Clink in 1609, though his occupation as an actor at the Globe did not continue after 1604:* his brother, Edmond Shakspeare, was buried in St. Saviour's church, 1607. The Globe was destroyed by fire June 29, 1613, when Ben Jonson was present; it was rebuilt in 1614, but is not mentioned after 1648: it was built on the site of Globe-alley, which led from Maid-lane to "the Bank," and is now included in the premises of Barclay and Perkins's Brewery (see the Map in Strype's *Stow*, 1720). The *Hope*, used both for bear-baiting and as a playhouse, was situated near the Rose: in 1614 Ben Jonson's *Bartholomew Fair* was first acted here; later it was used for prize-fighting, and in 1632 again for bear-baiting. The *Rose*, probably the oldest theatre upon Bankside, except Paris Garden (*Collier*), was built long before 1597: it was held for some years by Philip Henslowe, afterwards Alleyn's partner; it occupied the site of Rose-alley, west of Globe-alley (see Strype's Map). The *Swan* was in repute anterior to 1598. Both the Rose and Swan, after 1620, were only occupied occasionally by gladiators and fencers; and about 1648 all theatres were suppressed. (See the *Antwerp View of London*.)

BLACKFRIARS THEATRE was built in 1575, upon part of the site of the monastery of Blackfriars, between Apothecaries' Hall and Printing-house-square, and upon *Playhouse-yard*. The first proprietors were

* The Globe Theatre stood upon a spot of ground now occupied by four houses contiguous to the present Globe-alley, Maid-lane. (*Mirror*, March 31, 1832). We remember a large tavern, the *Globe*, in Chaingate, destroyed by fire about 1812. Pennant was told that the door of the Globe Theatre was very lately (1790) standing. See Knight's *Stratford Shakspere*, vol. i. 1854.

James Burbage and his fellows, who, with other players, had been ejected from the City by an act of Common Council: it was a winter theatre, arranged like an inn-yard (the earliest theatre), but with a roof over it. Shakspeare was a sharer in the Blackfriars playhouse in 1589; it was rebuilt in 1596; and was leased by Edward Alleyn in 1618 (see his *Diary*, at Dulwich College). It was taken down in 1655 (Collier's *Life of Shakspeare*), and dwelling-houses were built upon the ground. (See BLACKFRIARS, p. 48.)

BRUNSWICK THEATRE (the) was built upon the site of the Royalty Theatre (see p. 720), within seven months, by Stedman Whitwell, C.E. The façade resembled that of San Carlos at Naples. It was opened Feb. 25, 1828; but within three nights, on Feb. 28, during a day rehearsal, the whole theatre fell to the ground, and killed ten persons, among whom was a proprietor, D. S. Maurice, a tasteful printer, of Fenchurch-street. The catastrophe was caused by the unsafe iron roof and the great weights attached to it. A narrative of the accident was written from the evidence of one of the survivors, who was extricated from the ruins. See also *The Brunswick*, a poem, 1829.

COCKPIT or PHŒNIX THEATRE (from its sign), Drury-lane, occupied the site of Cockpit-alley, now Pitt-place, opposite the Castle Tavern, St. Giles's-in-the-Fields. It was altered from a cockpit, and when a theatre it was twice nearly destroyed by the London apprentices; and was pulled down in 1649 by soldiers, instigated by sectarian bigots. At the Restoration, Rhodes, a bookseller, rebuilt the theatre, but soon vacated it; and Sir W. Davenant, with Betterton and Kynaston in his company, performed here till 1662, when they removed to Portugal-row (see p. 624). At the Cockpit was performed the first play in print, *The Wedding*, by Shirley, printed in 1629, and expressly said to have been acted at Drury-lane.

COVENT GARDEN THEATRE, Bow-street, is the second theatre built here. The first theatre was built upon part of the Convent site, by Shepherd, architect of Goodman's Fields Theatre. Covent Garden was opened Dec. 7, 1732, by Rich, the celebrated harlequin; and Hogarth's caricature of "Rich's Glory," on his Triumphant Entry into Covent Garden," refers to his removal here: it shows one entrance, a magnificent Ionic archway, at the end of the eastern arcade of the Piazza. Here the Beefsteak Society was formed in 1735, by Rich and Lambert the scene-painter. In 1746 Garrick played here for the season. In 1803 John Kemble became a proprietor and stage-manager. On Sept. 20, 1808, the theatre was burned to the ground, and twenty persons killed in the ruins. It was rebuilt by R. Smirke, R.A. The first stone was laid by the Prince of Wales, Dec. 31, 1808; and the theatre was opened Sept. 18, 1809, when the "new prices" caused the O. P. (old prices) riot of seventy-seven nights, since which "a London audience has been found more captious than they previously had been" (*C. Dibdin*). In 1817 John Kemble here took leave of the public; and in 1840 retired his brother, Charles Kemble. The theatre was subsequently leased to Mr. C. Mathews and Madame Vestris, and Mr. Macready. In 1843-45 it was let to the Anti-Corn-Law League, who held a bazaar here in 1845 (see page 37). In 1847 the auditory was entirely reconstructed by Albano, and opened as an Italian Opera April 6. The exterior has a pure Grecian-Doric portico, copied from the Temple of Minerva at Athens; and statues of Tragedy and Comedy, and two panels of bas-relief figures, by Flaxman.

The *northern panel* has figures of Æschylus, Aristophanes, and Mæander; Thalia, Polyhymnia, Euterpe, and Clio; Minerva and Bacchus; Melpomone, two Furies, and Apollo. In the *southern panel* are figures of Shakspeare summoning

Caliban, Ferdinand, Miranda, Prospero, and Ariel; Hecate and Lady Macbeth. Also Milton, with Urania and Samson Agonistes, an incident from *Comus*, &c

First Appearances.—Incledon, the singer, 1790; Charles Kemble, 1794; Mrs. Glover, 1797; G. F. Cooke (Richard III.), Oct. 31, 1800; Miss Stephens (Countess of Essex), 1812; Miss O'Neill (Lady Beecher), 1814; Macready, 1816; W. Farren, 1818; Fanny Kemble, 1829; Adelaide Kemble, 1841. Here Edmund Kean last acted, 1833.

CURTAIN THEATRE (the), Holywell, is mentioned in 1577. Stow, speaking of the priory of St. John Baptist, says: " Near thereunto are builded *two publique houses* for the acting and showe of comedies, tragedies, and histories, for recreation; whereof the one is called *The Courtein*, the other *The Theatre*, both standing on the south-west side, towards the field " (*Stow*, 1st edit. 1599). Both theatres are mentioned in Northbrook's *Treatise against Diceing, Dancing, Vain Plays or Interludes*, 1577; by Stubbes in his *Anatomie of Abuses*, 1583; in a black-letter ballad, in the Pepysian collection, occurs " the Curtain at Holywell;" and in an epigram by Heath, 1610. Sir H. Herbert's office-book shows that in 1622 the Curtain was occupied by the servants of Prince Charles. Aubrey (1678) describes it as " a kind of nursery or obscure playhouse, called the Greene Curtain, situate in the suburbs towards Shoreditch." After it was abandoned as a playhouse, prize-fighters exhibited here. Sir Henry Ellis (*Hist. Shoreditch*, 1798) quotes from the parish books several entries of the marriage, burial, &c. of players. Maitland (*Hist. London*, 1772) mentions some remains of the Curtain standing at or near his time. It is said to have occupied the site of the curtain close (*curtis cenobii*) of the priory. The name survives in *Curtain-road.*

DRURY-LANE THEATRE, between Drury-lane and Brydges-street, forming the east side of Little Russell-street. The first theatre here was built precisely upon this site for Thomas Killigrew, and opened April 8, 1663; the company being called " the King's Servants," as Davenant's were " the Duke's Servants," both under patents granted by Charles II. in 1660. Drury-lane, " the King's Theatre," had the chief entrance in Little Russell-street. Pepys's *Diary* records many of his visits to " the King's House," and other London theatres, from 1660 to 1670. " The King's House" was burnt down Jan. 1671-72. It was rebuilt by Sir Christopher Wren, and opened March 26, 1674, with a prologue and epilogue by Dryden. Mr. Collier has printed in the *Shakespeare Society's Papers*, vol. iv. p. 147, an indenture showing Dryden to have been joined with Killigrew, Hart, Mohun, and others, in the speculation of this " new playhouse." In 1682 the King's and Duke's companies played here together. Rich, Steele, Dogget, Wilks, Cibber, and Booth were successively patentees; and Garrick in 1747, when he opened the theatre, Sept. 15, with the well-known prologue written by Dr. Johnson, and commenced the revival of Shakspeare's plays. On June 10, 1776, Garrick here took leave of the stage. Sheridan then became part-proprietor; and, in 1788, John Kemble manager. In 1791 the old theatre was taken down, rebuilt by Holland, and the new theatre opened March 12, 1794.

It was called by Mrs. Siddons "the Wilderness." The opening for the curtain was 43 feet wide and 38 feet high, or nearly seven times the height of the performers. There were seats for 3600 persons; but upwards of 5000 persons are known to have been squeezed into this theatre.

It was burnt down Feb. 24, 1809. The present house, built by B. Wyatt, from the plan of the great Bordeaux theatre, was opened Oct. 12, 1812, with a prologue by Lord Byron. In 1818 the theatre was let, at 10,200*l* per annum, to Elliston for whom Beazley reduced the auditory, added the Doric portico in Brydges-street, and the cast-iron colonnade in Little Russell-street in 1831. In the hall is a cast of Scheemakers's statue of Shakspeare, and a statue of Kean by S. Joseph. The staircases and rotunda are magnificent, and the interior circular roof of the auditory is geometrically fine.

First Appearances.—Nell Gwynne, at "the King's House," 1666; Barton Booth, 1701: Mrs. Siddons, 1775; John P. Kemble, 1783; Harriet Mellon (Duchess of St. Albans), 1795; Edmund Kean, 1814. Here Macready took leave of the stage, Feb. 26, 1851.

The first Drury-lane Theatre was sometimes called Govent Garden Theatre; and the late Mr. Richardson, of the Piazza Coffee-house, possessed a ticket inscribed, "For the Music at the Playhouse in Covent Garden, Tuesday, March 6, 1704."—*J. T. Smith.*

DORSET-GARDENS THEATRE (the) was built at the extremity of Salisbury-court, Fleet-street, and had a handsome front and stairs to the Thames. It was opened in 1671, under the management of Lady Davenant. Dryden, in his prologue to *Marriage à-la-Mode*, 1672, leaves contemptuously to the citizens "the gay shows and gaudy scenes" of Dorset-gardens. Here Shadwell's operatic version of Shakspeare's *Tempest* was produced with great splendour in 1673. After 1697 the theatre was let to wrestlers and fencers, but was taken down about 1720, and the site is now occupied by the City Gas-works. The theatre was designed by Wren, and the sculpture by Gibbons, including figures of Comedy and Tragedy surmounting the balustrade.

DUKE'S THEATRE, "the Opera," Lincoln's-Inn Fields. (See POR-TUGAL-STREET, pp. 624-5.) Here, May 10, 1735, Macklin killed his brother-actor Hallam, by accident, in a quarrel.

EAGLE TAVERN THEATRE, City-road, was built adjoining the tea-gardens, by Thomas Rouse, for regular dramatic entertainments (chiefly opera); and the audience were formerly allowed to enjoy their potations, in the pit, boxes, and gallery, during the performances.

FORTUNE THEATRE (the)—named from its sign,

"The picture of Dame Fortune
Before the Fortune playhouse" (*Heywood*)—

was built for Philip Henslowe and William Alleyn, in 1599-1600, on the east side of Golding-lane, without Cripplegate. It cost 1320*l.*, and was opened May 1601. It was a square timber and lath-and-plaster building, and was burnt Dec. 9, 1621 (Alleyn's *Diary*); but was rebuilt on a circular plan, of brick, and tiled. The interior was burnt in 1649—Prynne says by accident, but it was fired by sectarians. In the *Mercurius Politicus*, Feb. 14-21, 1661, the building, with the ground thereunto belonging, were advertised "to be lett to be built upon;" and it is described as standing between "Whitecross-street and Golen-lane," the avenue now known as Playhouse-yard.

GIBBON'S-COURT THEATRE, Clare Market. (See page 496.)

GOODMAN'S FIELDS THEATRE was first opened as a silk-throwster's shop, in 1729, by Thomas Odell, and was rebuilt by Henry Giffard; both of whom were, however, compelled to close the theatre by the puritanical clamour raised against it. Giffard returned to Goodman's Fields in 1737; and here, Oct. 19, 1741, David Garrick first appeared in London as Richard III. The town were "horn-mad" after Garrick's acting; but Walpole saw "nothing wonderful in it," and Gray was "stiff in opposition." The house was taken down about 1746. Garrick's first appearance at the Goodman's Fields Theatre arose from its proprietor being also manager of the Ipswich company, in which Garrick first appeared on the stage. In 1830 a "Garrick Theatre" was opened in Leman-street, Goodman's Fields.

HAYMARKET THEATRE, the "Little Theatre," was originally built by one Potter, and opened Dec. 29, 1720, by "the French comedians:" it was first called "the New French Theatre." In 1723 it was occupied by English actors; 1726, Italian operas, rope-dancing, and tumblers, by subscription; in 1727 the *Beggar's Opera* was produced here; 1731, gladiators and backswordsmen; 1732, English opera upon the Italian model; 1734-5, Fielding opened the theatre with "the Great Mogul's Company of Comedians," for whom he wrote his *Pasquin*, the satire of which upon the Walpole administration gave rise to the Licensing Act (10th of Geo. II. cap. 28). In 1738 a French company re-opened the theatre, but were driven from the stage the first night. In 1741, English operas were played here; 1744, Samuel Foote first appeared here as Othello; 1747, Foote became manager, and continued so for thirty years, commencing with his own Entertainments. Jan. 16, 1748-9, the Bottle Conjuror hoax and riot. 1762, the Haymarket was established as a regular summer theatre. 1777, it became a Theatre Royal, when Foote sold his interest to George Colman for a life annuity of 1600*l.*, and Foote died in the following October. Colman died in 1795, and was succeeded by his son, George Colman the younger, licenser of plays. Feb. 3, 1794, sixteen persons were trodden to death, or suffocated, in attempting to gain admission on a royal visit. The "Little Theatre" was taken down in 1820; the present theatre was built, at a few feet distant, by Nash, and opened July 14, 1821: it has a lofty Corinthian portico. In 1853, Mr. B. Webster concluded here a lesseeship of 16 years, and the theatre was let to Mr. Buckstone.

First Appearances.—Henderson, Bannister, Mathews, Elliston, Liston, and Young; Miss Fenton (Duchess of Bolton), Miss Farren (Countess of Derby), Miss Paton (Lady W. Lennox); Edmund Kean, in "little business," 1806. Here Macready gave his final performances.

ST. JAMES'S THEATRE (the), King-street, St. James's, was designed by Beazley, for John Braham, the singer, at a cost of 26,000*l.* The façade is Roman, of the middle ages; and the interior, by Crace, originally resembled the theatre of the Palace of Versailles. The St. James's Theatre was opened in 1835; and next year was produced here an operatic burletta written by Charles Dickens, the music by John Hullah.

LYCEUM THEATRE (the), Wellington-street, Strand, was originally built by James Payne, architect, in 1765, as an academy (or *lyceum*) for a society of artists; of whom, on the re-establishment of the Royal Academy, Garrick bought the lease of the premises, to prevent their becoming a theatre. They were next purchased by Mr. Lingham, a breeches-maker, in the Strand, and opened about 1790 for musical performances; in 1794 or 1795 Lingham leased the adjoining ground to Dr. Arnold, who built here a theatre, the license for which was suppressed, and it was let for music, dancing, and horsemanship, exhibition of paintings, &c.: a foreigner gained a large fortune by exhibiting here the first phantasmagoria seen in England; and here, in 1803-4, Winsor exhibited his experimental gas-lighting. In 1809, the theatre was enlarged by Mr. S. A. Arnold, and opened as the *English Opera-house:* it was rebuilt, in 1816, by Beazley; was destroyed by fire, Feb. 16, 1830; and rebuilt by Beazley somewhat further west, the site of the former theatre being included in the new street then formed from the Strand to Long Acre. The new theatre cost 35,000*l.*; it has an elegant Corinthian portico: it was opened with English opera, July 14, 1834; and was re-decorated in rich Italian taste, for Madame Vestris, in 1847.

MARIONETTE THEATRE, Agar-street, Strand, was originally the Adelaide Gallery, and was altered for the clever performances of *Marionettes*, or puppets, in 1852.

MARYLEBONE THEATRE, Church-street, Paddington, was built and opened in 1842, as "a penny theatre:" it was enlarged in 1854, to hold 2000 persons: Shakspeare's plays have been admirably performed here.

MILTON-STREET THEATRE, see GRUB-STREET, pp. 335-37.

NEWINGTON BUTTS: here was a theatre built before the Globe at Bankside: it is mentioned in the Diary of Philip Henslowe, which shows that from June 1594 the performances were jointly by the Lord Ad-miral's men and the Lord Chamberlain's men: here were acted *Titus Andronicus*, *Hamlet*, and the *Taming of a Shrew*.

NURSERY (the), in Golding-lane, was built by a patent of Charles II. as a school for the education of children for the stage:

> " Near these a Nursery erects its head,
> Where queens are formed, and future heroes bred,
> Where unfledged actors learn to laugh and cry,
> Where infant punks their tender voices try,
> And little Maximins the gods defy."—Dryden's *Mac Flecknoe.*

Bayes, in the *Rehearsal*, speaks of "the service of the Nursery;" and Pepys first went there 24th Feb. 1667-8. The house, with the royal arms and a figure of Charity, in plaster, on the front, existed to our time, and has been erroneously described as the Fortune Theatre. There was a similar *Nursery* in Hatton-garden, at which Joe Haynes, the dancer, performed.

OLYMPIC THEATRE (the), Wych-street, was originally erected by Philip Astley, upon the site of old Craven House, and was opened with horsemanship, Sept. 18, 1806: it was principally built with the timbers of *La Ville de Paris*, the ship in which William IV. served as midshipman; these materials were given to Astley, with a chandelier, by George III. The theatre was leased in 1813 to Elliston, who removed thence to Drury-lane; and subsequently to Madame Vestris, before she became lessee of Covent-garden; both which changes were ruinous. The Olympic Theatre was destroyed by fire, within an hour, March 29, 1849: it was rebuilt the same year, and opened Dec. 26.

First and last, at the Olympic Theatre have appeared Elliston and Mrs. Edwin; Oxberry and Power; Keeley and Fitzwilliam; Charles Kean and Ellen Tree; Madame Vestris, Mrs. Nisbett (Lady Boothby), Mrs. Keeley, and William Farren; Charles Mathews first appeared here; and Miss Foote (Countess of Harrington), Mrs. Orger, and Liston, last played here. In Craven-buildings, adjoining the theatre, have resided "three favourite actresses, from the time of Dryden to our own—Mrs. Bracegirdle, Mrs. Pritchard, and Madame Vestris."

PANTHEON THEATRE, Oxford-street (see p. 582).

PRINCESS' THEATRE (the), Oxford-street, was originally the Queen's Bazaar (see p. 36), was designed by Nelson, and opened Sept. 30, 1841, with promenade concerts. It cost 47,000*l.*; but the unique character of its Renaissance decoration, by Crace, has been spoiled: originally it consisted entirely of four tiers of boxes. This theatre, under the management of Mr. Charles Kean, has become noted for its dramas from the French; and its reproduction of Shakspeare's historic plays, with all the "pomp and circumstance" of modern art.

QUEEN'S THEATRE, Tottenham-street, Tottenham-court-road, was originally Francis Pasquali's Concert-room, enlarged for the Concerts of Ancient Music by Novosielski, who built here a superb box for George III. and Queen Charlotte (Dr. Rimbault, *Notes and Queries*, No. 10). It subsequently became the Tottenham-street, Regency, Royal, and West London, Theatre. It was the first theatre in London at which French plays were acted after the Peace of 1815. Here Young, the tragedian, first appeared upon the stage, in 1807, at a private performance.

RED BULL THEATRE (the), upon the site of Red Bull-yard, St. John-street, Clerkenwell, was originally an inn-yard, but rebuilt about 1633: here the King's Company, under Killigrew, acted until Drury-lane was ready for them. During the Interregnum, "Drolls" were performed here, and afterwards published by Kirkman, one of the players, with a frontispiece of the interior of the theatre. (See CLERKENWELL, p. 187.)

Sir William Davenant, to whom Charles I. granted a patent in 1639, continued recreation and music, after the manner of the ancients, at Rutland House, Bridgewater-square, and subsequently at the Cockpit, till the Restoration, when the few players who had not fallen in the wars or died of poverty assembled under Davenant at the Red Bull: the actors' clothes were " very poore, and the actors but common fellows."—*Pepys*, 1661.

ROYALTY THEATRE, Wells-street, Wellclose-square (named from *Goodman's Field Wells*, 1735), was built by subscription, and opened in 1787, when John Braham first appeared on the stage, as Cupid, and John Palmer was manager; Lee Lewis, Bates, Holland, and Mrs. Gibbs, were also of the company. It was purchased about 1820 by Mr. Peter Moore, M.P.; and was burnt down April 11, 1826.

SADLER'S WELLS, the oldest theatre in London, is on the S.W. side of Islington, and named in part from a mineral spring, which was superstitiously dispensed by the monks of the Priory of St. John of Jerusalem, probably from the time of Henry I. or Stephen. In the reign of Charles II., one Sadler built here a music-house, and in 1683 re-discovered in the garden the well of " excellent steel waters," which in 1684 was visited and drunk by hundreds of persons every morning. Evelyn, on June 11, 1686, went to "the New Spa Well, near Middleton's receptacle of water at the New River." Ned Ward describes the company as "inns of court beaux and lady bumsitters, mingled with the blue-frock order:" the entertainments were rope-dancing, tumbling, and gluttonous feats. The *well*, ceasing to attract, was covered over; and in 1764 the old music-house (engraved in the *Mirror*, No. 971,) was taken down, and the present theatre built by Rosoman. King (of Drury-lane) was long a partner and stage-manager; and Charles Dibdin and his sons, Thomas and Charles, were proprietors. Grimaldi, father, son, and grandson, were famous clowns at this theatre; and Belzoni was a posture-master here before he travelled to the East. In 1804 the New River water was introduced in a tank under the stage, where also is a mineral well: but the old well is between the stage-door and the New River. Wine was sold and drunk on the premises until 1807: under the old regulation, "for an additional sixpence, every spectator was allowed a pint of either port, Lisbon, mountain, or punch." But the more honourable distinction of Sadler's Wells Theatre is its admirable representations of Elizabethan plays, under the management of Mr. Phelps, by whom it has been made "the most popular retreat of the regular drama."

SALISBURY-COURT THEATRE (see p. 306).

SANS SOUCI THEATRE, Strand, was built by Dibdin, the song-writer, in the rear of his music-shop, and opened Feb. 16, 1793. Dibdin planned, painted, and decorated this theatre; wrote the recitations and songs, composed the music, and sang and accompanied them on an organised pianoforte of his own invention. He built another *Sans Souci* theatre in Leicester-place.

SOHO THEATRE was built for Frances Kelly, in 1840, as a school for acting, in the rear of No. 73 Dean-street. It will hold 800 persons.

STRAND THEATRE, No. 169 Strand, originally Barker's Panorama, was altered in 1831 for Rayner, the low comedian, and Mrs. Waylett, the singer. Here were produced Douglas Jerrold's early plays.

SURREY THEATRE (the), St. George's-fields, was first built by Charles Hughes and Charles Dibdin, the song-writer, and was opened Nov. 4, 1782, as the *Royal Circus*, for equestrianism. It was destroyed by fire Aug. 12, 1805, but was rebuilt in 1806 by Cabanel. Among its lessees were Elliston and Thomas Dibdin. Here Buckstone first appeared.

John Palmer was acting manager in 1790, when he was living within the Rules of the King's Bench; and Palmer's engagement here led to the abridgment, by Lord Chief-Justice Kenyon, of debtors' privileges in Surrey, by excluding all public-houses and places of amusement from the Rules.

"THE THEATRE" was built, in 1576, on the site of the Priory of St. John Baptist, at Holywell, Shoreditch; and is conjectured by Malone to have been "the first building erected in or near the metropolis purposely for scenic exhibitions:" it is noticed in John Stockwood's sermon at Paul's Cross, in 1578, as "the gorgeous playing-place erected in the fields." It was a wooden building; and in the Star-Chamber records is proof that, in 1598, "the Theatre" was taken down, and the wood removed to Bankside for rebuilding or enlarging the Globe Theatre.

VICTORIA THEATRE (the), New Cut, Lambeth, was originally named "the Cobourg," from the first stone having been laid by proxy for Prince Leopold of Saxe-Cobourg, Oct. 15, 1817: it has for its foundation part of the stone of the old Savoy Palace. The theatre was designed by Cabanel, a carpenter from Liege, who also constructed the stage of old Drury-lane Theatre, and invented a roof known by his name. The Cobourg Theatre was first opened May 13, 1818: for its *répertoire*, Clarkson Stanfield, now R.A., painted scenery; and here was constructed *a looking-glass curtain*, of large plates of glass, enclosed in a gilt frame. The house was leased to Egerton and Abbott in 1833, when the name was changed to "Victoria," and the Princess (her present Majesty) visited the theatre.

WHITEFRIARS THEATRE (the), was originally the hall of White-friars monastery, outside the garden-wall of Dorset House. From a survey in Mr. Collier's possession, we learn that the theatre was fitted up in 1586; it was taken down in 1613. Howes, in his continuation of *Stow*, describes "the erection of a new fair playhouse near the Whitefriars," 1629: this was "the Private House in Salisburie-court."

OPERA HOUSES, ITALIAN.—HER MAJESTY'S THEATRE. The first theatre for the performance of Italian operas in England was built by subscription, by Sir John Vanbrugh, at the south-west corner of the Haymarket, and was opened April 9, 1705; but operas were not performed here wholly in Italian until 1710, when *Almahide* was produced, and next year Handel's *Rinaldo*, in Italian, and by Italian singers. On June 17, 1789, the theatre was burnt down; and upon the same site, enlarged, April 3, 1790, was laid the first stone of the present Opera House, designed by Novosielski, who introduced the horse-shoe form of auditory, from the Italian theatres. In 1820 the exterior was altered by Nash and Repton in the Roman-Doric style, as we now see it, surrounded with arcade and colonnade: each of the iron columns is a single casting. The Haymarket front bears a basso-relievo, by Bubb, of lithargolite, or artificial stone, illustrating the progress of Music; Apollo and the Muses occupying the centre. The interior, at the time of its erection, was larger than that of La Scala at Milan, or the Théâtre Italien at Paris. The audience and stage ground are held on two distinct leases. The whole theatre is lined with thin wood in very long pieces, as the best conductor of sound. It was entirely re-

A A A

decorated in the Raphaelesque and Roman style in 1846. There are 177 boxes, the freehold of some of which has been sold for 7000 and 8000 guineas; the season-rent is 300 guineas; a small box, fourth tier, has been let for one night at 12 guineas. When Mr. Lumley purchased the theatre in 1844, he realised 90,000*l.* by selling boxes in perpetuity. The house will accommodate about 3000 persons. The drop-scene was painted by Stanfield, R.A. The decorations, after ancient masters, are extremely beautiful. Here is a model of the theatre, 10 feet high. Part of the scenery is deposited at "the Barn," James-street, Haymarket.

The Italian Opera House in the Haymarket has ever been a costly speculation. In 1720 George I. headed a subscription of 50,000*l.* for its support. Ebers lost 44,080*l* (see his *Seven Years of the King's Theatre*, 1829). For two seasons he paid 15,000*l.* rent per annum. One season's expenses:—Opera, 8636*l.*; ballet, 10,678*l.*; orchestra, 3261*l.*; scene-painting and wardrobes (50,000 dresses), 5372*l.*; lighting, 1281*l.*; salaries, 2578*l.*; servants, 403*l.*; military guard at the doors, 150*l.*; fittings of the king's box, in 1821, 300*l.*; nightly expenses from 700*l.* to 1000*l.* The largest receipts were in the seasons when Jenny Lind sang. Her Majesty's is stated to be the only theatre which has no lease. It claims the exclusive right to produce foreign operas, from a deed made in 1792, covenanting that "the patents of Drury Lane and Covent Garden shall never be exercised for the purpose of Italian operas." See an able account of Her Majesty's Theatre, by Shirley Brooks, *Morning Chronicle*, March 20, 1851.

ROYAL ITALIAN OPERA (the), Covent Garden Theatre, was designed by Albano, and executed at a cost of 40,000*l.* The greatest width of the internal area is 62 feet, two feet wider than Her Majesty's Theatre: the greatest height is 54 feet. The decorations are gold and white; and the ceiling is enriched with allegorical figures. There are six tiers of boxes (210), in part divided by caryatides. The house holds upwards of 3000 persons. It was opened April 6, 1847, with *Semiramide* (Grisi), and Costa as musical director. The originator of this second Italian Opera House was Mr. C. L. Grüneisen, with Mr. T. F. Beale as director. In the seasons of 1848 and 1849 were expended 60,000*l.*; and the salaries of Alboni, Viardot, Grisi, and Mario, were between 4000*l.* and 5000*l.* each. Here Madame Grisi took her farewell, Aug. 7, 1854.

The Opera Stage at night is an extraordinary scene. Place your back to the dark curtain, waving gently in the draught. Look up, and in the roof you distinguish a misty glare of gas, in which you can discover monstrous beams, extending like the lowest yards of a first-rate line-of-battle ship, and somewhat as loosely, dangling ropes, tackles with pulleys, &c. Blocks are creaking; you hear huge iron windlasses clicking rapidly; and you descry dingy phantoms of scenes, technically denominated "cloth," majestically rising, with a slow motion, like black clouds. These are ascending, one behind the other, in a lurid light; and you see on each side, at some distance, a tall ladder-looking series of deal frames in perspective, black with smoke and grimy with dust, leather hose, gas-pipes, bright lights, and brass apparatus; series of brilliant jets, starring in extended line, blue clouds and amber-water, columns with wreaths, *moresques*, and flat-nosed statues; traps and stray rocks are interjectionary in a confused assemblage of carpenters in paper caps and corduroy, dusky gasmen; gentlemen with their hats in their hands, and in black dress coats and white neckerchiefs; pot-boys; fairies with a silver star on their foreheads; burly gods, with broad faces red with ochre, roseate foreheads, raven ringlets, and gimlet eyes; kings displaying superb black whiskers, with crowns on their heads, and crimson draperies; one or two dressers in muslin caps, with perhaps a cracked teacup to be seen in the hand; and persecuted princesses in spangled gauze.—Cocks's *Musical Almanack*, 1851.

THREADNEEDLE-STREET,

Or *Three-Needle-street*, (*Stow*,) originally extended from Bishopsgate-street to Stocks Market, but now terminates at the Bank of England. The name is from three needles, the charge on the shield of the Needle-makers' Company's arms; but Pennant traces the final cause to the Hall of the Merchant-Taylors, Taylors, and Linen-armourers in this street. Hatton refers it to " such a sign." (See MERCHANT-TAILORS'. HALL, SOUTH-SEA HOUSE, and HALL OF COMMERCE.) Upon part of the site of the latter lived Sir William Sidney, one of the heroes of Flodden Field; and his son, Sir Henry Sidney, in whose arms died Edward VI. Sir Henry then retired to Penshurst, where was born, in 1554, his son, the famed Sir Philip Sidney. Upon the site of the present chief entrance to the Bank of England, in Threadneedle Street, stood the Crown Tavern, " behind the 'Change :" it was much frequented by Fellows of the Royal Society, when they met at Gresham College, hard by. The Crown was burnt in the Great Fire, but was rebuilt; and a century since, at this tavern, " it was not unusual to draw a butt of mountain; containing 120 gallons, in gills, in a morning." (Sir John Hawkins.) At No. 20 lived Alderman Moon, the eminent print-publisher: he was Lord-Mayor in 1854-5, and a worthy successor of Alderman Boydell.

TOKENS.

In the reign of Elizabeth (1558), the great want of halfpence and farthings led to private Tokens, or farthings, of lead, tin, latten, and leather, being *struck* for alehouse-keepers, chandlers, grocers, vintners, and other traders; the figure and devices being emblematical of the various trades, victuallers especially adopting their signs. They were made without any form or fashion; and some of them (as the leaden tokens of Elizabeth's reign) are now of extreme rarity. Every one issuing this useful specie was compelled to take it again when offered; and this practice continued until 1672, when Charles II. struck halfpence and farthings. Within the present century, however, many tokens obtained general circulation in London, by which means tradesmen advertised their business: such tokens also recorded great events, portraits of public men, views of places and of entertainments, which might otherwise have been lost. They mostly disappeared on Watt's new copper coinage of George III. The great national collection of tokens in the British Museum is the finest we possess. Mr. Roach Smith's Museum of London Antiquities, 5 Liverpool-street, also contains about 500 mediæval leaden tokens, and many tradesmen's tokens in brass, from about 1648 to 1674. (See *Catalogue*, 1854.) The Beaufoy Cabinet, presented to the Corporation Library, consists exclusively of *London* traders', tavern, and coffee-house tokens current in the 17th century, 1174 in number: they are well described and annotated in a Catalogue by Jacob Henry Burn, printed for the Corporation, 1853. See also the work on *Tradesmen's Tokens current in London*, 1648 to 1672, by J. Y. Akerman, F.S.A., 4to, 1849.

Token-house Yard, on the north side of Lothbury, is named from the Mint-house, or office for the issue and change of these farthings or tokens: it was built in the reign of Charles I., and occupied the site of the house and garden of the Earl of Arundel; and from its proximity to the brass-founders of Lothbury, they are thought to have minted the Tokens.

TOTTENHAM-COURT ROAD,

From Oxford-street to the Hampstead-road, was the old way from the village of St. Giles's to the prebendal manor of Totham, Toten, or Totten Hall (named in Domesday), and *temp.* Henry III. the mansion of William de Totenhall. It stood at the north-west extremity of the present road, and is mentioned as a house of entertainment in the parish-books of St. Giles's, in 1645, when Mrs. Stacye's maid and two others were fined " for drinking at Tottenhall Court, on the Sabbath daie," xij*d.* a-piece." It was then altered to the Adam-and-Eve pubic-house, which, with the King's Head and Tottenham Court turnpike, is shown in Hogarth's "March to Finchley," at the Foundling Hospital. At the Adam and Eve were a music-room and tea-gardens; here Lunardi descended in his balloon, May 16th, 1785. A portion of the old court-house remained to our time; the gardens were built upon between 1806 and 1810, and the public-house has been rebuilt. J. T. Smith, in his *Book for a Rainy Day*, remembers, in 1773, Cappers' Farm, behind the north-west end of Russell-street, noted for its garden-houses in Strype's time. From Cappers' Farm were straggling houses, but Tottenham-Court-road was then "unbuilt upon." The first house (No. 1) in Oxford-street bore on its front, cut in stone, "Oxford-street, 1725." "The Blue Posts," corner of Hanway-street, was once kept by Sturges, the famous draught-player, author of a Treatise on Draughts. The site of Gresse-street (named from Gresse, the painter), was then gardens, recommended by physicians for the salubrity of the air. Stephen-street was then built: George Morland, the painter, lived here, at No. 14, in 1780. Whitefield's chapel was built, in 1754 (see page 177), upon the site of "the Little Sea" pond; and a turnstile opened into Crab-tree Fields, which then extended to the Adam and Eve.

"Totten-Court, a mansion in the fields," is a scene in Ben Jonson's *Tale of a Tub*; and the scene of Thomas Nabs's *Tottenham-Court*, a pleasant comedy (1639), is laid in "Marrowbone Park."

TOWER OF LONDON (THE),

"The citadel to defend or command the City" (*Stow*), stands on the north bank of the Thames, about a mile below London Bridge, and in the oldest part of the metropolis; "between the south-east end of the City Wall and the river, though the west part is supposed within the City,* but with some uncertainty; and in what county the whole stands is not easy discovered." (*Hatton*, 1708.) It comprises within the walls an area of 12 acres 5 roods. Tradition has assigned its origin to Julius Cæsar, and our early poets have adopted this antiquity:

> "*Prince Edward.* I do not like the Tower, of any place.
> Did Julius Cæsar build that place, my lord?
>   *Buckingham.* He did, my gracious lord, begin that place,
> Which since succeeding ages have re-edified.
>   *Prince Edward.* Is it upon record, or else reported
> Successively from age to age, he built it?
>   *Buckingham.* Upon record, my gracious lord."
>   Shakspeare's *Richard III.* act iii. sc. 1.

This, however, is unsupported by records; but that the Romans had a fortress here in a subsequent age is probable, from the discovery of Roman remains upon the site (see page 651).

The oldest portion of the present fortress is the Keep, or *White Tower*, so named from its having been originally whitewashed, as appears from a Latin document of the year 1241. This tower was built about 1078, for William the Conqueror, by Gundulph, bishop of Rochester, who also erected Rochester Castle; and the two fortresses have points of resemblance. William Rufus greatly added to the Tower; Henry I. strengthened the fortress; and Stephen, in 1140, kept his court here, with all the rude splendour of the period.

Fitzstephen describes it as "the Tower Palatine, very large and very strong,

---

* "It was proved in the case of Sir Thomas Overbury, upon a question as to whether his murder was committed within the boundaries of the City or in the county of Middlesex, that the City Wall traversed the buildings contained within the Tower; and his apartment being on the west of it, the criminals came accordingly under the jurisdiction of the City."—Archer's *Vestiges*, part iii.

whose court and walls rise up from a deep foundation. The mortar is tempered with the blood of beasts. On the west are two castles, well fenced."

About 1190, the Regent Bishop Longchamp surrounded the fortress with an embattled stone wall and "a broade and deepe ditch:" for breaking down part of the City wall he was deposed, and besieged in the Tower, but surrendered after one night. King John held his court here. Henry III. strengthened the White Tower, and founded the Lion Tower and other western bulwarks; and in this reign the palace-fortress was alternately held by the king and the insurgent barons. Edward I. enlarged the moat, and on the west made the last additions of military importance prior to the invention of cannon. Edward II. retired here against his subjects; and here was born his eldest daughter, Joan of the Tower. Edward III. imprisoned here many illustrious persons, including David king of Scotland, and John king of France with Philip his son. During the insurrection of Wat Tyler, King Richard II. took refuge here, with his court and nobles, 600 persons: Richard was deposed whilst imprisoned here, in 1399. Edward IV. kept a magnificent court here. In 1460 Lord Scales was besieged here by the Yorkists, and was taken and slain in endeavouring to escape by water. Henry VI., twice imprisoned in the fortress, died here in 1471; but the tradition that George Duke of Clarence was drowned here in 1478, in a butt of malmsey-wine, is of little worth. The beheading of Lord Hastings, in 1483, by order of the Protector Gloucester (on a log of timber in front of the Chapel); the seizure of the crown by Richard; and the supposed murder of his nephews, Edward V. and the Duke of York,—are the next events in the annals of the fortress. Henry VII. frequently resided in the Tower, where also his queen sought refuge from "the society of her sullen and cold-hearted husband:" the king held a splendid tournament here in 1501; his queen died here in 1503. Henry VIII. often held his court in this fortress: here, in great pomp, Henry received all his wives previous to their espousals; here were beheaded his queens Anne Boleyn and Catherine Howard. About this time (1548) occurred a great fire in the Tower:

"ij A° (Edw. VI.) —Item the xxij day of November was in the nyghte a grete fyer in the tower of London, and a gret pesse burnyd, by menes of a Frencheman that sette a barrelle of gonnepoder a fyere, and soo was burnyd hymselfe, and no more persons, but moch hurte besyde."—*Chron. Grey Friars of London.*

Edward VI. kept his court in the Tower prior to his coronation: here his uncle, the Protector Somerset, was twice imprisoned before his decapitation on Tower Hill, in 1552. Lady Jane Grey entered the fortress as queen of England, but in three weeks became here a captive with her youthful husband: both were beheaded. Queen Mary, at her court in the Tower, first showed her Romish resolves: her sister, the Princess Elizabeth, was imprisoned here on suspicion of favouring Sir Thomas Wyatt's design; she was compelled to enter at the *Traitor's Gate*, when she exclaimed, "Here landeth as true a subject, being a prisoner, as ever landed at these stairs; and before Thee, O God, I speak it." Queen Elizabeth did not keep her court in the Tower, but at no period was the state prison more "constantly thronged with delinquents." James I. resided here, and delighted in combats of the wild beasts kept here. In Charles I's. reign many leading partisans were imprisoned here; and under the government of Oliver Cromwell, and in the reigns of Charles II. and James II., the Tower was filled with prisoners, the victims of state policy, intrigue, tyranny, or crime. Almost from the Conquest, our sovereigns, at their coronation, went in great state and procession from the Tower, through the City, to Westminster; the last observance being at the coronation of Charles II. All the domestic apartments of

A. White Tower.   B. Wardrobe Tower.   C. St. John's Chapel, in the White Tower.   D. Cold Harbour.   E. Bloody Tower.   F. St. Thomas's Tower.   G. Traitor's Gate.   H. Well Tower. I. Cradle Tower.   K. Hall Tower.   L. Lantern Tower.   M. Salt Tower.   N. Tower above the Iron Gate.   O. Tower leading to the Iron Gate.   P. Broad Arrow Tower.   Q. Constable Tower.   R. Martin Tower.   S. Brick Tower.   T. Bowyer's Tower.   U. Flint Tower.   V. Bell Tower.   W. Devill Tower.   X. Beauchamp Tower.   Y. Byward Tower.   Z. Middle Tower.

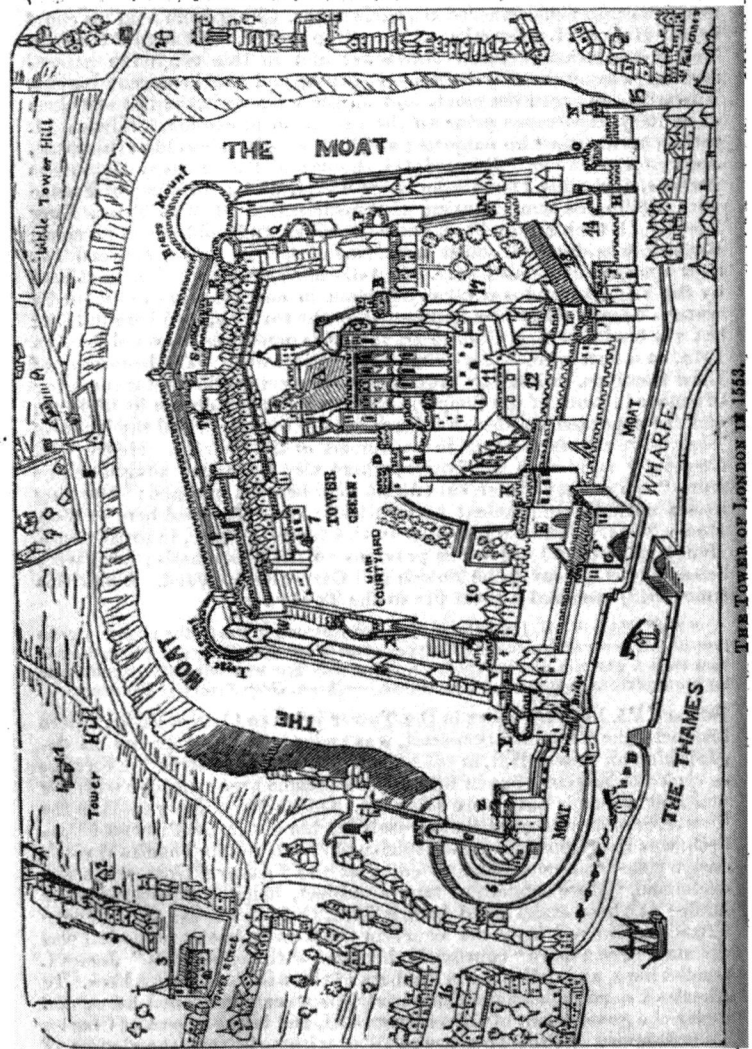

1. Posts of the Scaffold.   2. Cage.   3. Barkin Church.   4. The Bulwark Gate.   5. Lyon Tower.   6. Lyons Gate.   7. St. Peter's Church.   8. Postern Gate.   9. The Stone Kitchen.   10. Lieutenant's Lodgings.   11. Jewel House.   12. Hall decayed.   13. Queen's Gallery.   14. Private Gardens.   15. Iron Gate.   16. Thames-street.   17. Queen's Lodgings.

the ancient palace within the Tower were taken down during the reigns of James II. and William and Mary. In 1792 the garrison was increased:

"Several hundred men were employed in repairing the fortifications, opening the embrasures, and mounting cannon; and on the western side of the fortress a strong barrier was formed with old casks filled with earth and rubble; the gates were closed at an early hour, and no one but the military allowed to go on the ramparts."—*Bayley*.

The *Tower Palace* occupied the south-eastern portion of the inner ward, as shown in the opposite plan of the fortress in the reign of Elizabeth, within a century from which period much of its ancient character was obliterated by small buildings between its towers and courts. Northward of the White Tower was built, *temp*. James II. and William III., the *Grand Storehouse* for the Royal Train of Artillery, and the *Small Armoury* for 150,000 stand of arms: this building, 345 feet in length, was destroyed by fire October 30, 1841;* since which the Tower has been "remodelled," many small dwelling-houses have been cleared away, and several towers and defences have been rebuilt. The houses of Petty Wales and the outworks have been removed, with the Menagerie buildings at the entrance from the west.

The *Lion Tower* was built by Henry III., who commenced assembling here a menagerie with three leopards sent to him by the Emperor Frederic II., "in token of his regal shield of arms, wherein those leopards were pictured." Here, in 1255, the Sheriffs built a house "for the King's elephant," brought from France, and the first seen in England. Our early sovereigns had a mews in the Tower as well as a menagerie:

> "Merry Margaret, as Midsomer flowre,
> Gentyll as faucon and hawke of the Towre."—*Skelton*.

To the Lion Tower was built an emicircular enclosure, where lions and bears were baited with dogs, in which James I. and his court much delighted. A lion was named after the reigning king; and it was popularly believed that "when the king dies, the lion of that name dies after him" (see also Addison's *Freeholder*, No. 47). "Washing the Lions on the first of April" was another popular hoax. The menagerie greatly declined until 1822, when it revived under the management of Mr. Cops; the last of the animals was, however, transferred to the Zoological Society's Gardens, in the Regent's Park, in 1834: the Refreshment-room and Ticket-office occupy part of the site of the Lion Tower; but the buildings were not entirely removed until 1853. The animals are described in a work entitled *The Tower Menagerie*, with woodcut portraits cleverly drawn by William Harvey.

The *Tower Moat or Ditch* was drained in 1843, filled up, and turfed, for the exercise of the garrison: occasionally sheep feed here. The banks are clothed with thriving evergreens; and on the north-east is a pleasant shrubbery-garden.†

"In draining the moat were found several stone shot, which had probably been projected against the fortress during the siege of 1460, when Lord Scales held the Tower for the king, and the Yorkists cannonaded him from a battery on the Southwark side of the river."—*Hewitt*. (See page 725.)

The land entrance to the fortress is by the *Middle Tower*, and a

---

* There were 94,500 stands of arms, of which 4000 were saved: loss by the fire, about 250,000*l.* Among the objects destroyed and lost were a cannon of wood, and the state swords of Justice and Mercy carried before the Pretender when he was proclaimed in Scotland in 1715.

† In 1830 the Tower Ditch was filled with water, and cleansed, by order of the Duke of Wellington, as Constable; which measure has been gravely described as putting the fortress into a state of security against the Reform Bill agitation!

stone bridge, anciently a drawbridge, crossing the Moat, at the south-west angle, to the *Byward Tower* : these towers were strongly forti-fied, and provided each with a double portcullis. On the right, a small drawbridge crosses the Moat, and leads to the wharf fronting the Thames. Here is *St. Thomas's Tower*, and beneath it *Traitor's Gate*, with a cut which connected the ditch with the river: by this entrance state prisoners were formerly brought into the Tower, and through it

." Went Sidney, Russell, Raleigh, Cranmer, More."—Rogers.

"When it was found necessary, from any cause, to carry a prisoner through the streets, the Sheriffs received him from the king's lieutenants at the entrance to the City, gave a receipt for him, and took another on delivering him up at the gates of the Tower. The receipt of the Governor for the body of the Duke of Monmouth—his living body—is still extant."—Dixon's *Prisons.*

Eastward is the basement-story of the *Cradle Tower*, in good con-dition; the *Well Tower* is used as a warder's residence; and at the south-eastern angle is the *Iron-gate Tower*, used as a powder-magazine.

In the extreme angle, overhanging the ditch, is the *Devilin Tower*, which crowns "the Devil's Battery;" here is stored up gunpowder. The front wall is embattled, and mounted with cannon; and on the wharf were formerly fired the "Tower Guns." Hatton describes them, in 1708, as "62 guns, lying in a range, fast in the ground, always ready to be discharged on any occasion of victories, coronations, festivals, days of thanksgiving, triumphs, &c." The guns are now fired from a new "Saluting Battery," facing Tower-hill.

Between the outer and inner wards extends a narrow street, in part formerly occupied by the buildings of the Mint, removed to Tower Hill in 1810. The towers of the inner ward are—commencing from the south-east, the *Bell Tower*, containing the alarm-bell of the garrison; it is said to have been the prison-lodging of Fisher, Bishop of Rochester, and subsequently of the Princess Elizabeth: "at this point, in former times, were other gates, to prevent an enemy getting possession of the lines, and to guard the approaches to the inner ballium."—*Hewitt.*

Between the *Bell Tower* and the *Beauchamp Tower* was formerly a passage by the leads, used as a promenade for prisoners, of whom the walls bear memorials; among them is "*Respice finem, W. D.*"

Next, northward, is the *Beauchamp* or *Cobham Tower*, a curious specimen of the military architecture of the 12th and 13th centuries.

. This tower is named from Thomas Beauchamp, Earl of Warwick, being confined here in 1397, and the Cobhams in 1554. It was restored by Anthony Salvin in 1854; when lithographed copies of the Inscriptions, Memorials, and Devices cut on the walls of the several rooms and cells, were published by W. R. Dick.

· Upon the wall is a rebus of Dr. Abel, chaplain to Catherine Queen of Aragon; a bell inscribed TA, and Thomas above. Couplets, maxims, allegories, and spiritual truths are sometimes added: of these we can only select a few :

"Thomas Willyngar, goldsmithe. My hart is yours tel dethe." By the side is a figure of a bleeding "hart," and another of "dethe;" and "T. W." and "P. A."

"Thomas Rose,
Within this Tower strong
Kept close
By those to whom he did no wrong. May 8th, 1666."

The figure of man, praying, underneath "Ro. Bainbridge" (1587-8).

"Thomas Bawdewin, 1585, Jvly. As vertve maketh life, so sin cawseth death."
" Walter Paslew, dated 1569 & 1570. My hope is in Christ." Devices of the Peverels; and crucifix and bleeding heart. "J. C. 1538." "Learne to feare God." "Reprens . le . sage . et : il . te ; armera.—Take wisdom, and he shall arm you."

Over the fireplace is inscribed:

" Quanto plus afflictionis pro Christo in hoc sæculo,
Tanto plus gloriæ cum Christo in futuro.
Arundell, June 22, 1587."
" Gloria et honore eum coronasti Domine:
In memoria æterna erit justus. Atuch ....."

One of the most elaborate devices is that of John Dvdle, Earl of
Warwick, tried and condemned in 1553 for endeavouring to deprive Mary
of the crown; but being reprieved, he died in his prison-room, where
he had wrought upon the wall his family's cognizance, the lion, and
bear, and ragged staff, underneath which is his name; the whole surrounded by oak-sprigs, roses, geraniums, and honeysuckles, emblematic
of the Christian names of his four brothers, as appears from this unfinished inscription:

" Yow that these beasts do wel behold and se,
May deme with ease wherefore here made they be
Withe borders eke wherein (there may be found)
4 brothers' names, who list to serche the grovnd."

The names of the brothers were Ambrose, Robert, Guildford, and
Henry: thus, A, acorn; R, rose; G, geranium; and H, honeysuckle:
others think the rose indicates Ambrose, and the oak Robert (robur).
In another part is carved an oak-tree bearing acorns, signed R.D.; the
work of Robert Dudley, Earl of Leicester.

" I h s 1571, die 10 Aprilis. Wise men ought circumspectly to see what they
do, to examine before they speake, to prove before they take in hand, to beware
whose company they use, and above all things, to whom they truste. Charles
Bailly." Another of Bailly's apophthegms is: " The most vnhapy man in the
world is he that is not pacient in adversities; for men are not killed with the adversities they have, but with ye impacience which they svffer."

" O . Lord . whic . art . of . heavn . King . Graunt : gras . and . lvfe . everlastig :
to . Miagh . thy . servant . in . prison . alon . with * . * * Tomas Miagh." Again:

" Thomas Miagh, whiche lieth here alon,
That fayne wovld from hens be gon,
By tortyre straunge mi troth was
tryed, yet of my libertie denied. 1581, Thomas Myagh."

(A prisoner for treason, tortured with Skeffington's irons and the rack.)

" Hit is the poynt of a wyse man to try and then trvste, for hapy is he whome
yndeth one that is ivst. T. C." Again: " T. C. I leve in hope and I gave
credit to mi frinde in time did stande me moste in hande, so wovlde I never do
igaine, excepte I hade him sver in bande, and to al men wiche I so vnles, ye
ivssteine the leke lose as I do. Vnhappie is that mane whose actes doth procvre
he miseri of this hovs in prison to indvre. 1576, Thomas Clarke."

In the State Prison Room occurs twice the name of " IANE" (Lady
Jane Grey), probably inscribed by one of the Dudleys, who were all
imprisoned here in 1553, and one of whom, Guildford, was the lady's
husband: this is the only memorial preserved of Lady Jane in the Tower.

Wallace, the Scottish hero, is erroneously named among the prisoners here; for Wallace was not confined in any part of the Tower.

The memorial of Thomas Salmon, 1622, now let into the wall of the
middle room, was formerly in the upper prison-lodging:

A shield surrounded by a circle; above the circle the name " T. Salmon;" a
crest formed of three salmons, and the date 1622; underneath the circle the
motto Nec temere, nec timore—" Neither rashly nor with fear." Also a star containing the abbreviation of Christ, in Greek, surrounded by the sentence, Sic vive
ut vivas—" So live that thou mayest live." In the opposite corner are the words,
Et morire ne morteris—" And die that thou mayest die not." Surrounding a representation of Death's head, above the device, is the enumeration of Salmon's
confinement: " Close prisoner 8 moneths, 32 wekes, 224 dayes, 5376 houres."

On the ground-floor is:

> " The man whom this house can not mend,
> Hath evill becom, and worse will end."

"Round this (Beauchamp) chamber a secret passage has recently been discovered in the masonry, in which spies were, no doubt, set to listen, and report the conversation or soliloquies of prisoners, when they, poor souls, believed themselves alone. The men who live in the Tower have christened this passage the Whispering Gallery."—Dixon's *Prisons*, 1850, p. 70.

Raleigh was thrice imprisoned in the Tower; in 1592 (eight weeks), for winning the heart of Elizabeth Throgmorton, one of Elizabeth's maids of honour; "not only a moral sin, but in those days a heinous political offence." In 1604 he was again committed to the Tower, and in the frenzy of despair attempted to stab himself to the heart; he remained here a captive nearly thirteen years, part of the time with Lady Raleigh: here, 1605, was born Carew, their second son. Sir Walter's prison-lodging is thought to have been the second and third stories of the Beauchamp Tower; here he devoted much time to chemistry and pharmaceutical preparations. "He has converted," says Sir William Wade, Lieutenant of the Tower, "a little hen-house in the garden into a still-house, and here he doth spend his time all the day in distillations; . . . he doth show himself upon the wall in his garden to the view of the people:" here Raleigh prepared his "rare cordial,"* wrote his political discourses, and commenced his famous *History of the World.* He was at length liberated, but again committed to the Tower, about two months before his execution at Westminster.

North of the Beauchamp Tower is the *Devereux Tower,* which has been rebuilt under the direction of the Ordnance. The original tower, with walls 11 feet thick, was the prison-lodging of Robert Devereux, Earl of Essex; in the lower chambers were passages leading to the adjoining CHAPEL OF ST. PETER, described at pp. 155, 156.

Eastward are the *Flint, Bowyer,* and *Brick Towers,* which have also been rebuilt by the Ordnance. In the Bowyer Tower resided the Master and Provider of the King's Bows; and in a work-room over this tower originated the fire which destroyed the Grand Storehouse in 1841: the basement, strongly groined and vaulted, has been restored. Beneath the floor is a still more dreary vault, with a trap-door opening upon a flight of steps. The Brick Tower, the reputed prison-house of Lady Jane Grey, had its modernised superstructure destroyed in the fire of 1841; but the original basement and a dungeon beneath remained.

The *Martin Tower,* at the north-east angle, was formerly a prison-lodging, and next the Jewel Tower. Anne Boleyn was imprisoned here: on the walls is a coat-of-arms and "Boullen:" she slept in the little upper room. Robert Devereux, Earl of Essex, and Lord Southampton (Shakspeare's friend), were also prisoners in the Martin Tower; and here were confined, by James II., Archbishop Sancroft and the six bishops. Here resides the Keeper of the Regalia. Thence, southward, is the *Constable Tower,* rebuilt by the Ordnance. Next is the *Broad Arrow Tower,* in its original condition: Lady Jane Grey was a prisoner here: the Latin couplet which Fox states Jane scratched with a pin upon the walls of her chamber, can nowhere be found. The *Salt(petre) Tower* is called "Julius Cæsar Tower" in a survey *temp.* Henry VIII., and is supposed to be actually of the reign of William Rufus. It is circular, and has a vaulted dungeon: in the first-story

* Raleigh's " Rare Cordial," with other ingredients introduced by Sir Kenelm Digby and Sir A. Frazer, is the *Confectio aromatica* of the present London Pharmacopœia.

chamber, among the devices and inscriptions cut in the wall, is a sphere with the signs of the zodiac, and

"Hew : Draper : of : Bristow : made : thys : spheer : the : 30 : daye : of : Maye : anno 1561."

Draper was a wealthy tavern-keeper at Bristow, and was committed here "as suspect of a conjuror or sorceror," practising against "Sir William St. Lowe and my ladie;" but he affirmed that "longe since he soe misliked his science, that he burned all his books." A view of the Salt Tower, taken in 1846, is etched in Archer's *Vestiges*, part iii.

Next the Salt Tower, westward, was the *Lantern Tower*, removed for the *Ordnance Office*, greatly heightened in 1854. Further west is the *Record Tower*, also called *Wakefield*, from the imprisonment of the Yorkists here after the battle of Wakefield, 1460 : this was also anciently the *Hall Tower*, from its proximity to the great hall of the palace : the basement is Norman, probably of the reign of William Rufus ; the walls are 13 feet thick. The upper chamber has been a Record-room since the reign of Henry VIII. : here are the *cartæ antiquæ* and chancery rolls, chronologically ranged in presses. Opposite the chamber in which Henry VI. is supposed to have been murdered, is the Record-keeper's room, where hang some of the Keepers' portraits : William Lambarde, the topographer ; the learned Selden ; the Puritan, William Prynne ; and William Petyt, Samuel Lysons, and Henry Petrie, were distinguished Record-keepers. In the Octagon, " Edward the Confessor's Room," the last person confined was Ings, the Cato-street conspirator.

Adjoining the Record Tower, westward, is the *Bloody Tower* : here, in a dark windowless room, in which one of the portcullises was worked, George Duke of Clarence is said to have been drowned in malmsey ; in the adjoining chamber, the two princes are said to have been "smothered;" whence the name of Bloody Tower. This has been much disputed ; but in a tract *temp.* James I. we read that the above "turret our elders termed the *Bloody Tower ;* for the bloodshed, as they say, of those infant princes of Edward IV., whom Richard III., of cursed memory (I shudder to mention it), savagely killed, two together at one time." In the latter chamber was imprisoned Colonel Hutchinson, whose wife, daughter of Sir Allen Apsley, Lieutenant of the Tower, where she was born, relates the above traditions. This portion was formerly called the *Garden Tower ;* it was built *temp.* Edward III., and is the only ancient place of security, as a state prison, in the Tower : it is entered through a small door in the inner ballium ; it consists of a day-room and a bed-room, and the leads on which the prisoner was sometimes allowed to breathe the air. The last person who occupied these apartments was Arthur Thistlewood, the Cato-street conspirator. Westward are the *Lieutenant's Lodgings* (the Lieutenant's residence), chiefly timber-built, *temp.* Henry VIII. ; in 1610 was added a chamber having a prospect to all the three gates of the Tower, and enabling the lieutenant to call and look to the warders. In the "Council Chamber" the Commissioners examined Guy Fawkes and his accomplices, as commemorated in a Latin and Hebrew inscription upon a parti-coloured marble monument ; and elsewhere in the building there was discovered, about 1845, "an inscription carved on an old mantelpiece relating to the Countess of Lenox, grandmother of James I., 'commytede prysner to thys Logynge for the Marige of her Sonne my Lord Henry Darnle and the Queen of Scotlande.'" (Hewitt's *Tower*, &c.) Here a bust of James I. was set up, in 1608, by Sir William Wade, then Lieutenant ; the walls are painted with representations of men inflicting and suffering torture ; and the room is reputed to be haunted ! The last person confined in the lodgings here was Sir Francis Burdett, committed April 6, 1810, for writing in Cobbett's *Weekly Register.*

"Besides the 'prison-lodgings,' there were other still more terrible chambers in the Tower; chambers especially constructed with a view to the torture of their inmates. One of these was called 'Little Ease;' a cell so small in its dimensions, that it was impossible for the prisoner to stand erect or to lie down except in a cramped position (*Holinshed*, vol. iii. p. 825). Another was named 'The Pit.' Others are said to have been full of vermin, especially rats, which at high water were driven up in shoals from the Thames. The Devil's Tower probably took its name from some *contrivance of this kind.*"—*Hewitt.*

The *Place of Execution within the Tower on the Green* was reserved for putting to death privately; and the precise spot, nearly opposite the door of St. Peter's Chapel, is denoted by a large oval of dark flints: hereon perished Anne Boleyn and Catherine Howard, Margaret Countess of Salisbury, and Lady Jane Grey.

The *Bloody Tower gateway*, built *temp.* Edward III. (opposite *Traitor's Gate*), is the main entrance to the Inner Ward: it has massive gates and portcullis, complete, at the southern end; but those at the north end have been removed.

"The gates are genuine, and the portcullis is said to be the only one remaining in England fit for use. The archway forms a noble specimen of the Doric order of Gothic. For a prison-entrance we know of no more perfect model."— Weale's *London,* p. 160.

Westward of the White Tower, between the Chapel and Lieutenant's Lodgings, was the "Tower Green," now the parade-ground of the garrison. Northward, upon the site of the Grand Storehouse,* are the *Waterloo Barracks* (to receive 1000 men), in the "modern castellated style," its only ancient features being battlements and machiolations: the first stone was laid June 14, 1845, by the Duke of Wellington, of whom here is a pedestrian stone statue, by Milnes, upon a pedestal.

North-east of the White Tower is another "modern castellated" range of buildings for the officers of the garrison. South-eastward are the *Ordnance Office* and *Storehouses.*

THE WHITE TOWER, citadel, or keep (for many years of itself "the Tower of London," the other buildings having been added as outworks), was begun by Bishop Gundulph, in 1078, on the site of a work said to have been destroyed by floods. The external dimensions of the White Tower are 176 feet north and south by 96 feet east and west, with an eastern semicircular projection, the apsis of the chapel. The elevation is 92 feet; it is embattled; and its angles are finished with turrets, the vanes of which are surmounted with the royal crown. The north and south western turrets are square, with a slight projection; the south-eastern turret is built upon the summit of the wall; and that at the north-eastern angle is an irregular circle, and was pierced to receive four clock-dials in 1854. This tower was called the *Observatory,* and was employed by the "Astronomical Observator, John Flamstead," who had "an hundred poundes yearly payd him out of this office (of Ordnance):" it contains a staircase which communicates with each of the floors, from the vaults to the roof, which is covered with lead, and was once a promenade for the prisoners. Traces of a large archway on the north side indicate the original grand entrance, shown in the oldest views; the present entrances, north and south, are modern. The external walls are from 10 to 12 feet thick, and the internal walls 7 feet;

* The large pediment of the Storehouse, filled with bold sculptures of the royal arms, guns, and military trophies, was preserved, and has been set up opposite the Martin Tower.

of these there are only two, which divide each floor into three apartments. The White Tower was first considerably repaired about the middle of the 13th century; next, with Caen stone, in 1532; "it was almost new erected in 1637 and 1638, being built of boulder and square stone" (*Hatton*); and windows and other ancient features were obliterated in the reign of William III. On the eastern side is a wing occupied for Ordnance books and papers. Here, *circ.* 1708, were "3000 barrels of gunpowder at a time, with vast quantities of match; also swords and gin for mounting great guns; and on the east side is a place where the powder is proved before the surveyor and other officers."

On the first floor is *Queen Elizabeth's Armoury*, with a vaulted roof: on the north side a door opens to a cell, 10 feet by 8, in the thickness of the wall; this is said to have been the prison-lodging of Sir Walter Raleigh; near the cell entrance are inscribed Rudstone, Fane, and Culpeper, all implicated in Sir Thomas Wyatt's rebellion.

> "He that indvreth to the ende shal be savid
> M : 10 R. Rvdston. Dar. Kent. Ano. 1553."

> "Be faithfvl vnto the deth and I wil give thee a crowne of Life.
> T. Fane 1554."

> "T. Cvlpeper of Ailsford, Kent."

On the second floor, reaching to the roof, is the *Chapel of St. John the Evangelist*, the most perfect specimen of Norman architecture in the metropolis; it has an apsis, and a gallery supported by 12 massive round columns, united by semicircular arches: here our early sovereigns knelt before the King of kings. Three stained-glass windows were added to this chapel by Henry III.: it has long been used as a record depository. In the third floor is the Council Chamber, a state apartment, with a massive timber roof: here the Protector Gloucester ordered Lord Hastings to be led to instant execution in front of St. Peter's Chapel; and commanded the arrest of the Archbishop of York, the Bishop of Ely, and Lord Stanley. King John of France was lodged in the White Tower in 1357. The vaults underneath were occupied as prisons: among their inscriptions is one carved by Fisher, Bishop of Rochester. Throughout the building there is no trace of a fireplace or of a well.

A paper drawn up by a yeoman-warder, in 1641, shows the White Tower to have then been the Office of Ordnance; the Martin Tower to the Porter of the Mint; the Byward and Water-gate Towers to the warders; and eleven other towers to have been "prison-lodgings."

Imprisonments. — Upwards of 1000 prisoners have been confined in the chambers and cells of the Tower at one time. Among the celebrated persons imprisoned here, besides those already named, were: A.D. 1100. Ralph Flambard, the militant Bishop of Durham. 1296. Balliol, King of Scotland, and Scottish chieftains. 1307. Lady Badlesmere, for refusing the queen of Edward II. lodging in her castle of Leeds, Kent. 1347. Charles of Blois, and the twelve citizens of Calais with the governor. 1386. Geoffrey Chaucer, said to have here written his *Testament of Love*. (Chaucer was appointed clerk of the works, July 13, 1389, 13th Richard II.) 1415. The Duke of Orleans, father of Louis XII., composed here a volume of English poems, which contains the earliest view of the Tower. 1534. John Fisher, Bishop of Rochester; and Sir Thomas More. 1540. Thomas Cromwell, Earl of Essex. 1547. The Duke of Norfolk and his son, the poet Earl of Surrey.

"xxxviij°. A°. (Hen. VIII.) Thys yere the xijth day of December the dewke of Norffoke and the yerle of Sorré hys sonne ware comyttyd unto the tower of London, and the dewke went be watter from the lorde chaunselers place in Holborne that was sometyme the byshoppe of Ely's, and soo downe un to the watter syde, and so be watter un to the tower; and hys sonne the yerle of Sorré went thorrow the cytte of London, makynge grete lamentacion. * * Item the 13. day of Januarij was the yerle of Sorrey browte from the tower of London un to the yelde halle of London, and there he was from ix. unto yt was v. at nyght, and there had hys juggement to be heddyd; and soo the xix. day of the same month it was done at the Towre hylle."—*Chron. Grey Friars of London.*

1553. Cranmer, Latimer, and Ridley. Latimer was also a prisoner here from 1541 to 1547. 1554. Sir Thomas Wyatt. 1562. The Earl of Southampton, the friend of Shakspeare. 1606. Guy Fawkes and his fellow-conspirators. 1622. Lord Chancellor Bacon, "a broken reed;" Sir Edward Coke, a close prisoner. 1613. Sir Thomas Overbury, supposed to have been poisoned by his gaoler. 1616. The Countess of Somerset,* for Overbury's murder. 1626. "Mr. Moor was sent to the Tower for speaking (in Parliament) out of season; and Sir William Widdrington and Sir Herbert Price for bringing in candles against the desire of the House." (*Dwarris, on Statutes,* p. 83.) 1628. Felton, the assassin of the Duke of Buckingham; Sir John Elliot, second imprisonment; John Selden. 1641. Thomas Wentworth, Earl of Strafford; Archbishop Laud, and Bishop Hall. 1648. The pious Jeremy Taylor. 1651. Sir William Davenant, whose life was saved by Milton and Whitelocke. 1656. Lucy Barlow, mother of the Duke of Monmouth: she was liberated by Oliver Cromwell. 1661. Harrington, who wrote the *Oceana.* 1679. Viscount Stafford, beheaded 1680. 1679. Samuel Pepys, the diarist, suspected of connexion with the Popish Plot; liberated on bail for 30,000*l.* 1681. The Earl of Shaftesbury. 1683. William Lord Russell and Algernon Sidney. 1685. James Duke of Monmouth. 1688 (the Revolution). The infamous Lord Jeffreys; William Penn, for street preaching; the Seven Bishops. 1692. The great Duke of Marlborough. 1712. Sir Robert Walpole, for receiving bribes. 1715. Harley, Earl of Oxford; the Earls of Derwentwater and Nithsdale. 1717. William Shippen, "downright Shippen" (*Pope*). 1722. Bishop Atterbury and the Earl of Orrery. 1746. Lords Kilmarnock, Balmerino, and Lovat. 1760. Earl Ferrers, hanged for murder. 1762. John Wilkes; no charge specified. 1780. Lord George Gordon (Riots). 1794. John Horne Tooke, Hardy, Thelwall, Holcroft, and others. The Tower still remains the prison to which political offenders are committed by Parliament.

The *Constable of the Tower* was formerly styled the *Constable of London,* the *Constable of the Sea,* and the *Constable of the Honour of the Tower;* which post was conferred by William I. upon Geoffry de Mandeville, in reward of his services at the battle of Hastings. The Constable, besides his salary, privileges, and perquisites, *temp.* Edward II. received a custom of 2*d.* from each person going and returning by the Thames, on a pilgrimage to St. James's shrine. In the reign of Richard II. the Constable received yearly 100*l.*, with fees from his prisoners, according to their rank, "for the suit of his irons:" of every duke committed, 20*l.*; and for irons, earl, 20 marks; baron, 10*l.*; knight, 100 shillings. The Constable's salary is now 1000*l.* per annum: the great Duke of Wellington was Constable from 1820 to his death in 1852, and was succeeded by Viscount Combermere. The *Lieutenant of the Tower* is next in rank to the Constable; but the duties of both offices are performed by the *Deputy-Lieutenant* and the *Tower Major.* Colonel Gurwood, editor of the Duke of Wellington's *Despatches,* was long Deputy-Lieutenant. The *Gentleman Gaoler* had the custody and

* The Countess of Somerset's "only child, born in the Tower during her imprisonment, and named Anne, after the name of the Queen, in the hopes thereby of propitiating her majesty, was afterwards married to the Duke of Bedford, and was the mother of Lord William Russell."—*Amos.*

ocking-up of the state prisoners. The *Yeomen Warders,* of whom
here are now 45, originally kept watch over the prisoners : in the reign
f Edward VI., the Duke of Somerset, in return for the attention and
espect they paid him whilst in confinement, procured them, after his
iberation, " to be sworne extraordinary of the guard, and to weare the
ame livery they doe." Their uniform has not been changed since the
eign of Charles II.

Locking-up the Tower is an ancient, curious, and stately ceremony.
\ few minutes before the clock strikes the hour of eleven—on Tuesdays
nd Fridays, twelve—the Head Warder (Yeoman Porter), clothed in a
ong red cloak, bearing a huge bunch of keys, and attended by a brother
varder carrying a lantern, appears in front of the main guard-house,
nd loudly calls out, " Escort keys !" The sergeant of the guard, with
ve or six men, then turns out and follows him to the "Spur," or
uter gate ; each sentry challenging as they pass his post, " Who
oes there ?"—" Keys." The gates being carefully locked and barred,
he procession returns, the sentries exacting the same explanation, and
eceiving the same answer as before. Arrived once more in front of
he main guard-house, the sentry there gives a loud stamp with his foot,
nd asks, " Who goes there ?"—" Keys." " Whose keys ?"—" Queen
Victoria's keys." " Advance Queen Victoria's keys, and all's well."
The Yeoman Porter then exclaims, " God bless Queen Victoria!" The
nain guard respond, "Amen." The officer on duty gives the word,
' Present arms !" the firelocks rattle ; the officer kisses the hilt of his
word ; the escort fall in among their companions ; and the Yeoman
'orter marches across the parade alone to deposit the keys in the Lieu-
enant's Lodgings. The ceremony over, not only is all egress and ingress
otally precluded, but even within the walls no one can stir without
eing furnished with the countersign.

The Tower has a separate coroner ; and the public have access to the
ortress only by sufferance. When Horwood made his Survey of Lon-
lon, 1799, he was denied admission to the Tower ; and the refusal is thus
ecorded upon the map :—" The Tower : the internal parts not distin-
uished, being refused permission to take the survey."

The Tower is extra-parochial ; and in 1851 the population was 882,
nd the military in barracks 606.

THE ARMOURIES.—The fortress has been the depository of the na-
ional arms and accoutrements from the earliest ages of our monarchy ;
nd writs of various dates enumerate warlike stores contained in or
ssued from the Tower by " the Keeper of the Arms." In an inventory
emp. Edward VI. are mentioned many of the articles in the present col-
ection ; and Hentzner describes the Armouries in the reign of Eliza-
eth as one of the sights of London.

The Horse Armoury, 150 feet long, is on the south side of the White
Tower, and was built in 1826, when it was arranged by Sir Samuel
Meyrick. In the centre is a line of twenty-two equestrian figures, in
he armour of various reigns from Edward I. to James II. Over each
igure is a crimson banner bearing the name and time of the king or
night represented by the effigy below ; but only a few of the armours
ave been actually worn by the persons to whom they are assigned.
Around the room are ranged other figures in armour, interspersed with
nilitary trophies and emblems ; besides other mounted figures ; arms of
lifferent ages ; helmets, cuirasses, shields, &c. ; and on the ceiling are
lisplayed obsolete arms and accoutrements in fanciful devices. The
questrian figures are of the time of

Edward I. (1272).—Suit of a hauberk, with sleeves and chaussees, and a hood
rith camail ; square-topped shield ; prick-spurs ; surcoat and baudric, modern.

Henry VI. (1450).—Back and breast blates of flexible armour; chain-mail sleeves and skirt; fluted gauntlets; helmet à la Cade, with a frontlet and surmounting crest; the horse housing emblazoned with the arms of France and England; fluted chauffron.

Edward IV. (1465).—Tournament suit, with tilting lance; war saddle, somewhat later; horse housings, black, powdered with the king's badges—the white rose and sun; a spiked chauffron on horse's head.

Knight, temp. Richard III. (1483-1485).—Ribbed German armour; tilting apparel and original tilting lance: this suit was worn at the Eglinton Tournament by the Marquis of Waterford.

Knight, temp. Henry VII. (1485-1509).—Fluted (German) suit; burgonet helmet. Suit of fluted armour of the same reign; ancient sword, battle-axe, and war-saddle; horse armour fluted, and only wanting the flanchards.

Henry VIII. (1520).—Damasked armour actually worn by this king. Two suits of the same reign, worn by Charles Brandon, Duke of Suffolk, and Edward Clinton, Earl of Lincoln. In a recess is "*one of the most curious suits of armour in the world,*" of German workmanship, once gilt, and made to commemorate the marriage of Henry VIII. and Katherine of Arragon: it is most elaborately engraved with the rose and pomegranate, portcullis, fleurs-de-lis, and red dragon; "H. K.," united by a true-lover's-knot; saintly legends, mottoes, &c.

Edward VI. (1552).—Russet armour, covered with beautiful filagree-work; burgonet helmet; horse armour complete, embossed with the combined badges of Burgundy and Granada.

Francis Hastings, Earl of Huntingdon (1555).—Richly gilt suit, with indented slashes; weight of body armour exceeds 100 lbs.

Robert Dudley, Earl of Leicester (1560).—Tilting suit actually worn by Leicester, *temp.* Elizabeth: it bears the initials "R. D.," and the earl's cognizance of the bear and ragged staff: this suit "was kept in the tilt-yard, where it was exhibited on particular days" (*Meyrick*).

Sir Henry Lea (1570).—Suit of plate.

Robert Devereux, Earl of Essex (1581).—Suit of armour, richly engraved and gilt; burgonet helmet. This armour was worn by the King's Champion at the coronation of George II.

James I. (1605).—Plain suit of tilting armour. Of the same period are the suits of cap-à-pie armour assigned to Sir Horace Vere, and Thomas Howard, Earl of Arundel.

Henry Prince of Wales (1612).—Richly-gilt suit made for the prince; engraved with battles, sieges, &c.

George Villiers, Duke of Buckingham (1618).—Full suit of plate.

Charles Prince of Wales (1620).—Suit made for the prince when about twelve years old.

Thomas Wentworth, Earl of Strafford (1635).—Armour continued only to the knees.

Charles I. (1640).—Magnificent suit presented to Charles, when Prince of Wales, by the Armourers' Company of the City of London: it is richly gilt and arabesqued; face is carved by Gibbons. This suit was laid on the coffin of the great Duke of Marlborough, in his funeral procession.

James II. (1685).—Cuirass over a velvet coat; casque and pierced visor: the head was carved by Gibbons, as a portrait of Charles II.

Here also are: a swordsman (Henry VII.). A man-at-arms and foot-soldier (Henry VIII.). "Armour cap-a-pe, rough from the hammer, said to be King Henry ye 8ths." Suits belonging to the Princes Henry and Charles, sons of James I. Cavaliers and pikemen (*temp.* Charles I.). A fragment of "penny plate armour." Magnificent suit of Italian armour, engraved and gilt. Cuirasses from Waterloo. Ancient suits of chain-mail. Halbards,* shields, and helmets. "The Norman Crusader," really an Asiatic suit of mixed chain and plate. Very curious helmets. Pieces of a puffed and engraved suit of armour (*temp.* Henry VIII.), extremely rare. Ancient German bone saddle, with Teutonic inscription. The "Anticke Headpiece with rames Hornes and speckakels on it of Will Somers," jester to Henry VIII. Specimens of hand fire-

* The halbard remained in use among our troops till within 50 years, and may still be seen as an official weapon in our courts of justice. The warders of the Tower are still armed with the partisan: it is still carried by the watchmen in Denmark.

arms. Ancient warder's horn, of carved ivory. Chinese military dresses from Chusan. Helmet, belt, straight sword, and scimitars of Tippoo Saib. Concave rondelle with spiked boss, such as is seen in the picture of "Henry the Eighth's Embarcation at Dover," at Hampton Court. Part of a horse armour of *cuir bouilli*, extremely rare and curious. On the columns are groups of arms now in use among continental powers; arms employed in England from the time of James II. to the present reign; and projects for the improvement of war implements.

Here are celts; ancient British axes, swords, and spears, of bronze (one axe found near Hastings, supposed *temp.* Harold); a British battle-axe found in the Thames in 1829; Roman spear-head; Saxon daggers and battle-axes.

At the top of the stairs are two rudely-carved wood figures, "Gin" and "Beer," from over the buttery of the old palace at Greenwich. A very curious Indian suit of armour, sent to Charles II. by the Great Mogul. Ten small cannon, presented by the brass-founders of London to Charles II. when a boy.

Queen Elizabeth's Armoury, cased with wood in the Norman style, is entered at the eastern side of the White Tower: the windows are filled with stained glass, in part ancient. Here is an equestrian figure of Elizabeth, in a *fac simile* of the robe worn by her on going to St. Paul's to return thanks. The weapons collected here were brought originally from "The Spanish Weapon House," and were long called "The Spanish Armoury," misinterpreted as the spoils of the Spanish Armada. These weapons were mostly used *temp.* Elizabeth and Henry VIII. The collection of spears is interesting. Here is the Morning-star, or Holy-water (blood) Sprinkle, a spiked ball on a pole, used by infantry from the Conquest till *temp.* Henry VIII. The walls are hung with early shields. Two bows of yew, from the wreck of the Mary Rose, 1545; early kite shield; two cross-hilted swords, *temp.* Crusaders, authentic and rare. Thumb-screws, or thumbikins; the "Iron Coller of Torment, taken from ye Spanyard in ye yeare 1588;" the iron Cravat, "Scavenger's or Skeffington's Daughter." Ancient Cresset, with spear-head. Mace-cannon, carried at the saddle-bow. Long-pikes and boar-spears, in the Tower *temp.* Edward VI. Large pavoise, or archer's shield. "Great Holly-water Sprincle, with three gonnes in the top." Spontoon of the guard of Henry VIII. Guisarmes and glaives, partisans, lances, pikes, and halbards. On the floor is the heading-axe with which the Earl of Essex was executed, *temp.* Elizabeth. Heading-block on which Lords Balmerino, Kilmarnock, and Lovat were decapitated on Tower-hill, in 1746. The money received for admission to the Armouries is expended in adding to the collection; thus, in 1853, a beautiful suit of Greek armour, found in a tomb at Cumæ, was purchased for 200*l.*: it is shown in the Horse Armoury.

Among the *Curiosities* mentioned by Hatton, 1708, is the sword which Lord Kingsale took from a French guard, for which he and his posterity have the favour of being covered in the king's presence. On the stairs is part of the keel of the Royal George, sunk in 1782.

In the *Ante-room* added to Queen Elizabeth's Armoury, fitted up in 1851, from the plan of Mr. Stacey, Ordnance Storekeeper, are a group of cannon from Waterloo, two kettle-drums from Blenheim; and specimens, ancient and modern, of every description of weapon now in the Tower. Here are also the sword and sash of Field Marshal the Duke of York; and General Wolfe's cloak, on which he died before Quebec. In the centre of the room is a beautifully ornamented bronze gun. Here are two large brass guns taken at Quebec by General Wolfe, a stand of cross-bows, and four figures in armour. In the western compartment are chiefly oriental arms and armour: suit of chain-mail (reputed Bajazet, 1401); Asiatic iron boot; Saracenic and Indian armour; memorials from Tippoo Saib's armoury; collection of Chinese armour; brass gun taken from the Chinese in 1842, inscribed, "RICHARD: PHILIPS: MADE: THIS: PECE: AN: DNI: 1601;" arms from Kaffraria; hempen armour from the South Seas; New Zealand implements, and chief's robe; rich Indian and Moorish arms and accoutrements, from the Great Exhibition of 1851; and a cabinet of oriental armour, weapons, horse-furniture, &c., presented by the Hon. East India Company. Here is the large anchor taken at Camperdown by Admiral Duncan. In 1854 were added 2000 stands of arms from Bomarsund, the first spoils of the Russian war.

Outside the White Tower, on the south-east, are: an ancient gun for stone shot; two brass guns, *temp.* Henry VII. and Henry VIII.; French, Spanish, and Chinese guns; guns from the wreck of the Royal George; and several mortars, including one of 18 inches, used at the siege of Namur by William III.

Mr. Hewitt's work is by far the most accurate and illustrative guide to the Tower Armouries.

THE REGALIA, OR CROWN JEWELS, have been exhibited to the public for a fee since the Restoration of Charles II. They had been previously kept sometimes in the Tower, in the Treasury of the Temple or other religious house, and in the Treasury at Westminster. The Royal Jewels were several times pledged to provide for the exigences of our monarchs: by Henry III., Edward III., Henry V., Henry VI.; and Richard II. offered them to the merchants of London as a guarantee for a loan. The office of Keeper of the Regalia, conferred by the king's letters patent, became in the reigns of the Tudors a post of great emolument and dignity, and "the Master of the Jewel-house" took rank as the first Knight Bachelor of England: the office was sometime held by Cromwell, afterwards Earl of Essex. During the civil war under Charles I. the Regalia were sold and destroyed. On the Restoration of Charles II. new Regalia were made, for which was paid to the king's goldsmith, Sir Robert Vyner, 21,978*l.* 9*s.* 11*d.* (*Treasury Order,* 20 June, 1662.) The emoluments of the Master of the Jewel-house were now so reduced, that Sir Gilbert Talbot obtained permission to show the Regalia to strangers for a fee; which proved so profitable, that Sir Gilbert, upon the death of his servant who showed the jewels, was offered 500 gold broad-pieces for the place. In this reign, May 9, 1671, Colonel Blood made his daring attempt to carry off "the crown, globe, and sceptre." The Regalia were then kept in a strong vaulted chamber of the Martin Tower, and were shown behind strong iron bars: through these, in 1815, a woman forced her hands and tore the royal crown to pieces. The Regalia were next shown at one view, by the light of six argand lamps, with powerful reflectors.

In 1842, a new Jewel House was built in the late Tudor style, south of the Martin Tower: where the Regalia are shown upon a pyramidal stand, enclosed within plate-glass; and over the whole is an open iron frame, or cage, of Tudor design, surmounted by a regal crown of iron.

The *Regalia* are:—*St. Edward's Crown,* or the ancient Imperial Crown, made *temp.* Charles II., to replace that said to have been worn by Edward the Confessor: and with which the Sovereign is crowned at the altar. This is the crown which Blood stole: the arches, flowers, and fillets are covered with large multi-coloured jewels; and the purple velvet cap is faced with ermine.

The *New State Crown* was made with the jewels of the crown of George IV., for the coronation of Queen Victoria. The cap is of purple velvet; the nearly pointed arches are covered with diamonds, and support a mound and Maltese cross, also of brilliants (the mound was originally one stone, an aqua-marine); in the cross are 3 large pearls, the "inestimable sapphire," nearly 2 inches square, and the heart-shaped ruby, said to have been worn by the Black Prince, and presented to him by John King of Portugal. It has also an emerald 7 inches round; and in the front is a large Jerusalem cross, entirely fronted with brilliants. The four largest diamonds in the crown are valued at 40,000*l.*; the whole crown is estimated at 111,900*l.*: it weighs only 19 oz. 10 dwts.[*] There are correct woodcuts of the crown, by S. Williams, in Britton's *Dictionary of Architecture*, and Sharp's *Peerage*. Haydon, in his *Autobiography* (1830), vol. ii. p. 236, has this odd entry:

"The Crown at the Coronation was not bought, but borrowed. Rundell's price was 70,000*l.*; and Lord Liverpool told the King he could not sanction such an expenditure. Rundell charged 7000*l.* for the loan; and as some time elapsed before it was decided whether the crown should be bought or not, Rundell charged 3000*l.* or 4000*l.* more for the interval."

The Prince of Wales's Crown, of pure gold, plain, without jewels: it is placed upon a velvet cushion, in the House of Lords, before the seat of the Heir Apparent, when Her Majesty opens or prorogues Parliament; for which occasions it is conveyed with the imperial crown of the sovereign from the Tower, by the Keeper of the Jewel-office, attended by warders, in a coach.

The Queen Consort's Crown, of gold, set with diamonds, pearls, and other jewels; made for the queen of William III.

The Queen's Diadem, or Circlet of Gold, made for the coronation of Maria d'Este, consort of James II., at the cost of 111,000*l.* (*Sandford*): it is set with diamonds, and surmounted with a string of pearls.

St. Edward's Staff, of beaten gold, 4 feet 7 inches in length; surmounted by an orb and cross, and shod with a steel spike; the orb is said to contain a fragment of the true Cross. The staff weighs 9 lbs.

The Royal Sceptre, or Sceptre with the Cross, of gold: the pommel is set with rubies, emeralds, and diamonds; the *fleurs-de-lis* have been replaced by the rose, shamrock, and thistle, in gold; and the cross is covered with jewels, and has a large centre table-diamond.

The Rod of Equity, or Sceptre with the Dove, of gold, 3 feet 7 inches long, is set with diamonds, &c., and is surmounted with an orb, banded with rare diamonds, supporting a Jerusalem cross, on which is a gold dove with expanded wings.

The Queen's Sceptre and Cross, ornamented with large diamonds; made for the coronation of Mary, Queen of William III.

The Queen's Ivory Sceptre, made for Maria d'Este, mounted in gold, and bearing a golden cross, and a dove of white onyx: it is sometimes miscalled Queen Anne Boleyn's.

An ancient Sceptre, found behind the wainscoting of the old Jewel-office in 1814: it is set with jewels, and is supposed to have belonged to Mary, Queen of William III.

The Orb, of gold, 6 inches in diameter; the bands are set with precious stones and roses of diamonds, and edged with pearls; a very large amethyst supports the gold cross, set with diamonds, &c.

The Queen's Orb, resembling the former, but of smaller dimensions.

The Sword of Mercy, or Curtana, of steel, but pointless; ornamented with gold.

The Swords of Justice, Ecclesiastical and Temporal.

The Armillæ, or Coronation Bracelets, of gold, chased with the rose, fleur-de-lis, and harp, and edged with pearls.

The Royal Spurs, of curiously wrought gold: they are used at the coronation of king or queen.

[*] The State Crown of Charles I., found in the upper Jewel-house, contained 7 lbs. 7 oz. of gold: in one of the *fleur-de-lis* was "a picture of the Virgin Mary."

The Ampulla, of pure gold, in the form of an eagle; is used at coronations for the holy oil, which is poured from the beak into

The Gold Anointing Spoon, supposed to be the only relic of the ancient Regalia; its date is about the 12th century. The Ampulla is said to have been brought from Sens Abbey, in France, by Thomas à Becket.

The Gold Saltcellar of State, set with jewels, and chased with grotesque figures, is in the form of a round castle, and has been miscalled "a Model of the White Tower;" it has a central turret, and four at the angles, the tops of which are removed for the salt; around the base are curious figures. It was presented to the crown by the City of Exeter, and was last used at the coronation banquet of George IV.

The Baptismal Font, silver-gilt, elaborately chased, and formerly used at the christening of the Royal Family, but superseded by a new font of picturesque design. A large *Silver Wine Fountain*, presented by the Corporation of Plymouth to Charles II.; 12 *Golden Saltcellars*, chased; two massive gold "Coronation Tankards;" the Banqueting Dish, Gold Spoons, and other Coronation Plate. Also, a Service of Sacramental Plate, one dish bearing a fine *alto relievo* of the Last Supper; used at Coronations, and in the chapel of St. Peter in the Tower.

Admission daily (Sundays excepted), to the *Armouries*, 6d. each person; and to see the *Regalia*, 6d. each; in parties of twelve, conducted by a warder, every half-hour, from 12 to 4 o'clock inclusive.

TOWER HILL

Is described by Hatton (1708) as "a spacious place extending round the west and north parts of the Tower, where are many good new buildings, mostly inhabited by gentry and merchants. Upon this hill such persons as are committed to the Tower and found guilty of high treason are commonly executed. And Stow says the scaffolds were built at the charge of the City, but in the reign of Edward IV. the same was erected at the charge of the King's officers; and that many controversies have been between the City and Lieutenant of the Tower touching their liberties." A century previous the spot was noted for its salubrity:

> "The Tower Hill,
> Of all the places London can afford,
> Hath sweetest ayre."—Haughton's *Englishmen for my Money*, 1616, 4to.

The "bounds" of the Tower Liberties are perambulated triennially, when, after service in the church of St. Peter, a procession is formed upon the parade: including a headsman, bearing the axe of execution; a painter to mark the bounds; yeomen warders, with halbards; the Deputy Lieutenant and other officers of the Tower, &c.: when the boundary-stations are painted with a red "broad arrow" upon a white ground, while the chaplain of St. Peter's repeats, "Cursed be he who removeth his neighbour's landmark." Another old custom of lighting a bonfire on Tower Hill on Nov. 5th was suppressed in 1854.

Lady Raleigh lived on Tower Hill after she had been forbidden to lodge with her husband in the Tower. William Penn was born, April 14th, 1644, in a court on the east side of Tower Hill. At the Bull public-house died, April 14th, 1685, Otway the poet, it is said of hunger. "In a by cutler's shop of Tower Hill," says Sir Henry Wotton, "Felton bought a tenpenny knife (so cheap was the instrument of this great attempt)," with which he assassinated the Duke of Buckingham.

Postern-row, with a few posts set across the footpath (opposite about the middle of the Tower moat), denotes the site of the Postern-gate, at the south-eastern termination of the City Wall. Here is the rendezvous for enlisting sailors and soldiers, which formerly had its press-gangs. The shops display odd admixtures of marine stores, pea-jackets and straw-hats, "rope, hour-glasses, Gunter's scales, and dog-biscuits." *The Place of Execution*, on Great Tower Hill, is shown in the old plan of the Tower at page 726: the space eastward is *Little Tower Hill*.

Notable Persons Executed on Tower Hill.—June 22, 1535, Bishop Fisher. July 6, 1535, Sir Thomas More. July 28, 1540, Cromwell, Earl of Essex. May 27, 1541, Margaret Pole, Countess of Shrewsbury. Jan. 20, 1547, Earl of Surrey, the poet. March 20, 1549, Thomas Lord Seymour of Sudeley, by order of his brother, the Protector Somerset, who was beheaded Jan. 22, 1552. Feb. 12, 1553-4, Lord Guildford Dudley. April 11, 1554, Sir Thomas Wyatt. May 12, 1641, Earl of Strafford. Jan. 10, 1644-5, Archbishop Laud. Dec. 29, 1680, William Viscount Stafford, "insisting on his innocence to the very last." Dec. 7, 1683, Algernon Sydney. July 15, 1685, the Duke of Monmouth. Feb. 24, 1716, Earl of Derwentwater and Lord Kenmuir. Aug. 18, 1746, Lords Kilmarnock and Balmerino. Dec. 8, 1746, Mr. Radcliffe, who had been, with his brother Lord Derwentwater, convicted of treason in the Rebellion of 1715, when Derwentwater was executed; but Radcliffe escaped, and was identified by the barber who, 31 years before, had shaved him in the Tower. The late Chamberlain Clark, who died in 1831, aged 92, well remembered (his father then residing in the Minories) seeing the glittering of the executioner's axe in the sun as it fell upon Mr. Radcliffe's neck. April 9, 1747, Simon Lord Lovat, the last beheading in England, and the last execution upon Tower Hill, when a scaffolding built near Barking-alley fell with nearly 1000 persons on it, and 12 were killed.

On the west side of Tower Hill is *Great Tower-street:* No. 48, on the south side, is the *Czar's Head*, built upon the site of a former tavern, where Peter the Great (Czar of Muscovy) and his companions, after their day's work, used to meet, to smoke pipes and drink beer and brandy. In *Little Tower-street*, No. 12, was Watts's Academy, where Thomson was tutor when he wrote his *Summer*.

At the south-west corner of the Hill is *Tower Dock*, where Sir Walter Raleigh, disguised, embarked in a boat for Tilbury; but being betrayed, he was arrested on the Thames, and committed to the Tower.

TOWER ROYAL,

A short street or lane between St. Antholin's Church, Watling-street, and the south end of St. Thomas Apostle, was removed in 1853-4, in forming New Cannon-street West. It occupied the site of a building stated by Stow to have anciently belonged to the kings of England, as early as Stephen; but it was subsequently discastled, and held as a tenement by one Simon of Beauvais, surgeon to Edward I. Mr. Hudson Turner states it to be invariably called in early records *la Real, la Riole*, or *la Ryle* or *Ryole*, but not a tower; and he could not find it occupied by royalty until Edward III., in 1331, granted it to his Queen Philippa as a depository for her wardrobe; by whom *la Real* was externally repaired, if not rebuilt. In 1370, Edward bestowed it upon the canons of St. Stephen's, Westminster; but it reverted to the Crown, and was called "the Queen's Wardrobe" in the reign of Richard II. It was a place of strength; and the king's mother fled here for shelter when Wat Tyler had seized the Tower of London. Leon III., King of Armenia, when driven from his kingdom by the Turks, was lodged and entertained in Tower Royal by Richard II., in 1386. It was granted by Richard III. to the first Duke of Norfolk of the Howard family, as entered in that king's ledger-book. In Stow's time, Tower Royal had become stabling for the king's horses, and was let in tenements: the whole was destroyed in the Great Fire of 1666. In removing the modern houses upon the site, in 1852, were found the remains of a Roman villa: the earth was interspersed with horns, bones, teeth of goats and oxen; tusks of boars; fragments of flanged tiles, scored flue-tiles, amphorae, mortaria, urns, glass vessels, and Samian pottery. Some of these relics are engraved in the *Illustrated London News*, No. 554.

TREASURY (THE),

And other Government Offices, Whitehall, occupy a portion of the site of the old palace. To make way for the north wing, the last portion of old York House was taken down in 1846: it had been refronted, but the Tudor doorway was ancient. The principal Treasury building, however, faces the parade-ground, St. James's Park: it was built by Kent, in 1733; it consists of three stories, Tuscan, Doric, and Ionic. The Whitehall front consists of the Treasury, Board of Trade, and Privy Council Offices; designed by Barry, R.A., in 1846-8, partly in place of Sir John Soane's façade (the centre and south wing), decorated with three-quarter columns from those of the Campo Vaccino at Rome. Soane's exterior, exposed to the criticism of every passenger, was much censured; "whilst the interior, in which the skill and taste of the architect is most manifest, and particularly the Council Chamber, is but little seen, and known only to a few persons." (Britton.) Barry's design consists of a long series of attached Corinthian columns on rusticated piers, and carrying a highly-enriched entablature and frieze; the attics have carved drops of fruit and flowers, and the balustrade carries urn-shaped vases: the whole facade is 296 feet long. The Council Office occupies the site of the old Tennis-court.

At the Cockpit died General Monk, Duke of Albemarle, 4th Jan. 1670; and in the same month his duchess, Nan Clarges. Queen Anne, when Princess of Denmark, fled down the back stairs, in 1688, to join her father's enemies, Lord Dorset and Bishop Compton riding on each side of the hackney-coach as an escort. Hatton, in 1708, describes the Treasury Office kept at the Cockpit, "where the Lord High Treasurer sits to receive petitions, and give orders, warrants, &c." Here, March 8, 1711, Guiscard attempted to stab with a penknife Harley, Earl of Oxford, but was struck down by the swords of Lord Paulet and Mr. St. John. The Cockpit itself occupied nearly the site of the present Board of Trade Office, and it existed early in the present century: the King's speech was read "at the Cockpit" on the day before it was delivered at the opening of the session of Parliament; and the discontinuance of this practice was much complained of by the Opposition. The term "Given at the Cockpit at Westminster" was in use within the writer's recollection. The Lord High Treasurer formerly carried a staff of office (see the portrait of the great Lord Burghley); and he sat in a needlework chair, which is preserved at the Office of the Comptroller of the Exchequer, Whitehall-yard. "The sovereign occasionally presided at the Board of Treasury until the accession of George III.; and the royal throne still remains at the head of the table." (Notes, by F. S. Thomas, Record Office.) The Board of Treasury sits daily, but has long ceased to manage the revenue. An interesting series of Treasury Minutes, from 1667 to 1834, is appended to the "Seventh Report of the Deputy-Keeper of the Public Records."

TRINITY HOUSE (THE),

On the north side of Tower Hill, was built by Samuel Wyatt, 1793-5, for the ancient guild founded by Sir Thomas Spert, commander of the great ship Harry Grace de Dieu, and Comptroller of the Navy to King Henry VIII., and incorporated 1515. It has in charge the light-houses and sea-marks, and the licensing of pilots, tonnage, ballastage, beaconage, &c., producing about 300,000l. a-year: the net revenue, about one-fourth, is principally expended in maintaining poor disabled seamen and their widows and orphans, by pensions, in the Corporation hospitals at Deptford-Strond; which the Master, Deputy-Master, and Brethren visit in their state-yacht, in grand procession, on

Trinity Monday. The Master, Prince Albert, succeeded the late Duke of Wellington in 1852. The Trinity House is of the Ionic order ; upon its principal front are sculptured the arms of the Corporation, medallions of George III. and Queen Charlotte; genii with nautical instruments; the four principal lighthouses on the coast, &c. The interior has busts of Vincent, Nelson, Howe, and Duncan; W. Pitt and Capt. J. Cotton, by Chantrey; George III., by Turnerelli, &c. The Courtroom is decorated with impersonations of the Thames, Medway, Severn, and Humber ; and among the pictures is a large painting, 20 feet long, by Gainsborough, of the Elder Brethren of the Trinity House. In the Board-room are portraits of James I. and II., Elizabeth, Anne of Denmark, Earl Craven, Sir Francis Drake, Sir J. Leake, and General Monk. The Museum is noticed at page 545. The arms of the Corporation are a cross between four ships under sail.

The present is the *third* House built for the Corporation ; the first was destroyed in the Great Fire of 1666. Pepys records: "Sept. 4, I after supper walked in the dark down to Tower-street, and there saw it all on fire; at the Trinity House on that side, and the Dolphin Tavern on this side." The second House was erected in Water-lane in 1671, and is described by Hatton as "a stately building of brick and stone, and adorned with ten bustos:" the house, of fine red brick, in part remains.

TYBURN AND "TYBURN TREE."

Tyburn was anciently a manor and village west of London, on the *Tybourn* or brook, subsequently the West*bourn*, the western boundary of the district, now incorporated in the parish of Paddington. This stream (within memory a favourite resort of anglers) is shown descending from the high ground about Hampstead in the maps by Saxton, 1579; Speede, 1610; Seller, 1733; in Morden's and Seales's, and in Rocque's surveys. Upon its bank was the place of execution for criminals convicted in London and Middlesex as early as 1330, when Roger de Mortimer was "drawn and hanged" at "the Elms," described by Holinshed as "now Tiborne;" and Elms-lane, Bayswater, points out to this day where the fatal elm grew, and the gentle Tiborne ran :

> " Then fatal carts through Holborn seldom went,
> And Tyburn with few pilgrims was content."—Oldham's *Satire*, 1682.

Elms-lane is the first opening on the right hand after getting into the Uxbridge-road from the Grand-Junction-road, opposite the head of the Serpentine; the Serpentine itself being formed in the bed of the ancient stream, first called Tybourn, then Westbourn; then Ranelagh Sewer; while the stream which crossed Oxford-street, west of Stratford-place, first bore the name of Eyebourn, then Tybourn, then King's Scholars' Pond.—Robins's *Paddington*, 1853, page 8.

The gallows, "Tyburn-tree," was a triangle upon three legs, and is thus described in the 16th and 17th centuries. If Mr. Robins's location of the gibbet be correct, it was subsequently changed; for in the lease of the house No. 49 Connaught-square, the gallows is stated to have stood upon that spot. Smith (*Hist. St. Mary-le-Bone*) states it to have been for many years a standing fixture on a small eminence at the corner of the Edgware-road, near the turnpike, on the identical spot where a tool-house was subsequently erected by the Uxbridge-road Trust. Beneath this place lie the bones of Bradshaw, Ireton, and other regicides, which were taken from their graves after the Restoration, and buried under the gallows. It subsequently consisted of two uprights and a cross-beam, erected on the morning of execution across the Edgware-road, opposite the house at the corner of Upper Bryanstone-street and the Edgware-road, wherein the gallows was deposited after being used; and this house had curious iron balconies to the windows of the first and second floors, where the sheriffs attended the executions. After the place of execution was changed to Newgate in 1783, the gallows was bought by a carpenter, and made into stands for beer-butts in the cellars of the Carpenters' Arms public-house, hard by.

Around the gibbet ("the fatal retreat for the unfortunate brave") were erected open galleries like a race-course stand, wherein seats were let to spectators at executions: the key of one of them was kept by Mammy Douglas, "the Tyburn pew-opener." In 1758, when Dr. Henesey was to have been executed for treason, the prices of seats rose to 2s. and 2s. 6d.; but the doctor being "most provokingly reprieved," a riot ensued, and most of the seats were destroyed. The criminals were conveyed thither from Newgate:

> "thief and parson in a Tyburn cart."—*Prologue by Dryden*, 1682.

The oldest existing representation of the Tyburn gallows is in a German print in the *Crowle Pennant*, in the British Museum; wherein Henrietta-Maria, queen of Charles I., is kneeling in penance beneath the triple-tree: it is moonlight; the confessor is seated in the royal coach, drawn by six horses; and at the coach-door is a servant bearing a torch. The "pore queene," it is stated, walked afoot (some say barefoot) from St. James's to Tyburn, to do homage to the saintship of some recently executed papists: but this is denied by the Marshal de Bassompierre; and the above print is of later date than 1628, the year of the reputed pilgrimage.

Memorable Executions at Tyburn.—1330 (4th Edw. III.), Roger de Mortimer, for treason; 1388 (12th Richard II.), Judge Tresilian and Sir N. Brembre, treason; 1449 (14th Hen. VII.), Perkin Warbeck was executed here for plotting his escape from the Tower; 1534 (24th Hen. VIII.), the Holy Maid of Kent and her confederates; 1535, the last Prior of the Carthusian Monastery (Charter House); Robert Southwell, Elizabethan sacred poet; 1615, Mrs. Turner, hanged in a yellow-starched ruff, for the poisoning of Sir Thomas Overbury; 1628, John Felton, assassin of Villiers, Duke of Buckingham; 1660-1 (Jan. 30), the first anniversary of the execution of Charles I. after the Restoration: the disinterred bodies of Oliver Cromwell, Ireton, and Bradshaw hung in their shrouds and cerecloths at each angle of Tyburn gallows till sunset, when they were taken down and beheaded, and the bodies buried under the gallows, the heads being set on Westminster Hall; 1660-62, five persons who had signed the death-warrant of Charles I.; 1684, Sir Thomas Armstrong (Rye House Plot); 1705, John Smith, a burglar, having hung above a quarter of an hour, when a reprieve arrived, he was cut down, and being let blood, came to himself (*Hatton*, 1708). 1724, Jack Sheppard, housebreaker; 1725, Jonathan Wild, thief and thief-taker; 1726, Catherine Hayes, for the murder of her husband: she was burnt alive, for the indignant mob would not suffer the hangman to strangle her, as usual, before the fire was kindled. 1760, Earl Ferrers, for the murder of his steward: he rode from the Tower, wearing his wedding-clothes, in his landau drawn by six horses: he was indulged with a silken rope, and "the drop" was first used instead of the cart; the executioners fought for the rope, and the mob tore the black cloth from the scaffold as relics; the landau stood in a coach-house at Acton until it fell to pieces; and the bill for the silken rope has been preserved. 1767, Mrs. Brownrigg, for murder; 1774, John Rann (Sixteen-Stringed Jack), highwayman; 1775, the two Perraus, for forgery; 1777, Rev. Dr. Dodd, forgery; 1779, Rev. James Hackman, assassination of Miss Reay: he was taken from Newgate in a mourning-coach. 1783, Ryland, the engraver, for forgery. 1783, John Austin, the last person executed at Tyburn.

The road between St. Giles's Pound and Tyburn gallows was first called *Tyburn-road*, now *Oxford-street;* the lane leading from which to Piccadilly was called *Tyburn-lane*, now *Park-lane*. The original Turnpike-gate stood close to St. Giles's Pound; then at Tyburn, removed in 1825; then at Winchester-row; next at Pine-apple-place; and next at Kilburn. Strange have been the mutations in which the rural Tybourn "welled forth away" through pleasant fields to the Town, there became linked with the crimes of centuries, and lost in a murky sewer; but left its name to *Tyburnia*, the newly-built city of palaces northwest of Hyde Park. (See PADDINGTON, page 563.)

UNIVERSITY OF LONDON (THE),

omerset House, was instituted Nov. 28, 1836, for "rendering acade-
iical honours accessible, without distinction, to every class and every
enomination." The University consists of a chancellor, vice-chancel-
ir, and senate; and graduates. It is solely an examining body, and
onfers degrees on the graduates of University College and King's
iollege, London; and the colleges not belonging to the other univer-
.ties; besides all the medical schools in the empire, and most of the
illeges of the Roman Catholics, Baptists, Independents, and Wes-
iyans. The degrees are conferred, and the honours bestowed, in
ublic; and the senate first met for this purpose on May 1, 1850, in
ie large hall of King's College, Somerset House; the Earl of Burling-
in, Chancellor of the University, presiding.

VAUXHALL GARDENS,

he oldest existing place of public amusement in the metropolis, is
imed from its site in the manor of Fulke's Hall, or Faukeshall, from
ulke de Breauté, its possessor *temp.* King John. The manor-house,
bsequently called Copped or Copt Hall, was the prison-house of Ara-
illa Stuart. The tradition that it belonged to Guido or Guy Fawkes
ily rests upon the coincidence of names. The estate, in the manors of
ambeth and Kennington, belonged to the family of Fauxe, or Vaux, in
ie reigns of Elizabeth and James I.; and in 1615 it was held by Jane
aux, widow, erroneously supposed the relict of Guy Fawkes. The con-
iirators, however, hired a house at Lambeth for storing their powder,
c., in 1604, which has strengthened the tradition: this house was burnt
iwn by accident in 1635; its site is uncertain.

Vauxhall Gardens were first laid out about 1661. Evelyn records:
2 July, 1661, I went to see the *New Spring Gardens** at Lambeth, a
etty contrived plantation;" and Baltshazar Monconys, early in the
ign of Charles II., describes the Gardens well frequented in 1663.

Sir Samuel Morland "built a fine room at *Vaux-hall* anno 1667, the inside
of looking-glass, and fountains very pleasant to behold, which is much visited
strangers; it stands in the middle of the Garden." (Mr. Bray thought this
om to have been erected by Morland for the entertainment of Charles II. when
visited this place with his ladies.) "Without the *New Spring Garden* is the
mainder of a kind of horn-work, belonging to the lines of communication made
out 1643-4." (Aubrey's *Surrey,* vol. i. pp. 12, 13.)

A large mound of earth, said to have been thrown up for defence,
ill remains near the firework-shed. North of the Gardens is believed
have stood a Roman fort or camp; and Roman pottery has been
und here. Canute's Trench has been traced through the Gardens
its influx into the Thames (*Maitland*).

Morland's room is believed to have stood where the or-
estra was afterwards built; and in 1794 a leaden pump
as removed bearing Sir Samuel's mark:

<table>
<tr><td>1</td><td>S</td><td>6</td></tr>
<tr><td>9</td><td>M</td><td>4</td></tr>
</table>

In a plan dated 1681 the place is named Spring Garden, and "marked
planted with trees and laid out in walks." Pepys's *Diary* has en-
ies in 1665-8 of his visits to *Fox-hall* and the Spring Garden; and
" the humours of the citizens, pulling off cherries, and God knows
hat;" "to hear the nightingale and the birds, and here fiddlers, and
ere a harp, and here a Jew's trump; and here laughing, and there
ie people walking, is mighty diverting." Pepys also tells of "supper
an arbour," ladies walking " with their masks on," &c.; and—

* To distinguish it from Spring Garden, Charing Cross (see page 678).

"July 27, 1688. So over the water, with my wife and Deb, and Mercer, to Spring Garden, and there eat and walked; and observed how rude some of the young gallants of the town are become, to go into people's arbors where there are not men, and almost force the women, which troubled me to see the confidence of the vice of the age; and so we away by water with much pleasure home."

Wycherley refers to a cheesecake and a syllabub at New Spring Garden; and Tom Brown (in 1700) speaks of the close walks, and of the little wildernesses, which "are so intricate, that the most experienced mothers have often lost themselves in looking for their daughters." And in the *Spectator*, No. 383 (May 20, 1712), Addison describes his going with Sir Roger de Coverley on the water from the Temple Stairs to Spring Garden, "which is exquisitely pleasant at this time of year:" a mask tapped Sir Roger upon the shoulder, and invited him to drink a bottle of mead with her. The usual supper of that period was "a glass of Burton ale, and a slice of hung beef."

In 1728, Spring Gardens were leased by Elizabeth Masters, for 30 years, to Jonathan Tyers, of Denbies, Surrey, at the yearly rent of 250*l*. Tyers's lease enumerates the Dark Room, Ham Room, Milk-house, Pantry-room; and among the arbours, covered and paved with tiles, are the names of Checker, King's Head, Dragon, Oak, Royal Arbour, York, Queen's Head, Royal George, Ship, Globe, Phœnix, Swan, Eagle, and the Barge. The hatch at the Water-gate is of Tyers's time.

The Gardens were opened by Tyers, June 7, 1732, with a *Ridotto al fresco*. Frederick Prince of Wales was present, and the company wore masks, dominoes, and lawyers' gowns. The admission was one guinea: 400 persons were present; and there were 100 Foot-Guards posted round the Gardens to keep order. The admission-ticket was designed by the younger Laguerre.

The author of *A Touch at the Times, or a Trip to Vauxhall*, 1737,

"Sail'd triumphant on the liquid way,
To hear the fiddlers of Spring Garden play."

Tyers set up an organ in the orchestra; and in the garden, in 1738, a fine statue of Handel, as Orpheus playing a lyre, by Roubiliac, his first work in England.[*] Here was also a statue of Milton, by Roubiliac, cast in lead, and painted stone-colour. The season of 1739 was for three months, and the admission only by silver tickets, at 25*s*. each, to admit two persons. These silver tickets were struck after designs by Hogarth: the obverse bore the number, name of the holder, and date; and the reverse a figure of Euterpe, Erato, or Thalia.

Hogarth, who was then lodging in Lambeth-terrace,[†] suggested to Tyers the embellishment of the Gardens with paintings; in acknowledgment of which Tyers presented Hogarth with a *Gold Ticket* of perpetual admission: it bears on its obverse, "Hogarth," and beneath it, "*In perpetuam beneficii memoriam;*" on the reverse are two figures surrounded with the motto, "*Virtus voluptas felices una.*" This ticket (for the admission of six persons or "one coach") was last used in the season of 1836: it is now possessed by Mr. Frederick Gye, jun., who purchased it for 20*l*. Hogarth designed for the pavilions in the Gardens the Four Parts of the Day, which Hayman copied; besides other pictures. In 1745, Tyers added vocal to his instrumental music, and Dr. Arne composed ballads, duets, &c.; Mrs. Arne, Lowe, and the elder Reinhold were singers.

In England's *Gazetteer*, 1751, the entertainments are described as "the sweet song of numbers of nightingales, in concert with the best

* This statue was sold, in 1854, to the Sacred Harmonic Society for 200*l*., and is now in their committee-room at Exeter Hall, Strand.
† The house which Hogarth occupied is still shown; and a vine is pointed out which he planted.—Allan Cunningham, *Lives of British Painters, &c.*, 1829.

and of musick in England. Here are fine pavilions, shady groves, and most delightful walks illuminated with above 1000 lamps."

"At Vauxhall the artificial ruins are repaired; the cascade is made to spout with several additional streams of block-tin; and they have touched up all the pictures which were damaged last season by the fingering of those curious connoisseurs who could not be satisfied without feeling whether the figures were alive."—*Connoisseur*, May 15, 1755.

Goldsmith thus describes the Vauxhall of about 1760:

"The illuminations began before we arrived; and I must confess that upon entering the Gardens I found every sense overpaid with more than expected pleasure: the lights every where glimmering through scarcely moving trees; the full-bodied concert bursting on the stillness of night; the natural concert of the birds in the more retired part of the grove, vieing with that which was formed by art; the company gaily dressed, looking satisfied, and the tables spread with various delicacies,—all conspired to fill my imagination with the visionary happiness of the Arabian lawgiver, and lifted me into an ecstasy of admiration. ' Head of Confucius,' cried I to my friend, ' this is fine! This unites rural beauty with courtly magnificence."—*Citizen of the World*, Letter lxxi.

"The last gay picture in Goldsmith's life is of himself and Sir Joshua (Reynolds) at Vauxhall. And not the least memorable figures in that sauntering crowd,—though it numbered princes and ambassadors then; and on its tide and current of fashion floated all the beauty of the time; and through its lighted avenues of trees glided cabinet ministers and their daughters, royal dukes and their wives, agreeable ' young ladies and gentlemen of eighty-two,' and all the red-heeled macaronies,—were those of the President and the Ancient History Professor of the Royal Academy."—*Forster's Goldsmith*, p. 676.

Miss Burney also lays scenes of her *Evelina* and *Cecilia* in Vauxhall Gardens. Tyers subsequently bought the property: he died in 1767: so great was the delight he took in this place, that, possessing his faculties to the last, he caused himself to be carried into the Gardens a few hours before his death, to take a last look at them." They were called Spring Garden until 1785; and the license, every season, is to this day obtained for "Spring Garden, Vauxhall." The property remained with Tyers's family until it was sold in 1822, for 28,000*l.*, to Bish, Gye, and Hughes (the London Wine Company), who retained it till 1840. The most profitable season was in 1823; 133,279 visitors, 9,590*l.* receipts: the greatest number of persons in one night was Aug. 2, 1833, the second night of the revival of the shilling admission, when 20,137 persons paid for admission. In July 1841, the estate (about 11 acres), with its buildings, timber, covered walks, &c., was offered for sale by auction, but bought in at 20,200*l.* The estate is held under the Duchy of Cornwall; and subject only to an annual quit-rent of *l.* 3*s.* 7*d.*, and 5*s* a year for tithe.

The Gardens are well described in the *Ambulator*, 12th edition, 1820; where the paintings in the supper-pavilions, by Hogarth and Hayman, are enumerated. The Gardens have since been rented by various *entrepreneurs*. Their arrangement has been little altered from Tyers's plan, as may be seen by the old views; one of the earliest, attached to *A Trip to Vauxhall*, 1737. Tyers's rustic music-house was in 1758 replaced by a Gothic orchestra, built by a carpenter named Maidman, with niches, ornaments, &c. in compo'. The general plan is a quadangular grove, a colonnade, two semicircular sweeps of pavilions, a rotunda, detached theatre, &c.; octagon temples, set scenes, machinery, sculpture, a firework tower, myriads of cut-glass lamps, &c. The earliest lamps resembled the street-lamps of the last century.

A Vauxhall supper usually consisted of

" Lilliput chickens boil'd ;
Bucellas warm, from Vauxhall ice,
And hams that flit in airy slice,
And salads scarcely soil'd."—*Lond. Mag.* Sept. 1824.

To which should be added arrack-punch and "wax-lights." The old punch-bowls, plates, and mugs, bore a representation of the orchestra.

In 1827 was produced in the Gardens, by Mr. Farley, of Covent Garden Theatre, a representation of the Battle of Waterloo, with set scenes of La Belle Alliance, the wood and château of Hougomont; also, horse and foot soldiers, artillery, ammunition-wagons, &c.

Vauxhall Gardens were open from 1732 to 1840 without intermission; in the latter year they were closed; but were opened in 1841 by Mitchell and Andrews, of Bond-street, with great success, and this year, six summer fêtes were got up here by Bunn. The price of admission to the gardens was 1s. until 1792, except on particular nights, as on the celebration of the fiftieth anniversary, when it was 10s. 6d. After 1792 the admission was raised to 2s., including tea and coffee; in 1809 to 3s. 6d.; in 1850 reduced to 1s.; and since various. At the Vittoria Fête, July 1814 (admission one guinea), 1350 visitors dined in the rotunda, the Duke of York presiding; there were also present the Dukes of Clarence, Kent, Sussex, and Gloucester; the Princess of Wales, and the Duchess of York. The fireworks were by Colonel Congreve.

At the sale of the movable property, Oct. 1841, twenty-four pictures by Hogarth and Hayman produced but small sums: they had mostly been upon the premises since 1742; the canvass was nailed to boards, and much obscured by dirt. By Hogarth: Drunken Man, 4l. 4s.; a Woman pulling out an Old Man's grey hairs, 3l. 3s.; Jobson and Nell in the *Devil to pay*, 4l. 4s.; the Happy Family, 3l. 15s.; Children at Play, 4l. 11s. 6d. By Hayman: Children Bird's-nesting, 5l. 10s.; Minstrels, 3l.; the Enraged Husband, 4l. 4s.; the Bridal Day, 6l. 6s.; Blindman's Buff, 3l. 8s.; Prince Henry and Falstaff, 7l.; Scene from the Rake's Progress, 9l. 15s.; Merry-making, 1l. 12s.; the Jealous Husband, 4l.; Card-party, 6l.; Children's Party, 4l. 15s.; Battledore and Shuttlecock, 1l. 10s.; the Doctor, 4l. 14s. 6d.; Cherry-bob, 2l. 15s.; the Storming of Seringapatam, 8l. 10s.; Neptune and Britannia, 8l. 15s. Four busts of Simpson, the celebrated Master of the Ceremonies, were sold for 10s.; and a bust of his royal shipmate, William IV., 19s.

Music.—Among the Vauxhall composers were Arne, Boyce, Carter, Mountain, Hook (organist upwards of 40 years), and Signor Storace. Male singers: Beard, Lowe, Webb, Dignum, Vernon, Incledon, Braham, Pyne, Sinclair, Tinney, Robinson, Bedford, and Sharp. Females: Miss Brent, Mrs. Wrighten, Mrs. Weischel (mother of Mrs. Billington), Mrs. Mountain, Signora Storace, Mrs. Crouch, Mrs. Bland, Miss Tryrer (afterwards Mrs. Liston), Miss Graddon, Miss Love, Miss Tunstall, &c. Italian operas were performed here in 1829. The band were the last to wear the semicircular or cocked hat:

> " By that high dome that trembling glows
> With lamps, cock'd hats, and shiv'ring bows,
> How many hearts are shook!
> A feather'd chorister is there,
> Warbling some tender, grove-like air,
> Compos'd by Mr. Hook."—*London Magazine*, Sept. 1824.

Fireworks were first occasionally exhibited at Vauxhall in 1798. In 1802 the first *Balloon* ascent took place here, by Garnerin and two companions. In 1836 Green ascended in his new " Vauxhall Balloon," constructed in the Gardens (see p. 23). Mr. John Fillinham, of Walworth, possesses a large collection of Vauxhall bills of entertainment, engravings, and other interesting records of the Gardens.

WALBROOK,

A narrow street named from the stream or brook which, rising on the north of Moorfields, entered the City *through the walls*, between Bishopsgate and Moorgate, and proceeded nearly along the line of the new street of that name; thence, according to Stow, across Lothbury, beneath the kitchen of Grocers' Hall and St. Mildred's Church, through

Bucklersbury, past the sign of the " Old Barge" (from Thames barges being rowed up there); and thence through the present Walbrook-street, under which it still runs as a sewer, and discharges itself, by a part of Elbow-lane, down Greenwich-lane, into the Thames at Dow-gate. The Walbrook was crossed by a bridge connecting Budge-row and Cannon-street, and several other bridges, but was vaulted over with brick, and its banks built upon, long since; so that in Stow's time the course of Walbrook was "hidden under ground, and thereby hardly known.' The brook was navigable not merely to Bucklersbury but as far as Coleman-street, where a Roman boat-hook has been found; and with it was found a coin of Alectus, who ruled in Britain towards the close of the third century. In forming Prince's-street, the work-men came upon the course of the brook, which the Romans had em-banked with wooden piles; and the bed was thickly strewn with coins, brass scales, styli, knives, tools, pottery, &c. In Walbrook was one of the three taverns in London licensed to sell sweet wines in the reign of Edward III. Walbrook gives name to the ward: at its north-east corner is *St. Stephen's Church*, described at page 160. Lower down, upon the brook, at Dowgate-hill, was the church of Allhallows the Less, destroyed in the Great Fire, and not rebuilt; but its burial-ground, with a solitary altar-tomb, remains. Nearly opposite London Stone, in June 1852, was unearthed part of the cloister of the church of St. Mary Bothaw, which stood near Walbrook bank at Dowgate, and was named Boat-haw from being near a yard where boat-building was carried on: here was interred Fitzalwin, first Mayor of London.

WAPPING,

A hamlet of Stepney, is now a long street extending from Lower East Smithfield, on the north bank of the Thames, to New Crane. It was commenced building in 1571, to secure the manor from the depredations of the river, which made the whole site a great wash; the commis-sioners of sewers rightly thinking that " the tenants would not fail being attentive to their lives and property." Stow calls it " Wapping in the Wose," or Wash.

Here was *Execution Dock*, " the usual place for hanging of pirates and sea-rovers, at the low-water mark, and there to remain till three tides had over-flowed them; but since the gallows being after removed farther off, a continual street or filthy strait passage, with alleys of small tenements or cottages built, inhabited by sailors' victuallers, along by the river of Thames almost to Rad-cliffe, a good mile from the Tower."—*Stow*.

To Wapping, in 1689, Lord Chancellor Jefferies fled, disguised as a sailor, but was there identified in a public-house by a scrivener whom he had terrified when he was Lord Chief Justice. Joseph Ames, author of the *Typographical Antiquities*, F.R.S., and Secretary to the Society of Antiquaries, was a ship-chandler at Wapping, where he died in 1758: ' he was a person of vast application and industry in collecting old printed books, prints, and other curiosities, both natural and artificial" (*Cole*). John Day, with whom originated " Fairlop Fair," in Hainault Forest, was a block and pump maker at Wapping. Here the first Fuchsia brought to England from the West Indies, being seen by Mr. Lee, the nurseryman, became, in the next flowering season, the parent of 300 fuchsia-plants, which Lee sold at one guinea each.

Wapping is noted, as in Stow's time, for its nautical signs, its ship and boat builders, rope-makers, biscuit-bakers and provision-dealers; mast, oar, and block makers; ship-chandlers and sail-makers: and the name *Wapping* was probably derived from the ship's rope called a *wapp;* or from *wapin-schaw*, a periodical exhibition of arms, which may for-merly have been held upon this open ground.

Among the thirty-six taverns and public-houses in Wapping High-street and Wapping Wall, are the signs of the Ship and Pilot, Ship and Star, Ship and Punch-bowl, Union Flag and Punch-bowl, the Gun, North American Sailor, Golden Anchor, Anchor and Hope, the Ship, Town of Ramsgate, Queen's Landing, Ship and Whale, the Three Mariners, and the Prospect of Whitby.

Between Nos. 224 and 225 is the entrance to the THAMES TUNNEL (see p. 712); and between 288 and 304 are Wapping Old Stairs:.

> " Your Molly has always been true, she declares,
> Since last time we parted at Wapping Old Stairs."—Dibdin's *Waterman.*

Many of the wood-built wharf and house fronts towards the river are quaint and old.

WATER-SUPPLY OF LONDON.

The earliest water-supply was derived from the Thames, by direct carriage, or from the bournes or streams which flowed through the town, but are now covered sewers. The water was laid from these springs in leaden pipes, as early as the reign of Henry III., to CONDUITS in various parts of the town (see p. 228), whence it was conveyed in buckets and carts: from Tyburn in 1236; from Highbury in 1438; from Hackney in 1535; from Hampstead in 1543; and from Hoxton in 1546. In 1581, Morice threw a jet of the Thames over old St. Magnus' steeple, before which " no such thing was known in England as this raising of water." Next year were formed London Bridge Waterworks, described at page 55. In 1613 was opened the NEW RIVER (see page 550), when commenced the modern systems of supply, now executed by seven companies.

1. The NEW RIVER COMPANY (see page 550).
2. The EAST LONDON WATER-WORKS, supplied from the river Lea, near Old Ford, on each side of which are two reservoirs, with an aqueduct or conduit under the river to connect them all. " The pressure requisite to drive the water through the mains in the district is given by a column of water in a vertical iron *stand-pipe,* open at the top, about 130 feet high, 5 feet in diameter at the bottom, and 3 feet 6 in. at the top; the water being kept at a suitable level in the pipe by the action of the pumps in the steam-engine, the first Cornish engine used for other than mining purposes."—Weale's *London,* p. 852.
3. The GRAND JUNCTION WATER-WORKS, first projected in 1798, works commenced 1811, and first supplied from the rivers Colne and Brent, and the Ruislip springs, by way of the Paddington Canal; but since 1820 supplied from the Thames. The present works are above Kew Bridge, where the water is pumped from the middle of the river to the filter-beds. The great Cornish steam-engine is the largest of the kind ever made: it raises 3257 gallons of water per minute in a standpipe nearly 220 feet high: and the main which brings the water to London is between 6 and 7 miles in length, and 30 inches diameter. The Company's storing-reservoir on Camden Hill, Bayswater, contains 6,000,000 gallons.
4. The WEST MIDDLESEX WATER-WORKS, commenced in 1806, pump their water from the Thames at Barnes into two subsiding reservoirs of 16 acres area, whence the water is forced through a mainpipe under the Thames, Hammersmith, and thence to the elevated reservoirs, one of which, on Primrose Hill, contains 4,750,000 gallons: some of the houses supplied by this Company are ten miles from the spot whence the water is forced.
5. The CHELSEA WATER-WORKS were originally founded in 1724, and early supplied the palace and government-offices. Their present works, 20 acres, are north-east of Chelsea Reach; where the water, drawn from the bed of the Thames, is pumped into subsiding reser-

voirs, and then into filter-beds: the Company have also two elevated reservoirs in the Green Park and Hyde Park.

6. The SOUTHWARK AND VAUXHALL WATER-WORKS, in Battersea Fields, are supplied from the Thames, and have two depositing reservoirs of 32,000,000 gallons, and two filtering reservoirs of 11,000,000 gallons: the two stand-pipes are each 150 feet high. Until the destruction of Old London Bridge, Southwark was supplied with water from ponds at St. Mary Overie's, and works under one of the southern arches of the bridge. This Company, with the Grand Junction, and West Middlesex, have also Works at Hampton, opened in 1855.

7. The LAMBETH WATER-WORKS are described at page 439.

Daily average supply of water by the above Companies in 1853:

	Gallons.	Houses.
New River	17,537,396	90,510
East London	11,990,989	63,142
Grand Junction	5,115,675	10,019
West Middlesex	5,000,606	34,376
Chelsea	5,632,000	22,725
Southwark and Vauxhall	8,501,837	40,046
Lambeth	5,603,000	25,583
	59,381,503	286,401

The *Hampstead Water-works*, first established under 35 Henry VIII. ap. 10, supply Kentish Town and Camden Town from springs and wells.

The daily supply of water to the metropolis, when 44,000,000 gallons, was nearly twice as much as would fill St. Paul's Cathedral; "a quantity which, large as it is, could be delivered in twenty-four hours by a brook nine feet wide and three feet deep, running at the rate of three feet per second, or little more than two miles per hour. * * * If the mains (supply-pipes) were allowed to flow into the area of St. James's Park, they would in the course of the twenty-four hours flood its entire space with a depth of 30 inches of water; and the whole annual supply would be quite sufficient to submerge the City (one mile square) 10 feet."—*Quarterly Review*, No. cxc.

Five of the seven Companies draw their water from the Thames, adjacent to the outpouring of all the common-sewers;" and although the removal of the works from the town, higher up the stream, with subsidence and filtration, have modified the evil, the best water, and the best means of supply, remain undecided. Artesian Wells, sunk through the London clay into the chalk, produce excellent water, but fail in dry weather, and are affected if a deeper well be sunk in the neighbourhood. (See ARTESIAN WELLS, p. 20.) The *deepest Well* in London, 522 ft., is stated to be that at Combe and Co.'s brewery, Long Acre. The well on the site of the Excise Office is 300 feet.—*The Builder*.

Within the Bank of England an Artesian well was completed in 1852: it is 330 feet deep, 100 feet being in the chalk: the water is raised to tanks of 50,000 gallons, in the roof, by the same steam-engine that prints the bank-notes, &c. With these tanks is connected a fountain, which throws a column of water 30 feet high, amongst the branches of two of the finest lime-trees in London.*

The YORK BUILDINGS WATER-WORKS, formed in 1691, leased to the New River Company in 1818, and abolished 1829, are described at p. 694.

* The fountain is placed on the site of the churchyard of St. Christopher-le-stocks. The last funeral which took place here was that of Jenkins, a Bank clerk, who was 7½ feet in height, and his outer coffin was 8 feet in length: he was permitted to be buried within the walls of the Bank, to prevent the possibility of disinterment, on account of his unusual height.

WATLING-STREET,

Commencing at the north-east corner of St. Paul's-churchyard, and formerly extending through Budge-row and Cannon-street, is considered to have been the principal street of Roman London, and "one of the four grand Roman ways in Britain;"[*] as well as a British road before the arrival of the Romans: "with the Britons it was a forest-lane or trackway; with the Romans it became a stratum, street, or raised road, constructed according to their well-known manners" (A. J. Kempe, *Archæologia*, xxvi. 467). This is corroborated by the discovery of British remains on the line, in Cannon-street. The Romans made it part of their grand route from the point of their invasion, through a portion of Kent and the north-eastern corner of Surrey, and thence from Stoney-street over the Thames to Dowgate, north of the river, by the present Watling-street, to Aldersgate; where, quitting the City, it ran along Goswell-street to the west of Islington, through Hagbush-lane (the road in part remains), to Verulamium, or St. Alban's. Dr. Stukeley, however, maintains that the old Watling-street did not enter London, but, in its course from Verulam, crossed the Oxford-road at Tyburn, and thence ran over part of Hyde Park, and by May Fair through St. James's Park, to the Wool-staple at Westminster, and crossed the Thames by Stanegate-ferry, across St. George's Fields, and south of the Lock Hospital, Kent-street, to Deptford and Blackheath. Stukeley adds: "as London increased, passengers went through the City by Cannon-street, Watling-street, and Holborn, this being a vicinal branch of Watling-street." Wren, however, considers it to have been the centre or Prætorian way of the old Roman station; the principal gate being at Eastcheap. In 1853, in excavating Budge-row, there was discovered a fragment of Roman wall.

"Watling-street crossed the Walbrook by a bridge at the junction of Cannon-street and Budge-row; and then branching off at London Stone, in Cannon-street, ran along the Langbourne to Aldgate; whilst a smaller road ran from the ferry at Dowgate towards Cripplegate, one of the three City gates during the Roman rule. Enough of remains of houses have been found in Budge-row and Watling-street to show that the rudiments of a street, in continuation of the line from Aldgate, existed on the west side of the brook."—*National Miscell.* No. 6.

This street, says Leland, was formerly called *Atheling* (or *Noble*) street, from being near the Old Change (see page 283), where the Mint formerly was; and afterwards, corruptly, *Watheling* and *Watling* street: but from this Stow dissents. By another, Watling is traced to the ancient British words, *gwaith*, work, and *lea*, legion, whence *gwaith-lea*, i.e. legion-work (*Gent. Mag.* 1796). Dr. Jamieson states it to have been "called by the Romans *Via Lactea* (Milky Way), from its fancied resemblance to a broad street, or causeway, being as it were paved with stars." Moxon, in his *Tutor to Astronomy*, 1670, describing the Milky Way, observes: "some, in a sporting manner, call it Watling-street; but why they call it so I cannot tell, except it be in regard to the narrowness it seemeth to have." The south side has been almost entirely taken down and rebuilt; and the narrowness of Watling-street has disappeared in the fine broad thoroughfare of Cannon-street West. Watling-street has been, since Stow's time, inhabited by "wealthy drapers, retailers of woollen cloths, both broad and narrow, of all sorts." Hatton describes it as "much inhabited by wholesale grocers, tobacconists, and other great dealers." Several of the new buildings on the south side of Cannon-street are the mansion-like warehouses of wholesale stationers.

[*] The Watling-street Thistle (*Eryngium campestre*) is named from this ancient road being its only known habitat in England.—Baker's *Northants. Gloss.* ii. 386.

WAX-WORK SHOWS.

The oldest Exhibition of Wax-work in England of which we have any record was that at *Westminster Abbey*, called "the Play of the Dead Volks," and "the Ragged Regiment." Of this collection we find the following account in a description of the Abbey, "its monuments and curiosities," "printed for J. Newbery, at the Bible and Sun, in St. Paul's Churchyard, 1754;"

"Over this chapel (Islip, otherwise St. Erasmus) is a chantry in which are two large wainscot presses full of the effigies of princes and others of high quality, buried in this Abbey. These effigies resembled the deceased as near as possible, and were wont to be exposed at the funerals of our princes and other great personages in open chariots, with their proper ensigns of royalty or honour appended. Those that are here laid up are in a sad mangled condition; some stripped, and others in tattered robes, but all maimed or broken. The most ancient are the least injured, by which it would seem as if the costliness of their clothes had occasioned this ravage; for the robes of Edward VI., which were once of crimson velvet, but now appear like leather, are left entire; but those of Q. Elizabeth and K. James the First are entirely stript, as are all the rest, of every thing of value. In two handsome wainscot presses are the effigies of K. William and Q. Mary, and Q. Anne, in good condition, and greatly admired by every eye that beholds them." The figure of Cromwell is not here mentioned; but in the account of his lying-in-state, the effigies is described as made to the life, in wax, apparelled in velvet, gold lace, and ermine. This effigies was laid upon the bed-of-state, and carried upon the hearse in the funeral procession; both were then deposited in Westminster Abbey: but at the Restoration, the hearse was broken in pieces, and the effigies was destroyed after hanging from a window at Whitehall.

In the *Picture of London*, 1806, the collection is described as "a variety of figures in wax, in cases with glass doors, which are shown as curious to the stranger;" their exhibition was continued until 1839.

The NEW EXCHANGE, Strand, was also noted for its Wax-work shows.

MRS. SALMON'S WAX-WORK, in Fleet-street, is described at p. 308. The minor exhibitions of wax-work are too numerous to mention; but we may instance a collection of figures shown at the Queen's Bazaar, Oxford-street, in 1830; and Dubourg's Mechanical Exhibition, in Windmill-street, Haymarket; as admirable specimens of foreign ingenuity in wax-modelling. To these may be added the lifelike and spirited figures of costumed natives of Mexico, and American Indians, modelled in wax with surprising minuteness and artistic feeling, both in the position and grouping, varied expression, and anatomical development: these figures, at the Great Exhibition of 1851, gained for their artist, N. Montanari, a prize medal.

MADAME TUSSAUD AND SON'S Collection, Baker-street, Portman-square, is stated to be the oldest exhibition in Europe. It was commenced on the Boulevard du Temple at Paris in 1780, and was first shown in London, at the Lyceum, Strand, in 1802. It now consists of upwards of 200 figures in wax, in the costume of their time, and several in the dresses which they actually wore; besides a large collection of paintings and sculpture, arranged in superb saloons, the largest 240 feet by 49 feet.

Madame Tussaud was born at Berne, in Switzerland, in 1760. When a child she was taught to model figures in wax, by her uncle M. Curtius, at whose house she often dined with Voltaire, Rousseau, Dr. Franklin, Mirabeau, and La Fayette, of whose heads she took casts. She taught drawing and modelling to the Princess Elizabeth, and many of the French noblesse, just before the Revolution of 1789. She also modelled in wax Robespierre, Marat, and Danton; and often took models of heads severed on the scaffold. Thus she commenced her collection of royalists, revolutionists, generals, authors and men of science, and distinguished ladies; with which she came to London in 1802. She has left her *Memoirs and Reminiscences*, published in 1838; a very curious narrative of the old French Revolution, and its leading characters *en costume*. Madame Tussaud died in London, 15 April 1850, aged 90; her mother lived to the same age, her grandmother to 104, and her great-grandmother to 111.

The Tussaud Collection not only contains fine specimens of modelling in wax, but a curious assemblage of costume and personal decoration, memorials of celebrated characters, historical groups, &c. Among the most noteworthy are the costumed recumbent effigies of the Duke of Wellington; a group of Henry VIII. and his six queens; Edward VI. and Henry VII.; Queen Victoria and Prince Albert, and the royal children; Alexander Emperor of Russia, taken from life, in England, in 1814; Napoleon Bonaparte, from life, in 1815; Louis XVI., his queen and children, modelled from life, in 1790, and exhibited at La Petite Trianon; Lord Nelson, the cast taken from his face; the beautiful Madame l'Amaranthe; Madame Tussaud, taken by herself; William Cobbett, very like; Madame Grisi as Lucrezia Borgia; Richard III., from the portrait at Arundel Castle; Voltaire (taken from life a few months before his death), and a Coquette of the same period, both admirably characteristic; Loushkin, the Russian giant, 8 ft. 5 in. high; Jenny Lind, very like; Sir Walter Scott, modelled by Madame Tussaud, in Edinburgh, in 1828.

The Hall of Kings: the ceiling painted by Thornhill. Here are portraits of Queen Victoria (Hayter); Prince Albert (Patten); George IV. (Lawrence); William IV. (Simpson); George III. and Queen Charlotte (Reynolds); George II. (Hudson); Louis XIV. (Parosel). Also a group of figures of Queen Victoria (the throne from Carlton Palace); the Queen Dowager, the Dukes of Sussex and Cambridge, and the Princess Augusta, in coronation robes; George III. taken from life in 1809; William IV. as Lord High Admiral.

In the richly-gilt chamber adjoining is George IV. in his coronation robe, which, with two other robes, contain 567 feet of velvet and embroidery, and cost 18,000*l.*: the chair is the homage-chair used at the coronation; and the crown and sceptre, orb, orders, &c. are copies from the actual regalia. Here is a large picture of the Birth of Venus, by Boucher; and of the Marriage of George IV., with many portraits.

Napoleon Relics.—The camp-bedstead on which Napoleon died; the counterpane stained with his blood. Cloak worn at Marengo. Three eagles taken at Waterloo. Cradle of the King of Rome. Bronze posthumous cast of Napoleon, and hat worn by him. Whole-length portrait of the Emperor, from Fontainebleau; Marie Louise and Josephine, and other portraits of the Bonaparte family. Bust of Napoleon, by Canova. Isabey's Portrait Table of the Marshals. Napoleon's three Carriages: two from Waterloo, and a landau from St. Helena. His garden chair and drawing-room chair. "The flag of Elba." Napoleon's sword, diamond, tooth-brush, and table-knife; dessert knife, fork, and spoons; coffee-cup; a piece of willow-tree from St. Helena; shoe-socks and handkerchiefs, shirt, &c. Model figure of Napoleon in the clothes he wore at Longwood; and porcelain dessert-service used by him. Napoleon's hair and tooth, &c.

Miscellaneous Relics.—Nelson's Order of the Bath, and coat worn at the Nile. Snuff-box of James II. Shirt worn by Henry IV. of France when stabbed by Ravaillac (from Cardinal Mazarine's collection). Coat and waistcoat of the Duke of Wellington, given to Haydon, the painter. Model of Longwood, St. Helena.

The Chamber of Horrors contains portrait figures of the murderers Rush and the Mannings, Good and Greenacre, Courvoisier and Gould, Burke and Hare; Fieschi and the infernal machine; Marat, taken immediately after his assassination; heads of French Revolutionists; the decapitating knife and lunette; model of the guillotine, &c.: this being a class of models in which Madame Tussaud excelled in her youth.

Admission to the general collection, 1*s.*; Chamber of Horrors, 6*d.*

THE ORIENTAL AND TURKISH MUSEUM, St. George's Gallery, Knightsbridge, opened 1854, contains models from Eastern life, with costumes, arms, and implements; set scenes of Turkish baths, coffee-shops, and bazaars; a wedding, repasts, and councils; the palace, the harem, and the divan; street scenes, &c.: the figures are modelled in wax by James Boggi, with wonderful variety of expression and character. Admission 1s. In the same gallery was formerly exhibited the Chinese Collection, the figures of which were modelled in a kind of clay.

WESTMINSTER,

The general title of the western portion of the metropolis, but properly applying only to the City of Westminster, or "the parish of St. Margaret, including the ecclesiastical district of St. John the Evangelist; the other parishes constituting the Liberties of Westminster." (*Rev. M. E. C. Walcott.*) It is named from the founding of St. Peter's Minster on Thorney Island in the seventh century, which was called West Minster to distinguish it from St. Paul's, the church of the East Saxons: thus the town grew up around the monastery from which it took its name. The island site, "formed by the rude channel worn by the river tides," in a charter of King Offa, A.D. 785, is called "Torneia in loco terribili, quod dicitur æt. Westmunster." King Edgar's charter describes Westminster to extend from Fleet Ditch, next the City of London, to the Military Way, now the Horseferry-road; and from Tybourn and Holbourne to the Thames. Subsequently the boundary of the City of London was extended from Fleet Ditch to Temple Bar.

Thorney Island, 470 yards long and 370 yards broad, was insulated by a small stream, called in modern times Long Ditch, which has been traced from the Thames at Manchester-buildings, across King-street by Gardener's-lane, by Prince's-street (where it is the common sewer), to Tothill-street, and thence to the Thames at the end of Abingdon-st.

"This island comprised the precinct of the Abbey and Palace, which were further defended by lofty stone walls; those on the east and south of the College gardens being the last remains of such defences of a later date. They were pierced with four gateways: the first in King-street; the second near New Palace-yard, the foundations of which were seen in December A.D. 1838, in excavating for a sewer; the third opening into Tothill-street; and the fourth near the mill in College-street. The precinct was entered by two bridges: one crossed the water of Long Ditch, at the east end of Gardener's-lane, having been built by Queen Matilda, the consort of King Henry I., for foot passengers; the other still exists at the east end of College-street, underneath the pavement,—it connected Millbank with Dirty-lane."—Walcott's *Westminster,* p. 3.

In Domesday-Book, Westminster is designated a village, with about 50 holders of land, and "pannage for a hundred hogs," probably in part of the forest of Middlesex, on the north-west; so that the Liberty of Westminster thus early extended northward to Tyburn: the whole of the Abbey and Palace precinct, south of Pall Mall, was called by the Normans, "Thorney Island and tout le champ." In Domesday, also, is "the vineyard lately made by Bainard," a Norman follower of the Confessor or the Conqueror. Westward, the parish of St. Margaret's extends to Chelsea, and includes Kensington Palace. In 1174, Fitzstephen describes the Royal Palace as about two miles westward of the City of London, with an intervening suburb of gardens and orchards. Around the Old Palace the courtiers and nobility fixed their town residences. The establishment of the Wool-staple at Westminster made it the early resort of merchants; the Law Courts were fixed here, and thenceforth Parliaments were more frequently held; and in the reign of Henry VIII, Westminster obtained the title of City, from its having been for a short time the residence and see of a bishop. St. Martin's-in-the-Fields became a parish 1353-61.

Early in the reign of Queen Elizabeth, about 1560, a plan shows Westminster united to London by a double line of buildings, extending from the palace of Whitehall (built by Henry III.), by Charing Cross and along the Strand. Around Westminster Abbey and Hall, the buildings formed a town of several streets; and at the close of Charles II.'s reign they had extended westward along the south side of St. James's Park, and southward along Millbank to the Horseferry opposite Lambeth Palace. In the reign of Elizabeth, Westminster was the abode of great numbers of felons, masterless men, and cutpurses; and in the next reign, "almost every fourth house was an alehouse, harbering all sorts of lewd and badde people." To the church of St. Margaret (originally built by Edward the Confessor) was added, in 1728, St. John's near Millbank; and in 1747 was completed Westminster Bridge. The old streets were so narrow, that "opposite neighbours might shake hands out of the windows;" and a knot of wretched lanes and alleys were called "the desert of Westminster." For a century past these miserable abodes have been in course of removal.

Among the old Westminster Signs, mentioned in the parish books, are the Rose (the Tudor badge); the Lamb and the Saracen's Head (Crusades); and the White Hart (Richard II.), to this day the sign of Elliot's Ale-brewery at Pimlico.

Westminster is governed by a High-Steward and a High-Bailiff. The first High-Steward was the great Lord Burghley. The City has returned two members to Parliament since 1 Edward VI.

Abingdon-street has been built in place of Dirty-lane.

Almonry, the (see page 4), has disappeared.

St. Anne's-lane, named from the Chapel of the Mother of Our Lady, was part of the orchard and fruit-gardens of the Abbey. Henry Purcell and Dr. Heather, the famous musicians, lived here.

Artillery-place was the ground for the men of Westminster's shooting at "the butts;" and early in the last century it was "made use of by those who delight in military exercises."

Barton-street was built by Barton Booth, the celebrated actor; and *Cowley-street* is named from Cowley, in Middlesex, where Booth resided.

Broadway (the), west of Tothill-street, was granted as a hay-market by James I. and Charles II. Here were "the White Horse and Black Horse Inns; there being none in the parish of St. Margaret at Westminster for stage-coaches, waggons, or carriers." (*Survey, circ.* 1700.) In one of the Broadway courts lodged Turpin, the highwayman; and from his mare, Black Bess, a tavern took its sign. In the Broadway lived Sir John Hill, the empiric, of physic-garden fame. (See CHRISTCHURCH, Broadway, p. 122.)

Canon-row formerly extended from the Woolstaple northward to the south wall of the orchard of Whitehall. It is named from the dean and canons of St. Stephen's Chapel lodging there.

"'Twas the old way when the King of England had his house, there were canons to sing service in his chapel; so at Westminster is St. Stephen's Chapel (where the House of Commons sits). from which canons the street called Canon-row has its name, because they lived there."—Selden's *Table-talk.*

It has been vulgarly called Channel-row, and in our time Cannon-row. Upon the site of the canons' houses were built several mansions, the gardens of which reached to the Thames: for one of these houses the Comptroller of the Household of Edward VI. paid only 30s. annually. Here Anne Duchess of Somerset, sister-in-law to Queen Katherine Parr, built a stately house, wherein Anne Clifford, Countess of Dorset, was born in 1590: upon the site is Dorset-court. In 1618, William Earl of Derby built here a mansion, which was surrendered to Parliament *temp.* Charles I.; and here died, in 1643, John Pym, their patriotic leader;

the house was temporarily, in the reign of Charles II., the Admiralty Office; it occupied the site of Derby-court. In Canon-row lived Lady Wheler, to whom Charles I., two days before his execution, sent, by his attendant Herbert, a token-ring: the lady handed him a cabinet, with which he returned to the King, who opened it on the morning of his execution; it contained diamonds and jewels, most part broken Georges and garters : " You see," said he, " all the wealth now in my power to give my children." Here is the *Office of the Board of Control for the Affairs of India*, originally built for the Ordnance Office, by William Atkinson : " the Ionic portico of this chaste and fine building is one of the best proportioned and best applied in the metropolis" (*Elmes*). *Manchester-buildings* occupy the site of a mansion of the Montagues, Earls of Manchester. In Canon-row is the *Architectural Museum* (see Museums, page 532).

Charles-street : at No. 19 lived Ignatius Sancho, a negro, who had been butler to the Duke of Montague, and gave his last shilling to see Garrick play Richard III. Here Garrick and Sterne visited him; and Mortimer, the painter, often consulted him.

Dean's-yard, south-west of the Abbey, has a *green*, or playground, for the Westminster Scholars, whereon have played, in " careless childhood," Ben Jonson, George Herbert, Cowley, Dryden, Nat. Lee, Rowe, Prior, Churchill, Dyer, Cowper, and Southey ; Hackluyt, the voyager ; Sir Christopher Wren, Locke, South, Atterbury, Warren Hastings, and Gibbon. In Dean's-yard lived Sir Symonds d'Ewes, the antiquary, who delighted in bell-ringing. Bishop Wilcocks, whom Pope Clement VIII. called " the blessed heretic," was born in Dean's-yard in 1673; in the cloisters, in 1708, died the excellent Bishop Beveridge; Carte, the Jacobite historian, lived in Dean's-yard, where Mrs. Porter, Gibbon's aunt, built and occupied a boarding-house. In *Little Dean's-yard* is Ashburnham House, described at page 22.

Downing-street, see Whitehall.

Duke-street, " a spacious and pleasant street between St. James's Park N., and Long Ditch s., mostly (especially the w. side) inhabited by persons of quality" (*Hatton*, 1708). In a house facing Charles-street lived the poet Prior. Bishop Stillingfleet, author of *Origines Britannicæ*, died here 1699; Archbishop Hutton, 1758; and Dr. Arnold, the musical composer, 1802. At the north end of the street is the entrance to the State-Paper Office. Duke-street Chapel is described at page 167. At the corner of the south end of Delahay-street and Great George-street lived Lady Augusta Murray, " Duchess of Sussex."

Fludyer-street, between King-street and St. James's Park, is named from Sir Samuel Fludyer, Bart., the ground-landlord, who, when lord-mayor in 1761, entertained George III. and Queen Charlotte at Guildhall. Fludyer-street occupies the site of Axe-yard, from the Axe brewhouse, named in a document 23 Hen. VIII. Pepys had a house here.

Francis-street : here is the Victoria Lodging-house for the wives and children of soldiers.

Gardener's-lane extends from Duke-street to King-street: here died, in 1677, Wenceslaus Hollar, the celebrated engraver, aged 70, at the moment when he had an execution in his house; he desired of the sheriff's officers " only the liberty of dying in his bed, and that he might not be removed to any other prison but his grave" (*Oldys*). He was buried in the New Chapel yard, near the place of his death; and no monument was erected to his memory. Hollar engraved 2400 prints, and worked for the booksellers at 4*d.* per hour; yet his finest prints bring rare prices.

Gatehouse (the) is described at page 325.

Great George-street, named from the House of Hanover, was completed in 1750: the site was an arm of the Thames, when the tide flowed up from Bridge-street to the canal in St. James's Park. Here was Storey's Gate, named from Edward Storey, who constructed the decoys in St. James's Park for Charles II., and who lived upon the site: this gate was taken down in 1854. At No. 15 Great George-street died Lord Chancellor Thurlow, 1806. At No. 25 (then Sir Edward Knatchbull's) the body of Lord Byron lay in state two days, before it was removed, July 12, 1824, for interment at Hucknall, Notts. No. 25 Great George-street has a handsome architectural front, and is now the *Institution of Civil Engineers* (see LIBRARIES, p. 459; and MUSEUMS, p. 533). At No. 24 the Reform Club was commenced; and here subsequently lived Alderman Sir Matthew Wood, Bart., M.P.

Horseferry (the) is described at p. 377.

James-street is described at p. 421. It was partly taken down in 1854 for the Pimlico improvements.

In 1763 there were but few houses in James-street, and none behind it; nor any filthy courts between Petty France and the Park; nor any buildings in Palmer's Village, or in Tothill-fields, or on the Artillery-ground, or to the south of Market-street.—*Bardwell.*

King-street was the principal street of Westminster *temp.* Henry VIII., with Cockpit-gate at the north end, and High-gate south. Here the poet Spenser died "for lake of bread," in an obscure lodging, Jan. 16, 1599; here also died Sir Thomas Knevett, who seized Guy Fawkes. Cromwell lived here when member of parliament, north of Blue-Boar's-Head-yard. Dr. Sydenham lived upon the site of Ram's Mews. Near the south end, on the west side, was *Thieven-* (Thieves) *lane,** the passage for thieves to the Gatehouse prison, so that they might not escape into the Sanctuary. The roadway was so bad, that fagots were thrown into the ruts to facilitate the passage of the state-coach when the sovereign went to parliament. Here, at the Bell Tavern, met the October (Queen Anne) Club. Here lodged the poet Carew, who wrote the masque of *Cœlum Britannicum* for Charles I. Through King-street, Elizabeth and James and Charles I. proceeded to the Houses of Parliament in their state-coaches; and the republicans of Cromwell's days on foot and horseback. After the burning of Whitehall Palace, a broader road was made by Parliament-street. Cromwell, when he went to Ireland in 1649, took horse at his house in King-street. At the north end of King-street was built, by Henry VIII., the Westminster or King's Gate, of stone, as a communication, by a passage over it, of Whitehall Palace with the Park: it was of Tudor design, with four round-capped turrets: each front was enriched with Ionic pilasters and an entablature, roses, the portcullis, and the royal arms, and glazed biscuit-ware busts. In this Gatehouse lived the Earl of Rochester and Herr von Auls: it was taken down in 1723.

Millbank-street, in 1745 called the High-street at Millbank, was named from the Abbey water-mill, built by Nicholas Littlington, at the end the present College-street, and turned by the stream which flowed by the Infirmary garden-wall eastward into the Thames (*Walcott*). Upon the site of the mill was built Peterborough House, by the first Earl of Peterborough, in the reign of Charles I., and is shown in Hollar's Map of London, 1708. Stow describes the mansion with a large front court, and fine gardens behind: "but its situation was bleak in winter, and not over-healthful." The house was purchased by the Grosvenor family, and rebuilt: it was taken down in 1809. In the middle of Millbank lived Mr. Vidler, the Government contractor: hence the mail-coach procession started annually on the king's birth-

* *Thieven* or *Thieving lane* was also called Bow-street, from its bowed line; and Bow-street, Covent Garden, to this day the terror of thieves.

day. The *Penitentiary*, at Millbank, is described at page 633. In *New-way*, adjoining, was a chapel where Romaine preached.

Palace-yard, New, is named from William Rufus's intended new palace, of which the hall only was built: here was a beautiful Conduit, removed *temp.* Charles II. Opposite Westminster Hall gate, *temp.* Edward I., Lord Chief-Justice Hengham built a large stone clock-tower, taken down 1698. In this yard King Edward I. appealed to the loyalty of his people, from a platform erected against the front of Westminster Hall, in 1297; here Perkin Warbeck was set in the stocks, in 1498; Stubbs, the Puritan attorney, and his servant, had their hands cut off in New Palace-yard, in 1580, for a libel against Queen Elizabeth; and William Parry was here hung and quartered for high treason, in 1578; here Lord Sanquhar was hanged for murder, 1612; Archbishop Leighton's father was pilloried and publicly whipped for libel, 1630; William Prynne was pilloried here, and his *Histrio-Mastix* burned, 1634; here the Duke of Holland, the Earl of Holland, and Lord Capel, were put to death for treason, in 1649; Titus Oates was pilloried here in 1685; and John Williams in 1765, for publishing No. 45 of Wilkes's *North Briton*. Here was the Turk's Head, Miles's Coffee-house, where the noted Rota Club met, whose republican opinions Harrington has glorified in his *Oceana*. The Tudor buildings of the old Palace were principally taken down in 1793; but a range, including the *Star Chamber*,[*] on the eastern side of the court, were not removed until 1836 (see page 396). At his official residence, east of Westminster Hall porch, died William Godwin, the novelist, April 7, 1836, aged 81.

Palace-yard, Old, south-west of the Houses of Parliament, had on the west the old Lady Chapel of the Abbey, and abutting upon it the White Rose Tavern, and the house of Chaucer, in which he died (the site is now occupied by the mausoleum of Henry VII.); and in a house between the churchyard and the Old Palace died Ben Jonson; so that two greatest of England's poets died almost upon the same spot. At the south-east corner of Old Palace-yard stood the house through which the conspirators in the Gunpowder Plot carried their barrels into the vault; and in the yard, Guy Faukes, Winter, Rookwood, and Keyes, suffered death in 1606. Here, 29th Oct. 1618, Sir Walter Raleigh was executed at 8 in the morning of Lord Mayor's Day, "so that the pageants and fine shewes might draw away the people from beholding the tragedie of one of the gallantest worthies that ever England bred."[†]

Palmer's Village, west of the Almonry, was a low-lying district (12½ inches below high-water mark), consisting of straggling cottages around the twelve almshouses built in 1566 by the Rev. Edward Palmer, B.D., with a chapel and school attached. Thirty years since, here was an old wayside inn (the Prince of Orange), rows of cottages

---

[*] In 1830 a semi-political journal entitled the *Star-Chamber* was announced for publication, to be edited by Benjamin Disraeli, jun.

[†] In the Pepysian Collection at Cambridge is a Ballad with the following title: "Sir Walter Rauleigh his Lamentation, who was beheaded in the Old Pallace of Westminster the 29 of October, 1618. To the tune of Welladay." *Note to Raleigh's Imprisonment in the Tower*, see page 730: In 1603, "in the course of a few months Raleigh was first confined in his own house, then conveyed to the Tower, next sent to Winchester gaol, returned from thence to the Tower, imprisoned for between two and three months in the Fleet, and again removed to the Tower, where he remained until released thirteen years afterwards, to undertake his new expedition to Guiana." (Mr. J. Payne Collier; *Archæologia*, vol. xxxv. p. 218.) Mr. Collier possesses a copy of that rare tract, "A Good Speed to Virginia," 4to, 1609, with the autograph on the title-page, "W. Ralegh, Turr. Lond.;" showing that at the time this tract was published, and read by Ralegh, he recorded himself as a prisoner in the Tower of London.

with gardens, and the village-green, upon which the Maypole was annually set up: this rurality has now disappeared, and with it from maps and plans the name of "Palmer's Village."

Park-street, built *circ.* 1708, northward from *Carteret-street*, making it like a T, contains the house of Mr. Charles Towneley, who, in 1772, assembled here his first collection of marbles, terra-cottas, bronzes, &c., commenced in 1768 at Rome. See BRITISH MUSEUM, page 519.

Petty France (*Petit France*, Hatton, 1708), and now *York-street*, from Frederick Duke of York, son of George II., having temporarily resided here, extends from Tothill-street to James-street. In Petty France was Milton's pleasant garden-house, described at page 595.

Prince's-street was formerly *Long Ditch*: here was an ancient conduit, the site of which is now marked by a pump; at the bottom of the well is a black marble image of St. Peter, and some marble steps. The southern extremity of this street was called *Broken Cross*: here, about the middle of the last century, was the most ancient house in Westminster (*Walcott*). Upon the east side of the street was built *Her Majesty's New Stationery Office*, in neat Italian style, in 1854, upon the site of the Westminster Mews. In *Prince's-court*, at the south end of the street, lived John Wilkes in 1788.

Queen-square is described at page 684. In Queen-street was born, in 1642, James Tyrrell (a grandson of Archbishop Usher): he wrote a *History of England*, 3 vols. folio, valuable for its exact references to the ancient chronicles.

Rochester-row is named from the Bishops of Rochester, who were also Deans of Westminster. Here are Emery Hill's Almshouses; and opposite are the Church of St. Stephen, and Schools, built and endowed by the munificence of Miss Angela Burdett Coutts. (See page 160.)

Sanctuary (the) of Westminster Abbey is described as the space by St. Margaret's churchyard, between the old Gatehouse s.w., and King-street N.E. The right of sanctuary, *i. e.* protection to criminals and debtors from arrest, was retained by Westminster after the Dissolution in 1540; and "sanctuary men" were allowed to use a whittle only at their meals, and compelled to wear a badge. The privilege of sanctuary caused the houses within the precinct to let for high rents; but it was totally abolished by James I. in 1623: it is called by Fabyan, "the Seyntwary before the Abbey." Here were two cruciform churches, built one above the other, the lower a double cross: the upper, the Rev. Mr. Walcott thinks, for the debtors and inhabitants of the *Broad* and the *Little Sanctuaries;* the lower for criminals. "They could not leave the precinct without the dean's license, or between sunset and sunrise." In Little Sanctuary was the Three Tuns Tavern, built upon part of the church vaults, which served as the inn-cellar. The tower of the church, rebuilt by Edward II., contained three bells, the ringing of which "sowered all the drinke in the town." The church was demolished in 1750. Fifty years later was removed from Broad Sanctuary the old market-house, built in 1568; and upon the site was erected, in 1805, the present Guildhall, with a Doric vestibule, S. P. Cockerell architect. Here also are the *Office and Central Schools of the National Society;* the *Westminster Hospital*, built 1833 (see page 387); and the *New Stationery Office.* The Sanctuary churches are described by Dr. Stukeley, who remembered their standing (*Archæologia*, i. p. 39). There were other sanctuaries in London; but the Westminster site alone retains its ancient name.

Here Judge Tresilian (*temp.* Richard II.) fled, but was dragged to Tyburn and hanged. In 1441, Eleanor Cobham, Duchess of Gloucester, accused of witchcraft and treason, was denied refuge. In 1460, Lord Scales, as he was seeking sanctuary here, was murdered on the Thames. Elizabeth Woodville, queen of Edward IV., and her family, escaped from the Tower, and registered themselves "sanctuary women;" and here, "in great penury, forsaken of all friends," she gave birth to Edward V. More describes her sitting "alow on the rushes," in her grief. The Register of the Sanctuary, Gough states, was bought out of Sir Henry Spelman's Collection, by Wanley, for Lord Weymouth, and preserved in the library at Longleat.

The vacant ground was let, in 1821, to speculators in seats to view the coronation-procession of George IV., upon a raised platform, from Westminster Abbey to Westminster Hall. In 1854 was built, adjoining the west end of the Abbey, a block of houses in the Mediæval style, G. G. Scott architect; the centre opening being the entrance to Dean's-yard.

Tothill Fields, between Pimlico and the Thames, anciently the manor of Tothill, belonging to John Maunsel, chancellor, who, in 1256, entertained here Henry III. and his court, at a vast feast in tents and pavilions. The Normans called this district *tout le champ*, which is thought to have been clipped into *tout le*, and then corrupted into *outle* and *Tot-hill*. (*Bardwell.*) It occurs, however, in an ancient lease as Toot-hill or Beacon Field,* which Mr. Hudson Turner suggested to Mr. Cunningham as the probable origin. The Rev. Mr. Walcott restricts it within the sanctuary of the Abbey. At the Tothill were decided wagers of battle and appeals by combat. Necromancy, sorcery, and witchcraft were punished here; and "royal solemnities and goodly jousts were held here." In Culpeper's time the fields were famous for parsley. In 1642 a battery and breastwork were here erected. Here were built the "Five Houses," or "Seven Chimneys," as pest-houses for victims to the Plague; and in 1665 the dead were buried "in the open Tuttle Fields." The Fields are described as "of great use, pleasure, and recreation" to the king's scholars and neighbours; and in 1672 the parish made here a new Maze, which was "much frequented in summer time in fair afternoons." (*Aubrey.*) In Queen Anne's reign, here was William Well's bear-garden, upon the site of Vincent-square. St. Edward's Fair was removed from St. Margaret's churchyard to Tothill Fields, 34 Hen. III., who granted the Abbot of Westminster "leave to keepe a markett in the Tuthill every Munday, and a faire every yeare for three days;" and Edward III. granted a fair of thirty-one days. Both fairs were suppressed by James I. Here, in 1651, the Trained Bands were drawn out; and in the same year, Heath's *Chronicle* records, the Scotch prisoners "driven like a herd of swine through Westminster to Tuthill Fields, and there sold to several merchants, and sent to the Barbadoes." One of "the Civil War Tracts of Lancashire," printed by the Chetham Society, states there were 4000 Scots, Highlands, or Redshanks," many with their wives and bairns, of whom 1200 were buried in Tuttle Fields. They next became a noted duel-ground: here, in 1711, Sir Cholmeley Dering, M.P., was killed by the first shot of Mr. Richard Thornhill, who was tried for murder and acquitted, but found guilty of manslaughter, and was burnt in the hand. Here also was an ancient Bridewell (see page 637).

Tothill-street, extending from Broad Sanctuary to York-street, has lost most of its picturesque old houses. The Cock public-house (described at page 398) was taken down in 1854. In Tothill-street lived the Bishop of Chester, 1488; William Lord Grey of Wilton, "the greatest soldier of the nobility," died 1563; Sir George Carew, at Caron House, 1612; and Lincoln House was the Office of the Revels, 1664. Southern, the dramatic poet, lived ten years at No. 56, then as now, an oilman's: bears the date 1671. Betterton, the actor, was born in this street. In the reign of Elizabeth, the houses on the north side had gardens

* Others refer it to Toote Hill, shown in Rocque's map (1746), just at a bend the Horseferry-road, but now lost in the adjacent made ground.

extending to the park, and those on the south to Orchard-street, once the orchard-garden of the Abbey. Here, in 1789, died, aged 97, Thomas Amory, who wrote the *Memoirs of John Buncle.* Here is the Fleece public-house, of which a token exists, date 1666. The old Cock public-house, described at page 398, was taken down in 1853.

Tufton-street was built by Sir Richard Tufton (d. 1631): here was a cock-pit, which existed long after that in St. James's Park was deserted.

Victoria-street, commenced by the Westminster Improvement Commission in 1845, extends across the sites of the Almonry, Orchard-street, Duck-lane, New Pye-street, and part of Old Pye-street (named from Sir Robert Pye, who resided here), to Strutton-ground, named from Stourton-house, the mansion of the Lords Dacre of the South. Thence the new street crosses Artillery-place, through Palmer's Village, on the north-side of Westminster Bridewell, past Elliot's brewery to Shaftesbury-terrace, Pimlico. Victoria-street is above 1000 yards, or nearly five furlongs in length, and 80 feet wide: the houses are 82 feet in height; Henry Ashton architect. The ornamentation of the house-fronts, worked in cement, is extremely artistic: the interiors are mostly arranged in flats, as in Edinburgh and Paris. About the centre, on the north side, is a house of Jacobean design. In the line of street are the three churches of St. Mark, the Holy Trinity, and Christchurch; and at the north-west rear is St. Andrew's church, in the Geometrical style; the nave asles showing five gables on each side, filled with large and lofty windows; architect, G. G. Scott. Victoria-street was publicly opened Aug. 6, 1851. Here are the new Training-schools of the National Society, in the Mediæval style; Henry Clutton architect: the foundation-stone was laid by Prince Albert, 1852. Of the six other streets projected, the principal will be Albert-street, connecting Victoria-street with James-street, at Buckingham Gate.

Vine-street denotes the site of a vineyard, probably that of the Abbey. In the overseer's book, 1565, is rated "the vyne-garden" and "myll," next to Bowling-alley; the vine-garden called "because, perhaps, vines anciently were there nourished, and wine made." (*Stow.*) In Edward VIth's time it was inclosed with buildings. *Bowling street* and *alley* denote the site of the green where the members of the convent played at bowls. Opposite *Bowling-alley* is a house where the notorious Colonel Blood died, Aug. 24, 1680: upon the house-front was a shield with a coat of arms. (*Walcott.*)

Wood-street, described in 1720 as "very narrow, being old boarded hovels ready to fall," has disappeared. Here lived John Carter, the diligent antiquary. At No. 13 *North-street* lived Elliston, the comedian, who dearly loved his art: "wherever Elliston walked, sat, or stood still, there was the theatre."—*C. Lamb.*

Woolstaple (the) was, in 1353, appointed for weighing all the wool brought to London. The Long Staple (upon the site of *Bridge-street*) consisted of a strong round tower and a water-gate, which was destroyed to make room for the western abutment of Westminster Bridge, in 1741. Here was St. Stephen's Hospital, founded by Henry VIII. in 1548, and removed in 1745, when eight almshouses were rebuilt in St. Anne's-lane, inscribed "Woolstaple Pensioners, 1741." In 1628, in the overseers' books of St. Margaret's, is rated in the Wool-staple, "Orlando Gibbons, ijd."

WESTMINSTER HALL

Was originally added to the ancient Palace at Westminster by William Rufus, who held his first court herein, 1099. In 1394-9 Richard II. had its walls heightened two feet, the windows altered, and a new timber roof constructed, from the design of Henry Zeneley. During the repairs of 1835 the work of the two kings (William II. and Richard II.) was distinguishable, including a Norman arcade connecting the clerestory windows. The exterior is of modern design, except the north porch and window, which, with the internal stone-work (except the south end), is one of our earliest specimens of the Perpendicular style, and is thought to have been the work of William of Wykeham. The original walls (chiefly rubble and grout work) were then cased 1 foot 7 inches thick with stone, flying buttresses were erected as abutments on the east and west sides, and the embattled flanking towers and porch of the north front added: the towers were restored 1819-22. The roof was originally covered with lead; for which, on account of its immense weight, plates were substituted. The lantern, of cast-iron, is an exact copy of the original one erected near the end of the 14th century: it is glazed.

The interior dimensions of Westminster Hall are 239 feet by 68, and 92 feet high. The immense timber-framed roof is one of the finest existing examples of scientific construction in carpentry; its only bearing being at the extremities of the great ribs, which abut against the side walls, and rest upon twenty-six sculptured stone corbels. At half his height the timber arches spring from the stone string-course, sculptured with the white hart couchant under a tree, and other devices of Richard II.; so that the upper half of the height of the edifice is entirely of timber (oak),* unrivalled for its accurately moulded detail. The hammer-beams are sculptured with angels bearing shields of the arms of Richard II. or Edward the Confessor, which show the excellence that sculpture in wood had attained in England so early as the reign of Richard II. From the roof were formerly hung "guidons, colours and standards, ensigns and trophies of victory;" in Hatton's time (1708), 138 colours and 34 standards, from the battles of Neasby and Worcester, Preston and Dunbar, and Blenheim: Hatton describes fourteen, with their mottoes Englished. The roof was thoroughly repaired in 1820-21, when forty loads of oak, from old ships broken up in Portsmouth Dockyard, were used in renewing decayed parts, and completing the portion at the north end, where it had been left unfinished; the roof was also greatly strengthened by tension-rods added to the principals in 1851. Abutting on the southern end was the Galilee, finished by Edward III., and adapted by Richard II. with a flight of steps to the approach from the Great Hall to the Chapel of St. Stephen and the principal chambers of the Palace. Above the side line of windows are dormers (added in 1820-21), which improve the chiaroscuro; and above are apertures, opened in 1843, to aid the effect of an exhibition of cartoons. The Hall now forms the vestibule to the new Houses of Parliament; which Sir Charles Barry has effected by removing the large window from the south end to form an archway to St. Stephen's Porch, wherein he has fixed the Hall window, with an additional transom and row of lights. (See *St. Stephen's Porch*, pp. 600-2.)

The statues † flanking the archway in the Hall are:

WILLIAM II.	HENRY I.	STEPHEN.			HENRY II.	RICHARD I.	JOHN.

* The Roof is often stated to be of chestnut; but it is of the British oak, *quercus sessiflora*, which is so deficient in grain as not to be distinguishable at first sight from chestnut. The wood of the chestnut, though tolerably durable when young, is not at all so when it has attained the size of a timber-tree.— Loudon's *Arboretum et Fruticetum Britannicum*.

† These Statues, together with all the stone Statues in the interior and exterior the New Palace at Westminster, are by John Thomas.

Sir Charles Barry contemplates raising the roof fourteen feet, closing the doorways of the Law Courts, and adorning the walls with frescoes, &c. The heraldic decorations of the corbels and string-course are described by Mr. Willement in the *Collectanea Topogr. et Gen.* vol. iii. p. 55; and the architectural discoveries in 1835 are detailed by Mr. Sydney Smirke in *Archæologia*, vols. xxvi. and xxvii.

The floor of the Hall, from its low level, has often been flooded by the Thames: as in 1238, when the middle of the Hall might be passed in boats, and persons rode through it on horseback to their chambers; in 1555, when the Lord Mayor was rowed by a wherry-man into the Hall, to present the Sheriff to the Barons of the Exchequer; and in 1579, when the water rose so high in Westminster Hall, "that, after the fall thereof, some fishes were found there to remaine." (*Stow*).

The Coronation, Christmas, and other great Feasts of our sovereigns were held in Westminster Hall, the guests numbering thousands of all ranks. Edward I. was here proclaimed king, and for his coronation-feast the Hall was whitewashed. Here Edward III. feasted the captive John King of France. Richard II. celebrated the completion of the Hall with a "most royal" feast of 26 or 28 oxen, and 300 sheep, and fowls without number, several days; and here this king was solemnly deposed, and sentenced to perpetual imprisonment. After great part of the Palace was burnt in 1512, only the Great Hall was kept in repair; "and it serveth, as before it did, for feasts of coronations, arraignments of great persons charged with treasons, keeping of the courts of justice, &c." (*Stow*). Hither came 411 of the rioters on Evil May-day, 1517, each with a halter about his neck, crying to the king upon his throne for mercy; when "the general pardon being pronounced, all the prisoners showted at once, and cast their halters towards the roof of the Hall" (*Stow*).

Here Cromwell was inaugurated Lord Protector, 26th June, 1657, upon an elevated platform at the south end of the Hall, in the ancient coronation-chair, "under a prince-like canopy of state," with the Bible, sword, and sceptre of the Commonwealth before him; the Protector entering the Hall with the Lord Mayor bearing the City sword before him. On May 8th, 1660, King Charles II. was proclaimed at "Westminster Hall Gate." Upon the south gable were set up the heads of Cromwell, Ireton, and Bradshaw: Cromwell's head remained 20 years.

Abutting on the west side of Westminster Hall, and in part beneath it, were three taverns—*Heaven, Hell,* and *Purgatory.* They were anciently prisons, mentioned in a grant 1 Hen. VII. (1485). As taverns, they were much frequented by lawyers' clerks. In Ben Jonson's *Alchemist*, Dapper is forbidden to "break his fast in *Heaven* and *Hell.*"

"Faire Heaven at the end of Hell."—*Hudibras.*

Pepys records dining at Heaven, and spending the evening in one of these taverns with Lock and Purcell, and hearing Lock's new canon, *Domine salvum fac Regem.* "The prison-keys of Purgatory, attached to a leather girdle, are still preserved." (Walcott's *Westminster*, page 221.) Here were kept the "ducking-stools," with which the burgesses of Westminster (by statute 27 Eliz.) were empowered to punish common scolds, &c. Heaven and Purgatory were taken down about 1741.

Parliaments assembled in this Hall as early as 1248 (33 Hen. III.) and 1265 (49 Hen. III.), the latter being the first representation of the people in its present form.

Courts of Justice were held in this Hall almost from its first erection, the sovereign presiding: they are first noticed on the Placita Rolls, 10th Richard I.: thus for 7½ centuries it has been "the very Prætorium, or Hall of Justice for all England" (*Foss*). The arrangement of the courts is described at page 447. They are on the west side of the Hall, across which the Lord Chancellor and other judges proceed in state to open the courts on the first day of Term.

"In the reign of Charles I., the King's Servants, by His Majestie's special order, went to Westminster Hall in Term-time, to invite gentlemen to eat of the King's Acates or Viands; and in Parliament-time, to invite the Parliament-men thereunto."—Delaune's *Angliæ Metropolis*, 1690.

Memorable Trials in Westminster Hall.—1305, Sir William Wallace condemned for treason (in Rufus's Hall); 1417, Sir John Oldcastle the Wickliffite; 1522, Stafford, Duke of Buckingham, for treason; 1535, Sir Thomas More arraigned here; 1551, the Protector Somerset brought to trial, with "bills, halberts, and pole-axes attending him," the clamour of the people "heard to the Long Acre beyond Charing Crosse;" 1554, Sir Thomas Wyatt; 1557, Lord Stourton, for murder; 1600, Robert Devereux, Earl of Essex; 1606, Guy Fawkes and his fellow-conspirators; 1616, the profligate Earl and Countess of Somerset, for the murder of Sir Thomas Overbury; 1640 (18 days' trial), Wentworth, Earl of Strafford, before Charles I. and his queen; 1649, King Charles I. (in 1661, the Act for the King's Trial was burned by the common hangman in the Hall while the court was sitting); 1688, the Seven Bishops; 1710, Dr. Sacheverel; 1716, Viscount Kenmure and the Earl of Derwentwater; 1746-47, the rebel Lords Kilmarnock, Balmerino, and Lovat; 1760, Earl Ferrers, for murder; 1776, the Duchess of Kingston, for bigamy; 1788 to 1795, Warren Hastings's seven years' trial; 1806, Lord Melville.

Shops or *stalls*, chiefly of booksellers, sempstresses, and milliners, (resembling those in Old Exeter Change,) were kept in Westminster Hall: they are shown in Gravelot's print. "Counters and stalls for books (at one time sold by poor scholars of Westminster between school-hours), as well as other merchandise, were to be seen here in term-time, and during the session of Parliament, even in the beginning of the reign of King George III."—Walcott's *Westminster*, p. 250.

At the Great Fire of 1666 the Hall was filled with "the people's goods," for safety. The edifice narrowly escaped being burnt through a fire in the shops, Sunday, Feb. 20, 1630-31; and by the favourable direction of the wind, the Hall was saved in the great fire of 1834.

At the coronation-feast of Richard II. (July 16, 1377), Sir John Dymock, as successor of the Marmions, and in right of his wife, Margaret de Ludlow, claiming the privilege by his tenure of the manor of Scrivelsby, in Lincolnshire, having chosen the best charger save one in the king's stables, and the best suit of harness save one in the royal armoury, rode in armed to the teeth, and challenged, as the king's champion, all opposers of the young monarch's title to the crown; this picturesque ceremony was last performed at the coronation of George IV.

Haydon, the historical painter, describes the Coronation Festival of George V. (*Autobiography*, vol. ii.), which he witnessed from the Chamberlain's box: "The Hall doors were opened, and the flower-girls entered, strewing flowers. The distant trumpets and shouts of the people, the slow march, and at last the appearance of the King, crowned and under a golden canopy, and the universal burst of the assembly at seeing him, affected everybody. . . . . . After the banquet was over,* came the most imposing scene of all, the championship. Wellington, in his coronet, walked down the Hall, cheered by the officers of the Guards. He shortly returned, mounted, with Lords Anglesea and Howard. They rode gracefully to the foot of the throne, and then backed out. The Hall doors opened again; and outside, in twilight, a man in dark-shadowed armour appeared against the shining sky. He then moved, passed into darkness under the arch, and suddenly Wellington, Howard, and the champion stood in full view, with doors closed behind them. This was certainly the finest sight of the day. The herald then read the challenge; the glove was thrown down. They all then proceeded to the throne."

Westminster Hall is called the *Great Hall*, to distinguish it from the *Little* or *Lesser Hall*, the House of Commons after the fire of 1834. The Great Hall is erroneously stated to be the widest in Europe without any

* Among the items of the feast itself were 1700 lbs. of meat, 3000 fowls, 000 dozens of wine, 10,000 plates, and 17,000 knives and forks.

intermediate support, for there are two roofs in Italy which surpass it. The next largest ancient apartment in England is the dormitory attached to the great monastery of Durham.

WHITECHAPEL,

"A very extraordinary spacious street, between Whitechapel Bars (to which the freedom reaches) W., and the road to Mile-end E." (*Hatton*, 1708). It was, until the termination of the Eastern Counties Railway, the great Essex road: hence its numerous inns, some with old galleried yards. Upon the south side, west end, among the butchers' shops, is No. 76, a picturesque house-front, bearing the Prince of Wales's feathers and H. S. (Henry Stuart), the arms of Westminster, the fleur-de-lis of France, and the thistle of Scotland. On the north side was a prison for debtors, in the manor of Stepney, under 5l. per annum, of which there is in the Beaufoy Collection a Token, 1656; also a Whitechapel pawnbroker's Token, thought to be unique. Defoe lived here in safety during the Great Plague year; and he describes the richer sort of people thronging out of town from the City by this road, with their families and servants. Whitechapel contains 213 streets, and nearly 5000 inhabited houses: it has been sanitorily improved of late, especially by the furnaces of the factories consuming their own smoke. In Wentworth-street are the *Model Baths and Wash-houses*, established 1845. *St. Mary's Church*, Whitechapel, is described at page 146. Here was the offensive altar-piece, painted by W. Fellowes, in which Judas the traitor greatly resembled Dean Kennet (see the print in the Society of Antiquaries' Library): the picture is now in St. Alban's Abbey-church, and attributed to Sir James Thornhill. In Colchester-street, Leman-street, in 1854, was burnt the house No. 1, built 1667, and noted as the rendezvous of Claude Duval, the highwayman. Near the lower end of Whitechapel-lane was a Roman cemetery, in which was found, in 1776, a monumental stone inscribed to a soldier of the 24th legion. In 1854, there was living in the Whitechapel-road a corn-dealer aged 107, active in business as a man of 60. At No. 267 Whitechapel-road is the Bell-foundry of Chas. and Geo. Mears, where have been cast upwards of 188,000 single bells: they have often 30 tons of molten metal in their furnaces. Here were cast, in 1835, "the New Great Tom of Lincoln," 5 tons 8 cwt.; the Great Bell of Montreal, 13 tons 10 cwt.; Great Peter of York, 11 tons; the bells of the New Royal Exchange, &c.

WHITECROSS-STREET,

In the Ward of Cripplegate, is named from a white cross that stood formerly at the upper end of the street, mentioned in a presentment of 1275. Here is the *City Prison* (see page 631); and the *Green Yard*, where is kept the Lord Mayor's State-Coach (see page 688). "Whitecross-street and Wood-street were the last in the City to surrender their sign-boards; they retained them till 1773."—*J. H. Burn.*

WHITEFRIARS,

The streets, lanes, and alleys between Water-lane (now Whitefriars-street) and the Temple, and Fleet-street and the Thames; formerly the site of the house and gardens of a convent of Carmelites, or White Friars, founded by Sir Richard Gray in 1241, upon ground given by King Edward I. The church was rebuilt by Hugh Courtenay, Earl of Devon, about 1350; and Robert Marshall, Bishop of Hereford, about 1420, added the steeple, as shown in the Sutherland View of London, 1543. Stow gives a long list of benefactors and nobles buried in the hurch. At the Reformation, the chapter-house was given by Henry VIII. to his physician, Dr. Butts. In the next reign, the church, with ts stately tombs, was demolished; and in its place were "many fair iouses built, lodgings for noblemen and others" (*Stow*). Here lived Sir Iohn Cheke, Tutor and Secretary of State to Edward VI. The hall or refectory of the dissolved monastery was used as the Whitefriars Theatre. The precinct had long possessed the privileges of sanctuary, which were confirmed by charter of James I. in 1608; hence it became he asylum of characterless debtors, cheats, and gamblers, here proected from arrest: it acquired the cant name of "Alsatia," and is the cene of Shadwell's *Squire of Alsatia*, the characters of which "dare ot stir out of Whitefryers:" one of its cant-named portions, *Lombard-treet* (its "lewd women" were complained of by the Friars in the reign f Edward III.), exists to this day; as does *Lombard-street* in the Southvark Mint. Poets and players were attracted to Whitefriars by the ontiguous theatre in Dorset Gardens: dancing-masters and fencingnasters flocked here; and here, in the reign of James I., Turner the encing-master was assassinated by two villains hired by Lord Sanquhar, vhose eye Turner had put out during a fencing-lesson several years efore, but he had been forgiven the accident. The two assassins were anged opposite Whitefriars gates in Fleet-street; and Lord Sanuhar was hanged in Old Palace-yard. In the Friary-house, Selden ved with Elizabeth, countess-dowager of Kent, who bequeathed him he mansion: he died here, Nov. 30, 1654, and was buried in the Temple Church. The finest edition of Selden's works, by Wilkins, 3 vols. folio, vas printed in Whitefriars by William Bowyer, father and son; their rinting-office was the George Tavern, Dogwell-court, a scene in Shadvell's *Squire of Alsatia*; in this house, William Bowyer, jun. was born 1 1699. The premises are now the printing-office of Messrs. Bradbury nd Evans, who maintain the excellence of their predecessors. Few ther traces of old Whitefriars remain. *Hanging-Sword-alley*, east of Vater-lane, is named from "a house called the Hanging Sword," menoned by Stow. In Temple-lane are the *Whitefriars Glass-works*, stablished *circ.* 1700.

WHITEHALL,

hat part of Westminster which extends from near Charing Cross to owning-street, and from the Thames to St. James's Park. This was ie site of the royal Palace of Whitehall from 1530 to 1697. It was rmerly called *York Place*, from having been the town residence of ie Archbishops of York; one of whom, Walter de Grey, purchased it 1248 from the Convent of Black Friars of Holborn, to which it had een bequeathed by Hubert de Burgh, the Justiciary of England, and mous minister of Henry III., who had bought the inheritance from ie monks of Westminster for 140 marks of silver. The property was nveyed by Walter de Grey to his successors in the see of York. ardinal Wolsey was the last Archbishop of York by whom the palace as inhabited: he built extensively, and "lived a long season," here, sumptuous state:

> "Where fruitful Thames salutes the learned shore
>   Was this grave prelate and the muses plac'd,
> And by those waves he *builded* had before
>   A royal house with learned muses grac'd,
> But by his death imperfect and defac'd."
>
>   Storer's *Metrical History of Wolsey*, 1599.

bon the fall of Wolsey, in 1529, York Place was taken from him by enry VIII., and the broken-hearted prelate left in his barge on the ames for Esher. The name of the palace was then changed to White

Hall;* possibly from some new buildings having been constructed of white stone, at a time when bricks and timber were generally used.†

> "You must no more call it York Place—that is past:
> For since the Cardinal fell, that title's lost;
> 'Tis now the King's, and call'd White Hall."
> Shakspeare's *King Henry VIII.*, act iv. sc. 1.

Here Henry and Anne Boleyn were married in a garret of the palace; and here their coronation took place. Henry built a noble stone gallery, from which, in 1539, he reviewed 15,000 armed citizens; from this gallery also the court and nobility witnessed the jousts and tournaments in the Tilt-yard, now the parade-ground of the Horse Guards. The King "most sumptuously and curiously builded many beautiful, costly, and pleasant lodgings, buildings, and mansions;" and added a tennis-court, bowling-alleys, and a cock-pit, "for his pastime and solace."

The Palace was seven years in building; and in 1536 (the old palace of Edward the Confessor having been in utter ruin and decay since the fire in 1512), it was enacted by Parliament that all the ground, mansion and buildings, the park, and the entire space between Charing Cross and the Sanctuary at Westminster, from the Thames on the east side to the park-wall westward, should be cleared and called the King's Palace of Westminster. Here the King assembled many pictures, which afterwards became the nucleus of the splendid collection of Charles I. Henry made munificent proposals to Raphael and Titian, and the former painted for him a "St. George." The King also took into his service Hans Holbein, and gave him apartments at Whitehall, with a pension, besides paying him for his pictures. Holbein built, opposite the entrance to the Tilt-yard, a magnificent Gate-house, of small squared stones and flint boulder, glazed and tesselated. On each front were four terra-cotta busts, naturally coloured, and gilt. This gate was removed in 1750, when it was begged by William Duke of Cumberland, son of George II., with the intention of rebuilding it in the Great Park at Windsor; the stones were numbered for this purpose, which was never fulfilled. Three of the busts, Henry VII. and VIII. and Bishop Fisher, are now at Hatfield Priory, Essex. The Gatehouse was used as a State-Paper Office many years before its removal, and was known as the Cockpit Gate. At Whitehall, on Dec. 30, 1546, Henry signed his will, and on Jan. 28 expired.‡

Edward VI. held a Parliament here:

1553. "And this yere the furst day of (March was the) parlament, and kepte wythin the kynges pallys at Westmyster, Whythalle."—*Chron. Grey Friars Lond.*

Bishop Latimer preached before the Court in the Privy Garden, the King sitting at one of the palace windows. Queen Mary went from Whitehall by water to her coronation at Westminster, Elizabeth bearing the crown before her. Whitehall palace was attacked by Sir Thomas Wyatt's rebels, who "shotte divers arrowes into the courte,

* The "White Hall" was a name not unfrequently given by our ancestors to the festive halls of their habitations: there was a White Hall at Kenilworth; and the Hall formerly the House of Lords was the White Hall of the royal Palace of Westminster, and is so called by Stow.

† Portland-stone, now employed in nearly all the public buildings of London, was first used in the Whitehall Banquetting-house. Portland Isle is a mass of freestone rock, of which nearly 30,000 tons have been dug annually, in very large blocks: in Westminster Bridge are stones of 5 tons weight, and some have been dug 7 tons. Varieties of this stone soon become soft in the London atmosphere; but in Portland are buildings upwards of three centuries old, in perfect condition.

‡ Thursday was a fatal day to Henry VIII., and so also to his posterity. He died on Thursday, Jan. 28. King Edward VI. on Thursday, July 6. Queen Mary on Thursday, Nov. 17. Queen Elizabeth on Thursday, March 24.—*Aubrey.*

the gate beying open;" and looking out over the gate, the Queen pardoned the Kent men, with halters about their necks. From the palace the Princess Elizabeth was taken captive to the Tower on Palm Sunday, 1554. At Whitehall, Nov. 13, 1555, died Gardiner, Bishop of Winchester and Lord Chancellor of England, at midnight, exclaiming: "I have sinned, I have not wept with Peter." Hentzner describes, in 1598, Elizabeth's library of Greek, Latin, Italian, and French books; a little one in her own handwriting, addressed to her father; and a book of prayers written by Elizabeth in five languages, with her own miniature and that of her suitor, the Duc d'Anjou. In her 67th year, 'this day she appoints a Frenchman to doe feates upon a rope in the conduit court. To-morrow she hath commanded the bears, the bull, and the ape, to be bayted in the tilt-yard. Upon Wednesday she will have solemn dawncing." (*Rowland White*.) Elizabeth revived the pageants and joustings at Whitehall; and here she built " the Fortress or Castell of perfect Beautie," a large wooden banqueting-house on the north-west side of the palace. In 1561 Sackville and Norton's tragedy of *Ferrex and Pollex* was acted here by gentlemen of the Inner Temple. In the great gallery, Elizabeth received the Speaker and Common House, when they came " to move her grace to marriage." On March 24, 1603, " then deceased," from Richmond, " the Queen was brought by water to Whitehall."

In the Orchard of Whitehall the Lords in Council met; and in the Garden, James I. knighted 300 or 400 judges, sergeants, doctors-at-law, &c. Here the Lord Monteagle imparted to the Earl of Salisbury the warning letter of the Gunpowder Plot; and Guy Fawkes was examined in the King's bedchamber, and carried hence to the Tower. In 1617, when James visited Scotland, Lord Keeper Bacon resided at Whitehall. James I., in 1608, had " the old, rotten, slight-builded Banqueting House" removed, and next year rebuilt; but it was destroyed by fire in 1619. In this reign were produced many " most glorious masques" by Inigo Jones and Ben Jonson; and Inigo designed a new palace, the drawings for which are preserved in Worcester College, Oxford.

In magnitude, Inigo Jones's plan would have exceeded that of the palace of Diocletian, and would have covered nearly 24 acres. It was to have consisted of seven courts, and to have extended 874 feet fronting the Thames, and the same length along the foot of St. James's Park: presenting one front to Charing Cross, of 1200 feet long; and another, the principal, of similar dimensions towards Westminster Abbey. (See Fourdrinier's large print.) A more distinct idea may be formed of this extent by comparing it with that of other palaces: thus, Hampton Court covers 8 or 9 acres, St. James's 4, Buckingham 2½ acres.

Of Jones's magnificent design, only the *Banqueting-house* was completed. Charles I. commissioned Rubens to paint the ceiling, and by his agency obtained the Cartoons of Raphael. In the Cabinet-room of the palace, built also by Inigo Jones, fronting westward to Privy Garden, Charles assembled pictures of almost incalculable value; the royal collection containing 460 paintings, including 28 by Titian, 11 by Correggio, 16 by Julio Romano, 9 by Raphael, 4 by Guido, and 7 by Parmegiano. Upon the Civil War breaking out, Whitehall was seized by the Parliament, who, in 1645, had " the boarded masque-house" pulled down, sold great part of the paintings and statues, and burnt the " superstitious pictures." Here, Jan. 29, 1649, in the Cabinet-room Charles last prayed; in the Horn-chamber he was delivered to the officers, and thence led out to execution upon a scaffold in front of the Banqueting-house. (See page 166.)

Charles was taken on the first morning of his trial, Jan. 20, 1649, in a sedan-chair, from Whitehall to Cotton House, where he slept pending his trial in West-

D D D

minster Hall; after which the king returned to Whitehall; but on the night before his execution he slept at St. James's. On Jan. 30 he was "most barbarously murthered at his own door, about two a clock in the afternoon." (*Histor. Guide*, 3d imp., 1688.) Lord Leicester and Dugdale state that Charles was beheaded at Whitehall gate. The scaffold was erected in front of the Banqueting-house, in the street now Whitehall; and Herbert states that the king was led out by "a passage broken through the wall," on to the scaffold; but Ludlow states that it was out of a window, according to Vertue, of a small building north of the Banqueting house, whence the king stepped upon the scaffold. A picture of the sad scene, painted by Weesop, in the manner of Vandyke, shows the platform, extending only in length, before two of the windows, to the commencement of the third casement. Weesop visited England from Holland in 1641, and quitted England in 1649, saying "he would never reside in a country where they cut off their king's head, and were not ashamed of the action."

Cromwell, by vote of Parliament in 1650, had "the use of the lodging called the Cockpit, of the Spring Garden, and St. James's House, and the command of St. James's Park," for some time before he assumed the supreme power. To Whitehall, in 1653, April 20th, he returned with the keys in his pocket, after dissolving the Long Parliament, which he subsequently explained to the Little or Barebones Parliament assembled in the Council-chamber of Whitehall. Here the Parliament desired Cromwell to "magnify himself with the title of King;" here Milton was Cromwell's Latin Secretary, Andrew Marvell his frequent guest, with Waller his friend and kinsman, and sometimes the youthful Dryden. Cromwell repurchased the Cartoons and many other pictures, and in 1656 Evelyn found the palace "very glorious and well furnished." Here Cromwell expired, Sept. 3, 1658, "the double day of victory and death." Richard Cromwell resided here. Charles II., at the Restoration, came in grand procession of seven hours from the City to Whitehall. To the Lords Commissioners of the Treasury Charles assigned the Cockpit; and in this locality their chambers have ever since remained. Charles collected by proclamation the plate, hangings, and paintings, which had been pillaged from the palace: he also built a stone gallery to flank Privy Garden, and below it suites of apartments for his "Beauties." Evelyn describes the Duchess of Portsmouth's apartment, "twice or thrice pulled down and rebuilt to satisfy her prodigal and expensive pleasures;" its French tapestry, "Japan cabinets, screens, pendule clocks, great vases of wrought plate, table-stands, chimney-furniture, sconces, branches, brasenas, &c., all of massive silver, and out of number." Evelyn describes a Sunday evening in the palace:

"The king sitting and toying with his concubines, Portsmouth, Cleaveland, and Mazarine, &c.; a French boy singing love-songs in those glorious galleries; whilst about twenty of the great courtiers and other dissolute persons were at basset round a large table, a bank of at least 2000*l*. in gold before them. Six days after was all in the dust."

In Vertue's plan are shown the buttery, bakehouse, wood and coal yards, charcoal-house, spicery, cider-house; and, beneath the Banqueting-house, the king's privy cellar. Owing to its low level, Whitehall was liable to floods from the Thames. Pepys, in 1663, records a high tide having drowned the whole palace; and Charles II., when he received the Lords and Commons in the Banqueting-hall at the Restoration, desires them to mend the ways, so that his wife "may not find Whitehall under water."

At Whitehall Charles collected about 1000 volumes, dedicated or presented to him: including an illuminated Breviary given by Henry VII. to his daughter, Margaret Queen of Scots, with his autograph; a curious MS. in high Dutch on the Great Elixir; a French MS. 300 years old, with paintings of plants in miniature; and a journal, &c. in the handwriting of Edward VI. Charles II. died at Whitehall, Feb. 6, 1685; and his successor was immediately proclaimed at the palace-gate. James II. resided here: he washed the feet of the poor with his own hands on Maundy Thursday in the Chapel Royal: here he admitted Penn, the Quaker, to his private closet; and he rebuilt the chapel for Romish worship, with marble statues by Gibbons, and a fresco by Verrio. The King also erected upon the Banqueting-house a large weathercock, that he might calculate by the wind the probable arrival of the Dutch fleet. (See Canaletti's view.) On Dec. 18, 1688, James left Whitehall in the state-barge, never to return. In 1691 a destructive fire reduced the palace to "nothing but walls and ruins:" 150 houses were burned down, and twenty blown up with gunpowder. In 1697 a fire broke out in the laundry; all the pictures in the palace were destroyed, and twelve persons perished. The remaining portions of the site of Whitehall were given away by the Crown. Charles Duke of Richmond had a mansion on the south-east side of Privy Garden: it was rebuilt from a plan by the Earl of Burlington, and was burnt down in 1791; its site is now occupied by Richmond-terrace. In Privy Garden was also built *Pembroke House;* and subsequently, *Gwydir House,* now the Office of the Poor-Law Board.

Gardens and Dials.—The gardens were laid out in terraces and parterres, and ornamented with marble and bronze statues, a few of which are now at Hampton Court and Windsor. In Privy Garden was a dial set up by Edward Gunter, professor of astronomy at Gresham College (and of which he published a description), by command of James I., in 1624. A large stone pedestal bore four dials at the four corners, and "the great horizontal concave" in the centre; besides east, west, north, and south dials at the sides. In the reign of Charles II. this dial was defaced by a drunken nobleman of the Court:

> " This place for a dial was too unsecure,
>   Since a guard and a garden could not defend;
> For so near to the Court they will never endure
>   Any witness to show how their time they misspend."—*Marvell.*

In the court-yard facing the Banqueting-house was another curious dial, set up in 1669 by order of Charles II. It was invented by one Francis Hall, *alias* Lyne, a Jesuit, and professor of mathematics at Liège. This dial consisted of five stages rising in a pyramidal form, and bearing several vertical and reclining dials, globes cut into planes, and glass bowls; showing, "besides the houres of all kinds," "many things also belonging to geography, astrology, and astronomy, by the sun's shadow made visible to the eye." Among the pictures were portraits of the king, the two queens, the Duke of York, and Prince Rupert. Father Lyne published a description of this dial, which consisted of seventy-three parts: it is illustrated with seventeen plates. (The details are condensed in No. 400 of the *Mirror.*) About 1710, William Allingham, a mathematician in Canon-row, asked 500*l.* to repair this dial: it was last seen by Vertue at Buckingham House.

Remains of ancient Whitehall have been from time to time discovered. In 1831, Mr. Sydney Smirke, F.S.A., in the basement of "Cromwell House," Whitehall-yard, found a stone-built and groined Tudor apartment—undoubtedly a relic of Wolsey's palace, and corresponding with the wine-cellar in Vertue's plan,—which is characteristically larger than the chapel. Mr. Smirke also found a Tudor arched doorway, with remains of the arms of Wolsey and the see of York in the spandrels; a portion of the river-wall and circular bastions; and two stone mullioned Tudor windows, at the back of the Almonry-office, corresponding with the back wall of the apartments of "the Yeomen of the Wood-yard," in Vertue's plan. In 1847 were removed the last remains of York House, a Tudor embattled doorway, which had been built into a later façade of the Treasury. (*Archæologia*, vol. xxv.)

Upon the site of the small-beer cellar (engraved in No. 4 of Hollar's prints of Whitehall) is the house of the Earl of Fife. Here were some fine Gobelins tapestry; a marble picture of Mary Stuart, with her infant; and in Pennant's time here was a head of Charles I. when Prince of Wales, said to have been painted at Madrid by Velasquez, in 1625.* The mansion was sold, in 1809, for 12,000*l*. to the Earl of Liverpool, who possessed it until his death in 1828. In an adjoining wall is the Tudor arched entrance to the palace water-stairs. In Privy Garden was the celebrated Museum formed by the Duchess of Portland: here Pennant was shown a rich pearl surmounted with a crown, which was taken out of the ear of Charles I. after his head was struck off: here also was the Barberini or Portland Vase, purchased by the Duchess of Sir William Hamilton for 1800 guineas. The museum was sold by auction, in lots, April 24, 1786, when the vase was bought by the Duke of Portland for 1029 guineas, and deposited by his grace in the British Museum in 1810. (See page 523.)

In *Whitehall Yard* is the UNITED SERVICE INSTITUTION MUSEUM, described at page 545. No. 3 is the Office of the Comptroller General of the Exchequer, where is held "the Trial of the Pyx." (See pp. 99 and 508.)

In *Whitehall Gardens* (till recently called by the old name, *Privy Garden*) is MONTAGUE HOUSE (see page 491); No. 4 is LADY PEEL'S (see page 493). No. 1 is the *National Club House*, where is a noble saloon 80 feet in length, hung with large tapestry pictures in the manner of Teniers, of considerable age, yet fresh in colour. No. 7 is *Pembroke House* (formerly the Earl of Harrington's): in 1854, it was fitted up for the Minister-at-War.

WHITEHALL commences at *Scotland-yard*,† named from its having been the site of the palace "for receipt of the Kings of Scotland, when they came to the Parliament of England:" here is *Palace-row*, and a large Conduit-house. Milton, when Latin Secretary to Cromwell, had apartments in Scotland-yard, where died the poet's infant son. The Crown Surveyor had his official residence in Scotland-yard; and here lived Inigo Jones, Sir John Denham, and Sir Christopher Wren, who successively filled that office. Here Sir John Vanbrugh built himself a house out of the ruins of Whitehall Palace: Swift has ridiculed the house of "brother Van" for its resemblance to a goose-pie: Vanbrugh died here in 1726.

Near his house in Scotland-yard, Inigo Jones, uniting with Nicholas Stone, the sculptor, buried his money in a private place. "The Parliament published an order encouraging servants to inform of such concealments; and as four of the workmen were privy to the deposit, Jones and his friend removed it privately, and with their own hands buried it in Lambeth Marsh."—*Life* by Cunningham.

On the west side of Whitehall are the Government Offices: the ADMIRALTY (see page 1); HORSE GUARDS (p. 377); TREASURY (p. 742). Next is *Downing-street*, "between King-street E. and no thorow fair West" (*Hatton*). It was named from Sir George Downing, Bart., a political "sider with all times and changes," who, after serving Cromwell, became Secretary to the Treasury under Charles II., 1667. At the Revolution, the property, then belonging to Lee, Lord Lichfield,

* In 1845, Mr. Snare, of Reading, bought at a sale of pictures at Radley Hall a painting which he believes to be "the lost portrait" of Prince Charles by Velasquez, and so denoted by the Earl of Fife in his catalogue of his pictures at Fife House, in 1798. (See Account of the Picture, &c. Reading, 1847.)

† Northward, at No. 30 Charing Cross (now Parker & Co., military booksellers), Thomson the poet took lodgings when he first arrived in London, with the Ms. of his *Winter*: here he wrote part of his *Summer*.

was forfeited to the Crown. The largest house was, *temp.* George I., the office of the Hanoverian minister, Baron Bothmar, at whose death the mansion was given by George to Sir Robert Walpole, " who, in 1735, would only accept it for his office of First Lord of the Treasury, to which post he got it annexed for ever." (*Ædes Walpolianæ.*) It has accordingly since been the official residence of successive prime ministers: here Lady Hester Stanhope received Mr. Pitt's guests: but the rooms are ill adapted for state assemblies. The adjoining house has been purchased within the present century, for the Foreign Office, Colonial Office, and Office of the Chancellor of the Exchequer. To this *cul-de-sac* a street of smaller houses was added: the south side was taken down in 1828 : at the corner next King-street was the noted Cat and Bagpipes, used as a chop-house in early life by George Rose, subsequently Secretary of the Treasury, and the originator of Savings-banks.

In one of the above mansions, in 1763, died Aubrey de Vere, last Earl of Oxford. In the street lived, in 1723, John Boyle, Earl of Orrery, the friend of Swift. and contributor to *The World* and *Connoisseur.* Here resided Boswell, the biographer of Johnson; and Lord Sheffield, the friend of Gibbon, the historian.

WINDOWS OF PAINTED AND STAINED GLASS.

The following are the more noteworthy specimens in the metropolis, most of which are incidentally noticed in describing the edifices which contain them. First, in CHURCHES and CHAPELS:

All Saints', St. John's Wood—Chancel window, by Fairs: the head filled with figures and foliage; and the ten lights with emblematic devices of the evangelists, and the eucharistic service.

All Saints', Margaret-street—A large western Jesse window of 13 figures, ending with Christ crucified; painted by Gerente; the clerestory windows by O'Connor: all constructed in the ancient manner.

St. Andrew's, Holborn—A large east Palladian window in two stories, painted by Price, of York, in 1718, with the Last Supper and the Ascension. Also two aisle windows, with arms, one dated 1687, and the other a memorial to Thavie, of 1348.

St. Barnabas', Queen-street, Pimlico—All the windows are filled with scenes and incidents from the life of St. Barnabas, by Wailes.

St. Bride's, Fleet-street—Large eastern window, the Descent from the Cross ; copied by Muss, from Rubens's picture at Antwerp.

"This is a fine production, although it does not give a perfect idea of the original picture. The whole of the light is thrown upon the body of our Saviour, while the rest of the painting is quite obscure; producing the sort of effect that Rembrandt would have given to the subject had he treated it, rather than that with which Rubens has invested it. The fine group of women at the foot of the cross is quite undiscoverable."—Godwin's *Churches of London.*

St. Catherine's Cree, Leadenhall-street—East window, with Catherine-wheel mullions filled with brilliant glass ; above, the arms of Geo. I.

Christ Church, Woburn-square—One of the finest modern windows, representing Christ blessing little children, after Overbeck's print; and Moses giving the law to the Israelites, after Raphael.

St. Dunstan's in the West, Fleet-street—Eight clerestory windows, in each of which is one of the letters of the architect's name, *John Shaw.* Pointed altar-window, filled with subjects of antique design: full-length figures of the Evangelists, with their names—*S. Mattheus, S. Marcus, S. Lucas*, and *S. Johannes :* beneath which, respectively, are, a curious monogram of the Trinity, the crown of thorns and the nails, the spear and sponge upon a reed, and the Holy Lamb; and under all is: 𝔇𝔢𝔬 𝔢𝔱 𝔢𝔠𝔠𝔩𝔢𝔰𝔦𝔞𝔢 𝔣𝔯𝔞𝔦𝔯𝔢𝔰 𝔥𝔢𝔞𝔯𝔱 𝔟𝔦𝔠𝔞𝔟𝔢𝔯𝔲𝔫𝔱, 𝔞𝔫𝔫𝔬 𝔇𝔬𝔪𝔦𝔫𝔦 𝔐𝔇𝔠𝔠𝔠𝔵𝔵𝔵𝔦𝔦. These very fine windows are by Willement. When the old church of St. Dunstan was cleared away in 1830, a painted window was sold for 4*l.* 5*s.*, and subsequently built into the Elizabethan mansion at Gilston Park, Herts, which was taken down in 1853.

St. Dunstan's in the East, Tower-street—East window, by Backler, describing symbolically the Law and the Gospel; between two windows by E. Baillie: Christ blessing little children, and the Adoration of the Magi. The heads of the south-aisle windows contain arms of ancient benefactors of the parish, with scriptural scrolls, by Baillie.

St. George's, Hanover-square—Eastern window filled with painted glass not later than 1520, and originally brought from Flanders: it has been much repaired; and a head of a monarch, which antiquaries would seize on as giving the date, is modern. The glass originally represented a Stem of Jesse, and occupied a window of three lights: Jesse being at the foot of the second light, and above him Solomon, David, the Virgin Mary, the Holy Ghost, and God the Father; left-hand light, two prophets, and Isechias, Roboam, Argo, Jehosaphat, and Josias; right hand, two prophets, and Joram, Achaz, Manasses, and Jechonias. All these figures are in St. George's windows, except that of the Father; which figure has been transformed into a bishop, and is now in one of the windows of the new Byzantine church at Wilton, Wilts. (See also p. 127.)

St. George's, Southwark—Eastern Venetian window: whole-length of the Saviour, by Backler.

St. George's Roman Catholic Church, Lambeth—Great western window, containing figures of SS. George the Martyr, Richard, Ethelbert, Oswald, Edmund, and Edward the Confessor, with angels bearing scrolls and instruments. Great east window of nine lights, by Wailes, representing the Root of Jesse, or the genealogy of our Lord: the gift of the Earl of Shrewsbury. Three side windows, with figures of SS. George, Stephen, and Lawrence, by Hardman, under canopies, with angels bearing crowns and laurels. The windows of the aisles will also be eventually filled with painted glass. The Petre Chantry has three two-light windows, by Hardman, containing figures of St. George, our Blessed Lady, St. Edward the Confessor, St. Lawrence, St. Robert, and St. Germanus.

St. Giles's, Camberwell—East window, 13th-century style, a fine specimen of the symbolism of religious art; nave window, arms of the vicar and his wife, chiefly ancient glass imported from Cologne, with modern additions; south transept window, with figures of St. Peter and St. Paul, and sacred symbols. (This and the preceding are *grisailles, i. e.* windows with a white ground relieved by a running decorative pattern in positive colours; as distinguished from *mosaiques* (such as the chancel window), when the ground is of the same quality with the figures.) Also transept memorial window, with canopied figures of Moses and Christ, the donor's arms, and inscription: the modern glass by Ward and Nixon.

Immaculate Conception (Roman-Catholic) Church, Farm-street, Berkeley-square, has several fine works. East, a Jesse window: in the base of the centre opening is Jesse seated (usually represented recumbent); and from him springs a stem encircling in each opening one of the kings, the Virgin and Child immediately above Jesse. The tracery is filled with subjects from the history of the Virgin, and adoring angels. Immediately over the centre is a wall-painting of the Immaculate Conception. West, a Passion Window, containing emblems of our Lord's Passion, as the cross, dice, &c. The stonework is very fine. The side windows are chiefly filled with angels bearing crosses and palm-branches. The several windows were donations, and were painted by Wailes.

St. James's, Piccadilly—A two-storied east window. In 1809, Backler proposed to fill this window with a copy of Raphael's picture of the Transfiguration; John Martin next suggested the Baptism of the Saviour in Jordan; and the Birth and Death of our Saviour were then designed, in the modern style, by Corbould. But the Bishop of London preferred a more ancient style of art; and the window was filled by Wailes, in 1846, with the Resurrection and Ascension, the Agony and Bloody Sweat, the Passion, and the Bearing of the Cross. The borders are Italian, from Raffaelle, J. Romano, and others.

St. John the Evangelist's, Westminster. The eastern window represents our Lord bearing his cross, and is said to have been brought from an ancient church at Rouen in Normandy.

St. John's of Jerusalem, South Hackney—Chancel windows, with incidents in the life of our Saviour, figures of the apostles, &c.. by Wailes. Transept windows by Powell, representing Abraham offering up Isaac, and scenes in the life of Moses; and richly-diapered glass. Aisle windows, diapered and painted by Wailes and Castell. Clerestory memorial window, Christ blessing little children, and raising Jairus's daughter; and two other windows by Ward and Nixon. Also figures of Elias and John the Baptist; the Royal arms of England, and the arms of the sees of Canterbury, London, &c., by Powell.

St. Katherine's, Regent's Park, contains some very fine specimens of heraldic decorations.

St. Leonard's, Shoreditch, has an eastern window, 1634. The subject is the Last Supper: to the bread and wine usually placed *per se* on the table, the artist has added several articles, one of which has often been mistaken for a little pig, but represents a young kid. Had it been a pig, (to the Jews) forbidden food, it is averred that the painter might in justification have quoted the vision of St. Peter (Acts x. 12-15); for that, therefore, the pig was no longer prohibited by the law.

Lincoln's Inn Chapel windows are filled with glass, principally painted by Bernard and Abraham Van Linge, Flemish artists, between 1623 and 1626: others were executed "by Mr. Hall, a glass-painter in Fetter-lane; and in point of colour are as rich as the richest decorated glass of the best period." (Winston on *Glass-Painting*.) South side: three windows of four lights, each filled with a saint and his attribute, canopied and inscribed, surrounded by angels bearing the crests of the arms emblazoned upon the pedestals of the figures. North side: three windows of four lights, filled with King David playing the harp, Moses and the Prophets, St. John the Baptist, and St. Paul. The great eastern and western windows are filled with arms: in the latter are the arms of Henry Shirfield, Recorder of Salisbury, who was prosecuted and severely fined by the Star Chamber for breaking a painted window at Salisbury. (See *State Trials*, vol. i. p. 339.) The arms of his opponent, Noy, then Attorney-general of Charles I., are also in the Chapel. The several arms are minutely described in Spilsbury's *Lincoln's Inn.*

St. Margaret's, Westminster—East window, a very fine specimen of glass-painting *temp.* Henry VIII., and said to have been presented by the magistrates of Dort, in Holland, to Henry VII., whom the kneeling effigy of the king more resembles than his son. But the patron saintess, St. Catherine, over the kneeling figure of the queen, and the badge of the pomegranate in the tracery light, rather point to Henry VIII. than his father. It is possible that the king died before the window was completed, and that it was finished from a likeness of Henry VII. with which the people of Dort provided the painter. The glass is clearly of the time of Henry VIII. and not Henry VII., and is as late as 1526; but has been retouched, probably when put up in the church in 1758. The principal subject represented is the Crucifixion. Mr. Rickman, however, regarded the kneeling figures as Prince Arthur and the Princess Catherine; which is scarcely reconcilable with the *arched* crown on the male head. (See also pages 136 and 137.)

St. Mary's, Herne Hill—All the windows filled: east, the four evangelists; north and south, arms of the archbishop, the bishop, &c.; west, arms of Her Majesty; Prince Albert, and Queen Dowager; aisle windows, arms of subscribers.

St. Mary's, Rotherhithe—An east window by Collins, with a whole-length of St. Mary the Virgin.

St. Mary's, West Brompton, a picturesque church (G. Godwin, F.S.A., architect), contains a fine memorial window, by Wailes, to Mr. Robert Gunter, donor of the church-site, 1853. The window, in three principal compartments, is painted with the Ascension; the figures and colouring are fine: the oriels are filled with tracery and angels bearing scrolls.

St. Mary's, Wyndham-place, Marylebone—East window, the Ascension: poorly executed, though it cost 250*l.*

St. Stephen's, Rochester-row, Westminster—Windows by Wailes, representing scenes in the life of St. Stephen, in which the rude quaintness of early glass-painting is faithfully imitated.

St. Stephen's, Walbrook—Altar window erected in place of West's picture of the stoning of St. Stephen, and presented by the Grocers' Company, in 1852. The window was designed and executed by Willement, in the Roman style adopted by Raphael: central subjects, the ordination and stoning of St. Stephen; sides, the four evangelists, with their emblems; semicircular top, the figure of our Saviour, angels in devotional attitudes, and the Lamb bearing the banner of the cross.

St. Stephen's Chapel, Westminster, reputed to have been founded by King Stephen, rebuilt after the fire of 1298 by Edward I., and restored by Edward II. and III., had its windows filled with glass painted by John de Chester, at the weekly wages of 7*s.*! The Account Rolls, 25th and 26th Edward III., contain items of blue, red, and azure glass; drawings of several images; painters on glass, at 7*d.* per day: silver filings, geet (jet), arnement (orpiment, or yellow arsenic), among the painting materials. In 1548, the Chapel was fitted up for the Commons' House of Parliament; and when, in 1809, the window was enlarged, it was discovered that the elegant tracery of the windows had been painted with the stories of Adam and Eve; of Noah and his Family; of Abraham, Joseph, and the Israelites; and of the life of our Saviour.

Temple Church—Windows in the ancient manner, by Willement, described at page 163. Window in the "Round," next the door, fine.

Westminster Abbey (see page 112)—Five only of the original windows remain,—three of the apsis over St. Edward's Chapel, and two at the west ends of the side aisles. The former, coeval with the architecture, represent: 1. Our Saviour and the Virgin Mary; 2. St. Augustine and Bishop Mellitus; 3. Edward the Confessor giving his ring to the pilgrim. One of the small windows is in the north tower, and represents an ecclesiastic; the other, in the south tower, Edward the Black Prince (so says Walpole), in plate-armour, beneath a canopy, bearing a lance, and long sword by his side, and a surcoat with the arms of France and England, quarterly: below his feet are the Lancastrian rose, and the arms of Edward the Confessor. The north window, date 1722, represents in its sixteen compartments our Saviour and the Eleven, and the Evangelists. The west window, date 1735, has in the upper row Abraham, Isaac, and Jacob; next, seven of Jacob's sons; and beneath are five more, Moses and Aaron. The arms are those of George II., in the centre; King Sebert, Queen Elizabeth, Dean Wilcocks, and the College of Westminster. "There are many fragments of glass, coats of arms, &c. of the time of Edward I.," says Mr. Winston, "in the three east clerestory windows; but without going to the triforium, it is impossible to distinguish them from the fragments of all dates with which they are surrounded: the large figures in these windows are of the 15th century. The west window of the south aisle contains a large figure, much broken (face modern), of the time of Richard II. Henry the Seventh's Chapel contains remains of its original glazing: one of the figures in a clerestory window is entire." (*Communication*.) Here a stray rose and a stray letter (ℌ) occasionally occur. The crowns in bushes (Richard III. at Bosworth) have long since disappeared.

Crosby Hall, Bishopsgate-street—Oriel window with arms, executed and presented by Willement; including the arms and badges of St. Helen's Priory, Sir John Crosby, Richard III., Sir Thomas More, the House of York, "the rich Spencer," &c. The other windows are similarly enriched.

Field of Cloth-of-Gold, the largest specimen of modern Glass-painting, was exhibited at No. 15 Oxford-street, in 1830.

The subject was the Tournament of the Field of Cloth-of-Gold, between Henry VIII. and Francis I., at Ardres; the last tourney, June 25, 1520: painted by Thomas Wilmshurst (the horses by Woodward), from a sketch by R. T. Bone. This window was 432 square feet, or 18 by 24 feet; and consisted of 350 pieces, fitted into metal astragals, falling with the shadows, so that the whole picture appeared an entire sheet of glass: it was exhibited in a first-floor room, decorated in the taste of the time of Henry VIII. The picture was composed from the details of Hall's Chronicle, and contained upwards of 100 life-size figures (40 portraits, mostly after Holbein): including the two Queens, Wolsey, Anne Boleyne, and the Countess of Chateaubriant; Charles Brandon, Duke of Suffolk; Queen Mary, Dowager of France; the ill-fated Duke of Buckingham, &c. The gorgeous assemblage of costume, gold and jewels, waving plumes, glittering arms, velvet, ermine, and cloth-of-gold, with heraldic emblazonry, picturesquely managed. The work cost the artist 3000*l*. On the night of Jan. 31, 1832, the house was destroyed in an accidental fire, and with it the picture; not even a sketch or study was saved, and the property was wholly uninsured.

Guildhall, King-street, Cheapside—The upper compartments of the great pointed arched east and west windows are enriched by stained and painted glass, mostly modern. In the east window are the Royal arms and supporters, with the stars and jewels of the Orders of the Garter, Bath, Thistle, and St. Patrick; west window, the City arms and supporters. When these windows are illuminated with gas from the exterior, the effect in the hall is very gorgeous.

Inns of Court—The *Inner Temple Hall* has but few heraldic enrichments in its windows.* The windows of the *Middle Temple Hall* contain an almost perfect series of coats of arms of distinguished members, from Queen Elizabeth to the present reign: in the great bay-windows are conspicuous the arms of Hardwicke and

* Among the insignia are the arms of the Inner Temple, a horse striking the earth with his hoof, or "a Pegasus luna on a field argent;" assumed in the fifth year of the reign of Elizabeth, by the advice of Master Gerard Lee, a herald of the court, who was also a member of this Inn: the Society, though not entitled to arms, as not being a corporation, yet had been so long established that the College of Heralds did not object. He also emblazoned them with precious stones and planets, "as bye truly honourable societies they are often thereunto now." Master Lee suggested such singular arms, as signifying that the knowledge acquired at this learned seminary would raise the professors of the law to the highest honours, adding by way of motto, *Volat ad æthera virtus;* and he intended to allude to what are esteemed the more liberal sciences, by giving them Pegasus forming the fountain of Hippocrene, by striking his hoof against the rock, as a proper emblem of lawyers becoming poets,—as Chaucer and Gower, the fathers of English poetry, were both of the Inner Temple. Their other device is more ancient origin.

Somers; and opposite, those of Tenterden and Gifford, Eldon and Stowell. *Lincoln's Inn* has some fine heraldic glass, described at pages 410 and 411. *Gray's Inn Hall* has its windows richly emblazoned with arms; those of Burghley, Verulam, Sir Nicholas Bacon, and Jenkins, being conspicuous in the large and lofty bay-window. The *Hall of Staple Inn* has also a collection of armorial glass.

Jerusalem Chamber, Westminster Abbey—Remains of painted glass, *temp.* Henry VIII. and somewhat later (arms of Henry, and badges of some of his queens), in the windows of the passages and the ante-room. In the large north window of the chamber, in medallions, are the arms of the see of Lincoln, College of Westminster, and others, with seven small historical and scriptural subjects, referred to Richard II.'s reign. This is believed to be the oldest painted glass in London—the last half of the 12th century. Some of the glass has lately been repaired.

Lambeth Palace—The Great Hall, now the Library, contains specimens of olden glass collected from different parts of the house: they are described at page 444. The windows of the Picture Gallery contain the arms of many of the primates: in the bay-window are the arms of the Protestant Archbishops, from Cranmer to Cornwallis.

The Chapel windows, now filled with Powell's modern *pressed* glass, contained before the Civil Wars finely painted glass, bearing the device of Cardinal Morton, illustrating the History of Man from the Creation to the Day of Judgment, three lights in a window. The two side-lights contained the types in the Old Testament, and the middle light the anti-type and verity of the New: the outer chapel had two windows with the Day of Judgment; there was also represented the Crucifixion. Archbishop Laud, at his coming to Lambeth, found these windows "shameful to look on, all diversly patched, like a poor beggar's coat," and repaired them; when it was alleged against Laud, "that he did repair the story of those windows by their like in the *Mass-book:*" but this Laud denied, affirming that he and his secretary made out the story as well as they could by the unbroken remains. The windows were defaced May 1, 1643.

Archbishop Laud, in his *Defence*, mentions these "harmless goodly windows," as "set up new long since that statute of Edward VI."

Listowel House, Knightsbridge, contains in the conservatory a large window representing a garden scene, painted by John Martin, a pupil of Charles Muss, the celebrated enamel-painter.

Northumberland House, Strand, contains a copy of Martin's Belshazzar's Feast, executed by Hoadley and Oldfield for Collins; cost 400 guineas: it fills a cheval fire-screen.

Pedlar (the), St. Mary's Church, Lambeth, the painting in the middle aisle window, is described at page 145.

Soane Museum, No. 13 Lincoln's Inn Fields—Several specimens of ancient painted glass, chiefly scriptural subjects. Also the figure of Charity, executed by Collins from the celebrated window at New College, Oxford, designed and presented by Sir Joshua Reynolds, 1777.

St. Stephen's Porch, at the south end of Westminster Hall, has a large window by Hardman, representing the arms of the sovereigns of England, from William the Conqueror to the present time; a very brilliant combination of coloured and white glass. (See PARLIAMENT HOUSES.)

ZOOLOGICAL SOCIETY'S GARDENS (THE),

Upon the north-west side of the Regent's Park, consist of a triangular garden south of the outer road, and a northern garden upon the bank of the Regent's Canal: they are connected by a tunnel beneath the road, and their extent is about 17 acres. The soil being originally the London clay very near the surface, was cold and damp, and caused great mortality among the animals of the Menagerie; but the whole has been thoroughly drained and tastefully planted.

The Zoological Society was instituted in 1826, "for the general advancement of zoological science." It had been proposed

"The great objects should be, the introduction of new varieties, breeds, and races of animals, for the purpose of domestication or for stocking our farmyards, woods, pleasure-grounds, and wastes; with the establishment of a general zoological collection, consisting of prepared specimens in the different classes and orders, so as to afford a correct view of the Animal Kingdom at large, in as complete a series as may be practicable; and at the same time point out the analogies between the animals already domesticated and those which are similar in character, upon which the first experiments may be made. * * * * Should the Society flourish and succeed, it will not only be useful in common life, but would likewise promote the best and most extensive objects of the Scientific History of Animated Nature, and offer a collection of living animals such as never yet existed in ancient or modern times."—*Prospectus*, privately circulated, 1824.

Among the founders of the Society were Sir Stamford Raffles, Sir Humphry Davy, Earl Darnley, Sir Everard Home, Mr. Davies Gilbert, Dr. Horsfield, the Rev. W. Kirby, Mr. Sharpe Macleay, and Mr. N. A. Vigors; and into the new Society merged the Zoological Club. At the same time was commenced the formation of a Museum, at No. 33 Bruton-street, with the magnificent collection of Sir S. Raffles. A plot of ground in the Regent's Park was granted to the Society by the government, and laid out by Decimus Burton, who also built the first houses and inclosures for the animals. Sir Francis Chantrey took great interest in the Society, and the embellishment of the Gardens. In 1827, the lake in the Park, with its islands and water-fowl, and a site for breeding and rearing, were likewise granted to the Society; and the Gardens were first opened to the public in 1828, by members' orders, and one shilling each person; and during seven months there were upwards of 30,000 visitors: there were in the Menagerie 430 animals; and the year's expenses were 10,000*l*.

Among the earliest tenants of the Menagerie were a pair of emeus from New Holland; two Arctic bears and a Russian bear; a herd of kangaroos; Cuban mastiffs and Thibet watch-dogs; two llamas from Peru; a splendid collection of eagles, falcons, and owls; a pair of beavers; cranes, spoonbills, and storks; zebras and Indian cows; Esquimaux dogs; armadilloes; and a collection of monkeys. To the Menagerie have since been added an immense number of species of *Mammalia* and *Birds*, lists of which are appended to the several annual Reports. To these was added, in 1849, a collection of *Reptiles;* and in 1853, a collection of *Fish, Mollusca, Zoophytes*, and other *Aquatic Animals.* Among the royal donors to the collection are the Emperor of Russia, the late Queen of Portugal, the Viceroy of Egypt, and Queen Victoria. In 1830, the menagerie collected by George IV. at Sandpit-gate, Windsor, was removed to the Society's Gardens; and in 1834 the last of the Tower Menagerie was received here. The collection was also enriched by purchases from the menagerie of the late Earl of Derby (long President of the Zoological Society), at Knowsley. It is now the finest public Vivarium in Europe.

The Menagerie has been illustrated by W. Harvey, in 2 vols. 8vo; with descriptions by E. T. Bennett, late Vice-Secretary of the Society.

A picturesque description of the Gardens is appended to Landseer's *Characteristic Sketches of Animals*, edited by John Barrow, 1832. See also the Guide-book and Plan of the Gardens, and the Reports, Proceedings, and Catalogues, printed for the Society.

The Museum in 1841 was valued at 10,965*l*., and was then removed from Leicester-square to Broad-street, Golden-square. An extensive collection of birds and insects was bequeathed by the first Secretary, N. A. Vigors, who died in 1840. The MUSEUM, now in the south garden, is described at page 546.

We have only space to enumerate a few of the principal animals in the Gardens:—*Alligators*, a pair of the North American species, captured in Carolina. *Antelopes*, the great family of, finely represented. The beautiful *Elands* were bequeathed by the late Earl of Derby, and have bred freely since their arrival in 1851. The Leucoryx is the first of her race born out of Africa. *Ant-eaters, Giant*: the first was brought to England from Brazil in 1853, and was exhibited in Broad-street, St. Giles's, until purchased by the Zoological Society for 200*l.* (See an admirable paper by Professor Owen, *Literary Gazette*, No. 1916.) *Apteryx*, or *Kiwi* bird, from New Zealand; the first living specimen brought to England of this rare bird. The *Aquatic Vivarium*, built of iron and glass, in 1853, in the south garden, consists of a series of glass tanks, in which fish spawn, zoophytes produce young, and algæ luxuriate; crustacea and mollusca live successfully, and ascidian polypes are illustrated, together with sea anemones, jelly-fishes and star-fishes, rare shell-fishes, &c.: a new world of animal life is here seen as in the depths of the ocean, with masses of rock, sand, gravel, corallines, sea-weed, and sea-water; the animals are in a state of natural restlessness, now quiescent, now eating and being eaten. *Aurochs*, or *European Bisons*: a pair presented by the Emperor of Russia, in 1847, from the forest of Bialowitzca: the male died in 1848, the female in 1849 from pleuro-pneumonia. *Bears*: the collection is one of the largest ever made. *Elephants*: including an Indian elephant calf and its mother. In 1847 died here the great Indian elephant Jack, having been in the gardens sixteen years. Adjoining the stable is a tank of water, of a depth nearly equal to the height of a full-grown elephant. In 1851 the Society possessed a *herd of four Elephants*, besides a hippopotamus, a rhinoceros, and both species of tapir; being the largest collection of pachydermata ever exhibited in Europe. *Deer*, several species: the reindeer and wapiti have produced several fawns. *Flamingoes*, a numerous group. *Giraffes*: four received in 1836 cost the Society upwards of 2300*l.*, including 1000*l.* for steamboat passage: the female produced six male fawns here between 1840 and 1851. *Hippopotamus*, a young male (the first living specimen seen in England), received from Egypt in May 1850, when ten months old, seven feet long, and six and a half feet in girth; also a female hippopotamus, received 1854: they are provided with a bath. *Humming-birds*: Mr. Gould's matchless collection of 2000 examples was exhibited here in 1851 and 1852. *Iguanas*, two from Cuba and Carthagena, closely resembling, in every thing but size, the fossil Iguanodon. The *Lions* number generally from eight to ten, including a pair of cubs born in the gardens, in 1853; a pair of fine Indian lions, received in 1854; a noble old Nubian lion and lioness. *Orang-utan* and *Chimpanzee*: the purchase-money of the latter sometimes exceeds 300*l.* The orang "Darby," brought from Borneo in 1851, is the finest yet seen in Europe, very intelligent, and docile as a child. *Parrot-houses*, these sometimes contain from sixty to seventy species. *Rapacious Birds*, so extensive a series of eagles and vultures has never yet been seen at one view. The *Reptile-house* was fitted up in 1849; the creatures are placed in large plate-glass cases: here are pythons and a rattle-snake, with a young one born here; here is also a case of the tree frogs of Europe: a yellow snake from Jamaica has produced eight young in the gardens. *Arab Serpent-Charmers* exhibited here, in 1850, their feats with a group of cobras. *Cobra de Capello*, from India: in 1852, a keeper in the gardens was killed by the bite of this serpent. *A large Boa* in 1850 swallowed a blanket, and disgorged it in thirty-three days. A *one-horned Rhinoceros*, of continental India, was obtained in 1834, when it was about four years old, and weighed 26 cwt.; it died in 1850: it has been replaced by a female, about five years old. *Satin Bower-Birds*, from Sydney: a pair have built here a bower, or breeding-place. *Tapir* of the Old World, from Mount Ophir; the nearest existing form to the Paleotherium. *Tigers:* a pair of magnificent specimens, presented by the Guicoway of Baroda in 1851; a pair of clouded tigers, 1854. *Tortoise:* a gigantic land specimen, 7 feet long; circumference, 7 feet 8 inches; height when walking, 3 feet; age, 180 years. *Wapiti* (from Knowsley), and young.

Rent of the Gardens to the Crown, 337*l.* per annum; rates to Marylebone and St. Pancras parishes, 199*l.* Animals in the Gardens, about 1300: although reduced in number, they are much more valuable and interesting than when their number was higher. Cost of the keep of the animals in 1854, about 4000*l.* salt water and carriage in 1853 cost 83*l.*). Purchase of animals in the same year, 1234*l.* (the presents are numerous). The visitors to the Gardens in 1854 exceeded 400,000.

The Gardens are open from 9 a.m. till sunset; the Museum from 10 till 6. The public are admitted daily, for 1*s.* each person; except on Monday, 6*d.* On Whit-Monday, 1853, upwards of 22,000 were admitted. *President of the Society,* H.R.H. Prince Albert, K.G. *Secretary,* D. W. Mitchell, B.A. Office, 11 Hanover-square.

Admission of Members.—Fellows pay an admission-fee of 5*l.*; and an annual contribution of 3*l.*, or a composition of 30*l.* Annual subscribers, 3*l.* on Jan. 1st. Fellows have personal admission to the Gardens and Museum, with two companions, daily; on Saturday they admit two friends to the Gardens by written order, instead of by their personal introduction; on Sunday, two friends by written order, in addition to two by their personal introduction: they receive also 20 tickets annually. Annual subscribers have personal admission to the Gardens and Museum, with one companion, daily; on Saturdays and Sundays they may admit one friend as above: they also receive 20 tickets annually. The wife of a fellow or annual subscriber may exercise these privileges in his absence.

ZOOLOGICAL GARDENS (THE SURREY)

Were established in 1831, by Mr. Edward Cross, upon the demesne which had been attached to the manor-house at Walworth. Thither Cross removed his menagerie from the King's Mews, where it had been transferred from Exeter 'Change (see page 289). The Gardens were laid out by Henry Phillips, author of *Sylva Florifera;* when a glazed circular building, 100 feet in diameter, was built for the cages of the carnivorous animals (lions, tigers, leopards, &c.); and other houses for mammalia, birds, &c. Here, in 1834, was first exhibited a young Indian one-horned rhinoceros, for which Cross paid 800*l.*; it was the only specimen brought to England for twenty years: in 1836 were added three giraffes, one fifteen feet high. To the zoological attraction was added a large picture-model, upon the borders of the lake, three acres in length: the first picture, Mount Vesuvius (with the natural lake for the Bay of Naples), was produced in 1837, when fireworks were also first introduced, for the volcanic eruption; in 1839, Iceland and its volcanoes; 1841, the City of Rome; 1843, Temple of Ellora; 1844, London and the Great Fire of 1666; 1845, Edinburgh; 1846, Vesuvius, reproduced; 1848, Rome, reproduced; 1849, Storming of Badajoz. These picture-models, mostly painted by Danson, were of great extent; that of Rome occupying five acres, and a painted surface of 260,000 square feet. These pictures probably originated in the Ranelagh spectacles of the last century; for in 1792 was exhibited there Mount Etna, 80 feet high, with the flowing lava, and altogether a triumph of machinery and pyrotechnics. Balloon-ascents, flower-shows, and other sights, with out-door concerts, have been added to the attractions of these Gardens. Admission 1*s.*

ADDITIONS AND CORRECTIONS.

Page 15. *Amusements : Copenhagen House* was taken down in 1853.
P. 31. *Bartholomew Fair* was entirely extinct in 1854.
P. 51. *Chelsea : Apothecaries' Company's "Physic Garden :"* One
of the fine old cedar-trees was blown down in 1854.
P. 52. *Loddidge's Nursery*, Hackney : Most of the gigantic tropical
trees were removed in 1854.
P. 70. *Chelsea Hospital :* The remains of the great Duke of Wel-
lington lay in state in the Hall, Nov. 12-17, 1852.
P. 76. *Chelsea :* The Red House at Battersea was taken down 1854.
P. 77. For " view" read " vie."
P. 80. *Chess-clubs :* The St. George's Chess-club has removed to
No. 53 St. James's-street.
P. 91. *St. Paul's Cathedral :* For " Rivers" read " Riou." P. 92.
The remains of the great Duke of Wellington, interred here with great
state, Nov. 18, 1852, are placed within an altar-tomb in the Crypt, about
40 feet west of Nelson's remains. P. 93. Sir James Thornhill's paint-
ings in the dome have been restored by Mr. Parris. P. 94. The Outer
Golden Gallery was regilt in 1845, at a cost of 68*l.*, paid by the late
Dean of St. Paul's, the Bishop of Llandaff. P. 95. The admission-
charge of 2*d.*, to view the tombs, is discontinued.
P. 99. *Westminster College Hall :* The fire upon the middle circular
hearth has been discontinued since 1850.
P. 110. *Westminster Abbey : Poets' Corner :* For " Conolly" read
" Cowley." P. 112. The statue of the poet Campbell has not yet been
placed here. In 1853, Gibson's statue of Sir Robert Peel was placed in
the north transept; and in 1854, a sitting statue of Wordsworth by Theed.
P. 118. For " Bridge-row" read " Budge-row."
P. 129. *St. Giles's Church, Cripplegate :* The Diary of General
Murray, referred to in the above page, and describing the profanation
of Milton's remains in 1790, is incorrect; for the skeleton then shown
as that of the poet, on being subjected to a very accurate inspection
proved to be that of a female. (See Dr. Symmons's *Life of Milton*,
2d edit. p. 570, *note.* 1810.)
P. 144. *St. Mary's Church, Lambeth*, has been rebuilt, except the
tower, by P. C. Hardwick.
P. 155. *St. Pancras' Old Church :* for " after the Reformation"
read " before the Reformation."
P. 161. Second line, for " D.D." read " LL.D."
P. 162. *Temple Church :* last line, for " Gibbon, the historian,"
read " Edmund Gibbon, ancestor of the historian."
P. 166. *Whitehall Chapel Organ :* for " Stamford" read " Stanford."
P. 170. *L. Inn Chapel :* for " Marquis of" read " Marquis" Wellesley.
P. 117. *Margaret-street Chapel :* Upon the site has been erected
the church of All Saints (Butterfield, architect), with an elegantly pro-
portioned spire 220 feet high.
P. 176. *The Tabernacle, Moorfields :* for " Told" read " Todd."
P. 182. *The Oratory of St. Philip Neri* has removed to a new chapel
and college built at Brompton, next Holy Trinity church.
P. 192. *The Carlton Club-house*, Pall Mall, has been completed.
P. 193. *Club-houses : Coventry House ;* p. 194, *Erectheum ;* and p.
196, *Oriental ;* dissolved.
P. 199. *Jun. United Service Club-house* taken down 1854, to be rebuilt.
Pp. 199 and 699. The Whittington Club-house premises (formerly the
Crown and Anchor tavern), extending from Arundel-st. to Milford-lane,
in the rear of the Strand houses, were destroyed by fire, Dec. 3, 1854.

P. 201. *Chapter Coffee-house*, Paternoster-row, closed in 1854.

P. 206. *College for Civil Engineers*, Putney, dissolved.

P. 219. *St. Olave's and St. John's Free Grammar School* rebuilt at Horsleydown in 1854.

P. 253. *The Diorama* premises, Regent's Park, have been converted into a chapel for Baptists.

P. 259. *Doctors' Commons :* The Will of Napoleon I. has been transferred to Paris.

P. 267. *Egyptian Hall, Piccadilly :* Haydon's "Mock Election" picture was sold for 500, not 800 guineas.   P. 268. Her Majesty visited the Mont Blanc Exhibition, 1854.

P. 272. For "Seldon" read "Selden."

P. 289. *Excise Office* (the) was taken down in 1854.

P. 306. For "Davenent" read "Davenant."

P. 309. *Fleet-street :* Cowley was not born in Fleet-street, but in Chancery-lane, where his father was a law-stationer and engrosser.

P. 335. *Whittington's shield :* for "E. B. Prince" read "E. B. Price."

P. 355. *Haberdashers' Hall* was taken down in 1854, to be rebuilt.

P. 362. *Cutlers' Hall* was taken down in 1854, to be rebuilt.

P. 367. *Wax-chandlers' Hall* was taken down in 1853, to be rebuilt.

P. 372. *Jermyn-street :* The One Tun Tavern no longer exists.

P. 378. *Horse Guards :* The remains of the great Duke of Wellington were deposited in the Audience-room the night before his funeral.

P. 389. *Brookes's Menagerie :* The old wooden house not taken down.

P. 393. *Hale House*, Earl's-court, was taken down in 1853. *Lindsey House :* John Martin, the painter, died in 1854.

P. 397. *The Angel Inn*, St. Clement's, has been taken down. *Bell*, it. Carter-lane : before "for a loan of thirty pounds," insert "a letter."

P. 399. *The Cock* (properly the Cock and Tabard) public-house, Tothill-street, was taken down in 1854.

P. 435. *Kentish Town :* "Nelson's tree" has disappeared.

P. 454. *Leicester-square :* The statue of Geo. I. disappeared in 1854.

P. 455. *Leicester-square : The Panopticon* was opened in March 854. It was designed in the Saracenic style, by T. Hayter Lewis. The cubic contents of the great hall and recesses are about 500 feet. t is heated by Gurney's "warming battery." In the centre is a fountain, the water of which can be thrown up by a pneumatic apparatus 0 feet, from an artesian well 346 feet deep. The decorations are in enamelled slate, with glass mosaic enrichments; the fronts of the galleries being Saracenic arches : the gilding and emblazonry are very elegant; and when lighted by gas, in chandeliers of beautiful design, the effect is very superb. There is an ascending-room to the photographic gallery. The stupendous organ, by Hill and Co., in England, is exceeded in size, but not in power, by that at York only. The institution was originally projected by E. M. Clarke, the philosophical-instrument maker. Admission, 1s.

P. 457. *Libraries :* Under this head we may mention the *Clerical (or Metropolitan) Library* of James Darling, 81 Great Queen-street, Lincoln's Inn Fields. This library is, perhaps, the most complete of any in England in theology, besides cognate subjects and other branches of literature. The catalogue, the labour of ten years, and printed at a great expense, is equally adapted to any extensive library.

P. 461. *Royal Geographical Society* removed to 15 Whitehall-place.

P. 479. *Apsley House :* The bullet-proof iron Venetian blinds have been removed by the present Duke of Wellington.

P. 480. For "Stohard" read "Stothard."

P. 505. *Royal Mews*, Prince's-street, Westminster, taken down in 54, and a new Stationery Office built upon the site.

Pp. 547, 548. Mr. Bernal and Mr. Windus died in 1854.
P. 561. *Oxford-street :* The shop-front of No. 54 is *Renaissance.*
P. 585. *Hyde Park :* for "Lake House" read "Cake House."
P. 63L *Giltspur-street.Compter* was taken down in 1854.
P. 655. *Royal Society :* for "Dr. Williams" read "Dr. Wilkins."
P. 670. *Somerset House :* In the west wing of the Strand front are
the Offices of the Registrar-General.

THE CRYSTAL PALACE, SYDENHAM.

Although this stupendous structure is not, like its patronymic, the
Great Exhibition building in Hyde Park, placed within the limits of the
town, the "Curiosities of London" would scarcely be complete without
some notice of the contents of the Crystal Palace at Sydenham. It occupies the summit of a hill between the Brighton Railway and the Dulwich
Wood, the fall from its site to the railway being 200 feet. In its construction the materials of the Great Exhibition building have been employed; but it is larger than its predecessor by 1623 feet, and by nearly
one-half in cubic contents. It is almost entirely of iron and glass,
covers nearly three-quarters of a mile of ground; and its height from
the garden-front to the top of the louvres is 208 feet, 6 feet higher than
the Monument. The nave is covered with an arched roof, raising it 44 feet
higher than the nave in Hyde Park; and the centre and two end transepts
have similar roofs Nearly 10,000 tons of iron have been used in the main
building and wings; and the superficial quantity of glass is 25 acres.

The Nave is entered at the south end, through an ornamental screen
of niches filled with statues of kings and queens by John Thomas. In
the area, statues are picturesquely grouped with stupendous pines,
palms, and other tropical plants of luxuriant beauty, backed by the
brilliant façades of the various Industrial and Fine Arts Courts. East
and west are groups illustrating the ethnology, zoology, and botany
of the Old and New Worlds; and at each end is a spacious basin, for a
fountain to throw up water from 70 to 200 feet. In the Great Transept
are the works of French and Italian, German and English, Roman and
Greek sculptors; and models of celebrated ancient and modern edifices.
Throughout the whole building are galleries devoted to the exhibition
of objects of industry and fine art. The most beautiful works are the
Courts representing the architecture and sculpture of each nation:
Egyptian, Greek, Roman, Pompeian, Alhambra, Assyrian, Byzantine,
and Romanesque; German, English, French, and Italian mediæval; Renaissance, Elizabethan, Italian, &c.

Descending to the Italian and English Landscape Garden and the
Park (planned by Sir Joseph Paxton, F.L.S.), we find Science and
Philosophy teaching their sublime truths in a geological illustration of
the Wealden formation, "so well known in Kent, Surrey, and Sussex,
and formerly the great metropolis of the Dinosaurian orders, or the
largest of gigantic lizards:" the various strata are here represented;
and here Mr. Waterhouse Hawkins, under the guiding eye of Professor
Owen, has built up gigantic animals of a former world, and in some
instances restored them from fossil remains.

The Palace is approached by a branch from the Brighton Railway,
into its very arcades. The building was opened by her Majesty, June
10, 1854. It has already cost a million of money; and in grandeur of
purpose is a marvel of enlightened enterprise. (See the series of excellent Guide-books, by the late Samuel Phillips, D.C.L.)

INDEX.

THE END.

LONDON:
PRINTED BY ROBSON, LEVEY, AND FRANKLYN,
Great New Street and Fetter Lane.

Lightning Source UK Ltd.
Milton Keynes UK
UKHW022104240921
391136UK00006B/1153